Concepts

Concepts

Core Readings

Edited by Eric Margolis and Stephen Laurence

A Bradford Book
The MIT Press
Cambridge, Massachusetts
London, England

Second printing, 2000

This book was set in Palatino by Asco Typesetters, Hong Kong.
Printed and bound in the United States of America.

Library of Congress Cataloging-in-Publication Data

Concepts : core readings / edited by Eric Margolis and Stephen
  Laurence.
     p.   cm.
  "A Bradford book."
  Includes bibliographical references and index.
  ISBN 0-262-13353-9 (hardcover : alk. paper). — ISBN 0-262-63193-8
  (pbk. : alk. paper)
  1. Concepts. 2. Philosophy of mind. 3. Knowledge, Theory of.
I. Margolis, Eric, 1968–   . II. Laurence, Stephen.
BD418.3.C635   1999
121'.4—dc21   98-49117
                                                    CIP

Contents

Acknowledgments   ix

Introduction   1

Chapter 1
Concepts and Cognitive Science   3
Stephen Laurence and Eric Margolis

PART I
Origins of the Contemporary Study of Concepts   83

The Classical Theory   85

Chapter 2
Euthyphro   87
Plato

Chapter 3
The Process of Concept Attainment   101
Jerome Bruner, Jacqueline Goodnow, and George Austin

Chapter 4
On the General Character of Semantic Theory   125
Jerrold Katz

Philosophical Skepticism about the Classical Theory   151

Chapter 5
Two Dogmas of Empiricism   153
W. V. O. Quine

Chapter 6
Philosophical Investigations, sections 65–78   171
Ludwig Wittgenstein

The Probabilistic Turn: Stereotypes, Prototypes, Exemplars   175

Chapter 7
Is Semantics Possible?   177
Hilary Putnam

Chapter 8
Principles of Categorization   189
Eleanor Rosch

Chapter 9
The Exemplar View   207
Edward Smith and Douglas Medin

Critical Reactions to the Probabilistic Turn   223

Chapter 10
What Some Concepts Might Not Be   225
Sharon Lee Armstrong, Lila R. Gleitman, and Henry Gleitman

Chapter 11
On the Adequacy of Prototype Theory as a Theory of Concepts   261
Daniel N. Osherson and Edward E. Smith

Chapter 12
Concepts and Stereotypes   279
Georges Rey

PART II
Current Theories and Research   301

Neoclassical Theories   303

Chapter 13
What Is a Concept, That a Person May Grasp It?   305
Ray Jackendoff

Chapter 14
Précis of *A Study of Concepts*   335
Christopher Peacocke

Chapter 15
Resisting Primitive Compulsions   339
Georges Rey

Chapter 16
Can Possession Conditions Individuate Concepts?   345
Christopher Peacocke

Rethinking Prototypes   353

Chapter 17
Combining Prototypes: A Selective Modification Model   355
Edward E. Smith, Daniel N. Osherson, Lance J. Rips, and Margaret Keane

Chapter 18
Cognitive Models and Prototype Theory   391
George Lakoff

The Theory-Theory   423

Chapter 19
The Role of Theories in Conceptual Coherence   425
Gregory Murphy and Douglas Medin

Chapter 20
Knowledge Acquisition: Enrichment or Conceptual Change?   459
Susan Carey

Conceptual Atomism   489

Chapter 21
Against Definitions   491
Jerry A. Fodor, Merrill F. Garrett, Edward C. T. Walker, and Cornelia H. Parkes

Chapter 22
Information and Representation   513
Jerry Fodor

Chapter 23
A Common Structure for Concepts of Individuals, Stuffs and Real Kinds: More
Mama, More Milk, and More Mouse   525
Ruth Garrett Millikan

Chapter 24
How to Acquire a Concept   549
Eric Margolis

Concept Possession in Infants and Children   569

Chapter 25
The Object Concept Revisited: New Directions in the Investigation of Infants'
Physical Knowledge   571
Renée Baillargeon

Chapter 26
Insides and Essences: Early Understandings of the Non-Obvious   613
Susan A. Gelman and Henry M. Wellman

Index   639

Acknowledgments

We would like to thank all of the contributors to the volume as well as the people at MIT Press who have worked with us on this project, especially Wendy Drexler, Michael Sims, Betty Stanton, and Amy Yeager. We'd also like to thank Shelly Fitzgerald for last-minute help with the manuscript and two anonymous referees for their comments and suggestions.

Eric Margolis
Stephen Laurence

The editors and MIT Press acknowledge with thanks permission granted to reproduce in this volume the following materials previously published elsewhere. Every effort has been made to trace copyright holders, but if any have been inadvertently overlooked the publisher will be pleased to make the necessary arrangement at the first opportunity.

Plato, "Euthyphro" translated by G. Grube, in *Plato: Five Dialogues*, Hackett Publishing Company, Inc., 1981, © 1981 by Hackett Publishing Company, Inc., reprinted by permission of the publisher.

Bruner, J., Goodnow, J., and Austin, G. "The Process of Concept Attainment," chapter 3 of *A Study of Thinking*, 1956, © 1956 by Transaction Publishers, all rights reserved, reprinted by permission of the authors and the publisher.

Katz, J. Excerpt from his *Semantic Theory*, 1972, © 1972 by Jerrold J. Katz, reprinted by permission of the author and Addison-Wesley Educational Publishers Inc.

Quine, W. "Two Dogmas of Empiricism," in *From a Logical Point of View*, Harvard University Press, 1980, © 1953, 1961, 1980 by the Presidents and Fellows of Harvard College, reprinted by permission of the author and the publisher.

Wittgenstein, L., Excerpt from his *Philosophical Investigations*, 3d edition, translated by G. Anscombe, © 1953, reprinted by permission of Prentice-Hall, Inc., and Blackwell Publishers Ltd.

Putnam, H. "Is Semantics Possible?" in H. Kiefer and M. Munitz, eds., *Languages, Belief and Metaphysics*, vol. 1, 1970, © 1970 by State University of New York Press, reprinted by permission of the author and publisher.

Rosch, E. "Principles of Categorization," in E. Rosch and B. Lloyd, eds., *Cognition and Categorization*, 1978, © 1978 Lawrence Erlbaum Associates, Inc., Publishers, reprinted by permission of the author and the publisher.

Smith, E., and Medin, D., "The Exemplar View," chapter 7 of *Categories and Concepts*, 1981, © 1981 by the Presidents and Fellows of Harvard College, reprinted by permission of the authors and the publisher.

Armstrong, S., Gleitman, L., and Gleitman, H. "What Some Concepts Might Not Be," *Cognition*, 13, 1983 © 1983 Elsevier Science—NL, Sara Burgerhartstraat 25, 1055 KV Amsterdam, The Netherlands, reprinted with permission of the authors and the publisher.

Osherson, D., and Smith, E. "On the Adequacy of Prototype Theory as a Theory of Concepts" *Cognition* 9 (1981), © 1981 Elsevier Science—NL, Sara Burgerhartstraat 25, 1055 KV Amsterdam, The Netherlands, reprinted with permission of the authors and the publisher.

Rey, G. "Concepts and Stereotypes," *Cognition* 15 (1983), © 1983 Elsevier Science—NL, Sara Burgerhart-straat 25, 1055 KV Amsterdam, The Netherlands, reprinted with permission of the author and the publisher.

Jackendoff, R. "What Is a Concept, That a Person May Grasp It?" *Mind & Language*, 4, 1989, © 1989 Blackwell Publishers Ltd., reprinted by permission of the author and the publisher.

Peacocke, C. "Précis of *A Study of Concepts*," *Philosophy and Phenomenological Research*, LVI, 2, 1996, © 1996 by *Philosophy and Phenomenological Research*, reprinted by permission of the author and the publisher.

Rey, G. "Resisting Primitive Compulsions," *Philosophy and Phenomenological Research* 56, no. 2 (1996), © 1996 by *Philosophy and Phenomenological Research*, reprinted by permission of the author and the publisher.

Peacocke, C. Excerpt from his "Can Possession Conditions Individuate Concepts?" *Philosophy and Phenomenological Research* 56. no. 2 (1996): 433–440, © 1996 by *Philosophy and Phenomenological Research*, reprinted by permission of the author and the publisher.

Smith, E., Osherson, D., Rips, L., and Keane, M. "Combining Prototypes: A Selective Modification Model," *Cognitive Science* 12 (1988), © 1988 by Ablex Publishing Corporation, reprinted by permission of the authors and Ablex Publishing Corporation.

Lakoff, G. "Cognitive Models and Prototype Theory" in U. Neisser, ed., *Concepts and Conceptual Development: Ecological and Intellectual Factors in Categorization*, 1987, © 1987 Cambridge University Press, reprinted by permission of the author and the publisher.

Murphy, G., and Medin, D. "The Role of Theories in Conceptual Coherence" *Psychological Review* 92 (1985), © 1985 by the American Psychological Association, reprinted with permission of the authors and the publisher.

Carey, S. "Knowledge Acquisition: Enrichment or Conceptual Change?" in S. Carey and R. Gelman, eds., *The Epigenesis of Mind: Essays on Biology and Cognition*, 1991, © 1991 Lawrence Erlbaum Associates, Inc., Publishers, reprinted by permission of the author and the publisher.

Fodor, J., Garrett, M., Walker, E., and Parkes, C. Excerpt from their "Against Definitions," *Cognition* 8 (1980), © 1980 Elsevier Science—NL, Sara Burgerhartstraat 25, 1055 KV Amsterdam, The Netherlands, reprinted with permission of the authors and the publisher.

Fodor, J. "Information and Representation" in P. Hanson, ed., *Information, Language, and Cognition*, 1990, University of British Columbia Press, © 1991 by Oxford University Press, reprinted by permission of the author and Oxford University Press.

Millikan, R. "A Common Structure for Concepts of Individuals, Stuffs, and Real Kinds: More Mama, More Milk, and More Mouse," *Behavioral and Brain Sciences* 21 (1998), © 1998 Cambridge University Press, reprinted by permission of the author and the publisher.

Margolis, E. How to Acquire a Concept. *Mind and Language* 13 (1998), © 1996 by Blackwell Publishers Ltd., reprinted by permission of the author and the publisher.

Baillargeon, R. "The Object Concept Revisited: New Directions in the Investigation of Infants' Physical Knowledge," in C. Granrund, ed., *Visual Perception and Cognition in Infancy*, 1993, © 1993 Lawrence Erlbaum Associates, Inc., Publishers, reprinted by permission of the author and the publisher.

Gelman, S., and Wellman, H. "Insides and Essences: Early Understandings of the Non-Obvious," *Cognition* 38 (1991), © 1991 Elsevier Science—NL, Sara Burgerhartstraat 25, 1055 KV Amsterdam, The Netherlands, reprinted with permission of the authors and the publisher.

Introduction

Chapter 1

Concepts and Cognitive Science

Stephen Laurence and Eric Margolis

---

1. Introduction: Some Preliminaries

Concepts are the most fundamental constructs in theories of the mind. Given their importance to all aspects of cognition, it's no surprise that concepts raise so many controversies in philosophy and cognitive science. These range from the relatively local

> Should concepts be thought of as bundles of features, or do they embody mental theories?

to the most global

> Are concepts mental representations, or might they be abstract entities?

Indeed, it's even controversial whether concepts are objects, as opposed to cognitive or behavioral abilities of some sort. Because of the scope of the issues at stake, it's inevitable that some disputes arise from radically different views of what a theory of concepts ought to achieve—differences that can be especially pronounced across disciplinary boundaries. Yet in spite of these differences, there has been a significant amount of interdisciplinary interaction among theorists working on concepts. In this respect, the theory of concepts is one of the great success stories of cognitive science. Psychologists and linguists have borrowed freely from philosophers in developing detailed empirical theories of concepts, drawing inspiration from Wittgenstein's discussions of family resemblance, Frege's distinction between sense and reference, and Kripke's and Putnam's discussions of externalism and essentialism. And philosophers have found psychologists' work on categorization to have powerful implications for a wide range of philosophical debates. The philosopher Stephen Stich (1993) has gone so far as to remark that current empirical models in psychology undermine a traditional approach to philosophy in which philosophers engage in conceptual analyses. As a consequence of this work, Stich and others have come to believe that philosophers have to rethink their approach to topics in areas as diverse as the philosophy of mind and ethics. So even if disciplinary boundaries have generated the appearance of disjoint research, it's hard to deny that significant interaction has taken place.

We hope this volume will underscore some of these achievements and open the way for increased cooperation. In this introduction, we sketch the recent history of theories of concepts. However, our purpose isn't solely one of exposition. We also provide a number of reinterpretations of what have come to be standard arguments in the field and develop a framework that lends more prominence to neglected areas

---

This paper was fully collaborative; the order of the authors' names is arbitrary.

of the intellectual geography. Given the vast range of theories at play, it would be impossible to say anything substantive without offending some theoretical scruples. So we should say right now that we don't claim to be completely neutral. As we go along, we try to justify our choices to some extent, but inevitably, in a space as short as this, certain views will receive less attention. Our strategy is to present what we take to be the main theories of concepts and do this in terms of idealized characterizations that provide rather rough yet useful demarcations.

Before we begin, however, there are three preliminary issues that need to be mentioned. Two can be dealt with fairly quickly, but the third—concerning the ontological status of concepts—requires a more extended treatment.

Primitive, Complex and Lexical Concepts[1]

For a variety of reasons, most discussions of concepts have centered around *lexical concepts*. Lexical concepts are concepts like BACHELOR, BIRD, and BITE—roughly, ones that correspond to lexical items in natural languages.[2] One reason for the interest in lexical concepts is that it's common to think that words in natural languages inherit their meanings from the concepts they are used to express. In some discussions, concepts are taken to be just those mental representations that are expressed by words in natural languages. However, this usage is awkward, since it prohibits labeling as concepts those representations that are expressed by complex natural language expressions. One wouldn't be able to say, for example, that the concept BLACK CAT (corresponding to the English expression "black cat") is composed of the simpler concepts BLACK and CAT; only the latter would be concepts. Yet most of the reasons that one would have to single out BLACK and CAT and the like as concepts apply equally to complexes that have these as their constituents. There may be little difference between lexical concepts and other complex concepts apart from the fact that the former are lexicalized; indeed, on many views, lexical concepts are themselves complex representations. At the same time, it seems wrong to designate as concepts mental representations of any size whatsoever. Representations at the level of complete thoughts—that is, ones that may express whole propositions—are too big to be concepts. Accordingly, we will take *concepts* to be subpropositional mental representations.

Two other points of terminology should be mentioned. We'll say that *primitive concepts* are ones that lack structure. *Complex concepts*, in contrast, are concepts that aren't primitive. In the cognitive science literature, primitive concepts are sometimes called *atomic* concepts or *features*, although this terminology is confused by the fact that "feature" is sometimes used more permissively (i.e., to refer to any component of a concept) and is sometimes used more restrictively (i.e., to refer to only primitive sensory concepts). We'll adopt a permissive use of "feature" and say that unstruc-

1. Throughout, we will refer to concepts by using expressions in small caps. When quoting, we will adjust other people's notations to our own.
2. For present purposes, there is no need to insist on a more precise characterization, apart from noting that the concepts in question are ones that are usually encoded by single morphemes. In particular, we won't worry about the possibility that one language may use a phrase where another uses a word, and we won't worry about exactly what a word is (but for some alternative conceptions, see Di Sciullo and Williams 1987). Admittedly, the notion of a lexical concept isn't all that sharp, but it does help to orient the discussion toward the specific concepts that have been most actively subjected to investigation, for instance, BIRD as opposed to BIRDS THAT EAT REDDISH WORMS IN THE EARLY MORNING HOURS.

tured concepts are primitive or atomic. What exactly it means to say that a concept has, or lacks, structure is another matter. This brings us to our second preliminary point.

Two Models of Conceptual Structure

Most theories of concepts treat lexical concepts as structured complexes. This raises the issue of what it is for such representational complexes to have structure. Despite the important role that conceptual structure plays in many debates, there has been little explicit discussion of this question. We discern two importantly different models of structure that are implicit in these debates.

The first view we'll call the *Containment Model*. On this view, one concept is a structured complex of other concepts just in case it literally has those other concepts as proper parts. In this way, a concept C might be composed of the concepts X, Y, and Z. Then an occurrence of C would necessarily involve an occurrence of X, Y, and Z; because X, Y, and Z are contained within C, C couldn't be tokened without X, Y, and Z being tokened. For example, the concept DROPPED THE ACCORDION couldn't be tokened without ACCORDION being tokened. As an analogy, you might think of the relation that words bear to phrases and sentences. The word "accordion" is a structural element of the sentence "Tony dropped the accordion" in the sense that it is a proper part of the sentence. Consequently, you can't utter a token of the sentence "Tony dropped the accordion" without thereby uttering a token of the word "accordion."

The second view, which we'll can the *Inferential Model*, is rather different. According to this view, one concept is a structured complex of other concepts just in case it stands in a privileged relation to these other concepts, generally, by way of some type of inferential disposition. On this model, even though X, Y, and Z may be part of the structure of C, C can still occur without necessitating their occurrence. For example, RED might have a structure implicating the concept COLOR, but on the Inferential Model, one could entertain the concept RED without having to token the concept COLOR. At most, one would have to have certain dispositions linking RED and COLOR—for example, the disposition to infer X IS COLORED from X IS RED.

Thus, for any claim that a concept has such-and-such structure—or such-and-such *type* of structure (see sec. 7)—there will be, in principle, two possible interpretations of the claim: one in terms of the Containment Model and one in terms of the Inferential Model. The significance of these distinctions will become clearer once we present some specific theories of concepts. For now we simply want to note that discussions of conceptual structure are often based on an implicit commitment to one of these models and that a proper evaluation of a theory of concepts may turn on which model is adopted.

Concepts as Abstracta vs. Concepts as Mental Representations

The third and last preliminary point that we need to discuss concerns a more basic issue—the ontological status of concepts. In accordance with virtually all discussions of concepts in psychology, we will assume that concepts are mental particulars. For example, your concept GRANDMOTHER is a mental representation of a certain type, perhaps a structured mental representation in one of the two senses we've isolated. It should be said, however, that not all theorists accept as their starting point the thesis that concepts are mental particulars. In philosophy especially it's not uncommon to think of concepts as abstract entities.[3] Clarifying the motivations for this view and its relation to standard psychological accounts requires a digression.[4] We hope the reader will bear with us, however, since some of the distinctions that are at play in this dispute will be relevant later on.

Perhaps the best way to begin is by way of the nineteenth-century German philosopher Gottlob Frege and his distinction between *sense* and *reference*. Frege was primarily interested in language, in particular, artificial languages used in logic, mathematics, and science. But the distinctions he drew have analogues for natural language and theories about the nature of mental representation.

In the first instance, it helps to think of senses in terms of another technical notion in Frege—the *mode of presentation* for the referent of a term. Frege discussed a variety of cases where different terms refer to the same object but do so by characterizing the object in different ways. For instance, "two plus two" and "the square root of 16" both refer to the number four, but they incorporate different ways of characterizing it. This distinction—between referent and mode of presentation—is standardly applied to expressions of every size and semantic category. We can speak of the mode of presentation for a name, or a kind term, or even a whole sentence, just as we can for a phrase. "Mark Twain" and "Samuel Clemens" may refer to the same individual, but their modes of presentation for this individual aren't the same. Similarly, "gold" and "element with atomic number 79" may refer to the same stuff, but clearly under distinct modes of presentation.

The connection with senses is that Frege held that expressions have a sense, in addition to a referent, and that the sense of an expression "contains" the mode of presentation for its referent. We needn't worry about all of the details here, but to get clearer about senses, it pays to think of them as being characterized by the roles that Frege asked them to play. Three ought to be clearly distinguished (cf. Burge 1977):

> 1. *Senses are the cognitive content of linguistic expressions* This role is related to what has come to be known as *Frege's Puzzle*. Frege asks how two identity statements—"the morning star is the morning star" and "the morning star is the evening star"—could differ in cognitive content. Both are identity statements involving coreferential terms denoting the planet Venus, yet the first is a truism, the second a significant astronomical discovery. Frege's solution to the puzzle is to say that the expressions involved in these statements have senses, and the differences in cognitive content correspond to differences between the senses they express.
>
> 2. *Senses determine reference* For Frege, our linguistic and conceptual access to the world is mediated by the senses of the expressions in our language. A sense, as a mode of presentation, fixes or determines the referent of an expression. And it is through our grasp of a sense that we access the referent. The

---

3. Yet another alternative is the view that concepts are not particulars at all but are, instead, behavioral or psychological abilities. We take it that behavioral abilities are ruled out for the same reasons that argue against behaviorism in general (see, e.g., Chomsky 1959). However, the view that concepts are psychological abilities is harder to evaluate. The chief difficulty is that more needs to be said about the nature of these abilities. Without a developed theory, it's not even clear that an appeal to abilities is in conflict with the view that concepts are particulars. For example, such abilities might require that one be in possession of a mental particular that is deployed in a characteristic way.

4. A variety of theoretical perspectives treat concepts as abstracta, but we take the version we discuss to be representative.

expression "the morning star" refers to the object it does because this expression has the sense it does.

3. *Senses are the indirect referents of expressions in intensional contexts*   Certain linguistic contexts (e.g., "... believes that ...￼" and other propositional attitude reports) have distinctive and peculiar semantic properties. Outside of these contexts, one can freely substitute coreferential terms without affecting the truth value of the sentence ("the morning star is bright" → "the evening star is bright"), but within these contexts, the same substitutions are not possible ("Sue believes that the morning star is bright" ↛ "Sue believes that the evening star is bright"). Frege's explanation of this type of case is that in such contexts expressions do not refer to their customary referents, but rather to their customary *senses*. Since the expressions have different customary senses, they actually have different referents in these contexts. Thus Frege is able to maintain the principle that coreferring terms can be substituted one for the other without a change in truth value, despite what otherwise may have appeared to be a decisive counterexample to the principle.

Frege's semantic theory, and the phenomena he used to motivate it, have generated a great deal of controversy, and they have had an enormous influence on the development of semantic theories in philosophy and linguistics. For now, though, the important issue is the ontological status of senses. Frege argued that senses, construed in terms of these theoretical roles, cannot be mental entities. Since it's common in philosophy to hold that concepts just are Fregean senses, it would seem that Frege's case against mental entities is especially pertinent. The problem, in his view, is that mental entities are subjective, whereas senses are supposed to be objective. Two people "are not prevented from grasping the same sense; but they cannot have the same idea" (1892/1966, p. 60). (Note that for Frege, ideas are mental entities.)

If this is the argument against the view that concepts are mental representations, however, it isn't the least bit convincing. To see why, one has to be careful about teasing apart several distinctions that can get lumped together as a single contrast between the subjective and the objective. One of these concerns the difference between mental representations, thoughts, and experiences, on the one hand, and extra-mental entities on the other. In this sense, a stone is objective, but a mental representation of a stone is subjective; it's subjective simply because it's mental. Notice, however, that subjectivity of this kind doesn't preclude the sharing of a mental representation, since two people can have the same type of mental representation. What isn't possible is for two people to have the very same *token* representation. This brings us to a second subjective-objective distinction. It can be put this way: Mental representations are subjective in that their tokens are uniquely possessed; they belong to one and only one subject. Their being subjective in this sense, however, doesn't preclude their being shareable in the relevant sense, since, again, two people can have the same representation by each having tokens of the same type. When someone says that two people have the same concept, there is no need to suppose that she is saying that they both possess the same token concept. It would make as much sense to say that two people cannot utter the same sentence because they cannot both produce the same token sentence. Clearly what matters for being able to utter the same sentence, or entertain the same concept, is being able to have tokens of the same type. So while mental representations are subjective in the two senses we've isolated, this doesn't stop them from being objective in the sense of being shareable.[5]

In short, we see no reason why concepts can't be mental representations. And given the role of mental representations in theories of psychological processing, it would be entirely natural to follow psychological usage in calling these representations concepts. Still, this usage isn't meant to preclude a role for the abstracta that Fregeans mean to highlight. To see this, one need only consider the question of whether Frege himself could have it both ways, employing mental representations and senses. The answer, of course, is that he could. On this model, beliefs and other propositional attitudes would involve token mental representations that have other representations—concepts—as their constituents. Senses would come in as the semantic values of these representations. That is, in addition to having worldly objects and properties as their referents, mental representations (like words, on Frege's original account) would have senses too. In this way, senses help to type mental representation; they provide part of the conditions for individuating concepts.

Given this way of combining the more traditional philosophical account of concepts with the representationalism of psychology, it's little more than a terminological debate whether representations or the abstracta should be called concepts. Since we think there needn't be any confusion on this point—and since we are primarily interested in the mental representations—we'll continue to follow standard psychological usage, according to which concepts are representations.[6]

With these preliminaries out of the way, we can now turn to the theories of concepts themselves. We will work though five that figure prominently in discussions in linguistics, philosophy, and psychology. They differ in their motivations and the problems they face, but they aren't nearly as distinct from one another as is often assumed. We'll see, for example, that some problems aren't tied to a single theory; rather they present a general challenge to nearly any theory of concepts. Similarly, some of the resources that trace back to one account of concepts can be enlisted in surprising ways to help other accounts. In general, the theories that we will discuss differ in what they say about the structure of concepts. Along the way, we'll mention a number of respects in which the options regarding conceptual structure can be expanded. In the concluding section (sec. 7), we'll bring some of these strands together by discussing four ways of construing what theories of concepts have to say about the nature of concepts.

2. The Classical Theory of Concepts

2.1. Concepts and Definitions

In one way or another, most theories of concepts can be seen as reactions to, or developments of, what is known as the *Classical Theory of Concepts*.[7] The Classical

---

5. A third sense in which mental entities may be subjective—also suggested by Frege's text—is that they are highly idiosyncratic. Much of Frege's criticism of "ideas" is that they are too variable from one person to the next. "A painter, a horseman, and a zoologist will probably connect different ideas with the name 'Bucephalus'" (59). At best, however, Frege's observation establishes only that ideas aren't likely to be shared, not that they are, in principle, unshareable. Moreover, it's hard to see how the idiosyncrasy of ideas would motivate the claim that concepts are abstracta.

6. For further discussion on this point, see the appendix (sec. 8) and Margolis and Laurence (ms).

7. Also called the *Traditional Theory* or the *Definition View*.

Theory holds that most concepts—especially lexical concepts—have definitional structure. What this means is that most concepts encode necessary and sufficient conditions for their own application.[8] Consider, for example, the concept BACHELOR. According to the Classical Theory, we can think of this concept as a complex mental representation that specifies necessary and sufficient conditions for something to be a bachelor. So BACHELOR might be composed of a set of representations such as IS NOT MARRIED, IS MALE, and IS AN ADULT. Each of these components specifies a condition that something must meet in order to be a bachelor, and anything that satisfies them all thereby counts as a bachelor. These components, or features, yield a semantic interpretation for the complex representation in accordance with the principles of a compositional semantics.

This conception of concepts has a long history in philosophy. The seventeenth-century philosopher John Locke seems to be assuming a version of the Classical Theory when he gives his account of the concepts SUN and GOLD (1690/1975, pp. 298–299 and p. 317, respectively):

> [T]he *Idea* of the *Sun*, What is it, but an aggregate of those several simple *Ideas*, Bright, Hot, Roundish, having a constant regular motion, at a certain distance from us, and, perhaps, some other....

> [T]he greatest part of the *Ideas*, that make our complex *Idea* of *Gold*, are Yellowness, great Weight, Ductility, Fusibility, and Solubility, in *Aqua Regia, etc.* all united together in an unknown *Substratum*...[9]

On the Classical Theory, most concepts—including most lexical concepts—are complex representations that are composed of structurally simpler representations. What's more, it's natural to construe their structure in accordance with the Containment Model, where the components of a complex concept are among its proper parts.[10] Some of these components may themselves be complex, as in the case of BACHELOR. But eventually one reaches a level of primitive representations, which are undefined. Traditionally, these primitive representations have been taken to be sensory or perceptual in character, along broadly empiricist lines.

It is, of course, an oversimplification to speak of *the* Classical Theory of concepts, as though there were just a single, unitary theory to which all classical theorists subscribe. In reality, there is a diverse family of theories centered around the idea that

---

8. By "application" we mean a semantic relation; that is, a concept encodes the conditions that are singly necessary and jointly sufficient for something to be in its extension. Another sense of the term is to indicate a psychological process in which an object is judged to fall under a concept. We'll try to avoid this ambiguity by always using "application" in the semantic sense, unless the context makes it very clear that the psychological sense is intended. Notice, then, that in the first instance we have characterized the Classical Theory in semantic terms. This doesn't mean, however, that the theory is devoid of psychological import. See the discussion of concept acquisition and categorization, below.

9. Locke's views about natural kind concepts are complicated by the fact that he took natural kinds to have both a nominal and a real essence. For Locke, the real essence of a kind like gold isn't known, but the nominal essence is, and must be, in order to possess the corresponding concept. Arguably, however, he takes the nominal essence to give necessary and sufficient conditions for the application of a kind concept, since he holds that the nominal essence is defined relative to the real essence in such a way that the two track one another.

10. It's natural, but not mandatory. Alternatively, one could think of a classically structured concept as a node that stands in inferential relations to its defining features. The advantage of the Containment Model is that it makes especially clear which associated concepts are its defining features and which are incidental.

concepts have definitional structure. What we call the Classical Theory of concepts is an idealized account that abstracts away from many of their differences. To mention just one point on which classical theorists disagree: Many recent classical theorists have abandoned the strict empiricist view that concepts are ultimately composed of features expressing sensory properties.

It would be difficult to overstate the historical predominance of the Classical Theory. Aspects of the theory date back to antiquity (see Plato 1981 [chapter 2 in this volume]).[11] And the first serious challenges to its status weren't until the 1950s in philosophy, and the 1970s in psychology. Why has the Classical Theory been held in such high regard? The theory has powerful explanatory resources, offering unified accounts of concept acquisition, categorization, epistemic justification, analytic entailment, and reference determination, all of which flow directly from its basic commitments (see Fodor, J. A. et al. 1980 [chapter 21]). We will briefly review these accounts, since it helps to flesh out the Classical Theory and its substantial motivations.

Box 1

The Classical Theory

Most concepts (esp. lexical concepts) are structured mental representations that encode a set of necessary and sufficient conditions for their application, if possible, in sensory or perceptual terms.

Concept Acquisition   If a concept is a complex representation built out of features that encode necessary and sufficient conditions for its application, then the natural model of concept acquisition is one where the learner acquires a concept by assembling its features. If, in accordance with the empiricist version of the Classical Theory, we add the further stipulation that primitive features are sensory or perceptual, the model we arrive at is something like the following. Through perception, sensory properties are monitored so that their representations are joined in a way that reflects environmental contingencies. Having noticed the way these properties correlate in her environment, the learner assembles a complex concept that incorporates the relevant features in such a way that something falls under the new, complex concept just in case it satisfies those features. In this way, all concepts in the end would be defined in terms of a relatively small stock of sensory concepts. As John Locke put it in *An Essay Concerning Human Understanding* (1690/1975, p. 166),

> [E]ven *the most abstruse* Ideas, how remote soever they may seem from Sense, or from any operation of our own Minds, are yet only such, as the Understanding frames to it self, by repeating and joining together *Ideas*, that it had either from Objects of Sense, or from its own operations about them....

A somewhat more recent advocate of this position is the influential twentieth-century German philosopher Rudolf Carnap. In "The Elimination of Metaphysics through Logical Analysis of Language," Carnap writes (1932/1959, pp. 62–63),

---

11. When, for the first time, we refer to a chapter that is reprinted in the present volume, we'll indicate this with brackets. Subsequent references will omit the bracketed material.

> In the case of many words, specifically in the case of the overwhelming major-
> ity of scientific words, it is possible to specify their meaning by reduction to
> other words ("constitution," definition). E.g., "'arthropodes' are animals with
> segmented bodies and jointed legs." ... In this way every word of the language
> is reduced to other words and finally to the words which occur in the so-called
> "observation sentences" or "protocol sentences."[12]

In the face of repeated failures to analyze everyday concepts in terms of a purely
sensory base, contemporary theorists have often relaxed the strong empiricist assumption that all simple concepts must be sensory. For example, Eve Clark (1973)
sees the process of acquiring the meaning of a word like "brother" as comprising
several stages where semantic components get added to an initial representation. In
the earliest stage the representation consists of only two components: +MALE, −ADULT.
In subsequent stages, −ADULT is changed to ±ADULT, +SIBLING is added, and
+RECIPROCAL is added. In this way, a representation for "brother" is gradually constructed from its constituent representations, which collectively provide a definition
of the word and distinguish it from related words, such as "boy." Though these components may not be primitive, Clark isn't committed to the idea that further decomposition will always lead to purely sensory concepts. In fact, she says that many
words, especially relational terms, require possibly irreducible features that encode
"functional, social, or cultural factors" (p. 106). Similarly, the linguist and philosopher
Jerrold Katz writes (1972 [chapter 4 in this volume], p. 40),

> [T]he English noun "chair" can be decomposed into a set of concepts which
> might be represented by the semantic markers in (4.10):
>
> (4.10)   OBJECT, PHYSICAL, NON-LIVING, ARTIFACT, FURNITURE, PORTABLE, SOMETHING WITH
>   LEGS, SOMETHING WITH A BACK, SOMETHING WITH A SEAT, SEAT FOR ONE.

He adds that these semantic markers—or features—require further analysis, but, like
Clark, he isn't committed to a reduction that yields a purely sensory base.

No doubt, a component-by-component model of concept acquisition is compelling
even when it is detached from its empiricist roots. The simplicity and power of the
model provides considerable motivation for pursuing the Classical Theory.

Categorization   The Classical Theory offers an equally compelling model of categorization (i.e., the application of a concept, in the psychological sense; see note 8). In
fact, the model of categorization is just the ontogeny run backwards; that is, something is judged to fall under a concept just in case it is judged to fall under the features that compose the concept. So, something might be categorized as falling under
the concept CHAIR by noting that it has a seat, back, legs, and so on. Categorization on
this model is basically a process of checking to see if the features that are part of a
concept are satisfied by the item being categorized. As with the general model of
concept acquisition, this model of categorization is powerful and intuitively appealing, and it's a natural extension of the Classical Theory.

---

12. Throughout we'll ignore certain differences between language and thought, allowing claims about
words to stand in for claims about concepts. Carnap's account is about the semantics of linguistic items but
otherwise is a useful and explicit version of the Classical Theory.

Epistemic Justification   A number of philosophical advocates of the Classical Theory have also emphasized the role it could play as a theory of epistemic justification. The idea is that one would be justified in taking an item to fall under a given concept by determining whether its defining components are satisfied.

The quotation from Carnap (above) is part of a larger passage where he explains that we are justified in taking a thing, x, to be an arthropode if a sentence of the form "the thing x is an arthropode" is "deducible from premises of the form 'x is an animal,' 'x has a segmented body,' 'x has jointed legs' ..." (1932/1959, p. 63). Since the components that enter into the concept provide a definition of the concept, verifying that these components are satisfied is tantamount to verifying that the defined concept is satisfied as well. And since it's often assumed that the ultimate constituents of each concept express sensory properties, the verification procedure for a concept's primitive features is supposed to be unproblematic. The result is that justification for abstract or complicated concepts—including the "theoretical" concepts of science—reduces to a series of steps that implicate procedures with little epistemic risk.

Analyticity and Analytic Inferences   Another important motivation for the Classical Theory is its ability to explain a variety of semantic phenomena, especially analytic inferences. Intuitively, there is a significant difference between the inferences in (1) and (2):

(1)   Smith is an unmarried man. So Smith is a man.

(2)   Smith is a weight-lifter. So Smith is a man.

In (1), unlike (2), the conclusion that Smith is a man seems to be guaranteed by the premise. Moreover, this guarantee seems to trace back to the meaning of the key phrase in (1), namely, "unmarried man."

Traditionally, analytic inferences have been taken to be inferences that are based on meaning, and a sentence or statement has been taken to be analytic just in case its truth is necessitated by the meanings of its constituent terms. Much of this conception of analyticity is captured in Immanuel Kant's account of analyticity as conceptual containment. "Either the predicate B belongs to the subject A, as something which is (covertly) contained in this concept A; or B lies outside the concept A, although it does indeed stand in connection with it. In the one case I entitle the judgment analytic, in the other synthetic" (1787/1965, p. 48). One of the most widely cited examples in the contemporary literature is the concept BACHELOR. Consider (3):

(3)   Smith is a bachelor. So Smith is a man.

The inference in (3) is not only correct but seems to be guaranteed by the fact that it is part of the meaning of "bachelor" that bachelors are men. It's not as if one has to do a sociological study. The Classical Theory explains why one needn't look to the world in assessing (3), by claiming that the concept BACHELOR has definitional structure that implicates the concepts MAN, UNMARRIED, and so on. Thus (3) and (1) turn out to be similar, under analysis.

Katz (1972) gives much the same explanation of the validity of the inferences from (4.13)

(4.13)   There is a chair in the room.

to (4.14)–(4.21)

(4.14)   There is a physical object in the room.

(4.15)   There is something nonliving in the room.

(4.16)   There is an artifact in the room.

(4.17)   There is a piece of furniture in the room.

(4.18)   There is something portable in the room.

(4.19)   There is something having legs in the room.

(4.20)   There is something with a back in the room.

(4.21)   There is a seat for one person in the room.

According to Katz, all of these inferences are to be explained by reference to the concept CHAIR and its definition, given above as (4.10). The definition is supposed to be understood in Kantian terms, by supposing that the one concept—CHAIR—contains within it the other concepts that secure the inferences—ARTIFACT, PHYSICAL OBJECT, and so on. The only difference, then, between (1) and (3), or (1) and the inferences from (4.13) to (4.14–4.21), is that the logical form of (1) is manifest, whereas the forms underlying the other inferences are hidden.[13]

Reference Determination   One of the most important properties of concepts is that they are semantically evaluable. A thought may be true or false, depending on how things are with that portion of the world which the thought is about. In like fashion, an item may fall under a concept or not, depending on the concept's referential properties. When someone categorizes something as a bird, for example, she may or may not be right. This is perhaps the most basic feature of what is called the *normativity of meaning*. Just because she applies the concept BIRD to the item (in the sense that she judges it to be a bird) doesn't mean that the concept truly applies to the item (in the sense that the item is in the extension of the concept BIRD).

The referential properties of a concept are among its most essential properties. When one acquires the concept ROBIN, doing so crucially involves acquiring a concept that *refers* to robins. And when one draws an inference from ROBIN to IS A BIRD, or IS AN ANIMAL, one draws an inference *about* robins. This isn't to say that reference is sufficient to distinguish between concepts. TRIANGULAR and TRILATERAL refer to exactly the same class of mathematical objects, yet they are different concepts for all that. And in Plato's time, one might have believed that PIETY and ACTING IN A WAY THAT IS PLEASING TO THE GODS are coextensive—perhaps even necessarily coextensive—but that doesn't make them the same concept. Thus Plato can sensibly ask whether an action is pious because it is pleasing to the gods or whether it is pleasing to the gods because it is pious (1981).

That concepts have referential properties is a truism, but an important truism. A clear desideratum on a theory of concepts is that it should account for, or at least be

---

13. If (1) is considered to be a logical truth, then much the same point can be put by saying that the Classical Theory explains the other inferences by reducing informal validity to logical necessity.

compatible with, the referential properties of concepts.[14] According to the Classical Theory, a concept refers to those things that satisfy its definition. That is, a concept represents just those things that satisfy the conditions that its structure encodes. The appeal of this account is how nicely it meshes with the Classical Theory's other motivations. Concept acquisition, categorization, and so on are all explained in terms of the definitional structure that determines the reference of a concept. Its account of reference determination is what unifies the Classical Theory's explanatory power.

2.2. The Retreat from Definitions

Any theory that can do as much as the Classical Theory promises to do deserves serious consideration. In recent years, however, the theory has been subjected to intense criticism, and many feel that in spite of its obvious attractions the Classical Theory can't be made to work. We'll look at six of the main criticisms that have been raised against the Classical Theory.

Plato's Problem[15]   Perhaps the most basic problem that has been leveled against the Classical Theory is that, for most concepts, there simply aren't any definitions. Definitions have proven exceptionally difficult to come by, especially if they have to be couched in perceptual or sensory terms in accordance with empiricist strictures. Locke, in discussing the concept LIE, gives a sketch of what its components should look like (1690/1975, p. 166):

> 1. Articulate Sounds. 2. Certain *Ideas* in the Mind of the Speaker. 3. Those words the signs of those *Ideas*. 4. Those signs put together by affirmation or negation, otherwise that the *Ideas* they stand for, are in the mind of the Speaker.

He adds (p. 166),

> I think I need not go any farther in the Analysis of that complex *Idea*, we call a *Lye*: What I have said is enough to shew, that it is made up of simple *Ideas*: And it could not but be an offensive tediousness to my Reader, to trouble him with a more minute enumeration of every particular simple *Idea*, that goes into this complex one; which, from what has been said, he cannot but be able to make out to himself.

Unfortunately, it is *all but obvious* how to complete the analysis, breaking the concept down into simple, sensory components. As several authors have observed (Armstrong et al. 1983 [chapter 10 in this volume]; Fodor, J. A. 1981), it isn't even clear that definitions such as the one suggested by Locke bring us any *closer* to the level of sensory

---

14. We say that this is a clear desideratum, but others disagree. See, e.g., Ray Jackendoff (1991) and (1989 [chapter 13 in this volume]). Jackendoff's main objection is that he thinks that reference and truth and other related notions are tied to an incorrect metaphysics, one according to which the world exists entirely independently of our ways of conceptualizing it. Jackendoff's concerns tap into deep and controversial issues in philosophy, but they are misplaced in the present context. The main distinction that we want to insist on is the difference between true and false judgments. Sometimes you are right when you think that something is a bird, sometimes you are wrong. This distinction holds whether or not *bird* is a mind-independent kind or not. To put much the same point in Kantian terms, even if we only have epistemic access to the phenomenal world, we can still make incorrect judgments about what goes on there.
15. What we call Plato's Problem shouldn't be confused with an issue which is given the same name by Noam Chomsky (1986). Chomsky's concern is with how we can know as much as we do, given our limited experience. The concern of the present section, however, is that concepts are extremely hard to define.

concepts than the concept under analysis. Are the concepts SPEAKER, AFFIRMATION, NEGA-TION, or STANDING FOR really any closer to the sensory level than the concept LIE.[16]

Even putting aside the empiricist strictures, however, there are few, if any, examples of definitions that are uncontroversial. Some of the most intensively studied concepts are those connected to the central topics of philosophy. Following Plato, many philosophers have tried to provide definitions for concepts like KNOWLEDGE, JUS-TICE, GOODNESS, TRUTH, and BEAUTY. Though much of interest has come from these attempts, no convincing definitions have resulted.

One of the more promising candidates has been the traditional account of KNOWL-EDGE as JUSTIFIED TRUE BELIEF. But even this account is now widely thought to be inadequate, in particular, because of Gettier examples (named after Edmund Gettier who first put forward an example of this kind in his 1963 paper "Is Justified True Belief Knowledge?"). Here is a sample Gettier case (Dancy 1985, p. 25):

> Henry is watching the television on a June afternoon. It is Wimbledon men's finals day, and the television shows McEnroe beating Connors; the score is two sets to none and match point to McEnroe in the third. McEnroe wins the point. Henry believes justifiably that
>
>   1   I have just seen McEnroe win this year's Wimbledon final.
>
> and reasonably infers that
>
>   2   McEnroe is this year's Wimbledon champion.
>
> Actually, however, the cameras at Wimbledon have ceased to function, and the television is showing a recording of last year's match. But while it does so McEnroe is in the process of repeating last year's slaughter. So Henry's belief 2 is true, and surely he is justified in believing 2. But we would hardly allow that Henry knows 2.

Notice that the significance of the example is that each condition in the proposed analysis of KNOWLEDGE is satisfied yet, intuitively, we all know that this isn't a case of knowledge. Philosophers concerned with the nature of KNOWLEDGE have responded in a variety of ways, usually by supplementing the analysis with further conditions (see Dancy 1985 for discussion). One thing is clear, though: Despite a tremendous amount of activity over a long period of time, no uncontroversial definition of KNOWLEDGE has emerged.

Nor is the situation confined to concepts of independent philosophical interest. Ordinary concepts have resisted attempts at definition as well. Wittgenstein (1953/1958) famously argues that the concept GAME cannot be defined. His argument consists of a series of plausible stabs at definition, followed by clear counterexamples (see the excerpt reprinted as chapter 6 in this volume). For instance, he considers and rejects the proposal that a game must be an activity that involves competition (counterexample: a card game such as patience or solitaire), or that a game must involve winning or losing (counterexample: throwing a ball against a wall and catching it).

16. A related point is that many concepts seem to involve functional elements that can't be eliminated (e.g., it may be essential to chairs that they are designed or used to be sat upon). These preclude a definition in purely sensory terms. Cf. Clark (1973), quoted above, and Miller and Johnson-Laird (1976).

In much the same spirit, Jerry Fodor (1981) considers several proposals for the concept PAINT$_{tr}$, corresponding to the transitive verb "paint." Fodor's example is quite dramatic, as he tries to show that PAINT$_{tr}$ cannot be defined even using, among other things, the concept PAINT, corresponding to the noun "paint." The first definition he considers is: X COVERS Y WITH PAINT (based on Miller 1978). Fodor argues that one reason this definition doesn't work is that it fails to provide a sufficient condition for something falling under the concept PAINT$_{tr}$. If a paint factory explodes and covers some spectators in paint, this doesn't count as an instance of PAINTING—the factory or the explosion doesn't paint the spectators—yet the case is an instance of the original proposal. What seems to be missing is that an agent needs to be involved, and the surface that gets covered in paint does so as a result of the actions of the agent. In other words: X PAINT$_{tr}$ Y if and only if X IS AN AGENT AND X COVERS THE SURFACE OF Y WITH PAINT. But this definition doesn't work either. If you, an agent, kick over a bucket of paint, and thereby cover your new shoes with paint, you haven't painted them. We seem to need that the agent intentionally covers the surface with paint. Yet even this isn't enough. As Fodor says, Michelangelo wasn't painting the ceiling of the Sistine Chapel; he was painting a picture on the ceiling. This is true, even though he was intentionally covering the ceiling with paint. The problem seems to be with Michelangelo's intention. What he primarily intended to do was paint the picture on the ceiling, not paint the ceiling. Taking this distinction into account we arrive at something like the following definition: X PAINT$_{tr}$ Y if and only if X IS AN AGENT AND X INTENTIONALLY COVERS THE SURFACE OF Y WITH PAINT AND X'S PRIMARY INTENTION IN THIS INSTANCE IS TO COVER Y WITH PAINT. Yet even this definition isn't without its problems. As Fodor notes, when Michelangelo dips his paintbrush in the paint, his primary intention is to cover the tip of his paintbrush with paint, but for all that, he isn't painting the tip of his paintbrush. At this point, Fodor has had enough, and one may have the feeling that there is no end in sight—just a boundless procession of proposed definitions and counterexamples.[17]

Of course, there could be any number of reasons for the lack of plausible definitions. One is that the project of specifying a definition is much harder than anyone has supposed. But the situation is much the same as it may have appeared to Socrates' interlocutors, as portrayed in Plato's dialogues: Proposed definitions never seem immune to counterexamples. Even the paradigmatic example of a concept with a definition (BACHELOR = UNMARRIED MAN) has been contested. Is the Pope a bachelor? Is Robinson Crusoe? Is an unmarried man with a long-term partner whom he has lived with for years?[18] As a result of such difficulties, the suspicion in much of cognitive science has come to be that definitions are hard to formulate because our concepts lack definitional structure.

17. To be fair, Fodor's discussion may not do justice to the Classical Theory. In particular, it's not clear that the force of his counterexamples stems from the meaning of PAINT$_{tr}$, rather than pragmatic factors. Certainly there is something odd about saying that Michelangelo paints his paintbrush, but the oddness may not be owing to a semantic anomaly.

18. See Fillmore (1982) and Lakoff (1987 [chapter 18 in this volume]). We should add that Lakoff's position is more complicated than just insisting that BACHELOR and the like constitute counterexamples to the Classical Theory, though others may read these cases that way. Rather, he maintains that BACHELOR has a definition but that the definition is relativized to an "idealized cognitive model" that doesn't perfectly match what we know about the world. To the extent that such mismatches occur, problematic cases arise.

The Problem of Psychological Reality A related difficulty for the Classical Theory is that, even in cases where sample definitions of concepts are granted for the purpose of argument, definitional structure seems psychologically irrelevant. The problem is that definitional structure fails to turn up in a variety of experimental contexts where one would expect it to. In particular, the relative psychological complexity of lexical concepts doesn't seem to depend on their relative definitional complexity.[19]

Consider the following example of an experiment by Walter Kintsch, which has been used to try to locate the effects of conceptual complexity in lexical concepts (reported in Kintsch 1974, pp. 230–233).[20] It is based on a phoneme-monitoring task, originally developed by D. J. Foss, where subjects are given two concurrent tasks. They are asked to listen to a sentence for comprehension and, at the same time, for the occurrence of a given phoneme. When they hear the phoneme, they are to indicate its occurrence as quickly as they can, perhaps by pressing a button. To ensure that they continue to perform both tasks and that they don't just listen for the phoneme, subjects are asked to repeat the sentence or to produce a new sentence that is related to the given sentence in some sensible way.

In Foss's original study, the critical phoneme occurred either directly after a high-frequency word or directly after a low-frequency word. He found that reaction time for identifying the phoneme correlated with the frequency of the preceding word. Phoneme detection was quicker after high-frequency words, slower after low-frequency words (Foss 1969). The natural and by now standard explanation is that a greater processing load is introduced by low-frequency words, slowing subjects' response to the critical phoneme.

Kintsch adopted this method but changed the manipulated variable from word frequency to definitional complexity. He compared subjects' reaction times for identifying the same phoneme in the same position in pairs of sentences that were alike apart from this difference: In one sentence the phoneme occurred after a word that, under typical definitional accounts, is more complex than the corresponding word in the other sentence. The stimuli were controlled for frequency, and Kintsch used a variety of nouns and verbs, including the mainstay of definitional accounts, the causatives. For example, consider the following pair of sentences:

(1) The doctor was *convinced* o̲nly by his visitor's pallor.

(2) The story was *believed* o̲nly by the most gullible listeners.[21]

This first test word ("convince") is, by hypothesis, more complex than the second ("believe"), since on most accounts the first is analyzed in terms of the second. That is, "convince" is thought to mean *cause to believe*, so that CONVINCE would have BELIEVE as a constituent.

Kintsch found that in pairs of sentences like these, the speed at which the critical phoneme is recognized is unaffected by which of the two test words precedes it. So

19. The reason the focus has been on lexical concepts is that there is little doubt that the psychological complexity associated with a phrase exceeds the psychological complexity associated with one of its constituents. In other words, the psychological reality of definitions at the level of phrases isn't in dispute.
20. For related experiments and discussion, see J. A. Fodor et al. (1980 [chapter 21 in this volume]), and J. D. Fodor et al. (1975).
21. Italics indicate the words whose relative complexity is to be tested; underlines indicate the phoneme to be detected.

the words (and corresponding concepts) that definitional accounts predict are more complex don't introduce a relatively greater processing load. The natural explanation for this fact is that definitions aren't psychologically real: The reason definitions don't affect processing is that they're not there to have any effect.

It's not obvious, however, how worried defenders of the Classical Theory ought to be. In particular, it's possible that other explanations could be offered for the failure of definitions to affect processing; definitions might be "chunked," for instance, so that they function as a processing unit. Interestingly, a rather different kind of response is available as well. Classical theorists could abandon the model of conceptual structure that these experimental investigations presuppose (viz., the Containment Model). If, instead, conceptual structure were understood along the lines of the Inferential Model, then definitional complexity wouldn't be expected to manifest itself in processing studies. The availability of an alternative model of conceptual structure shows that the experimental investigation of conceptual structure has to be more subtle. Still, Kintsch's study and others like it do underscore the lack of evidence in support of the Classical Theory. While this is by no means a decisive point against the Classical Theory, it adds to the doubts that arise from other quarters.

The Problem of Analyticity   With few examples on offer and no psychological evidence for definitional structure, the burden for the Classical Theory rests firmly on its explanatory merits. We've seen that the Classical Theory is motivated partly by its ability to explain various semantic phenomena, especially analytic inferences. The present criticism aims to undercut this motivation by arguing that analyticities don't require explaining because, in fact, there aren't any. Of course, if this criticism is right, it doesn't merely challenge an isolated motivation for the Classical Theory. Rather, it calls into question the theory as a whole, since every analysis of a concept is inextricably bound to a collection of purported analyticities. Without analyticity, there is no Classical Theory.

Skepticism about analyticity is owing largely to W. V. O. Quine's famous critique of the notion in "Two Dogmas of Empiricism" [chapter 5 in this volume] and related work (see esp. Quine 1935/1976, 1954/1976). Quine's critique involves several lines of argument and constitutes a rich and detailed assessment of logical positivism, which had put analyticity at the very center of its philosophy in its distinction between meaningless pseudo-propositions and genuine (or meaningful) ones. Roughly, meaningful propositions were supposed to be the ones that were verifiable, where the meaning of a statement was to be identified with its conditions of verification. Verification, in turn, was supposed to depend upon analyticity, in that analyticities were to act as a bridge between those expressions or phrases that are removed from experience and those that directly report observable conditions. Since facts about analyticities are not themselves verifiable through observation, they needed a special epistemic status in order to be meaningful and in order for the whole program to get off the ground. The positivists' solution was to claim that analyticities are tautologies that are fixed by the conventions of a language and therefore known a priori. On this view, then, a priori linguistic analysis should be able to secure the conditions under which a statement would be verified and hence provide its meaning. This program is behind Carnap's idea that the definition or analysis of a concept provides a condition of justification for thoughts involving that concept. To be justified in thinking that spiders are arthropods one need only verify that spiders are animals, have jointed legs, segmented bodies, and so on.

The theory that analytic statements are tautologies also helped the positivists in addressing a long-standing difficulty for empiricism, namely, how to account for the fact that people are capable of a priori knowledge of factual matters even though, according to empiricism, all knowledge is rooted in experience. Mathematics and logic, in particular, have always been stumbling blocks for empiricism. The positivists' solution was to claim that logical and mathematical statements are analytic. Since they also held that analyticities are tautologies, they were able to claim that we can know a priori the truths of logic and mathematics because, in doing so, we don't really obtain knowledge of the world (see, e.g., Ayer 1946/1952; Hahn 1933/1959).

As is clear from this brief account of the role of analyticity in logical positivism, the positivists' program was driven by epistemological considerations. The problem was, assuming broadly empiricist principles, how to explain our a priori knowledge and how to account for our ability to know and speak of scientific truths that aren't directly observable. Considering the vast range of scientific claims—that atoms are composed of protons, neutrons, and electrons, that the universe originated from a cosmic explosion 10 to 20 billion years ago, that all animals on Earth descended from a common ancestor, etc.—it is clear that the positivists' program had truly enormous scope and ambition.

Quine's attack on the notion of analyticity has several components. Perhaps the most influential strand in Quine's critique is his observation, following Pierre Duhem, that confirmation is inherently holistic, that, as he puts it, individual statements are never confirmed in isolation. As a consequence, one can't say in advance of empirical inquiry what would confirm a particular statement. This is partly because confirmation involves global properties, such as considerations of simplicity, conservatism, overall coherence, and so on. But it's also because confirmation takes place against the background of auxiliary hypotheses, and that, given the available evidence, one isn't forced to accept, or reject, a particular statement or theory so long as one is willing to make appropriate adjustments to the auxiliaries. On Quine's reading of science, no statement has an isolatable set of confirmation conditions that can be established a priori, and, in principle, there is no guarantee that any statement is immune to revision.

Some examples may help to clarify these points and ground the discussion. Consider the case of Newton's theory of gravitation, which was confirmed by a variety of disparate and (on a priori grounds) unexpected sources of evidence, such as observations of the moons of Jupiter, the phases of Venus, and the ocean tides. Similarly, part of the confirmation of Darwin's theory of evolution is owing to the development of plate tectonics, which allows for past geographical continuities between regions which today are separated by oceans. This same case illustrates the dependency of confirmation on auxiliary hypotheses. Without plate tectonics, Darwin's theory would face inexplicable data. A more striking case of dependency on auxiliary hypotheses comes from an early argument against the Copernican system that cited the absence of annual parallax of the fixed stars. Notice that for the argument to work, one has to assume that the stars are relatively close to the Earth. Change the assumption and there is no incompatibility between the Earth's movement and the failure to observe parallax. There are also more mundane cases where auxiliary hypotheses account for recalcitrant data, for instance, when college students attempt to replicate a physical experiment only to arrive at the wrong result because of any number of interference effects. Finally, as Hilary Putnam has emphasized, a principle that appears to be immune from rejection may turn out to be one that it's rational to abandon in the context of unexpected theoretical developments. A classic example that draws from the history of science is the definition of a straight line as the shortest distance between two points—a definition that isn't correct, given that our universe isn't Euclidean. The connection between STRAIGHT LINE and THE SHORTEST DISTANCE BETWEEN TWO POINTS may have seemed as secure as any could be. Yet in the context of alternative geometries and contemporary cosmological theory, it not only turns out to be something that can be doubted, but we can now see that it is false (see Putnam 1962). What's more, Putnam and others have extended these considerations by imagining examples that illustrate the breadth of possible scientific discoveries. They've argued that we could discover, for instance, that gold or lemons aren't yellow or that cats aren't animals, thereby breaking what otherwise might have looked like the best cases of analyticities among familiar concepts.[22]

How does all this bear on the Classical Theory of concepts? Some philosophers hold that Quine has succeeded in showing that there is no tenable analytic-synthetic distinction and that this mean that concepts couldn't be definable in the way that the Classical Theory requires. However, the issue isn't so simple. Quine's critique is largely directed at the role that analyticity plays in the positivists' epistemological program, in particular, against the idea that there are statements that can be known a priori that are insulated from empirical test and that can establish specific, isolatable conditions of verification for the statements of scientific theories. If Quine is right that confirmation is holistic, then one can't establish these specific, isolatable conditions of verification. And if he is right that no statement is immune to revision, then there can't be statements that are known to be true a priori and therefore protected from future theoretical developments. So the positivist program falls flat. But the notion of analyticity needn't be tied to this explanatory burden. Analyticity simply understood as *true in virtue of meaning alone* might continue to be a viable and useful notion in describing the way that natural language and the human conceptual system works (Antony 1987; Horwich 1992). That is, for all that Quine says, there may still be a perfectly tenable analytic-synthetic distinction; it's just one that has none of the epistemological significance that the positivists took it to have. Purported analyticities are to be established on a posteriori grounds and are open to the same possibilities of disconfirmation as claims in any other part of science.

Still, Putnam's extension of Quine's considerations to examples like STRAIGHT LINE ($\neq$ SHORTEST DISTANCE ...) or GOLD ($\neq$ YELLOW METAL ...) may be disturbing to those who would like to defend the notion of analyticity. If theoretical developments allow for the rejection of these conceptual connections, then perhaps no purported analyticity will hold up to scrutiny. More or less, this direction of thought has led many philosophers to be skeptical of definitional analyses in any form, regardless of their epistemic status. The thought is that the potential revisability of nearly every statement—if only under conditions of a fantastical thought experiment—shows that the aim for definitions is futile. Yet it's hardly clear that this attitude is war-

22. For arguments that these considerations are, in fact, quite far-reaching, see Burge (1979). For arguments that we might turn out to be mistaken about the defining properties of even the paradigmatic classical concept, BACHELOR, see Lormand (1996) and Giaquinto (1996).

ranted. Its appeal may stem from paying too much attention to a limited range of examples. It may be that the cases Putnam and others have discussed are simply misleading; perhaps the concepts for the kinds in science are special. This would still leave us with thousands of other concepts. Consider, for example, the concept KILL. What surrounding facts could force one to revise the belief that killings result in death? Take someone who is honest and sincerely claims that although he killed his father, his father isn't dead or dying. No matter what the surrounding facts, isn't the plausible thing to say that the person is using the words "kill" and "dead" with anomalous meanings? At any rate, one doesn't want to prejudge cases like this on the grounds that other cases allow for revisions without changes in meaning.

In the first instance, Quine's critique of analyticity turns out to be a critique of the role of the Classical Theory in theories of justification, at least of the sort that the positivists imagined. To the extent that his arguments are relevant to the more general issue of analyticity, that's because the potential revisability of a statement shows that it isn't analytic; and many philosophers hold that this potential spans the entire language. Whether they are right, however, is an empirical question. So the issue of what analyticities there are turns on a variety of unresolved empirical matters.

The Problem of Ignorance and Error   In the 1970s Saul Kripke and Hilary Putnam both advanced important arguments against *descriptivist* views of the meaning of proper names and natural kind terms (Kripke 1972/1980; Putnam 1970 [chapter 7 in this volume], 1975).[23] (Roughly, a descriptivist view is one according to which, in order to be linguistically competent with a term, one must know a description that counts as the meaning of the term and picks out its referent.) If correct, these arguments would apparently undermine the Classical Theory, which is, in effect, descriptivism applied to concepts.[24] Kripke and Putnam also sketched the outlines of an alternative positive account of the meaning of such terms, which, like their critical discussions, has been extremely influential in philosophy.

Kripke and Putnam offer at least three different types of arguments that are relevant to the evaluation of the Classical Theory. The first is an argument from error. It seems that we can possess a concept in spite of being mistaken about the properties that we take its instances to have. Consider, for example, the concept of a disease, like SMALLPOX. People used to believe that diseases like smallpox were the effects of evil spirits or divine retribution. If any physical account was offered, it was that these diseases were the result of "bad blood." Today, however, we believe that such people were totally mistaken about the nature of smallpox and other diseases. Saying this, however, presupposes that their concept, SMALLPOX, was *about* the same disease that our concept is about. They were mistaken because the disease that their concept referred to—smallpox—is very different in nature than they had supposed. Presumably, then, their most fundamental beliefs about smallpox couldn't have been part of a definition of the concept. For if they had been, then these people wouldn't have been wrong about smallpox; rather they would have been thinking and speaking

23. For arguments that similar considerations apply to an even wider range of terms, again, see Burge (1979).
24. Again, we will move freely from claims about language to claims about thought, in this case adapting Kripke's and Putnam's discussions of natural kind terms to the corresponding concepts. For an interesting discussion of how these arguments relate to the psychology of concepts, see Rey (1983 [chapter 12 in this volume]).

about some other possible ailment. Closely related to this type of argument is another, namely, an argument from ignorance. Continuing with the same example, we might add that people in the past were ignorant about a number of crucial properties of smallpox—for example, that smallpox is caused by the transmission of small organisms that multiply in great numbers inside the body of a host, and that the symptoms of the disease are the result of the causal effect of these organisms on the host's body.

Arguments from ignorance and error present compelling reasons to suppose that it's possible to possess a concept without representing necessary or sufficient conditions for its application. The conditions that a person actually associates with the concept are likely to determine the wrong extension for the concept, both by including things that do not belong in the extension, and by excluding things that do belong. By failing to represent such crucial properties of smallpox as its real nature and cause, we are likely to be left with merely symptomatic properties—properties that real cases might lack, and noncases might have.

The third type of argument is a modal argument. If an internally represented definition provides necessary and sufficient conditions for the application of a concept, it determines not just what the concept applies to as things actually stand but also what it would apply to in various possible, nonactual circumstances. The problem, however, is that the best candidates for the conditions that people ordinarily associate with a concept are ones which, by their own lights, fail to do justice to the modal facts. Thus, to change the example, we can perfectly well imagine circumstances under which gold would not have its characteristic color or other properties that we usually associate with gold. Perhaps if some new gas were to diffuse through the atmosphere, it would alter the color—and maybe various other properties—of gold. The stuff would still be gold, of course; it would simply lack its previous color. Indeed, we don't even need to imagine a hypothetical circumstance with gold, as it does lose its color and other characteristic perceptual properties in a gaseous state, yet gold-as-a-gas is still gold for all that.

One of the driving motivations behind Kripke's and Putnam's work is the intuition that we can learn important new facts about the things we think about. We can discover that gold, under other circumstances, might appear quite different to us, or that our understanding of the nature of a kind, like smallpox, was seriously in error. Discussions of these ideas are often accompanied by stories of how we might be wrong about even the most unassailable properties that are associated with ordinary concepts like GOLD, CAT, or LEMON. These stories sometimes require quite a stretch of imagination (precisely because they attempt to question properties that we would otherwise never imagine that instances of the concept could lack). The general point, however, is that we don't know which concepts we might be wrong about, or how wrong we might be. Even if some of our concepts for natural kinds have internally represented definitions which happen to determine a correct extension, it seems likely that many others do not. And if the reference of these other concepts is not mediated by definitions, we need some other account of how it is determined. This suggests that, for natural kind concepts in general, classical definitions do not mediate reference determination.

Another example might be helpful. Consider the concept HUMAN BEING. As it happens, people's views on the nature and origin of humans vary immensely. Some people believe that human beings have an immaterial soul which constitutes their true essence. They believe that humans were created by a deity, and that they have an eternal life. Others believe that human beings are nothing but complex collections of physical particles, that they are the result of wholly physical processes, and that they have short, finite lives. And of course there are other views of humans as well.[25] Such beliefs about humans are held with deep conviction and are just the sort that one would expect to form part of a classical definition of HUMAN BEING. But presumably, at least one of these groups of people is gravely mistaken; notice that people from these different groups could—and do—argue about who is right.

How, then, is the reference of a concept to be fixed if not by an internalized definition? The Kripke/Putnam alternative was originally put forward in the context of a theory of natural language, but the picture can be extended to internal representations, with some adjustments. Their model is that a natural kind term exhibits a causal-historical relation to a kind and that the term refers to all and only members of the kind. In the present case, the assumption is that *human being* constitutes a kind and that, having introduced the term and having used it in (causal-historical) connection with humans, the term refers to all and only humans, regardless of what the people using it believe.[26]

This theory isn't without its problems, but for present purposes it pays to see how it contrasts with the Classical Theory.[27] One way to put the difference between the Kripke/Putnam account and the Classical Theory is that the Classical Theory looks to internal, psychological facts to account for reference, whereas the Kripke/Putnam account looks to external facts, especially facts about the nature of the paradigmatic examples to which a term has been historically applied. Thus much of the interest in Kripke's and Putnam's work is that it calls into question the idea that we have internally represented necessary and sufficient conditions that determine the extension of a concept.

Their arguments are similar in spirit to ones that came up in the discussion of analyticity. Here, too, classical theorists might question the scope of the objection. And, in fact, it does remain to be seen how far the Kripke/Putnam arguments for an externalist semantics can be extended. Even among the most ardent supporters of externalism, there is tremendous controversy whether the same treatment can extend beyond names and natural kind terms.

The Problem of Conceptual Fuzziness Another difficulty often raised against the Classical Theory is that many concepts appear to be "fuzzy" or inexact. For instance, Douglas Medin remarks that "the classical view implies a procedure for unambiguously determining category membership; that is, check for defining features." Yet, he adds, "there are numerous cases in which it is not clear whether an example belongs to a category" (Medin 1989, p. 1470). Are carpets furniture? One often buys carpet-

25. To mention just one, many people believe in reincarnation. Presumably, they take human beings to be something like transient stages of a life that includes stages in other organisms. It's also worth noting that past theoretical accounts of the nature of humans have been flawed. For example, neither "featherless biped" nor "rational animal" is sufficiently restrictive.
26. Michael Devitt and Kim Sterelny have done the most to develop the theory. See esp. Devitt (1981) and Devitt and Sterelny (1987).
27. The most serious of these problems has come to be known as the *Qua Problem*, that is, how to account for the fact that a word or concept has a determinate reference, despite being causally related to multiple kinds. For example, what accounts for the fact that CAT refers to cats and not to mammals, living things, or material objects? If the concept is causally related to cats, then it is automatically causally related to these other kinds too. For discussion, see Devitt and Sterelny (1987).

ing in a furniture store and installs it along with couches and chairs in the course of furnishing a home; so it may seem uncomfortable to say that carpets aren't furniture. At the same time, it may seem uncomfortable to say that they are. The problem for the Classical Theory is that it doesn't appear to allow for either indeterminacy in category membership or in our epistemic access to category membership. How can a Classical Theory account of FURNITURE allow it to be indeterminate whether carpets fall under FURNITURE, or explain how we are unable to decide whether carpets fall under FURNITURE?

Though this difficulty is sometimes thought to be nearly decisive against the Classical Theory, there are responses that a classical theorist could make. One resource is to appeal to a corresponding conceptual fuzziness in the defining concepts. Since the Classical Theory claims that concepts have definitional structure, it is part of the Classical Theory that a concept applies to all and only those things to which its definition applies. But definitions needn't themselves be perfectly sharp. They just have to specify necessary and sufficient conditions. In other words, fuzziness or vagueness needn't prohibit a definitional analysis of a concept, so long as the analysis is fuzzy or vague to exactly the same extent that the concept is (Fodor, J. A. 1975; Grandy 1990a; Margolis 1994). For instance, it is more or less uncontroversial that BLACK CAT can be defined in terms of BLACK and CAT: It is necessary and sufficient for something to fall under BLACK CAT that it fall under BLACK and CAT. All the same, we can imagine borderline cases where we aren't perfectly comfortable saying that something is or isn't a black cat (perhaps it's somewhere between determinately gray and determinately black). Admittedly, it's not perfectly clear how such a response would translate to the FURNITURE/CARPET example, but that seems more because we don't have a workable definition of either FURNITURE or CARPET than anything else. That is, the Problem of Fuzziness for these concepts may reduce to the first problem we mentioned for the Classical Theory—the lack of definitions.

The Problem of Typicality Effects   The most influential argument against the Classical Theory in psychology stems from a collection of data often called *typicality effects*. In the early 1970s, a number of psychologists began studying the question of whether all instances of a given concept are on equal footing, as the Classical Theory implies. At the heart of these investigations was the finding that subjects have little difficulty ranking items with respect to how "good they are" or how "typical they are" as members of a category (Rosch 1973). So, for example, when asked to rank various fruits on a scale of 1 to 7, subjects will, without any difficulty, produce a ranking that is fairly robust. Table 1.1[28] reproduces the results of one such ranking.

What's more, rankings like these are generally thought to be reliable and aren't, for the most part, correlated with the frequency or familiarity of the test items (Rosch and Mervis 1975; Mervis, Catlin, and Rosch 1976).[29]

Typicality measures of this sort have been found to correlate with a wide variety of other psychological variables. In an influential study, Eleanor Rosch and Carolyn Mervis (1975) had subjects list properties of members of various categories. Some

---

28. Based on Rosch (1973), table 3. For comparison, Malt and Smith (1984) obtained the following values: Apple (6.25), Strawberry (5.0), Fig (3.38), Olive (2.25), where on their scale, 7 indicates the highest typicality ranking.

29. However, see Barsalou (1987) for a useful critical discussion of the reliability of these results.

Table 1.1

Fruit	Typicality rating on a scale of 1–7 (with 1 being highest)
Apple	1.3
Plum	2.3
Pineapple	2.3
Strawberry	2.3
Fig	4.7
Olive	6.2

Table 1.2

Feature	Bird	Robin	Chicken	Vulture
Flies	yes	yes	no	yes
Sings	yes	yes	no	no
Lays eggs	yes	yes	yes	no
Is small	yes	yes	no	no
Nests in trees	yes	yes	no	yes
Eats insects	yes	yes	no	no

properties occurred in many of the lists that went with a category, others occurred less frequently. What Rosch and Mervis found was that independent measures of typicality predict the distribution of properties that occur in such lists. An exemplar is judged to be typical to the extent that its properties are held to be common among other exemplars of the same superordinate category.[30] For instance, robins are taken to have many of the properties that other birds are taken to have, and correspondingly, robins are judged to be highly typical birds, whereas chickens or vultures, which are judged to be significantly less typical birds, are taken to have fewer properties in common with other birds (see table 1.2).[31]

Importantly, typicality has a direct effect on categorization when speed is an issue. The finding has been, if subjects are asked to judge whether an X is a Y, that independent measures of typicality predict the speed of correct affirmatives. So subjects are quicker in their correct responses to "Is an apple a fruit?" than to "Is a pomegranate a fruit?" (Rosch 1973; Smith, Shoben, and Rips 1974). What's more, error rates correlate with typicality. The more typical the probe relative to the target category, the fewer errors.[32]

The problem these results pose for the Classical Theory is that it has no natural model for why they should occur. Rather, the Classical Theory seems to predict that

30. In the literature, *exemplar* is used to denote subordinate concepts or categories, whereas *instance* is used to denote individual members of a given category.
31. Based on Smith (1995), table 1.3.
32. Typicality measures correlate with a variety of other phenomena as well. See Rosch (1978 [chapter 8 in this volume]).

all exemplars should be on a par. If falling under BIRD is a matter of satisfying some set of necessary and sufficient conditions, then all (and only) birds should do this equally. And if categorizing something as a bird is a matter of determining that it satisfies each of the required features for being a bird, there is no reason to think that "more typical" exemplars should be categorized more efficiently. It's not even clear how to make sense of the initial task of rating exemplars in terms of "how good an example" they are. After all, shouldn't all exemplars be equally good examples, given the Classical Theory's commitment that they all satisfy the same necessary and sufficient conditions for category membership?

In an important and influential overview of the intellectual shift away from the Classical Theory, Edward Smith and Douglas Medin note that there are, in fact, classical models that are compatible with various typicality results (Smith and Medin 1981). As an example, they suggest that if we assume that less typical members have more features than typical ones, and we also assume that categorization involves an exhaustive, serial, feature-matching process, then less typical members should take longer to categorize and cause more processing errors. After all, with more features to check, there will be more stages of processing. But the trouble with this and related models is that they involve ad hoc assumptions and conflict with other data. For instance, there is no reason to suppose that atypical exemplars have more features than typical ones.[33] Also, the model incorrectly predicts that atypical exemplars should take longer to process in cases where the categorization involves a negated target (an X is not a Y). It should take longer, that is, to judge that a chicken is not a fish than to judge that a robin is not a fish, but this just isn't so. Finally, the account has no explanation of why typicality correlates with the distribution of features among exemplars of a superordinate category.

Also, it's worth noting that the features that are involved in the typicality data are not legitimate classical features since most are not necessary. A quick look at table 1.2 makes this clear: *none* of the features listed there is necessary for being a bird; none is shared by all three exemplars. So an explanation in terms of the number of features can't really get off the ground in the first place, since the features at stake aren't classical.

In sum, then, typicality effects raise serious explanatory problems for the Classical Theory. At the very least, they undermine the role of the Classical Theory in categorization processes. But, more generally, they suggest that the Classical Theory has little role to play in explaining a wide range of important psychological data.

The Classical Theory has dominated theorizing about concepts from ancient times until only quite recently. As we have just seen, though, the theory is not without serious problems. The threats posed by these objections are not all of the same strength, and, as we've tried to emphasize, the Classical Theory has some potential responses to mitigate the damage. But the cumulative weight against the theory is substantial and has been enough to make most theorists think that, in spite of its impressive motivations, the Classical Theory simply can't be made to work.

33. If anything, it would be the opposite, since subjects usually list more features for typical exemplars than for atypical ones. But one has to be careful about taking "feature lists" at face value, as the features that subjects list are likely to be governed by pragmatic factors. For instance, no one lists for BIRD that birds are objects. Most likely this is because it's so obvious that it doesn't seem relevant.

Box 2

Summary of Criticisms of the Classical Theory

1. **Plato's Problem**
   There are few, if any, examples of defined concepts.
2. **The Problem of Psychological Reality**
   Lexical concepts show no effects of definitional structure in psychological experiments.
3. **The Problem of Analyticity**
   Philosophical arguments against analyticity also work against the claim that concepts have definitions.
4. **The Problem of Ignorance and Error**
   It is possible to have a concept in spite of massive ignorance and/or error, so concept possession can't be a matter of knowing a definition.
5. **The Problem of Conceptual Fuzziness**
   The Classical Theory implies that concepts have determinate extensions and that categorization judgments should also yield determinate answers, yet concepts and categorization both admit of a certain amount of indeterminacy.
6. **The Problem of Typicality Effects**
   Typicality effects can't be accommodated by classical models.

3. The Prototype Theory of Concepts

3.1. The Emergence of Prototype Theory

During the 1970s, a new view of concepts emerged, providing the first serious alternative to the Classical Theory. This new view—which we will call the *Prototype Theory*—was developed, to a large extent, to accommodate the psychological data that had proved to be so damaging to the Classical Theory. It was the attractiveness of this new view, as much as anything else, that brought about the downfall of the Classical Theory.

There is, of course, no single account to which all prototype theorists subscribe. What we are calling the Prototype Theory is an idealized version of a broad class of theories, which abstracts from many differences of detail. But once again putting qualifications to the side, the core idea can be stated plainly. According to the Prototype Theory, most concepts—including most lexical concepts—are complex representations whose structure encodes a statistical analysis of the properties their members tend to have.[34] Although the items in the extension of a concept *tend* to have these properties, for any given feature and the property it expresses, there may be items in the extension of a concept that fail to instantiate the property. Thus the features of a concept aren't taken to be necessary as they were on the Classical Theory. In addition, where the Classical Theory characterized sufficient conditions for concept application in terms of the satisfaction of all of a concept's features, on the Prototype Theory application is a matter of satisfying a sufficient number of features, where some may be weighted more significantly than others. For instance, if BIRD is composed of such features as FLIES, SINGS, NESTS IN TREES, LAYS EGGS, and so on, then on the

---

34. More likely they are structured and interconnected sets of features (Malt and Smith 1984). For example, with the concept BIRD, features for size and communication might be linked by the information that small birds sing and large birds don't.

Prototype Theory, robins are in the extension of BIRD because they tend to have all of the corresponding properties: robins fly, they lay eggs, etc. However, BIRD also applies to ostriches because even though ostriches don't have all of these properties, they have enough of them.[35]

This rejection of the Classical Theory's proposed necessary and sufficient conditions bears an affinity to Wittgenstein's suggestion that the things that fall under a concept often exhibit a family resemblance. They form "a complicated network of similarities overlapping and criss-crossing: sometimes overall similarities, sometimes similarities of detail" (Wittgenstein 1953/1968 [chapter 6 in this volume], p. 32). In fact, Eleanor Rosch and Carolyn Mervis, two important and influential figures in the development of the Prototype Theory, explicitly draw the parallel to Wittgenstein's work (1975, p. 603):

> The present study is an empirical confirmation of Wittgenstein's (1953) argument that formal criteria are neither a logical nor psychological necessity; the categorical relationship in categories which do not appear to possess criterial attributes, such as those used in the present study, can be understood in terms of the principle of family resemblance.

For Wittgenstein, as for Rosch and Mervis, a word or concept like GAME isn't governed by a definition but rather by a possibly open-ended set of properties which may occur in different arrangements. Some games have these properties, some have those, but despite this variation, the properties of games overlap in a way that establishes a similarity space. What makes something a game is that it falls within the boundaries of this space.

Because the Prototype Theory relaxes the constraints that the Classical Theory imposes on a concept's features, it is immune to some of the difficulties that are especially challenging for the Classical Theory. First among these is the lack of definitions. Since the Prototype Theory claims that concepts don't have definitional structure, it not only avoids but actually predicts the difficulty that classical theorists have had in trying to specify definitions. Similarly, the Prototype Theory is immune to the problems that the Classical Theory has with analyticity. Given its rejection of the classical idea that concepts encode necessary conditions for their application, the Prototype Theory can wholeheartedly embrace the Quinean critique of analyticity. Additionally, the theory makes sense of the fact that subjects generally list nonnecessary properties in the generation of feature lists.

The rejection of necessary conditions also highlights the Prototype Theory's emphasis on nondemonstrative inference. This is, in fact, another advantage of the theory, since one function of concepts is to allow people to bring to bear relevant information upon categorizing an instance or exemplar. Yet encoding information isn't without its tradeoffs. As Rosch puts it, "[T]he task of category systems is to provide maximum information with the least cognitive effort...." (1978 [chapter 8 in this volume], p. 28). What this means is that representational systems have to strike

---

35. For convenience, it will be useful to refer to a such structure as a concept's "prototype." We should point out, however, that the term "prototype" doesn't have a fixed meaning in the present literature and that it's often used to refer to the exemplar that has the highest typicality ratings for a superordinate concept (as, e.g., when someone says that ROBIN is the prototype for BIRD).

a balance.[36] On the one hand, a concept should encode a considerable amount of information about its instances and exemplars, but on the other, it shouldn't include so much that the concept becomes unwieldy. The solution offered by the Prototype Theory is that a concept should encode the distribution of statistically prominent properties in a category. By representing statistically prominent properties, concepts with prototype structure generate many more inferences than do classical representations; they trade a few maximally reliable inferences for many highly reliable though fallible ones.[37]

The Prototype Theory also has an attractive model of concept acquisition—in fact, much the same model as the Classical Theory. In both cases, one acquires a concept by assembling its features. And, in both cases, it's often assumed that the features correspond to sensory properties. The main difference is that on the Prototype Theory, the features of a concept express statistically prominent properties. So on the Prototype Theory the mechanism of acquisition embodies a statistical procedure. It doesn't aim to monitor whether various properties always co-occur, but only whether they tend to. Of course, to the extent that the Prototype Theory inherits the empiricist program associated with the Classical Theory, it too faces the problem that most concepts resist analysis in sensory terms. The trouble with empiricism, remember, isn't a commitment to definitions but a commitment to analyzing concepts in purely sensory terms. If LIE was a problem for Locke, it's just as much a problem for prototype theorists. Assuming they can articulate some plausible candidate features, there is still no reason to think that all of these can be reduced to a sensory level. This is true even for their stock examples of concepts for concrete kinds, concepts like BIRD or FRUIT.[38] But, like the Classical Theory, the Prototype Theory can be relieved of its empiricist roots. When it is, its model of concept acquisition is at least as compelling as the Classical Theory's.

Probably the most attractive aspect of the Prototype Theory is its treatment of categorization. Generally speaking, prototype theorists model categorization as a similarity comparison process that involves operations on two representations—one for the target category and one for an instance or an exemplar. (For ease of expression, we'll frame the discussion in terms of instances only, but the same points go for exemplars as well.) On these models, an instance is taken to be a member of a category just in case the representation of the instance and the representation of the category are judged to be sufficiently similar. The advantage of this approach is that similarity-based categorization processes lay the groundwork for a natural explana-

36. Rosch, however, sharply distances herself from any psychological interpretation of this work (see Rosch 1978). But as we are interested in the bearing of research in this tradition on theories of concepts construed as mental particulars, we will not discuss nonpsychological interpretations.

37. For Rosch, much of the interest in the efficiency of a conceptual system concerns its hierarchical structure. "[N]ot all possible levels of categorization are equally good or useful; rather, the most basic level of categorization will be the most inclusive (abstract) level at which the categories can mirror the structure of attributes perceived in the world" (1978, p. 30). According to Rosch and her colleagues the basic level in a conceptual system is defined in terms of its informational potential relative to other levels in the hierarchy, and its effects are widespread and can be independently measured. For instance, basic level concepts appear early in cognitive and linguistic development, they have priority in perceptual categorization, and, in a hierarchy, they pick out the most abstract categories whose members are similar in shape. For discussion, see Rosch (1978) and Rosch et al. (1976).

38. Look at most discussions and you'll find that the sample features for BIRD are things like WINGS, FLIES, EATS WORMS, SINGS, and so on. Notice, though, that none of these is more "sensory" than BIRD itself.

tion of typicality effects. To see how this works, we need to take a closer look at the notion of similarity.

Prototype theorists have developed a number of different psychological measures for similarity. Perhaps the most commonly used is Amos Tversky's (1977) "Contrast Principle" (see, e.g., Smith et al. 1988 [chapter 17 in this volume]).[39] The idea behind this principle is that the judged similarity of any two items, i and j, is measured by comparing the sets of shared and distinctive features that are associated with them. Where I and J are the feature sets, the function can be defined as follows:

$$\text{Sim } (I, J) = af(I \cap J) - bf(I - J) - cf(J - I)$$

The constants a, b, and c allow for different weights to be assigned to the set of common features ($I \cap J$) and to each set of distinctive features ($I - J$ and $J - I$), and the function f allows for weights to be assigned to individual features. To illustrate how the principle works, consider the measure of similarity between BIRD and TWEETIE, where the latter is a representation that, for simplicity, incorporates just four features: FLIES, SINGS, IS SMALL, and LAYS EGGS. Also assume that the sets of common and distinctive features are each given an equal weight of 1 (i.e., a, b, and c are all 1) and that the function f assigns each of the individual features equal weight. Then, using the six features in table 1.2, the similarity of TWEETIE to BIRD is $4 - 2 - 0 = 2$. Presumably, this is sufficiently high to count Tweetie as a bird.[40]

Now the Contrast Principle measures the psychological similarity of two categories, but it doesn't specify the computational procedure that actually generates the judgment. For a sample processing model, consider this simple schematic account (see Smith and Medin 1981; Smith 1995): To compute the similarity of a given object to a target category, one compares the feature sets associated with the object and the category, possibly checking all the features in parallel. As each feature is checked, one adds a positive or negative value to an accumulator, depending on whether it is a common feature or not. When the accumulator reaches a certain value, the judgment is made that the item is sufficiently similar to the target category to count as a member; items that are computed to have a lower value are judged insufficiently similar— they are taken to be nonmembers.

This isn't the only model of categorization that is open to prototype theorists. Yet even one as straightforward as this generates much of the typicality data:

> *Graded Judgments of Exemplariness*   Recall the datum that subjects find it a natural task to rank exemplars for how typical they are for a given category. Apples are judged to be more typical of fruit than olives are. The accumulator model explains this phenomena under the assumption that the very same mechanism that is responsible for categorization is also responsible for typicality judgments. Since the mechanism results in a similarity judgment, and since similarity is itself a graded notion, it's no surprise that some exemplars are considered to be more typical than others. The ones that are more similar to the

39. For other measures of similarity, see Shepard (1974) and Estes (1994). For further discussion, see Medin et al. (1993), Gleitman et al. (1996), and *Cognition* 65, nos. 2–3—a special issue devoted to the topic of similarity.

40. The same measure also works in the comparison of a representation of an exemplar and a superordinate concept. For instance, using table 1.2 again, the similarity of ROBIN to BIRD is $6 - 0 - 0 = 6$, and the similarity of CHICKEN to BIRD is $1 - 5 - 0 = -4$.

target are the ones that are judged to be more typical; the ones that are less similar to the target are the ones that are judged to be less typical.

Typicality Correlates with Property Lists   The reason the distribution of features in subjects' property lists predicts the typicality of an exemplar is that the properties that are the most common on such lists characterize the structure of the concept that is the target of the similarity-comparison process. Taking the example of BIRD and its exemplars, the idea is that the properties that are commonly cited across categories such as *robin, sparrow, hawk, ostrich,* and so on, are the very properties that correspond to the features of BIRD. Since ROBIN has many of the same features, robins are judged to be highly typical birds. OSTRICH, on the other hand, has few of these features, so ostriches are judged to be less typical birds.

Graded Speed of Quick Categorization Judgments   Assuming that the individual feature comparisons in the similarity-comparison process take varying amounts of time, the outcome of each comparison will affect the accumulator at different times. As a result, items that are represented to have more features in common with a target will be judged more quickly to be members. A less thorough comparison is required before a sufficient number of shared features is registered.

Categorization Errors Are Inversely Correlated with Typicality   For less typical exemplars, more feature comparisons will be needed before a sufficient number of shared features is reached, so there are more chances for error.

The accumulator model also explains certain aspects of conceptual fuzziness. Prototype theorists often cite fuzziness as a point in favor of their theory, while not saying much about what the fuzziness of concepts consists in. One way of unpacking the notion, however, is that judgments about whether something falls under a concept are indeterminate, that is, the psychological mechanisms of categorization do not yield a judgment one way or the other.

> *Fuzziness*   To predict fuzziness in this sense, the model need only be supplemented with the following qualification: Where an exemplar isn't clearly similar enough to a target by a prespecified margin the result is neither the judgment that it falls under the target concept nor the judgment that it doesn't.

From this brief survey of the data, one can see why the Prototype Theory has been held in such high regard. Not only does it seem to be immune to some of the difficulties surrounding the Classical Theory, but it addresses a wide variety of empirical data as well. While there is virtually no doubt about the importance of these data, a number of problems have been raised for the theory, problems that are largely directed at its scope and interpretation. Some of these problems have been thought to be serious enough to warrant a radical reworking of the theory, or even its abandonment. We'll discuss four.

Box 3

The Prototype Theory

Most concepts (esp. lexical concepts) are structured mental representations that encode the properties that objects in their extension tend to possess.

3.2. Problems for the Prototype Theory

The Problem of Prototypical Primes   In an important early critical discussion of the Prototype Theory, Sharon Armstrong, Lila Gleitman, and Henry Gleitman investigated the question of whether well-defined concepts, such as EVEN NUMBER or GRANDMOTHER, exhibit typicality effects (Armstrong et al. 1983). ("Well-defined" here means that people know and can readily produce the concepts' definitions.) Armstrong et al. argued that if typicality effects reveal that a concept has statistical structure, then well-defined concepts shouldn't exhibit typicality effects. Using four well-defined concepts, they showed that people nonetheless find it natural to rank exemplars according to how good they are as members of such concepts.[41] Just as apples are ranked as better examples of fruit than figs are, the number 8 is ranked as a better example of an even number than the number 34 is. What's more, Armstrong et al. found that typicality rankings for well-defined concepts correlate with other data in accordance with some of the standard typicality effects. In particular, typicality correlates with speed and accuracy of categorization. Just as subjects produce correct answers for "Is an apple a fruit?" faster than for "Is a fig a fruit?" they produce correct answers for "Is 8 an even number?" faster than for "Is 34 an even number?" The conclusion that Armstrong et al. reached was that the considerations that are standardly thought to favor the Prototype Theory are flawed. "[T]o the extent that it is secure beyond doubt that, e.g., FRUIT and PLANE GEOMETRY FIGURE have different structures, a paradigm that cannot distinguish between responses to them is not revealing about the structure of concepts" (p. 280). In other words, Armstrong et al. took their findings to be evidence that typicality effects don't argue for prototype structure.

A common way of thinking about prototypes—and the one that Armstrong et al. assume—is to interpret a concept with prototype structure as implying that subjects represent its extension as being graded. On this view of prototypes, subjects think that robins are literally "birdier" than ostriches, just as Michael Jordan is literally taller than Woody Allen. The reason prototypes are read this way is because of the focus on typicality judgments. Typicality judgments are then explained as reflecting people's views about the degree to which the instances of an exemplar instantiate a category. Unsatisfied with the argument that moves from typicality judgments to prototype structure, Armstrong et al. asked subjects outright whether various categories are graded, including their four well-defined categories. What they found was that, when asked directly, people actually claim that well-defined concepts aren't graded—and many hold that other categories, such as *fruit*, aren't graded either—but even so they remain willing to rank exemplars for how good they are as members. Although Armstrong et al.'s subjects unanimously said that *even number* is an all-or-none category, the tendency was still to say 8 is a better example of an even number than 34 is.

Armstrong et al. took this to be further evidence that the arguments for prototype structure involve deep methodological problems. Yet this may be too strong of a conclusion. One could hold instead that typicality effects do argue for prototype

---

41. The four concepts Armstrong et al. investigated were EVEN NUMBER, ODD NUMBER, FEMALE, and PLANE GEOMETRY FIGURE. Though they didn't test the concept PRIME NUMBER, we feel it's safe to say that this concept would exhibit the same effects. For example, we bet that subjects would say that 7 is a better example of a prime number than 113 is.

structure but that prototype structure has no implications for whether subjects represent a category as being graded. In other words, the proposal is that typicality judgments reflect an underlying prototype; it's just that prototypes needn't involve a commitment to graded membership.

If typicality judgments aren't about degrees of membership, what are they about? We are not sure that there is a simple answer. Yet it's not unreasonable to think much of what's going on here relates back to properties that are represented as being highly indicative of a category. The difference between ROBIN and OSTRICH, on this view, is that robins are represented as possessing more of the properties that, for one reason or another, are taken to be the usual signs that something is a bird. But the usual signs needn't themselves be taken to be constitutive of the category. So long as one believes that they aren't, and that they merely provide evidence for whether something is a member of the category, the number of signs an item exhibits needn't determine a degree to which it instantiates the category.

The distinction between properties that are represented as being evidential and those that are represented as being constitutive is especially pertinent when categorization takes place under pressures of time and limited resources. In a pinch, it makes sense to base a categorization judgment on the most salient and accessible properties—the very ones that are most likely to be merely evidential. The conclusion that many psychologists have drawn from this observation is that categorization can't be expected to be a univocal affair. Given the correlations between judged typicality and quick category judgments for both accuracy and speed, the Prototype Theory provides a compelling account of at least part of what goes on in categorization. But considered judgments of category membership seem to tell a different story. This has prompted a variety of theorists to put forward *Dual Theories* of concepts, where one component (the "identification procedure") is responsible for quick categorization judgments and the other component (the "core") is called upon when cognitive resources aren't limited (Osherson and Smith 1981 [chapter 11 in this volume]; Smith et al. 1984; Landau 1982).[42] Such Dual Theories have often been thought to give the best of both worlds—the Prototype Theory's account of fast categorization and the Classical Theory's account of more thoughtful categorization, especially where the relevant properties are hidden or in some way less accessible. For instance, in discussing the merits of Dual Theories, Smith et al. (1984) are careful to insist that both the core and the identification procedure are accessed in categorization processes. The difference between them, they claim, can be illustrated with the concept GENDER. "Identification properties might include style of clothing, hair, voice, etc., while core properties might involve having a particular kind of sexual organs. As this example suggests, our distinction centers on notions like salience, computability, and diagnosticity..." (p. 267).

---

42. The division of labor between the core and the identification procedure hasn't been fully worked out in the literature. For instance, in the text we adopt the interpretation according to which the difference between cores and identification procedures is just a matter of how they enter into categorization processes. Another difference that's often cited is that cores are the primary, or perhaps the only, component that enters into the compositional principles that determine the semantics of complex concepts on the basis of their constituents. But it is at least open to question whether the components responsible for making considered judgments of category membership are also the ones that compositionally generate the semantics of complex concepts. We discuss this issue further below.

Unfortunately, such a view ignores the difficulties that are associated with the theories it tries to combine. For instance, if there was a problem before about specifying definitions, adding a prototype component to a classical component doesn't eliminate the problem. Nor does it help with the Problem of Ignorance and Error, which, as it turns out, arises for both theories in isolation and so can't help but arise for a Dual Theory.

The Problem of Ignorance and Error   Since the Prototype Theory requires a way of fixing the extensions of concepts, ignorance and error are still as much a problem as they were for the Classical Theory. Indeed, in some ways they are actually more of a problem for the Prototype Theory. Take, for example, the concept GRANDMOTHER. Prototypical grandmothers are old, they have gray hair and glasses, they are kind to children, and, let's suppose, they like to bake cookies. The problem is that someone can satisfy these properties without being a grandmother, and someone can be a grandmother without satisfying these properties. Tina Turner is a grandmother. So is Whoopi Goldberg.

Much the same point applies to concepts that lack definitions or whose definitions aren't generally known. Consider, once again, the concept SMALLPOX. The properties that most people associate with this disease, if any, are its symptoms—high fever, skin eruptions, and so on. And since symptoms are, in general, reliable effects of a disease, they are good candidates for being encoded in prototype representations. At the same time, the Prototype Theory faces a serious difficulty: Because symptoms aren't constitutive of a disease but are instead the effects of a variety of causal interactions, they aren't completely reliable guides to the presence of the disease. Someone could have the symptoms without having the disease, and someone could have the disease without the symptoms. As Armstrong et al. note, birds with all their feathers plucked are still birds, and "3-legged, tame, toothless, albino tigers" are still tigers (1983, p. 296). Nor is a convincing toy tiger a tiger. The point is that everyone knows this and is prepared to acknowledge it, so, by their own lights, prototype representations don't determine the correct extension for a concept like BIRD or TIGER. Prototype representations lack sufficient richness to include all birds or all tigers, and at the same time they are, in a sense, too rich in that they embody information that includes things that aren't birds or tigers.

One way to avoid these conclusions that some might find tempting is to claim that if something doesn't fit a concept's prototype, then it doesn't really fall under the concept. That is, one might make the radical move of denying that TIGER applies to our toothless, 3-legged creature. The idea behind this suggestion is that how a concept is deployed determines what items fall under it. Yet while this view may have some initial appeal, it can't be made to work—it's really far too crude. Not only would it imply that 3-legged albino tigers aren't tigers and that convincing tiger toys are, but in general, it would rule out the possibility of *any* misrepresentation. When Jane is nervously trekking through the Amazon jungle, fearful of snakes, and she is startled by what she takes to be a snake lying across her path just ahead, we want it to be possible that she could actually be mistaken, that it could turn out that she was startled by a snake-shaped vine, and not a snake at all. But if categorization processes determine the extension of the concept, then this item has to be a snake: Since it was categorized as falling under SNAKE, it *is* a snake. In short, on this suggestion there is no room for the possibility of a concept being misapplied, and this is just too high a price to pay.[43]

Notice that Dual Theories might help somewhat, if it's assumed that conceptual cores are involved in categorization. The core would provide Jane with a definition of SNAKE that would have the final word on whether something falls under the concept by providing a more substantial procedure for deciding whether something is a snake. Then her mistake could be credited to the deployment of an identification procedure; what would make it a mistake is that the outcome of the identification procedure fails to match the outcome of the core. Presumably, were Jane to deploy the core, she'd be in a position to recognize her own error. But as we've already noted, Dual Theories aren't much of an advance, since they reintroduce the difficulties that face the Classical Theory.

Another mark against the present form of a Dual Theory is that it inherits the difficulties associated with a verificationist semantics. For instance, people's procedures for deciding whether something falls under a concept are subject to change as they acquire new information, new theories, and (sometimes) new technologies. Yet this doesn't mean that the concept's identity automatically changes. To return to the example of a disease, when two people differ on the symptoms they associate with measles, they would appear to be in disagreement; that is, they appear to be arguing about the best evidence for deciding whether measles is present. But if the identity of MEASLES is given by the procedures under which one decides whether it is instantiated, then we'd have to say that the two couldn't genuinely disagree about the symptoms associated with measles. At best, they would be talking at cross purposes, one about one ailment, the other about another. The same goes for a single person over time. She couldn't come to change her mind about the best indications of measles, since in adopting a new procedure of verification she'd thereby come to deploy a new concept. We take it that these difficulties offer good prima facie grounds for shying away from a verificationist version of the Dual Theory.

The Missing Prototypes Problem   The strongest evidence in favor of the Prototype Theory is that subjects find it natural to rate exemplars and instances in terms of how representative they are of a given category and the fact that these ratings correlate with a range of psychological phenomena. But although this is true of many concepts, it is by no means true of all concepts. Many concepts aren't associated with typicality judgments, and for many concepts, people fail to represent any central tendencies at all. As Jerry Fodor has put it (1981, pp. 296–297):

> There may be prototypical *cities* (London, Athens, Rome, New York); there may even be prototypical *American cities* (New York, Chicago, Los Angeles), but there are surely no prototypical *American cities situated on the East Coast just a little south of Tennessee.* Similarly, there may be prototypical *grandmothers* (Mary Worth) and there may be prototypical *properties of grandmothers* (*good, old* Mary Worth). But there are surely no prototypical properties of, say, *Chaucer's grand-*

43. Note that nothing turns on the example being a natural kind (where it's plausible that science is the best arbiter of category membership). The point is just that, wherever there is representation, there is the potential for misrepresentation. An account that doesn't permit misrepresentation simply isn't an adequate theory of concepts.

mothers, and there are no prototypical properties of *grandmothers most of whose grandchildren are married to dentists.*

It's important to see that this is not at all an isolated problem, or an artifact of a few exotic examples. Indefinitely many complex concepts lack prototype structure. Some fail to have prototype structure because people simply don't have views about the central tendencies of the corresponding categories. This seems to be the case with many uninstantiated concepts:

- U.S. MONARCH
- 4TH CENTURY SAXOPHONE QUARTET
- 31ST CENTURY INVENTION
- GREAT-GREAT-GREAT GRANDCHILD OF CINDY CRAWFORD

Others lack prototype structure because their extensions are too heterogeneous:

- A CONSEQUENCE OF PHYSICAL PROCESSES STILL GOING ON IN THE UNIVERSE
- OBJECTS THAT WEIGH MORE THAN A GRAM
- NEW SPECIES
- NOT A WOLF
- FROG OR LAMP

Still others lack prototype structure for other reasons:

- BELIEF[44]
- THE RADIATION BEING THE SAME IN EVERY DIRECTION TO A PRECISION OF ONE PART IN ONE HUNDRED THOUSAND
- PIECE OF PAPER I LEFT ON MY DESK LAST NIGHT
- IF X IS A CHAIR, X IS A WINDSOR[45]

A related problem is that it's perfectly possible to have a concept without knowing a prototype, even if others who possess the concept do. Thus, for example, you could have the concept of a DON DELILLO BOOK or a FRISBEE-GOLF COACH without representing any properties as being statistically prominent in the corresponding categories, even though other people may have strong views about the matter. Delillo fans know that his books are usually funny, they have slim plots, and are laced with poignant observations of American popular culture. But if you haven't read a Delillo book, you may not know any of this. Still, what's to stop you from possessing the concept, using it to support inductive inferences, organize memory, or engage in categorization? If you know that Don Delillo's books are usually well stocked at Barnes and Noble, then you may infer that Barnes and Noble is likely to have Delillo's latest book. If you are told that his latest is *Underworld*, then you will remember it as a Delillo book. And later, when you go to Barnes and Noble and you see a copy of *Underworld*, you will categorize it as a Delillo book. It would seem, then, that concept possession doesn't require a representation with prototype structure.

---

44. Osherson and Smith (1981) suggest that concepts like BELIEF, DESIRE, and JUSTICE may lack prototype structure because they are too "intricate"—a somewhat vague yet intriguing idea.

45. For some discussion of concepts that involve Boolean constructions, see Fodor (1998). Fodor points out that these concepts are generally subject to what he calls the *Uncat Problem*, namely, they lack prototypes.

The objection that many concepts lack prototype structure is standardly presented as an issue about compositionality, since most of the concepts that lack prototypes are patently complex. Compositionality is certainly an important feature of the conceptual system, as it provides the best explanation for one of the most important and striking features of human thought—its productivity. Important as compositionality is, however, it's not really needed for the present objection. The force of the Missing Prototypes Problem is simply that many concepts lack prototype structure and that it's often possible to possess a concept without thereby knowing a prototype.

The implications of this objection aren't always given their full due. Edward Smith, for example, suggests that the Prototype Theory isn't intended to be a general theory of concepts. He says that some classes, such as *objects that weigh forty pounds*, are arbitrary and that "the inductive potential of a class may determine whether it is treated as a category" (1995, p. 7). The representation OBJECTS THAT WEIGH FORTY POUNDS, however, is a perfectly fine concept, which one can readily use to pick out a property. For any of a variety of purposes, one might seek to find an object that weighs forty pounds, categorize it as such, and reason in accordance with the corresponding concept. In any event, though there is nothing wrong with the idea that concepts divide into groups requiring different theoretical treatments, we still require an account of the concepts that aren't covered by the Prototype Theory. Given that there seem to be indefinitely many such concepts, the question arises whether prototypes are central and important enough to concepts generally to be considered part of their nature. Perhaps it is more appropriate to say that many lexical concepts have prototypes associated with them but that these prototypes aren't in any way constitutive of the concepts.

Another option—one that aims to mitigate the damage caused by the Missing Prototypes Problem—is (once again) to appeal to a Dual Theory. The idea might be that for some concepts it is possible to have the concept without having both components. So for these concepts, not knowing a prototype is fine. The advantage of this sort of Dual Theory would appear to be that it allows for a univocal treatment of all concepts; one needn't appeal to a completely distinct theory for those concepts that lack prototypes. Yet it's hardly clear that this is much of a gain, since the resulting Dual Theory fails to preserve the spirit of the Prototype Theory. It looks like what's essential to a concept, on this view, is the classical core, with the prototype being (in many cases) merely an added option. In short, the Dual Theory is beginning to sound more and more like a supplemented version of the Classical Theory.

The Problem of Compositionality   One of the most serious and widely discussed objections to the Prototype Theory is the charge that it's unable to account for the phenomenon of compositionality. This difficulty seems especially pressing in light of the importance of compositionality in accounting for our ability to entertain an unbounded number of concepts. To the extent that anyone can foresee an explanation of this ability, it's that the conceptual system is compositional.[46]

Early discussions of compositionality in the literature on Prototype Theory were concerned with explaining how graded extensions could be combined. Thus these discussions were based on the assumption that most categories are graded in the

46. Which isn't to say that the details have been completely worked out or that there is no controversy about the content of the principle of compositionality. For discussion, see Grandy (1990b).

sense that items are members of a category to varying degrees (i.e., membership isn't an all-or-none matter).[47] The standard model for composing graded categories was a version of fuzzy set theory—a modification of standard set theory that builds on the notion of graded membership (see esp. Zadeh 1965). A fuzzy set can be understood in terms of a function that assigns to each item in the domain of discourse a number between 0 and 1, measuring the degree to which the item is in the set. If an item is assigned the value 1, it is wholly and completely inside the set. If it is assigned the value 0, it is wholly and completely outside the set. All values between 0 and 1 indicate intermediate degrees of membership, with higher values indicating higher degrees. Under these assumptions, fuzzy set theory characterizes a variety of operations that are analogues of the standard set-theoretic operations of intersection, union, and so on. Fuzzy set intersection, for example, is given in terms of the *Min Rule*: An item is a member of the fuzzy intersection of two sets to the minimum of the degrees to which it is an element of the two sets. If Felix is a cat to degree 0.9 and is ferocious to degree 0.8, then Felix is a ferocious cat to degree 0.8.[48]

In a seminal discussion of the Prototype Theory's reliance on fuzzy sets, Daniel Osherson and Edward Smith presented a number of forceful objections to this treatment of compositionality (Osherson and Smith 1981). One is a straightforward counterexample to the Min Rule. Consider the intersective concept STRIPED APPLE (intersective in that intuitively its extension is determined by the intersection of the corresponding categories—something is a striped apple just in case it's striped and an apple). Fuzzy set theory reconstructs this intuition by saying that the concept's extension is determined by fuzzy set intersection. That is, something is a striped apple to the minimum of the degrees that it is striped and that it is an apple. A consequence of this view is that nothing should be counted as a striped apple to a higher degree than it is counted as an apple. But, as Osherson and Smith point out, a very good instance of a striped apple will inevitably be a poor instance of an apple. The Min Rule simply makes the wrong prediction.[49] Perhaps more worrying still, consider the concept APPLE THAT IS NOT AN APPLE. Clearly, the extension of this concept is empty; it's logically impossible for something that is not an apple to be an apple. Yet fuzzy set theory's account of compositionality doesn't deliver this result. APPLE THAT IS NOT AN APPLE is just another intersective concept, combining APPLE and NOT AN APPLE. According to the Min Rule, something falls under it to the minimum of the degrees to which it is an apple and to which it is not an apple. Taking again a highly representative striped apple, we may suppose that such an item is taken to be an apple to a fairly low degree (perhaps 0.3) and striped to some higher degree (perhaps 0.8). Taking the complement of the fuzzy set of apples, our item is not-an-apple to the degree $1 - 0.3 = 0.7$. Since it will be an instance of APPLE THAT IS NOT AN APPLE to the minimum of the degrees to which it is an instance of APPLE (0.3) and to which it is an instance of NOT AN APPLE (0.7), it will be an instance of APPLE THAT IS NOT AN APPLE to degree 0.3.

47. This assumption seemed plausible to many in light of the fact that subjects were so willing to rate instances or exemplars of a concept in terms of how representative they were of the concept. But again, the results of Armstrong et al. (1983) show that the inference from such ratings to graded membership is mistaken.

48. In like fashion, the complement of a fuzzy set may be defined by taking the value of $1 - x$ for each element of the set. E.g., if Felix is in the set of cats to degree 0.9, then Felix is in the set of non-cats to degree $1 - 0.9 = 0.1$.

49. For an argument against a broader class of proposals (of which the Min Rule is a special case), see Osherson and Smith (1982).

Though difficulties like these may seem to be decisive against fuzzy set theory's model of compositionality, we should note that fuzzy set theory doesn't provide the only model of compositionality that is compatible with the Prototype Theory.[50] Still, compositionality has proven to be a notable stumbling block for prototypes.

The general objection that Prototype Theory cannot provide an adequate account of conceptual combination has been pushed most vigorously by Jerry Fodor. In this context, Fodor has argued both that many complex concepts simply don't have prototypes and that, when they do, their prototypes aren't always a function of the prototypes of their constituents. We've already dealt with the first sort of case, under the heading of the Problem of Missing Prototypes. To get a feel for the second, consider the concept PET FISH. The prototype for PET FISH is a set of features that picks out something like a goldfish. Prototypical pet fish are small, brightly colored, and they live in fish bowls (or small tanks). How does the prototype for PET FISH relate to the prototypes of its constituents, namely, PET and FISH?[51] Presumably, the features that constitute the prototypes for PET pick out dogs and cats as the most representative examples of pets—features such as FURRY, AFFECTIONATE, TAIL-WAGGING, and so on. The prototype for FISH, on the other hand, picks out something more like a trout or a bass—features such as GRAY, UNDOMESTICATED, MEDIUM-SIZED, and so on. Thus prototypical pet fish make rather poor examples both of pets and of fish. As a result, it's difficult to see how the prototype of the complex concept could be a function of the prototypes of its constituents.

One of the most interesting attempts to deal with the composition of complex prototypes is Smith, Osherson, Rips, and Keane's (1988 [chapter 17 in this volume]) Selective Modification Model. According to this model, conceptual combinations that consist of an adjectival concept (e.g., RED, ROUND) and a nominal concept (e.g., APPLE, FRUIT) in the form Adj + N are formed by a process where the adjectival concept modifies certain aspects of the nominal concept's structure. The nominal concept is taken to decompose into a set of features organized around a number of attributes. Each attribute is weighted for diagnosticity, and instead of having default values, each value is assigned a certain number of "votes," indicating its probability. For simplicity, Smith et al. consider only adjectival concepts assumed to have a single attribute (see figure 1.1). The way conceptual combination works is that the adjectival concept selects the corresponding attribute in the nominal concept's representation, increases its diagnosticity, and shifts all of the votes within the scope of the attribute to the value that the adjectival concept picks out. For instance, in the combination RED APPLE, the attribute COLOR is selected in the representation APPLE, its diagnosticity is increased, and the votes for all of the color features are shifted to RED (see figure 1.2).

Smith et al. subjected this model to the following sort of experimental test. By asking subjects to list properties of selected items, they obtained an independent measure of the attributes and values of a range of fruit and vegetable concepts. They took the number of listings of a given feature to be a measure of its salience (i.e., its number of votes), and they measured an attribute's diagnosticity by determining how useful it is in distinguishing fruits and vegetables. This allowed them to generate

50. Indeed, Osherson and Smith have proposed an alternative model of their own, which we will discuss shortly. See also Hampton (1991).

51. We take it that the empirical claims made here about the prototypes of various concepts are extremely plausible in light of other findings, but the claims are not based on actual experimental results. Accordingly, the arguments ultimately stand in need of empirical confirmation.

```
┌─────────────────────────────────────────┐
│              APPLE                        │
│                                           │
│  1  COLOR          RED  25                │
│                    GREEN  5               │
│                    BROWN                  │
│                       ...                 │
│                                           │
│  .5  SHAPE         ROUND  15              │
│                    SQUARE                 │
│                    CYLINDRICAL  5         │
│                       ...                 │
│                                           │
│  .25  TEXTURE      SMOOTH  25             │
│                    ROUGH  5               │
│                    BUMPY                  │
│                       ...                 │
│                                           │
└─────────────────────────────────────────┘
```

Figure 1.1
A partial representation of the structure of the concept APPLE. Each attribute (COLOR, SHAPE, TEXTURE) is weighted for diagnosticity, represented by the number to the left of the attribute. The values (RED, GREEN, ROUND, etc.) are each assigned a certain number of "votes," indicating their probability.

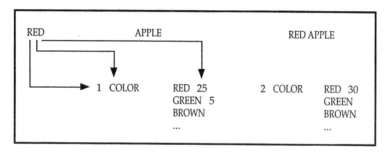

Figure 1.2
A schematic representation of the Selective Modification Model. RED combines with APPLE by selecting the attribute COLOR, increasing its diagnosticity, and shifting all of votes within its scope to RED (adapted from Smith et al. 1988, p. 493).

predictions for the typicality of exemplars for complex concepts such as RED VEGETABLE, ROUND FRUIT, and LONG VEGETABLE. Then they compared these predictions with the typicality ratings that subjects gave in an independent test. The average of the correlations between predictions and directly elicited typicality ratings was 0.70.[52]

Despite this success, the Selective Modification Model is highly limited—a point that Smith et al. themselves bring attention to. Even if we restrict the scope of a compositional theory to the simplest sorts of complex concepts, it doesn't cover nonintersective concepts (e.g., FAKE, ALLEGED, POSSIBLE) and it is especially unequipped to deal with cases where the modifier's effects transcend a single attribute, as, for example, with the concept WOODEN SPOON. (Wooden spoons are known to be larger

---

52. For vegetable concepts the average was 0.88. Abstracting from a few anomalous results which may have been due to a poor choice of exemplars, the average of all correlations would have been 0.87. See Smith et al. (1988) for details and further tests of the model.

than other spoons and used for cooking, not eating.)[53] It doesn't even cover the case we started with, namely, PET FISH.

Smith et al. suggest some ways in which the model might attempt to cope with these difficulties. One borrows an idea from James Hampton (1987), who notes that the prototypes for some complex concepts may be sensitive to real-world knowledge. For instance, your prototype for WOODEN SPOON may be more a result of experience with wooden spoons than your having constructed the concept from compositional principles. In Smith et al.'s hands, this suggestion emerges as a two-stage model. In the first stage, a prototype is constructed on a purely compositional basis, in accordance with the original mechanism of the Selective Modification Model; in the second, the prototype is subject to changes as world knowledge is brought into play. In principle, a more complicated model like this is capable of dealing with a fair number of the difficult examples we've mentioned. For instance, WOODEN SPOON needn't be so troublesome anymore. Perhaps people do construct a prototype in which just the MATERIAL COMPOSITION attribute for spoon is altered. Later, in the second stage, the attribute SIZE is altered as experience teaches that wooden spoons are typically larger than metal spoons. Perhaps PET FISH can be accommodated by a two-stage model as well.

The strongest objection to Hampton's suggestion is owing to Jerry Fodor and Ernest Lepore. They emphasize that one can't allow experience to fix the prototype of a complex concept without admitting that such prototypes are essentially idioms. But, they argue, if prototypes are idioms, then the Prototype Theory offers a wholly inadequate account of concepts (1996, p. 267):

> Prototypes aren't compositional; they work like idioms. Concepts, however, must be compositional; nothing else could explain why they are productive. So concepts aren't prototypes.

In addition, they argue that the two-stage model is implausible since as concepts get more complex (and we are less likely to have real-world knowledge about them), we don't default to a compositionally determined prototype. As an example, they point to the concept PET FISH WHO LIVE IN ARMENIA AND HAVE RECENTLY SWALLOWED THEIR OWNERS. Though no one has real-world knowledge for a concept like this—knowledge that might interfere with the effects of the Selective Modification Model—no one has a compositionally determined prototype either. Concepts like these simply lack prototypes.

Notice that the second of these objections is no more than a repetition of the Missing Prototypes Problem. The reply here will be much the same as it was there.[54]

---

53. For another example, consider MALE NURSE. Male nurses aren't taken to be just like other nurses, only male. Among other things, they wear different sorts of uniforms—slacks, not dresses. Thus the combination can't just be a matter of the modifier affecting the SEX attribute in NURSE, shifting all the votes to the value MALE. For some discussion of the significance of context effects in conceptual combination, see Medin and Shoben (1988).

54. Actually, we aren't so sure that highly modified concepts inevitably lack prototypes. For many cases it seems likely that people will have a sketchy idea of how to rank exemplars or instances for typicality. Take Fodor and Lepore's example: While we aren't prepared to say too much about these unusual fish, we do know they have to be fairly large if they are going to swallow people (who but a person owns a fish?). Among other things, this knowledge implies that goldfish are going to be extremely poor exemplars and that white sharks may be better. To the extent that one can make such judgments, this counts as evidence for a schematic prototype. If it's idiomatic, that's just to say that there are other ways to construct an idiomatic prototype than by having experience with members of the corresponding category. In this case, the idiom could derive from a reasoning process that incorporates information from the classical core and general background knowledge.

Smith et al. are free to adopt a Dual Theory.[55] Under a Dual Theory, concepts have two components—a classical core and an optional identification procedure with prototype structure. Since one can possess a concept while being in possession of just a core, the absence of a prototype is no problem at all. What's more, the absence of a prototype needn't prevent the concept from being compositional, so long as the core is compositional. And everyone agrees that if compositionality works anywhere, it works for classical conceptual components. In short, the failure of prototypes to compose doesn't argue against the Prototype Theory once it's admitted that concepts aren't *just* prototypes. Fodor and Lepore's arguments have no leverage against a Dual Theory.

On the other hand, we will need an account of how prototypes are constructed for those complex concepts that do have prototypes. Since people can generate prototypes for some novel complex concepts in the absence of any specific experience with members of the corresponding category, the implication is that at least part of the story will be compositional (cf. STRIPED APPLE, WOODEN BICYCLE, ORANGE ELEPHANT). This is the context in which the Selective Modification Model should be viewed. To the extent that compositional processes are responsible for the construction of prototypes, the model is pertinent. What the model doesn't aim to do is provide a comprehensive account of the composition of concepts. A theory of prototype composition is one thing, a theory of concept composition is another. Under a Dual Theory, concepts aren't (just) prototypes.

Fodor (1998) has another argument against Smith et al., but it too falls short once the implications of a Dual Theory are recognized. His argument is that PET FISH couldn't be an idiom, since it clearly licenses the inferences PET FISH → PET and PET FISH → FISH. In contrast, a paradigmatic idiom like KICKED THE BUCKET doesn't generate any such inferences. (If John kicked the bucket, it doesn't follow that there is something he kicked.) Fodor's gloss of this contrast is that the inferences in the case of PET FISH result from the compositional structure of the concept, in particular, its logical form. But, he claims, under the Prototype Theory, concepts don't have logical forms; they have prototype structure. By now the flaw in this reasoning should be fairly clear. A prototype theorist who opts for a Dual Theory can claim that concepts *do* have logical forms insofar as they have classical cores. PET FISH needn't be an idiom, even if its prototype is.[56]

Still, relying on a Dual Theory isn't unproblematic. Our main worry for the Prototype Theory in connection with the Smith et al. model of prototype combination is that prototypes seem more and more like cognitive structures that are merely associated with concepts rather than structures that are part of the nature of concepts. The more it's granted that prototypes are optional and that the prototypes for complex concepts act like idioms, the less essential prototypes seem to be. Once again,

---

55. Though they aren't perfectly explicit about the matter, it appears that they do adopt a Dual Theory when they claim that "prototypes do not exhaust the contents of a concept" (Smith et al. 1988, p. 486).

56. For this same reason, it won't do for Fodor and Lepore to argue that the weights assigned to the modified features aren't compositionally determined. "[W]hat really sets the weight of PURPLE in PURPLE APPLE isn't its prototype; it's its logical form" (1996, p. 264). Fodor and Lepore's point is that the modified feature in a simple construction is often given maximum weight, as if it didn't express a statistical property at all. True enough, but this needn't be anything more than a reflection of PURPLE APPLE's classical core. Alternatively, Smith et al. could add that their second stage of processing has access to the concept's core, letting classical modifiers adjust the corresponding features so that they receive a maximum weight.

with the core of a concept apparently doing so much work, the Dual theory beings to look more like a supplemented version of the Classical Theory. We should end this discussion, however, by emphasizing that the issues surrounding compositionality are extremely complicated and that there is much more to be said. We'll return to these issues in what we hope will be a new and illuminating context, when we examine some of the problems associated with Conceptual Atomism (sec. 6.2).

The Prototype Theory continues to be one of the dominant theories of concepts in psychology and cognitive science. This is understandable, given its ability to explain a wide range of psychological data. We've seen, however, that in the face of a number of problems related to concept possession and reference determination, prototype theorists are apt to fall back on the idea that concepts have classical cores. The result is that the Prototype Theory may inherit some of the difficulties that motivated it in the first place. This may be so, regardless of how strong the evidence is that concepts have prototype structure.

Box 4

Summary of Criticisms of the Prototype Theory

1. **The Problem of Prototypical Primes**
   Typicality effects don't argue for prototype structure, since even well-defined concepts exhibit typicality effects.
2. **The Problem of Ignorance and Error**
   Ignorance and error is as much a problem for the Prototype Theory as it is for the Classical Theory. Indeed, the problem is considerably worse for the Prototype Theory, since concepts with prototype structure fail to cover highly atypical instances and incorrectly include non-instances.
3. **The Missing Prototypes Problem**
   Many concepts lack prototypes.
4. **The Problem of Compositionality**
   The Prototype Theory does not have an adequate account of compositionality, since the prototypes of complex concepts aren't generally a function of the prototypes of their constituent concepts.

---

4. The Theory-Theory of Concepts

4.1. Theories, Explanations, and Conceptual Structure

In the past ten years or so, an increasing number of psychologists have gravitated to a view in which cognition generally is assimilated to scientific reasoning. The analogy to science has many strands. One is to distance the theory of categorization from early empiricist models, where categorization consisted of nothing more than a process of checking an instance against a list of sensory properties. Another is to liken concepts to theoretical terms, so that philosophical treatments of theoretical terms can be recruited in psychology. Yet another is to provide a characterization and explanation of conceptual change along the lines of theory change in science. Within the boundaries of these explanatory goals lies the *Theory-Theory of Concepts*.[57]

---

57. The terminology here is somewhat unfortunate, since "Theory-Theory" is also used in reference to a specific account of how people are able to attribute mental states to one another. The view is that they have an internalized theory of mind. See, e.g., Wellman (1990).

People who approach the Theory-Theory for the first time may find it somewhat confusing, because theory-theorists slip between talking about concepts being like theories and concepts being like theoretical terms—structures at entirely different levels. When theory-theorists say that concepts are mental theories, using expressions like the child's or the adult's "theory of number," the intended object of investigation is a body of propositions that articulate people's knowledge within a given domain. When theory-theorists say that concepts are like theoretical terms, they are concerned with the constituents of thoughts. The trouble, of course, is that the Theory-Theory can't at once be about concepts understood in both of these ways; that would amount to a mereological paradox.

A natural bridge between these two ways of appealing to theories is to give priority to the second notion (where concepts are likened to theoretical terms) but to explain their nature relative to the first notion. Susan Carey holds a view like this. The focus of much of Carey's research has been the characterization of how children understand things differently than adults in several important domains of cognition. In laying out the background to her investigations she is unusually explicit in isolating concepts from larger cognitive structures (Carey 1991 [chapter 20 in this volume], p. 258):

> Concepts are the constituents of beliefs; that is, propositions are represented by structures of concepts. Theories are complex mental structures consisting of a mentally represented domain of phenomena and explanatory principles that account for them.

And in her seminal book *Conceptual Change in Childhood*, she draws the connection between concepts and the mental theories in which they are embedded (1985, p. 198):

> One solution to the problem of identifying the same concepts over successive conceptual systems and of individuating concepts is to analyze them relative to the theories in which they are embedded. Concepts must be identified by the roles they play in theories.

In other words, the idea is that some bodies of knowledge have characteristics that distinguish them as analogues to scientific theories and that the concepts that occur in these bodies of knowledge are individuated by their cognitive roles in their respective "mental theories."

This view raises a number of questions, one of which is whether any cognitive structures warrant the designation of mental theory. Among theory-theorists, there is considerable disagreement about how lenient one should be in construing a body of representations as a theory. Most would agree that an important feature of theories is that they are used for explanatory purposes.[58] Yet this alone doesn't help, since it just raises the issue of how permissive one should be in treating something as an appropriate explanation. Carey, for one, is fairly restrictive, claiming that only a dozen or so cognitive structures should be counted as theories (1985, p. 201). On the other side of the spectrum, Gregory Murphy and Douglas Medin are so permissive that they count nearly any body of knowledge as a theory (1985 [chapter 19 in this volume]).[59] We

58. For this reason, the Theory-Theory is sometimes called the *Explanation-Based View* (see, e.g., Komatsu 1992).
59. "When we argue that concepts are organized by theories, we use *theory* to mean any of a host of mental 'explanations,' rather than a complete, organized, scientific account. For example, causal knowledge certainly embodies a theory of certain phenomena; scripts may contain an implicit theory of the entailment relations between mundane events; knowledge of rules embodies a theory of the relations between rule constituents; and book-learned, scientific knowledge certainly contains theories" (Murphy and Medin, 1985, 290).

don't want to have to settle this dispute here, so we'll opt for a more permissive understanding of theories. For our purposes, the point to focus on is that a concept's identity is determined by its role within a theory.

Now there would be little to argue about if the claim were merely that concepts are embedded in explanatory schemas of sorts. Few would deny this. The interesting claim is that a concept's identity is constituted by its role in an explanatory schema. To put this claim in a way that brings out its relation to other theories of concepts, we can say that according to the Theory-Theory concepts are structured mental representations and that their structure consists in their relations to other concepts specified by their embedding theories. Notice that put this way the Theory-Theory can't appeal to the Containment Model of conceptual structure. For any two concepts that participate in the same mental theory, the structure of each will include the other; but if the first contains the second, the second can't contain the first. What this shows is that the Theory-Theory is partial to the Inferential Model of structure. Concepts are individuated in virtue of the inferences they license based on their role in the theories that embed them.

When it comes to concept application, the Theory-Theory appeals to the structure of a concept, just as the Classical Theory and the Prototype Theory do. Generally, psychologists haven't been explicit about how the mechanism works, but their remarks about how they view scientific terms places them squarely in a tradition that is familiar from the philosophy of science (see, e.g., Kuhn 1962; Sellars 1956; and Lewis 1970, 1972). On this account the meaning of a theoretical term is determined by its role in a scientific theory. This can be given as a definite description that characterizes the role that the term plays in the theory.[60] Then the referent of the term is whatever unique entity or kind satisfies the description.[61]

One advantage of the Theory-Theory is in the models of categorization that it encourages. Many psychologists have expressed dissatisfaction with earlier theories of concepts on the grounds that they fail to incorporate people's tendency toward essentialist thinking—a view that Douglas Medin and Andrew Ortony (1989) have dubbed *psychological essentialism*. According to psychological essentialism, people are apt to view category membership for some kinds as being less a matter of an instance's exhibiting certain observable properties than the item's having an appropriate internal structure or some other hidden property. For instance, we all recognize the humor in the Warner Brothers cartoons involving Pepe LePew. In these sketches, a delicate and innocent black female cat is subjected to the inappropriate attention of a gregarious male skunk when she accidentally finds herself covered head to toe by a stripe of white paint. The joke, of course, is that she isn't a skunk, even though to all appearances she looks like one. As most people see it, what makes something a skunk isn't the black coat and white markings, but rather having the right biological history, or the right genetic make-up.

It's not just adults who think this. Prompted by an interest in the development of essentialist thinking, a number of psychologists have investigated its emergence in

60. See Lewis's papers, in particular, for an account based on the work of Frank Ramsey (1929/1990) which shows how one can provide definite descriptions for theoretical terms when their meanings are inter-defined.
61. An alternative account, which theory-theorists generally haven't explored, is to say that much of the content of a concept is given by its role in cognition but that its referent is determined independently, perhaps by a causal relation that concepts bear to items in the world. Cf. two-factor conceptual role theories in philosophy, such as Block (1986).

childhood. Susan Gelman and Henry Wellman, for instance, have found marks of psychological essentialism in children as young as four and five years old (Gelman and Wellman 1991 [chapter 26 in this volume]).[62] Young children, it turns out, are reasonably good at answering questions about whether a substantial transformation of the insides or outsides of an object affects its identity and function. When asked if an item such as a dog that has had its blood and bones removed is still a dog, Gelman and Wellman's young subjects responded 72% of the time that it no longer is. And when asked whether the same sorts of items change identity when their outsides are removed (in this case, the dog's fur), they responded 65% of the time that they do not.

The Theory-Theory connects with psychological essentialism by allowing that people access a mentally represented theory when they confront certain category decisions. Rather than passing quickly over a check-list of properties, people ask whether the item has the right hidden property.[63] This isn't to say that the Theory-Theory requires that people have a detailed understanding of genetics and chemistry. They needn't even have clearly developed views about the specific nature of the property. As Medin and Ortony put it, people may have little more than an "essence placeholder" (1989, p. 184). We gather that what this means is that people represent different sorts of information when they think of a kind as having an essence. In some cases they may have detailed views about the essence. In most, they will have a schematic view, for instance, the belief that genetic makeup is what matters, even if they don't represent particular genetic properties or have access to much in the way of genetic knowledge.

Earlier, in looking at the Prototype Theory, we saw that categorization isn't necessarily a single, unitary phenomenon. The mechanisms responsible for quick categorization judgments may be quite different from the ones responsible for more considered judgments. If anything, the Theory-Theory is responsive to people's more considered judgments. This suggests that a natural way of elaborating the Theory-Theory is as a version of the Dual Theory. As before, the identification procedure would have prototype structure, only now, instead of a classical core, concepts would have cores in line with the Theory-Theory. We suspect that a model of this sort has widespread support in psychology.

Apart from its ties to categorization, much of the attraction of the Theory-Theory has come from its bearing on issues of cognitive development. One source of interest in the Theory-Theory is that it may illuminate the cognitive differences between children and adults. In those cases where children have rather different ways of conceptualizing things than adults, such a difference may be due to children and adults' possessing qualitatively distinct theories. Cognitive development, on this view, mimics the monumental shifts in theories that are exhibited in the history of science (Carey 1985, 1991; Keil 1989; Gopnik and Meltzoff 1997). Some theorists would even go further, arguing that theory changes in development are due to the very same cognitive mechanisms that are responsible for theory change in science. On this view, the claim isn't merely that an analogy exists between scientists and children; the claim is rather that scientists and children constitute a psychological kind. As

62. See also Carey (1985), Keil (1989), and Gelman et al. (1994).

63. As a result, the Theory-Theory, like the Prototype Theory, is concerned with nondemonstrative inference. In conceptualizing an item as falling under a concept, the inferences that are licensed include all of those that go with thinking of it as having an essence. For example, in categorizing something as a bird, one is thereby licensed to infer that it has whatever essence is represented for birds and that its salient observable properties (e.g., its wings, beak, and so on) are a causal effect of its having this essence.

Alison Gopnik puts it, "Scientists and children both employ the same particularly powerful and flexible set of cognitive devices. These devices enable scientists and children to develop genuinely new knowledge about the world around them" (1996, p. 486; see also Gopnik and Meltzoff 1997). In other words, cognitive development and theory change (in science) are to be understood as two facets of the very same phenomenon.

In sum, the Theory-Theory appears to have a number of important advantages. By holding that concepts are individuated by their roles in mental theories, theory-theorists can tie their account of concepts to a realistic theory of categorization—one that respects people's tendency toward essentialist thinking. They also can address a variety of developmental concerns, characterizing cognitive development in terms of the principles relating to theory change in science. Despite these attractions, how-ever, the Theory-Theory isn't without problems. Some shouldn't be too surprising, since they've cropped up before in other guises. Yet the Theory-Theory also raises some new and interesting challenges for theorizing about concepts.

Box 5

The Theory-Theory

Concepts are representations whose structure consists in their relations to other concepts as specified by a mental theory.

4.2. Problems for the Theory-Theory
The Problem of Ignorance and Error   Let's start with the Problem of Ignorance and Error. Does it affect the Theory-Theory too? It certainly does, and in several ways. For starters, we've seen that theory-theorists typically allow that people can have rather sketchy theories, where the "essence placeholder" for a concept includes rela-tively little information. Notice, however, that once this is granted, most concepts are going to encode inadequate information to pick out a correct and determinate exten-sion. If people don't represent an essence for birds, apart from some thin ideas about genetic endowment, then the same goes for dogs, and bears, and antelopes. In each case, the theory in which the concept is embedded looks about the same. People have the idea that these creatures have some property in virtue of which they fall into their respective categories, but they don't have much to say about what the property is. How, then, will these concepts come to pick out their respective extensions?

When we faced a comparable problem in the context of the Prototype Theory, the natural solution was to rely on a Dual Theory that posited classical cores. If proto-types don't determine reference (because of the Problem of Ignorance and Error), then perhaps that isn't their job; perhaps they should be relegated to identification proce-dures. Within the context of the Theory-Theory, however, the analogous move is something of a strain. As we've noted, the Theory-Theory is generally under-stood to be about considered acts of categorization and hence is itself most naturally construed as giving the structure of conceptual cores. In any event, it's not likely that appealing to the Classical Theory can help, since it too faces the Problem of Igno-rance and Error.

A lack of represented information isn't the only difficulty for the Theory-Theory. In other cases, the problem is that people represent incorrect information. A simple example is that someone might incorporate a false belief or two into their essence placeholder for a concept. To return to our example from before, someone might hold that smallpox is caused by divine retribution. But, again, this shouldn't stop him from entertaining the concept SMALLPOX, that is, the very same concept that we use to pick out a kind that has nothing in particular to do with God. To the extent that Putnam and Kripke are right that we might be incorrect in our deeply held beliefs about a kind, the same point holds for the Theory-Theory.[64]

To take another example, consider people's concept PHYSICAL OBJECT. Elizabeth Spelke, Renée Baillargeon, and others have tried to characterize this concept, while engaging in a sustained and fascinating program of research which asks whether infants have it too (see, e.g., Spelke 1990; Baillargeon 1993 [chapter 25 in this volume]; Leslie 1994; and Gopnik and Meltzoff 1997). Generally speaking, the notion of a physical object that has emerged is one of a cohesive three-dimensional entity that retains its boundaries and connectedness over time. Among the principles that are widely thought to underlie people's understanding of such things is that qua physical objects, they can't act upon one another at a distance.[65] For example, were a moving billiard ball to come close to a stationary ball yet stop just short of touching it, one wouldn't view the subsequent movement of the stationary ball as being a causal effect of the first ball's motion, even if it continued in the same direction as the first ball. This principle—sometimes called the *principle of contact*—seems to encapsulate deeply held beliefs about physical objects, beliefs that can be traced back to infancy.

Notice, however, that the principle of contact is in direct conflict with physical principles that we all learn in the classroom. The first billiard ball may not crash into the other, but it still exerts a gravitational influence on it, however small. The implication is that most people's understanding of physical objects may be in error. The very entities that people are referring to in thinking about physical objects lack a property that is about as fundamental to their understanding of physical objects as one can imagine. In other words, their theory of physical objects is incorrect, yet this doesn't stop them from thinking about physical objects. Of course, one could try to maintain the stark position that prior to being educated in the science of physics such people aren't wrong about anything. They simply have a different concept than the rest of us. This position might be explored in more detail, but we don't think it's especially attractive. The reason is, once again, that one wants to say that these people could change their minds about the nature of objects or that they could be in a position of arguing with their educated counterparts. To the extent that such disagreements are possible, the concepts that are pitted against one another have to be in some sense the same. Otherwise, there wouldn't be any disagreement—just a verbal dispute.

The Problem of Stability   To be sure, whether two people are employing the same concept or not and whether the same person is employing the same concept over time are difficult questions. For purposes of setting out the Problem of Ignorance and Error, we've relied on a number of cases where intuitively the same concept is at play. We suspect, however, that many theorists would claim that it's simply inappropriate to insist that the very same concept may occur despite a difference in surrounding

64. Thus it's ironic that discussions of the Theory-Theory sometimes take it to be a development of Kripke's and Putnam's insights about natural kind terms.
65. The qualification is to preclude cases of psychological action at a distance. That is, objects understood as psychological entities may cause each other to move without being in contact with one another, but objects understood as purely physical bodies cannot.

beliefs. The alternative suggestion is that people need only have similar concepts. That is, the suggestion is to concede that differences in belief yield distinct concepts but to maintain that two concepts might be similar enough in content that they would be subsumed by the same psychological generalizations.

Suppose, for instance, that your theory of animals says that animals are entirely physical entities while your friend's theory of animals says that some animals (perhaps humans) have nonphysical souls. This might mean that you don't both possess the same concept ANIMAL. Still, by hypothesis, you both possess concepts with similar contents, and though strictly speaking they aren't the same, they are similar enough to say that they are both animal-concepts. Let's call the problem of explaining how the content of a concept can remain invariant across changes in belief, or how two people with different belief systems can have concepts with the same or similar content, the *Problem of Stability*. The suggestion that is implicit in many psychological discussions is that strict content stability is a misguided goal. Really what matters is content similarity. As Smith et al. (1984) put it, "[T]here is another sense of stability, which can be equated with similarity of mental contents (e.g., 'interpersonal stability' in this sense refers to situations where two people can be judged to have similar mental contents) ..." (p. 268).

As tempting as this strategy may be, it's not as easy to maintain as one might have thought. The difficulty is that the notion of content similarity is usually unpacked in a way that presupposes a prior notion of content identity (Fodor and Lepore 1992). Consider, for instance, Smith et al.'s explanation. They propose that two concepts are similar in content when they have a sufficient number of the same features. Moreover, they point out that subjects tend to cite the same properties in experiments where they are asked to list characteristics of a category. Following Rosch and others, they take this to be evidence that people's concepts, by and large, do incorporate the same features. The consequence is supposed to be that people's concepts are highly similar in content.

But notice the structure of the argument. Features are themselves contentful representations; they are just more concepts. Smith et al.'s reasoning, then, is that two concepts are similar in content when their structure implicates a sufficient number of concepts with the *same* content. But if these other concepts have to share the same content, then that's to say that the notion of content similarity is building upon the notion of content identity; the very notion that content similarity is supposed to replace is hidden in the explanation of how two concepts could be similar in content. What's more, Smith et al.'s proposal is hardly idiosyncratic. Content similarity is generally understood in terms of overlapping sets of features. But again, feature sets can't overlap unless they have a certain number of the same features, that is, representations with the same content. And if they have representations with the same content, then one might as well admit that concepts have to have the same content (not similar content), despite differences in belief. This brings us full circle.

The scope of this problem hasn't been absorbed in the cognitive science community, so perhaps it pays to consider another proposed solution. Here's one owing to Lance Rips (1995). He suggests that we think of concepts as being individuated along two dimensions. One is a mental theory; the other, a formally specified mental symbol. So the concept DOG is a formally individuated mental representation taken together with a collection of contentful states that incorporate salient information about dogs. Rips likens his model to a Dual Theory of concepts, but one that incorporates neither a classical core nor a prototype-based identification procedure. The advantage of the model is supposed to be that without postulating definitions for concepts, Rips's "cores" provide sufficient resources to solve a number of problems, including the problem of stability. They are supposed to generate stability, since states can be added or removed from the theory part of a concept while the core remains invariant. In this way, changes or differences in belief can still be tracked by the same mental representation. Consequently, there is a mechanism for saying that they are changes, or differences, with respect to the same theory.

Now Rips himself admits that his account doesn't have a fully developed explanation of stability. Yet he claims to have solved the problem for cases where the belief changes are relatively small (Rips 1995, p. 84):

> To take the extreme case, if there is *no* overlap in your previous and subsequent theories of daisies then does your former belief that Daisies cause hayfever conflict with your present belief that *Daisies don't cause hayfever*? The present proposal leaves it open whether a larger divergence in representations about a category [i.e., the theory component of a concept] could force a change in the representations-of the category [i.e., the formally individuated symbol]. What's clear is that less drastic differences in a theory do allow disagreements, which is what the present suggestion seeks to explain.

In other words, changes in a small number of the beliefs that make up a given theory needn't undermine stability, so long as the subsequent theory is associated with the very same formally identified symbol.

This is a novel and interesting suggestion, but unfortunately it can't be made to work as it stands. The reason is that incidental changes to a theory can't be tracked by a representation understood as a merely formal item. That's like tracking the content of a cluster of sentences by reference to a word form that appears throughout the cluster. Notice that whether the cluster of sentences continues to mean the same thing (or much the same thing) depends upon whether the invariant word form continues to mean the same thing (or much the same thing). If for some reason the word comes to have a completely different content, then the sentences would inherit this difference. If, for example, the word form starts out by expressing the property *electron* but later comes to express the property *ice cream*, the subsequent theory wouldn't conflict with the previous theory. In short, Rips's suggestion doesn't get us very far unless his "core" part of the concept, that is, the symbol, maintains its content over time. Then one could easily refer back to the content of that symbol in order to claim that the earlier theory and the subsequent theory are both about electrons. But Rips can't accept this amendment; it assumes that a concept's content is stable across changes in belief. Rather than explain stability, it presupposes stability.[66]

This isn't the last word on conceptual stability. We expect that other suggestions will emerge once the issue is given more attention. Nonetheless, stability is one of the key problems that a worked-out version of the Theory-Theory needs to face.[67]

66. Another way to make the main point here is to ask what makes something a *small* change in a theory. Intuitively, small changes are ones that don't affect the contents of the concepts involved, and Rips seems to be saying just that. His story amounts to the claim that concepts are stable (i.e., they don't change meaning) under relatively small changes in theories (i.e., changes that don't affect meaning). Clearly, without an independent account of when a change is small, this theory is vacuous.

67. That there are few discussions of stability is, we think, a reflection of the fact that the Theory-Theory hasn't been subjected to as much critical scrutiny as previous theories. Another respect in which the Theory-Theory remains relatively undeveloped is in its treatment of compositionality. On the face of it, theories are poor candidates for a compositional semantics.

The "Mysteries of Science" Problem   Not all theory-theorists claim that cognitive development mimics patterns in the history of science, but among those that do, another problem is specifying the mechanism responsible for cognitive development. Alison Gopnik and Andrew Meltzoff take up this burden by claiming that the very same mechanism is responsible for both scientific theory change and cognitive development. Yet this raises a serious difficulty: The appeal to science isn't informative if the mechanisms of theory change in science are themselves poorly understood.

Unfortunately, this is exactly the situation that we seem to be in. Gopnik and Meltzoff do their best to characterize in broad terms how one theory comes to give way to another in science. Some of their observations seem right. For instance, theories are often protected from recalcitrant data by ad hoc auxiliary hypotheses, and these eventually give way when an intense period of investigation uncovers more recalcitrant data, alongside a superior alternative theory. But how do scientists arrive at their new theories? Gopnik and Meltzoff have little more to say than that this is the "mysterious logic of discovery" (1997, p. 40). And what is distinctive about the transition from one theory to another? Here they emphasize the role of evidence and experimentation. It too is "mysterious, but that it plays a role seems plain" (p. 40). We don't doubt that experimentation is at the heart of science but without articulated accounts of how transitions between scientific theories take place, it simply doesn't help to claim that scientific and cognitive development are one and the same. Saying that two mysterious processes are really two facets of a single process is suggestive, but it hardly dispels either mystery. In other words, it's simply misleading to cite as an advantage of the Theory-Theory that it solves the problem of cognitive development when the mechanism that is supposed to do all the work is as intractable as the problem it's supposed to explain.

Like the other theories we've discussed so far, the Theory-Theory has substantial motivation and a number of serious challenges. Though it does well in explaining certain types of categorization judgments, it has trouble in allowing for stability within the conceptual system and in accounting for the referential properties of concepts. This isn't to say that there is no analogy between concepts and theoretical terms. But it does call into question whether the Theory-Theory can provide an adequate account of the nature of concepts.

Box 6

Summary of Criticisms of the Theory-Theory

1. **The Problem of Ignorance and Error**
   It is possible to have a concept in spite of its being tied up with a deficient or erroneous mental theory.
2. **The Problem of Stability**
   The content of a concept can't remain invariant across changes in its mental theory.
3. **The "Mysteries of Science" Problem**
   The mechanisms that are responsible for the emergence of new scientific theories and for the shift from one theory to another are poorly understood.

5. The Neoclassical Theory of Concepts

5.1. Updating the Classical Theory

Within psychological circles, the Classical Theory is generally considered to be a nonstarter except by those Dual Theorists who relegate classical structure to conceptual cores. In contrast, elements of the Classical Theory continue to be at the very center of discussion in other areas of cognitive science, especially linguistics and, to some extent, philosophy. We'll bring together a variety of theories emanating from these fields under the heading of the *Neoclassical Theory of Concepts*. In some ways, this family of views is the most heterogeneous in our taxonomy. Some neoclassical theorists are really just contemporary classical theorists who are sensitive to the objections we've already reviewed. Others depart from the Classical Theory on substantive points while expanding its resources in new directions. We'll say something about each of these two groups, but our focus will be on the second.

Much of the interest in the Neoclassical Theory is to be found among linguists investigating the meanings of words, especially verbs. Steven Pinker, for instance, is keenly aware that the project of specifying definitions for words is highly suspect. He notes that "[t]he suggestion that there might be a theory of verb meaning involving a small set of recurring elements might be cause for alarm" (1989, p. 167). Still, his proposal is that definitions of a sort are a perfectly viable goal for lexical semanticists (p. 168):

> I will not try to come up with a small set of primitives and relations out of which one can compose definitions capturing the totality of a verb's meaning. Rather, the verb definitions sought will be hybrid structures consisting of a scaffolding of universal, recurring, grammatically relevant meaning elements and slots for bits of [real-world knowledge]. . . .

This view has strong affinities with the Classical Theory, in spite of its admission about real-world knowledge entering into the definition of a word. Ray Jackendoff, another neoclassical theorist, emphasizes the Classical Theory's commitment to necessary conditions but adds that a word's meaning includes other information as well (Jackendoff 1983, p. 121):

> At least three sorts of conditions are needed to adequately specify word meanings. First, we cannot do without *necessary* conditions: e.g., "red" must contain the necessary condition COLOR and "tiger" must contain at least THING. Second, we need graded conditions to designate hue in color concepts and length-width ratio of cups, for example. These conditions specify a focal or central value for a continuously variable attribute. . . . Third we need conditions that are typical but subject to exceptions—for instance, the element of competition in games or a tiger's stripedness.

The commitment to necessary conditions ties Jackendoff to the Classical Theory, but, like Pinker, he thinks that there are different parts to a word's meaning. This is a characteristic view among lexical semanticists, even if there is a healthy amount of disagreement about what these different parts are. Abstracting from such internal disputes, we can say that what distinguishes the Neoclassical Theory is the idea that concepts have *partial definitions* in that their structure encodes a set of necessary conditions that must be satisfied by things in their extension. Following Jackendoff, one might hold, for example, that the structure of the concept RED embodies the condition that something can't be red without being colored. What makes this a partial definition is that this much structure encodes only a necessary condition and, at any rate, doesn't specify a sufficient condition for something's falling under the concept.

Though the appeal to partial definitions may be viewed by some as something of a cop-out, the situation isn't that lexical semanticists are just trying to put a happy face on Plato's Problem. Rather, neoclassical theorists begin with a variety of interesting linguistic phenomenon and argue that only concepts with neoclassical structure can explain this data. It may help to work through an example. Consider Jackendoff's explanation of causative constructions—a fairly standard treatment in the field of lexical semantics. Jackendoff's starting point is the observation that causatives exhibit a pronounced distributional pattern (1989 [chapter 13 in this volume], p. 50).

(16) a. x killed $y \rightarrow y$ died
      b. x lifted $y \rightarrow y$ rose
      c. x gave z to $y \rightarrow y$ received z
      d. x persuaded y that $P \rightarrow y$ came to believe that P

Now these inferences could all be treated as having nothing to do with one another. But they are strikingly similar, and this suggests that they have a common explanation. Jackendoff's suggestion is that the meaning of a causative implicates a proprietary event and that, under this assumption, the pattern of inferences can be explained by introducing a single rule that covers all these cases, namely,

(17) X cause E to occur $\rightarrow E$ occur

For instance, the proper analysis of (16d) is supposed to be: x cause [y came to believe that P]. This analysis, taken in conjunction with the inference rule (17) implies y came to believe that P. In the present context, however, this is just to say that the concept PERSUADE has structure. CAUSE TO BELIEVE gives a partial definition of PERSUADE. There may be more to persuading someone that P than causing them to believe P,[68] but at least this provides a necessary condition for the application of PERSUADE. Moreover, this necessary condition is one that is evidenced in the distributional pattern of English illustrated by (16a)–(16d).

The causatives are just one example of how the Neoclassical Theory finds support in linguistic phenomena. Neoclassical structure has also been invoked to explain a variety of data connected with polysemy, syntactic alternations, and lexical acquisition.[69]

In philosophy, too, neoclassical structure is taken to have explanatory support. Some of the data at stake include people's intuitions about the application of a concept. Georges Rey, for example, claims that Quine's arguments against the analytic-synthetic distinction are flawed and holds, as a consequence, that it is an open question how we are to understand what he calls the *analytic data*. The analytic data

68. For example, suppose you fall down the stairs when you are walking just a bit too fast. This might lead an observer to believe that one should approach the stairs with caution. Yet, intuitively, you didn't persuade the observer of this; you merely caused him to believe it.

69. On polysemy, see Jackendoff (1989); on syntactic alternations and lexical acquisition, see Pinker (1989). For a useful collection that shows the scope of contemporary lexical semantics, see Levin and Pinker (1991b).

concern our judgments about the constitutive conditions for satisfying a concept. For example, upon hearing a Gettier example (see sec. 2), most people can be relied upon to appreciate its force; knowledge can't be (just) justified true belief. Why is it that people have this intuition? Rey's claim is that we need a theory of why this is so. "[W]e need to ask here exactly the question that Chomsky asked about syntax: what explains the patterns and projections in people's judgments?" (1993, p. 83). Rey's answer is that, by and large, the analytic intuitions are best explained by the theory that they reflect constitutive relations among our concepts. A concept such as KNOWL- EDGE may have a definition after all, or at least a partial definition; it's just that the definition involves tacit rules that are extremely difficult to articulate.[70]

The Neoclassical Theory has an affinity with the Classical Theory because of its commitment to partial definitions. But the motivation for the Neoclassical Theory is largely independent of any desire to preserve the Classical Theory. The typical neo- classicist is someone who invokes partial definitions for explanatory reasons. With these motivations in mind, we turn now to some problems facing the Neoclassical Theory.

Box 7

The Neoclassical Theory

Most concepts (esp. lexical concepts) are structured mental representations that encode partial definitions, i.e., necessary conditions for their application.

5.2. Problems for the Neoclassical Theory
The Problem of Completers   Many of the problems facing the Neoclassical Theory aren't new. In fact, it's not clear that the Neoclassical Theory offers a truly distinctive perspective on concepts at all. This comes out most vividly when we consider the question of how the partial definitions offered by neoclassical theorists are supposed to be filled out. Here neoclassical theorists confront a dilemma. On the one hand, if the partial definitions are to be turned into full definitions, then all of the problems that faced the Classical Theory return.[71] On the other hand, if they are left as partial definitions, then the Neoclassical Theory is without an account of reference determination.

We suspect that this dilemma hasn't been much of a worry among some neo- classical theorists because they aren't interested in giving a theory of concepts per se.

---

70. Christopher Peacocke, who in some ways is a model classical theorist (see Peacocke 1996a, 1996b [chapters 14 and 16 in this volume]), holds a similar view in a recent elaboration of his theory of concepts. See Peacocke (1997).

71. A possible exception is Katz (1997), which explicitly addresses the Problem of Analyticity. Katz argues, e.g., that the discovery that cats aren't animals is consistent with its being analytic that cats are animals. He is able to do this by claiming that, contrary to most accounts, analyticity isn't tied up with the notions of reference and truth. For Katz, analyticity is simply a matter of the containment relations among concepts. If CAT contains ANIMAL, then it's analytic that cats are animals. Whether CAT *refers* to creatures that are animals is another matter.

They are interested, instead, in grammatically relevant aspects of word meaning. For instance, when Steven Pinker claims that his "definitions" aren't intended to capture all of a verb's meaning, we take it that his point is that he isn't aiming to provide a complete characterization of the concept that the verb encodes. Understandably, given his interest in natural language, his focus is on those aspects of conceptual structure that are manifested in grammatical processes. His slots for "bits of [real-world knowledge]" are a gesture toward the larger project outside of the study of grammar, yet this is a project that Pinker is under no obligation to pursue. Jane Grimshaw is perhaps even clearer on this point. For example, she states that the words "dog" and "cat," or "melt" and "freeze," are synonymous. She doesn't mean by this that, in all senses of the term, they have the same content. The point is rather that they have the same content insofar as content has grammatical influence. "Linguistically speaking pairs like these are synonyms, because they have the same structure. The differences between them are not visible to the language" (unpublished ms., p. 2). These remarks indicate a circumscribed yet sensible research program. Grimshaw is concerned with conceptual structure, but only from the point of view of its effects on grammar. Grammatically relevant structure she calls *semantic structure*; the rest she calls *semantic content*. "Semantic structure has linguistic life, semantic content does not" (p. 2).

Still, those of us who *are* interested in the nature of concepts can't be so indifferent to the Problem of Completers. Either partial definitions are fleshed out or they are not. If they are, then the problems associated with the Classical Theory return. If they are not, then we are left without an account of how concepts apply to their instances. What makes it the case that DOG applies to all and only dogs? The fact that the concept incorporates the feature ANIMATE may place a constraint on an explanation—DOG can only apply to animates—but it is a constraint that is far too weak to answer the question.

The Problem of Ignorance and Error   Because so many neoclassical theorists shy away from defending comprehensive theories of concepts, it's hard to say whether their theories are subject to the Problem of Ignorance and Error—a problem that we've seen crops up for just about everyone else. Among those neoclassical theorists who expect to complete their partial definitions, it's likely that they would have as much trouble with ignorance and error as classical theorists have. This is one respect in which the Neoclassical theory may be on the same footing as its predecessor. In both cases, there is the strong danger that the structure of a concept will encode insufficient information, or erroneous information, and so won't be able to fix the concept's reference.

Still, some neoclassical theorists may have views on reference determination that aren't readily assimilated to the Classical Theory. Ray Jackendoff's work in this area stands out. For while his theory is sensitive to grammatical indices of conceptual structure, it doesn't stop short with what Grimshaw calls semantic structure. Jackendoff's theory *is* about the nature of concepts. What's more, the structure that he takes concepts to have, in addition to their necessary conditions, isn't just a throwback to the Classical Theory. He has a number of interesting suggestions about other aspects of conceptual structure.

We won't be able to review all of his innovations, but one seems especially pertinent. Jackendoff asks the question of how to distinguish between the lexical entries for words that are closely related in meaning, such as "duck" and "goose." He notes that these words have much the same structure in that both exhibit such general features as ANIMATE and NONHUMAN. But what makes the two have different meanings? For Jackendoff the suggestion that they differ with respect to a single additional feature is absurd; it's not as if "duck" has −LONG NECK and "goose" +LONG NECK. "To put a +/− sign and a pair of brackets around any old expression simply doesn't make it into a legitimate conceptual feature" (1989, p. 44). Jackendoff's alternative suggestion is that the lexical entries for object words include spatial information organized around a 3-D model (understood along the lines of Marr 1982). A 3-D model is a sophisticated spatial representation, but in essence, Jackendoff's theory is an elaboration of the idea that "knowing the meaning of a word that denotes a physical object involves in part knowing what such an object looks like" (Jackendoff 1987, p. 201). Though the emphasis here is on word meanings, we take it that Jackendoff's view is really about the concepts that words express. Lexical concepts for objects have a structure that incorporates a 3-D model in addition to the more mundane features that are the stock and trade of lexical semantics.

That this is Jackendoff's view of lexical concepts seems clear. On the other hand, how the view is supposed to connect with issues of reference determination is less clear. The problem is that Jackendoff has a negative attitude toward truth-theoretic semantics and generally shies away from the notion of reference. But these reservations really are beside the point. What's at stake is that a theory of concepts needs to capture a normative dimension of meaning—at a minimum, by pulling apart cases of erroneous categorization from cases of veridical categorization (see note 14). The suggestion we are entertaining is that spatial representations supplement features for necessary conditions, and that the resulting structure determines which things fall under a concept.

Unfortunately, such structure isn't up to the task, and for much the same reason that prototype structure isn't. Something can satisfy the properties specified by the spatial representation without falling under the concept, and something can fall under the concept without satisfying the properties specified by the spatial representation. For instance, an animal that strongly resembles a goose needn't be one, and a goose may for whatever reason fail to look like one. People readily appreciate this fact. Recall our 3-legged, tame, toothless, albino tigers. They are, nonetheless, recognized to be tigers. A theory of concepts that can't do justice to this fact is simply inadequate.[72]

The Regress Problem for Semantic Field Features   Since the Neoclassical Theory is motivated by a diverse set of explanatory goals, its status, to a large extent, turns on how it meets the data. That is, a full evaluation of the theory would require a thorough evaluation of whether neoclassical structure is part of the best explanation of a host of linguistic phenomena. We can't provide anything of the sort here, but we will briefly discuss a methodological objection to some representative arguments in lexical semantics according to which the lexical concepts have semantic field features. These features are supposed to access patterns of inferences that are proprietary to a

---

72. Which isn't to say that the theory is entirely wrong. Just as prototypes might still be part of the nature of concepts even though they don't determine reference, so might 3-D representations. It's doubtful, however, that Jackendoff would want to accept a version of the Dual Theory, as many prototype theorists have.

particular field. For instance, concepts with a feature indicating the field "spatial location and motion" may license one body of inferences, while a feature indicating the field "scheduling of activities" may license another. Such differences are supposed to account for distributional patterns where lexical items that have similar meanings nonetheless permit distinct and characteristic inferences.

Ray Jackendoff, for example, argues for the existence of semantic field features on the basis of the following evidence, labeled according to four proposed fields (Jackendoff 1989, p. 37):

a. *Spatial location and motion*
    i.   The bird went from the ground to the tree.
    ii. The bird is in the tree.
    iii. Harry kept the bird in the cage.
b. *Possession*
    i.   The inheritance went to Philip.
    ii. The money is Philip's.
    iii. Susan kept the money.
c. *Ascription of properties*
    i.   The light went/changed from green to red.
         Harry went from elated to depressed.
    ii. The light is red.
         Harry is depressed.
    iii. Sam kept the crowed happy.
d. *Scheduling of activities*
    i.   The meeting was changed from Tuesday to Monday.
    ii. The meeting is on Monday.
    iii. Let's keep the trip on Saturday.

The intuition that is the basis of Jackendoff's argument is that "go," "be," and "keep" are polysemous whereby, in a given semantic field, each verb has a different though similar meaning to the one it has in any other semantic field. "The *go* sentences each express a change of some sort, and their respective terminal states are described by the corresponding *be* sentences. The *keep* sentences all denote the causation of a state that endures over a period of time. One has the sense, then, that this variety of uses is not accidental" (1989, p. 37). Jackendoff's suggestion is that these intuitions ought to be taken seriously and that the way to do this is by introducing two degrees of freedom. First, the similarities of meaning can be captured under the assumption that the similar items are associated with partially identical representations. Second, the differences in meaning can be captured under the assumption that their associated representations differ with respect to a constituent that picks out a semantic field. This constituent may then interact with inference rules that explain why a single word licenses different inferences depending on its context.

To take an example, Jackendoff's representation for the "keep" verbs all share this much structure:

(1) $[_{\text{Event}} \text{CAUSE} ([_{\text{Thing}} x], [_{\text{Event}} \text{STAY} ([\ ], [\ ])])]$

The way we are to understand the notation is that the word "keep" expresses a function (labeled "CAUSE") that takes two arguments (one labeled "Thing," the other labeled "Event") onto a value (labeled "Event"), where the second argument is itself a function (labeled "STAY").[73] Semantic fields may then be indicated as subscripts on the function labels. Thus the difference between "keep" in (a-iii) and "keep" in (b-iii) is to be indicated by the subscript on "CAUSE":

(2)   [$_{Event}$ CAUSE$_{Spatial}$ ([$_{Thing}$ x], [$_{Event}$ STAY ([ ], [ ])])]

(3)   [$_{Event}$ CAUSE$_{Poss}$ ([$_{Thing}$ x], [$_{Event}$ STAY ([ ], [ ])])]

A full elaboration of the sentences requires filling in the variables, as we've done here for a sample sentence, (a-iii):

(4)   [$_{Event}$ CAUSE$_{Spatial}$ ([$_{Thing}$ HARRY], [$_{Event}$ STAY ([$_{Thing}$ THE BIRD], [$_{Place}$ IN THE CAGE])])]

The thing to keep your eye on is how this notation makes explicit Jackendoff's explanation of why the different occurrences of "keep" seem both similar and different in meaning. To the extent that they are similar, this is because they share the same underlying structural template, namely, (1); to the extent that they are distinct, this is because their associated representations contain different semantic field features, as in (2) and (3).

The methodological objection that is associated with this type of explanation is one that Jerry Fodor (1998) pushes vigorously. Fodor's argument is that polysemy can't be accounted for by the interaction of a verb template and a semantic field feature because this type of explanation confronts a dilemma. Either it involves an endless regress or else the postulation of neoclassical structure is simply gratuitous. The source of the dilemma is the fact that for a verb like "keep" to retain part of its meaning across semantic fields, its semantic constituents must themselves be univocal across semantic fields. If, for example, CAUSE and THING change their meaning every time they occur in a new context, then "keep" couldn't be relied upon to retain any of its meaning. So the univocality of "keep" depends upon the univocality of, among other things, CAUSE. But are we to explain CAUSE's univocality by postulating that it too has a definition? If so, then when the same problem crops up again for its defining constituents, we'll have to postulate yet more definitions, with no end in sight. On the other hand, if CAUSE can retain its meaning across semantic fields without its having neoclassical structure, then so can "keep." "Why not say that 'keep' is univocal because it always means *keep*; just as, in order to avoid the regress, Jackendoff is required to say that 'CAUSE' is univocal because it always means *cause*" (Fodor 1998, p. 52).

This being a methodological objection, it will suffice to show that there is nothing inherently flawed in Jackendoff's strategy of argument. Whether he is right that "keep" and other verbs have neoclassical structure that implicates semantic field features is, ultimately, the question of the most interest. For present purposes, however, the primary issue is the methodological one, and on this score we see no reason why Jackendoff should be worried about Fodor's dilemma.

---

73. We've maintained Jackendoff's notation which may be a little confusing, since his use of capital letters resembles our use of small caps. We hope readers won't be misled into thinking that only the items designated by capitals are concepts. On the contrary, all of the items that Jackendoff's notation picks out are concepts. For example, his "Event" and "CAUSE" are both internal representations that express sub-propositional contents.

As we see it, Jackendoff should take hold of the second horn. He should admit that, in principle, a word can retain aspects of its meaning across semantic fields without having neoclassical structure. That is, just as CAUSE retains its meaning, so might "keep." But just because this is the case in principle, doesn't mean that the best explanation requires that one withhold the postulation of neoclassical structure. If one has an explanatory reason to invoke neoclassical structure in some cases (but not all), then the postulation of such structure isn't the least bit gratuitous. Nor need it lead to a regress. The reason for saying that "keep" has structure needn't be applicable at all levels of representation. Maybe it simply isn't valid once one gets to the level of the concept CAUSE. In short, polysemy doesn't require neoclassical structure, but there may still be an explanatory advantage to postulating the structure. It remains for Jackendoff to demonstrate this explanatory advantage. The main point, however, is that there is no a priori reason to think that there isn't one.

In general, the merits of postulating neoclassical structure depend upon the explanations that prove the most tenable for a variety of data—not just evidence of polysemy, but also data concerning syntactic phenomena, lexical acquisition, and our intuitions about the constitutive relations among concepts.[74] We see no reason why neoclassical structure shouldn't be implicated to explain these things, but just because it is doesn't mean we've been given a full account of the nature of concepts. How partial definitions are to be filled in and how their application is to be determined remain to be seen.

Box 8

Summary of Criticisms of the Neoclassical Theory

   1. **The Problem of Completers**
      If partial definitions are turned into full definitions, then the Neoclassical Theory has all the problems that are associated with the Classical Theory. If, instead, they are left incomplete, then the Neoclassical Theory has no account of reference determination.
   2. **The Problem of Ignorance and Error**
      Supplementing neoclassical structure with 3-D models won't help in accounting for reference determination.
   3. **The Regress Problem for Semantic Fields**
      Neoclassical structure can't explain how a word retains aspects of its meaning across different semantic fields. Either its conceptual constituents must themselves have neoclassical structure, and so on, or else no structure is needed at all.

---

6. Conceptual Atomism

6.1. Concepts Without Structure

All of the theories that we've covered so far disagree about the structure of concepts, but that most concepts have structure—especially lexical concepts—is an assump-

---

74. We've postponed the discussion of the latter until sec. 6.2, where we contrast neoclassical and atomistic accounts of the analytic data.

tion they all share. The last theory of concepts that we will discuss is unique in that it denies this assumption. As Jerry Fodor puts it (1998, p. 22; emphasis removed):

> "What is the structure of the concept DOG?" ... on the evidence available, it's reasonable to suppose that such mental representations have no structure; it's reasonable to suppose that they are atoms.

This view, which we will call *Conceptual Atomism*, is sometimes met with stark incredulity. How can lexical concepts have no structure at all? If they are atoms, wouldn't that rob them of any explanatory power? After all, in other theories, it's a concept's structure that is implicated in accounts of categorization, acquisition, and all the other phenomena that theories of concepts are usually taken to address. Defenders of Conceptual Atomism, however, are motivated by what they take to be grave failings of these other theories, especially the lack of definitions (for the Classical Theory) and the imposing difficulties of compositionality (for the Prototype Theory). In addition, conceptual atomists find support in the arguments first given by Kripke and Putnam against descriptivist theories of meaning.

As stated, Conceptual Atomism is largely a negative view. It doesn't posit concepts with classical or neoclassical structure, it doesn't posit concepts with prototype structure, and it doesn't posit concepts with theory structure. It posits concepts with no structure. This may leave one wondering what a developed version of Conceptual Atomism looks like. What's needed is a theory of how the reference of unstructured concepts is determined. For purposes of exposition, we will use Fodor's Asymmetric Dependence Theory, since it is one of the most developed in the field (see Fodor, J. A. 1990a [chapter 22 in this volume]; see also Fodor, J. A. 1990b, 1990c).

The Asymmetric Dependence Theory is a descendent of the causal-historical theories of Kripke and Putnam. The heart of the theory is the idea that the content of a primitive concept is determined by the concept's standing in an appropriate causal relation to things in the world. For Fodor, the causal relation is a nomic connection between types of concepts and the properties their tokens express. For example, the content of the concept BIRD isn't to be given by its relation to such concepts as ANIMAL, WINGS, and so on. Rather, BIRD expresses the property *bird*, in part, because there is a causal law connecting the property of being a bird with the concept BIRD.[75] This much of the theory places Fodor's account squarely in the information-based semantics tradition, according to which mental content is a species of informational content (see Dretske 1981). *Information* is basically a matter of reliable correlations. Where one type of event is a reliable cause of another, the second is said to carry information about the first. So mental content, for Fodor, requires that a concept carry information about the property it expresses. But there is more to mental content than information. As is widely recognized, there are a variety of cases where a concept is a reliable effect of things that are not in its extension. The standard case of this kind is a situation where an erroneous application of a concept is, for whatever reason, reliable. Take, for instance, a situation when viewing conditions are poor. It's a dark night, perhaps a bit foggy, and you think you see a cow in the field just beyond the road. That's to say, you apply the concept COW to the entity over there, and you do

---

75. The extension of the concept is then a trivial consequence of the property it expresses. Something falls under the concept BIRD just in case it instantiates the property *bird*.

so for understandable reasons—it looks like a cow. Nonetheless, it's a horse; you've misapplied your concept. That's to be expected in conditions like these, since under the conditions we are envisioning, the horse actually looks like a cow. The result is that your concept COW is the reliable effect of at least two causes: cows and horses. If, however, there is nothing more to content than information, we would not have a case of error here at all, but rather a veridical application of a concept expressing the disjunctive property *cow or horse*. In philosophical circles, this issue has come to be known as the *Disjunction Problem*.

Information-based semanticists have explored a number of ways to overcome the Disjunction Problem. Fodor's solution is to claim that certain informational relations are more basic than others and that this difference is what counts. His theory has two parts:

> (1) A concept—COW, for example—stands in a lawful relation, L, to the property it expresses, namely, *cow*.
>
> (2) Other lawful relations involving COW, L_1-L_n, are asymmetrically dependent upon the lawful relation between COW and *cow*. That is, L_1-L_n wouldn't hold but that L does, and not the other way around.

Thus the critical difference between the *cow*/COW law and the *horse*/COW law is that although both are reliable, the first is the more fundamental: It would obtain even if the *horse*/COW dependence did not, whereas the *horse*/COW dependence would not obtain without the *cow*/COW dependence. That's why COW expresses the property *cow* and not, as it might be, *cow or horse*.[76]

Notice that an advantage of the Asymmetric Dependence Theory is that it implies that no representation that is associated with a concept is essential to its having the content that it does. In principle, one might even have the concept COW without having the concept ANIMAL. All that is required is that there be some mechanism or other that secures the right mind-world relations. As a result, Conceptual Atomism is able to sidestep some of the most persistent difficulties that confront other theories. For instance, there needn't be a problem about ignorance and error. So long as COW is appropriately connected with *cow* (the property), it doesn't matter what you believe about cows. For much the same reason, there needn't be a problem about stability. So long as COW continues to stand in the same mind-world relation, variations in surrounding beliefs can have no effect on its content.[77]

---

76. We should emphasize that Conceptual Atomism shouldn't be conflated with any particular theory of reference determination and its way of dealing with the Disjunction Problem. Ruth Millikan, e.g., makes use of a theory that is similar to Fodor's but which requires certain historical facts as well. "A substance concept causally originates from the substance that it denotes. It is a concept of A, rather than B, not because the thinker will always succeed in reidentifying A, never confusing it with B, but because A is what the thinker has been conceptually, hence physically, tracking and picking up information about, and because the concept has been tuned to its present accuracy by causal interaction with either the members of A's specific domain or with A itself, during the evolutionary history of the species or through the learning history of the individual" (1998 [chapter 23 in this volume], p. 63; see also Millikan 1984). For a useful overview of theories of mental content, see Crane (1995).

77. To the extent that the mind-world relation is supported by varying sets of beliefs, these can be thought of as forming an equivalence class. Each set is semantically the same as all the others since they all converge on the same mind-world relation; it's this relation, however, and not the specific belief contents, that determine a concept's content.

No doubt, these are among the chief attractions of Conceptual Atomism.[78] But, like any other theory of concepts, Conceptual Atomism isn't without its own problems. We turn to these next.

Box 9

Conceptual Atomism

Lexical concepts are primitive; they have no structure.

6.2. Problems for Conceptual Atomism
The Problem of Radical Nativism   One of the most powerful motivations for developing nonatomistic accounts of concepts is a worry that is often lurking in the background, even if it is left unstated. This is the view that Conceptual Atomism involves far too strong of a commitment to innate concepts. The support for this view comes from Jerry Fodor's argument that primitive concepts have to be innate (Fodor, J. A. 1981; see also Fodor, J. A. et al. 1980). Since Conceptual Atomism says that lexical concepts are primitive, atomists would be committed to a huge stock of innate concepts, including such unlikely candidates as BROCCOLI, CARBURETOR, and GALAXY. Fodor is famous—or rather, infamous—for having endorsed this conclusion.

Now few people have been enthusiastic about embracing such a radical form of nativism, but the logic of his argument and the significance of the issue aren't to be dismissed so quickly. For example, Beth Levin and Steven Pinker speak for many people in cognitive science when they defend the need for conceptual structure (1991a, p. 4):

> Psychology ... cannot afford to do without a theory of lexical semantics. Fodor ... points out the harsh but inexorable logic. According to the computational theory of mind, the primitive (nondecomposed) mental symbols are the innate ones.... Fodor, after assessing the contemporary relevant evidence, concluded that most word meanings are not decomposable—therefore, he suggested, we must start living with the implications of this fact for the richness of the innate human conceptual repertoire, including such counterintuitive corollaries as that the concept CAR is innate. Whether or not one agrees with Fodor's assessment of the evidence, the importance of understanding the extent to which word meanings decompose cannot be denied, for such investigation provides crucial evidence about the innate stuff out of which concepts are made.

In even stronger terms, Ray Jackendoff claims to endorse the logic of Fodor's argument "unconditionally"; if a concept is unstructured, he says, it can't be learned (1989, p. 50).

---

78. Another is that conceptual atomists don't have to distinguish the relations among concepts that are constitutive of their content from those that merely express collateral information; for an atomist, no relations among concepts are constitutive of their content. This is one reason Fodor is such an ardent supporter of atomism. He thinks that once one admits that some relations among concepts are constitutive of their content, one is forced to admit that all are. The result is supposed to be an untenable holistic semantics (Fodor 1987; Fodor and Lepore 1992).

Let's put aside the question of whether nonatomic theories of lexical concepts are defensible. What is the reasoning behind the rest of Fodor's argument? Briefly, Fodor sees only one way that cognitive science can explain the learning of a concept. This is by postulating a mechanism whereby a new complex concept is assembled from its constituents. To take a simple example, suppose that the concept FATHER is the concept of a male parent and that the concept has the structure MALE PARENT, that is, it is literally composed of the concepts MALE and PARENT (and whatever logico-syntactic concepts may be involved). In this case, one can imagine that the acquisition of FATHER proceeds by noticing that some parents are male and by constructing a complex concept to reflect this contingency, namely, MALE PARENT (= FATHER). Notice that, in this way, the learning of FATHER takes place only on the condition that the agent previously possesses the concepts MALE and PARENT. Turning to the component concepts, MALE and PARENT, we can now ask the same question about how they are acquired. Perhaps they too decompose into simpler concepts and are acquired in much the same way as we are supposing FATHER is acquired. Yet clearly this process has to stop. Eventually decomposition comes to an end, and at that point we simply can't explain acquisition in terms of a constructive process. Since this is the only explanation of how a concept is learned, there is no explanation of how primitive concepts can be learned. Thus they must be innate.

In one form or another, this argument has led many people to be weary of Conceptual Atomism. After all, accepting the innateness of GALAXY and CARBURETOR is no small matter. Fortunately, Fodor's argument isn't sound, though not primarily for the reasons that are usually cited. What's really wrong with Fodor's position is that with his focus on conceptual structure, he fails to pose the issue of conceptual acquisition in its most fundamental terms. If to possess a concept is to possess a contentful representation, the issue of acquisition is how, given the correct theory of mental content, one can come to be in a state in which the conditions that the theory specifies obtain. To answer this question one needs to look at the acquisition process from the vantage point of a developed theory of content. One of the reasons atomistic theories may have appeared to prohibit learning is precisely because they have rarely been articulated to the point where one can ask how a mind comes to satisfy their constraints. Ironically, now that Fodor has provided a detailed atomistic theory, we can see by relation to the theory how an unstructured concept might be learned.

To explain acquisition on the Asymmetric Dependence Theory one needs an account of how the mind-world dependencies that are constitutive of content come to obtain. The key to the explanation is the notion of a *sustaining mechanism*. A sustaining mechanism is a mechanism that supports a mind-world dependency relation. For some concepts there will be sustaining mechanisms in terms of neurologically specified transducers, but the majority of concepts require sustaining mechanisms that take the form of inferential processes. The idea is that although specific inferences implicating a concept aren't constitutive of the concept's content, they nonetheless contribute to the explanation of why the concept is tokened in a variety of contexts.

Since having a concept involves having an appropriate sustaining mechanism, a psychological model of concept acquisition is to be directed at the question of how various sustaining mechanisms are acquired. Margolis (1998 [chapter 24 in this volume]) examines this question in detail and catalogs a number of distinct types of sustaining mechanisms. An interesting result of this work is that a typical sustaining mechanism for natural kind concepts implicates a *kind syndrome*—the sort of information that one might accumulate in encountering a kind—along with a more general disposition to treat instances as members of the category only if they have the same essential property that is a reliable cause of the syndrome. The significance of this account of the sustaining mechanisms for natural kind concepts is that it readily translates into a learning model. Concept learning—at least for some natural kind concepts—proceeds by accumulating contingent, largely perceptual, information about a kind. This information, together with the more general disposition, establishes an inferential mechanism that causes the agent to token her concept under the conditions which, according to the Asymmetric Dependence Theory, are constitutive of conceptual content. Since the acquisitional process relies on a relatively general process and reflects the contingencies of experience, we think it is fair to say that this is a learning model. Such a model shows how concepts might be learned in spite of lacking semantic structure.

The exact implications of a model of this kind have yet to be worked out. Most likely, it's not one that a strict empiricist would endorse, since it seems to rely upon considerable innate machinery. At the same time, it brings Conceptual Atomism together with the idea that specific concepts needn't themselves be innate. In this way, it undermines one of the chief points of resistance to atomistic theories.[79]

The Problem of Explanatory Impotence   For many theorists in cognitive science, it's close to a platitude that lexical concepts can't be primitive even if the issue of radical concept nativism is put to the side. The basis for this sentiment is the thought that Conceptual Atomism is incapable of providing illuminating accounts of psychological phenomena. Were concepts atoms, they'd lack the resources to explain anything. For instance, how can atomists make sense of categorization? Without any structure, it would seem that concepts have to be applied directly, that is, without any mediating processes. Surely this is unrealistic. But what alternatives does an atomist have?

This problem encapsulates a major challenge to Conceptual Atomism, and it is vital that atomists have a response to it. Perhaps the main thing that an atomist can say is that, for any given concept, as much structure as you like may be invoked to explain its deployment, but with one serious qualification: This structure is to be treated as being merely associated with the concept rather than constituting part of its nature.

The distinction between a representation's being merely associated with another and its being partly constitutive of the other isn't new. Just about every theory makes the same distinction, each drawing the line in its own characteristic way.[80] For instance, on the Classical Theory, a concept's constitutive structure is restricted to its relations to concepts that encode the necessary and sufficient conditions for its application. You may think that bachelors make good friends; you may even rely on this belief whenever you deploy the concept BACHELOR. But on the Classical Theory, FRIEND

79. Fodor (1998) abandons a commitment to radical concept nativism, but in a different way than we are suggesting and one that we think is ultimately inadequate. In focusing on the question of how a primitive concept can be occasioned by its instances, Fodor argues for a metaphysical view about the nature of the properties that primitive concepts express. In effect, he defines these properties relative to the effects they have on human minds. However, he says nothing about the nature of the cognitive mechanisms that are responsible for concept acquisition. That is, he doesn't say anything about how these properties have the effects on us that they do. To us, this is an unsatisfactory account, since it doesn't really address the question of how concepts are acquired. For an extended discussion of these issues, see Laurence and Margolis (ms).
80. An exception would be an extreme form of meaning holism, according to which the content of a mental representation is determined by its relation to every other representation in the cognitive system. See, e.g., Lormand (1996).

remains outside of the structure of BACHELOR simply because it's not part of the defini-tion of BACHELOR. Like any other theorist, the atomist holds that people associate a considerable amount of information with any concept they possess. The only differ-ence is that whereas other theorists say that much of the information is collateral (and that only a small part is constitutive of the concept itself), atomists say that *all* of it is collateral. Thus for conceptual atomists a lexical concept can be unstructured while retaining its links to the representational resources that explain how it functions.

We take it that a move like this is implicit in most discussions of Conceptual Atomism. For instance, in spite of Fodor's defense of the idea that lexical concepts are primitive, he fully acknowledges the importance of prototype structure. He writes (1981, p. 293):

> Now, what is striking about prototypes as opposed to definitions is that, whereas the evidence for the psychological reality of the latter is, as we've seen, exiguous, there is abundant evidence for the psychological reality of the former. Eleanor Rosch ... and her colleagues, in particular, have provided striking dem-onstrations that the prototype structure of a concept determines much of the variance in a wide variety of experimental tasks, chronometric and otherwise.... Insofar as theses get established in cognitive psychology, I think we can take the reality of prototype structures as read.

In other words, Fodor endorses the existence of prototype structure and its explana-tory significance, yet he denies that this structure is part of the nature of concepts; for him it's entirely collateral.[81] For Fodor, prototypes are related to their concepts in much the way that a classical theorist would say that FRIEND is related to BACHELOR. If there is any difference, it's just that prototypes involve cognitive relations that have more reliable and pervasive effects.

The Problem of the Analytic Data   As we noted earlier, one reason that philosophers cite for thinking that concepts have partial definitions is that this provides an expla-nation of the analytic data. People can feel the pull of a proposed definition or a counterexample and, more generally, they are able to form judgments about the con-stitutive conditions for satisfying a concept. George Rey (1993) has marshaled an argument against Conceptual Atomism based on this data. His claim is that quite apart from the question of whether there are any analytic truths, people certainly have intuitions about what's analytic. One explanation of these intuitions is that they reflect constitutive relations among the concepts at stake. So barring an alternative atomistic explanation, we have simultaneously an argument against Conceptual Atomism and an argument for the Neoclassical Theory. Rey's position is that no plausible atomistic alternative exists.

One atomistic proposal Rey considers is that intuitions of analyticity reflect the way that a concept is introduced. For instance, one might try to maintain that we learn a concept like BACHELOR by being told that bachelors are unmarried men. This explanation is inadequate, however, as it fails to address a range of cases where there

---

81. More precisely, he denies that prototypes are part of the semantic structure of concepts. Since he seems to assume that there is nothing more to the structure of a concept than its semantic structure, he doesn't distinguish between the two claims. We've seen, however, that some theorists do distinguish them (e.g., dual theorists), so one has to be careful. We'll return to the question of how to think about conceptual structure in sec. 7.

are intuitions of analyticity, and it implies that there should be intuitions of analyticity in cases where there are none. Thus, as Rey points out, few of us learned what knowledge is by being told that knowledge is (at least) justified true belief. And in spite of the fact that almost all of us had our first acquaintance with Christopher Columbus by being told that Columbus discovered America, no one has the intuition that "Columbus discovered America" is analytic.[82]

Another atomistic explanation of our intuitions of analyticity is that they merely reflect deeply held beliefs, perhaps ones that are so central to our thinking or so entrenched that we find it nearly impossible to abandon them. For instance, logical and mathematical truths have always been among the best candidates for analytic truths, and they are especially difficult to abandon. Once again, however, Rey argues that the explanation fails in both directions. On the one hand, the most compelling analyses of philosophically interesting concepts (e.g., KNOWLEDGE) are hardly entrenched; they don't even command widespread acceptance. On the other hand, many beliefs that are deeply entrenched don't seem in the least analytic (e.g., that the Earth has existed for more than five minutes).

In Rey's view it's unlikely that atomists have an adequate explanation of our intuitions of analyticity. Of course, atomists might insist that it's wrong to expect a single explanation of the intuitions. After all, from the point of view of Conceptual Atomism, the intuitions of analyticity are faulty (see, e.g., Fodor 1998). But we think there is a simpler atomistic response.

To a first approximation, the intuitions of analyticity might be explained by claiming that they reflect our entrenched beliefs about the constitutive conditions for satisfying particular concepts. That is, they don't reflect actual constitutive conditions, but rather our deeply held *beliefs* about such conditions. Notice that this theory addresses all of the cases that Rey cites. Thus we believe that it's constitutive of being a bachelor that the person be unmarried and male. But we don't believe that it's constitutive of being Columbus that he discovered America. We believe that it's constitutive of knowledge that it be at least justified true belief. But we don't believe that it's constitutive of anything that the Earth should have existed for more than five minutes.

Unfortunately, this first approximation isn't quite right. Notice that we can have entrenched beliefs about what's constitutive of what that do not seem analytic. For example, many people are totally convinced that water is H_2O—that it is constitutive of water that it has the chemical composition H_2O. Yet no one thinks it's analytic that water is H_2O. The amendment that our theory requires is that it should be intuitively or pretheoretically obvious that the condition is constitutive. That is, on our theory a belief that, say, bachelors are unmarried should seem obvious, whereas the comparable belief in the case of water/H_2O should not. And that does seem right. Even people who are thoroughly convinced that water is H_2O don't think it is obviously so; you have to know your chemistry.

So there is an atomistic alternative to the Neoclassical Theory. Moreover, our account has an advantage over the Neoclassical Theory. One of the interesting psychological facts surrounding the intuitions of analyticity is that they vary in the

82. A related suggestion, which is subject to the same counterexamples, is that intuitions of analyticity derive from a process of conditioning. That is, they aren't owing to a single introduction to a concept but to an extended process in which people are exposed to the same information, over and over again, until it's drilled in.

extent to which they hold our convictions. The examples involving BACHELOR are about as firm as they come. But other cases are less secure. Is it analytic that cats are animals? Here our own intuitions waver, and the controversies surrounding this case seem to suggest that other people's intuitions are less secure as well. Our account of the analytic data predicts this variability. Part of the variability traces back to the clause that the constitutive relation has to seem obvious; surely some things are less obvious than others. But another part traces back to the clause that the belief is entrenched. We need only add that not all such beliefs are equally entrenched. Those that are highly entrenched will give rise to firm intuitions of analyticity; those that are less entrenched will give rise to shakier intuitions. As far as we can tell, Rey has no comparable explanation. Since he relies upon actual analytic connections among concepts, they would seem to be all on a par. So at this point in the debate, Conceptual Atomism may have an advantage over the Neoclassical Theory.

The Problem of Compositionality   In a sense, an atomistic theory of concepts such as Fodor's doesn't have any problem with conceptual combination. Yet this is only because, as the theory is posed, it is restricted to lexical concepts.

Suppose, however, that we treat Fodor's theory of reference determination as a comprehensive theory of concepts, in the same way that we initially treated the Prototype Theory. Then his theory appears to have difficulties that will seem all too familiar. Consider, for example, a concept we discussed in connection with the Prototype Theory, an example that's owing to Fodor himself—GRANDMOTHERS MOST OF WHOSE GRANDCHILDREN ARE MARRIED TO DENTISTS. It is hardly likely that this concept stands in a lawful dependency relation with the property of being a grandmother most of whose grandchildren are married to dentists. Nor is it likely that any other dependency relations that it might stand in are asymmetrically dependent on this one (Laurence 1993).[83]

Earlier (in sec. 3.2) we quoted Fodor and Lepore arguing against Prototype Theory in the following way:

1. Prototypes aren't compositional.
2. Concepts are compositional.
3. So concepts aren't prototypes.

But asymmetric dependence relations are in exactly the same position. The asymmetric dependence relations of complex concepts aren't a function of the asymmetric dependence relations of their constituents. Thus one could adopt an argument against the Asymmetric Dependence Theory that runs parallel to Fodor and Lepore's argument against the Prototype Theory:

1. Representations in asymmetric dependence relations aren't compositional.
2. Concepts are compositional.
3. So concepts aren't representations in asymmetric dependence relations.

Fodor, of course, is aware of the difficulties surrounding complex concepts. His own way out has two parts. The first we've already noted: He stipulates that his theory applies to lexical concepts only. The second, which is just as important, is that he appeals to a different theory to account for complex concepts. This move on his part

---

83. Fodor's theory also has special difficulties with any complex concept that by definition picks out items that can't be detected, e.g., UNDETECTABLE STAR BIRTH.

is crucial, since he needs some way to account for complex concepts, and asymmetric dependence won't do. The theory he ends up using is the Classical Theory. Not implausibly, Fodor claims that patently complex concepts have classical constituents.

What, then, is to stop the prototype theorist from saying the same thing? The short answer is: nothing. Prototype theorists can also stipulate that, as a theory of reference determination, the Prototype Theory only covers lexical concepts. Then once the reference for these concepts is determined, they can compose into increasingly complex concepts in accordance with classical principles.[84] Of course, the Prototype Theory may still have trouble with explaining the reference determination of lexical concepts—a problem we discussed earlier. The point here, however, is that the problems specifically associated with conceptual combination needn't be understood as giving an independent argument against the Prototype Theory. In particular, they needn't favor Conceptual Atomism over the Prototype Theory.

Finally, it is worth remarking that the Asymmetric Dependence Theory may have difficulties with a variety of concepts that have received little attention, because their interest depends to a large extent on their contributions to complex concepts. For instance, it's not the least bit clear what the Asymmetric Dependence Theory says about the semantic properties of concepts for prepositions, verbs, or adverbs. How does asymmetric dependence apply to OF or IS or QUICKLY? We can highlight the problem by briefly noting the difficulties that a comparative adjectival concept like BIG presents for the theory. Since things aren't big absolutely, but big only relative to some comparison class, it's difficult to imagine the lexical concept BIG standing in the necessary asymmetric dependence relations to determine its content. One might be tempted to suppose, instead, that it derives its semantic properties by abstraction from the complex concepts in which it figures. Perhaps concepts like BIG DOG, BIG CAT, BIG TREE, and so on stand in asymmetric dependence relations to big dogs, big cats, and so on; DOG and CAT stand in such relations as well; and the semantic properties of BIG are identified with whatever mediates between these different asymmetric dependence relations. On this account, BIG itself doesn't have its semantic properties in virtue of standing in its own asymmetric dependence relations. Its content is derived from other representations that do. Unfortunately, this solution doesn't work. The problem is that since it is not just lexical concepts that can be modified by BIG, but any concept (e.g., BIG GRANDMOTHERS MOST OF WHOSE GRANDCHILDREN ARE MARRIED TO DENTISTS), we are left with the implication that the conditions of asymmetric dependence are supposed to apply directly to an unbounded number of complex concepts—a view we have already rejected.[85]

---

84. As we've already noted, if a complex concept has a prototype, we will still need an explanation of why this is so. But this is a completely separate issue, one which may have nothing to do with the determination of the semantic properties of the concept.

85. A further complication—but one we'll ignore—is that, in point of fact, even concepts like CAT and DOG don't stand in simple asymmetric dependence relations with the properties they express. The problem is that concepts are tokened in the context of thoughts, and in most thought contexts a concept needn't stand in *any* lawful relations to the property it expresses. Perhaps CAT stands in a lawful relation to the property of being a cat in the context of the thought THAT'S A CAT. But it's hardly obvious that it will in contexts like CATS ARE EXTINCT or THAT'S NOT A CAT or even CATS ARE ANIMALS. On the contrary, it seems pretty clear that it won't in these contexts. This is actually quite a serious problem for theories of content generally, but very little has been said about it. For Fodor's attempt to address these problems, see Fodor (1990a [chapter 22 in this volume]).

The Problem of Empty and Coextensive Concepts   Conceptual Atomism implies that the reference of a lexical concept isn't determined by its structure. This view contrasts with all the other theories we've looked at, in that on all the other theories, lexical concepts have structure and it's their structure that determines their reference. One way of putting the difference is that other theories of concepts are descriptivist; an item falls under a concept just in case it satisfies the description that is encoded by the concept's structure. We've seen that the advantage of a nondescriptivist theory is that it is better equipped to handle difficulties such as the Problem of Stability; but descriptivist theories have their advantages too. One is a point that will be familiar from our discussion of Frege. If all there is to the content of a concept is its reference, then there is no way to distinguish coreferential concepts. Descriptivist theories have no trouble here, since they distinguish coreferential concepts in terms of their differing structures; the structure of a concept acts as its mode of presentation. In contrast, atomic theories have considerable trouble with coreferential concepts.

To see the significance of this issue, consider a case where two concepts are coextensive as a matter of necessity. Take, for instance, the concepts TRIANGULAR and TRILATERAL. Since every geometrical object that instantiates the one must instantiate the other, it's hard to see how to pull apart the properties *triangular* and *trilateral*. Supposing that there is a law connecting *triangular* with TRIANGULAR, there must also be a law connecting *trilateral* with TRIANGULAR. But surely the latter isn't asymmetrically dependent on the former. If trilateral objects didn't cause tokenings of TRIANGULAR, how *could* triangular objects cause tokenings of TRIANGULAR?[86] To take another example, suppose, as many philosophers do, that the properties *water* and H_2O are identical. How, then, can the Asymmetric Dependence Theory distinguish between the concepts WATER and H_2O? Both would be nomically dependent upon the very same property. These considerations are all the more vivid if we consider the large stock of empty concepts that we all possess, concepts such as UNICORN and ELF. All of these concepts are correlated with the same thing, namely, nothing. Yet they are clearly distinct from one another.

Another sort of example may be of special interest to psychologists. Many species besides humans are selectively sensitive to stimuli in a way that argues that they should be credited with concepts. At the same time, it seems that the concepts they have are not always the same as our own, even when they apparently have the same extension. For instance, Richard Herrnstein and his colleagues have conducted a range of experiments where pigeons have proven to be highly skilled at sorting photographs into those that depict trees from those that do not (Herrnstein 1979, 1984). The photographs were taken from a variety of perspectives—some showing close-ups of the ends of a few branches, some showing tree-covered shores from a substantial distance, and so on. Contrasting photographs depicted close-ups of celery stalks and the like. Despite the vast differences among the photographs of trees and the existence of the tree-like items in the nontree photographs, pigeons are able to sort them with considerable accuracy. What's more, they are able to do much the same for a number of other categories, including *human*, *fish*, *flower*, and *automobile*. It looks as though they are causally responsive to groupings of objects that are very nearly coextensive with salient categories of human cognition. At the same time, it

---

86. Cf. also pairs of concepts such as BUY and SELL. Every event in which something is bought is also an event in which something is sold. How can Asymmetric Dependence distinguish the two?

seems unlikely that we should credit them with possessing the same concepts that we do. Does a pigeon really have the concept AUTOMOBILE?

The Asymmetric Dependence Theory does have some resources for dealing with these problems, though it doesn't have an easy time with them. Fodor (1990c) suggests that the theory can account for empty concepts like UNICORN, since laws can hold between properties even if they are uninstantiated. Though there aren't any unicorns, it may still be a law that unicorns cause UNICORN's. And laws between other types of things (e.g., horses with artificial horns) and UNICORN's may be asymmetrically dependent on the unicorn/UNICORN law.

Another suggestion of Fodor's helps with the WATER/H_2O case. Here he is willing to accept they are distinct concepts on the grounds that H_2O is actually a complex concept and, in particular, that its structure implicates the concepts HYDROGEN and OXYGEN (Fodor 1990c). So one can't have the concept H_2O without having the concept HYDROGEN, but one can have the concept WATER without having any chemical concepts. Fodor summarizes this position by saying that his theory permits that some concepts are distinguished by their inferential roles—it's just that these are ones where the complexity of the concept isn't in dispute.

Still, it remains to be seen whether the Asymmetric Dependence Theory can avoid a larger commitment to the idea that the relations among concepts are constitutive of their identity. Consider, again, the concepts TRIANGULAR and TRILATERAL. The obvious suggestion for distinguishing between them is to supplement the conditions of asymmetric dependence with a limited amount of inferential role. One could say that TRIANGULAR involves an inferential disposition that links it specifically to the concept ANGLE, whereas TRILATERAL involves a disposition that links it to the concept SIDE. Similarly, one might hold that the difference between the pigeon concepts that pick out automobiles and trees and the human concepts, AUTOMOBILE and TREE, is to be given in terms of their inferential roles. TREE and AUTOMOBILE may be tied up with other concepts (e.g., NATURAL KIND and ARTIFACT), concepts that may have no role in pigeon cognition.

We suspect that many theorists who are sympathetic to information-based semantics also want to allow that inferential roles are, to some extent, part of the nature of concepts. In a way, the suggestion is to combine the Neoclassical Theory with the theories of reference that, in the first instance, find their home among conceptual atomists.[87] From the point of view of the Neoclassical Theory, it makes perfect sense to co-opt the Asymmetric Dependence Theory, or some other information-based semantics, since as we've already seen neoclassical structure is far too limited to account for the reference of a concept. On the other hand, the sort of theory that we are imagining here departs considerably from the doctrine of Conceptual Atomism. To the extent that the relations among lexical concepts determine their identity, lexical concepts can no longer be treated as atoms. They'd have some structure, even if it's not that much.

---

87. In philosophy, two-factor conceptual role theories take this shape. However, not all two-factor theories develop around the same motivation. Some do emphasize the referential properties of concepts, where conceptual roles are added to solve the problems that arise with coreferential concepts (see, e.g., Rey 1996 [chapter 15 in this volume]). But others seem to emphasize conceptual roles, where a theory like Asymmetric Dependence is added only to deal with the problems that arise from so-called Twin Earth examples (see, e.g., Block 1986).

Not surprisingly, Fodor is reluctant to supplement his Asymmetric Dependence Theory with inferential roles. His alternative suggestion is that coextensive concepts can be distinguished in terms of their formal properties. Like words, concepts are objects with formal and semantic properties. So just as the words "trilateral" and "triangular" are to be distinguished by their spelling or their orthography (as well as their content), the concepts TRIANGULAR and TRILATERAL are to be distinguished by whatever properties account for their being of distinct formal types. Whether this proposal works remains to be seen. It's an interesting suggestion, however, since it pulls apart several strands in the Fregean response to coextensive concepts. In the Fregean tradition, coextensive concepts are handled by saying that they have different modes of presentations. But the notion of a mode of presentation is generally understood in terms of its relevance for semantic phenomena. Don't forget: Frege said that a mode of presentation is contained within the sense of an expression and determines its reference. Another way of looking at Fodor's treatment of coextensive concepts is that he, too, wants to say that coextensive concepts differ with respect to their modes of presentation. Fodor would only add that modes of presentation needn't be part of the content of a concept; they needn't even determine a concept's reference. They simply give us a means for dealing with Frege's puzzle. In this way, Fodor may be able to maintain the view that lexical concepts are primitive, while avoiding some of the pitfalls that go with purely referential theories of content.

This completes our survey of theories of concepts. While our discussion is by no means exhaustive, we have tried to touch on the advantages and the problems associated with the major theories of concepts that are currently under debate.[88] As we've left things, no theory stands out as providing the best comprehensive account of concepts. One reason for this may be that there are different ways for a theory of concepts to contribute to an understanding of their nature. We'll take up this question in the next section.

Box 10

Summary of Criticisms of Conceptual Atomism

1. **The Problem of Radical Nativism**
   Under Conceptual Atomism, most lexical concepts turn out to be innate, including such unlikely candidates as XYLOPHONE and CARBURETOR.
2. **The Problem of Explanatory Impotence**
   If lexical concepts are primitive, they can't explain psychological phenomena such as categorization.
3. **The Problem of the Analytic Data**
   Conceptual Atomism lacks an adequate explanation of why people have intuitions of analyticity.
4. **The Problem of Compositionality**
   Atomistic theories of concepts have as much difficulty with conceptual combination as the Prototype Theory.
5. **The Problem of Empty and Coextensive Concepts**
   If concepts are atoms and the content of a concept is just its reference, then coextensive concepts can't be distinguished. As a result, all empty concepts have the same content.

---

88. An important exception is the Exemplar Theory. See, e.g., the excerpt from Smith and Medin (1981 [chapter 9 in this volume]) and Estes (1994).

7. Concluding Remarks

To begin, consider some of the explanatory roles that have been assigned to concepts. Among other things, different theories address:

- Fast categorization
- Considered acts of categorization
- Semantic application
- The licensing of inductive inference
- Analytic inference
- Concept Acquisition
- Compositionality
- Stability

Notice that the theories we've discussed aren't equally equipped to deal with each of these. For example, the Classical Theory has trouble with categorization, especially fast categorization, even though it has a natural account of compositionality (i.e., with respect to the reference determination of complex concepts). On the other hand, the Prototype Theory does far better with fast categorization, but it has considerable trouble with compositionality. Given the diversity of these explananda—and the fact that no single theory does justice to them all—one may be tempted to abandon the hope of providing a single, comprehensive theory of concepts. We think, instead, that it would be better to step back and ask how to understand claims about the nature of concepts.

Undoubtedly, some theorists want to insist that the nature of a concept is to be given solely in terms of *compositional reference-determining structure*. On this view, the structure of a concept can consist in nothing more than its relations to those other concepts that determine its reference under a principle of semantic composition. This view is what's driving the inference from the claim that prototype structures don't compose to the claim that concepts themselves don't compose. We've seen, however, that the inference breaks down. If there is more to a concept than its prototype, then there is no reason why concepts can't compose even when their prototypes don't. In a similar vein, one of the main charges against the Classical Theory—the Problem of Typicality Effects—vanishes once it's acknowledged that not all of a concept's components need to contribute to its reference. Dual Theorists tend to suppose that a concept's identification procedure has nothing to do with reference. We might say that this other structure is *nonsemantic conceptual structure*. So we have at least two views about the nature of concepts. One is that a concept can only have structure that compositionally determines its reference. The other is that concepts can have nonsemantic structure as well.

But a commitment to nonsemantic structure raises an important question: Why think that something that purports to be part of the nonsemantic structure of a concept, like a concept's identification procedure, is in any way constitutive of its identity? Why think, for example, that the features HAS GRAY HAIR, WEARS GLASSES, etc., are constitutive of GRANDMOTHER, or that FLIES, SINGS, etc., are constitutive of BIRD? The question is motivated, in part, by the assumption that some of the information associated with a concept is irrelevant to its identity. Presumably, if people think that birds are smarter than rocks, it doesn't follow merely from this fact alone that BEING SMARTER THAN A ROCK is a feature of BIRD. What is the difference, then, between BEING SMARTER

THAN A ROCK and FLIES?[89] This challenge—to single out those relations among concepts that are constitutive of their identity—is especially difficult when one is concerned with nonsemantic components. Without the constraint that a concept's structure must contribute to its content, there may be no principled way to draw the line. One suggestion—though admittedly a sketchy one—is that a concept's structure has to be robust and theoretically significant. We aren't sure what to say in general terms about when a structure is theoretically significant. As a guideline, however, we'd suggest cases where it's universal, or nearly universal, or where its appearance is a matter of psychological necessity. To the extent that prototypes are good candidates for non-semantic structure, this is because their deployment in fast categorization does appear to be psychologically necessary, and because particular prototypes figure in robust explanations of a variety of data. So maybe the claim that concepts have nonsemantic structure can be made to stick.

Yet another view of conceptual structure is that a concept may have components that are relevant to its semantics but not to its reference. In much this spirit, Hilary Putnam suggests that a word's meaning includes a prototype-like structure even though it plays no part in the determination of the word's reference (Putnam 1970, p. 148):

> [T]here is somehow associated with the word "tiger" a *theory*; not the actual theory we believe about tigers, which is very complex, but an oversimplified theory which describes a, so to speak, tiger *stereotype*. It describes ... a *normal member* of the natural kind. It is not necessary that we believe this theory, though in the case of "tiger" we do. But it is necessary that we be aware that *this* theory is associated with the word: if our stereotype of tiger ever changes, then the word "tiger" will have changed its meaning.

This claim easily translates into a view about concepts. The suggestion is that a concept can have structure that is partly constitutive of its content even if the structure isn't implicated in an account of the concept's reference. The thing we want to emphasize is that this is a different position than the Fregean view that there is more to the meaning of a concept than its reference. After all, it was part of the Fregean program that sense determines reference. In contrast, the present suggestion is that in addition to a reference, concepts have another aspect to their content, but one that doesn't determine their reference.[90]

Finally, a fourth way of understanding conceptual structure is in terms of the sustaining mechanisms that support a reference-determining relation, such as asymmetric dependence. On this view, one concept may be part of another's structure if the first is part of a theoretically significant sustaining mechanism associated with the second. Again, what counts as theoretically significant is a hard question. But as before, it's plausible enough to include ones that are universal (or nearly universal), or ones that appear to be a matter of psychological necessity. This might be where Jackendoff's 3-D representations find their place. Perhaps they are part of the structure of object concepts. Though they have problems determining reference, there is no reason why they shouldn't be an important part of the sustaining mechanisms for many object concepts. The same goes for prototypes. (For some suggestions along these lines, see Margolis 1998.)

Box 11

> *Four Types of Conceptual Structure*[91]
>
>   1. *Compositional Reference-Determining Structure*—structure that contributes to the content and reference of a concept via a compositional semantics.
>   2. *Nonsemantic Structure*—structure that doesn't contribute to the content of a concept, but does contribute significantly to some other theoretically important explanatory function of concepts.
>   3. *Nonreferential Semantic Structure*—structure that contributes to the content of a concept but is isolated from referential consequences.
>   4. *Sustaining Mechanism Structure*—structure that contributes to the content of a concept indirectly by figuring in a theoretically significant sustaining mechanism, i.e., a mechanism that supports a relation such as asymmetric dependence.

An interesting implication of these different ways of thinking about conceptual structure is that theories that appear to be in conflict may actually turn out to be good partners. We'll end by mentioning one of these possibilities, a form of the Dual Theory. The twist is that instead of using classical or theory-like cores, our suggestion is that this is the place to insert Conceptual Atomism. What allows for this arrangement is a simple refinement. In light of the varying interpretations of conceptual structure, let's say that Conceptual Atomism is the view that lexical concepts lack compositional reference-determining structure (even though they may have other types of structure and *will*, in particular, have sustaining mechanism structure).

Now different theorists have specified a number of roles for conceptual cores:

(1) Cores enter into the compositional processes that generate complex concepts.
(2) Cores determine reference.
(3) Cores act as the ultimate arbiters of categorization.
(4) Cores provide stability.[92]

Surprisingly, Conceptual Atomism does fairly well by these standards.

Compositionality We've argued that Conceptual Atomism has no difficulty with conceptual combination, since it can ultimately appeal to the Classical Theory's account. Thus, as far as compositionality goes, atomic cores and classical cores are entirely on a par.

Reference Determination While no theory offers a fully satisfactory account of reference determination, atomic theories do seem to offer an advance over

91. For each of these types of structure, there will be in principle two possible interpretations—one along the lines of the Containment Model and one along the lines of the Inferential Model (see sec. 1).
92. We've already discussed (1)–(3) in connection with Osherson and Smith (1981) and Smith et al. (1984). On stability, see Smith (1989).

descriptivist theories, including the Classical Theory and the Theory-Theory, since these face the Problem of Ignorance and Error.

Ultimate Arbiters of Categorization   Atomic cores do not give a satisfactory account of our most considered judgments about category membership, so they aren't suited to be the ultimate arbiters of categorization. Arguably, however, classical cores and cores with theory structure can do no better. Given the implications of confirmation holism, it may be that nothing short of the entire belief system can act as the ultimate arbiter of categorization. At best, the Theory-Theory might allow for the claim that reflective category judgments implicate theoretical knowledge, including knowledge that implicitly involves a commitment to essentialism. And, of course, this information couldn't be part of an atomic core. But Conceptual Atomism can explain these judgments by appeal to the same theoretical beliefs, claiming they are merely associated with the concept in question or, alternatively, claiming that they are part of the nonsemantic structure of the concept, alongside its prototype. The fact that the information specified by such beliefs appears to be of great theoretical significance argues for the atomist taking the latter view.[93]

Stability   Since Conceptual Atomism is not a descriptivist account, the concepts it covers are largely unaffected by changes in the beliefs that are associated with them. In contrast, the Classical Theory can't provide stability until it first overcomes the Problem of Ignorance and Error, and the Theory-Theory is notoriously poor at providing stability.

In short, atomistic cores are the best of the lot. To the extent that a version of the Dual Theory is to be preferred, it's one that brings together atomic cores with prototypes and perhaps some theory structure too, all united by a nondescriptivist account of reference.

This brings us full circle. At the beginning of our discussion, we took pains to emphasize that the study of concepts has had a rich history of interdisciplinary interaction. Also, all along we've been careful to tease apart the different explanatory goals that have accompanied the major theories. The integration of these goals yields four general ways of construing the nature of a concept. In our view, each deserves to be explored in considerable detail. No doubt, this will require further cooperation across the disciplinary boundaries of cognitive science.

8. Appendix: More on Ontology

We suspect that some philosophers may be unsatisfied with our brief discussion of the ontology of concepts, since there are other reasons than Frege's for claiming that concepts can't be mental representations. Christopher Peacocke and Georges Rey may be more representative of contemporary theorists who hold that concepts are

---

93. We should note that the question of whether people's knowledge in a given domain is organized around a theory is distinct from the question of whether that theory determines the content of the concepts involved. Theory-theorists usually assume that the claim about content comes for free once it's established that people have internally represented theories. But it doesn't (see Margolis 1995). For instance, one could easily maintain that an internal theory of belief subserves commonsense psychological reasoning, while also maintaining that this theory fails to determine the contents for BELIEF, DESIRE, etc. Instead their contents may be determined, for example, in accordance with an information-based semantics.

abstracta (and not mental entities). For though they are both happy to allow that mental representations have their place in the scientific study of the mind, they hold out by claiming that concepts can't be identified with mental representations. Their worry, in brief, is that mental representations and concepts exhibit too loose of a connection; so they have to be distinguished. Toward the beginning of his *A Study of Concepts*, Peacocke insists on the distinction by claiming that "It is possible for one and the same concept to receive different mental representations in different individuals" (1992, p. 3). And in a recent overview of the literature on concepts, Rey remarks in much the same spirit (1994, p. 186):

> [M]any philosophers take the view that these internal representation types would no more be identical to concepts than are the type words in a natural language. One person might express the concept CITY by the word "city," another by the word "ville"; still another perhaps by a mental image of bustling boulevards; but, for all that, they might have the same concept CITY; one could believe and another doubt that cities are healthy places to live. Moreover, different people could employ the same representation to express different concepts: one person might use an image of Paris to express PARIS, another to express FRANCE.

Notice that there are two arguments here. The first is that just as different words can express the same content (e.g., the English "cat" and the French "chat"), mental representations of different types can correspond to the same concept. This is the heart of Peacocke's position. But Rey adds a second argument, going in the other direction: A single type of mental representation might correspond to multiple concepts. That is, tokens of the same representation type might turn out to express different concepts.[94]

In our view, neither of these arguments works. Despite their initial appeal, they fail to raise any difficulties for the view that concepts are mental representations.

Take the first argument. Suppose one were to grant that different types of mental representations can express the same concept—a point to which we'll return. Still, it doesn't follow that concepts can't be identified with types of mental representations. If two or more different representations of different types express the same concept, then, of course, that concept cannot be identified with one or the other of these two types. But there is no reason why the concept shouldn't be identified with a broader, more encompassing type—one that has the mental representations of these other two types among its tokens. Just as particular Persian cats can be cats alongside Siamese cats and tabbies, so tokens of different types of representations can all be instances of a broader representation type. In short, granting that different types of internal representations can express the same concept raises no difficulties for the view that concepts are mental representations.

On the other hand, it's hardly clear that one should grant that different types of mental representations can express the same concept. Perhaps a word-like mental representation and a mental image with the same, or similar, content express different concepts. Certainly they will have substantially different inferential roles. Whether

94. For ease of exposition, we will follow Rey in using the locution that a mental representation "expresses a concept." If concepts are mental representations, however, it would be better to say that a token mental representation is an instance of a mental representation type and is a concept by virtue of instantiating that type.

these two should be treated as the same concept would seem to be an open theoretical question, not one to be settled by fiat. For instance, one would face the question of whether inferential roles are constitutive of concepts and, to the extent that they are, the question of which inferential roles are relevant to conceptual identity. Given the tremendous controversy surrounding both of these issues, it makes no sense to assume from the outset that any particular difference in inferential role is irrelevant to the issue of conceptual identity.

What about Rey's second argument, that a given type of representation might be used to express different concepts by different individuals?[95] Here too the point can be granted without abandoning the claim that concepts are mental representations. If a given type of representation, M, can be used to express different types of concepts, then of course we cannot identify these different concepts with M. But nothing stops us from identifying each of the different types of concepts (e.g., PARIS and FRANCE) with other typings of mental representations, each of which can be instantiated by instances of M. For example, M might be a representation that is typed in terms of its orthographic or imagistic properties (or some other nonsemantic property). At the same time, M will represent one thing or another, depending upon various other facts about it—facts about its relations to other mental representations, or perhaps facts about its causal or nomic relations to things in the world. Which concept a given instance of M expresses will then depend not just on its being a token of M but also on its typing in virtue of these other facts. In other words, concepts can still be mental representations, so long as the conditions for typing representation tokens aren't confined to a highly limited set of formal properties.

As before, though, it's hardly clear that representationalists have to be so concessive. That is, it isn't obvious that as a matter of psychological fact, a given type of representation can be used to express different concepts by different individuals. For all we know, one's image of Paris might not be suited to serve as a concept of France, even if it seems on a given occurrence that it does. Why trust introspection in such cases? Perhaps what's really going on is that one consciously entertains an image of Paris and this occasions a (distinct) mental representation of France.[96]

In short, Peacocke's and Rey's arguments don't work. We haven't been given sufficient reason to think that concepts can't be mental representations, even if we accept the assumptions they ask us to make. Granting the psychological reality of mental representations, the implications are clear: Nothing is lost by saying that concepts *are* mental representations.[97]

References

Antony, L. (1987). Naturalized Epistemology and the Study of Language. In A. Shimony and D. Nails (Eds.), *Naturalistic Epistemology* (pp. 235–257). Dordrecht: D. Reidel.

95. Or, for that matter, that a single individual might use the same type of representation to express different concepts at different times.
96. That said, it does seem likely that for at least some typings of mental representations, representations so typed should be capable of instantiating more than one concept. For example, sometimes mental representations may acquire new meanings and thereby become different concepts. But even then there is no reason to say that the concepts—old and new—aren't mental representations.
97. We would like to thank Peter Carruthers, Richard Grandy, Jean Kazez, Daniel Osherson, Sarah Sawyer, Scott Sturgeon, and Jonathan Sutton for their comments on this chapter.

Armstrong, S., Gleitman, L., and Gleitman, H. (1983). What Some Concepts Might Not Be. *Cognition*, 13, 263–308. [Chapter 10, this volume.]

Ayer, A. (1946/1952). *Language, Truth and Logic*. New York: Dover.

Baillargeon, R. (1993). The Object Concept Revisited: New Directions in the Investigation of Infants' Physical Knowledge. In C. Granrund (Ed.), *Visual Perception and Cognition in Infancy* (pp. 265–315). Hillsdale, NJ: Lawrence Erlbaum Associates. [Chapter 25, this volume.]

Barsalou, L. (1987). The Instability of Graded Structure: Implications for the Nature of Concepts. In U. Neisser (Ed.), *Concepts and Conceptual Development: Ecological and Intellectual Factors in Categorization* (pp. 101–140). New York: Cambridge University Press.

Block, N. (1986). Advertisement for a Semantics for Psychology. In P. A. French, T. Uehling Jr., and H. Wettstein (Eds.), *Midwest Studies in Philosophy*, vol. 10: *Studies in the Philosophy of Mind* (pp. 615–678). Minneapolis: University of Minnesota Press.

Burge, T. (1977). Belief *De Re. Journal of Philosophy*, 74, 338–362.

Burge, T. (1979). Individualism and the Mental. In P. French, T. Uehling Jr., and H. Wettstein (Eds.), *Midwest Studies in Philosophy*, vol. 4: *Studies in Metaphysics* (pp. 73–121). Minneapolis: University of Minnesota Press.

Carey, S. (1985). *Conceptual Change in Childhood*. Cambridge, MA: MIT Press.

Carey, S. (1991). Knowledge Acquisition: Enrichment or Conceptual Change? In S. Carey and R. Gelman (Eds.), *The Epigenesis of Mind: Essays on Biology and Cognition* (pp. 257–291). Hillsdale, NJ: Lawrence Erlbaum Associates. [Chapter 20, this volume.]

Carnap, R. (1932/1959). Uberwindung der Metaphysik durch Logische Analyse der Sprache. *Erkenntnis*, vol. 2. Reprinted as "The Elimination of Metaphysics through Logical Analysis of Language" in A. Ayer (Ed.), *Logical Positivism* (pp. 60–81). New York: The Free Press.

Chomsky, N. (1959). Review of Skinner's *Verbal Behavior. Language*, 35, 26–58.

Chomsky, N. (1986). *Knowledge of Language: Its Nature, Origin, and Use*. New York: Praeger.

Clark, E. (1973). What's in a Word? On the Child's Acquisition of Semantics in His First Language. In T. Moore (Ed.), *Cognitive Development and the Acquisition of Language* (pp. 65–110). New York: Academic Press.

Crane, R. (1995). *The Mechanical Mind: A Philosophical Introduction to Minds, Machines and Mental Representations*. London: Penguin.

Dancy, J. (1985). *Introduction to Contemporary Epistemology*. Cambridge, MA: Blackwell.

Devitt, M. (1981). *Designation*. New York: Columbia University Press.

Devitt, M., and Sterelny, K. (1987). *Language and Reality: An Introduction to the Philosophy of Language*. Cambridge, MA: MIT Press.

Di Sciullo, A., and Williams, E. (1987). *On the Definition of Word*. Cambridge MA: MIT Press.

Dretske, F. (1981). *Knowledge and the Flow of Information*. Cambridge, MA: MIT Press.

Estes, W. (1994). *Classification and Cognition*. New York: Oxford University Press.

Fillmore, C. (1982). Towards a Descriptive Framework for Spatial Deixis. In R. Jarvella and W. Klein (Eds.), *Speech, Place, and Action* (pp. 31–59). London: Wiley.

Fodor, J. A. (1975). *The Language of Thought*. New York: Thomas Y. Crowell.

Fodor, J. A. (1981). The Present Status of the Innateness Controversy. In *Representations: Philosophical Essays on the Foundations of Cognitive Science* (pp. 257–316). Cambridge, MA: MIT Press.

Fodor, J. A. (1987). *Psychosemantics: The Problem of Meaning in the Philosophy of Mind*. Cambridge, MA: MIT Press.

Fodor, J. A. (1990a). Information and Representation. In P. Hanson (Ed.), *Information, Language, and Cognition* (pp. 175–190). Vancouver: University of British Columbia Press. [Chapter 22, this volume.]

Fodor, J. A. (1990b). A Theory of Content, I: The Problem. In *A Theory of Content and Other Essays* (pp. 51–87). Cambridge, MA: MIT Press.

Fodor, J. A. (1990c). A Theory of Content, II: The Theory. In *A Theory of Content and Other Essays* (pp. 89–136). Cambridge, MA: MIT Press.

Fodor, J. A. (1998). *Concepts: Where Cognitive Science Went Wrong*. New York: Oxford University Press.

Fodor, J. A., Garrett, M., Walker, E., and Parkes, C. (1980). Against Definitions. *Cognition*, 8, 263–367. [Excerpted as chapter 21, this volume.]

Fodor, J. A., and Lepore, E. (1992). *Holism: A Shopper's Guide*. Cambridge, MA: Basil Blackwell.

Fodor, J. A., and Lepore, E. (1996). The Red Herring and the Pet Fish: Why Concepts Still Can't Be Prototypes. *Cognition*, 58, 253–270.

Fodor, J. D., Fodor, J. A., and Garrett, M. (1975). The Psychological Unreality of Semantic Representations. *Linguistic Inquiry*, 6, 515–532.

Foss, D. (1969). Decision Processes during Sentence Comprehension: Effects of Lexical Item Difficulty and Position upon Decision Times. *Journal of Verbal Learning and Verbal Behavior*, 8, 457–462.

Frege, G. (1892/1966). On Sense and Reference. M. Black (Tr.). In P. Geach and M. Black (Eds.), *Translations from the Philosophical Writings of Gottlob Frege* (pp. 56–78). Oxford: Blackwell.

Gelman, S., Coley, J., and Gottfried, G. (1994). Essentialist Beliefs in Children: The Acquisition of Concepts and Theories. In L. Hirschfeld and S. Gelman (Eds.), *Mapping the Mind: Domain Specificity in Cognition and Culture* (pp. 341–365). New York: Cambridge University Press.

Gelman, S., and Wellman, H. (1991). Insides and Essences: Early Understandings of the Non-Obvious. *Cognition*, 38, 213–244. [Chapter 26, this volume.]

Gettier, E. (1963). Is Justified True Belief Knowledge? *Analysis*, 23, 121–123.

Giaquinto, M. (1996). Non-Analytic Conceptual Knowledge. *Mind*, 105, 249–268.

Gleitman, L., Gleitman, H., Miller, C., and Ostrin, R. (1996). Similar, and Similar Concepts. *Cognition*, 58, 321–376.

Gopnik, A. (1996). The Scientist as Child. *Philosophy of Science*, 63, 485–514.

Gopnik, A., and Meltzoff, A. (1997). *Words, Thoughts, and Theories*. Cambridge, MA: MIT Press.

Grandy, R. (1990a). Concepts, Prototypes, and Information. In E. Villanueva (Ed.), *Information, Semantics, and Epistemology*. Cambridge, MA: Blackwell.

Grandy, R. (1990b). Understanding and the Principle of Compositionality. In J. Tomberlin (Ed.), *Philosophical Perspectives*, vol. 4: *Action Theory and Philosophy of Mind* (pp. 557–572). Atascadero, CA: Ridgeview Publishing Company.

Grimshaw, J. (unpublished). Semantic Structure and Semantic Content. Rutgers University. Department of Linguistics and Center for Cognitive Science.

Hahn, H. (1933/1959). Logic, Mathematics and Knowledge of Nature. In A. Ayer (Ed.), *Logical Positivism* (pp. 147–161). New York: The Free Press.

Hampton, J. (1987). Inheritance of Attributes in Natural-Concept Conjunctions. *Memory and Cognition*, 15, 55–71.

Hampton, J. (1991). The Combination of Prototype Concepts. In P. Schwanenflugel (Ed.), *The Psychology of Word Meaning* (pp. 91–116). Hillsdale, NJ: Lawrence Erlbaum Associates, Inc.

Herrnstein, R. (1979). Acquisition, Generalization, and Discrimination Reversal of a Natural Concept. *Journal of Experimental Psychology: Animal Behavior Processes*, 5, 118–129.

Herrnstein, R. (1984). Objects, Categories, and Discriminative Stimuli. In H. Roitblat, T. Bever, and H. Terrace (Eds.), *Animal Cognition* (pp. 233–261). Hillsdale, NJ: Lawrence Erlbaum Associates.

Horwich, P. (1992). Chomsky versus Quine on the Analytic-Synthetic Distinction. *Proceedings of the Aristotelian Society*, 92, 95–108.

Jackendoff, R. (1983). *Semantics and Cognition*. Cambridge, MA: MIT Press.

Jackendoff, R. (1987). *Consciousness and the Computational Mind*. Cambridge, MA: MIT Press.

Jackendoff, R. (1989). What Is a Concept, That a Person May Grasp It? *Mind and Language*, 4, 68–102. Reprinted Jackendoff (1992), *Languages of the Mind: Essays on Mental Representation* (pp. 21–52). [Chapter 13, this volume.]

Jackendoff, R. (1991). The Problem of Reality. *Nôus*, 25. Reprinted Jackendoff (1992), *Languages of the Mind: Essays on Mental Representation* (pp. 157–176). Cambridge, MA: MIT Press.

Kant, I. (1787/1965). *Critique of Pure Reason*. N. Kemp Smith (Tr.). New York: St. Martin's Press.

Katz, J. (1972). *Semantic Theory*. New York: Harper and Row. [Excerpted as chapter 4, this volume.]

Katz. J. (1997). Analyticity, Necessity, and the Epistemology of Semantics. *Philosophy and Phenomenological Research*, 57, 1–28.

Keil, F. (1989). *Concepts, Kinds, and Cognitive Development*. Cambridge, MA: MIT Press.

Kintsch, W. (1974). *The Representation of Meaning in Memory*. Hillsdale, NJ: Lawrence Erlbaum Associates.

Komatsu, L. (1992). Recent Views of Conceptual Structure. *Psychological Bulletin*, 112, 500–526.

Kripke, S. (1972/1980). *Naming and Necessity*. Cambridge, MA: Harvard University Press.

Kuhn, T. (1962). *The Structure of Scientific Revolutions*. Chicago: University of Chicago Press.

Lakoff, G. (1987). Cognitive Models and Prototype Theory. In U. Neisser (Ed.), *Concepts and Conceptual Development: Ecological and Intellectual Factors in Categorization* (pp. 63–100). New York: Cambridge University Press. [Chapter 18, this volume.]

Landau, B. (1982). Will the Real Grandmother Please Stand Up? The Psychological Reality of Dual Meaning Representations. *Journal of Psycholinguistic Research*, 11(1), 47–62.

Laurence, S. (1993). *Naturalism and Language: A Study of the Nature of Linguistic Kinds and Mental Represen-tation*. Ph.D. thesis, Rutgers University.

Laurence, S., and Margolis, E. (ms). Concepts, Content, and the Innateness Controversy.

Leslie, A. (1994). ToMM, ToBy, and Agency: Core Architecture and Domain Specificity. In L. Hirschfeld and S. Gelman (Eds.), *Mapping the Mind: Domain Specificity in Cognition and Culture* (pp. 119–148). New York: Cambridge University Press.

Levin, B., and Pinker, S. (1991a). Introduction. In *Lexical and Conceptual Semantics*. Cambridge, MA: Black-well.

Levin, B., and Pinker, S. (1991b). *Lexical and Conceptual Semantics*. Cambridge, MA: Blackwell.

Lewis, D. (1970). How to Define Theoretical Terms. *Journal of Philosophy*, 67, 427–446.

Lewis, D. (1972). Psychophysical and Theoretical Identifications. *Australasian Journal of Philosophy*, 50, 249–258.

Locke, J. (1690/1975). *An Essay Concerning Human Understanding*. New York: Oxford University Press.

Lormand, E. (1996). How to Be a Meaning Holist. *Journal of Philosophy*, 93, 51–73.

Malt, B., and Smith, E. (1984). Correlated Properties in Natural Categories. *Journal of Verbal Learning and Verbal Behavior*, 23, 250–269.

Margolis, E. (1994). A Reassessment of the Shift from the Classical Theory of Concepts to Prototype Theory. *Cognition*, 51, 73–89.

Margolis, E. (1995). The Significance of the Theory Analogy in the Psychological Study of Concepts. *Mind and Language*, 10, 45–71.

Margolis, E. (1998). How to Acquire a Concept. *Mind and Language*, 13, 347–369. [Chapter 24, this volume.]

Margolis, E., and Laurence, S. (ms). Concepts as Mental Representations.

Marr, D. (1982). *Vision: A Computational Investigation into the Human Representation and Processing of Visual Information*. New York: W. H. Freeman and Company.

Medin, D. (1989). Concepts and Conceptual Structure. *American Psychologist*, 44, 1469–1481.

Medin, D., Goldstone, R., and Gentner, D. (1993). Respects for Similarity. *Psychological Review*, 100, 254–278.

Medin, D., and Ortony, A. (1989). Psychological Essentialism. In S. Vosniadou and A. Ortony (Eds.), *Simi-larity and Analogical Reasoning* (pp. 179–195). New York: Cambridge University Press.

Medin, D., and Shoben, E. (1988). Context and Structure in Conceptual Combination. *Cognitive Psychology*, 20, 158–190.

Mervis, C., Catlin, J., and Rosch, E. (1976). Relationships among Goodness-of-Example, Category Norms, and Word Frequency. *Bulletin of the Psychonomic Society*, 7, 283–284.

Miller, G. (1978). Semantic Relations among Words. In M. Halle, J. Bresnan, and G. Miller (Eds.), *Linguistic Theory and Psychological Reality* (pp. 60–118). Cambridge, MA: MIT Press.

Miller, G., and Johnson-Laird, P. (1976). *Language and Perception*. Cambridge, MA: Harvard University Press.

Millikan, R. (1984). *Language, Thought, and Other Biological Categories: New Foundations for Realism*. Cam-bridge, MA: MIT Press.

Millikan, R. (1998). A Common Structure for Concepts of Individuals, Stuffs, and Real Kinds: More Mama, More Milk, and More Mouse. *Behavioral and Brain Sciences*, 21, 55–65. [Chapter 23, this volume.]

Murphy, G., and Medin, D. (1985). The Role of Theories in Conceptual Coherence. *Psychological Review*, 92(3), 289–316. [Chapter 19, this volume.]

Osherson, D., and Smith, E. (1981). On the Adequacy of Prototype Theory as a Theory of Concepts. *Cognition*, 9, 35–58. [Chapter 11, this volume.]

Osherson, D., and Smith, E. (1982). Gradedness and Conceptual Combination. *Cognition*, 12, 299–318.

Peacocke, C. (1992). *A Study of Concepts*. Cambridge, MA: MIT Press.

Peacocke, C. (1996a). Précis of *A Study of Concepts*. *Philosophy and Phenomenological Research*, 56, 407–411. [Chapter 14, this volume.]

Peacocke, C. (1996b). Can Possession Conditions Individuate Concepts? *Philosophy and Phenomenological Research*, 56, 433–460. [Excerpted as chapter 16, this volume.]

Peacocke, C. (1997). Implicit Conceptions, Understanding and Rationality. Sociedad Filosofica Ibero Amer-icana (SOFIA), 10th Annual Conference, June 1997. Barcelona, Spain.

Pinker, S. (1989). *Learnability and Cognition: The Acquisition of Argument Structure*. Cambridge, MA: MIT Press.

Plato (1981). Euthyphro. In G. Grube (Ed. and tr.), *Five Dialogues* (pp. 5–22). Indianapolis: Hackett Publish-ing Co. [Chapter 2, this volume.]

Putnam, H. (1962). The Analytic and the Synthetic. In H. Feigl and G. Maxwell (Eds.), *Minnesota Studies in the Philosophy of Science*, vol. 3. Minneapolis: University of Minnesota Press.

Putnam, H. (1970). Is Semantics Possible? In H. Kiefer and M. Munitz (Eds.), *Language, Belief and Metaphysics* (pp. 50–63). New York: State University of New York Press. [Chapter 7, this volume.]

Putnam, H. (1975). The Meaning of Meaning. In K. Gunderson (Ed.), *Language, Mind and Knowledge*. Minneapolis: University of Minnesota Press.

Quine, W. (1935/1976). Truth by Convention. In *The Ways of Paradox and Other Essays* (pp. 77–106). Cambridge, MA: Harvard University Press.

Quine, W. (1951/1980). Two Dogmas of Empiricism. In *From a Logical Point of View: Nine Logico-Philosophical Essays* (pp. 20–46). Cambridge, MA: Harvard University Press. [Chapter 5, this volume.]

Quine, W. (1954/1976). Carnap and Logical Truth. In *The Ways of Paradox and Other Essays* (pp. 107–132). Cambridge, MA: Harvard University Press.

Ramsey, F. (1929/1990). Theories. In D. H. Mellor (Ed.), *Philosophical Papers* (pp. 112–136). New York: Cambridge University Press.

Rey, G. (1983). Concepts and Stereotypes. *Cognition*, 15, 237–262. [Chapter 12, this volume.]

Rey, G. (1993). The Unavailability of What We Mean: A Reply to Quine, Fodor, and Lepore. In J. A. Fodor and E. Lepore (Eds.), *Holism: A Consumer Update* (pp. 61–101). Atlanta: Rodopi B. V.

Rey, G. (1994). Concepts. In S. Guttenplan (Ed.), *A Companion to the Philosophy of Mind* (pp. 185–193). Cambridge, MA: Blackwell.

Rey, G. (1996). Resisting Primitive Compulsions. *Philosophy and Phenomenological Research*, 56, 419–424. [Chapter 15, this volume.]

Rips, L. (1995). The Current Status of Research on Concept Combination. *Mind and Language*, 10, 72–104.

Rosch, E. (1973). On the Internal Structure of Perceptual and Semantic Categories. In T. Moore (Ed.), *Cognitive Development and the Acquisition of Language* (pp. 111–144). New York: Academic Press.

Rosch, E. (1978). Principles of Categorization. In E. Rosch and B. Lloyd (Eds.), *Cognition and Categorization* (pp. 27–48). Hillsdale, NJ: Lawrence Erlbaum Associates. [Chapter 8, this volume.]

Rosch, E., and Mervis, C. (1975). Family Resemblances: Studies in the Internal Structure of Categories. *Cognitive Psychology*, 7, 573–605.

Rosch, E., Mervis, C., Gray, W., Johnson, D., and Boyes-Braem, P. (1976). Basic Objects in Natural Categories. *Cognitive Psychology*, 8, 382–439.

Sellars, W. (1956). Empiricism and the Philosophy of Mind. In H. Feigl and M. Scriven (Eds.), *The Foundations of Science and the Concepts of Psychology and Psychoanalysis: Minnesota Studies in the Philosophy of Science* (pp. 253–329). Minneapolis: University of Minnesota Press.

Shepard, R. (1974). Representation of Structure in Similarity Data: Problems and Prospects. *Psychometrika*, 39, 373–421.

Smith, E. (1989). Concepts and Induction. In. M. Posner (Ed.), *Foundations of Cognitive Science*. Cambridge, MA: MIT Press.

Smith, E. (1995). Concepts and Categorization. In E. Smith and D. Osherson (Eds.), *Thinking: An Invitation to Cognitive Science*, Vol. 3, second edition (pp. 3–33). Cambridge, MA: MIT Press.

Smith, E., and Medin, D. (1981). *Categories and Concepts*. Cambridge, MA: Harvard University Press.

Smith, E., Medin, D., and Rips, L. (1984). A Psychological Approach to Concepts: Comments on Rey's "Concepts and Stereotypes." *Cognition*, 17, 265–274.

Smith, E., Osherson, D,. Rips, L., and Keane, M. (1988). Combining Prototypes: A Selective Modification Model. *Cognitive Science*, 12, 485–527. [Chapter 17, this volume.]

Smith, E., Shoben, E., and Rips, L. (1974). Structure and Process in Semantic Memory: A Featural Model for Semantic Decisions. *Psychological Review*, 81(3), 214–241.

Spelke, E. (1990). Principles of Object Perception. *Cognitive Science*, 14, 29–56.

Stich, S. (1993). Moral Philosophy and Mental Representation. In M. Hechter, L. Nadel, and R. Michod (Eds.), *The Origin of Values* (pp. 215–228). Hawthorne, NY: Aldine de Gruyter.

Tversky, A. (1977). Features of Similarity. *Psychological Review*, 84(4), 327–352.

Wellman, H. (1990). *The Child's Theory of Mind*. Cambridge, MA: MIT Press.

Wittgenstein, L. (1953/1958). *Philosophical Investigations*. 3d edition. Anscombe (Tr.). Oxford: Blackwell. [Excerpted as chapter 6, this volume.]

Zadeh, L. (1965). Fuzzy Sets. *Information and Control*, 8, 338–353.

PART I

Origins of the Contemporary Study of Concepts

The Classical Theory

Chapter 2

Euthyphro

Plato

Euthyphro:[1] What's new, Socrates, to make you leave your usual haunts in the Lyceum and spend your time here by the king-archon's court? Surely you are not prosecuting anyone before the king-archon as I am?

Socrates: The Athenians do not call this a prosecution but an indictment, Euthyphro.

E: What is this you say? Someone must have indicted you, for you are not going to tell me that you have indicted someone else.

S: No indeed.

E: But someone else has indicted you?

S: Quite so.

E: Who is he?

S: I do not really know him myself, Euthyphro. He is apparently young and unknown. They call him Meletus, I believe. He belongs to the Pitthcan deme, if you know anyone from that deme called Meletus, with long hair, not much of a beard, and a rather aquiline nose.

E: I don't know him, Socrates. What charge does he bring against you?

S: What charge? A not ignoble one I think, for it is no small thing for a young man to have knowledge of such an important subject. He says he knows how our young men are corrupted and who corrupts them. He is likely to be wise, and when he sees my ignorance corrupting his contemporaries, he proceeds to accuse me to the city as to their mother. I think he is the only one of our public men to start out the right way, for it is right to care first that the young should be as good as possible, just as a good farmer is likely to take care of the young plants first, and of the others later. So, too, Meletus first gets rid of us who corrupt the young shoots, as he says, and then afterwards he will obviously take care of the older ones and become a source of great blessings for the city, as seems likely to happen to one who started out this way.

E: I could wish this were true, Socrates, but I fear the opposite may happen. He seems to me to start out by harming the very heart of the city by attempting to wrong you. Tell me, what does he say you do to corrupt the young?

S: Strange things, to hear him tell it, for he says that I am a maker of gods, and on the ground that I create new gods while not believing in the old gods, he has indicted me for their sake, as he puts it.

This chapter is translated by G. M. A. Grube; the footnotes are also his. [EM and SL]
1. We know nothing about Euthyphro except what we can gather from this dialogue. He is obviously a professional priest who considers himself an expert on ritual and on piety generally, and, it seems, is generally so considered. One Euthyphro is mentioned in Plato's *Cratylus* (396d) who is given to *enthousiasmos*, inspiration or possession, but we cannot be sure that it is the same person.

E: I understand, Socrates. This is because you say that the divine sign keeps coming to you.[2] So he has written this indictment against you as one who makes innovations in religious matters, and he comes to court to slander you, knowing that such things are easily misrepresented to the crowd. The same is true in my case. Whenever I speak of divine matters in the assembly and foretell the future, they laugh me down as if I were crazy; and yet I have foretold nothing that did not happen. Nevertheless, they envy all of us who do this. One need not worry about them, but meet them head-on.

S: My dear Euthyphro, to be laughed at does not matter perhaps, for the Athenians do not mind anyone they think clever, as long as he does not teach his own wisdom, but if they think that he makes others to be like himself they get angry, whether through envy, as you say, or for some other reason.

E: I have certainly no desire to test their feelings towards me in this matter.

S: Perhaps you seem to make yourself but rarely available, and not to be willing to teach your own wisdom, but I'm afraid that my liking for people makes them think that I pour out to anybody anything I have to say, not only without charging a fee but even glad to reward anyone who is willing to listen. If then they were intending to laugh at me, as you say they laugh at you, there would be nothing unpleasant in their spending their time in court laughing and jesting, but if they are going to be serious, the outcome is not clear except to you prophets.

E: Perhaps it will come to nothing, Socrates, and you will fight your case as you think best, as I think I will mine.

S: What is your case, Euthyphro? Are you the defendant or the prosecutor?

E: The prosecutor.

S: Whom do you prosecute?

E: One whom I am thought crazy to prosecute.

S: Are you pursuing someone who will easily escape you?

E: Far from it, for he is quite old.

S: Who is it?

E: My father.

S: My dear sir! Your own father?

E: Certainly.

S: What is the charge? What is the case about?

E: Murder, Socrates.

S: Good heavens! Certainly, Euthyphro, most men would not know how they could do this and be right. It is not the part of anyone to do this, but of one who is far advanced in wisdom.

E: Yes, by Zeus, Socrates, that is so.

S: Is then the man your father killed one of your relatives? Or is that obvious, for you would not prosecute your father for the murder of a stranger.

---

2. In Plato, Socrates always speaks of his divine sign or voice as intervening to prevent him from doing or saying something (e.g., *Apology* 31d), but never positively. The popular view was that it enabled him to foretell the future, and Euthyphro here represents that view. Note, however, that Socrates dissociates himself from "you prophets" (3e).

E: It is ridiculous, Socrates, for you to think that it makes any difference whether the victim is a stranger or a relative. One should only watch whether the killer acted justly or not; if he acted justly, let him go, but if not, one should prosecute, even if the killer shares your hearth and table. The pollution is the same if you knowingly keep company with such a man and do not cleanse yourself and him by bringing him to justice. The victim was a dependent of mine, and when we were farming in Naxos he was a servant of ours. He killed one of our household slaves in drunken anger, so my father bound him hand and foot and threw him in a ditch, then sent a man here to enquire from the priest what should be done. During that time he gave no thought or care to the bound man, as being a killer, and it was no matter if he died, which he did. Hunger and cold and his bonds caused his death before the messenger came back from the seer. Both my father and my other relatives are angry that I am prosecuting my father for murder on behalf of a murderer when he hadn't even killed him, they say, and even if he had, the dead man does not deserve a thought, since he was a killer. For, they say, it is impious for a son to prosecute his father for murder. But their ideas of the divine attitude to piety and impiety are wrong, Socrates.

S: Whereas, by Zeus, Euthyphro, you think that your knowledge of the divine, and of piety and impiety, is so accurate that, when those things happened as you say, you have no fear of having acted impiously in bringing your father to trial?

E: I should be of no use, Socrates, and Euthyphro would not be superior to the majority of men, if I did not have accurate knowledge of all such things.

S: It is indeed most important, my admirable Euthyphro, that I should become your pupil, and as regards this indictment challenge Meletus about these very things and say to him: that in the past too I considered knowledge about the divine to be most important, and that now that he says that I am guilty of improvising and innovating about the gods I have become your pupil. I would say to him: "If, Meletus, you agree that Euthyphro is wise in these matters, consider me, too, to have the right beliefs and do not bring me to trial. If you do not think so, then prosecute that teacher of mine, not me, for corrupting the older men, me and his own father, by teaching me and by exhorting and punishing him." If he is not convinced, and does not discharge me or indict you instead of me, I shall repeat the same challenge in court.

E: Yes, by Zeus, Socrates, and, if he should try to indict me, I think I would find his weak spots and the talk in court would be about him rather than about me.

S: It is because I realize this that I am eager to become your pupil, my dear friend. I know that other people as well as this Meletus do not even seem to notice you, whereas he sees me so sharply and clearly that he indicts me for ungodliness. So tell me now, by Zeus, what you just now maintained you clearly knew: what kind of thing do you say that godliness and ungodliness are, both as regards murder and other things; or is the pious not the same and alike in every action, and the impious the opposite of all that is pious and like itself, and everything that is to be impious presents us with one form[3] or appearance in so far as it is impious?

---

3. This is the kind of passage that makes it easier for us to follow the transition from Socrates' universal definitions to the Platonic theory of separately existent eternal universal Forms. The words *eidos* and *idea*, the technical terms for the Platonic Forms, commonly mean physical stature or bodily appearance. As we apply a common epithet, in this case pious, to different actions or things, these must have a common characteristic, present a common appearance or form, to justify the use of the same term, but in the early dialogues, as here, it seems to be thought of as immanent in the particulars and without separate existence. The same is true of 6d where the word "Form" is also used.

E: Most certainly, Socrates.

S: Tell me then, what is the pious, and what the impious, do you say?

E: I say that the pious is to do what I am doing now, to prosecute the wrongdoer, be it about murder or temple robbery or anything else, whether the wrongdoer is your father or your mother or anyone else; not to prosecute is impious. And observe, Socrates, that I can quote the law as a great proof that this is so. I have already said to others that such actions are right, not to favour the ungodly, whoever they are. These people themselves believe that Zeus is the best and most just of the gods, yet they agree that he bound his father because he unjustly swallowed his sons, and that he in turn castrated his father for similar reasons. But they are angry with me because I am prosecuting my father for his wrongdoing. They contradict themselves in what they say about the gods and about me.

S: Indeed, Euthyphro, this is the reason why I am a defendant in the case, because I find it hard to accept things like that being said about the gods, and it is likely to be the reason why I shall be told I do wrong. Now, however, if you, who have full knowledge of such things, share their opinions, then we must agree with them too, it would seem. For what are we to say, we who agree that we ourselves have no knowledge of them? Tell me, by the god of friendship, do you really believe these things are true?

E: Yes, Socrates, and so are even more surprising things, of which the majority has no knowledge.

S: And do you believe that there really is war among the gods, and terrible enmities and battles, and other such things as are told by the poets, and other sacred stories such as are embroidered by good writers and by representations of which the robe of the goddess is adorned when it is carried up to the Acropolis? Are we to say these things are true, Euthyphro?

E: Not only these, Socrates, but, as I was saying just now, I will, if you wish, relate many other things about the gods which I know will amaze you.

S: I should not be surprised, but you will tell me these at leisure some other time. For now, try to tell me more clearly what I was asking just now, for, my friend, you did not teach me adequately when I asked you what the pious was, but you told me that what you are doing now, prosecuting your father for murder, is pious.

E: And I told the truth, Socrates.

S: Perhaps. You agree, however, that there are many other pious actions.

E: There are.

S: Bear in mind then that I did not bid you tell me one or two of the many pious actions but that form itself that makes all pious actions pious, for you agreed that all impious actions are impious and all pious actions pious through one form, or don't you remember?

E: I do.

S: Tell me then what this form itself is, so that I may look upon it, and using it as a model, say that any action of yours or another's that is of that kind is pious, and if it is not that it is not.

E: If that is how you want it, Socrates, that is how I will tell you.

S: That is what I want.

E: Well then, what is dear to the gods is pious, what is not is impious.

S: Splendid, Euthyphro! You have now answered in the way I wanted. Whether your answer is true I do not know yet, but you will obviously show me that what you say is true.

E: Certainly.

S: Come then, let us examine what we mean. An action or a man dear to the gods is pious, but an action or a man hated by the gods is impious. They are not the same, but quite opposite, the pious and the impious. Is that not so?

E: It is indeed.

S: And that seems to be a good statement?

E: I think so, Socrates.

S: We have also stated that the gods are in a state of discord, that they are at odds with each other, Euthyphro, and that they are at enmity with each other. Has that, too, been said?

E: It has.

S: What are the subjects of difference that cause hatred and anger? Let us look at it this way. If you and I were to differ about numbers as to which is the greater, would this difference make us enemies and angry with each other, or would we proceed to count and soon resolve our difference about this?

E: We would certainly do so.

S: Again, if we differed about the larger and the smaller, we would turn to measurement and soon cease to differ.

E: That is so.

S: And about the heavier and the lighter, we would resort to weighing and be reconciled.

E: Of course.

S: What subject of difference would make us angry and hostile to each other if we were unable to come to a decision? Perhaps you do not have an answer ready, but examine as I tell you whether these subjects are the just and the unjust, the beautiful and the ugly, the good and the bad. Are these not the subjects of difference about which, when we are unable to come to a satisfactory decision, you and I and other men become hostile to each other whenever we do?

E: That is the difference, Socrates, about those subjects.

S: What about the gods, Euthyphro? If indeed they have differences, will it not be about these same subjects?

E: It certainly must be so.

S: Then according to your argument, my good Euthyphro, different gods consider different things to be just, beautiful, ugly, good, and bad, for they would not be at odds with one another unless they differed about these subjects, would they?

E: You are right.

S: And they like what each of them considers beautiful, good, and just, and hate the opposites of these?

E: Certainly.

S: But you say that the same things are considered just by some gods and unjust by others, and as they dispute about these things they are at odds and at war with each other. Is that not so?

E: It is.

S: The same things then are loved by the gods and hated by the gods, and would be both god-loved and god-hated.

E: It seems likely.

S: And the same things would be both pious and impious, according to this argument?

E: I'm afraid so.

S: So you did not answer my question, you surprising man. I did not ask you what same thing is both pious and impious, and it appears that what is loved by the gods is also hated by them. So it is in no way surprising if your present action, namely punishing your father, may be pleasing to Zeus but displeasing to Kronos and Ouranos, pleasing to Hephaestus but displeasing to Hera, and so with any other gods who differ from each other on this subject.

E: I think, Socrates, that on this subject no gods would differ from one another, that whoever has killed anyone unjustly should pay the penalty.

S: Well now, Euthyphro, have you ever heard any man maintaining that one who has killed or done anything else unjustly should not pay the penalty?

E: They never cease to dispute on this subject, both elsewhere and in the courts, for when they have committed many wrongs they do and say anything to avoid the penalty.

S: Do they agree they have done wrong, Euthyphro, and in spite of so agreeing do they nevertheless say they should not be punished?

E: No, they do not agree on that point.

S: So they do not say or do anything. For they do not venture to say this, or dispute that they must not pay the penalty if they have done wrong, but I think they deny doing wrong. Is that not so?

E: That is true.

S: Then they do not dispute that the wrongdoer must be punished, but they may disagree as to who the wrongdoer is, what he did and when.

E: You are right.

S: Do not the gods have the same experience, if indeed they are at odds with each other about the just and the unjust, as your argument maintains? Some assert that they wrong one another, while others deny it, but no one among gods or men ventures to say that the wrongdoer must not be punished.

E: Yes, that is true, Socrates, as to the main point.

S: And those who disagree, whether men or gods, dispute about each action, if indeed the gods disagree. Some say it is done justly, others unjustly. Is that not so?

E: Yes, indeed.

S: Come now, my dear Euthyphro, tell me, too, that I may become wiser, what proof you have that all the gods consider that man to have been killed unjustly who became a murderer while in your service, was bound by the master of his victim, and died in his bonds before the one who bound him found out from the seers what was to be done with him, and that it is right for a son to denounce and to prosecute his father on behalf of such a man. Come, try to show me a clear sign that all the gods definitely believe this action to be right. If you can give me adequate proof of this, I shall never cease to extol your wisdom.

E: This is perhaps no light task, Socrates, though I could show you very clearly.

S: I understand that you think me more dull-witted than the jury, as you will obviously show them that these actions were unjust and that all the gods hate such actions.

E: I will show it to them clearly, Socrates, if only they will listen to me.

S: They will listen if they think you show them well. But this thought came to me as you were speaking, and I am examining it, saying to myself: "If Euthyphro shows me conclusively that all the gods consider such a death unjust, to what greater extent have I learned from him the nature of piety and impiety? This action would then, it seems, be hated by the gods, but the pious and the impious were not thereby now defined, for what is hated by the gods has also been shown to be loved by them." So I will not insist on this point; let us assume, if you wish, that all the gods consider this unjust and that they all hate it. However, is this the correction we are making in our discussion, that what all the gods hate is impious, and what they all love is pious, and that what some gods love and others hate is neither or both? Is that how you now wish us to define piety and impiety?

E: What prevents us from doing so, Socrates?

S: For my part nothing, Euthyphro, but you look whether on your part this proposal will enable you to teach me most easily what you promised.

E: I would certainly say that the pious is what all the gods love, and the opposite, what all the gods hate, is the impious.

S: Then let us again examine whether that is a sound statement, or do we let it pass, and if one of us, or someone else, merely says that something is so, do we accept that it is so? Or should we examine what the speaker means?

E: We must examine it, but I certainly think that this is now a fine statement.

S: We shall soon know better whether it is. Consider this: Is the pious loved by the gods because it is pious, or is it pious because it is loved by the gods?

E: I don't know what you mean, Socrates.

S: I shall try to explain more clearly: we speak of something being carried[4] and something carrying, of something being led and something leading, of something being seen and something seeing, and you understand that these things are all different from one another and how they differ?

---

4. This is the present participle form of the verb *pheromenon*, literally *being-carried*. The following passage is somewhat obscure, especially in translation, but the general meaning is clear. Plato points out that this participle simply indicates the object of an action of carrying, seeing, loving, etc. It follows from the action and adds nothing new, the action being prior to it, not following from it, and a thing is said to be loved because someone loves it, not vice versa. To say therefore that the pious is being loved by the gods says no more than that the gods love it. Euthyphro, however, also agrees that the pious is loved by the gods because of its nature (because it is pious), but the fact of its being loved by the gods does not define that nature, and as a definition is therefore unsatisfactory. It only indicates a quality or affect of the pious, and the pious is therefore still to be defined (11a7).

E: I think I do.

S: So there is something being loved and something loving, and the loving is a different thing.

E: Of course.

S: Tell me then whether that which is being carried is being carried because someone carries it or for some other reason.

E: No, that is the reason.

S: And that which is being led is so because someone leads it, and that which is being seen because someone sees it?

E: Certainly.

S: It is not seen by someone because it is being seen but on the contrary it is being seen because someone sees it, nor is it because it is being led that someone leads it but because someone leads it that it is being led; nor does someone carry an object because it is being carried, but it is being carried because someone carries it. Is what I want to say clear, Euthyphro? I want to say this, namely, that if anything comes to be, or is affected, it does not come to be because it is coming to be, but it is coming to be because it comes to be; nor is it affected because it is being affected but because something affects it. Or do you not agree?

E: I do.

S: What is being loved is either something that comes to be or something that is affected by something?

E: Certainly.

S: So it is in the same case as the things just mentioned; it is not loved by those who love it because it is being loved, but it is being loved because they love it?

E: Necessarily.

S: What then do we say about the pious, Euthyphro? Surely that it is loved by all the gods, according to what you say?

E: Yes.

S: Is it loved because it is pious, or for some other reason?

E: For no other reason.

S: It is loved then because it is pious, but it is not pious because it is loved?[5]

E: Apparently.

S: And because it is loved by the gods it is being loved and is dear to the gods?

E: Of course.

S: The god-beloved is then not the same as the pious, Euthyphro, nor the pious the same as the god-beloved, as you say it is, but one differs from the other.

5. I quote an earlier comment of mine on this passage: "... it gives in a nutshell a point of view from which Plato never departed. Whatever the gods may be, they must by their very nature love the right because it is right." They have no choice in the matter. "This separation of the dynamic power of the gods from the ultimate reality, this setting up of absolute values above the gods themselves was not as unnatural to a Greek as it would be to us.... The gods who ruled on Olympus ... were not creators but created beings. As in Homer, Zeus must obey the balance of Necessity, so the Platonic gods must conform to an eternal scale of values. They did not create them, cannot alter them, cannot indeed wish to do so." (*Plato's Thought*, Indianapolis: Hackett Publishing Co., 1980, pp. 152–3.)

E: How so, Socrates?

S: Because we agree that the pious is beloved for the reason that it is pious, but it is not pious because it is loved. Is that not so?

E: Yes.

S: And that the god-beloved, on the other hand, is so because it is loved by the gods, by the very fact of being loved, but it is not loved because it is god-beloved.

E: True.

S: But if the god-beloved and the pious were the same, my dear Euthyphro, and the pious were loved because it was pious, then the god-beloved would be loved because it was god-beloved, and if the god-beloved was god-beloved because it was loved by the gods, then the pious would also be pious because it was loved by the gods; but now you see that they are in opposite cases as being altogether different from each other: the one is of a nature to be loved because it is loved, the other is loved because it is of a nature to be loved. I'm afraid, Euthyphro, that when you were asked what piety is, you did not wish to make its nature clear to me, but you told me an affect or quality of it, that the pious has the quality of being loved by all the gods, but you have not yet told me what the pious is. Now, if you will, do not hide things from me but tell me again from the beginning what piety is, whether loved by the gods or having some other quality—we shall not quarrel about that—but be keen to tell me what the pious and the impious are.

E: But Socrates, I have no way of telling you what I have in mind, for whatever proposition we put forward goes around and refuses to stay put where we establish it.

S: Your statements, Euthyphro, seem to belong to my ancestor, Daedalus. If I were stating them and putting them forward, you would perhaps be making fun of me and say that because of my kinship with him my conclusions in discussion run away and will not stay where one puts them. As these propositions are yours, however, we need some other jest, for they will not stay put for you, as you say yourself.

E: I think the same jest will do for our discussion, Socrates, for I am not the one who makes them go round and not remain in the same place; it is you who are the Daedalus; for as far as I am concerned they would remain as they were.

S: It looks as if I was cleverer than Daedalus in using my skill, my friend, in so far as he could only cause to move the things he made himself, but I can make other people's move as well as my own. And the smartest part of my skill is that I am clever without wanting to be, for I would rather have your statements to me remain unmoved than possess the wealth of Tantalus as well as the cleverness of Daedalus. But enough of this. Since I think you are making unnecessary difficulties, I am as eager as you are to find a way to teach me about piety, and do not give up before you do. See whether you think all that is pious is of necessity just.

E: I think so.

S: And is then all that is just pious? Or is all that is pious just, but not all that is just pious, but some of it is and some is not?

E: I do not follow what you are saying, Socrates.

S: Yet you are younger than I by as much as you are wiser. As I say, you are making difficulties because of your wealth of wisdom. Pull yourself together, my dear sir, what I am saying is not difficult to grasp. I am saying the opposite of what the poet said who wrote:

You do not wish to name Zeus, who had done it, and who made all things grow,
for where there is fear there is also shame.
I disagree with the poet. Shall I tell you why?

E: Please do.

S: I do not think that "where there is fear there is also shame," for I think that many
people who fear disease and poverty and many other such things feel fear, but are
not ashamed of the things they fear. Do you not think so?

E: I do indeed.

S: But where there is shame there is also fear. For is there anyone who, in feeling
shame and embarrassment at anything, does not also at the same time fear and dread
a reputation for wickedness?

E: He is certainly afraid.

S: It is then not right to say "where there is fear there is also shame," but that where
there is shame there is also fear, for fear covers a larger area than shame. Shame is a
part of fear just as odd is a part of number, with the result that it is not true that
where there is number there is also oddness, but that where there is oddness there is
also number. Do you follow me now?

E: Surely.

S: This is the kind of thing I was asking before, whether where there is piety there
is also justice, but where there is justice there is not always piety, for the pious is a
part of justice. Shall we say that, or do you think otherwise?

E: No, but like that, for what you say appears to be right.

S: See what comes next: if the pious is a part of the just, we must, it seems, find out
what part of the just it is. Now if you asked me something of what we mentioned just
now, such as what part of number is the even, and what number that is, I would say it
is the number that is divisible into two equal, not unequal, parts. Or do you not think
so?

E: I do.

S: Try in this way to tell me what part of the just the pious is, in order to tell
Meletus not to wrong us any more and not to indict me for ungodliness, since I have
learned from you sufficiently what is godly and pious and what is not.

E: I think, Socrates, that the godly and pious is the part of the just that is concerned
with the care of the gods, while that concerned with the care of men is the remaining
part of justice.

S: You seem to me to put that very well, but I still need a bit of information. I do
not know yet what you mean by care, for you do not mean the care of the gods in
the same sense as the care of other things, as, for example, we say, don't we, that not
everyone knows how to care for horses, but the horse breeder does.

E: Yes, I do mean it that way.

S: So horse breeding is the care of horses.

E: Yes.

S: Nor does everyone know how to care for dogs, but the hunter does.

E: That is so.

S: So hunting is the care of dogs.

E: Yes.

S: And cattle raising is the care of cattle.

E: Quite so.

S: While piety and godliness is the care of the gods, Euthyphro. Is that what you mean?

E: It is.

S: Now care in each case has the same effect; it aims at the good and the benefit of the object cared for, as you can see that horses cared for by horse breeders are benefited and become better. Or do you not think so?

E: I do.

S: So dogs are benefited by dog breeding, cattle by cattle raising, and so with all the others. Or do you think that care aims to harm the object of its care?

E: By Zeus, no.

S: It aims to benefit the object of its care?

E: Of course.

S: Is piety then, which is the care of the gods, also to benefit the gods and make them better? Would you agree that when you do something pious you make some one of the gods better?

E: By Zeus, no.

S: Nor do I think that this is what you mean—far from it—but that is why I asked you what you meant by the care of gods, because I did not believe you meant this kind of care.

E: Quite right, Socrates, that is not the kind of care I mean.

S: Very well, but what kind of care of the gods would piety be?

E: The kind of care, Socrates, that slaves take of their masters.

S: I understand. It is likely to be a kind of service of the gods.

E: Quite so.

S: Could you tell me to the achievement of what goal service to doctors tends? Is it not, do you think, to achieving health?

E: I think so.

S: What about service to shipbuilders? To what achievement is it directed?

E: Clearly, Socrates, to the building of a ship.

S: And service to housebuilders to the building of a house?

E: Yes.

S: Tell me then, my good sir, to the achievement of what aim does service to the gods tend? You obviously know since you say that you, of all men, have the best knowledge of the divine.

E: And I am telling the truth, Socrates.

S: Tell me then, by Zeus, what is that excellent aim that the gods achieve, using us as their servants?

E: Many fine things, Socrates.

S: So do generals, my friend. Nevertheless you could easily tell me their main concern, which is to achieve victory in war, is it not?

E: Of course.

S: The farmers too, I think, achieve many fine things, but the main point of their efforts is to produce food from the earth.

E: Quite so.

S: Well then, how would you sum up the many fine things that the gods achieve?

E: I told you a short while ago, Socrates, that it is a considerable task to acquire any precise knowledge of these things, but, to put it simply, I say that if a man knows how to say and do what is pleasing to the gods at prayer and sacrifice, those are pious actions such as preserve both private houses and public affairs of state. The opposite of these pleasing actions are impious and overturn and destroy everything.

S: You could tell me in far fewer words, if you were willing, the sum of what I asked, Euthyphro, but you are not keen to teach me, that is clear. You were on the point of doing so, but you turned away. If you had given that answer, I should now have acquired from you sufficient knowledge of the nature of piety. As it is, the lover of inquiry must follow his beloved wherever it may lead him. Once more then, what do you say that piety and the pious are? Are they a knowledge of how to sacrifice and pray?

E: They are.

S: To sacrifice is to make a gift to the gods, whereas to pray is to beg from the gods?

E: Definitely, Socrates.

S: It would follow from this statement that piety would be a knowledge of how to give to, and beg from, the gods.

E: You understood what I said very well, Socrates.

S: That is because I am so desirous of your wisdom, and I concentrate my mind on it, so that no word of yours may fall to the ground. But tell me, what is this service to the gods? You say it is to beg from them and to give to them?

E: I do.

S: And to beg correctly would be to ask from them things that we need?

E: What else?

S: And to give correctly is to give them what they need from us, for it would not be skillful to bring gifts to anyone that are in no way needed.

E: True, Socrates.

S: Piety would then be a sort of trading skill between gods and men?

E: Trading yes, if you prefer to call it that.

S: I prefer nothing, unless it is true. But tell me, what benefit do the gods derive from the gifts they receive from us? What they give us is obvious to all. There is for us no good that we do not receive from them, but how are they benefited by what they receive from us? Or do we have such an advantage over them in the trade that we receive all our blessings from them and they receive nothing from us?

E: Do you suppose, Socrates, that the gods are benefited by what they receive from us?

S: What could those gifts from us to the gods be, Euthyphro?

E: What else, do you think, than honour, reverence, and what I mentioned just now, gratitude?

S: The pious is then, Euthyphro, pleasing to the gods, but not beneficial or dear to them?

E: I think it is of all things most dear to them.

S: So the pious is once again what is dear to the gods.

E: Most certainly.

S: When you say this, will you be surprised if your arguments seem to move about instead of staying put? And will you accuse me of being Daedalus who makes them move, though you are yourself much more skillful than Daedalus and make them go round in a circle? Or do you not realize that our argument has moved around and come again to the same place? You surely remember that earlier the pious and the god-beloved were shown not to be the same but different from each other. Or do you not remember?

E: I do.

S: Do you then not realize now that you are saying that what is dear to the gods is the pious? Is this not the same as the god-beloved? Or is it not?

E: It certainly is.

S: Either we were wrong when we agreed before, or, if we were right then, we are wrong now.

E: That seems to be so.

S: So we must investigate again from the beginning what piety is, as I shall not willingly give up before I learn this. Do not think me unworthy, but concentrate your attention and tell the truth. For you know it, if any man does, and I must not let you go, like Proteus, before you tell me. If you had no clear knowledge of piety and impiety you would never have ventured to prosecute your old father for murder on behalf of a servant. For fear of the gods you would have been afraid to take the risk lest you should not be acting rightly, and would have been ashamed before men, but now I know well that you believe you have clear knowledge of piety and impiety. So tell me, my good Euthyphro, and do not hide what you think it is.

E: Some other time, Socrates, for I am in a hurry now, and it is time for me to go.

S: What a thing to do, my friend! By going you have cast me down from a great hope I had, that I would learn from you the nature of the pious and the impious and so escape Meletus' indictment by showing him that I had acquired wisdom in divine matters from Euthyphro, and my ignorance would no longer cause me to be careless and inventive about such things, and that I would be better for the rest of my life.

Chapter 3

The Process of Concept Attainment

Jerome Bruner, Jacqueline Goodnow, and George Austin

It is curiously difficult to recapture preconceptual innocence. Having learned a new language, it is almost impossible to recall the undifferentiated flow of voiced sounds that one heard before one learned to sort the flow into words and phrases. Having mastered the distinction between odd and even numbers, it is a feat to remember what it was like in a mental world where there was no such distinction. In short, the attainment of a concept has about it something of a quantal character. It is as if the mastery of a conceptual distinction were able to mask the preconceptual memory of the things now distinguished. Moreover, the transition experience between "not having" the distinction and "having it" seems to be without experiential content. From the point of view of imagery and sensory stuff the act of grasping a conceptual distinction is, if not *unanschaulich* or impalpable, to use the language of the Wurzburg investigators, at least unverbalizable. It is, if you will, an enigmatic process and often a sudden process. The psychologist's "aha experience" singles out this suddenness as does the literary man's "shock of recognition." Something happens quickly and one thinks one has found something. Concept attainment seems almost an intrinsically unanalyzable process from an experiential point of view: "Now I understand the distinction, before there was nothing, and in between was only a moment of illumination."

It is perhaps because of the inaccessibility of reportable experience that psychologists have produced such a relatively sparse yield of knowledge when they have sought to investigate concept attainment and the thought processes by techniques of phenomenological analysis. To say, as Graham Wallas (1926) did a generation ago, that thinking or invention is divided into the four stages of "preparation," "incubation," "illumination," and "verification" is helpful only in so far as it serves to indicate that while the experience of "grasping" (illumination or insight) is sudden, it is imbedded in a longer process—still to be described in analytic terms. We do well to heed the lesson of history and look to sources of data additional to the report of direct experience as a basis for understanding what is the process of concept attainment.

In the study of how people come to grasp conceptual or categorical distinctions, one may state these guiding questions (see Bruner, Goodnow, and Austin 1956 for further discussion). How do people *achieve* the information necessary for isolating and learning a concept? How do they *retain* the information gained from encounters with possibly relevant events so that it may be useful later? How is retained information *transformed* so that it may be rendered useful for testing an hypothesis still unborn at the moment of first encountering new information? People do manage these vastly complex tasks of achieving, retaining, and transforming information and they do so without exceeding the relatively narrow limits of human cognitive capacity. They do it in a manner that reflects with nicety the requirements of speed, accuracy, and the like that are imposed upon them by circumstances. We look about us and we see people constantly engaged in picking up and using information that enables them to make conceptual distinctions on the basis of appropriate defining attributes, doing it in such a way that they seem neither overwhelmed by the complexity of the task nor much endangered by maladaptive slowness or by reckless speed. People learn to distinguish conceptually between daylight color film and indoor color film, between different cuts of meat, between fresh vegetables and stale ones, between policemen and subway guards, between detergents and soap flakes, between honest and crooked politicians, between bashful children and less timid ones, between a flow of traffic that permits crossing the street safely and a flow that one should not risk. How may one go about analyzing the learning process that leads to such rational behavior?

The Investigation of Concept Attainment

It is more than a casual truism of the operational behaviorist that in order to study a psychological process one must externalize it for observation. Concept attainment is not an exception. How get it externalized into observable behavior? Verbal report, as we have noted, provides insufficient data for making generalizations about it. What then?

Consider the chain of events leading up to the learning of a concept, and we purposely choose an example from everyday life. Our hypothetical subject is a foreigner who has arrived in town and is being introduced around by an old resident who is a trusted friend of his. The people to whom he is being introduced are the instances. After each encounter with a new person—an "instance," in the jargon of concept studies—his friend remarks either, "He's an influential person" or "He's a nice fellow but not very influential." Our subject has reason to respect his friend's judgment and is, more or less intentionally, trying to learn the basis of his friend's distinction between "influential" people and "nice but not influential" people. Looked at more precisely, he encounters instances and then has them labelled categorywise as in one class or another by his tutor-friend. The instances that he encounters vary in the myriad of attributes by which human beings are marked. Some are more educated than others, better travelled, more facile conversationally, richer, more forceful, etc. His task is to determine which attributes lead reliably to membership in the class "influential people." Note one thing. Very early in the round of visits, our subject begins to make tentative judgments of his own, prior to his friend's advice, as to whether the person he is meeting is influential or not, perhaps on the basis of attributes that he would have difficulty in describing even to himself. With respect to these tentative hypotheses, several contingencies may arise: he may consider a person influential and have his judgment confirmed or infirmed by his friend, or he may consider a person not influential with the same two possible outcomes. And, of course, the tutor-friend can also resolve cases of doubt for him. If the friend were also able to give him the proper advice about the defining attributes of the class, the task would be finished. But let us assume that this is not to be the case, that the tutor-friend is somehow reticent on this score.

Our subject as we have described him thus far exists in something of a privileged enclave in which he is protected from the consequences of his own tentative judgments. This is how it is, of course, in most concept-attainment studies—whether a particular Chinese figure is called a CIV or a DAX by a subject is seemingly without consequence, save that miscalling may hurt one's self-esteem. But it is conceivable that our man may have to act on the basis of his tentative categorization before getting his friend's guidance, and his action may have serious consequences. To what extent will this lead to constant errors in his placement of people and in the tentative hypotheses he develops? Our man's position is privileged too in the sense that there is no limit of time on his learning activity. Suppose that his tutor-friend were only going to be in town for a few days and in that time he had to learn to recognize examples of the category "influential people" in order to carry out his future business. To what extent would this influence his approach to learning?

We must also ask a question about record-keeping. How does the person keep track? Each instance he encounters exhibits many attributes, and our man notes the value of some of these and not others upon encountering exemplars and non-exemplars of the class "influential people": that more of the "influentials" were rich than poor, but not that more of them were tall rather than short. He may also want to keep track of the fate of those tentative hypotheses that were checked and found wanting on subsequent encounters. Is the record-keeping (whether in his head or in a ledger) of such a kind that it ensures the ready utilization of informatin encountered?

Finally, how does the person know when he has learned the concept in a serviceable way? This is a deceptively simple question. The first thing that may come to mind is that the person knows he has learned the concept when he feels he is able to predict the status of new instances with a sufficiently high degree of certainty. But what is a "sufficiently high degree of certainty" when a person is working with a probabilistic concept where cues do not yield complete prediction of identity? We will find that some people will continue to explore obvious attributes and abstract not obvious ones to explore so long as they are not able to categorize perfectly. Others will stabilize in their behavior and will base their categorizations exclusively on partially predictive cues without any further effort to try out new, possibly relevant attributes. Even when a subject is working with a simple conjunctive concept whose defining attributes predict perfectly the status of all instances encountered, he may not be sure that he "has" the concept even though he is performing perfectly. He will go on testing new instances, "just to be sure." We do not mean to obscure what may seem to be a simple matter, but in fact it is very difficult to describe what it is that leads a subject to state that he has now learned the concept. For simplicity's sake, it is often better to by-pass the question and to ask instead whether the attributes that are criterial for the subject in his categorizing judgment are also the attributes that are defining of the concept. Let it be clear, however, that some people require many more encounters beyond this point before they feel any degree of certainty; others reach the stage of certainty before their behavior meets this criterion.

The first and most notable thing about the sequence of events set forth is that it can be described as a series of decisions. At the very outset, even before the person has so much as encountered a single instance, he must make a decision about the nature of the task. Will he try to learn the concept "influential people" or will he concentrate on remembering in rote fashion which people he met were and which people were not "influential"? There are then decisions to be made, important ones from the point of view of efficiency, as to which attributes and how many attributes he should attend to in attempting to find out how to spot an influential person without having to ask his friend or going through the difficult business of observing the exercise of influence in the community. And should a tentative hypothesis prove wrong, his next decision is how to change it. Indeed, if his hypothesis is correct on one encounter, should he hold to it *in toto*? The decisions, moreover, are always contingent on the consequences he foresees and he must also make decisions about what consequences seem reasonable. If you will, then, the steps involved in attaining a concept are successive decisions, earlier ones of which affect the degrees of freedom possible for later decisions.

In studying concept attainment, then, it has been our aim to externalize for observation as many of the decisions as could possibly be brought into the open in the hope that regularities in these decisions might provide the basis for making inferences about the processes involved in learning or attaining a concept. These regularities in decision-making we shall call *strategies*.

The phrase "strategies of decision-making" is not meant in a metaphoric sense. A strategy refers to a pattern of decisions in the acquisition, retention, and utilization of information that serves to meet certain objectives, i.e., to insure certain forms of outcome and to insure against certain others. Among the objectives of a strategy are the following:

a. To insure that the concept will be attained after the minimum number of encounters with relevant instances.

b. To insure that a concept will be attained with certainty, regardless of the number of instances one must test *en route* to attainment.

c. To minimize the amount of strain on inference and memory capacity while at the same time insuring that a concept will be attained.

d. To minimize the number of wrong categorizations prior to attaining a concept.

Other objectives can be stated (see Bruner, Goodnow, and Austin 1956). These suffice to illustrate what is intended by the objectives of a strategy.

Let it be said at the outset that a strategy as we are using the term here does not refer to a conscious plan for achieving and utilizing information. The question whether a person is or is not conscious of his strategy, while interesting, is basically irrelevant to our inquiry. Rather, a strategy is inferred from the pattern of decisions one observes in a problem-solver seeking to attain a concept. What instances does he seek to test, what hypotheses does he construct, how dose he change these when he meets certain contingencies? These are the data from which strategies are inferred. The manner in which one proceeds in analyzing a strategy can only be described here in general terms (see Bruner, Goodnow, and Austin 1956, chapters 4–7 for more detailed discussion). Essentially, what is required is that one construct an ideal strategy or a set of ideal strategies that have the formal properties necessary to meet certain demands or objectives with "maximum rationality." Such ideal strategies can be stated in quite strict logical terms. For any given concept-attainment task, for example, there is an ideal strategy that can be constructed having the property that by following it one can attain a concept with a minimum number of encounters—but without regard to the cognitive strain involved. There are other ideal strategies having the property of minimizing cognitive strain, but they often are wasteful of the number of instances one must encounter en route to solution. And, indeed, there are also ideal compromise strategies that serve both the purposes of cognitive economy and rapid solution. To put the matter perhaps too simply, the analysis of performance strategy consists in comparing the actual performance of a subject with a set of rational or ideal strategies and determining a best fit. We ask then which ideal strategy does the subject's performance conform to most closely.

Obviously, strategies as employed by people are not fixed things. They alter with the nature of the concept being sought, with the kinds of pressures that exist in the situation, with the consequences of behavior, etc. And this is of the essence. For what is most creative about concept-attainment behavior is that the patterning of decisions does indeed reflect the demands of the situations in which the person finds himself. We do not know how strategies are learned, and the matter does not concern us for the present. Presumably they are learned. "What" is learned, however, is not of the order of a set of simple responses. For the systematic behavior of subjects attaining concepts is a highly patterned, skilled performance. If contemporary theories of learning are to deal with such performances, it is our feeling that the unit of analysis now called the "response" will have to be broadened considerably to encompass the long, contingent sequence of acts that, more properly speaking can only be called a "performance." But such matters are not, as we have said, within the scope of this work. Our effort is directed to locating strategies for dealing with information and trying to understand the manner in which they reflect the person's adjustment to the complex environment in which he must move.

Conditions Affecting Concept-Attainment Behavior

The pattern of decisions involved in attaining a concept is affected by a host of factors. Without doing too much violence to this diversity of determinants, it is possible to group them under several rather broad headings.

1. *The definition of the task*   What does the person take as the objective of his behavior? What does he think he is supposed to do?
2. *The nature of instances encountered*   How many attributes does each exhibit, and how many of these are defining and how many noisy? Does he encounter instances at random, in a systematic order, and does he have any control over the order in which instances will be tested? Do instances encountered contain sufficient information for learning the concept fully?
3. *The nature of validation*   Does the person learn each time an instance is encountered whether it is or is not an exemplar of the concept whose definition he is seeking? Or is such validation only available after a series of encounters? Can hypotheses be readily checked or not?
4. *The consequences of specific categorizations*   What is the price of categorizing a specific instance wrongly and the gain from a correct categorization? What is the price attached to a wrong hypothesis? And do the various contingencies-rightness or wrongness of a categorization of "X" and "not-X"—have a different price attached to them?
5. *The nature of imposed restrictions*   Is it possible to keep a record of instances and contingencies? Is there a price attached to the testing of instances as a means of finding out in which category they belong? Is there pressure of time to contend with, a need for speedy decisions?

Consider each of these matters in turn.

The Definition of the Task

The first consideration here is whether or not the person is consciously or "reportedly" seeking to attain a concept. Consider our hypothetical subject mentioned in the preceding section. It makes a vast difference in behavior whether he is "set" to find out the extrapolatable properties of the class of people who are influential or whether he is merely trying to remember in rote fashion which of the people he met were and which were not influential. Many of the classic experiments in concept attainment, beginning with Hull's famous study (1920), have employed rote-memory instructions leading their subjects to believe that their task was to memorize the labels of different figures presented to them rather than to seek to discover what were the defining properties of instances bearing the same labels. Yet we know from the careful studies of Reed (1946) that this prior set of the subject makes a considerable difference, even when the concepts to be attained are simple in nature. When a subject is set only to learn names, the rate of success in discovering the basis for grouping was 67%; with instructions to discover the basis for grouping, the figure increased to 86%—and this, let it be noted, with very simple concepts.

In Brown (1956), Roger Brown proposes that one of the functions of words is to alert people to the possibilities of concept attainment. We say to a class of students in biological chemistry, "Consider now the substance *histamine.*" The function of such a word is to suggest that a concept is about to be presented and that one must be alert to the possible defining attributes in terms of which its exemplars can be differentiated from other things in the world. It may well be, as Goldstein (1940) has so vigorously and persuasively suggested, that people are differentially set to handle the events they encounter, some seeking constantly to form conceptual groupings, others to deal with events concretely in terms of simple identity categories, "This thing in all its appearances," rather than "This thing as a member of the class of things alpha." There are many deep and unsolved problems surrounding the question of what it is that alerts people to conceptualizing activity, and it is clear that the full picture of concept-attainment behavior will not emerge until these problems are solved.

A second question concerning the definition of the task is the person's expectancies concerning the nature of the concept with which he must deal. People in our culture dislike and do not have much skill in dealing with disjunctive concepts—a class of events defined by the presence of the appropriate values of one attribute *or* another attribute *or* both in conjunction (see Bruner, Goodnow, and Austin 1956, chapter 6 for more details). Some of our own studies have indicated that, when the nature of the concept to be sought is not specified, subjects will tend to assume that they are looking for a simple conjunctive concept of the certainty type. Is it indeed the case, as the late Alfred Korzybski (1951) urged, that Western man is burdened down by a preference for conjunctive classification stemming from the tradition of so-called Aristotelian logic? Does the difficulty of dealing with disjunctive, relational, and probabilistic concepts reflect the difficulty of such concepts or does the difficulty perhaps reflect certain cultural biases in problem-solvers?

These are questions that cannot presently be answered. Certainly, there are cultural factors at work, or subcultural ones. The organic chemist, if organic chemistry can be treated as a subculture, develops a taste for relational groupings, at least during his working hours. Benzene rings, for example, are essentially relational groupings. Presumably, the physicist who works in quantum mechanics and nuclear theory will develop a taste for probabilistic concepts by the very nature of the discipline he must use. Though the generalization requires a leap, it is probably the case that most modern science is moving in the direction of probabilistic-relational concepts: classes of events defined in terms of the probability that certain attribute values will represent a kind of relation to each other. In economics, one classes nations over a period of years in terms of an average state of their balance of payments, whether favorable or unfavorable. Botany, a field in which conjunctive classificatory schemata have been classical, now deals with concepts such as a habitat's "balance," or with approximations to certain forms of "climax" in which a special variety of soil, climate, and flora are in a quasi-stationary equilibrium.

Still another feature of "defining the task," already alluded to earlier, is the predilection for criterial attributes that a person brings to the task of concept attainment. This is particularly the case when the task is one of constructing a series of systematic categories for continuing use as in geology, zoology, or anthropology. What is striking about such "attribute-predilection" (and the Latin origin, *praedilegere*, "to choose in advance," is indeed the proper word) is that one finds both in the behavior of subjects and of scientists that preferred but nondefining attributes are not readily given up even when one's encounter with instances proves them to be noisy and useless. In so far as people define the task of attaining a concept as one of proving that their prior hunches about defining attributes were right, it will be reflected in the pattern of decisions about changes in one's hypotheses in the face of infirming contingencies.

One hidden feature of the definition of a task—one of the skeletons in the psychologist's closet—needs some publicity, for it most certainly affects the manner in which people in experiments go about the task of attaining a concept. It is the "two-man game" feature of most experimental research on the thought processes. Subjects in psychological experiments tend to define the task as one in which their abilities are under test. As a result, "error" may come to have a consequence that is different from and perhaps more severe than what usually prevails in more private cognitive activity. The effect may be to lead the subject to play safe in his choice of hypotheses or in the instances he chooses for testing. One countervailing factor, however, may make such a hedgehog strategy less attractive. For the subject in approaching a task also may operate on the assumption that the experimenter would not have chosen an easy task for testing his abilities. So one often finds subjects trying complicated approaches to a problem when easy ones would have served them better, and admitting it sheepishly after they discover that the talk was simpler than they thought. We cannot settle this vexing problem here, but wish only to point it out as a ubiquitous and important factor in determining the behavior of subjects in experiments on the thought processes.

One last point about the subject's definition of the task: his expectations about what constitutes successful solution or successful progress in a problem-solving task. Simmel (1953) reports that one of the subjects in her problem-solving experiment asked to be allowed to keep going after he had attained solution on the grounds that his solution was "inelegant." At the other extreme, Smedslund (1955) tells of one of his subjects in a multiple-cue probability experiment who was doing badly and showing no improvement. When queried, he replied that his "system" was quite satisfactory and that he was "performing as well as one could possibly do under the given circumstances, and that he was not responsible for his failures because they were unavoidable" (p. 39). The two contrasting cases illustrate nicely the extent to which the objectives of the systematic behavior adopted by a subject will differ as a function of how he defines his task. In one case, the subject wants an "elegant solution," in the other he wants to do only somewhat better than chance. What is interesting about these levels of aspiration is that they determine in considerable measure when the person will cease trying, where he will stabilize and end the strainful process of searching out relevant attributes and relations. Thus all the factors that have to do with the setting of the level of aspiration—situational and personological alike—will in some measure affect the definition of a task and in so doing affect the objectives that go into the forming of a behavior strategy.

One other feature of "aspiration level" is the depth of understanding that the subject seeks to achieve in his solution. We single out this point because it has special relevance to the matter of "knowing" a concept behaviorally and "knowing" it at the level of verbal report. The world of mathematics is rife with examples of people who could come up with correct solutions before ever they were able to describe the steps used in attaining them. Many experiments in concept attainment, including our own, have shown that subjects are able to distinguish correctly exemplars from non-exemplars of a concept before being able to name the defining features on which their judgments are based. The studies of Hull (1920), Smoke (1932), and Walk (1952) all provide examples. Indeed, Adkins and Lyerly (1951) indicate that different factors contribute to success on two forms of the Progressive Matrices Test, one form requiring the subject to recognize the answer, the other to furnish it. We do not know whether there is a difference in behavior that results when one sees one's task as "behavioral attainment" in contrast to "verbal attainment" of a concept. There is evidence, however, that the two forms of attainment come at different points in a sequence of behavior and that "good" problem-solvers show this separation more markedly than poor ones. At least Thurstone (1950) suggests, on the basis of Bouthilet's study (1948), that creative problem-solving may express itself in this way, with the more imaginative problem-solver being the one whose actual performance runs well ahead of his ability to state verbal justifications for it. It remains to be seen whether patterns of decisions in problem-solving reflect this kind of difference.

The Nature of Instances Encountered

Return for a moment to the hypothetical foreign visitor seeking to discover the defining attributes of an influential person. At the outset, he is armed with a certain amount of wisdom. While it is possible for him to distinguish many possible attributes of the people-instances he encounters, he is wise enough to know that certain of these are more likely to be important than others and will not waste his time considering whether shoe size is something worth attending to. But even after he strips the situation down to the most likely factors—factors, of course, that had proved useful in making distinctions between influential and other people in his own country—the number that remain to be tested will make a great deal of difference in terms of the nature of the task and, indeed, in the strategy he will adopt. First, in terms of the number of possible hypotheses he may entertain about the correct basis for inferring the influence of a person. Suppose, for argument's sake, that there were four likely attributes, each with three discriminable values. Let us say one is *age* (under 35, 35–50, over 50), *economic status* (high, medium, and low), *religion* (Catholic, Jew, Protestant), and *apparent aggressiveness* (high, medium, low). Assuming (quite in the manner of an Aristotle-ridden Western man!) that the concept "influential people" is conjunctive, the four attributes each with their three values could be compounded in a frighteningly large number of ways. For example, the influential people could be defined in terms of the values of all *four* attributes and include all those who are:

Over 50, rich, Protestant, and moderately aggressive.

Or they could be defined by values of only *two* attributes:

Rich and Protestant.

Rich and moderately aggressive.

Over 50 and highly aggressive, etc.

The larger the number of attributes exhibited by instances and the larger the number of discriminable values they exhibit, the greater will be the number of hypotheses to be entertained. This is the first constraining factor imposed on problem-solving by the nature of instances encountered.

Here we note that one of the principal differences between various strategies is the rate with which they eliminate alternative hypotheses about which attribute values are relevant for identifying exemplars of a concept (see also Bruner, Goodnow, and Austin 1956, chapter 4). Moreover, the larger the number of attributes being considered, and therefore the larger the number of alternative hypotheses to be eliminated, the greater will be the necessity for adopting a "quick elimination" strategy if time is short or if the number of encounters permitted is limited by their costliness. In sum, the number or richness of the attributes to be dealt with almost inevitably introduces a factor to be dealt with in attaining concepts.

The nature of the instances that one must bring under conceptual grouping may also vary in terms of the *kinds* of attributes they exhibit: their immediacy, their familiarity, their status as good systematic differentia, and their value in past conceptualizing. We remarked, for example, that our hypothetical foreigner in search of the defining attributes of "influence" would adopt certain "reasonable" attributes as good places for starting his search. This is indeed a rational procedure, although... the road to failure in concept attainment is often marked by a sense of verisimilitude created by past experience. These matters have already been discussed and all that need be said at this point is that they make a systematic difference (see Bruner, Goodnow, and Austin 1956).

The manner and order of encounter with instances is another factor in determining the behavior of subjects. Does the effort to isolate a conceptual grouping begin with a positive instance or exemplar of the concept being sought? If the concept to be discovered is conjunctive, then from a sheer informational point of view the problem-solver is in a position, if he knows how to utilize the information contained in this instance, to eliminate a very great majority of the possible hypotheses that were entertainable before such an encounter. If the concept is disjunctive, a first positive instance often proves the occasion for adopting an altogether incorrect approach to the problem (cf. Bruner, Goodnow, and Austin 1956, chapter 6). Hovland (1952) has provided an excellent analysis of the potential information to be gained from positive and negative instances of a conjunctive concept when such instances appear at different places in series of encounters (see Bruner, Goodnow, and Austin 1956).

The sheer frequency of positive and negative instances, whatever the order in which they are encountered, also governs the likelihood of encountering certain contingencies with respect to the tentative hypotheses one is trying out. That is to say, one may encounter positive or negative instances and each of these is capable of confirming or infirming an hypothesis the problem-solver may have tentatively developed concerning the correct concept. If, for example, one encounters a red instance at a time when one is considering the hypothesis that "red" is the correct basis for grouping, and if the instance encountered is positive or exemplifying of the concept, then we speak of this as a positive confirming contingency. Each contingency encountered requires an act of decision on the part of the problem-solver. Shall he maintain the hypothesis that he is holding tentatively or shall he change it, and if he changes it, how shall this be done? Now, a high proportion of negative instances (at least where conjunctive concepts are concerned) inevitably places a strain on inference capacity whether the instance confirms or infirms the hypothesis in force. (Lest the reader be puzzled, a negative instance, one not exemplifying the concept being sought, is confirming when it is predicted to be negative by the hypothesis in force.) And in so far as negative instances are infirming of an hypothesis, the change that is required in the hypothesis entails considerable strain on memory for reasons that will be apparent presently. Thus a long series of encounters with negative instances often requires the person to adopt modes of solution that are predominantly devoted to reduction on memory strain.

Smoke (1933) has made much of the role of negative instances in concept attainment. He contrasted the performance of subjects who worked with a series of instances composed half of positive and half of negative instances in contrast to subjects working with positive instances alone. Success in attainment did not seem affected by these two conditions, a questionable finding since the two series were not equated for the amount of information they contained, but a finding that has been properly established by the better controlled experiment of Hovland and Weiss (1953). Smoke makes an exceedingly interesting point about the subjects in the two groups. "There is a tendency for negative instances to discourage 'snap judgments.' ... The subjects ... tended to come to an initial wrong conclusion less readily and to subsequent wrong conclusions less frequently, than when they were learning from positive instances alone," (p. 588). This finding suggests that negative instances play some role, yet to be ascertained, in determining the feeling of confidence that leads the subject to believe he has attained the concept.

Are encounters with instances orderly or haphazard? Consider the matter in terms of our useful hypothetical foreigner. Suppose his friend had introduced him to residents of the community in a prearranged order somewhat as follows. He begins by meeting people who are rich, over 50, and Protestant, and who differ only in terms of aggressiveness. He then moves on to people who are rich, over 50, Catholic, and again only differing in aggressiveness, etc., until he has had a chance to sample each attribute systematically and see its relationship to influence in the community. A properly conscientious guide, if he were of an orderly turn of mind, would doubtless do something like this in educating his friend. If he did, he would find that his pupil arrived far more easily at the correct solution. For the patterns of solution that people adopt in attempting to attain concepts reflect very sensitively the order inherent in the instances they meet. Where order is systematic, the objective of minimizing memory strain becomes notably less, and with a reduction of strain, new modes of attack begin to appear.

The question of the orderliness of encounter and the effort to reduce cognitive strain brings us to a more general problem, one that has to do with methods of reducing disorder and confusion used by a subject in attaining or utilizing concepts. The reader will very soon become aware of the importance of what we will later call a "focus": an exemplar of a concept that the problem-solver uses as a reference point or *pied-à-terre*. Virtually all the effective strategies for attaining concepts depend upon the use of some sort of initial focus. Recall your own efforts in learning to distinguish prime numbers from other numbers. It is likely that you will recall the number 3 as your first association, and this number is very likely the focus point from which you began exploring other exemplars of that interesting class of integers divisible only by themselves and unity. So, too, we would expect that our hypothetical foreign visitor would be likely to take the first "positive instance" encountered of an influential person and use him as a basis for comparison with new members of the class. The use of such foci in concept attainment—usually positive instances although not universally so—represents one of the most direct and simple ways of reducing strain on memory and on inference. "Reference backward" to the focus is perhaps what suggests that under certain circumstances the attaining of a concept is like the construction of a composite photograph, although the image connoted is, we believe, a highly misleading one.

Indeed, *after* a concept has been attained, the process of keeping order continues by the use of two processes. One of them is represented by the phenomenon of the adaptation level: the formation of a "typical instance" of the category. This consists essentially of "summarizing" all exemplars of a class that have been encountered in terms of typical or average values of each of the defining attributes of the class. For example, the subjects in the experiment of Bruner and Rodrigues previously described found no difficulty in setting a color wheel to the typical color of an eating orange, less trouble, indeed, than they had in setting the extremes of the acceptable range. A typical instance of a category is, then, the adaptation level of the values of the defining attributes of the class, whether computed as a weighted geometric mean of instance values as Helson (1948) proposes or in some other way. A "typical orange," for example, has a typical color, typical size, typical shape, etc. As Helson suggests, such an adaptation level or typical instance permits one to evaluate exemplars in terms of their "fitness" in the category.[1]

Another order-preserving device used after a concept has been attained, akin in some respects to the typical instance, is the "generic instance," a representation of the concept in terms of idealized values of the defining attributes and stripped of all noisy attributes. It is perhaps the kind of schematized imagery that Fisher (1916) reports developing in her subjects as they move toward concept attainment. Often they become highly conventionalized, as, for example, the images of the different types of levers described by Archimedes which are represented by idealized fulcra, levers, and weights. The usual isosceles right-angled triangle that one thinks of when the class "right-angled triangle" is mentioned is another case in point. It is highly doubtful

---

1. An interesting study by D. R. Brown (1953) indicates the importance of identifying an instance as a member of a class of relevant instances as a condition for its affecting the adaptation level or typical instance of a category. Making a weight distinctively separate from a class of weights being judged by a subject reduces significantly its effect as an anchor on the series or its contribution to the adaptation level of the series. The role of categorial identity as a factor in adaptation level phenomena is discussed in Brown's paper.

whether the average right-angled triangle we see is indeed marked by two equal sides around the right angle. The function of the generic instance beyond its use as an ordering or simplifying device is obscure, but it may well be that it is used as a search model in problem-solving behavior when a subject is considering what classes of things would be relevant to fill a gap in an unsolved problem.

Another feature of the sequence of instances encountered now needs consideration. There is a specifiable point in any sequential array of information that, formally speaking, can be regarded as "informationally sufficient." One can illustrate this by reference to the amount of information necessary for deciding whether A is equal to, greater then, or smaller than C. The informationally sufficient array of information is

$A > B$

$B > C$

and any further data or any repetitions of these data would be redundant. The mystery story writer, Ellery Queen, uses the same technique when he informs the reader that at a certain point all the clues necessary are available if the reader wishes to solve the mystery. One can specify the minimum array of instances necessary in order for our hypothetical foreigner to solve the problem of who is influential. But however convincing this may sound as a logical matter, it is grossly misleading from a psychological point of view. Redundancy thus defined has very little to do with psychological redundancy. The point of *psychological* informational sufficiency depends upon the strategy of information utilization a person has adopted, and upon the manner and rate at which he is using the information contained in instances he is encountering. Since more than a few psychological experiments on concept attainment utilizing instances with multiple attributes have failed to take into account either the formal or the psychological point of informational sufficiency, the matter is worth noting in passing. For the way in which people will operate when insufficient information is provided them is not of the same order as their behavior when a sufficient series of instances has been permitted them (see Bruner, Goodnow, and Austin 1956, chapter 4).

A critical question in determining the kind of strategies that may be employed is whether or not the person can control the order of instances he will encounter or whether they come to him under the control either of chance factors or of some external agency. The difference can be caricatured as similar to that which separates the clinician and the experimentalist. Let us say that each is interested in finding out what areas of the brain mediate (i.e., are defining attributes of) intact pattern vision. The experimentalist goes systematically about the task of extirpating now this area, now that, all in a manner dictated by the canons of efficient experimental design, until he arrives at the point where he is ready to publish his paper. The clinician gets his cases as they come, testing for pattern vision and for brain damage. In principle (and if the clinician were patient enough and orderly enough to keep his records elegantly) there is no difference in the situations of the two men. But in fact, the difference in behavior is striking. It is not simply that the experimentalist has "cleaner data." When the data are, so to speak, "cleaned up" (as they are in Bruner, Goodnow, and Austin 1956, chapters 4 and 5), the difference in the kinds of decisions each must make is even more apparent. It is a matter worthy of scrutiny, and it will receive that in the appropriate place.

Another feature of "control" versus "no control" over the order of instances one encounters is whether or not one encounters instances when one is ready for them. In Hull's well-known study (1920) in which the defining attributes of the concepts to be attained were radicals imbedded in pseudo-Chinese ideograms, he contrasted two orders of presentation: one going from displays containing complex exemplars to ones with simple exemplars, the other from simple to complex. Simple and complex are defined by the number of what we have called "noisy attributes" contained in exemplars to be grouped. When subjects were allowed only a short and specified time to examine each exemplar, there was no difference in success rates for the two procedures. But if subjects were allowed to proceed at their own pace, "if each individual experience in the series is continued until the reaction to it is just perfected before passing on to the next, there is a distinct advantage in favor of the simple-to-complex method," (p. 38). The result of "readiness for the next instance" is not simply that one succeeds more readily, but that it also affects the manner in which a subject goes about the decisions required in his task (see Bruner, Goodnow, and Austin 1956, chapter 5).

One can go on almost endlessly about the critical role of the nature and order of instances encountered—for example, of the effect of successive encounters with instances as compared with simultaneous encounters with an array of instances that are either laid out in an orderly or in a random fashion (see Bruner, Goodnow, and Austin 1956 for general discussion). These are problems that are not simply technical in nature. They critically affect the manner in which concept-attainment behavior unfolds and they have notable implications for teaching practice as well. How, for example, should one expose a student to the bewildering array of instances that must be categorized in terms of the concepts of geology or botany or any of the other classificatory sciences? And with respect to the conduct of scientific research, when the scientist has control over the instances being scrutinized or must depend on a random intake as the clinician must, what is the optimal way of ordering one's contact with instances so that one can test them for defining attributes? When a neuroanatomist, using techniques of electrophysiology, attempts to collate the data on localization in order to map those brain areas associated with different behavioral processes, how shall he proceed? One neurologist, Karl Pribram (1953), proposes that one pay attention only to "positive instances," reported instances where a given area has been found to be related to the presence of a particular kind of behavior—related either by the evidence of extirpation or the evidence of electrophysiological activity. Is this the best procedure? The evidence in Bruner, Goodnow, and Austin (1956) indicates that it may not always be so.

The Nature of Validation

In Bruner, Goodnow, and Austin (1956) chapter 1 we examined the various sources of validation of one's categorizations: by reference to a pragmatic criterion, by "official" or consensual validation, by consistency, etc. Now we must introduce the question of *opportunity* for validation in the course of attaining a concept: the frequency of validation, how soon it occurs after a tentative categorization has been made, the ambiguity of validation (since it is not always clear whether we are "right" or "wrong"), and the extent to which the validation is direct or indirect.

Usually in psychological experiments we give subjects (be they animal or human) full knowledge of results. In a typical discrimination learning experiment, an animal must learn to make a distinction between, say, black doors and white doors in terms of the pragmatic criterion of whether they are in the class "go-throughable" or "blocked." If the correction method is used, the animal learns which door is correct and may also have an opportunity for checking the wrong door if he happens to try it first. Where noncorrection procedures are followed, the animal at least gets a chance to test one instance for its positive or negative status. So too in concept-attainment experiments. The subject is shown an instance, may be asked to give his best guess about its category membership (usually to be indicated by a label of some sort), and then told the correct label. Only in the test trials is validation withdrawn. To test the animals' conceptual learning, new instances are introduced, say, a light gray and a dark gray door, in place of the black and white ones, and both doors are left unlatched to see whether the animal has learned the relational concept of going to the darker (or the lighter) door. In concept-attainment experiments, the same procedure is followed. Instances other than those used in the original learning are introduced and these the subject must label without benefit of feedback from the experimenter who now changes his role from tutor to that of tester.

Much the same type of procedure prevails when the young child is being taught to distinguish the conceptual entities of the environment. At first, the word "cat" is uttered each time the child is exposed to this animal. Then there is a stage at which the child is asked to name it and if he is correct we validate by approbation; if not we correct him. Eventually, the child comes to operate on his own and validation by an external source is given only on an intermittent basis.

But there are many cases in everyday life where the course of validation is neither so regular, so benign, nor so well designed to help the struggling attainer of concepts. Validation may be absent, may in fact be prevented; it may be greatly delayed and frequently is. Indeed, it is often indirect and ambiguous as well. The pattern of validating clearly, immediately, frequently, and directly, so typical of psychological experimentation, does not by any means heed the *caveat* of Brunswik (1947) that psychological research designs be representative of the life situations to which their results will be generalized.

One feature of opportunity for validation is simply the frequency with which validation is available. Infrequent opportunity for validation may have the effect of increasing the reliance on preferred cues that are considerably less than certain. If in learning to categorize aircraft silhouettes attempted identifications are not frequently checkable against external information, the effect may be to lead the learner to utilize exessively some cues that have permitted him to make a few successful identifications in the past. One may under conditions of restricted opportunity for validation stabilize one's cue utilization too soon and end with a level of performance that is less efficient than warranted by the goodness of cues available. Or with reduced opportunity, one may turn to some other external criterion for checking one's categorizations. Experiments by Asch (1951) and Crutchfield (1954) indicate that, if correction is not readily available, subjects will turn to the group consensus as a basis for validation, even though the subject may be utilizing better bases for categorization than can be found in the consensus. In the Asch experiment, for example, the subject is asked to categorize the length of lines in terms of their height. Given no validation by the experimenter and given the fact that the group of which he is a member consists of "stooges" who are all primed to call out the wrong categorizing answer, the beleaguered subject soon comes to adopt the group norm as the basis of validation and begins to change his own pattern of calls. To be sure, Asch notes that few subjects were tricked to the extent of "seeing" length of lines in this distorted way. But the fact of the matter is that the actual categorizations made do suffer a marked change under these conditions. If external validation on the actual length of lines had been provided regularly, it is dubious indeed that the effect could have been produced, although Crutchfield's research indicates that even with some external validation, susceptibility to consensual pressures varies widely from subject to subject.

Frequency is only one feature of validation. Immediacy is another. In human relationships one quite often learns to make and continues to make groupings of people and events in the environment with considerably delayed validation. Consider such categorizations of other people as "honest" or "of high integrity" or as a "promising young man." Perhaps under the tutelage of parents and peers, we early learn to classify people as, say, "honest," "somewhat shifty," and "downright crooked" on the basis of a minimum number of defining attribute values. We are often a long time finding out the validity of such categorizations if indeed we ever fully do. "He seemed like an honest man from all I could tell, and I must say I'm surprised that ..." The "seeming" and the validation may be years apart.

It is likely that long delay in the validation of one's categorial inferences also leads to undue reliance on those few cues that have in the past paid off predictively or to reliance upon consensus in much the same manner discussed in connection with reduced frequency of validation. If we are unable to check immediately our bases for classification against a good external criterion, we are readier to use the vicarious criterion of consensus or to rely on rather nonrational cues.

It may also be characteristic of delayed validation that one reconstructs backward from the validation to possible defining attributes that "might have been." A man is suddenly found to be an embezzler who for the last ten years has been accepted as a pillar of the community. Immediately the "search backward" begins as we try to "recall" signs that might have led us to infer correctly that the man was going to behave in this way. The eventual effectiveness of the "search backward" will depend of course on...the ecological validity of labels. More likely than not, the cues that are honored in the consensus of folklore will be "found." "He did, after all, have shifty eyes," or "He did act rather too piously and one does well to suspect that sort of thing." Or a factor of vividness will operate. "That facial tic probably indicated a not very balanced person."

It is rather unfortunate that one must treat the subject of delayed validation by reference to intuitive examples from everyday life, for it seems apparent that it is a rich area for systematic psychological inquiry. The psychological literature yields little on the subject.

The same complaint can be made about work on the ambiguous validation of categorial inference. Everyday life abounds with examples, yet a literature of experimentation on the subject is virtually nonexistent. Without meaning to be flippant in illustration, we may take the heavily magical sphere of angling as a prime starting ground of examples. Consider the fly fisherman who is "learning" a stream, one of the principal components of which is learning to sort his flies into those that are "takers" on this stream and those that are not. His testing of instances consists of making a series of casts and determining whether the particular fly he is using will or will not raise a fish. If he is serious about his sport, his objective in learning is to be able to emerge with knowledge such as "a small pattern, tied sparsely, of a dark color, cast slightly upstream" will take fish (the presumed criterion) on Yellowjacket Brood. Consider what is involved in validation and what makes for ambiguous validation. There are some days when fish will rise to anything up to and including a discarded cigarette butt. There are other days when fish will rise for nothing that is offered. Somewhere between there are days when, to use the conventional phrase, the fish are "feeding selectively." Validation under these variable circumstances is hard to estimate. Is failure to get a strike on a particular fly an indication that the fly is inappropriate or simply that no fish are feeding that day? Does a strike mean that the fly used is in the category of "takers" or simply that the fish are striking at everything offered?

The essence of ambiguous validation is that the validating criterion provides uncertain information as in the example just cited. This may come about in one of two ways. The first is that the validating criterion—whether a pragmatic one, an official one, or what not—itself turns out to have a probabilistic relationship to the concept. Take the category "mentally ill" as a case in point. We seek prognostic signs of mental illness that may prove useful in predicting mental breakdown. Part of the difficulty in fixing upon useful anticipatory attributes of this sort is the difficulty of finding a validating criterion. Admission to a mental hospital? Clearly not, since many severe neurotics spend their lives without going into a mental hospital. Going to a psychiatrist for treatment? Again, the validating criterion is not certain, for many people seek the aid of a psychiatrist in times of personal troubles without being seriously ill and a good many neurotics avoid the psychiatrist on principle. Under these circumstances, one is faced with a category that is clearly accepted as "existing" by the society at large but about which there is a lack of full agreement concerning a properly valid criterion. As frequently happens, the consequences of the decision as to whether a particular person is or is not mentally ill are extremely grave, as in establishing responsibility for crimes or when it must be decided whether a will is valid or not. Under these circumstances societies maintain official organs for deciding. One must have recourse to a court of law.

A second condition of ambiguous validation is when the validating criterion is itself equivocal in the sense that it may not be clear whether it indicates one way or the other. The angling example given a moment ago is a sufficient illustration of this case. Does a strike or the absence of a strike provide sure information on whether or not a particular fly is a "taker"?

The effect of ambiguous validation on the process of concept attainment and concept utilization seems to be much as we have described it under conditions of reduced opportunity for or delay in validation. Quips about the fisherman being the easiest thing to catch are not without justification and the multimillion-dollar fishing-tackle industry is a tribute to the range of nonrational factors that affect the fisherman. The contending claims of laymen and experts alike concerning the predisposing factors leading to mental ailments bespeak the same type of failure to pin down the defining conditions associated with a category whose validating criterion is itself ambiguous.

One last matter remains in considering validation. It has to do with "direct" and "indirect" validation. By direct test we mean the chance to test one's hypothesis about what an exemplar of a category *is*. The child is seeking to find out what is meant by the concept "cat." An animal comes along. The child says, "That's a cat." The parent says either "yes" or "no." In either case, a direct test of the hypothesis has been made. An indirect test, of course, is the case in which the same child says,

"Oh, that's not a cat." Again the parent will answer in the affirmative or negative. But the child's hypothesis about what a cat *is* will not be tested directly, only his residual hypothesis about what a cat *is not*. Note that this is not a matter of positive and negative instances. It refers to the direct or indirect test of an hypothesis, regardless of the negative or positive status of the instance that occurs.

Consider a simple experimental procedure used by Goodnow (1955) in which the subject must bet either on the left key or the right key of a "two-armed bandit." He has an hypothesis that the right key will pay off. Each time, one or the other key pays off, so that which ever way he bets, he will know which one was correct. The subject has an hypothesis that the right key will pay off on the next trial. Under these circumstances, subjects prefer to "act out" their hypothesis by a choice of the right key, even though in doing so they risk losing by virtue of the fact that they have learned the left key does in fact pay off 70% of the time. To bet on the left and find that the right key paid off "does not give you the same information" as a straight choice of right, as one subject put it. We suspect that such indirect validation is more difficult for the subject because it requires transformation of information and risks the making of errors. Though the transformation is not great, the urge to avoid indirect tests may often lead to risk in the interest of making more direct tests. In Bruner, Goodnow and Austin (1956) chapter 7, we see that under many conditions this feature of validation can be a critical factor in determining decisions about what instances to test next.

So much, then, for problems raised by the nature of validation. We turn next to the critical question of the consequences of categorizing events in one class or in another while one is in process of learning a category and after learning has been completed and the category is being used for grouping the environment.

The Anticipated Consequences of Categorizing
The point has already been made that learning a new category can be fruitfully conceived of as the making of a series of interrelated sequential decisions. These decisions include such matters as what instance to test next, or what hypothesis to adopt next. It is in decisions such as these that the anticipated consequences become of major importance.

We begin by stating some of the assumptions we make about the relations between decisions and their expected consequences. The first assumption, already implicit in much of the previous discussion, is that each step in a performance can be usefully regarded as a choice or decision between alternative steps. The second assumption is that in analyzing the expected consequences of a decision it is necessary to consider the expected consequences not only of the step taken by the decision-maker but also of the step he did *not* take. The third assumption is that the expected consequences of a decision can be analyzed into two components. The first is the *estimated likelihood of occurrence of alternative outcomes*. The second is the *value* placed by the decision-maker on anticipated outcomes. So much by way of introduction. We turn now to the application of these notions, taken principally from outside psychology, to the process of categorization.[2]

2. The reader familiar with economic theory will see immediately that there is a fair similarity between the assumptions made here and those made in many economic theories of choice (cf. Arrow, 1951). We have in fact derived much stimulation from such theories and especially from the arguments of Knight (1921), Shackle (1949), and Marschak (1950, 1954), who appear to us to be most aware of the psychological features of choice and decision-making.

Consider first the question: what are the outcomes which have value for an individual in a concept-attainment situation? And how does the individual's performance reflect the value to him of certain kinds of outcome rather than others?

Which particular outcomes are valued depends essentially upon the objectives of the individual. Take as an example the objective of attaining a concept after encountering as few instances as possible. This is a common objective guiding subjects in their decisions about instances to test and hypotheses to try out. We may deliberately set this objective before them by insisting that the concept must be attained within a limited number of choices. Or we may say to a subject, often without realizing the consequences, "Try to discover the nature of the concept as quickly as you can." By either procedure we are telling the subject that *each encounter with an instance matters* and that as much information as possible must be extracted from each.

Suppose one is testing instances to find out whether or not they are exemplars of the concept one is trying to learn, as for example in the Vigotsky Test or the procedures used in the experiments in Bruner, Goodnow, and Austin (1956). One chooses an instance at the outset that turns out to be positive. It exhibits values of, say, six attributes. The next decision to be made by the person is: "What kind of instance to test next?"

This decision is informationally a crucial one. Concretely, shall the person choose an instance that is drastically different from the first positive instance encountered, or shall he choose one that differs only slightly? If our by now somewhat overworked foreigner had met first an influential person who was over 50, rich, Protestant, and aggressive, should he now ask to meet one who is over 50 but poor, Catholic, and meek? Or shall he choose a second case for testing who differs in only one respect from the original influential person encountered? Let us suppose the individual chooses as his second instance one who differs in all respects save one from the previous positive instance. This is a desperate measure in the sense that, should the instance chosen turn out to be negative, it will provide the individual with little of no information. He will not know which one or ones of the many attributes changed made the instance negative. If, however, the instance chosen turns out to be positive, then in one fell swoop the individual will have learned that only the one attribute left unchanged really mattered as far as influence is concerned—a very big yield indeed.

In contrast, what are the consequences if the individual chooses as the second instance to test one which differs in only one respect from the previous positive instance? Whether it turns out to be positive or negative, one is assured of being able to use the information it provides. If positive, the one attribute changed does not matter; if negative, the one attribute changed does matter. Whatever the result, however, only one attribute will have been checked. If there are six or more attributes which may be defining, the task of solution will barely have begun.

Faced with the need to attain the concept within a limited number of instances encountered, which step will the individual take? Shall he choose as his next instance one which differs in all respects save one from the previous positive instance, or one which differs in only one respect? In other words, will he take a chance or adopt the slow-but-sure method?

Presented with such a question, the reader will surely demur: "It all depends upon whether the individual expects the next instance to turn out to be positive or negative." If he thinks the instance is more likely to be positive, then he will be more prone to take a chance and choose a second instance which differs a great deal from

Table 3.1

Decision alternatives	Anticipated events and outcome values	
	Longer than 10 inches	Shorter than 10 inches
Categorize as "long"	Good	Bad
Categorize as "short"	Bad	Good
Estimated likelihood of events	0.60	0.40

the previous positive one. But if he thinks it is very likely to be negative, then he will be more prone to take the surer step and choose an instance which differs little from the previous positive instance. This is how our subjects do decide between alternative steps (see Bruner, Goodnow, and Austin 1956, chapter 4). The precise results can be ignored for the moment. We wish in this chapter simply to make the point that the step taken or the decision made rests upon a resolution of expectations about the values of positive and negative outcomes and the likelihood of occurrence of each of these.

We have introduced this discussion of anticipated consequences and of expected values and likelihoods by reference to a concrete problem. We wish now to talk about consequences in a more general and somewhat more formal manner. As our context, we take the case where the individual is presented with a choice of placing an object or event in one category or another under conditions of uncertainty, and we consider the consequences of placing the object or event in each category and being right or wrong in one's placement.

The basic device in such analysis is the *payoff matrix*. Suppose we start with as simple an example as possible: a psychophysical experiment in which a series of lines is being presented, each to be categorized as "long" or "short." The subject at the outset is given a reference line, 10 inches in length, all lines longer than which are to be called "long," all lines shorter to be called "short." The subject is told to be as careful as possible. He is told, moreover, that for every four short lines presented, there will be six long lines. The matrix can be specified as in table 3.1.

In this "accuracy" matrix, the outcome values of placement in either category are balanced. Categorizing correctly a line as "short" is as good as correctly categorizing it as "long." Both correct categories are equally valued, and both incorrect placements are equally negatively valued. Since the outcome values are balanced, we would expect to find that estimates of event probability would be the major factor biasing judgment whenever there is uncertainty. We would expect the subject in case of doubt to favor calls of "long," since he has been told that long lines are the more likely.

The fact of the matter is that the accuracy matrix with its balanced outcome values is only one of several highly interesting matrices that may govern categorizing decisions. Let us consider what the problems are like when the outcome values of placement in either category are not equal. There is, for example, a matrix that we have come to call a "sentry matrix" because it is so well illustrated by the plight of a sentry in a combat zone. A sentry is standing at his post. It is his task to categorize oncoming figures in the dark as friend or foe. Enemy intelligence and reconnaissance have been so good that enemy and friend alike now know the password and it can no

Table 3.2

Decision alternatives	Anticipated events and outcome values	
	Foe	Friend
Categorize "foe" and fire	Alive and highly regarded	Alive, regretful, but duty fulfilled
Categorize "friend" and not fire	Dead or wounded	Alive, but feels both lucky and neglectful
Estimated likelihood of events	0.50	0.50

longer be used as a basis of discrimination. The sentry estimates that the chances of any given figure being friend or foe are 50:50. Two alternatives are available to him. He may categorize the approaching figure as a foe and open fire. Or he may categorize it as a friend and hold fire. We represent the matrix as in table 3.2.

This is a matrix where the events being equally likely we can expect the decisions to be biased by the unequal outcomes of placement in the two categories. If the sentry categorizes an approaching figure as foe and is correct, the outcome is highly favorable (alive and highly regarded); if incorrect, the outcome is not too bad (alive, regretful, but duty fulfilled). If the sentry categorizes an approaching figure as friend and is correct, the outcome is middling in value (alive, feels both lucky and neglectful); if incorrect, the outcome is highly unfavorable (dead or wounded). The outcome values are all in favor of categorizing an uncertain figure as foe and acting accordingly. It is small wonder that sentries are regarded as so dangerous to men returning from patrol.

We have chosen so far two simple cases of categorizing decision: one where the expected outcome values are balanced, and where the differences in expected event probabilities sway decision; the other, where expected event probabilities are balanced, and where differences in outcome values bias decision. One need not be limited to such simple cases. In general, the argument can be made that, when outcome values are equal for placement in one category or another, categorizing decisions will correspond to the expected event probabilities; and when outcome values are not equal, categorizing decisions will be biassed in the direction of the most favorable alternative. See Bruner, Goodnow, and Austin 1956, chapter 7, for experimental studies supporting this argument.

It must be noted, however, that we are always limited to statements about the *direction* that bias will take as long as we remain on the descriptive level. We can make no predictions about the *amount* of bias or departure from expected event probabilities that will occur. Predictions of amount call first for replacing our descriptive statements of value with numerical statements. Once such numerical values have been assigned, one can follow the traditional mathematical technique of multiplying outcome values by probability estimates to obtain a measure of "expected utility," and one can also argue for a general principle such as "maximizing utility" to determine which alternative should be chosen. There are, however, a number of problems in determining how the expected values of an outcome for any given individual can be quantitatively stated. Again, these questions are more fully discussed in Bruner, Goodnow, and Austin 1956, chapter 7. Here we will only state the general conclusion we reach there. This is that we are not prepared to develop or utilize as yet any formal or mathematical model to predict the effect of anticipated consequences on categorizing judgments. We have chosen to be satisfied with less precise prediction and to concern ourselves with the psychological questions which must eventually underlie any model. The most important of these questions concern the objectives determining outcome values and the conditions affecting an individual's estimate of event probability.

For all its present limitation, the concept of a payoff matrix is a useful and a suggestive one. In the first place, it suggests problems that have far too long been overlooked. Psychophysics, concerned as it is with the categorization of magnitudes, could well be reexamined for the manner in which outcome values and likelihood estimates affect categorizing behavior. It could, we believe, thereby be brought much closer to the judgmental behavior of people in everyday situations.

Analysis of the effects of anticipated consequences in terms of payoff matrices may also serve as a link between motivational states and judgmental behavior. Specifically, one's set in judging is partially describable in such terms. Again we may benefit by examining the judging acts that prevail in everyday life. One example is the personnel officer who must categorize applicants into "acceptable" and "unacceptable" groups and who is punished only when his incorrect categorization takes the form of classing as acceptable a man who later fails. The practices of the progressive school provide another example: there the child is rewarded for his correct categorizations only, the others being overlooked. The situation in the basic training camp is yet another example: only errors are noted and punished, correct acts are overlooked. Each time a subject walks into an experimental room, he imposes a payoff matrix on the situation the experimenter presents to him and often the experimenter needs to set him straight.[3]

The Nature of Imposed Restrictions
We end with what may seem like a trivial problem in comparison with the one just discussed; the restrictions imposed upon concept-attainment strategies by the nature of one's working conditions. But in fact, the topic is anything but trivial. Concretely, for example, does the individual have to work toward concept attainment without such external aids as paper and pencil? Does he encounter instances visually and concretely or must he work entirely from verbal descriptions of instances? Are the instances with which he must cope concrete and palpable such as the stimulus cards of the psychologist, or are they abstract and only to be inferred like the data of the modern physicist? These are among the things that comprise the conditions of work that impose restrictions on the manner of attaining a concept.

A few words about the problems involved will suffice to introduce the subject and to foreshadow later chapters. In so far as one is forced to operate entirely "in the head" in solving a concept—on a "mental problem" rather than one in which concrete instances must be sorted—one's method of proceeding may have to take into account the added strain in some way or other. One may literally have to throw

3. An interesting example is provided in a recently reported experiment by Green (1955). His subjects operated in a kind of Skinner-box situation where, when a positive exemplar of a concept appeared, they were to hit a key as often as they could get points. The experimenter soon discovered that subjects had to be warned not to hit the key when a nonexemplar was shown. So long as there was no penalty for doing so they operated on the principle of not taking any chances: one *might* be wrong about an instance that seemed like a nonexemplar.

away information and proceed more slowly if one is to succeed at all. Indeed, there are certain strategies of concept attainment that are "informationally wasteful" but which make it possible to work under a restricting work condition (see Bruner, Goodnow, and Austin 1956). It has been our experience in studying the behavior of our subjects that people who have been trained in mathematics and theoretical physics, where systems of condensed notation make easy the task of carrying along a lot of information, frequently attempt solutions to conceptual problems that, while excellent in principle, cannot succeed because of the impositions they make upon memory.

More often, to be sure, ineffectiveness in concept attainment derives from the use of techniques that are too wasteful of information and do not utilize fully enough the cognitive capacities of our subjects. The use of the dramatic instance as a basis for arriving at the definition of a concept, overextrapolation of attributes found useful in the past with a failure to adopt an adequate information-gathering strategy—these and various other lapses from cognitive rigor are more notable.

In the end, the question reduces to one of choosing a mode of attack that is appropriate to the restrictions imposed by the conditions of work provided. The point is a simple one and an obvious one. Its importance for conceptual activity will be apparent.

Concluding Remarks

We have perhaps strained the reader's patience by lingering so long ... on the various ramifications and the conditions affecting the process of categorial inference. Our justification is threefold. Firstly, we wished to make it as clear as possible that the task of isolating and using a concept is deeply imbedded in the fabric of cognitive life; that indeed it represents one of the most basic forms of inferential activity in all cognitive life. Secondly, it was our wish to develop in some detail the great functional utility of this type of activity in the adjustment of organisms to their environment: the role of categorizing in the economy of knowing one's environment. And finally, perhaps of most importance, our object has been to sketch in outline some of the processes involved in pragmatically *rational* or *effective* behavior. Organisms do group the objects and events of their world into pragmatically useful concepts and they do so with regard to reality constraints. Psychology has been celebrating the role of "emotional factors" and "unconscious drives" in behavior for so long now that man's capacity for rational coping with his world has come to seem like some residual capacity that shows its head only when the irrational lets up. To account for the exquisite forms of problem-solving that we see in everyday life and may see in our laboratories any time we choose to give our subjects something more challenging than key-pressing to perform, highly simplified theories of learning have been invoked. One learns concepts by the association of external stimuli with internal mediating stimuli either by some simple law of frequency or contiguity or by a rather circular and overbegged law of effect. If we have at times portrayed conceptual behavior as perhaps overly logical, we will perhaps be excused on the ground that one excess often breeds its opposite. Man is not a logic machine, but he is certainly capable of making decisions and gathering information in a manner that reflects better on his learning capacity than we have been as yet ready to grant.

References

Adkins, D. C., and Lyerly, S. B. (1951) "Factor Analysis of Reasoning Tests." Adjutant General's Office: PR Rep. No. 878.

Arrow, K. J. (1951) "Alternative Approaches to the Theory of Choice in Risk-Taking Situations." *Econometrica*, 19, 404–37.

Asch, S. E. (1951) "Effects of Group Pressure Upon the Modification and Distortion of Judgments." In H. Guetzkow (ed.), *Groups, Leadership and Men*. Pittsburgh: Carnegie Press, pp. 177–90.

Bouthilet, L. (1948) "The Measurement of Intuitive Thinking." Unpublished Thesis, University of Chicago.

Brown, D. R. (1953) "Stimulus-Similarity and the Anchoring of Subjective Scales." *Amer J Psycho*, 66, 199–214.

Brown, R. (1956) "Language and Categories." In J. Bruner, J. Goodnow, and G. Austin, *A Study of Thinking*. New Brunswick, NJ: Transaction Publishers. pp. 247–312.

Bruner, J., Goodnow, J., and Austin, G. (1956) *A Study of Thinking*. New Brunswick, NJ: Transaction Publishers.

Brunswik, E. (1947) *Systematic and Representative Design of Psychological Experiments with Results in Physical and Social Perception*. Berkeley, CA: University of California Press.

Crutchfield, R. S. (1954) "Conformity and Character." Presidential Address, American Psychological Association, New York, Division of Personal and Social Psychology, September 1954.

Fisher, S. C. (1916) "The Process of Generalizing Abstraction; and its Product, the General Concept." *Psychol Monogr*, 21, No. 2 (Whole No. 90).

Goldstein, K. (1940) *Human Nature in Light of Psychopathology*. Cambridge, MA: Harvard University Press.

Goodnow, J. J. (1955) "Determinants of Choice-Distribution in Two-Choice Situations." *Amer J Psychol* 68, 106–16.

Green, E. J. (1955) "Concept Formation: A Problem in Human Operant Conditioning." *J Exp Psychol*, 49, 175–80.

Helsen, H. (1948) "Adaptation-Level as a Basis for a Quantitative Theory of Frames of Reference." *Psychol Rev*, 55, 297–313.

Hovland, C. I. (1952) "A 'Communication Analysis' of Concept Learning." *Psychol Rev*, 59, 461–72.

Hovland, C. I., and Weiss, W. (1953) "Transmission of Information Concerning Concepts Through Positive and Negative Instances." *J Exp Psychol*, 45, 175–82.

Hull, C. L. (1920) "Quantitative Aspects of the Evolution of Concepts." *Psychol Monogr*, 28, No. 1 (Whole No. 123).

Knight, F. H. (1921) *Risk, Uncertainty and Profit*. Boston: Houghton Mifflin.

Korzybski (1951) "The Role of Language in Perceptual Processes." In R. R. Blake and G. V. Ramsey (eds.), *Perception: An Approach to Personality*. New York: Ronald Press. pp. 170–205.

Marschak, J. (1950) "Rational Behavior, Uncertain Prospects and Measurable Utility." *Econometrica*, 18, 111–41.

Marschak, J. (1954) "Scaling of Utilities and Probabilities." Cowles Commission Discussion Paper: Econ. No. 216.

Pribram, K. (1953) Paper read at annual AAAS meeting, Boston.

Reed, H. B. (1946) "Factors Influencing the Learning and Retention of Concepts. IV. The Influence of the Complexity of the Stimuli." *J Exp Psychol*, 36, 71–87.

Shackle, G. L. S. (1949) Expectations in Economics. (1st ed.). Cambridge: CUP.

Simmel, M. L. (1953) "The Coin Problem: A Study in Thinking." *Amer J Psychol*, 66, 229–41.

Smedslund, J. (1955) *Multiple-Probability Learning: An Inquiry into the Origins of Perception*. Oslo: Akademisk Forlag.

Smoke, K. L. (1932) "An Objective Study of Concept Formation." *Psychol Monogr*, 42, No. 4 (Whole No. 191).

Smoke, K. L. (1933) "Negative Instances in Concept Learning." *J Exp. Psychol*, 16, 583–88.

Thurstone, L. L. (1950) "Creative Talent." Psychometric Lab.: University of Chicago. Rep. No. 61.

Walk, R. D. (1952) "Effect of Discrimination Reversal on Human Discrimination Learning." *J Exp Psychol*, 44, 410–19.

Wallas, Graham (1926) *The Art of Thought*. New York: Harcourt, Brace.

Chapter 4

On the General Character of Semantic Theory

Jerrold Katz

The Structure of the Theory of Language

A theory of the ideal speaker's linguistic competence to relate acoustic signals to meanings is broader than a theory of language: the latter comprises only that branch of linguistics whose aim is to state the universals of language, those aspects of the ideal speaker's linguistic competence that the ideal speaker of every natural language shares; the former encompasses the particular features of the natural language in question as well as whatever is common to all natural languages. The implicit knowledge that an ideal speaker has about the idiosyncracies of his language and the implicit knowledge that he has about every language together constitute the grammar of the language.

The theory of language that transformational grammar is now attempting to develop is a revival of the traditional rationalistic theory of *universal grammar* or *philosophical grammar*. Beattie, in the latter part of the eighteenth century, conceived its aim as follows:

> Languages ... resemble men in this respect, that, though each has peculiarities, whereby it is distinguished from every other, yet all have certain qualities in common. The peculiarities of individual tongues are explained in their respective grammars and dictionaries. Those things, that all languages have in common, or that are necessary to every language, are treated of in a science, which some have called *Universal* or *Philosophical* grammar.[1]

The qualification "that are necessary to every language" is somewhat vague, but it is clearly intended to exclude accidental linguistic regularities. A clarification of this vagueness in Beattie's characterization is provided by Chomsky and Halle (1968):

> The essential properties of natural languages are often referred to as "linguistic universals." Certain apparent linguistic universals may be the result merely of historical accident. For example, if only inhabitants of Tasmania survive a future war, it might be a property of all then existing languages that pitch is not used to differentiate lexical items. Accidental universals of this sort are of no importance for general linguistics, which attempts rather to characterize the range of possible human languages. The significant linguistic universals are those that must be assumed to be available to the child learning a language as an a priori, innate endowment. That there must be a rich system of a priori properties—of

---

This chapter is excerpted from chapter two of Katz's *Semantic Theory*. Displayed sentences and principles have been renumbered for this volume. [EM and SL]
1. Quoted in Chomsky (1965, p. 5).

essential linguistic universals—is fairly obvious from the following empirical observations. Every normal child acquires an extremely intricate and abstract grammar, the properties of which are much underdetermined by the available data. This takes place with great speed, under conditions that are far from ideal, and there is little significant variation among children who may differ greatly in intelligence and experience. The search for essential linguistic universals is, in effect, the study of the a priori *faculté de langage* that makes language acquisition possible under the given conditions of time and access to data (p. 4).

One unique feature of the transformationalist conception of linguistic theory is that it is framed as a specification of the class of grammars, so that its statements of the universal properties of languages are given in the form of constraints on grammars. The formulation of linguistic universals as necessary conditions on a formal system qualifying as a grammar is an extremely important departure from their traditional formulation as direct predications about languages. Its importance lies not only in the ease with which a formal statement of universals can be given, but, more significantly, in the fact that it makes possible the statement of a wider range of universals, including, for example, the definition of grammaticality as generation in an optimal grammar.

The theory of language, then, is a definition of 'grammar' and, alternatively, a definition of 'natural language', where a grammar is any system of rules consistent with the specified constraints and a natural language is anything represented by a grammar. The constraints are of three types: *formal universals, substantive universals,* and *organizational universals.* Formal universals constrain the form of the rules in a grammar; substantive universals provide a theoretical vocabulary from which the constructs used to formulate the rules of particular grammars are drawn; organizational universals, of which there are two subtypes, *componential organizational universals* and *systematic organizational universals,* specify the interrelations among the rules and among systems of rules within a grammar.

The categories of formal, substantive, and componential organizational universals cross-classify with the categories of *phonological universals, syntactic universals,* and *semantic universals.* This is to say that the former group of universals can be about phonological, syntactic, or semantic features of language and, conversely, that such features of language can concern form, content, or organization. Accordingly, linguistic theory consists of three subtheories: *phonological theory, syntactic theory,* and *semantic theory.* The first states the formal, substantive, and componential organizational universals at the phonological level; the second states the universals at the syntactic level; and the third states them at the semantic level. Each of these subtheories of linguistic theory is, then, a model of one of the components of a grammar: phonological theory defines the notion 'phonological component', syntactic theory defines the notion 'syntactic component', and semantic theory defines the notion 'semantic component'. The formal and substantive universals in each of the subtheories specify the requirements on the form and content of the rules in the component of the grammar that the subtheory defines. The requirement that grammars contain transformational rules is a formal universal, while the requirement that the constructs out of which phonological rules are formulated be chosen from a fixed vocabulary of distinctive features is a substantive universal. The componential organizational universals in each subtheory specify the way in which the rules of each component are organized. They determine the ordering conditions under which rules of certain kinds within a component apply with respect to one another and with respect to rules of other kinds. For example, the relation of the base to the transformational subcomponent of the syntactic component and the ordering of transformational rules are universals of this type.

The systematic organizational universals specify how the three components of a grammar are related to one other. They are thus what makes linguistic theory a model of a grammar, and they are the principal part of linguistic theory's explanation of how different speakers of a language are capable of making the same systematic sound-meaning correlations. The most significant of such universals in current linguistic theory is stated in (4.1):

(4.1)   The syntactic component is the generative source of a grammar. Its output is the input to both the phonological component and the semantic component. Its output consists of an infinite set of structural descriptions, one for each sentence of the language. Each structural description consists of a set of underlying phrase markers and a single superficial phrase marker. The semantic component operates on the former to provide a representation of the meaning of the sentence; the phonological component operates on the latter to provide a representation of its pronunciation.

Various aspects of (4.1) are quite controversial at this time (see Katz 1972, Chapter 8). But if (4.1) is accepted, we obtain the following explanation of the sound-meaning correlations. The phonological component interprets superficial phrase markers in terms of speech sounds and the semantic component interprets underlying phrase markers in terms of meaning. The superficial phrase marker of a sentence is related to its underlying phrase markers by sequences of intervening phrase markers. These phrase markers are determined by sequences of transformations that generate the first intervening phrase markers from the underlying phrase markers, the next from the first intervening phrase markers, and so on, until the superficial phrase marker is obtained from the last intervening phrase markers. Thus, the interpretation of the sentence's pronunciation is related to the interpretation of its meaning by virtue of the mediating transformation relation between the syntactic objects of which they are interpretations.

If linguistic theory is to provide this or some form of this explanation of the correlation of semantic and phonetic interpretations, it must have a means of representing the phonetic shape of utterances, the common structure of phrase structure and transformational relations, and the meaning paired with phonetic objects by such relations. Thus phonological theory is required to provide a representation scheme for perceptual correlates of acoustic signals, a definition of the notion 'possible utterance in a language' in terms of a recursive enumeration of the set of phonetic representations for possible utterances of natural languages.[2] Syntactic theory is required to provide a representation scheme for the syntactic organization within a sentence.

2. On the present account of phonological theory, such representations take the form of two-dimensional matrices in which the rows stand for particular constructs (i.e., distinctive features) from the substantive universals of the phonological level and the columns for the consecutive segments of the utterance being represented. (See Chomsky and Halle 1968, pp. 5, 165.)

That is, it will contain a universal theory of constituent structure and grammatical relations in which the notion 'possible sentence in a language' is defined by a recursive enumeration of the set of possible sentence structures.[3] We also require a semantic theory to provide a representation scheme for meanings, that is, a universal theory of concepts in which the notion 'possible (cognitive) meaning in a language' is defined by a recursive enumeration of the set of possible senses.[4]

The problem of constructing a universal scheme for semantic representation is thus one of the primary goals of semantic theory, just as the problem of constructing a universal scheme for phonetic representation is one of the primary goals of phonological theory. A solution to the latter problem would be a system of universal phonology in which the notion 'phonetic representation' is defined, and a solution to the former would be a system of universal semantics in which the notion 'semantic interpretation' is defined. Given such systems, the two interpretive components of grammars would have available phonetic and semantic representations to map onto underlying and superficial phrase markers.

Semantic theory must therefore contain (4.2):

(4.2)   A scheme for semantic representation consisting of a theoretical vocabulary from which semantic constructs required in the formulation of particular semantic interpretations can be drawn.

Semantic theory must also contain a model of the semantic component of a grammar which must describe the manner in which semantic interpretations are mapped onto underlying phrase markers. It must specify the contribution of both linguistic universals and language-specific information to this mapping. It must also explain the semantic competence underlying the speaker's ability to understand the meaning of new sentences chosen arbitrarily from the infinite range of sentences. This explanation must assume that the speaker possesses, as part of his system of internalized rules, semantic rules that enable him to obtain the meaning of any new sentence as a compositional function of the meanings of its parts and their syntactic organization. The model must prescribe that the semantic component of a grammar contain a dictionary that formally specifies the senses of every syntactically atomic constituent in the language. It must also prescribe rules for obtaining representations of the senses of syntactically complex constituents, which are formed from representations of the senses of their atomic constituents in the dictionary. The dictionary provides the finite basis and the rules provide the machinery for projection onto infinite range. Thus, semantic theory must also contain (4.3):

(4.3)   A specification of the form of the dictionary and a specification of the form of the rules that project semantic representations for complex syntactic constituents from the dictionary's representations of the senses of their minimal syntactic parts.

To complete this explanation of compositionality, semantic theory will also need to include certain componential organizational universals that relate the components of the dictionary, that relate the dictionary to the projection rules, and that specify

---

3. See Katz and Postal (1964) and Chomsky (1965).
4. See Katz and Fodor (1963).

the manner in which these rules operate in the process of going from less to more syntactically complex constituents. Thus, semantic theory must also contain (4.4):

(4.4)   A specification of the form of the semantic component, of the relation between the dictionary and the projection rules, and of the manner in which these rules apply in assigning semantic representations.

Requirement (4.2) concerns the substantive universals at the semantic level. The semantic vocabulary that meets this requirement will contain the analogues of syntactic substantive universals such as the constructs 'S', 'NP', 'V' and phonological substantive universals such as the features [± consonantal], [± strident]. Requirement (4.3) concerns the formal universals at the semantic level. Their analogues are the formal characterizations of phrase structure and transformational rules. Requirement (4.4) concerns the componential organizational universals at the semantic level. Their analogues are the statements of the relation between the base and transformational component and the ordering conditions on transformational rules.

Beyond (4.2)–(4.4), which determine the role semantic theory theory plays in the explanation of sound-meaning correlations given by linguistic theory, semantic theory has a special task of its own. Semantics is the area of linguistics that concerns itself with such phenomena as synonymy, semantic similarity, semantic ambiguity, antonymy, and meaningfulness and meaninglessness. The basic task of this theory, then, is to explain (explicate) each such semantic property and relation. Thus, (4.5) must be added as a requirement for a semantic theory:

(4.5)   A set of definitions for semantic properties and relations such as synonymy, antonymy, ambiguity, presupposition, analytic truth and contradictoriness.[5]

Semantic Theory's Model of a Semantic Component

How does the conception of semantic theory as a body of explications which meets (4.5) relate to the conception of semantic theory as an account of the manner in which semantic interpretations are assigned to underlying phrase markers? How do these two conceptions fit together into one coherent conception of semantic theory?[6] The answer is straightforward, stemming from the almost trivial observation that linguistic expressions have the semantic properties and relations they do by virtue of their meaning. Thus, since semantic properties and relations are aspects of the structure of the senses formed in the compositional determination of meaning, there is no problem in coalescing the two conceptions of semantic theory into one coherent whole.

Since the semantic properties and relations of an expression are determined by its meaning and since its meaning is given by semantic representations, it follows that the definitions of semantic properties and relations must be stated in terms of formal

5. For a more extensive list of semantic properties and relations, see Katz (1972) pp. 5–6. [EM & SL]
6. This situation is not unique to semantics. It also arises in phonology. Phonological theory not only must determine the general form of phonetic representations and the principles by which they are assigned to syntactic representations of surface structure; it must accomplish its own special task, dictated by its own subject matter, of explaining such phonological properties and relations as alliteration, rhyme, internal rhyme, metrical forms, etc.

features of semantic representations. If this is done, there will be an explanation of how the meaning of one expression makes it synonymous with another, or analytic, semantically ambiguous, semantically anomalous, and so on. It will be clear what features of its meaning determine that the expression has a particular semantic property or relation, because just these features will be the basis on which the definition of the particular property or relation will apply. Accordingly, the language-independent semantic properties and relations like those in (4.5) will be defined in terms of general features of semantic representations.

We will now try to spell out the requirements (4.2)–(4.5) in sufficient detail to make clear how a semantic component's description of a sentence represents its meaning as a compositional function of the meanings of its parts and how its semantic properties and relations are determined by this description, in conjunction with the definitions of the semantic properties and relations in semantic theory. (See Katz (1972) for a more detailed specification of (4.2)–(4.5).)

The most elementary syntactic components of a sentence are, in general, meaningful units of the language. These, the morphemes, can be divided into two types, grammatical morphemes, which are relatively rare and devoid of meaning, and the nongrammatical morphemes, each of which bears some fixed conceptual interpretation. The latter are meaningful in a sense which makes them contrast with nonsense syllables and nonce words. However, they cannot by themselves express full messages in linguistic communication, as do sentences, nor are they all meaningful in the same way. For example, common nouns like "boy," "table," and "car" are meaningful in a different way from affixes like "de-," "un-," and "-ed." This difference is sometimes described by saying that the latter are syncategorematic. We shall return to these two sorts of meaning at a later point.

Since morphemes are formed out of phonological elements having no intrinsic semantic content, and since higher level syntactic constituents are formed out of them, it is reasonable to think that the meaning of higher level syntactic constituents comes from the meanings of their component morphemes. If so, then a speaker's ability to understand any sentence depends in part on his knowing the meanings of its component morphemes. This can be seen from the fact that a speaker who does not know the meaning of certain morphemes in his language will miss something about the meaning of every sentence in which those unfamiliar morphemes appear— aside from cases where he can "guess" the meaning from the sentential or sociophysical context. That the incomprehensibility due to an unknown word can be transmitted to every constituent of the sentence of which that word is a part (up to and including the whole sentence) shows that the meaning of the sentence and each of its constituents containing the unknown word depends on the meaning of that word. This, in turn, shows that any constituent's meaning is a compositional function of the meanings of its parts and thus, ultimately, its morphemes. Idioms are the exceptions that prove this rule. Locutions like "shoot the breeze," "stir up trouble," "give hell to" make no sense whatever if construed compositionally.

The meaning of a complex constituent does not depend only on the meanings of its component morphemes, however. It also depends on syntactic structure, that is, the way the morphemes are syntactically related to one another in the complex constituent. The same set of morphemes can mean different things when put in different syntactic arrangements, as illustrated by (4.6), (4.7), and (4.8):

(4.6)   John thought he had left Mary alone

(4.7)   Mary alone thought he had left John

(4.8)   Had he alone thought Mary left John?

Rearranging the order of morphemes can also produce just a jumble of words, grammatical word salad such as (4.9):

(4.9)   Thought left John he Mary had alone

Such considerations clearly demonstrate the necessary role of syntactic organization in determining the meaning of complex constituents.

To explain how a speaker is able to understand sentences, we must explain how he goes from the meanings of morphemes in specific relations to each other to the meaning of sentences. We must reconstruct the semantic knowledge an ideal speaker-hearer has of the meanings of the morphemes in his language, the syntax of the sentences, and the compositional function that gives him the meaning of sentences in terms of both of these. This reconstruction attempts to formulate rules that formally reflect the structure of this knowledge by producing semantic representations of sentences from semantic representations of their elementary parts and the syntactic relations between these parts.

These considerations lead us to a first approximation of the internal organization of the semantic component. First, it is a device whose inputs are the underlying phrase markers produced by the syntactic component: the semantic component operates on underlying phrase marker(s) to obtain the syntactic information it requires about a sentence. Second, it is a device that contains a list of the meanings of the morphemes of the language (and the idioms). The meanings of the morphemes can be listed since there are only finitely many of them (and only finitely many idioms). Third, it is a device that contains rules that use information about the syntactic structure of a sentence and the meanings of its morphemes to assign the sentence a semantic interpretation that represents each semantic fact about it. Such semantic interpretations will be the outputs of the semantic component. In short, the semantic component consists of a list of the meanings of the morphemes of the language, which we will call a *dictionary*, and a set of rules that reconstruct the speaker's ability to project sentence meanings from morpheme meanings, which we will call *projection rules*. The inputs are underlying phrase markers and the outputs are *semantic interpretations*.

The process which ends with the assignment of a semantic interpretation to a sentence begins, as we have seen, with the assignment of a meaning to each of the morphemes of that sentence. The meaning of a morpheme is represented by what we shall call a *dictionary entry*. But many, perhaps almost all, morphemes are semantically ambiguous. We shall use the term *sense* in its customary usage to refer to one of the different meanings which a morpheme (or expression) may bear and reserve the term *meaning* for the collection of senses that a morpheme (or expression) has. Accordingly, the meaning of a morpheme, or, as we shall say, a *lexical item*, is the set of senses it has in the dictionary, and the meaning of a complex expression is the set of senses it has on the basis of the meanings of its parts and their mode of semantic composition. Thus, a dictionary entry will contain a semantic representation for each sense of its lexical item, and the semantic representation of the meaning of a lexical item will be taken to be the set of semantic representations of its senses.

We want a representation of a sense to formally distinguish it from other senses and to formally reflect the respects in which it is similar to other senses. The formal properties of a representation must be such that combinations of this representation with others will result in correct representations of the senses of complex expressions and sentences. To construct semantic representations that will satisfy these demands, it is essential to treat a sense neither as atomic nor as monolithic but as a composite of concepts that can be decomposed into parts and the relations in which they stand.[7] The representation of a sense must formalize the structure of a sense, reflecting in its formal structure the natural division of the sense into its conceptual parts and their interrelations. If these representations are built so that each is a formal analysis of the sense it represents, they will exhibit the structural complexity which displays the similarities and differences among senses and determines their compositional potentials.

We thus introduce a pair of technical terms that incorporate this design for the construction of semantic representations. We use the term *reading* to refer to a semantic representation of a sense of a morpheme, word, phrase, clause, or sentence. In addition, we use the term *semantic marker* to refer to the semantic representation of one or another of the concepts that appear as parts of senses. Semantic markers represent the conceptual constituents of senses in the same way in which phrase markers represent the syntactic constituents of sentences. They represent not only the atomic constituents of a sense, that is, the simplest concepts in the sense (analogous to the morphemes in a sentence), but also the complex ones. Accordingly, some semantic markers will have a highly complex internal structure, reflecting the highly complex internal structure of the concepts they represent. A reading, then, is a set of semantic markers. For present purposes, we make no distinction between semantic markers and distinguishers.[8] The latter constructs are treated as special cases of semantic markers. Finally, we differentiate between *lexical readings* and *derived readings*, the former being readings that occur in dictionary entries while the latter are formed from lexical readings by the operation of projection rules.

Let us consider the notion of a semantic marker further. First, it will occur to the reader that the semantic markers are collectively the theoretical vocabulary for semantic representation that was referred to in (4.2). This is roughly correct, except for two qualifications. One is that in a variety of cases semantic markers are introduced by the operation of projection rules. These rules can combine readings in such a manner that a semantic marker in one is fitted into a semantic marker in another or transformed into another, thus creating a partly new, partly old construct. Such semantic markers, which we discuss further at a later point, need not be included in the theoretical vocabulary of semantic theory. They are uniquely determined by the set of semantic markers occurring in dictionary entries and the projection rules. Moreover, they comprise an infinite set of semantic markers and so could not in principle be listed in the theoretical vocabulary. The other exception is those semantic markers that, although they occur in dictionary entries, can be defined in terms of primitives. This is a familiar case in theory construction. The treatment, too, is

---

7. For example, if we were to take the sense of a morpheme like "nude" as unanalyzable, we would then be unable to explain the semantic redundancy of an expression like "naked nude" as a case where the sense of the modifier is identical to a proper part of the sense of the head.

8. See Katz (1972) chapter 3, Section 5.

familiar: we include within our theoretical vocabulary only the *primitive semantic markers*. However, it must be clearly understood that an extensional distinction between primitive and defined constructs in semantic theory can be drawn only after semantic theory has reached a much more sophisticated state of formulation. Therefore, this distinction will be of little concern to us in these investigations. In the final statement of semantic theory, the theoretical vocabulary of semantic markers will consist of each and every primitive semantic marker that is required in the formulation of dictionary entries.[9]

We next turn to the question of the interpretation of semantic markers. As we have already indicated, a semantic marker is a theoretical construct which is intended to represent a concept that is part of the sense of morphemes and other constituents of natural languages. By a concept in this connection we do not mean images or mental ideas or particular thoughts. These, which we will refer to collectively as *cognitions*, form part of the conscious experience of some individual person, in the same way as do sensations, feelings, memories, and hallucinations. Cognitions are individuated in part by the persons who have them. If you and I both have the same thought that John will marry Mary, there are two cognitions, not one. Cognitions are datable: they occur within the time period marked out by their appearance and disappearance from the consciousness of the person who has them. Concepts, on the other hand, are abstract entities. They do not belong to the conscious experience of anyone, though they may be thought about, as in our thinking about the concept of a circle. They are not individuated by persons: you and I may think about the same concept. They are not, as Frege (1956) urged, elements in the subjective process of thinking, but rather the objective content of thought processes, which is "capable of being the common property of several thinkers." Nor are they datable: they cannot posses temporal properties or bear temporal relations.

Because abstract entities such as concepts and propositions differ in these ways from cognitions (and physical objects), they present a problem in regard to their individuation. How are we to decide when reference is being made to the same concept or proposition and when reference is being made to different ones? How do we differentiate one such abstract entity from others if it cannot be assigned differential spatio-temporal properties (as in the case of physical objects) and if it cannot be differentially related to persons who are antecedently individuated, in part, spatio-temporally (as in the case of cognitions)? The answer is that natural languages accomplish such individuation. Speakers, after all, communicate without confusion of reference about particular abstractions and use them to investigate the characteristics of concrete objects. What enables them to perform such individuations is that concepts and propositions are senses of expressions and sentences. That is, senses are concepts and propositions connected with the phonetic (or orthographic) objects in

9. In this connection, note the following remark by Frege (1952): "... my explanation is not meant as a proper definition. One cannot require that everything shall be defined, any more than one can require that a chemist shall decompose every substance. What is simple cannot be decomposed, and what is logically simple cannot have a proper definition. Now something logically simple is no more given us at the outset than most of the chemical elements are; it is reached only by means of scientific work. If something has been discovered that is simple, or at least must count as simple for the time being, we shall have to coin a term for it, since language will not originally contain an expression that exactly answers. On the introduction of a name for something logically simple, a definition is not possible; there is nothing for it but to lead the reader or hearer, by means of hints, to understand the words as is intended" (pp. 42–43).

natural languages. Since these objects have physical counterparts, we can look to the semantic and phonetic representations of sentences and the grammatical rules that systematically interconnect representations of meaning and sound to individuate concepts and propositions. If the grammar provides an account of the semantic content of each phonetic object in the language, then the pairing of sound and meaning will provide the required individuation in terms of phonetically specified features of stretches of speech. These features will differentiate the meanings with which they are correlated under this mapping. Therefore, the problem of individuating abstract conceptual entities is part of the general problem of grammar construction. Since the former problem is solved by speakers on the basis of their linguistic competence, the grammar's reconstruction of linguistic competence will have to explain their solution.

This, however, still leaves open the question of what the ontological status of concepts and propositions is, of what kinds of things senses and meanings are. This question will be left here without a final answer. The reason is twofold. On the one hand, the problem, pushed far enough, becomes the ancient philosophical puzzle about universals, which is best left out of attempts to carry on scientific investigations. On the other hand, even approximations to a serious solution cannot be developed until much more is known about semantic structure. The situation is comparable to the question in physics of what light is. Fruitful investigation into the structure of a phenomenon does not presuppose a definite knowledge of what that phenomenon really is, but, quite the reverse, eventually learning what that phenomenon is presupposes an extensive knowledge of its structure. Just as Maxwell's field theory explains many of the structural features of the propagation of light without explaining what light really is, so we can construct a semantic theory which explains the structure of complex meanings without resting this explanation on an ontological account of concepts and propositions.

It is quite unreasonable to insist at the outset, as some philosophers have,[10] that we provide a general definition of 'semantic marker' and 'reading' that clarifies the ontological status of the notions 'concept' and 'proposition' before these constructs are introduced, to insist, that is, on a clarification of the ontological underpinnings of the notions of concept and proposition as a precondition for accepting the explanations of semantic properties and relations given by a theory employing 'semantic marker' and 'reading'. The parody of this demand runs as follows. Mathematicians have defined notions like 'sum', 'product', 'square root' (the analogues of 'synonymy', 'semantic ambiguity', 'semantic anomaly', 'analyticity', etc.) in terms of 'number' (the analogue of 'proposition' and 'concept'). But no ontologically satisfactory definition of 'number' has been given, and so we must regard the definitions mathematicians give of 'sum', 'product', 'square root', etc., as suspect. How can mathematicians resist the demand for a definition of 'number' and at the same time claim to have supplied definitions of 'sum', 'product', 'square root'? This parody shows that such ontological clarifications, though highly desirable, are not preconditions for successful theory construction and theoretical explanation. A general definition of 'semantic marker' and 'reading' is, then, no more a prerequisite for definitions of 'semantic ambiguity',

10. Wilson (1967) argues that I have defined "'analytic' in terms of 'semantic marker', and on this account ... cannot honestly resist the demand for a general definition of 'semantic marker' and at the same time claim, as [I do], to have supplied a general definition of 'S is analytic in L'" (p. 67).

'semantic anomaly', 'synonymy', and other semantic properties and relations than a definition of 'number' is a prerequisite for defining arithmetic operations.

Of course, there must be some progress toward an explanation of the construct of a semantic marker in terms of an extensional characterization of the notion 'x is a semantic marker'. This is exactly the task of building a semantic theory of natural language, since the values of 'x' would be the empirical spelling out of (4.2). Therefore, the demand that we provide a general definition of 'semantic marker' and 'reading' is unreasonable if laid down as a condition for accepting a semantic theory, since it insists on a complete semantic theory in advance of the empirical and theoretical work required to construct it.

Some further intuitive considerations will clarify the notion of a semantic marker. When we consider semantic markers in their role of representing senses of constituents, we find that there are a few ways to think of them. A reading provides a decomposition of the sense it represents by breaking down that sense into its component concepts. The structure of a conceptually complex sense is thus reflected in the form of semantic markers, which serve as the formal elements to make this analysis possible. For example, the most common sense of the English noun "chair" can be decomposed into a set of concepts which might be represented by the semantic markers in (4.10):

(4.10) (Object), (Physical), (Non-living), (Artifact), (Furniture), (Portable), (Something with legs), (Something with a back), (Something with a seat), (Seat for one)

It is obvious that this analysis leaves out a considerable amount of information. Each of the concepts represented by the semantic markers in (4.10) can itself be broken into components. For example, the concept of an object represented by '(Object)' might be analyzed as *an organization of parts that are spatio-temporally contiguous which form a stable whole having an orientation in space*. On such further analysis, the semantic markers representing the concepts 'legs', 'back', and 'seat' could be formally related to the notion of parts in the analysis of the concept of an object so as to indicate that these are the parts of a chair. This would provide an aspect of the distinction between the meaning of "chair" and other closely related words like "table." Also, we might be able to formally represent the notion 'orientation in space' so that it could be specified here as inherently vertical, thus providing a basis for the difference in meaning between (4.11) and (4.12):[11]

(4.11) The chair is tall

(4.12) The cigarette is tall

As in the case of the concept 'object', we shall often leave concepts without a definition in terms of more primitive semantic markers. This means that certain relationships that depend on the internal structure of the concept cannot yet be formalized. Still, we can work with a reading that takes us part of the way toward a full analysis of the sense and try to determine to what extent the semantic markers found useful here are also useful in providing a means of representing senses of other expressions and stating semantic relations between them.

11. See Bierwisch (1967) and Teller (1969).

Another way of thinking of semantic markers is as the elements in terms of which semantic generalizations about senses can be made. Consider the word "chair" in connection with the words "hat," "planet," "shadow," "car," "molecule" and contrast these with words such as "breath," "truth," "ripple," "thought," "togetherness," "feeling." The senses of the words in the first group are in many ways quite different from one another, yet they are semantically similar in a way in which the senses of the words in the second group are not: each word in the first group contains the concept of an object as one component of its sense while no word in the second group has a sense containing this concept. The generalization about the intragroup similarities and intergroup differences can be expressed using the semantic marker '(Object)' as an element in the lexical reading of each of the words in the former group and excluding it from the lexical reading of any word in the latter. In general, then, semantic markers, by their inclusion or exclusion from readings in dictionary entries, enable us to state semantic generalizations about words.

A third way of thinking about semantic markers is as symbols that mark the components of senses of expressions on which inferences from sentences containing the expressions depend. They are, in this case, thought of as marking aspects of the logical form of the sentences in whose semantic representation they occur. The sentence (4.13) entails (4.14)–(4.21):

(4.13)   There is a chair in the room

(4.14)   There is a physical object in the room

(4.15)   There is something nonliving in the room

(4.16)   There is an artifact in the room

(4.17)   There is a piece of furniture in the room

(4.18)   There is something portable in the room

(4.19)   There is something having legs in the room

(4.20)   There is something with a back in the room

(4.21)   There is a seat for one person in the room

The semantic markers in (4.10), which comprise a reading for "chair," mark the elements in the sense of this word on which the inferences from (4.13) to (4.14)–(4.21) depend. Moreover, the absence of other semantic markers, such as '(Female)', explains why certain other sentences, such as (4.22), are not valid inferences from (4.13):

(4.22)   There is a woman in the room

It is worth noting here that Frege (1952) came close to having the notion of a semantic marker. He observed that instead of saying (4.23a,b,c), we can say (4.24):

(4.23)   (a)   2 is a positive number

          (b)   2 is a whole number

          (c)   2 is less than 10

(4.24)   2 is a positive whole number less than 10

Thus, 'to be a positive number', 'to be a whole number', and 'to be less than 10' are all, in Frege's terminology, *properties* of the number '2' and *marks* of the concept 'positive whole number less than 10'. If Frege had made the further observation—which, as far as I can tell, he did not make—that marks could be represented by formal symbols and that these symbols could be employed to provide a formal representation of the contribution that the senses of items in the descriptive vocabulary of a language make to the inference potentialities of sentences in which the items occur (Frege had the notion of compositionality), then he would have had the notion of a semantic marker. There is, after all, nothing basically different between this case of Frege's and cases where the relation 'is a mark of' holds between the subconcepts forming a composite concept, on the one hand, and that composite concept in the role of the sense of a syntactically simple noun, on the other—for example, between the subconcepts 'to be a physical object', 'to be human', 'to be male', 'to be an adult', and 'to never have married' and the composite concept 'physical object which is human, male, adult, and never married', which is the sense of the syntactically simple noun "bachelor."

Having considered the notion of a semantic marker in some detail, we return to our discussion of lexical and derived readings. Lexical readings are the basis of the compositional process which assigns semantic representations to syntactically complex constituents of sentences. Derived readings are the semantic representations that are assigned to syntactically complex constituents as a representation of the way their meaning is a function of the meanings of their syntactic parts. Succinctly, the process of forming and assigning derived readings works as follows. The phrase markers of a sentence that provide the information necessary for semantic interpretation are received as input by the semantic component. Its first operation is to assign lexical readings from the dictionary to each terminal element of the phrase marker that represents a meaningful element of the sentence. Lexical redings are then combined by the projection rule to form derived readings which are assigned to the lowest order syntactically complex constituents. The projection rule goes on to combine derived readings until a set of derived readings is associated with each syntactically complex constituent, including the whole sentence itself.

The process just sketched must not only construct readings, in must also prevent the construction of them. If we count the number of senses of lexical items in an ordinary fifteen- or twenty-word sentence and compute the total number of possible combinations that could be formed from these senses when they are paired up appropriately, the number of possible senses for the whole sentence usually runs into the hundreds. Since no sentence has anywhere near this many different senses, a rather severe form of selection must be at work in the process whereby derived readings are produced. Furthermore, the fact that some sentences have no sense, even though their individual words are meaningful, indicates that the absence of sense, i.e., meaninglessness, is the limit of whatever selectional process gives rise to multiplicity of senses, i.e., ambiguity. Both these considerations suggest that the account of this process of selection included in the semantic component of a grammar must be in terms of some mechanism that allows or blocks the formation of a derived reading.

Since the formation of derived readings begins with the combination of lexical readings, the latter must contain, besides a set of semantic markers, a *selection restriction*. This will state the condition under which the sense represented by the set of semantic markers can combine with other senses to form a sense of a syntactic complex constituent. The adjective "gold," for example, has at least two senses—that of being made of a certain malleable metallic element and that of having a deep yellowish color. Neither of these senses can combine with the senses of nouns like "truth," "thought," "virtue": expressions like "metal truth," "yellow thought," "yellow virtue" are senseless. The selection restriction reconstructs the distinction between the range of senses with which a given sense can unite to form a new sense and the range of senses with which it cannot unite. Whenever a constituent is formed from component constituents and the sense of one belongs to the range of senses excluded from combination with the sense of the other, then the constituent is meaningless (conceptually absurd) unless the component constituents have other senses that can combine. Both senses of "gold" can combine with the sense of "chair," giving the two senses of the semantically ambiguous expression "gold chair," namely, one of a metal chair and the other of a chair of a certain color. But only the first sense of "gold" can combine with the senses of the other constituents in "white-gold ring" to form a sense for the whole, whereas only the second sense of "gold" can combine with the sense of "mist" to form a sense for "gold mist." Were "gold" to have only the first sense, "gold mist" would be meaningless. Note, however, that were "gold" to have only the second sense, "white-gold ring" would not be meaningless but contradictory. The senses of words like "white," "red," "blue" are antonymous with "gold" in the sense of the color, as is "nongold," but they have the same range of combination with other senses that "gold" does. The same things that can be gold (in color) can be white, red, blue, etc., and the things that cannot literally be gold cannot literally be white, red, blue, etc. Thus there is something common in the senses of the words to which "gold," "white," "red," "blue," etc. apply that marks them off as a class from those words to which "gold," "white," "red," "blue," etc. cannot apply. This common semantic element will be stated in the selection restriction of "gold," "white," "red," "blue," etc., and the fact that each of these words has the same selection restriction will express this generalization about a common semantic element. Since, furthermore, as in the case of any element of a sense, such common semantic elements are represented by semantic markers, a selection restriction must be formulated as a requirement on the semantic marker content of readings. Thus the selection restriction in a reading specifies the semantic markers that other readings must have in order that they may combine with the first reading to form derived readings.

Let us consier a crude illustration of a dictionary entry. The adjective "handsome" appears to have one sense where it means 'beautiful with dignity', another where it means 'gracious or generous', and still another where it means 'moderately large'. The first applies to persons and artifacts, as in expressions like "a handsome woman" or "a handsome desk"; the second applies to some forms of conduct, as in the expression "a handsome welcome"; and the third applies to amounts, as in "a handsome sum of money." Thus, the dictionary entry for "handsome" might look like (4.25), where the semantic markers enclosed in angled brackets represent the selection restriction for that sense:

(4.25)   *handsome*; [+ Adj, . . .];   (Physical), (Object), (Beautiful), (Dignified in appearance), ⟨(Human) ∨ (Artifact)⟩
(Gracious), (Generous), ⟨(Conduct)⟩
(Moderately large), ⟨(Amount)⟩

One can see how, given something like (4.10) as the lexical reading of one sense of "chair," the derived reading for the noun "handsome chair" would be one on which the sense is 'a physical object which is a portable piece of furniture with legs, a back, and a seat which serves as a seat for one, and which is an artifact of beauty and dignity'. The other lexical readings of "handsome" would not combine with this lexical reading of "chair" because it contains neither the semantic marker '(Conduct)' nor the semantic marker '(Amount)'.

The dictionary consists of a complete list of dictionary entries, one for each lexical item in the lexicon of the syntactic component that represents a meaningful item of the language, and a list of what we may call *semantic redundancy rules*. These serve to simplify the formulation of dictionary entries by allowing us to eliminate any semantic markers from a lexical reading whose occurrence is predictable on the basis of the occurrence of another semantic marker in the same reading. The rules can be illustrated by (4.26):

(4.26) (a) (Furniture) $\rightarrow$ (Artifact)

(b) (Artifact) $\rightarrow$ $\left\{ \begin{array}{l} \text{(Object)} \\ \text{(Physical)} \\ \text{(Non-living)} \end{array} \right\}$

The rules in (4.26) would simplify the lexical reading for one sense of "chair" given in (4.10) by allowing the elimination of '(Object)', '(Physical)', '(Non-living)', '(Artifact)'. There will, of course, be many other redundancy rules that eliminate semantic markers such as '(Physical)' and '(Artifact)' from the dictionary, as, for example, rules (a) and (b) of (4.27):[12]

(4.27) (a) (Animal) $\rightarrow$ (Physical)

(b) (Vehicle) $\rightarrow$ (Artifact)

The dictionary is the base from which the semantic component works in forming derived readings to account for the compositional meaning of syntactically complex constituents. The projection rules are the mechanism for forming the derived readings. Let us now examine how the dictionary and the projection rules work together to provide readings for each constituent of a sentence.

As has already been observed, the compositional account of the meaning of a sentence requires two types of syntactic information, namely, a specification of the syntactic atomic constituents (that is, the lexical items) and a specification of their syntactic organization (that is, which items go together to form constituents of the sentence and by what relations they combine). Although information of this sort is included in all of the phrase markers in the structural description of a sentence, the underlying phrase markers seem to give it in its most complete form. The other phrase markers result from transformations, and transformational operations of deletion and permutation eliminate information about both lexical items and constituent structure.[13] Therefore, if the semantic component is to have the syntactic information it needs, it seems reasonable to require that the input to the semantic component for a sentence S is the underlying phrase marker(s) of S generated by the syntactic component.

12. For further discussion see Katz (1966, pp. 224–239).
13. See Katz and Postal (1964, Chapters 3 and 4).

The first step in the process of providing readings for the constituents of a sentence is to assign appropriate lexical readings from the dictionary to the lexical items in the terminal string of the underlying phrase marker. This can be done on the basis of the following convention: an occurrence of a lexical item in the terminal string is paired with the set of lexical readings in the dictionary entry for this item on the condition that the syntactic markers in the lexicon entry categorize it in the same way that it is categorized in the underlying phrase marker. The simplest form of this convention would be the stipulation that the set of lexical readings paired with a lexical item in a dictionary entry is carried along with the lexical item when the lexical rule of the syntactic component inserts that item in a preterminal string.[14]

Once lexical readings are assigned to lexical items in an underlying phrase marker, the semantic redundancy rules can operate to fill out compressed lexical readings by supplying the semantic markers which were excluded for purposes of economy in the formulation of lexical readings in dictionary entries. These semantic markers must be introduced at this stage because they will be required to determine whether or not lexical readings can combine to form derived readings. For instance, the sense of "hard" meaning 'not easily penetrated' can combine with the sense of "chair" represented by the lexical reading given in (4.10) only if the semantic marker '(Physical)' appears in the reading of "chair" in an underlying phrase marker. But, as was mentioned with regard to rule (4.26), this semantic marker does not actually appear in the lexical reading of "chair." Hence, it must be introduced by a semantic redundancy rule prior to the point at which the projection rules would combine readings of "hard" and "chair" to obtain a derived reading for "hard chair."

Once the semantic redundancy rules have done their work, we have what we will call *lexically interpreted underlying phrase markers*. These constitute the domain of the projection rules. The principles expressing the order of the operation of the subcomponents—the assignment of lexical readings first, then the application of the semantic redundancy rules, and finally the operation of the projection rules—constitute the main semantic universals under (4.4), that is, the main componential organizational universals at the semantic level.

The projection rules finish the job of giving the readings for the constituents of a sentence by assigning all of the derived readings. They convert lexically interpreted underlying phrase markers into *semantically interpreted underlying phrase markers*. Each of the constituents of these underlying phrase markers is associated with an optimal set of readings, that is, each reading in the set represents one sense of the constituent to which it is assigned and each sense of this constituent is represented by one reading in the set.

The projection rules first combine expanded lexical readings. They next combine the derived readings formed from the combination of expanded lexical readings and continue combining derived readings until the process terminates with the assignment of derived readings for the whole sentence. When the lexical readings were assigned to terminal symbols, the semantic component used the underlying phrase marker for information about what lexical items occurred in the deep structure of the sentence and what syntactic categorization they received. At the point when the projection rules apply, the semantic component again uses the underlying phrase marker, this time for information about how the lexical items concatenate to form

---

14. See Chomsky (1965, Section 2.3.3. of Chapter 2).

constituents, that is, information about the relation of subconstituent to constituent and about the syntactic categorization of constituents. The projection rules can then combine readings associated with subconstituents to form the readings for the full constituent. They do this by moving from smaller to larger constituents in accord with another semantic universal under (4.5).[15] In the course of their operation, the projection rules enforce selection restrictions at each step, thus preventing some readings from combining while allowing others to form derived readings which are assigned to constituents. In this manner, each constituent in an underlying phrase marker, including the whole sentence constituent, receives a set of readings to represent its meaning, and the lexically interpreted underlying phrase marker is converted into a semantically interpreted underlying phrase marker.

Projection rules, as they have been formulated,[16] differ from one another by their conditions of application and by the operations they perform in producing a derived reading. A projection rule applies to a set of readings associated with an n-tuple of constituents just in case the n-tuple satisfies the grammatical relation in terms of which the projection rule is defined. There is, then, a different projection rule for each distinct grammatical relation—one for the attribution relation, one for the subject-verb relation, one for the verb-direct object relation, one for the verb-indirect object relation, and so on. Which projection rule applies in a given step in forming a semantically interpreted underlying phrase marker thus depends on the grammatical relation that holds among the subconstituents (of the constituent at that step), which already have readings assigned to them, and the full complex constituent that these subconstituents form, which does not as yet have any readings assigned to it. If, for example, the relation is that of modifier to head, then the projection rule applies whose conditions of application are defined by the modification relation; if the relation is verb-object, then the projection rule defined for that grammatical relation applies, and so forth. Each such rule, moreover, performs a distinct operation on the readings to which it applies. The projection rule that applies to readings of a modifier and readings of its head forms a derived reading by taking the Boolean union of the semantic markers in both readings, while the projection rule that combines readings of a verb with readings of its direct object forms derived readings by embedding the reading of the direct object in the reading of the verb at a fixed position. Of course, such combinatorial operations are performed only if the readings in the domain of a projection rule meet the selection restriction governing their combination. Thus, the projection rules associate types of semantic combination with particular grammatical relations. They specify the semantic import of the grammatical relations defined in syntactic theory. Their full characterization is, then, a main item under (4.3), that is, a prime formal universal on the semantic level.

We now define the notion 'semantic interpretation of a sentence'. What is involved here is the concept of the full set of statements that can be made about the meaning of the sentence. The set of semantically interpreted underlying phrase markers for a sentence does not by itself specify the semantic properties and relations that the sentence has. This is what the semantic interpretation of the sentence provides over and

---

15. The universal in question here states that projection rules apply first to the innermost labeled bracketings of the terminal string of an underlying phrase marker, then to the next innermost, and so on, until they reach the outermost. In other words they proceed from the bottom to the top of a tree.

16. See Katz and Fodor (1963) and Katz (1966).

above representations of senses. Given definitions for each semantic property and relation (i.e., a complete specification of (4.5)) and semantically interpreted underlying phrase markers for a sentence S, it will be possible to enumerate the full list of *semantic predictions* about the semantic properties and relations of S. This list is the semantic interpretation of S.

Preliminary Definitions of Some Semantic Properties and Relations

The definitions of semantic properties and relations in semantic theory can be thought of as formal explications of our ordinary notions about semantic concepts. For example, our ordinary notions of semantic similarity, ambiguity meaningfulness, and synonymy are, roughly, that semantically similar expressions are ones whose senses share a feature, that an ambiguous expression is one that has more than one sense, that a meaningful expression is one that has a sense, and that two expressions are synonymous in case they have a common sense. To construct a semantic theory, we have to reformulate such ordinary, common sense notions within a formal theory of grammar which exhibits their interrelations and their connections to the expressions and sentences of natural languages. In each case the lines along which we are to construct the reformulation is to some extent suggested by the ordinary notion we are trying to explicate formally. But although these notions guide our efforts to arrive at formal definitions, they by no means determine them. As we shall see in the course of this study, the form in which the definitions are given is also influenced by considerations of other sorts, considerations having to do with the role these definitions play in semantic theory, their interrelations and their connection to other systematic aspects of the theory of language and semantic theory. The definitions to be presented in this section are the most direct conversion of our ordinary notions of semantic concepts into the formalism of semantic theory. This is so because, at the present early stage of theory construction, there is very little else available to influence the form such definitions take. Once we develop semantic theory more fully, other considerations will enter to change their statement. Accordingly, the definitions to be given here are called "preliminary" to acknowledge from the outset that they are not intended as final characterizations of semantic properties and relations.

We think of things as similar when they have some but not all features in common. Accordingly, we think of two expressions from a natural language as similar in meaning when their senses are built out of some of the same concepts. Since semantic markers represent the concepts out of which senses are built, we are immediately led to the definitions of 'semantic similarity' and 'semantic distinctness' in (4.28) and (4.29):

(4.28)   A constituent C_i is semantically similar to a constituent C_j on a sense just in case there is a reading of C_i and a reading of C_j which have a semantic marker in common. (They can be said to be semantically similar with respect to the concept ϕ in case the shared semantic marker represents ϕ.)

(4.29)   A constituent C_i is semantically distinct from a constituent C_j on a sense of C_i and a sense of C_j just in case the readings of these senses have no semantic markers in common.

Clearly, synonymy is the limiting case of semantic similarity: it is the case where two constituents are as similar as possible, where there is no difference in meaning between a sense of one and a sense of the other. Hence, the definition of 'synonymy' is as in (4.30) and of 'full synonymy' as in (4.31):

(4.30)   A constituent C_i is synonymous with another constituent C_j on a sense just in case they have a reading in common.

(4.31)   A constituent C_i is fully synonymous with C_j just in case the set of readings assigned to C_i is identical to the set of readings assigned to C_j.

Paraphrase can be taken as synonymy between sentences.

Closely tied in with these relations is 'meaning inclusion', defined as in (4.32) and (4.33):

(4.32)   A constituent C_i's sense is semantically included in a sense of a constituent of C_j just in case every semantic marker in a reading of C_i is also in a reading for C_j.

(4.33)   A constituent C_i is fully included semantically in a constituent C_j just in case, for each reading of C_i, there is a reading of C_j such that the semantic markers in the former are also in the latter.

If two constituents are synonymous, then they are each semantically included in the other, but if one is semantically included in the other, it does not follow that the two are synonymous.

The next semantic properties to be defined depend on the manner in which multiple senses of lexical items are carried up to constituents at higher phrase structure levels.

Ambiguity, as ordinarily understood, is a case where there is a problem telling one thing from another, and, accordingly, a semantic ambiguity is a case where there are (at least) the two senses required to pose this problem. Furthermore, given that readings represent sense of constituents and that the number of senses of a constituent is its degree of ambiguity, it follows that the number of readings assigned to a constituent should correctly reflect its degree of ambiguity. Thus, we define 'semantic ambiguity' as in (4.34):

(4.34)   A constituent C is semantically ambiguous just in case the set of readings assigned to C contains two or more members. (C's degree of ambiguity is given by the number of readings in the set.)

Normally selection restrictions filter out some potential readings and allow others to form and to be assigned to the appropriate higher level constituents. In the extreme case, however, the selection restriction will block all combinations and the higher level constituents will receive no reading. The constituents are then represented as having no senses, as being meaningless or, as we shall say here, semantically anomalous.[17] Hence, the definition of 'anomaly' is as in (4.35):

(4.35)   A constituent is semantically anomalous just in case it is assigned no readings (the set of readings assigned to it is null).

17. This term is chosen because "meaningless" has a stronger connotation than is desired.

144   Katz

If exactly one reading is assigned to a constituent, it is neither semantically anomalous nor semantically ambiguous. Thus the definition of 'uniqueness' is as in (4.36):

> (4.36) A constituent is semantically unique just in case the set of readings assigned to it contains exactly one member.

The Kantian notion of analyticity is that of the vacuous assertion that results when the meaning of a predicate contains only attributes that are components of the meaning of the subject. Analytic sentences are thus trivially true by virtue of the fact that the determination of the things to which their subject refers already guarantees that these things will have the attributes their predicate asserts of them. Since semantic markers represent the conceptual components that form the meaning of a subject and a predicate, the primary condition for 'analyticity' can be stated, as in (4.37) and (4.38), in terms of the formal condition that the semantic markers in the reading of the predicate also appear in the reading of the subject.[18] (The further defining condition in (4.37) will be explained in Katz 1972, Chapter 4.)

> (4.37) S is analytic on a reading $R_{1,2}$ if and only if every noncomplex semantic marker in R_2 occurs in R_1 and for any complex semantic marker $((M_1) \vee (M_2) \vee \cdots \vee (M_n))$ in R_2 there is an (M_i), $1 \leq i \leq n$, in R_1;

> (4.38) S is fully analytic if and only if S is analytic on each reading assigned to its sentence constituent; i.e., for each reading $R_{i,j}$ assigned to S, S is analytic (in the sense of (4.37)) on $R_{i,j}$;
>
> where the symbol 'R_i' or 'R_1' stands for a reading of the subject of a sentence in the range of 'S', the symbol 'R_j' or 'R_2' stands for a reading of the predicate of such a sentence, and the symbol '$R_{i,j}$' or '$R_{1,2}$' stands for a reading of the whole sentence which results from the semantic combination of 'R_i' and 'R_j' and of 'R_1' and 'R_2', respectively.

Analyticity is the counterpart on the sentence level of the semantic relation of redundancy at the level of nonsentential constituents. The analyticity of "Mothers are female" is thus the counterpart of the redundancy of "female mother." This leads to the definitions (4.39) and (4.40) of 'redundancy':

> (4.39) A constituent C is redundant on a reading $R_{i,j}$ if (a) C is syntactically formed from the constituents c_i and c_j, (b) c_i is a modifier and c_j is its head, (c) $R_{i,j}$ is a reading of C formed from R_i which is a reading of c_i and R_j which is a reading of c_j, (d) every noncomplex semantic marker in R_i occurs in R_j and for any complex semantic marker $((M_1) \vee (M_2) \vee \cdots \vee (M_n))$ in R_i, there is an (M_z), $1 \leq z \leq n$, in R_j.

> (4.40) C is fully redundant if and only if C is redundant on each of its readings.

Analogously, contradiction is the counterpart, on the level of sentences, of the semantic relation of meaning incompatibility at the level of lower order constituents. We thus seek definitions which are constructed in such a manner that the similarity

18. We assume throughout the remaining definitions that the variable 'S' ranges over sentences that are determinable, which means, in the case of (4.37), that S is determinable on $R_{1,2}$. This notion and the reason for the requirement are dealt with in Katz (1972) Chapter 4, where the concept of determinability is presented.

and difference between contradictoriness and incompatibility are explained. Further, these definitions must integrate with (4.37), (4.38), and the definitions of 'syntheticity' to provide the logical relationships among these concepts.

Linguistically, the concept of incompatibility appears as antonymy, which is a relation between expressions. Under the general notion there are many specific types of antonymy relations. One example is the sex-antonymy relation that holds between a pair of expressions just in case their senses are identical except that where one contains femaleness as one of its component concepts the other contains maleness. Some instances of sex-antonymy are given in (4.41):

> (4.41) bride/groom, aunt/uncle, cow/bull, girl/boy, actress/actor, doe/buck

The general case for antonymy relations is not pairs, but n-tuples. For example, there are species-antonymous n-tuples, an instance of which is presented in (4.42):

> (4.42) child/cub/puppy/kitten/cygnet

Besides there being many other types of antonymy relations, the extension of any one, i.e., the set of all and only the n-tuples of expressions of the language that bear that type of antonymy relation to one another, is infinite, since the process of constructing further expressions from the simplest cases by syntactic rules is recursive and generally preserves the antonymy relation. Thus, the set of antonymous n-tuples that contains the words listed in (4.41) also contains the more complex expressions listed in (4.43):

> (4.43) the nervous bride/the nervous groom, several aunts who talk far too much/several uncles who talk far too much, our beloved old cow/our beloved old bull

Note that the importance of obtaining an explication of the concept of antonymy—here understood in the broad sense which goes beyond the lexicographer's usage where "antonymy" is usually applied only to the relation when it holds of words—has to do not only with explaining this semantic relation between words and expressions as in (4.41) and (4.42) but also with explaining various other semantic properties.

Consider the sentences in (4.44):

> (4.44) (a) John is well and Mary's not sick either
>   (b) John is smart and Mary's not stupid either
>   (c) John is well and Mary's not $\left\{ \begin{array}{l} \text{in fair health} \\ \text{well, healthy} \\ \text{foolish} \\ \text{poor} \\ \text{dead} \end{array} \right\}$ either
>   (d) John is smart and Mary's not $\left\{ \begin{array}{l} \text{smart} \\ \text{bright} \\ \text{sick} \\ \text{dirty} \\ \text{alive} \end{array} \right\}$ either

The sentences represented in (a) and (b) of (4.45) are meaningful whereas those in (c) and (d) are semantically anomalous. The reason is clearly that when "either" operates together with a conjunction to conjoin a positive and negative sentence in order to say something about one person and then "ditto" about another, there is a semantic restriction that the expressions serving as predicates (the expressions that provide the content for what is said about the people) must be antonymous (members of the same antonymous n-tuple). Obviously, then, the formalism on which such semantic anomalousness is predicted and explained will require a definition of the antonymy relation.

The most natural way of defining the notion 'antonymous constituents' so that the definition will be adequate for antonymy sets containing infinitely many particular n-tuples of antonymous expressions is to group semantic markers into antonymous n-tuples on the basis of the incompatibilities they are supposed to represent. This can be accomplished by using some suitable formal device in the formulation of semantic markers in which they are so represented that the membership of any n-tuple of antonymous semantic markers can be uniquely determined on the basis of formal features of the symbols that comprise the semantic markers. For example, we could write the semantic markers that represent the concepts of maleness and femaleness, assuming them to be incompatible and jointly exhaustive of the sexual domain, in the form '(S^+)' and '(S^-)', respectively. Assuming, on the other hand, that the concepts are not jointly exhaustive (taking the term "hermaphrodite" into consideration, for example), we could write an antonymous n-tuple in the form '(S^m)', '(S^f)', and '(S^h)'. Actually, later we shall find reason to further modify this notation in certain ways, but, generally, the notation for X-antonymous n-tuples of semantic markers will be represented by a common base semantic marker with semantic marker superscripts that indicate the incompatible elements within the domain determined by the base semantic marker. Thus, the general form of an antonymous n-tuple of semantic markers is as shown in (4.45) and as specified in (4.46):

(4.45) $(M^{(\alpha_1)}), (M^{(\alpha_2)}), \ldots, (M^{(\alpha_n)})$

(4.46)   Two semantic markers belong to the same antonymous n-tuple of semantic markers if and only if one has the form $(M^{(\alpha_i)})$ and the other has the form $(M^{(\alpha_j)})$, where $i \neq j$ and $1 \leq i \leq n$ and $1 \leq j \leq n$.

We may now define 'antonymy' as in (4.47) and (4.48):

(4.47)   Two constituents C_i and C_j are antonymous (on a sense) if and only if they are not full sentences and they have, respectively, readings R_i and R_j such that R_i is identical to R_j except that R_i contains a semantic marker (M_i) and R_j contains a semantic marker (M_j) and the semantic markers (M_i) and (M_j) are distinct members of the same antonymous n-tuple of semantic markers.

(4.48)   Two constituents C_i and C_j are fully antonymous if and only if they are antonymous on every sense.

In earlier discussions,[19] we failed to single out the ordinary lexicographical notion of antonymy as we have done here. Instead, we included it under the general notion of incompatibility. Here we explicate the latter by (4.49) and (4.50):

19. See Katz (1964; 1966, pp. 118–224).

(4.49) Two constituents C_i and C_j are incompatible (on a sense) if and only if they are not full sentences and they have, respectively, readings R_i and R_j such that R_i contains a semantic marker (M_i) and R_j contains a semantic marker (M_j) and the semantic markers (M_i) and (M_j) are distinct members of the same antonymous n-tuple of semantic markers.

(4.50) Two constituents C_i and C_j are fully incompatible if and only if they are incompatible on every sense.

Lumping both notions under one definition and using the label 'antonymous expression' (as the defined term) caused some unnecessary confusion about antonymy and incompatibility. Cases like "cow" and "cowboy," which are not antonyms in the strict lexicographer's sense, were regarded as antonymous expressions on the former usage (incompatible expressions on the present usage). This led some to think that we were unable to explicate the lexicographer's notion of antonymy. The distinction we now make explicit in (4.47) and (4.48) should eliminate the occasion for such confusion and show that both the notion of lexicographical antonymy and the notion of incompatibllity can be explicated.

We may construct definitions for 'S is contradictory (on a sense)' and 'S is fully contradictory' that reveal the way in which these concepts reflect antonymy and incompatibility relations on the level of nonsentential constituents. Thus we have (4.51) and (4.52):

(4.51) S is contradictory on a sense represented by the reading $R_{1,2}$ if and only if the reading R_1 contains a semantic marker (M_i) and the reading R_2 contains a semantic marker (M_j) such that (M_i) and (M_j) are different semantic markers belonging to the same antonymous n-tuple of semantic markers.

(4.52) S is fully contradictory if and only if S is contradictory on every reading assigned to its sentence constituent.

What is asserted about a sentence when its semantic interpretation marks it as contradictory on a reading is that anything to which its subject refers possesses a property or properties incompatible with some property or properties attributed to it by the predicate. Thus, just as analytic statements are true by virtue of meaning alone, contradictory statements are false by virtue of meaning alone. The very condition that determines when something is correctly regarded as an instance of the subject concept guarantees the falsity of the predication.

In terms of the previous definitions, we can now define 'syntheticity' as in (4.53) and (4.54):

(4.53) S is synthetic on a sense if and only if there is a reading $R_{1,2}$ assigned to S's sentence constituent such that S is neither analytic nor contradictory on $R_{1,2}$.

(4.54) S is fully synthetic if and only if S is synthetic on each of the readings assigned to its sentence constituents.

These difinitions reconstruct the idea that a synthetic sentence is one whose truth or falsity cannot be decided on the basis of the meanings of its component words, but must be decided on the basis of consideration of whether or not what the sentence's subject refers to has the property that it is asserted to have.

Relative to the definitions of semantic properties and relations, the semantic component provides an explanation of how the semantic properties and relations of a constituent are determined by the senses of the constituents that comprise it. The form of such an explanation is as follows. A constituent of a sentence (perhaps the whole sentence itself) receives a set of readings in the semantically interpreted underlying phrase marker where the constituent occurs. Each reading in such a set formally represents one of the senses of the constituent in the sentence to which the semantically interpreted underlying phrase marker is assigned. Since the definitions of semantic properties and relations in semantic theory are formulated in terms of formal features of readings, whether a constituent C has the semantic property P or bears the relation H (to some other constituent) depends on whether the readings in the set assigned to C exhibit the formal features required by the definition for P or H. What explains the presence of the features of the readings in C's semantically interpreted underlying phrase marker by virtue of which C is marked as P (or H) are the projection rules, which reconstruct the way in which the meanings of complex constituents are a compositional function of the meanings of their component constituents, and the dictionary, which provides readings for noncomplex constituents of the language. Hence, what explains C being P (or H) is the application of the dictionary and the operation of the projection rules.

Not only do the definitions of semantic properties and relations complete the definition of the concept of a semantic interpretation, they also provide a basis for systematically testing the semantic component of a grammar. In accordance with these definitions, the semantic interpretation of a sentence S will contain a list of semantic predictions, each of which will say either that S has or does not have a certain semantic property P or that S does or does not bear a certain semantic relation H to some other constituent. These predictions can be tested against the judgments made by fluent speakers of the language. Fluent speakers make various judgments about aspects of the meaning of a constituent and the semantic interpretation makes predictions about the same aspects. If the judgments and predictions coincide, that is, if the statements in the semantic interpretation of the sentence about aspects of its meaning correctly predict the judgments of the speakers, then the semantic component from which the predictions come is confirmed; if not, it is disconfirmed. In this manner, the semantic component can be submitted to empirical tests that may either confirm or disconfirm its account of the meanings of expressions in the language. If there is confirmation over a wide range of empirical cases, it may be claimed that the semantic component reflects the linguistic competence of native speakers in regard to their knowledge of the semantic structure of their language. In the case of disconfirmation, the falsified predictions guide us in making suitable revisions in the dictionary or projection rules or definitions. Then the process of empirical test begins again.

As in the explication of any abstract concept, we assume in the explication of semantic properties and relations that we are, initially, in possession of a fairly representative set of the relevant facts. These take the form of examples of morphemes, words, phrases, and sentences of various natural languages that have one or another particular linguistic property or that bear one or another linguistic relation to some other construction. We assume, therefore, that such examples are substantiated on the basis of reliable linguistic intuitions on the part of fluent speakers of the language. That is, we assume that we can demonstrate, in one manner or another, that fluent speakers will make consistent intuitive judgments indicating that the example does exhibit the property or relation it has been taken to exhibit. Accordingly, these examples serve as clear cases for the explication of semantic concepts. We seek to construct a semantic theory that explains the clear cases in the simplest and most revealing way and to allow the theory to stand the challenge of predictive test as further clear cases are brought up. Not all cases will be clear cases. The unclear ones, those about which the intuitions of speakers are too weak or conflicting to determine linguistic properties and relations, have to be decided by the theory itself. This, however, is a familiar feature of explication. The fact that we can allow the theory to decide in some situations confers an enormous advantage on theory construction. It permits the linguist to postpone the obligation to provide a treatment of unclear cases until he has obtained the theoretical machinery for interpolating their treatment from the treatment he has given the available clear cases, thereby preventing unclear cases from standing in the way of further linguistic inquiry.

References

Bierwisch, M. (1967) "Some Semantic Universals of German Adjectivals," *Foundations of Language*, 3: 1–36.

Chomsky, N. (1965) *Aspects of the Theory of Syntax*. Cambridge, MA: MIT Press.

Chomsky, N., and Halle, M. (1968) *The Sound Pattern of English*. New York: Harper and Row.

Frege, G. (1952) "On Concept and Object." In P. Geach and M. Black (eds.), *Translations from the Philosophical Writings of Gottlob Frege*. Oxford: Basil Blackwell & Mott.

Frege, G. (1956) "The Thought: A Logical Inquiry." *Mind*, 65: 289–311. Reprinted in E. D. Klemke, (ed.) *Essays on Frege*. Urbana: University of Illinois Press.

Katz, J. (1964) "Analyticity and Contradiction in Natural Language." In Fodor and Katz (eds.), *The Structure of Language: Readings in the Philosophy of Language*. Englewood Cliffs, NJ: Prentice-Hall.

Katz, J. (1966) *The Philosophy of Language*. New York: Harper & Row.

Katz, J. (1972) *Semantic Theory*. New York: Harper & Row.

Katz, J., and Fodor, J. A. (1963) "The Structure of a Semantic Theory." *Language*, 39, 170–210. Reprinted in Fodor and Katz (eds.), *The Structure of Language: Readings in the Philosophy of Language*. Englewood Cliffs, NJ: Prentice-Hall.

Katz, J., and Postal, P. (1964) *An Integrated Theory of Linguistic Descriptions*. Cambridge, MA: MIT Press.

Teller, P. (1969) "Some Discussion and Extension of Bierwisch's Work on German Adjectivals." *Foundations of Language*, 5: 185–217.

Wilson, N. L. (1967) "Linguistic Butter and Philosophical Parsnips." *Journal of Philosophy*, 64: 55–67.

Philosophical Skepticism about the Classical Theory

Chapter 5

Two Dogmas of Empiricism

W. V. O. Quine

Modern empiricism has been conditioned in large part by two dogmas. One is a belief in some fundamental cleavage between truths which are *analytic*, or grounded in meanings independently of matters of fact, and truths which are *synthetic*, or grounded in fact. The other dogma is *reductionism*: the belief that each meaningful statement is equivalent to some logical construct upon terms which refer to immediate experience. Both dogmas, I shall argue, are ill-founded. One effect of abandoning them is, as we shall see, a blurring of the supposed boundary between speculative metaphysics and natural science. Another effect is a shift toward pragmatism.

1. Background for Analyticity

Kant's cleavage between analytic and synthetic truths was foreshadowed in Hume's distinction between relations of ideas and matters of fact, and in Leibniz's distinction between truths of reason and truths of fact. Leibniz spoke of the truths of reason as true in all possible worlds. Picturesqueness aside, this is to say that the truths of reason are those which could not possibly be false. In the same vein we hear analytic statements defined as statements whose denials are self-contradictory. But this definition has small explanatory value; for the notion of self-contradictoriness, in the quite broad sense needed for this definition of analyticity, stands in exactly the same need of clarification as does the notion of analyticity itself. The two notions are the two sides of a single dubious coin.

Kant conceived of an analytic statement as one that attributes to its subject no more than is already conceptually contained in the subject. This formulation has two shortcomings: it limits itself to statements of subject-predicate form, and it appeals to a notion of containment which is left at a metaphorical level. But Kant's intent, evident more from the use he makes of the notion of analyticity than from his definition of it, can be restated thus: a statement is analytic when it is true by virtue of meanings and independently of fact. Pursuing this line, let us examine the concept of *meaning* which is presupposed.

Meaning, let us remember, is not to be identified with naming.[1] Frege's example of 'Evening Star' and 'Morning Star', and Russell's of 'Scott' and 'the author of *Waverley*', illustrate that terms can name the same thing but differ in meaning. The distinction between meaning and naming is no less important at the level of abstract terms. The terms '9' and 'the number of the planets' name one and the same abstract entity but presumably must be regarded as unlike in meaning; for astronomical observation was

---

1. See Quine (1948/1953), p. 9.

needed, and not mere reflection on meanings, to determine the sameness of the entity in question.

The above examples consist of singular terms, concrete and abstract. With general terms, or predicates, the situation is somewhat different but parallel. Whereas a singular term purports to name an entity, abstract or concrete, a general term does not; but a general term is *true of* an entity, or of each of many, or of none.[2] The class of all entities of which a general term is true is called the *extension* of the term. Now paralleling the contrast between the meaning of a singular term and the entity named, we must distinguish equally between the meaning of a general term and its extension. The general terms 'creature with a heart' and 'creature with kidneys', for example, are perhaps alike in extension but unlike in meaning.

Confusion of meaning with extension, in the case of general terms, is less common than confusion of meaning with naming in the case of singular terms. It is indeed a commonplace in philosophy to oppose intension (or meaning) to extension, or, in a variant vocabulary, connotation to denotation.

The Aristotelian notion of essence was the forerunner, no doubt, of the modern notion of intension or meaning. For Aristotle it was essential in men to be rational, accidental to be two-legged. But there is an important difference between this attitude and the doctrine of meaning. From the latter point of view it may indeed be conceded (if only for the sake of argument) that rationality is involved in the meaning of the word 'man' while two-leggedness is not; but two-leggedness may at the same time be viewed as involved in the meaning of 'biped' while rationality is not. Thus from the point of view of the doctrine of meaning it makes no sense to say of the actual individual, who is at once a man and a biped, that his rationality is essential and his two-leggedness accidental or vice versa. Things had essences, for Aristotle, but only linguistic forms have meanings. Meaning is what essence becomes when it is divorced from the object of reference and wedded to the word.

For the theory of meaning a conspicuous question is the nature of its objects: what sort of things are meanings? A felt need for meant entities may derive from an earlier failure to appreciate that meaning and reference are distinct. Once the theory of meaning is sharply separated from the theory of reference, it is a short step to recognizing as the primary business of the theory of meaning simply the synonymy of linguistic forms and the analyticity of statements; meanings themselves, as obscure intermediary entities, may well be abandoned.[3]

The problem of analyticity then confronts us anew. Statements which are analytic by general philosophical acclaim are not, indeed, far to seek. They fall into two classes. Those of the first class, which may be called *logically true*, are typified by:

(1)   No unmarried man is married.

The relevant feature of this example is that it not merely is true as it stands, but remains true under any and all reinterpretations of 'man' and 'married'. If we suppose a prior inventory of *logical* particles, comprising 'no', 'un-', 'not', 'if', 'then', 'and', etc., then in general a logical truth is a statement which is true and remains true under all reinterpretations of its components other than the logical particles.

2. See Quine (1948/1953), p. 10, and Quine (1953a), pp. 107–115.
3. See Quine (1948/1953), pp. 11f, and Quine (1953b), pp. 48f.

But there is also a second class of analytic statements, typified by:

(2) No bachelor is married.

The characteristic of such a statement is that it can be turned into a logical truth by putting synonyms for synonyms; thus (2) can be turned into (1) by putting 'unmarried man' for its synonym 'bachelor'. We still lack a proper characterization of this second class of analytic statements, and therewith of analyticity generally, inasmuch as we have had in the above description to lean on a notion of "synonymy" which is no less in need of clarification than analyticity itself.

In recent years Carnap has tended to explain analyticity by appeal to what he calls state-descriptions.[4] A state-description is any exhaustive assignment of truth values to the atomic, or noncompound, statements of the language. All other statements of the language are, Carnap assumes, built up of their component clauses by means of the familiar logical devices, in such a way that the truth value of any complex statement is fixed for each state-description by specifiable logical laws. A statement is then explained as analytic when it comes out true under every state description. This account is an adaptation of Leibniz's "true in all possible worlds." But note that this version of analyticity serves its purpose only if the atomic statements of the language are, unlike 'John is a bachelor' and 'John is married', mutually independent. Otherwise there would be a state-description which assigned truth to 'John is a bachelor' and to 'John is married', and consequently 'No bachelors are married' would turn out synthetic rather than analytic under the proposed criterion. Thus the criterion of analyticity in terms of state-descriptions serves only for languages devoid of extralogical synonym-pairs, such as 'bachelor' and 'unmarried man'—synonym-pairs of the type which give rise to the "second class" of analytic statements. The criterion in terms of state-descriptions is a reconstruction at best of logical truth, not of analyticity.

I do not mean to suggest that Carnap is under any illusions on this point. His simplified model language with its state-descriptions is aimed primarily not at the general problem of analyticity but at another purpose, the clarification of probability and induction. Our problem, however, is analyticity; and here the major difficulty lies not in the first class of analytic statements, the logical truths, but rather in the second class, which depends on the notion of synonymy.

2. Definition

There are those who find it soothing to say that the analytic statements of the second class reduce to those of the first class, the logical truths, by *definition*; 'bachelor', for example, is *defined* as 'unmarried man'. But how do we find that 'bachelor' is defined as 'unmarried man'? Who defined it thus, and when? Are we to appeal to the nearest dictionary, and accept the lexicographer's formulation as law? Clearly this would be to put the cart before the horse. The lexicographer is an empirical scientist, whose business is the recording of antecedent facts; and if he glosses 'bachelor' as 'unmarried man' it is because of his belief that there is a relation of synonymy between those forms, implicit in general or preferred usage prior to his own work. The notion of synonymy presupposed here has still to be clarified, presumably in terms relating to

4. Carnap (1947), pp. 9ff; (1950a), pp. 70ff.

linguistic behavior. Certainly the "definition" which is the lexicographer's report of an observed synonymy cannot be taken as the ground of the synonymy.

Definition is not, indeed, an activity exclusively of philologists. Philosophers and scientists frequently have occasion to "define" a recondite term by paraphrasing it into terms of a more familiar vocabulary. But ordinarily such a definition, like the philologist's, is pure lexicography, affirming a relation of synonymy antecedent to the exposition in hand.

Just what it means to affirm synonymy, just what the interconnections may be which are necessary and sufficient in order that two linguistic forms be properly describable as synonymous, is far from clear; but, whatever these interconnections may be, ordinarily they are grounded in usage. Definitions reporting selected instances of synonymy come then as reports upon usage.

There is also, however, a variant type of definitional activity which does not limit itself to the reporting of preëxisting synonymies. I have in mind what Carnap calls *explication*—an activity to which philosophers are given, and scientists also in their more philosophical moments. In explication the purpose is not merely to paraphrase the definiendum into an outright synonym, but actually to improve upon the definiendum by refining or supplementing its meaning. But even explication, though not merely reporting a preëxisting synonymy between definiendum and definiens, does rest nevertheless on *other* preëxisting synonymies. The matter may be viewed as follows. Any word worth explicating has some contexts which, as wholes, are clear and precise enough to be useful; and the purpose of explication is to preserve the usage of these favored contexts while sharpening the usage of other contexts. In order that a given definition be suitable for purposes of explication, therefore, what is required is not that the definiendum in its antecedent usage be synonymous with the definiens, but just that each of these favored contexts of the definiendum, taken as a whole in its antecedent usage, be synonymous with the corresponding context of the definiens.

Two alternative definientia may be equally appropriate for the purposes of a given task of explication and yet not be synonymous with each other; for they may serve interchangeably within the favored contexts but diverge elsewhere. By cleaving to one of these definientia rather than the other, a definition of explicative kind generates, by fiat, a relation of synonymy between definiendum and definiens which did not hold before. But such a definition still owes its explicative function, as seen, to preëxisting synonymies.

There does, however, remain still an extreme sort of definition which does not hark back to prior synonymies at all: namely, the explicitly conventional introduction of novel notations for purposes of sheer abbreviation. Here the definiendum becomes synonymous with the definiens simply because it has been created expressly for the purpose of being synonymous with the definiens. Here we have a really transparent case of synonymy created by definition; would that all species of synonymy were as intelligible. For the rest, definition rests on synonymy rather than explaining it.

The word 'definition' has come to have a dangerously reassuring sound, owing no doubt to its frequent occurrence in logical and mathematical writings. We shall do well to digress now into a brief appraisal of the role of definition in formal work.

In logical and mathematical systems either of two mutually antagonistic types of economy may be striven for, and each has its peculiar practical utility. On the one hand we may seek economy of practical expression—ease and brevity in the statement of multifarious relations. This sort of economy calls usually for distinctive concise notations for a wealth of concepts. Second, however, and oppositely, we may seek economy in grammar and vocabulary; we may try to find a minimum of basic concepts such that, once a distinctive notation has been appropriated to each of them, it becomes possible to express any desired further concept by mere combination and iteration of our basic notations. This second sort of economy is impractical in one way, since a poverty in basic idioms tends to a necessary lengthening of discourse. But it is practical in another way: it greatly simplifies theoretical discourse *about* the language, through minimizing the terms and the forms of construction wherein the language consists.

Both sorts of economy, though prima facie incompatible, are valuable in their separate ways. The custom has consequently arisen of combining both sorts of economy by forging in effect two languages, the one a part of the other. The inclusive language, though redundant in grammar and vocabulary, is economical in message lengths, while the part, called primitive notation, is economical in grammar and vocabulary. Whole and part are correlated by rules of translation whereby each idiom not in primitive notation is equated to some complex built up of primitive notation. These rules of translation are the so-called *definitions* which appear in formalized systems. They are best viewed not as adjuncts to one language but as correlations between two languages, the one a part of the other.

But these correlations are not arbitrary. They are supposed to show how the primitive notations can accomplish all purposes, save brevity and convenience, of the redundant language. Hence the definiendum and its definiens may be expected, in each case, to be related in one or another of the three ways lately noted. The definiens may be a faithful paraphrase of the definiendum into the narrower notation, preserving a direct synonymy[5] as of antecedent usage; or the definiens may, in the spirit of explication, improve upon the antecedent usage of the definiendum; or finally, the definiendum may be a newly created notation, newly endowed with meaning here and now.

In formal and informal work alike, thus, we find that definition—except in the extreme case of the explicitly conventional introduction of new notations—hinges on prior relations of synonymy. Recognizing then that the notion of definition does not hold the key to synonymy and analyticity, let us look further into synonymy and say no more of definition.

3. Interchangeability

A natural suggestion, deserving close examination, is that the synonymy of two linguistic forms consists simply in their interchangeability in all contexts without change of truth value—interchangeability, in Leibniz's phrase, *salva veritate*.[6] Note that synonyms so conceived need not even be free from vagueness, as long as the vaguenesses match.

But it is not quite true that the synonyms 'bachelor' and 'unmarried man' are everywhere interchangeable *salva veritate*. Truths which become false under substitu-

5. According to an important variant sense of 'definition', the relation preserved may be the weaker relation of mere agreement in reference; see Quine (1953c), p. 132. But definition in this sense is better ignored in the present connection, being irrelevant to the question of synonymy.
6. Cf. Lewis (1918), p. 373.

tion of 'unmarried man' for 'bachelor' are easily constructed with the help of 'bachelor of arts' or 'bachelor's buttons'; also with the help of quotation, thus:

'Bachelor' has less than ten letters.

Such counterinstances can, however, perhaps be set aside by treating the phrases 'bachelor of arts' and 'bachelor's buttons' and the quotation "bachelor" each as a single indivisible word and then stipulating that the interchangeability *salva veritate* which is to be the touchstone of synonymy is not supposed to apply to fragmentary occurrences inside of a word. This account of synonymy, supposing it acceptable on other counts, has indeed the drawback of appealing to a prior conception of "word" which can be counted on to present difficulties of formulation in its turn. Nevertheless some progress might be claimed in having reduced the problem of synonymy to a problem of wordhood. Let us pursue this line a bit, taking "word" for granted.

The question remains whether interchangeability *salva veritate* (apart from occurrences within words) is a strong enough condition for synonymy, or whether, on the contrary, some heteronymous expressions might be thus interchangeable. Now let us be clear that we are not concerned here with synonymy in the sense of complete identity in psychological associations or poetic quality; indeed no two expressions are synonymous in such a sense. We are concerned only with what may be called *cognitive* synonymy. Just what this is cannot be said without successfully finishing the present study; but we know something about it from the need which arose for it in connection with analyticity in §1. The sort of synonymy needed there was merely such that any analytic statement could be turned into a logical truth by putting synonyms for synonyms. Turning the tables and assuming analyticity, indeed, we could explain cognitive synonymy of terms as follows (keeping to the familiar example): to say that 'bachelor' and 'unmarried man' are cognitively synonymous is to say no more nor less than that the statement:

(3)   All and only bachelors are unmarried men

is analytic.[7]

What we need is an account of cognitive synonymy not presupposing analyticity—if we are to explain analyticity conversely with help of cognitive synonymy as undertaken in §1. And indeed such an independent account of cognitive synonymy is at present up for consideration, namely, interchangeability *salva veritate* everywhere except within words. The question before us, to resume the thread at last, is whether such interchangeability is a sufficient condition for cognitive synonymy. We can quickly assure ourselves that it is, by examples of the following sort. The statement:

(4)   Necessarily all and only bachelors are bachelors

is evidently true, even supposing 'necessarily' so narrowly construed as to be truly applicable only to analytic statements. Then, if 'bachelor' and 'unmarried man' are interchangeable *salva veritate*, the result:

---

7. This is cognitive synonymy in a primary, broad sense. Carnap (1947), pp. 56ff and Lewis (1946), pp. 83ff have suggested how, once this notion is at hand, a narrower sense of cognitive synonymy which is preferable for some purposes can in turn be derived. But this special ramification of concept-building lies aside from the present purposes and must not be confused with the broad sort of cognitive synonymy here concerned.

(5)   Necessarily all and only bachelors are unmarried men

of putting 'unmarried man' for an occurrence of 'bachelor' in (4) must, like (4), be true. But to say that (5) is true is to say that (3) is analytic, and hence that 'bachelor' and 'unmarried man' are cognitively synonymous.

Let us see what there is about the above argument that gives it its air of hocus-pocus. The condition of interchangeability *salva veritate* varies in its force with variations in the richness of the language at hand. The above argument supposes we are working with a language rich enough to contain the adverb 'necessarily', this adverb being so construed as to yield truth when and only when applied to an analytic statement. But can we condone a language which contains such an adverb? Does the adverb really make sense? To suppose that it does is to suppose that we have already made satisfactory sense of 'analytic'. Then what are we so hard at work on right now?

Our argument is not flatly circular, but something like it. It has the form, figuratively speaking, of a closed curve in space.

Interchangeability *salva veritate* is meaningless until relativized to a language whose extent is specified in relevant respects. Suppose now we consider a language containing just the following materials. There is an indefinitely large stock of one-place predicates (for example, 'F' where 'Fx' means that x is a man) and many-place predicates (for example, 'G' where 'Gxy' means that x loves y), mostly having to do with extralogical subject matter. The rest of the language is logical. The atomic sentences consist each of a predicate followed by one or more variables 'x', 'y', etc.; and the complex sentences are built up of the atomic ones by truth functions ('not', 'and', 'or', etc.) and quantification.[8] In effect such a language enjoys the benefits also of descriptions and indeed singular terms generally, these being contextually definable in known ways.[9] Even abstract singular terms naming classes, classes of classes, etc., are contextually definable in case the assumed stock of predicates includes the two-place predicate of class membership.[10] Such a language can be adequate to classical mathematics and indeed to scientific discourse generally, except in so far as the latter involves debatable devices such as contrary-to-fact conditionals or modal adverbs like 'necessarily'.[11] Now a language of this type is extensional, in this sense: any two predicates which agree extensionally (that is, are true of the same objects) are interchangeable *salva veritate*.[12]

In an extensional language, therefore, interchangeability *salva veritate* is no assurance of cognitive synonymy of the desired type. That 'bachelor' and 'unmarried man' are interchangeable *salva veritate* in an extensional language assures us of no more than that (3) is true. There is no assurance here that the extensional agreement of 'bachelor' and 'unmarried man' rests on meaning rather than merely on accidental matters of fact, as does the extensional agreement of 'creature with a heart' and 'creature with kidneys'.

For most purposes extensional agreement is the nearest approximation to synonymy we need care about. But the fact remains that extensional agreement falls far

8. Quine (1937/1953), pp. 81ff contain a description of just such a language, except that there happens there to be just one predicate, the two-place predicate 'ε'.
9. See Quine (1948/1953), pp. 5–8; also Quine (1937/1953), pp. 85f and Quine (1953d) pp. 166f.
10. See Quine (1937/1953), p. 87.
11. On such devices see also Quine (1953c).
12. This is the substance of Quine (1940), *121.

short of cognitive synonymy of the type required for explaining analyticity in the manner of §1. The type of cognitive synonymy required there is such as to equate the synonymy of 'bachelor' and 'unmarried man' with the analyticity of (3), not merely with the truth of (3).

So we must recognize that interchangeability *salva veritate*, if construed in relation to an extensional language, is not a sufficient condition of cognitive synonymy in the sense needed for deriving analyticity in the manner of §1. If a language contains an intensional adverb 'necessarily' in the sense lately noted, or other particles to the same effect, then interchangeability *salva veritate* in such a language does afford a sufficient condition of cognitive synonymy; but such a language is intelligible only in so far as the notion of analyticity is already understood in advance.

The effort to explain cognitive synonymy first, for the sake of deriving analyticity from it afterward as in §1, is perhaps the wrong approach. Instead we might try explaining analyticity somehow without appeal to cognitive synonymy. Afterward we could doubtless derive cognitive synonymy from analyticity satisfactorily enough if desired. We have seen that cognitive synonymy of 'bachelor' and 'unmarried man' can be explained as analyticity of (3). The same explanation works for any pair of one-place predicates, of course, and it can be extended in obvious fashion to many-place predicates. Other syntactical categories can also be accommodated in fairly parallel fashion. Singular terms may be said to be cognitively synonymous when the statement of identity formed by putting '=' between them is analytic. Statements may be said simply to be cognitively synonymous when their biconditional (the result of joining them by 'if and only if') is analytic.[13] If we care to lump all categories into a single formulation, at the expense of assuming again the notion of "word" which was appealed to early in this section, we can describe any two linguistic forms as cognitively synonymous when the two forms are interchangeable (apart from occurrences within "words") *salva* (no longer *veritate* but) *analyticitate*. Certain technical questions arise, indeed, over cases of ambiguity or homonymy; let us not pause for them, however, for we are already digressing. Let us rather turn our backs on the problem of synonymy and address ourselves anew to that of analyticity.

4. Semantical Rules

Analyticity at first seemed most naturally definable by appeal to a realm of meanings. On refinement, the appeal to meanings gave way to an appeal to synonymy or definition. But definition turned out to be a will-o'-the-wisp, and synonymy turned out to be best understood only by dint of a prior appeal to analyticity itself. So we are back at the problem of analyticity.

I do not know whether the statement 'Everything green is extended' is analytic. Now does my indecision over this example really betray an incomplete understanding, an incomplete grasp of the "meanings," of 'green' and 'extended'? I think not. The trouble is not with 'green' or 'extended', but with 'analytic'.

It is often hinted that the difficulty in separating analytic statements from synthetic ones in ordinary language is due to the vagueness of ordinary language and that the distinction is clear when we have a precise artificial language with explicit "semantical rules." This, however, as I shall now attempt to show, is a confusion.

---

13. The 'if and only if' itself is intended in the truth functional sense. See Carnap (1947), p. 14.

The notion of analyticity about which we are worrying is a purported relation between statements and languages: a statement S is said to be *analytic for* a language L, and the problem is to make sense of this relation generally, that is, for variable 'S' and 'L'. The gravity of this problem is not perceptibly less for artificial languages than for natural ones. The problem of making sense of the idiom 'S is analytic for L', with variable 'S' and 'L', retains its stubbornness even if we limit the range of the variable 'L' to artificial languages. Let me now try to make this point evident.

For artificial languages and semantical rules we look naturally to the writings of Carnap. His semantical rules take various forms, and to make my point I shall have to distinguish certain of the forms. Let us suppose, to begin with, an artificial language L_0 whose semantical rules have the form explicitly of a specification, by recursion or otherwise, of all the analytic statements of L_0. The rules tell us that such and such statements, and only those, are the analytic statements of L_0. Now here the difficulty is simply that the rules contain the word 'analytic', which we do not understand! We understand what expressions the rules attribute analyticity to, but we do not understand what the rules attribute to those expressions. In short, before we can understand a rule which begins 'A statement S is analytic for language L_0 if and only if ...', we must understand the general relative term 'analytic for'; we must understand 'S is analytic for L' where 'S' and 'L' are variables.

Alternatively we may, indeed, view the so-called rule as a conventional definition of a new simple symbol 'analytic-for-L_0', which might better be written untendentiously as 'K' so as not to seem to throw light on the interesting word 'analytic'. Obviously any number of classes K, M, N, etc. of statements of L_0 can be specified for various purposes or for no purpose; what does it mean to say that K, as against M, N, etc., is the class of the "analytic" statements of L_0?

By saying what statements are analytic for L_0 we explain 'analytic-for-L_0' but not 'analytic', not 'analytic for'. We do not begin to explain the idiom 'S is analytic for L' with variable 'S' and 'L', even if we are content to limit the range of 'L' to the realm of artificial languages.

Actually we do know enough about the intended significance of 'analytic' to know that analytic statements are supposed to be true. Let us then turn to a second form of semantical rule, which says not that such and such statements are analytic but simply that such and such statements are included among the truths. Such a rule is not subject to the criticism of containing the un-understood word 'analytic'; and we may grant for the sake of argument that there is no difficulty over the broader term 'true'. A semantical rule of this second type, a rule of truth, is not supposed to specify all the truths of the language; it merely stipulates, recursively or otherwise, a certain multitude of statements which, along with others unspecified, are to count as true. Such a rule may be conceded to be quite clear. Derivatively, afterward, analyticity can be demarcated thus: a statement is analytic if it is (not merely true but) true according to the semantical rule.

Still there is really no progress. Instead of appealing to an unexplained word 'analytic', we are now appealing to an unexplained phrase 'semantical rule'. Not every true statement which says that the statements of some class are true can count as a semantical rule—otherwise *all* truths would be "analytic" in the sense of being true according to semantical rules. Semantical rules are distinguishable, apparently, only by the fact of appearing on a page under the heading 'Semantical Rules'; and this heading is itself then meaningless.

We can say indeed that a statement is *analytic-for-L_0* if and only if it is true according to such and such specifically appended "semantical rules," but then we find ourselves back at essentially the same case which was originally discussed: '*S* is analytic-for-L_0 if and only if....' Once we seek to explain '*S* is analytic for *L*' generally for variable '*L*' (even allowing limitation of '*L*' to artificial languages), the explanation 'true according to the semantical rules of *L*' is unavailing; for the relative term 'semantical rule of' is as much in need of clarification, at least, as 'analytic for'.

It may be instructive to compare the notion of semantical rule with that of postulate. Relative to a given set of postulates, it is easy to say what a postulate is: it is a member of the set. Relative to a given set of semantical rules, it is equally easy to say what a semantical rule is. But given simply a notation, mathematical or otherwise, and indeed as thoroughly understood a notation as you please in point of the translations or truth conditions of its statements, who can say which of its true statements rank as postulates? Obviously the question is meaningless—as meaningless as asking which points in Ohio are starting points. Any finite (or effectively specifiable infinite) selection of statements (preferably true ones, perhaps) is as much a set of postulates as any other. The word 'postulate' is significant only relative to an act of inquiry; we apply the word to a set of statements just in so far as we happen, for the year or the moment, to be thinking of those statements in relation to the statements which can be reached from them by some set of transformations to which we have seen fit to direct our attention. Now the notion of semantical rule is as sensible and meaningful as that of postulate, if conceived in a similarly relative spirit—relative, this time, to one or another particular enterprise of schooling unconversant persons in sufficient conditions for truth of statements of some natural or artificial language *L*. But from this point of view no one signalization of a subclass of the truths of *L* is intrinsically more a semantical rule than another; and, if 'analytic' means 'true by semantical rules', no one truth of *L* is analytic to the exclusion of another.[14]

It might conceivably be protested that an artificial language *L* (unlike a natural one) is a language in the ordinary sense *plus* a set of explicit semantical rules—the whole constituting, let us say, an ordered pair; and that the semantical rules of *L* then are specifiable simply as the second component of the pair *L*. But, by the same token and more simply, we might construe an artificial language *L* outright as an ordered pair whose second component is the class of its analytic statements; and then the analytic statements of *L* become specifiable simply as the statements in the second component of *L*. Or better still, we might just stop tugging at our bootstraps altogether.

Not all the explanations of analyticity known to Carnap and his readers have been covered explicitly in the above considerations, but the extension to other forms is not hard to see. Just one additional factor should be mentioned which sometimes enters: sometimes the semantical rules are in effect rules of translation into ordinary language, in which case the analytic statements of the artificial language are in effect recognized as such from the analyticity of their specified translations in ordinary language. Here certainly there can be no thought of an illumination of the problem of analyticity from the side of the artificial language.

From the point of view of the problem of analyticity the notion of an artificial language with semantical rules is a *feu follet par excellence*. Semantical rules determining

---

14. The foregoing paragraph was not part of the present essay as originally published. It was prompted by Martin (see References).

the analytic statements of an artificial language are of interest only in so far as we already understand the notion of analyticity; they are of no help in gaining this understanding.

Appeal to hypothetical languages of an artificially simple kind could conceivably be useful in clarifying analyticity, if the mental or behavioral or cultural factors relevant to analyticity—whatever they may be—were somehow sketched into the simplified model. But a model which takes analyticity merely as an irreducible character is unlikely to throw light on the problem of explicating analyticity.

It is obvious that truth in general depends on both language and extralinguistic fact. The statement 'Brutus killed Caesar' would be false if the world had been different in certain ways, but it would also be false if the word 'killed' happened rather to have the sense of 'begat'. Thus one is tempted to suppose in general that the truth of a statement is somehow analyzable into a linguistic component and a factual component. Given this supposition, it next seems reasonable that in some statements the factual component should be null; and these are the analytic statements. But, for all its a priori reasonableness, a boundary between analytic and synthetic statements simply has not been drawn. That there is such a distinction to be drawn at all is an unempirical dogma of empiricists, a metaphysical article of faith.

5. The Verification Theory and Reductionism

In the course of these somber reflections we have taken a dim view first of the notion of meaning, then of the notion of cognitive synonymy, and finally of the notion of analyticity. But what, it may be asked, of the verification theory of meaning? This phrase has established itself so firmly as a catchword of empiricism that we should be very unscientific indeed not to look beneath it for a possible key to the problem of meaning and the associated problems.

The verification theory of meaning, which has been conspicuous in the literature from Peirce onward, is that the meaning of a statement is the method of empirically confirming or infirming it. An analytic statement is that limiting case which is confirmed no matter what.

As urged in §1, we can as well pass over the question of meanings as entities and move straight to sameness of meaning, or synonymy. Then what the verification theory says is that statements are synonymous if and only if they are alike in point of method of empirical confirmation or infirmation.

This is an account of cognitive synonymy not of linguistic forms generally, but of statements.[15] However, from the concept of synonymy of statements we could derive the concept of synonymy for other linguistic forms, by considerations somewhat similar to those at the end of §3. Assuming the notion of "word," indeed, we could explain any two forms as synonymous when the putting of the one form for an occurrence of the other in any statement (apart from occurrences within "words") yields a synonymous statement. Finally, given the concept of synonymy thus for linguistic forms generally, we could define analyticity in terms of synonymy and logical

15. The doctrine can indeed be formulated with terms rather than statements as the units. Thus Lewis describes the meaning of a term as "a criterion in mind, by reference to which one is able to apply or refuse to apply the expression in question in the case of presented, or imagined, things or situations" (1946), p. 133.—For an instructive account of the vicissitudes of the verification theory of meaning, centered however on the question of meaningfulness rather than synonymy and analyticity, see Hempel (1950).

truth as in §1. For that matter, we could define analyticity more simply in terms of just synonymy of statements together with logical truth; it is not necessary to appeal to synonymy of linguistic forms other than statements. For a statement may be described as analytic simply when it is synonymous with a logically true statement.

So, if the verification theory can be accepted as an adequate account of statement synonymy, the notion of analyticity is saved after all. However, let us reflect. Statement synonymy is said to be likeness of method of empirical confirmation or infirmation. Just what are these methods which are to be compared for likeness? What, in other words, is the nature of the relation between a statement and the experiences which contribute to or detract from its confirmation?

The most naïve view of the relation is that it is one of direct report. This is *radical reductionism*. Every meaningful statement is held to be translatable into a statement (true or false) about immediate experience. Radical reductionism, in one form or another, well antedates the verification theory of meaning explicitly so called. Thus Locke and Hume held that every idea must either originate directly in sense experience or else be compounded of ideas thus originating; and taking a hint from Tooke we might rephrase this doctrine in semantical jargon by saying that a term, to be significant at all, must be either a name of a sense datum or a compound of such names or an abbreviation of such a compound. So stated, the doctrine remains ambiguous as between sense data as sensory events and sense data as sensory qualities; and it remains vague as to the admissible ways of compounding. Moreover, the doctrine is unnecessarily and intolerably restrictive in the term-by-term critique which it imposes. More reasonably, and without yet exceeding the limits of what I have called radical reductionism, we may take full statements as our significant units—thus demanding that our statements as wholes be translatable into sense-datum language, but not that they be translatable term by term.

This emendation would unquestionably have been welcome to Locke and Hume and Tooke, but historically it had to await an important reorientation in semantics— the reorientation whereby the primary vehicle of meaning came to be seen no longer in the term but in the statement. This reorientation, seen in Bentham and Frege, underlies Russell's concept of incomplete symbols defined in use;[16] also it is implicit in the verification theory of meaning, since the objects of verification are statements.

Radical reductionism, conceived now with statements as units, set itself the task of specifying a sense-datum language and showing how to translate the rest of significant discourse, statement by statement, into it. Carnap embarked on this project in the *Aufbau*.

The language which Carnap adopted as his starting point was not a sense-datum language in the narrowest conceivable sense, for it included also the notations of logic, up through higher set theory. In effect it included the whole language of pure mathematics. The ontology implicit in it (that is, the range of values of its variables) embraced not only sensory events but classes, classes of classes, and so on. Empiricists there are who would boggle at such prodigality. Carnap's starting point is very parsimonious, however, in its extralogical or sensory part. In a series of constructions in which he exploits the resources of modern logic with much ingenuity, Carnap succeeds in defining a wide array of important additional sensory concepts which, but

16. See Quine (1948/1953), p. 6.

for his constructions, one would not have dreamed were definable on so slender a basis. He was the first empiricist who, not content with asserting the reducibility of science to terms of immediate experience, took serious steps toward carrying out the reduction.

If Carnap's starting point is satisfactory, still his constructions were, as he himself stressed, only a fragment of the full program. The construction of even the simplest statements about the physical world was left in a sketchy state. Carnap's suggestions on this subject were, despite their sketchiness, very suggestive. He explained spatio-temporal point-instants as quadruples of real numbers and envisaged assignment of sense qualities to point-instants according to certain canons. Roughly summarized, the plan was that qualities should be assigned to point-instants in such a way as to achieve the laziest world compatible with our experience. The principle of least action was to be our guide in constructing a world from experience.

Carnap did not seem to recognize, however, that his treatment of physical objects fell short of reduction not merely through sketchiness, but in principle. Statements of the form 'Quality q is at point-instant $x; y; z; t$' were, according to his canons, to be apportioned truth values in such a way as to maximize and minimize certain over-all features, and with growth of experience the truth values were to be progressively revised in the same spirit. I think this is a good schematization (deliberately over-simplified, to be sure) of what science really does; but it provides no indication, not even the sketchiest, of how a statement of the form 'Quality q is at $x; y; z; t$' could ever be translated into Carnap's initial language of sense data and logic. The connective 'is at' remains an added undefined connective; the canons counsel us in its use but not in its elimination.

Carnap seems to have appreciated this point afterward; for in his later writings he abandoned all notion of the translatability of statements about the physical world into statements about immediate experience. Reductionism in its radical form has long since ceased to figure in Carnap's philosophy.

But the dogma of reductionism has, in a subtler and more tenuous form, continued to influence the thought of empiricists. The notion lingers that to each statement, or each synthetic statement, there is associated a unique range of possible sensory events such that the occurrence of any of them would add to the likelihood of truth of the statement, and that there is associated also another unique range of possible sensory events whose occurrence would detract from that likelihood. This notion is of course implicit in the verification theory of meaning.

The dogma of reductionism survives in the supposition that each statement, taken in isolation from its fellows, can admit of confirmation or infirmation at all. My counter-suggestion, issuing essentially from Carnap's doctrine of the physical world in the *Aufbau*, is that our statements about the external world face the tribunal of sense experience not individually but only as a corporate body.[17]

The dogma of reductionism, even in its attenuated form, is intimately connected with the other dogma—that there is a cleavage between the analytic and the synthetic. We have found ourselves led, indeed, from the latter problem to the former through the verification theory of meaning. More directly, the one dogma clearly supports the other in this way: as long as it is taken to be significant in general to

---

17. This doctrine was well argued by Duhem (1906), pp. 303–328. Or see Lowinger (1941), pp. 132–140.

speak of the confirmation and infirmation of a statement, it seems significant to speak also of a limiting kind of statement which is vacuously confirmed, *ipso facto*, come what may; and such a statement is analytic.

The two dogmas are, indeed, at root identical. We lately reflected that in general the truth of statements does obviously depend both upon language and upon extra-linguistic fact; and we noted that this obvious circumstance carries in its train, not logically but all too naturally, a feeling that the truth of a statement is somehow ana-lyzable into a linguistic component and a factual component. The factual component must, if we are empiricists, boil down to a range of confirmatory experiences. In the extreme case where the linguistic component is all that matters, a true statement is analytic. But I hope we are now impressed with how stubbornly the distinction between analytic and synthetic has resisted any straightforward drawing. I am impressed also, apart from prefabricated examples of black and white balls in an urn, with how baffling the problem has always been of arriving at any explicit theory of the empirical confirmation of a synthetic statement. My present suggestion is that it is nonsense, and the root of much nonsense, to speak of a linguistic component and a factual component in the truth of any individual statement. Taken collectively, science has its double dependence upon language and experience; but this duality is not significantly traceable into the statements of science taken one by one.

The idea of defining a symbol in use was, as remarked, an advance over the impossible term-by-term empiricism of Locke and Hume. The statement, rather than the term, came with Bentham to be recognized as the unit accountable to an empiricist critique. But what I am now urging is that even in taking the statement as unit we have drawn our grid too finely. The unit of empirical significance is the whole of science.

6. Empiricism without the Dogmas

The totality of our so-called knowledge or beliefs, from the most casual matters of geography and history to the profoundest laws of atomic physics or even of pure mathematics and logic, is a man-made fabric which impinges on experience only along the edges. Or, to change the figure, total science is like a field of force whose boundary conditions are experience. A conflict with experience at the periphery occasions readjustments in the interior of the field. Truth values have to be redis-tributed over some of our statements. Reëvaluation of some statements entails reëvaluation of others, because of their logical interconnections—the logical laws being in turn simply certain further statements of the system, certain further elements of the field. Having reëvaluated one statement we must reëvaluate some others, which may be statements logically connected with the first or may be the statements of logical connections themselves. But the total field is so underdetermined by its boundary conditions, experience, that there is much latitude of choice as to what statements to reëvaluate in the light of any single contrary experience. No particular experiences are linked with any particular statements in the interior of the field, except indirectly through considerations of equilibrium affecting the field as a whole.

If this view is right, it is misleading to speak of the empirical content of an indi-vidual statement—especially if it is a statement at all remote from the experiential periphery of the field. Furthermore it becomes folly to seek a boundary between syn-thetic statements, which hold contingently on experience, and analytic statements, which hold come what may. Any statement can be held true come what may, if we make drastic enough adjustments elsewhere in the system. Even a statement very close to the periphery can be held true in the face of recalcitrant experience by pleading hallucination or by amending certain statements of the kind called logical laws. Conversely, by the same token, no statement is immune to revision. Revision even of the logical law of the excluded middle has been proposed as a means of simplifying quantum mechanics; and what difference is there in principle between such a shift and the shift whereby Kepler superseded Ptolemy, or Einstein Newton, or Darwin Aristotle?

For vividness I have been speaking in terms of varying distances from a sensory periphery. Let me try now to clarify this notion without metaphor. Certain statements, though *about* physical objects and not sense experience, seem peculiarly germane to sense experience—and in a selective way: some statements to some experiences, others to others. Such statements, especially germane to particular experiences, I picture as near the periphery. But in this relation of "germaneness" I envisage nothing more than a loose association reflecting the relative likelihood, in practice, of our choosing one statement rather than another for revision in the event of recalcitrant experience. For example, we can imagine recalcitrant experiences to which we would surely be inclined to accommodate our system by reëvaluating just the statement that there are brick houses on Elm Street, together with related statements on the same topic. We can imagine other recalcitrant experiences to which we would be inclined to accommodate our system by reëvaluating just the statement that there are no centaurs, along with kindred statements. A recalcitrant experience can, I have urged, be accommodated by any of various alternative reëvaluations in various alternative quarters of the total system; but, in the cases which we are now imagining, our natural tendency to disturb the total system as little as possible would lead us to focus our revisions upon these specific statements concerning brick houses or centaurs. These statements are felt, therefore, to have a sharper empirical reference than highly theoretical statements of physics or logic or ontology. The latter statements may be thought of as relatively centrally located within the total network, meaning merely that little preferential connection with any particular sense data obtrudes itself.

As an empiricist I continue to think of the conceptual scheme of science as a tool, ultimately, for predicting future experience in the light of past experience. Physical objects are conceptually imported into the situation as convenient intermediaries—not by definition in terms of experience, but simply as irreducible posits[18] comparable, epistemologically, to the gods of Homer. For my part I do, qua lay physicist, believe in physical objects and not in Homer's gods; and I consider it a scientific error to believe otherwise. But in point of epistemological footing the physical objects and the gods differ only in degree and not in kind. Both sorts of entities enter our conception only as cultural posits. The myth of physical objects is epistemologically superior to most in that it has proved more efficacious than other myths as a device for working a manageable structure into the flux of experience.

Positing does not stop with macroscopic physical objects. Objects at the atomic level are posited to make the laws of macroscopic objects, and ultimately the laws of experience, simpler and more manageable; and we need not expect or demand full

18. Cf. Quine (1948/1953) pp. 17f.

definition of atomic and subatomic entities in terms of macroscopic ones, any more than definition of macroscopic things in terms of sense data. Science is a continuation of common sense, and it continues the common-sense expedient of swelling ontology to simplify theory.

Physical objects, small and large, are not the only posits. Forces are another example; and indeed we are told nowadays that the boundary between energy and matter is obsolete. Moreover, the abstract entities which are the substance of mathematics— ultimately classes and classes of classes and so on up—are another posit in the same spirit. Epistemologically these are myths on the same footing with physical objects and gods, neither better nor worse except for differences in the degree to which they expedite our dealings with sense experiences.

The over-all algebra of rational and irrational numbers is underdetermined by the algebra of rational numbers, but is smoother and more convenient; and it includes the algebra of rational numbers as a jagged or gerrymandered part.[19] Total science, mathematical and natural and human, is similarly but more extremely underdetermined by experience. The edge of the system must be kept squared with experience; the rest, with all its elaborate myths or fictions, has as its objective the simplicity of laws.

Ontological questions, under this view, are on a par with questions of natural science.[20] Consider the question whether to countenance classes as entities. This, as I have argued elsewhere,[21] is the question whether to quantify with respect to variables which take classes as values. Now Carnap (1950b) has maintained that this is a question not of matters of fact but of choosing a convenient language form, a convenient conceptual scheme or framework for science. With this I agree, but only on the proviso that the same be conceded regarding scientific hypotheses generally. Carnap (1950b, p. 32n) has recognized that he is able to preserve a double standard for ontological questions and scientific hypotheses only by assuming an absolute distinction between the analytic and the synthetic; and I need not say again that this is a distinction which I reject.[22]

The issue over there being classes seems more a question of convenient conceptual scheme; the issue over there being centaurs, or brick houses on Elm Street, seems more a question of fact. But I have been urging that this difference is only one of degree, and that it turns upon our vaguely pragmatic inclination to adjust one strand of the fabric of science rather than another in accommodating some particular recalcitrant experience. Conservatism figures in such choices, and so does the quest for simplicity.

Carnap, Lewis, and others take a pragmatic stand on the question of choosing between language forms, scientific frame-works; but their pragmatism leaves off at the imagined boundary between the analytic and the synthetic. In repudiating such a boundary I espouse a more thorough pragmatism. Each man is given a scientific heritage plus a continuing barrage of sensory stimulation; and the considerations which guide him in warping his scientific heritage to fit his continuing sensory promptings are, where rational, pragmatic.

19. Cf. Quine (1948/1953) p. 18.
20. "L'ontologie fait corps avec la science elle-même et ne peut en être separée." Meyerson (1932), p. 439.
21. Quine (1948/1953), pp. 12f; Quine (1953a), pp. 102ff.
22. For an effective expression of further misgivings over this distinction, see White (1950).

References

Carnap, Rudolf (1928) *Der Logische Aufbau der Welt* (Berlin).

Carnap, Rudolf (1947) *Meaning and Necessity* (Chicago: University of Chicago Press).

Carnap, Rudolf (1950a) *Logical Foundations of Probability* (Chicago: University of Chicago Press).

Carnap, Rudolf (1950b) "Empiricism, Semantics and Ontology." *Revue Internationale de Philosophie* 4, 20–40.

Duhem, Pierre (1906) *La Théorie Physique: Son Objet et sa Structure* (Paris).

Hempel, C. G. (1950) "Problems and Changes in the Empiricist Criterion of Meaning." *Revue Internationale de Philosophie* 4, 41–63.

Lewis, C. I. (1918) *A Survey of Symbolic Logic* (Berkeley).

Lewis, C. I. (1946) *An Analysis of Knowledge and Valuation* (LaSalle, Ill: Open Court).

Lowinger, Armand (1941) *The Methodology of Pierre Duhem* (New York: Columbia University Press).

Martin, R. M. (1952) "On 'Analytic'." *Philosophical Studies*, 3, 42–7.

Meyerson, Émile (1932) *Identité et Realité* (Paris, 1908; 4th ed.).

Quine, W. V. O. (1937/1953) "New Foundations for Mathematical Logic," in Quine, *From a Logical Point of View*. Cambridge, Mass.: Harvard University Press, pp. 80–101.

Quine, W. V. O. (1948/1953) "On What There Is," in Quine, *From a Logical Point of View*. Cambridge, Mass.: Harvard University Press, pp. 1–19.

Quine, W. V. O. (1940) *Mathematical Logic* (New York: Norton, 1940; Cambridge, MA: Harvard University Press, 1947; rev. ed., 1951).

Quine, W. V. O. (1953a) "Logic and the Reification of Universals," in Quine, *From a Logical Point of View*. Cambridge, Mass.: Harvard University Press, pp. 102–129.

Quine, W. V. O. (1953b) "The Problem of Meaning in Linguistics," in Quine, *From a Logical Point of View*. Cambridge, Mass.: Harvard University Press, pp. 47–64.

Quine, W. V. O. (1953c) "Notes on the Theory of Reference," in Quine, *From a Logical Point of View*. Cambridge, Mass.: Harvard University Press, pp. 130–138.

Quine, W. V. O. (1953d) "Meaning and Existential Inference," in Quine, *From a Logical Point of View*. Cambridge, Mass.: Harvard University Press, pp. 160–167.

Quine, W. V. O. (1953e) "Reference and Modality," in Quine, *From a Logical Point of View*. Cambridge, Mass.: Harvard University Press, pp. 139–159.

White, Morton (1950) "The Analytic and the Synthetic: An Untenable Dualism," in Hook (ed.), *John Dewey: Philosopher of Science and Freedom* (New York: Dial Press), pp. 316–30.

Chapter 6

Philosophical Investigations, Sections 65–78

Ludwig Wittgenstein

---

65.   Here we come up against the great question that lies behind all these considerations.—For someone might object against me: "You take the easy way out! You talk about all sorts of language-games, but have nowhere said what the essence of a language-game, and hence of language, is: what is common to all these activities, and what makes them into language or parts of language. So you let yourself off the very part of the investigation that once gave you yourself most headache, the part about the *general form of propositions* and of language."

And this is true.—Instead of producing something common to all that we call language, I am saying that these phenomena have no one thing in common which makes us use the same word for all,—but that they are *related* to one another in many different ways. And it is because of this relationship, or these relationships, that we call them all "language." I will try to explain this.

66.   Consider for example the proceedings that we call "games." I mean board-games, card-games, ball-games, Olympic games, and so on. What is common to them all?—Don't say: "There *must* be something common, or they would not be called 'games'"—but *look and see* whether there is anything common to all.—For if you look at them you will not see something that is common to *all*, but similarities, relationships, and a whole series of them at that. To repeat: don't think, but look!—Look for example at board-games, with their multifarious relationships. Now pass to card-games; here you find many correspondences with the first group, but many common features drop out, and others appear. When we pass next to ball-games, much that is common is retained, but much is lost.—Are they all 'amusing'? Compare chess with noughts and crosses. Or is there always winning and losing, or competition between players? Think of patience. In ball-games there is winning and losing; but when a child throws his ball at the wall and catches it again, this feature has disappeared. Look at the parts played by skill and luck; and at the difference between skill in chess and skill in tennis. Think now of games like ring-a-ring-a-roses; here is the element of amusement, but how many other characteristic features have disappeared! And we can go through the many, many other groups of games in the same way; can see how similarities crop up and disappear.

And the result of this examination is: we see a complicated network of similarities overlapping and criss-crossing: sometimes overall similarities, sometimes similarities of detail.

67.   I can think of no better expression to characterize these similarities than "family resemblances"; for the various resemblances between members of a family: build, features, colour of eyes, gait, temperament, etc. etc. overlap and criss-cross in the same way.—And I shall say: 'games' form a family.

And for instance the kinds of number form a family in the same way. Why do we call something a "number"? Well, perhaps because it has a—direct—relationship with several things that have hitherto been called number; and this can be said to give it an indirect relationship to other things we call the same name. And we extend our concept of number as in spinning a thread we twist fibre on fibre. And the strength of the thread does not reside in the fact that some one fibre runs through its whole length, but in the overlapping of many fibres.

But if someone wished to say: "There is something common to all these constructions—namely the disjunction of all their common properties"—I should reply: Now you are only playing with words. One might as well say: "Something runs through the whole thread—namely the continuous overlapping of those fibres."

68.   "All right: the concept of number is defined for you as the logical sum of these individual interrelated concepts: cardinal numbers, rational numbers, real numbers, etc.; and in the same way the concept of a game as the logical sum of a corresponding set of sub-concepts."—It need not be so. For I *can* give the concept 'number' rigid limits in this way, that is, use the word "number" for a rigidly limited concept, but I can also use it so that the extension of the concept is *not* closed by a frontier. And this is how we do use the word "game." For how is the concept of a game bounded? What still counts as a game and what no longer does? Can you give the boundary? No. You can *draw* one; for none has so far been drawn. (But that never troubled you before when you used the word "game.")

"But then the use of the word is unregulated, the 'game' we play with it is unregulated."—It is not everywhere circumscribed by rules; but no more are there any rules for how high one throws the ball in tennis, or how hard; yet tennis is a game for all that and has rules too.

69.   How should we explain to someone what a game is? I imagine that we should describe *games* to him, and we might add: "This *and similar things* are called 'games'." And do we know any more about it ourselves? Is it only other people whom we cannot tell exactly what a game is?—But this is not ignorance. We do not know the boundaries because none have been drawn. To repeat, we can draw a boundary—for a special purpose. Does it take that to make the concept usable? Not at all! (Except for that special purpose.) No more than it took the definition: 1 pace = 75 cm. to make the measure of length 'one pace' usable. And if you want to say "But still, before that it wasn't an exact measure," then I reply: very well, it was an inexact one.—Though you still owe me a definition of exactness.

70.   "But if the concept 'game' is uncircumscribed like that, you don't really know what you mean by a 'game'."—When I give the description: "The ground was quite covered with plants"—do you want to say I don't know what I am talking about until I can give a definition of a plant?

My meaning would be explained by, say, a drawing and the words "The ground looked roughly like this." Perhaps I even say "it looked *exactly* like this."—Then were just *this* grass and *these* leaves there, arranged just like this? No, that is not what it means. And I should not accept any picture as exact in *this* sense.

Someone says to me: "Shew the children a game." I teach them gaming with dice, and the other says "I didn't mean that sort of game." Must the exclusion of the game with dice have come before his mind when he gave me the order?

71.   One might say that the concept 'game' is a concept with blurred edges.—"But is a blurred concept a concept at all?"—Is an indistinct photograph a picture of a person at all? Is it even always an advantage to replace an indistinct picture by a sharp one? Isn't the indistinct one often exactly what we need?

Frege compares a concept to an area and says that an area with vague boundaries cannot be called an area at all. This presumably means that we cannot do anything with it.—But is it senseless to say: "Stand roughly there"? Suppose that I were standing with someone in a city square and said that. As I say it I do not draw any kind of boundary, but perhaps point with may hand—as if I were indicating a particular *spot*. And this is just how one might explain to someone what a game is. One gives examples and intends them to be taken in a particular way.—I do not, however, mean by this that he is supposed to see in those examples that common thing which I—for some reason—was unable to express; but that he is now to *employ* those examples in a particular way. Here giving examples is not an *indirect* means of explaining—in default of a better. For any general definition can be misunderstood too. The point is that *this* is how we play the game. (I mean the language-game with the word "game.")

72.   *Seeing what is common.*   Suppose I shew someone various multicoloured pictures, and say: "The colour you see in all these is called 'yellow ochre'."—This is a definition, and the other will get to understand it by looking for and seeing what is common to the pictures. Then he can look *at*, can point *to*, the common thing.

Compare with this a case in which I shew him figures of different shapes all painted the same colour, and say: "What these have in common is called 'yellow ochre'."

And compare this case: I shew him samples of different shades of blue and say: "The colour that is common to all these is what I call 'blue'."

73.   When someone defines the names of colours for me by pointing to samples and saying "This colour is called 'blue', this 'green'....." this case can be compared in many respects to putting a table in may hands, with the words written under the colour-samples.—Though this comparison may mislead in many ways.—One is now inclined to extend the comparison: to have understood the definition means to have in one's mind an idea of the thing defined, and that is a sample or picture. So if I am shewn various different leaves and told "This is called a 'leaf'," I get an idea of the shape of a leaf, a picture of it in my mind.—But what does the picture of a leaf look like when it does not shew us any particular shape, but 'what is common to all shapes of leaf'? Which shade is the 'sample in my mind' of the colour green—the sample of what is common to all shades of green?

"But might there not be such 'general' samples? Say a schematic leaf, or a sample of *pure* green?"—Certainly there might. But for such a schema to be understood as a *schema*, and not as the shape of a particular leaf, and for a slip of pure green to be understood as a sample of all that is greenish and not as a sample of pure green—this in turn resides in the way the samples are used.

Ask yourself: what *shape* must the sample of the colour green be? Should it be rectangular? Or would it then be the sample of a green rectangle?—So should it be 'irregular' in shape? And what is to prevent us then from regarding it—that is, from using it—only as a sample of irregularity of shape?

74.   Here also belongs the idea that if you see this leaf as a sample of 'leaf shape in general' you *see* it differently from someone who regards it as, say, a sample of this

particular shape. Now this might well be so—though it is not so—for it would only be to say that, as a matter of experience, if you *see* the leaf in a particular way, you use it in such-and-such a way or according to such-and-such rules. Of course, there is such a thing as seeing in *this* way or *that*; and there are also cases where whoever sees a sample like *this* will in general use it in *this* way, and whoever sees it otherwise in another way. For example, if you see the schematic drawing of a cube as a plane figure consisting of a square and two rhombi you will, perhaps, carry out the order "Bring me something like this" differently from someone who sees the picture three-dimensionally.

75.   What does it mean to know what a game is? What does it mean, to know it and not be able to say it? Is this knowledge somehow equivalent to an unformulated definition? So that if it were formulated I should be able to recognize it as the expression of my knowledge? Isn't my knowledge, my concept of a game, completely expressed in the explanations that I could give? That is, in my describing examples of various kinds of games; shewing how all sorts of other games can be constructed on the analogy of these; saying that I should scarcely include this or this among games; and so on.

76.   If someone were to draw a sharp boundary I could not acknowledge it as the one that I too always wanted to draw, or had drawn in my mind. For I did not want to draw one at all. His concept can then be said to be not the same as mine, but akin to it. The kinship is that of two pictures, one of which consists of colour patches with vague contours, and the other of patches similarly shaped and distributed, but with clear contours. The kinship is just as undeniable as the difference.

77.   And if we carry this comparison still further it is clear that the degree to which the sharp picture *can* resemble the blurred one depends on the latter's degree of vagueness. For imagine having to sketch a sharply defined picture 'corresponding' to a blurred one. In the latter there is a blurred red rectangle: for it you put down a sharply defined one. Of course—several such sharply defined rectangles can be drawn to correspond to the indefinite one.—But if the colours in the original merge without a hint of any outline won't it become a hopeless task to draw a sharp picture corresponding to the blurred one? Won't you then have to say: "Here I might just as well draw a circle or heart as a rectangle, for all the colours merge. Anything—and nothing—is right."——And this is the position you are in if you look for definitions corresponding to our concepts in aesthetics or ethics.

In such a difficulty always ask yourself: How did we *learn* the meaning of this word ("good" for instance)? From what sort of examples? in what language-games? Then it will be easier for you to see that the word must have a family of meanings.

78.   Compare *knowing* and *saying*:

how many feet high Mont Blanc is—
how the word "game" is used—
how a clarinet sounds.

If you are surprised that one can know something and not be able to say it, you are perhaps thinking of a case like the first. Certainly not of one like the third.

The Probabilistic Turn: Stereotypes, Prototypes, Exemplars

Chapter 7

Is Semantics Possible?

Hilary Putnam

In the last decade enormous progress seems to have been made in the syntactic theory of natural languages, largely as a result of the work of linguists influenced by Noam Chomsky and Zellig Harris. Comparable progress seems *not* to have been made in the semantic theory of natural languages, and perhaps it is time to ask why this should be the case. Why is the theory of meaning so *hard*?

The Meaning of Common Nouns

To get some idea of the difficulties, let us look at some of the problems that come up in connection with general names. General names are of many kinds. Some, like *bachelor*, admit of an explicit definition straight off ('man who has never been married'); but the overwhelming majority do not. Some are derived by transformations from verbal forms, e.g. *hunter = one who hunts*. An important class, philosophically as well as linguistically, is the class of general names associated with *natural kinds*—that is, with classes of things that we regard as of explanatory importance; classes whose normal distinguishing characteristics are 'held together' or even explained by deep-lying mechanisms. *Gold, lemon, tiger, acid*, are examples of such nouns. I want to begin this paper by suggesting that (1) *traditional* theories of meaning radically falsify the properties of such words; (2) logicians like Carnap do little more than formalize these traditional theories, inadequacies and all; (3) such semantic theories as that produced by Jerrold Katz and his co-workers likewise share all the defects of the traditional theory. In Austin's happy phrase, what we have been given by philosophers, logicians, and 'semantic theorists' alike, is a 'myth-eaten description'.

In the traditional view, the meaning of, say 'lemon', is given by specifying a conjunction of *properties*. For each of these properties, the statement 'lemons have the property P' is an analytic truth; and if $P_1, P_2, \ldots, P_n$ are all the properties in the conjunction, then 'anything with all of the properties $P_1, \ldots, P_n$ is a lemon' is likewise an analytic truth.

In one sense, this is trivially correct. If we are allowed to invent unanalyzable properties *ad hoc*, then we can find a single property—not even a conjunction—the

This chapter originally appeared in H. Kiefer and M. Munitz (eds.) *Languages, Belief and Metaphysics*, Volume 1 of *Contemporary Philosophic Thought: The International Philosophy Year Conferences at Brockport* by permission of the State University of New York Press. Copyright © 1970 by State University of New York.

While responsibility for the views expressed here is, of course, solely mine, they doubtless reflect the influence of two men who have profoundly affected my attitude towards the problems of language: Paul Ziff and Richard Boyd. I owe them both a debt of gratitude for their insight, their infectious enthusiasm, and for many happy hours of philosophical conversation.

possession of which is a necessary and sufficient condition for being a lemon, or being gold, or whatever. Namely, we just postulate *the property of being a lemon*, or *the property of being gold*, or whatever may be needed. If we require that the properties $P_1, P_2, \ldots, P_n$ *not* be of this *ad hoc* character, however, then the situation is very different. Indeed, with any natural understanding of the term 'property', it is just *false* that to say that something belongs to a natural kind is just to ascribe to it a conjunction of properties.

To see why it is false, let us look at the term 'lemon'. The supposed 'defining characteristics' of lemons are: yellow color, tart taste, a certain kind of peel, etc. Why is the term 'lemon' *not* definable by simply conjoining these 'defining characteristics'?

The most obvious difficulty is that a natural kind may have *abnormal members*. A green lemon is still a lemon—even if, owing to some abnormality, it *never* turns yellow. A three-legged tiger is still a tiger. Gold in the gaseous state is still gold. It is only normal lemons that are yellow, tart, etc.; only normal tigers that are four-legged; only gold under normal conditions that is hard, white or yellow, etc.

To meet this difficulty, let us try the following definition: X is a *lemon = df*; X belongs to a natural kind whose normal members have yellow peel, tart taste, etc.

There is, of course, a problem with the 'etc.' There is also a problem with 'tart taste'—shouldn't it be *lemon* taste? But let us waive these difficulties, at least for the time being. Let us instead focus on the two notions that have come up with this attempted definition: the notions *natural kind* and *normal member*.

A natural kind *term* (so shift attention, for the moment, from natural kinds to their preferred designations) is a term that plays a special kind of role. If I describe something as a *lemon*, or as an *acid*, I indicate that it is likely to have certain characteristics (yellow peel, or sour taste in dilute water solution, as the case may be); but I also indicate that the presence of those characteristics, if they are present, is likely to be accounted for by some 'essential nature' which the thing shares with other members of the natural kind. What the essential nature is is not a matter of language analysis but of scientific theory construction; today we would say it was chromosome structure, in the case of lemons, and being a proton-donor, in the case of acids. Thus it is tempting to say that a natural kind term is simply a term that plays a certain kind of role in scientific or pre-scientific theory: the role, roughly, of pointing to common 'essential features' or 'mechanisms' beyond and below the obvious 'distinguishing characteristics'. But this is vague, and likely to remain so. Meta-science is today in its infancy: and terms like 'natural kind', and 'normal member', are in the same boat as the more familiar meta-scientific terms 'theory' and 'explanation', as far as resisting a speedy and definitive analysis is concerned.

Even if we *could* define 'natural kind'—say, 'a natural kind is a class which is the extension of a term P which plays such-and-such a methodological role in some well-confirmed theory'—the definition would obviously embody a theory of the world, at least in part. It is not *analytic* that natural kinds are classes which play certain kinds of roles in theories; what *really* distinguishes the classes we count as natural kinds is itself a matter of (high level and very abstract) scientific investigation and not just meaning analysis.

That the proposed definition of 'lemon' uses terms which themselves resist definition is not a fatal objection however. Let us pause to note, therefore, that if it is correct (and we shall soon show that even it is radically oversimplified), then the traditional idea of the force of general terms is badly mistaken. To say that something is a lemon is, on the above definition, to say that it belongs to a natural kind whose normal members have certain properties; but not to say that it necessarily has those properties itself. There are no *analytic* truths of the form *every lemon has* P. What has happened is this: the traditional theory has taken an account which is correct for the 'one-criterion' concepts (i.e. for such concepts as 'bachelor' and 'vixen'), and made it a general account of the meaning of general names. A theory which correctly describes the behavior of perhaps three hundred words has been asserted to correctly describe the behavior of the tens of thousands of general names.

It is also important to note the following: if the above definition is correct, then knowledge of the properties that a thing has (in any natural and non 'ad hoc' sense of property) is not enough to determine, in any mechanical or algorithmic way, whether or not it is a lemon (or an acid, or whatever). For even if I have a description in, say, the language of particle physics, of what are in fact the chromosomal properties of a fruit, I may not be able to tell that it is a lemon because I have not developed the theory according to which (1) those physical-chemical characteristics are the chromosomal structure-features (I may not even have the notion 'chromosome', and (2) I may not have discovered that chromosomal structure is the *essential* property of lemons. Meaning does not determine extension, in the sense that given the meaning and a list of all the 'properties' of a thing (in any particular sense of 'property') one can simply *read off* whether the thing is a lemon (or acid, or whatever). Even given the meaning, whether something is a lemon or not, is, or at least sometimes is, or at least may sometimes be, a matter of what is the best conceptual scheme, the best theory, the best scheme of 'natural kinds'. (This is, of course, one reason for the failure of phenomenalistic translation schemes.)

These consequences of the proposed definition are, I believe, correct, even though the proposed definition is itself still badly oversimplified. Is it a necessary truth that the 'normal' lemons, as we think of them (the tart yellow ones) are really normal members of their species? Is it logically impossible that we should have mistaken what are really very atypical lemons (perhaps diseased ones) for normal lemons? On the above definition, if there is no natural kind whose normal members are yellow, tart, etc., then even these tart, yellow, thick-peeled fruits that I make lemonade from are *not literally lemons*. But this is absurd. It is clear that they are lemons, although it is not analytic that they are *normal* lemons. Moreover, if the color of lemons changed—say, as the result of some gases getting into the earth's atmosphere and reacting with pigment in the peel of lemons—we would not say that lemons had ceased to exist, although a natural kind whose normal members were *yellow* and had the other characteristics of lemons *would* have ceased to exist. Thus the above definition is correct to the extent that what it says *isn't* analytic indeed isn't; but it is incorrect in that what would be analytic if it were correct isn't. We have loosened up the logic of the natural kind terms, in comparison with the 'conjunction of properties' model; but we have still not loosened it up enough.

Two cases have just been considered: (1) the normal members of the natural kind in question may not really be the ones we *think* are normal; (2) the characteristics of the natural kind may change with time, possibly due to a change in the conditions, without the 'essence' changing so much that we want to stop using the same word. In the first case (normal lemons are blue, but we haven't seen any normal lemons), our theory of the natural kind is false; but at least there is a natural kind about which we have a false theory, and that is why we can still apply the term. In the second case, our theory was at least once true; but it has ceased to be true, although the natural kind has not ceased to exist, which is why we can still apply the term.

Let us attempt to cover both these kinds of cases by modifying our definition as follows:

> X is a *lemon* = *df* X belongs to a natural kind whose ... (as before) OR X belongs to a natural kind whose normal members used to ... (as before) OR X belongs to a natural kind whose normal members were formerly believed to, or are now incorrectly believed to ... (as before).

Nontechnically, the trouble with this 'definition' is that it is slightly crazy. Even if we waive the requirement of sanity (and, indeed, it is all too customary in philosophy to waive any such requirement), it still doesn't work. Suppose, for example, that some tens of thousands of years ago lemons were unknown, but a few atypical oranges were known. Suppose these atypical oranges had exactly the properties of peel, color, etc., that lemons have: indeed, we may suppose that only a biologist could tell that they were really queer oranges and not normal lemons. Suppose that the people living at that time took them to be normal members of a species, and thus thought that oranges have exactly the properties that lemons in fact do have. Then all now existing oranges would be lemons, according to the above definition, since they belong to a species (a natural kind) of which it was once believed that the normal members have the characteristics of yellow peel, lemon taste, etc.

Rather than try to complicate the definition still further, in the fashion of system-building philosophers, let us simply observe what has gone wrong. It is true—and this is what the new definition tries to reflect—that one possible use of a natural kind term is the following: to refer to a thing which belongs to a natural kind which does *not* fit the 'theory' associated with the natural kind term, but which was believed to fit that theory (and, in fact, to be *the* natural kind which fit the theory) when the theory had not yet been falsified. Even if cats turn out to be robots remotely controlled from Mars we will still call them 'cats'; even if it turns out that the stripes on tigers are painted on to deceive us, we will still call them 'tigers'; even if normal lemons are blue (we have been buying and raising very atypical lemons, but don't know it), they are still lemons (and so are the yellow ones.) Not only will we still *call* them 'cats', they are cats; not only will we still call them 'tigers', they are tigers; not only will we still call them 'lemons', they are lemons. But the fact that a term has several possible uses does not make it a disjunctive term; the mistake is in trying to represent the complex behavior of a natural kind word in something as simple as an analytic definition.

To say that an analytic definition is too simple a means of representation is not to say that no representation is possible. Indeed, a very simple representation is possible, namely:

> *lemon*: natural kind word   associated characteristics:
> yellow peel, tart taste, etc.

To fill this out, a lot more should be said about the linguistic behavior of natural kind words: but no more need be said about *lemon*.

Katz's Theory of Meaning

Carnap's view of meaning in natural language is this: we divide up logical space into 'logically possible worlds'. (That this may be highly language-relative, and that it may presuppose the very analytic-synthetic distinction he hopes to find by his quasi-operational procedure are objections he does not discuss.) The informant is asked whether or not he would say that something is the case in each logically possible world: the assumption being that (1) each logically possible world can be described clearly enough for the informant to tell; and (2) that the informant can say that the sentence in question is *true/false/not clearly either* just on the basis of the description of the logically possible world and the meaning (or 'intension') he assigns to the sentence in question. The latter assumption is false, as we have just seen, for just the reason that the traditional theory of meaning is false: even if I know the 'logically possible world' you have in mind, deciding whether or not something is, for example, a lemon, may require deciding what the best *theory* is; and this is not something to be determined by asking an informant yes/no questions in a rented office. This is not to say that 'lemon' has no meaning, of course: it is to say that meaning is not *that* simply connected with extension, even with 'extension in logically possible worlds'.

Carnap is not my main stalking-horse, however. The theory I want to focus on is the 'semantic theory' recently propounded by Jerrold Katz and his co-workers. In main outlines this theory is as follows:

(1) Each word has its meaning characterized by a string of 'semantic markers'.
(2) These markers stand for 'concepts' ('concepts' are themselves brain processes in Katz's philosophy of language; but I shall ignore this *jeu d'esprit* here). Examples of such concepts are: *unmarried, animate, seal*.
(3) Each such concept (concept for which a semantic marker is introduced) is a 'linguistic universal', and stands for an *innate* notion—one in some sense-or-other 'built into' the human brain.
(4) There are recursive rules—and this is the 'scientific' core of Katz's 'semantic theory'—whereby the 'readings' of whole sentences (these being likewise strings of markers) are derived from the meanings of the individual words and the deep structure (in the sense of transformational grammar) of the sentence.
(5) The scheme as a whole is said to be justified in what is said to be the manner of a scientific theory—by its ability to explain such things as our intuitions that certain sentences have more than one meaning, or the certain sentences are queer.
(6) Analyticity relations are also supposed to be able to be read off from the theory: for example, from the fact that the markers associated with 'unmarried' occur in connection with 'bachelor', one can see that 'all bachelors are unmarried' is analytic; and from the fact that the markers associated with 'animal' occur in connection with 'cat', one can see (allegedly) that 'all cats are animals' is analytic.

There are internal inconsistencies in this scheme which are apparent at once. For example, 'seal' is given as an example of a 'linguistic universal' (at least, 'seal' occurs as part of the 'distinguisher' in one reading for 'bachelor'—the variant reading: *young male fur seal*, in one of Katz's examples); but in no theory of human evolution is contact with seals universal. Indeed, even contact with *clothing*, or with *furniture*, or with *agriculture* is by no means universal. Thus we must take it that Katz means that whenever such terms occur they could be further analyzed into concepts which really are so primitive that a case could be made for their universality. Needless to say, this program has never been carried out, and he himself constantly ignores it in giving examples. But the point of greatest interest to us is that this scheme is an unsophisticated translation into 'mathematical' language of precisely the traditional theory that it has been our concern to criticize! Indeed, as far as general names are concerned, the only change is that whereas in the traditional account each general name was associated with a list of properties, in Katz's account each general name is associated with a list of *concepts*. It follows that each counterexample to the traditional theory is at once a counterexample also to Katz's theory. For example, if Katz lists the concept 'yellow' under the noun 'lemon', then he will be committed to 'all lemons are yellow'; if he lists the concept 'striped' under the noun 'tiger', then he will be committed to the analyticity of 'all tigers are striped'; and so on. Indeed, although Katz denies that his 'semantic markers' are themselves *words*, it is clear that they can be regarded as a kind of artificial language. Therefore, what Katz is saying is that:

(1) A mechanical scheme can be given for translating any natural language into this artificial 'marker language' (and this scheme is just what Katz's 'semantic theory' is).
(2) The string of markers associated with a word has exactly the meaning of the word.

If (1) and (2) were true, we would at once deduce that there exists a possible language—a 'marker language'—with the property that every word that human beings have invented or could invent has an analytic definition in that language. But this is something that we have every reason to disbelieve! In fact: (1) We have just seen that if our account of 'natural kind' words is correct, then none of these words has an analytic definition. In particular, a natural kind word will be analytically translatable into marker language only in the special case in which a marker happens to have been introduced with its exact meaning. (2) There are many words for which we haven't the foggiest notion what an analytic definition would even look like. What would an analytic definition of 'mammoth' look like? (Would Katz say that it is analytic that mammoths are extinct? Or that they have a certain kind of molar? These are the items mentioned in the dictionary!) To say that a word is the name of an extinct species of elephant is to exactly communicate the use of that word; but it certainly isn't an analytic definition (i.e. an analytically necessary and sufficient condition). (3) *Theoretical terms* in science have no analytic definitions, for reasons familiar to every reader of recent philosophy of science; yet these are surely items (and not atypical items) in the vocabulary of natural languages.

We have now seen, I believe, one reason for the recent lack of progress in semantic theory: you may dress up traditional mistakes in modern dress by talking of 'recursive rules' and 'linguistic universals', but they remain the traditional mistakes. The problem in semantic theory is to get away from the picture of the meaning of a word as something like a *list of concepts*; not to formalize that misguided picture.

Quine's Pessimism

Quine has long expressed a profound pessimism about the very possibility of such a subject as 'semantic theory'. Certainly we cannot assume that *there is* a scientific subject to be constructed here just because ordinary people have occasion to use the word 'meaning' from time to time; that would be like concluding that there must be a scientific subject to be constructed which will deal with 'causation' just because ordinary people have occasion to use the word 'cause' from time to time. In one sense, *all* of science is a theory of causation; but not in the sense that it uses the word *cause*. Similarly, any successful and developed theory of language-use will in one sense be a theory of meaning; but not necessarily in the sense that it will employ any such notion as the 'meaning' of a word or of an utterance. Elementary as this point is, it seems to be constantly overlooked in the social sciences, and people seem constantly to expect that psychology, for example, must talk of 'dislike', 'attraction', 'belief', etc., simply because ordinary men use these words in psychological description.

Quine's pessimism cannot, then, be simply dismissed; and as far as the utility of the traditional notion of 'meaning' is concerned, Quine may well turn out to be right. But we are still left with the task of trying to say what are the real problems in the area of language-use, and of trying to erect a conceptual framework within which we can begin to try to solve them.

Let us return to our example of the natural kind words. It is a fact, and one whose importance to this subject I want to bring out, that the use of words can be taught. If someone does not know the meaning of 'lemon', I can somehow convey it to him. I am going to suggest that in this simple phenomenon lies the problem, and hence the *raison d'être*, of 'semantic theory'.

How do I convey the meaning of the word 'lemon'? Very likely, I show the man a lemon. Very well, let us change the example. How do I convey the meaning of the word 'tiger'? *I tell him what a tiger is.*

It is easy to see that Quine's own theoretical scheme (in *Word and Object*) will not handle this case very well. Quine's basic notion is the notion of *stimulus meaning* (roughly this is the set of nerve-ending stimulations which will 'prompt assent' to *tiger*). But: (1) it is very unlikely that I convey exactly the stimulus-meaning that 'tiger' has in my idiolect; and (2) in any case I don't convey it directly, i.e. by describing it. In fact, I couldn't describe it. Quine also works with the idea of *accepted sentences*; thus he might try to handle this case somewhat as follows: 'the hearer in your example already shares a great deal of language with you; otherwise you couldn't tell him what a tiger is. When you "tell him what a tiger is," you simply tell him certain sentences that you accept. Once he knows what sentences you accept, naturally he is able to use the word, at least observation words.'

Let us, however, refine this last counter somewhat. If conveying the meaning of the word 'tiger' involved conveying the totality of accepted scientific theory about tigers, or even the totality of what I believe about tigers, then it would be an impossible task. It is true that when I tell someone what a tiger is I 'simply tell him certain sentences'—though not necessarily sentences I *accept*, except as descriptions of linguistically stereotypical tigers. But the point is, *which* sentences?

In the special case of such words as 'tiger' and 'lemon', we proposed an answer earlier in this paper. The answer runs as follows: there is somehow associated with the word 'tiger' a *theory*; not the actual theory we believe about tigers, which is very complex, but an oversimplified theory which describes a, so to speak, tiger *stereotype*. It describes, in the language we used earlier, a *normal member* of the natural kind. It is not necessary that we believe this theory, though in the case of 'tiger' we do. But it is necessary that we be aware that *this* theory is associated with the word: if our stereotype of a tiger ever changes, then the word 'tiger' will have changed its meaning. If, to change the example, lemons all turn blue, the word 'lemon' will not immediately change its meaning. When I first say, with surprise, 'lemons have all turned blue', lemon will still mean what it means now—which is to say that 'lemon' will still be associated with the stereotype *yellow lemon*, even though I will use the word to deny that lemons (even normal lemons) are in fact yellow. I can refer to a natural kind by a term which is 'loaded' with a theory which is known not to be any longer true of that natural kind, just because it will be clear to everyone that what I intend is to refer to *that* kind, and not to assert the theory. But, of course, if lemons really did turn blue (and stayed that way) then in time 'lemon' would come to have a meaning with the following representation:

> *lemon*: natural kind word   associated characteristics:
> *blue* peel, tart taste, etc.

Then 'lemon' would have changed its meaning.

To sum this up: there are a few facts about 'lemon' or 'tiger' (I shall refer to them as *core facts*) such that one can convey the use of 'lemon' or 'tiger' by simply conveying those facts. More precisely, one cannot convey the approximate use *unless* one gets the core facts across.

Let me emphasize that this has the status of an empirical hypothesis. The hypothesis is that there are, in connection with almost any word (not just 'natural kind' words), certain core facts such that (1) one cannot convey the normal use of the word (to the satisfaction of native speakers) without conveying those core facts, and (2) in the case of many words and many speakers, conveying those core facts is sufficient to convey at least an approximation to the normal use. In the case of a natural kind word, the core facts are that a normal member of the kind has certain characteristics, or that this idea is at least the stereotype associated with the word.

If this hypothesis is false, then I think that Quine's pessimism is probably justified. But if this hypothesis is right, then I think it is clear what the problem of the theory of meaning is, regardless of whether or not one chooses to call it 'theory of *meaning*': the question is to explore and explain this empirical phenomenon. Questions which naturally arise are: what different kinds of words are associated with what different kinds of core facts? and by what mechanism does it happen that just conveying a small set of core facts brings it about that the hearer is able to imitate the normal use of a word?

Wittgensteinians, whose fondness for the expression 'form of life' appears to be directly proportional to its degree of preposterousness in a given context, say that acquiring the customary use of such a word as 'tiger' is coming to share a form of life. What they miss, or at any rate fail to emphasize, is that while the acquired disposition may be sufficiently complex and sufficiently interlinked with other complex dispositions to warrant special mention (though hardly the overblown phrase 'form of life'), what *triggers* the disposition is often highly discrete—e.g. a simple lexical definition frequently succeeds in conveying a pretty good idea of how a word is used. To be sure, as Wittgenstein emphasizes, this is only possible because we have a shared human nature, and because we have shared an acculturation process—there has to be a great deal of stage-setting before one can read a lexical definition and guess how a word is used. But in the process of 'debunking' this fact—the fact that something as simple as a lexical definition *can* convey the use of a word—they forget to be impressed by it. To be sure there is a great deal of stage-setting, but it is rarely stage-setting specifically designed to enable one to learn the use of *this* word. The fact that one *can* acquire the use of an indefinite number of new words, and on the basis of simple 'statements of what they mean', is an amazing fact: it is *the* fact, I repeat, on which semantic theory rests.

Sometimes it is said that the key problem in semantics is: how do we come to understand a new sentence? I would suggest that this is a far simpler (though not unimportant) problem. How logical words, for example, can be used to build up complex sentences out of simpler ones is easy to describe, at least in principle (of course, natural language analogues of logical words are far less tidy than the logical words of the mathematical logician), and it is also easy to say how the truth-conditions, etc., of the complex sentences are related to the truth-conditions of the sentences from which they were derived. This much *is* a matter of finding a structure of recursive rules with a suitable relation to the transformational grammar of the language in question. I would suggest that the question, How do we come to understand a new *word*? has far more to do with the whole phenomenon of giving definitions and writing dictionaries than the former question. And it is this phenomenon—the phenomenon of writing (and needing) dictionaries—that gives rise to the whole idea of 'semantic theory'.

Kinds of Core Facts

Let us now look a little more closely at the kind of information that one conveys when one conveys the meaning of a word. I have said that in the case of a 'natural kind' word one conveys the associated *stereotype*: the associated idea of the characteristics of a normal member of the kind. But this is not, in general, enough; one must also convey the extension, one must indicate *which* kind the stereotype is supposed to 'fit'.

From the point of view of any traditional meaning theory, be it Plato's or Frege's or Carnap's or Katz's, this is just nonsense. How can I 'convey' the extension of, say 'tiger'? Am I supposed to give you all the tigers in the world (heaven forfend!). I can convey the extension of a term only by giving a description of that extension; and then that description must be a 'part of the meaning', or else my definition will not be a meaning-statement at all. To say: 'I gave him certain conditions associated with the word, *and* I gave him the extension' (as if that weren't just giving *further* conditions) can only be nonsense.

The mistake of the traditional theorist lies in his attachment to the word 'meaning'. If giving the meaning is *giving* the *meaning*, then it is giving a definite thing; but giving the meaning isn't, as we shall see in a moment, giving some one definite thing. To drop the word 'meaning', which is here extremely misleading: there is no *one* set of facts which has to be conveyed to convey the normal use of a word; and taking account of this requires a complication in our notion of 'core facts'.

That the same stereotype might be associated with different kinds seems odd if the kind word one has in mind is 'tiger'; but change the example to, say, 'aluminum' and it will not seem odd at all. About all *I* know about aluminum is that it is a light metal, that it makes durable pots and pans, and that it doesn't appear to rust (although it does occasionally discolor). For all I know, every one of these characteristics may also fit molybdenum.

Suppose now that a colony of English-speaking Earthlings is leaving in a spaceship for a distant planet. When they arrive on their distant planet, they discover that no one remembers the atomic weight (or any other defining characteristic) of aluminum, nor the atomic weight (or other characteristic) of molybdenum. There is some aluminum in the spacecraft, and some molybdenum. Let us suppose that they guess which is which, and they guess wrong. Henceforth, they use 'aluminum' as the name for molybdenum, and 'molybdenum' as the name for aluminum. It is clear that 'aluminum' has a different meaning in this community than in ours: in fact, it means *molybdenum*. Yet how can this be? Didn't they possess the normal 'linguistic competence'? Didn't they all 'know the meaning of the word "aluminum"'?

Let us duck this question for a moment. If I want to make sure that the word 'aluminum' will continue to be used in what counts as a 'normal' way by the colonists in my example, it will suffice to give them some test for aluminum (or just to give them a carefully labelled sample, and let them discover a test, if they are clever enough). Once they know how to *tell* aluminum from other metals, they will go on using the word with the correct extension as well as the correct 'intension' (i.e. the correct stereotype). But notice: it does not matter *which* test we give the colonists. The test isn't part of the meaning; but that there be some test or other (or something, e.g. a sample, from which one might be derived), is necessary to preservation of 'the normal usage'. Meaning indeed determines extension; but only because extension (fixed by *some* test or other) is, in some cases, 'part of the meaning'.

There are two further refinements here: if we give them a test, they mustn't make it part of the stereotype—that would be a change of meaning. (Thus it's better if they don't all *know* the test; as long as only experts do, and the average speaker 'asks an expert' in case of doubt, the criteria mentioned in the test can't infect the stereotype.) Asking an expert is enough of a test for the normal speaker; that's why we don't give a test in an ordinary context.

We can now modify our account of the 'core facts' in the case of a natural kind word as follows: (1) The core facts are the stereotype *and the extension*. (2) Nothing normally need be said about the extension, however, since the hearer knows that he can always consult an expert if any question comes up. (3) In special cases—such as the case of colonists—there may be danger that the word will get attached to the wrong natural kind, even though the right stereotype is associated with it. In such cases, one must give some way of getting the extension right, but no one *particular* way is necessary.

In the case of 'lemon' or 'tiger' a similar problem comes up. It is logically possible (although empirically unlikely, perhaps) that a species of fruit biologically unrelated to lemons might be indistinguishable from lemons in taste and appearance. In such a case, there would be two possibilities: (1) to call them *lemons*, and thus let 'lemon' be a word for any one of a number of natural kinds; or (2) to say that they are not lemons (which is what, I suspect, biologists would decide to do). In the latter case, the problems are exactly the same as with *aluminum*: to be sure one has the 'normal usage' or 'customary meaning' or whatever, one has to be sure one has the right extension.

The problem: that giving the extension is part of giving the meaning arises also in the case of names of sensible qualities, e.g. colors. Here, however, it is normal to give the extension by giving a sample, so that the person learning the word learns to recognize the quality in the normal way. Frequently it has been regarded as a defect of *dictionaries* that they are 'cluttered up' with color samples, and with stray pieces of empirical information (e.g. the atomic weight of aluminum), not sharply distinguished from 'purely linguistic' information. The burden of the present discussion is that this is no defect at all, but essential to the function of conveying the core facts in each case.

Still other kinds of words may be mentioned in passing. In the case of 'one-criterion' words (words which possess an analytical necessary and sufficient condition) it is obvious why the core fact is just the analytical necessary and sufficient condition, e.g. 'man who has never been married', in the case of 'bachelor'). In the case of 'cluster' words (e.g. the name of a disease which is known not to have any one underlying cause), it is obvious why the core facts are just the typical symptoms or elements of the cluster; and so on. Given the *function* of a kind of word, it is not difficult to explain why certain facts function as core facts for conveying the use of words of that kind.

The Possibility of Semantics

Why, then, is semantics so hard? In terms of the foregoing, I want to suggest that semantics is a typical social science. The sloppiness, the lack of precise theories and laws, the lack of mathematical rigor, are all characteristic of the social sciences today. A general and precise theory which answers the questions (1) why do words have the different sorts of functions they do? and (2) exactly how does conveying core facts enable one to learn the use of a word? is not to be expected until one has a general and precise model of a language-user; and that is still a long way off. But the fact that Utopia is a long way off does not mean that daily life should come to a screeching halt. There is plenty for us to investigate, in our sloppy and impressionistic fashion, and there are plenty of real results to be obtained. The first step is to free ourselves from the oversimplifications foisted upon us by the tradition, and to see where the real problems lie. I hope this paper has been a contribution to that first step.

Chapter 8

Principles of Categorization

Eleanor Rosch

The following is a taxonomy of the animal kingdom. It has been attributed to an ancient Chinese encyclopedia entitled the *Celestial Emporium of Benevolent Knowledge*:

> On those remote pages it is written that animals are divided into (a) those that belong to the Emperor, (b) embalmed ones, (c) those that are trained, (d) suckling pigs, (e) mermaids, (f) fabulous ones, (g) stray dogs, (h) those that are included in this classification, (i) those that tremble as if they were mad, (j) innumerable ones, (k) those drawn with a very fine camel's hair brush, (l) others, (m) those that have just broken a flower vase, (n) those that resemble flies from a distance. (Borges 1966, p. 108)

Conceptually, the most interesting aspect of this classification system is that it does not exist. Certain types of categorizations may appear in the imagination of poets, but they are never found in the practical or linguistic classes of organisms or of manmade objects used by any of the cultures of the world. For some years, I have argued that human categorization should not be considered the arbitrary product of historical accident or of whimsy but rather the result of psychological principles of categorization, which are subject to investigation. This chapter is a summary and discussion of those principles.

The chapter is divided into five parts. The first part presents the two general principles that are proposed to underlie categorization systems. The second part shows the way in which these principles appear to result in a basic and primary level of categorization in the levels of abstraction in a taxonomy. It is essentially a summary of the research already reported on basic level objects (Rosch et al., 1976). Thus the second section may be omitted by the reader already sufficiently familiar with that material. The third part relates the principles of categorization to the formation of prototypes in those categories that are at the same level of abstraction in a taxonomy. In particular, this section attempts to clarify the operational concept of prototypicality and to separate that concept from claims concerning the role of prototypes in cognitive processing, representation, and learning for which there is little evidence. The fourth part presents two issues that are problematical for the abstract principles of categorization stated in Part I: (1) the relation of context to basic level objects and prototypes; and (2) assumptions about the nature of the attributes of real-world objects that underlie the claim that there is structure in the world. The fifth part is a report of initial attempts to base an analysis of the attributes, functions, and contexts of objects on a consideration of objects as props in culturally defined events.

It should be noted that the issues in categorization with which we are primarily concerned have to do with explaining the categories found in a culture and coded by the language of that culture at a particular point in time. When we speak of the formation of categories, we mean their formation in the culture. This point is often misunderstood. The principles of categorization proposed are not as such intended to constitute a theory of the development of categories in children born into a culture nor to constitute a model of how categories are processed (how categorizations are made) in the minds of adult speakers of a language.

The Principles

Two general and basic principles are proposed for the formation of categories: The first has to do with the function of category systems and asserts that the task of category systems is to provide maximum information with the least cognitive effort; the second has to do with the structure of the information so provided and asserts that the perceived world comes as structured information rather than as arbitrary or unpredictable attributes. Thus maximum information with least cognitive effort is achieved if categories map the perceived world structure as closely as possible. This condition can be achieved either by the mapping of categories to given attribute structures or by the definition or redefinition of attributes to render a given set of categories appropriately structured. These principles are elaborated in the following.

Cognitive Economy   The first principle contains the almost common-sense notion that, as an organism, what one wishes to gain from one's categories is a great deal of information about the environment while conserving finite resources as much as possible. To categorize a stimulus means to consider it, for purposes of that categorization, not only equivalent to other stimuli in the same category but also different from stimuli not in that category. On the one hand, it would appear to the organism's advantage to have as many properties as possible predictable from knowing any one property, a principle that would lead to formation of large numbers of categories with as fine discriminations between categories as possible. On the other hand, one purpose of categorization is to reduce the infinite differences among stimuli to behaviorally and cognitively usable proportions. It is to the organism's advantage not to differentiate one stimulus from others when that differentiation is irrelevant to the purposes at hand.

Perceived World Structure   The second principle of categorization asserts that unlike the sets of stimuli used in traditional laboratory-concept attainment tasks, the perceived world is not an unstructured total set of equiprobable co-occurring attributes. Rather, the material objects of the world are perceived to possess (in Garner's, 1974, sense) high correlational structure. That is, given a knower who perceives the complex attributes of feathers, fur, and wings, it is an empirical fact provided by the perceived world that wings co-occur with feathers more than with fur. And given an actor with the motor programs for sitting, it is s fact of the perceived world that objects with the perceptual attributes of chairs are more likely to have functional sit-on-able-ness than objects with the appearance of cats. In short, combinations of what we perceive as the attributes of real objects do not occur uniformly. Some pairs, triples, etc., are quite probable, appearing in combination sometimes with one, sometimes another attribute; others are rare; others logically cannot or empirically do not occur.

It should be emphasized that we are talking about the perceived world and not a metaphysical world without a knower. What kinds of attributes *can* be perceived are, of course, species-specific. A dog's sense of smell is more highly differentiated than a human's, and the structure of the world for a dog must surely include attributes of smell that we, as a species, are incapable of perceiving. Furthermore, because a dog's body is constructed differently from a human's, its motor interactions with objects are necessarily differently structured. The "out there" of a bat, a frog, or a bee is surely more different still from that of a human. What attributes *will* be perceived given the ability to perceive them is undoubtedly determined by many factors having to do with the functional needs of the knower interacting with the physical and social environment. One influence on how attributes will be defined by humans is clearly the category system already existent in the culture at a given time. Thus, our segmentation of a bird's body such that there is an attribute called "wings" may be influenced not only by perceptual factors such as the gestalt laws of form that would lead us to consider the wings as a separate part (Palmer 1977) but also by the fact that at present we already have a cultural and linguistic category called "birds." Viewing attributes as, at least in part, constructs of the perceiver does not negate the higher-order structural fact about attributes at issue, namely that the attributes of wings and that of feathers do co-occur in the perceived world.

These two basic principles of categorization, a drive toward cognitive economy combined with structure in the perceived world, have implications both for the level of abstraction of categories formed in a culture and for the internal structure of those categories once formed.

For purposes of explication, we may conceive of category systems as having both a vertical and horizontal dimension. The vertical dimension concerns the level of inclusiveness of the category—the dimension along which the terms collie, dog, mammal, animal, and living thing vary. The horizontal dimension concerns the segmentation of categories at the same level of inclusiveness—the dimension on which dog, cat, car, bus, chair, and sofa vary. The implication of the two principles of categorization for the vertical dimension is that not all possible levels of categorization are equally good or useful; rather, the most basic level of categorization will be the most inclusive (abstract) level at which the categories can mirror the structure of attributes perceived in the world. The implication of the principles of categorization for the horizontal dimension is that to increase the distinctiveness and flexibility of categories, categories tend to become defined in terms of prototypes or prototypical instances that contain the attributes most representative of items inside and least representative of items outside the category.

The Vertical Dimension of Categories: Basic-Level Objects

In a programmatic series of experiments, we have attempted to argue that categories within taxonomies of concrete objects are structured such that there is generally one level of abstraction at which the most basic category cuts can be made (Rosch et al. 1976a). By *category* is meant a number of objects that are considered equivalent. Categories are generally designated by names (e.g., *dog, animal*). A *taxonomy* is a system by which categories are related to one another by means of class inclusion. The greater the inclusiveness of a category within a taxonomy, the higher the level of abstraction. Each category within a taxonomy is entirely included within one other category (unless it is the highest level category) but is not exhaustive of that more inclusive category (see Kay 1971). Thus the term *level of abstraction* within a taxonomy refers to a particular level of inclusiveness. A familiar taxonomy is the Linnean system for the classification of animals.

Our claims concerning a basic level of abstraction can be formalized in terms of cue validity (Rosch et al. 1976a) or in terms of the set theoretic representation of similarity provided by Tversky (1977, and Tversky and Gati 1978). Cue validity is a probabilistic concept; the validity of a given cue x as a predictor of a given category y (the conditional probability of y/x) increases as the frequency with which cue x is associated with category y increases and decreases as the frequency with which cue x is associated with categories other than y increases (Beach 1964a, 1964b; Reed 1972). The cue validity of an entire category may be defined as the summation of the cue validities for that category of each of the attributes of the category. A category with high cue validity is, by definition, more differentiated from other categories than one of lower cue validity. The elegant formulization that Tversky (1978) provides is in terms of the variable "category resemblance," which is defined as the weighted sum of the measures of all of the common features within a category minus the sum of the measures of all of the distinctive features. Distinctive features include those that belong to only some members of a given category as well as those belonging to contrasting categories. Thus Tversky's formalization does not weight the effect of contrast categories as much as does the cue validity formulation. Tversky suggests that two disjoint classes tend to be combined whenever the weight of the added common features exceeds the weight of the distinctive features.

A working assumption of the research on basic objects is that (1) in the perceived world, information-rich bundles of perceptual and functional attributes occur that form natural discontinuities, and that (2) basic cuts in categorization are made at these discontinuities. Suppose that basic objects (e.g., chair, car) are at the most inclusive level at which there are attributes common to all or most members of the category. Then both total cue validities and category resemblance are maximized at that level of abstraction at which basic objects are categorized. This is, categories one level more abstract will be superordinate categories (e.g., furniture, vehicle) whose members share only a few attributes among each other. Categories below the basic level will be bundles of common and, thus, predictable attributes and functions but contain many attributes that overlap with other categories (for example, kitchen chair shares most of its attributes with other kinds of chairs).

Superordinate categories have lower total cue validity and lower category resemblance than do basic-level categories, because they have fewer common attributes; in fact, the category resemblance measure of items within the superordinate can even be negative due to the high ratio of distinctive to common features. Subordinate categories have lower total cue validity than do basic categories, because they also share most attributes with contrasting subordinate categories; in Tversky's terms, they tend to be combined because the weight of the added common features tend to exceed the weight of the distinctive features. That basic objects are categories at the level of abstraction that maximizes cue validity and maximizes category resemblance is another way of asserting that basic objects are the categories that best mirror the correlational structure of the environment.

We chose to look at concrete objects because they appeared to be a domain that was at once an indisputable aspect of complex natural language classifications yet at the same time were amenable to methods of empirical analysis. In our investigations of basic categories, the correlational structure of concrete objects was considered to consist of a number of inseparable aspects of form and function, any one of which could serve as the starting point for analysis. Four investigations provided converging operational definitions of the basic level of abstraction: attributes in common, motor movements in common, objective similarity in shape, and identifiability of averaged shapes.

Common Attributes   Ethnobiologists had suggested on the basis of linguistic criteria and field observation that the folk genus was the level of classification at which organisms had bundles of attributes in common and maximum discontinuity between classes (see Berlin 1978). The purpose of our research was to provide a systematic empirical study of the co-occurrence of attributes in the most common taxonomies of biological and man-made objects in our own culture.

The hypothesis that basic level objects are the most inclusive level of classification at which objects have numbers of attributes in common was tested for categories at three levels of abstraction for nine taxonomies: tree, bird, fish, fruit, musical instruments, tool, clothing, furniture, and vehicle. Examples of the three levels for one biological and one nonbiological taxonomy are shown in Table 8.1. Criteria for choice of these specific items were that the taxonomies contain the most common (defined by word frequency) categories of concrete nouns in English, that the levels of abstraction bear simple class-inclusion relations to each other, and that those class-inclusion relations be generally known to our subjects (be agreed upon by a sample of native English speakers). The middle level of abstraction was the hypothesized basic level: For nonbiological taxonomies, this corresponded to the intuition of the experimenters (which also turned out to be consistent with Berlin's linguistic criteria); for biological categories, we assumed that the basic level would be the level of the folk generic.

Subjects received sets of words taken from these nine taxonomies; the subject's task was to list all of the attributes he could think of that were true of the items

Table 8.1
Examples of taxonomies used in basic object research

Superordinate	Basic Level	Subordinate
Furniture	Chair	Kitchen chair
		Living-room chair
	Table	Kitchen table
		Dining-room table
	Lamp	Floor lamp
		Desk lamp
Tree	Oak	White oak
		Red oak
	Maple	Silver maple
		Sugar maple
	Birch	River birch
		White birch

included in the class of things designated by each object name. Thus, for purposes of this study, attributes were defined operationally as whatever subjects agreed them to be with no implications for whether such analysis of an object could or could not be perceptually considered prior to knowledge of the object itself. Results of the study were as predicted: Very few attributes were listed for the superordinate categories, a significantly greater number listed for the supposed basic-level objects, and not significantly more attributes listed for subordinate-level objects than for basic-level. An additional study showed essentially the same attributes listed for visually present objects as for the object names. The single unpredicted result was that for the three biological taxonomies, the basic level, as defined by numbers of attributes in common, did not occur at the level of the folk generic but appeared at the level we had originally expected to be superordinate (e.g., *tree* rather than *oak*).

Motor Movements   Inseparable from the perceived attributes of objects are the ways in which humans habitually use or interact with those objects. For concrete objects, such interactions take the form of motor movements. For example, when performing the action of sitting down on a chair, a sequence of body and muscle movements are typically made that are inseparable from the nature of the attributes of chairs—legs, seat, back, etc. This aspect of objects is particularly important in light of the role that sensory-motor interaction with the world appears to play in the development of thought (Bruner, Olver, and Greenfield 1966; Nelson 1974; Piaget 1952).

In our study of motor movements, each of the sets of words used in the previous experiment was administered to new subjects. A subject was asked to describe, in as much finely analyzed detail as possible, the sequences of motor movements he made when using or interacting with the object. Tallies of agreed upon listings of the same movements of the same body part in the same part of the movement sequence formed the unit of analysis. Results were identical to those of the attribute listings; basic objects were the most general classes to have motor sequences in common. For example, there are few motor programs we carry out to items of furniture in general and several specific motor programs carried out in regard to sitting down on chairs, but we sit on kitchen and living-room chairs using essentially the same motor programs.

Similarity in Shapes   Another aspect of the meaning of a class of objects is the appearance of the objects in the class. In order to be able to analyze correlational structures by different but converging methods, it was necessary to find a method of analyzing similarity in the visual aspects of the objects that was not dependent on subjects' descriptions, that was free from effects of the object's name (which would not have been the case for subjects' ratings of similarity), and that went beyond similarity of analyzable, listable attributes that had already been used in the first study described. For this purpose, outlines of the shape of two-dimensional representations of objects were used, an integral aspect of natural forms. Similarity in shape was measured by the amount of overlap of the two outlines when the outlines (normalized for size and orientation) were juxtaposed.

Results showed that the ratio of overlapped to nonoverlapped area when two objects from the same basic-level category (e.g., two cars) were superimposed was far greater than when two objects from the same superordinate category were superimposed (e.g., a car and a motorcycle). Although some gain in ratio of overlap to nonoverlap also occurred for subordinate category objects (e.g., two sports cars), the gain obtained by shifting from basic-level to subordinate objects was significantly less than the gain obtained by shifting from superordinate to basic-level objects.

Identifiability of Averaged Shapes   If the basic level is the most inclusive level at which shapes of objects of a class are similar, a possible result of such similarity may be that the basic level is also the most inclusive level at which an averaged shape of an object can be recognized. To test this hypothesis, the same normalized superimposed shapes used in the previous experiment were used to draw an average outline of the over-lapped figures. Subjects were then asked to identify both the superordinate category and the specific object depicted. Results showed that basic objects were the most general and inclusive categories at which the objects depicted could be identified. Furthermore, overlaps of subordinate objects were no more identifiable than objects at the basic level.

In summary, our four converging operational definitions of basic objects all indicated the same level of abstraction to be basic in our taxonomies. Admittedly, the basic level for biological objects was not that predicted by the folk genus; however, this fact appeared to be simply accounted for by our subjects' lack of knowledge of the additional depth of real-world attribute structure available at the level of the folk generic (see Rosch et al. 1976a).

Implications for Other Fields

The foregoing theory of categorization and basic objects has implications for several traditional areas of study in psychology; some of these have been tested.

Imagery   The fact that basic-level objects were the most inclusive categories at which an averaged member of the category could be identified suggested that basic objects might be the most inclusive categories for which it was possible to form a mental image isomorphic to the appearance of members of the class as a whole. Experiments using a signal-detection paradigm and a priming paradigm, both of which have been previously argued to be measures of imagery (Peterson and Graham 1974; Rosch 1975c), verified that, in so far as it was meaningful to use the term *imagery*, basic objects appeared to be the most abstract categories for which an image could be reasonably representative of the class as a whole.

Perception   From all that has been said of the nature of basic classifications, it would hardly be reasonable to suppose that in perception of the world, objects were first categorized either at the most abstract or at the most concrete level possible. Two separate studies of picture verification (Rosch et al. 1976a; Smith, Balzano, and Walker 1978) indicate that, in fact, objects may be first seen or recognized as members of their basic category, and that only with the aid of additional processing can they be identified as members of their superordinate or subordinate category.

Development   We have argued that classification into categories at the basic level is overdetermined because perception, motor movements, functions, and iconic images would all lead to the same level of categorization. Thus basic objects should be the first categorizations of concrete objects made by children. In fact, for our nine taxonomies, the basic level was the first named. And even when naming was controlled, pictures of several basic-level objects were sorted into groups "because they were the same type of thing" long before such a technique of sorting has become general in children.

Language From all that has been said, we would expect the most useful and, thus, most used name for an item to be the basic-level name. In fact, we found that adults almost invariably named pictures of the subordinate items of the nine taxonomies at the basic level, although they knew the correct superordinate and subordinate names for the objects. On a more speculative level, in the evolution of languages, one would expect names to evolve first for basic-level objects, spreading both upward and downward as taxonomies increased in depth. Of great relevance for this hypothesis are Berlin's (1972) claims for such a pattern for the evolution of plant names, and our own (Rosch et al. 1976a) and Newport and Bellugi's (1978) finding for American Sign Language of the Deaf, that it was the basic-level categories that were most often coded by single signs and super- and subordinate categories that were likely to be missing. Thus a wide range of converging operations verify as basic the same levels of abstraction.

The Horizontal Dimension: Internal Structure of Categories: Prototypes

Most, if not all, categories do not have clear-cut boundaries. To argue that basic object categories follow clusters of perceived attributes is not to say that such attribute clusters are necessarily discontinuous.

In terms of the principles of categorization proposed earlier, cognitive economy dictates that categories tend to be viewed as being as separate from each other and as clear-cut as possible. One way to achieve this is by means of formal, necessary and sufficient criteria for category membership. The attempt to impose such criteria on categories marks virtually all definitions in the tradition of Western reason. The psychological treatment of categories in the standard concept-identification paradigm lies within this tradition. Another way to achieve separateness and clarity of actually continuous categories is by conceiving of each category in terms of its clear cases rather than its boundaries. As Wittgenstein (1953) has pointed out, categorical judgments become a problem only if one is concerned with boundaries—in the normal course of life, two neighbors know on whose property they are standing without exact demarcation of the boundary line. Categories can be viewed in terms of their clear cases if the perceiver places emphasis on the correlational structure of perceived attributes such that the categories are represented by their most structured portions.

By prototypes of categories we have generally meant the clearest cases of category membership defined operationally by people's judgments of goodness of membership in the category. A great deal of confusion in the discussion of prototypes has arisen from two sources. First, the notion of prototypes has tended to become reified as though it meant a specific category member or mental structure. Questions are then asked in an either-or fashion about whether something is or is not the prototype or part of the prototype in exactly the same way in which the question would previously have been asked about the category boundary. Such thinking precisely violates the Wittgensteinian insight that we can judge how clear a case something is and deal with categories on the basis of clear cases in the total absence of information about boundaries. Second, the empirical findings about prototypicality have been confused with theories of processing—that is, there has been a failure to distinguish the structure of categories from theories concerning the use of that structure in processing. Therefore, let us first attempt to look at prototypes in as purely structural a fashion as possible. We will focus on what may be said about prototypes based on operational definitions and empirical findings alone without the addition of process-ing assumptions.

Perception of typicality differences is, in the first place, an empirical fact of people's judgments about category membership. It is by now a well-documented finding that subjects overwhelmingly agree in their judgments of how good an example or clear a case members are of a category, even for categories about whose boundaries they disagree (Rosch 1974, 1975b). Such judgments are reliable even under changes of instructions and items (Rips, Shoben, and Smith 1973; Rosch 1975b, 1975c; Rosch and Mervis 1975). Were such agreement and reliability in judgment not to have been obtained, there would be no further point in discussion or investigation of the issue. However, given the empirical verification of degree of prototypicality, we can pro-ceed to ask what principles determine which items will be judged the more proto-typical and what other variables might be affected by prototypicality.

In terms of the basic principles of category formation, the formation of category prototypes should, like basic levels of abstraction, be determinate and be closely related to the initial formation of categories. For categories of concrete objects (which do not have a physiological basis, as categories such as colors and forms apparently do—Rosch 1974), a reasonable hypothesis is that prototypes develop through the same principles such as maximization of cue validity and maximization of cate-gory resemblance[1] as those principles governing the formation of the categories themselves.

In support of such a hypothesis, Rosch and Mervis (1975) have shown that the more prototypical of a category a member is rated, the more attributes it has in com-mon with other members of the category and the fewer attributes in common with members of the contrasting categories. This finding was demonstrated for natural language superordinate categories, for natural language basic-level categories, and for artificial categories in which the definition of attributes and the amount of experience with items was completely specified and controlled. The same basic principles can be represented in ways other than through attributes in common. Because the present theory is a structural theory, one aspect of it is that centrality shares the mathematical notions inherent in measures like the mean and mode. Prototypical category mem-bers have been found to represent the means of attributes that have a metric, such as size (Reed 1972; Rosch, Simpson, and Miller 1976).

In short, prototypes appear to be just those members of a category that most reflect the redundancy structure of the category as a whole. That is, if categories form to maximize the information-rich cluster of attributes in the environment and, thus, the cue validity or category resemblance of the attributes of categories, prototypes of categories appear to form in such a manner as to maximize such clusters and such cue validity still further within categories.

It is important to note that for natural language categories both at the super-ordinate and basic levels, the extent to which items have attributes common to the category was highly negatively correlated with the extent to which they have attrib-utes belonging to members of contrast categories. This appears to be part of the

---

1. Tversky formalizes prototypicality as the member or members of the category with the highest summed similarity to all members of the category. This measure, although formally more tractable than that of cue validity, does not take account, as cue validity does, of an item's dissimilarity to contrast categories. This issue is discussed further later.

structure of real-world categories. It may be that such structure is given by the correlated clusters of attributes of the real world. Or such structure, may be a result of the
human tendency once a contrast exists to define attributes for contrasting categories
so that the categories will be maximally distinctive. In either case, it is a fact that both
representativeness within a category and distinctiveness from contrast categories are
correlated with prototypicality in real categories. For artificial categories, either principle alone will produce prototype effects (Rosch et al. 1976b; Smith and Balzano,
personal communication) depending on the structure of the stimulus set. Thus to
perform experiments to try to distinguish which principle is the *one* that determines
prototype formation and category processing appears to be an artificial exercise.

Effects of Prototypicality on Psychological Dependent Variables
The fact that prototypicality is reliably rated and is correlated with category structure
does not have clear implications for particular processing models nor for a theory of
cognitive representations of categories (see the introduction to Part III of Rosch and
Lloyd 1978 and Palmer 1978). What is very clear from the extant research is that the
prototypicality of items within a category can be shown to affect virtually all of the
major dependent variables used as measures in psychological research.

Speed of Processing: Reaction Time   The speed with which subjects can judge statements about category membership is one of the most widely used measures of processing in semantic memory research within the human information-processing
framework. Subjects typically are required to respond true or false to statements of
the form: X item is a member of Y category, where the dependent variable of interest
is reaction time. In such tasks, for natural language categories, responses of true are
invariably faster for the items that have been rated more prototypical. Furthermore,
Rosch et al. (1976b) had subjects learn artificial categories where prototypicality was
defined structurally for some subjects in terms of distance of a gestalt configuration
from a prototype, for others in terms of means of attributes, and for still others in
terms of family resemblance between attributes. Factors other than the structure of
the category, such as frequency, were controlled. After learning was completed, reaction time in a category membership verification task proved to be a function of
structural prototypicality.

Speed of Learning of Artificial Categories (Errors) and Order of Development in Children
Rate of learning of new material and the naturally obtainable measure of learning
(combined with maturation) reflected in developmental order are two of the most
pervasive dependent variables in psychological research. In the artificial categories
used by Rosch et al. (1976b), prototypicality for all three types of stimulus material
predicted speed of learning of the categories. Developmentally, Anglin (1976)
obtained evidence that young children learn category membership of good examples
of categories before that of poor examples. Using a category-membership verification
technique, Rosch (1973) found that the differences in reaction time to verify good
and poor members were far more extreme for 10-year-old children than for adults,
indicating that the children had learned the category membership of the prototypical
members earlier than that of other members.

Order and Probability of Item Output   Item output is normally taken to reflect some
aspect of storage, retrieval, or category search. Battig and Montague (1969) provided

a normative study of the probability with which college students listed instances of superordinate semantic categories. The order is correlated with prototypicality ratings (Rosch 1975b). Furthermore, using the artificial categories in which frequency of experience with all items was controlled, Rosch et al. (1976b) demonstrated that the most prototypical items were the first and most frequently produced items when subjects were asked to list the members of the category.

Effects of Advance Information on Performance: Set, Priming   For colors (Rosch 1975c), for natural superordinate semantic categories (Rosch 1975b), and for artificial categories (Rosch et al. 1976b), it has been shown that degree of prototypicality determines whether advance information about the category name facilitates or inhibits responses in a matching task.

The Logic of Natural Language Use of Category Terms: Hedges, Substitutability into Sentences, Superordination in ASL   Although logic may treat categories as though membership is all or none, natural languages themselves possess linguistic mechanisms for coding and coping with gradients of category membership.

1. *Hedges.* In English there are qualifying terms such as "almost" and "virtually," which Lakoff (1972) calls "hedges." Even those who insist that statements such as "A robin is a bird" and "A penguin is a bird" are equally true, have to admit different hedges applicable to statements of category membership. Thus it is correct to say that a penguin is technically a bird but not that a robin is technically a bird, because a robin is more than just technically a bird; it is a real bird, a bird par excellence. Rosch (1975a) showed that when subjects were given sentence frames such as "X is virutally Y," they reliably placed the more prototypical member of a pair of items into the referent slot, a finding which is isomorphic to Tversky's work on asymmetry of similarity relations (Tversky & Gati 1978).

2. *Substitutability into sentences.* The meaning of words is initimately tied to their use in sentences. Rosch (1977) has shown that prototypicality ratings for members of superordinate categories predict the extent to which the member term is substitutable for the superordinate word in sentences. Thus, in the sentence "Twenty or so birds often perch on the telephone wires outside my window and twitter in the morining," the term "sparrow" may readily be substituted for "bird" but the result turns ludicrous by substitution of "turkey," an effect which is not simply a matter of frequency (Rosch 1975d).

3. *Productive superordinates in ASL.* Newport and Bellugi (1978) demonstrate that when superordinates in ASL are generated by means of a partial fixed list of category members, those members are the more prototypical items in the category.

In summary, evidence has been presented that prototypes of categories are related to the major dependent variables with which psychological processes are typically measured. What the work summarized does not tell us, however, is considerably more than it tells us. The pervasiveness of prototypes in real-world categories and of prototypicality as a variable indicates that prototypes must have some place in psychological theories of representation, processing, and learning. However, prototypes themselves do not constitute any particular model of processes, representations, or learning. This point is so often misunderstood that it requires discussion:

1. To speak of *a prototype* at all is simply a convenient grammatical fiction; what is really referred to are judgments of degree of prototypicality. Only in some artificial categories is there by definition a literal single prototype (for example, Posner, Goldsmith, and Welton 1967; Reed 1972; Rosch et al. 1976b). For natural-language categories, to speak of a single entity that is the prototype is either a gross misunderstanding of the empirical data or a covert theory of mental representation.

2. Prototypes do not constitute any particular processing model for categories. For example, in pattern recognition, as Palmer (1978) points out, a prototype can be described as well by feature lists or structural descriptions as by templates. And many different types of matching operations can be conceived for matching to a prototype given any of these three modes of representation of the prototypes. Other cognitive processes performed on categories such as verifying the membership of an instance in a category, searching the exemplars of a category for the member with a particular attribute, or understanding the meaning of a paragraph containing the category name are not bound to any single process model by the fact that we may acknowledge prototypes. What the facts about prototypicality do contribute to processing notions is a constraint—process models should not be inconsistent with the known facts about prototypes. For example, a model should not be such as to predict equal verification times for good and bad examples of categories nor predict completely random search through a category.

3. Prototypes do not constitute a theory of representation of categories. Although we have suggested elsewhere that it would be reasonable in light of the basic principles of categorization, if categories were represented by prototypes that were most representative of the items in the category and least representative of items outside the category (Rosch and Mervis 1975; Rosch 1977), such a statement remains an unspecified formula until it is made concrete by inclusion in some specific theory of representation. For example, different theories of semantic memory can contain the notion of prototypes in different fashions (Smith, 1978). Prototypes can be represented either by propositional or image systems (see Kosslyn 1978 and Palmer 1978). As with processing models, the facts about prototypes can only constrain, but do not determine, models of representation. A representation of categories in terms of conjoined necessary and sufficient attributes alone would probably be incapable of handling all of the presently known facts, but there are many representations other than necessary and sufficient attributes that are possible.

4. Although prototypes must be learned, they do not constitute any particular theory of category learning. For example, learning of prototypicality in the types of categories examined in Rosch and Mervis (1975) could be represented in terms of counting attribute frequency (as in Neuman 1974), in terms of storage of a set of exemplars to which one later matched the input (see Shepp 1978 and the introduction to Part II of Rosch and Lloyd 1978), or in terms of explicit teaching of the prototypes once prototypicality within a category is established in a culture (e.g., "Now that's a *real* coat.")

In short, prototypes only constrain but do not specify representation and process models. In addition, such models further constrain each other. For example, one could not argue for a frequency count of attributes in children's learning of prototypes of categories if one had reason to believe that children's representation of attributes did not allow for separability and selective attention to each attribute (see Garner 1978 and the introduction to Part II of Rosch and Lloyd 1978).

Two Problematical Issues

The Nature of Perceived Attributes   The derivations of basic objects and of prototypes from the basic principles of categorization have depended on the notion of a structure in the perceived world—bundles of perceived world attributes that formed natural discontinuities. When the research on basic objects and their prototypes was initially conceived (Rosch et al. 1976a), I thought of such attributes as inherent in the real world. Thus, given an organism that had sensory equipment capable of perceiving attributes such as wings and feathers, it was a fact in the real world that wings and feathers co-occurred. The state of knowledge of a person might be ignorant of (or indifferent or inattentive to) the attributes or might know of the attributes but be ignorant concerning their correlation. Conversely, a person might know of the attributes and their correlational structure but exaggerate that structure, turning partial into complete correlations (as when attributes true only of many members of a category are thought of as true of all members). However, the environment was thought to constrain categorizations in that human knowledge could not provide correlational structure where there was none at all. For purposes of the basic object experiments, perceived attributes were operationally defined as those attributes listed by our subjects. Shape was defined as measured by our computer programs. We thus seemed to have our system grounded comfortably in the real world.

On contemplation of the nature of many of the attributes listed by our subjects, however, it appeared that three types of attributes presented a problem for such a realistic view: (1) some attributes, such as "seat" for the object "chair," appeared to have names that showed them not to be meaningful prior to knowledge of the object as chair; (2) some attributes such as "large" for the object "piano" seemed to have meaning only in relation to categorization of the object in terms of a superordinate category—piano is large for furniture but small for other kinds of objects such as buildings; (3) some attributes such as "you eat on it" for the object "table" were functional attributes that seemed to require knowledge about humans, their activities, and the real world in order to be understood (see Miller 1978). That is, it appeared that the analysis of objects into attributes was a rather sophisticated activity that our subjects (and indeed a system of cultural knowledge) might well be considered to be able to impose only *after* the development of the category system.

In fact, the same laws of cognitive economy leading to the push toward basic-level categories and prototypes might also lead to the definition of attributes of categories such that the categories once given would appear maximally distinctive from one another and such that the more prototypical items would appear even more representative of their own and less representative of contrastive categories. Actually, in the evolution of the meaning of terms in languages, probably both the constraint of real-world factors and the construction and reconstruction of attributes are continually present. Thus, given a particular category system, attributes are defined such as to make the system appear as logical and economical as possible. However, if such a system becomes markedly out of phase with real-world constraints, it will probably tend to evolve to be more in line with those constraints—with redefinition of attributes ensuing if necessary. Unfortunately, to state the matter in such a way is to provide no clear place at which we can enter the system as analytical scientists. What is the unit with which to start our analysis? Partly in order to find a more basic real-world unit for analysis than attributes, we have turned our attention to the contexts in which objects occur—that is, to the culturally defined events in which objects serve as props.

The Role of Context in Basic Level Objects and Prototypes   It is obvious, even in the absence of controlled experimentation, that a man about to buy a chair who is standing in a furniture store surrounded by different chairs among which he must choose will think and speak about chairs at other than the basic level of "chair." Similarly, in regard to prototypes, it is obvious that if asked for the most typical African animal, people of any age will not name the same animal as when asked for the most typical American pet animal. Because interest in context is only beginning, it is not yet clear just what experimentally defined contexts will affect what dependent variables for what categories. But it is predetermined that there will be context effects for both the level of abstraction at which an object is considered and for which items are named, learned, listed, or expected in a category. Does this mean that our findings in regard to basic levels and prototypes are relevant only to the artificial situation of the laboratory in which a context is not specified?

Actually, both basic levels and prototypes are, in a sense, theories about context itself. The basic level of abstraction is that level of abstraction that is appropriate for using, thinking about, or naming an object in most situations in which the object occurs (Rosch et al. 1976a). And when a context is not specified in an experiment, people must contribute their own context. Presumably, they do not do so randomly. Indeed, it seems likely that, in the absence of a specified context, subjects assume what they consider the normal context or situation for occurrence of that object. To make such claims about categories appears to demand an analysis of the actual events in daily life in which objects occur.

The Role of Objects in Events

The attempt we have made to answer the issues of the origin of attributes and the role of context has been in terms of the use of objects in the events of daily human life. The study of events grew out of an interest in categorizations of the flow of experience. That is, our initial interest was in the question of whether any of the principles of categorization we had found useful for understanding concrete objects appeared to apply to the cutting up of the continuity of experience into the discrete bounded temporal units that we call *events*.

Previously, events have been studied primarily from two perspectives in psychology. Within ecological and social psychology, an observer records and attempts to segment the stream of another person's behavior into event sequences (for example, Barker and Wright 1955; Newtson 1976). And within the artificial intelligence tradition, Story Understanders are being constructed that can "comprehend," by means of event scripts, statements about simple, culturally predictable sequences such as going to a restaurant (Shank 1975).

The unit of the event would appear to be a particularly important unit for analysis. Events stand at the interface between an analysis of social structure and culture and an analysis of individual psychology. It may be useful to think of scripts for events as the level of theory at which we can specify how culture and social structure enter the individual mind. Could we use events as the basic unit from which to derive an understanding of objects? Could we view objects as props for the carrying out of events and have the functions, perceptual attributes, and levels of abstraction of objects fall out of their role in such events?

Our research to date has been a study rather than an experiment and more like a pilot study at that. Events were defined neither by observation of others nor by a priori units for scripts but introspectively in the following fashion. Students in a seminar on events were asked to choose a particular evening on which to list the events that they remembered of that day—e.g., to answer the question what did I do? (or what happened to me?) that day by means of a list of the names of the events. They were to begin in the morning. The students were aware of the nature of the inquiry and that the focus of interest was on the units that they would perceive as the appropriate units into which to chunk the days' happenings. After completing the list for that day, they were to do the same sort of lists for events remembered from the previous day, and thus to continue backwards to preceding days until they could remember no more day's events. They also listed events for units smaller and larger than a day: for example, the hour immediately preceding writing and the previous school quarter.

The results were somewhat encouraging concerning the tractability of such a means of study. There was considerable agreement on the kinds of units into which a day should be broken—units such as making coffee, taking a shower, and going to statistics class. No one used much smaller units: That is, units such as picking up the toothpaste tube, squeezing toothpaste onto the brush, etc., never occurred. Nor did people use larger units such as "got myself out of the house in the morning" or "went to all my afternoon classes." Furthermore, the units that were listed did not change in size or type with their recency or remoteness in time to the writing. Thus, for the time unit of the hour preceding writing, components of events were not listed. Nor were larger units of time given for a day a week past than for the day on which the list was composed. Indeed, it was dramatic how, as days further and further in the past appeared, fewer and fewer events were remembered although the type of unit for those that were remembered remained the same. That is, for a day a week past, a student would not say that he now only remembered getting himself out of the house in the morning (though such "summarizing" events could be inferred); rather he either did or did not remember feeding the cat that day (an occurrence that could also be inferred but for which inference and memory were introspectively clearly distinguishable). Indeed, it appeared that events such as "all the morning chores" as a whole do not have a memory representation separate from memory of doing the individual chores—perhaps in the way that superordinate categories, such as furniture, do not appear to be imageable per se apart from imaging individual items in the category. It should be noted that event boundaries appeared to be marked in a reasonable way by factors such as changes of the actors participating with ego, changes in the objects ego interacts with, changes in place, and changes in the type or rate of activity with an object, and by notable gaps in time between two reported events.

A good candidate for the basic level of abstraction for events is the type of unit into which the students broke their days. The events they listed were just those kinds of events for which Shank (1975) has provided scripts. Scripts of events analyze the event into individual units of action; these typically occur in a predictable order. For example, the script for going to a restaurant contains script elements such as entering, going to a table, ordering, eating, and paying. Some recent research has provided evidence for the psychological reality of scripts and their elements (Bower 1976).

Our present concern is with the role of concrete objects in events. What categories of objects are required to serve as props for events at the level of abstraction of those listed by the students? In general, we found that the event name itself combined most readily with superordinate noun categories; thus, one gets dressed with clothes and needs various kitchen utensils to make breakfast. When such activities were analyzed into their script elements, the basic level appeared as the level of abstraction of objects necessary to script the events; e.g., in getting dressed, one puts on pants, sweater, and shoes, and in making breakfast, one cooks eggs in a frying pan.

With respect to prototypes, it appears to be those category members judged the more prototypical that have attributes that enable them to fit into the typical and agreed upon script elements. We are presently collecting normative data on the intersection of common events, the objects associated with those events and the other sets of events associated with those objects.[2] In addition, object names for eliciting events are varied in level of abstraction and in known prototypicality in given categories. Initial results show a similar pattern to that obtained in the earlier research in which it was found that the more typical members of superordinate categories could replace the superordinate in sentence frames generated by subjects told to "make up a sentence" that used the superordinate (Rosch 1977). That is, the task of using a given concrete noun in a sentence appears to be an indirect method of eliciting a statement about the events in which objects play a part; that indirect method showed clearly that prototypical category members are those that can play the role in events expected of members of that category.

The use of deviant forms of object names in narratives accounts for several recently explored effects in the psychological literature. Substituting object names at other than the basic level within scripts results in obviously deviant descriptions. Substitution of superordinates produces just those types of narrative that Bransford and Johnson (1973) have claimed are not comprehended; for example, "The procedure is actually quite simple. First you arrange things into different groups. Of course, one pile may be sufficient [p. 400]." It should be noted in the present context that what Bransford and Johnson call context cues are actually names of basic-level events (e.g., washing clothes) and that one function of hearing the event name is to enable the reader to translate the superordinate terms into basic-level objects and actions. Such a translation appears to be a necessary aspect of our ability to match linguistic descriptions to world knowledge in a way that produces the "click of comprehension."

On the other hand, substitution of subordinate terms for basic-level object names in scripts gives the effect of satire or snobbery. For example, a review (Garis 1975) of a pretentious novel accused of actually being about nothing more than brand-name snobbery concludes, "And so, after putting away my 10-year-old Royal 470 manual and lining up my Mongol number 3 pencils on my Goldsmith Brothers Formica

2. This work is being done by Elizabeth Kreusi.

imitation-wood desk, I slide into my oversize squirrel-skin L. L. Bean slippers and shuffle off to the kitchen. There, holding *Decades* in my trembling right hand, I drop it, *plunk*, into my new Sears 20-gallon, celadon-green Permanex trash can [p. 48]."

Analysis of events is still in its initial stages. It is hoped that further understanding of the functions and attributes of objects can be derived from such an analysis.

Summary

The first part of this chapter showed how the same principles of categorization could account for the taxonomic structure of a category system organized around a basic level and also for the formation of the categories that occur within this basic level. Thus the principles described accounted for both the vertical and horizontal structure of category systems. Four converging operations were employed to establish the claim that the basic level provides the cornerstone of a taxonomy. The section on prototypes distinguished the empirical evidence for prototypes as structural facts about categories from the possible role of prototypes in cognitive processing, representation, and learning. Then we considered assumptions about the nature of the attributes of real-world objects and assumptions about context—insofar as attributes and contexts underlie the claim that there is structure in the world. Finally, a highly tentative pilot study of attributes and functions of objects as props in culturally defined events was presented.

References

Anglin, J. Les premiers termes de référence de l'enfant. In S. Ehrlich and E. Tulving (Eds.), *La memoire sémantique*. Paris: Bulletin de Psychologie, 1976.

Barker, R., and Wright, H. *Midwest and its children*. Evanston, Ill.: Row-Peterson, 1955.

Battig, W. F., and Montague, W. E. Category norms for verbal items in 56 categories: A replication and extension of the Connecticut category norms. *Journal of Experimental Psychology Monograph*, 1969, *80* (3, Pt. 2).

Beach, L. R. Cue probabilism and inference behavior. *Psychological Monographs*. 1964, *78*, (Whole No. 582). (a)

Beach, L. R. Recognition, assimilation, and identification of objects. *Psychological Monographs*, 1964, *78*, (Whole No. 583). (b)

Berlin, B. Speculations on the growth of ethnobotanical nomenclature. *Language in Society*, 1972, *1*, 51–86.

Berlin, B. Ethnobiological Classification. In E. Rosch and B. B. Lloyd (Eds.), *Cognition and Categorization*. Hillsdale, NJ: Lawrence Erlbaum Associates, Inc., 1978.

Borges, J. L. *Other inquisitions 1937–1952*. New York: Washington Square Press, 1966.

Bower, G. *Comprehending and recalling stories*. Paper presented as Division 3 presidential address to the American Psychological Association, Washington, D.C., September 1976.

Bransford, J. D., and Johnson, M. K. Considerations of some problems of comprehension. In W. Chase (Ed.), *Visual information processing*. New York: Academic Press, 1973.

Bruner, J. S., Olver, R. R., and Greenfield, P. M. *Studies in cognitive growth*. New York: Wiley, 1966.

Garis, L. The Margaret Mead of Madison Avenue. *Ms.*, March 1975, pp. 47–48.

Garner, W. R. *The processing of information and structure*. New York: Wiley, 1974.

Garner, W. R. Aspects of a Stimulus: Features, Dimensions, and Configurations. In E. Rosch and B. B. Lloyd (Eds.), *Cognition and Categorization*. Hillsdale, NJ: Lawrence Erlbaum Associates, Inc., 1978.

Kay, P. Taxonomy and semantic contrast. *Language*, 1971, *47*, 866–887.

Kosslyn, S. M. Imagery and Internal Representation. In E. Rosch and B. B. Lloyd (Eds.), *Cognition and Categorization*. Hillsdale, NJ: Lawrence Erlbaum Associates, Inc., 1978.

Lakoff, G. Hedges: A study in meaning criteria and the logic of fuzzy concepts. *Papers from the eighth regional meeting, Chicago Linguistics Society*. Chicago: University of Chicago Linguistics Department, 1972.

Miller, G. A. Practical and Lexical Knowledge. In E. Rosch and B. B. Lloyd (Eds.), *Cognition and Categorization*. Hillsdale, NJ: Lawrence Erlbaum Associates, Inc., 1978.

Nelson, K. Concept, word and sentence: Interrelations in acquisition and development. *Psychological Review*, 1974, *81*, 267–285.

Neuman, P. G. An attribute frequency model for the abstraction of prototypes. *Memory and Cognition*, 1974, *2*, 241–248.

Newport, E. L., and Bellugi, U. Linguistic Expression of Category Levels in a Visual-Gestural Language: A Flower Is a Flower Is a Flower. In E. Rosch and B. B. Lloyd (Eds.), *Cognition and Categorization*. Hillsdale, NJ: Lawrence Erlbaum Associates, Inc., 1978.

Newtson, D. Foundations of attribution: The perception of ongoing behavior. In J. Harvey, W. Ickes, and R. Kidd (Eds.), *New directions in attribution research*. Hillsdale, N.J.: Lawrence Erlbaum Associates, 1976.

Palmer, S. Hierarchical structure in perceptual representation. *Cognitive Psychology*, 1977, *9*, 441–474.

Palmer, S. E. Fundamental Aspects of Cognitive Representation. In E. Rosch and B. B. Lloyd (Eds.), *Cognition and Categorization*. Hillsdale, NJ: Lawrence Erlbaum Associates, Inc., 1978.

Peterson, M. J., and Graham, S. E. Visual detection and visual imagery. *Journal of Experimental Psychology*, 1974, *103*, 509–514.

Piaget, J. *The origins of intelligence in children*. New York: International Universities Press, 1952.

Posner, M. I., Goldsmith, R., and Welton, K. E. Perceived distance and the classification of distorted patterns. *Journal of Experimental Psychology*, 1967, *73*, 28–38.

Reed, S. K. Pattern recognition and categorization. *Cognitive Psychology*, 1972, *3*, 382–407.

Rips, L. J., Shoben, E. J., and Smith, E. E. Semantic distance and the verification of semantic relations. *Journal of Verbal Learning and Verbal Behavior*, 1973, *12*, 1–20.

Rosch, E. On the internal structure of perceptual and semantic categories. In T. E. Moore (Ed.), *Cognitive development and the acquisition of language*. New York: Academic Press, 1973.

Rosch, E. Linguistic relativity. In A. Silverstein (Ed.), *Human communication: Theoretical perspectives*. New York: Halsted Press, 1974.

Rosch, E. Cognitive reference points. *Cognitive Psychology*, 1975, *7*, 532–547. (a)

Rosch, E. Cognitive representations of semantic categories. *Journal of Experimental Psychology: General.*, 1975, *104*, 192–233. (b)

Rosch, E. The nature of mental codes for color categories. *Journal of Experimental Psychology: Human Perception and Performance*, 1975, *1*, 303–322. (c)

Rosch, E. Universals and cultural specifics in human categorization. In R. Brislin, S. Bochner, and W. Lonner (Eds.), *Cross-cultural perspectives on learning*. New York: Halsted Press, 1975. (d)

Rosch, E. Human categorization. In N. Warren (Ed.), *Advances in cross-cultural psychology* (Vol. 1). London: Academic Press, 1977.

Rosch, E., and Lloyd, B. B. *Cognition and Categorization*. Hillsdale, NJ: Lawrence Erlbaum Associates, Inc., 1978.

Rosch, E., and Mervis, C. B. Family resemblances: Studies in the internal structure of categories. *Cognitive Psychology*, 1975, *7*, 573–605.

Rosch, E., Mervis, C. B., Gray, W. D., Johnson, D. M., and Boyes-Braem, P. Basic objects in natural categories. *Cognitive Psychology*, 1976, *8*, 382–439. (a)

Rosch, E., Simpson, C., and Miller, R. S. Structural bases of typicality effects. *Journal of Experimental Psychology: Human Perception and Performance.* 1976, *2*, 491–502. (b)

Shank, R. C. The structure of episodes in memory. In D. G. Bobrow and A. Collins (Eds.), *Representation and understanding: Studies in cognitive science*. New York: Academic Press, 1975.

Shepp, B. E. From Perceived Similarity to Dimensional Structure: A New Hypothesis About Perspective Development. In E. Rosch and B. B. Lloyd (Eds.), *Cognition and Categorization*. Hillsdale, NJ: Lawrence Erlbaum Associates, Inc., 1978.

Smith, E. E. Theories of semantic memory. In W. K. Estes (Ed.), *Handbook of learning and cognitive processes* (Vol. 5). Hillsdale, N.J.: Lawrence Erlbaum Associates, 1978.

Smith, E. E., and Balzano, G. J. Personal communication, April 1977.

Smith, E. E., Balzano, G. J., and Walker, J. H. Nominal, perceptual, and semantic codes in picture categorization. In J. Cotton and R. Klatzky (Eds.), *Semantic factors in cognition*. Hillsdale, N.J.: Lawrence Erlbaum Associates, 1978.

Tversky, A. Features of similarity. *Psychological Review*, 1977, *84*, 327–352.

Tversky, A., and Gati, I. Studies of Similarity. In E. Rosch and B. B. Lloyd (Eds.), *Cognition and Categorization*. Hillsdale, NJ: Lawrence Erlbaum Associates, Inc., 1978.

Wittgenstein, L. *Philosophical investigations*. New York: Macmillan, 1953.

Chapter 9

The Exemplar View

Edward Smith and Douglas Medin

In this chapter we take up our third view of concepts, the exemplar view. Since this view is quite new and has not been extensively developed, we will not give separate treatments of featural, dimensional, and holistic approaches. Instead, we will sometimes rely on featural descriptions, other times on dimensional ones.

Rationale for the Exemplar View

As its name suggests, the exemplar view holds that concepts are represented by their exemplars (at least in part) rather than by an abstract summary. This idea conflicts not only with the previous views but also with common intuitions. To talk about concepts means for most people to talk about abstractions; but if concepts are represented by their exemplars, there appears to be no room for abstractions. So we first need some rationale for this seemingly bold move.

Aside from a few extreme cases, the move is nowhere as bold as it sounds because the term *exemplar* is often used ambiguously; it can refer either to a specific instance of a concept or to a subset of that concept. An exemplar of the concept clothing, for example, could be either "your favorite pair of faded blue jeans" or the subset of clothing that corresponds to blue jeans in general. In the latter case, the so-called "exemplar" is of course an abstraction. Hence, even the exemplar view permits abstractions.[1]

A second point is that some models based on the exemplar view do not exclude summary-type information (for example, the context model of Medin and Schaffer, 1978). Such models might, for example, represent the information that "all clothing is intended to be worn" (this is summary information), yet at the same time represent exemplars of clothing. The critical claim of such models, though, is that the exemplars usually play the dominant role in categorization, presumably because they are more accessible than the summary information.

These rationales for the exemplar view accentuate the negative—roughly speaking, the view is plausible because its representations are *not* really restricted to specific exemplars. Of course, there are also positive reasons for taking this view. A number of studies in different domains indicate that people frequently use exemplars when making decisions and categorizations. In the experiments of Kahneman and Tversky (1973), for example, it was found that when subjects try to estimate the relative frequencies of occurrence of particular classes of events, they tend to retrieve a few

---

1. While "your favorite pair of faded blue jeans" is something of an abstraction in that it abstracts over situations, it seems qualitatively less abstract than blue jeans in general, which abstracts over different entities.

exemplars from the relevant classes and base their estimates on these exemplars. To illustrate, when asked if there are more four-letter words in English that (1) begin with *k* or (2) have *k* as their third letter, subjects consistently opt for the former alternative (which is incorrect); presumably they do so because they can rapidly generate more exemplars that begin with *k*. In studies of categorization, subjects sometimes decide that a test item is *not* an instance of a target category by retrieving a counterexample; for example, subjects base their negative decision to "All birds are eagles" on their rapid retrieval of the exemplar "robins" (Holyoak and Glass, 1975). And if people use exemplar retrieval to make negative decisions about category membership, they may also use exemplars as positive evidence of category membership (see Collins and Loftus, 1975; Holyoak and Glass, 1975).

The studies mentioned above merely scratch the surface of what is rapidly becoming a substantial body of evidence for the use of exemplars in categorical decisions (see, for example, Walker, 1975; Reber, 1976; Brooks, 1978; Medin and Schaffer, 1978; Kossan, 1978; Reber and Allen, 1978. This body of literature constitutes the best rationale for the exemplar view.

Concept Representations and Categorization Processes

The Critical Assumption

There is probably only one assumption that all proponents of the exemplar view would accept: The representation of a concept consists of separate descriptions of some of its exemplars (either instances or subsets). Figure 9.1 illustrates this assumption. In the figure the concept of bird is represented in terms of some of its exemplars. The exemplars themselves can be represented in different ways, partly depending on whether they are themselves subsets (like robin, bluejay, and sparrow) or instances (the pet canary "Fluffy"). If the exemplar is a subset, its representation can consist either of other exemplars, or of a description of the relevant properties, or both (these possibilities are illustrated in Figure 9.1). On the other hand, if the exemplar is an instance, it must be represented by a property description. In short, the representation is explicitly disjunctive, and the properties of a concept are the sum of the exemplar's properties.

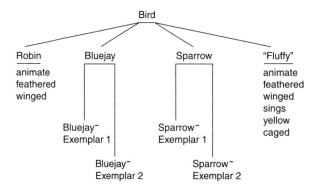

Figure 9.1
An exemplar representation

This assumption conflicts with that of a summary representation, and it is useful to pinpoint the extent of the conflict. Recall that we use three criteria for a summary representation: it is the result of an abstraction process, it need not correspond to a specific instance, and it is always applied when a question of category membership arises. To what extent is each of these criteria violated by the above assumption? We can best answer this by considering each criterion in turn.

The representation in Figure 9.1 shows a clear-cut lack of abstraction in two respects. First, it contains a specific instance, "Fluffy"; second, it contains subsets (for example, robin and bluejay) whose properties overlap enough to permit some amalgamation. Note, however, that the very fact that some exemplars are subsets means that some abstraction has taken place. Thus lack of abstraction is a matter of degree, and our safest conclusion is that exemplar-based representations show a substantially greater lack of abstraction than representations based on the classical or the probabilistic view. This aspect, as we shall see, is the only thing common to all present models based on the exemplar view; so it is the real meat of the critical assumption.

The representation in Figure 9.1 also seems at odds with our second criterion, for it contains a component corresponding to a specific instance. Again, the offender is our friend "Fluffy." But if we remove this instance, the representation still qualifies as an exemplar one. That is, some models based on the exemplar view (for example, Medin and Schaffer, 1978) permit representations with no specific instances. Thus, whether or not part of a representation corresponds to a instance is a point on which various exemplar models vary, not a criterion for being an exemplar model.

Finally, there is the summary-representation criterion that the same information is always accessed when category membership is being determined. This issue concerns categorization processes, so the sample representation in Figure 9.1 is neutral on this point. Once we consider categorization models based on the exemplar view, it turns out that some violate this criterion (for example, different test items would access different exemplars in the representation in Figure 9.1), while others are consistent with the criterion (for example, the entire representation in Figure 9.1 would always be accessed when there is a question of birdhood). Again, then, the criterion is really a choice point for various exemplar models.

The Proximity Model as an Extreme Case

We have seen that the critical assumption behind the present view is that the representation lacks abstraction and is "needlessly disjunctive." All exemplar models violate this criterion of a summary representation. Exemplar models differ among themselves, however, with respect to the other two criteria of summary representations; consequently some exemplar models depart from previous views more than others. To appreciate this, it is useful to consider briefly an extreme case of the exemplar view, the *proximity* model (see Reed, 1972). This model violates all three criteria of a summary representation.

In the proximity model each concept is represented by all of its instances that have been encountered. When a novel test item is presented along with a target category, the test item automatically retrieves the item in memory that is most similar to it. The test item will be categorized as an instance of the target concept if and only if the retrieved item is a known instance of that concept. Thus: (1) the concept representation is lacking entirely in abstraction; (2) every exemplar in the representation is realizable as an instance; and (3) the information retrieved in making a decision about a particular concept varies with the test item presented.

Since the proximity model leaves no room at all for abstraction, it conflicts with the intuitions we mentioned earlier. There is another obvious problem with the model. Adults have experienced an enormous number of instances for most natural concepts, and it seems highly implausible that each instance would be a separate part of the representation; the memory load seems too great. For an exemplar model to be plausible, then, there must be some means of restricting the exemplars in the representation. The models that we now consider attempt to do this.

Models of Categorization

Best-Examples Model

Assumptions Though Rosch explicitly disavows a concern with models (1975, 1978), her work—and that of her collaborator, Mervis, (1980)—points to a particular kind of categorization model. In the following discussion, we will try to develop it.

In addition to the assumption of exemplar descriptions, the best-examples model assumes that the representation is restricted to exemplars that are typical of the concept—what Rosch often refers to as the *focal instances* (1975). More specifically:

> (1) The exemplars represented are those that share some criterial number of properties with other exemplars of the concept; that is, the exemplars have some criterial family resemblance score. (Since family resemblance is highly correlated with typicality, this amounts to assuming that the exemplars represented meet some criterial level of typicality.)

This assumption raises some questions. First, why leave room for multiple typical exemplars rather than restricting the representation to the single best example? A good reason for not using such a restriction comes directly from data. Inspection of actual family resemblance scores indicates that usually a few instances share the highest score (Rosch and Mervis, 1975; Malt and Smith, 1981). Similarly, inspection of virtually any set of typicality ratings (for example, Rips, Shoben, and Smith, 1973; Rosch, 1975) shows that two or more instances attain comparable maximal ratings. Another reason for permitting multiple best examples is that some superordinate concepts seem to demand them. It is hard to imagine that the concept of animal, for instance, has a single best example; at a minimum, it seems to require best examples of bird, mammal, and fish.

A second question about our best-examples assumption is, How does the learner determine the best exemplars? This question is difficult to answer; all we can do is to mention a few possibilities. At one extreme, the learner might first abstract a summary representation of the concept, then compare this summary to each exemplar, with the closest matches becoming the best exemplars, and finally discard the summary representation. Though this proposal removes any mystery from the determination of best examples, it seems wildly implausible. Why bother with determining best examples when you already have a summary representation? And why ever throw the latter away? A second possibility seems more in keeping with the exemplar view. The learner stores whatever exemplars are first encountered, periodically computes the equivalent of each one's family resemblance score, and maintains only those with high scores. The problem with this method is that it might attribute more computations to the learner than are actually necessary. Empirical data indicate that the initial exemplars encountered tend to have high family resemblance scores; for instance, Anglin's results (1977) indicate that parents tend to teach typical exemplars before atypical ones. This suggests a very simply solution to how best examples are learned—namely, they are taught. The simplicity is misleading, however; for now we need an account of how the teachers determine the best examples. No doubt they too were taught, but this instructional regress must stop somewhere. At some point in this account there must be a computational process like the ones described above.

In any event, given a concept representation that is restricted to the most typical exemplars, we can turn to some processing assumptions that will flesh out the model. These assumptions concern our paradigm case of categorization—an individual must decide whether or not a test item is a member of a target concept. One possible set of assumptions holds that:

(2a) All exemplars in the concept representation are retrieved and are available for comparison to the test item.

(2b) The test item is judged to be a concept member if and only if it provides a sufficient match to at least one exemplar.

If the matching process for each exemplar is like one of those considered in previous chapters [of Smith and Medin 1981—EM&SL]—for example, exemplars and test item are described by features, and a sufficient match means accumulating a criterial sum of weighted features—then our exemplar-based model is a straightforward extension of models considered earlier. Since few new ideas would arise in fleshing out this proposal, we will adopt an alternative set of processing assumptions.

The alternative is taken from Medin and Schaffer's context model (1978). (Since this is the only exemplar model other than the best-examples model that we will consider, it simplifies matters to use the same set of processing assumptions.) The assumptions of interest are as follows:

(3a) An entity X is categorized as an instance or subset of concept Y if and only if X retrieves a criterial number of Y's exemplars before retrieving a criterial number of exemplars from any contrasting concept.

(3b) The probability that entity X retrieves any specific exemplar is a direct function of the similarity of X and that exemplar.

To illustrate, consider a case where a subject is given a pictured entity (the test item) and asked to decide whether or not it is a bird (the target concept). To keep things simple, let us assume for now that categorization is based on the first exemplar retrieved (the criterial number of exemplars is 1). The presentation of the picture retrieves an item from memory—an exemplar from some concept or other. Only if the retrieved item is a known bird exemplar would one categorize the pictured entity as a bird (this is assumption 3a). The probability that the retrieved item is in fact a bird exemplar increases with the property similarity of the probe to stored exemplars of bird (this is assumption 3b). Clearly, categorization will be accurate to the extent that a test instance is similar to stored exemplars of its appropriate concept and dissimilar to stored exemplars of a contrast concept.

The process described above amounts to an induction based on a single case. Increasing the criterial number of exemplars for categorization simply raises the number of cases the induction is based on. Suppose one would classify the pictured entity as a bird if and only if k bird exemplars are retrieved. Then the only change in the process would be that one might retrieve a sample of n items from memory $(n > k)$ and classify the pictured item as a bird if and only if one samples k bird exemplars before sampling k exemplars of another concept. Categorization will be accurate to the extend that a test instance is similar to several stored exemplars of the appropriate concept and dissimilar to stored exemplars of contrasting concepts; these same factors will also govern the speed of categorization, assuming that the sampling process takes time.

Note that processing assumptions 3a and 3b differ from the previous ones (2a and 2b) in that the present assumptions postulate that different information in the concept is accessed for different test items. This is one of the theoretical choice points we mentioned earlier.

One more issue remains: How is the similarity between a test instance and an exemplar determined? The answer depends, of course, on how we describe the properties of representation—as features, dimension values, or templates. In keeping with the spirit of Rosch's ideas (for example, Rosch and Mervis, 1975; Rosch et al., 1976), we will use feature descriptions and assume that the similarity between a test instance and an exemplar is a direct measure of shared features.

Explanations of Empirical Phenomena   In this section we will briefly describe how well the model of interest can account for the seven phenomena that troubled the classical view.

> *Disjunctive concepts*   Each concept representation is explicitly disjunctive—an item belongs to a concept if it matches this exemplar, *or* that exemplar, and so on.
> *Unclear cases*   An item can be an unclear case either because it fails to retrieve a criterion number of exemplars from the relevant concept, or because it is as likely to retrieve a criterion number of exemplars from one concept as from another.
> *Failure to specify defining features*   There is no reason why the feature of one exemplar should be a feature of other exemplars; that is, the features need not be necessary ones. And since the concept is disjunctive, there is no need for sufficient features.
> *Simple typicality effect*   There are two bases for typicality ratings. First, since the representation is restricted to typical exemplars, a typical test item is more likely to find an exact match in the concept. Second, for cases where a test item is not identical to a stored exemplar, the more typical the test item the greater is its featural similarity to the stored exemplars. Both factors should also play a role in categorization; for example, since typical instances are more similar to the stored exemplars of a concept, they should retrieve the criterial number of exemplars relatively quickly. And the same factors can be used to explain why typical items are named before atypical ones when concept members are being listed. That is, the exemplars comprising the concept representation function as retrieval cues, and the cues themselves should be named first, followed by instances most similar to them. As for why typical exemplars are learned earlier, we have already considered means by which this could come about; for example, the learner may use a kind of family-resemblance computation to decide which exemplars to maintain.

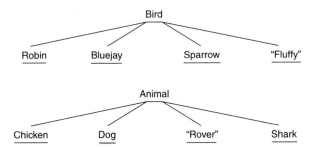

Figure 9.2
Representations that can explain similarity ratings for nested triples.

Determinants of typicality   The fact that typical instances share more features with other concept members is essentially presupposed by the present model.

Use of nonnecessary features   As already noted, there is no requirement that the features of one exemplar be true of all other exemplars.

Nested concepts   Figure 9.2 illustrates why some instances (for example, robin) are judged more similar to their immediate than their distance superordinates, while other instances (for example, chicken) manifest the reverse similarity relations. In this illustration robin is one of the represented exemplars for bird, but not for animal. This alone makes it likely that robin is rated more similar to bird than to animal. On the other hand, chicken is a represented exemplar of animal but not of bird, thereby making it likely that chicken is rated as being more similar to animal. In essence, the set of exemplars in a concept may shift with the level of concept.

Context Model
The context model of Medin and Schaffer (1978) differs from the preceding proposal in two critical respects. One concerns the learning of exemplar representations; the other deals with the computation of similarity in categorization processes. We will consider each issue in turn.

Nature of the representation   To understand the representational assumptions of the context model, we will begin with a simple case. Suppose that subjects in an experiment on artificial concepts have to learn to classify schematic faces into two categories, A and B; the distribution of facial properties for each category is presented abstractly at the top of Figure 9.3. Here the relevant properties will be treated as dimensions. They correspond to eye height (EH), eye separation (ES), nose length (NL), and mouth height (MH). Each dimension can take on one of two values, for example, a short or a long nose; these values are depicted by a binary notation in Figure 9.3. For example, a nose length of 0 indicates a short nose, a value of 1 signals a long nose. The structure of concepts A and B is presumably that of natural concepts—though A and B lack defining conditions, for each concept there are certain dimension values that tend to occur with its instances. The instances of A, for example, tend to have large noses, while those of B favor small noses.

How, according to the context model, is this information represented by the concept learner? The answer depends on the strategies employed. If our concept learner

Category A					Category B				
Instances	Dimension values				Instances	Dimension values			
	EH	ES	NL	MH		EH	ES	NL	MH
1	1	1	1	0	1	1	1	0	0
2	1	0	1	0	2	0	1	1	0
3	1	0	1	1	3	0	0	0	1
4	1	1	0	1	4	0	0	0	0
5	0	1	1	1					

Category A				Category B			
Instances	Dimension values			Instances	Dimension values		
	EH	ES	NL		EH	ES	NL
1'	1	1	1	1'	1	1	0
2'	1	0	1	2'	0	1	1
3'	1	1	0	3'	0	0	0
4'	0	1	1				

Category A	Category B
.8[a] high eyes	.75[a] low eyes

a = weight associated with dimension value.

Figure 9.3
Representational assumptions of the context model.

attends equally to all instances and their dimension values, her final representation should be isomorphic to what is depicted in the top part of Figure 9.3—each exemplar would be represented by its set of values. However, if our concept learner selectively attends to some dimensions more than others—say she ignores mouth-height entirely—her representation should be isomorphic to the middle part of Figure 9.3. Here instances 2 and 3 of concept A have been collapsed into a single exemplar, and the same is true for instances 3 and 4 of concept B (remember, exemplars can be abstract). This strategy-based abstraction can be even more extensive. To take the extreme case, if our learner attends only to eye height, she will end up with concept representations like those at the bottom of Figure 9.3. Here there is no trace of exemplars; instead, the representations are like those in models based on the probabilistic view.

The notion of strategy-based abstraction gives the context model a means of restricting representations to a limited number of exemplars when natural concepts are at issue. (Recall that a plausible exemplar model needs such a restriction.) In particular, suppose that a learner when acquiring a natural concept primarily attends to properties that occur frequently among concept members; then the learner will end up with detailed representations of typical exemplars, which contain the focused properties, but with only incomplete or collapsed representations of atypical exemplars, which do not contain the focused properties. In this way the context model can derive the notion that typical exemplars dominate the representation, rather than assuming this notion outright as is done in the best-examples model. In addition, the context model can assume that in the usual artificial concept study, where there are very few items, each exemplar is fully represented (unless instructions encourage otherwise). Hence in artificial-concept studies, the context model's representations may differ substantially from those assumed by the best-examples model.

Similarity Computations in Categorization   The general assumptions about categorization processes in the present model are identical to those in the best-examples model (this is no accident, since we deliberately used the context model's assumptions in developing the best-examples proposal). To reiterate these assumptions:

(3a) An entity X is categorized as an instance or subset of the concept Y if and only if X retrieves a criterial number of Y's exemplars before retrieving a criterial number of exemplars from any constrasting concept.

(3b) The probability that entity X retrieves any specific exemplar is a direct function of the similarity of X and that exemplar.

There is, however, an important difference between the context model and the previous one with regard to how these assumptions are instantiated. The difference concerns how similarity, the heart of assumption 3b, is computed.

Thus far, whenever we have detailed a similarity computation we have used an *additive* combination. In featural models, the similarity between a test item and a concept representation (whether it is summary or an exemplar) has been some additive combination of the individual feature matches and mismatches. In dimensional models, similarity between test item and concept representation has been measured by an additive combination of differences on component dimensions. This notion of additivity is rejected by the context model. According to the present model, computing the similarity between test instances and exemplar involves *multiplying* differences along component dimensions.

This process is illustrated in Figure 9.4. The top half repeats some representations given in the previous figure. Associated with each dimensional difference is a similarity parameter, α_i, with high values indicating high similarity. Thus α_{NL} is a measure of the similarity between a long and a short nose. Two factors can decrease the size of each parameter, that is, decrease the similarity between the values of a dimension. One factor is the psychophysical difference between the two values of a dimension; the other is the salience of the dimension, which is itself determined by the attentional and strategy considerations that we discussed earlier. Given a fixed set of parameters, one computes similarity between test item and exemplar by multiplying the four parameters. As examples, the similarity between a test item and exemplar that have different values on every dimension would be $\alpha_{EH} \cdot \alpha_{ES} \cdot \alpha_{NL} \cdot \alpha_{MH}$, while the similarity between a test item and exemplar that have identical values on all dimensions would be $1 \cdot 1 \cdot 1 \cdot 1 = 1$. Some intermediate cases are shown in the middle part of Figure 9.4. The bottom part of Figure 9.4 shows how these similarity computations between test item and exemplar are cumulated over all relevant exemplars to derive a final categorization of the test item. The probability of assigning test item to, say, concept A is equal to the sum of the similarities of the test items to all stored exemplars of A, divided by the sum of the similarities of the test item to all stored exemplars of both A and B (this instantiates assumption 3b).

How much hinges on computing similarity by a multiplicative rule rather than by an additive one? Quite a bit, as the two cases illustrated in the middle part of Figure

Sample representations

Category A					Category B				
Instances	Dimension values				Instances	Dimension values			
	EH	ES	NL	MH		EH	ES	NL	MH
1	1	1	1	0	1	1	1	0	0
2	1	0	1	0	2	0	1	1	0
3	1	0	1	1	3	0	0	0	1
4	1	1	0	1	4	0	0	0	0
5	0	1	1	1					

Sample compulations for Category A exemplars

$S(A1, A1)^* = 1 \cdot 1 \cdot 1 \cdot 1 = 1.0$ $\qquad$ $S(A2, A1) = 1 \cdot \alpha_{ES} \cdot 1 \cdot 1 = \alpha_{ES}$

$S(A1, A2) = 1 \cdot \alpha_{ES} \cdot 1 \cdot 1 = \alpha_{ES}$ $\qquad$ $S(A2, A2) = 1 \cdot 1 \cdot 1 \cdot 1 = 1.0$

$S(A1, A3) = 1 \cdot \alpha_{ES} \cdot 1 \cdot \alpha_{MH}$ $\qquad$ $S(A2, A3) = 1 \cdot 1 \cdot 1 \cdot \alpha_{MH}$
$\qquad\quad = \alpha_{ES} \cdot \alpha_{MH}$ $\qquad\qquad\qquad = \alpha_{MH}$

$S(A1, A4) = 1 \cdot 1 \cdot \alpha_{NL} \cdot \alpha_{MH}$ $\qquad$ $S(A2, A4) = 1 \cdot \alpha_{ES} \cdot \alpha_{NL} \cdot \alpha_{MH}$
$\qquad\quad = \alpha_{NL} \cdot \alpha_{MH}$ $\qquad\qquad\qquad = \alpha_{ES} \cdot \alpha_{NL} \cdot \alpha_{MH}$

$S(A1, A5) = \alpha_{EH} \cdot 1 \cdot 1 \cdot \alpha_{MH}$ $\qquad$ $S(A2, A5) = \alpha_{EH} \cdot \alpha_{ES} \cdot 1 \cdot \alpha_{MH}$
$\qquad\quad = \alpha_{EH} \cdot \alpha_{MH}$ $\qquad\qquad\qquad = \alpha_{EH} \cdot \alpha_{MH}$

Final categorization

$P(A1 \subset \text{Category A})^{**}$

$$= \frac{1.0 + \alpha_{ES} + \alpha_{ES} \cdot \alpha_{MH} + \alpha_{NL} \cdot \alpha_{MH} + \alpha_{EH} \cdot \alpha_{MH}}{\sum_X S(A1, X)}$$

$P(A2 \subset \text{Category A})$

$$= \frac{\alpha_{ES} + 1.0 + \alpha_{MH} + \alpha_{ES} \cdot \alpha_{NL} \cdot \alpha_{MH} + \alpha_{EH} \cdot \alpha_{ES} \cdot \alpha_{MH}}{\sum_X S(A2, X)}$$

*$S(i, j)$ = Similarity between i and j
**$P(i \subset \text{Category A})$ = Probability that i is
$\qquad\qquad\qquad\qquad\quad$ assigned to Category A

Figure 9.4
How the context model computes similarity.

9.4 demonstrate. Following the multiplicative rule, instance 2 should be easier to learn and categorize than instance 1. This essentially reflects the fact that instance 2 is highly similar (that is, differing on only one dimension) to two exemplars of category A (instances 1 and 3) but is not highly similar to any exemplar of concept B; instance 1, on the other hand, is highly similar to only one exemplar in A (instance 2) but to the first two exemplars in B. Had we computed similarity by an additive rule, this prediction would reverse. This can be seen by noting that instance 1 shares an average of more than two values with other exemplars of A, while instance 2 shares an average of exactly two values with other A exemplars. (Both instances share the same average number of values with B exemplars.) These contrasting predictions were tested in a number of artificial-concept experiments by Medin and Schaffer (1978), and the results uniformly supported the multiplicative rule: instance 2 was learned faster and categorized more efficiently than instance 1. In a follow-up study

(Medin and Smith, 1981) we found that the superiority of instance 2 held across widely different instructions, including ones that implicitly suggested an additive rule to subjects.

Admittedly, this particular contrast between multiplicative and additive similarity computations is highly specific, and is probably only realizable with artificial materials. Still, it provides some basis for favoring the context model's way of instantiating the exemplar-based processing assumptions over that specified by the best-examples model. Other reasons for favoring the multiplicative rule will be given later in the chapter.

Explanations of Empirical Phenomena   There is no need to detail how the context model handles our standard list of phenomena, since these accounts are virtually identical to those given for the best-examples model. Again, the explicitly disjunctive nature of an exemplar-based representation immediately accounts for the existence of disjunctive concepts, the failure to specify defining properties, and the use of non-necessary properties during categorization. And to the extent that the learning strategies posited by the context model eventuate in a representation dominated by typical exemplars, the model would explain typicality effects in the same manner as the best-examples model.

Criticisms of the Exemplar View

Having discussed some of the strengths of the exemplar view, we now consider its weaknesses. We will first take up those difficulties that the present view shares with the probabilistic one; that is, problems in (1) representing all the knowledge in concepts, (2) constraining possible properties, and (3) accounting for context effects. Then we will consider a fourth set of problems—those that are specific to the exemplar view's critical assumption that a concept is represented by a disjunction of exemplars.

Representing More Knowledge in Concepts

To return to our standard example, how can we represent the knowledge that the properties "small" and "sings" tend to be correlated across exemplars of the concept of bird? Note that the solutions we considered in conjunction with the probabilistic view, such as labeling relations between properties, are irrelevant here. For in the present view exemplars tend to be represented separately, so how can we represent something that pertains to all exemplars?

The most promising solution appears to be this: knowledge about a correlation between properties is *computed* from an exemplar-based representation when needed, rather than *prestored* in the representation. We can illustrate with the kind of representation used in the best-examples model. Suppose that the concept of bird is represented by two best examples, one corresponding to robin, the other to eagle. Then one can compute the negative correlation between size and singing ability by noting that the best example that is small (robin) also sings, while the best example that is large (eagle) does not. More generally, to the extent that each best example contains properties that characterize a particular cluster of instances (for example, many of a robin's properties also apply to bluejays and sparrows), then property differences between best examples reflect correlations among properties in the instances at large.

Another kind of additional knowledge that we have routinely been concerned with has to do with variability in properties associated with a concept. Some knowledge of this sort is implicit in any exemplar representation. The different exemplars represented must manifest some differences in their features or dimension values, and one can use these differences to compute estimates of property variability. The problem, though, is that these computations would probably yield smaller estimates of variability than those actually obtained in relevant experiments (Walker, 1975). This would clearly be the case for computations based on best-examples representations, since only a few highly typical exemplars are represented here, and typical exemplars show only limited variation in their properties (see Rosch and Mervis, 1975). The situation seems more promising for the contest model: it is at least compatible with a concept representation containing multiple exemplars, some of which may be atypical, and its representations therefore permit a more realistic computation of property-variability.

Lack of Constraints
There really are two problems involving constraints with the exemplar view: a lack of constraints on the properties associated with any exemplar, and a lack of constraints on the relations between exemplars included in the same representation. We will treat only the first problem here, saving the second for our discussion of problems specific to the exemplar view.

We start with the obvious. For exemplars corresponding to instances, there is no issue of specifying constraints in the form of necessary or sufficient properties, since we are dealing with individuals. So the following applies only to exemplars that correspond to subsets of a concept, for example, the exemplars "chair" and "table" of the concept "furniture." With regard to the latter kind of exemplar, the problem of unconstrained properties *vis-à-vis* an exemplar is identical to that problem *vis-à-vis* a summary representation. This is so because a subset-exemplar is a summary representation of that subset—there need be no difference between the representation of chair when it is included as one component of an exemplar representation of furniture and when it stands alone as a probabilistic representation. Hence, all our suggestions about how to constrain properties in probabilistic representations apply *mutatis mutandis* to exemplar representations. For the best-examples model, then, there may be a need to specify some necessary features, *or* some sufficient ones, for each exemplar represented in a concept; otherwise we are left with problems such as the exemplar permitting too great a degree of disjunctiveness.

The same, of course, holds for the context model, but here one can naturally incorporate necessary properties via similarity parameters and the multiplicative rule for computing similarity. Specifically, a dimension is a necessary one to the extent that its similarity parameter goes to zero when values on the dimension increasingly differ; and given a near-zero value on one parameter, the multiplication rule ensures that the product of all relevant parameters will also be close to zero. An illustration should be helpful: a creature 90 feet tall might possibly be classified as a human being, but one 9,000 feet tall would hardly be. In the former case, the parameter associated with the height difference between the creature and known human beings would be small but nonzero; in the latter case, the parameter for height difference might be effectively zero, and consequently the overall, multiplicative similarity between creature and human being would be effectively zero regardless of how many other properties they shared. In essence, we have specified a necessary range of values along the height dimension for human beings. To the extent that this is a useful means of capturing property constraints, we have another reason for favoring multiplicative over additive rules in computing similarity.

Context Effects
Thus far little has been done in analyzing context effects of the sort we described in conjunction with the probabilistic view. We will merely point out here what seems to us to be the most natural way for exemplar models to approach context effects.

The basic idea is that prior context raises the probability of retrieving some exemplars in representation. To return to our standard example of "The man lifted the piano," the context preceding "piano" may increase the availability of exemplars of heavy pianos (that is, exemplars whose representations emphasize the property of weight), thereby making it likely that one of them will actually be retrieved when "piano" occurs. This effect of prior context is itself reducible to similarity consideration; for example, the context in the above sentence is more similar to some piano exemplars than to others. Retrievability is thus still governed by similarity to stored exemplars, and our proposal amounts to increasing the factors that enter into the similarity computation.

The above proposal seems workable to the extent that a representation contains numerous exemplars. If there are only a few exemplars, then many contexts will fail to activate a similar exemplar. To illustrate, consider the sentence "The holiday platter held a large bird," where the context seems to activate a meaning of bird akin to chicken or turkey. If the representation of bird is restricted to a few typical exemplars, like robin and eagle, there is no way the preceding context effect can be accounted for. Since the best-examples model is restricted in just this way, it will have difficulty accounting for many context effects through differential retrievability of exemplars. The context model is less committed to this kind of restriction, and thus may fare better.

Problems Specific to Exemplar Representations
We see two major problems that stem from the assumption that a concept is represented by a disjunction of exemplars. The first concerns the relation between the disjunctions; the second, the learning of summary information. Both can be stated succinctly.

According to the ideas presented thus far, the only relation between the exemplars in a given representation is that they all point to the same concept. But "exemplars that point to the same concept" can be a trait of totally unnatural concepts. For example, let FURDS be the "concept" represented by the exemplars of chair, table, robin, and eagle; again each exemplar points to the same "concept," but this collection of exemplars will not meet anyone's pretheoretical notion of a concept. The point is that the exemplar view has failed to specify principled constraints on the relation between exemplars that can be joined in a representation.

Since any added constraint must deal with the relation between concept exemplars, the constraint must be something that applies to all exemplars. For the concept of furniture, it might be that all the exemplars tend to be found in living spaces, or are likely to be used for some specific purpose. Positing such a constraint therefore amounts to positing something that *summarizes* all exemplars. In short, any added constraint forces a retreat from a pure exemplar representation toward the direction of a summary representation. The retreat, however, need not be total. The summary constraints may be far less accessible than the exemplars themselves (perhaps because the former are less concrete than the latter), and consequently categorization might be based mainly on exemplars. This proposal would leave the currently formulated exemplar models with plenty of explanatory power; it also seems compatible with Medin and Schaffer's statement of the context model (1978), which does not prohibit properties that apply to the entire concept. But whether our proposal is compatible with the spirit behind the best-examples model (that is, the work of Rosch and her colleagues) is at best debatable.

With regard to learning summary information, we are concerned with the situation where someone (say, an adult) tells a concept learner (say, a child) something like "All birds lay eggs." What, according to the exemplar view, is the learner to do with such information—list it separately with each stored bird exemplar and then throw away the summary information? This seems implausible. What seems more likely is that when one is given summary information, one holds onto it as such. Again, we have a rationale for introducing a bit of a summary representation into exemplar-based models.

Conclusions

With regard to those problems it shares with probabilistic approaches, the exemplar view offers some new ideas about potential solutions. Thus computing property correlations from exemplars that represent different clusters is an interesting alternative to prestoring the correlation, say, by means of a labeled relation. Similarly, accounting for context effects via differential retrieval of exemplars seems a viable alternative to the context-sensitive devices proposed for the probabilistic view. And the context model's multiplicative rule for computing similarity offers a particularly natural way of incorporating necessary properties into representations that can also contain nonnecessary ones. But the exemplar view has two unique problems—specifying relations between disjuncts and handling summary-level information—and the solution to these problems seems to require something of a summary representation. This suggests that it would be a useful move to try to integrate the two views.

References

Anglin, J. M. (1977) *Word, Object and Conceptual Development*. New York: Norton.
Brooks, L. (1978) "Nonanalytic Concept Formation and Memory for Instances." In *Cognition and Categorization*, ed. E. Rosch and B. Lloyd. Hillsdale, NJ: LEA.
Collin, A., and Loftus, E. (1975) "A Spreading Activation Theory of Semantic Processing." *Psychological Review*, 82: 407–28.
Holyoak, K., and Glass, A. (1975) "The Role of Contradictions and Counterexamples in the Rejection of False Sentences." *Journal of Verbal Learning and Verbal Behavior*, 14: 215–39.
Kahneman, D., and Tversky, A. (1973) "On the Psychology of Prediction." *Psychological Review*, 80: 237–51.
Kossan, N. (1978) "Structure and Strategy in Concept Acquisition." Ph.D. Dissertation, Stanford University.
Malt, B., and Smith, E. (1981) "Correlations Structure in Semantic Categories."
Medin, D., and Schafer, M. (1978) "A Context Theory of Classification Learning." *Psychological Review*, 85: 207–38.
Medin, D., and Smith, E. (1981) "Strategies and Classification Learning." *Journal of Experimental Psychology: Human Learning and Memory*.

Mervis, C. (1980) "Category Structure and the Development of Categorization." In *Theoretical Issues in Reading Comprehension*, ed. R. Spiro, B. Bruce, and W. Brewer. Hillsdale, NJ: LEA.

Reber, A. (1976) "Implicit Learning of Synthetic Languages: The Role of Instructional Set." *Journal of Experimental Psychology: Human Memory and Learning*, 2: 88–94.

Reber, A., and Allen, R. (1978) "Analogical and Abstraction Strategies in Synthetic Grammar Learning: A Functionalist Interpretation." *Cognition* 6: 189–221.

Reed, S. (1972) "Pattern Recognition and Categorization." *Cognitive Psychology* 3: 382–407.

Rips, L., Shoben, E., and Smith, E. (1973) "Semantic Distance and the Verification of Semantic Relations." *Journal of Verbal Learning and Verbal Behavior*, 12: 1–20.

Rosch, E. (1975) "Cognitive Representations of Semantic Categories." *Journal of Experimental Psychology: General*, 104: 192 233.

Rosch, E. (1978) "Principles of Categorization." In: *Cognition and Categorization*, ed. E. Rosch and B. Lloyd, 27–48. Hillsdale, NJ: LEA.

Rosch, E., and Mervis, C. (1975) "Family Resemblance Studies in the Internal Structure of Categories." *Cognitive Psychology*, 7: 573–605.

Rosch, E., Mervis, C. Gray, W. Johnson, D., and Boyes-Braem, P. (1976) "Basic Objects in Natural Categories." *Cognitive Psychology*, 3: 382–439.

Smith, E., and Medin, D. (1981) *Categories and Concepts*. Cambridge, MA: Harvard University Press.

Walker, J. (1975) "Real World Variability, Reasonableness Judgements, and Memory Representations for Concepts." *Journal of Verbal Learning and Verbal Behavior*, 14: 241–52.

Critical Reactions to the Probabilistic Turn

Chapter 10

What Some Concepts Might Not Be

*Sharon Lee Armstrong, Lila R. Gleitman, and
Henry Gleitman*

Introduction

Recently, psychologists have renewed their interest in mental categories (concepts) and their learning. As always, part of the basis for this rekindling of interest has to do with some apparently positive findings that seem to make a topic investigatable. In this case, what seems positive are some recent discussions of cluster concepts (as first described by Wittgenstein, 1953) and powerful empirical demonstrations of proto-typicality effects by E. Rosch and others (McCloskey and Glucksberg, 1979; Mervis and Rosch, 1981; Rips, Shoben, and Smith, 1973; Rosch, 1973, 1975; Tversky and Gati, 1978; and for an excellent review of the field, see Smith and Medin, 1981). We continue in this paper discussion and interpretation of the prototypicality theory of mental categories, in light of further experimental findings we will report. To summarize at the beginning where we think these findings lead, we believe that the cluster descriptions are a less satisfactory basis for a theory of human conceptual structure than might have been hoped.

Holistic and Decompositional Descriptions of Mental Categories
The central question addressed by the work just cited has to do with everyday categories of objects. For example, over an impressively wide range of instances, people can divide the world of objects into the dogs and the nondogs. They can form and use a category that includes the poodles, the airedales, and the chihuahuas, but excludes the cats, the bears, and the pencils. The clearest demonstration that people do acquire and use such a category is that all of them, in a linguistic community, standardly use the same word, 'dog', to refer to more or less the same creatures.

In detail, we distinguish the extension of *dog* from its category (concept) and from its linguistic title. As the terms are here used, all the real and projected creatures in

We are indebted to quite a large number of colleagues for discussion of the issues addressed in this paper, and for reading and commenting on prior drafts of this manuscript. Particularly, we wish to thank B. Armstrong, D. Bolinger, J. A. Fodor, J. D. Fodor, R. Gallistel, F. W. Irwin, R. Jackendoff, J. Jonides, J. Katz, L. Komatsu, B. Landau, J. Levin, J. Moravschik, E. Newport, S. Peters, M. Posner, M. Seligman, E. Shipley, E. Spelke, E. Wanner, K. Wexler, M. Williams, and an anonymous reviewer. All of us, but especially Lila Gleitman, particularly thank Scott Weinstein for his long and patient attempts to explicate the issues in philosophical semantics for us; this service, as well as reading drafts of the current paper, he has heroically extended over two years; nevertheless, he is not accountable for the manner of review of these, nor for the positions we take here, quite obviously. The work reported was funded in part by a National Institutes of Health postdoctoral Fellowship to S. L. Armstrong, and by a grant to L. R. Gleitman and B. Landau from the National Foundation of the March of Dimes. We thank these agencies for their support of this work. Felice Bedford, Manuel Ayala, and Jordan Klemes are thanked for helping us collect the data for these studies.

the world that properly fall under the category *dog* form the extension of the category *dog*; the English word 'dog' is standardly used both to refer to dogs out there (the extensions), and to the category *dog*; the category *dog* is the mental representation, whatever this will turn out to be, that fixes the conditions under which we use the word 'dog'.[1]

Cognitive psychologists have asked: What are the mental bases for such categorizations; and, What is the internal structure of such categories? Related questions have traditionally been asked within philosophical and linguistic semantics: What is the relation between linguistic expressions (say, 'dog') and things in the world (say, the dogs) such that 'dog' conventionally refers to dogs?

A possible answer is that the relations between words and mental categories is simple, one-to-one; i.e., the word 'dog' refers to the category *dog*, which is unanalyzable. Such holistic theories have hardly even been considered until very recently. One reason for their unpopularity, as Fodor (1975; 1981) has discussed, is the desire to limit the set of atomic categories or elementary discriminations with which each human must be assumed to be endowed. Instead, traditional theories have assumed that only a very few of the words code unanalyzable concepts; rather, even most common words such as 'dog' are cover labels for mental categories that are themselves bundles of simpler mental categories (in this context, usually called *features*, *properties*, or *attributes*). Knowledge of the complex categories is then built up by recognizing that some sensible elements (simple categories) recur together in the encounters of the sensorium with the external world and so, by association, get bundled together. Maybe, for example, what we call in English 'a bird' is mentally represented as an *animal*, that *flies*, has *wings*, *feathers*, lays *eggs*, etc. (cf., Locke, 1968/1690). According to many proponents of feature theories, then, it is the structure of the real world as observed by the learner that gives rise to such categorizations: it is the fact that what has feathers tends to fly and lay eggs, in our world, which gives rise to (perhaps 'is') the complex category *bird*.

Despite the beguiling appearance of simplicity of semantic feature theory, this general approach looks more tangled on closer inspection. For example, our description of the possible features of *bird* has already run into a problem for actually a bird *is* an animal, *has* wings, *lays* eggs, and so forth. Not all these putatively simpler categories are related to the category *bird* in the same way. Some models of categorization that employ feature descriptions have further apparatus specifically designed to respond to such defects. For instance, the Collins and Loftus spreading activation model (1975) connects features by labelled links (such as *have*, *is*, etc.), thus at least acknowledging (though not explaining) the complexity of feature relations.

---

1. However, whether or not the mental category/concept 'properly' fixes the extension of the English term is left open, though this issue will come up in later discussion. It could be that there is a fact of the matter about the extension of the term unknown to the users (i.e., not given as a consequence of the structure of the mental representation). For example, on at least some views (cf., Locke, 1968/1690) there are *real essences* ("to be found in the things themselves," p. 288) and *nominal essences* (that "the mid makes," p. 288). Our use of concept/category, then, has to do with the nominal essences, the 'mental structure' of the concept which may or may not properly fix the extension. That is, our concept of gold may have the consequence for sorting that we pick out only certain yellow metal in the world to call 'gold', but the internal structure of the sort of thing we mean to be talking about when we talk about gold may exclude some of the instances we identified as gold on the basis of their yellowness, and include some other instances that were white in appearance, but still—really—gold (see Kripke, 1972, for discussion).

Another difficulty is that the empiricist program as articulated by Locke and his heirs had gained much of its explanatory force by postulating that the simple categories (or at least the nominal essences, leaving aside the unknowable real essences, cf., note 1) were sensory categories; that all categories, no matter how complex, could be built up as combinations of these sensory categories. It is a pretty sure bet that this strong form of the empiricist program won't work. The features (e.g., *wing*) of words that have no simple sensory description do not turn out to be noticeably more sensory than the words (e.g., 'bird') of which they are to be the features, again a point that has been made by Fodor (1975; see also Bolinger, 1965). The weaker version of this position, that recognizes nonsensory categories among the elementary ones often seems lame in practice, as the features one has to countenance to make it work grow increasingly implausible (e.g., *wing* for 'bird' but also *never married* for 'bachelor').[2]

But problems and details aside, we have just sketched the distinction between holistic theories, in which the unit of analysis is a category with scope something like that of the word itself; and feature (or decompositional) theories, in which analysis is on units more molecular than the word. We now turn to a major subdivision among the feature theories.

The Definitional View
We take up here two major subtypes of the feature theory of mental categories (and, hence, lexical semantics): the classical *definitional* view, and the *prototype* or cluster concept view. On the definitional variant, a smallish set of the simple properties are individually necessary and severally sufficient to pick out all and only, say, the birds, from everything else in the world. Membership in the class is categorical, for all who partake of the right properties are in virtue of that equally birds; and all who do not, are not. No other distinctions among the class members are relevant to their designation as birds. For example, the familiar creature in Figure 10.1 is a bird because it has the feathers, the wings, and so on. But the grotesque creature of Figure 10.2 is no more nor less a bird despite its peculiarities, again because it exhibits the stipulated properties.

It is reasonable to ask why this definitional theory has seemed attractive for so long (see Fodor, Garrett, Walker, and Parkes, 1980, for discussion of the history of ideas on this topic and illuminating analyses, which we roughly follow here). The central reason is that this theory gives hope of explaining how we reason with words and solve the problem of compositional meaning: how the words take their meanings together in a linguistic structure, to yield the meanings of phrases and sentences. For example, programmatically, this theory has an explanation of word-to-phrase synonymy, for how 'bachelor' and 'man who has never married' could be recognized to mean the same thing. The claim is that, in the language of the mind, the category *bachelor* decomposes into its list of features, including *man* and *never married*—just

---

2. Recent versions of (nonfuzzy) decompositional semantics respond to some of these difficulties both by radically increasing the internal complexity of lexical entries—and thus parting company with any recognizable associationist position on mental structure—or by asserting that an appropriate semantic theory is not psychologistic anyway, but rather formal and nonempirical (Katz, 1981, and personal communication; see also Bever, 1982). Whatever the real causes of semantic structure will turn out to be, we reiterate that the present discussion is of human representation of this structure—the nominal essence. Hence the Platonic descriptions, defensible or not, are not relevant here.

Figure 10.1
A prototypical bird.

Figure 10.2
A marginal bird.

the same items that occur in the semantic representation of the phrase. On this view, then, semantic interpretation is on the feature level vocabulary, not the word level vocabulary (Katz and Fodor, 1963).

The potential for explaining compositional meaning would be a formidable virtue indeed for a theory of categories; in fact, there seems little point to any theory of concepts or categorization that lacks this potentiality, for there is no way to commit to memory all the categories we can conceive, and that can be expressed by phrases (e.g., 'all the spotted ostriches on Sam's farm'). So the question now becomes: why do so many doubt the validity of the definitional view?

The only good answer is that the definitional theory is difficult to work out in the required detail. No one has succeeded in finding the supposed simplest categories (the features). It rarely seems to be the case that all and only the class members can be picked out in terms of sufficient lists of conjectured elemental categories. And eliminating some of the apparently necessary properties (e.g., deleting *feathers*, *flies*, and

Figure 10.3
The Smith Brothers.

eggs so as to include the down-covered baby male ostriches among the birds) seems not to affect category membership. Generally speaking, it is widely agreed today in philosophy, linguistics, and psychology, that the definitional program for everyday lexical categories has been defeated—at least in its pristine form (cf., note 2; and for a very informative review of recent philosophical discussion of these issues, see Schwartz, 1979).

The Prototype View

However, as is also well known, there is another class of feature descriptions that gives up the necessary and sufficient claim of the classical theory. This is the family resemblance description, first alluded to by Wittgenstein (1953), though he might be surprised at some of its recent guises. Wittgenstein took as an important example the word 'game'. He defied anyone to think of a definition in virtue of which all and only the possible games could be picked out. This being impossible on the face of it, Wittgenstein conjectured that *game* was a cluster concept, held together by a variety of gamey attributes, only some of which are instantiated by any one game. His analogy was to the structure of family resemblances. It is such a position that Rosch and her co-workers have adapted and refined, and brought into psychology through a series of compelling experimental demonstrations.

We can sketch the properties of such a theory by using the example of the Smith Brothers, of cough-drop fame, as shown in Figure 10.3. All these Brothers have features in common—the eyeglasses, the light hair, the bushy moustache, and so forth. But not all Smith Brothers have the same Smith-features, and no one criterial feature defines the family. The equal membership assumption of the definitional view is not an assumption of recent family resemblance descriptions. Instead, we can distinguish among the Smith Brothers according to the number of Smith-family attributes each embodies. The Brother at 11 o'clock in Figure 10.3 is a poor exemplar of *Smithness* for he has only a few of the attributes and thus will share attributes with the Jones family or the James family. But the Brother in the middle is a prototypical Smith for he has all or most of the Smith attributes. Finally, there is no sharp boundary delimiting where the Smith family ends and the Jones family starts. Rather, as the Smiths' biographers could probably tell you, the category boundary is indistinct.

A large class of models theoretically is available that expand upon this general structure.[3] Particularly appealing is one in which the representation is "in the form of an abstract ordered set of inclusion probabilities ordered according to the internal structure of the category" (Rosch, 1975a). If we understand correctly, Rosch's idea here is that there are distinctions among the properties, themselves, relative to some category. There are privileged properties, manifest in most or even all exemplars of the category; these could even be necessary properties. Even so, these privileged properties are insufficient for picking out all and only the class members, and hence a family resemblance description is still required. Prototypical members have all or most privileged properties of the categories. Marginal members have only one or a few. Possession of a privileged property from another category (e.g., the water-bound nature of whales or the air-borne nature of bats) or failure to exhibit a privileged property (e.g., the featherlessness of baby or plucked robins) may also relegate some members to the periphery.

But it should be emphasized that proponents of cluster-prototype theories of categories are not committed to defend this particular realization of such a model, nor to make detailed claims of a particular sort about the nature of the hypothesized properties themselves (as Rosch has pointed out, they may be imagelike or not, or imagelike for some concepts, less so for other concepts; see note 3), nor about how they are stored or accessed from memory, learned, etc. Finally, it need not be claimed that all mental categories have this structure, or this structure only, i.e., some models incorporate a paired logical and prototypical structure for single concepts (we return to discussion of this variant in the conclusions to this chapter, Part I). A large variety of cluster, nondefinitional, models currently contend in the psychological literature. As Smith and Medin (1981) elegantly describe, the models fare variously well in describing subjects' categorization behavior in various tasks. Of course, a mixed

---

3. But we are restricting discussion to models that interpret prototype theory decompositionally rather than holistically; and featurally in particular. The major reason is that a featural interpretation is at least implicit in most of the experimental literature on prototype theory, and it is this literature that we specifically address in this chapter. Nevertheless it is important to note here that some prototype theorists have a different, nonfeatural, account in mind. At the extreme, such a nondecompositional prototype theory would involve a holistic mental representation (perhaps imagistic) of a designated prototypical category member, some metric space into which other members of the category are placed, relative to the prototypical member, and some means of computing distance of members from the prototype such that the more prototypical members are those closest in the space to the prototype itself. It is hard to see how any such holistic view would allow a general theory of concepts to be stated. This is because a notion of 'general similarity', suitable for comparing all things against all other things is not likely to be found. Most nonfeatural prototype discussions, then, assume that the metric space into which category members are organized is dimensionalized in ways specifically relevant to the categories in question (e.g., comparisons of wave lengths for colors, but of lines and angles for geometric figures, etc., the dimensions of comparison now being fewer than the object types that must be compared). Osherson and Smith, 1981, have described this kind of prototype model formally, and distinguished it from the featural interpretations of prototype theory. For both types of models, these authors demonstrate that prototype theory, amalgamated with combinatorial principles from fuzzy-set theory (Zadeh, 1965), cannot account for our intuitions about conceptual combination. More to our present point, and as Osherson and Smith also point out, it is not obvious that the required designated prototypes, the dimensionalized metric space for each semantic field, or the function that computes similarity of arbitrary member to prototypical member within each field, etc., can ever be found. To us, then, the nonfeatural prototype theories escape the problems of the featural ones only by being less explicit. Moreover, whatever we say of the problems of 'features' we also assert to have closely related problems within a theory that employs 'dimensions'.

model, such as the one these latter authors finally defend, describes more of the data than any one of the other contending models, but at cost of expanding the postulated formal apparatus.

What are the virtues of this class of proposals about the organization of mental categories? To the extent that the prototype views are still componential, they still give hope of limiting the primitive basis, the set of innate concepts. If correct, they allow the empiricist program to go through in detail for the complicated concepts: in Rosch's version of the position, it is the "correlated structure of the world," the observed cooccurrence of the basic attributes out there that leads to these. Second, and most usefully, the cluster-prototype theories programmatically have an account, in terms of various available measures of feature overlap and/or feature organization, for the apparent fact that membership in a category may be graded; for example, to explain why the bird in Figure 10.1 seems a birdier bird than the one in Figure 10.2.

Moreover, there is an extensive body of empirical research that seems to provide evidence for the psychological validity of this position. For example, Table 10.1 shows four everyday superordinate categories—*fruit, sport, vegetable,* and *vehicle*— and some exemplars of each. (We follow Rosch's use of the term *exemplar*: By an exemplar we shall mean a category, e.g., *table*, that falls under some superordinate category, e.g., *furniture*. When speaking of some real table—of an extension of the category *table*—we shall use the term *instance*).

In one experiment, Rosch (1973) asked subjects to indicate how good an example each exemplar was of its category by use of an appropriate rating scale. It turns out that people will say that apples are very good examples of *fruit*, and deserve high ratings, while figs and olives are poor examplars, and deserve lower ratings. Rosch and her colleagues have interpreted such findings as evidence that membership in a category is graded, rather than all or none; and thus as support for a cluster-prototype theory while inconsistent with a definitional theory of the mental representation of these categories.

The robustness and reliability of these effects is not in question.[4] Prototype theorists have devised a large number of plausible paradigms, and in each shown that the same kinds of results crop up. As one more case, subjects respond faster in a verification task to items with high exemplariness ratings than to those with lower ones. That is, the verification time for 'A ROBIN IS A BIRD' is faster than the verification time for 'AN OSTRICH IS A BIRD' with word frequency controlled across the list (Rips *et al.*, 1973; Rosch, 1975a). In the face of such findings, one might well conclude, as have many cognitive psychologists, that the psychological validity of the cluster-prototype descriptions of everyday categories has been demonstrated beyond reasonable doubt.

---

4. This is not to say that these findings have not been questioned on methodological grounds. For example, Loftus (1975) questioned the peculiarity of some of the exemplars subjects were asked to rate: The presentation, e.g., of *foot* among the list of *weapon* exemplars might account for much of the intra-subject disagreement, generating the fuzzy outcome as a statistical artifact of these item choices (which in turn were ultimately selected from responses in an exemplar-naming task devised by Battig and Montague, 1969). But Rosch (1975b) showed that the graded responses recur in lists from which such problematical items have been removed. Furthermore, McCloskey and Glucksberg (1978) have demonstrated empirically that inter- and intra-subject variability, where each subject at each time is assumed to have a nonfuzzy definitional concept in mind, is an unlikely explanation of the graded responses.

Table 10.1
Categories, category exemplars, and exemplariness ratings for prototype and well-defined categories

Prototype categories				Well-defined categories			
Fruit				*Even number*			
apple	1.3	orange	1.1	4	1.1	2	1.0
strawberry	2.1	cherry	1.7	8	1.5	6	1.7
plum	2.5	watermelon	2.9	10	1.7	42	2.6
pineapple	2.7	apricot	3.0	18	2.6	1000	2.8
fig	5.2	coconut	4.8	34	3.4	34	3.1
olive	6.4	olive	6.5	106	3.9	806	3.9
Sport				*Odd number*			
football	1.4	baseball	1.2	3	1.6	7	1.4
hockey	1.8	soccer	1.6	7	1.9	11	1.7
gymnastics	2.8	fencing	3.5	23	2.4	13	1.8
wrestling	3.1	sailing	3.8	57	2.6	9	1.9
archery	4.8	bowling	4.4	501	3.5	57	3.4
weight-lifting	5.1	hiking	4.6	447	3.7	91	3.7
Vegetable				*Female*			
carrot	1.5	peas	1.7	mother	1.7	sister	1.8
celery	2.6	spinach	1.7	housewife	2.4	ballerina	2.0
asparagus	2.7	cabbage	2.7	princess	3.0	actress	2.1
onion	3.6	radish	3.1	waitress	3.2	hostess	2.7
pickle	4.8	peppers	3.2	policewoman	3.9	chairwoman	3.4
parsley	5.0	pumpkin	5.5	comedienne	4.5	cowgirl	4.5
Vehicle				*Plane geometry figure*			
car	1.0	bus	1.8	square	1.3	square	1.5
boat	3.3	motorcycle	2.2	triangle	1.5	triangle	1.4
scooter	4.5	tractor	3.7	rectangle	1.9	rectangle	1.6
tricycle	4.7	wagon	4.2	circle	2.1	circle	1.3
horse	5.2	sled	5.2	trapezoid	3.1	trapezoid	2.9
skis	5.6	elevator	6.2	ellipse	3.4	ellipse	3.5

Note: Under each category label, category exemplars and mean exemplariness ratings are displayed for both Set A (N = 31, shown on the left) and Set B (N = 32, shown on the right).

We believe, however, that there are grounds for caution before embracing a particular interpretation of these findings. Some of the reasons have to do with the logic of the prototype position. To the extent the prototype theory is asserted to be a feature theory, it shares many of the woes of the definitional theory. For example, it is not notably easier to find the prototypic features of a concept than to find the necessary and sufficient ones. But to the extent the prototype theory is asserted not to be a feature theory—that is, to be a holistic theory—it must share the woes of that kind of theory (as pointed out by Fodor, 1975); namely, massive expansion of the primitive categorial base. (We will return in later discussion to general problems with feature theories of lexical concepts; see Discussion, Part II).

Even more damaging to prototype theories is that they render the description of reasoning with words—for example, understanding lexical entailments of the vixen-is-a-fox variety—titanically more difficult. And understanding compositional (phrase and sentence) meaning looks altogether hopeless. One reason is that if you combine, say 'foolish' and 'bird' into the phrase 'foolish bird' it is no longer a fixed matter—rather it is indeterminate—which *foolish* elements and which *bird* elements are intended to be combined. It goes almost without saying that, to fix this, one couldn't envisage the phrasal categories (e.g., *foolish bird*) to be mentally represented in terms of their own prototype descriptions, there being indefinitely many of these.[5] Speaking more generally, one need only consider such attributes as *good, tall,* and the like, and the trouble they make even for the classical view (i.e., what makes a knife a good knife is not what makes a wife a good wife; for discussion, see Katz, 1972; G. A. Miller, 1977) to realize how many millenia we are away from a useful theory of the infinitely combining lexical concepts. The problems become orders of magnitude more difficult still when the classical approach is abandoned.

In the light of these difficulties, it seems surprising that psychologists have usually been pleased, rather than depressed, by experimental findings that tend to support a cluster-prototype theory. Since we speak in whole sentences rather than in single words, the chief desideratum of a theory of categories (coded by the words) would seem to be promise of a computable description for the infinite sentence meanings. These apparent problems with a prototype theory provide some impetus to reconsider the empirical outcomes obtained by the Rosch group and others. Do these findings really commit us to the prototype theory of conceptual structure?

In the experiments we will report, we will first revisit these outcomes by extending the category types under investigation. After all, the current basis for claiming that certain categories have a prototypical, nondefinitional, feature structure is the finding

---

5. Notice that we are speaking of the combinatorial structure of the concepts (the mental representations), not of extensions. Indeed there might be a fuzzy set of foolish birds out there; but it doesn't follow that concepts, even concepts concerning foolish birds, themselves have to be fuzzy. (We particularly thank J. A. Fodor for discussion of this point). It may very well be that there are limits on humanly natural concepts, and that not all the sundry objects and events in the world fit neatly under those that we have. (For an important discussion of natural and unnatural concepts, in the sense we here intend, see Osherson, 1978). In that case, we might not be able to make a neat job of naming everything in the world. Notice that the experimental findings we have been discussing (family-resemblance type responses to exemplars and instances) would arise artifactually in case humans really do have only certain concepts, and ways of expressing these in natural language, but must willy nilly name all the gadgets in the world, whether or not these truly fit under those concepts. (See Osherson and Smith, 1981, for a formal demonstration of related problems for prototype theory in describing lexical entailments).

of graded responses to their exemplars in various experimental paradigms. But if you believe certain concepts are nondefinitional because of graded responses to their exemplars, that must be because you also believe that if the categories *were* definitional (all-or-none) in character, and if the subjects *knew* these definitions, the graded responses would *not* have been achieved. But this remains to be shown. A necessary part of the proof requires finding some categories that *do* have definitional descriptions, and showing as well that subjects patently know and assent to these definitions; and, finally, showing that these categories *do not* yield the graded outcomes.[6]

Are there definitional concepts? Of course. For example, consider the superordinate concept *odd number*. This seems to have a clear definition, a precise description; namely, *an integer not divisible by two without remainder*. No integer seems to sit on the fence, undecided as to whether it is quite even, or perhaps a bit odd. No odd number seems odder than any other odd number. But if so, then experimental paradigms that purport to show *bird* is prototypic in structure in virtue of the fact that responses to 'ostrich' and 'robin' are unequal should fail, on the same reasoning, to yield differential responses to 'five' and 'seven', as examples of *odd number*. Similarly, such well-defined concepts as *plane geometry figure* and *female* ought not to yield the graded response patterns that were the experimental basis for the claim that the concept *bird* has a family resemblance structure.

As we shall now show, the facts are otherwise. For graded responses are achieved regardless of the structure of the concepts, for both *fruit* and *odd number*.

Experiment I

Experiment I asks what happens when subjects are required to rate "how good an exemplar is" as an example of a given category. In part, this experiment represents a replication of Rosch (1973), but it goes beyond it for the subjects had to rate exemplars of two kinds of categories: well-defined ones, such as *even number*, and the allegedly prototypic ones, such as *sport*.

Method

Subjects   The subjects were 63 University of Pennsylvania undergraduates, 22 male and 41 female, all of whom were volunteers and were native speakers of English.

Stimuli   The stimuli were items that fell into eight categories. Four of these were prototype categories chosen from among those previously used by Rosch (Rosch,

---

6. A possibly supportive demonstration to those we will now describe, one that adopts a similar logic, has appeared after the present chapter was written, and we thank an anonymous reviewer for putting us on to it. Bourne (1982) reports findings from a concept learning experiment which he interprets as demonstrating that prototype-like responses can arise from sources other than "fuzzy concepts" in the subject. However, the materials used by Bourne were artificial categories, designed to be simple-featural, thus finessing the question whether natural categories are featural. Even more difficult for his interpretations, it is ambiguous from the reported results what structure(s) the experimental subjects thought described the categories whose members they learned to identify. Nonetheless, Bourne's interpretation of his experiments and their outcomes formally parallels aspects of those we are about to report: that prototypelike responses from subjects can coexist with manifest knowledge, in the same subjects, of the logical structure of those categories. In concord with Osherson and Smith (1981), Bourne accepts something like a 'core/identification procedure' distinction as the appropriate account of the findings (for discussion of this position, see Conclusions, Part I, following).

1973; 1975a): *fruit, sport, vegetable,* and *vehicle.* Four other categories were of the kind we call well-defined: *even number, odd number, plane geometry figure,* and *female.*

Each category was represented by two sets of six exemplars each. For the proto-type categories, the first sets of exemplars (set A) were those used by Rosch pre-viously (Rosch, 1973). Their choice was determined by using norms established by Battig and Montague (1969) who asked subjects to provide exemplars of everyday categories and then computed frequencies of the responses. The choice of the six exemplars was such as to approximate the following distribution of frequencies on these norms: 400, 150, 100, 50, 15, and 4 or less. Our second sets of exemplars for prototype categories (set B) were selected according to these same criteria. Since there are no previously collected norms for the well-defined categories we used here, two sets of six exemplars were generated for each category on the basis of an intuitive ranking made by the experimenters. The eight categories with both sets of exemplars are shown in Table 10.1.

Procedure   The subjects were asked to rate, on a 7-point scale, the extent to which each given exemplar represented their idea or image of the meaning of each category term. Each category name (e.g., *fruit*) was typed on a separate page. Approximately half of the subjects (31) rated one set of exemplars (set A) of each of the eight cate-gories; the rest (32) rated the other sets of exemplars (set B). Within these sets, each subject was assigned randomly to a different order of the eight categories. The ex-emplar stimuli themselves (e.g., *apple*) were typed below their category names. They were presented in two different random orders within each category, with about half of the subjects receiving one order and the other half receiving the other order.

The specific instructions for the rating task were taken verbatim from Rosch's study (Rosch, 1975a). The following is an extract that gives the general idea of what the subjects were asked to do (The instructions from Rosch, that we repeated verbatim in our replication, do not distinguish *exemplar* from *instance,* as is obvious; for the purposes of instructing naive subjects, at least, marking the distinction seemed irrelevant):

> This study has to do with what we have in mind when we use words which refer to categories.... Think of dogs. You all have some notion of what a "real dog," a "doggy dog" is. To me a retriever or a German Shepherd is a very doggy dog while a Pekinese is a less doggy dog. Notice that this kind of judg-ment has nothing to do with how well you like the thing.... You may prefer to own a Pekinese without thinking that it is the breed that best represents what people mean by dogginess. On this form you are asked to judge how good an example of a category various instances of the category are.... You are to rate how good an example of the category each member is on a 7-point scale. A *1* means that you feel the member is a very good example of your idea of what the category is. A *7* means you feel the member fits very poorly with your idea or image of the category (or is not a member at all). A *4* means you feel the member fits moderately well.... Use the other numbers of the 7-point scale to indicate intermediate judgments.
>
> Don't worry about why you feel that something is or isn't a good example of the category. And don't worry about whether it's just you or people in general who feel that way. Just mark it the way you see it.

Table 10.2
Comparison of mean exemplariness ratings

	Rosch, 1973	Armstrong et al., 1982
Fruit		
apple	1.3	1.3
strawberry	2.3	2.1
plum	2.3	2.5
pineapple	2.3	2.7
fig	4.7	5.2
olive	6.2	6.4
Sport		
football	1.2	1.4
hockey	1.8	1.8
gymnastics	2.6	2.8
wrestling	3.0	3.1
archery	3.9	4.8
weight-lifting	4.7	5.1
Vegetable		
carrot	1.1	1.5
celery	1.7	2.6
asparagus	1.3	2.7
onion	2.7	3.6
pickle	4.4	4.8
parsley	3.8	5.0
Vehicle		
car	1.0	1.0
boat	2.7	3.3
scooter	2.5	4.5
tricycle	3.5	4.7
horse	5.9	5.2
skis	5.7	5.6

Results and Discussion

Our subjects, like Rosch's, found the task readily comprehensible. No one questioned or protested about doing what they were asked to do. The results on the categories and exemplars that were used by both us and Rosch (Rosch, 1973) were virtually identical, as Table 10.2 shows. Our subjects, like Rosch's, felt that certain exemplars are good ones for certain categories (as in *apple* for *fruit*) while others are poor (as in *olive* for *fruit*). Moreover, there was considerable agreement among subjects about which items are good and which bad exemplars. To test for such inter-subject agreement, Rosch used split-group correlations, correlating the mean ratings obtained by a randomly chosen half of the subjects with the mean ratings of the other half (Rosch,

1975*a*). Rosch reports split-group correlations above 0.97; our own split-group rank correlations were 1.00, 0.94, 0.89, and 1.00 for the categories *fruit, vegetable, sport,* and *vehicle,* respectively, using the same exemplars employed by Rosch (that is, our stimulus sets A). Here too, our pattern of results is essentially identical with that obtained by Rosch.

The important question concerns the results for the well-defined categories. Keep in mind that we here asked subjects, for example, to distinguish *among* certain odd numbers, *for* oddity, and common sense asserts one cannot do so. But the subjects could and did. For example, they judged *3* a better odd number than *501* and *mother* a better female than *comedienne.* The full pattern of these results is shown in Table 10.1, which presents mean exemplariness ratings for all the exemplars of all alleged prototype and well-defined categories in our study.

What is more, just as with the prototype categories, the subjects seemed to agree as to which exemplars are good and which poor examples of the categories. To prove this point, we used the same method employed by Rosch, and calculated split-group correlations for both sets in each of the categories. The correlations are quite high. Combining sets A and B, the median split-group rank correlations were 0.94, 0.81, 0.92, and 0.92, for *even number, odd number, female,* and *plane geometry figure,* respectively. (In retrospect, the choice of *odd number* as one of the categories was bound to cause some trouble and yield the slightly lower rank correlation just because the subjects could, and sometimes did, take the liberty of interpreting *odd* as *peculiar;* this kind of ambiguity clearly will contaminate the correlations, as McCloskey and Glucksberg, 1978, have demonstrated).

Taken as a whole, the results for the well-defined categories look remarkably like those that have been said to characterize fuzzy categories—those that are said in fact to be the basis on which the categories are termed nondefinitional. Just as some fruits are judged to be fruitier than others, so some even numbers seem more even than other even numbers. In addition, there is considerable inter-subject agreement about these judgments.

To be sure, there are some differences between the judgments given to exemplars of prototypic and well-defined categories. Pooling all the prototype categories, we obtain a mean exemplariness rating of 3.4, as compared to 2.5 for all the well defined categories, ($t = 18.4$, df $= 62$, p < 0.001). This means that, overall, the subjects were more likely to judge a given exemplar of a prototype category as less than perfect than they were to render this judgment on an exemplar of a well-defined category.

One interpretation of this result is that it is a simple artifact of the way the category exemplars were selected. The prototype sets were constructed following Rosch's procedures, and included some rather unlikely exemplars (such as *skis* as an instance of *vehicle*). The lower mean ratings for the well-defined categories could have been a consequence of the fact that we made no attempt here to think of atypical exemplars. But they could also be reflections of a true difference in the category types. Maybe there is no such thing as a perfectly ghastly even number that is an even number all the same.

We did make an attempt to check the manipulability of these ratings, by developing new lists of the well-defined categories that included exemplars we thought 'atypical'. The very fact that one can consider doing this, incidentally, is further proof that there is some sense in which exemplars of well-defined categories must be rankable. For the category *female,* we replaced such stereotypical female items as *housewife* with what seemed to us more highly charged items; specifically, the new list was: *mother, ballerina, waitress, cowgirl, nun,* and *lesbian.* For the category *even number,* we substituted a list whose cardinality increased more, and at the same time which contained more and more odd digits among the even ones. Specifically, the list was: *2, 6, 32, 528, 726,* and *1154.*

We ran 20 volunteers at Wesleyan University on these new lists, using the same procedures. In fact we did get a weak increase in the means for the even numbers (the overall mean for *even number* in Experiment I was 2.4 and it increased to 2.9 for the new list, though not significantly ($t = 1.51$, df $= 49$, $p < 0.10$). For the category *female,* we got a surprise. It is obvious from Table 10.1 that the rankings of females follow a fairly strict sexism order. It was this dimension we tried to exploit in adding such items as *lesbian.* But now the mean rankings went down (to 2.8 from 2.9), not a significant difference and not in the expected direction. Perhaps the choice of new items was injudicious or perhaps there are no exemplars for *female* that fall at the lowest points on the scale.

To summarize, the central purpose of our experiment has been to show that responses to well-defined categories are graded. Graded responses to everyday concepts in precisely this experimental paradigm have heretofore been taken as demonstrating that these everyday concepts are nondefinitional. That this interpretation was too strong, *for the everyday concepts,* is shown by the fact that the formal concepts yield the same response patterns, on the same tasks. This new finding says nothing about the structure of everyday concepts for it is a negative result, pure and simple. Its thrust is solely this: to the extent it is secure beyond doubt that, e.g., *fruit* and *plane geometry figure* have different structures, a paradigm that cannot distinguish between responses to them is not revealing about the structure of concepts. A secondary point in this first experiment was that subjects may not find any even number or female quite so atypical of their categories as some fruit or some vehicle is atypical of their categories. But what has to be confronted head on is the finding that *some* even numbers are said to be *any* evener than *any* others, and that subjects are in accord on such judgments. The next experiments are designed to clarify what this strange outcome might mean.

Experiment II

It is possible to suppose that the graded responses to all-or-none categories in the experiment just reported are epiphenomena. After all, we asked subjects to judge odd numbers for oddity, and the like. They might have been reacting to silly questions by giving silly answers. The task (rating exemplars) is a reflective one, without time and difficulty constraints, so the subjects might well have developed *ad hoc* strategies quite different from those used by subjects in previous prototype experiments, yielding superficially similar results, but arising from utterly different mental sources. To see whether such an explanation goes through, we performed another experiment, this time one in which there is a premium on speed and in which the subject is not asked explicitly to reflect on the way exemplars fit into mental category structures. This experiment again replicates prior work with prototype categories.

Rosch and others have shown that subjects respond more quickly in a category verification task given items of high as opposed to low exemplariness (Rips, Shoben, and Smith, 1973; Rosch, 1973; for general reviews see Danks and Glucksberg, 1980;

Mervis & Rosch, 1981; Smith, 1978). It takes less time to verify sentences such as 'A ROBIN IS A BIRD' than sentences such as 'AN OSTRICH IS A BIRD' with word frequency controlled across the list of sentences. This result fits in neatly with the prototype view. For example, if a concept is mentally represented by a prototype, and if processing time is some function of feature matching, then one might well expect that the more features a word has in common with a prototype, the more quickly that word will be identified as a category exemplar (The varying models of fuzzy concept structure have appropriately varying accounts of why the typical exemplars are verified the faster; it is not for us to take a stand among them, but see Smith and Medin, 1981, for a lucid comparative discussion).

The present study uses the same basic verification task. But the sentences that have to be verified here include instances of both the well-defined and the alleged proto-type categories. The question is whether the differential verification times that had been used as an argument for the prototype structure of categories such as *sport* or *vegetable* will be found for categories such as *even number*.

Method

Subjects   The subjects were ten undergraduate volunteers, 5 male and 5 female, at the University of Pennsylvania.

Stimuli   The stimuli were 64 sentences of the form 'AN *A* IS A *B*' in which B was a category of which A was said to be an exemplar. Thirty-two of the sentences were true (e.g., 'AN ORANGE IS A FRUIT'); 32 were false (e.g., 'AN ORANGE IS A VEHICLE'). To construct the true sentences, we used the eight categories employed in Experiment I (four prototype categories and four well-defined ones). Each of the categories had four exemplars. These varied along two dimensions: category exemplariness and word frequency. Two exemplars had previously (that is, in earlier test-ing) been rated to be relatively good category members and two were rated to be relatively poor (as indicated by mean ratings below and above 2.0, respectively). Fol-lowing Rosch, we also controlled for word frequency (Rosch, 1973). Thus one of the two highly rated exemplars was a high frequency word, while the other was of low frequency. The same was true of the two low-rated exemplars. The word-frequencies were determined by reference to the Thorndike and Lorge (1944) and Kucera and Francis (1967) word counts. (In case you're wondering: there *are* frequency counts for some numbers in Kucera and Francis, 1967, and we limited our choices to those for which such frequency counts were available). The categories and their exemplars used in the 32 true sentences are shown in Table 10.3. To construct the 32 false sen-tences, each of the 32 exemplars was randomly paired with one of the seven cate-gories to which it did *not* belong. There was one constraint: each category had to be used equally often; that is, four times.

Procedure   The sentences were displayed on the screen of a PET microprocessor. Each trial was initiated by the subject, who pressed the space bar to indicate he or she was ready. This led to appearance of one of the 64 sentences on the screen. The trial ended when the subject pressed one of two keys to indicate 'true' or 'false'. The sub-jects were instructed to respond as quickly and as accurately as possible. The 64 sen-tences were presented twice in a different random order for each subject. The testing session was preceded by ten practice trials using other exemplars and other cate-gories. Both the response and the reaction time were recorded by the microprocessor.

Table 10.3
Categories and category exemplars used in sentence verification study[*,§]

	Good exemplars	Poorer exemplars
Prototype categories		
fruit	orange, banana	fig, coconut
sport	baseball, hockey	fishing, archery
vegetable	peas, spinach	onion, mushroom
vehicle	bus, ambulance	wagon, skis
Well-defined categories		
even number	8,22	30, 18
odd number	7,13	15, 23
female	aunt, ballerina	widow, waitress
plane geometry figure	rectangle, triangle	ellipse, trapezoid

[*] Under each rubric (e.g., fruit, good exemplar), high-frequency exemplars are listed first, low-frequency ones second.
[§] The prototype exemplars were taken from Rosch (1975a). The well-defined exemplars were taken from Experiment 1 of this chapter, and some previous pilot studies. The criterion of exemplariness was that used in Rosch's original verification study (Rosch, 1973); good exemplars had ratings of 2 or less, poorer exemplars had ratings above this.

Results and Discussion

Table 10.4 shows the mean verification times for the true sentences, displayed by category and by exemplariness. The data are based on correct responses only with errors excluded. Since the error rate was reasonably low (5%), this had little effect.

As the table shows, we found that exemplariness affects verification time. The better exemplars of a category were more readily identified as category members. This result was found for the prototype categories, where the mean verification times were 977 msec and 1127 msec for good and poorer exemplars respectively (t = 2.36, df = 9, p < 0.05). But it was found also for the well-defined categories, in which the mean verification times were 1074 msec and 1188 msec for good and poorer exemplars respectively (t = 3.19, df = 9, p < 0.01). An overall analysis of variance yielded a marginally significant main effect due to kind of category (members of well-defined categories required longer verification times than those of the prototype categories; F = 3.20, df = 1/27, p < 0.10) and a main effect due to exemplariness (good exemplars led to shorter verification times than poorer exemplars, F = 12.79, df = 1/27, p < 0.005). There was no trace of an interaction between these two factors (F < 1).

Summarizing these results, differential reaction times to verification (just like exemplariness ratings) are as reliable and often as powerful for well-defined, even mathematical, concepts as they are for the everyday concepts that seem to be ill-defined or prototypical. Moreover, this is not simply a case of subjects responding haphazardly to questions that make no sense, for such an explanation cannot account for why the subjects agreed with each other in rating and reacting. The prototype theories have ready accounts for why it takes longer to say 'yes' to 'A COCONUT IS A FRUIT' than to 'AN ORANGE IS A FRUIT', in terms of differential numbers of, or access to, features for typical and atypical exemplars of fuzzy categories. But

Table 10.4
Verification times for good and poorer exemplars of several prototype and well-defined categories (in msec)

	Good exemplars	Poorer exemplars
Prototype categories		
fruit	903	1125
sport	892	941
vegetable	1127	1211
vehicle	989	1228
Well-defined categories		
even number	1073	1132
odd number	1088	1090
female	1032	1156
plane geometry figure	1104	1375

how can such a theory explain that it takes longer to verify that '18 IS AN EVEN NUMBER' than that '22 IS AN EVEN NUMBER'?

Some have responded to these findings very consistently, by asserting that the experimental findings are to be interpreted as before: that, psychologically speaking, odd numbers as well as birds and vegetables are graded concepts. But this response to us proves only that one man's *reductio ad absurdum* is the next man's necesary truth (J. M. E. Moravcsik, personal communication). We reject this conclusion just because we could not explain how a person could compute with integers who truly believed that 7 was odder than 23. We assert confidently that the facts about subjects being able to compute and about their being able to give the definition of odd number, etc., are the more important, highly entrenched, facts we want to preserve and explain in any theory that purports to be 'a theory of the conceptual organization of the integers; particularly, of the conceptual organization of the notion odd number'. A discordant note possibly defeating such a description has been struck by the finding that some odd numbers are rated as odder than other odd numbers and verified more slowly as being odd numbers. Of all the facts about the mental structure of oddity that one would want the psychological theories to explain, however, this seems one of the least crucial and the least connected to the other facts; certainly, unimportant compared to the fact that all odd numbers, when divided by two, leave a remainder of one. Since one cannot have both facts simultaneously in the theory of the mental representation of oddity, we ourselves are prepared to give up the seeming fact that some odd numbers appear, as shown by their behavior in certain experimental paradigms, to be odder than others. As we shall later discuss, we do not give it up by saying it was no fact; rather, by saying it must have been a fact about something other than the structure of concepts. (For a theoretical treatment that turns on notions of the entrenchment and connectedness of predicates in a related way, see Goodman, 1965; and also relatedly, see Osherson, 1978, for the position that natural concepts are "'projectible' in the sense that [they] can figure in law-like generalizations that support counterfactuals" p. 265).

Reiterating, then, we hold that *fruit* and *odd number* have different structures, and yet we obtain the same experimental outcome for both. But if the same result is achieved regardless of the concept structure, then the experimental design is not pertinent to the determination of concept structure.

Experiment III

Despite our conclusion, our subjects and previous subjects of Rosch were orderly in their response styles to these paradigms, so they must be telling us something. If not about the structure of concepts, what *are* they telling us about? As a step toward finding out, we now frankly asked a new pool of subjects, for a variety of the definitional and putatively prototypical concepts, to tell us straight out whether membership in the class was graded or categorical. After all, the results for Experiments I and II are puzzling only if we assume the subjects were really rating category membership (an assumption that it seems to us is made by prior investigators). But suppose the subjects are not really rating category membership; that is, suppose category exemplariness is psychologically not identical to category membership. To test this idea, we now asked subjects whether you could be a more-or-less-birdish bird, a more-or-less-odd odd number, or whether each was an all-or-none matter, as the classical theory would have it.

Method

Subjects   The subjects were 21 undergraduate volunteers, 10 male and 11 female, at the University of Pennsylvania, all run in individual sessions.

Stimuli   Each subject was given two test booklets constructed in the same manner as those used for set A in Experiment I. The instructions differed, however, from those of Experiment I and were printed on a separate sheet. The two tasks are described below:

Procedure, Task 1   The subjects were given the first booklet and asked to go through it page by page. The booklets were just like those of Experiment I. At the top of each page was typed a category name. Four of the prototype variety and four of the definitional variety were used, in fact just the categories used in Experiment I. Under each category name was typed its six exemplars; these were the set A items from Experiment I. The subjects' first task was to tell us whether they believed that membership in a given class is graded or categorical. The actual question they were posed (which they had to answer for each category by writing 'Yes' or 'No' on each page) was:

> Does it make sense to rate items in this category for *degree of membership* in the category?

To explain what we meant, the instruction sheet provided the following statements (on later inquiry, all subjects indicated that they had understood the question):

> What we mean by degree of membership: It makes sense to rate items for degree of membership in a category if the items meet the criteria required for membership to a *different degree*.
>
>   It does *not* make sense to rate items for degree of membership in a category if all the items meet the criteria required for membership to the *same degree*; that is, if the items are literally either in or out of the category.

Procedure, Task 2   Having told us whether they believed that membership in the various categories is graded or categorical, the subjects were given a new task. They were presented with a second set of booklets. These contained the same categories and the same exemplars as the first booklet, except that the order of the categories (as before, each on a separate page) and the order of exemplars within categories was randomly varied. They also contained a new set of instructions that described the subjects' new task.

These new instructions first told the subjects to "disregard the previous question in answering this one. This is a new and different question." They were then asked to rate the exemplariness of each item in each category—the same task, posed with the identical instructions, that we (following Rosch) had given to the subjects in Experiment I. Their job was the same regardless of how they had performed on the first task. They had to rate the exemplariness of the category items even if they had previously stated that membership in this category is all-or-none. Thus the selfsame subject who had, say, denied that some odd numbers could be odder than others, was now asked to rate odd numbers according to which was a good example of odd numbers, which not so good, and so on, on the usual 7-point scale.

Results and Discussion

The results of Task 1 are displayed in Table 10.5, which shows the percentage of subjects who said that items in a given category could *not* be rated by degree of membership, that an item is either in or out with no in between. As the table shows, 100% felt this way about *odd number*, *even number*, and *plane geometry figure* and a substantial percentage (86%) felt this way about *female*. Mildly surprising is that about half of the subjects felt similarly about such presumably fuzzy categories as *fruit*, *vegetable*, *sport*, and *vehicle*.

Notice that this result accords ill with that of Experiment I, if the latter is interpreted as a test of category structure. Subjects in Experiment I could (by hypothesis) rate exemplars of varying category types for degree of membership, but subjects in

Table 10.5
Subjects' responses when asked: "Does it make sense to rate items in this category for degree of membership in the category?" (N = 21)

	Percent of subjects who said "NO"
Prototype categories	
fruit	43
sport	71
vegetable	33
vehicle	24
Well-defined categories	
even number	100
odd number	100
female	86
plane geometry figure	100

the present experiment say it is often absurd to rate for degree of membership. To solidify this result, we had to determine whether the selfsame subjects would behave in these two different ways. That is the central point of Task 2 of the present experiment, in which the subjects were asked to go back to the same categories they had just described as all-or-none and rate their members according to how good an example of this category each was. The results are shown in Table 10.6, which presents the mean ratings for all items on all categories. Each mean is based on the ratings of *only those subjects who had previously said 'No' when asked whether it makes sense to rate membership in this particular category*. For purposes of comparison, the table also shows the mean ratings for the same items obtained from the subjects in Experiment I.

As the table shows, there is still an exemplariness effect. *Apples* are still ranked higher than *olives*, and by subjects who say that being a *fruit* is a definite matter, one way or the other. By and large, the same exemplars judged to be better or worse in Experiment I were similarly rated in Experiment III. For example, in both experiments the best two *vegetables* were *carrot* and *celery* while the worst three were *onion*, *parsley*, and *pickle*. The numbers *4* and *8* were still the best *even numbers*, and *34* and *106* were still the worst. As in Experiment I, these new subjects generally agreed with each other as to which exemplar is better and which worse, as shown by median split-group correlations of 0.87 and 0.98 for prototype and well-defined categories, respectively.

Another similarity to Experiment I was the fact that the mean ratings were lower for instances of the well-defined categories than for the prototype categories. To document this point statistically, we compared overall mean ratings to exemplars of the two types. We considered only exemplars in categories that had previously been judged all-or-none. In addition, we restricted our analysis to subjects who had given such an all-or-none judgment for at least two of the prototype categories, since we wanted to have a reasonable data base for comparing ratings given to both kinds of categories and made by the same subjects. These restrictions left 12 subjects. They produced a mean rating of 1.4 for the well-defined categories and 2.3 for the prototype categories ($t = 4.4$, df $= 11$, $p < 0.001$).

It is clear then that, even under very extreme conditions, an exemplariness effect is still found; and even for well-defined categories, and even for subjects who had said that the membership in question is all-or-none. We regard this as a strong argument that category membership is not psychologically equivalent to category exemplariness. This is not to say that the exemplariness effect cannot be muted, for we have certainly decreased its magnitude by our various manipulations. The overall means found for the relevant categories rated in Experiment I were 3.5 and 2.6 for the prototype and well-defined categories, respectively; in Experiment III, the means are 2.3 and 1.4, as we just stated. These differences are highly significant (the two t-values are 4.3 and 7.4 respectively, with df's of 41, and p-values of less than 0.001).

This difference may indicate that the subjects genuflected slightly in Task 2 to their behavior in Task 1. The subjects as a group surely have no consciously held theory that distinguishes between class membership and exemplariness and indeed many of them may have thought their one set of responses contradicted the other. Even so, the graded responses remain, only diminished in magnitude. On the other hand, this magnitude difference may be due to differential selection, since the mean ratings here are based only on those subjects who previously said these categories are all-or-none. Such subjects may generally provide lower ratings in tests of this sort. For all we

Table 10.6
Mean exemplariness ratings

	Experiment I all subjects		Experiment III subjects who said NO (out of 21)	
	n	$\bar{X}$	n	$\bar{X}$
Prototype categories				
Fruit				
apple	31	1.3	9	1.3
strawberry		2.1		1.7
plum		2.5		1.9
pineapple		2.7		1.3
fig		5.2		3.3
olive		6.4		4.2
Vegetable				
carrot	31	1.5	7	1.1
celery		2.6		1.1
asparagus		2.7		1.4
onion		3.7		3.1
pickle		4.8		4.1
parsley		5.0		3.1
Sport				
football	31	1.4	15	1.1
hockey		1.8		1.5
gymnastics		2.8		1.6
wrestling		3.1		1.9
archery		4.8		2.5
weight-lifting		5.1		2.6
Vehicle				
car	31	1.0	5	1.0
boat		3.3		1.6
scooter		4.5		3.8
tricycle		4.7		2.6
horse		5.2		2.8
skis		5.6		5.2
Well-defined categories				
Even number				
4	31	1.1	21	1.0
8		1.5		1.0
10		1.7		1.1
18		2.6		1.2
34		3.4		1.4
106		3.9		1.7

Table 10.6 (continued)

	Experiment I all subjects		Experiment III subjects who said NO (out of 21)	
	n	$\bar{X}$	n	$\bar{X}$
Odd number				
3	31	1.6	21	1.0
7		1.9		1.0
23		2.4		1.3
57		2.6		1.5
501		3.5		1.8
447		3.7		1.9
Female				
mother	31	1.7	18	1.1
housewife		2.4		1.8
princess		3.0		2.1
waitress		3.2		2.4
policewoman		3.9		2.9
comedienne		4.5		3.1
Plane geometry figure				
square	31	1.3	21	1.0
triangle		1.5		1.0
rectangle		1.9		1.0
circle		2.1		1.2
trapezoid		3.1		1.5
ellipse		3.4		2.1

know, both factors may be involved in lowering the mean ratings in this condition, and other factors as well.

But none of this affects our main point. Superficially subjects seem to have contradicted themselves, asserting that a category is all-or-none in one condition and then regarding it as graded in the next. But as we see it, the contradiction is only apparent. The subjects responded differently because they were asked to judge two different matters: exemplariness of exemplars of concepts in the one case, and membership of exemplars in a concept in the other.

General Discussion

The results of our studies suggest that it has been premature to assign a family-resemblance structure to certain natural categories. The prior literature has shown that exemplars from various categories receive graded responses, in a variety of paradigms. But graded responses to exemplars of such categories as *fruit* do not constitute evidence for the family resemblance structure of these categories without—at minimum—a further finding: all-or-none responses to exemplars of categories that are known to have definite, all-or-none, descriptions and whose all-or-none descriptions are known to be known to the subjects. And this is precisely what we failed to find. Our subjects were tested in two of the well-known paradigms, with such categories as *odd number*. But they then gave graded responses.

These results do not suggest that categories such as *fruit* or *vehicle* are well-defined in the classical or any other sense—no more than they suggest that *odd number* is fuzzy. What they do suggest is that we are back at square one in discovering the structure of everyday categories *experimentally*. This is because our results indicate that certain techniques widely used to elicit and therefore elucidate the structure of such categories are flawed. This being so, the study of conceptual structure has not been put on an experimental footing, and the structure of those concepts studied by current techniques remains unknown.

Over and above this negative and essentially methodological conclusion, we want to know why the graded responses keep showing up, if they do not directly reflect the structure of concepts. We will now try to say something about why. Specifically, in Part I below, we will present a suitably revised description of how featural prototypes relate to concepts. This description, similar to many now in the literature of cognitive psychology, superficially seems to handle our findings rather appealingly, mitigating some of their paradoxical quality. That is the happy ending. But as the curtain reopens on Part II of this discussion, we will acknowledge that without a theory of what is to count as a 'feature' (or 'relevant dimension'), the descriptive victory of Part I was quite hollow. That is our sad ending. Part III closes with some speculations about likely directions for further investigation into concepts.

Part I. Exemplariness and Prototypes
One enormous phenomenon stands firm: subjects do give graded responses when queried, in any number of ways, about concepts. So powerful is this phenomenon that it survives even confrontation with the very concepts (*odd number*) it could not possibly illuminate or even describe. A graded view of odd numbers could not explain how we compute with integers, how we know (finally) that each integer is odd or not odd, how we know that to find out about the oddness of an integer we are quite free to look at the rightmost digit only, and so forth. These facts are among those we care about most passionately, among the various oddness-competencies of human subjects. The mischievous finding of graded responses to the odd numbers makes mysterious, inexplicable, perverse, all these essential matters about the mental representation of the odds *just in case the graded findings say something about the concept of oddness*. We have concluded, therefore, and even before the findings of Experiment III were in, and bolstered the position, that the category *odd* is determined, exact, and nonfuzzy, as known to human subjects. So the question still remains to be answered: where do the graded responses come from?

In presenting the results of our experiments, we suggested that the prototype descriptions apply to an organization of 'exemplariness' rather than to an organization of 'class membership'. Perhaps the graded judgments and responses have to do with a mentally stored *identification function* used to make quick sorts of things, scenes, and events in the world. On this formulation, instances of a concept share some rough and ready list of perceptual and functional properties, to varying degrees (just as Rosch argues and as her experiments elegantly demonstrate). For example, grandmothers tend to have *grey hair, wrinkles, a twinkle* in their eye. Some of these properties may be only loosely, if at all, tied to the criteria for membership in the class (for example, *twinkles* for grandmotherliness) while others may be tightly, systematically, tied to the criteria for membership (for example, being *adult* for grandmotherliness). But in addition to this identification function, there will be a mentally stored *categorial description* of the category that does determine membership in it. For *grandmother*, this will be *mother of a parent*.

For some concepts, by hypothesis, there may be very little beyond the identification function that is stored in memory. For example, few, other than vintners and certain biologists, may have much in the way of a serious description of *grape* mentally represented. For other concepts, such as *grandmother*, there might be a pair of well-developed mental descriptions that are readily accessed depending on the task requirements: the exemplariness or identification function, and the sytematic categorial description, the *sense* (cf., Frege, 1970/1892). This latter seems to be essentially what Miller (1977) and some others have called the conceptual core. We adopt this term, *core*, to distinguish the systematic mental representation of the concept from yet another, third, notion, the *real essence* (cf., Kripke, 1972), or factual scientific description of natural categories, apart from the fallible mental descriptions of these. Notice that in principle, then, *gold* might have a rough and ready identification heuristic (the *yellow, glittery* stuff), a core description that is different from this at least in recognizing that all that glitters is not gold, and also a scientific description (at the present moment in the history of inorganic chemistry, atomic number such-and-such).

Even if this general position about concepts is correct, the present authors, clearly, take no stand about the nature of the conceptual cores; only, we will argue in the end that cores for the various concepts would be likely to differ massively from each other both formally and substantively. For the concepts whose internal structure seems relatively transparent, sometimes a classical feature theory seems natural, as for the kin terms. For other concepts, such as *noun or prime number*, it seems to us that although these concepts have substructure, that substructure cannot be featural and may not be list-like. (But see Maratsos, 1982, for the opposing idea, that lexical categories such as *noun* may be distributional feature bundles; and Bates and MacWhinney, 1982, for the view that such categories may be prototypical).

The dual position on concepts, of conceptual core and identification function, seems attractive on many grounds. Most centrally, it allows us to resolve some apparent contradictions concerning well-defined categories such as the kinship terms. To return to the present example, all it takes to be a grandmother is being a mother of a parent, but the difficulty is that all the same some grandmothers seem more grandmotherly than others. This issue is naturally handled in terms of a pair of representations: the first, the function that allows one to pick out likely grandmother candidates easily (it's probably that kindly grey haired lady dispensing the chicken soup) and the second, the description that allows us to reason from *grandmother* to *female*. In short, this dual theory seems at first glance to resolve some of the paradox of our experimental findings: subjects were able to distinguish among, e.g., the plane geometry figures or the females, simply by referring to some identification function; but when asked about membership in the class of *plane geometry figures* or *females*, they referred instead to the core description. As for the everyday concepts, such as *fruit* and *vehicle*, they too would have identification functions, whether or not for them there is also a distinct core.[7]

One could think of further reasons to be optimistic about the dual description just sketched. There even seems to be a story one could tell about how the list of identifying properties would arise necessarily as part of the induction problem for language learning. They would arise whether the properties in question were themselves part of the primitive base, or were learned. This is because a whole host of properties such as *grey hair, grandmother, kindly, elderly, female,* all or most will present themselves perceptually (or at least perceptibly) the first time you are confronted with a grandmother and introduced to her and to the word: "This is grandmother" or "This is Joey's grandmother." Favorable as this set of circumstances is, it is insufficient for learning that 'grandmother' means *a kindly grey haired elderly female* and all the more insufficient for learning that 'grandmother' means *mother of a parent.* For 'grandmother' might mean any one (or two, or three) of these properties, rather than all together. Hence, the problem that presents itself with Joey's grandmother is which among the allowable concepts (we leave aside the awesome problem of which concepts are allowable) is being coded by the term 'grandmother' that has been uttered in her presence to refer to her—is she the female in front of you, the grandmother in front of you, the grey haired one; which? Best to make a list, and wait for exposure conditions that dissociate some of these conjectures (for example, it may be helpful to meet little Howie Gabor's grandma, ZsaZsa). To the extent that certain properties occur repeatedly (e.g., *grey haired*) these remain the longer, or remain near the top of the list, as conjectures about the meaning of 'grandmother'.

If this plausible tale is part of the true story of lexical-concept attainment, a question remains. Why isn't the rough and ready attribute list torn up when it is discovered that 'grandmother' really means *mother of a parent, and chicken soup be damned*? (The discovery, to the extent this description goes through, would be that *mother of parent* is the only attribute that always is present in the 'grandmother'- utterance situation; and the discovery, insofar as this description *doesn't* go through, would be that the core is discovered in some totally different way.) The answer, as Landau (1982) and others have argued, would have to do with the sheer convenience of the identification function; it is easier, when seeking grandmothers or attempting to identify present entities, to check such a list of properties than to conduct geneological inquiries. So the list of properties that is constructed in the natural course of language learning hangs on to do a variety of identifying chores in later life. To keep matters in perspective, however, it will require quite a different organization for such kinship terms so as to reason with them—for example, as to whether some of the grandmothers could be virgins, or not. Landau has shown experimentally that even

---

7. We are leaving many ends loose here, that we will try to tie up in later discussion. The present discussion is by way of a last ditch attempt to salvage a featural description of the mental concepts, in light of our experimental findings. But we have already overstated the work any feature theory we know of can do in this regard, even when viewed as a heuristic identification scheme, operating on features. Notice that having lots of odd digits or being of low cardinality doesn't really help, in any known or imaginable rough-and-ready sense, to identify odd numbers. What makes these easier than divisible by two, leaving one? A good question, one that at least limits, perhaps defeats, even the restricted role we have outlined for feature theories of conceptual structure. (We thank E. Wanner and E. Newport for pointing out these challenges to the dual feature story).

young children will switch from the one description of grandmothers to the other, as the task is changed from one of identification to one of justification.

To summarize, we have just discussed our results in terms of a dual theory of the description of concepts, one that seems to have considerable currency among cognitive psychologists today. This theory asserts that there is a core description, relevant to compositional meaning and informal reasoning; and an identification procedure that is a heuristic for picking out concept-instances in the world. In terms of this dual theory, it is not surprising that concepts of quite different kinds (at their core) all have identification functions. And it is less paradoxical by far to say that some *females* are 'better' as *females*, some *plane geometry figures* better as *figures*, than others, once the role of prototypes in mental life is limited to the topic of exemplariness, removed from class membership or structure. What is more, it is not surprising that the identification functions are sometimes quite tangential to the core meanings themselves. After all, their utility does not rest on their sense, nor on the tightness of their relation to the conceptual core. Finally, such a position does not even require the belief that all concepts have a *conceptual* core, distinct from that identification function. For example, it is possible to believe with Kripke and others that the mass of everyday concepts are quasi-indexical; that is, that their extensions are determined quasi-indexically by human users.

Part II. Can We Make Good on the Feature Descriptions?
Without denying that some progress can be made by acknowledging the distinction between core and identification procedure, we would not want to paint too rosy a picture about current knowledge of concepts. We have argued so far only that our subjects' graded responses can be better understood as pertaining to a relatively unprincipled identification metric, thought to consist of a set of features prototypically organized, in the terms of one of the extant models, or some other. So understood, the role of prototypes in mental life would be more limited. But many serious problems remain. For to the extent that they are understood as feature theories, both prototype theories and nonprototype theories inherit many of the difficulties of all feature theories, including the classical definitional position; namely, that the features are hard to find, organize, and describe in a way that illuminates the concepts. And this is so even if the main use—or even the only use—of prototypes is to provide an identification procedure. Alarmingly, we must return to the question whether prototype plus core has solved anything.

A. What Are the Identification Features?   Our prior discussion had one central explanatory aim. We wanted to hold onto the feature-list descriptions, as relevant to mental representations, in light of the orderly outcomes of the experimental literature on prototypes. At the same time, we had to find a method of preservation that encompassed our new findings for the well-defined concepts. A dual theory might accomplish these twin goals, and in fact dual theories for concepts have been widely considered recently (see, e.g., Miller, 1977; Osherson and Smith, 1981; Smith and Medin, 1981, for very interesting discussions). Even in the now limited sense, however, the featural descriptions have grave problems. For one thing, as we noted earlier (see again note 3), it is not obvious *how* the proposed identification schemes are to work, for the various concepts, even if we are able (a matter independently in doubt) to describe the featural substrate *on which* they are to operate.

1. Are there coreless concepts?   One problem concerns the extent to which the identification function approach can be pushed. Prototype theorists might be tempted to assert that the identification function for most natural concepts *is* the structure of each of these concepts. They would probably argue that for such concepts the core and identification function are essentially alike (or perhaps that those concepts have no core at all). In that case, to describe the identification function would, minutia and a few sophisticated concepts aside, be tantamount to description of the 'psychological organization' of most concepts. But things can't be quite as simple as this. For if this argument is accepted—if *apple* and *sport* and *bird* and *tiger* are nothing but heuristic identification schemes for carving up the real world—shouldn't subjects throw in the conceptual towel when asked whether a bird is still a bird even when plucked (or dewinged, or debeaked, or whatever) or a tiger still a tiger without its stripes? But on the contrary, subjects seem to be quite sanguine about having these identification features (if that is what they are) removed, and even for the concepts that allegedly consist of nothing else. That is, it's not at all hard to convince the man on the street that there are three legged, tame, toothless albino tigers, that are tigers all the same. Of course the tigers are growing less prototypical, but what keeps them tigers?

A trivializing answer is that we simply haven't asked subjects to discard sufficient of these constituent tiger-features. After all, though the Cheshire cat was smug about his continuing existence, *qua* Cheshire cat, when only his smile remained, Alice was by her own admission 'disconcerted'. This question requires formal experimentation to resolve; but Komatsu (in progress), has preliminary evidence that subjects will give up most of their cherished features, while still maintaining that the tiger remains. If this is true, then whatever the case for the identification function, it is no substitute for the concept's core, even in the case of natural—family resemblance—concepts. Subjects often respond with surprise and some dismay when they are asked to describe what it is to be a *tiger*, and find they cannot. But they tend, in spite of this, to hold on to the commonsense notion that there *is* an essence, common to and definitive of *tiger*, though it is unknown to themselves; known, perhaps, to experts— biologists, maybe, for the present tiger-question (for this position, concerning the 'division of linguistic labor' between ordinary and expert users of a term, see Putnam, 1975).

2. What are the identification features?   Up to now we've assumed we know or can find out the rough-and-ready attributes by which an exemplar of a given category is to be identified—stripes for tigers, brownie-dispensing for grandmothers, and so on. But the specification of the identification function poses many problems. After all, the argument is standard and irrefutable that there's no end to the descriptions that can apply to any one stimulus or to all or some of its parts (see, for example, Quine on rabbits; 1960). All hope of an economical theory of categorization, even rough and ready categorization, is gone unless we can give an account of the feature set that learners and users will countenance. If this set is unconstrained, then the list of primitive discriminations burgeons. This argument (cf., Fodor, 1975) applies to definitional feature theories of concepts, but it applies no less to the supposed lists of identification features. Moreover, as Fodor has reminded us, the combinatorial problem that we discussed in introductory remarks for a theory of prototypical concepts arises in exactly the same way if we are to have a featural description of identification functions: it's not clear at all that the identification features for a complex concept can be inherited in any regular way from the identification features for its constituents. To use an example of Fodor's (personal communication), if you have an identification procedure for both *house* and *rich man*, this gives you no obvious productive system that yields an identification procedure for *rich man's house*. But if that is so, then the explanatory role of identification procedures is catastrophically reduced, for mainly we talk and understand more than one word at a time.

One problem at least is clear: the rough-and-ready attributes that determine whether a given item is a good or a bad exemplar differ from one category to another. In our study, the 'good' odd and even numbers were the *smaller* ones (as inspection of Table 10.1 shows). That makes sense, since cardinality and the notion *smallest* are surely relevant to arithmetic. But even in the domain of integers, smallness or even cardinality doesn't always enter into the prototype patterns that subjects reveal. Thus Wanner (1979) found that the prototypical prime numbers are those that go through certain heuristic decision procedures easily, and these aren't necessarily the smallest prime numbers. For example, 91 'looks primy' partly because it is odd, indivisible by 3, etc., properties that are connected only rather indirectly to primeness. When we move to a more distant domain, the relevant features are more different still. For instance, inspection of Table 10.1 shows that the *smallest females* are not taken to be the prototypical females. Smallness probably is not central to the female prototype even though certainly it is possible to ascertain the sizes of the females (and in fact size is even a rough distinguisher of *female* from *male*, at least for the mammals; that is, size has some cue validity in this case). As a matter of fact, we have previously remarked that it is something like a sexism metric that organizes the rankings of the female (with *mother* on the top and *comedienne* the lowest of all), as inspection of the Table also shows. None of this is really surprising, for given that the categories differ, the way in which one can identify their exemplars should surely differ too. But will we ever be able to specify how? On what limited bases? Is there any great likelihood that the list of needed identifying features will converge at a number smaller than that of the lexical items (see Fodor, 1975)?

So far as we can see, the prototype theories are not explicit, except in the claim for variability around a central value, for each concept. But that central value potentially is defined on different dimensions or features for each concept. Without stating these, there is close to no explanatory contribution in the assertion that each concept has 'a central value' in terms of feature composition, for this latter is differently composed in the case of each concept. What is likely is that 'heuristic identification schemes' like that uncovered by Wanner for spotting the prime numbers, and revealed in our experiments for spotting and ranking the odd numbers—and, quite likely, the fruits and vehicles!—are not merely matters of consulting lists of perceptual features; but something else: computation schemes, relevantly different for different concepts, in terms of which certain instances are more easily computable than others. There seems no special reason to think these schemes implicate sublexical features.

The problems we have discussed do not seem to exhaust the list of difficulties for feature list searches as identification functions—even if the features in question are just rough-and-ready ones. Suppose we knew, for *grandmother*, *rhubarb*, etc., the relevant features of their identification function. But surely, since this feature list is designed so that we can recognize new grandmothers, new rhubarbs, the features have to be cast in some relatively abstract form, and so must be marked also for the degree of allowable latitude on each. But allowable latitude, too, is hard to describe either in general or in particular. If (a big if) both tables and dogs are said to be identifiable by four *legs* in the same sense of legs, then what is the outside leg-to-body ratio allowed? Forty-yard legs on a two-inch body? The same for dogs and tables? Must we distinguish artifact legs from organism legs; worse, dog legs?

B. Features and Concept Cores   The arguments that we reviewed above are familiar enough: once having said 'feature theory', the job is to name which features with which latitudes for which concepts. What we argued in particular is that the difficulty of carrying out such an enterprise seems formidable even if limited to identification functions and to prototype organizations. But there is little doubt that the difficulties for a feature approach to concepts is even worse for describing the concept's core than for describing its identification function.

1. The search for the featural substrate   Enormous efforts have gone into the attempt to identify a featural substrate. For the most notable recent attempt, see Katz and Fodor (1963) and continuing work from Katz (1972; 1977). This enterprise was an attempt to infer the features of word meaning in terms of judgments of sentences in which the words occurred. The judgments were on such properties as synonymy, entailment, contradiction, anomaly, and so forth. For example, the judged anomaly of *I met a two year old bachelor yesterday* is a first basis for postulating a feature *adult* for *bachelor*. The approach has the great merit of tailoring the word-meaning description so that it directly serves the purposes of composing the phrase and sentence meanings, and determining the lexical and phrasal entailments. But for all its elegance, the approach has not been notoriously successful for the mass of ordinary words that, unlike the kin terms, are not so obviously definitional. In fact Fodor, Garrett, Walker, and Parkes (1980) present evidence, from sentence comprehension and verification studies, against the hypothesis that even *bachelor* literally decomposes into features, on which units comprehension is to take place. (At the opposite position, Katz, 1981, has recently argued that such psychological reactions—or even certain muddy judgments—are not the appropriate data on which to build a semantic theory, thus disconnecting formal semantics from any responsibility in accounting for human knowledge or behavior).[8]

A number of other empirical approaches to finding the feature set grew out of the traditions of experimental psychology and psychophysics. Here too the main lines of

8. A recent tradition in philosophy to which we earlier alluded supposes that for at least some terms—the natural kind terms—the systematic description (the real, not the psychologically real, essence of the terms) is the preserve of experts within the linguistic community; for example, these could be the biologists, physicists, chemists, etc., who describe *tiger, gold,* etc. in terms of scientific state-of-the-art microscopic features that correctly fix the extension of each (Putnam, 1975). An optimistic view for semantics would be that the conceptual cores are, ultimately, related to these real essences. However, Dupre (1981) gives a compelling, if depressing, discussion of the possible relations between the scientifically discoverable categories, and the mental categories underlying our lexical usages. He does this by considering how biological taxa (as developed by the biologists) map onto ordinary language terms. He points out that the biological taxa crosscut the linguistic categories extensively; that it is not only at the margins of category boundaries that biologists and ordinary language users part company. An example cited by Dupre concerns the onion, which, as it happens, is (from an expert point of view) just one more lily. If, in general, the scientists and the speakers part company at the centers, and not only at the margins, of the categories in which they traffic, we can't look to the scientific taxonomies as explications of the natural language categories. In sum, if there is a feature set for the conceptual core (or the identification function, for that matter) we can't look to the natural scientists to do the semantic work of uncovering them for psychologists concerned with human categorization.

attack have been indirect. The features (or dimensions) were inferred, for example, through a factor analysis of the ratings of words on a set of polar adjectives (Osgood et al., 1957) or through multidimensional scaling (Caramazza et al., 1976; Rips et al., 1973). But the results here are somewhat disheartening for the feature set (or set of dimensions) that emerges from such manipulations is simply too impoverished to do justice to the phenomena of categorization, or lexical semantics.

2. *The attribute-listing paradigm*   It has remained for Rosch and Mervis (1975) to attack this problem head on. In effect, they asked their subjects to act as the lexicographers. Given a word, the subjects were to provide the attributes (that is, the features) that described it. This experiment has been extremely influential, and justly so for it seemed to be one of the most direct demonstrations of prototype structure.[9] But it is doubtful that it succeeded in discovering the relevant feature set for various natural concepts that others had failed to find. To document this point, we will consider the Rosch and Mervis paradigm and its usual interpretations more closely.

Rosch and Mervis' (1975) subjects were simply presented with various exemplars from a number of superordinate concepts (e.g., *chair, sofa, bed*, from the category *furniture*) and asked to list "all the attributes" they could think of for each of these items. Their rationale was straightforward: If there is a set of necessary and sufficient attributes that defines, say, *furniture*, then every item that falls under the concept *furniture* necessarily has all the required attributes. Rosch and Mervis found that "very few" (sometimes no) attributes were listed for all the items that presumably are exemplars of their superordinate categories. Given this result, the investigators concluded that the superordinate itself (e.g., *furniture*) was properly described as a family resemblance category rather than as a definitional category. We have already argued that such descriptions are more easily interpreted as pertaining to exemplariness than to category structure. But there is a prior issue that has to do with what the Rosch and Mervis task asks, for it is by no means clear that the subjects could really comply with the instructions to come up with the appropriate features that describe a given word (or concept). After all, why should one expect them to succeed where generations of lexicographers before them failed?

2a. *The Suppression of Features*   One problem concerns the suppression of features. Suppose a subject is asked to list all the features of a given term (and suppose there are such features). Would he really list them all even if he knew them? Clearly not. Some of the reasons are quite systematic, and have to do with lexical redundancy rules. So for example most subjects don't mention *living thing* let alone *physical object* for *canary*. The features of the superordinate are simply presumed to apply to the

---

9. As mentioned earlier (see note 4), some methodological and technical objections have been mounted against this experiment. But we believe such difficulties are minor, and at any rate Rosch (1975b) has answered most of them. Even so, one problematical point is that judges intervened between the subjects' responses and the scoring. As we understand the report of the study, the judges crossed out any absurd attributes subjects listed and added some (this latter under a severe constraint) that they may have forgotten. It is a bit puzzling how to interpret the subjects' responses as filtered through this correction procedure, though it has plausibility, and though the authors report that "the changes made by the judges were infrequent". We are assuming none of these technicalities affect the reported outcomes very seriously, though subjects have on occasion been reported to be quite unruly in this procedure. For example, in a partial replication run by Komatsu (unpublished manuscript), one subject's total entry for *lettuce* was (1) throw away outside leaves, (2) eat inside leaves.

items that fall under it, and don't have to be listed as such. For related reasons, people tend to tell you what they think you need to know, suppressing the obvious. For example, a standard dictionary defines a *zebrula* as a *cross between a zebra and a horse*; but no dictionary would ever define a *horse* as a *cross between a horse and a horse*. This could be because the lexicographer has a pretty good idea of what you know about horses, organisms, etc. What holds of lexicographers doubtless holds for subjects in attribute-listing experiments as well so the level of response, and hence the particular attributes listed, may vary from item to item. These problems are all quite obvious. Still they seem to us cause to wonder just what is happening when subjects "list the attributes."

2b. The Expression of Features   An even more troublesome problem is whether the subjects could express the features anyway—again assuming such features exist, and assuming redundancy rules and context determinants, etc., will not keep the subjects from listing them all. How do we know the subject can access the features in the first place, and express them in words? For if the feature theory is the correct theory, few of the words in the language represent a feature bare. Assuming the correctness of this theory, most words must represent a bundle of features—each of which presumably is writ in Mentalese. If so, how could the subjects tell us about the features, unless each of these is expressable by one word only (which is unlikely) and that a word which carries no excess featural baggage of its own (more unlikely still)? The point is that the more the theory is correct that words are bundles of features, the less likely that the subjects' responses in whole words would be single-feature responses.

Some empirical basis for this particular worry comes from an examination of subjects' responses in an attribute-listing experiment. In a partial replication of the Rosch and Mervis study, Komatsu obtained some interesting reactions that indicate a mismatch between query (about features) and answers (in words). Take the subjects' responses to *grapefruit* and *tractor*. The subjects varied. Some said grapefruits are sweet while others said sour. Some said tractors had four wheels, while others said two wheels. To this extent the concepts *tractor* and *grapefruit* seem to vary among members of the linguistic community, much as the prototype theory would have it. But this interpretation seems shaky, just because it's not clear that *sweet* and *two wheels* are attributes of the appropriate scope. For while the subjects differed they also agreed up to a point: none of them said how many wheels a grapefruit had and none of them said how sweet a tractor was. (A tractor *can* be sweet, by the way. Taste one: it might surprise you. This means the absence of this feature can't be explained on grounds of an ontological category violation, as described by Keil, 1979. Sweetness is obviously irrelevant, of tractors; but this doesn't make it a category error). In short, the subjects seemed to share some common conceptions of the categories, but were unable to come up with the right level of description—perhaps they should have said 'bewheeled' or 'sweet/sour dimension' but they could not or would not. We conclude that even if categories are describable in terms of some featural vocabulary, it will be difficult to expose this by direct inquiry. But, as described earlier, more indirect methods have not fared much better.

3. *The sum of the features is not the whole concept*   The preceding discussion tried to highlight some difficulties in making explicit a feature account of concepts, whether fuzzy or definable. But even more damaging to such a theory is the kind of Gestalt problem that has been discussed again and again (e.g., Fodor, 1975; 1981). The simple

fact is that a bird is not a sum of features, whatever these may be. All the features in the world that are characteristic of and common to all birds don't make a bird—that is, not unless these properties are held together in a bird structure. To paraphrase a famous example from Quine (used, of course, to urge a different point), without the bird-Gestalt all the bird features might as well be undetached bird parts. This is to say, though, that the crucial feature of bird is: essence of *bird*.

Symmetrically, not all feature assemblies add up to good Gestalts. An old riddle asks: What looks like a box, smells like lox, and flies? The answer is a flying lox-box. *Feathers, wings, flies, animalness* (etc.) compose on the featural view to a natural complex, *bird*. On the other hand, to the extent *lox, box,* and *flies* are features too (or bundles of features, it doesn't matter here) how come their conjunction doesn't yield a natural complex? That is, what's so funny about a flying lox-box? A good feature theory would be one that could engage this problem, it seems to us.

In addition to the fact that separable bird features don't seem to do the job in describing the bird concept, there is the question of whether proposed bird-features are, as required by a feature theory, somehow more primitive components of the concepts they describe—little meaning atoms that combine in differing ways to form the multitude of concepts in our mental world. But if so, why hasn't anyone found them? Shouldn't one expect the many words in the language to be describable by a (smaller) set of more primitive words, corresponding, however crudely, to these meaning atoms? Perhaps we should, but dictionaries seem to tell us otherwise. Most of the words in the language are defined there in terms of one another, with most words—unfamiliar ones excepted—acting as defined on some occasions and definers on others. It is as if all the words made their living by taking in each others' washing.

Part III. Final Thoughts in Favor of Not Studying the Concepts All at Once, at Least Not Now

We have been advancing a series of arguments that seem to us, taken together, to weaken the case for attribute or feature theories of at least most ordinary concepts, even if the features are to be relevant 'only' to an identification procedure. The problem is ultimately that the concepts don't seem to decompose, except into each other. There must be rich and intricate relations among the lexical concepts, to be sure, but it isn't clear that some small number of them are the basic ones. Giving up the feature story does not, as again Fodor has argued, make the job of describing compositional meaning any harder (networks of relations *among* the whole words will do the job as well or as badly).

However, giving up the idea of features makes it more difficult than ever even to envisage a *general* theory of concepts. This is because, quite possibly, a nonfeatural account of the concepts would have to countenance the huge number of natural categories (for example, those that are lexicalized in the everyday vocabulary of a natural language) each as an item in the primitive base, none of them in any natural ways arising from or reduceable to each other (Fodor, 1975).

More optimistically, we might hope for discovery of a set of *principles*—some set of interrelated rules—that, applied to our experiences with the world, would yield the variety of lexical concepts as the inevitable outcomes (see Chomsky, 1975, ch. 2, for discussion). Such principles might be general across conceptual domains (for contributions that seem to adopt this perspective, see, e.g., Garner, 1978; Markman, 1979; E. Smith and Medin, 1981; and L. Smith and Kemler, 1978). On the other hand, these principles may be different in each of the conceptual domains. Perhaps we have linguistic principles that inevitably, on exposure to linguistic data, yield such linguistic categories as *noun*; and perceptual principles of other kinds that, on exposure to, say, the visible world, yield such categories as *object* (e.g., Spelke, 1982). At any rate, positive results in these terms, even if possible, seem a long way away. For ourselves, we can only dimly envisage what kinds of principled approach to the organization of concepts might be taken. Nor can we envisage the precise sense in which generative principles of organization, for conceptual domains, might be more than terminologically different from 'features', as these latter were never made very precise by their proponents.

In the current state of affairs in cognitive psychology, we ourselves are not optimistic that a general theory of categorization, one that will answer to the serious problems (explication of functions from words to the world, and of the units that figure in phrasal meanings and in lexical entailments) is just around the corner. To the contrary, the continuing failure of the search for such units leads us to doubt whether there is a general psychological domain encompassing 'all concepts' parallel, say, to a general cognitive domain of 'all sensory experiences', 'all emotions', and so forth. In our opinion, cognitive psychology has made progress precisely where it has attempted to identify and investigate singly rich and highly structured conceptual domains. A paradigm recent example has been the study of universal grammar.

We do not think that discoveries concerning the various important conceptual domains will reveal that any of them are organized as simple feature structures. Rather, in each domain, the units, their patterning, the principles that organize them, their development, their environmental dependence, are all likely to be different and likely to be complex, rewarding serious study. As for the minor everyday concepts, such as *rhubarb*, *slipper*, *pebble*, *sofa*, it is possible we are fooling ourselves that the question of their single or joint structure is interesting, or fundamental to psychology. Even if it is, there may be no general theory of categorization that will subsume and therefore explain them all.

In sum, a host of thinkers have shown us that there is enormous difficulty in explicating even so simple and concrete a concept as *bird*. They've shown that the difficulty becomes greater by orders of magnitude when confronted with an abstract functional concept like *game*. Perhaps psychologists are more than a little over-exhuberant in supposing it will be easier to explicate the concept *concept*.

References

Bates, E., and MacWhinney, B. (1982) Functionalist approaches to grammar in E. Wanner and L. R. Gleitman (eds.), *Language Acquisition: State of the Art*. Cambridge, Cambridge University Press.

Battig, W. R., and Montague, W. E. (1969) Category norms for visual items in 56 categories. A replication and extension of the Connecticut Category Norms. *J. exper. Psychol. Mono., 80*, (3, pt. 2).

Bever, T. G. (1982) Some implications of the nonspecific bases of language, in E. Wanner and L. R. Gleitman (eds.), *Language Acquisition: State of the Art*. Cambridge, Cambridge University Press.

Bolinger, D. L. (1965) The atomization of meaning. *Lange., 41*, 555–573.

Bourne, L. E., Jr. (1982) Typicality effects in logically defined categories, *Mem. Cog., 10* (1), 3–9.

Caramazza, A., Hersch, H., and Torgerson, W. S. (1976) Subjective structures and operations in semantic memory. *J. verb. Learn. verb. Behav., 15*, 103–118.

Chomsky, N. (1975) *Reflections on Language*, New York, Random House.

Collins, A., and Loftus, E. F. (1975) A spreading activation theory of semantic processing. *Psychol. Rev., 82* (6), 407–428.

Danks, J. H., and Glucksberg, S. (1980) Experimental psycholinguistics. *An. Rev. Psychol., 31,* 391–417.

Dupre, J. (1981) Natural kinds and biological taxa. *Phil. Rev., 40* (1), 66–90.

Fodor, J. A. (1975) *The Language of Thought.* Cambridge, Harvard University Press.

Fodor, J. A. (1981) *Representations.* Cambridge, Mass, MIT Press.

Fodor, J. A., Garrett, M. F., Walker, E. T., and Parkes, C. (1980) Against definitions. *Cog., 8* (3), 1–105.

Fodor, J. D., Fodor, J. A., and Garrett, M. F. (1975) The psychological unreality of semantic representations. *Ling. Inq., 6* (4), 515–53.

Frege, G. (1970) On sense and reference, translated by M. Black, in P. Geach and M. Black (eds.), *Philosophical Writings of Gottlob Frege.* Oxford, Basil Blackwell, Original publication, 1892.

Garner, W. R. (1978) Aspects of a stimulus: Features, dimensions, and configurations. In E. Rosch and B. B. Lloyd (eds.), *Cognition and categorization.* Hillsdale, NJ, Erlbaum.

Goodman, N. (1965) *Fact, Fiction, and Forecast.* New York, Bobbs-Merrill.

Katz, J. J. (1972) *Semantic Theory.* New York, Harper and Row.

Katz, J. J. (1977) The real status of semantic representations. *Ling. Inq., 8* (3), 559–584.

Katz, J. J. (1981) *Language and Other Abstract Objects.* Totowa, NJ, Rowman and Littlefield.

Katz, J. J., and Fodor, J. A. (1963) The structure of a semantic theory. *Lang., 39,* 170–210.

Keil, F. C. (1979) *Semantic and Conceptual Development.* Cambridge, Mass., Harvard University Press.

Kripke, S. (1971) Identity and necessity. In M. K. Munitz (ed.), *Identity and Necessity.* New York, New York University Press.

Kripke, S. (1972) Naming and necessity, In D. Davidson and G. Harman (eds.), *Semantics of Natural Language.* Dordrecht, Holland, Reidel.

Kucera, H. K., and Francis, W. N. (1967) *Computational Analysis of Present-day American English.* Providence, RI, Brown University Press.

Landau, B. (1982) Will the real grandmother plesase stand up. *J. Psycholing. Res., 11* (2), 47–62.

Locke, J. (1968) *An Essay concerning Human Understanding.* Cleveland, Ohio, World Publishing Co. Original publication 1690.

Loftus, E. F. (1975) Spreading activation within semantic categories: Comments on Rosch's "Cognitive representation of semantic categories." *J. exper. Psychol.: Gen., 104* (3), 234–240.

Maratsos, M. (1982) The child's construction of grammatical categories in E. Wanner and L. R. Gleitman, (eds.), *Language Acquisition: State of the Art* Cambridge, Cambridge University Press.

Markman, E. M. (1979) Classes and collections: Conceptual organization and numerical abilities. *Cog. Psychol., 11,* 395–411.

McCloskey, M., and Glucksberg, S. (1978) Natural categories: Well defined or fuzzy sets? *Mem. Cog., 6* (4), 462–472.

McCloskey, M., and Glucksberg, S. (1979) Decision processes in verifying category membership statements: implications for models of semantic memory, *Cog. Psychol., 11,* 1–37.

Mervis, C. B., and Rosch, E. (1981) Categorization of natural objects. *An. Rev. Psychol., 32,* 89–115.

Miller, G. A. (1977) Practical and lexical knowledge, In P. N. Johnson-Laird and P. C. Wason (eds.), *Thinking: Readings in Cognitive Science.* Cambridge, Cambridge University Press.

Miller, G. A., and Johnson-Laird, P. N. (1976) *Language and Perception.* Cambridge, Harvard University Press.

Osgood, C. D., Suci, G. J., and Tannenbaum, P. H. (1957) The measurement of meaning. Urbana, University of Illinois Press.

Osherson, D. N. (1978) Three conditions on conceptual naturalness, *Cog., 6,* 263–89.

Osherson, D. N., and Smith, E. F. (1981) On the adequacy of prototype theory as a theory of concepts. *Cog., 9* (1), 35–58.

Putnam, H. (1975) *Mind, Language, and Reality: Philosophical Papers, Volume 2.* Cambridge, Cambridge University Press.

Quine, W. V. O. (1960) *Word and Object.* Cambridge, MIT Press.

Rips, L. J., Shoben, E. J., and Smith, E. E. (1973) Semantic distance and the verification of semantic relations. *J. verb. Learn. verb. Behav., 12,* 1–20.

Rosch, E. (1973) On the internal structure of perceptual and semantic categories. In T. E. Moore (ed.), *Cognitive Development and the Acquisition of Language.* New York, Academic Press.

Rosch, E. (1975a) Cognitive representations of semantic categories. *J. exper. Psychol.: Gen., 104,* 192–233.

Rosch, E. (1975b) Reply to Loftus. *J. exper. Psychol.: Gen., 104* (3), 241–243.

Rosch, E. (1978) Principles of categorization. In E. Rosch and B. B. Lloyd (eds.), *Cognition and Categorization.* Hillsdale, NJ, Erlbaum.

Rosch, E., and Mervis, C. B. (1975) Family resemblances: Studies in the internal structure of categories. *Cog. Psychol.*, *7*, 573–605.

Rosch, E., Mervis, C. B., Gray, W. D., Johnson, D. M., and Boyes-Braem, P. (1976) Basic objects in natural categories. *Cog. Psychol.*, *8*, 382–439.

Schwartz, S. P. (1979) Natural kind terms. *Cog.*, *7* (3), 301–315, 382–439.

Smith, E. E. (1978) Theories of semantic memory. In W. K. Estes (ed.), *Handbook of Learning and Cognitive Processes, Vol. 6.* Potomac, Md., Erlbaum.

Smith, E. E., and Medin, D. L. (1981) *Categories and concepts.* Cambridge, Harvard University Press.

Smith, L. B., and Kemler, D. G. (1978) Levels of experienced dimensionality in children and adults. *Cog. Psychol.*, *10*, 502–532.

Spelke, E. S. (1982) Perceptual knowledge of objects in infancy. In J. Mehler, M. Garrett, and E. Walker (eds.), *On Mental Representation.* Hillsdale, NJ, Erlbaum.

Thorndike, E. L., and Lorge, I. (1944) *The Teacher's Word Book of 30,000 words.* New York, Teacher's College.

Tversky, A., and Gati, I. (1978) Studies of similarity. In E. Rosch and B. B. Lloyd (eds.), *Cognition and Categorization.* Hillsdale, NJ, Erlbaum.

Wanner, E. (1979) False identification of prime numbers. Paper presented at the 1979 meeting of *The Society for Philosophy and Psychology*, New York, N.Y.

Wittgenstein, L. (1953) *Philosophical Investigations.* New York, MacMillan.

Zadeh, L. (1965) Fuzzy sets. *Information and control*, *8*, 338–53.

Chapter 11

On the Adequacy of Prototype Theory as a Theory of Concepts

Daniel N. Osherson and Edward E. Smith

A novel and ambitious theory has emerged from the last ten years of psychological research into the concepts that underlie "kind" terms like "animal," "tree," "tool," and "clothing." The distinguishing doctrine of the new theory is that entities fall neither sharply in nor sharply out of a concept's extension. Rather, an object instances a concept only to the extent that it is similar to the prototype of the concept; the boundary between membership and nonmembership in a concept's extension is thus fuzzy. We'll call the new theory (really, class of theories) *prototype theory*. In this paper we consider two aspects of concepts relevant to choosing between prototype theory and its more traditional rivals. One concerns conceptual combination, that is, the process whereby relatively complex concepts are forged out of relatively simple ones. The other deals with truth conditions for thoughts, that is, the circumstances under which a thought corresponding to a declarative proposition is true. For both aspects, we argue that the new theory of concepts fares worse than the old.

The organization of this paper is as follows. We first present one version of prototype theory. We then show how it might be extended to account for conceptual combination by means of principles derived from *fuzzy-set theory* (e.g., Zadeh, 1965). This extension is demonstrated to be fraught with difficulties. We then move on to the issue of truth conditions for thoughts, again using fuzzy-set theory as a means of implementing the prototype approach, and again demonstrating that this implementation won't work. In a final section, we establish that our analysis holds for virtually any version of prototype theory, and consider ways of reconciling previous evidence for this theory with the wisdom of the older kind of theory of concepts.

Section 1. Prototype Theory

The version of prototype theory expounded in this section appears implicitly and explicitly in several well known papers (e.g., Posner and Keele, 1968; Rosch, Simpson and Miller, 1976), and it is the simplest account we know. However, other work within the prototype theory tradition (e.g., Reed, 1972) directly contradicts it, and there are numerous alternative formulations of the theory that differ from our version in various details. Nevertheless, the version about to be specified is "prototypical" of prototype models in that it captures key ideas of prototype theory more successfully than rival versions; and it is only these key ideas that are crucial for our analysis, as we demonstrate later (see section 4.2).

This research was partly supported by U.S. Public Health Service Grant MH-19705. We thank Ned Block, Susan Carey, David Israel, Louis Narens, Gary Olson, Molly Potter, Lance Rips, William Salter, and Ken Wexler for helpful discussion of the ideas in this paper.

1.1. Formal Characterization

According to the present version of prototype theory, many concepts can be identified with (mental) representations of quadruples like (∗),

$$(*) \quad \langle A, d, p, c \rangle$$

where

A is a set of readily envisionable objects (real or imagined) called a *conceptual domain*;

d is a function from $A \times A$ into the positive real numbers, called a *distance metric*;

p is a member of A, called the concept's *prototype*; and

c is a function from A into [0, 1], called the concept's *characteristic function*; and such that the following two conditions hold:

(1.1) $\langle A, d \rangle$ is a *metric space*, i.e.,
             $(\forall x \in A)(\forall y \in A)$
    (1a) $d(x, y) = 0$ iff $x = y$
    (1b) $d(x, y) = d(y, x)$
    (1c) $d(x, y) + d(y, z) \geq d(x, z)$

(1.2) $(\forall x \in A)(\forall y \in A)$
             $d(x, p) \leq d(y, p) \rightarrow c(y) \leq c(x)$.

The second condition requires that the closer an object is to its prototype, the more characteristic it is of the concept.

We can illustrate with the concept *bird*. According to prototype theory it is identical to a mental representation of the quadruple

$$\langle B, d_{bird}, p_{bird}, c_{bird} \rangle,$$

where

B is the set of all readily envisionable birds (including robins, sparrows, and penguins);[1]

d_{bird} is a function on pairs of such birds into real numbers (assigning smaller numbers to pairs of similar objects, e.g., robin-sparrow, than to pairs of dissimilar ones, e.g., robin-penguin, thereby reflecting relative psychological similarity among elements of B);

p_{bird} is some particular bird in B (usually taken to be the bird that has the average value on each dimension of the underlying metric space); and

c_{bird} is a function assigning numbers in [0, 1] to members of B in such a way that closeness to the prototype reflects greater "birdiness."

---

1. If you come across an ordinary robin that is new to your experience, is the theory committed to a change in your bird concept, in light of the new element added to B? No, the new robin was already envisionable, so it was in B to begin with. On the other hand, if you happen upon a very queer bird (e.g., one with tusks), not so readily envisioned, your concept may well change by expansion of B.

When construed in this way, the concept *bird* appears to meet conditions (1.1) and (1.2). And this construal is consistent with a number of empirical findings. In particular, consider the case where subjects give similarity ratings for pairs including either two instances of bird (e.g., "robin-sparrow") or one instance and the term "bird" itself (e.g., "robin-bird"), and then these ratings are converted into a multidimensional metric space. Assuming that the point in the space for the term "bird" corresponds to the prototype, the following findings emerge:

> (a) The value of the prototype on each dimension is roughly equal to the average value of all scaled instances on this dimension (Rosch and Mervis, 1975). This provides some justification for identifying the prototype with an average, though it is not really critical for the present version of prototype theory.
>
> (b) In general, the less the metric distance between any bird and the prototype, the more characteristic or prototypical of the concept that bird is judged to be (e.g., Rips, Shoben and Smith, 1973). Since different groups of subjects make the initial pairwise similarity ratings and prototypicality judgments, these results provide good evidence for condition (1.2) above, i.e., for the psychological reality of a function mapping distance from a prototype into a characteristic function that reflects "birdiness."
>
> (c) In general, the more characteristic or prototypical a particular bird: (i) the more efficiently it can be categorized, efficiency being measured by both accuracy and speed (e.g., Rips *et al.*, 1973); (ii) the earlier it will be output when subjects list instances of the concept (e.g., Rosch *et al.*, 1976); and (iii) the earlier a child will learn that it is an instance of the concept (e.g., Rosch, 1973). Thus, the value of the characteristic function for an object can be used to predict aspects of real-time processing and conceptual development.

1.2. Some Gaps in the Theory

While the above findings provide some support for one version of prototype theory, there are currently two substantial gaps in this or any other extant version of the theory. First, not all natural concepts succumb to the kind of construal we have given for *bird*. Prototype theory, as thus far developed, is best suited to "kind" notions (like *dog*, *tree*, and *animal*), to "artifact" notions (like *tool* and *clothing*), and to simple descriptive notions like *triangular* and *red*. What remains outside the theory's purview are intentional or otherwise intricate concepts like *belief*, *desire*, and *justice*, as well as the meanings of prepositions, sentence connectives, and a host of other ideas. It is an open question whether or not the theory can be extended to cover these cases, and in this paper we shall say no more about them.

The second gap is the inverse of the first; namely, many nonnatural concepts do succumb to the kind of construal we have given for *bird*. According to the present version of prototype theory, each concept is identical to some quadruple, with distinct concepts being identical to distinct quadruples (i.e., quadruples differing in at least one component).[2] But many such quadruples will have bizarre domains (and perhaps other defects as well). It is possible, for example, to use a single metric space to represent objects as diverse as dogs, chairs and toothpaste (thereby satisfying

---

2. More precisely, different concepts are to be identified with *mental representations* of different quadruples (we'll count different mental representatons of the same quadruple to be variants of the same concept). In what follows, we will occasionally suppress this mental-representation qualifier.

condition (1.1), to define a prototype in this space, and to then map distances from this prototype into values of a characteristic function so that small distances go with larger characteristic values (thereby satisfying condition (1.2)). This state of affairs reveals an important incompleteness in the theory. We need to know more about the entities A, d, p, and c than is revealed by conditions (1.1) and (1.2), so that we can limit the theoretically possible concepts to those that are psychologically natural. Again it is an open question whether such an extension of the theory can be made, and again we shall say no more about the issue here.

Section 2. Prototype Theory and Conceptual Combination

Despite the gaps just mentioned, it is useful to evaluate prototype theory by means of facts about conceptual combination, where the concepts are natural ones and restricted to kind terms. Though there has been some experimental work on this issue (e.g., Hersch and Caramazza, 1976; Oden, 1977), the present analysis provides a more general outlook. In what follows, we first briefly describe the issue of conceptual combination, then relate this issue to legitimate demands upon prototype theory, next spell out the principles of fuzzy-set theory on which prototype theorists rely in order to deal with conceptual combination, and lastly show that this enterprise eventuates in a snarl of contradictions.

2.1. The Issue

One or more concepts combine to form another whenever the latter has the former as constituents. Grammatical constituency can often serve as a guide to conceptual constituency. Thus, the words "red" and "table" are constituents of the grammatical structure "red table," and in parallel fashion the concepts *red* and *table* are constituents of the conceptual structure *red table*. The same parallel holds for many other conceptual combinations, e.g., *square window* and *tasty onion*.[3] There are, of course, cases where the parallelism breaks down. Thus, the concept *dark horse* (as in political contests) does not have *dark* and *horse* as conceptual constituents. Such idioms notwithstanding, it seems safe in what follows to frequently rely on grammatical structure as a guide to conceptual structure.

The phenomena surrounding conceptual combination can be used to evaluate prototype theory in the following way. Let's say that this theory is *compatible* with conceptual combination if principles can be supplied that correctly predict the relation between complex concepts and their constituents, when concepts are construed as specified by the theory. Or at least, many such conceptual combinations accord with the theory's principles and few violate them.

2.2. Criteria of Adequacy Regarding Conceptual Combination

Suppose a given concept C has concepts C_1 and C_2 as constituents. For prototype theory to be compatible with this case of conceptual combination, principles must be

---

3. It is unclear whether the parallel holds for grammatical structures like "very happy". It may be that *very happy* has only one conceptual constituent, namely, *happy*. That is, the word "very" may not denote a concept in *very happy*, since it may not correspond to a constituent in the language of thought, but instead be represented syncategorematically. Similar remarks apply to *unhappy*. We'll extend the ordinary usage of "combination" to allow a single concept to be "combined" into another concept by the use of such devices.

available to specify the quadruple associated with C on the basis of the quadruples associated with C_1 and C_2.[4] Actually, these principles ought to specify the (*mental*) *representation* of the former quadruple on the basis of the (mental) representations of the latter quadruples; but in the present era of psychological understanding, we shall settle for a specification, not of the representation (i.e., not of C itself), but of the associated quadruple (i.e., of what C represents).

The desired principles, then, will characterize C's domain, distance metric, prototype, and characteristic function on the basis of the entities from the quadruples for C_1 and C_2. However, we shall restrict attention to the problem of specifying C's characteristic function on the basis of those of C_1 and C_2. There are two reasons to so narrow the present inquiry. First, a solution to the characteristic function problem is necessary for a general solution to the problem of conceptual combination, and it may be close to sufficient as well.[5] Second, the only explicit account of conceptual combination within the prototype theory tradition (given below) restricts *its* attention to the characteristic functions of C, C_1, and C_2.

We may now investigate the compatibility of prototype theory with the facts of conceptual combination, in particular, with the relationship between the characteristic functions of complex concepts and the characteristic functions of their conceptual constituents. Combinatorial principles germane to this problem have been supplied by Zadeh (e.g., 1965) under the name of *fuzzy-set theory*, and prototype theorists (e.g., Oden, 1977; Rosch and Mervis, 1975) cite fuzzy-set theory in this connection. It is possible that principles other than those provided by Zadeh can better serve prototype theory in accounting for conceptual combination, but no suitable alternative has yet been suggested (so far as we know).[6] Since, in addition, fuzzy-set theory is a natural complement to prototype theory, and the former is an appealing theory in its own right, we shall evaluate prototype theory exclusively in the context of fuzzy-set theory. If this ensemble is at variance with the facts of conceptual combination, there is some reason to doubt the compatibility of prototype theory with these facts.

2.3. Fuzzy-Set Theory

The principles of fuzzy set theory are straightforward generalizations of elementary principles of standard set theory.[7] We start by enumerating the relevant principles of standard set theory.

Let D be the domain of discourse, and A a subset of D. In standard set theory, the *characteristic function for A* is defined to be that unique function

(2.1) $c_A : D \to \{0, 1\}$

such that

4. Additionally, it must be true that prototype theory successfully construes C, C_1, and C_2 as mental representations of quadruples of form (∗) in the first place. We'll assume so in what follows.
5. For: (a) C's domain is likely just the union of those for C_1 and C_2, (b) C's distance metric can be highly constrained by its characteristic function if condition (1.2) is strengthened in any of several empirically plausible ways (we omit the details), and (c) C's prototype can be taken as the "average" member of C's domain according to its distance metric.
6. In Sections 3.5 and 4.3 we discuss alternatives to Zadeh's (1965) proposals.
7. Zadeh (1965) develops fuzzy-set theory beyond the limits imposed here, e.g., to deal with the composition of relations. However, we will present enough of the theory to assess its empirical adequacy.

$$(2.2) \quad (\forall x \in D) c_A(x) = \begin{cases} 1 \text{ if } x \in A \\ 0 \text{ if } x \notin A. \end{cases}$$

Set membership is thus strictly binary; there are no liminal cases of objects falling neither precisely in nor precisely out of a set.

The characteristic functions for intersections, unions, and complements of sets can be standardly defined as follows (where A and B are arbitrary subsets of D).

$(2.3) \quad (\forall x \in D) c_{A \cap B}(x) = \min(c_A(x), c_B(x))$ (Intersection)

$(2.4) \quad (\forall x \in D) c_{A \cup B}(x) = \max(c_A(x), c_B(x))$ (Union)

$(2.5) \quad (\forall x \in D) c_{\text{non}A}(x) = 1 - c_A(x)$ (Complement)

The characteristic functions for the empty and universal sets, $\varnothing$ and D, meet conditions (2.6) and (2.7), respectively.

$(2.6) \quad (\forall x \in D) c_\varnothing(x) = 0$ (Empty set)

$(2.7) \quad (\forall x \in D) c_D(x) = 1$ (Universal set)

Thus, in the domain of animals, suppose that $c_{\text{dog}}(\text{Rover}) = 1$ and $c_{\text{female}}(\text{Rover}) = 0$. Then:

$$c_{\text{dog} \cap \text{female}}(\text{Rover}) = \min(c_{\text{dog}}(\text{Rover}), c_{\text{female}}(\text{Rover}))$$
$$= \min(1, 0) = 0;$$

$$c_{\text{dog} \cup \text{female}}(\text{Rover}) = \max(c_{\text{dog}}(\text{Rover}), c_{\text{female}}(\text{Rover}))$$
$$= \max(1, 0) = 1;$$

$$c_{\text{nondog}}(\text{Rover}) = 1 - c_{\text{dog}}(\text{Rover}) = 1 - 1 = 0;$$

$$c_{\text{nonfemale}}(\text{Rover}) = 1 - c_{\text{female}}(\text{Rover}) = 1 - 0 = 1.$$

Fuzzy set theory results from expanding the range of characteristic functions from $\{0, 1\}$ to $[0, 1]$, i.e., from the set whose only elements are 0 and 1 to the set of all real numbers between 0 and 1, inclusive. Set membership thus becomes continuously graded, an element, e, belonging to A to the extent that $c_A(e)$ approximates 1. Instead of (2.1) and (2.2), we now have

$(2.8) \quad c_A : D \to [0, 1]$

(2.9) The larger $c_A(x)$, the more x belongs to A;
       the smaller $c_A(x)$, the less x belongs to A;
       1 and 0 are limiting cases (for all $x \in D$).

The definitions given by (2.3)–(2.7) remain unchanged, but the characteristic functions therein are now taken to be of the fuzzy-set type, (2.8), rather than of the standard type, (2.1). To illustrate, if $c_{\text{dog}}(\text{Rover}) = 0.85$ and $c_{\text{female}}(\text{Rover}) = 0.10$, then:

$$c_{\text{dog} \cap \text{female}}(\text{Rover}) = \min(c_{\text{dog}}(\text{Rover}), c_{\text{female}}(\text{Rover}))$$
$$= \min(0.85, 0.10) = 0.10;$$

$$c_{\text{dog} \cap \text{female}}(\text{Rover}) = \min(c_{\text{dog}}(\text{Rover}), c_{\text{female}}(\text{Rover}))$$
$$= \max(0.85, 0.10) = 0.85;$$

$$c_{\text{nondog}}(\text{Rover}) = 1 - c_{\text{dog}}(\text{Rover}) = 1 - 0.85 = 0.15;$$

$$c_{\text{nonfemale}}(\text{Rover}) = 1 - c_{\text{female}}(\text{Rover}) = 1 - 0.10 = 0.90.$$

2.4. Is Prototype Theory Compatible with Conceptual Combination?

We are ready to demonstrate that prototype theory in conjunction with fuzzy-set theory contradicts strong intuitions we have about concepts. Three problem areas are considered: conjunctive concepts, logically empty and logically universal sets, and disjunctive concepts.[8]

2.4.1. Conjunctive Concepts

Let the domain of discourse be the set, F, of all fruit, and consider the characteristic functions for the (fuzzy) concepts *apple*, *striped*, and *striped apple*. The concept *striped apple* stands in the same relation to *striped* and *apple* as does *red house* to *red* and *house*, *square field* to *square* and *field*, and so on. *Striped apple* thus qualifies as a conjunctive concept. Within fuzzy-set theory, conjunctive concepts are most naturally represented as fuzzy intersections, as in (2.3). At least, they clearly are not fuzzy unions, nor any yet more complex fuzzy Boolean function of their constituents. So, if there is to be any account of the conceptual combination *striped apple* within fuzzy-set theory, it will likely rest upon (2.10).

$$(2.10) \quad (\forall x \in F) \quad c_{\text{striped apple}}(x) = \min(c_{\text{striped}}(x), c_{\text{apple}}(x))$$

Equation (2.10) exhibits *striped apple* as a familiar kind of combination of the concepts *striped* and *apple*. Without (2.10) it is doubtful that fuzzy-set theory can secure the compatibility of prototype theory with this elementary case of conceptual combination.

But (2.10) cannot be maintained. Let (a) in Figure 11.1 be a particular apple in F. There can be no doubt that it is psychologically less prototypical of an apple (whose prototype looks more like (b)) than of an apple-with-stripes; so,

$$(2.11) \quad c_{\text{striped apple}}(a) > c_{\text{apple}}(a).$$

The inequality (2.11) asserts, simply, that (a) is a better illustration of the concept *striped apple* than it is of the concept *apple* (just as the reverse is true of (b)). But (2.11) contradicts (2.10) since the latter implies

$$c_{\text{striped apple}}(a) = \min(c_{\text{striped}}(a), c_{\text{apple}}(a))$$

which in turn implies

$$(2.12) \quad c_{\text{striped apple}}(a) \leqslant c_{\text{apple}}(a).$$

And (2.11) and (2.12) are inconsistent.

Given the above, it becomes clear that prototype theory conjoined to fuzzy-set theory will lead to a contradiction whenever an object is more prototypical of a con-

---

8. A comment is in order about the kinds of problems that we will *not* consider. One kind involves counterexamples to fuzzy intersections that can be generated with concepts like *counterfeit*, *bogus*, *imitation*, etc. For example, a "good" counterfeit dollar, d, might be a "good" counterfeit, but it will be a "bad" dollar; hence, the characteristic function for the relevant fuzzy intersection between *counterfeit* and *dollar* will mistakenly declare d to be a "bad" counterfeit dollar, since the intersection function yields the minimum value of the constituents. We will pass over this kind of objection, however, in view of our earlier agreement to treat only simple concepts, among which *counterfeit* and the like cannot be found.

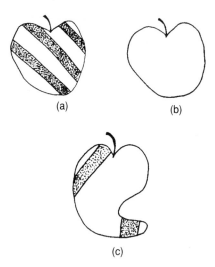

(a)   (b)

(c)

Figure 11.1
Some apples.

junction than of its constituents. When phrased this way, numerous familiar conjunctions seem to provide counterexamples, e.g., a guppie is more prototypical of the conjunctive concept *pet fish* than it is of either *pet* or *fish*.[9] We conclude that prototype theory *cum* fuzzy-set theory is not compatible with strong intuitions about conjunctive concepts.

2.4.2. Logically Empty and Logically Universal Concepts   The concept *apple that is not an apple* is logically empty since it can apply to nothing.[10] Its characteristic function within fuzzy-set theory should reflect this peculiar property; that is, its function should conform to condition (2.6), which in this case can be written as:

(2.13) $(\forall x \in F)c_{\text{apple that is not an apple}}(x) = 0.$

However, within fuzzy-set theory, the concept *apple that is not an apple* would be represented as the (fuzzy) intersection of *apple* and *nonapple* yielding (by (2.3) and (2.5)):

(2.14) $(\forall x \in F)c_{\text{apple that is not an apple}}(x) = \min(c_{\text{apple}}(x), 1 - c_{\text{apple}}(x)).$

9. In deriving our counterexample, we chose to work with an unfamiliar conjunction (*striped apple*) rather than with a familiar one (e.g., *pet fish*) so as to make it less likely that the reader would have represented the conjunction as a single conceptual constituent. The latter could be the case for many familiar conjunctions (Bolinger, 1975; Potter and Faulconer, 1979), and for such cases representation in terms of intersection is misleading.
10. Some might object on the grounds that people frequently use locutions of the form "——— and not a ———" to describe some object. For example, one might describe tomatoes by saying:

    (i) They are both fruit and not fruit.

But (i) seems to be a case in which grammatical structure is a misleading guide to conceptual structure; (i) is probably idiomatic for asserting that tomatoes have some properties of fruit but lack others. More generally, all locutions of the form "——— is a — — — and not a — — —" that we can think of seem to be idiomatic.

Consider again apple (a) of Figure 11.1. Since (a) is a "better" apple than (c), but a "worse" one than (b), we have, by condition (1.2):

(2.15) $c_{\text{apple}}(c) < c_{\text{apple}}(a) < c_{\text{apple}}(b)$.

(2.15) implies (2.16) in the presence of (2.8).

(2.16) $0 < c_{\text{apple}}(a) < 1$.

But if the appleness value of (a) is between 0 and 1, then so is one minus that value. Therefore both $c_{\text{apple}}(a)$ and $1 - c_{\text{apple}}(a)$ exceed 0; so the minimum cannot be 0, which contradicts the condition stated in (2.13). That is, (2.16) in conjunction with (2.14) implies

$$c_{\text{apple that is not apple}}(a) \neq 0,$$

thereby contradicting (2.13).[11]

In the above, the contradiction rested critically on the fuzzy-set theory assumption that the value of a conjunctive combination cannot be less than that of its minimum-valued constituent. We now derive a similar contradiction for logically universal concepts, this time using the fuzzy-set theory assumption that the value of a disjunctive combination cannot exceed that of its maximum-valued constituent.

The concept *fruit that either is or is not an apple* is logically universal (with respect to the domain F), and therefore its characteristic function should conform to (2.7), which in this case can be written as:

(2.17) $(\forall x \in F) c_{\text{fruit that either is or is not an apple}}(x) = 1$.

Within fuzzy-set theory the concept *fruit that either is or is not an apple* is represented as the (fuzzy) union of *apple* and *nonapple*, yielding (by (2.4) and (2.5)):

(2.18) $(\forall x \in F) c_{\text{fruit that either is or is not an apple}}(x) = \max(c_{\text{apple}}(x), 1 - c_{\text{apple}}(x))$.

Again, consider apple (a). Since its characteristic function value for *apple*, and one minus that value, both lie between 0 and 1 (as shown by (2.15)), the maximum of these two values must be less than 1. Hence (2.18) must be less than 1, which contradicts the condition stated in (2.17).

Similar counterexamples are easily generated. We conclude that fuzzy-set theory does not render prototype theory compatible with strong intuitions pertaining to logically empty and logically universal concepts.

2.4.3. Disjunctive Concepts   As an example of a disjunctive concept, consider (financial) wealth. It seems clear that wealth is conceptually connected to liquidity and investment in this way: the degree to which one enjoys either or both of the latter determines the degree to which one is wealthy. In particular, it is clear that of the three persons whose assets are given in Table 11.1, person (A) enjoys the greatest liquidity, person (C) the greatest investment, and person (B) the greatest wealth. Given the appropriate domain, D, and subsets for *liquidity*, *investment*, and *wealth*, we thus have:

---

11. Indeed, since in the case depicted by Figure 11.1, apple (a) falls to neither extreme of appleness, $c_{\text{apple that is not an apple}}(a)$ appreciably exceeds 0. So $c_{\text{apple that is not an apple}}$ does not come close to meeting condition (2.13).

Table 11.1
Wealth of three persons

	Liquidity	Investment
A.	$105,000	$5,000
B.	$100,000	$100,000
C.	$5,000	$105,000

(2.19) $c_{\text{liquidity}}(A) > c_{\text{liquidity}}(B)$

(2.20) $c_{\text{investment}}(C) > c_{\text{investment}}(B)$

(2.21) (i) $c_{\text{wealth}}(B) > c_{\text{wealth}}(A)$
         (ii) $c_{\text{wealth}}(B) > c_{\text{wealth}}(C).$

Now if fuzzy-set theory is to represent the conceptual connections among liquidity, investment, and wealth, it would seem that its only option is to employ fuzzy union, as in (2.22).

(2.22) $(\forall x \in D)c_{\text{wealth}}(x) = c_{\text{liquidity} \cup \text{investment}}(x).$

In light of (2.4), defining union,

(2.23) $(\forall x \in D)c_{\text{wealth}}(x) = \max(c_{\text{liquidity}}(x), c_{\text{investment}}(x)).$

But (2.19)–(2.23) are inconsistent. To see this, focus on c_{wealth} (B). According to (2.23), $c_{\text{wealth}}(B)$ is the larger of $c_{\text{liquidity}}(B)$ and $c_{\text{investment}}(B)$. Suppose that $c_{\text{liquidity}}(B)$ is the larger, then:

(2.24) $c_{\text{liquidity}}(B) = c_{\text{wealth}}(B).$

Now focus on $c_{\text{wealth}}(A)$. Since, by (2.23) again, $c_{\text{wealth}}(A)$ cannot be smaller than $c_{\text{liquidity}}(A)$,

(2.25) $c_{\text{wealth}}(A) \geqslant c_{\text{liquidity}}(A).$

Combining this information with (2.19) yields:

(2.26) $c_{\text{wealth}}(A) \geqslant c_{\text{liquidity}}(A) > c_{\text{liquidity}}(B) = c_{\text{wealth}}(B).$

And (2.26) implies

$c_{\text{wealth}}(A) > c_{\text{wealth}}(B),$

contradicting (2.21) (i). The only alternative is that $c_{\text{investment}}(B)$ is equal to or larger than $c_{\text{liquidity}}(B)$, making the former the value of $c_{\text{wealth}}(B)$. But then, by a parallel argument to that just given, we have:

$c_{\text{wealth}}(C) > c_{\text{wealth}}(B),$

which contradicts (2.21) (ii). Hence fuzzy-set theory does not properly represent the relation between *wealth* on the one hand, and *liquidity* and *investment* on the other. We conclude that fuzzy-set theory renders prototype theory incompatible with strong intuitions about disjunctive conceptual combination.

Section 3. Prototype Theory and the Truth Conditions of Thoughts

3.1. The Issue

We take concepts to be the immediate constituents of thoughts. Given this, it seems reasonable to ask a prototype theory of concepts for principles that informatively characterize the circumstances under which thoughts are true, (when the thoughts correspond to declarative propositions). In particular we are concerned with whether prototype theory, coupled with fuzzy-set theory, can offer a correct account of simple quantificational thoughts like *All A's are B's, Some A's are B's, No A's are B's,* and so forth. We can restrict attention to *All A's are B's* since our remarks will apply *mutatis mutandis* to other simple quantificational thoughts.

3.2. Criteria of Adequacy Regarding Truth Conditions

Let A and B be concepts compatible with the claims of prototype theory, and let T be the thought expressed by (3.1).

(3.1)   All A's are B's.

On prototype theory, T consists, in part, of (mental) representations of the quadruples for A and B. A fully adequate version of the theory would supply principles that specify the truth conditions of T on the basis of these latter representations. Since so little is known about (such mental) representations, we shall require only that prototype theory specify the truth conditions of T on the basis of the quadruples themselves, i.e., on the basis of A and B's domains, distance metrics, prototypes, and characteristic functions. And for reasons similar to those advanced in Section 2.2, we shall focus on the availability of principles that relate A and B's characteristic functions to T's truth conditions. In summary, then, we require of prototype theory a specification of what makes (3.1) true on the basis of the characteristic functions for A and B.

Once again it is fuzzy-set theory that saves prototype theory from inexplicitness. Zadeh (1965) offers an explicit principle relating inclusions like (3.1) to the characteristic functions for A and B. Since Zadeh's principle naturally extends the principles reviewed earlier, since his proposal has interest in its own right, and since no alternative principle has been advanced to fill the present theoretical need (so far as we know), we feel justified in pinning the hopes of prototype theory to the fuzzy inclusion principle. If this ensemble is at variance with strong intuitions pertaining to the truth conditions of thoughts, there is reason to doubt the compatibility of prototype theory with those intuitions.

3.3. Fuzzy-set Theory Again

Fuzzy inclusion is a straightforward generalization of standard inclusion. Standardly, the inclusion (3.1) is assigned the truth condition (3.2).

(3.2) $(\forall x \in D)(c_A(x) \leqslant c_B(x))$

To illustrate in the domain of animals,

(3.3)   All females are dogs

is true just in case (3.4) is true.

(3.4) $(\forall x \in \text{animals})(c_{\text{female}}(x) \leqslant c_{\text{dog}}(x))$.

(3.4) comes out false in light of a female nondog, a, for whom $c_{female}(a) = 1$ and $c_{dog}(a) = 0$.

The fuzzy inclusion principle results, as before, from generalizing the notion of a characteristic function from (2.1) and (2.2) to (2.8) and (2.9). The fuzzy truth condition on (3.1) may still be stated as (3.2). Then, (3.3) remains false in fuzzy-set theory, in the light of a female rabbit, r, for whom $c_{female}(r) = 0.80$ and $c_{dog}(r) = 0.20$, contradicting (3.4).

3.4. Is Prototype Theory Compatible with the Truth Conditions of Inclusion?
We now present a counterintuitive result to which prototype theory, in the context of the fuzzy inclusion principles, is committed.[12] In this example, we use the domain, A, of animals, and the subsets associated with *grizzly bear* and *inhabitant of North America*. Consider the following inclusion.

(3.5)   All grizzly bears are inhabitants of North America.

Within fuzzy-set theory, the truth condition of (3.5) is

(3.6) $(\forall x \in A)(c_{grizzly\ bear}(x) \leqslant c_{inhabitant\ of\ North\ America}(x))$.

One thing we want from (3.6) is that it capture our intuitions about what conditions insure the falsehood of the inclusion (3.5). But (3.6) fails to do this. For, according to (3.6), the existence of a squirrel on Mars in sufficient to falsify the proposition that all grizzly bears live in North America. The argument unfolds as follows.

The characteristic function for *grizzly bear* is supposed to represent the degree to which animals count as grizzly bears. Thus, polar bears will be assigned a number close to 1, frogs a number closer to 0, and earthworms a number yet closer to 0. Let Sam be a squirrel, and suppose that

(3.7) $c_{grizzly\ bear}(Sam) = p$ (where $p > 0$).

The characteristic function for *inhabitant of North America*, if it is to accord with our intuition, must assign progressively smaller numbers to locations that are progressively further from the North American continent. Thus, it assigns Cuba a higher number than Scotland, which in turn is assigned a higher number than is Egypt. Now, is there a place that Sam could live so that $c_{inhabitant\ of\ North\ America}$ would assign Sam a number smaller than p? If so, we will contradict (3.6) and hence falsify (3.5). Surely, if Sam lived far enough from North America, the value of $c_{inhabitant\ of\ North\ America}(Sam)$

---

12. Another comment about kinds of problems *not* to be considered: It is possible to produce counterexamples to fuzzy inclusions by suitable choice of the domain of discourse. In a domain including both galaxies and radishes, for example, the false inclusion

All small galaxies are small things

would be declared true by fuzzy set theory because it is a theorem of the theory that for all subsets A, B, of D, and all $x \in D$,

$c_{A \cap B}(x) \leqslant c_A(x)$.

We choose not to rely on this class of counterexample since the problem of relative adjectives like *small* is too severe a burden to impose on a theory with so few competitors. Consequently, in the examples to follow, we employ natural (in particular, intuitively homogeneous) domains.

would be forced below p.[13] Perhaps a home in Egypt would suffice; if not, we can imagine he lives in Pakistan or Indonesia, or, if necessary, on Mars or Pluto, in the vicinity of a nearby star, or within some distant galaxy. Let's suppose that Mars is far enough. Then we have:

(3.8) $c_{\text{inhabitant of North America}}(\text{Sam}) < p.$

Putting (3.7) and (3.8) together, we have:

(3.9) $c_{\text{grizzly bear}}(\text{Sam}) > c_{\text{inhabitant of North America}}(\text{Sam}),$

which contradicts (3.6). Since it is easy to generate an indefinite number of examples like this, it seems that fuzzy-set theory does not render prototype theory compatible with the truth conditions of inclusions.[14]

3.5. Partial Falsification to the Rescue?

One response to the difficulty just exhibited for fuzzy inclusion is to embrace fuzzy truth, that is, an (uncountable) infinity of truth-values between 0 and 1. On this view, the inclusion (3.5) is not outrightly falsified by Martian squirrels but only slightly weakened, some scheme being envisioned for computing the falsifying effects of counterexamples to truth conditions of form (3.2). To support this proposal it is pointed out that the discovery of Martian squirrels would indeed lower our confidence that all grizzly bears inhabit North America (if Martian squirrels, why not other Martian mammals?). So, psychologically, at least, (3.5) is partly falsified by (3.9), as the new approach predicts.

Note of this is well taken. We give three reasons for our distrust of a fuzzy-truth remedy to the problems associated with fuzzy inclusion.

Note first that the new proposal is no mere adjustment of truth condition (3.2), found inadequate in the last subsection. To replace (3.2) with a "partial falsification" scheme so as to allow for truth values between *truth* and *falsity* requires nontrivial theory construction of a kind apparently not yet undertaken. Such a theory will need to include principles governing the degrees of falsification associated with (partial) counterexamples to inclusions. Reverting to our example, the theory must decide (a) how much additional falsification is engendered by the existence of $n + 1$ Martian squirrels instead of n (for all n), (b) whether some number of Martian squirrels falsify (3.5) as much as one European grizzly bear, (c) whether, if giraffes counts as grizzly bears no more nor less than do squirrels, then a Martian squirrel and a Martian giraffe falsify (3.5) to the same extent as two Martian squirrels or two Martian giraffes, and so forth for many obvious questions. Until such a calculus of partial falsification is

---

13. Unless $c_{\text{inhabitant of North America}}$ asymptotes above p. But this is an arbitrary and counterintuitive restriction on the behavior of $c_{\text{inhabitant of North America}}$; it would moreover, complicate the representation of subjects' relative similarity judgments, since the psychological distance between objects far away from North America does not seem sufficiently foreshortened compared to those nearby for such an elevated asymptote.

14. An interesting class of examples results from considering inclusions, $A \subseteq B$, such that A is a very atypical kind of B, e.g.,

   All penguins are birds.
   All tomatoes are fruit.
   All bats are mammals, etc.

For, there may well be some quintessential penguin that is a better examplar of *penguin* than of *bird*, thereby falsifying the generalisation that all penguins are birds (and similarly for the other cases).

offered that provides principled answers to questions like these, no explicit alternative to truth condition (3.2) is available to conjoin to prototype theory.

Second, and in the same vein, allowing propositions to admit of an infinity of possible truth values raises problems for the interpretation of sentential connectives and quantifiers. This issue is analogous to that for conceptual combination, only now it is the combination of simple propositions into complex propositions that concerns us, instead of the combination of simple concepts into complex concepts. In particular, the familiar semantical apparatus of classical logic needs to be replaced since standard semantics is appropriate for interpreting its connectives and quantifiers only in the context of binarily valued propositions. To interpret, e.g., the conjunction of infinitarily-valued propositions, an appropriate *infinite-valued logic* needs to be invoked. Many such logics have been devised; see Rescher (1969, pp. 36–45) for a survey, as well as Zadeh's (1975) own preliminary paper. The problem is that infinite valued logics generally violate strong intuitions about truth, validity, and consistency.[15] At the least, their psychological suitability is not obvious. The advocate of fuzzy-truth, then, incurs the responsibility of selecting and defending an appropriate infinite-valued logic, and this promises to be a nontrivial undertaking. But until such a logic is presented, a serious alternative to fuzzy-set theory is not available to conjoin to prototype theory.

Finally, we suspect that the partial falsification proposal results from mistaking degrees of belief for degrees of truth. We share the intuition that the discovery of Martian squirrels should lower confidence in the truth of (3.5), but it is the confidence that is partially weakened, not the truth. Analogously, evidence might be adduced that alters our confidence in some as yet undecided mathematical assertion; but the assertion, irrespective of our doubts and conjectures, is either flatly true or flatly false. In other words, the effect on our beliefs of the discovery of Martian squirrels is a problem relevant to *inductive logic*, not to the analysis of the truth conditions of inclusions. The "supporting intuition" of the fuzzy-truth advocate thus explained away, it is helpful to appeal to another intuition, namely, that it is logically possible *both* for all grizzly bears, without exception, to dwell in North America, *and* for Mars to be teeming with squirrels; the irrelevance of Martian squirrels to the inclusion (3.5)—*pace* fuzzy-set theory and partial falsification schemes—is thereby revealed.

We conclude that programmatic suggestions about partial falsification do not rescue prototype theory from its dependence on fuzzy-set theory; in particular, truth condition (3.2) is still the most natural and explicit interpretation of the inclusion relation within the prototype theory tradition; and (3.2), we saw, has unwelcome consequences.

---

15. To illustrate with an influential system, consider Łukasiewicz's infinite valued logic Ł-aleph. The intuitively valid sentence

> If John is happy, and if John is happy only if business is good, then business is good.

is ruled nontautologous in Ł-aleph. (A tautology within Ł-aleph is any formula that assumes maximal truth value under all truth assignments to atomic subformulas.) Also, explicit contradictions (of the form (p and -p)) may differ in truth-value. Many other counterintuitive results issue from Ł-aleph. The rival infinite valued logics in the literature appear to yield similar paradoxes.

None of these paradoxical results are features of classical (two valued) logic, although it is well known that classical logic yields some counterintuitive results of its own (for discussion, see Kreuger and Osherson, forthcoming).

Section 4. Implications

In this final section we consider three issues: (1) the "immunity" of standard set theory from the contradictions we derived, (2) the susceptibility of all versions of prototype theory to the derived contradictions, and (3) what can be salvaged from prototype theory in the light of these difficulties.

4.1. Standard Set Theory and Traditional Theories of Concepts
Standard set theory, with its binarily valued characteristic functions, is the natural complement of traditional theories of concepts—at least insofar as those theories enforce a sharp boundary between membership and nonmembership in a concept's extension. We now wish to point out that this amalgamation does not lead to the contradictions we derived from the amalgamation of fuzzy-set theory and our version of prototype theory. Hence, the former amalgamation is superior to the latter when it comes to accounting for conceptual combination and the truth conditions of thoughts.

The point is trivial to demonstrate. For, every contradiction we derived rests partly on the assumption that constituents of complex concepts can be assigned characteristic function values that fall between 0 and 1, i.e., this assumption is necessary (though not sufficient) for all our derivations. To take the most obvious example, consider the concept we used in discussing logically empty sets, namely, *apple that is not an apple*. Recall that in fuzzy-set theory the characteristic function of this concept meets (2.14):

$$(2.14) \quad (\forall x \in F) c_{\text{apple that is not an apple}}(x) = \min(c_{\text{apple}}(x), 1 - c_{\text{apple}}(x))$$

Recall further that the contradiction arose because there exists an apple whose appleness value is between 0 and 1, thereby insuring that one minus this value is also between 0 and 1, which in turn insures that the minimum is greater than 0. In standard set theory the characteristic function of *apple that is not an apple* must also meet (2.14), but since the appleness value of any apple must be either 0 or 1, for any x, one of $c_{\text{apple}}(x)$, $1 - c_{\text{apple}}(x)$ equals 0, thereby insuring that the minimum will be 0. A similar analysis in terms of standard set theory will remove the contradiction in the other cases we considered.

4.2. Extension of the Present Results to Other Versions of Prototype Theory
It was noted at the outset that there are versions of prototype theory alternative to the one we presented; indeed, some of these alternative versions enjoy greater empirical confirmation than that we presented. There is, however, good reason to believe that the contradictions we derived apply to other versions of prototype theory as well.

In the version we chose, concepts were identified with mental representations of quadruples like (*),

(*) $\langle A, d, p, c \rangle$,

where A is a conceptual domain of envisionable objects, d is a metric function, p is a particular object in A, and c is a characteristic function. Most other versions of prototype theory differ from the above in their choices for the second and third coordinates of (*). Instead of a function that measures the psychological similarity between objects in terms of distance, many prototype theorists favor a function that measures this similarity in terms of number of common features (e.g., Rosch and Mervis, 1975; Smith, Shoben, and Rips, 1974), or in terms of a weighted contrast between common and distinctive features (Tversky, 1977). (The latter function has the virtue of not requiring that the similarity between two objects be symmetric.) And instead of the prototype being a particular envisionable object in the domain, some have assumed it is an abstraction from objects in the domain, e.g., a collection of features that occur most frequently in the domain (Smith et al., 1974).

But such variations would not influence the contradictions we derived. For as long as a version of (∗) postulates that (a) there is some proximity function that computes similarity between an object and a prototypical description, and (b) this computation results in graded similarity values that are mapped into a characteristic function such that high similarity goes with high characteristic values, then (c) the characteristic functions associated with the constituents of complex concepts can assume values between 0 and 1. And point (c), in conjunction with the formalism of fuzzy-set theory, is what produced all our contradictions.

This can again be seem most easily by considering the logically empty concept: *apple that is not an apple*. Even if the prototypical apple is an abstraction, and even if similarity to a particular apple is computed by summing common features, it will still be the case that a particular apple can have an intermediate similarity value that results in a characteristic function value betwen 0 and 1. And this is all it takes to insure that the minimum constituent of *apple that is not an apple* is greater than 0, which in turn insures that this logically empty concept is not associated with a characteristic function that is identically zero. Similar remarks apply to other cases of conceptual combination we considered, and to inclusion. As best we can tell, then, no current version of prototype theory is immune from the problems we have raised in this paper.

4.3. General Implications for Prototype Theory
One thing is clear. Amalgamation of any of a number of current versions of proto-type theory with Zadeh's (1965) rendition of fuzzy-set theory will not handle strong intuitions about the way concepts combine to form complex concepts and proposi-tions. This is an important failing because the ability to construct thoughts and com-plex concepts out of some basic stock of concepts seems to lie near the heart of human mentation.

Where does this leave prototype theory? Three answers are worth considering. The first is that the theory is a sound rendition of concepts, but that it should beware of associating with Zadeh's (1965) specific version of fuzzy-set theory since the latter brings with it the kinds of problems we have discussed. This possibility receives some support in Oden's (1977) work. He noted that within the general class of fuzzy-set theories (i.e., a set theory that conforms to (2.8) and (2.9)) there are alternatives to Zadeh's characterization of fuzzy intersection and union. Thus, instead of the mini-mum rule for fuzzy intersection, (2.3), we can use a multiplicative expression (due to Gougen, 1969):

$$(\forall x \in D)(c_{A \cap B}(x) = c_A(x) \cdot c_B(x)).$$

And applying DeMorgan's law to the above yields an alternative to the minimum rule for union, (2.4), namely,

$$(\forall x \in D)(c_{A \cup B}(x) = c_A(x) + c_B(x) - c_A(x) \cdot c_B(x)).$$

Oden (1977) showed that these alternative formulations provide a better account of subjects judgments of truthfulness of complex statements than do Zadeh's formulations.

But the above alternatives still yield almost all the contradictions we derived; e.g., as long as the two constituents of a logically empty set have characteristic function values between 0 and 1, their product must be greater than 0. Similar remarks apply to all the contradictions we derived, with the sole exception of that concerning the disjunctive concept of wealth (Section 2.4.3). (Referring back to Table 11.1, given a reasonable choice of characteristic function values corresponding to the various liquidity and investment amounts, the above expression for union correctly selects B as the wealthiest individual.) In short, we know of no alternative set theory that can be joined with prototype theory to account for all the evidence about conceptual combinations and truth conditions. Nor does it seem promising to fuzz the notion of truth to allow for partial falsification of thoughts, as was seen in Section 3.5. Perhaps a novel set theory and logic can be developed whose association with prototype theory will be free of the difficulties raised in this paper; such a development would be of considerable theoretical interest, in our opinion. Until a viable alternative to fuzzy-set theory materializes, however, prototype theory cannot be suitably extended; and the possibility that no such alternative can be developed ought not to be minimized.

A second possibility is to forget about prototype theory entirely. We count this as too extreme. For one thing, the empirical research that has resulted from prototype theorizing points to the use of similarity in establishing membership for many simple concepts. We mentioned some of the relevant findings in Section 1.1, and there are many other interlocking results of this kind (see, e.g., Rosch, 1978). So prototype theory seems to capture something about the natural use of simple concepts. Furthermore, the leading intuition behind prototype theory—that concepts are often vague and apply to different objects to different extents—is quite compelling, and central to theories of reasoning. It is well known, for example, that the principle of mathematical induction cannot be reliably applied to vague predicates. To see this, define F to be the numerical predicate

———— grains of sand brought together do not constitute a heap.

Note that F(0), and if F(k) then F(k + 1) (0 grains of sand brought together do not constitute a heap, and if k grains won't do the job neither will k + 1). So mathematical induction leads to the false conclusion that no matter how large k gets, k grains of sand brought together do not constitute a heap. An adequate theory of concepts should provide an illuminating characterization of the class of vague predicates, and this is the goal of prototype theory.

The third possibility is that prototype theory is by its nature incomplete because it is about only a limited aspect of concepts. To make this clearer, we can distinguish between a concept's *core* and its *identification procedure*; the core is concerned with those aspects of a concept that explicate its relation to other concepts, and to thoughts, while the identification procedure specifies the kind of information used to make rapid decisions about membership. (This distinction is similar to one proposed by Miller and Johnson-Laird, 1976). We can illustrate with the concept *woman*. Its core might contain information about the presence of a reproductive system, while its identification procedures might contain information about body shape, hair length, and voice pitch. Given this distinction it is possible that some traditional theory of concepts correctly characterizes the core, whereas prototype theory characterizes an important identification procedure. This would explain why prototype theory does well in explicating the real-time process of determining category membership (a job for identification procedures), but fares badly in explicating conceptual combination and the truth conditions of thoughts (a job for concept cores). This seems to us to offer the most satisfactory reconciliation of the present failures of prototype theory with its previous successes.

References

Bolinger, D. L. (1975) *Aspects of Language*, (2nd Edition). New York, Harcourt Brace Jovanovich.

Gougen, J. A. (1969) The logic of inexact concepts, *Synthese*, *19*, 325–373.

Hersch, H. M. and Caramazza, A., (1976) A fuzzy set approach to modifiers and vagueness in natural language. *J. exper. Psychol.: Gen.*, *105*, 254–276.

Miller, G. A. and Johnson-Laird, P. N. (1976) *Language and Perception*. Cambridge, Harvard University Press.

Oden, G. C. (1977) Integration of fuzzy logical information. *J. exper. Psychol.: Hum. percep. perform.*, *3*, 365–575.

Posner, M. I. and Keele, S. W. (1968) On the genesis of abstract ideas. *J. exper. Psychol.*, *77*, 353–363.

Potter, M. and Faulconer, B. (1979) Understanding noun phrases, *J. verb. Learn. verb. Behav.*, *18* (5), 509–522.

Reed, S. K. (1972) Pattern recognition and categorization, *Cog. Psychol.*, *3*, 382–407.

Rescher, N. (1969) *Many-valued logics*, McGraw-Hill.

Rips, L. J., Shoben, E. J. and Smith, E. E. (1973) Semantic distance and the verification of semantic relations. *J. verb. Learn. verb. Behav.*, *12*, 1–20.

Rosch, E. (1973) On the internal structure of perceptual and semantic categories. In T. E. Moore (Ed.) *Cognitive development and the acquisition of Language*. New York, Academic Press.

Rosch, E. (1978) Principles of categorization. In E. Rosch and B. B. Lloyd (Eds.) *Cognition and categorization*. Potomac, MD, Erlbaum.

Rosch, E. and Mervis, C. B. (1975) Family resemblance: Studies in the internal structure of categories. *Cog. Psychol.*, *7*, 573–605.

Rosch, E. H., Simon, C. and Miller, R. S. (1976) Structural bases of typicality effects. *J. exper. Psychol.: Hum. Percep. Perform.*, *2*, 491–502.

Smith, E. E., Shoben, E. J. and Rips, L. J. (1974) Structure and process in semantic memory: A featural model for semantic decisions. *Psychol. Rev.*, *81*, 214–241.

Tversky, A., (1977) Features of similarity, *Psychol. Rev.*, *84*, 327–352.

Zadeh, L. (1965) Fuzzy sets. *Inform. control*, *8*, 338–353.

Zadeh, L. A. (1975) Calculus of fuzzy restrictions, in L. A. Zadeh, K. Fu, K. Tanada and M. Shimura (Eds.), *Fuzzy sets and their applications to cognitive and decision processes*, Academic Press.

Chapter 12

Concepts and Stereotypes

Georges Rey

I

Concepts seem to be the very stuff of which cognitions are made. At any rate, cognitive states like beliefs and preferences, with which many of us hope to explain behavior, seem to involve relations between agents and, roughly speaking, *conceptual contents*.[1] For example, someone's slowing her car in the desert might be explained by her (mistaken) belief that there is water on the road ahead and her preference not to skid in it. Such an explanation seems to proceed by positing relations between the agent and such contents as [There's water on the road ahead], [Cars skid in water], and [Skidding cars can be dangerous]. But it is hard to see how the agent might enjoy those relations without having *inter alia* the concepts [water], [car], [skids] and [dangerous]. Indeed, it would appear to be precisely such things as these concepts that would provide the basis for the relevant *connections* between those cognitive states whereby they might realize the familiar patterns of 'rationality' that so much of cognitive explanation exploits: e.g., it is the [water] that connects the belief about the road with the belief about skidding cars and so rationally explains her act of slowing. But, one well might ask, (1) precisely *what is a concept?* and (2) *what is it for an agent to have one?*

Traditionally, these questions were addressed almost exclusively by philosophers. They are responsible for what has come to be called 'the Classical View', which associates with (most) concepts necessary and sufficient, 'defining' conditions that an agent must appreciate in order properly to have the concept. Lately, a number of psychologists—notably, Eleanor Rosch and her associates—have been adducing considerable experimental evidence that appears to conflict with the Classical View, and to support views that associate concepts instead with such things as 'prototypes', typical features, and individual exemplars. Much of this latter work is perspicuously

Critical Discussion of Edward Smith and Douglas Medin (1981) *Categories and Concepts*. This paper was written while I was a Research Affiliate at the Center for Cognitive Science at the Massachusetts Institute of Technology. I'd like to thank the Center, particularly Jay Kayser, for its hospitality, and also Jonathan Adler, Louise Antony, Jerry Fodor, David Israel, Michael Lipton, and Ed Smith for many helpful discussions.
1. I shall refer to the thing that has cognitive states—be it person, animal, or machine—as the 'agent' of the state. By 'conceptual content' I mean to refer, as innocuously as possible, to whatever it is that the agent is in general related to in being in a cognitive state—be it proposition, thought, set of possible worlds, or inscriptions in a language of thought. I intend my use of 'concept' to be just as neutral, referring centrally to those conceptual contents associated with 'open class' items such as nouns, verbs, and adjectives. In order to maintain this neutrality, it will be important to distinguish conceptual contents from the words that might express them, and so I shall refer (even when quoting from Smith and Medin) to the former by enclosing the latter in square brackets, and to the latter by the usual device of single quotes.

reviewed in *Categories and Concepts* by Edward Smith and Douglas Medin (hereinafter 'S&M'). In the remainder of the present section I will briefly summarize the main conclusions S&M draw about concepts from this work. In section II, I will distinguish a number of different functions concepts have traditionally been invoked to perform, proceeding in section III to consider which of these functions S&M can be taken to be addressing. I will argue that there is no reasonable function that their conception of concepts does serve, in particular that their account, as a theory of *concepts*, hopelessly confuses metaphysical issues of conceptual *identity* with (roughly speaking) epistemological issues of conceptual *access*. Nevertheless, their discussion does point to needed revisions especially in some of the more implicit assumptions of the Classical View, revisions that are independently motivated in the work of a number of recent philosophers, notably Wittgenstein, Putnam, Kripke, and Burge. I shall discuss these revisions and some of their implications for cognitive science in sections IV and V.

I should emphasize from the start that I do not for a moment intend to undermine what I take to be the important and somewhat surprising results of work on prototypes and exemplars. I think that the work reviewed by S&M reveals important features of people's *access* to the system of their beliefs. All that I shall be disputing is the relevance of those features to a theory of *concepts*, to the identity conditions of them, even to the conditions under which someone is competent to use one. A theory of either of these different sorts of conditions, I shall conclude in section V, is not affected by the evidence S&M adduce in the way that they appear to believe. It may not be a piece of psychology at all.

Cognitive psychologists were originally inclined to answer our questions—what is a concept? What is it for an agent to have one?—in the Classical way: a concept is (1) a summary representation of some set of things in terms of (2) conditions that are singly necessary and jointly sufficient for membership in that set. These two conditions are what S&M regard as the 'heart of the Classical View' (p. 23). A further, more implicit assumption is (3) that *having a concept* consists in *knowing* the defining conditions.[2] S&M provide as an example, [square], which is certainly definable by the following features (p. 24):

> square: (s1) a closed, plane figure;
>   (s2) has four sides;
>   (s3) all sides are equal in length;
>   (s4) all interior angles are equal.

Each of (s1)–(s4) is by itself *necessary* for something's being a square, and together they are *sufficient*. Moreover, it is plausible to suppose that were someone not to know these conditions, at least implicitly, she couldn't rightly be said to have the concept [square]. The aim of the Classical View is to provide such analyses for at least the preponderance of our concepts.[3]

---

2. S&M do not explicitly include this third claim as one of the assumptions of the Classical View. But, as I shall discuss at length below, it is everywhere implicit, particularly given their view of the chief 'categorization' function concepts are supposed to play) (p. 7). A third claim that they do explicitly associate with the Classical View—that the defining features of a set are included in those for any subset (p. 24–25)—I ignore since nothing in my discussion will turn upon it.

3. Most defenders of the Classical View would not require such analyses to be provided for *all* concepts, since the view naturally allows that there are *atomic* concepts (e.g., sensory ones) in terms of which all others are to be analyzed, but which are not analyzable themselves. More about this in section V.

There are four main difficulties S&M raise for the Classical View.[4]

(1) Necessary and sufficient conditions do not seem to be available for any but a very small set of concepts. Most people cannot produce them for most of the concepts they employ; philosophers have generally failed to produce them even after nearly a century of concerted reflection; and they do not seem to be generally available for the familiar concepts of even so developed a science as biology (pp. 30–32).[5] Moreover

(2) There are the 'unclear cases': competent users of the concepts [tomato] and [fruit] are frequently confused and unable to decide whether tomatos are fruit (pp. 29–30). If the Classical View were correct, there would seem to be clear answers to such questions, and competent users of the concepts ought to know them.

(3) A now considerable body of experimental evidence suggests that what competent users of a concept know is instead better expressed in terms of typicalities: it can be shown quite reliably that typical[6] members of a concept can be categorized more efficiently than atypical ones (e.g., robins and sparrows are categorized as birds more quickly than are eagles or hawks); typical members are learned first by children; they are named first when subjects are asked the members of a concept; and they serve as cognitive reference points (an ellipse is almost a circle, but not *vice versa*) (pp. 33–35). S&M conclude:

> typicality effects reveal that not all members of a concept are equal, or to put it more positively, that concepts possess an internal structure that favors typical members over less typical ones. (p. 35)

And this seems *prima facie* incompatible with the Classical View, since defining conditions presumably apply to all members equally. Lastly,

(4) these typicalities are highly correlated with 'family resemblance', or the degree to which a member of a concept shares properties shared by other members, properties, however, that may not be shared by all members, nor even be remotely defining of the concept. Thus, [made of wood] and [has four legs] contribute highly to family resemblance among chairs, but are obviously not necessary conditions, much less defining ones for [chair] (pp. 39–41). The necessary and sufficient conditions of the Classical View simply do not appear to play a role in peoples' actual acts of categorization.

The bulk of S&M's book is devoted to considering alternatives to the Classical View that might better accommodate these difficulties. They discuss four such views: three of them, what they call the 'Probabilistic Views'—the 'Featural', the 'Dimensional', and the 'Holistic'—seek alternatives to defining conditions, attempting to capture in different ways the family resemblance structure correlated with the typicalities; the fourth, the 'Exemplar View' attempts to go right to the typicalities them-

---

4. S&M actually count eight (pp. 32, 50). Some of these I combine; some (e.g., 'exclusion of functional features') involve errors that they do not endorse (e.g., p. 25); some (e.g., 'categorization of nested concepts') are secondary to the concerns here (see note 2 above); and some (e.g., 'disjunctive concepts') involve peripheral misunderstandings that are best sorted out later (note 21 below).

5. So far as the Classical View is concerned, the situation in biology seems to be even worse than S&M describe, given the on-going competition between the phenetic, cladistic, and evolutionary taxonomies.

6. I shall use 'typical' and 'atypical' to mean what is always intended in these discussions, 'judged to be (a)typical', since no claims are ever made about what might be actually typical or atypical. My uses of 'typicality' bear no intended relation to Tversky's use of that term.

selves, including 'instances' in a concept's representation, and so denying the first assumption of the Classical View as well, that the representations be a summary description.

S&M offer as their 'main conclusion' the claim that 'the facts about object categorization fit the probabilistic and exemplar views better than they do the Classical View' (p. 175). They do qualify this conclusion with a discussion of the more classical-looking tree structures associated with *some* general ('ontological') categories that are explored in the work of Sommers (1965) and Keil (1979) (pp. 176–179); and they call attention to the significant problems for the Probabilistic and Exemplar Views posed by conceptual combination (it is not clear how on those views the representation of a complex concept, e.g., [pet fish], is computed as a function of its components, pp. 180–182). These are important difficulties, particularly the last. But they seem to me to be manifestations of even more important ones. It is unclear to me what the actual significance of these facts about object categorization is. In particular, it is not at all clear how people's responses to categorization queries bear upon the question of the identity of concepts, or even on the conditions under which they are competent to use one. Is it the sole function of concepts only to aid people in their acts of categorization? Could any of S&M's four alternatives to the Classical View actually do all the work the Classical View was intended to perform? A proper discussion of these questions requires a fuller discussion of the concept of a concept that S&M anywhere provide, to which therefore I now turn.

II

The following is a breakdown of what I take to be the main (but not necessarily exclusive or exhaustive) functions that concepts have been invoked to perform (examples follow):

I. *Stability* Functions:
 (a) *intrapersonal:* the basis for conceptual competence and for comparisons of cognitive states *within* a given agent.
 (b) *interpersonal:* the basis for comparisons of cognitive states *across* agents.

II. *Linguistic* Function: the meanings of open class linguistic items, whereby they enjoy relations of translation, synonymy, antinomy, and semantic implication.

III. *Metaphysical* Functions:
 (a) *metaphysically taxonomic:* that by virtue of which things are the kinds of things they are (by virtue of which they are *correctly* classified).
 (b) *metaphysically modal:* the basis for claims of counterfactuality, possibility, and necessity.

IV. *Epistemological Functions:*
 (a) *epistemologically taxonomic:* the means by which an agent categorizes things, decides whether or not something is of a certain kind.
 (b) *epistemologically combinatorial:* the means by which an agent categorizes things into complex kinds.
 (c) *epistemologically modal:* the basis for claims to 'a priori knowledge', or knowledge justifiable 'completely independently of any experience'.

The Stability functions are essentially those with which our discussion began. Concepts are posited as part of an explanation of cognitive processes. This explanation seems committed to claiming that a single agent can be in the same (type) cognitive state at different times, and that different agents can be in the same (type) such state at the same and different times: such a typology provides the relevant kinds out of which a cognitive explanation is constructed (rather as the Periodic Table provides the kinds for chemical explanation). Concepts, themselves, are simply a reasonable basis for constructing that typology, providing the commonalities between different contents, the links between different cognitive states that are 'about the same thing'[7] (cf., the atoms and their structures as the basis for the Periodic Table). Thus, a theory of concepts fulfilling this function ought to provide a basis for characterizing the relations, e.g., between a belief in some generalization ([Cars can skid in puddles]) and beliefs in its instances ([My car can skid in that puddle]); between a belief ([Skidding cars can be dangerous]) and a preference ([to avoid skidding cars]); and between the beliefs of different people ([There is/is not a puddle ahead]).

The Linguistic function is, of course, closely allied with the Stability functions, since the most efficient way of representing concepts seems to be by way of a language, which fact is well exploited by people when they use language systematically to express the content of their cognitive states. A happy story here is that the semantic structure of, for example English, mirrors the structure of concepts, as they fulfill their Stability roles. Thus, when someone says, sincerely and fully knowing 'the rules of English', 'There's water on the road' she is expressing her belief, [There's water on the road], and that is true because the rules of English, *inter alia*, associate 'water' with [water] and 'road' with [road]; and *she has those concepts*. Since the present discussion is not particularly concerned with the semantics of natural language, and since this happy story is presupposed by S&M (p. 7), I shall presuppose it here as well.[8]

So much is relatively uncontroversial. Where the real controversy begins is over which of the remaining functions on our list are to be joined to the primary Stability

---

7. There is an ambiguity that pervades our ordinary semantic and psychological talk that needs to be borne in mind throughout any discussion of concept ascription, and that is between 'transparent' and 'opaque', or *de re* and *de dicto* ascriptions. For our purposes, it might be characterized as the difference between those ascriptions of cognitive states that *do not* entail that the agent shares the concepts employed in the ascription and those ascriptions that *do*. When a physicist says of her young son, 'He thinks the cyclotron is a hamburger stand', she presumably does not intend to credit him with the concept [cyclotron]: that is the 'transparent', or *de re* reading of the ascription (with respect to 'cyclotron'). Were she to intend to so credit him (say, because he had some theory linking particle physics and hamburgers), the reading would be opaque, or *de dicto*. (For an introduction to the surprising intricacies of this distinction, see Quine [1956], Kaplan [1968], and Burge [1978].) Claims about what a cognitive state is 'about' share in this ambiguity: two cognitive states can be about the same thing, transparently, so long as the concepts they employ, no matter how different they may otherwise be, pick out the same things in the world; to be about the same thing opaquely, they had better also employ the very *same* concepts. *Throughout the present discussion, I shall be restricting myself to opaque readings of cognitive ascriptions and claims about what the ascribed states are 'about'.*

8. Notice that the Linguistic and Stability functions go hand in hand not only positively: scepticism about either function is often linked to scepticism about the other. Thus there is Quine's (1960) notorious thesis of the 'indeterminacy of translation', which can be read as an attack not only on the notion of meaning, but on the scientific legitimacy of *any* talk of concepts and cognitive states (see also Davidson [1970] and Stich [1981]). I fear, though I am not yet convinced, that this scepticism might find some support in the tentative conclusions I present in section V below.

and Linguistic ones. The division I draw between these remaining functions corresponds to a crucial, if very battered distinction in philosophy between *metaphysics* and *epistemology*, or between issues surrounding *how the world is* (what exists, what is true) and issues surrounding *how we know, believe, infer, how the world is*. Although this distinction is not everywhere perfectly sharp (e.g., in describing our own cognitions), and despite the fact that some people (e.g., various sorts of relativists and idealists) are inclined to *argue* that the distinction is ultimately only apparent, it should seem on its face pretty plausible: there is, after all, all the difference in the world between the issue of *whether there actually is a cow on the road* and the issue of *whether anyone knows, believes, has inferred, or even cares whether there is*. Similarly, then, there would seem to be all the difference in the world between *something being a cow* and *someone knowing, believing, or inferring that it is*.

The metaphysical function that concepts have often been asked to perform consists in providing a basis for such metaphysical claims as e.g., that Elsie is a cow; i.e., specifying the facts about Elsie in *virtue of which* she is a cow.[9] Presumably not just any facts about Elsie will do: the fact that she is an animal seems relevant, the fact that she has fleas does not. To put it in more traditional terms, what is wanted is a characterization of the 'universal' [cow]. Concepts in this role may be regarded *in isolation*, as providing the principles of classification for what is to count as their instances (their 'metaphysically taxonomic function') and they may be regarded as entering into complexes, as in [not a cow], [a contented cow], [a cow that was black only in the falling of the dusk] (the 'metaphysically combinatorial function'). The metaphysical role is most striking, however, in its modal aspect: it is presumably by virtue of the constraints imposed by the concept [cow] that certain possibilities and not others are open to cows (as cows), e.g., that they may grow fatter or thinner, but that they may not be made of papier mâché, or survive their disintegration into dust.[10]

How we *tell* whether something is an instance of a concept may be quite another matter. Take gender. There are presumably fairly well defined conditions by virtue of which something *is* (metaphysically) male or female. But it is thought impolite to ascertain those conditions in public. Instead we go by features that we know full well are not at all part of the metaphysical concept of [male] or [female], but which are nevertheless reliable indicators, e.g., style of clothing, hair, voice, etc.; and we might do so not only for concepts individually, but also in combination, deciding whether someone is an instance of [married woman], i.e., of [woman] and [married], by noticing her dress and ring. Insofar as concepts are those things playing *these* sorts of roles, aiding in such decisions, they are playing a role distinct from the metaphysical ones, *viz.* the (taxonomic and combinatorial) epistomological ones. (*Whether* anything that played this role would be a concept, or only something that played this role in a certain 'ultimate' way, is an issue to which we shall return.) Moreover, in playing these roles, they have often been thought to be available also for the traditionally important role of providing a basis for claims to *a priori* knowledge. At any rate, the

9. I hope it is clear that my use of 'metaphysical' here is uncommitted to the historical use of the term for, roughly, researches into the nature of reality that were somehow supposed to go beyond mere empirical science. On the present use—common to recent philosophy—the sciences may provide a good part, and perhaps all there is to know, of metaphysics.
10. I hasten to caution the reader from conflating these *metaphysical* modal claims with *epistemological* modal claims to be discussed at length below.

question, 'How do you know x is F?' is sometimes answered by specifying a way of *telling* whether x is F; and that way of telling sometimes consists in specifying conditions that are constitutive of being (an) F, i.e., of the concept [F]. Anyone who has the concept (in this role) must appreciate those conditions, which they thereby know, independently of any experience of Fs, that all Fs *must* satisfy.

Roughly since Hume and Kant, it has been widely presumed that the epistemologically and metaphysically modal coincide: what was necessarily true was knowable *a priori*, and what was *a priori* was necessarily true. But recently this presumption has been challenged by a number of philosophers, notably Saul Kripke (1972).[11] Many of his examples are (as we shall see) a little controversial, but it is worth considering some of them as a way of at least *allowing* for a possible divergence between the epistemologically and metaphysically modal roles concepts may be required to play. Perhaps the clearest example is the mathematical one of Goldbach's Conjecture ('every even number is the sum of two primes'). Despite centuries of effort, this conjecture has never been proved to be a consequence of the axioms of arithmetic; but neither has any counterexample been found. From Gödel's Incompleteness Theorem, we know that there are truths of arithmetic that cannot be proved in it. Perhaps Goldbach's conjecture is among them. If it is, then it would appear not to be knowable *a priori*, since what is *a priori* ought to be knowable by reasoning, i.e., proof procedures, alone. Yet, if it were true, then like all mathematical truths, it would be *necessarily* true; and if false, then its negation would be necessarily true. So there may be at least one necessary truth that is not knowable *a priori*. Moreover, what is *epistemologically possible* ('conceivable', compatible with all we know), in the way that Goldbach's Conjecture and its negation appear to be, may not be *metaphysically possible* (true in any possible world). Whether and how concepts actually play these different modal roles will be an issue that we shall pursue in section IV.

These, then, are the main roles concepts have traditionally been asked to play. Whether there actually *are* any such things that *could* play *all* these roles—or even *any* of them—is not a question I want to prejudge. That it might be at least tempting to suppose that some one sort of thing might play all these roles is perhaps best brought out by recalling the Logical Positivists, who made a point of identifying all these roles in their 'Verification Principle': the meaning of a sentence consists in the methods people employ in verifying it; a concept is specified by the methods by which people determine what does and does not belong to it. This tempting view is not without its problems. Before discussing those problems, however, it is worth considering its affinities with, of all things, the views of S&M. For they, too, tend to identify the metaphysical and epistemological roles, in ways that (perhaps needlessly) burden their views with very similar problems.

III

Epistemology is conflated with metaphysics almost entirely throughout S&M's discussion. It begins right at the beginning, in *their* characterization of the functions of concepts. They list four: two 'taxonomic' functions—'categorization' and 'combination'—and two, roughly, Linguistic ones—'propositional' and 'interrogating' (pp. 7–

---

11. But independently by Amélie Rorty (1972); and earlier by John Locke (1690; bk. III. vi, 6).

8).[12] No distinction whatever is advanced between epistemological and metaphysical ways of understanding these functions. Instead, the crucial terms are left almost perfectly ambiguous between the two. Consider the 'categorization' function, upon which they 'will focus almost exclusively' (p. 8):

> *Categorization.* This function involves determining that a specific instance is a member of a concept (for example, this particular creature is a guppy) or that one particular concept is a subset of another (for example, guppies are fish). (p. 7)

'Categorization', 'determining', like 'taxonomic' itself, can refer either to issues surrounding how the things of the world are *correctly* classified, or to issues surrounding how people actually engage in the *process* of classifying, categorizing, taxonomizing —correctly or incorrectly. S&M do, further on, attempt to address this distinction, setting out a distinction between the 'core' and the 'identification procedure' of a concept, or between 'the features ... primarily responsible for revealing certain relations between concepts' and 'perceptual features like height and weight ... used for categorizing real-world objects' (p. 20). But, quite aside from the vagueness and inadequacy of this formulation, they rarely take this distinction very seriously.[13] On the one hand, they claim:

> Since the views of concepts we are interested in, particularly the Classical View, are mainly concerned with concept cores, we will emphasize experimental studies that either use a semantic task or use a perceptual one where there is good reason to believe the core consists entirely of perceptual features. (p. 21)

But, on the other, as they quite correctly make explicit from the start:

> In almost all cases we will be concerned with object concepts—animals, plants, human artifacts, and so on.... This domain is a particularly interesting test case for the three views. Had we chosen geometric concepts like [square] as a target domain, we might have prejudiced things in favor of the Classic view.... Similarly, had we chosen as our domain abstract concepts like [love] or [brilliance], we might have prejudiced things against the Classical View.... Natural objects and human artifacts offer an in-between case—between concepts any schoolboy can define and concepts that no scholar can grapple with. (p. 5)

But at least *natural kind* concepts, like those of biology, are precisely *not* the sorts of concepts for which we might expect the 'perceptual' and the 'core' features to coin-

---

12. They only briefly mention the 'interrogating' role. It is a little unclear, from their use of 'propositional', how much this role is part of what I call the 'Linguistic' role (e.g., supporting 'semantic implications'), and how much a part of what I included in the 'Stability' role (e.g., supporting chains of 'inferences' between different contents). Since the role is not further discussed in the book, and is included in one or another of the roles I set out, I shall disregard it.

13. Notice that some 'relations among concepts', e.g., coextensiveness (e.g. the relation between [rational animal] and [featherless biped]) might not involve, intuitively, the 'core' of a concept, while some 'identification procedures' might not really be perceptual (e.g., 'found on farms' (p. 71)). Also, given the very great importance of Frege's discussion of these matters, it is worth pointing out that S&M quite incorrectly identify their distinction between core and identification procedure with his distinction between 'sense' and 'reference' (pp. 20–21). Frege's distinction is, rather, the distinction between what we have been calling a *concept*, in its Linguistic role, and the (set of) *things in the world* picked out by the concept, i.e., the extension of the concept.

cide. After all, we all know full well that something might share all the usual perceptual features of a kind of plant or animal, but nevertheless fail quite definitely to *be* of that kind: we all have had our run-ins with silk flowers, wax figures, and fancy mechanical toys. That is, these are precisely the sorts of cases in which we would expect the epistemological and the metaphysical roles of concepts to diverge (cf., the gender examples mentioned earlier). Either S&M need to stick to examples in which the two roles coincide, or they need more scrupulously to observe this distinction in their interpretation of experimental results. But they do neither. By far the preponderance of their examples is of animal kinds, and the experiments generally involve rapid classification tasks, such as answering 'Are robins birds?', in which it would seem perfectly reasonable to suppose that people might well go by precisely such familiar and/or easily accessible perceptual features as [moves], [winged], [feathered], [flies] (p. 71).

S&M do at one point consider a defense of the *Classical View* along these lines. But they argue that, what with the lack of defining conditions and the presence of unclear cases anyway, this demonstrated reliance of subjects upon the identification procedures prevents the Classical View from playing any real psychological role. A retreat to the core

> seems to save the Classical View by shifting all the theoretical action away from the defining features of the core.... We may raise the question, why bother to posit Classical View concepts at all? (p. 59)

But quite independently of this question with regard merely to the Classical View, there is the larger question of positing any 'core' at all, distinct from the identification procedure, Classical or otherwise. That is, what is really at issue here is not whether there are defining conditions, but whether there is any reason to distinguish the metaphysical from the epistemological roles concepts might play. What S&M share with the Verificationists is their dismissal of the utility of this distinction (in S&M's case, perhaps only for the psychology of categorization).

But there are quite a number of reasons to insist upon it. There is first of all the point that it does appear to be a *psychologically real* distinction: people do distinguish [looking like a bird] from [actually being a bird]. At any rate, as we have already noted, most adults know that something might exhibit the outward, 'perceptible' and/or 'accidental' features of a bird, but be in fact a mechanical toy and so not any sort of bird at all. And conversely, as S&M everywhere presuppose, people do count things that *do not* look like birds—e.g., penguins—as nevertheless real birds. Perhaps the clearest case is that of numbers. As S&M mention in a footnote (p. 186), Armstrong *et al.* (1983) have demonstrated typicality effects even with [even number]. Here, there are quite obviously sharp defining conditions (being divisible by 2 without remainder) that any competent user knows, whether or not they deploy them in actual identification tasks. Indeed, we and they know full well why they might, under time pressure, mis-identify '246801', since they, as we, can distinguish the core from the identification procedures and realize that the latter can mislead.

In a related vein, people can generally distinguish—although S&M in their book do not—between something's *probably* being an F and something's being a *borderline case* of an F; or being an F *with probability n*, and being an F *to degree n*. Consider [bald], a concept that is 'graduated', or admits of degree, if there ever was one. Most things are more or less bald, i.e., bald to a certain degree n (say, between 0 and 1).

Someone might *be* bald to degree *n*, but be judged to be so, given a certain glimpse, with only probability *m* ($\neq n$): if I see a middle-aged man with a toupé, I might well hazard the guess that there's a 0.9 probability that he is half bald (i.e., bald to degree 0.5), and perhaps only a 0.6 probability that he is almost entirely bald (i.e., bald to degree 0.9). I would, that is, distinguish the metaphysical fact of a certain degree of baldness from the epistemological one of the likelihood, given my evidence, that he enjoys that degree. For all their 'probabilistic' conclusions regarding the concept [bird], I doubt very much whether S&M want to claim that a penguin is a bird only to a relatively small degree, *much less that anyone actually thinks so.* I strongly suspect that most people consider penguins to be (metaphysically) *bona fide* birds—i.e., birds to degree 1—despite their slight hesitation in judging them to be so, i.e., despite the somewhat low (epistemological) probabilities that something with merely the perceptual features of penguins might be so.

Indeed, a corresponding distinction needs to be drawn between two sorts of 'unclear cases': those, like that of *euglena* (p. 31), which may well *be* on the borderline between animal and plant; and those, like that of *tomatoes* (p. 59), which may *be* (metaphysically) clear cases of fruit (check the dictionary!), even though people may be (epistemologically) confused about them. The fact that subjects might be unclear about whether something falls under a particular concept will not show anything one way or another about whether there are metaphysically defining conditions for that concept unless it can be shown that the unclarity is metaphysical and not merely epistemological. But neither S&M nor we, for that matter, have yet considered what might establish *that*.

Not only is the distinction between metaphysics and epistemology psychologically real for people, but perhaps most important, it would seem to play a crucial role in fixing the Stability functions of concepts. Consider what can happen to those functions if we ignore that distinction. S&M write:

> A concept is stable within an individual to the extent that once a person has a concept, then, except for early developmental changes or physiological ones, that person will always have the same set of properties in mind. A concept is stable across individuals to the extent that when any two people have the same concept they have the identical sets of properties in mind. (p. 10)

But if, as we found S&M later recommending, the distinction between the 'core' and the 'identification procedure' of a concept is to have no psychological significance, then any two people who use different procedures, or one person who uses different procedures at different times, would *ipso facto* have different concepts. If the features by which I identify birds have to do with their songs, while those you go by have to do with their feathers, then, since you and I have different sets of properties 'in mind', you and I have different concepts associated with 'bird'. That is—to recall precisely the work concepts are to do in their Stability and Linguistic roles—you and I could not have beliefs and preferences with the same content [bird]; our uses of the word 'bird' would be mere homonyms; our agreements and disputes about *birds* illusory. And how much worse off would we all be in these respects on the *Exemplar* view, since we probably all do have at least slightly (but usually very) different exemplars in mind when we think. Finally, as several generations of philosophers have pointed out against Verificationism (see e.g., Putnam, 1966), identifying a concept with its identification procedure precludes discovering new identification procedures, or abandoning old ones: for any such change in a method of verification would *ipso facto* constitute a change in the concept.

All of this seems, of course, a needless encumbrance of scientific practice, and of intra- and inter-personal comparisons of conceptual content. Not just any belief ought to count as a change in concept. In particular, not just any change in a belief about how you *tell* whether something satisfies a concept ought to count as a change in that concept. This is surely part of the purpose in separating the 'core' from the 'identification procedure', the metaphysics from the epistemology, in the way that S&M, following what seems to be a psychologically real distinction, were originally inclined to do. The fact that the core might not turn out to consist of *necessary and sufficient defining conditions*, that *it* might even turn out to be 'graduated', ought not to deter them. That is quite another matter from whether a concept ought to be regarded as having any core at all.

It might be tempting to suppose at this point that there are simply *two* concepts of concepts, one metaphysical, the other epistemological, and that the work of S&M ought properly be construed as addressing only the latter. This is the temptation behind the view of meaning as 'conceptual role' (see Grice and Strawson, 1956; and especially Field, 1977). But once the distinction is fully clear, there would seem to be serious obstacles to positing a concept of concept's playing a purely epistemological role. First, as S&M remark in their introduction:

> Concepts give our *world* stability.... They capture the notion that many objects and events are alike in important respects. (p. 1, my italics)

Concepts, that is, would seem—at least in the first instance—to be about the world and how *it* divides up; not about how we might divide up our methods of investigating it. The interest is in the ducks themselves, not in our ways of knowing them.[14] Indeed, one ought to expect to find the latter *not* very well divided up at all: in determining what's what, surely people ought to use (as they do) whatever works. The richer one's ingenuity and theory of the world, the more diverse the methods that will work. Thus does spectroscopy tell us what's what on distant stars, and carbon-dating what was what at distant times.

Second, as Duhem (1906) and Quine (1953) have emphasized, claims about the world are not confirmed or disconfirmed by experimental methods in isolation. Methods (e.g., of spectroscopy, carbon-dating, or just taking in the feathers and song) are reasonable ways of finding out what's what only in conjunction with the theories that support them. Those theories in turn receive support from other theories and claims about the world in such a way that 'our statements about the external world face the tribunal of sense experience not individually but only as a corporate body' (Quine, 1953, p. 42). Separating off from that body some particular procedure as a distinct concept would seem wholly arbitrary, both rationally and historically. Certain methods and the features associated with them may emerge as particularly stable for some people at some times, due to their believed reliability against the background of those peoples' other beliefs. But change some even remote portion of that

---

14. This point could be exaggerated. Once one is focused upon a particular (sort of) thing in the world, how one is thinking about it—what sorts of evidence one accepts—could be *additionally* relevant to concept identification, as it seems to be in such cases as [the morning star] *versus* [the evening star], cf. section V below.

background—some belief about the wave structure of light, about the precise rate of radioactive carbon's decay, about the local imitability of feathers and songs—and they might quite readily alter those methods and their faith in those features. What purpose would be served by singling out occasional stability of some method for some special concept of concept? Not, so far as I can see, any of the other purposes for which concepts seem intended.

But perhaps among the many changing methods whereby one determines what satisfies a concept, some method does play a central role. That method might be singled out as the 'core' of a concept. That is, while the metaphysical and epistemological roles might not coincide for the whole identity of the concept, they might coincide in the core. This 'core' method might be not just how one tells what's what given this or that theory of the world, but how one would tell what's what *ultimately,* given any theory. It is this idea that lies behind the suggestion that the core be regarded as a kind of 'backup procedure' (p. 59, see also Katz (1977)), a suggestion over which we will linger a little longer than do S&M.

IV

Regarding the core as a backup procedure obviously affords a way of protecting the Classical View from much of S&M's 'probabilistic' data. It does not, however, protect it from the other two difficulties we mentioned at the start: the fact that people cannot even after prolonged reflection, seem to produce defining conditions for most of the concepts they employ, and the fact that they are stymied by 'unclear cases', like those of both [tomato] and [euglena]. Nor does it protect it from the sorts of counterexamples frequently raised against plausible definitions: e.g., if cats are 'by definition' animals, then how are we to account for such apparent possibilities as that they might turn out to be robots controlled from Mars (Putnam, 1970)? Moreover, research on sentence comprehension (Fodor, *et al.,* 1975; Fodor *et al.,* 1980) strongly suggests that defining conditions have no role to play there. And Carey (1980) points out that there is no evidence that they play any role in semantic development. If there are Classical cores, they certainly seem to make themselves scarce in peoples' actual psychological processing.

But all of these facts pose problems for the Classical View only on what I presented as the third, entirely implicit assumption attached by S&M to the Classical View: what it is for someone to *have* a particular concept is for her to *know* its defining conditions. Perhaps concepts do have Classical cores, but competent users of the concepts do not always know what they are. It is worth at least considering this possibility before abandoning the Classical View altogether.

The suggestion that competent users of a concept may not know defining conditions for its application emerges from recent work in the philosophy of language on the definitions of terms. Given the linguistic function of concepts that we are assuming as uncontroversial, we can, I think, take claims about the definability of terms to be interchangable with claims about the cores of the concepts those terms express.

Perhaps the best known attack on definability can be found in those passages of Wittgenstein that served as the inspiration of much of the original research on stereotypicality effects. There is his notorious example of 'game' (discussed by S&M, p. 30), for which he claims, after a cursory examination of several candidates, that no defining features can be found; and there are the frequent admonitions throughout his later work against supposing that there are any strict rules at all that people follow in their use of language. But these claims are standardly taken to be aimed at the Classical View as a whole.[15] The more restricted suggestion that, *whether or not there actually are defining conditions*, competent users of a concept may still not know them is a suggestion that emerges from the work of Putnam (1966, 1970, 1975) and Kripke (1971, 1972).[16]

Essentially what Putnam and Kripke do is to insist more strenuously still on the distinction between metaphysics and epistemology. Focusing upon proper names and natural kind terms in natural language, they try to show that whatever defining conditions such terms might have is entirely a matter of metaphysics, of how the world is; whether anyone actually knows those conditions is quite inessential to the identity of those conditions, and even to whether someone is a competent user of such a term.

Kripke and Putnam argue for their view primarily on the basis of ordinary linguistic intuitions regarding 'natural kind terms',[17] or terms that purport to refer to kinds of things that are the subject matter of some science, e.g., 'multiple sclerosis', 'acid', 'gold', 'tiger'. Take 'gold'. Kripke and Putnam claim that we are prepared to discover that the descriptions many of us presently believe to be individuating of gold—e.g., 'the precious, yellow metal mined in the Sierras', 'the metal used in wedding rings', 'the international monetary standard'—might turn out not to be so. These without contradiction could turn out to be lies, half-truths, tall stories (perhaps it is actually white, pyrites are used for rings, and the monetary standard is a hoax). Or, even if they are true, it is *metaphysically* possible that they not be: had the geological history of the earth been different, gold might never have even been discovered or used by anyone for anything. Still no contradiction. Thus, the information most of us are in a position to associate with gold—as with, Kripke and Putnam would claim, most any natural kind—is not in any way necessarily tied to it, and so would seem inadequate as any definition of 'gold'.

But none of this implies that the term has no definition at all. Indeed, 'gold' seems to have: try 'basic chemical element with atomic number 79'. At any rate, this chemical description, if true, would appear to provide us with nomologically necessary and sufficient conditions for the proper use of the term, those facts in virtue of which something qualifies as being (made of) gold. And it would also seem to capture our *metaphysically* modal intuitions: again, if the description is *true*, then only something having atomic number 79 *would* be gold; even something yellow, mined in the Sierras, used in wedding bands and as a monetary standard, but lacking that atomic number,

15. As would seem to be Wittgenstein's intention except for certain passages in Wittgenstein (1965, pp. 25–26) in which, discussing how the 'symptoms' and 'criteria' of, e.g., *angina* can vary over time, he seems to anticipate the sort of view I ascribe to Putnam below.

16. The view also seems available in Locke (1690, bk. III, vi, 6). I should emphasize that in what follows I am reading the remarks of Kripke and Putnam in a more heavily Lockean way than either of them may have intended. Concerned as they are more with reference than actually with meaning, they should by no means be held to the application I make of their remarks to a theory of *concepts*.

17. Kripke actually first considered proper names in this regard. And, indeed, the linguistic intuitions appealed to in these arguments are perhaps sharpest with regard to proper names (substitute 'Aristotle' for 'gold' and common beliefs about Aristotle for the common beliefs about gold in the discussion that follows). But since S&M are not concerned with names, and since in any case it is not clear in what way a *concept* may be associated with one, I shall pass over this portion of Kripke's argument.

would not be. In short, the description would appear to provide much that has been standardly asked of a definition.

With one conspicuous exception: it might well not be *known* even to most competent users of the term. And so it would not serve any of the epistemological functions concepts have sometimes been asked to serve. For all that competent users of 'gold' might know, its proper definition might involve atomic number 89, or 2, or no atomic number at all (presumably the early theorists did not already know the appropriate theory and definitions that they were trying to find!). But this is just the assumption that the work of Kripke and Putnam challenges: the assumption that competent users of a term need to know its proper definition, that the proper definition of a term need play some epistemological role.

S&M do consider these views of Kripke and Putnam in a brief footnote. But, consistent with their disregard of the distinction between epistemology and metaphysics generally, they miss this latter crucial point. They regard Kripke and Putnam as having delivered the 'death blow' to the Classical View, since, according to them, Kripke and Putnam

> have argued that there is no property of an object that we refer to by the name X that the object must necessarily have in order for us properly to call it an X. (p. 186, fn. 1, ch. 3)

But Kripke and Putnam have argued no such thing, much less delivered any such blow. First of all, they have quite explicitly claimed that there *are* properties that, for example, gold must necessarily have in order for us properly to call it 'gold': e.g., having atomic number 79. That, according to them, is a metaphysical necessity. But this metaphysical necessity is entirely compatible with the epistemological possibility that it *not* have that property, just as, as we observed earlier, the (let us suppose) metaphysical necessity of Goldbach's conjecture is compatible with the epistemological possibility that it is false. To be epistemologically possible is to be something like 'imaginable', 'conceivable', 'compatible with a certain set of beliefs', and, as such, is relative to the state of a person's beliefs and imagination at a time; metaphysical possibilities have nothing to do with *us*, but only with the nature of the things being described or conceived. Perhaps the distinction might best be drawn by regarding metaphysical necessities to be of the form, 'if p then necessarily p' (e.g., 'if gold has atomic number 79 then necessarily it does'), whereas epistemological possibilities have the form, 'Given what little I know about chemistry, I am prepared to discover that gold has atomic number 89'. And these claims are then more evidently compatible: e.g., 'Given how little I know about chemistry, I am prepared to discover that gold has atomic number 89, even though, if it in fact has atomic number 79, then necessarily it does'.

By insisting upon this distinction between metaphysical and epistemological possibilities, and denying definitions any essential epistemological role, Putnam and Kripke, far from dealing the Classical View any sort of 'death blow', may actually have afforded it its only chance of survival. For now it is no longer at the mercy of the often capricious epistemological possibilities—nor S&M's purported psychological evidence—that have been raised against it. That is, it is no longer an objection to the Classical View (on which, say, cats and penguins are 'by definition' living things) that we can *imagine* cats to be robots or penguins to be fancy Swiss toys; nor is it an objection that competent users of these concepts might not be able to provide defining conditions for them, nor even be able to decide 'unclear cases' like that of either [tomato] or [euglena]. All of these latter facts are explainable on the plausible assumption that, while at least many such natural kind terms do in fact have definitions, competent users may simply be ignorant of what they might be.

The proper definitions of natural kind of terms, on this view, are provided by the portion of science that deals with the respective natural kind. Putnam treats this fact as an instance of a general 'hypothesis of the universality of the division of linguistic labor':

> Every linguistic community ... possesses at least some terms whose associated 'criteria' are known only to a subject of the speakers who acquire the terms, and whose use by other speakers depends upon a structured cooperation between them and the speakers in the relevant subsets. (Putnam, 1975, p. 228)

In the case of 'gold' and 'acid', the appropriate subset appears to be the experts in chemical theory; for 'multiple sclerosis', presumably medical doctors; for 'tiger', as for S&M's 'robin', 'sparrow', 'bird', zoologists.[18]

Especially in these scientistic days, there probably are experts who can define a great many of our ordinary terms. But *need* there be? Even Putnam's hypothesis would seem to be too epistemological. Prior to atomic theory presumably *no-one* could correctly define 'gold'—perhaps no one actually can today either (atomic theory might be wrong) or *ever*. There is, after all, no guarantee that anyone really is smart enough to figure out any *true* theories of anything.[19] In order therefore properly to divorce the issue of definitions from the issue of *anyone's* ability to provide them (and, moreover, to permit agents outside of any communities to have access if not to language, at least to *concepts*), it seems to me that we would do well to substitute for Putnam's hypothesis the more general:

> *Hypothesis of External Definitions:* the correct definition of a concept is provided by the optimal account of it, which need not be known by the concept's competent users.

By 'optimal account' I mean an account of a concept, all relevant issues and possible evidence considered, than which no account (metaphysically) could be better. (For realists, that might be the *true* account; for those more idealistically inclined, it may simply be the account human beings will eventually agree upon.) Since, as we mentioned earlier, relevance seems to be distributed holistically across our system of beliefs and evidence, definitions on this view are no different than any other claim to knowledge, and are continually revisable in the light of further argument and

---

18. Notice that, *pace* Schwartz (1977), this hypothesis is by no means confined to proper names and natural kind terms. Similar intuitions are readily available for artifactual terms ('carburator', 'viola da gamba'), mathematical terms ('number', 'ellipse'), logical terms ('proof', 'validity', 'only if', 'or'), and even the terms of philosophy and psychology ('belief', 'thought', and, not to put too fine a point upon it, 'concept' itself). I have developed this hypothesis with regard to a variety of psychological terms in Rey (1977, 1980*b*, 1983). For a quite subtle discussion of how people might be mistaken about the meanings of even entirely non-theoretical terms like 'sofa', see Burge (1978, 1979).

19. Locke, who proposed a similar position about the 'real essences' of things, also believed that they were unknowable (see Locke, *op. cit.*).

research.[20] The appeal to experts for the correct definition simply becomes a piece of the appeal to experts on behalf of *any* knowledge.

So the core of a concept may well be what we would ultimately use to decide whether or not something satisfies it. But a competent user of the concept may not know that core and so simply be unable to make any such ultimate decision. The cores of concepts may have at best only a *hypothetical* epistemological role to play, and none whatsoever if certain sorts of optimal knowledge are impossible.

Notice that this hypothetical role may not be without its psychological reality. Indeed, it is every bit as psychologically real as the Hypothesis of External Definitions: if the latter is true *and believed to be so by competent users of concepts*, then we should expect an agent's representation of a concept to have, as it were, specially marked 'slots' for defining conditions, slots that may or may not be filled, depending upon the agent's knowledge. This latter hypothesis is presumably not entirely untestable. Fairly strong *prima facie* evidence for it is provided by the very arguments and intuitions of Kripke and Putnam that I have discussed, intuitions of philosophers and other conceptually competent psychological agents that need to be explained just as much as any other data in psychology.

Of course, nothing that has been said so far in the least constitutes a *positive* argument for a Classical View of the core of a concept, or even for the ultimate truth of the intuitions of Kripke and Putnam or of any other philosophers. What I do believe has been established, however, is a negative claim, *viz.* that the Classical View is not refuted by the kinds of evidence and arguments advanced by S&M. What might be called the 'External Classical View' can withstand all the evidence in the world regarding peoples' *ignorance* of what may for all that be a concept's necessary and sufficient defining conditions.

The Classical View does, however, have problems *related* to the epistemological problems raised by S&M. There are the problems about providing necessary and sufficient conditions for concepts *even on the best candidates for optimal views* that anyone has yet been able to think of. Family resemblance structures seem to crop up even there (see Sibley (1966) for aesthetic concepts; Coleman and Kay (1981) for ethical ones); *sufficient* conditions can seem impossible to find (are there really sufficient conditions for, for example, being a sparrow *other than* being a sparrow? Why is it important that there be?); and there is the endlessly vexing problem of what seems to be an unavoidable 'fuzziness' in all our concepts: all our concepts, as they apply to

20. The common expression 'true by definition' can be misleading in this regard. As Quine (1954) has pointed out, this expression is best understood as an expository convenience, selecting out of a body of belief certain claims for the moment as fixed, rather in the way certain sentences of geometry may be selected as axioms, or certain points in Ohio as points of departure. As any further claim to *truth*, such claims are indistinguishable from general claims to simplicity and conservativism of theory (see especially Quine [1954, p. 121]). In any case, the claims to definitions being considered here are better regarded not as 'truths *by* definition' so much as 'truths *and* definitions'. It is in this way that this account of meaning is immune from one of Quine's chief attacks on the notion, as it is used in marking an 'analytic/synthetic' distinction and providing a basis for *a priori* knowledge. For no claim is being made about any special set of sentences that are 'true by definition' or in any way *a priori* or unrevisable in the light of further research. Of course, it is not immune from his scepticism about modality generally. But it seems to me that *that* is a scepticism that much of our science and ordinary intuitions are quite strong enough to withstand.

concrete objects in space and time, seem upon close inspection to be graduated in just the way that [is bald] is.[21] But these issues take us far from the kinds of issues raised by S&M. They would seem to involve much more general issues of logic and definition as, moreover, they apply to the particular optimal accounts (e.g., the particular sciences) in which the concept occurs. They would seem to involve, that is, issues well beyond the scope of psychology alone.

V

But how, it might well be asked, could the proper characterization of what would seem to be the very stuff of cognition be beyond the scope of cognitive science? Indeed, how possibly could the Hypothesis of External Definitions be correct? For it would appear on this hypothesis that someone could be a competent user of a concept she doesn't really understand, a competent user of words whose meanings she does not know. How can the stability functions of concepts be so divorced from both the metaphysical and epistemological roles?

A satisfactory answer to these questions would require a fuller theory of semantic and conceptual competence, and in general of the stability function, than anyone has yet provided, and, in any case, than could possibly be provided here. The point of the preceding discussion has only been to cast doubt upon the theory that has been too uncritically assumed both by proponents of the Classical View and by many of its critics, e.g. S&M. But it may be worth mentioning some considerations that point towards positive alternatives. Whether they actually point to a single, unified, and principled basis for the ascription of conceptual content is a question that awaits much further work.

In the first place, a competence may often be more than a purely 'intrinsic' affair, involving matters beyond the internal constitution of the agent. While the ability to sing, for example, may be entirely intrinsic in this way, the ability to be a senator from New York obviously is not (there must exist, for example, a state of New York with a certain form of government). Conceptual structures may be more like structures outside one's skin to which one bears certain sorts of, for example, causal rela-

---

21. The problem of finding necessary and sufficient conditions however need not be quite as difficult as S&M make it out to be. In particular, it is hard to see why one ought to insist, as they do, on conditions that are *both* 'singly necessary and jointly sufficient' (p. 23) in the manner of conventional, 'tree structure' taxonomies. Perfectly useful definitions in mathematics, for example, do not observe any such stricture: [is a natural number] can be defined as [either zero or the successor of a natural number], in which either condition is sufficient, but neither of them necessary. Presumably S&M would not be happy with this as a Classical definition, since it is disjunctive, which they claim no Classical definition ought to be. But this demand, too, seems arbitrary. Indeed, since any disjunction ('F or G') is logically equivalent to a negated conjunction of negations ('not (not-F and not-G)'), such a stricture would also seem to rule out the standard functions out of which definitions are constructed. Perhaps the point is this: 'family resemblance' concepts are essentially 'open-ended'. Ever new objects sharing ever new properties with merely *some* of the old objects could be regarded as members of a concept (Wittgenstein's example of [game] looks like it might be open-ended in just this way). Consequently, no *finite* disjunction could provide a defining condition. Finitude is, of course, a reasonable demand to place on a Classical definition. But this issue is quite independent of mere disjunctiveness itself.

tions, than as structures entirely within it.[22] It may seem uncomfortably Platonistic to conceive of concepts in this way; but it is not obviously false, no more obviously false, anyway, than the claim that 'mankind has a common store of thoughts which is transmitted from one generation to another' (Frege 1892/1960) (cf., the stability functions of concepts).

Second, conceptual competence could turn out not to involve any substantial knowledge-*that* at all. Many competencies—bicycling, playing the violin—seem to involve mostly know-how, which may or may not involve the possession of any propositional attitudes. The extent to which even so seeming a rule-governed competence as the appreciation of grammar actually involves the agent's representation of explicit rules is a subtle question to which, I gather, there is as yet no clear answer. Insofar as conceptual competence might involve merely an ability to make certain sorts of discriminations (say, being able to sort, under certain circumstances, things that do from things that do not satisfy the concept), we can certainly imagine mechanisms that do this without any representations whatsoever: consider *detecting* devices (metal detectors, light detectors).[23] Even on the aforementioned Verificationist View (on which agents make categorization decisions on the basis of defining features), competence with the primitive (e.g., sensory) concepts often consisted merely in being able to make certain sorts of discriminations, presumably on the basis of non-representational processes of transduction. Perhaps more of our concepts than we might expect are primitive in this way (see Fodor [1987, 1990]).

Lastly, even if conceptual know-how does sometimes consist in part in some explicitly represented knowledge-that, still that knowledge-that might be of merely evidential, inferential, or simply popularly believed conditions, not defining ones. That is, for at least some concepts, like [bird], [bee], [elm], [beech], [owl], [penguin], it may be enough to know that, for example, birds chirp, bees buzz, elms and beeches are kinds of trees, owls go 'whoo' and penguins live in the cold looking as though they wear tuxedos. Certainly the sort of information S&M's subjects know seems to be precisely of this sort (see Table 9, pp. 90–92, for particularly amusing evidence). And, of course, none of this need be genuine *knowledge*, since, as we observed in the previous section, these sorts of beliefs may well be false. At best, what a competent user of a word is sometimes required to know is something like its *dictionary* definition; but, as inspection of the *Oxford English Dictionary* should reveal, what is provided there is rarely genuinely defining conditions, more usually simply commonly held beliefs.

22. This is a way I am inclined to read Fodor's thesis of 'methodological solipsism' (see Fodor (1980) and my accompanying commentary, Rey (1980a)). On this view, the task of psychology is only the description of the formal, or purely 'syntactic', features of an agent's system of representation and computation. The *semantic* features, i.e., the features involving the ascription of content, involve the relations the agent bears to its particular environment. Unlike Fodor, I suspect that this will be true not only for *extensional* semantics, but also—for the sorts of reasons adduced in the previous section—for *intensional* semantics as well. The beginnings of a discussion of the causal relation that may be involved can be found in the same discussions of Putnam and Kripke, as well as in Devitt (1980).
23. This is not to say that just *any* detector can be credited with the corresponding concept [metal]. There are doubtless other conditions (e.g., being a system that manipulates symbols in some rational fashion) that something must satisfy in order to be credited with any concepts *at all*. The view that having a specific concept consists in (besides satisfying these other conditions) being able to make certain sorts of discriminations under certain circumstances has its source in Classical Learning Theory, but has also been advanced in more sophisticated ways by Stampe (1979), Dretske (1979), and Fodor (1987, 1990).

Looking to the inferential role of a concept can seem like looking back to the very epistemological role for concepts that I earlier abjured. I argued that the holistic character of the evidence relation undermined identifying a concept with any particular evidence or inference that might at some time be associated with it. And in the previous section I argued that even any ultimate inferential relation that may attach to a concept may emerge only from an ideal account of the concept, an account that competent users well might not know. The role of inference and evidence here, however, is more modest than was earlier being proposed. Although inferential relations may not be *constitutive* of either conceptual identity or competence, still they could *bear* particularly upon the latter. Knowing *some* of the inferential relations of a concept— i.e., knowing something of the role it plays in our thought—may well be necessary, and in some cases perhaps sufficient for being competent with that concept, even though those relations may actually be false, and in any case not defining.[24]

Even here, however, the sort of knowledge (or belief) that might be required still need not be *stereotypical*. From the fact that competent users of a concept may have to share some inferential beliefs or others, it does not follow that there is some particular inferential belief, whether ultimate or stereotypical, that all competent users must share. Surely people with different stereotypes of birds, and different inferential beliefs, can still have the concept, [bird]. So even as a proposal about the inferential component of conceptual competence, S&M's claims about the roles of exemplars and probabilistic data seem needlessly restrictive (as do Putnam's (1970, p. 148) similar remarks about the role of 'stereotypical' information in the meanings of terms).

If it is not the conditions either for conceptual identity or conceptual competence that S&M's discussion can be taken to be addressing, what *is* its import? Perhaps it is merely this. People rely, more heavily than we might have originally supposed, on stereotypical information in making category judgments. The methods, that is, that people are often criticized for employing in making judgments of e.g., racial or sexual category ('Muggers are Black', 'Doctors are male') seem to be instances of a cognitive strategy people employ in making category judgments generally. They tend to access what they take to be typical properties, remembered examples, perhaps even constructed 'paradigms', or 'exemplars', in deciding what's what. However, as most of them would readily admit, they are hardly committed to those properties or exemplars being defining of those concepts. To the contrary: it is a happy fact about racist and sexist judgments, as about the sorts of judgments that concern S&M, that people *argue* about them and can sometimes be persuaded to give them up. They may still have different *conceptions* of Blacks, women, doctors, birds; and they quite probably have different sorts of experiences when they think about them. But it is still [Blacks],

24. In his account of proper names, Kripke discusses the role that the identifying descriptions that accompany usages of the name may play in 'fixing the reference' of the name, even though the description is patently not synonymous with it. The analogous suggestion here would be that the inferential role—the evidential conditions, the popular beliefs—that someone may associate with, say, a particular expression in her language of thought, might 'fix the meaning' of that expression i.e., be enough to attach it to some concept, even though that role might not provide the defining conditions for it. This might occur as a result of that evidence or those beliefs marking some salient contrast in the local environments of the agent. For example, someone might use 'F' to designate some observed birds that 'look like they're wearing tuxedos', which description, given the contrasts in the context, might be sufficient to fix the meaning of 'F' as [penguin]. But this suggestion needs of course to be worked out in a great deal more detail than is possible here.

[women], [doctors], [birds] that comprise part of the *conceptual content* of those disagreements, different conceptions, experiences, and later more enlightened beliefs; it is still those concepts that determine what those mental states are *about*. If S&M advance their proposals as claims about conceptual identity or competence, they would seem to deprive us of any basis for the coherent ascription of these sorts of mental states, and would leave us with no recognizable concept of concept that their 'probabilistic' theories could be taken to be addressing. As a theory, however, of how people generally *access* concepts they are independently competent to use, of peoples' *conceptions* of the world, their claims may well be true, and, if true, surprising.

This way of understanding their results would also free them from worries about the work of Sommers and Keil, and from the problem of conceptual combination. There is no bar to concepts that are merely standardly accessed by stereotype also having a tree structure, nor to agents thinking that they do. Nor is it difficult to see how an agent could engage in conceptual combination: being competent with concepts A and B, and with 'and' and 'or' and 'not', agents could presumably come to be competent with indefinitely many concepts that are combinations of these. The extension of the combination could still be a function of the extension of the parts. In particular, the defining conditions of an AB may simply be the conjunction of the defining conditions for A and the defining conditions for B. But, of course, a competent user may no more know how to determine that extension than how to determine the extension of those parts; for she may not know what those defining conditions might be.

References

Armstrong, S. L., Gleitman, L., and Gleiman, H. (1983) What some concepts might not be, *Cog.*, *13* (3), 263–308.

Burge, T. (1977) Belief *de re*, *J. Phil.*, *74* (6), 338–362.

Burge, T. (1978) Belief and synonymy, *J. Phil.*, *75* (3), 119–138.

Burge, T., (1979) Individualism and the Mental, *Midwest Studies in Philosophy*, Vol. 4 (Studies in Metaphysics), Minneapolis, Univ. of Minnesota Press.

Carey, S. (1980) Semantic development: State of the art. In Gleitman and Wanner. (eds.) *Language Acquisition: State of the Art.* Hillsdale, N.J. Erlbaum.

Coleman, L., and Kay, P. (1981) Prototype semantics: The English word 'lie'. *Lang.*, *57* (1), 26–44.

Davidson, D. (1970) Mental events. In L. Foster and J. Swanson (eds.) *Experience and Theory*. Amherst, MA, University of Massachusetts Press.

Devitt, M. (1980) *Designation*. New York, Columbia University Press.

Dretske, F. (1979) *Knowledge and the Flow of Information*. Cambridge, MA, Bradford Books.

Duhem, P. (1906) *La Théorie physique: son Objet et sa Structure*. Paris.

Field, H., (1977) Logic, meaning, and conceptual role, *J. Phil.* *74* (7) 379–409.

Fodor, J. A. (1987) *Psychosemantics: The Problem of Meaning in the Philosophy of Mind*. Cambridge, MA, Bradford Books.

Fodor, J. A. (1990) Psychosemantics, or: Where Do Truth Conditions Come From? In W. Lycan (ed.) *Mind and Cognition: A Reader*. Oxford, Basil Blackwell.

Fodor, J. A., Garrett, M. F., Walker, E. C. T., and Parkes, C. H. (1980) Against definitions. *Cog. 8* (3), 265–367.

Fodor, J. D., Fodor, J. A., and Garrett, M. F. (1975) The psychological unreality of semantic representations, *Ling. Inq. 6*, 515–531.

Frege, G. (1892/1966) On sense and reference. In P. Geach and M. Black (eds.) *Translations from the Philosophical Writings of Gottlob Frege*. London, Blackwells.

Grice, H. P., and Strawson, P. (1956) In defense of a dogma, *Phil. Rev.*, *65* (2), 141–158.

Kaplan, D. (1968) Quantifying in, *Synthese*, *19* (1/2), 178–214.

Katz, J. (1977) A proper theory of names. *Philosophical Studies, 31*, 1–80.

Keil, F. (1979) *Semantic and Conceptual Development*. Cambridge, MA, Harvard University Press.

Kripke, S. (1971) Identity and Necessity. In M. Munitz (ed.) *Identity and Individuation*. New York, New York University Press.

Kripke, S. (1972) Naming and Necessity. In D. Davidson and G. Harman (eds.) *Semantics of Natural Language*. Dordrecht, Netherlands, D. Reidel.

Locke, J. (1690) *An Essay Concerning Human Understanding*. New York, Dutton (1961).

Putnam, H. (1966) The Analytic and the Synthetic. In H. Feigl and G. Maxwell (eds.) *Minnesota Studies in the Philosophy of Science*, Vol. III. Minneapolis, University of Minnesota Press.

Putnam, H. (1970) Is Semantics Possible. In H. Keifer and M. Munitz (eds.) *Language, Belief, and Metaphysics*. New York, State University of New York Press.

Putman, H. (1975) the Meaning of 'Meaning'. In K. Gunderson (ed.) *Language, Mind, and Knowledge*. Minneapolis, University of Minnisota Press.

Quine, W. (1953) Two dogmas of empiricism. In *From a Logical Point of View*. Cambridge, MA, Harvard University Press.

Quine, W. (1954) Carnap and logical truth. In *Ways of Paradox*. Cambridge, MA, Harvard University Press (1976).

Quine, W. (1956) Quantifiers and propositional attitudes. In *Ways of Paradox*. Cambridge, MA, Harvard University Press.

Quine, W. (1960) *Word and Object*. Cambridge, MA, MIT Press.

Rey, G. (1977) Survival. In A. O. Rorty (ed.) *The Identities of Persons*. Berkeley, University of California Press.

Rey, G. (1980a) The formal and the opaque, *Beh. Br. Sci.*, *3*, 290–292.

Rey, G. (1980b) Functionalism and the emotions. In A. Rorty (ed.) *Explaining Emotions*. Berkeley, University of California Press.

Rey, G. (1983) A reason for doubting the existence of consciousness. In Davidson, Schwartz, and Shapiro (eds.) *Consciousness and Self-regulation*, Vol. 3. New York, Plenum.

Rorty, A. (1972) Essential possibilities and the actual world, *Rev. Metaphys.*, *XXV*, 607–624.

Schwartz, S. (1978) Putnam on artifacts, *Phil. Rev.*, 88, 566–574.

Sibley, F. (1966) Aesthetic concepts. In C. Barrett (ed.) *Collected Papers on Aesthetics*. New York Barnes and Noble.

Smith, E., and Medin, D. (1981) *Categories and concepts*. Cambridge, MA, Harvard University Press.

Sommers, F. (1965) Predicability. In M. Black (ed.) *Philosophy in America*. Ithaca, NY, Cornell University Press.

Stampe, D. (1979) Toward a causal theory of linguistic representation. In P. French *et al.* (eds.) *Contemporary Perspectives in the Philosophy of Language*. Minneapolis, University of Minnesota Press.

Stich, S. (1981) On the ascription of content. In A. Woodfield (ed.) *Thought and Object*. London, Oxford University Press.

Wittgenstein, L. (1953/1965) *Philosophical Investigations*. (3rd edn.). New York, Macmillan.

PART II

Current Theories and Research

Neoclassical Theories

Chapter 13

What Is a Concept, That a Person May Grasp It?

Ray Jackendoff

1. Prologue

Asking a psychologist, a philosopher, or a linguist what a concept is is much like asking a physicist what mass is. An answer cannot be given in isolation. Rather, the term plays a certain role in a larger world view that includes the nature of language, of meaning, and of mind. Hence the notion of a concept cannot be explicated without at the same time sketching the background against which it is set; and the "correctness" of a particular notion of concept cannot be evaluated without at the same time evaluating the world view in which it plays a role.

In turn, the evaluation of a world view is at least in part dependent on one's purposes. A world view incorporating a geocentric universe evidently was well suited for the purposes of the Church of the sixteenth century; a world view incorporating the Newtonian notions of mass and energy is perfectly adequate for building bridges. On the other hand, a world view incorporating a heliocentric planetary system is more suitable for the purpose of unifying the theories of terrestrial and celestial motion; a world view incorporating relativistic notions of mass and energy is more suitable if our purpose is building nuclear weapons.

My purpose is to better understand human nature. My method is to attempt to characterize the mental resources that make possible the articulation of humans' knowledge and experience of the world.

2. E-Concepts and I-Concepts

There is a fundamental tension in the ordinary language term *concept*. On one hand, it is something out there in the world: "the Newtonian concept of mass" is something that is spoken of as though it exists independently of who actually knows or grasps it. Likewise, "grasping a concept" evokes comparison to grasping a physical object, except that one somehow does it with one's mind instead of one's hand. On the other hand, a concept is spoken of as an entity within one's head, a private entity, a product of the imagination that can be conveyed to others only by means of language, gesture, drawing, or some other imperfect means of communication.

This chapter was originally prepared as the keynote lecture for the April 1989 meeting of Generative Linguists of the Old World, in Utrecht. It was first published in *Mind and Language* 4.1/2 (1989), as part of a special issue devoted to the topic "What Is a Concept?" It is reprinted here by permission. Much of it appears also in chapter 1 of Jackendoff 1990. The title owes apologies to Warren McCulloch. I am grateful to Noam Chomsky, John Macnamara, and Jerry Fodor for comments on an earlier version. I do not, however, intend to imply by this that they endorse my approach; in particular, Fodor doesn't believe a word of it.

This research was supported in part by NSF Grant IST 84-20073 to Brandeis University.

Precisely the same tension has been discussed by Chomsky (1986) with respect to the term *language*. He differentiates the two poles as "E-language" (externalized language, the language seen as external artifact) versus "I-language" (internalized language, the language as a body of internally encoded information). I will adopt Chomsky's terminology and speak of "E-concepts" versus "I-concepts."

For Chomsky's purpose—the characterization of the mental resources that make possible human knowledge of language—the notion of I-language rather than E-language is the appropriate focus of inquiry. Chomsky argues this point at length in Chomsky 1986, and he has in fact been quite explicit on this point at least since Chomsky 1965. The new terminology only helps make clearer an old and forceful position.

However, the choice of I-language as the focus of Chomsky's linguistic theory does not rest on a priori argumentation alone. It rests primarily on the suitability of this notion to support scientific investigation into the issues that flow from the over-arching goals of the inquiry. To the extent that generative linguistics has indeed been successful in increasing our understanding of the human language capacity, the choice of I-language as the object of inquiry has been vindicated. (And notice that disagreement—even violent disagreement—among its practitioners does not diminish the fact that progress has been made. It stands to reason that, at any particular moment, the most time and energy is being spent at the frontiers of understanding, not in the areas that have been settled. Any linguist will acknowledge that the frontiers have expanded considerably over the past three decades.)

My purposes—the characterization of the mental resources that make possible human knowledge and experience of the world—is conceived as an extension of Chomsky's goals. Accordingly, an important boundary condition on my enterprise is that it be compatible with the world view of generative linguistics.

In particular, if we think very roughly of language as a vehicle for expressing concepts, an integrated theory of language and the mind must include a way for linguistic expressions to be related to concepts. If, for my purposes and Chomsky's, the notion of I-language rather than E-language is the suitable focus of inquiry, then on the face of it one should also choose I-concepts rather than E-concepts as the focus for a compatible theory of knowledge.

In this chapter I hope to accomplish two things. First, I will ground a theory of I-concepts called Conceptual Semantics in first principles parallel to those of generative syntax and phonology, and show how other approaches are incompatible with this outlook. Second, since I have stressed that a world view is evaluated by how well it suits one's purposes, I will demonstrate some actual empirical results that flow from adopting my approach. (Most of the arguments are elaborated in greater detail in Jackendoff 1983, 1987, 1990.)

3. First Principles of I-Conceptual Knowledge

The fundamental motivation behind generative syntax is of course the creativity of language—the fact that speakers of a language can understand and create an indefinitely large number of sentences that they have never heard before. If follows from this observation that a speaker's repertoire of syntactic structures cannot be characterized just as a finite list of sentences. Nor, of course, can it be characterized as an infinite set of possible sentences of the language, because it must be instantiated in a finite (albeit large) brain. Rather, one's potential repertoire of syntactic structures must be mentally encoded in terms of a finite set of primitives and a finite set of principles of combination that collectively describe (or generate) the class of possible sentences. In speaking or understanding a sentence, then, a language user is taken to be creating or invoking a mental information structure, the syntactic structure of the sentence, which is organized in conformance with the principles of syntactic structure.

Parallel arguments obtain of conceptual knowledge, in two different ways. First, a language user presumably is not gratuitously producing and parsing syntactic structures for their own sake: a syntactic structure expresses an I-concept (or a "thought"). On the basis of this concept, the language user can perform any number of tasks, for instance checking the sentence's consistency with other linguistic or extralinguistic knowledge, carrying out inferences, formulating a response, or translating the sentence into another language. Corresponding to the indefinitely large variety of syntactic structures, then, there must be an indefinitely large variety of concepts that can be invoked in the production and comprehension of sentences. It follows that the repertoire of concepts expressed by sentences cannot be mentally encoded as a list, but must be characterized in terms of a finite set of mental primitives and a finite set of principles of mental combination that collectively describe the set of possible concepts expressed by sentences. For convenience, I will refer to these two sets together as the *grammar of sentential concepts*.

It is widely assumed, and I will take for granted, that the basic units out of which a sentential concept is constructed are the concepts expressed by the words in the sentence, that is, *lexical* concepts. It is easy to see that lexical concepts too are subject to the argument from creativity. For instance, consider the concept expressed by the word *dog*. Someone who knows this concept, upon encountering an indefinitely large variety of objects, will be able to judge whether they are dogs or not. Thus the concept cannot be encoded as a list of the dogs one has previously encountered; nor, because the brain is finite, can it be a list of all dogs there ever have been and will be, or of all possible dogs. Rather, it must be some sort of finite schema that can be compared with the mental representations of arbitrary new objects to produce a judgment of conformance or nonconformance.

Two immediate qualifications. First, there may well be objects for which people's judgments disagree. This does not entail that there is no concept *dog* or that people do not know the meaning of the word. Rather, since our concern is with people's internalized schemas, we simply conclude that people may have schemas for *dog* that differ in various details and that these differences too may bear examination.

Second, there may be novel objects such that one cannot judge clearly whether they are dogs or not. ("It's sort of a dog and sort of a wolf.") Again, this does not necessarily challenge the idea that one has an internalized schema. Rather, from such examples we may conclude that there is a potential degree of indeterminacy either in the lexical concept itself, or in the procedure for comparing it with mental representations of novel objects, or in both. Such indeterminacies are in fact rampant in lexical concepts; section 7 will discuss the characteristics of conceptual knowledge that give rise to them.

To sum up so far: Paralleling the argument from creativity to the necessity for principles or rules in syntactic knowledge, we have argued (1) that sentential concepts cannot be listed, but must be mentally generated on the basis of a finite set of primitives and principles of combination; (2) that lexical concepts cannot consist of a list of instances, but must consist of finite schemas that can be creatively compared (i.e. in rule-governed fashion) to novel inputs.

The second major issue in the foundation of syntactic theory flows from the problem of acquisition: How can a child acquire the rules of syntax on the basis of the fragmentary evidence available? In particular, how does the child induce *rules* from *instances* of well-formed sentences? This question is rendered especially pointed by the fact that the community of generative linguists (and cognitive psychologists and computational linguists and logicians), with all their collective intelligence, have not been able to fully determine the syntactic rules of English in over thirty years of research, supported by many centuries of traditional grammatical description—yet of course every normal child exposed to English masters the grammar by the age of ten or so. This apparent paradox of language acquisition motivates the central hypothesis of generative linguistics: that children come to the task of language learning equipped with an innate Universal Grammar that narrowly restricts the options available for the grammar they are trying to acquire. The driving issue in generative linguistics, then, is to determine the form of Universal Grammar, consonant both with the variety of human languages and also with their learnability.

The parallel argument can be made for the logical problem of concept acquisition, in both the sentential and lexical domains. For the sentential case, consider that the language learner must acquire not only the principles for constructing syntactically well formed sentences, but also the principles for constructing the corresponding sentential concepts. Like the rules of syntax, these principles must be acquired on the basis of some combination of linguistic experience, nonlinguistic experience, and innate constraints on possible principles. As in syntax, then, an important part of our task is to determine what aspects of the grammar of sentential concepts are learned and what aspects are innate, the innate parts must be sufficiently rich to make it possible to acquire the rest. (See Jackendoff 1992, chapter 3, for some further discussion of innateness.)

Turning to lexical concepts, consider that one is capable of acquiring during one's life an indefinitely large number of concepts, each of them on the basis of rather fragmentary evidence. (What evidence might be involved in learning the concepts expressed by such words as *bevel, prosaic, phonology, justice,* or *belief*?) Again since lexical concepts must be encoded as unconscious schemas rather than lists of instances—in the case of the words above it is not even clear what *could* be presented as instances —lexical concept acquisition too presents a problem parallel to the acquisition of syntax. As in syntax, we adopt the hypothesis that lexical concepts are constructed from an innate basis of possible concepts, modulated by the contribution of linguistic and nonlinguistic experience.

But now the argument from creativity applies in a new way. If there is an indefinitely large stock of possible lexical concepts, and the innate basis for acquiring them must be encoded in a finite brain, we are forced to conclude that the innate basis must consist of a set of generative principles—a group of primitives and principles of combination that collectively determine the set of lexical concepts. This implies in turn that most if not all lexical concepts are composite, that is, that they can be decomposed in terms of the primitives and principles of combination of this innate *grammar of lexical concepts*. Learning a lexical concept, then, is to be thought of as constructing a composite expression within the grammar of lexical concepts, associating it with phonological and syntactic structures, and storing them together in long-term memory as a usable unit. (This contrasts sharply with Jerry Fodor's view that lexical concepts are cognitively primitive monads linked with each other by meaning postulates. Section 8 compares the two positions.)

Given the parallelism in first principles, I therefore believe that the central issue of the theory of conceptual knowledge ought to parallel that of the theory of syntax: What are the innate units and principles of organization that make human lexical and sentential concepts both possible in all their variety and also learnable on the basis of some realistic combination of linguistic and nonlinguistic experience?

4. Three Models for the Description of Meaning

The preceding section used the expression *concept* operationally to mean essentially 'a mental representation that can serve as the meaning of a linguistic expression'. In the present framework, then, the act of understanding a sentence S—recovering its meaning—is to be regarded as placing S in correspondence with a concept C, which has internal structure derivable from the syntactic structure and lexical items of S. On the basis of C, one can draw inferences, that is, construct further concepts that are logical entailments of C. One can also compare C with other concepts retrieved from memory ("Do I know this already?"; "Is this consistent with what I believe?") and with conceptual structures derived from sensory modalities ("Is this what's going on?"; "Is that what I should be looking for?"). That is, the meaning of the sentence can be evaluated with respect to what one believes and perceives.

The idea that a meaning is a sort of mental representation is, of course, not universally accepted. Perhaps the most prestigious tradition in the study of meaning grows out of Frege's "Sense and Reference" (1892), where he very carefully disassociates the "sense" of an expression—what he takes to be an objective, publicly available entity—from the "ideas" that users of the expression carry in their heads, which are subjective and variable. Frege's notion of "sense" underpins the approach to meaning in truth-conditional semantics (including model-theoretic semantics and Situation Semantics as subcases). This is seen clearly, for instance, in the following quotation from David Lewis's foundational paper "General Semantics":

> I distinguish two topics: first, the description of possible languages or grammars as abstract semantic systems whereby symbols are associated with aspects of the world; and second, the description of the psychological and sociological facts whereby a particular one of these abstract semantic systems is the one used by a person or population. Only confusion comes of mixing these two topics. This paper deals almost entirely with the first. (Lewis 1972, 170)

It is hard to find a clearer statement that the purposes of truth-conditional semantics are different from those of generative linguistics, and that their world views are incompatible. To be sure, both generative grammar and truth-conditional semantics treat language as a formal system. But they differ radically in the goals they wish to accomplish through such treatment. The avowed purpose of truth-conditional semantics is to explicate Truth, a relation between language and "the world," independent of language users. In turn, the truth-conditions of sentences can be treated as speaker-independent only if both "the world" *and* the language that describes it are speaker-independent as well. Hence a truth-conditional semantics in the Tarskian or

Davidsonian sense requires a theory of E-language, of language as an abstract artifact extrinsic to speakers.

As stressed in section 2, the purpose of generative grammar has always been to explicate I-language, the principles internalized by speakers that constitute knowledge of a language. A typical statement of generative linguistic theory, say "Sentence S is grammatical in Language L because of Principle P," is taken to be shorthand for a psychological claim, roughly "Speakers of Language L treat Sentence S as grammatical because their knowledge of Language L includes Principle P," subject to the usual caveats about attentional and processing limitations. A compatible theory of meaning must therefore concern the principles internalized in speakers that permit them to understand sentences, draw inferences from them, and judge their truth: it must be a theory of I-semantics, not E-semantics. Within a theory of I-semantics, a statement in the Tarskian vein like "Sentence S in Language L is true if and only if Condition C is met" is taken as shorthand for something like "Speakers of Language L treat Sentence S as true if and only if their construal (or mental representation) of the world meets Condition C," and it is subject to similar caveats about attentional and processing limitations. This is the basis of the approach of Conceptual Semantics, in which a level of mental representation called *conceptual structure* is seen as the form in which speakers encode their construal of the world.

It is sometimes proposed that there is no inherent conflict between the two approaches. One is about the way the world *is*, and the other is about the way we *grasp* the world. They might lead to altogether different, though hopefully complementary, insights. I see nothing wrong with this conclusion in principle: you go your way, I'll go mine. The difficulty is one of terminological imperialism, as exemplified by Lewis's (1972) widely quoted slogan to the effect that the study of "Mentalese"— in effect I-semantics—isn't *really* semantics. Along with this goes the implication that what the I-semanticist and the psychologist are doing isn't really anything worth doing. As stressed in section 1, whether it's worth doing cannot be determined until the results are in; as promised, I will present some. I don't care what the enterprise is called; but notice that relativistic physics is a way of doing physics, not some curious nonenterprise, and it did make use of most of the basic terminology of Newtonian physics despite a radical conceptual restructuring. Such, I suggest, is the case in the contrast of E-semantics and I-semantics.

It is also sometimes suggested that my characterization of model-theoretic semantics is unfair. In principle, model-theoretic semantics is neutral between E-semantics and I-semantics; even if Davidson and Lewis designed the theory with E-semantics in mind, nothing stops us from choosing a model that conforms to psychological constraints and thereby producing a model-theoretic I-semantics. Again I agree—in principle. But to my knowledge, all model-theoretic semantics, other than a few exceptions such as the work of Bach (1986a) and Verkuyl (1989), has in practice been E-semantics. And of course, the project of determining a psychologically defensible model theory is pretty much equivalent to the enterprise of Conceptual Semantics, that is, finding out how human beings actually encode their construal of the world. Again, I don't want to make heavy weather of the terminology. If some readers are more comfortable thinking of Conceptual Semantics as a very particular and eccentric brand of model-theoretic semantics, I have no objection. It is the *psychological* claim, not the name of the theory, that is crucial. (See Jackendoff 1983, chapters 2, 3, 5 and Jackendoff 1987, chapter 7, for amplification of these points. Verkuyl and Zwarts

1990 recasts some of the leading formal innovations of Conceptual Semantics in model-theoretic terms, stressing the potential compatibility of the approaches.)

It is next necessary to differentiate Conceptual Semantics from Fodor's (1975) "Language of Thought" Hypothesis. On the face of it Fodor's position seems closer to mine: his purpose is to understand the character of mind. Unlike the model theorists, he is committed to a combinatorial mental representation in terms of which language users make inferences and formulate responses. Moreover, Fodor stresses that the performance of these tasks must be explained purely by virtue of the form of the representations. There can be no appeal to what the representations "mean." His argument is that the buck has to stop somewhere: if one is to characterize the brain as a computational device, driven by the syntax of internal representations, an appeal to meaning in the outside world amounts to an invocation of magic.

So far Fodor's story is altogether compatible with Conceptual Semantics. But now it splits in two directions. On one hand, Fodor argues (1980) for "methodological solipsism"—the idea that the only causal determinants of behavior (including inference) are the formal properties of internal representations. This is again consistent with Conceptual Semantics, in which rules of inference do not reach out from conceptual structures to "the world" but are rather confined to examining conceptual structures themselves.

However, another thread in Fodor's work (seen especially in Fodor 1987) is his insistence on "Intentional Realism," the idea that the mental representations over which these computations take place still *do* nonetheless have further semantic content—that they are representations of propositions with real-world reference and truth-value. This view allegedly makes contact with Chomsky's notion of Universal Grammar in the following way:

> It is, however, important to the Neocartesian [i.e. Chomskian] story that what is innately represented should constitute a bona fide object of propositional attitudes.... Now, the notion of computation is intrinsically connected to such semantical concepts as implication, confirmation, and logical consequence. Specifically, a computation is a transformation of representations which respects these sorts of semantic relations.... So, Chomsky's account of language learning is the story of how innate endowment and perceptual experience interact *in virtue of their respective contents* [Fodor's italics]. (Fodor 1983, 4–5)

I find this a serious misconstrual of generative grammar. Look at the representations of, say, generative phonology. It makes little sense to think of the rules of phonology as propositional; for instance, it is strange to say that English speakers know the proposition, *true in the world independent of speakers of English*, that syllable-initial voiceless consonants aspirate before stress. This amounts to an appeal to the properties of E-language. In generative phonology as it is conducted by its practitioners, this rule of aspiration is regarded as a principle of internal computation, not a fact about the world. "Such semantical concepts as implication, confirmation, and logical consequence" seem curiously irrelevant. In short, the notion of computation need not have anything to do with "respecting semantic relations," at least in the domains of phonology and syntax.

If you have hesitations about this argument with respect to phonology, consider a slightly more exotic cognitive domain, the understanding of music. As shown in Lerdahl and Jackendoff 1983, the factors that make a piece of music cohere for a listener into something beyond a mere sequence of notes involve complex internal computations over abstract mental representations of the piece. Fodor's insistence on respecting semantic relations seems totally out of place here: these abstract structures are part of mental life, but one would hardly want to make a metaphysical claim about there being something "real" in the world, propositional or otherwise, that they are representations *of*.

The question at issue, then, is whether conceptual structure is somehow different from phonology, syntax, and music—whether, when we enter the domain of meaning, the rules of the game should be changed, so that propositional content rather than computational form ought to be the focus of inquiry. Fodor's position, as I understand it, is that the generalizations (or laws) of psychology are intentional (that is, concern the propositional content of representations, outside the head), but that the mental mechanisms that instantiate these generalizations are merely formal computations that have no access to propositional content. For Fodor, the fact that these mental computations preserve semantic properties comes from the fact that the formal structures mimic the structure of the (nonmental) content in considerable detail. In fact, Fodor argues for the combinatorial character of mental representations precisely on the grounds that they must mimic what he takes to be the undeniable combinatoriality of propositional content. Put in present terms, his position is that we *grasp* the world the way we do precisely because that is the way the world *is*. (This argument is perhaps clearest in the Appendix to Fodor 1987.) What Fodor appears to require, then, is a marriage between the Realism of truth-conditional semantics and the mentalism of generative grammar—that is, a unified theory of E-semantics and I-semantics, mediated by the relation of intentionality, which even to Fodor is mysterious.[1]

Conceptual Semantics, on the other hand, is concerned most directly with the form of the internal mental representations that constitute conceptual structure and with the formal relations between this level and other levels of representation. The theory of conceptual structure is thus taken to be entirely parallel to the theory of syntactic or phonological structure. The computation of inference, like for instance the computation of rhyme in phonology, is a matter internal to the organism.

For Fodor, as for the model theorists, such an inquiry does not count as semantics: a theory of semantics must include a Realist account of truth-conditions and inference. Once again, I don't care too much about terminology. I would prefer that the enterprise be judged on its merits rather than being summarily dismissed because it doesn't address issues that someone calls the True Issues of Semantics. If you would rather call the enterprise logical or conceptual syntax, or the "Syntax of Thought" Hypothesis, that's fine with me. We should be clear, though, that it is as different from "straight" syntax (the grammar of NPs, VPs, etc.) as straight syntax is from phonology.

Given the meager positive empirical results of Fodor's approach, I submit that the merits of the Language of Thought Hypothesis over the Syntax of Thought Hypothesis have yet to be demonstrated.

How do the two approaches differ empirically? The difference is that Fodor insists that all combinatorial properties of concepts must be mirrored in Reality, whereas a

---

1. My interpretation here is confirmed by Dennett's (1987, 288) revealing anecdote, in which Fodor explicitly endorses Searle's position on the "intrinsic intentionality" of mental states.

theory of pure I-semantics is not necessarily subject to that constraint. As will be shown below, there are many structural properties of Conceptual Semantics that make little sense as properties of Reality, but a great deal of sense as properties of mind. I will therefore conclude that Fodor's insistence on Intentional Realism is misguided for the purpose of doing scientific psychology. (See also Jackendoff 1992 chapter 8.)

(Note that this conclusion is not inconsistent with Fodor's observation, seconded by Dennett [1987], that Intentional Realism is an extremely useful stance for dealing with people in ordinary life. But "folk physics" is a good stance for ordinary life, too. That does not make it a productive constraint for doing scientific physics. So why get mired in "folk psychology" when studying the mind?)

To conclude this section, I should mention the relation of Conceptual Semantics to a program of research called *Cognitive Grammar* or *Cognitive Semantics* (e.g. Fauconnier 1985; Langacker 1986; Herskovits 1986; Lakoff 1987). This work, like Conceptual Semantics, is concerned with the mental representation of the world and its relation to language. It shares with Conceptual Semantics a concern with the encoding of spatial concepts and their extension to other conceptual fields (see section 6). Some work in this tradition, especially that of Talmy (1980, 1983, 1985), has provided important insights and analyses to the present framework. Conceptual Semantics differs from Cognitive Grammar, however, in that (1) it is committed to an autonomous level of syntactic representation rather than its abandonment; (2) it is committed to rigorous formalism, insofar as possible, on the grounds that formal treatment is the best way of rendering a theory testable; (3) it makes contact with relevant results in perceptual psychology rather than leaving such relationships tacit; (4) it is committed to exploring issues of learnability and hence to the possibility of a strong innate formal basis for concept acquisition (see Jackendoff 1992 chapter 3).

5. *Organization of Language*

Next I must spend a little time sketching the relation of the putative level of conceptual structure to language. For concreteness, I will assume an overall organization of the information structure involved in language as diagrammed in figure 13.1. This organization includes three autonomous levels of structure: phonological, syntactic, and conceptual. Each of these has its own characteristic primitives and principles of combination and its own organization into subcomponents, such as segmental phonology, intonation contour, and metrical grid in phonology, and D-Structure, S-Structure, Phonetic Form (PF), and Logical Form (LF) (or counterparts in other theories) in syntax. Each of the levels is described by a set of *formation rules* that generates the well-formed structures of the level.

The grammar also contains sets of *correspondence rules* that link the levels. The correspondence of phonological structure to syntactic structure is specified by one such set. This is, for instance, the locus of "readjustment rules" such as cliticization. The correspondence of syntactic and conceptual structures is specified by what used to be called "projection rules" (Katz and Fodor 1963), which determine the relation of syntactic structure to meaning.

Figure 13.1 also includes correspondence rules between the linguistic levels and nonlinguistic domains. On one end, there must be a mapping from the acoustic analysis provided by the auditory system into phonological structure; this mapping is the

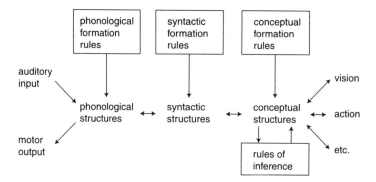

Figure 13.1

subject matter of acoustic phonetics. There must also be a mapping from phonological structure into motor commands to the vocal tract, the domain of articulatory phonetics. On the other end, there must be mappings between conceptual structure and other forms of mental representation that encode, for instance, the output of the visual faculty and the input to the formulation of action. One such representation will be discussed briefly in section 7 (see Jackendoff 1992 chapter 6 for a more extensive discussion).

Since conceptual structure is the domain of mental representation over which inference can be defined, figure 13.1 also includes a component called *rules of inference*, which maps conceptual structures into conceptual structures. As argued in Jackendoff 1983, chapters 5 and 6, I include in this component not only rules of logical inference but also rules of invited inference, pragmatics, and heuristics: whatever differences there may be among these categories of principles, they are all defined over the same level of mental representation. That is, there is no proprietary level of "semantic representation" at which only logical properties of sentences are encoded, with other "pragmatic" properties reserved for a different level. (This is an important point of commonality between Conceptual Semantics and Cognitive Grammar.)

It should be pointed out that, under the view being laid out here, the level of conceptual structure is not language-dependent, since it serves as an interface between linguistic information and information germane to other capacities such as vision and action. I assume, on grounds of evolutionary conservatism, that nonlinguistic organisms—both higher animals and babies—also possess a level of conceptual structure in their mental repertoire, perhaps not as rich as ours, but formally similar in many respects. The difference between us and the beasts is that we have evolved a capacity to process syntactic and phonological structures, as well as the mappings from them to conceptual structure and to the auditory and motor peripheries. These mappings are what permit us a relatively overt realization of conceptual structure—language— that is unavailable to other organisms.

Figure 13.1 as it stands contains no explicit lexical component. Where is the lexicon in this picture? Under the standard view of the lexicon, a lexical item establishes a correspondence between well-formed fragments of phonological, syntactic, and conceptual structure; that is, the lexicon is a part of the correspondence rule component. Thus we can regard each component in figure 13.1 as divided into lexical principles (those that apply within words) and extralexical principles (those that apply to domains larger than the word level). However, the basic alphabet of primitives and principles of combination is shared by the two subcomponents. For instance, Selkirk (1982) has argued that the syntactic part of morphology (word formation) consists essentially of an extension of the principles of syntax down below the word level. Similarly, in phonology, the lexical and extralexical principles of stress assignment, though different in details, deal in exactly the same kinds of formal entities.

In parallel fashion, we can ask about the relation between the grammar of sentential concepts and the grammar of lexical concepts, both of which are subsumed under the rubric "conceptual formation rules" in figure 13.1. Gruber (1965/1976) Jackendoff (1983), and indeed the generative semanticists (McCawley 1968; Postal 1970; Lakoff 1971) argue that the semantic combinations that can be expressed through syntactic phrases can in many cases also be incorporated into lexical conceptual structures. For instance, to the extent that *two times* paraphrases *twice*, or *cause to die* paraphrases *kill*, or *break violently* paraphrases *smash*, or *give away in exchange for money* paraphrases *sell*, the extralexical conceptual structures expressed by the paraphrases must be reproduced internal to unitary lexical items.[2] That is, the grammars of sentential concepts and of lexical concepts interpenetrate in much the same way as do the grammars of, say, sentential and lexical stress: they share many of the same primitives and principles of combination, even if they differ in details. In short, the division of the overall grammar into three independent levels linked by correspondence rules is crosscut by a subsidiary division in each component into lexical versus extralexical principles.

6. Feature-Based Aspects of Conceptual Structure

Section 3 argued that the central issue for a theory of I-conceptual knowledge ought to be the innate units and principles of organization that underlie human lexical and sentential concepts. I have now presented enough background to be able to sketch out three major subsystems within conceptual structure. The first involves the major category system and argument structure; the second involves the organization of semantic fields; the third involves the conceptualization of boundedness and aggregation.

6.1. Ontological Categories and Argument Structure
Jackendoff 1983, chapters 3 and 4, proposes a basic organization of major conceptual categories. Instead of a division of formal entities into such familiar logical types as constants, variables, predicates, and quantifiers, each of which has nothing in common with the others, it is argued that the major units of conceptual structure are *conceptual constituents*, each of which belongs to one of a small set of major ontological categories (or conceptual "parts of speech") such as Thing, Event, State, Place, Path, Property, and Amount. These are obviously all quite different in the kind of reference they

---

2. Generative Semantics used this observation as motivation for assimilating semantics to syntactic principles. The central program of the theory was to reduce *all* semantic compositionality to syntax. As more and more was discovered about semantic structure, it became clear that this program was not feasible. For at least some generative semanticists, the conclusion was that syntax should be abandoned altogether. As seen in figure 13.1, the approach here is to retain syntax for its proper traditional purposes, but to invest semantic expressivity in a different component with appropriate expressive power: conceptual structure.

pick out, but formally (algebraically) they have a great deal in common. Here are six points of similarity.

1. Each major syntactic constituent of a sentence (excluding contentless constituents such as epenthetic *it* and *there*) corresponds to a conceptual constituent in the meaning of the sentence. For example, in *John ran toward the house*, *John* and *the house* correspond to Thing-constituents, the PP *toward the house* corresponds to a Path-constituent, and the entire sentence corresponds to an Event-constituent.

Note that this correspondence is stated very carefully. As will be seen presently, the converse of this correlation does not hold. That is, not every conceptual constituent in the meaning of a sentence corresponds to a syntactic constituent, because (for one thing) many conceptual constituents of a sentence's meaning are completely contained within lexical items. In addition, note that the matching is by *constituents*, not by *categories*, because the mapping between conceptual and syntactic categories is many-to-many. For instance, and NP can express a Thing (e.g. *the dog*), an Event (*the war*), or a Property (*redness*); a PP can express a Place (*in the house*), a Path (*to the kitchen*), or a Property (*in luck*); and an S can express a State (*Bill is here*) or an Event (*Bill ran away*).

2. Each conceptual category supports the encoding of units not only on the basis of linguistic input, but also on the basis of the visual (or other sensory) environment. For example, (1a) points out a Thing in the environment; (1b) points out a Place; (1c) accompanies the demonstration of an Action; (1d) accompanies the demonstration of a Distance, independent of the object whose length it is.

(1) a. *That* is a robin.
    b. *There* is your hat.
    c. Can you do *this*?
    d. The fish was *this* long.

3. Many of the categories support a type-token distinction. For example, just as there are many individual tokens of the Thing-type expressed by *a hat*, there may be many tokens of the Event-type expressed by *John ate his hat*, and there may be many different individual Places of the Place-type expressed by *over your head*. (Properties and Amounts, however, do not appear to differentiate tokens and types.)

4. Many of the categories support quantification.

(2) a. Every dinosaur had a brain. (Things)
    b. Everything you can do, I can do better. (Actions)
    c. Anyplace you can go, I can go too. (Places)

5. Each conceptual category has some realizations in which it is decomposed into a function-argument structure; each argument is in turn a conceptual constituent of some major category. The standard notion of "predicate" is a special case of this, where the superordinate category is a State or Event. For instance, in (3a), which expresses a State, the arguments are *John* (Thing) and *tall* (Property); in (3b), also a State, both arguments are Things; and in (3c), an Event, the arguments are *John* (Thing) and ⟨*PRO*⟩ *to leave* (Event or Action).[3]

3. A point of notation: I will use angle brackets ⟨ ⟩ to enclose an optional constituent in a formal expression, the traditional parentheses being reserved to notate arguments of a function.

(3) a. John is tall.
     b. John loves Mary.
     c. John tried to leave.

But in addition a Thing may have a Thing as argument, as in (4a) or (4b); a Path may have as argument a Thing, as in (5a), or a Place, as in (5b); a Property may have as argument a Thing (6a) or an Event/Action (6b).

(4) a. father of the bride
     b. president of the republic

(5) a. to the house
     b. from under the table

(6) a. afraid of Harry
     b. ready to leave

6. The conceptual structure of a lexical item is an entity with zero or more open argument places; empirically, the maximum number of argument places seems to be three. The meanings of the syntactic complements of the lexical item fill in the values of the item's argument places in the meaning of the sentence. For instance, the verb *be* in (3a) expresses a function whose arguments are found in the subject and predicate adjective positions; *love* in (3b) expresses a function whose arguments are found in subject and object positions; *try* in (3c) expresses a function whose arguments are the subject and the complement clause; *father* and *president* in (4) express functions whose arguments are in the NP complement; *from* in (5b) expresses a function whose argument is a complement PP; *afraid* in (6a) expresses a function whose argument is the complement NP.

These observations should convey the general picture: though none of the major conceptual categories can be insightfully reduced to the others, they share important formal properties. Thus a basic formation rule for conceptual categories can be stated along the lines in (7).

$$
(7) \quad \text{Entity} \rightarrow \begin{bmatrix} \text{Event/Thing/Place/} \dots \\ \text{Token/Type} \\ F(\langle \text{Entity}_1, \langle \text{Entity}_2, \langle \text{Entity}_3 \rangle \rangle \rangle) \end{bmatrix}
$$

(7) decomposes each conceptual constituent into three basic feature complexes, the third of which, the argument structure feature, allows for recursion of conceptual structure and hence an infinite class of possible concepts.

In addition, observation 1 above—the fact that major syntactic phrases correspond to major conceptual constituents—can be formalized as a general correspondence rule of the form (8); and observation 6—the basic correspondence of syntactic and conceptual argument structure—can be formalized as a general correspondence rule of the form (9). (XP stands for any major syntactic constituent; X^0 stands for any lexical item whose complements are (optionally) YP and ZP.)

(8) XP corresponds to Entity.

$$
(9) \quad \begin{bmatrix} X^0 \\ \underline{\quad} \langle YP \langle ZP \rangle \rangle \end{bmatrix} \text{ corresponds to } \begin{bmatrix} \text{Entity} \\ F(\langle E_1 \rangle, \langle E_2, \langle E_3 \rangle \rangle) \end{bmatrix}
$$

where YP corresponds to E_2, ZP corresponds to E_3, and the subject (if there is one) corresponds to E_1.

The examples given for observations 1–6 show that the syntactic category and the value of the conceptual n-ary feature Thing/Event/Place ... are irrelevant to the general form of these rules. The algebra of conceptual structure and its relation to syntax is best stated cross-categorially.

6.2. Organization of Semantic Fields

A second cross-categorial property of conceptual structure forms a central concern of the "localistic" theory of Gruber (1965/1976) and others. The basic insight of this theory is that the formalism for encoding concepts of spatial location and motion, suitably abstracted, can be generalized to many other semantic fields. The standard evidence for this claim is the fact that many verbs and prepositions appear in two or more semantic fields, forming intuitively related paradigms. (10) illustrates some basic cases.

(10) a. *Spatial location and motion*
        i.   The bird went from the ground to the tree.
        ii. The bird is in the tree.
        iii. Harry kept the bird in the cage.
     b. *Possession*
        i.   The inheritance went to Philip.
        ii. The money is Philip's.
        iii. Susan kept the money.
     c. *Ascription of properties*
        i.   The light went/changed from green to red.
             Harry went from elated to depressed.
        ii. The light is red.
             Harry is depressed.
        iii. Sam kept the crowd happy.
     d. *Scheduling of activities*
        i.   The meeting was changed from Tuesday to Monday.
        ii. The meeting is on Monday.
        iii. Let's keep the trip on Saturday.

Each of these sets contains a verb *go* or *change* (connected with the prepositions *from* and/or *to*), the verb *be*, and the verb *keep*. The *go* sentences each express a change of some sort, and their respective terminal states are described by the corresponding *be* sentences. The *keep* sentences all denote the causation of a state that endures over a period of time. One has the sense, then, that this variety of uses is not accidental.

On the other hand, the generalization of lexical items across semantic fields is by no means totally free. Each word is quite particular about what fields it appears in. For instance, *go* cannot be substituted for *change* in (10d), and *change* cannot be substituted for *go* in (10a). *Travel* occurs as a verb of change only in the spatial field; *donate* only in possessional; *become* only in ascriptional; and *schedule* only in scheduling.

Gruber's *Thematic Relations Hypothesis*, as adapted in Jackendoff 1972, 1976, and 1983, chapter 10, accounts for the paradigms in (10) by claiming that they are each realizations of the basic conceptual functions given in (11). (The ontological category feature is notated as a subscript on the brackets; nothing except convenience hangs on this notational choice as opposed to that in (7).)

$$(11) \quad \text{a.} \quad \left[_{\text{Event}} \text{GO}\left([\ ], \left[_{\text{Path}} \begin{array}{l} \text{FROM } ([\ ]) \\ \text{TO } ([\ ]) \end{array} \right]\right)\right]$$

$$\text{b.} \quad [_{\text{State}} \text{BE } ([\ ]), [_{\text{Place}} \quad])]$$

$$\text{c.} \quad [_{\text{Event}} \text{STAY } ([\ ], [_{\text{Place}} \quad])]$$

The paradigms are distinguished from one another by a *semantic field feature* that designates the field in which the Event or State is defined. In the cited works, the field feature is notated as a subscript on the function: $\text{GO}_{\text{Spatial}}$ (or, more often, plain GO) versus GO_{Poss} versus GO_{Ident} (using Gruber's term *Identificational*) versus GO_{Temp}. Again, not much hangs on this particular notation. The point is that at this grain of analysis the four semantic fields have parallel conceptual structure. They differ only in what counts as an entity being in a Place. In the spatial field, a Thing is located spatially; in Possessional, a Thing belongs to someone; in ascriptional, a Thing has a property; in scheduling, an Event is located in a time period.

This notation captures the lexical parallelisms in (10) neatly. The different uses of the words *go, change, be, keep, from,* and *to* in (10) are distinguished only by the semantic field feature, despite the radically different sorts of real-world events and states they pick out. However, the precise values of the field feature that a particular verb or preposition may carry is a lexical fact that must be learned. Thus *be* and *keep* are unrestricted; *go* is marked for spatial, possessional, or ascriptional; and *change* is marked for ascriptional or scheduling. On the other hand, *travel, donate, become,* and *schedule* are listed with only a single value of the field feature. Similarly, *from* and *to* are unrestricted, but *across* is only spatial and *during* is only temporal.

Recall that in each paradigm in (10), the *be* sentence expresses the end state of the *go* sentence. This can be captured in the informally stated inference rule (12), which is independent of semantic field.

(12)   At the termination of $[_{\text{Event}} \text{GO}([X], [_{\text{Path}} \text{TO}([Y])])]$,
         it is the case that $[_{\text{State}} \text{BE}([X], [_{\text{Place}} \text{AT}([Y])])]$.

A variety of such inference rules appear, in slightly different formalism, in Jackendoff 1976. In particular, it is shown that many so-called implicative properties of verbs follow from generalized forms of inference rules developed to account for verbs of spatial motion and location. Thus inferential properties such as "factive," "implicative," and "semifactive" need not be stated as arbitrary meaning postulates. This is exactly the sort of explanatory power one wants from a theory of lexical decomposition into conceptual features.

Each semantic field has its own particular inference patterns as well. For instance, in the spatial field, one fundamental principle stipulates that an object cannot be in two disjoint places at once. From this principle plus rule (12), it follows that an object that travels from one place to another is not still in its original position. But in the field of information transfer, this inference does not hold. If Bill transfers information to Harry, by (12) we can infer that Harry ends up having the information. But since information can be in more than one place at a time, Bill still may have the information too. Hence rule (12) generalizes from the spatial field to information transfer, but the principle of exclusive location does not. Thus inference rules as well as lexical entries benefit from a featural decomposition of concepts: the Thematic Relations Hypothesis and the use of the semantic field feature permit us to generalize just those aspects that are general, while retaining necessary distinctions.[4]

Notice how this treatment of the paradigms in (10) addresses the issues of learnability discussed in section 3. The claim is that the different concepts expressed by *keep*, for example, are not unrelated: they share the same functional structure and differ only in the semantic field feature. This being the case, it is easier for a child learning English to extend *keep* to a new field than to learn an entirely new word. In addition, the words that cross fields can serve as scaffolding upon which a child can organize new semantic fields of abstract character (for instance scheduling), in turn providing a framework for learning the words in that field that are peculiar to it. Thus the Thematic Relations Hypothesis, motivated by numerous paradigms like (10) in English and many other languages, forms an important component of a mentalistic theory of concepts and how humans can grasp them. (See Jackendoff 1992, chapter 3, for further discussion of learnability.)

6.3. *Aggregation and Boundedness*

The phenomena discussed so far in this section involve areas where the syntactic category system and the conceptual category system match up fairly well. In a way, the relation between the two systems serves as a partial explication of the categorial and functional properties of syntax: syntax presumably evolved as a means to express conceptual structure, so it is natural to expect that some of the structural properties of concepts would be mirrored in the organization of syntax.

On the other hand, there are other aspects of conceptual structure that display a strong featural character but are not expressed in so regular a fashion in syntax (at least in English). One such aspect (discussed in Vendler 1957; Verkuyl 1972, 1989; Talmy 1978; Declerck 1979; Dowty 1979; Platzack 1979; Mourelatos 1981; Link 1983; Hinrichs 1985; and Bach 1986b, among many others) can be illustrated by the examples in (13).

(13) $\begin{cases} \text{For hours,} \\ \text{Until noon,} \end{cases}$

    a.   Bill slept.
    b.   the light flashed.   *(repetition only)*
    c.   lights flashed.
    d.   *Bill ate the hot dog.
    e.   Bill ate hot dogs.
    f.   *Bill ate some hot dogs.
    g.   Bill was eating the hot dog.

---

4. See Jackendoff 1983, sections 10.3–5, for further discussion of the Thematic Relations Hypothesis, and why it justifies the approach of Conceptual semantics as opposed to model-theoretic (E-)semantics. These sections also implicitly answer Dowty's (1988) charge that the "metaphorical extension" of thematic relations to nonspatial fields is incoherent. Basically, the cross-field generation of thematic relations probably only makes sense in terms of I-semantics, but Dowty is seeking an explication based on E-semantics.

Lakoff and Johnson (1980) and Lakoff (1990) subsume the facts accounted for by the Thematic Relations Hypothesis under a theory of "metaphor." In particular, Lakoff (1990) deals with almost exactly the same facts as Jackendoff 1983, chapter 10, without attribution; his "Invariance Hypothesis" appears quite close in its specifics to the Thematic Relations Hypothesis. However, Jackendoff and Aaron (1991) show that thematic parallelism is quite distinct from metaphor as traditionally conceived, and that Lakoff and Johnson's extended sense of the term glosses over important differences.

h.   ?Bill ran into the house.   (*repetition only*)
i.   people ran into the house.
j.   ?some people ran into the house.   (*repetition only*)
k.   Bill ran toward the house.
l.   Bill ran into houses.
m.   Bill ran into some houses.   (*repetition only*)
n.   Bill ran down the road.
o.   *Bill ran 5 miles down the road.   (OK only on reading where 5 miles down the road is where Bill was, not where 5 miles down the road is how far he got.)

The question raised by these examples is why prefixing *for hours* or *until noon* should have such effects: sometimes it leaves a sentence acceptable, sometimes it renders it ungrammatical, and sometimes it adds a sense of repetition. The essential insight is that *for hours* places a measure on an otherwise temporally unbounded process, and that *until noon* places a temporal boundary on an otherwise temporally unbounded process. *Bill slept*, for instance, inherently expresses an unbounded process, so it can be felicitously prefixed with these expressions. On the other hand, *Bill ate the hot dog* expresses a temporally bounded event, so it cannot be further measured or bounded.

In turn, there are two ways in which a sentence can be interpreted as a temporally unbounded process. One is for the sentence to inherently express a temporally unbounded process, as is the case in (13a, c, e, g, i, k, l, n). We will return to these cases shortly. The other is for the sentence to be interpreted as an indefinite repetition of an inherently bounded process, as in (13b, h, j, m). (*Bill ate the hot dog*, like *Bill died*, is bounded but unrepeatable, so it cannot be interpreted in this fashion.) This sense of repetition has no syntactic reflex in English, though some languages such as Hungarian and Finnish have an iterative aspect that does express it.

How should this sense of iteration be encoded in conceptual structure? It would appear most natural to conceive of it as an operator that maps a single Event into a repeated sequence of individual Events of the same type. Brief consideration suggests that in fact this operator has exactly the same semantic value as the plural marker, which maps individual Things into collections of Things of the same type. That is, this operator is not formulated specifically in terms of Events, but rather should be applicable in cross-categorial fashion to any conceptual entity that admits of individuation. The fact that this operator does not receive consistent expression across syntactic categories should not obscure the essential semantic generalization.

Returning to the inherently unbounded cases, it has often been observed that the bounded/unbounded (event/process, telic/atelic) distinction is strongly parallel to the count/mass distinction in NPs. An important criterion for the count/mass distinction has to do with the description of parts of an entity. For instance, a part of *an apple* (count) cannot itself be described as *an apple*; but any part of a body of *water* (mass) can itself be described as *water* (unless the part gets too small with respect to its molecular structure). The same criterion applies to the event/process distinction: a part of *John ate the sandwich* (event) cannot itself be described as *John ate the sandwich*. By contrast, any part of *John ran toward the house* (process) can itself be described as *John ran toward the house* (unless the part gets smaller than a single stride). These similarities suggest that conceptual structure should encode this distinction cross-

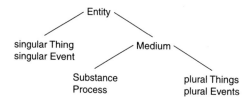

Figure 13.2

categorially too, so that the relevant inference rules do not care whether they are dealing with Things vs. Substances or Events vs. Processes.

It has also often been observed that plurals behave in many respects like mass nouns and that repeated events behave like processes. (Talmy [1978] suggests the term *medium* to encompass them both.) The difference is only that plural nouns and repeated events fix the "grain size" in terms of the singular individuals making up the unbounded medium, so that decomposition of the medium into parts is not as arbitrary as it is with substances and processes. Thus the structure of the desired feature system is organized as in figure 13.2. That is, the features that distinguish Things from Events are orthogonal to the features that distinguish individuals from media, and within media, homogeneous media from aggregates of individuals.

The examples in (13) provide evidence that Paths also participate in the system shown in figure 13.2. For instance, *to the house* is a bounded Path; no subparts of it except those including the terminus can be described as *to the house*. By contrast, *toward the house* and *down the road* are unbounded Paths, any part of which can also be described as *toward the house* or *down the road*. *Into houses* describes multiple bounded Paths, one per house. Thus the cross-categorial feature system in figure 13.2 extends to yet another major ontological category.

Here is an example that illustrates some of the explanatory power achieved through the system of features in figure 13.2: the meaning of the word *end*. For a first approximation, an *end* is a 0-dimensional boundary of an entity conceived of as 1-dimensional. So, for the simplest case, the end of a line is a point. A beam is conceived of (as in Marr 1982) as a long axis elaborated by a cross section. The end of a beam is a point bounding the long axis, elaborated by the same cross section; this makes it 2-dimensional. A table can be said to have an end just in case it can be seen as having a long axis (e.g. it is rectangular or oval but not square or circular); the end is then just the boundary of the long axis elaborated by the short axis. In the expected cross-categorial fashion, we can also speak of the end of a week (a point bounding a 1-dimensional period of time) and the end of a talk (a 0-dimensional State bounding an Event that extends over time).

However, there is an apparent difficulty in this account of *end*. If the end of a talk is a point in time, how can one felicitously say "I am now giving the end of my talk" or "I am now finishing my talk"? The progressive aspect in these sentences implies the existence of a process taking place over time and therefore seems to attribute a temporal extent to the end.

An answer is provided by looking at the treatment of the boundaries of Things. Consider what is meant by *Bill cut off the end of the ribbon*. Bill cannot have cut off the geometrical boundary of the ribbon. Rather, the sense of this sentence shows that the notion of end premits an optional elaboration: the end may consist of a part of the object it bounds, extending from the actual boundary into the object some small distance ϵ.

There are other boundary words that *obligatorily* include this sort of elaboration. For instance, a *crust* is a 2-dimensional boundary of a 3-dimensional volume, elaborated by extending it some distance ϵ into the volume. *Border* carries a stronger implication of such elaboration than does *edge*: consider that the *border of the rug* is likely to include a pattern in the body of the rug, whereas the *edge of the rug* is more likely to include only the binding.

The claim, then, is that *end* includes such an elaboration as an optional part of its meaning. Going back to the case of Events, I can therefore felicitously say "I am giving the end of my talk" or "I am finishing my talk" if I am within the region of time that extends backward the premissible destance ϵ from the actual cessation of speech. In other words, the featural machinery of dimensionality and boundaries, with which we characterize Things and the regions of space they occupy, extends to Events as well. That's why the word *end* is so natural in either context. The main difference in the systems is that Things have a maximum dimensionality of 3, whereas Events have a maximum dimensionality of only 1, so that certain distinctions in the Thing system are leveled out or unavailable in the Event system. Only in a theory of conceptual structure that permits this sort of cross-categorial generalization can even the existence of a word like *end* be explained, much less the peculiarities of its use in so many different contexts—and the fact that these peculiarities are evidently learnable. (This subsystem of conceptual structure is treated in more detail in Jackendoff 1991.)

A general conclusion emerges from these three brief case studies. Beneath the surface complexity of natural language concepts lies a highly abstract formal algebraic system that lays out the major parameters of thought. The distinctions in this system are quite sharp and do not appear to be based on experience. Rather, I would claim, they are the machinery available to the human mind to channel the ways in which all experience can be mentally encoded—elements of the Universal Grammar for conceptual structure.

Significantly, the primitives of this system cannot appear in isolation. Rather, they are like phonological features or the quarks of particle physics: they can only be observed in combination, built up into conceptual constituents, and their existence must be inferred from their effects on language and cognition as a whole. This result militates against Fodor's Intentional Realism, in that one should not expect constant counterparts in reality for every aspect of the conceptual system. Roughly speaking, concepthood is a property of conceptual *constituents*, not conceptual *features*. (See Verkuyl and Zwarts 1990 for a formal treatment of this distinction.)

7. Where Traditional Features Fail

One of the abiding reasons for skepticism about feature-based semantics, even among those who believe in semantic decomposition, is that binary or n-ary features are clearly inadequate to the full task of conceptual description. These suspicions have been voiced since the earliest days of semantics in generative grammar (Bolinger 1965; Weinreich 1966) and continue to the present day (e.g. Lakoff 1987). This section will briefly mention some of the problems and the forms of enrichment proposed within Conceptual Semantics to deal with them.

7.1. Spatial Structure of Objects and Actions

The first problem has to do with specifying the shapes of objects. For instance, consider the lexical entries for *duck* and *goose*. Both of these presumably carry features to the effect that they are animate, nonhuman categories of Things, that they are types of birds, perhaps types of waterfowl. But what comes next? How are they distinguished from one another? One possible factor, which clearly enters into learning the words in the first place, is how ducks and geese *look*, and how they differ in appearance. But to encode this difference in binary features, say [±long neck], is patently ridiculous. Similarly, how is a *chair* to be distinguished from a *stool*? Do they differ in a feature [±has-a-back]? What sort of feature is this? It is surely not a primitive. But, if composite, how far down does one have to go to reach primitives—if one can at all? To put a ± sign and a pair of brackets around any old expression simply doesn't make it into a legitimate conceptual feature.

This problem is addressed in Jackendoff 1987, chapter 10, in the context of the connection between the linguistic and visual faculties. In order for an organism to accomplish visual identification and categorization, independent of language, there must be a form of visual representation that encodes geometric and topological properties of physical objects. The most plausible proposal I have encountered for such a representation is the *3D model structure* of Marr 1982. In turn, this structure can be interfaced with conceptual structure via a set of correspondence rules, as suggested in figure 13.1. This correspondence effects a translation of visual information into linguistic format, enabling us to talk about what we see.

Marr's approach is interesting because of the way it goes beyond a simple template theory of visual recognition. The 3D model is much more than a "statue in the head." It is an articulated structure that encodes the decomposition of objects into parts, the geometric systems of spatial axes around which objects are organized, and the relations among the parts. Within this framework, it is possible to represent not just single objects in single positions, but ranges of sizes, ranges of angles of attachment of parts, and ranges of detail from coarse- to fine-grained. Thus it is admirably suited to encoding just those geometric aspects of an object's appearance that are an embarrassment to any reasonable feature system.

Jackendoff 1987 suggests, therefore, that the lexical entry for a physical object word includes a 3D model representation in addition to its phonological, syntactic, and conceptual structures. The 3D model in fact plays the role sometimes assigned to an "image of a stereotypical instance," except that it is much more highly structured, along the lines suggested by Marr, and it can include parameters of variation among instances. The distinctions between *duck* and *goose* and between *chair* and *stool*, then, can appear in the 3D model instead of conceptual structure. We thereby eliminate the need for a plethora of objectionable conceptual features in favor of a geometric representation with entirely different primitives and principles of combination. It is shown that this natural division of labor is of benefit not only to the theory of the lexicon but also to the theory of visual categorization; I will not repeat the arguments here.

I should however add that the use of the 3D model need not pertain just to objects and the nouns that denote them. Marr and Vaina (1982) propose a natural extension of the 3D model to encode action patterns such as throwing and saluting. This can be used to address a parallel problem in the verbal system: how is one to distinguish, say, *running* from *jogging* from *loping*, or *throwing* from *tossing* from *lobbing*? If the lexical entries for these verbs contain a 3D model representation of the action in question, no distinction at all need be made in conceptual structure. The first set of verbs will all simply be treated in conceptual structure as verbs of locomotion, the second set as verbs of propulsion. Thus again we are relieved of the need for otiose feature analyses of such fine-scale distinctions. (Chapter 6 elaborates on the relation between conceptual structure and spatial cognition, especially in the domain of spatial relations among objects.)

7.2. Focal Values in a Continuous Domain

A second area in which a simple feature analysis fails concerns domains with a continuous rather than a discrete range of values. Consider the domain expressed by temperature words (*hot, warm, tepid, cool, cold,* etc.) or the domain of color words. One cannot decompose *hot* and *red* exhaustively into discrete features that distinguish them from *cold* and *yellow* respectively. The proper analysis seems to be that these words have a semantic field feature (Temperature or Color) that picks out a "cognitive space" consisting of a continuous range of values. In the case of Temperature, the space is essentially linear; in the case of Color, it is the familiar 3-dimensional color solid (Miller and Johnson-Laird 1976). For a first approximation, each temperature or color word picks out a point in its space, which serves as a focal value for the word.

According to this analysis, a percept is categorized in terms of its relative distance from available focal values. So, for example, a percept whose value in color space is close to focal red is easily categorized as red; a percept whose value lies midway between focal red and focal orange is categorized with less certainty and with more contextual dependence. Thus color categorization is a result of the interaction between the intrinsic structure of the color space—including physiologically determined salient values—and the number and position of color values for which the language has words (Berlin and Kay 1969).

Refinements can be imagined in the structure of such spaces. For example, the field of temperature has both positive and negative directions, so one can ask either *How hot?* or *How cold?* By contrast, the field of size words has only a positive direction from the zero point, so that *How big?* asks a neutral question about size but *How small?* is intended in relation to some contextually understood small standard. I will not pursue such refinements here. The point is that the introduction of continuous "cognitive spaces" in which words pick out focal values is an important enrichment of the expressive power of conceptual structure beyond simple binary or n-ary feature systems.

7.3. Preference Rule Systems

A different challenge to feature systems arises in the treatment of so-called cluster concepts. Consider the following examples:

(14) a. Bill climbed (up) the mountain.
      b. Bill climbed down the mountain.
      c. The snake climbed (up) the tree.
      d. ?*The snake climbed down the tree.

Climbing appears to involve two independent conceptual conditions: (1) an individual is traveling upward; and (2) the individual is moving with characteristic effortful grasping motions, for which a convenient term is *clambering*. On the most likely interpretation of (14a), both these conditions are met. However, (14b) violates the first condition, and, since snakes can't clamber, (14c) violates the second. If *both* conditions are violated, as in (14d), the action cannot at all be characterized as climbing. Thus neither of the two conditions is necessary, but either is sufficient.

We do not want to say that the meaning of *climb* is just the disjunction of these two conditions. That would in effect claim that there are two unrelated senses of the word. If this were so, we would have the intuition that (14a) is as ambiguous as *Bill went down to the bank*, which may refer equally to a riverbank or a savings bank. But in fact we do not. Rather, (14a), which satisfies both conditions at once, is judged more "stereotypical" climbing. Actions that satisfy only one of the conditions, such as (14b,c), are somewhat more marginal but still perfectly legitimate instances of climbing. In other words, the two conditions combine in the meaning of a single lexical item *climb*, but not according to a standard Boolean conjunction or disjunction. Jackendoff 1983, chapter 8, calls a set of conditions combined in this way a *preference rule system*, and the conditions in the set *preference rules* or *preference conditions*.[5]

A similar paradigm can be displayed for the verb *see*:

(15) a. Bill saw Harry.
     b. Bill saw a vision of dancing devils.
     c. Bill saw the tree, but he didn't notice it at the time.
     d. *Bill saw a vision of dancing devils, but the didn't notice it at the time.

The two preference conditions for *x sees y* are roughly that (1) x's gaze makes contact with y, and (2) x has a visual experience of y. Stereotypical seeing (i.e. veridical seeing) satisfies both these conditions: x makes visual contact with some object and thereby has a visual experience of it. (15b) violates condition (1) and (15c) violates condition (2), yet both felicitously use the word *see*. But if both are violated at once, as in (15d), the sentence is extremely odd. Again, we don't want to say that there are two homonymous verbs *see* and hence that (15a) is ambiguous. The solution is to claim that these two conditions form a preference rule system, in which stereotypical seeing satisfies both conditions and less central cases satisfy only one—but either one.[6]

Similar phenomena arise in the lexical entries for nouns that denote functional categories: form and function often are combined in a preference rule system. For instance, a stereotypical *chair* has a stereotypical form (specified by a 3D model) and a standard function (roughly "portable thing for one person to sit on"). Objects that have proper function but the wrong form—say beanbag chairs—are more marginal instances of the category; and so are objects that have the right form but cannot fulfill the function—say chairs made of newspaper or giant chairs. An object that violates both conditions—say a pile of crumpled newspaper—is by no stretch of the imagination a chair. This is precisely the behavior we saw in *climb* and *see*.

5. This analysis of *climb* was to my knowledge first proposed in Fillmore 1982; a formal treatment in terms of preference rules appears in Jackendoff 1985a.
6. This analysis of *see* is adapted from Miller and Johnson-Laird 1976 and appears in more detail in Jackendoff 1983, chapter 8.

A further aspect of preference rule systems is that when one lacks information about the satisfaction of the conditions, they are invariably assumed to be satisfied as *default values*. Thus the reason (14a) and (15a) are interpreted as stereotypical climbing and seeing is that the sentences give no information to the contrary. It is only in the (b) and (c) sentences, which *do* give information to the contrary, that a condition is relinquished.

The examples of preference rule systems given here have all involved only a pair of conditions. Systems with a larger number of conditions are likely to exist, but are harder to ferret out and articulate without detailed analysis. A preference rule system with only one condition degenerates to a standard default value. More generally, preference rule systems are capable of accounting for "family resemblance" categories such as Wittgenstein's (1953) well-known example *game*, for Rosch's (1978) "prototypes," and for other cases in which systems of necessary and sufficient conditions have failed because all putative conditions have counterexamples, but not all at once.

Still more broadly, Jackendoff 1983 shows that preference rule systems are an appropriate formalism for a vast range of psychological phenomena, from low-level visual and phonetic perception to high-level operations such as conscious decision-making. The formalism was in fact developed originally to deal with phenomena of musical cognition (Lerdahl and Jackendoff 1983a) and was anticipated by the Gestalt psychologists in their study of visual perception (Wertheimer 1923). There seems every reason, then, to believe that preference rule systems are a pervasive element of mental computation; we should therefore have no hesitation in adopting them as a legitimate element of conceptual structure. (See Jackendoff 1983, chapters 7 and 8, for extended discussion of preference rule systems, including comparison with systems of necessary and sufficient conditions, prototype theory, and fuzzy set theory, and for a rejoinder to Armstrong, Gleitman, and Gleitman's (1983) criticisms of cluster concepts.)

To sum up, this section has suggested three ways in which the decomposition of lexical concepts goes beyond simple binary or n-ary feature oppositions. These mechanisms conspire to make word meanings far richer than classical categories. Each of them creates a continuum between stereotypical and marginal instances, and each can create fuzziness or vagueness at category boundaries. Moreover, each of them can be motivated on more general cognitive grounds, so we are not multiplying artifices just to save the theory of lexical decomposition. And indeed, they appear collectively to go a long way toward making a suitably expressive theory of word meaning attainable.

8. Lexical Composition versus Meaning Postulates

Section 3 used the creativity of lexical concept formation to argue that lexical conceptual structures must be compositional and that one must have an innate "Universal Grammar of concepts" that enables one to construct new lexical concepts as needed. An important aspect of Fodor's work on the Language of Thought Hypothesis has been to deny lexical compositionality. Not that Fodor has offered any alternative analysis of lexical concepts that deals with any of the problems discussed in the last two sections; indeed his arguments are almost exclusively negative. Nevertheless, for completeness I had better address his concerns.

Fodor's first set of arguments (Fodor 1970; Fodor et al. 1980) builds on the virtual impossibility of giving precise definitions for most words. If definitions are impossible, Fodor argues, there is no reason to believe that words have internal structure. But in fact, this observation shows only that if there are principles of lexical conceptual composition, they are not entirely identical with the principles of phrasal conceptual composition. If the principles are not identical, it will often be impossible to build up an expression of conceptual structure phrasally that completely duplicates a lexical concept. As it happens, it appears that the nondiscrete elements of concepts discussed in section 7 play a role only in lexical semantics and never appear as a result of phrasal conbination. Hence phrasal expansions of these aspects of lexical meaning cannot be constructed. Yet they are indubitably compositional. So this argument of Fodor's does not go through; it is founded on the false assumption that lexical and phrasal principles of composition are homogeneous.

The second set of arguments concerns processing. Fodor's supposition is that if lexical concepts are composite, a more complex word ought to induce a greater processing load and/or take more time to access or process than a less complex word. Finding no experimental evidence for such effects (Fodor, Fodor, and Garrett 1975), Fodor concludes again that lexical items cannot have compositional structure.[7] I see no reason to accept the premise of this argument. As is well known, the acquisition of complex motor concepts (such as playing a scale on the piano) *speeds up* performance over sequential performance of the constituent parts. Nevertheless, such motor concepts must still be compositional, since in the end the same complex motor pattern must be invoked. It stands to reason, then, that acquisition of a lexical concept might also speed up processiong over a syntactically complex paraphrase, without in any way reducing conceptual complexity: a lexical item is "chunked," whereas a phrasal equivalent is not.

Because Fodor can find no system of lexical composition that satisfies his criteria of intentionality and of decomposition into necessary and sufficient conditions (both of which are abandoned in Conceptual Semantics), he decides that the enterprise is impossible, and that lexical concepts must be indissoluble monads. He recognizes two difficulties in this position, having to do with inference and acquisition, and he offers answers. Let me take these up in turn.

The first issue is how inference can be driven by lexical concepts with no internal structure. If one is dealing with inferences such as (P & Q) → P, as Fodor does in most of his discussion, there is little problem, assuming principles of standard logic. But for inferences that involve nonlogical lexical items, such as *John forced Harry to leave* → *Harry left* or *Sue approached the house* → *Sue got closer to the house*, there can be no general principles. Rather, each lexical item must be accompanied by its own specific meaning postulates that determine the entailments of sentences it occurs in. This is the solution Fodor advocates, though he does not propose how it is to be accomplished except perhaps in the most trivial of cases, such as *Rover is a dog* → *Rover is an animal*.

The trouble with such an approach, even if it can succeed observationally, is that it denies the possibility of generalizing among the inferential properties of different lexical items. Each item is a world unto itself. Thus, for instance, consider the entail-

7. Actually, he finds evidence but disregards it; see Jackendoff 1983, 125–127 and 256, note 8.

ment relationship between the members of causative-noncausative pairs such as those in (16).

(16) a. x killed y → y died
     b. x lifted y → y rose
     c. x gave z to y → y received z
     d. x persuaded y that P → y came to believe that P

In a lexical meaning postulate theory, these inferences are totally unrelated. Intuitively, though, they are all instances of a schema stated roughly as (17), where E is an Event.

(17) x cause E to occur → E occur

In order to invoke a general schema like (17), the left-hand verbs in (16) must have lexical meaning postulates like (18), in which the bracketed expressions are Events.

(18) a. x kill y → x cause [y die]
     b. x lift y → x cause [y rise]
     c. x give z to y → x cause [y receive z]
     d. x persuade y that P → x cause [y come to believe that P]

But this is a notational variant of the analysis of causative in a lexical decomposition theory: it claims that there is an element *cause* that (1) is mentioned in the analysis (here, the lexical meaning postulates) of many lexical items and (2) gives access to more general-purpose rules of inference.

I suggest that, for fans of lexical meaning postulates, lexical decomposition can be regarded systematically in this light: each element in a lexical decomposition can be regarded as that item's access to more general-purpose rules of inference. The problem of lexical decomposition, then, is to find a vocabulary for decomposition that permits the linguistically significant generalizations of inference patterns to be captured formally in terms of schemas like (17) and rule (12) in section 6.2. (See Jackendoff 1976 for a range of such rules of inference.)

I conclude therefore that a lexical meaning postulate approach to inference either misses all generalizations across inferential properties of lexical items or else is essentially equivalent to a decomposition theory. Thus Fodor has correctly identified a problem for his approach but has proposed a nonsolution.

The second difficulty Fodor sees for noncompositional lexical concepts is how one could possibly acquire them. In any computational theory, "learning" can consist only of creating novel combinations of primitives already innately available. This is one of the fundamental arguments of Fodor 1975, and one that I accept unconditionally. However, since for Fodor all lexical concepts are primitive, they cannot be learned as combinations of more primitive vocabulary. It follows that all lexical concepts must be innate, including such exotica as *telephone*, *spumoni*, *funicular*, and *soffit*, a conclusion that strains credulity but that Fodor evidently embraces.

Notice how Fodor's position is different from saying that all lexical concepts must be within the innate expressive power of the grammar of conceptual structure, as advocated here. The difference is that in the present approach it is the *potential* of an infinite number of lexical concepts that is inherent in the grammar of conceptual structure—just as the potential for the syntactic structures of all human languages is inherent in Universal Grammar. Lexical acquisition then requires constructing a particular lexical concept and associating it with a syntactic and phonological structure.

Fodor notes of course that not every speaker has a phonological realization of every lexical concept. Since his notion of "realization" cannot include learning, he advocates the idea that somehow the attachment of an innate lexical concept to a phonological structure is "triggered" by relevant experience, perhaps by analogy with the way parameter settings in syntax are said to be triggered. However, the analogy is less than convincing. The setting of syntactic parameters is determined within a highly articulated theory of syntactic structure, where there is a limited number of choices for the setting. The supposed triggering of lexical concepts takes place in a domain where there is by hypothesis *no* relevant structure, and where the choices are grossly underdetermined. As far as I know, then, Fodor has offered no account of lexical concept realization other than a suggestive name. By contrast, real studies of language acquisition have benefited from decompositional theories of lexical concepts (e.g. Landau and Gleitman 1985; Pinker 1989), so the decomposition theory has empirical results on its side in this area as well.

An especially unpleasant consequence of Fodor's position is that, given the finiteness of the brain, there can be only a finite number of possible lexical concepts. This seems highly implausible, since one can coin new names for arbitrary new types of objects and actions ("This is a glarf; now watch me snarf it"), and we have no sense that we will someday run out of names for things. More pointedly, the number of potential category concepts is at least as large as the number of concepts for individuals (tokens), since for every individual X one can form a category of "things just like X" and give it a monomorphemic name. Thus if we can encode only a finite number of categories, we must be able to encode only a finite number of individuals as well. However, it is hard to believe that nature has equipped us with an ability to recognize individual things in the world that is limited to a finite number. So far as I know, Fodor has not addressed this objection. (See Jackendoff 1983, section 5.2, for a more detailed version of this argument.)

From these considerations I conclude that Fodor's theory of lexical concepts cannot deal at all with the creativity of concept formation and with concept acquisition. Nor can any other theory that relies on monadic predicates linked by meaning postulates. By contrast, a compositional theory in principle offers solutions parallel to those for the creativity and acquisition of syntax. (See Jackendoff 1992 chapter 3 for more discussion of learnability of concepts.)

9. Ending

So what is a concept? I have shown here that for the purpose of understanding the mind, the apposite focus of inquiry is the notion of I-concept, a species of mental information structure. The program of Conceptual Semantics provides a theoretical realization of this notion that unifies it in many ways with a mentalistic theory of the language faculty and with the theories of perception, cognition, and learning. In particular, I have identified the notion of *I-concept* with the formal notion of *conceptual constituent* as developed in Conceptual Semantics. Furthermore, I have sketched a number of the major elements of the internal structure of concepts, showing how the approach accounts for various basic phenomena in the semantics of natural language, and how it meets various well-known objections to theories of lexical decomposition.

In evaluating this approach, I think two things must be borne in mind. First, it does not address what are taken to be some of the standard hurdles for a theory of concepts, for example Putnam's (1975) Twin Earth problem. What must be asked with respect to such problems, though, is whether they are at all relevant to a theory of I-concepts, or whether they are germane only to the theory of E-concepts, as I believe is the case with the Twin Earth problem. If they are problems only for E-conceptual theory, they play no role in evaluating the present approach.

Second, what I find appealing about the present approach is that is leads one into problems of richer and richer articulation: What are the ontological categories, and do they themselves have internal structure? What sorts of fundamental functions are there that create Events, States, Places, and Paths? How are various semantic fields alike in structure, and how do they diverge? How do nondiscrete features interact with each other in phrasal combination? What are the conceptual primitives underlying social cognition and "folk psychology"? How are conceptual systems learnable? And so forth. The fact that Conceptual Semantics begins to provide a formal vocabulary in which such questions can be couched suggests to me that, despite its being at odds with most of the recent philosophical tradition, it is a fruitful framework in which to conduct scientific inquiry.

References

Bach, E. (1986a) "Natural Language Metaphysics." In R. Barcan-Marcus, G. Dorn, and P. Weingartner, eds., *Logic, Methodology and Philosophy of Science.* pp. 573–95. Amsterdam: North-Holland.

Bach, E. (1986b) "The Algebra of Events." *Linguistics and Philosophy*, 9, 5–16.

Berlin, B., and P. Kay (1969) *Basic Color Terms: Their Universality and Evolution.* Berkeley: University of California Press.

Bolinger, D. (1965) "The Atomization of Meaning." *Language*, 41, 555–73.

Chomsky, N. (1965) *Aspects of the Theory of Syntax.* Cambridge, Mass.: MIT Press.

Chomsky, N. (1986) *Knowledge of Language.* New York: Praeger.

Declerck, R. (1979) "Aspect and the Bounded/Unbounded (Telic/Atelic) Distinction." *Linguistics*, 17, 761–94.

Dennett, D. (1987) *The Intentional Stance.* Cambridge, Mass.: MIT Press.

Dowty, D. (1979) *Word Meaning and Montague Grammar.* Dordrecht: Reidel.

Dowty, D. (1988) "On the Semantic Content of the Notion 'Thematic Role.'" In G. Chierchia, B. Partee, and D. Turner, eds., *Properties, Types and Meaning.* Vol. 2: *Semantic Issues*, 69–130. Dordrecht: Kluwer.

Fauconnier, G. (1985) *Mental Spaces.* Cambridge, Mass.: MIT Press.

Fillmore, C. (1982) "Toward a Descriptive Framework for Spatial Deixis." In R. Jarvella and W. Klein, eds., *Speech, Place and Action.* 31–59. New York: Wiley.

Fodor, J. A. (1975) *The Language of Thought.* Cambrige, Mass.: Harvard University Press.

Fodor, J. A. (1980) "Methodological Solipsism Considered as a Research Strategy in Cognitive Science." *Behavioral and Brain Sciences*, 3, 63–73.

Fordor, J. A. (1983) *The Modularity of Mind.* Cambridge, Mass.: MIT Press.

Fodor, J. A. (1987) *Psychosemantics.* Cambridge, Mass.: MIT Press.

Fodor, J. D., J. A. Fodor, and M. Garrett (1975) "The Psychological Unreality of Semantic Representations." *Linguistic Inquiry*, 6, 515–32.

Frege, G. (1892) "On Sense and Reference." Reprinted in D. Davidson and G. Harman, eds., *The Logic of Grammar*, 116–28. Encino, Calif.: Dickenson (1975).

Gruber, J. S. (1965/76) "Studies in Lexical Relations." Ph.D. Dissertation, MIT. Reprinted as part of *Lexical Structures in Syntax and Semantics.* Amsterdam: North-Holland (1976).

Herskovits, A. (1986) *Language and Spatial Cognition: An Interdisciplinary Study of the Prepositions in English.* Cambridge: CUP.

Hinrichs, E. (1985) "A Compositional Semantics for Aktionsarten and NP Reference in English." Ph.D. Dissertation, Ohio State University.

Jackendoff, R. (1972) *Semantic Interpretation in Generative Grammar.* Cambridge, Mass.: MIT Press.

Jackendoff, R. (1976) "Toward an Explanatory Semantic Representation." *Linguistic Inquiry,* 7: 89–150.

Jackendoff, R. (1983) *Semantics and Cognition.* Cambridge, Mass.: MIT Press.

Jackendoff, R. (1985) "Multiple Subcategorization and the θ-Criterion: The Case of *Climb.*" *Natural Language and Linguistic Theory* 3: 271–95.

Jackendoff, R. (1987) *Consciousness and the Computational Mind.* Cambridge, Mass.: MIT Press.

Jackendoff, R. (1990) *Semantic Structures.* Cambridge, Mass.: MIT Press.

Jackendoff, R. (1991) "Parts and Boundaries." *Cognition* 41: 9–45.

Jackendoff, R. (1992) *Languages of the Mind: Essays on Mental Representation.* Cambridge, Mass.: MIT Press.

Jackendoff, R., and D. Aaron (1991) "Review of Lakoff and Turner (1989)." *Language* 67: 320–38.

Katz, J. J., and J. A. Fodor (1963) "The Structure of a Semantic Theory." *Language* 39: 170–210.

Lakoff, G. (1971) "On Generative Semantics." In D. Steinberg and L. Jakobovits, eds., *Semantics: An Interdisciplinary Reader,* 232–96. New York: Cambridge University Press.

Lakoff, G. (1987) *Women, Fire and Dangerous Things.* Chicago: University of Chicago Press.

Lakoff, G. (1990) "The Invariance Hypothesis: Is Abstract Reasoning Based on Image Schemas?" *Cognitive Linguistics* 1: 39–74.

Lakoff, G., and M. Johnson (1980) *Metaphors We Live By.* Chicago: University of Chicago Press.

Landau, B., and L. Gleitman (1985) *Language and Experience: Evidence from the Blind Child.* Cambridge, Mass.: Harvard University Press.

Langacker, R. (1986) *Foundations of Cognitive Grammar,* vol. 1. Stanford, Calif.: Stanford University Press.

Lehrdahl, F., and R. Jackendoff (1983) *A Generative Theory of Tonal Music.* Cambridge, Mass.: MIT Press.

Lewis, D. (1972) "General Semantics." In D. Davidson and G. Harman, eds., *Semantics of Natural Language,* 169–218. Reidel: Dordrecht.

Link, G. (1983) "The Logical Analysis of Plurals and Mass Terms: A Lattice-Theoretic Approach." In R. Bauerle, C. Schwarze, and A. von Stechow, eds., *Meaning, Use, and Interpretation of Language,* 302–23. Berlin: de Gruyter.

Marr, D. (1982) *Vision.* San Francisco: Freeman.

Marr, D., and Vaina, L. (1982) "Representation and Recognition of the Movements of Shapes." *Proceedings of the Research Society of London B* 214: 501–24.

McCawley, J. (1968) "Lexical Insertion in a Transformational Grammar without Deep Structure." In B. Darden, C.-J. N. Bailey, and A Davison, eds., *Papers from the Fourth Regional Meeting, Chicago Linguistic Society.* Chicago Linguistic Society, University of Chicago.

Miller, G., and P. Johnson-Laird (1976) *Language and Perception.* Cambridge, Mass.: Harvard University Press.

Mourelatos, A. P. D. (1981) "Events, Processes and States." In P. J. Tedeshi and A. Zaenen, eds., *Syntax and Semantics,* vol. 14: 191–212. New York: Academic Press.

Pinker, S. (1989) *Learnability and Cognition: The Acquisition of Argument Structure.* Cambridge, Mass.: MIT Press.

Platzack, C. (1979) *The Semantic Interpretation of Aspect and Aktionsarten.* Dordrecht: Foris.

Postal, P. (1970) "On the Surface Verb 'Remind.'" *Linguistic Inquiry* 1: 37–120.

Putnam, H. (1975) "The Meaning of 'Meaning.'" In K. Gunderson, ed., *Language, Mind and Knowledge,* 131–93. Minneapolis. University of Minnesota Press.

Rosch, E. (1978) "Principles of Categorization." In E. Rosch and B. Lloyd, eds., *Cognition and Categorization,* 27–48. Hillsdale, N.J.: LEA.

Selkirk, E. (1982) *The Syntax of Words.* Cambridge, Mass.: MIT Press.

Talmy, L. (1978) "The Relation of Grammar to Cognition." In D. Waltz, ed., *Proceedings of TINLAP-2: Theoretical Issues in Natural Language Processing.* New York: Association for Computing Machinery.

Talmy, L. (1980) "Lexicalization Patterns: Semantic Structure in Lexical Forms." In T. Shopen et al., eds., *Language Typology and Syntactic Description,* vol 3. New York: Cambridge University Press.

Talmy, L (1983) "How Language Structures Space." In H. Pick and L. Acredolo, eds., *Spatial Orientation: Theory, Research and Application.* New York: Plenum.

Talmy, L. (1985) "Force Dynamics in Language and Thought." In *Papers from the Twenty-First Regional Meeting, Chicago Linguistic Society.* Chicago Linguistic Society, University of Chicago. Also in *Cognitive Science* 12: 49–100 (1988).

Vendler, Z. (1957) "Verbs and Times." *Philosophical Review,* 56: 143–60. Reprinted in *Linguistics in Philosophy,* 97–121. Ithaca, N.Y.: Cornell University Press (1967).

Verkuyl, H. (1972) *On the Compositional Nature of Aspects.* Dordrecht: Reidel.

Verkuyl, H. (1989) "Aspectual Classes and Aspectual Composition." *Linguistics and Philosophy* 12: 39–94.

Verkuyl, H., and Zwarts, J. (1990) "Time and Space in Conceptual and Logical Semantics: The Notion of Path." Paper given at Max Planck Conference on Space, Time and the Lexicon, Nijmegen. Manuscript, University of Utrecht-OTS.

Weinreich, U. (1966) "Explorations in Semantic Theory." In T. Seebok, ed., *Current Trends in Linguistics*, vol. 3. The Hague: Mouton. Reprinted in *On Semantics*, 99–201. Philadelphia: University of Pennsylvania Press (1980).

Wittgenstein, L. (1953) *Philosophical Investigations*. Oxford: Blackwell.

Chapter 14

Précis of *A Study of Concepts*

Christopher Peacocke

The principal thesis of *A Study of Concepts* is that a concept is individuated by its possession condition. Concepts are here understood to be sliced as finely as epistemic possibility. So *now* and *6 o'clock* are different concepts, even if, in context, they pick out the same time; likewise for the observational concept *circular* and the complex concept *locus of coplanar points equidistant from a given point*. In the simplest cases, a possession condition is stated by giving a true, individuating statement of the form

> *F* is the unique concept *C* to possess which a thinker must meet the condition
> *A(C)*

where *A( )* meets certain restrictions. Within *A( )*, the concept *F* must not be mentioned as such within the scope of the thinker's propositional attitudes. In general, the condition *A( )* will speak of certain canonical ways of coming to accept contents containing the given concept, and/or of certain canonical conclusions that can be drawn from contents containing that concept. For instance, it is plausible that the concept of conjunction is that concept *C* to possess which a thinker must find transitions of these forms compelling, and do so because they are of these forms:

$$\frac{ACB}{A} \qquad \frac{ACB}{B} \qquad \frac{\begin{array}{c}A\\B\end{array}}{ACB}.$$

These transitions are not inferred from anything else; nor is it required for possession of the concept in question (here, conjunction) that the thinker take their correctness as answerable to anything else. This combination of characteristics I summarized by saying that the transitions are found primitively compelling.

Concepts are constituents of complete contents which are evaluable as true or as false. A concept, if necessary with some contribution from the world, fixes a semantic value. If a concept is individuated by its possession condition, that condition must equally fix a semantic value. I called a theory of the way in which a given concept's semantic value is fixed from its possession condition a *determination theory* for that possession condition. I also put forward the general hypothesis that for any concept, its semantic value is fixed in such a way as to make the belief-forming practices mentioned in its possession condition always yield true beliefs, and to make the inferential principles mentioned therein always truth-preserving.

It is a requirement for some formulation genuinely to pick out a possession condition for a concept that there exist a determination theory for the proposed possession condition. Without that, the alleged concept would have no referential properties, and no intelligible role in complete truth-evaluable contents. I also argued that possessing a concept can be identified with knowing what it is for something to be its semantic value, and that various properties of concepts, such as their recombinability and productivity, are consequences of this identification. This approach stands opposed both to theories which regard such phenomena as empirical, and to those which regard them as in some way stipulatively definitional of concepts. The phenomena necessarily hold for concepts, but they have a non-definitional explanation which draws upon the nature of concepts.

The relation between observational concepts and the experiences which make reasonable their application has long been a crux, both for theories of perception and for theories of concepts. Two notions of nonconceptual representational content of experience were distinguished in *A Study of Concepts* (henceforth, *SoC*). The first is that of scenario content. A perceptual experience with spatial content represents the world around the subject as being a certain way. A partial specification of that way is fixed by saying how the space around the subject must be filled in for the experience to be veridical. This notion of content is essentially that of a spatial type—a type under which a region of space may or may not fall, once origin and axes have been fixed. Scenario content can be used in a noncircular explanation of certain aspects of the first-person, and of perceptual demonstratives such as *that direction*. These concepts have a constitutive relation to the experiences which can justify their use in such thoughts as *It's foggy in that direction* or *I am in a sunny location*. Attribution of scenario content also gives a natural explanation of such phenomena as the unit-free character of perceptual experience. When you see how long something is, you do not in general see its length in meters, or any other unit. A spatial type is equally unit-free. It is important to emphasize that content at this level is given by the type itself, not by descriptions of the type. The fact that the type is described by unit-involving vocabulary does not mean that the type itself distinguishes one particular unit. *SoC* also argued that scenario content is not autonomous: it enters the content of experiences only of creatures who are also capable of at least rudimentary conceptual thought.

The other kind of nonconceptual content distinguished was that of protopropositional content, built up from objects, properties and relations (not concepts thereof), and of the form: objects $x_1, \ldots, x_n$ stand in relation R_n. This is more discriminating than scenario content, and is needed for the description of what is involved in, for instance, seeing a two-dimensional array as grouped in columns rather than rows. It also applies in non-spatial cases, and is needed to explain the difference between hearing an interval between two notes as an augmented fourth rather than as a diminished fifth. Many observational concepts will have as an element of their mastery sensitivity to experiences with a kind of content captured at the level of protopropositional content.

Concepts are abstract objects. Anyone who has read Frege's descriptions of what the called the Third Realm is likely to feel queasy at the use of an unelaborated ontology of concepts taken as abstract objects. *SoC* aims to give the required elaboration by developing a general account of *legitimation by application*. An ontology of abstract objects is legitimate if an account is given of how that ontology is applied in classifying the natural, nonabstract world. In the case of numbers, a mixed statement like 'There are nine planets' is equivalent to a conjunction. The first element of the conjunction is the individuating condition "Nine is the unique number n such that necessarily there are n Fs iff there exist distinct objects $a, b, c, \ldots i$ which are Fs and which exhaust the Fs." The other element of the conjunction is the wholly nonabstract condition that there are distinct objects a, . . . , i which are planets, and which exhaust the planets. So the first element of the conjunction specifies the role of the number 9 in classifying concepts (or properties), while the second says that the condition for its correct application in this case is fulfilled. The abstract ontology of concepts is equally legitimized by its role in classifying mental and linguistic states. (The parallel is not exact: each domain of abstract objects has its own distinctive character.) The possession condition for a concept spells out its contribution to this classificatory role. The role required of a state for it to be a belief that p is given by the requirements derived from the totality of the possession conditions for the constituent concepts in p, together with their mode of combination. On this approach to the legitimacy of the ontology of concepts, it is no more required that concepts be identified with objects of some other kind than it is required for numbers.

A theory of concepts must also explain their normative properties. Their normative character covers a family of properties. What are good reasons for accepting a content depends upon the identity of the concepts composing that content. The conditions for the correctness of a content, which is a normative notion, also depend on the identity of its constituents. Natural-teleological theories of content offer one approach to some normative properties, but in *SoC* I raised for these approaches what I called *the problem of reduced content*. Teleological theories have difficulty in distinguishing between a state's having the full content that p, and its having a reduced content which requires merely the truth of all the consequences of p which have a causal impact on the organism (and possibly its descendants). I aimed to explain normative properties rather by appeal to the property of determination theories of making true, or truth-preserving, the belief-forming (respectively, inferential) practices mentioned in the concept's possession condition. If determination theories have that property, consider the case in which a thinker judges a content on the basis of reasons mentioned in its constituents' possession condition as outright sufficient for acceptance of the content. In these circumstances, necessarily, and for a priori reasons, a judgement made for such reasons will be true. This underwrites the status of those reasons as good reasons. Other normative properties can be explained using the same resource.

The concept of belief was treated as a case study for the general approach of *SoC*. A possession condition was developed for the concept of belief which has two clauses, one dealing with first-person ascriptions and the other with third-person ascriptions. The first clause requires the thinker to be willing to self-ascribe the belief that p when he has a conscious belief that p. This goes hand-in-hand with a conception of the consciousness of a belief as not consisting merely in its being a belief the thinker believes he has. The other clause states that in ascribing the belief that p to another, the thinker incurs a commitment to the other being a state which has the same content-dependent role as his own belief that p, were he to believe it. The content-dependent role is given by the possession conditions of the constituents of p, together with their mode of combination in that content. Under this treatment, the concept of belief is said to be first-personal in a sense analogous to that in which an observational concept can be said to be experience-dependent, because one of the clauses of its possession condition has to deal specially with the case in which it is applied on the basis of perception. Consideration of these possession conditions also leads to the formulation of a requirement of referential coherence on possession conditions with multiple clauses.

The question arises of the relation between the philosophical theory of concepts and psychological theories of concept possession. *SoC* argues for the Simple Account of this relation, according to which an empirical psychology can and should explain why a thinker meets a concept's possession conditions (when she does). This explanation will be at the subpersonal and subrational level, and in the nature of the case must not mention states which presuppose that the thinker has the concept whose possession is to be empirically explained. Various Wittgensteinian views of meaning and rule-following are sometimes thought to be incompatible with the Simple Account. Insofar as those views state that how a thinker is inclined to go on must be mentioned in an account of concept-possession (or grasp of meaning), far from being incompatible, they are actually a consequence of the account in *SoC*. Possession conditions in general must at some point mention what thinkers find it compelling to judge. Other aspects of some readings of the rule-following considerations are indeed incompatible with the treatment in *SoC*, notably those theses which state or entail that the correctness of a new application of a concept is not fixed jointly by the way the world is and the thinker's prior use of the concept. If we look at what explains previous uses, and if *SoC* is right about the way semantic values are fixed from possession conditions, correctness conditions will be fixed by previous uses. *SoC* also argues that none of this involves a commitment to verificationism.

A good theory of concepts should also explain what is wrong with spurious concepts, and here too should do so without any commitment to verificationism. *SoC* argues that various hypotheses widely accepted as spurious, such as extreme forms of absolute space, or of inverted spectrum hypotheses, can be shown to be spurious by considerations in the theory of conceptual content. More particularly, every such hypothesis uses some (alleged) notion, like that of absolute location, or absolute cross-subject sameness of experience-type, for which it is impossible to give a possession condition. Any attempt to give a possession condition runs up against the difficulty that, on the spurious hypothesizer's own terms, it fails to distinguish the alleged concept in question from some other. The final chapter of *SoC* develops this form of argument in detail for several examples, without reliance on verificationist premises. The conclusion is that it is *not* true that if verificationism is dead, then everything is permitted.

Reference

Peacocke, C. (1992) *A Study of Concepts.* Cambridge, Mass.: MIT Press.

Chapter 15

Resisting Primitive Compulsions

Georges Rey

I'm sympathetic to a great deal of Peacocke's project: that possession of a concept should require it playing a certain role in thought; that semantic determination should be treated separately from concept possession; that certain (purported) concepts are defective by virtue of eluding sufficient determination or specification: such claims seems to me right, important, and too little appreciated on my side of the Atlantic.

One reason for this insufficient appreciation, I suspect, is that philosophers here fear that philosophers there underestimate the difficulty of projects like Peacocke's meeting the naturalistic challenges that have been raised against them. In this short note, I'll confine my remarks to indicating why Peacocke's attempts do seem in this regard inadequate.

The most significant naturalistic challenges to a project like Peacocke's arise from Quine's attack on the analytic/synthetic distinction: if there is no principled basis for distinguishing matters of meaning from mere matter of factual belief, then there can be no basis for selecting some and not other conditions as constitutive of possession of a particular concept. What would provide a sufficiently principled basis? Quine flirts with verificationist suggestions, but I think that the best version of his argument is that there is no serious, non-question-begging *explanatory* basis for drawing the distinction, rather as a defender of Relativity Theory might claim that there is no serious explanatory basis for selecting one frame of spatial reference as privileged or "absolute." For reasons I have discussed elsewhere (Rey 1993), I don't think this attack of Quine's is quite as devastating as many have supposed. But I do think it raises some deep and important challenges that any defender of a mentalistic psychology must ultimately confront.

Quine's attack on the analytic can be regarded as involving at least two, orthogonal challenges that are too seldom distinguished: there is a *"vertical"* challenge to "naturalize" intentional and related mental properties, showing how they can be "reduced" to non-intentional, non-mental properties independently available from the other sciences. This challenge harks back to Brentano and is most recently advanced by Kripke in his reading of Wittgenstein, which is the form in which Peacocke addresses it.

Quine's other challenge is more peculiarly his own: this is what might be called a *"horizontal"* challenge to specify *a principled distinction within psychology* (or philosophy) between matters of meaning and matters of mere factual belief, between connections in thought that are *constitutive* of concept possession and those that are incidental. Quine argued that all the ways that had been proposed for drawing this distinction were arbitrary: appeals to necessity, synonymy, etc., formed a vicious circle with the analytic itself; and Carnapian appeals to convention were indistinguishable from conventional appeals that science regularly makes on behalf of any hypothesis.

Peacocke mentions this horizontal challenge, noting the problem of distinguishing "between those liaisons that are supposed to be constitutive of a concept and those that depend upon collateral information" (1992, 126). He claims (p. 127) that this problem will be solved if we can specify the "normative liaisons" of a concept, or reasons whose status as "good reasons is dependent upon the identity of one of the constituents of the complete content in question" (p. 126).

A crucial notion on which Peacocke's enlistment of normative liaisons rests is that of someone finding a certain transition in thought "primitively compelling." This he characterizes early on:

> To say that a thinker finds such transitions primitively compelling is to say this: (1) he finds them compelling; (2) he does not find them compelling because he has inferred them from other premises and/or principles; and (3) for possession of the concept C in question ... he does not need to take the correctness of the transitions as answerable to anything else.—(1992, 6)

Thus, in reply to Kripke's version of the vertical challenge, Peacocke first identifies what he regards as the normative liaisons of *plus*, viz. the standard recursive specification of the addition function, and then claims that:

> finding instances of [these clauses] primitively compelling and doing so because they are of [those] forms ... are constitutive of a grasp of *plus*. This ... seems plausible. In normal circumstances of the sort on which propositional attitude psychology relies, it seems that a thinker is not thinking of the addition function in the way of *plus* unless he finds those instances compelling and does so in part because of their form.—(1992, 137)

This is supposed to meet Kripke's (our vertical) challenge, since:

> That a thinker finds certain transitions and principles primitively compelling and does so from certain causes is a naturalistically kosher claim.—(1992, 138)

But it's hard to see how this account begins to meet either the vertical or the horizontal challenge. For starters, it's by no means clear how Peacocke's third condition on primitive compulsions is all that kosher: a lack of "need to take correctness of transitions as answerable to anything else" would appear to be as normative a claim as any the compulsions are meant to ground (or does 'answerable to' not mean '*justifiable* by'?) Of course someone is adding and not quadding if her responses are answerable to the laws of addition; but the question is what kosher fact makes them answerable to those and not some other laws? A naturalistic diet surely requires that this condition be dropped; which leaves primitively compelling transitions being merely ones unmediated by inference.

But these won't satisfy Kripke's vertical sceptic. For surely errors can be as unmediatedly compelling as any correct applications of a rule. Someone who agrees with the rest of us about "addition" up to 57, but not thereafter, could be quadding, or she could be adding and making errors—compulsively. They might be errors like those studied in the extensive psychological literature on human reasoning: people seem surprisingly compelled by e.g. the gambler, confirmatory biases towards positive and salient instances, disregard of background probabilities, disregard of laws of large numbers. Some of these cases may be hard-wired and/or modularized in our brains, perhaps selected for some local advantage; others may simply be faults the ways our brains work. Still others could be due to conditioning, wishful thinking, lust (thoughts of Garbo can compel a multitude of bad ideas). Such transitions can be as primitive as any, as free as any of "intervening premises or principles." The role of inference would seem merely to get us to *resist* such compulsions.

But even if Peacocke could in some way meet meet the vertical challenge,[1] he would still need to face the horizontal one. *Pace* his presumption at p. 127 of *A Study of Concepts*, a solution to one *doesn't* bring with it a solution to the other. A naturalistic basis for distinguishing correct from erroneous applications of a rule need not be a basis for distinguishing differences of meaning from differences in belief.[2] Kripke's vertical challenge *takes for granted the analyses* of *plus* and *quus* and asks what determines which of these concepts someone has in mind; Quine's horizontal one questions *the status of analyses*, Peacocke's "normative liaisons," themselves.

What is the basis for Peacocke's proposed liaisons? It is striking that he provides no motivation for his analysis of *plus* other than saying that it "seems plausible." And of course it *is* plausible. But the Quinian challenge demands more than plausibility: it requires a serious *explanatory reason* for thinking that such conditions are indeed constitutive, and that someone who failed to be guided by them would therefore fail to have the concept *plus*. The horizontal challenge is to specify some explanatorily interesting fact that makes it true that the person diverging from us after 57 has *a different concept* than we do, and not merely *a different belief* involving *the same concept*.

This horizontal challenge of Quine's is given a special bite in view of the fact that the role of a concept in *overt* thought can be so *promiscuous*, forming liaisons with *most anything*. People, after all, seem to be capable of *believing* most anything. This is most evident is the case of philosophers, who have variously claimed that all is water, fire, ideas or texts; that truth is relative, nothing exists, and even that some contradictions are true. But it is also evident in comparing people across widely different cultures, different times, and different sub-groups (children, the senile, the insane). Moreover, I see no reason why the transitions sanctioned by these various beliefs mightn't be, or, if they are sufficiently routine, come to be felt to be as primitively compelling as any (as in memorization of a text or repetition of a lie). The important point here is that in many such cases we could have *explanatorily significant* reasons to suppose that the agent possesses the concept despite her deviant thoughts—which, of course, is precisely the possibility raised by our deviant "adder." Consequently there is a significant burden of proof to be borne by anyone like Peacocke who would tie concept possession to someone's finding certain liaisons compelling, and would consequently rule such cases out *a priori*.

One reply Peacocke might offer is to appeal to roles in *reason*: it can seem constitutive of someone's possessing a particular concept that she accept some but not other considerations as reasons for applying the concept. Indeed:

---

1. Note that determination theory, which Peacocke discusses at length in connection with naturalization (1992, 136–39), is of no help here: such a theory is obviously available for both *plus* and *quus*. Nor is the exclusion of non-supervenience (1992, 141–42) germane, since the vertical challenge is directed against the claim that *there is any fact of the matter at all* whose supervenience needs to be established.
2. A purely "atomistic" conception of content, such as in Fodor (1990), might meet the vertical challenge while cheerfully acquiescing to the horizontal one.

According to the theory in this book, that possession condition will involve states individuated in terms of their reason-giving relations.—(1992, 180)

But it is precisely here that Quine will, of course, remind us of his "confirmation holism": reasons for any particular claim consist in the coherency the claim brings to one's beliefs as a whole. Indeed, for Quine, rejecting local confirmation conditions is of a piece with rejecting the analytic/synthetic distinction. Now perhaps his holism is too strong. But if Peacocke is to meet the horizontal challenge, he needs to say where and how, and provide reasons for thinking that reasons can be identified locally in an explanatorily principled way.[3]

One trouble with "primitive compulsions" performing any of this theoretical work is that they are too much at the *surface* of our psychology: as the examples I have mentioned suggest, there can be a wide variety of underlying causes to these feelings.[4] What Peacocke wants is a *specific explanation* of these compulsions; but then the problem is how to pick *the right explanation* without presupposing the very claims about concept possession that the compulsions were supposed to explain.[5]

Let me conclude with a suggestion of an *approach* to Quine's challenges that some of us on this side of the Atlantic think promising. Recent "locking" theories of content identify the constitutive conditions for a simple, internal representation's having a certain content in some fact about the co-variant relations of tokenings of that representation with some external condition.[6] The ur-idea that seems to me to drive such theories is Dennis Stampe's (1977), that the co-variation be one that occurs under *ideal epistemic circumstances*: at least to a first approximation, what a person means by an expression has to do with what she'd apply it to were her knowledge of the world otherwise complete. You and I have the same concept [alligator] iff were our information about the world otherwise complete, we would agree about what are and what aren't alligators. If even under complete information about other matters, we were still to disagree about what are alligators, that would seem constitutive of our talking past each other, expressing different concepts by our words. Locking theories in this way begin to suggest precisely what I have been arguing Peacocke's account needs: a principled explanatory basis for isolating an interesting *semantic stability* from issues of *epistemic* differences. In particular, a locking theory allows us to capture what in the world an agent is "getting at" in her use of a symbol, isolating that from her relative epistemic success or failure in reaching it. It provides a basis for beginning to explain and predict how an agent will react to evidence and argument, enabling us to distinguish cases alterable by such processes from those not so alter-

3. In Rey (1993: §IV) I argue that Quine's holism is too strong, that he has no argument for his claim that our beliefs are confirmed "*only* as a corporate whole," or for ruling out the possibility of *both* global *and* local confirmatory means.

4. In Rey (1993) I complain that a tendency to what I call "superficialism"—the insistence that matters of meaning be somehow superficially available in either behavior or introspection—has plagued theories of mind and meaning from Russell through (and, alas, past) Quine.

5. Peacocke does at one point seem to have a deeper account in mind, adverting to the "*form* of the transitions and principles relied upon in counting that explains their compellingness" (1992, 145). Though this seems intuitively right, he unfortunately nowhere explains what "form" is or why it would be relevant. Do co-possessors of a concept need to make their transitions by rules that are *spelt* the same?

6. See the work of Dennis Stampe (1977), Robert Stalnaker (1984), Fred Dretske (1981, 1988), and Jerry Fodor (1981/1990, 1987, 1990). 'Locking' comes from Loewer and Rey (1991), which provides a short summary of much of this work.

able, cases in which one needs to get the agent to deploy a different concept. As the "locking" metaphor is intended to convey, insisting on such distinctions is like insisting on a distinction between guided missiles that end up at a certain location because that's where they are aimed, from those that, aimed elsewhere, end up there because of errors in navigation.

In Rey (1993) I argued that a number of considerations (e.g. familiar issues of necessarily co-instantiated predicates) show that such theories need to take account of the *way in which such covariation would be brought about*, in particular, that the ideal covariation would need to be brought about by a certain *rule*. There is, however, no reason to assume that this rule is *ordinarily* available at the introspectible or behavioral surface, or even manifested at that surface in any direct way. The rule might be "sub-doxastic," not only in the sense that it is not itself believed, but in that its manifestation in behavior or introspection might be mediated by other sub-systems of the mind that could conceal or distort the reasonings to which it would otherwise give rise. The existence of such a rule would in this way be compatible with the facts about the unlimited divergences and revisabilty of beliefs so stressed by Quine, and even with reasonable versions of his confirmation holism. "Primitive compulsions" might well provide *evidence*, but they would not be *constitutive* of such underlying rules.

Of course, much more needs to be said by way of specifying what's *special* about the role such meaning constitutive rules must play. In this respect, this approach hasn't yet fully met Quine's challenge. But, in appealing to sub-doxastic rules that determine ideal covariation in the way I have sketched, it has, I think, begun to avoid some of the difficulties Quine raised, but to which I have argued Peacocke's account still seems prey. It is not impossible, however, that there might be a way of fruitfully integrating his otherwise rich account into this approach.

References

Dretske, F. (1981) *Knowledge and the Flow of Information.* Cambridge, Mass.: MIT Press.

Dretske, F. (1988) *Explaining Behavior.* Cambridge, Mass.: MIT Press.

Fodor, J. (1981/1990) "Psychosemantics; or, Where Do Truth Conditions Come From?" In William Lycan, ed., *Mind and Cognition.* Oxford: Basil Blackwell.

Fodor, J. (1987) *Psychosemantics.* Cambridge, Mass.: MIT Press.

Fodor, J. (1990) "A Theory of Content, II." In his *A Theory of Content and Other Essays.* Cambridge, Mass.: MIT Press.

Loewer, B. and G. Rey (1991) "Introduction" to Barry Loewer and Georges Rey, eds., *Meaning in Mind: Fodor and his Critics.* Oxford: Blackwell.

Peacocke, C. (1992) *A Study of Concepts.* Cambridge, Mass.: MIT Press.

Rey, G. (1993) "The Unavailability of What We Mean I: A Reply to Quine, Fodor and LePore." In J. Fodor and E. LePore, eds., *Holism: a Consumer Update. Grazer Philosophica Studien*, 46: 61–101.

Stampe, D. (1977) "Toward a Causal Theory of Linguistic Representation." *Midwest Studies in Philosophy.* Minneapolis: University of Minnestoa Press, pp. 42–63.

Stalnaker, R. (1984) *Inquiry.* Cambridge, Mass.: MIT Press.

Chapter 16

Can Possession Conditions Individuate Concepts?

Christopher Peacocke

1. A Challenge about Answerability

Georges Rey draws a helpful distinction between vertical and horizontal challenges that might be made to projects like that of *A Study of Concepts* (henceforth *SoC*). The vertical challenge is to show how "intentional and related mental properties" "can be 'reduced' to non-intentional, non-mental properties independently available from the other sciences" (1996, 419). The horizontal challenge is to specify a principled distinction, within psychology or philosophy, between matters of meaning (or concept-identity) on the one hand, and matters of mere factual belief on the other. In particular, Rey worries about the third clause of my characterization of a transition's being primitively compelling. This states that for possession of the concept in question, the thinker does not need to take the correctness of the given transition as answerable to anything else. Rey remarks, "Of course someone is adding and not quadding if her responses are answerable to the laws of addition; but the question is what kosher fact makes them answerable to those and not some other laws? A naturalistic diet surely requires that this condition be dropped ..." (1996, 421).

The theory of *SoC* is not, and does not aim to be, strongly naturalistic in the reductive sense the vertical challenge presupposes. The possession conditions of *SoC* employ the intentional vocabulary of belief, judgement and reasons throughout. There is no commitment to the reducibility of these notions to vocabulary of some other kind. Nonetheless, Rey's question is still apposite. For *SoC* certainly aims to show how the normative properties of concepts are founded in the apparently non-normative possession conditions and determination theories. If I am found to be employing normative notions in the characterization of the primitively compelling, the part of the theory dealing with the normative dimension of concepts would still be in trouble.

I agree with Rey that if someone is adding, then her responses are answerable to the laws of addition. I agree too that this is a normative matter. But the crucial notion I am employing in characterizing the primitively compelling is that of *taking* the correctness of a transition as answerable to something else; and this seems to me not to be a normative notion. Suppose someone was taught, by an elementary school teacher whom he trusts implicitly, that $12 \times 12 = 154$. He may find this false identity compelling, and not because he has inferred it from anything else. But it seems to me that, if he really is employing the concept of multiplication, then when he counts up

---

This chapter is an excerpt of a longer paper of Peacocke's in which he addresses several responses to chapter 14 (this volume). We've included only the section that is directed to Rey's response, chapter 15 (this volume). [EM and SL]

12 steps from 12×11, which, let us suppose, he believes to be 132, and gets the answer 144, then he will—no doubt after checking—be willing to revise his belief about what number 12×12 is. This is a non-normative truth about the thinker. It is an example of the sort of phenomenon I wanted to capture within the general case of taking the correctness of a transition as answerable to something else.

As the example suggests, the class of transitions which are found primitively compelling, in my sense, is much more restricted than the class which are non-inferentially compelling. The theory of *SoC* is compatible with a thinker's being in radical error in the principles and transitions which he finds merely non-inferentially compelling. My account of concept possession requires only that he take these (erroneous) principles as answerable to others which, given the rest of the theory in *SoC*, will not be erroneous. Even one who has accepted his pre-Socratic teacher's doctrine that all is fire as a belief will take the correctness of his belief as answerable to the existence of certain properties common to any arbitrary thing and to real fires. Without that, we could not regard him as believing that all is fire.

Rey says that meeting the vertical challenge does not bring with it a solution to the horizontal challenge: "A naturalistic basis for distinguishing correct from erroneous applications of a rule need not be a basis for distinguishing differences of meaning from differences in belief" (1996, 421). Fundamentally, I agree. An objector might protest that anyone who meets the vertical challenge has a reduction of the notion of possessing particular concepts F and G, and so could give a non-intentional equivalent of the condition required for someone to have both these concepts and yet not believe *All F's are G's*. This objector does not meet the intended point. Our normal evidential basis for distinguishing differences in concept from differences in belief is at the intentional, not the non-intentional level. Rey is right that it must be possible to give a horizontal answer to the question. My own position is that in any case in which two thinkers are employing distinct concepts, there will at some point be differences in what they take as primitive reasons for their judgements, or what their judgements give primitive reasons for thinking, or what they take their judgements as answerable to. These bases for distinguishing difference of concept from difference of belief are at the intentional level, and so do aim to give a horizontal answer.

There is more to be said on answerability and concept-attribution, and I return to the topic in Peacocke 1996, §8.

2. A Quinean Challenge

Rey rightly notes that on my views, concepts are individuated in terms of what gives reasons for judging that they apply, and what such judgements themselves reasonably support. (The possession conditions speak of what the thinker takes as reasons of a certain kind; and the account of determination theories ensures that these reasons are good reasons.) Rey is worried that this treatment will commit me to local confirmation conditions, so that it will inevitably clash with what is right in Quine's confirmational holism.

For present purposes, let us set aside logical and mathematical concepts, for which local confirmation conditions are much more plausible (as I expect Rey would not want to dispute). We can confine our attention to thoughts and sentences about the natural world, and take confirmation holism as the thesis that these sentences are, quite generally, not confirmed by single or small sets of sentences or mental states with contents, but by very large sets of sentences and mental states. Confirmational holism so understood is not in conflict with the theory that concepts are individuated by their possession conditions. Indeed, in two salient kinds of example, confirmational holism is actually a consequence of the possession conditions for the concepts in question.

The first kind of case is that in which grasp of a concept, or concepts, is explained by its (their) role in a certain theory, or in a certain kind of theory. The cases of the concepts of belief and desire; or of mass and force; or of one's own location and the way the world is around one—all these have been argued to be instances of this first type. In a case of this first type, the grounds provided in the possession condition for judging that a given concept of this sort applies to a particular object will in the nature of the case be those for judging that the object has a property with a certain more or less complex role—the role captured in the Ramsification of the theory or theory-type. That the object has a property with this role can in general be confirmed only by large sets of sentences or thoughts, or by taking for granted in the background some such large set. Local confirmation is indeed impossible, because there is no necessary correlation between simple conditions not involving the concepts in question, and possession of the complex role. It is worth pointing out that in cases of this first kind, confirmational holism is present for constitutive reasons relating to the nature of the concepts. We are concerned with something more specific than the general, but not obviously meaning-relevant, doctrine that, in the context of suitable auxiliary hypotheses, virtually anything can be evidence for virtually anything.

The second kind of case is that of perceptually-based judgements. These cannot be straightforwardly assimilated to the first kind of case, since what is in question here is the role of perceptual experience itself as a reason for making a judgement, not thoughts or propositions about those experiences. (It is of course an important and interesting question whether less straightforward assimilations are possible.) No doubt there is a rational default structure in the possession conditions in the simplest cases, a default structure that again presupposes a massive background is in place. Other things equal, a perceptual experience as of something's being the case gives a reason for judging that it is so. But when things are not equal, all sorts of evidence may be relevant to the issue of whether to take experience at face value. What unifies such evidence is that, given the thinker's other attitudes, it gives reason to think his perceptual states are properly in contact with the world. The possession condition for an observational concept should in some way incorporate the point that suitable perceptual experience gives a thinker reason for applying the concept to a perceived object not only in the default case, but also when he needs, and has, a set of reasons which support the thought that he is in proper perceptual contact with the world. In the nature of the case, such sets of reasons cannot be listed one-by-one, and will often themselves be quite extensive. Confirmational holism can be expected to ensue. Outside the default case, the reasonability of making a judgement on the basis of perceptual experience is relative to the set of background beliefs which give the subject some reason to think he is in perceptual contact with the world.

Though I would not myself assimilate judgements made on the basis of scientific instruments to the use of observational concepts, nevertheless such judgements in science do provide a third kind of case in which some of the considerations which apply in the perceptual case also get a grip. Data from radio telescopes support claims that pulsars exist only relative to the background assumption that the telescope is properly focussed and connected in a way that means that it is giving information about objects in outer space. Confirmation that this background assumption is fulfilled cannot be a purely local matter either.

3. Too Much at the Surface?

Rey is concerned that the distinction between what is primitively compelling and what is not is "too much at the *surface* of our psychology" to perform significant theoretical work (1996, 422). I reply that whatever is involved in the individuation of a concept *needs* to be at the surface of our psychology, on pain of otherwise leaving the subject-matter of concepts behind. The notion of a concept has its home within the domain of reason-based explanation of thought and action. Nothing not having to do with reason-based explanation should be included in an account of what individuates a particular concept.

In *SoC*, the possession conditions for particular concepts do indeed require not merely that the thinker be willing to make a certain judgement involving the concept in specified circumstances, but also that the judgement be explained by those circumstances. But here, explanation always means reason-giving explanation: the requirement does not involve moving outside the defining domain of rational explanation.[1]

Could there be a pair of distinct concepts C_1 and C_2 which are the same in respect of which transitions involving them are found primitively compelling and why (at the personal level), but which are different solely because their possession conditions differ in their requirements on the explanation at the subpersonal level of certain judgements involving C_1 and C_2? For example, might it be required that for possession of C_1, certain subpersonal computations be carried out in one order, while for possession of C_2, they be carried out in the reverse order? It seems to me that under those conditions, the concepts could not be different. To think there could be two such distinct concepts is slicing finer than can be justified in the domain to which concept-identity is answerable. Certainly it would be slicing finer than the Fregean criterion for identity of sense. Such subpersonal differences could be present even though there were no circumstances in which it is rational to judge a content $A(C_1)$ and not rational to judge the (allegedly different) corresponding content $A(C_2)$.

There would be other, related problems too if it were claimed that the possession-conditions for our actual concepts contain such subpersonal requirements. How could we account for the fact that the perceptions and beliefs which normally give you good reasons for judging a content containing a concept can equally, for another

---

1. For some concepts, my account requires that thinkers find certain transitions involving the concept compelling because the transition is of a certain form. Rey says this is intuitively right, and he very reasonably asks for further specification of what I mean by the 'form' of a transition. He writes "Do co-possessors of a concept need to make their transitions by rules that are *spelt* the same?" (1996, his note 5). The notion of form I intended was not that of lexical type, but rather a notion of type which classifies the intentional contents expressed by sentences (a classification applying to the Thoughts themselves, as an enthusiast for Frege's third realm might say). It is a notion of type which takes into account semantic constituency, scope and binding, but allows that the same content, or type of content, may be expressed not only in many different words, but also with different surface orderings. On the intended notion, a transition "p, q, hence p & q" expressed in standard notation, and a transition "p, q, hence Kpq" expressed in Polish notation are transitions of the same form. This view is a commitment of anyone who holds that users of '&' and 'K' mean the same, and that what they mean is determined in part by the form of the corresponding inferences involving their respective operators which they find primitively compelling.

thinker similarly situated, and other things equal, give him a good reason for making the judgement too? For if the other thinker differs in the subpersonal explanation of some of his judgements, the corresponding perceptions and beliefs in him would not give good reason for applying the concept, if it had a possession condition containing such subpersonal materials. But they do in fact give good reasons.

Nothing in these remarks is intended in any way to be hostile to the possibility of empirical, subpersonal explanations of rational judgements, including those of the kinds mentioned in possession conditions for particular concepts. These remarks are intended only to insist on a proper division of the subject-matter, and on the distinction of goals appropriate to different levels of theoretical enterprise. It is one task to individuate a concept; another to give empirical explanations of how a particular thinker is capable of such mastery.

4. The Contrast with Covariation or "Locking" Theories

Rey favours an ideal covariation, or "locking," theory of concepts: "what a person means by an expression has to do with what she'd apply it to were her knowledge of the world otherwise complete. You and I have the same concept [alligator] iff were our information about the world otherwise complete, we would agree about what are and what aren't alligators" (1996, 423). Rey, rightly in my view, adds a further layer: the identity of a concept is also sensitive to the particular rule by which ideal covariation is brought about. Once we bring in these rules, a first question which arises is: how different is his favoured approach is from that of *SoC*? Certainly the possession conditions will equally mention rules governing the canonical applications of concepts.

Rey hints at one difference: he would allow the rule to be subdoxastic. But it is unclear how much of a difference there is, or needs to be, between us at this point. I certainly agree that some possession-conditions should mention the thinker's tacit knowledge of a certain rule. Normal mastery of the concept *chair* involves such knowledge. It is manifested, in accordance with the demands of the previous point, at the personal and reason-giving level by the thinker's finding some examples clearly instances of, and others clearly non-instances, of the concept *chair*. What a thinker can find hard to articulate—as very early AI efforts showed all too painfully—is which rule is governing his response to examples. When a subdoxastic rule does not have any distinctive impact at the reason-giving level, there would still be a divergence between Rey's position and mine. But for the reasons given in §3 above, I doubt that such rules can be constitutive of the identity of a concept.

A second question immediately arises: once we include a condition about rules in concept-individuation, do we any longer need the requirement about what thinkers would apply a concept to if their information were otherwise complete?

Two very different kinds of case can motivate this question. In some cases, fulfilment of this ideal-agreement requirement for a given concept seems simply to be a consequence of the thinkers' use of the concept being governed by the same rule. The reference to circumstances in which the thinkers' information is otherwise complete serves, in this class of cases, simply to sweep away ignorance, or misapprehension, of whether the conditions mentioned in the rule governing the concept are fulfilled or not. In cases of this first type, agreement in the improved circumstances described is consequential upon the concepts being governed by the same rule. The concepts *alligator* and *chair* are plausibly of this first kind.

In another type of case, a requirement of agreement in applications in the presence of otherwise complete information does not appear to be correct (let alone consequential on other rules). Particularly is this so for concepts for which truths not involving that concept do not settle the extension of the concept. Let us take a relatively uncontroversial case, that of universal quantification. Two thinkers may agree, of every actual object which is F, that it is also G. This does not commit them to agreeing that all F's are G's, since one thinker may hold that there are other things that are F, while the second thinker holds that the individual instances on which they have agreed exhaust the F's. This is just a reflection in the theory of concepts of Ramsey's objection to Wittgenstein's treatment in the *Tractatus* of universal quantification. For agreement to be ensured, one would have to add the condition that the two thinkers agree that the F's they have considered are all the F's. But this condition employs the concept of universal quantification *within* the scope of the two thinkers' attitudes. So it does not fall within the scope of the phrase "otherwise complete" information about the world.

Of course it is open to the locking theorist not to aim at total generality, and to say that his theory is not meant to apply to logical concepts (thus leaving open the nature of a fully general theory, if such be possible). The problem, though, is not confined to logical concepts. I mention two other sorts of case. One concerns concepts of the past—let us fix on the concept *yesterday* for illustration. Is it true that in the presence of otherwise complete information, you and I must agree on what was the case yesterday at a particular location in Bosnia? To avoid circularity, we are not given outright what was the case there then. But some of the indirect evidence may point in one direction, and some of it in another. There may be nothing conclusive (in the way that satellite photographs can be empirically conclusive). It seems to me that in these circumstances, you and I may reasonably disagree about what was the case at that place in Bosnia yesterday, and that our disagreement does not show that we do not mean the same by 'yesterday', 'Bosnia' or any of the other expressions involved. My own view would be that this shows that a rather different model of understanding past-tense discourse is required.

Another problem area worthy of extended investigation of the ideal-agreement requirement is that of moral concepts. It does not seem to me that two people who have complete information not involving the concept *morally wrong* must thereby agree on whether gambling for small sums of money is wrong. I suspect the same may be true for some moral disagreements about abortion.

This discussion is perforce, and manifestly, much briefer than the subject-matter merits. We would need to think more about various different general types of case. In the case of universal quantification, and perhaps the moral cases, it is plausible that we are dealing with concepts which are individuated by the consequences of their applications. When concepts are individuated that way, rather than on the basis of canonical evidence for applying them, it should not be surprising that agreement on application in ideal (non-circularly specified) circumstances is not required. All that is required by sameness of meaning or concept is agreement in (canonical) consequences when there *is* agreement on the universal quantification. The case of the past is rather different again, and a more full-blooded realism and causal epistemology seems correct in this case.

This brief discussion does seem to me to support the following conclusion. When a requirement of ideal agreement is correct, it follows from a specification of a rule which has anyway to be mentioned in an account of mastery of the relevant concept. For other concepts the requirement is not correct, and for reasons of which we have at least a rudimentary understanding.

References

Peacocke, C. (1992) *A Study of Concepts*. Cambridge, Mass.: MIT Press.

Peacocke, C. (1996) "Can Possession Conditions Individuate Concepts?" *Philosophy and Phenomenological Research* 56.2: 433–60.

Rey, G. (1996) "Resisting Primitive Compulsions" *Philosophy and Phenomenological Research* 56.2: 419–424.

Rethinking Prototypes

Chapter 17

Combining Prototypes: A Selective Modification Model

Edward E. Smith, Daniel N. Osherson, Lance J. Rips, and Margaret Keane

Research on natural concepts, such as *apple* and *fish*, has led to the conclusion that part of the mental representation of a concept consists of a "prototype," roughly, a description of the best examples or central tendency of a concept. Specifically, research has shown that the instances of any concept vary in how typical they are rated, and that such ratings predict how quickly and accurately an instance can be categorized, how readily it can be retrieved from memory, how early it can be learned, how efficiently it can be coded linguistically, and so on (see e.g., Mervis and Rosch, 1981). In light of such findings, is seems reasonable to posit that experience, direct or indirect, with exemplars of a concept gives rise to a prototype for that concept, that the rated typicality of an instance is a good predictor of its similarity to its prototype, and that similarity-to-prototype plays some role in categorization, memory and communication (see, e.g., Smith and Medin, 1981).

Such is the account commonly advanced within the prototype tradition for "simple" concepts, that is, concepts denoted by single words. But what about "composite" concepts, such as *striped apple* and *literary politician* (i.e., concepts formed from simpler constituents)?[1] For many such concepts, their instances seem to vary in typicality; yet we cannot have induced a prototype for each composite concept on the basis of experience with its exemplars, because many composite concepts are novel combinations and hence unfamiliar. There must therefore be some means of computing the typicality of an instance in a composite concept from knowledge about its constituents, some way of determining, say, that Lassie is not a very good example of *ferocious animal*, given what we know about Lassie and the concepts *ferocious* and *animal*.

More generally, if prototype theory is to be extended to composite concepts, principles of conceptual composition must be supplied. This is the concern of the present paper. In particular, we will focus on adjective-noun conjunctions such as *striped apple* and *not very red fruit*, and specify how prototypes for such conjunctions can be composed from prototypes for their constituents. While the specifics of our claims apply to only adjective-noun compounds, some of the broader principles we espouse may also characterize noun-noun compounds such as *dog house*.[2]

We thank Susan Carey, Allan Collins, Dedre Gentner, David Israel, Michael Lipton, and Mary Potter for their many suggestion that helped shape this research. The research was supported by U.S. Public Health Service Grant MH37208 and by the National Institute of Education under Contract No. US-HEW-C-400-82-0030.

1. We use italics to indicate concepts, and reserve quotes for the words that denote these concepts.
2. Fodor (1981) has argued that some composite concepts do not have prototypes, and hence there must be more to concepts than prototypes. This argument in no way conflicts with the present analyses. We are concerned only with those composite concepts that do have prototypes, and we have argued elsewhere that such prototypes do not exhaust the contents of a concept (see, e.g., Osherson and Smith, 1981).

Our exposition is arranged as follows: First, we motivate and present a model of how adjectives modify noun prototypes to form prototypes for conjunctions. Second, we describe in detail an initial experimental test of this model. Third, we present two subsequent tests of assumptions of the model. Fourth, we extend the model to handle conjunctions involving adverbs. Fifth, we provide an experimental test of the extended model. Sixth and finally, we take up a number of outstanding issues.

A Model for Adjective-Noun Conjunctions

Rationale for the Model

General Aspects of Prototypes   The term "prototype" has sometimes been used to mean a representation of the best example for a given concept (e.g., Medin and Schaffer, 1978; Mervis and Rosch, 1981). In this sense, a prototype for *apple* might be an image or a mental description of an especially good *apple* instance. Our own theory generalizes this idea to allow a prototype to be a more abstract description of the concept. In our view, a prototype is a prestored representation of the usual properties associated with the concept's instances (much as in schema or frame theory— see, e.g., Minsky, 1975; Rumelhart and Ortony, 1977). Thus, an *apple* prototype will include properties such as having seeds, properties that are part of our commonsense knowledge about apples. Earlier work on prototypes indicated that a concept's prototype includes properties that are not strictly necessary for concept membership (e.g., Rosch, 1973; Smith, Shoben, and Rips, 1974). The prototype of *apple*, for example, includes the nonnecessary properties of red, round, and smooth. Subsequent work has shown that the contents of a prototype must include far more than a list of properties.

For one thing, we need to decompose the notion of a property into two components: *attribute* and *value*. Thus the *apple* prototype includes attribute-value pairs such as color-red, shape-round, and texture-smooth. The reason for including attributes in prototypes is simply that there are numerous cases where people use attribute knowledge in categorization. Consider categorization with negative concepts, such as *nonred fruit*. Without the notion of an attribute, how can one ever know that a blueberry is an instance of *nonred fruit*? To know that blue counts as *nonred* while round does not, one must know that a certain set of values (the colors) constitutes an attribute.

A prototype also includes some indication of the salience of each relevant value. A couple of lines of evidence point to this conclusion. For one thing, when asked to verify that a property is true of a particular concept, people respond faster to properties that have previously been rated as more related or associated to the concept than to those rated less related (e.g., Glass and Holyoak, 1975). Thus, people are faster at deciding that *apples are red* than *apples are round*, suggesting that red is more salient than round in the prototype for *apple*. Another line of evidence for salience is that the nature of a value seems to be relative to a concept, the red in *apple*, for example, being redder than that in *brick* but less than that in a *fire engine* (Halff, Ortony, and Anderson, 1976). This suggests that the red in *apple* is more salient than that in *brick*, though less salient than the red in *fire engine*.

Finally, a prototype may also include some indication of the diagnosticity of each attribute, that is, a measure of how useful the attribute is in discriminating instances of the concept from instances of contrasting concepts. The importance of diagnosticity was demonstrated by Rosch and Mervis (1975); when subjects have to decide whether or not an item belongs to a target concept, they consider not only the item's attribute-by-arrtibute similarity to the target concept but also its attribute-by-attribute dissimilarity to concepts that contrast with the target.

In short, any model of prototype composition would do well to start with prototypes that include: (1) an attribute-value structurc, (2) indications of value salience, and (3) indications of attribute diagnosticity.

Conjunction Effects   In addition to the above three general aspects, the development of our model was guided by three specific findings that involve typicality judgments for adjective-noun combinations. The most important of these findings we call the "conjunction effect." To illustrate the effect, consider the typicality of a particular red apple as an instance of the concepts *apple* and *red apple*. Several experiments have found that the rated typicality of the instance in the conjunction exceeds that in the simple concept. Our red apple is judged more typical of *red apple* than of *apple* (Hampton, 1982; Osherson and Smith, 1982; Smith and Osherson, 1984; Shafir, Smith, and Osherson, 1988; for a related effect, see Tversky and Kahneman, 1983).[3]

Smith and Osherson (1984) uncovered a second phenomenon of interest. They investigated "incompatible" conjunctions, such as *brown apple*, where the adjective denotes an unlikely value of the object denoted by the noun, and "compatible" conjunctions, such as *red apple*, where the adjective denotes a likely value of the object denoted by the noun. They found that the conjunction effect is greater for incompatible than compatible conjunctions. For example, the extent to which a brown apple is judged more typical of *brown apple* than of *apple* is greater than the extent to which a red apple is judged more typical of *red apple* than of *apple*. A third finding arises when the item to be categorized is not a true member of the conjunction (e.g., a brown apple paired with the conjunction *red apple*). Unsurprisingly, here there is a "reverse conjunction" effect, the item being judged less typical of the conjunction than of the noun constituent (Smith and Osherson, 1984).

The Selective Modification Model

The model that we propose is an extension of one discussed in Smith and Osherson (1984). The current model has three major components: (1) a prototype representation for simple noun concepts, (2) procedure for modifying such a prototype, and (3) a means for determining the typicality of an instance vis-a-vis a prototype. We begin by describing the first and third components. The descriptions in this section are illustrative, more precision being supplied in the next section.

Typicality and Simple Concepts   A prototype for the concept *apple* is illustrated in the left-most panel of Figure 17.1, and it includes the three general aspects discussed earlier. The representation specifies: (1) A set of relevant attributes (color, shape, texture, etc.), and for each attribute a set of possible values that instances of the concept can assume (e.g., for color, the values include red, green, and brown); (2) The diag-

---

3. We follow Tversky and Kahneman (1983) in calling adjective–noun phrases "conjunctions." However, we do not mean to imply that phrases such as "red apple" are equivalent in meaning to explicit conjunctions such as "both red and apple." Indeed, in "red apple," the adjective seems to modify the noun concept rather than combine with it conjunctively (Oden, 1984), an intuition that lies at the heart of the model we develop.

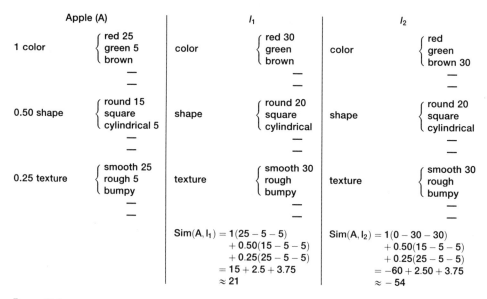

Figure 17.1
Illustration of attribute-value representations for a prototype (*apple*) and relevant instances (a red apple and a brown apple); beneath each instance representation is the similarity between the instance and prototype.

nosticity of each attribute for the concept, as indicated by the number to the attribute's left, and (3) The salience of each value of an attribute, as indicated by the number to the value's right (we refer to these numbers as "votes" for the value). With regard to a value's salience, we suspect that it reflects at least two contributing factors: the subjective frequency with which the value occurs in instances of the concepts, and the perceptibility of the value. Thus, red apples are encountered more frequently than green ones, and that may be why the red in *apple* is more salient (has more votes) than the green is *apple*. Also, the red of an apple is more perceptible than the red of a brick, and that may be why the red in *apple* is more salient (has more votes) than the red in *brick*.

The remaining panels of Figure 17.1 illustrate representations for two specific objects (or "instances"), I_1 and I_2, a typical red apple and a brown apple. We assume that an object representation is like a prototype except that is does not contain any indication of an attribute's diagnosticity. (We let the prototype alone determine attribute diagnosticity because it is being used as a standard against which the object is compared.) For simplicity, we have assumed further that for I_1 and I_2 all votes for an attribute are on one value (but this need not be generally true of object representations).

To determine an instance's typicality in a concept, we assume that typicality rests on similarity. To measure similarity, we use Tversky's (1977) "contrast" rule, which assesses similarity by a contrast between common and distinctive features. In our application of this model, each vote counts as a feature. In essence, n votes on a value (say, red) is equivalent to there being n copies of that value (n reds). The similarity between the features of a prototype ("P") and the features of an instance ("I") is given by:

$$(1) \quad \text{Sim}(P, I) = af(P \cap I) - bf(P - I) - cf(I - P),$$

where $P \cap I$ designates the set of votes or features common to the prototype and instance, $P - I$ designates the set of features distinct to the prototype, and $I - P$ designates the set of features distinct to the instance. In addition, f is a function that measures the importance of each of these three set of features, and a, b, and c are parameters that determine the relative contributions of the three sets. The basic idea is that similarity is an increasing function of the features common to the prototype and instance, and a decreasing function of the features distinct to the prototype and of those distinct to the instance.

For purposes of making computations, it is convenient to use a version of Equation (1) that specifies the common and distinctive features on an attribute-by-attribute basis. This is given by:

$$(2) \quad \text{Sim}(P, I) = \sum_i [af_i(P \cap I) - bf_i(P - I) - cf_i(I - P)],$$

where i indexes the relevant attributes, and now $P \cap I$ designates the set of features or votes on attribute i common to the prototype and instance, $P - I$ designates the set of features of attribute i distinct to the prototype, and $I - P$ designates the set of features of attribute i distinct to the instance. Beneath each object representation in Figure 17.1, we have used Equation (2) to calculate the object's similarity to the *apple* prototype. We have assumed that a, b and c are equal to one (just to keep things simple for now). We have further assumed that f_i multiplies the number of votes for attribute i in a set by the diagnosticity of i. To illustrate, to determine the similarity between the typical red apple (designated "I_1") and the prototype for *apple* (designated "A") on the color attribute, we note that *apple* and the red apple share 25 red votes, that *apple* has 5 distinct green votes, that the red apple has 5 distinct red votes, and that each component of the contrast is multiplied by the diagnosticity of 1.0 (see Figure 17.1). The computations are similar for the other attributes. For the examples provided in Figure 17.1, the contrast rule correctly predicts that the red apple, I_1, should be judged to be more typical of *apple* than is the brown apple, I_2.

Note that the only representational difference between I_1 and I_2 is on the color attribute. This difference eventuates in a large typicality difference between I_1 and I_2 because color has a substantial number of features (votes) and is a very diagnostic attribute. To appreciate the importance of diagnosticity, consider a third possible instance, I_3, which is identical to I_1 except that all its texture votes are on bumpy. The typicality of I_3 in *apple* is:

$$\text{Sim}(A, I_3) = 1(25 - 5 - 5) + .5(15 - 5 - 5) + .25(0 - 30 - 30)$$

$$= 15 + 2.5 - 15$$

$$= 2.5$$

Hence, I_3 is more typical of *apple* than is I_2, solely because I_3's mismatching attribute (texture) is less diagnostic than that of I_2 (color). This version of the contrast rule thus nicely captures differences in diagnosticity as well as differences in features or salience.

Adjective Modification   To extend this account to adjective–noun conjunctions, we need to specify how the adjective interacts with the noun. Two general ideas about the nature of this interaction have been proposed (see Cohen and Murphy, 1984, for

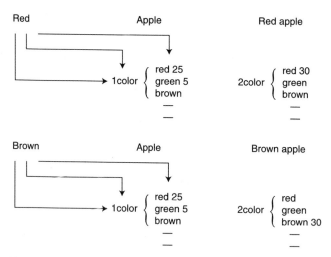

Figure 17.2
Illustration of three aspects of adjective modification.

discussion). One possibility is that the adjective and noun play symmetrical roles and that in forming a conjunction the features of the two concepts are somehow intersected. The other possibility is that the adjective and noun concepts play different and asymmetrical roles, the noun being the basic frame to be operated on and the adjective being the operator of modifier. We opt for the latter, "modification" approach. One reason for doing so is that there can be a striking change in meaning when the order of an adjective-noun combination is reversed—consider *red apple* versus *apple red*—and it is not obvious why this sort of change should occur if the conjunction is some kind of symmetrical intersection of the two prototypes. Other reasons for favoring a modification approach over an intersection one are discussed by Cohen and Murphy (1984).[4]

Our basic proposal about the modification process is as follows: Each attribute in the adjective concept selects the corresponding attribute in the noun concept; then, for each selected attribute in the noun, there is an increase in the salience (or votes) of the value given in the adjective, as well as an increase in the diagnosticity of the attribute. Consider *shriveled apple* as an example. Presumably *shriveled* contains attributes pertaining to shape and texture; accordingly, it would select these attributes in the *apple* prototype, boost their diagnosticities, and shift their votes away from round and smooth and toward irregular and bumpy.

In developing a precise account of the model, however, we will consider only those adjectives that presumably contain a single attribute, for example, *red* or *brown*. Figure 17.2 illustrates our specific assumptions for such cases. The adjective: (1) selects the relevant attribute in the noun (e.g., color), (2) shifts all votes on that attri-

4. Another approach to modification is possible if one adopts the view that a prototype consists of the best examples of a concept. Modification might amount to a change in the examples; for example, in the prototype for *apple* two of the three best examples might be red, while in the prototype for *red apple* all three best examples might be red. A serious problem with this approach is that it offers no principled account of how the best examples are chosen.

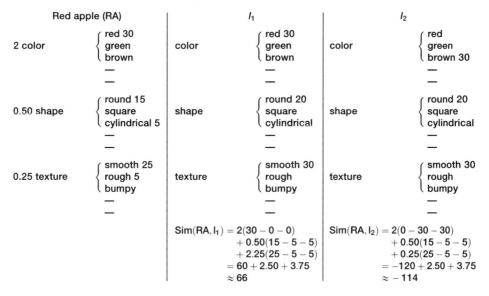

Figure 17.3
Illustration of attribute-value representations of *red apple* and relevant instances; beneath each instance representation is the similarity between the instance and prototype.

bute into the value named by the adjective, and (3) boosts the diagnosticity associated with the attribute. In the example at the top of Figure 17.2, most of the color votes already were on the value specified by the adjective, so few votes have to be shifted; this is the hallmark of compatible conjunctions. In the example at the bottom of Figure 17.2, all color votes have to be shifted, which is the hallmark of incompatible conjunctions.[5]

The above proposals hinge on two distinct intuitions about modification: roughly, that color is more important for determining typicality in *red apple* than in *apple* (the diagnosticity boost), and that a typical *red apple* is redder than a typical *apple* (the salience change). The rationale for the salience change is obvious: The change from *apple* to *red apple* unequivocally signals a change in the color of typical instances. The rationale for the boost in diagnosticity is more subtle. The boost is likely mediated by a change in the perceived contrast class of the concept. As we change from *apple* to *red apple*, the contrast class may change from *oranges* to *green apple*; if so, then color is the only distinguishing attribute for the conjunction, and that is why its diagnosticity increases.

Figure 17.3 illustrates the implications of the above changes in salience and diagnosticity for typicality ratings with compatible conjunctions. The left-most panel of the figure contains the prototype for *red apple*. The only differences between this representation and that of *apple* involve the color attribute. Now, all votes are on red, and the diagnosticity of color has increased by a factor of two (*two* being an arbitrary

5. Instead of shifting all votes to the value specified by the adjective, the votes might be distributed so that the more similar a value to that specified by the adjective the more votes that value receives. For example, in composing *brown apple* most votes may shift to brown, but some may remain on red because that value is similar to brown. While this seems plausible, for purposes of simplicity we ignore this possibility in what follows.

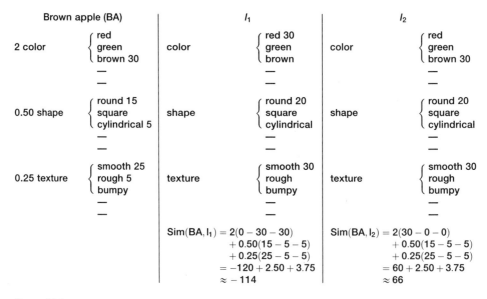

Figure 17.4
Illustration of attribute-value representations of *brown apple* and relevant instances; beneath each instance representation is the similarity between the instance and prototype.

choice on our part). The effects of these differences for typicality are illustrated in the remaining panels of Figure 17.3. There we have repeated the representations for our red and brown apples, and computed the similarity for each of these objects in the conjunction. When these similarity scores are compared with those in Figure 17.1, the results are that (1) The red apple is more similar to *red apple* than it is to *apple*, while (2) the brown apple is less similar to *red apple* than it is to *apple*. Result (1) is the conjunction effect, result (2) is the reverse conjunction effect.

Figure 17.4 illustrates a comparable analysis for incompatible conjunctions. The prototype for *brown apple* differs from that of *apple* only in that now all color votes are on brown and color has doubled in diagnosticity. The effect of these changes for typicality are shown in the remaining panels. Now, in comparison with our original computations in Figure 17.1, we find that the brown apple is more similar to *brown apple* than it is to *apple*, while the red apple is less similar to *brown apple* than it is to *apple*. Again we have reconstructed the conjunction effect and its reverse. Note further than the conjunction effect predicted in this case exceeds that in the previous case, which reconstructs the third effect described earlier. That is, the extent to which the brown apple is judged more typical of *brown apple* than *apple* $(66 - (-54) = 120)$ is greater than the extent to which the red apple is judged more typical of *red apple* than *apple* $(66 - 21 = 45)$.

Further Implications   The selective modification model incorporates the three general aspects of prototypes discussed earlier, and accounts in detail for the three conjunction effects. The model also has two additional implications that deserve to be spelled out.

One implication concerns a subtle prediction about conjunction effects. The typicality of, say, a brown apple in *brown apple* should be roughly equal to that of a red apple in *red apple*. That is, with regard to determining typicality in conjunction, what matters is the attribute not the value. This prediction follows because the total number of brown votes in *brown apple* or red votes in *red apple* is simply the total number of color votes that *apple* has. The data reported in Smith and Osherson (1984) support the prediction.

The second implication of the model is our assumption that during modification a simple adjective, such as *red* or *long*, selectively influences a single attribute of the noun representation. All things considered, this "selective influence" assumption may be too strong. There are relations between attributes, and some of these relations may be part of a prototype (see, e.g., Malt and Smith, 1984). Among apples, for example, there are relations between color, shape, and sweetness—compared with a red apple, a brownish one is usually more shriveled and less sweet. Hence, *brown* applied to *apple* may change more than just the color attribute. Medin and Shoben (1988) have recently reported findings that appear to demonstrate such additional changes.[6]

These additional changes, though, may not be as profound as the primary change (e.g., in *brown apple*, only a few of the shape or taste votes may be shifted, and there may be only small increases in the diagnosticities of these attributes). Also, the additional changes may be made subsequent to the primary one so that the additional changes are in effect part of another process. That is, initial judgments about membership in conjunctive concepts may conform with our selective-influence assumption. This possibility is supported by the evidence that we present in subsequent sections where we demonstrate how well our model predicts typicality ratings for conjunctions. The issue of selective modification is sufficiently controversial, though, that we return to it at the end of the paper.

A First Test of the Model: Study 1

The preceding account was highly illustrative. We used but a single noun concept, had no basis for the attributes, values, or votes that were included in the noun's prototype, and no rationale for the diagnosticity weights nor for how much they were boosted by modification. Study 1 remedied these deficiencies. In part 1, subjects listed properties of various instances of the concepts *fruit* and *vegetable*; these listings were used to determine the attributes, values, votes, and diagnosticities for the instances and concepts. With such representations in hand, we could use our modification procedures to produce representations for conjunctions, and then employ the contrast rule to predict the typicalities of the instances in the simple concepts and conjunctions. These predicted typicalities were compared with actual ratings obtained in part 2 of the study.

---

6. Medin and Shoben (1988) showed, for example, that a small spoon is judged more typical than a large spoon of *spoon*, while the reverse obtains for *wooden spoon*. This suggests that the adjective *wooden* has affected the size attribute. This argument seems plausible, but an alternative account should also be kept in mind. One's knowledge about the size of wooden spoons may have little to do with composition processes, but instead reflects prior experience with known instances of *wooden spoon*. That is, *wooden spoon* is not an unfamiliar concept, hence experience with its instances may figure in typicality judgments (Hampton, 1987). This consideration indicates that research on conceptual composition has not paid sufficient attention to the familiarity of the concepts involved, a criticism that applies to parts of the present paper as well.

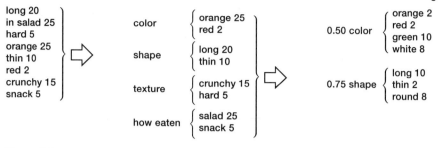

Figure 17.5
Illustration of coding of listed properties into attribute-value structures of instance *carrot* and concept *vegetable*.

Part 1

Method   The instances used were basic-level concepts, such as *apple, peach, carrot,* and *onion*, rather than specific objects like those employed by Smith and Osherson (1984) and used to illustrate the model in the previous section. This change in level allowed us to dispense with pictures or models of instances, in favor of one-word descriptions.

Thirty subjects listed properties for *fruit* instances and 30 listed properties for *vegetable* instances. All subjects were Harvard-Radcliffe undergraduates who were paid for their participation. Each subject was given a booklet that consisted of a page of instructions followed by 15 test pages, each of the latter containing the name of one *fruit* or one *vegetable* instance. The instructions were essentially the same as those used by Rosch and Mervis (1975). They informed subjects that, for each instance, they were to write down all its properties they could think of, and that they had 90 seconds to do this. The order of instances was randomly determined for each subject.

Results   First, any property that was mentioned by only one subject was eliminated. Then, for each instance, two raters (two of the authors) inspected the resulting set of listed properties for ones that intuitively seemed to be values of the same attribute. Wherever there was any disagreement between the raters, the properties were dropped from consideration. Only 12% of the listed properties was eliminated by these criteria.

For each attribute selected, the number of mentions of each property, or value, was taken as a measure of its number of votes. Part of this coding for the instance *carrot* is presented in Figure 17.5. While the figure shows only 4 attributes, there were in fact a total of 15 attributes for *carrot*. Most importantly, the attributes that emerged for this instance also appeared with other *vegetable* and *fruit* instances, as only 26 different attributes emerged across all 30 instances. This communality makes it reasonable to determine the attribute-value representation for the concepts *fruit* and *vegetable* by averaging over all relevant instances on each attribute, as illustrated on the right-hand side of Figure 17.5. Such averaging is in keeping with the idea of a prototype as a measure of central tendency. Our prototype for *fruit*, then, consisted of 25 attributes with an average of 7.16 values per attribute, while our prototype for *vegetable* contained 25 attributes with an average of 7.28 values per attribute. All of these attributes are listed in Table 17.1, along with the total number of votes cast for each,

Table 17.1
Attributes of *fruit* and *vegetable*, along with total votes and diagnosticities (Study 1)

Attribute	Total votes for fruit	Total votes for vegetable	Diagnosticity v
Outside color	503	462	.44
Outside texture	261	206	.61
Taste	252	167	.69
How eaten	238	397	.84
How grown	203	90	.82
Seeds	191	48	.13
Shape	157	158	.70
Juiciness	146	34	.61
Inside color	119	30	.37
Size	109	34	.12
Pit	55	0	.43
Inside texture	51	44	.52
Original identity	44	18	.55
Where grown	41	19	.96
Skin	39	25	.50
Stem	38	15	.24
Varieties	37	83	.71
Side-effects	27	47	.95
When grown	22	2	.34
Container	21	12	.53
Nutritional value	18	138	.83
Leaf	14	68	.67
Favorite consumer	9	47	.90
Nonfood uses	7	10	.79
Cost	4	2	1.00
Smell	0	36	.41

separately for *fruit* and *vegetable*. (Other ways of determining attribute-value representation for *fruit* and *Vegetable* are discussed in connection with Experiment 4.)

To estimate the diagnosticity weights for the concepts' attributes, we assumed that the diagnosticity of an attribute would be largely a matter of how useful it was for discriminating between fruits and vegetables. Accordingly, for each attribute we formed an n by 2 table; the two columns designated *fruit* and *vegetable*, the n rows designated every value of the attribute listed for any fruit of vegetable, and the cell entries were the numbers of votes for that value of *fruit* of *vegetable*. We then calculated the statistic v, a close cousin of chi-square (specifically, the square root for chi-square divided by the total number of votes in the table). This statistic varies between 0 and 1 and indicates the extent to which the values of the attribute are associated with *fruit* but not *vegetable*, or vice versa. We took the value of v as an estimate of the attribute's diagnosticity. These diagnosticity weights are given in the last column of Table 17.1.[7]

We now have sufficient information to predict typicalities for each of the 15 instances in the simple concepts *fruit* and *vegetable*, as well as in certain adjective-noun conjunctions. With regard to the simple concepts, earlier we presented Equation (2), which, computes similarity on an attribute-by-attribute basis. However, the computing equation that we actually used iterates not only over attributes, but over values of an attribute as well:

$$(3)\quad \text{Sim}(P,I) = \sum_i v_i \sum_j [a \min(n_{ij}(P), n_{ij}(I))$$
$$- b(n_{ij}(P) \dot{-} n_{ij}(I)) - c(n_{ij}(I) \dot{-} n_{ij}(P))].$$

Again i indexes the attributes, and now v_i is the diagnosticity of attribute i. Also, j indexes the values on an attribute, and $n_{ij}(\cdot)$ is the number of votes on value j of attribute i. The expression in brackets denotes a contrast between common and distinctive features for each value of each attribute, where the dot over the minus sign indicates the difference must be positive (i.e., $n_{ij}(P) \dot{-} n_{ij}(I) = n_{ij}(P) - n_{ij}(I)$ if $n_{ij}(P) > n_{ij}(I)$, and 0 otherwise). To illustrate, suppose the prototype had 20 red votes and the instance 15 red votes. Then the number of common features would be 15 (the minimum of the 2 vote counts), the number of features distinct to the prototype would be 5, the number distinct to the instance would be 0, these three numbers would be multiplied by a, b, and c, respectively, and the outcome of the contrast would be multiplied by the diagnosticity of color.

To predict typicalities in conjunctions, we have to augment our computing equations in the following way:

$$(4)\quad \text{Sim}(P,I) = \sum_j e_i v_i \sum_j [a \min(n_{ij}^*(P), n_{ij}(I))$$
$$- b(n_{ij}^*(P) \dot{-} n_{ij}(I)) - c(n_{ij}(I) \dot{-} n_{ij}^*(P))]$$

Equation (4) differs from its predecessor in two respects. First, for the prototype, the number of votes on value j of attribute i is now $n_{ij}^*(P)$, which is defined as follows:

$$n_{ij}^*(P) = \begin{cases} \sum_j n_{ij}(P), & \text{if the adjective in the conjunction matches value } j. \\ 0, & \text{if the adjective in the conjunction is a value of attribute } i \text{ other than } j. \\ n_{ij}(P), & \text{otherwise.} \end{cases}$$

7. The general formula for v is:
$$v = [X^2/N \min(I-1), (J-1)]^{1/2},$$
where X^2 is chi square, N is the total number of observations in the table, I is the number of rows, and J is the number of columns (Bishop, Feinberg, and Holland, 1975, Chap. 11). Because in our case there are always just two columns, the above formula reduces to:
$$v = [X^2/N]^{1/2}$$
Unlike X^2, v is not correlated with N.

For example, if the adjective in the conjunction is "red," then the number of red votes in the prototype would be the sum of all color votes, the number of green votes in the prototype would be zero, and the number of votes on the value of any other attribute in the prototype would be as usual. The other novelty in Equation (4) is the addition of e_i, which multiples v_i, the diagnosticity of attribute i; e_i is defined as follows:

$$e_i = \begin{cases} d, & \text{if the adjective in the conjunction encodes } i. \\ 1, & \text{otherwise.} \end{cases}$$

Thus, the diagnosticity of an attribute is boosted by a factor of d ($d > 1$) if that attribute is encoded by the adjective in the conjunction. Note that d, the "booster," is the only free parameter in (4) apart from the contrast weights a, b, and c. Equations (3) and (4) were used to predict the typicalities of the relevant instances in the simple concepts *fruit* and *vegetable* and in the eight conjunctions described below. (To estimate parameters, we used the program STEPIT [Chandler, 1969], and maximized average correlations between predicted and obtained ratings.)

Part 2
Method Thirty subjects, drawn from the same population as in the previous part of the study, rated the typicality of instances in 10 different concepts. These concepts included the simple concepts *fruit* and *vegetable* and the conjunctions formed by combining them with *red, white, round,* and *long*. Every subject was given a booklet which included instructions and test pages; each of the latter contained the name of one of the 10 concepts followed by a list of 15 relevant instances. Subjects were instructed to rate each instance "... for how good an example it is of the category." The ratings were made on an 11-point scale, where *10* means the instance "is about as good an example as you can get of your idea or image of what the category is and *0* means you think the item does not fit at all with your idea or image of the category."

The same 15 instances were used with *fruit* and with the 4 conjunctions involving *fruit*; all of these were technically fruits though two—*tomato* and *pickle*—were sometimes classified as vegetables. There were also 15 instances that were used with *vegetable* and the 4 conjunctions involving *vegetable*; 13 of them were technically vegetables while the remaining 2 were *tomato* and *pickle*. (All *fruit* and *vegetable* instances are listed in Table 17.2). For a given subject, the instances were listed in the same order when they appeared with different concepts (to ease the subject's rating task), but the order of instances and concepts varied randomly across subjects.

Results: Evaluation of the Model For each of the 10 concepts, we determined the average typicality ratings for the 15 instances. These ratings are presented in Table 17.2. Then, for each concept, we correlated the obtained ratings with those predicted by the model. These correlations are presented in the last row of Table 17.2. The model does a reasonable job with most of the concepts—the average r is about .70—and particularly with the *vegetable* concepts where the average r for the four conjunctions is .88.[8]

8. There may have been some contribution of an instance's frequency to its predicted typicality (Nosofsky, personal communication, April, 1987). Because subjects tended to list fewer properties for very infrequent instances such as *pomegranate* and *avocado* than for other instances, more properties of frequent than infrequent instances appeared in the prototypes of *fruit* and *vegetable*. Consequently, infrequent instances may have ended up being deemed less similar to their prototype.

Table 17.2
Average typicality ratings for 10 concepts (Study 1)

	Vegetable	Red vegetable	White vegetable	Round vegetable	Long vegetable
String beans	8.70	.54	1.13	.54	8.03
Carrot	8.44	2.27	.50	.64	8.17
Spinach	8.44	.33	.30	.40	2.30
Lettuce	7.64	1.10	1.84	5.77	1.37
Squash	7.44	1.34	2.17	3.87	5.30
Cauliflower	7.37	.17	9.04	4.43	1.34
Potato	7.20	1.83	6.77	6.37	2.27
Lima bean	6.87	.84	2.80	2.80	1.97
Turnip	6.60	3.17	5.37	4.47	2.64
Onion	6.40	2.80	7.53	7.87	1.10
Tomato	6.40	8.50	.30	7.70	.60
Mushroom	6.07	.40	6.17	2.70	.67
Pickle	3.93	.60	1.37	1.60	4.93
Seaweed	3.10	1.04	.93	.17	3.50
Garlic	2.74	1.07	5.47	3.00	.87
Correlation between observed and predicted typicalities	.40	.94	.84	.87	.85

	Fruit	Red fruit	White fruit	Round fruit	Long fruit
Apple	9.77	9.34	4.23	9.27	.67
Peach	9.23	3.33	.93	8.70	.67
Strawberry	9.14	8.57	.74	4.50	.97
Pear	9.04	1.37	3.84	3.67	2.94
Grape	8.40	3.60	3.23	8.14	1.04
Blueberry	8.34	.47	.53	8.60	.33
Watermelon	7.27	5.44	.80	4.57	5.44
Pomegranate	6.94	6.07	.70	7.00	1.37
Lemon	6.70	.30	1.20	4.93	1.64
Fig	4.73	1.07	.70	3.37	1.17
Raisin	4.64	.77	.87	3.30	1.07
Coconut	4.10	.24	5.37	6.90	1.14
Avocado	3.37	.44	.54	3.77	2.24
Tomato	3.33	6.37	.34	7.04	.50
Pickle	1.37	.27	.97	.73	2.17
Correlation between observed and predicted typicalities	.75	.91	.35	.92	.11

Table 17.3
Obtained and predicted (in parentheses) typicality ratings for nouns and conjunctions (Study 1)

Adjectives	Vegetable rating		Adjective vegetable rating	
Good members				
Red	6.40	(5.63)	8.50	(11.89)
White	5.84	(5.54)	6.72	(6.65)
Round	6.67	(5.79)	7.23	(7.99)
Long	7.02	(5.48)	7.04	(7.88)
Poor members				
Red	6.31	(5.35)	0.86	(0.22)
White	6.71	(5.38)	1.68	(0.13)
Round	6.47	(5.35)	1.84	(2.56)
Long	6.65	(5.50)	1.86	(3.30)

However, the model appears to fail with *white fruit* and *long fruit*. Further inspection of the obtained ratings for *white fruit* and *long fruit*, however, suggests that the problem is not in the model but in our selection of instances. First, and most important, our fruit instances showed little variation with respect to whiteness and length, which greatly limits the possible correlations. With regard to the obtained ratings for *white fruit* and *long fruit*, 11 of the 15 instances were rated less than 2.0 on our 11-point scale (see Table 17.2). Another problem with the instances is specific to *white fruit*. The three instances that subjects rated most typical of *white fruit* were *coconut*, *apple*, and *pear*; all three of these objects are white on the inside but not on the outside, yet it was outside color that subjects were instructed to rate and that our model considered in its predictions. The only other low correlation in Table 17.2 is for the simple concept *vegetable*. Again, the problem can be traced to a lack of variation in the instances: 12 of the 15 *vegetable* instances had typicality ratings between 6.07 and 8.70. The *fruit* instances showed substantially more variation.

The parameter values obtained in fitting the model were estimated separately for *fruit* and *vegetable* concepts. Three of the four parameters were intrinsic to the contrast model: a, the weight given to common features; b, the weight of features distinct to the concept; and c, the weight of features distinct to the instance. For *vegetable* concepts, $a = .88$, $b = .50$, and $c = .20$; for *fruit* concepts, $a = 1.84$, $b = .50$, and $c = .20$. The parameters are similar for the two kinds of concepts, and the ordering of the parameters is in agreement with prior results (Gati and Tversky, 1984; Tversky, 1977; Tversky and Gati, 1982). The fourth parameter, d, measures how much the diagnosticity of an attribute is boosted by modification. For *vegetable* concepts, $d = 8.36$, for *fruit* concepts, $d = 4.21$. Clearly, the attribute encoded by the adjective plays a major role.

Results: Conjunction Effects Lastly, we want to examine the data for conjunction effects. Table 17.3 presents the relevant data and predictions for *vegetable* concepts; we ignore the data for *fruit* concepts in light of the problems with *fruit* instances noted above. The top half of the table contains the data for instances that were "good" members of their corresponding conjunctions; for *white vegetable*, for example, just those instances that had at least five color votes on white. The bottom half of Table 17.3 contains the data for instances that were "poor" members of the conjunction; for *white vegetable*, those instances that had zero white votes. The data are presented separately for each conjunction. The obtained data replicate all our previous results: For good members, an instance is judged more typical of the conjunction than of the noun constituent; the conjunctions effect is greater for the incompatible conjunction (*red vegetable*) than for the compatible ones (the other three conjunctions); and for poor members, reverse-conjunction effects occur as an instance is judged less typical of the conjunction than of the noun constituent. Moreover, the predicted data, presented in parentheses, show exactly the same effects.[9]

Subsequent Tests of the Model: Studies 2 and 3

In study 1, subjects rated the typicality of instances with respect to nouns and adjective–noun conjunctions. It is of interest, however, to also determine the typicality of the instances vis-à-vis adjective constituents (e.g., *red* and *round*), and we did this in studies 2 and 3. Obtaining adjective ratings (along with noun and conjunction ratings) allowed us to evaluate two important assumptions that were left implicit in the previous study. One is that adjectives, such as *red* and *round*, are represented by only a single attribute; if this is the case, we should be able to fit the model to the adjective ratings by assuming that *red*, say, contains only the attribute of color with all votes being on the value red. The second assumption of interest is that subjects base their typicality ratings for a conjunction (e.g., the typicality of *apple* in *red fruit*) on all attributes of the noun concept (e.g., color, shape, and texture), not just on the attribute singled out by the adjective (color). To check this, for each set of instances, we correlated the ratings in the conjunction separately with those in the noun and with those in the adjective, to determine whether each constituent was contributing to the conjunction's ratings.

The only differences between studies 2 and 3 is that in the latter study some noninstances of *vegetable* (*fruit*) were included among the items paired with the *vegetable* (*fruit*) concepts. For example, subjects had to rate the typicality of apple in *vegetable*, *red*, and *red vegetable*. The purpose of this change was to make the variability of the items paired with the noun concept more comparable with the variability of the items paired with the adjective concept; we need such comparability to compare the correlation between noun and conjunction ratings with that between adjective and conjunction ratings. Also, because the *fruit* instances in study 1 hardly varied with respect to *white* and *long*, in studies 2 and 3 we used the same instances, but only the conjunctions *red fruit*, *round fruit*, *red vegetable*, and *round vegetable*. Because studies 2 and 3 are similar and produced comparable results, we treat them together in what follows.

Method
Study 2   The subjects were 30 students drawn from the same population as in the previous study. All subjects rated the typicality of instances in three types of con-

---

9. The predicted ratings in Table 17.3 have been rescaled to have the same mean and standard deviation as the obtained ratings in Table 17.3. This rescaling preserves the correlations reported in Table 17.2 because in fitting our model we maximized the average correlations between predicted and obtained ratings rather than minimized predicted-observed deviations.

cepts: noun concepts, including *fruit* and *vegetable*, adjective concepts, including *red* and *round*, and conjunctions, including *red fruit, round fruit, red vegetable*, and *round vegetable*. The 15 instances used with the *fruit* concepts were the same as those used in study 1, and so were the 15 instances used with *vegetable* concepts. In addition, both kinds of instances were used with *red* and *round*. Subjects thus made 10 sets of ratings. The order of the instances within each of these sets was randomized anew for each subject.

Again subjects worked with booklets, where the first pages gave instructions and subsequent pages contained the names of concepts followed by lists of 15 relevant instances. Concepts were blocked, so that all concepts of one type—noun, adjective, of conjunction—appeared on consecutive pages. All possible orders of the concept types were used. Other procedural details—rating scale, general content of instructions—were the same as in the previous study.

Study 3   The subjects were 30 students drawn from the usual population. The only change from the preceding study was in the nature of the *fruit* and *vegetable* "instances." The set of *fruit* "instances" now included our usual 15 fruits, plus 8 vegetables. Similarly, the set of *vegetable* "instances" included our usual 15 vegetables, plus 8 fruits.

Results: Studies 2 and 3
Evaluation of the Model   For each of the 10 concepts, we determined the average typicality ratings for the 15 critical instances. Then, for each concept, we correlated the obtained ratings with those predicted by the model. Applying our model to the data for adjective-noun conjunctions and their noun constituents involved nothing new. To apply the model to the data for adjective concepts, we assumed that the representation for an adjective consists of a single attribute, with all its votes on the value named by the adjective. Consider *red*: The only attribute is color, and all 30 votes are on the value red (*30* because that is the maximum number of votes that any value had in our noun representations).

Table 17.4
Correlations between obtained and predicted typicalities (Studies 2 and 3)

Concepts	Study 2	Study 3
Vegetable	.37	.80
Red	.97	.98
Round	.89	.88
Red vegetables	.96	.70
Round vegetables	.88	.74
Fruit	.70	.87
Red	.98	.97
Round	.96	.92
Red fruit	.97	.91
Round fruit	.95	.88

372   Smith, Osherson, Rips, and Keane

The results of these fits are in Table 17.4. In study 2, there is a relatively poor fit for the simple concept *vegetable* (just as we found in study 1), but now all other correlations between observed and predicted typicalities are very high. The average correlation for the adjective–noun conjunctions is a resounding .94. The results for study 3 lend further credence to the model, as the average correlation for the adjective-noun conjunctions is .81. Also, the correlations for the simple concepts, *vegetable* and *fruit*, have increased, presumably because of the increase in variability that resulted from including noninstances as well as instances of the concept.

In study 2 the three contrast-rule parameters were as follows: for *fruit* concepts, $a = .80$, $b = .50$, $c = .20$; for *vegetable* concepts, $a = .92$, $b = .50$, $c = .20$. In study 3, for *fruit* concepts, $a = 2.01$, $b = .50$, $c = .20$; for *vegetable concepts*, $a = 1.44$, $b = .56$, $c = .20$. The values are similar in the two studies and close to those obtained in the previous study. The remaining parameter is the booster, d. In study 2, d was 8.06 for *fruit* concepts and 8.46 for *vegetable* concepts; in study 3, d was 4.24 for *fruit* concepts and 2.70 for *vegetable* concepts. Again, these values are comparable with those obtained in study 1.

Correlations between Conjunctions and Constituents   The above findings support our claim that the problematical results of study 1 were due to a lack of variation in the instances, and that the adjectives *red* and *round* can be represented by a single attribute. What remains to be checked is our assumption that subjects base their typicality ratings for a conjunction on all attributes of a noun concept. We checked this for each conjunction by determining the correlation (across instances) between ratings in a conjunction and ratings in a particular constituent (with any contribution of the other constituent partialed out). These partial correlations are presented in Table 17.5. In study 2, ratings in a conjunction are more correlated with the adjective than the noun constituent, but the correlations with the noun are substantial and in two cases significant. In study 3, where the variability of instances in the noun concepts is comparable with that in the adjective concepts, all correlations are significant, and ratings in conjunctions are almost as correlated with the noun as the adjective constituents. Clearly, then, subjects ratings for conjunctions consider more than just the attribute singled out by the adjective.

Table 17.5
Partial correlations between typicality ratings in conjunctions and typicality ratings in the constituents (Studies 2 and 3)

Concepts	Study 2	Study 3
Red fruit—red	.99	.93
Red fruit—fruit	.52	.65
Round fruit—round	.97	.78
Round fruit—fruit	.80	.87
Red vegetable—red	.99	.72
Red vegetable—vegetable	.35	.54
Round vegetable—round	.99	.72
Round vegetable—vegetable	.31	.77

Note: For $p < .05$, $r = .50$; for $p < .01$, $r = .62$

Extension of the Model to Adverbs

In this section we extend the model to conjunctions that include the adverbs *very*, *slightly*, and *non*. Again the fundamental idea is that of modification. Now, however, the modifiers of interest are adverbs, and the frame that is altered is itself the outcome of a modification process (namely, the composite prototype that results when an adjective modifies a noun).

Single Adverbs

"Hedges" are a large class of adverbial modifiers whose major function seems to be that of qualifying predicates and which have previously figured in analyses of concept membership (e.g., Lakoff, 1973; Smith et al., 1974). As Lakoff (1973) notes, one subset of hedges includes terms like *very*, *slightly*, and *non*, where these terms seem to intensify aspects of the concepts or prototypes on which they operate (see also Clark and Clark, 1979; Cliff, 1959; Zadeh, 1971). While the principles by which such "intensifiers" operate are simpler than those characterizing most hedges (such as *technically speaking* or *loosely speaking*), intensifiers provide a useful starting point for extending a model of composite prototypes to include adverbs.

To illustrate how *very*, *slightly*, and *non* work, in *very red fruit*, *very* appears to augment the redness in *red fruit*; while in *slightly red fruit* or *nonred fruit*, the adverbs diminish the redness in *red fruit*. To capture these intuitions, we assume that:

> 1. *very* augments the modified value in a conjunction (e.g., the red in *red fruit*) by multiplying the votes on that value by some scalar greater than 1;
> 2. *slightly* diminishes the modified value in a conjunction by multiplying the votes on that value by some scalar between 0 and 1, thereby ensuring that there is a decrease in votes on the value but still some votes left; and
> 3. *non* diminishes the modified value in a conjunction by multiplying the votes on that value by a scaler less than or equal to 0, thereby ensuring that there are no (positive) votes left on the value.

Possible scalars for the three adverbs are:

> *very*: k_v, where $k_v > 1$
> *slightly*: $1 - k_s$, where $0 < k_s < 1$
> *not (non)*: $1 - k_n$, where $k_n \geq 1$

Our reasons for using the format $1 - k_s$ and $1 - k_n$ will become apparent when we describe more complicated adverb combinations.

To illustrate the above scheme, suppose that the number of red votes in *red fruit* is 10. When *very* is applied to *red fruit*, the number of red votes is increased by $10 k_v - 10$. When *slightly* is applied to *red fruit*, the number of red votes is decreased by $10 k_s$ (since k_s must be less than 1, the resulting number of red votes will always be greater than 0). When *non* is applied to *red fruit* the resulting number of red votes is decreased by $10 k_n$ (since k_n can never be less than 1, there can never be any red votes left). Thus *very red fruit* has more red than *red fruit*; *slightly red fruit* has less red than *red fruit* but more than zero red; and *nonred fruit* has no red at all. All of this is compatible with our intuitions.

A further comment is in order about our treatment of *non*. It might seem plausible that k_n should always be 1, thereby ensuring that $1 - k_n$ is always 0. As we will see, though, our results indicate that k_n exceeds 1, which means that $1 - k_n$ has a negative value. This in turn results in there being negative votes. Negative votes are to be treated as follows in computing similarity. Given a concept with negative votes on value j of attribute i, and an instance with some votes on value j' of attribute i, then the votes on j' can be converted to negative votes on j as long as $j' \neq j$. We can illustrate with the concept *nonred fruit*; *blueberry's* blue votes can be converted to negative red votes, thereby increasing its common color features with the concept; and the more salient the color of a particular nonred fruit, the more typical it will be of the concept *nonred fruit*.

Dual Adverbs

We can extend our model one step further by considering conjunctions that involve two adverbs such as *very nonred fruit* and *slightly nonround vegetable*. Combining adverbs comes down to combining scalars for single adverbs. One proposal for doing this is as follows:

> *slightly not*: $1 - [(1 - k_s)k_n]$
> *very not*: $1 - (k_v k_n)$
> *very slightly*: $1 - (k_v k_s)$

In *slightly not*, *not* applies first to yield $1 - k_n$, and then *slightly* operates directly on the value of k_n, resulting in $1 - [(1 - k_s)k_n]$. Hence the first-mentioned adverb has smaller scope than the second. Similarly, in *very not*, *not* applies first yielding $1 - k_n$, and the *very* augments the value of k_n, resulting in $1 - (k_v k_n)$. In *very slightly*, *slightly* applies first yielding $1 - k_s$, and then *very* augments the value of k_s, resulting in $1 - (k_v k_s)$. To illustrate, *slightly nonred fruit* has more red than *nonred fruit* because we have diminished the negation; in contrast, *very nonred fruit* has even less red than *nonred fruit* as we have augmented the negation, and *very slightly red fruit* has less red than *slightly red fruit* because we have augmented *slightly*. All of this seems in line with our intuitions.

There are other schemes for combining scalars that are consistent with our assumptions about *very*, *slightly*, and *non*. One obvious possibility is to simply multiply scalars; for example, the scalar for *slightly non* would be $(1 - k_s)(1 - k_n)$. It turns out, though, that this proposal does not do as well at predicting typicality ratings as the scheme we have proposed. Thus, part of the rationale for our proposal is *post hoc*. Still, our scheme captures basic intuitions about the interpretations of adverbs in conjunctions and offers some interesting claims about combining adverbs (e.g., the first-mentioned adverb has smaller scope than the second-mentioned one), in addition to doing as reasonable job of predicting typicality ratings in complex concepts as other schemes we have tried. (For some related proposals from a fuzzy-set theory perspective, see Hersh and Carmazza, 1976; Lakoff, 1973; and Zadeh, 1971; 1972).

To predict the typicality of an instance in a complex conjunction such as *nonred fruit*, we used a simple extension of Equation (4):

$$(5) \quad \text{Sim}(P, I) = \sum_i e_i v_i \sum_j [a \min(A_i n_{ij}^*(P), n_{ij}(I))$$
$$- b(A_i n_{ij}^*(P) \doteq n_{ij}(I)) - c(n_{ij}(I) \doteq A_i n_{ij}^*(P))]$$

Now we multiply the number of votes on the modified value, $n_{ij}^*(P)$, by the scalar associated with the adverb, A_i, where $A_i = k_v$ if the adverb is *very*, $A_i = 1 - k_s$ if the adverb is *slightly*, and so on. (Strictly speaking, Equation (5) is correct only when $A_i n_{ij}^*(\text{P})$ is nonnegative). Equation (5) involves seven parameters: four are the same as in Equation (4), namely, a, b, c, and e; the three new parameters are embedded in the A_i term and are the scalars k_v, k_s, and k_n.[10]

A Test of the Extended Model: Study 4

In study 4, we obtained typicality ratings for conjunctions involving the adverbs of interest, and then compared these ratings with those predicted by Equation (5). Study 4 was performed along with study 1 and it used the same *fruit* and *vegetable* instances. As a consequence, the ratings for concepts involving *white fruit* and *long fruit* again showed hardly any variability which once more resulted in artifactually low correlations between observed and predicted typicalities. In view of this, we will focus on the ratings for concepts that involved *red* or *round*.

Method

The subjects were drawn from the same population as in previous studies, and were divided into three groups of 30 each. Each group rated the typicality of instances in 16 different complex conjunctions. For group 1, the 16 conjunctions were generated by taking the basic 8 conjunctions from study 1 (*red fruit*, *white fruit* ..., *long vegetable*), and then modifying each one by *very* or *non*; for group 2, the 16 conjunctions were formed by modifying the basic 8 conjunctions by *slightly* or *slightly non*; and for group 3, the basic 8 conjunctions were modified by *very slightly* or *very non*. The 15 instances used with *fruit* concepts were the same as those in study 1, and similarly for the 15 instances used with *vegetable* concepts. Again subjects worked with booklets, where the first pages gave instructions and subsequent pages contained the names of concepts followed by a list of the 15 relevant instances. Other procedural details—rating scale, general content of instructions—were the same as in previous studies.

Results

A Preliminary Look at the Data   For each concept, we determined the average typicality rating for the 15 relevant instances. Before assessing how well these ratings agree with those predicted by the model, it is instructive to display a sample of the obtained ratings. In Table 17.6, the first column lists the 15 *fruit* instances ordered by their number of red votes, while the second, third, and fourth columns give the obtained typicality ratings of each instance in three conjunctions: *red fruit* (these data are from study 1), *nonred fruit* (data from study 4), and *very red fruit* (study 4). The ratings for instances in *red fruit* increase roughly monotonically with the number of red votes in the instance (*watermelon* is a clear outlier, presumably because subjects rated inside rather than outside color). More importantly for present purposes, the

10. Lakoff (1973) has argued that characterizing *very* and *slightly* solely by numerical values runs into trouble when the adjective to be modified is *similar*. Thus, in contrasting "Richard Nixon and Warren Harding are similar" and "Richard Nixon and Warren Harding are very similar," *very* seems to do more than just raise the degree of similarity. In particular, *very* seems to increase the number of attributes that are taken into consideration. However, our numerical proposals for *very* and *slightly* seem to work well with most other adjectives.

376   Smith, Osherson, Rips, and Keane

Table 17.6
Obtained typicality ratings for 3 sample conjunctions (Studies 1 and 4)

Instances	Red fruit	Nonred fruit	Very red fruit
Tomato	6.37	.07	9.24
Strawberry	8.57	.34	9.40
Apple	9.37	1.03	9.14
Pomegranate	6.07	3.34	6.60
Grape	3.60	5.24	4.20
Peach	3.33	5.60	3.37
Pear[a]	1.37	8.03	1.70
Fig	1.07	7.07	1.17
Raisin	.77	7.14	1.67
Coconut	.24	8.64	.07
Avocado	.44	8.70	.47
Watermelon	5.44	2.84	6.90
Pickle	.27	7.77	.30
Lemon	.30	9.44	.27
Blueberry	.47	9.00	.37

[a] All instances from pear through blueberry had zero red votes.

ordering of the instances in *nonred fruit* is essentially the reverse of that in *red fruit*. This reversal is in line with our assumption that *not* multiplies the votes on red by a scalar less than zero, for then instances that were typical of *red fruit* (because they "had a lot of red") are likely to become atypical of *nonred fruit* (because they have too much red), and vice versa. Turning to *very red fruit*, the ratings are again roughly monotonic with the number of red votes in the instance. This is compatible with our assumption that *very* multiplies the votes on *red* by a positive scalar, for then instances with more votes on the adjective will be more typical of *very red fruit*.

Evaluation of the Model   To assess the adequacy of our model quantitatively, again we correlated the obtained ratings with those predicted by the model. (In fitting the model we included the data from study 1, as studies 1 and 4 essentially constitute a single experiment.) A summary of the correlations is presented in Table 17.7. The results are broken down by: (1) *vegetable* or *fruit*; (2) the form of the concept—adjective-noun conjunctions (these data are from study 1), or adverb-adjective-noun conjunctions, or adverb-adverb-adjective-noun conjunctions; and (3) the specific adverbs involved—*very*, *slightly*, and so on.

For *vegetable* concepts, the model captures a good portion of the data, as almost all the correlations are above .60 and the overall average correlation is .70. However, the goodness of fit depends on the complexity of the concept: The correlation drops from .90 to .73 when an adverb is added to an adjective-noun conjunction, and drops further to .59 when a second adverb is added. Another thing to note is how correlations vary with the specific adverbs. For conjunctions with single adverbs, the model does best with concepts that involve *very* ($r = .86$) and worst with those that involve

Table 17.7
Correlations between obtained and predicted typicality ratings, separately for different kinds of *vegetable* and *fruit* concepts (Studies 1 and 4)

		VEGETABLE CONCEPTS		
	red			
		vegetable	.90	(.87)
	round			
	red			
Very		vegetable	.86	(.87)
	round			
	red			
Slightly		vegetable	.63	(.68)
	round			
	red			
Non		vegetable	.70	(.60)
	round			
	red			
Average for adverb		vegetable	.73	(.72)
	round			
	red			
Very slightly		vegetable	.44	(.47)
	round			
	red			
Slightly non		vegetable	.64	(.48)
	round			
	red			
Very non		vegetable	.70	(.60)
	round			
	red			
Average for adverb-adverb		vegetable	.59	(.52)
	round			

Note: The entries in parentheses give the correlation when all concepts are included, i.e., those involving *white* and *long* as well as those involving *red* and *round*. While the correlations are much reduced, particularly for *fruit*, even these tainted data show the usual effects of complexity and specific adverbs.

Table 17.7 (continued)

		FRUIT CONCEPTS		
	red			
		fruit	.92	(.54)
	round			
	red			
Very		fruit	.90	(.57)
	round			
	red			
Slightly		fruit	.74	(.52)
	round			
	red			
Non		fruit	.70	(.39)
	round			
	red			
Average for adverb		fruit	.78	(.49)
	round			
	red			
Very slightly		fruit	.28	(.20)
	round			
	red			
Slightly non		fruit	.70	(.41)
	round			
	red			
Very non		fruit	.64	(.34)
	round			
	red			
Average for adverb adverb		fruit	.54	(.32)
	round			

Note: The entries in parentheses give the correlation when all concepts are included, i.e., those involving *white* and *long* as well as those involving *red* and *round*. While the correlations are much reduced, particularly for *fruit*, even these tainted data show the usual effects of complexity and specific adverbs.

slightly ($r = .63$); for concepts with dual adverbs, the model does best with concepts that involve *very non* ($r = .70$) and worst with those that involve *very slightly* ($r = .44$).

A comment is in order about the decrease in correlation with the increase in concept complexity. There are two factors that contribute to this "complexity" effect. First, the effect is partly a consequence of the effects of specific adverbs. The model does poorest with concepts involving *slightly*, and the average correlation for single-adverb concepts includes one case with *slightly* while the average for dual-adverb concepts includes two cases with *slightly*. Inspection of Table 17.7 indicates that if we ignore concepts involving *slightly*, the complexity effect is substantially reduced. The second factor contributing to the complexity effect is reliability—subjects were less reliable in their ratings for dual-adverb concepts than for single-adverb or adjective–noun conjunctions. Split-half reliabilities were .93 and .95 for adjective-noun and single-adverb conjunctions, respectively, versus .88 for dual-adverb concepts. Apparently, subjects had some difficulty composing concepts that involved more than one adverb—possibly because of ambiguities in the scope of the adverbs—and when their performance became less systematic the model of course faltered.

Turning now to the data for *fruit* concepts in study 4, the results mirror the preceding ones in most important respects (see Table 17.7). The model captures a reasonable amount of the data, with the overall average correlation again being .70. Once more correlations decrease as the concepts become increasingly complex, dropping from .92 to .78 when a single adverb is added to an adjective–noun conjunction, and dropping further to .54 when a second adverb is added. Again this complexity effect can be attributed to the effects of *slightly* (see Table 17.7) and to a breakdown in reliability; with regard to the latter, the split-half reliabilities were .96 and .94 for adjective–noun and single-adverb conjunctions, respectively, versus .80 for dual-adverb conjunctions. With regard to the effects of specific adverbs, once more the model does best with *very* for single-adverb concepts, and worst with *very slightly* for dual-adverb concepts.

In sum, the selective modification model does an excellent job of accounting for ratings in adjective-noun conjunctions (the average correlation for the data in Table 17.7 is .91), a good job of accounting for ratings in adverb-adjective-noun conjunctions (the average correlation is .76), and at best a moderate job of accounting for ratings in dual-adverb concepts (the average correlation is about .56). There is, however, a blatant trouble spot for the model, namely concepts involving *slightly*, as correlations between predicted and observed ratings are routinely lower for such concepts than for other conjunctions. We return to the *slightly* problem soon, after we have taken a look at the parameters obtained in fitting the model.

Parameter Estimates   The top half of Table 17.8 gives the parameters obtained when the model is fit to *vegetable* concepts, and the bottom half gives the parameters for *fruit* concepts. The different rows give the parameters for the different studies (to facilitate comparisons, we have repeated the parameters obtained in studies 1–3). The three parameters of the contrast model are very stable. In virtually every case, the weight given to common features, *a*, exceeds that given to features distinct to the concept, *b*, which in turn exceeds that given to features distinct to the instance, *c*. The booster parameter is somewhat more variable, *d* being quite low for *vegetable* concepts in study 3 and extremely large for *vegetable* concepts study 4. The remaining

Table 17.8
Parameter values, separately for *vegetable* and *fruit* concepts

	Parameters						
Vegetable concepts	a	b	c	d	k_n	k_s	k_v
study 1	.88	.50	.20	8.36	—	—	—
study 2	.92	.50	.20	8.46	—	—	—
study 3	1.44	.56	.20	2.70	—	—	—
study 4 (& 1)	1.71	.50	.20	39.35	1.66	.74	1.04
Fruit concepts							
study 1	1.84	.50	.20	4.21	—	—	—
study 2	.80	.50	.20	8.06	—	—	—
study 3	2.01	.50	.20	4.24	—	—	—
study 4 (& 1)	.41	.50	.20	12.92	1.59	.56	3.63

three parameters pertain to the adverbs, and generally these values are stable and reasonable. Thus k_n averages about 1.60. This results in a scalar for *not* of roughly −.60, which eliminates all positive votes on the modified value of a conjunction. Similarly, k_s averages about .65. This results in a scalar of about .35, which substantially reduces the votes on the modified value of a conjunction but does leave some votes there. The remaining parameter, k_v, is a bit more variable being 1.04 for *vegetables* and 3.63 for *fruits*. This reflects the fact that there was little difference between, say, concepts involving *very red* and those involving *red* or *vegetable*, but a noticeable difference between the two kinds of concepts for *fruit*.

Note that the parameters common to all four studies—*a, b, c,* and *d*—provide support for two fundamental assumptions of the model. The fact that the similarity parameters *b* and *c* were always greater than zero attests to the contrast rule's assumption that similarity depends on distinctive features, not just common ones. And the fact that the booster parameter *d* was always substantial supports the claim that an adjective modifier boosts the diagnosticity of the associated attribute in the noun.[11]

In addition to the above, there are many "hidden" parameters in our model—namely, the attributes, values, and votes of the instances and concepts that were estimated by empirical means. For these hidden parameters, the critical question is whether their values depend on the methods used to obtain them. In particular, are our attribute-value representations for *fruit* and *vegetable*—which enter into every single prediction of the model—biased by the fact that they were determined by averaging over instances? To answer this, we had a new group of 30 subjects list properties for *fruit* and *vegetable* and used these listings to determine directly the attribute-value structures for the two simple concepts. The new *fruit* and *vegetable* prototypes contained fewer attributes than the old ones (an average of 13 attributes rather than 25), but the vast majority of attributes in the new prototypes were among

11. Note that in Table 17.8 the parameters *b* and *c* virtually always equaled .50 and .20, respectively. These constancies reflect the fact that, in fitting the model, we relied on the outcomes of preliminary fits and set the initial values of *a, b, c* and *d* to 1.00, .50, .20, and 6.0, respectively.

those attributes of the old prototypes that had the largest numbers of votes. Most importantly, when the new representations for *fruit* and *vegetable* were used to recompute all predictions for studies 1–4, there was hardly any decrease in how well the model fit the data (in study 4, for example, the average overall correlation change from .70 to .68).

Further Analysis of Slightly   Because the model did relatively poorly with concepts involving *slightly*, it is useful to take a closer look at the data obtained with such concepts. An analysis of the ratings for *slightly* concepts is presented in Figure 17.6. We have plotted the observed typicality of an instance in a conjunction involving *slightly* as a function of the instance's votes on the modified value. Thus the data entering into the curve labeled "slightly" include the typicality of the *fruit* instances in *slightly red fruit* as a function of how many red votes they have, the typicality of the *fruit* instances in *slightly round fruit* as a function of how many round votes they have, and similarly for the typicality of the *vegetable* instances in *slightly red vegetable* and *slightly round vegetable*. Each curve therefore averages over results of conjunctions involving *red fruit*, *round fruit*, *red vegetable*, and *round vegetable* (with different instances contributing the different points). There are separate curves for the three kinds of conjunctions involving *slightly*, and a fourth curve for adjective-noun conjunctions that serves as a frame of reference.

Compared with the curve for adjective–noun, all functions involving *slightly* are relatively flat. This uniformity sheds some light on the problems we have had with *slightly*—though the model is compatible with more uniform ratings for *slightly* than for the other adverbs, the fact that the obtained ratings vary so little makes it difficult for correlations with predicted scores to emerge. This statistical problem notwithstanding, the functions for *slightly* and *slightly non* manifest several trends that are congruent with the modification model.

The function for *slightly* initially rises and then levels off. The model is compatible with the rising trend (e.g., because *slightly red fruit* has a few red votes, it is more similar to *peach* than to *blueberry*). The model further suggests that the *slightly* function should decline at instances that contain many votes on the adjective (e.g., because *slightly red fruit* has only a few red votes, it is quite dissimilar to *strawberry*), thereby resulting in an overall nonmonotonic curve. (Lakoff's, 1973, analysis of *sort of* provides a similar argument.) There is some evidence for this nonmonotonicity in the *slightly* function in Figure 17.6. There might have been more evidence for this nonmonotonicity were it not for the case that the word "slightly" has a pragmatic ambiguity common to all quantitative words (Gazdar, 1979; Horn, 1972). Quantitative terms can be used to mean either N *or at least* N. Thus, *slightly red* can mean either $(1 - k_s)red$ or *at least* $(1 - k_s)red$, and under the latter interpretation even *strawberry* is *slightly red*.

The function for *slightly non* is remarkably similar to that for *slightly*. This similarity may seem surprising, but it is compatible with the model (because a particular relation obtained among the parameters for *slightly* and *non*, namely that $k_s = k_n/1 + k_n$). The remaining function in Figure 17.6 is for *very slightly* and here there is a serious discrepancy from the model. While *very slightly* resembles *slightly*, the model would have it behave more like *non*, being relatively high for instances that lack votes on the adjective and relatively low for instances that have many votes on the adjective.

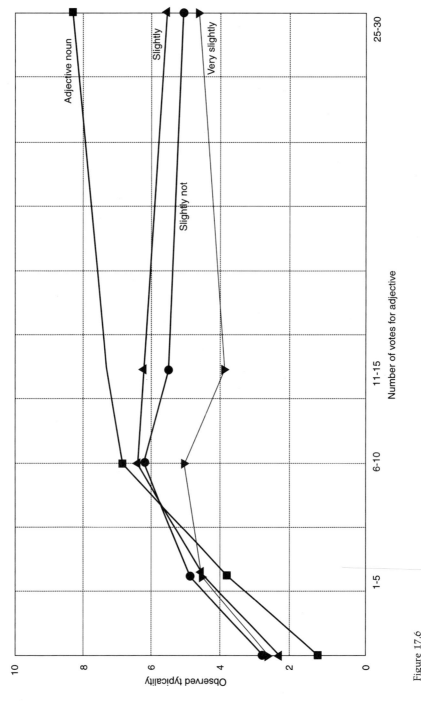

Figure 17.6
Obtained typicality of instances in conjunctions involving *slightly*, as a function of the instances' votes on the relevant value in the conjunction (Study 4).

The preceding qualitative analyses clarify the trouble spots that emerged in our quantatitive modeling. For all concepts involving *slightly*, typicality ratings were uniformly low; though compatible with our model, this uniformity restricts the correlations with predicted scores. Furthermore, because of the ambiguity of "slightly," the predicted nonmonotonicity of the function for *slightly* might have been obscured. And for concepts involving *very slightly*, the obtained data are at odds with some aspects of the model, which explains why these concepts yielded the lowest correlations between observed and predicted scores.

Summary and Other Issues

Summary

We began with three general aspects of a prototype—attribute-value structure, salience, and diagnosticity—and three specific findings about typicality effects in conjunctions—the conjunction effect, a greater conjunction effect for incompatible than compatible conjunctions, and the reverse conjunction effect. These aspects and findings guided our development of the selective modification model. One component of the model is a prototype representation for simple noun concepts, which specifies the relevant attributes and values for a concept along with numerical indicators of the diagnosticities of the attributes and the salience or votes for each value. The second component of our model specifies procedures for modifying prototypes. The procedure for adjectival modification consists of: (1) selecting the relevant attribute(s) in the noun prototype, (2) shifting all votes on that attribute(s) into the value(s) denoted by the adjective, and (3) boosting the diagnosticity of the attribute(s). The third component of the model is Tversky's (1977) contrast rule for determining typicality. The resulting package not only readily accounts for the three specific effects that started us off, but also allows us to elaborate each simple effect into a continuum; for example, the magnitude of the conjunction effect for an instance of *red fruit* depends on the number of red votes in the instance.

Study 1 provided an initial test of the model. First we used property listings to construct attribute-value representations for the noun concepts *fruit* and *vegetable* and for various instances of these concepts. Then we applied the model to produce representations for conjunctions, and to predict typicalities for the instances in the simple concepts and conjunctions. These predicted ratings were highly correlated with obtained ratings for most of the adjective-noun conjunctions that we tested.

There were, however, three concepts where the model's predictions failed to correlate highly with the obtained ratings. These concepts included *long fruit*, *white fruit*, and *vegetable*. We attributed the apparent failures of the model to a lack of variability in length, whiteness, and vegetableness among the instances paired with the relevant concepts (e.g., the instances paired with *long fruit* were all about the same size). To circumvent these variability problems, in studies 2 and 3 we used the same instances as in study 1 but employed only those conjunctions that involved *red* or *round*. Also, in study 3 we increased the variability of the items paired with *fruit* and *vegetable* concepts by including some noninstances of these concepts. In study 2, predicted scores were highly correlated with obtained scores for all concepts save *vegetable*, while in study 3 the model's predictions worked for all concepts. Moreover, the results of studies 2 and 3 provided support for two additional assumptions of the model; namely, that adjectives such as *red* and *round* contain only a single attribute, and that subjects base their typicality ratings for a conjunction on all attributes of the noun concept.

Next we extended the model to conjunctions that involve the adverbs *very*, *slightly*, or *non*, which seem to function as intensifiers. We added to the modification component of our model procedures for adverbial modification. The basic procedure consists of multiplication-by-a-scalar of the votes on a modified value. There are different scalars for the different adverbs, the scalar for *very* increases the votes on the values, that for *slightly* decreases the votes on the value but does not eliminate all votes on the value, and that for *non* eliminates all votes on the value. We extended the modification component further by proposing a means of combining scalars, thereby enabling the model to deal with concepts that involved dual adverbs.

Study 4 provided a test of the extended model. We generally found reasonable correlations between obtained typicality ratings for concepts involving single or dual adverbs and ratings predicted by the extended model. The exceptions were concepts involving *slightly*. Further analyses indicated that the obtained typicality ratings for *slightly* concepts were uniformly low, which restricted correlations with predicted scores, and that some aspects of the ratings for *very slightly* were not captured by the model.

Taken together these four studies provide evidence for many of the assumptions that make up the model. Moreover, the model is among the only theories of prototype combination to offer quantitative predictions about typicality, these predictions being based on data obtained from a paradigm (property listing) that is entirely different from rating typicalities. Of course, our case for the model is limited by our having dealt only with typicality ratings. But, as we noted at the outset, research with simple concepts has demonstrated that such ratings can be used to predict typicality effects on many kinds of performance, and there is good reason to expect the situation to turn out similarly with composite concepts.

Some Qualitative Implications
In addition to providing quantitative predictions about typicality, the selective modification model also offers qualitative insights about some important phenomena, including the generation of goal-derived concepts and apparent changes of concept structure with changing context.

Following Barsalou (1985), some concepts are created "on the fly" during one's efforts to achieve a goal. Examples of such "goal-derived" concepts include *foods not to eat on a diet* and *possessions to save in the event of fire*. Thus far researchers have treated goal-derived concepts as disconnected from natural concepts, such as *fruit* and *vegetable*. From the perspective of the selective modification model, however, many goal-derived concepts may be modified concepts like the ones discussed in this paper. *Foods not to be eaten on a diet*, for instance, may be roughly synonymous with *high-calorie foods*, a modification of *food* where all votes on the calories attribute have been shifted to the high end. Similarly, *possessions to save in the event of a fire* may be roughly synonymous with *valuable possessions*, a modification of *possession* where all votes on the worth attribute have been shifted to the high end.

Along with suggesting a mechanism for *how* goal-derived concepts are constructed, our approach provides a new account of some of Barsalou's (1985) major results. In particular, consider the finding that the typicality of an instance in a goal-derived concept is a function not of its similarity to other instances (or to a prototype summarizing those instances), but rather of its value on the dimension most relevant to the concept. For *foods not to eat on a diet*, for example, chocolate is more typical than bread and it also has a higher value on the relevant dimension of calories. All of this is intelligible in terms of the selective modification model. In composing *high-calorie foods*, if the diagnosticity of the calories attribute is boosted sufficiently high, this attribute will dominate typicality decisions and the effect of the instance's overall similarity to its prototype will be minimized. What looks like a qualitative switch in the process underlying typicality judgments may thus turn out to be just a quantitative change in one parameter of the process.

A similar story can be told about Roth and Shoben's (1983) proposal that context can change the basic structure of a concept. In one relevant experiment, subjects were timed as they read pairs of sentences in succession, such as (1a) and (2), or (1b) and (2):

(1a) Stacy milked the animal on the farm.
(1b) Fran wanted to ride the animal.

(2) She was very fond of the cow.

To understand (2), the reader must determine that "cow" refers to the same entity as "animal" does in the preceding sentence. Roth and Shoben found that this determination of coreference was easier when (2) was preceded by (1a) than (1b), and concluded that the context in (1) changed the meaning of the concept *animal*. The selective modification model, however, offers an alternative explanation. The different contexts in (1a) and (1b) lead the reader to construct different modified concepts, roughly, *milkable farm animal* and *ridable animal*, and it is these composites that the reader must relate to *cow* when reading the second sentence. (Alternatively, the modified concepts may strongly suggest particular instances—*milkable farm animal* suggests *cow*—which are then related to *cow* when reading the second sentence.) More generally, the basic claim of the selective modification model is that the meaning of a simple concept is relatively fixed and apparent meaning changes are due to modification.

Relations to Other Proposals
It is worth commenting briefly on the relation of the qualitative aspects of the selective modification model to some related proposals about prototype combination due to Thagard (1984) and Cohen and Murphy (1984). These researchers represent prototypes as "frames" (in the sense of Minsky, 1975). Our prototype representations can also be interpreted as frames. Our *attributes* are *slots*, our *values* are *slot-fillers*, and the distribution of votes over values is a *distribution of defaults*. Once this interpretation is made, it is easy to see that our model is compatible with the proposals of Thagard (1984) and Cohen and Murphy (1984).

Thagard (1984) treats simple concepts as frames, and notes that a slotfiller can be either a default value or an actual value. He then goes on to argue that in an adjective-noun conjunction, often there is at least one slot that is common to the two constituents (say, color), and the slot-filler for the adjective will dominate because it is interpreted as an actual value while the corresponding filler for the noun is only a default. Thagard's critical assumption, then, is that "actual values drive out defaults." All of this is completely in line with the modification component of our model. In the latter, it is the value named by the adjective (which corresponds to a slot-filler) that determines the final locus of the votes on the relevant attribute (slot) of the noun representation. In essence, we capture the same intuition as Thagard by letting the adjective direct the noun's votes.

Cohen and Murphy (1984) assume that: (1) Simple noun concepts are represented by frames like those discussed above; and (2) Slots are restricted to particular values —for example, at a minimum, the values that fill the shape slot for *fruit* cannot also fill its color slot. Adjective-noun conjunction is treated as a further restriction on values. In *red fruit*, for example, the color slot of *fruit* is restricted to red, and in *expert repair* the agent slot of *repair* is restricted to experts (these notions are adapted from the KL-ONE system of knowledge representation—see, e.g., Brachman and Schmolze, 1985). Cohen and Murphy's ideas have their obvious counterparts in the selective modification model: Attributes (slots) are restricted to the values (fillers) listed for them, and adjectival modification results in all votes for an attribute (slot) being restricted to one value (filler).

The point of the above is not that there are no distinct aspects of the work of Thagard or of Cohen and Murphy—Thagard considers context effects in adjectival modification, while Cohen and Murphy consider far more complex cases of modification than we do. Rather, the point is that there are no basic incompatibilities between our work and that of others using frame representations to model conceptual combination (see Murphy, 1988, for an extended comparison of models).

Limitations of the Selective Modification Model
Having made the case for our model, it seems judicious to close with some discussion of its limitations.

For one thing, there is a problem of "neutral" adjectives (as opposed to compatible and incompatible ones). Our modeling considered only those cases where the adjective encoded an attribute that presumably was part of the noun representation (*red* and *round*, say, encode the attributes color and shape, which are prestored in the prototype for *fruit*). What about cases like *upside-down fruit*, where the adjective encodes an attribute (orientation) that is unlikely to be part of the prototype for *fruit*? In Smith and Osherson (1984), we showed that such neutral conjunctions gave rise to the usual conjunction effects and their reverse. Our problem is how to model such effects. A possible solution is outlined in Cohen and Murphy (1984). In cases such as *upside-down fruit*, the relevant attribute must temporarily be added to the noun representation; then perhaps the value, votes, and boosted diagnosticity can be filled in (the value is that named by the adjective, the votes may be the maximum possible, and the boosted diagnosticity may be a constant). Of course this suggestion raises further questions—for example, how one determines the relevant attribute given only the adjective—but the suggestion seems worth pursuing.

A related difficulty is that the adjectives we have treated are all simple ones like *red*, which plausibly affect only a single attribute of a noun's representation. But many adjectives have more complex consequences for the noun phrases in which they appear. For starters, there are adjectives like *shriveled*, which we used in an earlier example and which require the model to operate simultaneously on two or more attributes (e.g., texture and shape). Although we believe the model is adequate for most multiattribute adjectives of this sort, we lack empirical evidence to support this claim. A more serious challenge comes from adjectives that produce more sweeping changes to the nouns they modify. Consider, for example, a combination such as *fake apple*. Although *fake* seems to leave some of the attributes of *apple* intact, it negates many others; thus, a fake apple might be of roughly the same color and shape as a real apple, but has a different texture, origin, and taste. R. Clark (1970) provides a useful catalog of these nonstandard adjectives (see also Kamp, 1975) that comprises the following types: *negators* (e.g., *fake*), *enlargers* (e.g., *possible*), *fictionalizers*, (e.g., *mythical*), *defictionalizers* (e.g., *simulated*), and *neutralizers* (e.g., *alleged*). Adjectives of each type can be distinguished by the inferences that they license; a *fake apple*, for instance, is necessarily a nonapple, whereas an *alleged apple* may be an apple. Presumably, the prototypes of these noun phrases differ in corresponding ways, but the task of characterizing these prototypes goes beyond what we can accomplish by means of our selective modification model.

Another limitation of our model is that it might be restricted to conjunctions of a certain syntactic form. Consider the contrast between (1) *red fruit* and (2) *red and fruit*. We have produced evidence that the adjective and noun play different roles (modifier and frame) in the first construction, but it is by no means obvious that this is true for the second construction (Oden, 1984, makes a similar point). In *red and fruit*, perhaps *red* is treated as a concept like *fruit*, rather than as a procedure for operating on *fruit*, and conceptual combination involves determining the intersection of the two concepts. This is an idea that we rejected for adjective-noun constructions, but it might work for the explicit *and* construction. These reservations about the generality of our proposals are amplified when we consider constructions even further removed, say explicit disjunction as in *red or fruit*. In short, complex concepts can be composed in different syntactic forms and it remains an open question whether different forms use different modification procedures.

Another limitation of our model is that it does not offer a convincing account of a phenomenon involving adjective-noun conjunctions that has figured centrally in previous discussions of conceptual combination (Osherson and Smith, 1982). Consider an object whose shape is midway between that of a block and that of a ball, and which is considered equally typical of the simple concepts *block* and *ball*. Intuitively, it seems that the object will be considered more typical of the conjunction *round block* than of the conjunction *round ball* because it is round for a block but not for a ball. This phenomenon rules out a large class of models of the fuzzy-set theory type. The most plausible way to account for this phenomenon in terms of the selective modification model is to assume that *ball* and *block* differ appreciably in their number of shape votes (to the extent these numbers are the same, the object in question should be equally typical of *round block* and *round ball*). But this assumption seems very dubious.

However, a slight revision of the model makes it compatible with the above phenomenon. When an adjective is applied to a noun, instead of all votes on the relevant attribute being shifted to the value denoted by the adjective, perhaps some votes are left in their original position. Thus, in forming *round block*, while most of the shape votes are shifted to round, some are left on square. Consequently, the object in question, which also has shape votes on both round and square, will find more matching shape votes in *round block* that in *round ball* (in the latter, all shape votes are round). While this revision of the model introduces another free parameter (the proportion of votes shifted), it leads to an interesting prediction. In an incompatible conjunction, typicality should be less for objects that maximally exemplify the adjective than for those that moderately exemplify it. The most typical *round block* is not perfectly round, and the most typical *square cantelope* is probably a bit round. This prediction remains to be tested.

Our last reservation about the model is that it deals with only the knowledge contained in prototypes, yet sometimes people bring to bear their general knowledge in making a decision about concept membership (see, e.g., Lakoff, 1987; Murphy and Medin, 1985; Rips, 1988). To illustrate with an example from Murphy and Medin, if at a party you see a person jump into a pool fully clothed, probably you would categorize him or her as *drunk*. This categorization is almost certainly not based on similarity to a prototype, because your prototype for *drunk* is unlikely to include any mention of jumping into pools clothed. Rather, your categorization is probably based on your general knowledge about parties, liquor, and erratic behavior.

In addition to influencing categorization processes, general knowledge may also affect the processes involved in constructing a composite prototype. Murphy (1988) points out that one may need general knowledge to determine which attributes of the noun are to be modified as well as to fill in the complex concept so that it is coherent (see also Hampton, 1987). Given the conjunction, *apartment dog*, for example, one needs general knowledge to: (1) know that *apartment* modifies the habitat attribute of *dog*, and (2) refine the composite by adding that an apartment dog is likely to be smaller, quieter, and better-behaved than dogs in general.

The above arguments indicate that the selective modification model offers an incomplete picture of the composition and use of modified concepts. Several considerations, however, suggest that the model will form an important component of any more general theory of conceptual combination. For one thing, the model may be adequate to handle many adjective-noun combinations, for the examples used to show the role of general knowledge typically involve noun-noun composites (such as *apartment dog*). Another matter is that even in cases where general knowledge is used, it may not come into play until after the procedures specified in the selective modification model. That is, our model may describe a rapid composition process, which is sometimes followed by a slower composition process that uses general knowledge. A third consideration is that, even if it turns out that the processing of general knowledge must be interleaved with the procedures of the selective modification model, the model still tells us the basic subtasks that modification must accomplish, such as finding the relevant attributes in the noun, boosting their diagnosticities and altering the saliences of their constituent values, and so on.

References

Barsalou, L. W. (1985). Ideals, central tendency, and frequency of instantiation as determinants of graded structure in categories. *Journal of Experimental Psychology: Learning, Memory, and Cognition, 11*, 629–654.

Bishop, Y. M. M., Feinberg, S. E., and Holland, P. W. (1975). *Discrete multivariate analyses*. Cambridge, MA: MIT Press.

Brachman, R. J., and Schmolze, J. G. (1985). An overview of the KL-ONE Knowledge Representation System. *Cognitive Science, 9*, 171–216.

Chandler, J. P. (1969). STEPIT—Finds local minimum of a smooth function of several parameters. *Behavioral Science, 14*, 81–82.

Clark, H. H., and Clark, E. V. (1979). *Psychology and language: An introduction to psycholinguistics*. New York: Harcourt Brace Jovanovich.

Clark, R. (1970). Concerning the logic of predicate modifiers. *Noûs, 4*, 311–336.

Cliff, N. (1959). Adverbs as multipliers. *Psychological Review, 66*, 27–44.

Cohen, B., and Murphy, G. L. (1984). Models of concepts. *Cognitive Science, 8*, 27–60.

Fodor, J. A. (1981). The present status of the innateness controversy. In J. A. Fodor (Ed.), *Representations: Philosophical essays on the foundations of cognitive science*. Cambridge, MA: MIT Press.

Gati, I., and Tversky, A. (1984). Weighting common and distinctive features in perceptual and conceptual judgements. *Cognitive Psychology, 16*, 341–370.

Gazdar, G. (1979). *Pragmatics: Implicature, presupposition and logical form*. New York: Academic.

Glass, A. L., and Holyoak, K. J. (1975). Alternative conceptions of semantic memory. *Cognition, 3*, 313–339.

Halff, H. M., Ortony, A., and Anderson, R. C. (1976). A context-sensitive representation of word meaning. *Memory and Cognition, 4*, 378–383.

Hampton, J. A. (1982). A demonstration of intransitivity in natural categories. *Cognition, 12*, 151–164.

Hampton, J. A. (1987). Inheritance of attributes in natural-concept conjunctions. *Memory and Cognition, 15*, 55–71.

Hersh, H. M., and Carmazza, A. (1976). A fuzzy set approach to modifiers and vagueness in natural language. *Journal of Experimental Psychology: General, 105*, 254–276.

Horn, L. R. (1972). *On the semantic properties of logical operators in English*. Unpublished doctoral dissertation, University of California, Los Angeles.

Kamp, J. A. W. (1975). Two theories about adjectives. In E. L. Keenan (Ed.), *Formal semantics of natural language*. Cambridge, England: Cambridge University Press.

Lakoff, G. (1973). Hedges: A study in meaning criteria and the logic of fuzzy concepts. *Journal of Philosophical Logic, 2*, 458–508.

Lakoff, G. (1987). *Women, fire, and dangerous things*. Chicago: University of Chicago Press.

Malt, B. C., and Smith, E. E. (1984). Correlated properties in natural categories. *Journal of Verbal Learning and Verbal Behavior, 23*, 250–269.

Medin, D. L., and Schaffer, M. M. (1978). A context theory of classification learning. *Psychological Review, 85*, 207–238.

Medin, D. L., and Shoben, E. J. (1988). Context and structure in conceptual combination. *Cognitive Psychology, 20*, 158–190.

Mervis, C. B., and Rosch, E. (1981). Categorization of natural objects. *Annual Review of Psychology, 32*, 89–115.

Minsky, M. (1975). A framework for representing knowledge. In P. H. Winston (Ed.), *The psychology of computer vision*. New York: McGraw-Hill.

Murphy, G. L. (1988). Constructing complex concepts: A cognitive science case study. *Cognitive Science, 12*, 529–562.

Murphy, G. L., and Medin, D. L. (1985). The role of theories in conceptual coherence. *Psychological Review, 92*, 289–316.

Oden, G. C. (1984). *Everything is a good example of something, and other endorsements of the adequacy of a fuzzy theory of concepts* (WHIPP 21, Wisconsin Human Information Processing Progress Report). Madison, WI.

Osherson, D. N., and Smith, E. E. (1981). On the adequacy of prototype theory as a theory of concepts. *Cognition, 9*, 35–58.

Osherson, D. N., and Smith, E. E. (1982). Gradeness and conceptual combination. *Cognition, 12*, 299–318.

Rips, L. J. (1988). Similarity, typicality, and categorization. In S. Vosniadou and A. Ortony (Eds.), *Similarity, analogy, and thought*. New York: Cambridge University Press.

Rosch, E. H. (1973). On the internal structure of perceptual and semantic categories. In T. E. Moore (Ed.), *Cognitive development and acquisition of language* (pp. 111–144). New York: Academic.

Rosch, E., and Mervis, C. B. (1975). Family resemblances: Studies in the internal structure of categories. *Cognitive Psychology, 7*, 573–605.

Roth, E. M., and Shoben, E. J. (1983). The effect of context on the structure of categories. *Cognitive Psychology, 15*, 346–378.

Rumelhart, D. E., and Ortony, A. (1977). The representation of knowledge in memory. In R. C. Anderson, R. J. Spiro, and W. E. Montaque (Eds.), *Schooling and the acquisition of knowledge*. Hillsdale, NJ: Erlbaum.

Shafir, E. B., Smith, E. E., and Osherson, D. N. (1988). *Typicality and reasoning fallacies*. Unpublished manuscript, University of Michigan, Ann Arbor.

Smith, E. E., and Medin, D. L. (1981). *Categories and concepts*. Cambridge, MA: Harvard University Press.

Smith, E. E., and Osherson, D. N. (1984). Conceptual combination with prototype concepts. *Cognitive Science, 8*, 357–361.

Smith, E. E., Shoben, E. J., and Rips, L. J. (1974). Structure and process in semantic memory: A featural model for semantic decisions. *Psychological Review, 81*, 214–241.

Thagard, P. (1984). Conceptual combination and scientific discovery. In P. Asquith and P. Kitcher (Eds.), *PSA*, 1. East Lansing, MI: Philosophy of Science Association.

Tversky, A. (1977). Features of similarity. *Psychological Review, 84*, 327–352.

Tversky, A., and Gati, I. (1982). Similarity, separability, and the triangle inequality. *Psychological Review, 89*, 123–154.

Tversky, A., and Kahneman, D. (1983). Extensional versus intuitive reasoning. The conjunction fallacy in probability judgment. *Psychological Review, 90*, 293–315.

Zadeh, L. A. (1971). Quantitative fuzzy semantics. *Information Sciences, 3*, 159–176.

Zadeh, L. A. (1972). A fuzzy-set theoretic interpretation of hedges. *Journal of Cybernetics, 2*, 4–34.

Chapter 18

Cognitive Models and Prototype Theory

George Lakoff

My purpose in this paper is to point out what I think is a deep misunderstanding of the nature of prototype theory. In well-replicated experiments, Eleanor Rosch and her coworkers have demonstrated the existence of *prototype effects:* scalar goodness-of-example judgments for categories. Thus, for a category like *bird,* subjects will consistently rate some kinds of birds as better examples than others. The best examples are referred to as *prototypes.* Such effects are superficial. They show nothing *direct* about the nature of categorization. As Rosch (1978) has observed,

> The pervasiveness of prototypes in real-world categories and of prototypicality as a variable indicates that prototypes must have some place in psychological theories of representation, processing, and learning. However, prototypes themselves do not constitute any particular model of processes, representations, or learning. This point is so often misunderstood that it requires discussion ... to speak of a *prototype* at all is simply a convenient grammatical fiction; what is really referred to are judgments of degree of prototypicality.... Prototypes do not constitute a theory of representation for categories....

Despite Rosch's admonitions to the contrary, prototype effects have often been interpreted as showing something *direct* about the nature of human categorization. There are two common interpretations of prototype effects:

> *The Effects = Structure Interpretation*: Goodness-of-example ratings are a direct reflection of degree of category membership.

According to the Effects = Structure interpretation, scalar goodness-of-example ratings occur if and only if category membership is not all-or-none, but a matter of degree. The Effects = Structure interpretation thus makes a claim that Rosch has explicitly denied—that category membership is scalar whenever goodness-of-example ratings are scalar.

> *The Prototype = Representation Interpretation*: Categories are represented in the mind in terms of prototypes (that is, best examples). Degrees of category membership for other entities are determined by their degree of similarity to the prototype.

There are at least two variations on the Prototype = Representation interpretation: one in which the prototype is an abstraction, say a schema or a feature bundle, and another in which the prototype is an exemplar, that is, a particular example.

A fuller account of the issues discussed in this chapter can be found in the author's book *Women, Fire, and Dangerous Things: What Categories Tell Us About the Nature of Thought*, University of Chicago Press, 1986.

Despite the fact that Rosch has specifically disavowed both of these interpretations, and despite the fact that they are incompatible with much of what is
known about prototype effects, they have remained popular. In fact, a whole school
of research has developed within cognitive psychology that takes these interpretations as defining prototype theory. Smith and Medin (1981) is a survey of research
based on these interpretations.

The purpose of this chapter is to suggest a different interpretation of prototype
effects: Prototype effects result from the fact that knowledge is organized in terms of
what I will call *cognitive models*. There are various kinds of cognitive models, and
hence prototype effects come from a variety of sources.

Interactional Properties

Before we proceed, there is one more common misconception about prototype theory that ought to be cleared up. In her early work, Rosch claimed that prototypes
could be characterized by clusters of real-world attributes. She later recanted (Rosch
1978:29, 41–42):

> When research on basic objects and their prototypes was initially conceived
> (Rosch et al. 1976), I thought of such attributes as inherent in the real world....
> On contemplation of the nature of many of our attributes listed by our subjects,
> however, it appeared that three types of attributes presented a problem for such
> a realistic view. (1) some attributes, such as "seat," for the object "chair," appear
> to have names which showed them not to be meaningful prior to the knowl-
> edge of the object as chair; (2) some attributes, such as "large" for the object
> "piano" seem to have meaning only in relation to categorization of the object in
> terms of a superordinate category—piano is large for furniture, but small for
> other kinds of objects such as buildings; (3) some attributes, such as "you eat on
> it" for the object "table" were functional attributes that seemed to require
> knowledge about humans, their activities, and the real world in order to be
> understood.

As I have argued elsewhere (Lakoff 1986), the properties that are relevant for the
characterization of human categories are not objectively existing properties that are
"out there" in the world, Rather they are "interactional properties," what *we* understand as properties by virtue of our interactive functioning in our environment. The
properties mentioned in cognitive models are properties of this sort, not objectively
existing properties of objects completely external to human beings.

This view is in keeping with results on basic-level categorization. The determinants
of basic-level categorization are all interactional in this respect: perception of overall
shape, motor movements relative to objects, mental images. Each of these is a matter
of interaction between people and objects. They are neither wholly objective nor
wholly subjective.

With this in mind, we can turn to the role of cognitive models in prototype theory.

Cognitive Models

The study of cognitive models of a certain sort has been fashionable in cognitive
science for some years now. Rumelhart's "schemas," Minsky's "frames," and Schank

and Abelson's "scripts" are tools for representing knowledge that are used by a wide range of cognitive scientists. To my knowledge, all of these developed out of Fillmore's earlier concept of a "case frame," which has been superseded by his frame semantics. Cognitive models of this sort are all roughly equivalent and I will refer to them as *propositional models*. Four other types of cognitive models are now being investigated within cognitive linguistics. These are: image-schematic, metaphoric, metonymic, and symbolic models (for detailed discussion, see Lakoff 1986). Cognitive models in general are used to structure and make sense of our experience, and each element in such a model can correspond to a category of mind.

Graded Models

A cognitive model characterizing a concept may be either graded or ungraded. A concept such as *rich* is characterized in part by a scale with gradations; individuals are rich to some degree, and not all individuals are clearly rich or not rich. This is the sort of category described by Zadeh (1965), and fuzzy-set theory has been set up to deal with such graded categories. I find them relatively uninteresting and will not discuss them any further. Prototype effects of the sort discovered by Rosch can occur in the case of such graded categories. They can also occur in a wide variety of other cases, and it is those cases that I will primarily be addressing.

The Idealized Character of Cognitive Models

Fillmore has observed that prototype effects can occur even when a cognitive model fits the classical definition of a category—that is, when the model is defined as having clear boundaries and necessary-and-sufficient conditions. Such prototype effects arise because cognitive models are *idealized*—that is, they may be defined relative to idealized circumstances rather than circumstances as they are known to exist. Fillmore (1982a) gives the example of the concept *bachelor*:

> The noun *bachelor* can be defined as an unmarried adult man, but the noun clearly exists as a motivated device for categorizing people only in the context of a human society in which certain expectations about marriage and marriageable age obtain. Male participants in long-term unmarried couplings would not ordinarily be described as bachelors; a boy abandoned in the jungle and grown to maturity away from contact with human society would not be called a bachelor: John Paul II is not properly thought of as a bachelor.

As a result of the background conditions with respect to which a bachelor is defined, certain fuzzy cases arise: homosexuals, Moslems who are permitted four wives but only have three, and so on. The fuzziness is not due to any gradience in the model of the concept *bachelor*. It is instead due to the inexactness of fit between the background conditions of that model and other knowledge that we have about the world. Thus, we can find cases where an individual might appropriately be described as "sort of a bachelor," "a bachelor to a degree." These are prototype effects, but they are not due to any graded category. In such cases, even classically defined models may give rise to prototype effects.

The moral is clear: Prototype effects are real, but superficial. They may arise from a variety of sources. It is important not to confuse prototype effects with the structure of the category as given by cognitive models.

Cognitive Models versus Feature Bundles

One of the most common versions of the P = R interpretation is the theory of weighted feature bundles. According to this theory, the prototype can be represented by a collection of features with associated weights indicating their importance. An example of such an analysis of prototype effects is the classic study by Coleman and Kay (1981), of the use of the verb *lie*. Coleman and Kay found that their informants did not appear to have necessary-and-sufficient conditions for characterizing the meaning of *lie*. Instead they found a cluster of three conditions, not one of which was necessary, and which varied in relative importance:

> a consistent pattern was found: falsity of belief is the most important element of the prototype of *lie*, intended deception the next most important element, and factual falsity is the least important. Informants fairly easily and reliably assigned the word *lie* to reported speech acts in a more-or-less, rather than all-or-none, fashion, ... [and] ... informants agree fairly generally on the relative weights of the elements in the semantic prototype of *lie*.

Thus, there is agreement that if you, say, steal something and then say you didn't, that's a good example of a lie. A less representative example of a lie is when you compliment a hostess when you hated her dinner, or if you say something true but irrelevant, like "I'm going to the candy store, Ma," when you're really going to the poolhall but will be stopping by the candy store on the way.

An important anomaly, however, turned up in the Coleman-Kay study. When informants were asked to define a lie, they consistently said it was a false statement, even though actual falsity turned out consistently to be the least important element by far in the cluster of conditions. Sweetser (1986) provides an important argument against the feature-bundles model and in favor of a cognitive-models account of lying. What she shows is that there are independently needed cognitive models of communication and belief that are used in understanding what a lie is. Sweetser shows that these cognitive models automatically predict the weightings found in the Coleman-Kay study and, moreover, permit one to define a lie as a false statement relative to these models, and still get the correct results. For details, see Sweetser (1984, 1986) or Lakoff (1986). Sweetser's study shows that it is the structure of the cognitive models that permits an adequate explanation of the Coleman-Kay findings, and that weighted feature bundles do not even constitute an adequate description, much less an explanation. As we will see below, feature bundles cannot account for most of the prototype phenomena discussed by cognitive linguists.

Mother

Some categories are characterized by *clusters* of cognitive models. There is an all-important difference between clusters of models and clusters of features: models have an internal structure that features do not have. An example of a concept characterized by a cognitive model cluster is the concept *mother*. According to the classical theory of categorization, it should be possible to give clear necessary-and-sufficient conditions for *mother* that will fit all the cases and apply equally to all of them. Such a definition might be something like: *a woman who has given birth to a child*. But as we will see, no such definition will cover the full range of cases. *Mother* is a concept that is based on a complex model in which a number of individual cognitive models converge, forming an experiential cluster. The models in the cluster are as follows.

The birth model: the person giving birth is the *mother*.

The birth model is usually accompanied by a genetic model, although, since the development of egg and embryo implants, they do not always coincide.

The genetic model: the female who contributed the genetic material is the *mother*.

The nurturance model: the female adult who nurtures and raises a child is the *mother* of that child.

The marital model: the wife of the father is the *mother*.

The genealogical model: the closest female ancestor is the *mother*.

The concept *mother* normally involves a complex model in which all of these individual models converge to form a cluster. There have always been divergences from this cluster; stepmothers have been around for a long time. But because of the complexities of modern life, the models in the cluster have come to diverge more and more. Still, many people feel the pressure to pick one model as being the right one, the one that "really" defines what a mother is. But, although one might try to argue that only one of these characterizes the "real" concept of *mother*, the linguistic evidence does not bear this out. As the following sentences indicate, there is more than one criterion for "real" motherhood:

I was adopted and I don't know who my real mother is.

I am not a nurturant person, so I don't think I could ever be a real mother to any child.

My real mother died when I was an embryo, and I was frozen and later implanted in the womb of the woman who gave birth to me.

I had a genetic mother who contributed the egg that was planted in the womb of my real mother, who gave birth to me and raised me.

By genetic engineering, the genes in the egg my father's sperm fertilized were spliced together from genes in the eggs of twenty different women. I wouldn't call any of them my real mother. My real mother is the woman who bore and raised me, even though I don't have any single genetic mother.

In short, more than one of these models contributes to the characterization of a *real mother*, and any one of them may be absent from such a characterization. Still, the very idea that there is such a thing as a *real mother* seems to require a choice among models where they diverge. It would be bizarre for someone to say:

I have four real mothers: the woman who contributed my genes, the woman who gave birth to me, the woman who raised me, and my father's current wife.

When the cluster of models that jointly characterize a concept diverge, there is still a strong pull to view one as the most important. This is reflected in the institution of dictionaries. Each dictionary, by historical convention, must list a primary meaning when a word has more than one. Not surprisingly, the human beings who write dictionaries vary in their choices. Dr. Johnson chose the birth model as primary, and many of the applied linguists who work for the publishers of dictionaries, as is so often the case, have simply played it safe and copied him. But not all. Funk and Wagnall's *Standard Dictionary* chose the nurturance model as primary, while the *American College Dictionary* chose the genealogical model. Though choices made by dictionary-makers are of no scientific importance, they do reflect the fact that, even among people who construct definitions for a living, there is no single, generally accepted cognitive model for such a common concept as "mother."

When the situation is such that the models for *mother* do not pick out a single individual, we get compound expressions like *stepmother, surrogate mother, adoptive mother, foster mother, biological mother, donor mother*, and so on. Such compounds, of course, do not represent simple subcategories, that is, kinds of ordinary mothers. Rather, they describe cases where there is a lack of convergence of the various models.

Not surprisingly, different models are used as the basis of different extended senses of *mother*. For example, the birth model is the basis of the metaphorical sense in

Necessity is the mother of invention.

whereas the nurturance model is the basis for the derived verb in

He wants his girlfriend to mother him.

The genealogical model is the basis for the metaphorical extension of *mother* and *daughter* used in the description of the tree diagrams that linguists use to describe sentence structure. If node A is immediately above node B in a tree, A is called the *mother* and B, the *daughter*. Even in the case of metaphorical extensions, there is no single privileged model for *mother* on which the extensions are based. This accords with the evidence cited above, which indicates that the concept *mother* is defined by a cluster of converging models.

This phenomenon is beyond the scope of the classical theory. The concept *mother* is not clearly defined, once and for all, in terms of common necessary-and-sufficient conditions. There need be no necessary-and-sufficient conditions for motherhood shared by normal biological mothers, donor mothers (who donate an egg), surrogate mothers (who bear the child, but may not have donated the egg), adoptive mothers, unwed mothers who give their children up for adoption, and stepmothers. They are all mothers by virtue of their relation to the ideal case, where the models converge. That ideal case is one of the many kinds of cases that give rise to prototype effects.

So far we have seen three sources of prototype effects: models with a graded scale (e.g., *rich*), classical models with background conditions (e.g., *bachelor*), and cluster models (e.g., *mother*). But there are two other types of sources of prototype effects that are even more interesting: metonymic models and radial categories. Let us begin with metonymic models.

Metonymic Models

Metonymy is one of the basic characteristics of cognition. It is extremely common for people to take one well understood or easy-to-perceive aspect of something and use it to stand either for the thing as a whole, or for some other aspect or part of it. The best-known cases are those like the following:

One waitress says to another: The ham sandwich just spilled beer all over himself.

Here *the ham sandwich* is standing for the person eating the sandwich. Another well-known example is the slogan:

Don't let El Salvador become another Vietnam.

Here the place is standing for the events that occurred at that place. As Lakoff and Johnson (1980) showed, such examples are instances of general patterns; they do not just occur one-by-one. We will refer to such patterns as *metonymic models*.

A particularly interesting case of metonymy occurs in giving answers to questions. It is common to give an answer that evokes the information requested, and there seem to be language-particular metonymic models used to do so. Take, for example, the case described by Rhodes (1976). Rhodes is a linguist who does field work on Ojibwa, a Native American language of central Canada. As part of his field work, he asked speakers of Ojibwa who had come to a party how they got there. He got answers like the following (translated into English):

I started to come.

I stepped into a canoe.

I got into a car.

He figured out what was going on when he read Schank and Abelson's *Scripts, Plans, Goals, and Understanding*. Going somewhere in a vehicle involves a structured scenario (or in our terms, an Idealized Cognitive Model, or ICM):

Precondition: You have (or have access to) the vehicle.
Embarcation: You get into the vehicle and start it up.
Center: You drive (row, fly, etc.) to your destination,
Finish: You park and get out.
End Point: You are at your destination.

What Rhodes found was that in Ojibwa it is conventional to use the embarcation point of an ICM of this sort to evoke the whole ICM. That is, in answering questions, part of an ICM is used to stand for the whole. In Ojibwa, that part is the embarcation point.

Ojibwa does not look particularly strange when one considers English from the same point of view. What are possible normal answers to a question such as "How did you get to the party?"

I drove. (Center stands for whole ICM)
I have a car. (Precondition stands for whole ICM)
I borrowed my brother's car. (This entails the Precondition, which in turn stands for the whole ICM)

English even has special cases that look something like Ojibwa.

I hopped on a bus. (Embarcation stands for whole ICM)
I just stuck out my thumb. (Embarcation stands for whole ICM)

In short, English can use the Embarcation metonymically to stand for the whole ICM, just in case there is no further effort involved, as in taking a bus or hitchhiking.

There are many metonymic models in a rich conceptual system, and they are used for a wide variety of purposes. The kind of most interest for our present purposes are those in which a member or subcategory can stand metonymically for the whole category for the purpose of making inferences or judgments.

Metonymic Sources of Prototype Effects

As Rosch observed, prototype effects are surface phenomena. A major source of such effects is metonymy—a situation in which some subcategory or member or sub-model is used (often for some limited and immediate purpose) to comprehend the category as a whole. In other words, these are cases where a part (a subcategory or member or submodel) stands for the whole category—in reasoning, recognition, and so on. Within the theory of cognitive models, such cases are represented by metonymic models.

The Housewife Stereotype

We have seen how the clustering of cognitive models for *mother* results in prototype effects. However, an additional level of prototype effects occurs in the *mother* category. The source of these effects is the stereotype of the mother as housewife. Social stereotypes are cases of metonymy—where a subcategory has a socially recognized status as standing for the category as a whole, usually for the purpose of making quick judgments about people. The housewife-mother subcategory, though unnamed, exists. It defines cultural expectations about what a mother is supposed to be. Because of this, it yields prototype effects. On the whole in our culture, housewife-mothers are taken as better examples of mothers than nonhousewife-mothers.

Such goodness-of-example judgments are a kind of prototype effect. But this effect is not due to the clustering of models, but rather to the case of a metonymic model in which one subcategory, the housewife-mother, stands for the whole category in defining cultural expectations of mothers. Other kinds of metonymic models will be discussed below.

Working Mothers

A *working mother* is not simply a mother who happens to be working. The category *working mother* is defined in contrast to the stereotypical housewife-mother. The housewife-mother stereotype arises from a stereotypical view of nurturance, which is associated with the nurturance model. According to the stereotypical view, mothers who do not stay at home all day with their children cannot properly nurture them. There is also a stereotypical view of work, according to which it is done away from the home, and housework and child-rearing do not count. This is the stereotype that the bumpersticker "Every Mother Is a Working Mother" is meant to counter.

The housewife-mother stereotype is therefore defined relative to the nurturance model of motherhood. This may be obvious, but it is not a trivial fact. It shows that metonymic models like stereotypes are not necessarily defined with respect to an entire cluster. In this case, the metonymic model is characterized relative to only one of the models in the cluster—the nurturance model. Here is some rather subtle evidence to prove the point:

Consider an unwed mother who gives up her child for adoption and then goes out and gets a job. She is still a mother, by virtue of the birth model, and she is working—but she is not a *working mother*!

The reason is that it is the nurturance model, not the birth model, that is relevant for the interpretation of the phrase. Thus, a biological mother who is not responsible for nurturance cannot be a working mother, though an adoptive mother, of course, can be one.

This example shows the following:

A social stereotype (e.g., the housewife-mother) may be defined with respect to only one of the base models of an experiential cluster (e.g., the nurturance model).

Thus, a metonymic model where a subcategory stands for the whole category may be defined relative to only one model in a complex cluster.

A subcategory (e.g., working mother) may be defined in contrast with a stereotype (e.g., the housewife-mother).

When this occurs, it is only the relevant cognitive model (e.g., the nurturance model) that is used as a background for defining the subcategory (e.g., working mother).

Thus, only those mothers for whom nurturance is an issue can be so categorized. Stepmothers and adoptive mothers may also be working mothers, but biological mothers who have given up their children for adoption and surrogate mothers (who have only had a child for someone else) are not working mothers—even though they may happen to be holding down a job.

Such models of stereotypes are important for a theory of conceptual structure in a number of ways. First, as we have seen, they may be used to motivate and define a contrasting subcategory like *working mother*. This is important because, according to the classical theory, such cases should not exist. In the classical theory, social stereotypes, by definition, play no role in defining category structure because they are not part of any necessary and sufficient conditions for category membership! In the classical theory, only necessary and sufficient conditions can have a real cognitive function in defining category membership. For this reason, the classical theory permits no cognitive function at all for social stereotypes. But the fact that the conceptual category *working mother* is defined by contrast with the housewife-mother stereotype indicates that stereotypes do have a role in characterizing concepts.

Second, stereotypes define a normal expectation that is linguistically marked. For example, the word *but* in English is used to mark a situation that is in contrast to some model that serves as a norm. Stereotypic models may serve as such a norm:

NORMAL: She is a mother, but she isn't a housewife.
STRANGE: She is a mother, but she's a housewife.

The latter sentence could only be used if stereotypical mothers were not housewives. Conversely, a category defined in contrast to a stereotype has the opposite properties:

NORMAL: She is a mother, but she has a job.
STRANGE: She is a mother, but she doesn't have a job.

In summary, we have seen two kinds of models for *mother*:

A cluster of converging cognitive models.
A stereotypic model, which is a metonymic model in which the housewife-mother subcategory stands for the category as a whole and serves the purpose of defining cultural expectations.

Both models give rise to prototype effects, but in different ways. Together, they form a structure with a composite prototype: the best example of a mother is a biological mother who is a housewife, principally concerned with nurturance, not working at a paid position, and married to the child's father. This composite prototype imposes what is called a *representativeness structure* on the category: the closer an individual is to the prototype, the more representative a mother she is.

Representativeness structures are linear. They concern nothing but closeness to the prototypical case, and thus they hide most of the richness of structure that exists in the cognitive models that characterize the category. Representativeness structures, though real, are mere shadows of cognitive models.

It is important to bear this in mind, as prototype theory is sometimes thought of as involving only such linear representativeness structures and not cognitive models.

The study of representativeness structures has played an important role in the history of prototype theory—largely in demonstrating that prototypes do exist and in making a bare first approximation to finding out what they are and what properties they have. But a full study of category structure must go well beyond just isolating a prototype and giving a linear ranking of how close nonprototypical cases are. At the very least, it must provide an account of the details of the cognitive models that give rise to the representativeness structure.

Radial Structures

Here are some kinds of mothers:

The central case, where all the models converge. This includes a mother who is and always has been female, and who gave birth to the child, supplied her half of child's genes, nurtured the child, is married to the father, is one generation older than the child, and is the child's legal guardian.
Stepmother: She didn't give birth or supply the genes, but she is currently married to the father.
Adoptive mother: She didn't give birth or supply the genes, but she is the legal guardian and has the obligation to provide nurturance.
Birth mother: This is defined in contrast to *adoptive mother*: given an adoption ICM, the woman who gives birth and puts the child up for adoption is called the *birth mother*.
Natural mother: This used to be the term used to contrast with *adoptive mother*, but it has been given up owing to the unsavory inference that adoptive mothers were, by contrast, "unnatural." This term has been replaced by *birth mother*.
Foster mother: She is being paid by the state to provide nurturance.
Biological mother: She gave birth to the child, but is not raising it, and there is someone else who is and who qualifies to be called a mother of some sort.
Surrogate mother: She has contracted to give birth and that's all. She may or may not have provided the genes, and she is not married to the father and is

not obligated to provide nurturance. Also, she has contractually given up the right to be legal guardian.

Unwed mother: She is not married to the father at the time of the birth.

Genetic mother: This is a term I have seen used for a woman who supplies an egg to be planted into someone else's womb, and has nothing else whatever to do with the child. It has not yet to my knowledge become conventional.

These subcategories of mother are all understood as deviations from the central case. But not all possible variations on the central case exist as categories. There is no category of mothers who are legal guardians but do not personally supply nurturance, hiring someone else to do it. There is no category of transsexuals who gave birth but have since had a sex-change operation. Moreover, some of the above categories are products of the twentieth century, and simply did not exist earlier: The point is that the central case does not productively generate all of these subcategories. Instead, the subcategories are defined by convention as variations on the central case. There is no general rule for generating kinds of mothers. They are culturally defined and have to be learned. They are by no means the same in all cultures. In the Trobriands, a woman who gives birth often gives the child to an old woman to raise. In traditional Japanese society, it was common for a woman to give her child to her sister to raise. Both of these are cases of kinds of mothers of which we have no exact equivalent.

The category of *mother* in this culture has what we will call a *radial structure*. A radial structure is one where there is a central case and conventionalized variations on it that cannot be predicted by general rules. Categories that are generated by central cases plus general principles—say, the natural numbers—are not radial structures, as we are defining the term. We are limiting radial structures only to cases where the variations are conventionalized and have to be learned. We are also ruling out cases where the central case is just more general than the noncentral case—that is, where the noncentral cases just have more properties than the central case, but no different ones. Radial structures are extremely common, and we will discuss them in very great detail below.

Some Kinds of Metonymic Models

So far, we have looked at one case of a metonymic model: the housewife-mother stereotype. It defines a subcategory that is used to stand for the entire category of mothers in defining social expectations. Any time a subcategory (or an individual member of a category) is used for some purpose to stand for the category as a whole, it is a potential source of prototype effects. For this reason, metonymic models play an important role in prototype theory. Let us look at them a bit more closely.

In general, a metonymic model has the following characteristics:

There is a "target" concept A to be understood for some purpose in some context.

There is a conceptual structure containing both A and another concept B.

B is either part of A, or is closely associated with it in that conceptual structure. Typically, a choice of B will uniquely determine A, within that conceptual structure.

Compared to A, B is either easier to understand, easier to remember, easier to recognize, or more immediately useful for the given purpose in the given context.

A metonymic model is a model of how A and B are related in a conceptual structure; the relationship is specified by a function from B to A.

When such a conventional metonymic model exists as part of a conceptual system, B may be used to stand, metonymically, for A. If A is a category, the result is a metonymic model of the category, and prototype effects commonly arise.

Most metonymic models are, in fact, *not* models of categories; they are models of individuals. Lakoff and Johnson (1980, Ch. 8) have shown that there are many types of metonymic models for individuals. There are also many types of metonymic models for categories; each type is a different *kind* of source for prototype effects. There are as many types of metonymic prototype effects as there are kinds of metonymic models for categories. Following are some of the types I have come across so far.

Social Stereotypes

As we saw in the case of the housewife-mother, social stereotypes can be used to stand for a category as a whole. Social stereotypes are usually conscious and are often the subject of public discussion. They are subject to change over time, and they may become public issues. Because they define cultural expectations, they are used in reasoning and especially in what is called "jumping to conclusions." However, they are usually recognized as not being accurate, and their use in reasoning may be overtly challenged.

Here are some examples of contemporary American stereotypes:

> The stereotypical politician is conniving, egotistical, and dishonest.
> The stereotypical bachelor is macho, dates a lot of different women, is interested in sexual conquest, hangs out in singles' bars, etc.
> The stereotypical Japanese is industrious, polite, and clever.

Since social stereotypes are commonly used to characterize cultural expectations, they tend to be exploited in advertising and in most forms of popular entertainment.

Incidentally, the *bachelor* stereotype provides a second level of prototype effects in addition to those that are a consequence of the *bachelor* ICM not fitting certain situations. Let us take a situation where the background conditions of the *bachelor* ICM do fit, a situation in which there are no cases that the concept was not defined to deal with: no priests, no gays, no Moslems with only three wives, no Tarzans. In these situations, there can still be prototype effects, but the effects will arise *within the clear boundaries of the category*. In such cases, the social stereotype of a *bachelor* will characterize the best examples, and those undisputed bachelors who do not fit the social stereotype will be less good examples.

A bachelor who is macho, promiscuous, and nondomestic fits the stereotype of *bachelor* better than, say, a nonmacho man who likes to take care of children, prefers stable relationships with one person, is not interested in sexual conquest, loves housework and does it well, and so on. Stereotypes are used in certain situations to define expectations, make judgments, and draw inferences. Thus, for example, if all one knew about someone was that he was a bachelor, one might be surprised to find that he loves housework and does it well, likes to care for children, and so on. Even though the *bachelor* ICM is defined within the classical theory and has clear boundaries in situations that conform to the background assumptions, prototype effects may still occur *internal* to the category boundaries because of the presence of a social stereotype.

Incidentally, we often have names for stereotypes, for example, Uncle Tom, Jewish Princess, stud. These are categories that function as stereotypes for other categories.

Typical Examples

Examples of typical cases are as follows:

> Robins and sparrows are typical birds.
> Apples and oranges are typical fruits.
> Saws and hammers are typical tools.

Social stereotypes are usually conscious and subject to public discussion—and may even have names. However, the use of typical category members is usually unconscious and automatic. Typical examples are not the subject of public discussion, and they seem not to change noticeably during a person's lifetime. They are not used to define cultural expectations. They are used in reasoning, as Rips (1975) showed, in the case where subjects inferred that if the robins on a certain island got a disease, then the ducks would, but not the converse. Such examples are common. It is normal for us to make inferences from typical to nontypical examples. If a typical man has hair on his head, we infer that atypical men (all other things being equal) will have hair on their heads. Moreover, a man may be considered atypical by virtue of not having hair on his head. There is nothing mysterious about this. An enormous amount of our knowledge about categories of things is organized in terms of typical cases. We constantly draw inferences on the basis of that kind of knowledge. We do it so regularly and automatically that we are rarely aware that we are doing it.

Reasoning on the basis of typical cases is a major aspect of human reason. Our vast knowledge of typical cases leads to prototype effects. The reason is that there is an asymmetry between typical and nontypical cases. Knowledge about typical cases is generalized to nontypical cases, but not conversely.

Ideals

Many categories are understood in terms of abstract ideal cases—which may be neither typical nor stereotypical. For example:

> The ideal husband: a good provider, faithful, strong, respected, attractive.
> The stereotypical husband: bumbling, dull, pot-bellied, ...

Naomi Quinn (personal communication) has observed, based on extensive research on American conceptions of marriage, that there are many kinds of ideal models for a marriage: *successful* marriages, *good* marriages, *strong* marriages, and so on. *Successful* marriages are those where the goals of the spouses are fulfilled. *Good* marriages are those where both partners find the marriage beneficial. *Strong* marriages are those likely to last. Such types of ideals seem to be of great importance in culturally significant categories—categories where making judgments of quality and making plans are important.

A lot of cultural knowledge is organized in terms of ideals. We have cultural knowledge about ideal homes, ideal families, ideal mates, ideal jobs, ideal bosses, ideal workers, and so on. Cultural knowledge about ideals leads to prototype effects. There is an asymmetry between ideal and nonideal cases: we make judgments of quality and set goals for the future in terms of ideal cases, rather than nonideal cases. This asymmetry is a consequence of a pattern of inference that we use with ideals. Ideals are assumed to have all the good qualities that nonideal cases have, but not conversely.

Paragons

We also comprehend categories in terms of individual members who represent either an ideal or its opposite. Thus, we have institutions like the ten-best and ten-worst lists, the Halls of Fame, Academy Awards, and the Guinness book of World Records. We have baseball paragons: Babe Ruth, Willie Mays, Sandy Koufax. Paragons are made use of in constructions in the language: *a regular Babe Ruth, another Willie Mays, the Cadillac of vacuum cleaners,* and so on. Scientific paradigms are also characterized by paragons. Thus, for example, The Michaelson-Morley Experiment is the paragon of physics experiments—and is used by many people to comprehend what a great experiment in physics is.

A great many of our actions have to do with paragons. We try to emulate them. We are interested in the life stories of great men and women. We use paragons as models to base our actions on. We have a great deal of interest in experiencing paragons: we watch All-Star games, go to Academy Award-winning movies, travel to the Seven Wonders of the World, and seek to own the paragons of consumer goods. We are constantly acquiring knowledge of paragons, and regularly base our actions on that knowledge. Incidentally, we also commonly base inferences on a folk theory that people who are paragons in some domain are paragons *as people*. Thus, people are shocked to find great baseball players or powerful politicians engaging in normal rotten human behavior.

Generators

There are cases where the members of a category are defined, or "generated," by the central members plus some general rules. The natural numbers are perhaps the best-known example. The natural numbers are, for most people, characterized by the integers between zero and nine, plus addition and multiplication tables and rules of arithmetic. The single-digit numbers are central members of the category *natural number*; they generate the entire category, given general arithmetic principles. In our system of numerical representation, single-digit numbers are employed in comprehending natural numbers in general. Any natural number can be written as a sequence of single-digit numbers. The properties of large numbers are understood in terms of the properties of smaller numbers, and ultimately in terms of the properties of single-digit numbers.

The single-digit numbers, together with addition and multiplication tables and rules of arithmetic, constitute a model that both generates the natural numbers and is metonymic in our sense: the category as a whole is comprehended in terms of a small subcategory.

The natural numbers, in addition, have other models that subdivide the numbers according to certain properties—odd and even, prime and nonprime, and so on. Such models are not metonymic. They work by classical Aristotelian principles. But they only define *subcategories* of the natural numbers. The category as a whole is defined metonymically and generatively by the single-digit numbers plus rules of arithmetic.

To make matters more complicated, other kinds of numbers are also defined by metonymic generative models: the rationals, the reals, the imaginaries, the transfinite cardinals, and so on. Thus rational numbers are understood as ratios of natural numbers, and real numbers are understood as infinite sequences of natural numbers. In other words, the rationals and the reals are understood metonymically in terms of the natural numbers—a subcategory used to generate the larger categories.

Submodels

Another way to comprehend a category is via a submodel. Take the category of natural numbers again. The most common submodel used is the subcategory of powers of ten: ten, a hundred, a thousand, and so on. We use this submodel to comprehend the relative size of numbers. The members of such a submodel are among what Rosch refers to as *Cognitive Reference Points*, which have a special place in reasoning, especially in making approximations and estimating size. Cognitive reference points within a submodel show prototype effects of the following sort: Subjects will judge statements like *98 is approximately 100* as being true more readily than statements like *100 is approximately 98*.

Some submodels have a biological basis: the primary colors, the basic emotions, etc. Others are culturally stipulated, for example, the Seven Deadly Sins.

Salient Examples

It is common for people to use familiar, memorable, or otherwise salient examples to comprehend categories. For example, if your best friend is a vegetarian and you don't know any others well, you will tend to generalize from your friend to other vegetarians. After a widely publicized DC-10 crash in Chicago, many people refused to fly DC-10s, choosing other types of planes despite the fact that they had overall worse safety records than DC-10s. Such people used the salient example of the DC-10 that crashed to stand metonymically for the entire category of DC-10s with respect to safety judgments.

Similarly, California earthquakes are salient examples of natural disasters. A. Tversky and Kahneman (1983) demonstrated that people use such salient examples in making probability judgments about the category of natural disasters. The reasoning used is what Tversky and Kahneman refer to as the *conjunction fallacy*. We know from probability theory that the probability of two events, A and B, occurring is always less than the probability of just one of the events, say B. Thus the probability of coins A and B both coming down heads is less than the probability of just B coming down heads.

The theory of probability is defined for events A and B, which are not related to one another. Cognitive models may, however, relate events in our minds that are unrelated in the external world. What Tversky and Kahneman found was that when we have a salient cognitive model relating events A and B, it affects our judgments of the probability of A and B both occurring.

The following is a typical example of the kind Tversky and Kahneman used. One group of subjects was asked to rate the probability of

> A massive flood somewhere in North America in 1983, in which more than 1000 people drown.

A second group was asked to rate the probability of

> An earthquake in California sometime in 1983, causing a flood in which more than 1000 people drown.

The estimates of the conjunction of earthquake and flood were considerably higher than the estimates of the flood. Tversky and Kahneman conclude:

> The attempts to predict the uncertain future, like the attempts to reconstruct the uncertain past, which is the domain of history and criminal law, are commonly based on the construction of hypothetical scenarios, These scenarios, or "best guesses," tend to be specific, coherent, and representative of our mental model of the relevant worlds.

In short, a cognitive model may function to allow a salient example to stand metonymically for a whole category. In such cases, our probability judgments about the category are affected.

To summarize, we have seen the following kinds of metonymic models: social stereotypes, typical examples, ideal cases, paragons, generators, submodels, and salient examples. They have a cognitive status, that is, they are used in reasoning. And they all yield prototype effects of some sort.

Radial Categories

Radial categories are perhaps the most interesting source of prototype effects. Radial categories have the following properties:

1. There can be no single cognitive model that represents the entire category.
2. There is a central submodel characterizing a central subcategory.
3. Representations for noncentral subcategories cannot be predicted either by rule or by a general principle such as similarity.
4. There are nonarbitrary *links* between the central and noncentral subcategories. These links are other cognitive models existing independently in the conceptual system.
5. Though the noncentral subcategories cannot be predicted from the central subcategory, they are *motivated* by the central subcategory plus other, independently existing cognitive models.
6. Motivated subcategories can be learned, remembered, and used more efficiently than arbitrary, unmotivated subcategories.

Elsewhere I have given a number of very detailed examples of radial categories (Lakoff 1986). Although there is no room here to go through all those examples in sufficiently convincing detail, I will provide one relatively short example, using data provided by Pamela Downing (Downing 1984) and Haruo Aoki (personal communication).

Japanese hon

The Japanese classifier, *hon*, in its most common use, classifies long, thin, rigid objects: sticks, canes, pencils, candles, trees, and so on. Not surprisingly, it can be used to classify dead snakes and dried fish, both of which are long and rigid. But *hon* can be extended to what are presumably less representative cases:

> martial arts contests, with staffs or swords (which are long and rigid)
> hits (and sometimes pitches) in baseball (straight trajectories, formed by the forceful motion of a solid object, associated with baseball bat, which is long, thin, and rigid)
> shots in basketball, serves in volleyball, and rallies in Ping-Pong
> judo matches (a martial arts contest, but without a staff or sword)
> a contest between a zen master and student, in which each attempts to stump the other with zen koans
> rolls of tape (which can be unrolled into something long and thin)
> telephone calls (which come over wires and which are instances of the CONDUIT metaphor as described by Reddy 1979 and Lakoff and Johnson 1980)
> radio and television programs (like telephone calls, but without the wires)
> letters (another instance of communication: moreover, in traditional Japan, letters were scrolls and hence sticklike)
> movies (like radio and television; moreover they come in reels like rolls of tape)
> medical injections (done with a needle, which is long, thin, and rigid)

These cases, though not predictable, are nonetheless not arbitrary. They do not all have something in common with long, thin rigid objects, but it *makes sense* that they might be classified in the same way. Let us ask exactly what kind of sense it makes.

Let us begin with martial arts contests using staffs or swords. Staffs and swords are long, thin, rigid objects, which are classified by *hon*. They are also the principal functional objects in these matches. A win in such a match can also be classified by *hon*. That is, the principal goal in this domain of experience is in the same category as the principal functional object.

Baseball bats are central members of the *hon* category. They are one of the two most salient functional objects in the game, the other being the ball. Baseball is centered on a contest between the pitcher and the batter. The batter's principal goal is to get a hit. When a baseball is hit solidly, it forms a trajectory—that is, it traces a long, thin path along which a solid object travels quickly and with force. The image traced by the path of the ball is a *hon* image—long and thin.

The extension of the *hon* category from bats to hits is another case of an extension from a principal functional object to a principal goal. It is also an extension from one principal functional object with a *hon* shape to a *hon*-shaped path formed by the other principal functional object. Incidentally, in the small amount of research done on *hon* to date, it appears that, whereas base hits and home runs are categorized with *hon*, foul balls, pop flies, ground balls, and bunts appear not to be. This is not surprising because these are not principal goals of hitting, nor do their trajectories form a *hon* shape.

The relationship between the shape of the hat and the trajectory formed by the batted ball—between a long, thin thing and a trajectory—is a common relationship between image-schemas that forms the basis for the extension of a category from a central to a noncentral case. Let us consider three examples from English.

The man ran into the woods.
The road ran into the woods.

In the first case, *run* is used for a case where there is a (long, thin) trajectory. In the second case, *run* is used for a long, thin object, a road.

The bird flew over the yard.
The telephone line stretched over the yard.

In the first case, *over* is used for a (long, thin) trajectory. In the second case, *over* is used for a long, thin object, a telephone line.

The rocket shot up.
The lamp was standing up.

In the first case, *up* is used for a trajectory. In the second case, *up* is used for a long, thin object, a standing lamp.

Such relationships are common and suggest that there exists what might be called an *image-schema transformation* of the following sort:

TRAJECTORY SCHEMA ↔ LONG, THIN OBJECT SCHEMA

This image-schema transformation is one of the many kinds of cognitive relationships that can form a basis for the extension of a category.

Some speakers of Japanese extend the *hon* category to baseball pitches, as well as hits—again on the basis of such an image-schema relationship within the same domain of experience. Some speakers extend *hon* to pitches using both the trajectory and the contest-perspective, in which the hitter and pitcher are engaged in a contest. These speakers use *hon* only for pitches seen from the point of view of the hitter. There are also speakers who classify pitches with *hon* only if they achieve the principal goal of pitching. Since getting strikes is the principal goal of pitching, such speakers can classify strikes, but not balls, with *hon*. No speakers have been found who use *hon* to classify balls but not strikes. Similarly, no speakers have been found who classify bunts and foul balls with *hon*, but not home runs and base hits.

There are similar motivations behind the extensions of *hon* to other concepts in sports. Thus, *hon* can classify shots and free throws in basketball, but not passes. And it can classify serves in volleyball and rallies in Ping-Pong. These are cases where there is both a trajectory and a possibility of scoring (achieving a principal goal).

There are several morals to be drawn from these examples:

1. What are taken to be the central cases for the application of *hon* appear to be concrete basic-level objects: sticks, pencils, bamboo staffs, baseball bats, etc. The direction of extension appears to go from concrete basic-level objects to other things, like hits and pitches.

2. A theory of motivations for the extension of a category is required. Among the things we need in such a theory are image-schema transformations and conceptual metonymies—cases where a principal object like a staff or bat can stand for a principal goal like a win or hit.

3. Hits in baseball and long, thin rigid objects do not have anything objective in common. The relationship between the bat and the hit is given by an image-schema transformation and a metonymy. Hence the classical theory, which requires that categorization be based on common properties, is inadequate.

4. The application of *hon* to hits in baseball may make sense, but it is not predictable. It is a matter of convention—not an arbitrary convention, but a *motivated* convention. Thus, the traditional view that everything must be either predictable or arbitrary is inadequate here. There is a third choice: motivation. In this case, the independently needed image-schema transformation and the object-for-goal metonymy provide the motivation.

Ideally, each instance of the use of a classifier outside the central sense should have a motivation. The motivation cannot be ad hoc—one cannot make up a metonymy or image-schema just to handle that case. It must be justified on the basis of other cases. This imposes a criterion of adequacy on the analysis of classifier languages.

Some investigators have suggested that such a criterion of adequacy is too strong; they have claimed that some classifications simply are arbitrary and that no non–ad hoc motivation exists. That is an empirical question, and the facts are by no means all in. But arbitrariness is a last resort. Even if there are some completely unmotivated cases, one can still apply a slightly weakened criterion of adequacy. Find out which extensions "make sense" to speakers and which extensions seem "senseless," and account for those that make sense. Each sensible extension of a category needs to be independently motivated. No analysis of a classifier system is complete until this is done.

So far, we have seen that metonymies and image-schema transformations can provide motivation for the extension of a category. Another important kind of motivation comes from conventional mental images. Take the example of a roll of tape, which can be classified by *hon*. We know what rolls of tape look like, both when they are rolled up and when they are being unrolled. That is, we have conventional mental images of tape, both when it is in storage form and when it is being put to use. We also know that we unroll tape when we are about to use it, and that the tape is functional when it is unrolled. A conventional image of tape being unrolled has two parts: the rolled part and the unrolled, functional part. The image of the unrolled, functional part fits the long, thin object image-schema associated with the central sense of *hon*. The image of the nonfunctional rolled part does not fit the central *hon* image-schema. Metonymy is involved here; the functional part of the conventional image is standing for the whole image, for the sake of categorization. The functional part fits the *hon* schema. This is, presumably, the motivation for the use of *hon* to classify rolls of tape. Again, we cannot predict the use of *hon* for rolls of tape; but we can do something that is extremely important. We can show why it makes sense. Making sense of categorization is no small matter. And doing so in a manner that shows in detail how basic cognitive mechanisms apply is anything but trivial. If the cognitive aspects of categorization are to be understood, it will require attention to detail at this level. For example, *hon* can be used to classify medical injections. Why does this make sense?

Medical injections are another case where the principal functional object (the needle) is long and thin; the needles can be classified with *hon* and, by metonymy, so can the injections.

So far we have seen how image-schema transformations, conventional mental images, and metonymy all enter into categorization by a classifier. Let us turn to a case that involves all of these plus metaphor. Recall that *hon* can be used to classify telephone calls. The conventional mental image of engaging in a telephone call involves using the most functional part of the telephone—the receiver, which is a long, thin, rigid object and fits the central image-schema for *hon*. The other principal conventional image related to telephone calls involves telephone wires. These are understood as playing a principal functional role in telephonic communication. These fit the long, thin object image-schema. They also fit the CONDUIT of the CONDUIT metaphor—the principal metaphor for communication. In short, there are two related but different motivations for the use of *hon* for telephone calls. That is, there are two ways in which this use of *hon* fits the conceptual system, and, where motivation is concerned, the more kinds of motivation, the better. That is, it is not a matter of finding which is right; both can be right simultaneously.

So far, we have seen that extended senses of *hon* can be based on the central sense of *hon*. But extended senses may themselves serve as the basis for further extensions via category chaining. Recall that letters are classified with *hon*. There are a number of considerations that motivate such a categorization. First, letters were originally in the form of scrolls, often wound around long, thin, wooden cylinders. They have been categorized with *hon* ever since, and that image remains very much alive in Japanese culture through paintings and the tradition of calligraphy. Second, the conventional image of writing a letter involves the use of a pen, which plays a principal functional role, and is also a long, thin object. Third, letters are a form of communication, and therefore an instance of the CONDUIT metaphor. These diverse motivations allow *hon* with all these senses to fit the ecology of the Japanese classifier system.

Letters and telephone calls are intermediate steps in a chain. Radio and television programs are also classified with *hon*. They are forms of communication at a distance, like letter-writing and telephone communication. They too are motivated by the CONDUIT metaphor for communication. Given that letters and telephone calls are classified by *hon*, radio and television programs constitute a well-motivated extension. Movies are also classified by *hon*. They are also instances of communication at a distance; in addition, one of the principal conventional images associated with movies is the movie reel, which looks like a spool of tape, which is classified with *hon*.

The phenomenon of category-chaining shows very clearly that the classical account of categorization is inadequate. Sticks and television programs are both in the *hon* category, but they share no relevant common properties. They are categorized in the same way by virtue of the chain structure of the *hon* category.

Finally, let us turn our attention to judo matches and contests between Zen masters and students. Judo matches are in the same domain of experience as martial arts contests with staffs or swords. A win in judo match can also be classified as a *hon*. Similarly, Zen contests are, in Japanese culture, in the same experiential domain as martial arts contests, and a win there also can be classified as a *hon*.

Incidentally, the noncentral cases of the *hon* category vary in some cases from speaker to speaker. Thus some speakers do not include baseball pitches and some do not include wins in Zen contests. But to my knowledge, every speaker of Japanese includes the central members—the candles, staffs, baseball bats, and so on. Moreover, many of the extensions have become conventionalized for speakers in general: letters, telephone conversations, home runs, spools of thread. The variation just displayed involves chaining that has not yet stabilized but which shows the same principles at work as in the stable conventionalized extensions.

Categories of Mind, or Mere Words

A possible objection to the kind of analyses we have been discussing is that classifiers are mere linguistic devices and do not reflect conceptual structure. That is, one might object that, say, the things categorized by *hon* in Japanese do not form a single conceptual category. Thus, one might suggest that the analysis of *hon* may show something about rules of language, but that it shows nothing about our conceptual system.

Let us, for the sake of argument, consider such a suggestion. Whatever their precise cognitive status is, rules of language are some part or other of our cognitive apparatus. Just what would such "rules of language" involve? In particular, they would involve all the things we discussed above in the analysis of *hon*:

Central and peripheral members
Basic-level objects at the center
Conventional mental images
Knowledge about conventional mental images
Image-schema transformations
Metonymy applied to mental imagery
Metonymy applied to domains of experience
Metaphors (which map domains into other domains)

These mechanisms are needed, no matter whether one calls them linguistic or not. Moreover, they appear to be the kinds of things that one would tend to call conceptual—mental images and image transformations do not appear to be merely linguistic. Moreover, linguistic categories can be used in nonlinguistic tasks, as Kay and Kempton (1984) have demonstrated. But whether they are used in nonlinguistic tasks or not, linguistic categories *are* categories—and they are part of our overall cognitive apparatus. Whether one wants to dignify them with the term "conceptual" or not, linguistic categories are categories within our cognitive system and a study of *all* categories within our cognitive system will have to include them.

What Is Prototype Theory?

From the point of view of a theory of cognitive models, prototype theory is a theory of how prototype effects arise. The claim implicit in the theory of cognitive models is that *prototype effects are a consequence of conceptual structure*. In some cases, they arise directly: when cognitive models contain scales, for example, a scale of wealth for the concept *rich*. They may also arise directly as a consequence of the radial structure of a category. On the other hand, they may arise indirectly, as in the case of metonymic and classical models that are idealized (cf. the *bachelor* example). All of these are cases where conceptual structure results in prototype effects.

The Core + Identification Procedure Proposal

Within recent years there has been a reactionary movement on the part of certain cognitive psychologists to return to the classical theory of categorization. The principal works are papers by Osherson and Smith (1981) and Armstrong, Gleitman, and Gleitman (1983). These papers purport to present arguments against prototype theory. Instead, they really present arguments—correct arguments—against two clearly incorrect interpretations of prototype effects: the Effects = Structure and Prototype = Representation interpretations.

These papers claim that prototype effects have nothing whatever to do with conceptual structure. Instead, they claim that all such effects result from procedures for *identifying* category members. They claim that the classical theory of categories can be kept if such procedures are postulated. Both papers make the following assumptions:

> The classical theory is workable for all phenomena having to do with reasoning.
> Prototype phenomena have nothing to do with reasoning.
> Prototype effects result only from identification procedures and not from anything in conceptual structure.

Before we turn to examining these papers in detail, it would be worthwhile to recall how the core versus identification procedure idea came into cognitive psychology. Oddly enough, the source was a paper of mine.

A bit of history is in order. In my 1972 paper, "Hedges," I began by taking for granted the Effects = Structure Interpretation, and I observed that Zadeh's fuzzy-set theory could represent degrees of category membership. Later in the paper, I observed that the Effects = Structure Interpretation was inadequate to account for hedges like *strictly speaking, loosely speaking, technically,* and *regular*. To account for the use of *regular* one must distinguish *definitional* properties from *characteristic but incidental* properties. This corresponds to the semantics-pragmatics distinction in the objectivist paradigm, the distinction between what the word "really means" and encyclopedic knowledge that you happen to have about the things the word refers to.

However, my observation that the distinction is necessary was not in the service of supporting the semantics-pragmatics distinction; my purpose was to provide a counterexample. Here is the relevant passage (Lakoff 1972:197–198):

> But hedges do not merely reveal distinctions of degree of category membership. They can also reveal a great deal more about meaning. Consider (6).
>
> (6) a. Esther Williams is a fish.
>   b. Esther Williams is a regular fish.
>
> (6a) is false, since Esther Williams is a human being, not a fish. (6b), on the other hand, would seem to be true, since it says that Esther Williams swims well and is at home in water. Note that (6b) does not assert that Esther Williams has gills, scales, fins, a tail, etc. In fact, (6b) presupposes that Esther Williams is not literally a fish and asserts that she has certain other characteristic properties of a fish. Bolinger (1972) has suggested that *regular* picks out certain "metaphorical" properties. We can see what this means in an example like (7).
>
> (7) a. John is a bachelor.
>   b. John is a regular bachelor.
>
> (7b) would not be said of a bachelor. It might be said of a married man who acts like a bachelor—dates a lot, feels unbound by marital responsibilities, etc. In short, *regular* seems to assert the connotations of "bachelor," while presupposing the negation of the literal meaning.

Edward Smith (personal communication) has remarked that this passage started him on a line of research that he has pursued ever since. What interested him was the distinction between definitional and incidental properties. The passage had provided counterevidence to the objectivist view of his distinction, which *absolutely requires* that "semantics" be kept independent of "pragmatics"; that is, definitional properties are completely independent of incidental properties. The use of the hedge *regular* violates this condition, since it makes use of incidental properties in *semantics*. Kay (1979, see also 1983) has argued that the definitional-incidental distinction is not objectively correct, but rather part of our folk theory of language. The hedge *regular* makes use of this folk theory. If Kay's argument is correct, then the semantics-pragmatics and definitional-incidental distinctions are invalidated in even a deeper way than I first suggested.

Smith seems not to have been aware that this example was in conflict with the theory of semantics in which the classical theory of categorization is embedded. He drew from the distinction a way to keep the classical theory of categories, while still accounting for prototype effects. His idea was that the definitional properties fit the classical theory and that the incidental properties gave rise to prototype effects. This idea is developed in Osherson and Smith's classic 1981 paper. That paper claims that the definitional properties characterize the conceptual "core" of a category, that which permits reasoning; incidental properties, on the other hand, have nothing to do with reasoning, but are used only to *identify* category members. Prototype effects, they claim, have to do with identification and not with reason or conceptual structure.

I find it ironic that a passage providing counterevidence to the classical view should provide the impetus for a defense of that view.

Osherson and Smith

Osherson and Smith begin their paper with the following definition of prototype theory:

> Prototype theory construes membership in a concept's extension as graded, determined by similarity to the concept's "best" exemplar (or by some other measure of central tendency).

Here Osherson and Smith are assuming both the Effects = Structure Interpretation and the Prototype = Representation Interpretation. Their paper is an argument against these interpretations. Osherson and Smith also make additional assumptions:

> They assume that fuzzy-set theory in the earliest of its many versions (Zadeh 1965) is the appropriate way of modeling the Effects = Structure Interpretation. They assume *atomism*, that is, that the meaning of the whole is a regular compositional function of the meaning of its parts. As a consequence, gestalt effects in semantics (cf. Lakoff 1977) are eliminated as a possibility.
> They assume *objectivist semantics*, that is, that meaning is based on truth.
> They assume that all noun modifiers are to be treated via conjunction. This is commonly done in objectivist semantics, though as we will see it is grossly inadequate.

In the light of the previous discussion, we can see that these assumptions are not well founded. As we have pointed out, almost all prototype and basic-level effects are in-consistent with objectivist semantics. However, the Effects = Structure Interpretation is not inconsistent with objectivist semantics. The reason is that it treats all categories as graded categories, and as we have seen, graded categorization is consistent with most of the objectivist assumptions.

If we grant all of Osherson and Smith's assumptions, their argument follows. The examples they give are well worth considering. Like classical set theory, classical fuzzy-set theory has only three ways of forming complex categories: intersection, union, and complementation. Osherson and Smith take each of these and show that they lead to incorrect results. Their first counterexample involves three drawings:

> a. A line drawing of a normally shaped apple with stripes superimposed on the apple.
> b. A line drawing of a normally shaped apple.
> c. A line drawing of an abnormally shaped apple with only a few stripes.

They now consider three concepts: *apple*, *striped*, and *striped apple*. They correctly observe that within classical fuzzy-set theory there is only one way to derive the complex category *striped apple* from the categories *apple* and *striped*, namely, by inter-section of fuzzy sets—which is defined by taking the minimum of the membership values in the two-component fuzzy sets. They assume the following:

> (a) is a good example of a striped apple.
> (a) is not a good example of an apple, since apples generally aren't striped.
> (a) is not a good example of a striped thing, since apples are not among the things that are typically striped.

It follows that:

> (a) will have a high value in the category *striped apple*.
> (a) will have a low value in the category *apple*.
> (a) a will have a low value in the category *striped*.

But since the minimum of two low values is a low value, it should follow from fuzzy-set theory that (a) has a low value in the category *striped apple*. Thus fuzzy-set theory makes an incorrect prediction. It predicts that an excellent example of a striped apple will have a low value in that category because it has low values in the component categories *apple* and *striped*.

There is a general moral here:

GOOD EXAMPLES OF COMPLEX CATEGORIES ARE OFTEN BAD EXAMPLES OF COMPONENT CATEGORIES.

Osherson and Smith cite a similar example: *pet fish*. A guppy might be a good example of a pet fish, but a bad example of a pet and a bad example of a fish. Set intersection in classical fuzzy-set theory will give incorrect results in such cases.

Osherson and Smith also use some of what might be called "logicians' examples":

P AND NOT P: an apple that is not an apple

P OR NOT P: a fruit that either is, or is not, an apple

They assume the correctness of the usual logician's intuitions about such cases: There is no apple that is not an apple, and so the first category should have no members to any degree; and all fruits either are or are not apples, so the second category should contain all fruits as full-fledged members. Such intuitions have been disputed: a carved wooden apple might be considered an apple that is not an apple. And a cross between a pear and an apple might be considered a bad example of a fruit that clearly either is, or is not, an apple. Osherson and Smith do not consider such possibilities. They correctly argue that classical fuzzy-set theory cannot account for the usual logician's intuitions in such cases.

The argument goes like this. Take an apple that is not a representative example of an apple, say a crabapple. According to classical fuzzy-set theory, this would have a value in the category *apple* somewhere in between zero and 1. Call the value c. Its value in the category *not an apple* would then be $1 - c$, according to the definition of set complementation in fuzzy-set theory. If c is in between zero and 1, $1 - c$ will also be between zero and 1. And both the maximum and the minimum of c and $1 - c$ will be in between zero and 1. Thus, according to fuzzy-set theory, a nonrepresentative apple, like a crabapple, would have a value greater than zero in the category *an apple that is not an apple*, and it would have a value less than 1 in the category *a fruit that either is, or is not, an apple*. This is inconsistent with the intuitions assumed to be correct by Osherson and Smith. If we accept their intuitions, their argument against fuzzy-set theory is correct.

Osherson and Smith's last major argument depends on their assumption of the Prototype = Representation Interpretation, namely, that in prototype theory, degree of membership is determined by degree of similarity to a prototypical member. They correctly produce a counterexample to this interpretation. It is based on the following use of the Prototype = Representation Interpretation. Consider grizzly bears and squirrels. Since one can find some (possibly small) similarities between grizzly bears and squirrels, it follows on the Prototype = Representation Interpretation that squirrels are members of the category *grizzly bear* to some degree greater than zero. Now consider the statement:

All grizzly bears are inhabitants of North America.

Suppose someone were to find a squirrel on Mars. Because that squirrel is a member of the category *grizzly bear* to some extent, and because Mars is far from North America, the discovery of a squirrel on Mars would serve as disconfirmation of the claim that all grizzly bears are inhabitants of North America. But this is ridiculous. The existence of squirrels on Mars should have nothing to do with the truth or falsity of that statement. Given Osherson and Smith's assumptions, this is indeed a counterexample to the Prototype = Representation Interpretation of prototype effects.

What Osherson and Smith have correctly shown is that, given all their assumptions, the Effects = Structure and Prototype = Representation Interpretations are incorrect. Of course, each one of their assumptions is questionable. One need not use the classical version of fuzzy-set theory to mathematicize these interpretations. The assumption that noun modifiers work by conjunction is grossly incorrect. And objectivist semantics and atomism are, as we have seen above, inadequate to handle the kinds of prototype phenomena that we have discussed. But, most importantly, the Effects = Structure and Prototype = Representation Interpretations are wildly inaccurate ways of understanding prototype and basic-level effects. To show that they are wrong is to show virtually nothing about any reasonable version of prototype theory. In addition, their argument shows nothing whatever about the Cognitive Models Interpretation that we are suggesting. But Osherson and Smith seem unaware of all this, and conclude (p. 54) that they have provided arguments against *all* versions of prototype theory.

Osherson and Smith then endorse a proposal reminiscent of that suggested by Miller and Johnson-Laird (1976) for saving the classical theory while accounting for the experimental results of prototype theory. What they adopt is a hybrid theory: each concept has a *core* and an *identification procedure*. The core works according to the traditional theory; the identification procedure accounts for the prototype effects that show up in experiments. As they put it:

> The core is concerned with those aspects of a concept that explicate its relation to other concepts, and to thoughts, while the identification procedure specifies the kind of information used to make rapid decisions about membership.... We can illustrate this with the concept *woman*. Its core might contain information about the presence of a reproductive system, while its identification procedures might contain information about body shape, hair length, and voice pitch.

The core, in other words, would be where the real work of the mind—thought—is done. The identification procedure would link the mind to the senses, but not do any real conceptual work. As they say,

> Given this distinction it is possible that some traditional theory of concepts correctly characterizes the core, whereas prototype theory characterizes an important identification procedure. This would explain why prototype theory does well in explicating the real-time process of determining category membership (a job for identification procedures), but fares badly in explicating conceptual combination and the truth conditions of thoughts (a job for concept cores).

This hybrid theory assumes that traditional theories actually work for complex concepts. The fact is that this is one of the most notorious weaknesses of traditional theories. The only traditional theories in existence are based on classical set theory. Such theories permit set-theoretical intersection, union, and complement operations, and occasionally a small number of additional operations. But on the whole they do very badly at accounting for complex categorization. We can see the problems best by looking first at the classical theory, without any additional operations. The traditional set-theoretical treatment of adjective-noun phrases is via set intersection. That is the only option the traditional theory makes available. So, in the classical theory, the complex concept *striped apple* would denote the intersection of the set of striped things and the set of apples.

The literature on linguistic semantics is replete with examples where simple set intersection will not work. Perhaps we should start with some that Osherson and Smith themselves mention (1981:43, fn 8; 50, fn 12).

> small galaxy—not the intersection of the set of small things and the set of galaxies
> good thief—not the intersection of the set of good things and the set of thieves
> imitation brass—not the intersection of the set of imitations and the set of brass things

Other classic examples abound:

> electrical engineer—not the intersection of the set of electrical things and the set of engineers
>
> mere child—not the intersection of the set of mere things and the set of children
>
> red hair—because the color is not focal red, it is not merely the intersection of the set of red things and the set of hairs
>
> happy coincidence—not the intersection of the set of happy things and the set of coincidences
>
> topless bar—not the intersection of the set of topless things and the set of bars
>
> heavy price—not the intersection of the set of heavy things and the set of prices
>
> past president—not the intersection of the set of past things and the set of presidents

Such examples can be multiplied indefinitely. There is nothing new about them, and no serious student of linguistic semantics would claim that such cases could be handled by intersection in traditional set theory. At present there is no adequate account of most kinds of complex concepts within a traditional framework, though a small number of isolated analyses using nonstandard set-theoretical apparatus have been attempted. For example, various logicians have attempted a treatment of the "small galaxy" cases using Montague semantics, and there have been occasional attempts to account for the "good thief" cases, and a couple of the others. But the vast number have not even been seriously studied within traditional approaches, and there is no reason whatever to think that they could be ultimately accounted for by traditional set theory, or any simple extension of it.

Let us turn now from the adequacy of the traditional set-theoretical core of the Osherson and Smith hybrid theory to the identification procedures. They do not give an indication as to what such identification procedures might be like. But what is more important is that Osherson and Smith do not consider the question of what the identification procedures for complex concepts would be like and how they would be related to the identification procedures for component concepts. Take, for example, Osherson and Smith's case of *pet fish*. As Osherson and Smith correctly observe, "A guppy is more prototypical of *pet fish* than it is of either *pet* or *fish*." In the hybrid theory, the identification procedure for *pet* would not pick out a guppy as prototypical, nor would the identification procedure for *fish*. How does the hybrid theory come up with an identification procedure for the complex concept *pet fish* that will pick out a guppy as prototypical? In short, the hybrid theory has not solved the problem of how to account for the prototypes of complex concepts. It has just given the problem a new name.

Perhaps the most inaccurate part of the hybrid theory is that it views prototype phenomena as involving no more than "identification." But metonymic cases of prototypes function to a large extent in the service of reasoning; in general, what Rosch calls *reference-point reasoning* has to do with drawing conclusions, and not mere identification. For example, arithmetic submodels are used for doing computations and making approximations; social stereotypes are used to make rapid judgments about people; familiar examples are used to make probability judgments; paragons are used to make comparisons, and ideals are used to make plans. Moreover, generative prototypes are not used just for identification; they are necessary to define their categories. Radial structures characterize relationships among subcategories, and permit category extension, which is an extremely important rational function. Most actual cases of prototype phenomena simply are not used in "identification." They are used instead in thought—making inferences, doing calculations, making approximations, planning, comparing, making judgments, and so on—as well as in defining categories, extending them, and characterizing relations among subcategories. Prototypes do a great deal of the real work of the mind, and have a wide use in rational processes.

In short, Osherson and Smith have said nothing whatever that bears on the version of prototype theory that we have given. Nor have they provided any reason to believe that their proposal for saving the classical theory will work. Indeed, the fact that prototypes are used widely in rational processes of many kinds indicates that the classical theory will not account for all those aspects of rational thought.

Armstrong, Gleitman, and Gleitman

The hybrid theory, despite all the arguments against it, is not likely to disappear. The classical theory that it incorporates as its "core" has two thousand years of tradition behind it. Within the past hundred years, theories of the form *core + everything else* have appeared repeatedly as attempts to preserve the classical theory of categories. A particularly interesting recent attempt to argue for some form of the Osherson and Smith core + identification procedure theory has been made by Armstrong, Gleitman, and Gleitman (1983). Armstrong et al. argue that the very ubiquity of prototype phenomena provides support for a classical theory over a prototype theory.

Like Osherson and Smith, Armstrong et al. equate prototype theory with the Effects = Structure Interpretation. That is, they assume that every version of prototype theory would have to claim that all categories are graded, and that goodness-of-example ratings correspond to degrees of membership. The form of their argument is roughly as follows:

(a) *Basic assumption*: Prototype theory assumes that whenever there are prototype effects for a category that category is graded. Goodness-of-example ratings correspond to degrees of membership. Conversely, it is assumed that prototype theory claims that ungraded categories would not yield prototype effects, since it is assumed that prototype effects only reflect degrees of membership.

(b) *Secondary assumption*: Concepts from formal mathematics are defined in terms of the classical theory, that is, by necessary and sufficient conditions, and therefore are not graded. By assumption (a), they should not show prototype effects. "Odd number" is an example.

(c) Armstrong et al. perform Rosch's experiments using the concept "odd number." They show that Rosch's prototype results appear, and that subjects give graded responses when asked if some numbers are better examples of the category "odd number" than other numbers.

(d) From (a), they reason that prototype theory must interpret these results as indicating that the category "odd number" is graded. But (b) shows that it is not graded.

(e) Since we know that (b) is true, prototype effects cannot show that a category is graded. Therefore, (a) must be false, and so prototype theory does not show anything about the real structure of categories.

(f) But Rosch's results must show something. The "core + indentification procedure" theory gives a plausible answer. Rosch's reproducible experiments reflect the identification procedure, but not the core, that is, the real cognitive structure of a category.

Like Osherson and Smith, Armstrong et al. assume the Effects = Structure Interpretation, and it is this interpretation that they, very reasonably, find wanting. They do not even consider the possibility of anything like the Cognitive Models Interpretation. But in the Cognitive Models Interpretation, their results make perfect sense.

To see why, let us first distinguish natural numbers as they are defined technically in formal arithmetic from natural numbers as ordinary people understand them. In formal arithmetic, the natural numbers are defined recursively. "0" is taken as a generator and "successor" as an operator. "1" is a name given to the successor of 0, "2" is a name given to the successor of the successor of 0, and so on. In mathematics, it is important to distinguish numbers from their names. We have a naming systems for numbers that takes 10 as a base; that is, we have ten single-digit number names— $0, 1, \ldots, 9$—and form multiple-digit number names thereafter. There are an indefinitely large number of possible naming systems. The best-known one after the base 10 system is the binary system, which takes 2 as a base and has only two single-digit number names: 0 and 1.

Most nonmathematicians do not distinguish numbers from their names. We comprehend numbers in terms of our base 10 naming system. The single-digit numbers are all generators. Multiple-digit numbers are understood as sequences of single-digit numbers. In order to compute with numbers, we must learn the generators—0 through 9—plus the addition and multiplication tables, plus algorithms for adding, multiplying, dividing, and so on. Computation with large numbers is understood in terms of computation with smaller numbers—ultimately single-digit numbers. Without understanding large numbers in terms of single-digit numbers, we could not do arithmetic computations.

Thus, single-digit numbers have a privileged place among the numbers. Double-digit numbers, especially those in the multiplication and addition tables, are somewhat less privileged. Larger numbers in general are less privileged still. A model for understanding all natural numbers in terms of single-digit numbers is, by our definition, a metonymic model. We would therefore expect that all other things being equal, single-digit numbers should be judged as better examples than double-digit numbers, which should be judged as better examples than larger numbers.

However, our understanding of numbers is more complicated than that. To aid in computation, and in judging the relative size of numbers, we have learned to comprehend numbers using various submodels. The most common submodel consists of powers of ten—ten, a hundred, a thousand, and so on. Another common subsystem consists of multiples of five; the American monetary system is based on these submodels and it is helpful in doing monetary calculations. Other common submodels are multiples of two, powers of two, and so on. As we pointed out above, each such submodel produces prototype effects. Taking all such sub-models together, we would expect prototype effects of complex sorts.

On the Cognitive Models Interpretation, such prototype effects for numbers would not correspond to degrees of membership. All numbers are equal with respect to membership in the category *number*. But with respect to the various models we use to comprehend numbers, certain numbers have privileged status.

Another submodel we use with numbers is one in which numbers are divided into odd numbers and even numbers; the even numbers are those divisible by 2, while the odd numbers are those of the form $2n + 1$. The odd-even submodel has no gradations; all numbers are either odd or even.

Let us now consider all the models together: the model used to generate the numbers, the powers-of-ten-model, the multiples-of-five model, the powers-of-two model, the prime number model, the odd-even model, and any others that we happen to have. Each model, by itself, produces prototype effects, except for the odd-even and prime number models. If we superimpose the all-or-none odd-even model on all the integers, we would expect to get prototype effects within the odd numbers and other prototype effects within the even numbers. We would expect these effects to be complex, since they would be the product of all the models together.

If we then asked subjects if the odd-even distinction was all-or-none or graded, we would expect them to say it was all-or-none. If we then asked them to give good-ness-of-example ratings for odd numbers and for even numbers, we would expect them to be able to perform the task readily, and to give rather complex ratings. This is exactly what Armstrong et al. did, and those were the results they got. It is exactly what prototype theory would predict—under the Cognitive Models Interpretation.

Unfortunately, Armstong et al. were using the Effects = Structure Interpretation of prototype theory, and the results they got were, not surprisingly, inconsistent with that interpretation. They assumed that, since the odd-even distinction was all-or-none, there should be no prototype effects, since there was no degree-of-membership gradation. When they found prototype effects in a nongraded category, they concluded that prototype effects occurred in all categories regardless of structure, and therefore reflected nothing about the structure of the category. Thus, the same experiment that confirms prototype theory under the Cognitive Models Interpretation disconfirms it under the Effects = Structure Interpretation.

Conclusion

Osherson and Smith, together with Armstrong, Gleitman, and Gleitman, have provided even more evidence that the incorrect Effects = Structure and Prototype = Representation interpretations of prototype theory are indeed incorrect. They have not shown that the core plus identification procedure theory *is* correct. In fact, the considerations we discussed above indicate that such a view is not viable for a number of reasons.

1. The classical theory of categories is hopelessly inadequate for complex concepts.
2. There is a correspondence between prototype effects and metonymically based reasoning. Such prototype effects can be accounted for by metonymic models, which are needed independently to account for what Rosch has called "reference point reasoning." Thus, prototype effects are not independent of reasoning.

3. There do exist direct correlations between conceptual structure and proto-type effects. They are of two types: (a) cognitive models containing scales that define gradations of category membership, and (b) radial categories.

The best way to account for prototype effects in general seems to be via a theory of cognitive models.

References

Armstrong, S. L., Gleitman, L., and Gleitman, H. (1983). What some concepts might not be. *Cognition, 13*, 263–308.

Coleman, L., and Key, P. (1981). Prototype semantics: The English verb *lie*. *Language, 57*, 1.

Downing, P. (1984). *Japanese numerical classifiers: Syntax, semantics, and pragmatics.* Unpublished doctoral dissertation, University of California, Berkeley.

Fillmore, Charles. (1982). Towards a descriptive framework for spatial deixis. In R. Jarvella and W. Klein (Eds.), *Speech, place, and action.* London: Wiley.

Kay, P. (1979). *The role of cognitive schemata in word meaning: Hedges revisited.* Unpublished manuscript, Department of Linguistics, University of California, Berkeley.

Kay, P. (1983). Linguistic competence and folk theories of language: Two English hedges. In *Proceedings of the Ninth Annual Meeting of the Berkeley Linguistics Society* (pp. 128–137).

Kay, P., and Kempton, W. (1984). What is the Sapir-Whorf hypothesis? *American Anthropologist 86*, 1, 65–79.

Lakoff, G. (1972). Hedges: A study in meaning criteria and the logic of fuzzy concepts. In *Papers from the Eighth Regional Meeting of the Chicago Linguistic Society.* Also in *Journal of Philosophical Logic* (1973), *2*, 458–508.

Lakoff, G. (1977). Linguistic gestalts. In *Proceedings of the Thirteenth Regional Meeting of the Chicago Linguistic Society*.

Lakoff, G. (1986). *Women, fire, and dangerous things: What categories tell us about the nature of thought.* Chicago: University of Chicago Press.

Lakoff, G., and Johnson, M. (1980). *Metaphors we live by.* Chicago: University of Chicago Press.

Miller, G., and Johnson-Laird, P. (1976). *Language and perception.* Cambridge, MA: Harvard University Press.

Osherson, D., and Smith, E. (1981). On the adequacy of prototype theory as a theory of concepts. *Cognition 9*, 1, 35–58.

Reddy, M. (1979). The Conduit metaphor. In A. Ortony (Ed.), *Metaphor and thought.* Cambridge, England: Cambridge University Press.

Rhodes, R. (1976). The morphosyntax of the central Ojibwa verb. Unpublished doctoral dissertation, University of Michigan, Ann Arbor.

Rips, L. J. (1975). Inductive judgments about natural categories. *Journal of Verbal Learning and Verbal Behavior, 14*, 665–681.

Rosch, E. (1978). Principles of categorization. In E. Rosch and B. B. Lloyd (Eds.), *Cognition and categorization.* Hillsdale, NJ: Erlbaum.

Smith, E. E., and Medin, D. E. (1981). *Categories and concepts.* Cambridge, MA: Harvard University Press.

Sweetser, E. E. (1984). *Semantic structure and semantic change.* Unpublished doctoral dissertation, University of California, Berkeley.

Sweetser, E. E. (1986). The definition of *lie*: An examination of the folk theories underlying a semantic prototype. In D. Holland and N. Quinn (Eds.), *Cultural models in language and thought.* Cambridge, England: Cambridge University Press.

Tversky, A., and Kahneman, D. (1983). Probability, representativeness, and the conjunction fallacy. *Psychological Review, 90*(4), 293–315.

Zadeh, L. (1965). Fuzzy sets. *Information and Control, 8*, 338–353

The Theory-Theory

Chapter 19

The Role of Theories in Conceptual Coherence

Gregory L. Murphy and Douglas L. Medin

Why is a given set of objects grouped together to form a category? That is, why is it that some groupings are informative, useful, and efficient, whereas others are vague, absurd, or useless? The current surge of interest in people's concepts has provided much information about conceptual structure and content. Yet, the central question of what makes a category seem coherent has only been sketchily addressed and incompletely answered.

A somewhat unusual, but nonetheless useful, example arises from an old puzzle of biblical scholarship, the dietary rules associated with the abominations of Leviticus, which produce the categories *clean animals* and *unclean animals*. Why should camels, ostriches, crocodiles, mice, sharks, and eels be declared unclean, whereas gazelles, frogs, most fish, grasshoppers, and some locusts be clean? What could chameleons, moles, and crocodiles have in common that they should be listed together? That is, what is there about clean and unclean animals that makes these categories sensible or coherent?

The main thesis of this article is that current ideas, maxims, and theories concerning the structure of concepts are insufficient to provide an account of conceptual coherence. All such accounts rely directly or indirectly on the notion of similarity, and we argue that the notion of similarity relationships is not sufficiently constraining to determine which concepts will be coherent or meaningful. These approaches are inadequate, in part, because they fail to represent intra- and inter-concept relations and more general world knowledge. We propose a different approach in which attention is focused on people's theories about the world.

The keystone of our explanation is that people's theories of the world embody conceptual knowledge and that their conceptual organization is partly represented in their theories. At one level, this statement is trivially true: For example, one's understanding of chemistry influences one's concept of substances like *water*. It would be very odd for a person to believe, for example, that water is animate, and yet to understand the phase relations between water, ice, and steam. Surely there is some consistency between people's concepts and their understanding of interacting objects and forces in the world, but the connection between the two has very seldom been spelled out. We attempt to specify the connection between theoretical and conceptual knowledge and to recast conceptual theory in that light.

This research was supported by United States Public Health Service Grant MH32370 (to DLM) and by National Science Foundation Grant 83-15145 (to GLM). This article is a fully collaborative venture, and the order of authorship is arbitrary.

The authors wish to acknowledge the helpful comments of Lawrence Barsalou, Maureen Callanan, Eve Clark, Sarah Hampson, Reid Hastie, Robert Macauley, Barbara Malt, Glenn Nakamura, Andrew Ortony, Elissa Newport, Brian Ross, Ed Shoben, Richard Shweder, and Ed Smith on an earlier draft.

Current theories of conceptual structure, including those we have proposed ourselves, represent concepts in ways that fail to bring out this relation between conceptual and theoretical knowledge. For example, one theory treats concepts[1] as
exemplars organized around a central prototype (see B. Cohen and Murphy 1984;
Osherson and Smith 1981). It is difficult to see how these concepts might be related
to or constrained by one's knowledge of the world. Another influential model (actually, a set of models) treats concepts as collections of features of some sort (see Smith
and Medin 1981).[2] Although this model may be broad enough to involve theoretical
knowledge, it does not particularly promote it, nor does it suggest what concepts
people are likely to have and why. In particular, the features suggested by most theories of concepts have excluded the theoretical connections we will discuss.

In this article, we do not propose a new model of conceptual representation.
Rather, we present a theory of what the glue is that holds a concept together and an
account of what sorts of concepts are easy to learn, use, and remember, with the
understanding that conceptual models must build appropriate structures to account
for the facts discussed.

When we argue that concepts are organized by theories, we use *theory* to mean
any of a host of mental "explanations," rather than a complete, organized, scientific
account. For example, causal knowledge certainly embodies a theory of certain phenomena; scripts may contain an implicit theory of the entailment relations between
mundane events; knowledge of rules embodies a theory of the relations between
rule constituents; and book-learned, scientific knowledge certainly contains theories.
Although it may seem to be glorifying some of these cases to call them theories, the
term connotes a complex set of relations between concepts, usually with a causal
basis. Furthermore, these examples are similar to theories used in scientific explanation (Achinstein 1968). Later on, we offer a list of some general properties of people's
theories and review examples illustrating the utility of thinking of concepts as being
embedded in theories.

The philosopher W. V. O. Quine was one of the first to make a case for the use of
theories in determining category membership. In his classic article, "Natural Kinds,"
Quine (1977) argued for both a psychological and a societal progression from an
innate, similarity-based conception of kinds to a theoretically oriented, more objective basis. Whereas early societies could only depend on perceptual and functional
qualities to differentiate objects into classes, modern society can use techniques of
chemical, physical, and genetic analysis in order to classify. Quine further argued
that, in a true case of ontogeny recapitulating phylogeny, modern children begin
with innate, perceptually based similarity metrics to define their kinds, only to have
them successively replaced by scientific knowledge (to the limits of their education
and our scientific progress). As Quine (1977, p. 171) puts it:

> One's sense of similarity or one's system of kinds develops and changes and
> even turns multiple as one matures, making perhaps for increasingly dependable

---

1. Many authors do not clearly distinguish between *concepts* and *categories*. We use *concepts* to refer to
mental representations of a certain kind, and *categories* to refer to classes of objects in the world. Past
writers seem to have used category to mean the mental representation of a class of objects, or both the
representation and the objects themselves. However, this distinction is important to account for deviations
between the two, as when someone's concept of *animal* does not actually include all animals.
2. Throughout this article, we use the terms *feature*, *attribute*, and *property* interchangeably.

prediction. And at length standards of similarity set in which are geared to theoretical science. This development is a development away from the immediate, subjective, animal sense of similarity to the remoter objectivity of a similarity determined by scientific hypotheses and posits and constructs. Things are similar in the later or theoretical sense to the degree that they are interchangeable parts of the cosmic machine revealed by science.

Although we do not subscribe to Quine's claims about societal progression (or the view that the use of scientific theories is necessarily more objective), we agree with his conclusion that one's theories explicate the world and differentiate it into kinds. We also concur with him that the notion of similarity must be extended to include theoretical knowledge. Although we focus on explicit theories as a source of conceptual coherence, it is likely that a broader view of theoretical knowledge will be needed to provide a complete account. People use some kinds of theoretical knowledge implicitly, only becoming aware of doing so when confronted with a mismatch or failure of that knowledge (as may arise in cross-cultural contact). Furthermore, even people's explicit theories may often not reach the rigor and consistency expected from a scientific theory (Nisbett and Ross 1980; A. Tversky and Kahneman 1980). Thus, the kind of theory Quine had in mind (an explicit, scientific one) is too narrow to fully explain coherence. The next section reviews previous approaches to conceptual coherence and their limitations.

Approaches to Conceptual Coherence—The Insufficiency of Similarity

We have already hinted at what we mean by a coherent category. It is one whose members seem to hang together, a grouping of objects that makes sense to the perceiver. We do not give an operational definition of coherence because we do not wish to tie it to a particular theoretical framework. There are a number of measures that might reflect coherence, including how easily the concept is learned and used, and there may be others that are not known yet.

It is important to distinguish this notion of coherence from the related one of *naturalness*, as used by Keil (1981) and others. Natural concepts are said to be those formed out of basic ontological categories, such as *living thing* or *intelligent being*. For example, a category that included only thoughts and fish would cross ontological boundaries improperly and would therefore form an unnatural concept. However, as we show later, a concept that is unnatural (according to this definition) may be coherent because people have some theory that it plays a part in. In short, most of people's concepts are probably natural and coherent, but the issue of what makes a concept hang together cannot be solved solely by recourse to such ontological categories.

Perhaps the most powerful explanation of conceptual coherence is that objects, events, or entities form a concept because they are similar to one another. The basic idea is that objects fall into natural clusters of similar kinds (that are dissimilar to other clusters), and our concepts map onto these clusters. Thus, similarity may be the glue that makes a category learnable and useful. Although it is true that category members seem similar, Quine (1977) pointed out that using similarity as the basis for concepts may raise the very questions it was meant to answer. Without some explanation of why things seem similar, we are left with an equivalent problem; many things appear to be similar just because they are members of the same category. In more practical terms, estimates of similarity may be influenced by people's knowledge that the things being compared are in the same (or different) categories.

To use a rough analogy, winning basketball teams have in common scoring more points than their opponents, but one must turn to more basic principles to explain why they score more points. In the same way, similarity may be a by-product of conceptual coherence rather than its determinant—having a theory that relates objects may make them seem similar. Goodman (1972, p. 437) goes so far as to say, "Similarity, ever ready to solve philosophical problems and overcome obstacles, is a pretender, an imposter, a quack. It has, indeed, its place and its uses, but is more often found where it does not belong, professing powers it does not possess."

We shall argue that, at its best, similarity only provides a language for talking about conceptual coherence. Certainly, objects in a category appear similar to one another. But does this similarity explain why the category was formed (instead of some other) or its ease of use? Suppose we follow A. Tversky's (1977) influential theory of similarity, which defines it as a function of common and distinctive features weighted for salience or importance. If similarity is the sole explanation of category structure, then an immediate problem is that the similarity relations among a set of entities depend heavily on the particular weights given to individual features. A barber pole and a zebra would be more similar than a horse and a zebra if the feature "striped" had sufficient weight. Of course, if these feature weights were fixed, then these similarity relations would be constrained. But as Tversky (1977) demonstrated convincingly, the relative weighting of a feature (as well as the relative importance of common and distinctive features) varies with the stimulus context and experimental task, so that there is no unique answer to the question of how similar one object is to another. To further complicate matter, Ortony, Vondruska, Jones, and Foss (1984) argued persuasively that the weight of a feature is not independent of the entity in which it inheres. The situation begins to look very much as if there are more free parameters than degrees of freedom, making similarity too flexible to explain conceptual coherence.

A further major complication derives from the fact that no constraints have been provided on what is to count as a feature or property in analyses of similarity. Suppose that one is to list the attributes that *plums* and *lawnmowers* have in common in order to judge their similarity. It is easy to see that the list could be infinite: Both weight less than 10,000 kg (and less than 10,001 kg, ...), both did not exist 10,000,000 years ago (and 10,000,001 years ago, ...), both cannot hear well, both can be dropped, both take up space, and so on. Likewise, the list of differences could be infinite. Furthermore, there are some attributes that are true of only a small number of the category members—perhaps there are some orange plums or some lawnmowers run by robots. What is the cutoff for excluding attributes that are not universal, or must they all be included (Murphy 1982a)? The point is that any two entities can be arbitrarily similar or dissimilar by changing the criterion of what counts as a relevant attribute. Unless one can specify such criteria, then the claim that categorization is based on attribute matching is almost entirely vacuous (see Goodman 1972).

These arguments about attributes fly in the face of perceptual experience that seems to naturally partition at least some entities into categories. Of course, there are some categorizations that blatantly contradict perceptual similarity (e.g., categorizing whales as *mammals*), which indicates that one's theories can override or at least select from perceptual information. Yet, it is true that the perceptual system has some built-in constraints on what will count as an attribute and which attribute relations are salient (see Ullman 1979, for elegant work that gets at some of these constraints). The problem with the abstract notion of similarity is that it ignores both the perceptual and theory-related constraints on concepts, when in fact they are doing most of the explanatory work. How much of our conceptual system is based on perceptually determined features and how much on theoretical features has yet to be determined. In general, people seem to be flexible about similarity (even perceptual similarity), and we know relatively little about nonperceptual constraints. Thus, we attempt to provide part of the answer to how people choose relevant attributes for concepts and how they weight those attributes in their conceptual processes. However, we wish to reduce the importance of individual attributes in conceptual representations and to emphasize the interaction of concepts in theory-like mental structures.

We now consider some candidate principles for category coherence that rely directly or indirectly on the notion of similarity. We begin by considering some standard maxims about what makes a good category and then turn our attention to particular categorization theories and their implications for category structure. Finally, we examine the widespread assumption that category judgments are based on some form of attribute matching that maps directly onto similarity. There are serious problems and limitations associated with each of these principles.

The Insufficiency of Similarity-Based Measures of Category Structure
Although we have already argued that similarity does not sufficiently constrain concepts, it may be that there are some general processing principles that are based on similarity that have greater explanatory power. For example, there is considerable evidence that the most useful concepts are neither the most specific nor the most abstract, but are at an intermediate level of abstraction (Rosch, Mervis, Gray, Johnson, and Boyes-Braem 1976). Although we would not want to equate concept coherence with these basic level concepts, such concepts are obviously highly coherent. Finding a metric that picks out these intermediate level categories is nontrivial.

Rosch and her colleagues argued that basic-level categories maximize cue validity (Rosch 1978; Rosch et al. 1976), the conditional probability that an object is in a category, given that it has some cue (or attribute) associated with the category. A coherent category should have many such cues, whereas a poor category has only inconsistent cues, or very few good ones. Categories with the highest cue validity would be expected to be particularly useful in perceptual categorization. Unfortunately, this measure incorrectly predicts that superordinate (i.e., the most inclusive) categories are always more coherent than any of their subordinates, inasmuch as anything that cues membership in one category also cues membership in its superordinates. For example, if something has feathers, it is likely to be a bird, but it is at least equally likely to be an animal. (See Murphy 1982a, 1982b, for details and consideration of similar measures.)

Perhaps coherent or useful categories are the ones that allow the most inferences to be made—after all, one purpose of categories is to enable inferences that may not be apparent from individual exemplars. If an object is a *dog*, for example, one can infer that it has ears, barks, has fur, and so forth, even if those properties have not been observed, whereas a vague category like *thing* or *object* enables few if any inferences to be made. Actually, this measure, which could be called *category validity*, is the reverse of cue validity, as it might be represented as the conditional probability that something has various attributes given its category membership. Accordingly, it has the reverse problem: Medin (1983) noted that the more specific a category, the more inferences it allows—individual objects being the limiting case for which one can specify the greatest number of correct "inferences."

It may well be possible to find measures that pick out intermediate levels of abstraction. For example, some weighting function combining cue validity and max-imizing inferences surely would (e.g., Jones 1983). But even here, there is little ground for confidence that we can measure coherence formally because the basic level appears to change with expertise (e.g., Rosch et al. 1976). One could reflect such changes by adding features or modifying feature weights, but again, these additions and modifications are doing the explanatory work. Similarity may be able to describe such facts, but it does not explain them.

The Insufficiency of Correlated Attributes

Another organizing principle for categories is the notion of correlated attributes. Rosch et al. (1976; Rosch 1978) proposed that natural categories divide the world up according to clusters of features, that they "cut the world at its joints." That is, attributes of the world are not randomly spread across objects, but rather appear in clusters. Furthermore, basic categories (which are the most useful and efficient) are said to maximize the correlational structure of the environment by preserving these attribute clusters.

Another motivation for the correlated attributes principle is the idea that organ-isms are constantly "going beyond the information given" to draw inferences and make predictions. For example, on the basis of seeing a round object in a gymnasium, one might predict with considerable confidence that it would bounce (though this inference would be wrong in the case of a medicine ball). In general, these predictions or inferences prove to be accurate to the extent that people correctly perceive such attribute correlations.

This *correlational structure* account implies that some version of the similarity models considered above is correct at a descriptive level because categories develop to group objects with a cluster of features and to exclude objects with different fea-tures. Yet, this account also makes a stronger claim than do those previous models: It is not undifferentiated similarity that holds a concept together, but some more elabo-rated structure of correlations. In this sense, the correlated attributes principle is deeper than are general notions of similarity. That is, an organism programmed to take advantage of attribute correlations will tend to form categories that have high within-category and low between-category similarity as a *consequence* of detecting correlations.

One problem with the correlated attributes notion is that there are so many possi-ble correlations that it is not clear how the correct ones get picked out (see Keil 1981, for an elaboration of this point). It would seem that some additional principle is needed to provide further constraints on category cohesion (e.g., perhaps correlations are more readily noticed if the parts are spatially contiguous or subserve the same function). A cause and its effect may be highly correlated, but they would probably be placed in different categories. Another problem is that the mental representation of correlated features needs to be specified further, including a specific mechanism that results in their making concepts more coherent.

We will not criticize this account because we believe that concepts that preserve correlations are in fact more coherent. However, we also believe that there are further principles that explain this fact—that correlated attributes do not provide a full account of conceptual cohesiveness. To anticipate our later arguments, we believe that feature correlations are partly supplied by people's theories and that the causal mechanisms contained in theories are the means by which correlational structure is represented.

The Insufficiency of Categorization Theories

Smith and Medin (1981) divided theories of category representation into three basic approaches: the classical view, the probabilistic view, and the exemplar view. It is natural to ask whether these theories imply useful constraints on concept or category goodness. For the most part, they do not.

Classical View   The classical view has it that categories are defined by singly necessary and jointly sufficient features. The major problems with this view as a structural principle are that many categories may not conform to the classical view (see Medin and Smith 1984; Mervis and Rosch 1981; Smith and Medin 1981, for reviews) and, equally seriously, that defining attributes do not ensure coherence. This theory does not pick out some defining feature sets as better or more appropriate than others. For example, a category consisting of striped things that have more than one leg and that weigh between 11 and 240 kg satisfies a classical view definition, but does not seem sensible or cohesive.[3]

Probabilistic View   The probabilistic view denies that there is a common core of criterial properties and argues that concepts may be represented in terms of features that are typical or characteristic, rather than defining. First, we should note that the criticism just made for the classical theory applies here as well: Without supplementation, the probabilistic view cannot tell which combinations of features form possible concepts and which form incoherent ones. It would not rule out the following combination of typical features: bright red, swims, has wings, eats mealworms, is found in Lapland, and is used for cleaning furniture. Clearly the mere fact that this combination is probabilistic does not mean that it is coherent (see Murphy and Wisniewski 1985).

Second, many processing models associated with the probabilistic view have the general constraint that the summary representation coupled with appropriate processing assumptions should accept all members and reject all nonmembers. The formal term for the constraint that categories be partitionable on the basis of a summing of evidence (i.e., the presence of features) is that the categories be separable by a linear discriminant function (Sebetsyen 1962). That is, categories should be separable on the basis of a weighted, additive combination of their features: Categories that are not linearly separable should be difficult to learn and use.

---

3. One might argue that this concept does not seem coherent simply because few objects actually contain all these features. (This objection could also apply to our first criticism of the probabilistic view below.) However, other empty concepts are fully coherent; in fact, our culture is full of fictional or mythical concepts that are perfectly coherent without having any members. The classical view does not explain why some empty categories seem reasonable and others do not. Furthermore, if we could provide a context in which our example *became* coherent (e.g., perhaps a stage prop with those characteristics is needed), the classical view would have nothing to say about this change.

Is linear separability important for actual concepts? One way of evaluating its importance is to set up two categorization tasks that are similar in major respects, except that in one task the categories are linearly separable and in the other categorization task they are not. Although this question has not received much attention, what little evidence there is is negative. In a series of four experiments varying instructions, category size, and stimulus materials, Medin and Schwanenflugel (1981) found no evidence that linearly separable categories were easier to learn than categories that were not linearly separable. Thus, linear separability does not appear to be a necessary property of "good" concepts.

Exemplar View   The exemplar view agrees with the probabilistic view in holding that concepts need not have criterial properties and, further, claims that categories may be represented by their individual exemplars rather than by some unitary description of the class as a whole (see Medin and Schaffer 1978). Obviously, such a view offers no principled account of conceptual structure because it does not constrain what exemplars are concept members. Although most exemplar theories assume that category members are similar, we have already argued that this alone is not a full explanation of coherence.

In brief, it seems that none of the three major views of category representation provides a principled account of category cohesiveness.

General Insufficiency of Attribute Matching and Similarity
Our claim is not only that approaches to category coherence based on similarity have to date been unsuccessful, but that, in principle, they will prove to be insufficient. We see three major problems with an exclusive focus on similarity and the associated practice of breaking concepts into constituent attributes or components: First, it leads naturally to the assumption that categorization is based solely on attribute matching; second, it ignores the problem of how one decides what is to count as an attribute; and third, and more generally, it engenders a tendency to view concepts as being little more than the sum of their constituent components. All of these problems derive directly or indirectly from failing to view concepts in terms of the relations between exemplar properties and the categorization system: Human interests, needs, goals, and theories are ignored.

Categorization as Attribute Matching   Our objection to the idea that categorization derives from attribute matching is that it may prove to be too limited. For example, the attributes associated with higher level concepts may be more abstract than those of lower level concepts or exemplars. Instead of attribute matching, categorization may be based on an inference process (see Collins 1978). For example, jumping into a swimming pool with one's clothes on is, in all probability, not associated with the concept *intoxicated*, yet that information might well be used to decide that a person is drunk. That is, categorizing the person as intoxicated may explain his or her behavior, even though the specific behavior was not previously a component of the concept. This inference process must be fairly complex, taking into account the context: In our example, the behavior could imply drunkenness in one context and heroism in another (e.g., jumping into the pool to save someone from drowning). Concepts may represent a form of shorthand for a more elaborate theory, and a concept may be invoked when it has a sufficient explanatory relation to an object, rather than when it matches an object's attributes.

A major respect in which attribute matching may be too limited is that our representations may include information concerning operations, transformations, and (indirectly) relations among attributes (see also Hampton 1981). Much of our reasoning about concepts may be based on contraints about operations that are permissible. Consider the following situation:[4] Suppose that all the soda cans you have come into contact with have been 7.5 cm in diameter and that all the silver dollars you have seen have been 4.0 cm in diameter. Suppose further that you are told that some entity has a diameter of 5.0 cm and you are asked whether it is more likely to be a soda can or a silver dollar. To our minds, it is more likely to be the can. One reason for this guess is that we know that silver dollars are mandated by law to be a particular size, whereas soda cans just happen to be of a uniform size. Alternatively, one might have made the opposite conjecture based on the knowledge that soda cans have to be a particular size to fit soda machines, whereas there is little reason for the particular size of silver dollars (other than in casinos). The point is that, whichever choice is made, it clearly does not derive solely from attribute matching or size similarity judgments, but rather from our knowledge about transformations and operations associated with concepts, and this, in turn, relies heavily on our general world knowledge.

This case could be recast as an example of attribute matching in which the attributes are higher order properties. For example, one's concept of *silver dollar* could have the attribute "used in machines sensitive to exact size." Although this is technically true, it misses the important point that the explanatory work is again being done by the theory-constrained processes that generate these complex attributes, rather than by attribute matching per se. Thus, although attribute matching could be made to be consistent with these facts, it does not explain or predict them by itself.

Although we believe that theoretical factors are important in people's categorizations, it seems likely that people can develop automatic routines for identifying objects as members of concepts when the concepts have consistent perceptual features. For example, one probably does not usually invoke much theoretical knowledge in categorizing something as a *robin*. The main influence of theories on perceptual categorization may be on novel objects and borderline cases, and when the categorization must be justified or explained. In short, we emphasize the theoretical aspects of categorization, but we do not mean to exclude the use of primarily perceptual information. Current research on categorization gives evidence that both are important (Kelter et al. 1984; Murphy and Smith 1982).

Selecting Attributes   Frequently, attributes are treated as givens or at least as sufficiently transparent that all one has to do is to ask experimental subjects to list them. As we have noted, this largely ignores the problem of what can count as an attribute. The formal models of category coherence mentioned above gain credence from their precise formulation of coherence, but they have no precise way in which to choose or exclude the attributes that form their basis.

More recently, some work has begun to be directed at this issue. Barsalou and Bower (1983), for example, showed that two types of properties are likely to be activated during processing. First, properties that have high diagnosticity may be active inasmuch as they are useful for distinguishing instances of a concept from instances of

4. The example is based on an idea provided by Lance Rips.

other conepts. Second, properties relevant to how people typically interact with instances of a concept are likely to be frequently active (see also Barsalou 1982, for further arguments). Note that forms of typical interaction themselves vary with context (see Roth and Shoben 1983).

Barsalou and Bower's (1983) research reinforces our thesis that the explanatory work is on the level of determining which attributes will be selected, with similarity being at least as much a consequence as a cause of conceptual coherence. In addition, their reference to typical interactions with objects suggests the causal schemata and scripts that we have said are important in conceptual representations. The properties that distinguish concepts may be greatly determined by people's goals, which are linked to their theories about the objects.

Concepts as Equivalent to Their Components   The more general problem associated with viewing concepts as equivalent to the sum of their components has a long history. Consider the following quote from John Stuart Mill (1843/1965):

> The laws of the phenomena of the mind are sometimes analogous to mechanical, but sometimes also to chemical laws. When many impressions or ideas are operating in the mind together, there sometimes takes place a process of a similar kind to chemical combination. When impressions have been so often experienced in conjunction, that each of them calls up readily and instantaneously the ideas of the whole group, those ideas sometimes melt and coalesce into one another, and appear not several ideas but one; in the same manner as when the seven prismatic colors are presented to the eye in rapid succession, the sensation produced is that of white. But in this last case it is correct to say that the seven colors when they rapidly follow one another *generate* white, but not that they actually *are* white; so it appears to me that the Complex Idea, formed by the blending together of several simpler ones, should, when it really appears simple, (that is when the separate elements are not consciously distinguishable in it) be said to *result from*, or be *generated by*, the simple ideas, not to *consist of* them.... These are cases of mental chemistry: in which it is possible to say that the simple ideas generate, rather than that they compose, the complex ones. (p. 29)

Although many investigators would agree that mental chemistry is a more apt metaphor for understanding concepts than is mental composition, the core of this distinction does not appear to have taken hold. Again, one would have thought that mental chemistry would convey a concern with *relations* (and constraints associated with them), *operations*, and *transformations* on components, as opposed to an exclusive focus on components (i.e., features) as independent entities.

One defense of the attribute-matching perspective is that relations and operations themselves might be treated as attributes. To take this step, however, is to concede that attributes may have a complex internal structure. Relations need arguments, and arguments and relations mutually constrain one another. This internal structure means that one is working with more than a list of simple attributes and that constraints and explanatory power will derive from this richer structure.

It also seems likely that the listing of category attributes, although helpful for certain methodological uses (e.g., Rosch and Mervis 1975), may drastically underestimate people's categorical knowledge, because part of their knowledge is about relations of category features to each other and of category members to the world. Thus, a person who simply *memorized* the attributes of some categories without knowing more about the object domain might have very different concepts than does a person with elaborated theories. These differences would show up in the uses of categories in language understanding, naming, problem solving, and other situations (some described below), but perhaps not in feature listings.

Summary of the Two Approaches

In our discussion, we have lumped together a number of accounts of concept representation and categorization under the general heading of *similarity-based approaches to concepts*. Although they differ in many respects, these accounts have in common the characteristic that they treat concepts as collections of attributes. In our critique of this approach, we argued that it is *insufficient* to explain conceptual coherence and the richness of conceptual structure. (In later sections we review more empirical data on this issue.) We emphasize *insufficient* here because we do not want to imply that this approach is completely wrong or misleading. It is clear that category members seem similar to one another, but we have argued that similarity is too flexible to give any specific, natural explanation of conceptual coherence. One could see our approach as supplying the constraints missing from the similarity explanation, rather than simply contradicting it.

Table 19.1 summarizes the differences of the similarity-based approach and the theory-based approach on a number of dimensions (some of which we have yet to address). The entries for the similarity-based approach uses *attribute* as a general term

Table 19.1
Comparison of two approaches to concepts

Aspect of conceptual theory	Similarity-based approach	Theory-based approach
Concept representation	Similarity structure, attribute lists, correlated attributes.	Correlated attributes plus underlying principles that determine which correlations are noticed.
Category definition	Various similarity metrics, summation of attributes.	An explanatory principle common to category members.
Units of analysis	Attributes.	Attributes plus explicitly represented relations of attributes and concepts.
Categorization basis	Attribute matching.	Matching plus inferential processes supplied by underlying principles.
Weighting of attributes	Cue validity, salience.	Determined in part by importance in the underlying principles.
Interconceptual structure	Hierarchy based on shared attributes.	Network formed by causal and explanatory links, as well as sharing of properties picked out as relevant.
Conceptual development	Feature accretion.	Changing organization and explanations of concepts as a result of world knowledge.

Table 19.2
General properties of theories and their potential role in understanding conceptual coherence

Property of theories	Speculation about role in conceptual coherence
"Explanations" of a sort, specified over some domain of observation.	Constrains which properties will be included in a concept representation.
	Focuses on certain relationships over others in detecting feature correlations.
Simplify reality.	Concepts may be idealizations that impose more structure than is "objectively" present.
Have an external structure—fit in with (or do not contradict) what is already known.	Stresses intercategory structure. Attributes are considered essential to the degree that they play a part in related theories (external structures).
Have an internal structure—defined in part by relations connecting properties.	Emphasizes mutual constraints among features. May suggest how concept attributes are learned.
Interact with data and observations in some way.	Calls attention to inference processes in categorization and suggests that more than attribute matching is involved.

for features, propositions, and other simple chunks of knowledge. Under the theory-based approach, *underlying principle* is used to refer to the causal connections, script links, and explanatory relations that we have been invoking as parts of theories.

In general, it can be seen that the similarity-based approach requires a minimum of conceptual organization and relations, whereas the theory-based approach emphasizes both. One way to describe this difference is to say that the theory-based approach expands the boundaries of conceptual representation: In order to characterize knowledge about and use of a concept, we must include all of the relations involving that concept and the other concepts that depend on it. To explain conceptual coherence, the processes that operate on a concept must be considered in addition to the information directly stored with it.

Concepts as Embedded in Theories
We have no illusions about having solved the problem of concept coherence. Unless one can specify constraints on what a theory is, it may not help at all to claim that conceptual coherence derives from having a theory. Table 19.2 lists five general properties that many theories manifest, along with some suggested roles that these properties may play in thinking about conceptual coherence. Because theories are flexible, conceptual coherence may also be. For example, the category *apple-or-prime number* does not appear to be a very coherent concept. In our view, this lack would derive mainly from the lack of clear internal or external structure in a theory about such a category. The relations that apples participate in (e.g., eating, biological relations) overlap very little with the relations that prime numbers participate in.

One could develop a scenario, however, in which this category might make sense.[5] For example, suppose that one of our colleagues in the math department, Wilma, has only two interests: prime numbers and apple farming. We might, then, form the con-

5. Larry Barsalou helped to develop this example.

cept *prime numbers-or-apples*, which is explained as "topics of conversation with Wilma." This explanation provides very little structure, however, so that it would probably be less coherent than the concept *apples-or-oranges*. By adding more explanatory links, one could make the concept more coherent. For example, one could try to explain why Wilma has only those two interests. Through reference to naive personality theory and by exploring the properties of apples and prime numbers, one could elaborate a theory about why a person would have just these interests. If this theory were consistent with one's other world knowledge, then it would also supply external structure to the concept. Whether this concept could ever become very coherent is an open question, depending on the status of the theory itself and the plausibility of competing theories. The point is that one might have a theory that could connect (to some degree) objects that seem to share very few features.

The rest of this article can be viewed as an amplification of the entries in Table 19.2 and in the right half of Table 19.1. In the following sections, we discuss how considering theories improves on the simple similarity accounts of these issues.

The Role of Theories in Cognition

Our claim is that representations of concepts are best thought of as theoretical knowledge or, at least, as embedded in knowledge that embodies a theory about the world. In this section, we reconsider some of the issues raised in the previous section and show how the addition of theoretical knowledge fills many of the gaps in explaining conceptual coherence.

Theories and Attribute Selection

Earlier we raised the issue of what is to count as an attribute. One answer is to rely on consensual validation: If several experimental subjects list some property as an attribute of some concept, then that attribute is included in the concept. Rosch and Mervis (1975) have shown that these listed attributes can be used to predict goodness of example ratings and times to verify that an exemplar is a member of a category (see Mervis and Rosch 1981, for a review).

Although this technique has generated important data for theories of categorization to explain, we may wish to consider the question of how people choose attributes to list. One might think that participants can simply retrieve the most important features of the target concept and report them. However, there are reasons to believe that the process of generating attributes is more complex.

First of all, most of the research involving attribute listing employs judge-amended tallies. The reason for this is that participants may list attributes at one level of abstraction and fail to include them at a lower level of abstraction. For example, they may list "two-legged" for *bird*, but not for *robin*, *eagle*, and other specific birds. B. Tversky and Hemenway (1984) analyzed this behavior in terms of cooperative rules of communication (Grice 1975) and implicit contrast sets (e.g., "two-legged" does not distinguish between *robin* and *eagle*, and so it may not be listed). The idea of implicit contrast sets may also explain why "does not fly" is much more likely to be listed for *penguin* than for *rainbow trout*. Thus, the subject's conception of the relevant contrast set, as well as the desired level of specificity, influences the choice of which features to list. It appears, then, that attribute listings may be quite constrained by factors that are only beginning to be studied.

We submit that attribute listings and the representations behind them are further constrained by the theories that the categories are involved in. Subjects list not everything they know about a concept, but rather those features that are particularly salient and diagnostic in their background knowledge (and that seem most relevant in the situation, as B. Tversky and Hemenway 1984 noted). For example, most people realize, upon reflection, that the attribute, "flammable," applies to wood, money, certain plastics, and (sadly) even animals. Yet, it probably would be found only in the conceptual representation (and the listings) for the first of these categories, presumably because of the known role of wood in human activities. Some attributes are prominent in our concepts because of their importance in our other knowledge about the world, and others are excluded because of their irrelevance to our theories. The concept *money* is central to our theories of economic and social interaction, in which the attribute of flammability plays no role. Thus, it is apparently not part of our representation of *money* even though it may easily be inferred as true of most money.

Miller and Johnson-Laird (1976) also noted the importance of theories in specifying attributes of lexical concepts. They contrast a concept's *core*, which contains theory-based attributes, with attributes that are perceptually salient and therefore useful in identification, but with little connection to the intrinsic nature of the concept. They describe the concept's core as being "an organized representation of general knowledge and beliefs about whatever objects or events the words [in a lexical field] denote—about what they are and do, what can be done with them, how they are related, what they relate to" (p. 291). They make the explicit equation: "A conceptual core is an inchoate theory about something" (p. 291). Although it is often difficult to draw the line between core features and more peripheral features, Miller and Johnson-Laird's description emphasizes the importance of external and internal structure of a concept's features in the core.

Theories and Correlated Attributes

We raised the possibility earlier that coherent concepts have clusters of correlated features. We then raised the question of how conceptual representations take advantage of these clusters. In other words, what is the difference between representations of categories with feature correlations and those without feature correlations that result in the former being more coherent than the latter?

Smith and Medin (1981, pp. 84–86) discussed two possibilities. One is to represent correlated features as one single feature. For example, the features "flies," "has wings," and "has a beak" might be combined into one global feature. Smith and Medin pointed out that this solution is unprincipled and counterintuitive, in that the compound feature really corresponds to three independent features that must be separated in other representations (e.g., bats and penguins have only two of the three features). The other possibility they mentioned is to link and label features that are correlated. So, all three pairs of the above features would have arcs labeled CORRELATED connecting them.[6] This has more intuitive appeal—its main drawback being the explosion of feature links it would engender—and Smith and Medin tentatively accept it.

---

6. The links would not have to be labeled as CORRELATED—they might simply be associations that simultaneously activate two features, and this pattern of activation could be used to infer that the features are correlated. That is, the correlations might be computed rather than specifically stored. However, this version is also subject to the objections we raise to the more explicit representation of correlated attributes.

This feature-linking solution has computational tractability. It can adequately represent feature correlations that might be accessed by processes using the concept. However, this solution misses an important insight. Features in categories are not correlated by virtue of random combinations. Rather, correlations arise from logical and biological necessity: Animals and artifacts have structural properties in order to fulfill various functions, so that some structural properties tend to occur with others, and certain structures occur with certain functions. It is no accident that animals with wings often fly or that objects with walls tend to have roofs. Even less obvious correlations, such as the one between furniture being made of wood and also having a flat top (Malt and Smith 1984), usually have clear explanations.

Suppose that people are not only sensitive to feature correlations, but that they can deduce *reasons* for those correlations, based on their knowledge of the way the world works. Perhaps, then, the connection between those features is not a simple link, but a whole causal explanation for how the two are related. For example, one can connect "has wings" to "flies" by one's intuitive knowledge of the use of wings to support a body on air pressure; "has walls" and "has a roof" are connected by their common function of protection from the elements. This approach avoids the explosion of CORRELATED links because it draws on previously existing knowledge about the attributes to connect them: The links are already in memory. Furthermore, memory research has shown that it is difficult to remember correlated facts through simple associations; when the facts are tied together by a theme of previous knowledge, memory interference is reduced (Bower and Masling 1978; Day and Bellezza 1983; Smith, Adams, and Schorr 1978).

Medin, Altom, Edelson, and Freko (1982) found in experiments with novel categories that people are, in fact, sensitive to feature correlations and that they use them in their categorization judgments (see also L. B. Cohen and Younger 1983; Younger and L. B. Cohen 1984). This was true even when overall typicality was controlled for. Thus, people do spontaneously use feature correlations to aid their judgments. Notably, during the debriefing, participants frequently offered reasons for *why* the correlation was present. They were not simply computing correlations but were developing and using theories to explain the correlations and to structure the concept.

Theories and Concept Use

So far, we have argued on theoretical grounds that people's concepts must be integrally tied to their theories about the world. A large part of this discussion has been somewhat abstract, dealing with various measures of conceptual coherence and accounts of category structure. This approach to conceptual coherence also has empirical implications for concept *use*. Although many process models of concept use involve attribute matching or similarity judgments, we argue that a number of lines of research give evidence of the use of causal knowledge, rules, theoretical consistency, and other theory-like knowledge. This section reviews evidence pertaining to how theories are involved in specific uses of concepts.

Correlated Attributes

We have already suggested that theories are necessary for people to explain feature correlations. Medin et al. (1982) showed that people are sensitive to empirical correlations of features in their category judgments, as Rosch et al. (1976) suggested they should be. However, features that are correlated in people's mental representations may not always reflect empirical relations in the world, but may derive instead from people's theories about the relations between the features. Although these theory-driven relationships may actually exist, people may never have empirical data to confirm or disconfirm their expectancies. Examples of these feature pairs are amount of education and income, zodiac sign and personality, rate of speech and intelligence, and amount of rehearsal and strength in long-term memory. Again, we rush to point out that some of these pairs may be truly correlated, but others probably are not. The property that they have in common is that they are predicted by (some) people's theories about the world, rather than being suggested by observation. In fact, some of them are so theory laden that it would be difficult to see how one could detect them without the theory to direct measurement. When a correlation is perceived to exist on the basis of one's theories, but has no basis in empirical fact, it is called an *illusory correlation.*

Chapman and Chapman (1967, 1969) presented evidence that therapists and naive subjects using certain psychodiagnostic tests perceived correlations between test results and psychological disorders when in fact there were none—or even when the opposite correlation obtained. They concluded that people's expectancies prevented them from objectively evaluating the relation between the test and mental illness. Other studies have confirmed the effects of theories on perception of correlations, although not always to the same degree (Crocker 1981; Wright and Murphy 1984). Bower and Masling's (1978) research suggested that the important factor may be that people be able to construct a causal explanation for a correlation, rather than that it match their current knowledge. Murphy and Wisniewski (1985) provided some preliminary evidence that theory-based correlations are actually used to form conceptual representations.

One could imagine a case opposite to the illusory correlation one, in which the observer perceived a correlation but could find no explanation for it; there might be no way to connect the two attributes in one's mental scheme of things. One of us (DLM) has recently completed a set of studies in which people were asked to sort descriptions of entities into categories. For example, in one case, the descriptions were symptoms and the categories were hypothetical diseases. The task was set up so that people could sort on the basis of two different sets of correlated attributes. The two sets of correlated attributes differed in terms of how readily people might think of a causal association between them. Although people are flexible enough that they can link many pairs of symptoms, pilot work suggested that it is easier to link some pairs (e.g., dizziness to earaches, and weight gain to high blood pressure) than others (e.g., dizziness to weight gain, or earaches to high blood pressure). People showed a strong tendency to cluster on the basis of correlated attributes for which a causal link could readily be made. Furthermore, subjects mentioned such linkages to justify their sorting. For example, they might say that an ear infection could disturb the vestibulary organ and produce both dizziness and earaches. Thus, feature correlations may be important in conceptual representations primarily when they can be represented as theoretical knowledge.

There is also evidence that a prior theory can facilitate perception or learning of contingencies and correlations. For example, in processing numerical information involving possible correlations, performance may be improved dramatically simply by the addition of meaningful labels for the variables that suggest their theoretical significance (e.g., Adelman 1981; Camerer 1981; Miller 1971; Muchinsky and Dudycha 1974; Wright and Murphy 1984). Camerer (1981) showed that people could learn an interaction between variables when they were labeled in accordance with prior beliefs (i.e., factors thought to affect wheat futures in the commodity market), but failed to learn when the same problem was given as an abstract task involving arbitrary labels.

Linear Separability in Categorization

We mentioned earlier that linear separability does not appear to be a natural constraint on human categorization. One reason for this may be that people's theories, and hence their categories, typically have more internal structure than can be captured by an independent summing of evidence or by similarity to a prototype. If this is true, then if a prior theory suggests that summing or similarity matching is appropriate, linear separability may in fact become important for categorization.

Recent work by Wattenmaker, T. Murphy, Dewey, Edelson, and Medin (1984) supported this idea. In one study the descriptions were properties of objects, and the categories were structured such that the typical attributes for one category would all be desirable properties if one were searching for a substitute for a hammer (e.g., flat surface, easy to grasp). In one condition subjects were given the notion of hammer substitutes, and in another condition they were not. The idea was that a hammer would act as an ideal standard and that subjects could judge how similar examples were to the hammer prototype (through independent summing of features).

When prior theories were developed or suggested, linearly separable categories were in fact easier to learn than were nonlinearly separable categories. The reverse held when no theory was suggested. This result depends on the theory evoked being compatible with a summing of evidence. By suggesting a different form of theory, one should be able to reverse this pattern of results. For example, if one category corresponded to psychologists, one might discourage people from summing up component information by alerting them to the fact that there are both experimental and clinical psychologists and that their traits may differ considerably. The attribute "likes computers" might predict category membership for experimental but not clinical psychologists. In a close analogue of this example, Wattenmaker et al. (1984) found a differential facilitation in learning categories that were not linearly separable.

The point of these examples is quite simple. One cannot describe some abstract conceptual structure as simple or complex, independent of the form of theory that might be brought to bear on it. When theory and structure match, the task becomes simple; when there is a mismatch between theory and structure, the task becomes difficult.

Theories and Prototype Structure

Assuming that most concepts have a typicality structure, people must discover this structure when they learn a new concept. When they encounter a new object, they must judge how typical it is of a variety of concepts. Both of these tasks may require use of a theory. Barsalou's (1983, 1985) research on goal-derived categories presents a particularly clear example in which theories are crucial to deriving conceptual structure. He investigated categories such as *things to do at a convention*. He found, first, that people are less likely to discover that four objects are in one of these categories when they do not know the goal that relates them (Barsalou 1983, Experiment

4). Second, he showed that the typicality structure of goal-derived categories was not simple family resemblance (similarity of the category members), but rather how well each instance satisfies the goal (Barsalou 1985). The reader may wish to introspect on what the category is that includes the objects children, jewelry, portable TVs, paintings, manuscripts, and photograph albums. Furthermore, which of the items mentioned is the most typical? Because the objects have low family resemblance, the task is nearly impossible. However, once the theme *taking things out of one's home during a fire* is known, these judgments become easy. Notice that this concept is not a "natural" one according to the criteria given by Keil (1981), yet it does seem to hang together in its context. Such examples suggest that theories can elucidate the relations among very different objects and thereby form them into a coherent category, even if they do not form a "natural" class.

A third interesting aspect of Barsalou's (1985) research involves some comparisons he made between natural and goal-derived concepts. In the process of showing that the exemplars of goal-derived categories had typicality ratings that correlated with the degree to which they satisfied the relevant goal, Barsalou performed similar computations on common concepts. Although the underlying dimensions for natural categories were speculative (e.g., for *fruit*, how much people like it), they proved to be significantly correlated with exemplar goodness even after the effects of frequency and family resemblance had been partialed out. This observation suggests that natural concepts may be partly organized in terms of underlying dimensions that reflect how the concept normally interacts with people's goals and activities.

Fillmore (1982) made a related suggestion about the source of typicality structures. He argued that lexical concepts are represented in terms of *idealized cognitive models*. For example, the concept *bachelor* can be defined as an unmarried adult male, in the context of human society in which certain (idealized) expectations about marriage and marriageable age are realized. The existence of "poor examples" of this concept —for example, Catholic priests, homosexual men, men cohabiting with a girlfriend— does not mean, Fillmore argued, that the concept itself is ill-defined. Rather, the claim is that the idealized cognitive model does not fit the actual world perfectly well. An entity may deviate from the concept (i.e., may be atypical) either because it fails to satisfy "unmarried, adult male" or because the idealized model is imperfectly realized. Clearly, such a model is an example of what we have been calling *theories*, inasmuch as it provides a means of connecting many concepts in order to explain diverse facts. Mohr (1977) argued that this is the correct way to view Platonic universals, and Lakoff (1982) developed this notion of idealized models in some detail.

In this view, the relation between concepts and exemplars is analogous to the relation between theory and data. Not only may data be somewhat noisy, but theories also typically involve simplifying assumptions that trade parsimony for power. As Kuhn (1962) argued, theories depend on a particular background of accepted beliefs and assumptions that is taken for granted—until contradictory data begin to accumulate. Fillmore's (1982) point was that categorizing objects also depends on background assumptions about the world, and our concepts have developed in the context of those assumptions. To some degree, then, it may be these simplified models that give rise to unclear cases, and when anomalous or unclear cases arise, our background assumptions become more salient.

We may underestimate the importance of implicit theories or background assumptions about the world because of their very implicitness. Ziff (1972) provided some delightful examples of the importance of implicit conceptual schemes in understanding. For example, it seems sensible to say "a cheetah can outrun a man." But what about a 1-day old cheetah, or an aged cheetah with arthritis, or a healthy cheetah with a 100-pound weight on its back? What we mean when we say that a cheetah can outrun a man is that under some tantalizingly difficult-to-specify conditions, a cheetah would outrun a man. Ziff referred to this set of conditions as a conceptual scheme and made the point that two people understand each other to the extent to which these conceptual schemes are shared. These implicit theories heavily constrain our understanding of relations among concepts.

Expertise

The prevailing view of expertise with regard to concepts seems to be that experts differ from novices primarily in making finer distinctions (as implicitly expressed by Dougherty 1978; Rosch et al. 1976). In that view, experts have many more specific categories than do novices, and they see those categories as being very distinct. It has often been suggested that experts should have different concepts from novices, but few studies have actually investigated their conceptual structure. Much of the relevant work has involved cross-cultural comparisons in anthropological studies of lexical structure (e.g., Berlin, Breedlove, and Raven 1973; Dougherty 1978; others are cited by Mervis and Rosch 1981). For example, members of agricultural societies are experts on plants and animals and have many names for specific animal concepts, whereas Berkeley undergraduates are novices and have few such names (Dougherty 1978; Rosch et al. 1976).

However, there may well be differences between experts and novices besides the *amount* they know about a category and the *number* of categories they can differentiate. Certainly, experts have better developed theories about the domain than do novices. How would this affect their conceptual structure? A reasonable null hypothesis would be that experts simply know more: They have more information about each category, and they know more categories. Although these quantitative predictions seem likely, we do not believe that they are the only differences. Experts in some domain probably know more relations between the objects in the domain. They can see connections where novices notice none because their theories lead them to look for certain similarities, regularities, and cause–effect relations. For example, biologists notice crucial similarities between shrimps, moths, grasshoppers, spiders, and crabs, putting them together in one class (the arthropods). We assume that naive observers would make more pragmatic distinctions, probably separating the flying, crawling, and water-living animals. The biologist's theories of evolution and physiological structures express themselves in the concept of the arthropods and would come into play explicitly when categorizing unfamiliar objects.

There is increasing evidence for the view that experts make far-reaching connections that affect their concepts, in addition to having greater specific knowledge. Murphy and Wright (1984) examined the concepts of experts and novices in child psychopathology. The novices were college undergraduates with no experience in abnormal psychology. Three other groups ranged in expertise from beginning counselors at a summer camp for disturbed children to clinical psychologists with extensive experience in the field. All of the subjects listed attributes of the three major categories of emotionally disturbed children. Surprisingly, experts' concepts were not more distinctive—in fact, the more expert the subjects, the more their categories seemed to overlap.

This result is somewhat counterintuitive because experts in clinical psychology are expected to classify people into different groups, and the more distinctive their concepts of the groups, the easier this would be. This finding points out that classification is not the only purpose for concepts. Like all psychologists, these experts wanted to find *explanations* for behavior, and those explanations point out commonalities to all cases of child psychopathology (analogous to the zoologist's search for organizing features in biological classifications). For example, the professional psychologists listed "feels angry" and "feels sad" for all categories, presumably because of their theories about the motivational and cognitive concomitants of psychopathology. Novices also have theories of psychopathology, but they are apparently more superficial, accounting for surface differences between the categories. For example, they listed "feels sad" as an attribute of depressed children only, and "feels angry" exclusively for aggressive children.

One interpretation of these findings is to attribute them to the fuzziness or even invalidity of psychopathological categories. However, similar evidence was reported in the realm of physics problems by Chi, Feltovich, and Glaser (1981), who noticed that novices classify physics problems using "surface features" that are only roughly correlated with physical principles. Experts, on the other hand, apparently categorized problems on the basis of the major principles used in their solutions. Consequently, "experts are able to 'see' the underlying similarities in a great number of different problems, whereas novices 'see' a variety of problems that they consider different" because the surface features differ (Chi et al. 1981, p. 130). As a result, the experts made fewer, larger classes than did the novices. Chi et al.'s results also highlight the fact that similarity is in the eyes—and theories—of the beholder.

It seems safe to assume that the physicists' classifications were not simply fuzzier than the novices' (as one might argue for the clinical psychology case). Similarly, the biologist's class of *arthropods* is accepted as valid, even though it is much more inclusive than preferred novice concepts (see Berlin et al. 1973; Rosch et al. 1976). These examples provide evidence that people's theories may lead them to form concepts that they would not normally have and to alter the content of other categories.

Cross-Cultural Research
An intriguing possible implication of the approach we have proposed has to do with cross-cultural differences in concepts. Clearly, people in different cultures have different theories about the world, which should cause them to have different concepts. In fact, there are a number of tantalizing examples of cultural differences in classification tasks (see the review by Cole and Scribner 1974). One well-documented culturally dependent phenomenon is the assignment of the basic level of categorization. Rosch et al. (1976) first noted that the basic level of their American subjects was more general than that of people from agricultural, nonindustrial societies (as described by Berlin et al. 1972). Dougherty (1978) and Geoghegan (1976) discussed these differences in depth and suggested that domains that are important to a culture are more fully individuated and elaborated both in the language and conceptual system. The basic level is more specific in such domains than in others. Such cultural dependence is evidence against the idea that the basic level is purely determined by features in the environment. In our view, this happens because the greater salience of a domain

promotes more elaborate knowledge structures in the domain, which in turn can differentiate more specific concepts.

However, these differences in salience do not exhaust the effects of cultural knowledge on concepts. One example is that the Karam of New Guinea do not consider a cassowary a bird. Bulmer (1967) argued that this is not merely because the cassowary does not fly, but because of its special role as a forest creature and its resulting participation in an elaborate antithesis in Karam thought between forest and cultivation. This antithesis is further related to basic concerns with kinship roles and rights. Apparently, the Karam's theories about forest life and cultivation produce different classifications than do our culture's biological theories. (For other similar examples, see Luria 1976; Tambiah 1969; and the review by Cole and Scribner 1974.) For categories that are more conceptual than perceptual, cross-cultural differences may be even more evident. Shweder and Miller (1985) demonstrated the importance of cultural presuppositions in social categories involved in person perception, in a strong parallel to the position of this article.

Linguistic Innovations and Complex Concepts
Because people's representations of word meanings are probably closely tied to their concepts (see E. Clark 1983), our theory should also have implications for semantic interpretation. This influence can probably best be seen in the understanding of innovative uses of language, which require modification of existing word meanings in order to be interpreted. A similar problem is the formation of complex concepts, in that existing concepts must be modified in order to create a new meaning.

Clark and Clark (1979) discussed the creation and interpretation of denominal verbs, which are often innovative—created for a single use by a particular speaker—rather than conventional like most word uses. Examples include *Max teapotted the dean*, and *the boy porched the newspaper*, in which the concepts *teapot* and *porch* must be modified to produce verb interpretations. To explain how people understand such innovations, Clark and Clark referred to people's "generic theories" of objects: their physical characteristics, ontogeny, and potential roles. For example, one's knowledge of boys, newspapers, and porches allows one to conclude that *the boy porched the newspaper* refers to throwing a paper on the porch (rather than making it into a porch or pasting it on the porch). The same denominal verb in a different sentence frame would involve a different interpretation, as in *the builder porched the house*. People's conceptual knowledge is heavily involved in producing and constructing interpretations of such sentences, and that knowledge apparently includes the origins and usual roles of such objects, as we have argued.

Combining simple concepts into compound concepts may involve similar processes.[7] For example, how does one generate the concept *pet fish* from the concepts *pet* and *fish*? One possibility is the "classical" method of set intersection (Osherson and Smith 1981). For example, *pet fish* would be formed by taking the intersection of all things that are *pets* and all things that are *fish*. Much of the early concept acquisition literature assumes such an account.

---

7. It is difficult to give operational criteria to separate simple from complex concepts. One clue is whether the concept has a single-word name or requires multiple words (Berlin et al. 1973). Yet, some compound noun phrases name unitary concepts, for example, *washing machine*. Rather than argue for an operational distinction here, we have used simple and complex concepts that are intuitively clear: The simple concepts are described by a single word, and they combine to form apparently complex concepts.

Unfortunately, this view has a great deal of trouble with many complex concepts. Consider, for example, *ocean drive, expert repair,* or *horse race.* These concepts are not intersective at all. *Ocean drives* are not both *oceans* and *drives; horse races* are not both *horses* and *races.* Linguists discussing nominal compounds have argued that the meaning of these terms is determined by a *mediating relation* between the two nouns (Kay and Zimmer 1976), but there is no single relation that will construct any complex concept (see Adams 1973). For example, a *horse race* is a race of horses, but an *ocean drive* is not a drive of oceans. An *expert repair* is a repair done by an expert, but an *engine repair* is probably not a repair done by an engine. So, no single relation (like set intersection) can describe all or even most compound concepts. Furthermore, the construction of complex concepts is not a simple operation on the features of the two concepts, such as feature overlap or projection. Although some of the features of *finger* get carried over onto *finger cup,* considerable knowledge is needed to specify which features are affected and how they are combined with the features of *cup.* Whenever people form complex concepts or understand compound nouns, they must be using their background knowledge of the way the world works in order to create the correct concept. In short, the formation of complex concepts requires mental chemistry rather than the simple addition of components.

B. Cohen and Murphy (1984) argued that it is impossible to explain how people form such compound concepts using only *knowledge independent* operations. That is, they said that it is impossible to say in advance what a complex concept XY means knowing only the meaning of X and Y, but that extensive knowledge relating X and Y comes into play in order to arrive at just the right compound. In the context of our discussion, this point translates into the use of people's implicit theories and operations on concepts. For example, one's knowledge of the use of vehicles, their parts and what they do, and mishaps that happen to them can lead one to combine *engine* and *repair* to get "repair of an engine." One's knowledge about *experts* leads one to combine *expert* and *repair* differently. The interpretation of a compound concept may be thought of as a hypothesis generated by background theories.

Related Ideas

The notion that people's concepts are tied up with their theories is not totally new to psychology (note the earlier discussion of Miller and Johnson-Laird 1976). Rumelhart (1980) made a related analogy in describing his theory of knowledge representation. Schemata, he suggested, are like theories in that they embody expectations of what things cooccur and how properties are related (pp. 37–38). Unfortunately, the actual schemata he presented are not rich enough to express people's knowledge about those relations and co-occurrences. For example, the schema for *buy* includes agents, an object being sold, the transfer of money, and so forth, which expresses a simple theory about financial transactions. However, people's full understanding of buying events includes information about the motives and desires of the seller and buyer, expectations about the relation between the money and the purchase (that they should be of near-equivalent worth), and a number of legal and cultural requirements. Our intent here is not to criticize Rumelhart's representations: It is possible that a complete schematic representation could contain all the necessary theoretical knowledge, especially when the relations among various schemata are included. Our point is that the full knowledge people have about concepts goes beyond that normally given in such discussions.

In memory research, the shift from emphasis on memory traces (the Ebbinghaus tradition) to processes of memory construction and reconstruction (the Bartlett tradition) has been well documented. Whereas early memory researchers investigated the passive laying down and decay of traces, more recent investigators have posited active encoding and reconstructive processes (Bransford, Barclay, and Franks 1972; Cofer 1973; Jenkins 1974). These processes are based on the relation of the material to the rest of the knowledge base, rather than on abstract learning rules.

In the area of judgment and inferences, A. Tversky and Kahneman (1980) considered the specific place of causal knowledge in decision making, implicating it in a number of judgment situations. Other work suggested that people give great weight to their theories about people and the world relative to statistical evidence (see Nisbett and Ross 1981; Wright and Murphy 1984, for reviews). In particular, abstract rules of judgment and decision making (e.g., Bayes's theorem or Luce's choice axiom) apparently do not characterize people's decisions. Although this field has engendered much controversy (e.g., L. J. Cohen 1981), it seems clear that people use specific theories of the world, sometimes inappropriately, to make predictions and decisions.

In the area of language comprehension, people's use of theoretical knowledge has been reflected in two ways. First, there has been increasing interest in people's theories of communication itself (although this factor is not usually described in this way). Grice (1975) first pointed out that speakers and hearers use their beliefs about the purposes of a conversation in order to make and understand implications. H. Clark and Carlson (1982) and H. Clark and Murphy (1982) discussed how listeners and readers use their beliefs about the purposes and methods of communication to understand reference and various aspects of meaning. In essence, these discussions have dealt with how implicit theories of communication come into play in everyday language use (we have already mentioned that they may affect the listing of concept attributes). Second, psycholinguists have begun to emphasize how people's knowledge of the discourse topic allows them to fully understand the discourse. In this case, people use their theories about the domain being discussed to rule out anomalous interpretations and to resolve ambiguities and vagaries. Simple models of lexical decomposition and inference no longer seem adequate to the task of explaining the range and depth of language understanding—see Collins, Brown, and Larkin (1980), Johnson-Laird (1981), Rumelhart (1981), and Schank and Abelson (1977).

Finally, the area of problem-solving has embraced the notion of mental models in people's reasoning about complex systems (see articles in Gentner and Stevens 1983). Content-free reasoning strategies such as means-ends analysis or logical deduction seem unable to account for the relative difficulty of different problems or for individual differences. Instead, investigators have suggested that subjects form a simplified mental model of a system and simulate its behavior in order to make a prediction or evaluation. Clearly, the subject's theory about the system and the domain it operates in will greatly determine his or her problem solution. Furthermore, concepts in the domain are determined to a great extent by the whole model in which they operate.

Although the psychological domains we have discussed are disparate, there is a clear theme running through them. In each case, a simple model based on invariant principles of organization or process has been found too inflexible to account for human abilities. People appear to use content-specific knowledge or theories to process information and to represent new knowledge. The importance of these constructive, knowledge-based processes appears to be well established for these fields.

It is interesting to note that procedural approaches to categorization from artificial intelligence have sometimes depended on theory-like structures. For example, the sorting algorithm that seems to best capture people's free sorting of entities into categories is not an exclusively bottom-up processor (Michalski 1983; Michalski, Stepp, and Diday 1981). Rather, the basic procedure of Michalski's program operates on the level of *descriptions* of clusters and aims to maximize criteria having to do with what represents a good description. These criteria include such factors as simplicity, the fit between descriptions and the entities, and a bias for conjunctive descriptions. Therefore, a good description can be thought of as having the character of a good theory (the former is a consequence of the latter).

Philosophy of science has long considered the question of whether concepts are integrally bound up with theories. Unfortunately, there is little agreement on the answer, with opinions ranging across the extremes. Philosophers such as Kuhn and Feyerabend argued that scientists with different theories about a domain must have different concepts in the domain, even if their concepts have the same names. For example, physicists who held the wave theory of light had concepts of *light, color,* and the like that differed from those of physicists who held the particle theory. Other philosophers have downplayed this possibility or have argued that any such conceptual differences are usually insignificant; Suppe (1977) provides a complete discussion of both sides. Although this issue remains controversial, it does seem clear that present-day scientific concepts are quite different from past understanding of the same concepts as a result of new theories and knowledge. Current work in philosophy of science focuses on the boundaries of such conceptual differences.

Conceptual Development

The study of children's concepts and semantic development may be a crucial area for showing the importance of theories in conceptual structure. Not only do children lack words for many of the entities, events, and situations that adults have words for, they may have quite different theories about how those entities, events, and situations are related. Although there is still no consensus on children's cognitive and linguistic representations, we believe that some of the accepted findings speak to the issues we have raised.

The most influential theory of semantic development in recent years has been Eve Clark's Semantic Feature Hypothesis (E. Clark 1973a, 1973b; Richards 1979). Following accepted linguistic analyses, Clark used sets of components or features as semantic representations. She suggested that children's first semantic representations of a word are a subset of the adult features (although occasionally completely incorrect features will sneak in) and that development consists primarily of adding features as they are learned. The Semantic Feature Hypothesis successfully described much of the data, including the order of acquisition of words in many domains and common naming errors (see E. Clark 1973a, 1973b, 1983).

For a variety of reasons, this theory is no longer widely accepted in its original form (see Carey 1982; E. Clark 1983; Richards 1979), a trend that is consistent with our previous arguments about the insufficiency of feature-based models of concepts. It is not our purpose to review the literature in semantic development here, but we would like to highlight the studies that shed light on how theories might influence conceptual development and that contrast with the featural view.

One of the first studies was E. Clark's (1973b) demonstration of nonlinguistic "biases." Previous data had suggested that children learned locative prepositions in the order, *in, on, under*. For some time, they treated *under* as if it meant *in* or *on*. One explanation for these data was that all three words had the same semantic representation at first, and that with increasing experience, children added features to differentiate them. However, Clark showed that children had biases about spatial arrangements that influenced their performance in comprehension tasks. That is, if told, "Put the block under the crib," they might put it in the crib instead, because of their knowledge of usual spatial relations. In fact, they made the same error even when imitating nonverbal actions. Clark suggested that the youngest children tested (about 21 months old) know only that *in, on* and *under* are spatial terms and that they use spatial strategies to respond to those words. Children depend on their knowledge of supporting surfaces and containers, and the usual orientation of objects to interpret utterances with locative prepositions (see also H. Clark 1973). In a sense, they are depending on implicit theories of spatial relations to understand and learn new words. Semantic development, therefore, consists of coordinating one's conceptual knowledge with the conventions of word use. As E. Clark (1973b) remarked, in this view it becomes very difficult to determine when a child knows the correct meaning of a word: One must try to access linguistic knowledge separately from the conceptual basis, which may be impossible in practice.

Carey (1982) also provided a critique of the notion of feature accretion as an explanation of semantic development. The acquisition of spatial adjectives like *big, little, tall, short, thick,* and *thin* had been taken to be evidence for the Semantic Feature Hypothesis: *Big–little* were analyzed as having relatively few semantic components, *tall–short* as having additional features specifying orientation, and *thick–thin* as having yet more features (see below). The order of acquisition followed this analysis. Carey, however, argued that the difficulty of learning *thick–thin* was not the mere number of features it contains, but rather that it requires attending to "theory-laden" features specifying that the dimension being referred to is "tertiary." In order to resolve the meaning of these terms, Carey claimed that children must learn the complex spatial system we use in our culture to assign such spatial adjectives, and that this system is not part of their beginning theories about the world. Presumably, the learning of this spatial system goes hand in hand with learning the language. We would add that the child must also have extensive background knowledge about individual objects in order to determine their primary and tertiary dimensions. This knowledge is necessary to interpret the use of *thick* when applied to objects as diverse as doors, lines drawn on a page, people, and bicycle tires.

Keil and Carroll (1980) provided a demonstration that children do not represent spatial terms as abstract features, but that their understanding of them was inextricably bound up in their knowledge of the world. They demonstrated that children's willingness to describe something as *tall* depended on what they believed they were naming. A child might be able to pick out the tallest of a trio of mountains, but not the tallest of a trio of blanket piles—even though the same picture was used for both. Keil and Carroll proposed that the children had not yet extracted the abstract meaning of *tall*, but they did know some things that *tall* is used to describe (e.g., people, houses, mountains). Until they learn the full meaning, they depend on some primitive theory of what tall things are like.

The work of Ellen Markman and her colleagues (see Markman and Callanan 1984) is also suggestive in this context. It is known that young children have difficulty learning and using superordinate concepts (Horton & Markman 1980; Mervis and Crisafi 1982; Rosch et al. 1976), which is not surprising, given their loose structure. Presumably, it is difficult for children to infer the functional relationship that often characterizes superordinates (*furniture, tool, vehicle, weapon,* etc.). Callanan and Markman (1982) suggested that 2- and 3-year-old children understand superordinates not as *classes*, but as *collections* of objects. That is, rather than thinking of *furniture* as a name that applies to individual objects, they think of it as a name for a group or configuration of a number of objects. They may believe that *furniture* refers to an arrangement of chairs and couches around a table in the living room. However, children do not seem to have the same problem with most basic concepts, which are much more perceptually based (Callanan and Markman 1982).

These results are consistent with the interpretation that children cannot simply memorize that couches, chairs, tables, and bureaus are all *furniture*—they seem to need an explanation for this grouping, which might otherwise be incoherent. For them, the most reasonable explanation may be a spatial configuration rather than the more abstract functional explanation that adults use. If this is true, then it demonstrates the importance of underlying relationships in learning concepts. (See Gentner 1983, for a similar claim concerning analogical transfer.)

Finally, in considering children's errors in learning noun and verb meanings, Carey (1982) argued that children's problems arise not from faulty linguistic abilities, but rather from an impoverished conceptual structure. For example, to fully understand a word like *buy* may require a sophisticated understanding of monetary exchange. But children may interpret *buy* merely as "get at a store." More generally,

> The components revealed by semantic analyses of the adult lexicon cannot be expected to be the primitives over which the child forms his hypotheses about the meanings of words. Often those components are theoretical terms in theories the child has not yet encountered, and they therefore require theory building on his part before they are available to his conceptual system. (Carey 1982, p. 374)

Of course, the relation cuts both ways: An impoverished conceptual structure might prevent someone from learning a word fully, but in other cases, language learning influences the conceptual structure. A child may learn about monetary exchanges through learning the meaning of *buy* and *sell* rather than through direct experience or lessons in economics. As the child learns about the distinction between *buy, sell, trade, give,* and so forth, he or she learns complex concepts that are central to understanding society.

In her own studies of biological concepts (as described in Carey 1982), Carey followed the development of concepts like *animal* and *living thing*. She attempted to empirically test Quine's theory that an innate similarity metric is replaced by a scientific metric as the basis of concepts. She did find some evidence for such a shift; children first organize properties of animals around their applicability to humans, but later develop a more systematic organization based on biological functions. However, even the youngest children (4 years old) showed some use of biological knowledge in their categorizations. Adults and children both rated a toy monkey as being more similar to people than a worm was. However, adults and children also agreed that the worm was more likely to have a spleen than was the toy monkey (a spleen was described as "a green thing inside people"). Apparently, even the youngest children differentiated surface similarity from category membership. Although worms may be less similar to people than are toy monkeys, they are more similar *in some respects*, namely, common biological functions. Carey's results demonstrate that it is those respects that determine category membership, rather than similarity as a whole. As Carey (1982, p. 386) put it, "The child's rudimentary biological knowledge influences the structure of his concept *animal* in several ways, even for children as young as 4. To that extent, *animal* functions as a natural kind concept by Quine's characterization."

A crucial question that arises in considering theories in conceptual development is when they make their first appearance. One might argue that children form their first concepts through perceptual similarity; then, as they learn more about the world, they incorporate knowledge into their concepts, where it has increasing importance. On this view, the similarity-based accounts of coherence are correct for early concepts, at least, to the extent that we can ascertain built-in constraints on the perception of similarity. The question, then, is just when theories begin to have an effect. Our view is that theories are important very early: E. Clark's (1973b) results showed that children under 2 years old demonstrated a variety of spatial biases. Other researchers have found that very young children can distinguish the sorts of objects that receive proper names from those that do not, presumably reflecting a theory of individuality (Gelman and Taylor 1984; Katz, Baker, and Macnamara 1974). As we argued earlier, these biases and preconceptions may be biologically determined to some extent through perceptual and cognitive structures (see H. Clark 1973; Keil 1981). Although young children may not have scientific theories or sophisticated schemata, they may well use their understanding of their world, or proto-theories, in forming concepts (see Karmiloff-Smith and Inhelder 1974/1975, for more direct evidence). Rather than a shift from similarity-based concepts to more theoretically-based concepts, perhaps all concepts are integrated with theories, but children's theories change radically.

Some studies of infants' categories have shown prototype structures in children a few months old (e.g., L. B. Cohen and Younger 1983). The age of the children and the structure of the stimuli leave little doubt that the infants are forming concepts based on perceptual similarity. However, as we have already noted, similarity itself is not an unanalyzable relation, and perceived similarity also changes with development (see Kemler 1982). It is certainly possible that children's prototheories of the functions, relations, and importance of objects have effects quite early. Exactly when they do is an empirical question, one that we hope will get some attention.

The Classical Theory of Concepts

A major bone of contention in the theory of concepts has been the question of whether concepts can be specified by necessary and sufficient features. Wittgenstein (1953) sparked the debate among philosophers, which continues today among psychologists and linguists as well. Although this classical theory appeared to be dead (see, e.g., Smith and Medin 1981), a number of hybrid theories have arisen. Osherson and Smith (1981), for example, suggested that the conceptual core is all or none, and that prototypes and other nonessential information about a concept are used mainly for identification, but are not strictly part of the concept. McNamara and Sternberg (1983) argued for a mixed theory, in which concepts are represented by both defining (necessary and sufficient) and characteristic features.

We do not mean to resolve the philosophical issues here. Regardless of one's theory of concepts, it is a fact that most people believe that there are necessary and sufficient features that define concepts. McNamara and Sternberg (1983) documented this fact convincingly, and informal questioning reveals that naive subjects are loathe to admit that there are no truly defining features, even when they cannot produce any (Rosch and Mervis 1975). Armstrong, Gleitman, and Gleitman (1983) asked subjects whether they thought certain categories were all or none or had graded membership. For their natural categories, the percentage of subjects who responded "all or none" ranged from 24% (for *vehicle*) to 71% (for *sport*). People apparently have a strongly held belief that there are defining attributes for categories, in spite of the failure of psychologists, linguists, and philosophers to find any. (Suggestions for necessary features have been made, but these never seem to define the concept sufficiently; e.g., perhaps all *trips* involve motion, but this does not separate them from innumerable other events.) What we will try to explain is, where do these beliefs come from?

A natural prediction from our previous discussion is that naive theories in a domain suggest that certain features are "defining." We have already claimed that theoretical and conceptual knowledge are closely intertwined. Perhaps, then, the reason that people believe in a necessary basis for their concepts is that much of their knowledge of the world depends on correctly differentiating things into categories. Suggesting that concepts are ill-defined or fuzzy might cast doubt on much of one's knowledge.

However, not all features are perceived as defining; "defining" features, on our account, are those that are most central to our understanding of the world. In Fillmore's (1982) terms, those features that are most integrally involved with our idealized cognitive models will appear to be defining. For example, if it turned out that *carrots* weren't made of cells, then we would have to reconsider most of our other beliefs about carrots as well as about plants in general (for example, our theories of plant growth). Or if it turned out that some diamonds are really quite soft, then we would have to re-explain our past experiences with diamonds (or things we believed to be diamonds), the numerous claims people make about diamond hardness, our beliefs about diamond formation, and anything we might have known about crystal structures. Thus, being made of cells for carrots might be considered a defining feature, as might hardness for diamonds, because these features are so closely tied to other information about those categories.

If some of our characteristic features turned out to be wrong, a much smaller change in the knowledge base would be required. For example, if carrots weren't really orange, one could just assume they have been systemantically dyed by unscrupulous grocers or farmers. This new information would probably not affect our concepts of plant life in general. If diamonds weren't really found in below-ground mines, none of the knowledge mentioned above would need to be reconsidered. One could assume that jewelers or diamond suppliers had lied in order to protect their market. In short, *defining features* are those at the meeting point of much of our knowledge.[8] *Characteristic features* are those toward the periphery of our knowledge base. More precisely, when a feature is involved in many causal links, rules, or scripts, it is perceived as "more defining" than a feature that is involved in few of them. The features at either end of the spectrum appear to be clearly defining or characteristic; those in the middle (involved in a moderate number of theoretical links) are the ones that cause arguments.

It is important here to separate the psychological question of defining and characteristic features from the philosophical-semantic issue. We think that, on reflection, most people would agree that it might be possible to find (or make) a soft diamond. Therefore, hardness is in some sense only a characteristic feature. Yet McNamara and Sternberg (1983) found that people say that being the hardest substance known is necessary for being a diamond. It seems likely that when people list such defining features, they are answering the question of which attributes are most central to their concepts, rather than which include all (potential) members and exclude all non-members. (An examination of other features given by McNamara and Sternberg's subjects reinforces this view.) Even if no feature is truly defining in a semantic-theoretical sense, people may put great weight on those that are tied up with much of their knowledge.

Conclusion

We have been arguing that people's theories and knowledge of the real world play a major role in conceptual coherence. This tendency to relate concepts and theories may be such that people impose more structure on concepts than simple similarity would seem to license.

Consider again the abominations of Leviticus, in which the animals that are clean and unclean for the people of Israel are listed in great detail. Over the years there have been many speculations concerning what properties of animals gave rise to their being listed as clean or unclean, as the overall similarity of the animals in each group is so low. To our minds, the most cogent speculation concerning this classification rule, developed in Mary Douglas's (1966) intriguing book, *Purity and Danger*, is that there should be a correlation between type of habitat, biological structure, and form of locomotion. Creatures of the water should have fins and scales, and swim; creatures of the land should have four legs and jump or walk; and creatures of the air should fly with feathered wings. Any class of creature not equipped for the right kind of locomotion in its element is unclean. For example, ostriches would be unclean because they do not fly. Crocodiles are unclean because their front appendages look like hands, and yet they walk on all fours. If this analysis is correct, then there was a theory of appropriate physiological structure associated with each type of environ-

---

8. Quine (1961) used a similar line of reasoning to argue against the existence of analytic truths, that is, statements that are necessarily true by virtue of the language. A prime candidate for such analytic truths has been to ascribe defining features to a concept, like "carrots are made of cells." Quine (1961, p. 43) pointed out that virtually *any* feature can be taken away from a category (e.g., hardness could be taken away from *diamonds*), but when some features are removed, a global reorganization of one's knowledge base is necessary. The larger this reorganization, the more analytic (defining) the feature is. Thus, he argued for a continuum of analytic to synthetic truths rather than a dichotomy. This philosophical argument parallels our psychological argument for why people perceive some features to be defining, although the two issues are potentially independent.

ment, and any animal that did not meet its standards was unclean. The category *clean animals*, then, comprises a coherent set of entities, even though the overall similarity of the members is very low. Although most categories probably have a better similarity structure than these examples, the point is clear that theories can impose coherence even when similarity is low.[9]

We think that there are two components to conceptual coherence. The first component involves the internal structure of a particular conceptual domain (see Table 19.2). Concepts that have their features connected by structure-function relationships or by causal schemata of one sort or another will be more coherent than those that do not. Although these correlations may be strictly empirical, in most cases they will be driven by expectations and hypotheses. In this way, the concept is integrated with the rest of the knowledge base. Other properties such as high within-category similarity and low between-category similarity may be by-products of this internal structure.

The second component of coherence has to do with the position of the concept in the complete knowledge base, rather than its internal structure (see Table 19.2). This component is the question of how the concept fits into "the cosmic machine revealed by science" (Quine 1977, p. 171)—or, more accurately, the cosmic machine represented in people's heads. Concepts that have no interaction with the rest of the knowledge base will be unstable and probably soon forgotten. This component is also important in the formation of new concepts.

One objection to the theory-based approach that might be raised is that it is circular. How can mental theories explain concepts, the objection goes, when theories themselves are made out of concepts? The answer is that we are not attempting to *reduce* issues of conceptual representation to theoretical representation. On the contrary, we believe that the influence is bidirectional—one cannot talk about theories or knowledge representation in a domain without specifying the concepts people have in the domain. (In fact, research on people's naive theories has typically included discussion of their relevant concepts; see Gentner and Stevens 1983.) Concepts and theories must live in harmony in the same mental space; they therefore constrain each other both in content and in representational format. Our point is that these constraints will provide insight into the structure of both areas, not that one can be replaced by the other. We agree that theories are made up of concepts (to a great extent) and urge that this fact be employed in our theories of concepts.

In our criticism of similarity as the sole basis of conceptual coherence, we pointed out that similarity needs to be greatly constrained before it makes any predictions. However, we should point out that the notion of a good theory is not yet fully constrained: We gave some idea in Tables 19.1 and 19.2 of what constitutes a good theory, but there is clearly more work to be done here. In fact, the point of this article is not to provide a complete account of the use of theories in conceptual structure, but is rather to demonstrate that theories are indeed important and to encourage future research to detail exactly how they are involved in concept formation and use.

We do *not* wish to suggest that previous studies on novel concepts that are divorced from real-world knowledge have no worth, nor that future such studies will

9. We are guilty of oversimplifying here. No doubt the conceptual scheme associated with the division of clean and unclean animals is more elaborated and more intertwined with the culture that gave rise to these concepts than this example implies.

be of little interest. These studies have provided the basis for our own theorizing, and they represent a necessary technique for studying conceptual structure. Our main point is that these studies and associated categorization theories relying exclusively on similarity relations are insufficient to provide a theory of concepts. We have argued that a coherent concept is one that we have a good theory about and that fits well with our other knowledge. This approach raises a number of empirical questions, many of them related to the question of how concepts are initially acquired and how expertise in a domain affects the concepts of that domain. The exact details of how theories affect internal and external conceptual structure have yet to be specified. Future research on concepts and categories can help answer these questions not by controlling the effects of world knowledge and experience, but by exploiting them— by bringing the concepts into contact with the whole cognitive system that created them.

References

Achinstein, P. (1968). *Concepts of science*. Baltimore: Johns Hopkins Press.

Adams, V. (1973). *An introduction to modern English word-formation*. London: Longman.

Adelman, L. (1981). The influence of formal, substantive, and contextual task properties on the relative effectiveness of different forms of feedback in multiple-cue probability learning tasks. *Organizational Behavior and Human Performance, 27*, 423–442.

Armstrong, S. L., Gleitman, L. R., and Gleitman, H. (1983). What some concepts might not be. *Cognition, 13*, 263–308.

Barsalou, L. W. (1982). Context-independent and context-dependent information in concepts. *Memory and Cognition, 10*, 82–93.

Barsalou, L. W. (1983). Ad hoc categories. *Memory and Cognition, 11*, 211–227.

Barsalou, L. W. (1985). Ideals, central tendency, and frequency of instantiation as determinants of graded structure in categories. *Journal of Experimental Psychology: Learning, Memory and Cognition, 11*, 625–654.

Barsalou, L. W., and Bower, G. H. (1983). *A priori determinants of a concept's highly accessible information*. Unpublished manuscript, Emory University.

Berlin, B., Breedlove, D. E., and Raven, P. H. (1973). General principles of classification and nomenclature in folk biology. *American Anthropologist, 75*, 214–242.

Bower, G. H., and Masling, M. (1978). *Causal explanations as mediators for remembering correlations*. Unpublished manuscript, Stanford University, Psychology Department.

Bransford, J. D., Barclay, J. R., and Franks, J. J. (1972). Sentence meaning: A constructive versus interpretive approach. *Cognitive Psychology, 3*, 193–209.

Bulmer, R. (1967). Why is the cassowary not a bird? A problem of zoological taxonomy among the Karam of the New Guinea Highlands. *Man, 2*, 5–25.

Callanan, M. A., and Markman, E. M. (1982). Principles of organization in young children's natural language hierarchies. *Child Development, 53*, 1093–1101.

Camerer, C. F. (1981). *The validity and utility of expert judgment*. Unpublished doctoral dissertation, University of Chicago.

Carey, S. (1982). Semantic development: The state of the art. In E. Wanner and L. R. Gleitman (Eds.), *Language acquisition: The state of the art* (pp. 347–389). Cambridge, England: Cambridge University Press.

Chapman, L. J., and Chapman, J. P. (1967). Genesis of popular but erroneous diagnostic observations. *Journal of Abnormal Psychology, 72*, 193–204.

Chapman, L. J., and Chapman, J. P. (1969). Illusory correlation as an obstacle to the use of valid psychodiagnostic signs. *Journal of Abnormal Psychology, 74*, 272–280.

Chi, M. T., Feltovich, P. J., and Glaser, R. (1981). Categorization and representation of physics problems by experts and novices. *Cognitive Science, 5*, 121–152.

Clark, E. V. (1973a). What's in a word? On the child's acquisition of semantics in his first language. In T. E. Moore (Ed.), *Cognitive development and the acquisition of language* (pp. 65–110). New York: Academic Press.

Clark, E. V. (1973b). Non-linguistic strategies and the acquisition of word meanings. *Cognition, 2,* 161–182.

Clark, E. V. (1983). Meanings and concepts. In J. H. Flavell and E. M. Markman (Eds.), *Manual of child psychology: Cognitive development* (Vol. 3, pp. 787–840). New York: Wiley.

Clark, E. V., and Clark, H. H. (1979). When nouns surface as verbs. *Language, 55,* 767–811.

Clark, H. H. (1973). Space, time, semantics and the child. In T. E. Moore (Ed.), *Cognitive development and the acquisition of language* (pp. 28–63). New York: Academic Press.

Clark, H. H., and Carlson, T. B. (1982). Speech acts and hearers' beliefs. In N. V. Smith (Ed.), *Mutual knowledge* (pp. 1–36). London: Academic Press.

Clark, H. H., and Murphy, G. L. (1982). Audience design in meaning and reference. In J.-F. LeNy and W. Kintsch (Eds.), *Language and comprehension* (pp. 287–299). Amsterdam: North-Holland.

Cofer, C. N. (1973). Constructive processes in memory. *American Scientist, 61,* 537–543.

Cohen, B., and Murphy, G. L. (1984). Models of concepts. *Cognitive Science, 8,* 27–58.

Cohen, L. B., and Younger, B. A. (1983). Perceptual categorization in the infant. In E. K. Scholwick (Ed.), *New trends in conceptual representation: Challenges to Piaget's theory?* (pp. 197–220). Hillsdale, NJ: Erlbaum.

Cohen, L. J. (1981). Can human irrationality be experimentally demonstrated? *Behavioral and Brain Sciences, 4,* 317–370.

Cole, M., and Scribner, S. (1974). *Culture and thought.* New York: Wiley.

Collins, A. (1978). Fragments of a theory of human plausible reasoning. In D. Waltz (Ed.), *Proceedings of the conference on Theoretical Issues in Natural Language Processing II* (pp. 194–201). Urbana: University of Illinois Press.

Collins, A., Brown, J. S., and Larkin, K. M. (1980). Inferences in text understanding. In R. J. Spiro, B. C. Bruce, and W. F. Brewer (Eds.), *Theoretical issues in reading comprehension* (pp. 385–407). Hillsdale, NJ: Erlbaum.

Crocker, J. (1981). Judgment of covariation by social perceivers. *Psychological Bulletin, 90,* 272–292.

Day, J. C., and Bellezza, F. S. (1983). The relation between visual imagery mediators and recall. *Memory and Cognition, 11,* 251–257.

Dougherty, J. W. D. (1978). Salience and relativity in classification. *American Ethnologist, 5,* 66–80.

Douglas, M. (1966). *Purity and danger.* London: Routledge & Kegan Paul.

Fillmore, C. (1982). Towards a descriptive framework for spatial deixis. In R. J. Jarvella and W. Klein (Eds.), *Speech, place and action: Studies in deixis and related topics* (pp. 31–59). Chichester, England: Wiley.

Gelman, S. A., and Taylor, M. (1984). How two-year-old children interpret proper and common names for unfamiliar objects. *Child Development, 55,* 1535–1540.

Gentner, D. (1983). Structure-mapping: A theoretical framework for analogy. *Cognitive Science, 7,* 155–170.

Gentner, D., and Stevens, A. L. (Eds.). (1983). *Mental models.* Hillsdale, NJ: Erlbaum.

Geoghegan, W. H. (1976). Polytypy in folk biological taxonomies. *American Ethnologist, 3,* 469–480.

Goodman, N. (1972). Seven strictures on similarity. In N. Goodman, *Problems and projects* (pp. 437–447). Indianapolis: Bobbs-Merrill.

Grice, H. P. (1975). Logic and conversation. In P. Cole and J. L. Morgan (Eds.), *Syntax and semantics, Vol. 3: Speech acts* (pp. 41–58). New York: Academic Press.

Hampton, J. A. (1981). An investigation of the nature of abstract concepts. *Memory and Cognition, 9,* 149–156.

Horton, M. S., and Markman, E. M. (1980). Developmental differences in the acquisition of basic and superordinate categories. *Child Development, 51,* 708–719.

Jenkins. J. J. (1974). Remember that old theory of memory? Well, forget it! *American Psychologist, 29,* 785–795.

Johnson-Laird, P. N. (1981). Mental models of meaning. In A. K. Joshi, B. L. Webber, and I. A. Sag (Eds.), *Elements of discourse understanding* (pp. 106–126). Cambridge, England: Cambridge University Press.

Jones, G. V. (1983). Identifying basic categories. *Psychological Bulletin, 94,* 423–428.

Karmiloff-Smith, A., and Inhelder, B. (1974/1975). If you want to get ahead, get a theory. *Cognition, 3,* 195–212.

Katz, N., Baker, E., and Macnamara, J. (1974). What's in a name? A study of how children learn common and proper names. *Child Development, 45,* 469–473.

Kay, P., and Zimmer, K. (1976). On the semantics of compounds and genitives in English. *Sixth California Linguistics Association Proceedings* (pp. 29–35). San Diego: Campile Press.

Keil, F. C. (1981). Constraints on knowledge and cognitive development. *Psychological Review, 88,* 197–227.

Keil, F. C., and Carroll. J. J. (1980). The child's conception of "tall": Implications for an alternative view of semantic development. *Papers and Reports on Child Language Development, 19,* 21–28.

Kelter, S., Grotzbach, H., Freiheit, R., Hohle, B., Wutzig, S., and Diesch, E. (1984). Object identification: The mental representation of physical and conceptual attributes. *Memory and Cognition, 12*, 123–133.

Kemler, D. G. (1982). Classification in young and retarded children: The primacy of overall similarity relations. *Child Development, 53*, 768–779.

Kuhn, T. S. (1962). *The structure of scientific revolutions.* Chicago: University of Chicago Press.

Lakoff, G. (1982). *Categories and cognitive models* (Cognitive Science Rep. No. 2). Berkeley: University of California, Cognitive Science Program.

Luria, A. R. (1976). *Cognitive development: Its cultural and social foundations.* Cambridge, MA: Harvard University Press.

Malt, B. C., and Smith, E. E. (1984). Correlated properties in natural categories. *Journal of Verbal Learning and Verbal Behavior, 23*, 250–269.

Markman, E. M., and Callanan, M. A. (1984). An analysis of hierarchical classification. In R. Sternberg (Ed.), *Advances in the psychology of human intelligence* (Vol. 2, pp. 345–365). Hillsdale, NJ: Erlbaum.

McNamara, T. P., and Sternberg, R. (1983). Mental models of word meaning. *Journal of Verbal Learning and Verbal Behavior, 22*, 449–474.

Medin, D. L. (1983). Structural principles in categorization. In T. J. Tighe and B. E. Shepp (Eds.), *Perception, cognition, and development: Interactional analyses* (pp. 203–230). Hillsdale, NJ: Erlbaum.

Medin, D. L., Altom, M. W., Edelson, S. M., and Freko, D. (1982). Correlated symptoms and simulated medical classification. *Journal of Experimental Psychology: Learning, Memory, and Cognition, 8*, 37–50.

Medin, D. L., and Schaffer, M. M. (1978). Context theory of classification learning. *Psychological Review, 85*, 207–238.

Medin, D. L., and Schwanenflugel, P. L. (1981). Linear separability in classification learning. *Journal of Experimental Psychology: Human Learning and Memory, 7*, 355–368.

Medin, D. L., and Smith, E. E. (1984). Concepts and concept formation. *Annual Review of Psychology, 35*, 113–138.

Mervis, C. B., and Crisafi, M. A. (1982). Order of acquisition of subordinate, basic, and superordinate level categories. *Child Development, 53*, 258–266.

Mervis, C. B., and Rosch, E. (1981). Categorization of natural objects. *Annual Review of Psychology, 32*, 89–115.

Michalski, R. S. (1983). A theory and methodology of inductive learning. *Artificial Intelligence, 20*, 111–161.

Michalski, R. S., Stepp, R. E., and Diday, E. (1981). A recent advance in data analysis: Clustering objects into classes characterized by conjunctive concepts. In L. Kanal and A. Rosenfeld (Eds.), *Progress in pattern recognition* (Vol. 1, pp. 33–55). Amsterdam: North-Holland.

Mill, J. S. (1965). *On the logic of the moral sciences.* New York: Bobbs-Merrill. (Originally published 1843)

Miller, G. A., and Johnson-Laird, P. N. (1976). *Language and perception.* Cambridge, MA: Harvard University Press.

Miller, P. McC. (1971). Do labels mislead? A multiple-cue study within the framework of Brunswik's probabilistic functionalism. *Organizational Behavior and Human Performance, 6*, 480–500.

Mohr, R. D. (1977). Family resemblance, platonism, universals. *Canadian Journal of Philosophy, 7*, 593–600.

Muchinsky, P. M., and Dudycha, A. L. (1974). The influence of a suppressor variable and labeled stimuli on multiple cue probability learning. *Organizational Behavior and Human Performance, 12*, 429–444.

Murphy, G. L. (1982a). Cue validity and levels of categorization. *Psychological Bulletin, 91*, 174–177.

Murphy, G. L. (1982b). *Note on measures of category structure.* Unpublished manuscript, Brown University, Psychology Department.

Murphy, G. L., and Smith, E. E. (1982). Basic-level superiority in picture categorization. *Journal of Verbal Learning and Verbal Behavior, 21*, 1–20.

Murphy, G. L., and Wisniewski, E. J. (1985). *Feature correlations in conceptual representations.* Unpublished manuscript, Brown University, Department of Psychology.

Murphy, G. L., and Wright, J. C. (1984). Changes in conceptual structure with expertise: Differences between real-world experts and novices. *Journal of Experimental Psychology: Learning, Memory, and Cognition, 10*, 144–155.

Nisbett, R., and Ross, L. (1980). *Human inference: Strategies and shortcomings of social judgment.* Englewood Cliffs, NJ: Prentice-Hall.

Ortony, A., Vondruska, R. J., Jones, L. E., and Foss, M. A. (1984). *Salience, similes, and the asymmetry of similarity.* Unpublished manuscript, University of Illinois, Department of Psychology.

Osherson, D. N., and Smith, E. E. (1981). On the adequacy of prototype theory as a theory of concepts. *Cognition, 9*, 35–58.

Quine, W. V. O. (1961). Two dogmas of empiricism. In W. V. O. Quine, *From a logical point of view* (2nd ed., pp. 20–46). New York: Harper & Row.

Quine, W. V. O. (1977). Natural kinds. In S. P. Schwartz (Ed.), *Naming, necessity, and natural kinds* (pp. 155–175). Ithaca, NY: Cornell University Press.

Richards, M. M. (1979). Sorting out what's in a word from what's not: Evaluating Clark's semantic features acquisition theory. *Journal of Experimental Child Psychology, 27,* 1–47.

Rosch, E. (1978). Principles of categorization. In E. Rosch and B. B. Lloyd (Eds.), *Cognition and categorization* (pp. 27–48). Hillsdale, NJ: Erlbaum.

Rosch, E., and Mervis, C. B. (1975). Family resemblances: Studies in the internal structure of categories. *Cognitive Psychology, 7,* 573–605.

Rosch, E., Mervis, C. B., Gray, W. D., Johnson, D. M., and Boyes-Braem, P. (1976). Basic objects in natural categories. *Cognitive Psychology, 8,* 382–439.

Roth, E. M., and Shoben, E. J. (1983). The effect of context on the structure of categories. *Cognitive Psychology, 15,* 346–378.

Rumelhart, D. E. (1980). Schemata: The building blocks of cognition. In R. J. Spiro, B. C. Bruce, and W. F. Brewer (Eds.), *Theoretical issues in reading comprehension* (pp. 33–58). Hillsdale, NJ: Erlbaum.

Rumelhart, D. E. (1981). Understanding understanding (CHIP Rep. No. 100). San Diego: University of California, Center for Human Information Processing.

Schank, R. C., and Abelson, R. P. (1977). *Scripts, plans, goals and understanding: An inquiry into human knowledge structures.* Hillsdale, NJ: Erlbaum.

Sebetsyen, G. S. (1962). *Decision-making processes in pattern recognition.* New York: Macmillan.

Shweder, R. A., and Miller, J. G. (1985). The social construction of the person: How is it possible? In K. J. Gergen and K. Davis (Eds.), *The social construction of the person.* Berlin: Springer-Verlag.

Smith, E. E., Adams, N., and Schorr, D. (1978). Fact retrieval and the paradox of interference. *Cognitive Psychology, 10,* 438–464.

Smith, E. E., and Medin, D. L. (1981). *Categories and concepts.* Cambridge, MA: Harvard University Press.

Suppe, F. (1977). The search for philosophic understanding of scientific theories. In F. Suppe (Ed.), *The structure of scientific theories* (2nd ed., pp. 3–241). Urbana: University of Illinois Press.

Tambiah, S. J. (1969). Animals are good to think and good to prohibit. *Ethnology, 8,* 424–459.

Tversky, A. (1977). Features of similarity. *Psychological Review, 84,* 327–352.

Tversky, A., and Kahneman, D. (1980). Causal schemas in judgments under uncertainty. In M. Fishbein (Ed.), *Progress in social psychology* (pp. 49–72). Hillsdale, NJ: Erlbaum.

Tversky, B., and Hemenway, K. (1984). Objects, parts, and categories. *Journal of Experimental Psychology: General, 113,* 169–193.

Ullman, S. (1979). *The interpretation of visual motion.* Cambridge, MA: MIT Press.

Wattenmaker, W., Murphy, T. D., Dewey, G. I., Edelson, S. E., and Medin, D. L. (1984). Linear separability, knowledge structures, and concept naturalness. Unpublished manuscript, University of Illinois, Department of Psychology.

Wittgenstein, L. (1953). *Philosophical investigations.* New York: Macmillan.

Wright, J. C., and Murphy, G. L. (1984). The utility of theories in intuitive statistics: The robustness of theory-based judgments. *Journal of Experimental Psychology: General, 113,* 301–322.

Younger, B. A., and Cohen, L. B. (1984). Infant perception of correlations among attributes. *Child Development, 54,* 858–867.

Ziff, P. (1972). *Understanding understanding.* Ithaca, NY: Cornell University Press.

Chapter 20

Knowledge Acquisition: Enrichment or Conceptual Change?

Susan Carey

There is a broad consensus that learning requires the support of innate representations (cf. Carey and Gelman 1991, Hirschfeld and Gelman 1994, Johnson and Morton 1992, but see also Elman et al. 1996). Further, recent data allow the characterization of some of the innate representations that guide cognitive development (see especially Gallistel et al. 1991, Marler 1991, and Spelke 1991). Spelke (1991) defends a stronger thesis: The initial representations of physical objects that guide *infants'* object perception and *infants'* reasoning about objects remain the core of the *adult* conception of objects. Spelke's thesis is stronger because the existence of innate representations need not preclude subsequent change or replacement of these beginning points of development. Her argument involves demonstrating that infants young as 2 1/2 to 4 months expect objects to move on continuous paths and that they know that one object cannot pass through another. She concludes by making a good case that these principles (spatiotemporal continuity and solidity) are central to the adult conception of objects as well. In the case of the concept of a physical object, cognitive development consists of enrichment of our very early concept, not the radical change Piaget posited.

I do not (at least not yet) challenge Spelke's claim concerning the continuity over human development of our conception of physical objects. However, Spelke implies that the history of the concept of an object is typical of all concepts that are part of intuitive adult physical reasoning. Further, she states that in at least one crucial respect, the acquisition of commonsense physical knowledge differs from the acquisition of scientific knowledge: The development of *scientific* knowledge involves radical conceptual change. Intuitive conceptions, in contrast, are constrained by innate principles that determine the entities of the mentally represented world, thus determining the entities about which we learn, leading to entrenchment of the initial concepts and principles. She suggest that going beyond these initial concepts requires the meta-conceptually aware theory building of mature scientists. To the degree that Spelke is correct, the scope for a constructivist genetic epistemology as envisioned by Piaget is correspondly small; normal cognitive development would involve minimal conceptual change and no major conceptual reorganizations.

Spelke's claim is implausible, on the widely held assumption of the continuity of science with commonsense explanation (e.g., Nersessian 1992). Of course, Spelke rejects the continuity assumption. In this chapter, I deny Spelke's conjecture that ordinary, intuitive, cognitive development consists only of enrichment of innate structural principles. The alternative that I favor is that conceptual change occurs during normal cognitive growth. Let me begin by settling some terminological matters. By *concept, belief,* and *theory,* I mean mentally represented structures. Concepts are units of mental representation roughly the grain of single lexical items, such as *object*, *matter*, and *weight*. Beliefs are mentally represented propositions taken by the believer to be true, such as *Air is not made of matter*. Concepts are the constituents of beliefs; that is, propositions are represented by structures of concepts. Theories are complex mental structures consisting of a mentally represented domain of phenomena and explanatory principle that account for them.

The debate between the enrichment and conceptual change views of cognitive development touches some of the deepest problems of developmental psychology. One such problem is the origin of human concepts. Theories of the origin of concepts are organized around two poles: the extreme nativist view that all concepts of the grain of single lexical items are innate (see Fodor 1975 for an argument in favor of this position) and the empiricist view that new concepts arise by combination from innate primitives (see Jackendoff 1989 for a modern statement of this position). As regards knowledge acquisition, both views are enrichment views, although the type of enrichment envisioned differs. On Fodor's view, knowledge acquisition consists of addition and changes of beliefs; on Jackendoff's, new concepts may also come into being, but these are defined in terms of innate primitives. Like Piaget's constructivism, the conceptual change position stakes out a third possibility, that new concepts may arise that are not definable in terms of concepts already held. Another problem touched by the debate concerns the origin of knowledge. Is knowledge acquisition merely a matter of belief revision? For example, when a child says that a piece of rice weighs nothing at all, is he or she merely expressing a false belief that he or she will eventually revise, or is the child expressing a true belief in terms of a concept of weight that differs from the adult's?

In keeping with current theorizing in cognitive psychology, I take concepts to be structured mental representations (see Smith 1989 for a review). A theory of human concepts must explain many things, including concepts' referential and inferential roles. Concepts may differ along many dimensions, and no doubt there are many degrees of conceptual difference within each dimension. Some examples of how concepts change in the course of knowledge acquisition follow:

1. What is periphery becomes core, and vice-versa (see Kitcher 1988). For example, what is originally seen to be the most fundamental property of an entity is realized to follow from even more fundamental properties. Example: in understanding reproduction, the child comes to see that being small and helpless are derivative properties of babies, rather than the essential properties (Carey 1985b, 1988).

2. Concepts are subsumed into newly created ontological categories or reassigned to new branches of the ontological hierarchy (see Thagard 1990). Example: Two classes of celestial bodies—stars and planets/moons—come to be conceptualized, with the sun and the earth as examples, respectively (Vosniadou and Brewer 1992).

3. Concepts are embedded in locally incommensurable theories. Example: the concepts of the phlogiston and oxygen theories of burning (Kuhn 1982).

According to Spelke, knowledge acquisition involving all three sorts of conceptual change contrasts with knowledge acquisition involving only enrichment. Enrichment consists in forming new beliefs stated over concepts already available. Enrichment:

New knowledge about entities is acquired, new beliefs represented. This knowledge then helps pick out entities in the world and provides structure to the known properties of the entities. Example: the child acquires the belief "unsupported objects fall" (Spelke 1991). This new belief influences decisions about object boundaries.

In this chapter, I explore the possibility of conceptual change of the most extreme sort.[1] I suggest that, in some cases, the child's physical concepts may be incommensurable with that of the adult's, in Kuhn's (1982) sense of local incommensurability. It is to the notion of local incommensurability that I now turn.[2]

1. Local Incommensurability

Mismatch of Referential Potential

A good place to start is with Philip Kitcher's analysis of local incommensurability (Kitcher 1988). Kitcher outlined (and endorsed) Kuhn's thesis that there are episodes in the history of science at the beginnings and ends of which practitioners of the same field of endeavor speak languages that are not mutually translatable. That is, the beliefs, laws, and explanations that are statable in the terminology at the beginning, in language 1 (L1), cannot be expressed in the terminology at the end, in language 2 (L2). As he explicated Kuhn's thesis, Kitcher focused on the referential potential of terms. He pointed out that there are multiple methods for fixing the reference of any given term: definitions, descriptions, and theory-relative similarity to particular exemplars. Each theory presupposes that for each term, its multiple methods of reference fixing pick out a single referent. Incommensurability arises when an L1 set of methods of reference fixing for some term is seen by L2 to pick out two or more distinct entities. In the most extreme cases, the perspective of L2 dictates that some of L1's methods fail to provide any referent for the term at all, whereas others provide different referents from each other. For example, the definition of "phlogiston" as "the principle given off during combustion" fails, in our view, to provide any referent for "phlogiston" at all. However, as Kitcher pointed out, in other uses of "phlogiston," where reference is fixed by the description of the production of some chemical, it is perfectly possible for us to understand what chemicals are being talked about. In various descriptions of how to produce "dephlogisticated air," the referent of the phrase can be identified as either oxygen or oxygen-enriched air.

Kitcher produced a hypothetical conversation between Priestley and Cavendish designed to show that even contemporaries who speak incommensurable languages can communicate. Kitcher argued that communication is possible between two parties, if one can figure out what the other is referring to and if the two share *some* language. Even in cases of language change between L1 and L2, the methods of reference fixing for many terms that appear in both languages remain entirely constant. Further, even for the terms for which there is mismatch, there is still some overlap, so that in many

---

1. Spelke points out that Piaget's claim for changes in the conception of objects during infancy are more extreme than any of the four enumerated here. Piaget denies the infant any *conception* of objects at all, granting only ephemeral sensory experiences. I endorse Spelke's counterarguments to Piaget's position; see also Leslie (1988) and Mandler (1988).

2. My explication of local incommensurability closely follows Carey (1988) though I work through different examples here.

contexts the terms will refer to the same entities. Also, agreement on reference is possible because the two speakers can learn each others' language, including mastering the other's methods of reference fixing.

The problem with Kitcher's argument is that it identifies communication with agreement on the referents of terms. But communication requires more than agreement on referents; it requires agreement on what is said about the referents. The problem of incommensurability goes beyond mismatch of referential potential.

Beyond Reference

If speakers of putatively incommensurable languages can, in some circumstances, understand each other, and if we can, for analogous reason, understand texts written in a language that is putatively incommensurable with our own, why do we want to say that the two languages are incommensurable? In answering this question, Kuhn moved beyond the referential function of language. To figure out what a text is referring to is not the same as to provide a translation for the text. In a translation, we replace sentences in L1 with sentences in L2 that have the same meaning. Even if expressions in L1 can be replaced with coreferential expression in L2, we are not guaranteed a translation. To use Frege's example, replacing "the morning star" with "the evening star" would preserve reference but would change the meaning of a text. In cases of incommensurability, this process will typically replace an L1 term with one L2 term in some contexts and other L2 terms in other contexts. But it matter to the meaning of the L1 text that a single L1 term was used. For example, it mattered to Priestley that all of the cases of "dephlogisticated" entities were so designated; his language expressed a theory in which all dephlogisticated substances shared an essential property that explained derivative properties. The process of replacing some uses of "dephlogisticated air" with "oxygen," others with "oxygen-enriched," and still others with other phrases, yields what Kuhn called a disjointed text. One can see no reason that these sentences are juxtaposed. A good translation not only preserves reference; a text makes sense in L1, and a good translation of it into L2 will make sense in L2.

That the history of science is possible is often offered as prima facie refutation of the doctrine of incommensurability. If earlier theories are expressed languages that are incommensurable with our own, the argument goes, how can the historian understand those theories and describe them to us so that we understand them? Part of the answer to this challenge has already been sketched herein. Although parts of L1 and L2 are incommensurable, much stays the same, enabling speakers of the two language to figure out what the other must be saying. What one does in this process is not *translation*, but rather *interpretation* and *language learning*. Like the anthropologist, the historian of science interprets, and does not merely translate. Once the historian has learned L1, he or she can teach it to us, and then we can express the earlier theory as well.

On Kuhn's view, incommensurability arises because a language community learns a whole set of terms together, which together describe natural phenomena and express theories. Across different languages, these sets of terms can, and often do, cut up the world in incompatible ways. To continue with the phlogiston theory example, one reason that we cannot express claims about phlogiston in our language is that we do not share the phlogiston theory's concepts *principle* and *element*. The phlogiston theory's *element* encompassed many things we do not consider elements, and modern chemistry has no concept at all that corresponds to phlogiston theory's *principle*. But we cannot express the phlogiston theory's understanding of combustion, acids, airs, and so on, without using the concepts *principle, element*, and *phlogiston*, for these concepts are all interdefined. We cannot translate sentences containing "phlogiston" into pure 20th-century language, because when it comes to using words like "principle" and "element" we are forced to choose one of two options, neither of which leads to a real translation:

1. We use "principle" and "element" but provide a translator's gloss before the text. Rather than providing a translation, we are changing L2 for the purposes of rendering the text. The translator's gloss is the method for teaching L1 to the speakers of L2.
2. We replace each of these terms with different terms and phrases in different contexts, preserving reference but producing a disjointed text. Such a text is not a translation, because it does not make sense as a whole.

Conceptual Differentiation

As is clear from the preceding text, incommensurability involves change at the level of individual concepts in the transition from one language to the other. There are several types of conceptual change, including:

1. Differentiation, as in Galileo's drawing the distinction between *average velocity* and *instantaneous velocity*; see Kuhn (1997).
2. Coalescences, as when Galileo saw that Aristotle's distinction between *natural* and *violent* motion was a distinction without a difference and collapsed the two into a single notion.
3. Simple properties being reanalyzed as relations, as when Newton reanalyzed the concept *weight* as a relation between the earth and the object whose weight is in question.

Characterizing change at the level of individual concepts is no simple matter. We face problems both of analysis and evidence. To explore these problems, take just one type of conceptual change—conceptual differentiation. Developmental psychologists often appeal to differentiation when characterizing conceptual change, but not all cases in which distinctions that are undrawn come to be drawn imply incommensurability. The 2-year-old may not distinguish collies, German shephards, and poodles and therefore may have an undifferentiated concept of *dog* relative to adults, but the concept *dog* could well play roughly the same role in both the 2-year-old's and the adult's conceptual system. The cases of differentiation involving incommensurability are those in which the undifferentiated parent concept from L1 is incoherent from the point of view of L2.

Consider McKie and Heathcote's (1935) claim that before Black, *heat* and *temperature* were not differentiated. This would require that thermal theories before Black represented a single concept, fusing our concepts *heat* and *temperature*. Note that in the language of our current theories, there is no superordinate term that encompasses both of these meanings—indeed, any attempt to wrap heat and temperature together would produce a monster. Heat and temperature are two entirely different types of physical mangnitides; heat is an extensive quantity, whereas temperature is an intensive quantity. Extensive quantities, such as the amount of heat in a body (e.g., 1 cup of water), are additive—the total amount of heat in two cups of water is the sum of that in each. Intensive quantities are ratios and therefore not additive—if one cup of water at 80 °F is added to 1 cup at 100 °F, the resultant temperature is 90 °F, not 180 °F. Furthermore, *heat* and *temperature* are interdefined—for example, a calorie is the amount of heat required to raise the temperature of 1 gram of water 1 °C. Finally, the two play completely different roles in explaining physical phenomena such as that of heat flow. Every theory since Black includes a commitment to thermal equilibrium, which is the principle that temperature differences are the occasion of heat flow. This commitment cannot be expressed without distinct concepts of *heat* and *temperature*.

To make sense of McKie and Heathcote's claim, then, we must be able to conceive how it might be possible for there to be a single undifferentiated concept fusing *heat* and *temperature*, and we must understand what evidence would support the claim. Often, purely linguistic evidence is offered; L1 contains only one term, whereas L2 contains two. However, more than one representational state of affairs could underlie any case of undifferentiated language. Lack of differentiation between *heat* and *temperature* is surely representationally different from mere absence of the concept *heat*, even though languages expressing either set of thermal concepts might have only one word, e.g., "hot." A second representational state that might mimic non-differentiation is the false belief that two quantities are perfectly correlated. For example, before Black's discoveries of specific and latent heat, scientist might have believed that adding a fixed amount of heat to a fixed quantity of matter always leads to the same increase in temperature. Such a belief could lead scientists to use one quantity as a rough and ready stand-in for the other, which might produce texts that would suggest that the two were undifferentiated.

The only way to distinguish these two alternative representational states of affairs (false belief in perfect correlation and absence of one or the other concept) from conceptual nondifferentiation is to analyze the roles that the concepts played in the theories in which they were embedded. Wiser and Carey (1983) analyzed the concept *heat* in the thermal theory of the 17th-century Academy of Florence, the first group to systematically study thermal phenomena. We found evidence supporting McKie and Heathcote's claim of nondifferentiation. The Academy's heat had both causal strength and qualitative intensity—that is, aspects of both modern *heat* and modern *temperature*. The "Experimenters" (their own self-designation) did not separately quantify heat and temperature and, unlike Black, did not seek to study the relations between the two. Furthermore, they *did* relate a single thermal variable, *degree of heat*, to mechanical phenomena. By analyzing contexts we now see *degree of heat* sometimes referred to temperature and sometimes to amount of heat. You may think of this thermal variable, as they did, as the *strength* of the heat and relate it to the magnitude of the physical effects of heat. The Experimenters used thermometers to measure degree of heat, but they did so by noting the rate of change of level in the thermometer, the interval of change, and only rarely the final level attained by the alcohol in their thermometers (which were not calibrated to fixed points such as the freezing and boiling points of water). That is, they did not quantify either temperature or amount of heat, and they certainly did not attempt to relate two distinct thermal variables. Finally, their theory provided a different account of heat exchange from that of the caloric theory of modern thermodynamics. The Experimenters did not formulate the principle of thermal equilibrium; their account needed no distinct concepts of heat and temperature. For all these reasons, we can be confident in ascribing a single undifferentiated concept that conflated *heat* and *temperature* to these 17th-century scientists. No such concept as the Experimenters' *degree of heat* plays any role in any theory after Black.

The Experimenters' concept, which is incoherent from our point of view, led them into contradictions that they recognized but could not resolve. For example, they noted that a chemical reaction contained in a metal box produced a degree of heat that was insufficient to melt paraffin, whereas putting a solid metal block of the same size on a fire induced a degree of heat in the block that was sufficient to melt paraffin. That is, the *latter* (the block) had a greater degree of heat. However, they also noted that if one put the box with the chemical reaction in ice water, it melted more ice than did the heated metal block, so the *former* (the box) had a greater degree of heat. Although they recognized this as a contradiction, they threw up their hands at it. They could not resolve it without differentiating temperature from amount of heat. The chemical reaction generates more heat but attains a lower temperature than does the block; the melting point of paraffin is a function of temperature, whereas how much ice melts is a function of amount of heat generated.

Summary

When we ask whether the language of children (L1) and the conceptual system it expresses (C1) might sometimes be incommensurable with the language (L2) and conceptual system (C2) of adults, where C1 and C2 encompass the same domain of nature, we are asking whether there is a set of concepts at the core of C1 that cannot be expressed in terms of C2, and vice-versa. We are asking whether L1 can be translated into L2 without a translator's gloss. Incommensurability arises when there are simultaneous differentiations or coalescences between C1 and C2, such that the undifferentiated concepts of C1 can no longer play any role in C2, and the coalesced concepts of C2 can play no role in C1.

2. Five Reasons to Doubt Incommensurability between Children and Adults

I have encountered five reasons to doubt that children's conceptual systems are incommensurable with adults':

1. Adults communicate with young children just fine.
2. Psychologists who study cognitive development depict children's conceptions in the adult language.
3. Where's the body? Granted, children cannot express all of the adult conceptual system in their language, but this is because L1 is a subset of L2, not because the two are incommensurable. Incommensurability requires that L2 not be able to express L1, as well as L1 not being able to express L2. Just as we cannot define "phlogiston" in our language, so holders of the phlogiston theory could not define "oxygen" in theirs. Where do children's conceptual systems provide any phenomena like those of the phlogiston theory? Where is a preschool child's "phlogiston" or "principle?"
4. There is no way incommensurability could arise (empiricist version). Children learn their language from the adult culture. How could children establish sets of terms that are interrelated differently from adult interrelations?

5. There is no way incommensurability could arise (nativist version). Intuitive conceptions are constrained by innate principles that determine the objects of cognition and that become entrenched in the course of further learning.

Those who offer one or more of the preceding objections share the intuition that although the young child's conceptual system may not be able to express all that the adult's can, the adult can express the child's ideas, that is, can translate the child's language into adult terms. Cognitive development, in this view, consists of enrichment of the child's conceptual system until it matches that of the adult.

Adults and Young Children Communicate

The answer to this objection should, by now, be familiar. Incommensurability does not require complete lack of communication. After all, the early oxygen theorists argued with the phlogiston theorists, who were often their colleagues or teachers. Locally incommensurable conceptual systems can share many terms that have the same meaning in both languages. This common ground can be used to fix referents for particular uses of nonshared terms, for example, a use of "dephlogisticated air" to refer to oxygen enriched air. Anyway, it is an empirical question just how well adults understand preschool children.

Developmental Psychologists Must Express Children's Beliefs in the Adult Language: Otherwise, How Is the Study of Cognitive Development Possible?

I discussed earlier how it is possible for the historian of science to express in today's language an earlier theory that was expressed in an incommensurable language. We understand the phlogiston theory, to the extent that we do, by *interpreting* the distinctive conceptual machinery and enriching our own language. To the extent that the child's language in incommensurable with the adult's, psychologists do not express the child's beliefs in the adult language. Rather, they interpret the child's language, learn it, and teach it to other adults. This is possible because of the considerable overlap between the two, enabling the psychologist, like the historian, to be interpreter and language learner.

Where's the Body?

As mentioned above, those who raise these objections believe that the child's concepts are a subset of the adult's; the child cannot express all adult concepts, but the adult can express all the child's. The body we seek, then, is a child's concept that cannot be expressed in the adult's language.

There are two cases of the subset relation that must be distinguished. If concept acquisition solely involves constructing new concepts out of existing ones, then the child's concepts will be a subset of the adult's, and no incommensurability will be involved. However, in some cases in which one conceptual system is a subset of another, *one-way* incommensurability obtains. For example, Newtonian mechanics is a subset of the physics of Maxwell. Maxwell recognized forces that Newton did not, but Maxwell did not reconceptualize mechanical phenomena. That is, Maxwell's physics could express Newton's. The reverse is not so. It is not possible to define electromagnetic concepts in terms of Newtonian concepts.

Although I certainly expect that there are cases of conceptual change in childhood that involve one-way incommensurability, full two-way incommensurability is the focus of the present analysis. In the most convincing cases of incommensurability from the history of science, some of the concepts of C1, such as "phlogiston" and "principle," have no descendents at all in C2. The body we seek is such a case in which the child's C1 contains concepts that are absent from the adult's C2—concepts that cannot be defined in C2. Note that *concepts* are the issue, not terms. Since children learn language from adults, we would not expect them to invent terms like "phlogiston" or "principle" that do not appear in the adult lexicon. However, two-way incommensurability does not require terms in L1 with no descendents in L2. Newtonian mechanics is incommensurable with Einsteinian mechanics, but Newton's system contains no bodies in this sense. Similarly, although the Florentine Experimenters' source-recipient theory of thermal phenomena is incommensurable with our thermal theory, there is no Florentine analog of "phlogiston." Their "degree of heat" is the ancestor of our "temperature" and "heat." In these cases, incommensurability arises from sets of core concepts being interrelated in different ways, and from several simultaneous differentiations and coalescences. Thus, although there may be no bodies such as "phlogiston" or "principle" in the child's language it remains an open empirical question whether cases of two-way incommensurable conceptual systems between children and adults are to be found.

How Would Incommensurability Arise (Empiricist Version)?
The child learns language from adults; the language being spoken to the child is L2; why would the child construct a L1 incommensurable with L2? This is an empiricist objection to the possibility of incommensurability because it views the child as a blank state, acquiring the adult language in an unproblematic manner. But although children learn language from adults, they are not blank slates as regards their conceptual system. As they learn the terms of their language, they must map these onto the concepts they have available to them. Their conceptual system provides the hypotheses they may entertain as to possible word meanings. Thus, the language they actually construct is constrained both by the language they are hearing and the conceptualization of the world they have already constructed. Incommensurability could arise when this conceptualization is incommensurable with the C2 that L2 expresses.

Presumably, there are no phlogiston-type bodies in the child's L1, because the child learns language from adults. The child learning chemistry and the explanation for combustion would never learn words like "principle" or "phlogiston." However, it is an open empirical question whether the child assigns meanings to terms learned from adult language that are incommensurable with those of the adult.

How Would Incommensurability Arise (Nativist Version)?
Empiricists question why the child, learning L2 from adults, might ever construct an incommensurable L1. Nativists worry how the developing mind, constrained by innate principles and concepts, would ever construct an L2 that is incommensurable with L1. This is Spelke's challenge, cited in the opening of the present chapter. Spelke does not deny the phenomenon of conceptual change in the history of science. That is, Spelke grants that innate constraints do not preclude the shift from the phlogiston theory to the oxygen theory, nor does she deny that this shift involves incommensurable concepts. Innate constraints do not preclude incommensurability *unless* children are different from scientists. Thus, Spelke's nativist objection requires the noncontinuity position, which is why she speculates that conceptual change requires

mature scientists' explicit scrutiny of their concepts and their striving for consistency. Of course, merely positing noncontinuity begs the question.

In considering these speculations, we must remember that the child develops his or her conceptual system in collaboration with the adult culture. Important sources of information include the language of adults, the problems adults find worthy and solvable, and so on. This is most obvious in the case of explicit instruction in school, especially in math and science, but it is no less true of the commonsense theories of the social, biological, and physical worlds constructed by cultures. Not all common-sense knowledge of the physical, social, and biological worlds develops rapidly and effortlessly. One source of difficulty may be incommensurability between the child's conceptual system and that which the culture has constructed. Again, it is an open empirical issue whether commonsense conceptual development is continuous with scientific conceptual development in the sense of implicating incommensurability.

In this section, I have countered five arguments that we should not expect incommensurability between young children's and adult's conceptual systems. Of course, I have not shown that local incommensurability actually ever obtains. That is the task of the next section.

3. The Evidence

I have carried out case studies of children's conceptualization of two domains of nature, and in both cases some of the child's concepts are incommensurable with the adult's. One domain encompasses the child's concepts of *animal, plant, alive, person, death, growth, baby, eat, breathe, sleep,* and so forth (Carey 1985b, 1988). The other encompasses the child's concepts of *matter, material kind, weight, density,* and so on. (Carey, Smith, Sodian, Zaitchik, and Grosslight unpublished manuscript; Smith, Carey, and Wiser 1985; see also Piaget and Inhelder 1941). Here, I draw my examples from the latter case, for it includes physical concepts and thus bears more directly on Spelke's conjecture that commonsense physical concepts develop only through enrichment.

The central phenomenon that suggests developmental cases of incommensurability is the same as the one that suggests historical cases as well. The child makes assertions that are inexplicable to the adult, for example, that a particular piece of styrofoam is weightless or that the weight of an object changes when the object is turned on its side. Of course, such assertions do not in themselves demonstrate incommensurability. They raise three possibilities as to the relations between the child's conceptual system and the adult's:

1. The child is expressing false beliefs represented in terms of the same concept of weight as the adult's.
2. The child is expressing beliefs in terms of a different concept of weight from the adult, but the child's concept is definable in the adult vocabulary.
3. The child is expressing beliefs in terms of a different concept of weight from the adult; the child's and adult's concepts are incommensurable.

The only way to decide among these three alternatives is to analyze the child's and the adult's concepts of weight in the context of related concepts and the intuitive theories in which they are embedded.

Spelke's work on infants' conceptions of objects tells us that, from the earliest moment at which these conceptions have been probed, children represent objects as solid, in the sense that no part of one objects can pass through the space occupied by any part of another (see Spelke 1991). Work by Estes, Wellman, and Woolley (1989) shows that 3-year-olds draw a distinction between real physical objects, such as a real cookie, and mentally represented objects, such as an image of a cookie or a dream of a cookie. These very young children know that only the former can be seen and touched by both the child and other people, and only the latter can be changed by thought alone. The young child distinguishes physical objects from other entities in terms of properties that are at least precursors to those that adults use in drawing the distinction between material and immaterial entities. We shall see, however, that the child does not draw the material/immaterial distinction on the same basis as does the adult. Furthermore, the child's conceptual system represents several concepts undifferentiated relative to the adult's, and the differentiations are of the type that implicate incommensurability, that is, are like the *heat/temperature* case rather than the *poodle/collie* case. One example is the undifferentiated concept of *weight/density*. Like the concept of *heat/temperature* before Black, an undifferentiated *weight/density* concept does not remain a useful superordinate concept in the conceptual systems of those who have drawn the distinction.[3]

Like heat and temperature, weight and density are different sorts of physical magnitudes; weight is an extensive quantity, and density is an intensive quantity, and the two are interdefined. A single concept undifferentiated between the two is incoherent from the later point of view.

4. Weight, Density, Matter, and Material Kind

Undifferentiated Concept: Weight/Density

We require evidence in two steps to support the claim that weight and density are not differentiated by young children. To rule out the possibility that young children simply lack the concept *density*, we must show that heaviness relativized to size plays some role in their judgements. Indeed, Smith et al. (1985) found that many young children (3- to 5-year-olds) appear to lack the concept of density at all. Older children, in contrast, relativized weight to size in some of their judgments of heaviness. Secondly, once we have shown that *density* is not entirely absent, we must show that the child does not relate density to some physical phenomena and weight to others, but rather accounts for all heaviness-related phenomena in terms of an undifferentiated weight/density concept. Of course, one can never establish this beyond doubt; it is always possible that tomorrow somebody will find some limited contexts in which the child has systematically distinguished the two. But we (Smith et al. 1985) devised a series of tasks, both verbal and nonverbal, that probed for the distinction in the simplest ways we could think of. For example, we presented children with pairs of objects made of different metals, and asked "Which is heavier?" or "Which is made of the heavier kind of metal?" Nonverbal versions of the same task

3. The concept of *density* at issue here is a ratio of *weight* and *volume* and is a property of material kinds. We are not probing the more general abstract concept of density expressing the ratio of any two extensive variable, such as population density (people per area).

involved the child predicting which objects would make a sponge bridge collapse (weight being the relevant factor) and sorting objects into steel and aluminum families (density being the relevant factor). In the steel and aluminum family task, for example, the child was first shown several pairs of identically sized cylinders, and it was pointed out that steel is a much heavier kind of stuff than is aluminum. Children with an undifferentiated concept showed intrusion of absolute weight on judgments we would base on density; in this case, this meant sorting large aluminum cylinders into the steel family because they were heavy.

Smith, Snir, Grosslight, and Unger (1988) corroborated these results with other simple tasks. They provided children with scales and with sets of objects that varied in volume, weight, and material kind and asked them to order the objects by size, by absolute weight, and by density (explained in terms of heaviness of the kind of stuff). The ordering required no calculations of density; for instance, if one object is larger than another, but they weigh the same or the smaller is heavier, we can infer without calculation that the smaller is denser. Prior to instruction, few children as old as age 12 are able to correctly order the same set of items differently on the basis of absolute weight and density. Mistakes reveal intrusions of weight into the density orderings, and vice-versa. These results are underscored when children are asked to depict in a visual model the size, weights, and densities of a set of such objects. Only children who show in other tasks that they have at least partially differentiated weight and density produce models that depict, in some way or another, all three physical magnitudes.

Just as the Experimenters' undifferentiated *heat/temperature* concept led them into contradictions, children's *weight/density* concept leads them into outright contradiction. Smith et al. (1985) presented children in this conceptual state with two bricks, one of steel and one of aluminum. Though the steel brick was smaller, the two weighed the same, and children were shown that they balanced exactly on a scale. Children were probed: "How come these weigh the same, since one is so much bigger?" They answered, "Because that one (the steel) is made of a heavier kind of stuff," or "Because steel is heavier," or some equivalent response. They were then shown two bricks of steel and aluminum, now both the same size as each other, and asked to predict whether they would balance or whether one would be heavier than the other. Now they answered that they would weigh the same, "because the steel and aluminum weighed the same before" (Fig. 20.1).

Children give this pattern of responses because they do not realize that the claim that a given steel object weighs the same as a given aluminum object is not the same as that steel and aluminum weigh the same, even though they also understand that if a small steel object weighs the same as a large aluminum one, this is possible because steel is heavier than aluminum. It is not that children are unmoved by the contradiction in these assertions. They can be shown the contradiction, and because they, as well as adults, strive for consistency, they are upset by it. Drawing out contradictions that are inherent in current concepts is one of the functions of thought experiments (see Kuhn 1977; Nersessian 1992). Here, we have produced a concrete instantiation of a thought experiment for the child. Just as the Experimenters were unable to resolve the contradictions due to their undifferentiated *heat/temperature* concept, so too children cannot resolve the contradictions due to their undifferentiated *weight/density* concept.

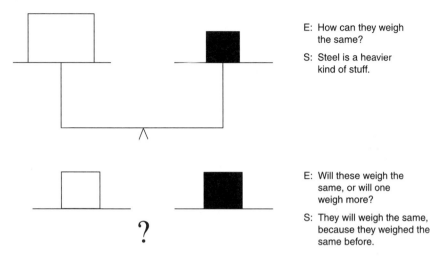

E: How can they weigh
   the same?

S: Steel is a heavier
   kind of stuff.

E: Will these weigh the
   same, or will one
   weigh more?

S: They will weigh the same,
   because they weighed the
   same before.

Figure 20.1
Concrete thought experiment.

How an Undifferentiated Weight/Density Concept Functions

The previous section outlined some of the evidence that 6- to 12-year-old children have a concept that is undifferentiated between weight and density. But how could such a concept function in any conceptual system, given the contradictions it leads the child into? The short answer is that the contexts in which the child deploys his or her weight/density concept do not, in general, elicit these contradictions. This is the same answer as for the Experimenter's *degree of heat* (undifferentiated between heat and temperature; Wiser and Carey 1983), or for Aristotle's *speed* (undifferentiated between average and instantaneous velocity; Kuhn 1997).

A sketch of the purposes for which children *do* use their concept provides a slightly longer answer. Like the Experimenters' *degree of heat*, the child's concept is *degree of heaviness*. Children appeal to heaviness of objects to explain some aspects of those objects' effects on themselves or on other objects. The greater an object's heaviness, the more difficult it is to lift, the more likely to hurt if dropped on one's toes, the more likely to break something else if dropped on it, and so on. Notice that "heavy," like other dimensional adjectives such as "big," is a relative term. Something is heavy relative to some standard, and the child can switch fluidly from one way of relativizing heaviness to another. An object can be heavy for objects of that type (e.g., a heavy book), heavy for the objects on the table, heavy for me but not my mother, or heavy for objects of that size. For the child with an undifferentiated weight/density concept, relativizing heaviness to a standard determined by size is no different from their ways of relativizing heaviness. Children differentiate *weight* and *density* as they realize that relativizing weight to size produces an independent physical magnitude, that is, one related in systematic ways to distinct phenomena in the world.

The full answer to how children can have an undifferentiated weight/density concept that functions effectively within their conceptual system will require a description of their conceptual system. The claim that weight and density are not differentiated does not exhaust the differences between the child's concept and the adult's; indeed, it could not. Because an undifferentiated weight/density concept is incoherent from the adult's point of view, it must be embedded in a very different conceptual system to function coherently in the child's. We should expect, therefore, that the child's concept of heaviness differs from the adult's in many ways, beyond it's being undifferentiated between weight and density.

The Material/Immaterial Distinction

The concepts of weight and density are embedded in an intuitive theory of matter. Weight is an extensive property of material entities; density an intensive property of material entities. Weight is proportional to quantity of matter; density is the ratio of quantity of matter to volume. The concepts of weight, density, matter, and quantity of matter have a long intellectual history (see Toulmin and Goodfield 1962; Jammer 1961, for comprehensive reviews). As Jammer (1961) told the story, the late 19th century saw the flowering of the substantial concept of matter, which identified matter and mass. The concept of inertial mass had been formulated by Kepler and systematized by Newton, who also fused it with the medieval concept of "quantity of matter." A typical statement from the turn of the century was, "If I should have to define matter, I would say: Matter is all that has mass, or all that requires force in order to be set in motion" (Charles de Freycinet 1896, quoted in Jammer 1961, p. 86). According to this view, mass is the essential property of matter and provides a measure of quantity of matter. In a given gravitational field, weight is an extensive quantity proportional to mass.

Clearly, prior to the formulation of the concept of mass, having mass could not be taken as the essence of material entities. And indeed, prior to the formulation of the concept of mass, weight was not seen as a candidate measure of quantity of matter, nor was having weight (even on Earth) seen as necessary and sufficient for an entity's being material (Jammer 1961). The Greeks and the medieval scholastics had different concepts of matter and weight from post-Newtonian physicists. According to Jammer, Aristotle had no concept of quantity of matter, and he saw weight as an accidental property of some material entities, akin to odor. Even if the Greeks had a concept of quantity of matter, weight could not have served as its measure, because some material entities, such as air, were thought to possess intrinsic levity. For the Greeks, weight was not an extensive quantity. There were no fixed units of weight; in practical uses, even within the same nation, different substances were weighed in terms of different standards. The weight of material particles were thought to depend on the bulk of the object in which they were embedded. That is, Aristotle thought that a given lump of clay would itself weigh more when part of a large quantity of clay than when alone. Neither did the alchemists consider weight to reflect quantity of matter; they fully expected to be able to turn a few pounds of lead into hundreds of pounds of gold (Jammer 1961).

Density also was taken to be an irreducible intensive quality, like color, odor, and other accidents of matter. Density was not defined as mass/volume until Euler did so; what was actually quantified by the ancients was specific gravity (the ratio of a substance's density to that of water), not density. For example, Archimedes never used a term for density in his writings (Jammer 1961).

If weight was not an essential property of material entities, what was? There were many proposals. Euclid proposed spatial extent—length, breadth, and depth. This was one dominant possibility throughout Greek and medieval times. Galileo listed shape,

size, location, number and motion as the essential properties of material entities—
spatial, arithmetic, and dynamic properties. The spatial notions included impenetrability; that is, material entities were seen to uniquely occupy space. In another thread
of thought, material entities were those that could physically interact with other
material entities (Toulmin and Goodfield 1962). Again, weight was seen as irrelevant; according to this view, heat while weightless, is certainly material. Finally,
another line of thought posited being inert, or passive, as the essence of matter. This
was the precursor to the concept of mass; material entities are those that require
forces for their movement (Kepler) or forms for their expression (Aristotle and the
scholastics).

The substantial conception of matter (the identification of matter with mass), occupied a brief moment in the history of science. Since Einstein, the distinction between
entities with mass and those without is not taken to be absolute, because mass and
energy are intraconvertible. It is not clear that the distinction between material and
immaterial entities plays an important role in today's physics, given the existence of
particles with no rest mass, such as photons, which are nevertheless subject to gravity, and, as Jammer (1961) pointed out, the concept of mass itself is far from unproblematic in modern physics.

Given the complex history of the concept of matter, what conception of matter
should we probe for in the child? *Ours* would be a good bet, i.e., that of the non-
scientific adult. What is the adult's intuitive conception of matter, and how is it
related to the commonsense concepts of weight and density? Although this is an empirical question, I shall make some assumptions. I assume that commonsense intuitive
physics distinguishes between clearly material entities, such as solid objects, liquids,
and powders, on the one hand, and clearly immaterial entities, such as abstractions
(height, value) and mental entities (ideas), on the other. I also assume that adults conceptualize quantity of matter. Probably, the essential properties of matter are thought
to include spatial extent, impenetrability, weight, and the potential for interaction
with other material entities. Probably, most adults do not realize that these four
properties are not perfectly coextensive. Weight is probably seen as an extensive
property of material entities, proportional to quantity of matter, whereas density is
an intensive property, seen as a ratio of quantity of matter and size. This view is
closely related to the substantial conception of matter achieved at the end of the 19th
century, but it differs from that in not being based on the Newtonian conception of
mass and being unclear about the status of many entities (e.g., gasses, heat, etc.).

There are two reasons why commonsense physics might be identified so closely
with one moment in the history of science. First, commonsense science is close to the
phenomena; it is not the grand metaphysical enterprise of the Greek philosophers.
For example, in two distinct cases, commonsense science has been shown to accord
with the concepts employed in the first systematic exploration of physical phenomena. Commonsense theories of motion share much with medieval impetus theories
(e.g., McKloskey 1983), and commonsense thermal theories share much with the
source-recipient theory of the Experimenters (see Wiser 1988). Both of these theories
require a concept of quantity of matter. For example, the impetus theory posits a resistance to impetus that is proportional to quantity of matter, and the source-recipient
theory of heat posits a resistance to heat that is proportional to quantity of matter.
That untutored adults hold these theories is one reason I expect them to have a pre-
Newtonian conception of quantity of matter. Second, the developments of theoretical

physics find their way into commonsense physics, albeit at a time lag and in a watered down and distorted version. The mechanisms underlying this transmission include assimilating science instruction (however badly), making sense of the technological achievements made possible by formal science, and learning to use the measuring devices of science, such as scales and thermometers.

The Child's Material/Immaterial Distinction
We have four interrelated questions. Do young children draw a material/immaterial distinction? If yes, what is the essence of this distinction? And finally, do they conceptualize "amount of matter?" If so, what is its measure?

Estes et al. (1989) claimed that preschool children know that mental entities are immaterial; Piaget (1960) claimed that, until age 8 or so, children consider shadows to be substantial, a claim that was endorsed by DeVries (1987). These works credit the young child with a material/immaterial distinction and with one true belief (ideals are immaterial) and one false belief (shadows are material) involving the concept of materiality. Assuming that children realize that shadows are weightless, this latter belief would indicate that, like Aristotle, they consider weight to be an accidental property of material entities. But is it true they draw a material/immaterial distinction, and if so, on what grounds?

The claim of Estes et al. is based on the fact that children distinguish physical objects, such as cookies, from mental entities, such as dreams and pictures in one's head. Estes et al. probed this distinction in terms of the properties of objective perceptual access (can be seen both by the child and others) and causal interaction with other material entities (cannot be moved or changed just by thinking about it). The clever studies of Estes et al. certainly show that the child distinguishes objects from mental representations of objects in terms of features relevant to the material/immaterial distinction. But many distinctions will separate some material entities from some immaterial entities. Before we credit the child with a *material/immaterial* distinction, we must assess more fully the extension of the distinction, and we must attempt to probe the role the distinction plays in the child's conceptual system.

Shadows' materiality would be consistent with the essential properties of material entities being public perceptual access and immunity to change as a result of mental effort alone. Piaget's and DeVries' claim is based on children's statements like the following: "A shadow comes off you, so it's made of you"; "If you stand in the light, it can come off you"; "It's always there, but the darkness hides it"; or "The light causes the shadow to reflect, otherwise it is always on your body" (DeVries 1987). Such statements show that children talk as if shadows are made of some kind of substance and that they attribute to shadow some properties of objects, such as permanent existence. DeVries studied 223 children, ages 2 to 9, and only 5% of the 8- and 9-year-olds understood that shadows do not continue to exist at night, in the dark, or when another object blocks the light source causing the shadow. In discussing the question of the continued existence of shadows, virtually all children spoke of one shadow being covered by another, or of the darkness of two shadows being mixed together, making it impossible to see the shadow, even though it was still there. A similar problem arises in interpreting these data as arises in interpreting those of Estes et al. These studies show that the child attributes to shadows some properties of material entities (i.e., independent existence and permanance), but what makes these properties tantamount to *substantiality*? It is not enough that these properties differentiate some entities we consider substantial, or material, from some we do not. Many properties do that.

We must assess whether the distinction between material and immaterial entities plays any role in the child's conceptual system. One reflection of such a role would be that children would find it useful to lexicalize the distinction. Preschool children surely do not know the word "matter" or "material," but they probably do know "stuff" and "kind of stuff." Have they mapped these words onto the distinction studied by Estes et al.? Do they consider shadows made of some kind of stuff, as Piaget and De Vries claimed? In the context of an interview about kinds of stuff such as wood, metal, and plastic, Smith et al. (1985) asked 4- to 9-year-olds whether shadows are made of some kind of stuff. About three fourths of the 4- to 7-year-olds replied "Yes," and most volunteered, "Out of you and the sun." Although this may reflect their considering shadows material, it seems more likely to reflect their understanding the question to be whether and how one can make a shadow.

In a recent study, my colleagues and I attempted to address directly whether the child distinguishes between entities made of some kind of stuff and entities not made of some kind of stuff, and if so, on what basis. We introduced children from the ages of 4 through 12 to the issue by telling them that some things in the world, such as stones and tables and animals, are made of some kind of stuff, are material, and are made of molecules, whereas other things that we can think of, like sadness and ideas, are not made of anything, are not material, and are not made of molecules (Carey et al. unpublished manuscript). We encouraged children to reflect on this distinction and to repeat our examples of material and immaterial entities. We then asked them to sort the following into two piles: (a) material things, like stones, tables, and animals and (b) immaterial things, like sadness and ideas: car, tree, sand, sugar, cow, worm, styrofoam, Coca Cola, water, dissolved sugar, steam, smoke, air; electricity, heat, light, shadow, echo, wish, and dream. We will credit children with the distinction if they sort objects, liquids, and powders in the material piles and wish and dream in the immaterial pile. Where they place the remaining items will provide some information concerning the properties they consider central to the distinction.

As can be seen from Table 20.1, our instructions led to systematic sorting at all ages. At all ages, over 90% of the placements of the car, the tree, and Styrofoam were into the material pile, and at all ages except age 6, less than 15% of the placements of wish and dream were into this pile. Children understood something of the introductory instruction and certainly distinguish solid inanimate objects from abstract entities and mental representations. Shadows were not considered material; at all ages except age 4, shadows and echos patterned with wishes and dreams. These data do not support Piaget's and DeVries' claim that young children consider shadows to be substantial. Nonetheless, many of the younger children revealed very different bases for their sorts than did the older children. Around one tenth of the 4- and 6-year-olds answered randomly. In addition, half of the preschool children took only solid inanimate objects plus powders as material. That is, 50% of the 4-year-olds denied that animals and liquids are material, including a few who also denied that sand and sugar are; 13% of the 6-year-olds also showed this pattern; see Table 20.2. These data are striking, because the introduction of the material/immaterial distinction explicitly mentioned animals as examples of material entities. These children seemed to focus on the locution "made of some kind of stuff" and therefore answered affirmatively either if they could think of the material of which something is made (many commented

Table 20.1
% judged material

	Age			
	4	6	10	12
Car, tree, styrofoam	93	96	91	100
Sand, sugar	65	94	95	100
Cow, worm	55	81	95	100
Coca Cola	30	88	100	100
Water	40	25	90	100
Dissolved sugar	63	63	55	88
Steam, smoke, air	20	25	30	61
Electricity	40	75	73	63
Heat, light	30	38	41	31
Echo, shadow	25	25	9	13
Wish, dream	5	19	5	13

Table 20.2
Individual pattern analysis (%)

	Age 4 $n = 10$	Age 6 $n = 8$	Age 10 $n = 11$	Age 12 $n = 8$
adult, mass criterial	0	0	9	0
mass, critical; gasses massless	0	0	9	38
physical consequences—includes gasses, electricity, light, etc.	0	0	0	63
physical consequences—excludes gasses	40	75	82	0
denies liquids, animals, gasses, and immaterial entities	50	13	0	0
random	10	13	0	0

that trees are made of wood) or if they thought of the entities as constructed artifacts. Another reflection of this construal is seen in the 6-year-olds' responses to Coke (88% sorted as material) compared to water (25% sorted as material). Children could think of ingredients of Coke (sugar and syrup), but saw water as a primitive ingredient, thus not made of any kind of stuff. This construal also contributed to the 6-year-old's affirmative judgments on wish and dream; some children commented that dreams are made of ideas. Thus, among the youngest children there were considerable problems understanding or holding onto what distinction was being probed. Sixty percent of the 4-year-olds and 25% of the 6-year-olds showed no evidence of a conception of matter that encompassed inanimate objects, animal, liquids, and powders. These children had not mapped the properties probed by Estes et al. onto their notion of "stuff."

However, 40% of the 4-year-olds, 75% of the 6-year-olds, and 100% of the 10–11-year-olds provided systematic sorts that clearly reflect a concept of matter. Clearly, weighing something, or having mass, is not coextensive with the entities children judge material. It is only the oldest children who sometimes claimed that all weightless entities were not material (38% of the oldest group, Table 20.2). As can be seen in Table 20.2, only one child in the whole sample had an adult pattern of judgments.

Three groups of entities are reflected in the sorts: (solids, liquids and powders on the one hand, and echo, shadow, wish and dream on the other, with all others firmly in between). For children under 12, electricity, heat, and light are equally or more often judged material than are dissolved sugar, steam, smoke, and air (Table 20.1). Further, all children under 12 judged some immaterial entities (such as heat) material *and* some material entities (such as air) immaterial. In their justifications for their judgments, children mainly appealed to the perceptual effects of the entities—they mentioned that one can see and touch them. One child in a pilot study articulated the rule that one needs two or more perceptual effects for entities to be material. You can see shadows, but cannot smell, feel, or hear them; you can hear echos but cannot see, smell, or touch them; therefore, shadows and echos are not material. Nor is air. But heat can be seen (heat waves) and felt, so heat is material.

To sum up the data from the sorting task, of the youngest children (ages 4 to 6), a significant portion do not know the meaning of "stuff" in which it is synonymous with "material." This leaves open the question of whether they draw the material/immaterial distinction, even though this task failed to tap it. However, about half of the younger children and all of the older ones did interpret "stuff" in the sense intended, revealing a material/immaterial distinction. Up through age 11, the distinction between material and immaterial entities is not made on the basis of weight. Only at ages 11–12 are there a few children who take all and only entities that weigh something as material.

Weight and Materiality, Continued

The sorting data show that early elementary children do not take an entity's weighing something as necessary for materiality (in the sense of being make of some kind of stuff). From ages 4 through 11, virtually all children who deemed solids, liquids, and powders material also judged some weightless entities (electricity, heat, light, echoes, or shadow) material. However, they might hold a related belief. They may see weight as a property of all prototypical material entities (solids, liquids and powders). Smith et al. (1985) provided data that suggest that young children do not expect even this relation between materiality and weight. When given a choice between "weighs a lot, a tiny amount, or nothing at all," children judged that a single grain of rice, or a small piece of Styrofoam, weighed nothing at all. We probed for a similar judgment from those children who had participated in the material/immaterial sorting task. Virtually all had judged Styrofoam to be material (Table 20.1). We began with a sheet of Styrofoam that measured 12" by 12" by 1/2" and asked whether it weighed a lot, a little, a tiny amount, or nothing at all. If children judged that it weighed a little, we showed a piece half that size and asked again. If that was judged as weighing at least a tiny amount, a small piece the size of a fingertip was produced, and the question was repeated. Finally, the child was asked to imagine the piece being cut again and again until we had a piece so small we could not see it with our eyes, and asked if that would weigh a lot, a little, or nothing at all—whether we could ever get to a piece so small it would weigh nothing at all.

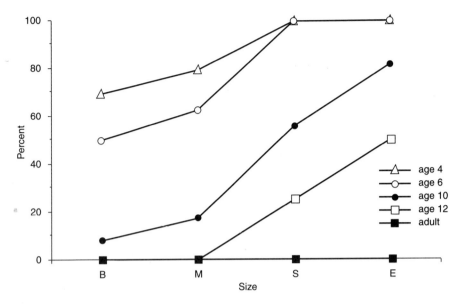

Figure 20.2
Weight of Styrofoam. Percent judging piece of Styrofoam weighs nothing at all as a function of size of piece. B, big; M, medium; S, small; E, ever, if one kept cutting it in half, repeatedly.

Smith et al.'s results were confirmed (Fig. 20.2). More than half of the 4-year-olds and fully half of the 6-year-olds judged that the *large* piece of Styrofoam weighed nothing at all, and all 4- to 6-year-olds judged that the small piece weighted nothing. Half of the 10–11-year-olds judged that the small piece weighed nothing at all, and almost all judged that if one kept dividing the Styrofoam, one would eventually obtain a piece that weighed nothing. Not until age 12 did half of the children maintain that however small the piece, even one so small one could no longer see it, it would weigh a tiny, tiny amount.

These data are important beyond showing that children consider an entity's weighing something as unrelated to its being material. They show that children, like the Greeks, do not take weight as a truly extensive property of substances. They do not conceive of the total weight of an object as the sum of weights of arbitrarily small portions of the substance from which it is made. This is one very important way in which the child's *degree of heaviness* differs from the adult's *weight*. The child's *degree of heaviness* is neither systematically intensive nor systematically extensive, as is required if the child's concept is undifferentiated between *weight* and *density*.

Physical Objects' Occupying Space
We do not doubt that even 4-year-olds know some properties that solids, liquids, and powders share, even if being "made of some kind of stuff" and having weight are not among these properties. Presumably, young children extend the properties of physical objects studied by Estes et al. (1989) to liquids and powders: public access and nonmanipulation by thought alone, for example. Another place to look might be a generalization of the infants' solidity constraint (see Spelke 1991). Infants know that one physical object cannot pass through the space occupied by another; we would

Table 20.3
Occupy space: Can steel and X fit in box at same time?

	No (%)		
	Steel and wood	Steel and water	Steel and air
Age 4 ($n = 10$)	100	90	0*
1st grade ($n = 8$)	100	100	25
5th grade ($n = 11$)	100	100	55
7th grade ($n = 8$)	100	100	62.5

*$n = 5$; The remaining five 4-year-olds denied there was air in the box.

certainly expect 4-year-olds to realize the related principle that no two objects can occupy the same space at the same time, and they might extend this principle to liquids and powders. We assessed this question by asking our subjects to imagine two pieces of material, one wood and one metal, cut to fill entirely the inside of a box. They were then asked whether we could put the wood and the metal in the box at the same time. No children had any doubts about this question; they answered that they both could not fit in at the same time (Table 20.3). When asked to imagine the box filled with water and then probed as to whether the steel piece and the water could be in the box at the same time, they all (except one 4-year-old who said that both could be in the box at the same time because the water would become compressed) again said no, that the water would be pushed out (Table 20.3).

Children are confident that solids and liquids (and, I am sure, though we did not probe it, materials such as sand as well) uniquely occupy space. However, it is unlikely that this property defines a material/immaterial distinction for them. To assess that, we would have to see whether those that think electricity, heat, light, echos, or shadows to be material also consider these to occupy space. Still, these data confirm our suspicion that children see physical objects, liquids, and powders as sharing properties relevant to the material/immaterial distinction. Having weight is simply not one of these properties.

A Digression: An Undifferentiated Air/Nothing Concept

The last questions about the box concerned air. Children were asked, of the apparently empty box, whether there was anything in it at the moment, and when they said no, we said, "What about air?" Except for half of the 4-year-olds, who denied there was air in the box and insisted that there was nothing in it, all children agreed that the box contained air. All who agreed were asked whether one could put the steel in the box at the same time as the air. If they said yes, they were further probed as to whether the steel and air would be in the box, then, at the same time. As can be seen from Table 20.3, the vast majority of the 4-year-olds and 6-year-olds thought that air and steel could be in the box at the same time, explaining, "Air doesn't take up any space," "Air is all over the place," "Air is just there—the metal goes in, air is still there," "Air isn't anything," and so on. One child said baldly, "Air isn't matter." Almost half of the 10–12-year-olds also provided this pattern of response.

The sorting task also suggests that young children consider air not material—air was judged to be made of some kind of stuff by none of the 4-year-olds, 10% of the

6-year-olds, and 36% of the 10–11-year-olds. Only 12-year-old subjects judged air to be made of some kind of stuff (75%) and also maintained that the steel would push the air out, just as it would the water (65%). Although the characterization of the child as believing air to be immaterial is easy enough to write down, a moment's reflection reveals it to be bizarre. If air is not material, what is it? Perhaps children consider air to be an immaterial physical, entity, like a shadow or an echo. But several children said outright, "Air is nothing; Air isn't anything." However, "air" is not simply synonymous with "nothing," or "empty space," for children this age know that there is no air on the moon or in outer space, that one needs air to breathe, that wind is made of air, and so on. Indeed, in a different interview in which we probed whether children of this age considered dreams and ideas to be made of some kind of stuff, an interview in which "air" was never mentioned, several different children spontaneously offered "air" as the stuff of which dreams and ideas are made of. This set of beliefs reflects another undifferentiated concept, *air/nothing* or *air/vacuum* incommensurable with the concepts in the adult conceptualization of matter.

Interim Conclusions—the Material/Immaterial Distinction
Children distinguish solids, liquids, and powders, on the one hand, from entities such as wishes and dreams, on the other, in terms of properties related to the distinction between material and immaterial entities. These include uniquely occupying space, and (probably) public perceptual access and not being manipulable by thought alone. Not all 4–6-year-olds have related this distinction to the notion of "stuff," so the data available at this point provide no evidence that these properties determine a *material/immaterial* distinction, rather than, for example, an undifferentiated *real/unreal* distinction. Some children of these ages, and all children in our sample of ages 10 and older, have related this distinction to the notion of "stuff" but do not yet see weight as one criterion for materiality.

Taking up Space: Matter's Homogeneity
Although young children may not draw a distinction between material and immaterial entities, they do conceptualize kinds of stuff such as plastic, glass, wood, sand, and water. They distinguish objects from the stuff of which they are made, realizing that the identity of an object does not survive cutting it into many small pieces, but the identity of the stuff is not affected. However, there is some question as to the limits of their ability to preserve identity of stuff as it is broken into smaller and smaller pieces. Smith et al. (1985) suggested that perhaps young children cannot conceive of substances as composed of *arbitrarily* small portions, each of which maintains the identity of the substance and some of its substance-relevant properties. In other words, they may not grasp that stuff is homogeneous. This could underly their lack of understanding that the total weight of an object is the sum of the weights of small portions. Alternatively, the problems young children have with conceptualizing the weight of tiny portions of matter could be independent of a homogeneous conception of substance.

Children's commitment to solids and liquids occupying space led us to probe their understanding of homogeneity in this context (Carey et al. unpublished manuscript). Our first method of doing so drew on the weight probes described before. We asked children whether the big piece of Styrofoam took up a lot of space, a little space, or no space at all. We then repeated that question concerning the small piece, the tiny

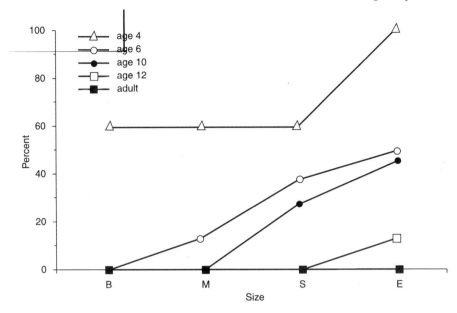

Figure 20.3
Styrofoam's taking up space. Percent judging piece of Styrofoam takes up no space at all as a function of size of piece. B, big; M, medium; S, small; E, ever, if one kept cutting it in half, repeatedly.

piece, and imagined halves and halves again until we got a piece so small one could not see it with one's eyes.

Compare Fig. 20.3 to Fig. 20.2. At all ages, children revealed a better understanding of homogeneity in the context of the question of whether a piece of Styrofoam occupies space than they did in the context of the question of whether a piece of styrofoam weighs anything. Twelve-year-olds were virtually perfect on the task; only one said that one could arrive at a piece of Styrofoam so small that it would not take up any space at all. More significantly, fully half of the 6- and 10–11-year-olds made these adult judgments. Only 4-year-olds universally failed; all said that if one arrived, by cutting, at a piece too small to see with one's eyes, that piece would not take up any space. By this measure then, almost all 12-year-olds, and half of the children between ages 6 and 12, understand that solid substances are continuously divisible, and that an arbitrarily small piece of substance still occupies a tiny tiny amount of space. They understand substances to be homogeneous. Equally important, by this measure, 4-year-olds do not have this understanding.

Not all children understood the locution "take up space." As Nussbaum (1985) pointed out, children lack the Newtonian conception of space as a geometric construction that defines points that may or may not be occupied by material bodies. Because we could see that some children were not understanding what we were getting at, we devised another question to probe children's understanding of the homogeneity of matter. We presented an iron cylinder, told children that it was made of iron, and asked whether they could see *all* the iron in the bar. If children responded "no," they were then shown a much smaller cylinder, and the question was repeated. Next they were shown an iron shaving, and the question repeated, and finally were

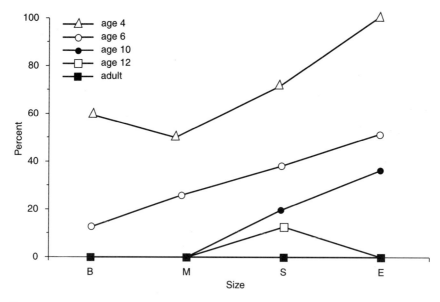

Figure 20.4
Visibility of all the iron. Percent judging one can see all the iron as a function of the size of the piece of iron. B, big; M, medium; S, shaving; E, ever, if one kept cutting it in half, repeatedly.

asked to imagine halving the iron repeatedly, probed as to whether one could ever get a piece small enough so that (with a microscope) one could see all the iron. A commitment to the continuity and homogeneity of matter is revealed in the response that however small the piece, there will always be iron inside. Of course, matter is particulate, not continuous. In principle, one could arrive, by the process of dividing, at a single atom of iron, in which there would be no iron inside. Children are often taught the particulate theory of matter beginning in seventh to ninth grades; work by science educators shows that children of these ages are deeply committed to a continuous theory of matter (e.g., Novick and Nussbaum 1978, 1981; Driver et al. 1987).

There were two types of answers that showed children to be thinking about the iron as an object, rather than as a continuous substance: "Yes, you can see all the iron," or "No, because you can't see the bottom," or "Because there is some rust on it." This probe for an understanding of homogenity and continuity of matter reveals the same developmental pattern as did the questions of whether small pieces of matter occupy space (Fig. 20.4; compare with Fig. 20.3.) All of the 12-year-olds said that one could never see all the iron, no matter how small the piece, because there would always be more iron inside. More than half of the 6–11-year-olds also gave this pattern of responses. Only 4-year-olds universally failed. A majority of the preschool children claimed that one could see all the iron in two large cylinders, more said so for the shaving, and virtually all said that one would eventually get to a speck small enough so one could see all the iron.

Figures 20.3 and 20.4 reveal nearly identical patterns. An analysis of consistency within individuals corroborates this result. Those children who revealed an understanding of continuity and homogeneity on the "see all the iron" task also did so on the "Styrofoam occupies space" task, and those who failed on one failed on the other.

The relationship holds even when the 4-year-olds (almost all failing both tasks) and the 12-year-olds (almost all succeeding at both tasks) are removed from the analysis ($p < .05$, chi-square). The two tasks are really quite different from each other, so this within-child consistency strengthens our conclusion that 4-year-olds do not grasp the continuity and homogeneity of solid substances, that half of early elementary aged children do, and that by age 12 virtually all children have constructed such an understanding of solid substance.

An understanding of substances as continuous and homogeneous may well be a conceptual prerequisite to an extensive understanding of weight. If children cannot think of a piece of iron as composed of arbitrarily small portions of iron, then they would not be able to think of the weight of an object as the sum of weights of arbitrary portions of the substance from which it is made. The data in Figs. 20.3 and 20.4 show that all 4-year-olds and half of the 6–11-year-olds lack this prerequisite for an extensive understanding of weight. But the comparisons between these data and those in Fig. 20.2 show that more is required for a reconceputalization of *degree of heaviness* as true *weight*. What might that be?

My answer is speculative, going well beyond the data at hand. My guess is that an understanding of substance as continuous and homogenous is a prerequisite for a concept of *quantity of substance* or *quantity of matter*. Even after one has formulated the concept of *quantity of matter*, the question of heaviness being an accidental property of matter is open. In the course of differentiating *weight* and *density*, the child will see that volume cannot be a measure of quantity of matter, leading the child to be open to an extensive conception of weight as a measure of quantity of matter.

Mathematical Prerequisites
Like the Experimenters' *degree of heat*, the child's *degree of heaviness* is not a fully quantitative concept. The child's *degree of heaviness* is certainly ordered. Children understand that one object (A) can be heavier than another (B), and they expect relative heaviness to be reflected in measurements of weight—if A weighs 250 grams, then B will weigh less than 250 grams. They take this relation to be transitive and asymmetric. However, the limits of children's quantification of degree of heaviness are revealed in their willingness to judge that a piece of substance 250 grams could be broken into 10 parts, each of which weighs nothing.

A true understanding of the extensivity of weight requires an understanding of division, a mathematical concept that is very difficult for most elementary school children (see Gelman 1991). And a quantitative, extensive conception of weight is clearly required for a quantitative conception of density. This further requires an understanding of ratios and fractions, also conceptually difficult for children in these age ranges (see Gelman 1991). Thus, as Piaget and Inhelder (1941) argued cogently, a quantitative understanding of density requires mathematical concepts that do not emerge in most children until early adolescence.

Black differentiated heat from temperature in the course of attempting to measure each independently from each other and relating each quantified magnitude to distinct thermal phenomena. The full differentiation of weight and density is achieved by children during science instruction, in the course of similar activities. Unlike Black, the young elementary-school-aged child lacks the mathematical tools for this achievement. The experimenters faced theory-specific conceptual barriers to differentiating heat and temperature. Similarly, the child faces theory-specific conceptual barriers to differentiating weight and density. But the child also lacks tools of wide application (Carey 1985a)—here, mathematical tools—important for the reconceptualization. In this sense, there is domain-general limitation on the young child's understanding of matter, just as Piaget and Inhelder (1941) argued.

5. Conclusions

Concepts change in the course of knowledge acquisition. The changes that occur can be placed on a continuum of types—from enrichment of concepts that maintain their core to evolution of one set of concepts into another that is incommensurable with the original. In this chapter, I have explored Spelke's conjecture that spontaneous development of physical theories involves only enrichment. I argued, contra Spelke, that the child's intuitive theory of physical objects is incommensurable with the adult's intuitive theory of material entities.

As in cases of conceptual change in the history of science, this case from childhood includes differentiations where the undifferentiated concepts of C1 play no role in the adult C2 and are even incoherent from the vantage point of C2. *Weight/density* and *air/nothing* were the examples sketched here. The child's language cannot be translated into the adult's without a gloss. One cannot simply state the child's beliefs in terms of adult concepts—the child believes that air is not material, but the "air" in that sentence as it expresses the child's belief is not our "air," and the "material" is not our "material." Similarly, the child believes that heavy objects sink, but the "heavy" in that sentence as it expresses the child's belief is not our "heavy." I can communicate the child's concepts to you, but have provided a gloss in the course of presenting the patterns of judgments the child makes on the tasks I described. To communicate the child's concept of *degree of heaviness*, I had to show its relation to the child's concepts of *density* and *substance*, for all these differ from the adult's concepts and are interrelated differently than in the adult conceptual system. These are the hallmarks of incommensurable conceptual systems.

Spelke might reply that the conceptual change described here was *originally* achieved by metaconceptually aware scientists, and that children only achieve it, with difficulty, as a result of schooling. Thus, it does not constitute a counterexample to her claim that spontaneous knowledge acquisition in childhood involves only enrichment. This (imaginary) reply misses the mark in two ways. First, even if the original development of the lay adult's concept of matter was achieved by metaconceptually sophisticated adults, and only gradually become part of the cultural repetoire of lay theorists, it is still possible that spontaneous (in the sense of unschooled) conceptual change occurs as children make sense of the lay theory expressed by the adults around them. Second, the construction of a continuous, homogeneous conception of substances occurs spontaneously between ages 4 and 11, in at least half of children in our sample. This is not taught in school; indeed, this theory is known to be false by science teachers. Similarly, in Smith et al. (1985), roughly half of the children had differentiated weight from density by age 9, before they encountered the topic in the school curriculum. True, many children require intensive instruction to achieve this differentiation (see Smith et al. 1988). What we have here is analogous to Gelman's findings on fractions; some elementary-aged children construct a conceptually deep understanding of fractions from minimal exposure to the topic, and others do not (Gelman 1991).

Spelke's speculations concerning spontaneous knowledge acquisition include two nested theses. She argues that conceptual change that is more extreme than enrichment (a) does not occur in the course of spontaneous development of physical concepts, in general, and (b) does not occur in the spontaneous development of the concept *physical objects*, in particular. It is the first thesis I have denied in this chapter. Let us now turn to the second. True, babies and adults see the world as containing objects that obey the solidity and spatio-temporal continuity principles. But for adults, these principles follow from a more abstract characterization of objects as material, and in the adult version of the principles, liquid, powders, and even gasses obey the same principles. At the very least, conceptual change of the second and their degrees has occured—what the baby takes as the core properties of objects are seen by the adult to be derived from more fundamental properties. And adults have constructed a fundamental theoretical distinction, material/immaterial, unrepresented by babies.

I would speculate that the conceptual evolution between the baby's concepts and the adult's passes through at least two major hurdles. Objects, for babies, are bounded, coherent, wholes and, as such, are totally distinct from liquids, gels, powder, and other nonsolid substances. The distinction between objects and nonsolid substances is very salient to young children; it conditions hypotheses about word meanings and relates to the quantificational distinction between entities quantified as individuals and entities not quantified as individuals (Soja, Carey, and Spelke 1991; Bloom 1990). It seems possible that young children believe that objects can pass through the space occupied by liquids, because they experience their own bodies passing through water and objects sinking through water. The first hurdle is the discovery that, in spite of these differences, physical objects and nonsolid substances share important properties, making liquids and powers *substantial* in the same sense as are objects. By age 4, children apparently understand that liquids uniquely occupy space; it is not clear whether younger children do.

Liquids and powders are not quantified as individuals precisely because they have no intrinsic boundaries; they can be separated and recoalesced at will. The quantificational distinction between nonsolid substances and objects supports seeing nonsolid substances as homogeneous and continuous and not seeing objects in this light. The second hurdle involves extending this conception of nonsolid substances to solid substances. The data reviewed heretofore shows that by ages 6 to 11, only half of the children in our sample had achieved this extension.

Changes of this sort go beyond mere enrichment. New ontological distinctions come into being (e.g., material/immaterial), and in terms of this distinction, entities previously considered ontologically distinct (e.g., objects and water) are seen to be fundamentally the same. The acquisition of knowledge about objects involves more than changes in beliefs about them. The adult can formulate the belief that "Objects are material"; the infant cannot.

References

Bloom, P. (1990). *Semantic structure and language development*. Unpublished doctoral dissertation, Massachusetts Institute of Technology, Cambridge, MA.
Carey, S. (1985a). Are children fundamentally different thinkers and learners from adults? In S. F. Chipman, J. W. Segal, and R. Glaser (Eds.), *Thinking and learning skills* (Vol. 2, pp. 486–517). Hillsdale, NJ: Lawrence Erlbaum Associates.

Carey, S. (1985b). *Conceptual change in childhood*. Cambridge, MA: MIT Press.

Carey, S. (1988). Conceptual differences between children and adults. *Mind and Language, 3*, 167–181.

Carey, S., and Gelman, R. (1991). *The Epigenesis of Mind: Essays on Biology and Cognition*. Hillsdale, NJ: Lawrence Erlbaum Associates, Publishers.

Carey, S., Smith, L., Sodian, B., Zaitchik, D., and Grosslight, L. (unpublished manuscript). *On some relations between children's conceptions of matter and weight*.

DeVries, R. (1987). Children's conceptions of shadow phenomena. *Genetic Psychology Monographs, 112*, 479–530.

Driver, R. (and members of CLIS). (1987): *Approaches to teaching the particulate theory of matter*. Leeds University: Children's Learning in Science Project.

Elman, J. L., Bates, E., Johnson, M. H., Karmiloff-Smith, A., Parisi, D., and Plunkett, K. (1996). *Rethinking Innateness: A Connectionist Perspective on Development*. Cambridge, Mass.: MIT Press.

Estes, D., Wellman, H. M., and Woolley, J. D. (1989). Children's understanding of mental phenomena. In H. Reese (Ed.), *Advances in child development and behavior* (pp. 41–87). New York: Academic Press.

Feyerabend, P. (1962). Explanation, reduction, empiricism. In H. Feigl and G. Maxwell (Eds.), *Minnesota studies in the philosophy of science* (Vol. 3, pp. 41–87). Minneapolis: University of Minnesota Press.

Fodor, J. (1975). *The language of thought*. New York: Thomas Y. Crowell.

Gallistel, C. R., Brown, A. L., Carey, S.,, Gelman, R., and Keil, F. C. (1991). Lessons From Animal Learning for the Study of Cognitive Development. In S. Carey and R. Gelman (Eds.), *The Epigenesis of Mind: Essays on Biology and Cognition* (pp. 3–36). Hillsdale, NJ: Lawrence Erlbaum Associates, Publishers.

Gelman, R. (1991). Epigenetic Foundations of Knowledge Structures: Initial and Transcendent Constructions. In S. Carey and R. Gelman (Eds.), *The Epigenesis of Mind: Essays on Biology and Cognition* (pp. 293–322). Hillsdale, NJ: Lawrence Erlbaum Associates, Publishers.

Hirschfeld, L. A., and Gelman, S. A. (1994). *Mapping the Mind: Domain Specificity in Cognition and Culture*. Cambridge: Cambridge University Press.

Jackendoff, R. (1989). What is a concept, that a person may grasp it? *Mind and Language, 4*, 68–102.

Jammer, M. (1961). *Concepts of mass*. Cambridge, MA: Harvard University Press.

Johnson, M. H., and Morton, J. (1991). *Biology and Cognitive Development: The Case of Face Recognition*. Oxford: Blackwell.

Kitcher, P. (1988). The child as parent of the scientist. *Mind and Language, 3*, 217–228.

Kuhn, T. S. (1997). A function for thought experiments. In T. S. Kuhn (Ed.), *The essential tension* (pp. 240–265). Chicago: University of Chicago Press.

Kuhn, T. S. (1982). Commensurability, comparability, communicability. *PSA 1982* (Vol. 2, pp. 669–688). East Lansing: Philosophy of Science Association.

Leslie, A. (1988). The necessity of illusion. In L. Weisenkranz (Ed.), *Thought without language* (pp. 185–210). Oxford: Oxford University Press.

Mandler, J. (1988). How to build a baby: On the development of an accessible representational system. *Cognitive Development, 3*, 113–126.

Marler, P. (1991). The Instinct to Learn. In S. Carey and R. Gelman (Eds.), *The Epigenesis of Mind: Essays on Biology and Cognition* (pp. 37–66). Hillsdale, NJ: Lawrence Erlbaum Associates, Publishers.

McKie, D., and Heathcote, N. H. V. (1935). The *discovery of specific and latent heat*. London: Edward Arnold.

McCloskey, M. (1983). Intuitive physics. *Scientific American, 4*, 122–130.

Nersessian, N. (1992). How do scientists think? Capturing the dynamics of conceptual change in science. In R. Giere (Ed.), *Minnesota studies in the philosophy of science* (Vol. 15). *Cognitive models of science*. Minneapolis, MN: University of Minnesota Press.

Novick, S., and Nussbaum, J. (1978). Junior high school pupils' understanding of the particulate nature of matter: An interior study. *Science Education, 62*, 273–281.

Novick, S., and Nussbaum J. (1981). Pupils' understanding of the particulate nature of matter: A cross-age study. *Science Education, 65* (2), 187–196.

Nussbaum, J. (1985). The particulate nature of matter in the gaseous phase. In R. Driver, E. Guesner, and A. Tiberghien (Eds.), *Children's ideas in science*. Philadelphia: Milton Keynes.

Piaget, J. (1960). *The child's conception of physical causality*. Paterson, NJ: Littlefleld, Adams, and Co.

Piaget, J., and Inhelder, B. (1941). *Le developpment des quantities chez l'enfant*. Neuchatel: Delchaux et Niestle.

Smith, C., Carey, S., and Wiser, M. (1985). On differentiation: A case study of the development of the concepts of size, weight, and density. *Cognition, 21*, 177–237.

Smith, C., Snir, Y., Grosslight, L., and Unger, C. (1988). Using conceptual models to facilitate conceptual change: Weight and density (Tech. Rep.). Cambridge, MA: Harvard University, Center for Educational Technology.

Smith, E. (1989). Concepts and induction. In M. Posner (Ed.), *Foundations of cognition science*. Cambridge, MA: MIT Press.

Soja, N., Carey S., and Spelke, E. (1991). Ontological constraints on early word meanings. *Cognition, 38*, 179–211.

Spelke, E. (1991). Physical Knowledge in Infancy: Replections on Piaget's Theory. In S. Carey and R. Gelman (Eds.), *The Epigenesis of Mind: Essays on Biology and Cognition* (pp. 133–169). HIllsdale, NJ: Lawrence Erlbaum Associates, Publishers.

Thagard, P. (1990). Concepts and conceptual change. *Synthese, 82*, 255–274.

Toulmin, S., & Goodfield, J. (1962). *The architecture of matter*. Chicago, IL: The University of Chicago Press.

Vosniadou, S., & Brewer, W. (1992) Mental Models of the Earth: A Study of Conceptual change in childhood. *Cognilive Psychology, 24*, 535–585.

Wiser, M. (1988). The differentiation of heat and temperature: history of science and novice-expert shift. In S. Strauss (Ed.), *Ontogeny, philogeny, and historical development* (pp. 28–48). Norwood, NJ: Ablex.

Wiser, M., and Carey, S. (1983). When heat and tempetature were one. In D. Gentner & A. Stevens (Eds.), *Mental models* (pp. 267–297). Hillsdale, NJ: Lawrence Erlbaum Associates.

Conceptual Atomism

Chapter 21

Against Definitions*

Jerry A. Fodor, Merrill F. Garrett, Edward C. T. Walker, and Cornelia H. Parkes

There existed an adult male person who had lived a relatively short time, belonging or pertaining to St. Johns (a college of Cambridge University), who desired to commit sodomy with the large webfooted swimming birds of the genus Cygnus *or subfamily* Cygninae *of the family* Anatidae, *characterized by a long and gracefully curved neck and a majestic motion when swimming.*

So he moved into the presence of the person employed to carry burdens, who declared: "Hold or possess as something at your disposal my female child! The large web-footed swimming birds of the genus Cygnus *or subfamily* Cygninae *of the family* Anatidae, *characterized by a long and gracefully curved neck and a majestic motion when swimming, are set apart, specially retained for the Head, Fellows and Tutors of the College."*
Gavin Ewart, 'Two Semantic Limericks'

The idea that there are definitions—that the morphemes of a natural language typically have internal structure at the 'semantic level'—has fascinated philosophers and psychologists at least since Plato. Epistemologists, to be sure, have recently shown signs of disaffection (see note 1). But in the 'cognitive sciences' the notion of definition remains one of those ideas that hardly anybody ever considers giving up. Perhaps for that very reason, there have been relatively few attempts to provide direct empirical evidence for the psychological reality of definitions. Still rarer are discussions of theoretical alternatives to definitional treatments of language and mind.

We think that a general reconsideration is long overdue; not only because the empirical basis of the definition construct is exiguous, but also because the whole theoretical superstructure in which it plays a central role has commenced to wobble. This paper has three parts and an Appendix. In Part I, we discuss, in some detail, the way that the notion of definition has served to connect several aspects of classical theories of language with one another and with widely credited accounts of concept acquisition. We will call this complex of views 'The Standard Picture (TSP)'. We are particularly interested in two issues: to what extent is TSP plausible independent of questions about the empirical status of the definition construct; and in what ways would TSP have to be revised if the definition construct were to be abandoned. Part II presents informally an experimental investigation directed toward determining whether claims for the psychological reality of definitions can be sustained. This is not, of course, a 'crucial experiment'; probably nothing could be. But we believe we

This chapter is an excerpt of a longer paper published under the same title. We've omitted section II and the appendix. [EM and SL]

can make a case that some important predictions which flow naturally from the view that definition is a basic notion in the theory of language are strikingly disconfirmed. The methods, materials, and statistical treatment of the results of the experiments are reserved for the Appendix, q.v. Finally, Part III returns briefly to The Standard Picture. We try to suggest in outline what cognitive psychology might look like in the post-definitional era.

Part I: The Standard Picture

Why do so many people think that there are definitions? Not, according to us, because there's much direct evidence that there are. Still less because there are many persuasive examples of the kind. Rather, there are several *other* theories that people hold about language and mind, and these other doctrines either rest upon, or anyhow closely comport with, the definitional account. There are, in fact, five such theories in which the notion of definition plays a significant—if not ineliminable—role. We will consider four of them.[1]

I.a. Language and the World: The Definition of a Word Determines Its Extension
According to TSP, the definition of a word makes explicit what is true of a thing if and only if the word applies to it. Consider the word "bachelor." It's often said that the definition of "bachelor" is "unmarried man." Suppose that this is true. Then the intended consequence is that:

1. Every bachelor is a man.
2. Every bachelor is unmarried.
3. Whatever is both unmarried and a man is a bachelor.

Or, to put the same point slightly differently, the idea is that the set of bachelors and the set of unmarried men are coextensive *in virtue* of the definition of "bachelor." In some sense or other, the fact that the definition of "bachelor" is "unmarried man" is supposed to explain the coextensivity of these sets.

It's important to see just how the explanation is supposed to go. Assume that the extension of the phrase "unmarried man" is determined somehow. Then, it's a consequence of the intended interpretation of the notion *definition* that if "unmarried man" is the definition of "bachelor," then "bachelor" has the *same* extension as "unmarried man," whatever that extension may be. That is: the definition of "bachelor" as "unmarried man" fixes the extension of "bachelor" relative to the extension of "unmarried man."[2]

If the definition of "bachelor" fixes its extension relative to the extension of "unmarried man," what fixes the extension of "unmarried man"? Patently, there are

---

1. The fifth is the epistemological doctrine according to which definitions guarantee the necessity (or unrevisability, etc.) of certain general truths, e.g., that bachelors are unmarried or that $F = MA$. We put this view aside because (a) it leads further into the philosophy of science than we propose to go, and (b) it is pretty thoroughly discredited as the result of work by such philosophers as Duhem, Putnam, and especially, Quine. For an airing of these issues, see Katz (1975) and Putnam (1975).

2. This situation is not materially altered if, for example, we think of definitions in the way that many linguists do: viz., as couched in a universal metalanguage. On such a view, a definition fixes the extension of an object language expression *relative to an interpretation of the metalanguage*. This is a nicety which we will henceforth ignore (but see J. A. Fodor 1975 and J. D. Fodor 1977 for extensive discussion).

two possibilities: (a) the extension of "unmarried man" is determined by the definition of *its* constituents, or (b) it is determined in some other way. It is also patent that we'll have to get to option (b) eventually, since exploiting option (a) raises the question: what fixes the extensions of the expressions in terms of which "unmarried" and "man" are defined? Definitions have to stop somewhere.

These considerations suggest the following view (which is itself part and parcel of TSP). The lexicon[3] of a natural language can be partitioned into (1) definable terms, and (2) a primitive basis. Definitions relate the definable terms to expressions in the vocabulary of the primitive basis.[4] They thereby fix the extensions of definable expressions relative to an interpretation of the primitive basis. Definition is thus viewed as an *asymmetric* relation in that there is a preferred direction of analysis for expressions in a language: analysis runs from definable expressions into the primitive vocabulary. Definitions typically apply in chains, and the further along a chain we go, the closer we get to expressions couched in the vocabulary of the primitive basis. The primitive basis is where definitions stop.

It should be emphasized that this view would be *vacuously* satisfied if *all* (or practically all) of the morphemically simple expressions in a natural language belonged to the primitive basis of that language. This is, of course, not what TSP intends. For TSP, the primitive basis of a natural language is *notably* smaller than the lexicon. Moreover, TSP has it in mind that definitions should exhibit the systematic articulation of the lexicon into semantic subsystems. In virtue of shared features of their definitions, morphemes should fall together into such families as action words, person words, color words, causatives, etc. (See, for example, Clark and Clark 1977).

Definitions fix the extensions of definable expressions relative to an interpretation of the primitive basis. What fixes the interpretation of the primitive basis? TSP provides no unequivocal answer to this question, but one version of the doctrine deserves special notice as historically venerable and currently influential. According to this (Empiricist) reading of TSP, items in the primitive vocabulary express sensory/motor properties. The extensions of these items are thus fixed by a causal account of the sensory/motor transducers. So, for example, the extension of "red" is that set of objects which do (or, more plausibly, would) appropriately activate the red-transducers; the extension of "angular" is that set of objects which do or would trigger appropriate motor-tracking responses; and so forth. According to this view, then, all non-primitive expressions are definable in a sensory/motor vocabulary whose items are, in turn, related to their extensions by a specifiable causal hook-up. Taken together, the definitions and the causal account of the transducers fix the interpretation of the entire lexicon. We believe that, insofar as the problem of interpreting the primitive basis has been faced at all by contemporary adherents of TSP (especially in AI and psychology) it has usually been something like the Empiricist version of the doctrine that they have had in mind. (Showing this would require more textual exegesis than we have space for here, but see J. A. Fodor, *op. cit.*).

---

3. Strictly, the morphemic inventory. We won't distinguish between morphemes and lexical items; the former are always intended.

4. Another pedantic note: Definitions relate definable terms to expressions in a vocabulary consisting of items in the primitive basis *together with logico-syntactic vocabulary*. So, for example, "bachelor" means "man *and not* married," where "and" and "not" belong to the logico-syntactic apparatus. We'll distinguish between primitive terms and logico-syntactic terms only where the distinction makes a difference.

Suffice it for present purposes that any theory which appeals to definitions to answer the question 'what relates words to the world?' must cope with the problem of intepreting the primitive basis *somehow*. One hasn't *got* a theory of language and the world unless that problem has been adequately addressed: all one has is a theory of a relation between uninterpreted linguistic forms. (Note that such formulae as "the definition of 'bachelor' is 'unmarried man'" assert relations between forms of words, not between forms of words and their extensions.) We stress this point in aid of dispelling an illusion. It's easy to suppose that, if one gives up the notion of definition—if, for example, one assumes that the entire lexicon is primitive—one thereby loses an account of the relation between language and the world; an account which exploitation of the definition relation would otherwise secure. On the contrary: for purposes of specifying the relation between a word and its extension, there is no *principled* difference between a theory which says that "unmarried" and "man" are primitive while "bachelor" is defined, and a theory which says that they're *all* primitive. It's just that the former sort of theory delays the question of interpretation till it gets to the primitive basis, while the latter sort faces the question straight off.

One further point under this general head. If the Empiricist version of TSP were plausible, that would be a *strong* argument for the strategy of using definitions to delay the question of interpretation. For, as we've seen, the Empiricist *does* have a (schematic) account of how a sensory/motor basis is to be interpreted; viz., by reference to the causal structure of the sensory/motor transducers. So, if he can use definitions to provide sensory/motor equivalents for each of the non-primitive items in a language, he really will have a theory of how the expressions in the lexicon of that language are related to their extensions.

It's thus important to emphasize that the Empiricist version of TSP is *not* plausible. If there are few convincing examples of definitions, there are literally *no* convincing examples of definitions which take *prima facie* non-sensory/motor terms into a sensory/motor vocabulary. There is, indeed, no reason to believe even that the definitions we have examples of generally exhibit an epistemically interesting direction of analysis. On the contrary, the 'right hand' (definiens) side of standard examples of definitions does not tend, by and large, to be more sensory/motor than the 'left hand' (definendum) side. So, for example, the conventional wisdom has it that "grandmother" means "mother of father or mother"; "ketch" means "two masted sailing vessel such that the aft (or 'mizzen') mast is stepped forward of the helm"; "bachelor" means "unmarried man"; "kill" means "cause to die," etc. It's hard to discern a tendency toward the sensory/motor in these examples, and these examples are quite typical. Surely, no one could seriously argue that words like "mother, father, mast, vessel, cause, die, married and man," all of which occur in the definiens, are somehow closer to transducer language, than say, "grandmother," "ketch," "kill" or "bachelor" are.[5]

---

5. We are *not* denying that natural languages like English contain a vocabulary of sensory/motor terms, where sensory/motor terms are those whose extensions can be specified solely by reference to the causal structure of transducer mechanisms. Perhaps, for example, "red" is in this sense a sensory/motor term (though recent work on color perception makes this seem unlikely). Our claim, in any event, is that even if there *are* sensory motor terms, the lexicon is not reducible to expressions containing only such terms and logico-syntactic vocabulary.

To summarize: definitions provide a useful part of a theory of language and the world *only if* they empty into a primitive basis which is independently interpreted. That is, definitions figure seriously in theories of language and the world only if: (a) all the expressions of a language are equivalent to expressions in the vocabulary of its primitive basis; (b) the primitive basis is notably smaller than the lexicon; and (c) the extensions of expressions in the primitive basis can be fixed without further appeal to the notion of definition. The only primitive basis which has so far been seriously alleged to satisfy (a)–(c) is sensory/motor, and it is morally certain that that allegation cannot be sustained. It may well be that definition plays *no* serious role in theories of language and the world, TSP to the contrary notwithstanding.

I.b. Intersentential Relations: Definitions Underwrite the Validity of Informally Valid Arguments

There are lots of ways of thinking about logic; here's one. People have pre-theoretic intuitions about the validity of arguments. These are intuitions to the effect that the conclusion of an argument does (or doesn't) 'follow from' its premises; that the truth of the premises does (or doesn't) guarantee the truth of the conclusions, etc. Logic provides a 'rational reconstruction' of these intuitions by systematizing, correcting, extrapolating and extending them.

Or, at least, it does so insofar as validity intuitions turn upon the *logical form* of the sentences which constitute the premises and conclusions of an argument. Logical form is that representation of a sentence which remains invariant under substitution for items in its *non-logical vocabulary*; and the non-logical vocabulary is specified by enumeration. Roughly, it's anything except such expressions as "all, some, not, or, equals, if then," and "and." In effect, according to this view, logic provides an account of the validity of an argument insofar as validity is mediated by the behavior of expressions in the logical vocabulary. One might go further and say something like this: logic provides an account of the validity of an argument insofar as its validity turns upon the *meanings* of items in its logical vocabulary. On this view, one has said what there is to say about the meaning of a word like "and" when one has said (for example) that *(P is true and Q is true) ≡ (P and Q is true)* is valid.

If one *does* think about logic this way, one might well be led to ask: what's so special about the logical vocabulary? Suppose that argument 4 is valid in virtue of the meaning of "and" (and "therefore"). Isn't it equally plausible that argument 5 is valid in virtue of the meaning of "bachelor"? If the goal of logic is to reconstruct pre-theoretic intuitions of validity, isn't the second case as apt for treatment as the first?

4. John left and Mary wept, therefore Mary wept.
5. John is a bachelor, therefore John is unmarried.

In short, it's possible to view standard logic as providing a reconstruction of validity for only a rather arbitrary selection of the intuitively valid arguments. It then becomes natural to seek a more extended treatment; one which provides an account of the *in*formally valid arguments. Informally valid arguments are those whose validity turns, at least in part, upon the meaning of items in the *non*-logical vocabulary.

The appeal to definitions comes in here. Suppose we assume that there is a 'semantic level' of linguistic representation and that at that level definable expressions are represented by their definitions. So, for example, the semantic-level representation of sentence 6 is something like formula 7.[6]

6. John is a bachelor.
7. John is a man and John is unmarried.

Assume further that *principles of valid inference* (including, for example, simplification of conjuction, the rule which allows us to infer *P* from *P and Q*) *apply to the semantic representations of sentences rather than to their surface forms*. On these assumptions, we need postulate no principled difference between arguments 4 and 5; in the extended sense of 'formally valid' where validity is a relation over semantic-level representations, both these arguments instantiate the formally valid scheme $P \& Q \rightarrow P$. Or, to put the same point slightly differently, given the present assumptions about semantic representations, we need not alter the standard logical apparatus in order to exhibit the validity of arguments which turn on the meaning of "bachelor"; for, on these assumptions, the word "bachelor" doesn't even occur at the level of representation for which validity is formally defined. All that occurs there is the (conjunctive) definition of that word. Similarly, *mutatis mutandis*, for other definable expressions.

The idea that systematic exploitation of the notion of definition might provide for an account of intuitions of informal validity enters the modern linguistic literature with Katz and Fodor (1963) and has been widely influential in 'linguistic semantics' (for a review, see J. D. Fodor, *op. cit.*). It connects in obvious ways with the definitional theory of language and the world sketched in I.a. For example, if the argument from "bachelor" to "unmarried" is valid in virtue of the meaning of "bachelor," it's hardly surprising that the extension of the former is included in the extension of the latter.

There are, nevertheless, several reasons for viewing the definitional account of informal validity with considerable suspicion. We will consider three. First, it's by no means certain that all informally valid arguments *will* be revealed as formally valid (as subsumed by the inferential apparatus of standard logic) even if couched at the (putative) level of semantic representation. In this respect, the "bachelor → unmarried" case may be quite misleading. Consider, for example, a kind of case which we will presently return to at length: the informal validity of arguments like 8. According

8. John killed Mary → Mary died.

to the conventional wisdom, the definition of "kill" is "cause to die," so that "John killed Mary" comes out as "John caused Mary to die" at the level of semantic representation. There is, however, no rule of *standard* logic which underwrites the validity of arguments like 9; this latter inference appears

9. John caused Mary to die → Mary die(d)

to turn essentially on the meaning of "cause,"[7] which is not itself a logical word. Of course, it's *conceivable* that we could make 9 formally valid by replacing "cause" by its

---

6. There's every reason to believe that, if there are such things as semantic representations, they must be syntactically analyzed formulae; perhaps they are something like tree structures, as practically all linguists have assumed. For present purposes we can ignore this, but it will be important further on.
7. Compare the *in*valid argument "John wanted Mary to die → Mary die(d)"

definition. But, as things now stand, nobody knows whether "cause" has a definition;[8] or, if it does, how it ought to be defined. And there is certainly no reason at all to believe that such a definition, if somebody could find it, would render arguments like 9 formally valid.

In short, the idea that informally valid arguments will prove to be formally valid when couched at the semantic level is equivalent to the idea that only their logical form is relevant to determining the validity of semantic-level arguments; and, as things now stand, there is simply no reason to believe that this is true. If it is not, then a reconstruction of informal validity may require an enrichment of the inferential apparatus of standard logic (e.g., the incorporation of rules which govern the behavior of formulae containing words like "cause") even if it *also* assumes the existence of definitions.[9]

The second consideration which militates against definitional accounts of informal validity is that there appear to be at least *some* informally valid arguments which *cannot* be reconstructed by appeal to the definition relation.[10] The point turns upon the symmetry of the inferences which definitions license. Suppose that "bachelor → unmarried" is valid in virtue of the definition of "bachelor." Then we can be sure that there will be some predicate P (in fact, the predicate "man") such that "unmarried & P → bachelor" is also valid.[11] Quite generally, if an informally valid argument turns on a definition, then there will be some clause that we can conjoin to the consequent which will make the corresponding bi-conditional true. Any informally valid argument which does not meet this condition can't be a definitional argument.

The problem is that there appear to be informally valid arguments which *don't* meet this condition. The standard examples are formulae like "if x is red then x is colored." A moment's reflection should serve to make clear that there is no predicate P such that "x is P and colored → x is red" is valid; hence that the validity of the first formula can't follow from the definition of 'red'.[12]

The moral here parallels the one we drew from the validity of arguments like 9. Even given the apparatus of definitional analysis, it looks as though some informally

---

8. If you just caught yourself thinking: 'but, surely, *every* word has a definition', that shows that you are in the grip of TSP. Words in the primitive basis are not definable, by assumption. Perhaps "cause" is one of these.

9. There is, of course, nothing incoherent about the proposal that a theory of informal validity requires *both* the existence of a semantic level *and* the extension of the logic. It's our impression, in fact, that most linguists who opt for definitions opt for an extended logic as well (barring, perhaps, Prof. Katz). We'll see, however, that there's a *prima facie* parsimony argument against such 'mixed' theories since it's adequately clear that any argument whose validity can be expressed by an extended logic plus definitions can equally be expressed by an appropriately extended logic *without* definitions.

10. For discussion, see J. D. Fodor (*op. cit.*) and also Geach (1957) where this point is made the basis of an argument against 'abstractionist' accounts of concept acquisition.

11. If the definition of "bachelor" were just "unmarried," then the condition is satisfied vacuously; i.e. "bachelor → unmarried" and "unmarried → bachelor" would *both* be valid. It is not, by the way, required that P be an *atomic* predicate in "unmarried & P → bachelor."

12. Of course "x is red and colored → x is red" is valid, but it's presumably not a candidate, since definable expressions (including, by assumption, "red") are not available at the semantic level. Alternatively, we could take "colored" to be the defined term, so that the semantic representation of "x is colored" is something like "x is red, or green, or purple, or brown...." This treatment *would* give "red → colored" as valid, but it will not commend itself to anyone who wants a psychologically plausible semantics; e.g. who wants the semantic representation of a sentence to be what is internally displayed when tokens of the sentence are understood.

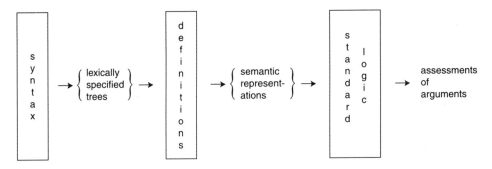

Figure 21.1
Sentence understanding systems in TSP.

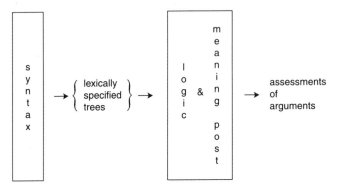

Figure 21.2
Sentence understanding systems on meaning postulates view.

valid arguments can't be captured within the inferential apparatus of standard logic. Rather, to get "red → colored" we will need a special rule of inference that does for "red" what the standard logical rules do for the operators, connectives and quantifiers. "Red" shows what "cause" suggests: assuming a semantic level won't, all by itself, buy you a theory of informal validity.

This brings us to our third point, which is that there is a serious alternative to appealing to definitions as part of an account of informal validity. TSP proposes a theoretical apparatus that looks like Fig. 21.1: definitions apply to syntactically analyzed natural language formulae to provide domains for the inferential apparatus of standard logic. The alternative account looks like Fig. 21.2: syntactically analyzed representations provide domains for an *enriched* inferential apparatus; one which contains rules which govern the behavior (not just of the logical vocabulary but also) of such non-logical words as "bachelor," "cause," "red" and the rest. In point of terminology, such non-standard rules of inference are traditionally called "meaning postulates." (See Carnap 1947, Kintsch 1974, Fodor, Fodor and Garrett 1975.)

There's an inclination to argue as follows: if your theory is willing to acknowledge an inference rule (meaning postulate) of the form "x is a bachelor iff x is unmarried and a man," isn't your theory really indistinguishable from one which acknowledges

"bachelor" means "unmarried man" as a definition? The answer to this question is
certainly "no." Looked at from the linguist's point of view, the two theories disagree
on what levels of representation there are (levels of linguistic representation are
individuated, *inter alia*, by their vocabulary. According to the definitional view, there
is a level of description at which "bachelor" is unavailable for the representation of
"John is a bachelor"; whereas, the meaning postulate account denies that this is so.)
Looked at from the psychologist's point of view, the theories disagree on what representation of tokens of "John is a bachelor" is recovered when they are understood.
The definitional view holds that such representations have the form "... unmarried
man ..."; whereas the meaning postulate view holds that such representations have
the form "... bachelor...." In short, the two theories differ in just about every way
that two theories can, given that they both assume a datum that "bachelor ↔
unmarried man" is valid.

As things now stand, it's hard to see any very decisive reason for preferring
the TSP account to the meaning postulate alternative. It's sufficiently obvious, for
example, that if the validity of an argument *can* be captured by the former sort of
theory, then it can also be captured by the latter. This is because, so far as questions
of validity are concerned, definitions just *are* a special case of meaning postulates.
Roughly, they're the symmetrical ones.[13] On the other hand, we've seen reason to
suppose that even if you have definitions, you will have to have meaning postulates
as well: arguments like "cause die → die" and "red → colored" probably aren't
formally valid *even* at the semantic level.[14]

So, the best that can be said for TSP, in the present context, is that definitions *may*
form part of the theory of informal validity. On the other hand, there are alternative
structures for such a theory and these may be able to do the job without appeal to
definitions; for that matter, without appeal to *any* 'semantic level' as that notion is
popularly understood. Moreover, the whole discussion proceeds *modulo* the uncertain
assumption that there is such a thing as informal validity; that there's some sense of
"valid" such that both simplification of conjunction and "bachelor → unmarried" are
usefully so stigmatized. If, in short, the phenomenon of informal validity is our best
reason for believing that there are definitions, then we have no very compelling
reason for that belief and TSP is in trouble.

I.c. Sentence Comprehension: To Understand a Word Is to Recover Its Definition
If a definition gives the meaning of a word, then it's natural to assume (a) that knowing what a word means is knowing its definition; and (b) that understanding a (token)
utterance/inscription of a word is, or involves, having the definition 'in mind'. We
reserve (a) for section I.d.

The natural way to understand (b) is to situate it in the context of a 'computational'
account of higher mental processes. According to such accounts, perception (including language perception) involves the assignment of 'internal representations' to distal
stimuli. These representations specify salient and/or task relevent properties of the

13. More precisely, they're the ones that are both symmetrical and eliminative.
14. This may well be a special case of the general principle that problems 'solved' by appeal to definitions
tend to recur in the form of problems about the primitive basis. In the present case, it looks as though 'red'
and 'cause' are good candidates for membership in the primitive basis of English. What, then, shall we do
about the informal validity of arguments which turn on the meaning of "red" and "cause"?

stimulus. A theory of perception for a given stimulus domain must say: what these properties are, what format is employed for their mental representation and what mental operations are involved in the assignment of the representations to the stimuli.

Viewed in this context, TSP claims that understanding a sentence involves the recovery of its representation at the semantic level[15] where, as we have seen, a semantic level representation is one in which definable expressions are replaced by their definitions. So, according to TSP, to understand a token of "John is a bachelor" involves representing the token as something like "John is an unmarried man."[16]

There are several preliminary points to make about this claim. To begin with, like any interesting theory, it operates only *modulo* suitable idealizations. Nobody has to maintain that *every* case of understanding a sentence token involves recovering definitions, even where the sentence contains definable terms; there might be any number of heuristic procedures for avoiding the recovery of definitions in special circumstances. All that has to be claimed is that understanding a sentence token involves recovering the definitions in, as it were, the systematic cases. It follows that —here as elsewhere—bringing about circumstances relevant to testing the theory (in particular, by eliminating the possibility of reliance upon heuristic short-cuts) might well require elaborate experimental manipulation. We will return to this point presently.

Second, there's the by now familiar point that the theory can at best be *vacuously* satisfied for sentences which draw their vocabulary entirely from the primitive basis. Perhaps understanding a sentence of the form "... bachelor ..." involves computing an internal representation of the form "... man...." But if "man" belongs to the primitive basis, then all that the definitional theory of understanding can say is that "man" *is its own internal representation*; that is, so far as the definitional theory is concerned, to understand an utterance of a sentence of the form "... man ..." is just to compute a token of a semantic representation of the form "... man...."

We stress this point because it's part of the intuitive appeal of the definitional theory that it avoids the necessity of saying things like *"bachelor" is defined as "bachelor,"* or *the internal representation of "bachelor" is "bachelor."* Progress appears to be made when tokens of "bachelor" are internally represented by tokens of some *other* formula (like "unmarried man"). Once again, however, this is only progress towards the primitive basis; once one gets there, some notion of understanding a word *other than recovering its definition* will have to be invoked.

As usual, then, reflection leads to the moral that nothing *principled* changes if we consider the entire vocabulary to be primitive, so that each word functions as its own internal representation for purposes of sentence comprehension. In fact, the account

---

15. It also claims that the semantic level representation of a sentence is the one that the speaker has in mind and which primarily (causally) explains his producing the token. We'll concentrate on the TSP model of the hearer for purposes of simplifying the exposition but cf. Fodor and Fodor (unpublished).

16. TSP doesn't, of course, claim that understanding tokens of "John is a bachelor" involves hearing them as tokens (of the sentence) "John is an unmarried man." TSP allows that sentence comprehension requires the recovery of morphological and syntactic as well as semantic representations, and the two sentences are morphologically and syntactically distinct, however much they may converge at the semantic level.

The reader may, by the way, be getting rather tired of bachelors and unmarried men, and we apologize for the paucity of our examples. Practically all the plausible examples of definitions come from jargon vocabularies ("ketch"), kinship vocabularies ("grandmother") and axiomatized systems ("triangle"). This rather limits one's range of choices and is a fact which should cause adherents of TSP to ponder.

of the lexical aspect of sentence comprehensions that emerges from such treatment is actually quite attractive; it's a serious alternative to TSP.

Any theory of sentence comprehension must somehow license a distinction between processes involved in understanding a token and processes involved in exploiting the information which the token carries. According to TSP, this distinction is drawn at the semantic level. That is, the output of the sentence comprehension system is the semantic representation of the sentence. This output, in turn, provides a domain for such further transformations as logical and inductive inferences, comparison with information in memory, comparison with information simultaneously available from other perceptual channels, etc. Since these 'extra-linguistic' transformations are defined over the semantic representations, they have access to the definitions of the lexical items that the sentence contains.

Whereas, on the alternative theory, extra-linguistic transformations are defined directly over the grammatical form of the sentence, roughly, over its syntactic structural description (which, of course, includes a specification of its lexical items.)[17] To say that the output of the syntax provides the domain for extra-linguistic transformations is, to all intents and purposes, to suggest that understanding a sentence *token* is just assigning it to a sentence *type*. The specification of a sentence type requires an ambiguity-free notation, but that is precisely what syntax (together with appropriate subscripting for ambiguous lexical items) ought to provide.

Notice that, on either account, the sentence comprehension system functions to provide domains for the extra-linguistic transformations. Both accounts thus postulate a sharp distinction between the mechanisms of sentence comprehension and those which determine the consequences (inductive, logical, plausible, etc.) of information that sentence tokens convey. The theories differ only in respect of the character of the representations that the sentence comprehension system provides; one alleges, and the other denies, that the system has access to (putatively) definable expressions like "bachelor."

There is, in fact, some rather tentative experimental evidence in favor of the non-definitional view. TSP entails that representations which specify definitions are internally displayed in the process of sentence comprehension; but experiments which have sought to test the psychological reality of such representations have not, thus far, met with notable success. In general, the tactics of such experiments involve (a) bringing about a situation in which it seems plausible to claim that S has understood a stimulus sentence; and then (b) attempting to show that some parameter of S's response is sensitive to properties of the *definitions* of items in the sentence. For example, Kintsch (*op. cit.*) used the phoneme monitor task (and other) experimental procedures in an attempt to show that RT to lexical items in a sentence is a function of the relative complexity of their definitions; and Fodor, Fodor and Garrett (*op. cit.*) used a speed-of-inference task to determine whether words which contain "negative" in their definitions (such as "bachelor," which means "*not* married man") show typical chronometric effects of the presence of negative morphemes.

---

17. We shan't consider the possibility that understanding a sentence involves recovering a representation which specifies its logical form in the *traditional* sense of that notion; roughly, a specification which formally determines such properties of the sentence as quantifier and operator scope, variable binding, etc. but which provides no access to internal structure in lexical items. This, in fact, seems to us quite a plausible view, but it's independent of the issues about definition which are our primary concern.

Both experiments were unsuccessful as, indeed, untutored intuition might have predicted. There is, for example, no intuitive support for the following entailment of TSP: given two otherwise identical sentences which are respectively of the form "... L_i ..." and "... L_j ..." and such that the definition of L_i is a proper part of the definition of L_j, the second sentence should be more complex than the first. For example, TSP predicts that "John is a bachelor" should be more complex than "John is unmarried" since the definition of "unmarried" is a proper part of the definition of "bachelor." And it predicts that "John broke the glass" is more complex than "the glass broke" since, according to the conventional wisdom, "break$_{transitive}$" is defined as "cause to break$_{intransitive}$." Neither prediction appears to have much intuitive warrant, and, as we remarked in the preceding paragraph, attempts at experimental vindication have, in general, not proved successful.

Such experimental studies have, however, been roundly criticized for their reliance upon chronometric measures. For example, Katz (1977) has argued that they show *at most* that subjects employ heuristic shortcuts to avoid the recovery of semantic representations when they are placed under time pressure. Katz doesn't offer any direct evidence that this is true, nor does he offer any suggestions as to what sort of task might have construct validity for testing the psychological reality of definitions. We'll return to this worry in section II where we consider evidence from some non-chronometric measures.

To summarize. In section I.b., we say that there is a trade-off between, on the one hand, theories which propose to save the inferential apparatus of standard logic by constructing a level of linguistic representation at which definitional structure is displayed; and, on the other, theories which dispense with a semantic level but propose to capture informal validity by a suitable enrichment of the inferential apparatus of standard logic. Not suprisingly, we now see that there is the possibility of the same sort of trade-off in theories of sentence comprehension. 'Deep' theories of comprehension (like TSP) require definitional analysis as part of the process of decoding tokens. In effect, they say that *some* inferences (like "bachelor → unmarried man") *must* be drawn on pain of failure to understand the sentence. Whereas, 'shallow' theories claim that the *entire* inferential apparatus is extra-linguistic (in the sense that there are *no* inferences which *must* be drawn in the course of understanding a sentence; including, NB, inferences which turn on definitions.) It's an open, and interesting, question how to choose between these views. But what should be clear from our discussion is that this is entirely an *empirical* question; there's no *a priori* reason why theories of sentence comprehension need to assume that definitions express important linguistic relations. Theories of sentence comprehension—at least in modern cognitive psychology—are functions from sentences onto internal representations. Internal representations are themselves expressions in a formal language. Nothing principled hinges on the size of the primitive vocabularies that this formalism exploits; *a fortiori*, nothing principled requires that it do without "bachelor."

I.d. Definitions and Theories of Concept Learning: Definitions Express the Decomposition of Concepts into Their Elements
The discussion in the last three sections has tended to exhibit TSP as one approach among others to a variety of problems about language and mind. We haven't yet found any *very* persuasive reason for preferring the definitional account to its alternatives, and we've suggested some reasons for supposing that TSP might be seriously

flawed. If this is correct, it raises a question which has some interest from the point of view of intellectual history: Why has the definition story been taken so seriously by so many theorists? In this section, we seek to provide part of the answer.

It's natural—perhaps it's mandatory—to speak of words as expressing concepts. Two consequences are implied thereby. First, the child's task of mastering the lexicon of his language is bifurcated into learning the concepts that lexical items express and learning which morpho-phonological forms are used to express those concepts in this language community. Second, the distinction between *defined and primitive lexical items* generates a corresponding distinction between *complex and basic concepts.*[18]

Given this presumptive parallelism between the lexical and conceptual systems, we can think of the definitions themselves as expressing not only the relations between definable expressions and the primitive vocabulary, but also the relations between complex and basic concepts. That is, we can say *both*: the meaning of "bachelor" is constructed from the meanings of "unmarried" and "man" *and* the concept BACHELOR is a construct out of the concepts UNMARRIED and MAN. The rule of definition supplies the principle of construction in both cases; definitions articulate both lexical decompositions and conceptual analyses.

This is a point of some significance since, so far as we can tell, practically all of the influential theories of concept learning in philosophy and psychology have relied heavily upon the possibility of constructing complex constructs from a primitive conceptual basis.[19] There is, in this respect, a direct line which runs from Locke and Hume, through Vygotsky and Bruner, to Winston and Miller and Johnson-Laird. We'll try to say, in outline, what it is that the views of such theorists have in common.

1. There is a presumed distinction between basic and complex concepts (paralleling, as we've seen, the presumed distinction between primitive and definable expressions.)

2. The *potential conceptual repertoire* of the organism is the closure of the primitive basis under some specified set of combinatorial operations.[20] In early versions of TSP, this combinatorial apparatus was implicit in the formal properties of the presumed associative principles. Recent versions (of which Miller and Johnson-Laird (1976) provide an unusually instructive example) typically assume much richer formalisms taken from logic, set theory or computer mathematics. In either case, however, the form of the theory is quite straightforward: the concepts you can have are the ones that can be constructed out of an inventory of basic concepts by the application of an inventory of combinatorial principles.

3. Given this account of the space of *potentially* available concepts, the theory of *concept learning* consists of a set of inductive procedures—to all intents and purposes, and inductive logic—which determines the availability of a complex concept relative to (a) the availability of appropriate basic concepts (in

18. In fact, this puts the matter slightly backwards since TSP is wont to view the distinction between complex and basic concepts as fundamental (e.g., as epistemologically principled) and the distinction between definable and primitive terms as merely derived (primitive terms being the ones which express basic concepts ... etc.).

19. The glaring exception is the work of the Cartesians and their followers, for whom concept acquisition is not assumed to be a *learning* process at all. We'll return to this presently.

20. Just as, *mutatis mutandis*, the *potential lexicon* is the closure of the primitive vocabulary under whatever logico-syntactic apparatus definitions are assumed to have access to.

particular, the ones from which the complex concept is constructed) and (b) the experience of the organism.

So, in its most familiar form, the theory has it that concept acquisition is a matter of framing and confirming hypotheses. In the Vygotsky/Bruner paradigm, for example, the concept BIK is said to have been learned when some such generalizations as "x is Bik iff x is round and red" controls the subject's sorting behavior. In such accounts, the inventory of basic concepts (together, as usual, with the logico-syntactic apparatus) provides the vocabulary in which the hypotheses are couched.[21] And the presumed laws of learning (problem solving strategies, principles of association, or whatever) operate to determine the degree of subjective confirmation of each hypothesis (the extent to which S believes it) as a function of environmental inputs, possibly including error-signals.

We are, in fact, inclined to believe that *all* standard theories of concept learning are variations on this model; that they all consist, fundamentally of an inventory of basic concepts, a combinatorial apparatus and an inductive logic. We'd be pleased to hear if the reader can think of a counter-example; we cannot. (For further discussion, see J. A. Fodor (1975), especially Chapters 1 and 2.)

The point of present concern is this: if our account of concept learning models is correct, then all such models are theories of the inductive acquisition of complex concepts *relative to the presumed availability of a primitive basis*. WHAT THEN OF THE ACQUISITION OF THE CONCEPTS IN THE PRIMITIVE BASIS? It seems to us that there is only one possible answer: theories of concept learning *presuppose* the availability of the primitive conceptual basis; they don't explain it. If, however, the primitive basis is presupposed in concept learning, then it cannot itself be learned. If it is not learned, then, presumably, it is innate.

The claim, then, is that all standard theories of concept learning require the innateness of the primitive basis and explain *at most* the acquisition of complex concepts relative to the availability of that basis. This claim may seem quite radical, but if it does that is only because the logical structure of theories of concept learning has not been widely appreciated in the modern literature. In fact, the idea that *everyone* has *always* been committed to the innateness of the basic concepts was common ground in many of the early discussions. William James, for example, who can hardly be viewed as a wild-eyed Nativist, comments as follows: "The first thing I have to say is that all schools (however they otherwise differ) must allow that the *elementary qualities* of cold, heat, pleasure, pain, red, blue, sound, silence, etc. are original, innate or *a priori* properties of our subjective nature, even though they should require the touch of experience to waken them into actual consciousness, and should slumber to all eternity without it." (*Principles of Psychology*, Vol. 2, p. 618). In fact, James is here quite close to Descartes; they both realize that concept acquisition presupposes a primitive basis, hence that the basic concepts cannot themselves be learned. On the other hand, neither thinks that the availability of basic concepts is causally independent of experience (of, for example, the activation of the sensorium). From the

---

21. Strictly speaking, the operation of the inductive procedures requires not only a source of hypotheses, but also a canonical formal for the representation of the (dis)confirming data. The inventory of basic concepts serves both functions; RED and ROUND, for example, occur both in the subject's hypotheses ("x is Bik iff it's red and round") and also in his internal memory representation of the experimental trials and their outcomes ("on trial *n*, the distal object was red and round and the hypothesis that it was Bik was rewarded").

contemporary point of view, one might say that James is a *triggering theorist* vis-à-vis the primitive basis and a constructivist (of the Associationist variety) about complex concepts. Whereas Descartes is a triggering theorist about practically *everything*: if the acquisition of concepts requires sensory stimulation, that is not because "... these extraneous things [distal stimuli] transmitted the ideas themselves to our minds through the organs of sense, but because they transmitted something which gave the mind occasion to form these ideas, by means of an innate faculty, at this time rather than at another.... Hence it follows that the ideas of ... movements and figures are themselves innate in us. So much the more must be the ideas of pain, colour, sound and the like be innate, that our mind may, on the occasion of certain corporeal movements envisage these ideas" (quoted by Adams 1975, pp. 76–77).[22]

These reflections put a rather significant twist on how one construes the traditional Rationalist-Empiricist debate. If all parties are committed to the innateness of the primitive basis, then the residual dispute must be over *how much* of the (potential or actual) conceptual repertoire is primitive. Here, surely, is one source of the widespread commitment to the existence of definitions. If there are no definitions then presumably the entire lexicon is primitive. If the entire lexicon is primitive, then presumably all the concepts that lexical items express are primitive. If all the concepts that lexical items express are primitive, then presumably all the concepts that lexical items express are innate. If that does not precisely amount to the innateness of *all* concepts, it is quite enough to give an Empiricist the willies.[23]

The moral, then, is this: what is not definable must be innate. Most of us are inclined to assume that it just *can't* be the case that *all* concepts are innate; most of us have therefore thought that many—indeed, *very* many—concepts must be definable. This is a persuasive line of argument *if Empiricism is true*. But what if Empiricism *isn't* true?

In short, the argument cuts both ways; if there is evidence that there are no definitions, then that is evidence *against* the standard views of concept learning. Since the standard views are the only ones we've got and since the only alternative to concepts being learned is that concepts are innate, it appears that the substance of the Rationalist-Empiricist debate turns quite centrally on the empirical status of the definition construct. That makes the empirical status of the definition construct a matter of very considerable interest. We are about to turn to it.

I.e. Summary
We've sought to show, in the preceding discussion, how the assumption that there are definitions plays a variety of roles in the conglomerate of theories that we've

22. What, according to Descartes, *shows* that sensory stimulations are at best 'occasions' (viz. triggers) for the formation of concepts is the *dissimilarity* between our concepts and their distal causes. A modern way of making this (very perceptive) point is that our experience does not, in general, provide a good inductive sample for the concepts we acquire. (See Chomsky 1975 on the relation between the corpus which triggers language acquisition and the grammar thereby induced.)

23. There is, of course, an infinity of concepts if one uses "concept" to denote not just what is expressed by words but also what is expressed by phrases. So, in particular, even if one claims that all *lexically encoded* concepts are primitive—hence innate—there will be infinitely many *phrasally encoded* concepts that are not primitive, hence learnable; even if the concepts expressed by "tin" and "trumpet" are basic, the concept expressed by "tin trumpet" is complex. Much of what modern theories of language (since Frege) are about is exhibiting the mechanisms in virtue of which a finite, lexically encoded primitive basis is projected onto an infinity of phrasally excoded forms which express complex concepts.

called "The Standard Picture." We've seen, in particular, that theories of concept learning are more heavily invested in the psychological reality of definitions than might at first appear; indeed, that the dispute between Empiricist and Rationalist accounts of the acquisition of concepts turns largely upon this issue.

If TSP were clearly true, that would in itself be a conclusive argument for endorsing the definition construct; if you accept a theory, you must accept its entailments. But, as we hope we've convinced the reader, there are plausible alternatives to TSP, and these alternatives are not committed to definitions. It would obviously be desirable if the question could be brought to empirical test.

Equally obviously, no single experiment could validate (or refute) the whole of TSP. The goal of Part II is to discuss experimental evidence relevant to assessing just one aspect of the standard picture: the doctrine (discussed in I.c.) that understanding a sentence token involves recovering (e.g., displaying in working memory) the definition of such lexical items as the sentence contains. This is part (though by no means all; see Part III) of what one might mean by saying that definitions are 'psychologically real'[24] for purposes of sentence comprehension.

... [Part II omitted] ...

Part III. TSP Revised

What does all this show? We review the situation in respect of each of the four aspects of TSP discussed in Part I.

III.a. Language and the World
TSP never did provide a plausible theory of the relation between terms and their extensions. It still doesn't.

As we saw in I.a, the appeal to definitions would provide for such a theory only *modulo* an account of the interpretation of the primitive basis. Only the Empiricist version of TSP does offer a reconstruction of the relation between primitive terms and their extensions, and it seems quite certain that the Empiricist version of TSP is indefensible. Even if there are definitions, it is wildly unlikely that they can be couched in a vocabulary of sensory/motor terms in any important number of cases.

This leaves us without a theory of language and the world. The best current hope for such a theory is perhaps to accept that aspect of the Empiricist treatment of primitive terms which claims that the relation between words and their extensions is somehow mediated by causal chains, but to abandon the condition that the relevant chains are exhaustively specifiable by reference to the behavior of sensory/motor mechanisms. (For contemporary discussions of 'causal theories' of reference, see Schwartz 1977). What is left is thus the very weak suggestion that the relation between, say, "Chicago" and Chicago, in virtue of which tokens of the one refer to the other, involves *some sort of* causal connection between the tokens and the city.

---

24. We assume throughout that "there are definitions" and "definitions are psychologically real" are just two ways of saying the same thing; more generally, that psychological states and processes provide the truth conditions on existential claims in linguistics. We realise that this view is sometimes denied, but we are quite unmoved thereby. For discussion, see the section entitled *Psychological Reality of Grammars* in Block (1981).

This kind of view seems reasonably plausible for names, intriguing but under-whelming for some kinds of descriptions, and only possibly defensible for kind terms. It clearly has deep troubles with abstract reference, reference to fictions and the like. Nor will a psychologist find it really satisfying even where it works best. What a psychologist wants to understand is *what kind* of causal chains fix extensions, and what the nomologically necessary and sufficient conditions for the existence of such chains are. About these questions, nothing worth reporting is known.[25]

To summarize: psychologists have wanted very much to have a theory of language and the world. Many of them have thought that appeals to definitions contribute substantially to the development of such a theory, but that was largely—perhaps solely—an Empiricist illusion. There is, as things now stand, no theory of language and the world and it seems most unlikely that one will be forthcoming in the foreseeable future. A methodological principle first enunciated by the philosopher Frank Ramsey applies here: what can't be said can't be said, and it can't be whistled either.

III.b. Informally Valid Arguments

In I.b we saw reason to believe that at least some informally valid inferences are inherently asymmetric; hence that meaning postulates will have to play a role in theories of informal validity even if definitions are endorsed. There is, however, a deeper point to be made in the light of such results as those in Part II.

Definitional theories of informal validity start out as attempts to break down the distinction between the logical and non-logical vocabularies. Paradoxically, however, they end up by exalting it. For, according to such accounts, the difference between a form of argument like, say, $P \rightarrow not\ (not\ P)$ and a form of argument like *bachelor* $\rightarrow$ *unmarried* actually implicates a difference of *linguistic levels*; whereas the validity of the former turns on the logical apparatus, the validity of the latter is determined by relations (e.g., of 'containment'; see Katz 1972) among semantic representations. No wonder theorists committed to definitions have claimed a basic intuitive distinction between 'analytic' (viz. definitional) truths and mere truths of logic.

In fact, we doubt that the intuitions are actually there. Even if they are, however, the results of Part II suggest that they are *not* intuitions of relations specified over definitional representations. If Part II is right, subjects don't compute definitional relations in situations where linguistic intuitions are elicited; not even when the intuitions elicited implicate semantic properties of the stimulus.

If intuitions of informal validity aren't intuitions of definitional relations, what *are* they intuitions of? There is a plethora of possibilities, all about equally plausible and all about equally unattractive. We mention a few by way of a shopping list.

   1. Intuitions of informal validity are just reports of empirical beliefs. This view has the virtue of compatibility with a post-Quinean epistemology. It explains

---

25. Though many false accounts are widely believed. For example, the kindest way of thinking about the Skinnerian account of language is perhaps to view it as an attempt to provide a model of just such causal connections. "Chicago" refers to Chicago because the latter is a discriminative stimulus for the production of tokens of the former; the laws of operant conditioning determine when, in general, a given discriminative stimulus controls a given discriminated response. This would appear to be the right *kind* of story to flesh out a causal theory of reference; all we have against it is its palpable untruth.

why we seem to be able to imagine rejecting putative informally valid arguments, given suitably bizarre contingencies. (*Cats are animals* is supposed to be informally valid; but suppose cats turned out to be robots manipulated by Martians; suppose they turned out to have a silicon-based biochemistry; etc.)

2. Intuitions of informal validity are *not* just reports of empirical beliefs; they're intuitions of deductive relations determined by the logical apparatus. On this story, there will have to be standard logical rules *and* meaning postulates, and the distinction between the logic (which contains both) and the body of empirical generalizations (which contains neither) will have to be principled. The putative counter-examples to informal validities will have to be explained away somehow (presumably by appeal to notions like change of meaning; to discover that cats are Martian robots would be to discover that there are no cats. To claim that cats are Martian robots would be implicitly to recommend redefining "cat").

3. The distinction between empirical generalizations and informally valid ones *is* principled, and so is the distinction between informal validity and formal validity. This might be the case if, for example, the distinction between meaning postulates and standard logical rules is itself principled. Then informally valid arguments might be ones which involve *only* the meaning postulates (or only the meaning postulates together with some designated subset of the logical rules). This is apparently the view that Carnap held; but see Quine (1963).

4. The distinction between informally valid arguments and analytic arguments is also principled. Analytic arguments might, for example, be the ones which implicate no more than precisely *n* of the meaning postulates under some canonical formalization.

5. The distinction between informally valid arguments and analytic arguments is *not* principled; there are degrees of analyticity with very analytic arguments corresponding to very short routes through the meaning postulates (and, perhaps, designated logical rules as per 3 above).

Etc. ... The reader who finds himself not much caring which, if any, of 1–5 is true has all our sympathy. There is, however, one point we want to emphasize: what all the non-definitional approaches to informal validity have in common is that they assume that the domain for the logical apparatus (including meaning postulates) is the output of the syntax; there is no semantic level (no level of logical form) except what may be required for the representation of such relations as quantifier binding, operator scope, etc. In particular, there is no logical form *inside lexical items*. It seems to us that the weight of the current evidence is that this latter claim is plausible.

If we had to bet, we'd bet on the following story and we'd stick to small sums:

a) The logical apparatus is defined over representations of logical form in something like the traditional sense (scope, binding, etc. are formally specified in the domain of the logical rules).

b) The logical apparatus contains standard rules and meaning postulates indifferently.

c) There is no semantic level in the sense of 'linguistic semantics'; the logical apparatus has access to the surface morphological inventory of the language.

This picture comports nicely with the results of Part II; it's compatible with the notion that logical form is determined solely or in large part by surface structure; it permits ambiguities of quantifier order (and other phenomena of traditional logical syntax) to be psychologically real; it provides room for a principled notion of informal validity in case somebody should happen to find a use for one; there appears to be no solid *a priori* or *a posteriori* reason for supposing that it is false. We are available for small wagers.

III.c. Sentence Comprehension without Definitions

Understanding a sentence is recovering a representation that provides a domain for relevant inferential processes. If there are no definitions, then understanding a sentence is recovering its logical form. If there are no logical forms, then understanding a sentence is recovering its syntactic structural descriptions. There must be syntactic structural descriptions; the ambiguity arguments prove it. In short, you won't be far wrong, on the present view, if you think of a sentence comprehension system as a function from tokens to types.

Here are two possible objections:

> 1. How could understanding a sentence be recovering a type-individuating representation of that sentence? Such representations are just formulae in some other (e.g., meta-) language. Answer: we doubt that this objection buys much in this context.[26] What's certain is that it buys nothing in aid of the definitional account: DEFINITIONS ARE ALSO JUST REPRESENTATIONS IN SOME OTHER LANGUAGE! The disagreement over the psychological reality of definitions is a dispute *within* versions of the representational theory of mind.
>
> 2. Understanding is a graded notion; different performances count as understanding depending on the circumstances; understanding can't be *formally* defined. Answer: if this is an argument at all, it's an argument against *both* definitional *and* non-definitional accounts. Both claim that there is a level of representation whose recovery is constitutive of (or at least necessary for) sentence comprehension. They disagree only about *which* level it is.

No doubt the ordinary notion of understanding *is* graded for all that. This is primarily because nobody (except academics) is ordinarily interested in understanding *sentences*; what we ordinarily want is to understand *what people say and what they meant by saying it*, and it's perfectly clear that all sorts of contextual, background and inferential apparatus is brought to bear in this latter undertaking.

This is not, however, an argument for studying understanding what people say and what they mean *instead* of studying understanding sentences. On the contrary, you can't do the former without doing the latter, since it's patent that the computational apparatus involved in understanding sentences is normally used in understanding people. That's why it is, in general, easier to understand somebody who's talking a language you know than to understand somebody who's talking a language you don't. A theory of understanding sentences is thus *part* of a theory of understanding

---

26. What it does is force a distinction between theories of sentence comprehension and semantic theories. Since the failure to grasp this distinction is epidemic among procedural semanticists, this is no small matter. See J. A. Fodor (1978).

people and, for all we now know, it may be the only part that's sufficiently systematic to reward specifically scientific scrutiny.

Briefly: if the ordinary notion of understanding is graded, so much the worse for the ordinary notion of understanding. We don't make physics out of the ordinary notion of energy.

III.d. The Innateness Controversy

Whatever is not *definable* must be innate. This is, however, weaker than: whatever is not internally represented by its definition must be innate. For example, it may be that while *adults* represent "kill" as *kill*, children learn "kill" as *cause to die*. After a while, one might imagine, *cause to die* consolidates and *kill* comes to act as a *derived* primitive. Derived primitives are representations which (a) have no computationally relevant internal structure, but (b) are introduced into the representational system by adding eliminative bi-conditionals to the logic. Rules which introduce derived primitives are, as it were, the diachronic equivalents of definitions.

This suggests (what we believe to be correct) that the case for a rich, innate primitive conceptual system can't be made just by demonstrating the psychological unreality of definitions in adults. The psychological reality of definitions in the adult provides a sufficient, but not a necessary, condition for the analyzability of concepts.

If you want to show that a concept which is psychologically unanalyzed for the adult is, nevertheless, only a *derived* primitive (hence definable, hence presumably, not innate) there are at least three things you can try.

1. Show that the concept is, in principle, analyzable. The existence of a possible analysis is *prima facie* evidence that the concept actually *is* analyzed somewhere in ontogeny. This card is not, however, easy to play; there are, as we have several times remarked, very few examples of plausible definitions.

2. Show that the concept is internally complex for the child; e.g., show that the child represents "kill" as *cause to die*. We think that the developmental literature which purports to demonstrate that the child's concepts are typically learned by assembling complex arrays of primitives (e.g., of semantic features) is thus far unpersuasive; if one approaches the data without Empiricist preconceptions, the striking fact is the *lack* of evidence for 'bottom up' processes in concept acquisition. We won't argue this here, however; our present concern is just to acknowledge the relevance of such data to the sorts of issues we have raised.

3. Show that the concept is expressed by a phrase (rather than a morphemically simple expression) in some natural language or other.

We've argued that morphemically simple expressions are typically undefined, that undefined expressions typically express primitive concepts; and that primitive concepts must be innate. The presumption that a concept expressed by a morpheme is primitive cannot, however, be right if there are actually languages in which that *same* concept is expressed by a phrase. For (a) if a concept *can* be expressed by a phrase, then it is *ipso facto* definable; and (b) if a concept is in fact primitive (hence innate) for any human, it must surely be primitive (hence innate) for all humans.

It would thus be extremely interesting to know how much different languages agree as to which concepts are expressed by morphemically simple expressions. Given, however, the notorious difficulty of making sense out of the translation relation, we aren't likely to find out by, say, next week.

All this should suggest—what is clearly true—that if you don't like *trumpet* being innate, you still have a plenty of room to wriggle. Dismantling TSP, if it is to be done at all, will surely be the work of generations, just as constructing it was. Since, however, TSP has been so widely endorsed, and since even the *possibility* that it is deeply wrong opens such startling vistas of speculation, it may be a good idea to end with the following considerations:

1. TSP has *never* worked. The appeal to definitions has been central to projects ranging from the theory of visual perception to axiomatic ethics; from linguistic semantics to the operational analysis of theoretical terms in science; from theories about how children might learn concepts to theories about how computers might understand newspapers. In each case, the underlying assumption has been that the primitive conceptual repertoire *cannot* be as rich as the available reportoire of categories; hence that many concepts *must* be analyzable. These assumptions have governed research in the Anglo-American tradition for some three hundred years; almost, in our view, totally without success. The definitions and analyses haven't been forthcoming and there is no prospect that they will turn up in the foreseeable future. Perhaps the world is trying to tell us something. Perhaps there is something wrong with our assumptions.

2. If we are finally forced to the view that people have a rich endowment of innate (e.g. triggered) concepts, that ought not to outrage intuition all *that* much; it would only be to accept for us a kind of doctrine that we take to be quite plausible for most of the rest of animate creation.

3. The true theory doesn't have to be boring. The theoretical reach of physics stretches to embrace the possibility of worlds in which the time arrow points backwards. Surely a little nativism ought not be more than psychologists can bear.

References

Adams, R. M. (1975) Where do our ideas come from? In Stitch (ed.), *Innate Ideas*. University of California Press.

Block, N. J. (1981) (ed.), *Readings in Philosophy of Psychology*, Vol. 2, Harvard Univ. Press, Cambridge, Mass.

Carnap, R. (1947) *Meaning and Necessity*. University of Chicago Press, Chicago.

Clark, E. and Clark, H. (1977) *Psychology and Language: An Introduction to Psycholinguistics*. Harcourt Brace Jovanovich, New York.

Chomsky, N. (1972) *Studies on semantics in Generative Grammar*. Mouton, The Hague.

Chomsky, N. (1975) *Reflections on Language*. Pantheon Books, New York.

Dowty, D. (1976) Montague grammar and the lexical decomposition of causative verbs. In B. Partee (ed.), *Montague Grammar*. Academic Press, New York.

Davidson, D. (1970) Mental events. In Forster L. and Swanson, J. (eds.), *Experience and Theory*. University of Massachusetts, Amherst.

Fodor, J. A. (1975) *The Language of Thought*. Crowell, New York.

Fodor, J. A. (1978) Tom Swift and his procedural grandmother. *Cog.*, *6*, 229–247.

Fodor, J. A., Bever, T. G. and Garrett, M. F. (1974) *The Psychology of Language*. McGraw-Hill, New York.

Fodor, J. A. and Fodor, J. D. (unpublished). *Language, Mind and Communication*, Harvard University Press, Cambridge. Mass.

Fodor, J. D. (1977) *Semantics: Theories of Meaning in Generative Grammar*. Crowell, New York.

Fodor, J. D., Fodor, J. A. and Garrett, M. F. (1975) The psychological unreality of semantic representations. *Linguistic Inquiry*, *VI*, 515–531.

Geach, P. (1957) *Mental Acts*. Routledge & Keegan Paul, London.

Katz, J. J. (1972) *Semantic Theory*. Harper, New York.

Katz, J. J. (1977) The real status of semantic representations. *Linguistic Inquiry, VIII*, 559–584.

Katz, J. J. (1975) in Gunderson (ed.), *Minnesota Studies in the Philosophy of Science*. University of Minnesota Press, Minneapolis, Minnesota.

Katz, J. J. and Fodor, J. A. (1963) The Structure of a Semantic Theory. *Language, 39*, 176–210.

Kintsch, W. (1974) *The Representation of meaning in Memory*. Wiley, New York.

Lakeoff, G. (1970) Linguistics and Natural Logic. *Studies in Generative Semantics, No. 1*, Phonetics Laboratory, University of Michigan. Also *Synthese* (1970) *22*, 151–271.

Levelt, W. M. (1970) A scaling approach to the study of syntactic relations. In G. B. Flores d'Arcais and W. J. M. Levelt (eds.), *Advances in Psycholinguistics*. North Holland, Amsterdam.

Levelt, W. M. (1974) *Formal Grammars in Linguistics and Psycholinguistics*. Mouton, The Hague.

McCawley, J. D. (1971) Preiexical Syntax. In R. S. O'Brien (ed.), *Monograph Series on Language and Linguistics*, No. 24, Georgetown University, Washington, D.C.

Miller, G. A. and Johnson-Laird, P. N. (1976) *Perception and Language*. Belknap, Cambridge, Mass.

Putnam, H. (1975) in Gunderson (ed.), *Minnesota Studies in the Philosophy of Science*. University of Minnesota Press, Minneapolis, Minnesota.

Quine, W. V. D. (1963) *From a Logical Point of View*. Harper and Row, New York.

Schwartz, S. (1977) Introduction. In B. Schwartz (ed.), *Naming, Necessity, and Natural Kind*. Cornell University Press, Ithaca, N.Y.

Schank, R. (1975) *Conceptual Information Processing*. North Holland, Amsterdam.

Walker, E. (1976) Some grammatical relations among words. In Wales, R. and Walker, E. (eds.), *New Approaches to Language Mechanisms*, North Holland, Amsterdam.

Chapter 22

Information and Representation

Jerry Fodor

This chapter has two parts. The first part says: "Look, there is this terrible problem about information-based semantic theories" (often hereafter "IBSTs"). The second part sketches a solution to the problem that the first part raises. I'm sure the first part is right: there really *is* this terrible problem about IBSTs. I'm far from sure that the second part is right, but I guess I think it's worth considering.

1. A Terrible Problem About IBSTs

I want to take some things for granted.

First, I assume that information-based semantics is primarily an attempt to *naturalize* the fundamental semantic relations; that is, to say in *non*semantic and *non*intentional (with a "t") terms what makes a thing a symbol. IBSTs thus play the same role in our theories of language and mind that Hume's suggestion that Ideas are about what they resemble played in his. In both cases, the point is to break out of the "intentional circle"; to show how to replace semantical/intentional talk with talk couched in the familiar vocabulary of the natural sciences *salve* the explanatory power of semantic/intentional theories.

Second, I assume that mental representations are the appropriate domain for IBSTs. Hume was right: it's Ideas (in the sense of mental particulars) that have semantic properties in the first instance. Mental states (beliefs, desires, and so on) are typically relational, and they derive their semantical properties from the Ideas that are their immediate objects; forms of words in natural languages derive their semantical properties from the mental states that they are standardly used to express. So, for example, "It's raining" means what it does because it is the form of words that English speakers standardly use to express the belief that it's raining; and the belief that it's raining has the intentional content it does because its object is a mental representation that means that it's raining. The question thus arises what the fact that a certain mental representation means that it's raining consists in. An information-based semantics purports to provide naturalistic answers to this sort of question.

But though I assume that mental representations are par excellence the symbols of whose intensional properties information-based semantics provides a naturalistic theory, *none of what I'm about to say depends on that assumption*. Though I almost always have mental representations in mind when I speak of symbols,[1] all the

---

1. I shall often use quoted English expressions as names for their counterparts in the language of thought. Thus "'rain'" will sometimes refer to the symbol that encodes the concept *rain* in Mentalese, and sometimes to the English word which translates that symbol. It should usually be clear from the context which is intended; and for most present purposes it won't matter. In fact, for most present purposes, one might as well assume that English *is* Mentalese.

For similar reasons, much of what I'm about to say about thinking holds just as well for talking and vice versa. In what follows, "say" will almost always mean *say or think*, and "think" will almost always mean *think or say*.

following applies equally well to the view that it is forms of words that have semantical properties in the first instance and that therefore provide the primary candidates for naturalization. I am told that there actually are philosophers who hold this view. Since there is the duck-billed platypus, this may well be so.

Third, I take it that all IBSTs claim that the fundamental intensional property of a symbol is that of *carrying information*.[2] "Carrying information" is a relation that is best introduced by examples, so here are some popular ones. In typical cases: smoke carries the information that there is fire; a tree's rings carry information about its age; a falling thermometer carries the information that it is getting cold; utterances of the form of words "that is a platypus" carry the information that that is a platypus; and so forth.

Finally, I assume that it's common ground among IBSTs that "carrying information" is to be naturalized by reference to relations of *causal covariance* between symbols (viz. the information carriers) and things symbolized (viz. the things that the information carried is about). For our purposes, the Ur-version of IBST is: As carry information about Bs iff the generalization "Bs cause As" is true and counterfactual-supporting. A couple of words about alternative formulations of IBST, and then we'll be ready to go.

> (1) There's a (Stanford) version of IBST according to which *causing* is viewed as just a special case of constraining, the general principle being that things carry information about whatever they constrain or are constrained by. So, for example, smoke carries the information that there is fire; but also, fire carries the information that there will be smoke, and the proposition that P&Q carries the information that Q. I shall be concerned with this generalized notion of information-carrying only insofar as it overlaps the narrower one.
>
> (2) Dretske has a very highly constrained notion of information-carrying according to which it's false that As carry information about Bs unless the probability that an arbitrary A is B-caused is always one. The main argument for this constraint is this: Suppose we allow that As carry information about Bs even when the probability that As are B-caused is *less* than one; suppose, for example, we accept a probability of .9. Then there could be a situation where "P" carries the information that P, "Q" carries the information that Q, but "P&Q" does *not* carry the information that P&Q (because the probability that P&Q is less than .9).

But I think this argument is ill-advised. There's no reason why an IBST should assign informational content independently to each expression in a symbol system. It will do if contents are assigned only to the *atomic* expressions, the semantics for syntactically complex expressions being built up recursively, by techniques familiar from the construction of truth definitions. So, if we have a (naturalistic) way of saying that "P" carries the information that P and that "Q" carries the information that Q, we can leave it to a recursive schema to assign the information that P&Q to "P&Q." I will therefore stick with the version of IBST that makes As informative about Bs

---

2. Carrying information is supposed to be an intensional relation in at least the technical sense that "a carries the information that S" and "S iff T" are supposed not to entail "a carries the information that T." Just *how* intensional "carries the information is"—whether, for example, it's as intensional as "believes that"—is moot.

whenever the causal connection from Bs to As is backed by a counterfactually supporting generalization, albeit one that may be statistically imperfect.

So much for preliminaries: Now for the terrible problem. Here, by way of introducing it, is a very small argument against information-based semantics.

Information-based semantics is the idea that "means" is univocal in "'smoke' means
smoke" and "smoke means fire" (viz. "means" means "carries information about" in
both cases). It is, in fact, because they hold that smoke really does *mean* fire, that
informational semanticists are inclined to insist on how much meaning there is
around. It's a favourite refrain of IBST theorists that there is nothing *all that* special
about linguistic or mental representation; they are just species of the sort of causal
constraint that is ubiquitous in the nonlinguistic, nonmental world.

But prima facie this can't be right. If "means" means "carries information about" in
"'smoke' means smoke" and "smoke means fire," then since *carries information about* is
transitive, it would follow from these premises that "smoke" means fire. Which, of
course, it doesn't. So something must be wrong.

I wouldn't be inclined to push this very small argument very hard except that it
seems to me that its conclusion is perfectly clearly true. The point about "smoke" is
that—most of the time, at least—it doesn't *carry information* about smoke; what
it does is it *represents* smoke (stands for it; refers to it; means it in *that* sense). And
similarly, *mutatis mutandis*, for the "mental representation" SMOKE. Notice that—
unlike *carries information about*—represents, stands for, refers to, and the like are *not*
transitive. If the first word on this page is "Granny," then the expression "the first
word on this page" represents (stands for, refers to) the expression "Granny." And, of
course, the expression "Granny" stands for, represents, and refers to Granny. It does
not follow that the expression "the first word on this page" itself stands for, represents, or refers to Granny; it doesn't follow and, indeed, it isn't true. The expression
"the first word on this page" refers (etc.) to the first word on this page, and nobody's
Granny is a word.

It is not, to put it mildly, clear how, or even whether, the relation between a symbol and what it represents is to be reduced to the relation between a symbol and
what it carries information about. I want to spend some time rubbing this in.

Consider two ways in which a symbol—"platypus," as it might be—can be used
to say something true. (I'm sticking to truths at this point because causal covariance
theories have notorious problems with errors, falsehoods, mistakes, and the like. I'll
have more to say about that in the next section.) Paradigmatic of one kind of case
is the use of the symbol in platypus-spotting. A platypus gallumphs by and one
says "Platypus!" (where, let's suppose, the utterance has the force: "There goes a
Platypus!"). An old-fashioned sort of analysis of this situation would have it that the
symbol-type "platypus" has an associated extension and one way to generate a true
utterance (thought) is to apply a token of the symbol to something that is *in* its
extension. You get a truth when you say *of* a platypus that it *is* one. I shall call the
uses of symbols that generate such truths "labelling" uses—for want of something
better to call them.

Now consider another way that "platypus" might be used to say something true.
Somebody says: "The platypus has webbed feet." There is no question, in this sort of
case, of applying a "platypus" token to something that's in the extension of the
"platypus" type; perhaps it would be closer to say that such tokens serve to *represent*
the extension associated with the corresponding type. The point is: when I use

"platypus" to say that platypai are webfooted, I'm not applying the term to anything; rather, I'm using it to stand for the things that it applies to.

Universal generalizations aren't, of course, the only cases where the function of a symbol appears to be representation rather than labelling. Other examples are occurrences in existentials ("there are platypuses"), occurrences in hypotheticals ("if there are platypuses, there may be anything"; "if there is anything, there may be platypuses"), occurrences embedded to verbs of propositional attitudes ("No one can really believe that there are platypuses"), and so forth. The point to keep your eye on is that in none of these cases is anything being *called* a platypus. Yet all these tokens of "platypus" are symbols; they are all paradigms of things that have bona fide intensional properties.

What, then, is the relation between cases where symbols are used to label and cases where they are used to represent? Notice that this is a question for which old-fashioned, unnaturalized semantics has a plausible answer: a symbol *has the same meaning* in both uses. Indeed, on Grandmother's view of semantics, symbols apply to things in virtue of the very meanings that they express when they are used to represent things. Or, to put it the other way around, the property that a symbol expresses when it represents is the very property that things have to have in order to be in its extension. So it's the very property that a thing has to have for an application of the symbol to it to be true.

But although I am an enthusiast for this grandmotherly analysis,[3] it isn't a story that a *naturalized* semantics is in a position to tell—reeking, as it does, of appeals to intensional notions like having a meaning and expressing a property.

OK, I can now say what the terrible problem is. It's that, although IBSTs provide at least a first fling at a naturalistic story about the cases where symbols are applied to things, they provide no story at all—or, worse, they provide a demonstrably wrong story—about representational uses of symbols. I now need to convince you first that this is so and second that it matters that it is so.

IBSTs say, in effect, that symbol tokenings carry information about what causes them; specifically, they carry the information that their causes have the property to which the tokenings are linked by a counterfactual supporting covering generalization. In consequence, there's a certain structural symmetry between the case where, as Grandmother Semantics would have it, *the symbol S applies to the object O in virtue of O's having the property P that S expresses*; and the case where, as IBSTs would have it, *the symbol S carries the information that O is P in virtue of a covering generalization that causally connects P-instances with S-tokenings*. In effect, Granny says that S applies to O because S expresses P and O is P. Correspondingly IBSTs say that S applies to O because O is P and Ss carry information about Ps. It is this structural symmetry that makes it not-utterly-unreasonable to identify the property that IBST says a symbol's tokenings *carry information about the instantiation of* with the property that Grandmother semantics says that the symbol *expresses*. So we get the much-wanted reduc-

---

3. It is sometimes said that Grandmother semantics will not do because "intensions don't determine extensions." But this is preposterous on the face of it. Nothing could be more clearly true—indeed, nothing could be more clearly a *semantic truth*—than that, on the one hand, "platypus" means platypus, and that, on the other, it is true for all values of x that "platypus" applies to x iff x is a platypus.

Philosophers get into no end of trouble by confusing the question whether intensions determine extensions (answer: of course they do) with the question whether words like "platypus" have *definitions* (answer: of course they don't).

tion: First of "the property expressed" to "the property about whose instantiation S-tokens carry information"; and then of "the property about whose instantiation S-tokens carry information" to the (naturalistic) notion of the "covering" property (viz. the property of Os in virtue of which "Os cause S-tokens" is counterfactual-supporting). Home free.

This is, no doubt, much too simple as it stands. For example, the relevant covering generalizations can't be of the form "Os cause S-tokens" simplicitar; some (e.g., unobserved) platypuses don't cause "platypus"s, and some (e.g., misguided) "platypus"s aren't platypus-occasioned. Almost equally depressing, *applying* "platypus" to a platypus doesn't uncomplicatedly reduce to having the platypus in question cause you to token "platypus." Think of the chap whose habit it is to use "platypus!" as an ejaculation expressing extreme surprise (where the rest of us would say "S'blood!" or "Blow me down!"). In this chap's case, a token of "platypus!" that happens to be platypus-occasioned would nevertheless not count as an application of the term to the animal, and would not count as the saying of something true. Other sorts of examples will, no doubt, suggest themselves; the moral is that, at best, only the right kind of platypus-caused tokens counts as applications of "platypus." Still, as previously remarked, I'm inclined to think that it's not utterly unreasonable to hope for a naturalistic account of labelling in terms of causal relations between symbols and the things they apply to.

There is, however, no plausibility at all to the proposal that *representing* uses of symbols be naturalized in this way. Clearly, there need be—to put it crudely—no platypus around, none in the local causal history of the tokens that do the representing—when, for example, I write "platypai astound me" or "would that there were not the platypus" or, more prosaically, "platypuses lay eggs." The proximal causes of such tokenings—the causes to which they are presumably connected by covering generalizations, *and which the tokenings therefore carry information about*—aren't platypuses; they're *thoughts*. It's, as it might be, recollections of Melbourne that cause me to token "would that I had a platypus!" or its Mentalese counterpart; and if, as we may suppose, the generalization that such recollections give rise to such tokens is counterfactual-supporting, then it's the thoughts, and not the platypuses, that these tokens carry information about.

I want to make this as clear as I can. It may be that there are causal connections to platypuses *somewhere* in the historical background of platypus-representing tokenings of "platypus." But they haven't the sort of causal roles that IBSTs construe information-carrying in terms of.[4] According to IBSTs, symbols carry information about the things that causally control their tokenings; and the current worry in a nutshell is that the representing tokens of a symbol—as contrasted with its labelling tokens—typically aren't caused by things that belong to its extension. If you are inclined to doubt this, notice the following: Whenever there is a true application of "platypus" there is (assuming IBST) an answer to the question "*which* platypus caused the tokening?" Viz., it's the platypus to which the token was truly applied. But which platypus caused the "platypus" in "Would that I had a platypus?" Answer: none.

---

4. If you take seriously the idea that carrying information about is a *statistical* relation (so that, for example, As carry information about Bs when there is a statistically reliable covariance between Bs and As), you could break the semantic relation between "platypus" and platypuses just by inflating the relative frequency of representating to labelling tokens; e.g., by saying (or thinking) "Up the platypus!" over and over again when there isn't a platypus around.

As for why all this matters, the examples may already have made that clear: The typical use of symbols *in thinking* is representation, not labelling.

No doubt, I do sometimes think "Hello, platypus here"; thoughts of this kind are, I suppose, the usual product of perceptual processes. And, again no doubt, such thoughts must sometimes play a role in reasoning. But it is as silly to think of thinking as *primarily* consisting in labelling as it would be to think of talking as consisting *primarily* in crying "Gavagai!" Much—very much—of what goes on in thinking is a movement from representation to representation; we put to ourselves ways that the world might be, and then we figure out what follows. It's this sort of figuring out which, together with remembering, extends the reach of the mental life beyond what is locally given to perception; and, unlike labelling, we can do it with our eyes shut.

It wouldn't be very misleading to say that IBST gives us *at best* a naturalistic theory of representation in perception, but *no theory at all* of representation in thought. This helps explain the infestations of frogs by which IBSTs are repeatedly plagued. Say to an informational semanticist: "Please, how does representation work?" and you are likely to get a song and dance about what happens when frogs stick their tongues out at flies. "There is," so the song goes, "a state of the frog's central nervous system that is (1) reliably caused by flies (in normal circumstances); and which (2) is the (normal) cause of an ecologically appropriate, fly-directed response. This state resonates, as one might say, to flies; and it is, for this reason, a paradigm of natural intentionality." If you then ask how this story about frogs and flies is supposed to apply to the case where one thinks to oneself, as it might be, "alack for the ungainly platypus" you will be told, in effect, that sorry but the theory is out to lunch.

The point, of course, is that frogs don't *think* about flies except, perhaps, when in the course of arranging to ingest one. So the question of how the frog represents flies *in thought* doesn't much arise. Still, there had better be an answer to such questions in the case of mental lives that are richer than the frog's. And, as we've seen, the terrible problem is that IBSTs haven't the slightest idea what this answer might be.

2. On the Nature of Representation

Recapitulation: We are assuming—in a spirit of be nice to IBSTs—that labelling occurrences of "platypus" are *adverbially* caused by local platypai. (What you put in the adverb position depends on which version of IBST you like best; candidates include "always," "normally," "ideally," "statistically significantly," "counterfactual-supportingly," etc.; and you're allowed to choose more than one adverb.) But representational occurrences of "platypus" are typically not so caused since they are typically not caused by platypai at all. Tokens of "platypus" that occur in the course of thinking about Melbourne, for example, are typically caused by *thoughts of Melbourne*. Presumably such tokens carry the information that their causes are thoughts about Melbourne; anyhow, they don't carry the information that their causes are platypai.

Let's collect together the kinds of events that are *adverbal* causes of representing occurrences of "platypus"; call them T-events. Then it's a way of putting our problem that "platypus" tokens at large have *two* kinds of causes: the labelling occurrences are, by hypothesis, platypus-occasioned; and the representing occurrences are, by hypothesis, T-occasioned. Our problem is therefore: WHY DOES "PLATYPUS" MEAN *PLATYPUS* AND NOT *PLATYPUS-OR-T*? After all, what its tokens are adverbially caused by, and hence carry information about are events that are (not platypus instantiations tout court, but) *either* platypus instantiations or T-instantiations.

This way of formulating the representation problem exhibits it as rather like—but much worse than—a worry that has sometimes been raised about the treatment of *errors* in IBSTs, and that is known, in that context, as "the disjunction problem." Let's suppose that *true* applications of "platypus" are *adverbially* caused by platypai. Still, it must be possible—either in thought or in speech—occasionally to *mis*apply "platypus"; and, presumably, misapplications of "platypus" are ipso facto *not* caused by platypai.[5] Suppose that there are circumstances under which I would regularly mistake—as it might be—a cow for a platypus. Then, *prima facie*, the generalization "if platypus or cow-in-those-circumstances, then 'platypus'" token is true and counterfactual-supporting. So it appears that, on standard accounts of "carries the information" my "platypus" tokens carry the information that they are occasioned by *either* platypai or cows-in-certain-circumstances. From which it presumably follows that "platypus" doesn't mean *platypus*, and that cow-occasioned "platypus" labellings are *true*.

Now various people (including, for example, David Israel and the Stanford crowd, Ruth Millikan, Georges Rey, Robert Stalnaker, and me)[6] have tried to get out of this by fooling with the adverb. The idea is that, though "platypus" tokenings may *sometimes* be cow-occasioned, still they aren't *adverbially* cow-occasioned. *Adverb* tokenings are, *ipso facto, always* occasioned by *platypai* (and are therefore always *true*). The problem, of course, is to find an adverb that will do this job *but that is not itself semantic/intentional*. "Normally" or "counterfactual-supportingly" presumably won't do since, at least in any unquestion-begging sense of these terms, it looks as though error is a perfectly normal feature of the use of symbols, and there appears to be no reason why the statement that such-and-such circumstances regularly cause errors shouldn't be counterfactual-supporting. Other adverbs are, however, frequently proposed. Maybe you don't ever get errors in "ideal" or "ecologically valid" circumstances; or in circumstances where the mechanisms of belief fixation are behaving "in the way that God or The Forces of Selection designed them to ..." etc. And maybe it's possible to say without circularity what "ideal" or "ecologically valid" or "designed to" means in these constructions. But I doubt it. Philosophers who pay for their semantics by drawing checks on Darwin are in debt way over their heads. Or so it seems to me. (For an extended discussion of these sorts of points, see my 1990a, "A Theory of Content, I".)

And, anyhow, even if idealization, natural selection, and the like will break the disjunction problem for the case of *error*, they clearly won't help for the corresponding problem about *representation*. Idealizing away from sources of error won't work for representation because representational occurrences of "platypus" don't covary with platypai *even when they're true*. Nothing has gone *wrong* when thinking about Melbourne causes me to think about platypai; even Omniscience could entertain such chains of thought. Well, maybe you can idealize away from mislabelling; but surely you can't idealize away from *thinking*. (And unless you're prepared to suppose that

5. Or, if they happen to be caused by platypai, then they must be so caused in not "the right way"; i.e., not in the way that's required for them to count as labelling their causes platypai.
6. In Fodor (1981/1990) "Psychosemantics." Not to be confused with the book of the same name, also by me, for a discussion of which see below.

evolution designed folks to label but *not* to think, God and Darwin won't help you either.)

The upshot is that—contrary to what a number of philosophers (including me) have supposed—the disjunction problem has nothing in particular to do with error. Or, rather, it has to do with error only insofar as misapplications of symbols share with lots of other kinds of symbol tokenings the property of not being caused by things in the symbol's extension. As long as there are such cases there will be a disjunction problem for IBSTs.

Now for some ancient history. Back in the days when I was still thinking of the disjunction problem as just the form that the problem of error takes in causal covariance theories of meaning, I published a book called *Psychosemantics* (one of the best-kept secrets of MIT Press). *Psychosemantics* contained a discussion of the disjunction problem, of which the following is the gist.

Platypuses and cows-on-occasions both cause "platypus" tokenings. But since "platypus" doesn't mean anything disjunctive, either meaning isn't reducible to causation or there must be something relevantly different between the ways that platypuses cause "platypus"s and the ways that cows-on-occasions do; some difference that would, inter alia, explain why tokens whose etiology runs along the second route are *false*. This difference is, of course, exactly what all the adverb-mongering theories are looking for when they suggest that cows, unlike platypuses, don't cause "platypus"s *normally*, or *under ideal circumstances*, or that *ecologically valid* cows don't. But, even when I was thinking of the disjunction problem just in the context of theories of error, these sorts of solutions struck me as pretty unconvincing. I tried, but I couldn't convince myself that, *ceteris paribus*, we're all infallible.

The idea that error is an accident won't wash; but there's an idea with which it's easily confused that may do the job: the Platonic doctrine that error is (ontologically) parasitic on truth. In particular, according to *Psychosemantics* it's true that some "platypus"s are causally dependent on cows, just as it's true that some "platypus"s are causally dependent on platypuses. But there is nevertheless a difference between the cases: The causal dependence of "platypus"s on cows is itself dependent on the causal dependence of "platypus"s on platypuses in a way that the causal dependence of "platypus"s on platypuses is *not* dependent on the causal dependence of "platypus"s on cows. Intuitively: But that one calls platypai "platypai," one's misidentifications of cows would not lead one to call *them* "platypai"; but that one uses "platypai" to label platypai, one would not use it to *mis*label cows. And this doesn't go the other way around. The use of "platypus" to label platypai does *not* depend upon its use to mislabel cows; you would call platypai "platypai" even if you never mistook a cow for one. It's because of this asymmetry that "platypus" means *platypus* and not *platypus or cow*. And it's because of this asymmetry that cow-caused "platypus"s are mislabellings.

So *Psychosemantics* said; but *Psychosemantics* suffered from the delusion that "platypus" tokens that don't carry the information that their causes are platypuses are ipso facto *false*. Whereas, we've now seen that there is a whole nother species of such tokens, viz. the representational uses. These are *not* ipso facto false, but they do raise a disjunction problem. So, clearly, there is something wrong with the *Psychosemantics* picture.

To summarize; Standard IBSTs offer us an exhaustive distinction between tokenings that are caused by what they apply to (platypus-occasioned "platypai") and false tokenings (cow-occasioned "platypai"). But, as it turns out, false tokenings are just a special case of tokenings of a symbol that are not caused by things in its extension. The taxonomy we are required to naturalize is therefore:

all Tokenings of "S"
that express the property P

true applications; i.e., tokens
caused by things that have P;
i.e., caused by things in the
extension of "S."

tokens are not caused by things
that have P; i.e., not caused by
things in the extension of S.

false applications   representations   ?

And there's a disjunction problem for every category on the right-hand side of the tree.

Here is what I now propose (but tune in for further revisions).

(1) I assume that IBST is right about true labellings: True labellings carry information about their causes. So, part of the story about applying "platypai" to platypai is that tokens of the symbol are under the causal control of instances of the property *platypus*.

(2) But the IBST story about true labelling doesn't, in and of itself, tell us what it is for "platypus" to mean *platypus*; it doesn't reconstruct the relation between a symbol and the property it expresses. Tokens of "platypus" are sometimes applied to cows (mislabelling) and they're sometimes deployed in thought (representation) and they do not thereby cease to express the property *platypus*. *The relation between a symbol and the property that it expresses* is not, therefore, directly reconstructed by a story about information carried, contrary to what IBST theorists have generally supposed. Outbreaks of the disjunction problem are indicative of an epidemic confusion between the analysis of the relation between a symbol and the property it expresses and the analysis of true labelling.

(3) Here's a first approximation to a story about the relation between symbols and the properties they express (for second and third approximations, see my *Psychosemantics* and "A Theory of Content, II"): Tokens of platypus mean *platypus* if (a) some tokens of "platypus" carry the information that they are caused by platypai; and (b) tokenings of "platypus" that do *not* carry this information are asymmetrically dependent on tokenings that do.[7] I'm inclined to think that that's what there is to representation, and that, au fond, that's all that there is. No doubt it's wrong of me to be inclined to think this.

7. One reason why this is *only* a first approximation is that you might have words which are *never* truly applied (i.e., never occasioned by things that they apply to). E.g., "unicorn." Presumably representational tokenings of "unicorn," and its misapplication to cows, are dependent upon counterfactual applications to unicorns. More precisely, they're dependent on the fact that "unicorns cause 'unicorns'" is counterfactual-supporting and (hence) can be true in the absence of unicorns.

Another reason is that, as stated, 3 is no good if "platypus" is ambiguous (as opposed to meaning something disjunctive); see *Psychosemantics*. Clearly there is a lot of tidying up to be done to make 3 work. That, however, does not mean that it's unworkable.

Note that:

(1) On this story, applications of "platypus" to platypuses express the property *platypus*; they carry the information that their causes are platypai, and all other tokenings of "platypus" are asymmetrically dependent upon them.

(2) Representational tokenings of "platypus" express the property *platypus*, and so do (mis)applications of "platypus" to cows; both are asymmetrically dependent upon there being (actual or possible) tokenings of 'platypus' that carry the information that their causes are platypai.

(3) Cow-occasioned tokenings of "platypus" do *not* express the property *platypus or cow* since it is platypus-occasioned "platypus" tokenings (and not platypus-or-cow-occasioned "platypus" tokenings) on which they asymmetrically depend. So the disjunction problem is solved. In this view, what was wrong with previous treatments of error in IBSTs is that they all tried to make erroneous tokenings of a symbol carry the same information that true labellings do. This doesn't work and it violates the basic tenet of IBST; viz. that symbol tokens carry information about their causes. According to the present version, by contrast, what platypus-occasioned "platypus"s share with cow-occasioned ones is (not the information they carry, but) *what they mean*: both express the property *platypus*. Granny wins again.

If any of this is right, then we now know what the relation is between "carrying the information" that so and so and meaning that so and so. A symbol that carries information about P-instantiation means P if its *other* information-carrying (the other causal covariances into which it enters) depends asymmetrically on its carrying information about P-instantiation. However, we still haven't got a theory of error. Or to put it another way, we know how false applications of "platypus" can mean *platypus* even though they aren't platypus-occasioned. What we don't know, however, is what makes them different from other tokens of "platypus" that also don't carry the information that platypai cause them; e.g., representing tokens.

Moreover (and here's where I depart from the intuitions that drove *Psychosemantics*), it seems reasonable to doubt that any variation on the theme of asymmetric dependency will throw light on this issue.[8] The point about errors, after all, is that they are things that we want to *avoid*; and their asymmetrical dependency on true labellings doesn't, in and of itself, explain why this is so. (To put it another way, Plato's attempt to derive the *normative* objection to false beliefs from the *ontological* priority of true ones simply doesn't work.) This is immediately apparent when we notice that representational tokenings are also asymmetrically dependent on true labellings, though we feel no pressure to avoid *them*. The current position is that, having solved the disjunction problem, we need a story about error not because error raises the disjunction problem, but just because we need a story abut error. And it would be very desirable if the story we tell explained why calling something a mistake has the normative force that it does.

I don't have a worked-out naturalistic story to tell about error; but I propose to close this paper with some suggestions about how to get started on constructing one.

---

8. This rest of this paragraph is owing to a conversation with Paul Boghossian; I'm greatly indebted to him for making me think about the error problem in these terms.

For these purposes, I'll stick to erroneous applications—i.e., to mislabellings. I expect that there's an extension to nonlabelling tokens (for example, to a naturalistic story about what's wrong with "platypuses sing"), but I'm not going to worry about that here.

From the current perspective, the point to emphasize about error is that it involves *misrepresentation*. Here I'm just following Granny: What she says is wrong with applying "platypus" to a cow is that one thereby represents the cow as having the property which "platypus" expresses; viz. the property of being a platypus. Which, of course, the cow doesn't; only platypuses do.

Now, this formulation relys on two key notions: the notion of *applying* a symbol to a thing, and the notion of a symbol *expressing* a property. We have (see above) a story about what it is for a symbol to express a property; what needs working on is the notion of application. Here, in roughest outline, is how I think such a story ought to go.

Applying the symbol S to the object O isn't just a matter of having O cause a token of S (see the discussion in section 1). So, what more is required? An old-fashioned suggestion is that applying a symbol to a thing involves having a disposition to reason and to act in certain ways, both in respect of the symbol and in respect of the thing you apply it to. So, for example, if you apply "platypus" to Bossie and you accept (i.e., believe-true) "platypai lay eggs," then *ceteris paribus* you are prepared to accept "Bossie lays eggs" and *ceteris paribus* you are prepared to act towards Bossie in whatever ways you are disposed to act towards platypai and egg-layers.

That, surely, is what Grandmother would have said. The question is: are *we*, qua naturalists, allowed to say it? Answer: maybe. It depends on whether we can get a naturalistic construal of notions like believing-true, being prepared to reason/act in such and such a way, etc. Well *can* we? Answer: maybe again. There are, after all, ideas floating around for functionalist reconstructions of these sorts of notions, and I'm prepared to view these ideas as not altogether crazy.[9]

So, for example: there is a symbol (viz. "Bossie is a platypus") which expresses a property that is instantiated by and only by states of affairs that are constituted by Bossie's being a platypus. One way to apply "is a platypus" to Bossie is to have a token of this symbol in your "believe-true box."[10] The believe-true box is defined by reference to the causal roles of the symbols it contains; that is, a symbol is said to be in the believe-true box if certain of its tokens have certain causes and effects. Among the consequences of this functional characterization is that, *ceteris paribus*, if "Bossie is a platypus" and "platypai lay eggs" are both in the believe-true box, then so too is "Bossie lays eggs." A further consequence is that some symbols in the believe-true box have specified causal relations to tokens of symbols located in a "desire-true box" (as per your favourite decision theory.) Among the causal consequences of having "Bossie is a platypus" and "platypai lay eggs" in your believe-true box and

9. I'm on record as holding that function plays no role in the determination of *content*. But, of course, that's quite compatible with holding that notions like *believing-true, accepting, inferring, acting on,* and other relations that agents bear *towards* contents should be functionally defined. For discussion, see *Psychosemantics*.
10. Other ways of doing so are distinguished by how Bossie is picked out (e.g., by a definite description, an anchored indexical), etc.

having "I get to eat a platypus omelette" in your desire-true box is that *ceteris paribus* you beat the fields[11] around Bossie for platypus eggs.[12]

But, as a matter of fact, *ceteris paribus you don't find any* because, of course, Bossie isn't a platypus (applications of "platypus" to Bossie are ispso facto *mis*applications) and it is in the nature of platypus eggs to be laid by, and only by, platypuses. That, in microcosim, is what's wrong with false beliefs. Show me a man who applies "platypus" to a cow and (*ceteris paribus*) I will show you a man who doesn't get any platypus eggs.

According to this view, the Naturalistic answer to "what's wrong with false beliefs?" is primarily that false beliefs lead to abortive actions. And if somebody wants to know what's wrong with abortive actions, the answer is that they lead to not getting what you want. And if somebody wants to know what's wrong with not getting what you want, the answer is that explanation has to stop somewhere.

This explanation stops here.[13]

References

Fodor, Jerry (1968) "The Appeal to Tacit Knowledge in Psychological Explanations." *Journal of Philosophy*, 65, 627–40.

Fodor, Jerry (1975) *The Language of Thought*. Cambridge, MA: Harvard University Press.

Fodor, Jerry (1981/90) "Psychosemantics; or, Where Do Truth Conditions Come From?" In William Lycan, (ed.), *Mind and Cognition*. Oxford: Basil Blackwell.

Fodor, Jerry (1987) *Psychosemantics*. Cambridge, MA: MIT Press.

Fodor, Jerry (1990a) "A Theory of Content, I." In his *A Theory of Content and Other Essays*. Cambridge, MA: MIT Press.

Fodor, Jerry (1990b) "A Theory of Content, II." In his *A Theory of Content and Other Essays*. Cambridge, MA: MIT Press.

Rey, Georges (1997) *Contemporary Philosophy of Mind*. Oxford: Blackwell.

11. Here, "beat the fields for" means indulging in a form of behaviour which is caused in a certain way by interactions between what's in the accept box and what's in the desire box; which, *ceteris paribus*, terminates when a token of "here are some platypus eggs" appears in the accept box ... and so forth. The general program for converting a belief/desire theory account of mental processes into a computational account is familiar from the literature in philosophy of mind. For early versions, see Fodor (1968, 1975); for a recent one, see Rey (1997).

12. This sketch of an account is "functionalist" about the notion of *applying* a symbol but, not, notice, about the notion of content per se. Applying a symbol involves a disposition to reason and act in certain ways; but representation itself requires only the asymmetric dependencies of some relations of information-carrying upon others. This is important in relation to the—frequent—philosophical claims that content is per se holistic; for discussion, see *Psychosemantics*.

13. Unless perhaps it doesn't. It may well be that this story about what's wrong with making mistakes concedes too much to vulgar Pragmatism. For example, it suggests that a being that lacked practical concerns could have *no* reason for preferring true labellings to false ones; indeed, that such a being could find nothing to choose between mind/world *correspondence* and any other mind/world relation. There is, on this view, nothing special about truth except that, for some reason, true beliefs are the ones that it usually turns out that it pays to act on. For *what* reason, one wonders.

Deep down, I think I don't believe any of this. But the question what to put in its place is too hard for me.

Chapter 23

A Common Structure for Concepts of Individuals, Stuffs, and Real Kinds: More Mama, More Milk, and More Mouse

Ruth Garrett Millikan

1. Introduction

Frank Keil observes mildly, "it is difficult to design and motivate empirical studies on concept acquisition without first committing oneself to a set of assumptions about what concepts are and how they are represented" (Keil 1989, p. 25). Indeed so! Concepts, taken as items that the psyche "acquires," are highly theoretical entities. Clearly it is not possible to study them empirically without committing oneself to substantial preliminary assumptions about their nature.

One aim of this target article is to show how, throughout the changing variety of competing theories of concepts and categorization developed by psychologists in the last half century, the theoretical assumption that the extensions of concepts (the set of things that fall under the concept) are determined by descriptions has managed to go unchallenged. This is true despite the fact that Putnam's (1975) and Kripke's (1972) famous arguments against descriptionism (or at least their conclusions) have been rehearsed numerous times in the core psychological literature, and despite the fact that there have been a number of brave attempts to integrate these insights into the psychological tradition (Gelman and Coley 1991; Keil 1989; Komatsu 1992; Lakoff 1987; Markman 1989; Neisser 1987, Ch. 2). The difficulty is that these insights were almost entirely negative. Moreover, the tentative positive views offered have concerned not the nature of concepts (something in the mind) but rather the extensions of words in a public language. Putnam and Kripke left obscure the nature of the psychological states or processes that would constitute an understanding of the meanings of the words they discussed, thus offering no aid to psychologists. I will try to help remedy that situation.

I will present a nondescriptionist theory of the nature of concepts of what (following Aristotle's *Categories*) I will call "substances." The category of substances includes (1) things we would ordinarily call "substances," namely, stuffs such as gold, milk, and mud, (2) things designated "primary substances" by Aristotle, namely, individuals such as Bill Clinton, Mama, and the Empire State Building, along with (3) things designated "secondary substances" by Aristotle, namely, real (as opposed to nominal) kinds. Real kinds include, paradigmatically, both "natural kinds" and the correspondents of what Eleanor Rosch called "basic level" categories (Rosch 1975)—those intermediate level categories such as *shoe* and *mouse* and *house* that children in all cultures learn first (Angelin 1977; Mervis and Crisafi 1982; Nelson 1974). My claim will be that these apparently quite different types of concepts have an identical root structure, and that this is possible because the various kinds of "substances" I have listed have an identical ontological structure when considered at a suitably abstract level. That is, surprisingly to us moderns, the Aristotelian term "substance" is univocal (having one meaning only). Unlike the Aristotelian tradition, in modern times concepts of stuffs and real kinds have traditionally been treated as predicate concepts. That is, to call a thing "gold" or "mouse" has been taken to involve saying or thinking that it as bears a certain description. One understands it as being gold or a mouse by representing it having a certain set or appropriate sample of properties, or certain relations to other things, or a certain kind of inner nature or structure, or a certain origin or cause. I will argue that, on the contrary, the earliest and most basic concepts we have of *gold* and *mouse* and so forth are subject concepts. Their structure is exactly the same as for concepts of individuals like Mama and Bill Clinton.

To call a person "Mama" is not to attribute to her any properties, relations, or inner or outer causes. It is not to classify her but to identify her. Similarly, Putnam argued, to call a thing "gold" or "mouse" is not to describe it. Neither concept consists of a representation of properties. Rather the extensions of "gold" and "mouse," like the extension of "Mama," are natural units in nature, units to which the concepts *gold* and *mouse* do something like "pointing," and to which they can continue to point despite large changes in the properties the thinker represents them as having. For example, large changes can occur in the way a child identifies gold, hence in the things the child is willing to call "gold," without affecting the extension of the child's word "gold." The difficulty, of course, is to cash in the metaphor of "pointing" (Putnam said "indexicality"). Speaking literally, what is the structure of a substance concept in this view?

Having substance concepts need not depend on knowing words. Preverbal humans, indeed, any animal that collects practical knowledge over time of how to relate to specific stuffs, individuals, and real kinds, must have concepts of them. On the other hand, language interacts with substance concepts in vigorous ways to completely transform the conceptual repertoire. Putnam (1975) argued for what he called "the division of linguistic labor." On the basis of rather different reasons, I will argue similarly, that public language plays a crucial role both in the acquisition of substance concepts and in their completed structure.

I will begin with a positive statement of what I take substances and substance concepts to be (sects. 2 and 3). From this nondescriptionist vantage it will be easier to see just how descriptionism continues to be an ingredient in contemporary experimental work on concepts (sect. 4). Then I will discuss the nature of concept development from a nondescriptionist perspective (sect. 5) and finally the crucial involvement of language in the acquisition and use of substance concepts (sect. 6).

2. Substances

The bulk of a child's earliest words are concrete nouns, including names of individuals, names of basic-level kinds, and some names for stuffs (milk, juice). These are acquired in a rush by the dozens between about one-and-a-half and two years of age: "this vocabulary spurt is often called the *naming* explosion to reflect the large preponderance of nouns that are learned" (Markman 1991, p. 81; see Gentner 1982 and Ingram 1989 for reviews, Dromi 1987 for some reservations.)[1] Adjectives come later and more slowly and abstract nouns later still. This suggests that the ability to distinguish

---

1. There is evidence that Korean children have a "verb spurt" a month or two before their "noun spurt" begins. The number of nouns nevertheless soon overtakes the number of verbs (Choi and Gopnik 1993).

concrete individuals in thought and the ability to distinguish basic kinds and stuffs may have something in common, and that concepts of properties and of other abstract objects may not be required for these tasks. There is much independent evidence that children come to appreciate separable dimensions, such as color, shape, and size only after a considerable period in which "holistic similarities" dominate their attention (see Keil 1989 for discussion). Thus concepts of properties again appear as less fundamental than those expressed with simple concrete nouns. I propose that individuals, basic-level kinds, and stuffs have something in common that makes them all knowable in a similar way, and prior to properties.

We can begin with kinds. In recent years, a number of researchers have been interested in the structure of concepts of "natural kinds" and in the development of children's understanding of these kinds (e.g., Carey 1985; Gelman and Coley 1991; Keil 1989; Markman 1989). Natural kinds are said to be distinguished in part by the fact that many true generalizations can be made about them. Concepts of natural kinds thus provide an indispensable key to the acquisition of inductive knowledge. According to Gelman and Coley (1991), people develop natural kind concepts

> with the implicit ... goal of learning as much as possible about the objects being classified.... For example, if we learn that X is a "cat," we infer that it has many important properties in common with other cats, including diet, body temperature, genetic structure, and internal organs. We can even induce previously unknown properties. For example, if we discover that one cat has a substance called "cytosine" inside, we may then decide that other cats also contain this substance. (p. 151)

Gelman and Coley (1991) call this feature "rich inductive potential." They, and especially Keil and Markman, are explicit, however, that "natural kinds" are not sharply set apart from artifactual or even, in Markman's view, purely nominal kinds. "Bird" and "white thing," Markman tells us

> should be viewed as endpoints on a continuum from natural kind categories, which have rich correlated structure and are embedded in scientific theories, to arbitrary categories, which have impoverished correlated structure. Many other categories fall somewhere between these two extremes. "Chair," for example, is an intermediate type of category. Once we know an object is a chair, we know a fair amount about its physical appearance, construction and typical function. (1989, p. 114)

If there is indeed such a continuum, basic-level categories would seem to be closer to the "natural kind" end. Thus Mervis tells us,

> [basic-level] categories are based on large clusters of (subjectively) correlated attributes that overlap very little from category to category. In our world, these basic-level categories are the most general categories whose members share similar overall shapes (or similar parts in particular configurations; Tversky and Hemenway 1984) and similar functions and characteristic actions. (Mervis 1987, p. 202, citing Rosch et al. 1976)

Many basic level kinds do not figure in scientific theories, however, because they do not figure in universal laws. They are of special interest because they afford so many inductive inferences, not because they afford totally reliable ones. In this way they differ from "natural kinds" in the strong sense intended by some philosophers (e.g., Putnam 1975). I will lump these two varieties of kinds together, speaking only of "real kinds" as opposed to "nominal kinds." There are two continua from richer to poorer among real kinds, reflecting (1) the multiplicity of inferences supported, and (2) their reliability.

What I want to do, now, is to generalize the notion of "rich inductive potential," showing how it applies not just to real kinds but also to stuffs and individuals.

Classically, induction is described as a movement from knowledge about certain instances of a kind to conclusions about other instances of the same kind. Consider, now, generalizations made over instances of the second order kind *encounters with kind K*, for example, over the kind *encounters with mice*. Compare this with making generalizations over *encounters with the stuff milk* and *encounters with the individual Mama*. These are equally easy and equally productive ways to generalize.

The ontological category "substances," as I use this term, is roughly (more precision later) that extensive category consisting of items about which it is possible to learn from one encounter something about what to expect on other encounters.[2] Thus, I can discover in one encounter (temporal or spatial) that cats eat fish, and that knowledge will remain good on other encounters with cats. Or I can discover that Xavier knows Greek, and this will remain good on other encounters with Xavier. Or I can discover that ice is slippery and this will remain good when I encounter ice again in that other puddle over there or next winter. For cats, I can also discover numerous other anatomical, physiological, and behavioral facts that will carry over: there is the entire subject of cat physiology and behavior studied by those attending veterinary schools. Even more carries over for Xavier, including all or most of what can be discovered about humans, along with many of his own stable properties. For any determinate kind of stuff, there is a vast array of questions, such as "What is its chemistry?", "What is its melting point?", "What is its specific gravity?", "What is its tensile strength?" that can sensibly be asked and answered, once and for all, on the basis of one careful observation. For these reasons, cat (kind), Xavier, and ice are each "substances." Besides stuffs, real kinds, and individuals, the category "substances" may include such things as certain event types,[3] cultural artifacts, musical compositions, and so forth, but I will ignore these in the present essay.

It is not a matter of logic, of course, but rather of the makeup of the world, that I can learn from one observation what color Xavier's eyes are or, say, how the water spider propels itself. It is not a matter of logic that these things will not vary from meeting to meeting. And indeed, the discovery on one meeting that cats are black does not carry over; next time a cat may be striped or white. Nor does the discovery that Xavier is talking or asleep carry over; next time he may be quiet or awake. Nor does discovering that ice is cubical or thin carry over. Although substances are items about which enduring knowledge can be acquired from one or a few encounters, for each substance or broad category of substances only certain types of knowledge are available. Moreover, most of the knowledge that carries over about ordinary substances is not certain knowledge, but merely probable knowledge. Some cats don't

2. An in-depth discussion of the ontological category of substances can be found in Millikan 1984, Chapters 16 and 17.

3. "There appears to be a basic or generic level of categorization for events, again just as for object categories (see Abbot et al. 1985; John 1985; Rifkin 1985; Rosch 1978; Tversky and Hemenway 1984)" (Clark 1991, p. 39).

like fish, perhaps, and a stroke could erase Xavier's Greek. But no knowledge whatever carries over about nonsubstance kinds, such as *the red square* or *the two-inch malleable object* or *the opaque liquid*, except what applies to one or another of the analytical parts of these complexes taken separately. (Similarly for Markman's "white thing" above. It is not on the scale with substances, for there is nothing to be learned about it.)

There are various contemporary interpretations of the underlying reasons why there are such things as real kinds in nature, including, especially, more than one thesis on the nature of "natural kinds" (Boyd 1989; 1991; Hacking 1991; Kornblith 1993; Putnam 1975). Everyone agrees, however, that what makes something a natural kind is that there is some such reason: kinds are not natural if they yield inductive knowledge by accident. Similarly, I suggest, for real kinds generally. If a term is to have genuine "rich inductive potential" it had better attach not just to a pattern of correlated properties, but to an univocal explanatory ground of correlation.

My own position (Millikan 1984, Ch. 16; forthcoming) is that there are many different reasons for the existence of real kinds. These reasons account for successes in generalizing over encounters in a variety of different ways. Sometimes there is a single underlying cause or inner structure (cf. Putnam's "natural kinds") that results, always, or under common conditions, in a certain selection of surface properties, as in the case of the various chemical substances. In such cases, the kinds have real essences, not merely nominal ones, discoverable by empirical investigation. Sometimes, rather than having a single unifying essence, the properties of a real kind may cluster because of a sort of homeostasis among them or their causes (Boyd 1991). Then there is no essence at all, nothing in common to all members of the kind. Nor is there an essence in the other cases I shall now mention.

Sometimes the unifying cause of a real kind may be largely external, as in the case of many artifact categories. Keil tells us,

> Chairs have a number of properties, features, and functions that are normally used to identify them, and although there may not be internal causal homeostatic mechanisms of chairs that lead them to have these properties, there may well be external mechanisms having to do with the form and functions of the human body and with typical social and cultural activities of humans. For example, certain dimensions of chairs are determined by the normal length of human limbs and torsos ... the causal homeostatic mechanisms for natural kinds are closely related to various domains of science, such as biology, chemistry, and physics, whereas those for artifacts and natural kinds involve more social and psychological domains of causality. (Keil 1989, pp. 46–47)

Another very common explanatory ground determining similarities among members of a real kind is copying or reproduction. For example, a factor often accounting for limited variety within artifact categories is that the same design is copied over and over. Similarly, the animals or plants in a species are alike, not only because of homeostasis in the gene pool, but because they (their genes) are reproduced from one another. Another variety of real kinds is the (fully or partially) socially constructed kind, for example, school teacher, doctor, and father. People falling in these categories act similarly as a result of similar training handed down from person to person (reproduction), custom (more reproduction), social pressures to conform (reproduction again), or law. Sometimes members form a social kind only because people class them together, but the "because" here may be causal not logical, hence the kind may be real not nominal (Millikan, forthcoming).

Turning now to what holds individuals together over encounters (over time), Xavier today is much like Xavier yesterday because Xavier today resulted directly from Xavier yesterday, in accordance with certain kinds of conservation laws and certain patterns of homeostasis.

Similarly, Ghiselin and Hull have claimed that a species is really just a big scattered individual, causing itself to continue over time much as a standard individual does (Ghiselin 1974; 1981; Hull 1978). A dog is a member of the species *dog* because it was born of a dog, not because it is like other dogs. Conversely, some philosophers have thought of Xavier as a class consisting of Xavier time-slices, each of which causes the next. Either way, there is a deep similarity between individuals and many real kinds, and either way, neither individuals nor real kinds need have essences.

Philosophers interested in such questions have thought up numerous bizarre examples where it would not be clear whether we should say that this individual thing was numerically the same as that individual thing occurring later in time. However, in the usual case we assume, quite rightly, that whether or not a correct identification of an individual has been made depends on how the world is, not on how we humans (or we English speakers) like to identify things. Similarly, the question whether a seemingly marginal item is or is not of a certain real kind is most often a straightforward substantive question about how the world is, not a question about how we humans (or English speakers) like to classify things. If it is not like other members of the kind for the reason the other members are like one another, it is not a member of the kind. On the other hand, because the occurrence of causal factors accounting for similarities among members of a group can be more or less irregular, and because numbers of causally grounded similarities can be larger or smaller, whether a real kind exists at all is sometimes a marginal matter.

In sum, a "substance" is something about which one can learn from one encounter things to apply on other occasions *where this possibility is not coincidental but grounded*. That is, there is an explanation or cause of the samenesses.

I now wish to show that it is plausible that despite the many different kinds of groundings that account for the unity of various types of substances, the basic structure of a concept of a substance is always the same. This is possible because there is no need to understand what the ground of a substance is, or even that a substance has a ground, in order to have a concept of that substance. Throughout the history of philosophy and psychology, the tendency has been to project into the mind itself the structure of the object grasped by thought. I will argue the contrary, namely that substances are grasped not by understanding the structures or principles that hold them together but by knowing how to exploit these substances for information gathering purposes. Knowing how to use a thing is not knowing facts about its structure.

3. Concepts of Substances

The "concept" of a substance, as I use that term,[4] is the capacity to represent the substance in thought for the purpose of information gathering and storage, inference,

---

4. I do not recommend generalizing this description of a concept indiscriminately, for example, to "mathematical concepts," "logical concepts," "modal concepts," and so forth. The idea that every word corresponds to a concept in some univocal sense of the term "concept" is surely mistaken.

and ultimately the guidance of action. We wish to know the structure of this ability. To describe the structure of an ability is to say what it is an ability to do, what sub-abilities are contained in it and, ultimately, by what means it is exercised, that is, how exactly it accomplishes what it does. Using largely a priori means we cannot hope to travel vary far, but Frank Keil was surely right that in order to engage in empirical research, one must have some idea of what one is looking for. Experimental results are worthless without an approximation, at least, to a sound theoretical framework in which to interpret them.

From the standpoint of an organism that wishes to learn, the most useful and accessible subjects of knowledge are things that retain many of their properties, hence potentials for theoretical or practical use, over numerous encounters with them. This makes it possible for the organism to store knowledge about the thing collected on earlier encounters for use on later occasions, the knowledge retaining its validity over time. Substances are (by definition) what afford this sort of opportunity to a learner. In the experience of a child, for example, *Mama* retains many of her properties over various encounters with her just as *milk* and *mouse* do. Given this, we might expect the child, indeed we might expect any animal, to learn how to relate to, and what to expect from, these various items in much the same way. For example, onto-logically speaking, individuals are space-time worms while real kinds are collections of similar space-time worms, but to have the capacity to understand this ontological distinction would require a grasp of space-time structure and temporal relations of a sort not acquired by children until years after they are proficient in the use of both proper and common names (Nelson 1991). Putting it Quine's way, the child's (and the dog's) first recognitions must be merely of *more Mama, more milk*, and *more mouse* (Quine 1960, p. 92). Children observe things about *Mama* when they encounter her, not about samples or instances of Mama. Similarly, to learn things about milk, they need not understand what it would be to think of or keep track of portions of milk as individuals. And the very point of having the concept *mouse* would seem to be that using it, one does not distinguish Amos from Amos's brother; one conceives them as the same. Note that I am talking here about applying substance concepts, not about acquiring them. My claim here is only that early substance concepts, even when what they are concepts of, ontologically, is kinds, need not be predicate concepts applied to prior subject concepts. They need not be understood as descriptions of anything.

The various substances differ, of course, in the types of knowledge they afford. The child's individual *highchair* retains its overall shape, hence its affordance of sittability-upon, across multiple encounters, but *Mama* does not (you cannot sit on Mama when she is standing). *Milk* and *Mama* retain their color while *cat* does not. But these primitive subjects of knowledge are grouped into rough ontological cate-gories. Even for the very young child, a casual look at a new piece of furniture on the one hand and a new uncle on the other easily reveals which can be counted on to retain its current climbing-up-on affordance and which may grow tired of the sport. Similarly, preschoolers know that what is sleepy might also be hungry, but not made of metal or in need of fixing (Keil 1983). An important question for psychologists, of course, is when and why and how these basic ontological category distinctions are grasped by the developing child.

Now think why a child, or animal, needs to carry knowledge of the properties of a substance from one encounter to another. If all of a substance's properties were immediately manifest to the child upon every encounter there would be no need to learn and remember what these properties were. Carrying knowledge of substances about is useful only because most of a substance's properties are not manifest but hidden from us most of the time. This is not, in general, because they are "deep" or "theoretical" properties, but because observing a property always requires a particular relation to it. To observe that the sugar is sweet it must be in your mouth, to observe that the milk is drinkable and filling you must tip the glass and drink. You do not find out that the cat scratches until you disturb it, or that the fire burns unless you near it; and the pretty design on the front of the quilt is not seen from the back. Different properties and utilities of a substance show themselves on different encounters. That is *why* it is useful to collect knowledge of a substance over time.

Yet there is a sort of paradox here. It won't help to lug knowledge of a substance about with you unless you can recognize that substance when you encounter it again as the one you have knowledge about. If different properties of a substance show themselves at different encounters, how is one to know when one has encountered the same substance again? The very reason you needed to carry knowledge about in the first place shows up as a barrier to applying it. Moreover, not only substances but their properties reveal themselves differently at different encounters. The enduring properties of substances are distal, not proximal, and they affect the external senses quite differently under different conditions and when bearing different relations to the perceiver.

Clearly, then, a most complex but central skill required for any organism that uses knowledge of substances will be the ability to reidentify these substances with fair reliability under a wide variety of conditions. This will be necessary, first, in order to develop practical skills in the use of various substances. It will be necessary, also, for any animal that uses representations of facts about substances as a basis for practical and theoretical inference. For example, suppose I am hungry and I know that yogurt is good to eat and that there is yogurt in the refrigerator. This is of no use unless I also grasp that these two bits of knowledge are about the same thing (yogurt). To caricature,[5] if I represent yogurt to myself in one way, with a mental heart, as I store away the knowledge that yogurt is good to eat, but represent it another way, with a mental diamond, as I store away the information that it is in the refrigerator, these bits of information will not help me when I am hungry. A fundamental subcapacity involved in having a concept of any substance must be the capacity to store away information gathered about it such that it is always represented again with what one understands to be another representation with the same semantic value. This capacity is the capacity to maintain a coherent inner representational system, which means that it is essential for representing something in thought at all!

The ideal capacity to identify a substance would allow reidentification under every physically possible condition, regardless of intervening media and the relation of the substance to the perceiver. The ideal capacity would also be infallible. Obviously there are no such capacities. If the cost of never making an error in identifying Mama or milk or mice is almost never managing to identify any of them at all, it will pay to be less cautious. If one is to recognize a substance when one encounters it a reasonable proportion of the time, one needs to become sensitive to a variety of *relatively* reliable indicators of the substance—indeed, to as many as possible, so as to recog-

5. To model the act of reidentifying a substance in thought as using the same mental term again, as I do here, is actually a crude and misleading expedient (see Millikan 1991; 1993b; 1994; 1997).

nize the substance under as many conditions as possible. Counted as indicators here would be, in the first instance, the various appearances of the substance to each of the various senses, under varying conditions, at varying distances, given varying intervening media, or resulting from various kinds of probing and testing. In the second instance indicators would be pieces of information about the presented substance— that it has this or that property that marks it reliably enough.

In the case of familiar substances, we typically collect numerous means of identification over time, all of them fallible, and certainly none of them "definitional" of the substances being identified. The purpose of a substance concept is not to sustain what Wettstein (1988) aptly calls "a cognitive fix" on the substance, but the practical one of facilitating information gathering and use for an organism navigating in a changing and cluttered environment. Consider, for example, how many ways you can recognize each of the various members of your immediate family: by the look of various body parts from each of dozens of angles, by characteristic postures, by voice, by footsteps, by handwriting, by various characteristic activities, by clothes and other possessions. None of these ways, nor any subset, *defines* for you any family member, and probably all are fallible. There are, for example, conditions under which you would fail to identify even your spouse, conditions under which you would misidentify him and conditions under which you might mistake another for him. The same is true of your ability to identify squirrels or wood. To be skilled in identifying a substance no more implies that one never misidentifies it than skill in walking implies that one never trips.

It follows that it cannot be one's dispositions to apply a substance term that determines what its extension is. In a passage characteristic of the literature, Lakoff remarks, "It is known, for example, that two-year-olds have different categories than adults. Lions and tigers as well as cats are commonly called "kitty" by two-year-olds" (1987, p. 50). How does Lakoff know that two-year-olds are not thinking of lions and tigers that they *are* kitties—kitties grown big? A little more experience and children may change their minds—not on the question what "cat" means, but on reliable ways to recognize cats. At age three, my mother stoutly insisted that her father was "Uncle Albert" when he came home one night without his beard. Surely it does not follow that "Uncle Albert," for her, referred also to her father? A child who has got only part way toward knowing how to ride a bicycle has not learned something other than bicycle riding, but *partially* learned how to ride a bicycle. The same is true of a child who has got only part way toward recognizing cats, or father, or Uncle Albert.

The practical ability to reidentify a substance when one encounters it, so as to collect information about it over time, and so as to know when it is possible to apply that information, has to be complemented, however, with another equally important ability. Having a concept of a substance also requires that one have some grasp of what kinds of things can be learned about it. For example, one must have some ability to tell which kinds of practical successes can be expected to carry over to new encounters with the substance. If the concept is to be used for gathering theoretical knowledge, one must know something of the range of predicates, that is, "determinables," that are applicable to the substance. That is, one must understand what are some of the meaningful questions to ask about it (see Millikan 1984, Ch. 15, pp. 252ff., and Chs. 16 and 17). You can ask how tall Mama is, but not how tall gold is. You can ask at what temperature gold melts, but not at what temperature chairs (as such) do. The latter is a question that can be answered only for (some) individual chairs. There is much that you can find out about the internal organs of each species of animal but not about the (visible) internal parts of gold or mud. Having a concept of a substance is not knowing an essence, but it must involve understanding something of what recognizing the substance might be good for in the context of developing either practical skills or theoretical knowledge.

4. Contrast with Descriptionism

In contrast to the position just sketched, the descriptionist is one who holds that the referent or extension of a substance term is determined by its falling under a description associated with the term by the user. Certain properties, relations, facts about origins, facts about causes, similarities to prototypes, similarities to given exemplars, and so fort—certain "information" about each portion of the extension—determine it to be a portion of the extension, and the thinker or the thinker's "mental representation" determines which information is to play this role. In the psychological literature, this view is frequently found caricatured in the statement that concepts *are* features or properties: "many properties are concepts themselves" (Barsalou 1987, p. 129). But it takes many other forms as well.

Thus, using the concept *chair* as his example, Komatsu (1992) describes the most general question that psychological theories of concepts have attempted to answer as follows: "what information, very generally, is represented by the concept chair, so that people are able to reason about chairs, recognize instances of chairs, and understand complex concepts" (1992, p. 500). Building on Medin and Smith (1981; 1984), Komatsu applies this formula to each of five accounts of concepts:

> the classical view (e.g., Katz 1972; Katz and Fodor 1963) ... the family resemblance view (e.g., Rosch and Mervis 1975) ... the exemplar view (e.g., Medin and Schaffer 1978) ... the schema view [Komatsu later cites Bartlett 1932; Minsky 1975; Neisser 1975; Piaget 1926; Rumelhardt 1980; Schank and Abelson 1977; Winograd 1975] ... the explanation-based view (e.g., Johnson-Laird 1983; Lakoff 1987; Murphy and Medin 1985) [later he cites Carey 1985; Gelman 1988a; 1988b; Gelman and Markman 1987; Keil 1989].

Descriptionism is most obviously compatible with "nominalism," the view that the members of the kinds that words name are grouped together either conventionally according to the dictates of culture, or according to patterns natural to human perception and thought. For example, heavily sprinkled throughout the literature we find references to "learning about people's categorization decisions." On this view, the descriptions that govern concepts have their source either in the conventions of society, or in peculiarities of human perceptual and cognitive systems, in ways it is natural to us to generalize. For example, in classical studies of concept learning, subjects were typically set the task of learning imaginary categories defined by arbitrarily chosen sets of properties, and many studies exploring family resemblance or prototype or exemplar views of categorization have also set arbitrary tasks. The view that the human mind has its own ways of imposing various groupings of things into kinds, ways that languages must respect in order to be learnable, has been evident especially since Rosch's work on color categories (e.g., Rosch 1973; 1975). In this tradition, the psychological problem concerning categorization is understood to be that of ferreting out exactly what these psychologically imposed principles are—those principles in accordance with which children or adults "prefer to sort" (Markman 1989). Thus Lakoff subtitles his 1987 book, "What categories reveal about the mind."

But descriptionism is not always allied with nominalism or conventionalism. It has also been combined with realism about human categories. The realist holds that many of our categories correspond to kinds that are grouped together by nature independently of the mind. As we acquire categories we learn not merely, say, how to communicate with others, but how to grasp structures that were already there in nature. The view of substances that I am advocating is a realist view. Realism and descriptionism might seem incompatible. If the extension of a category is determined by nature, then it is not determined by fitting a certain description associated with a word. But in fact there are a number of ways in which realism and descriptionism have been combined.

The simplest way to combine them is to take the extent of a substance term to be fixed by one, or a set, of definite descriptions of the substance.[6] Thus the classical twentieth century view was that Aristotle himself was a natural unit in nature, and that to have a concept of Aristotle was to capture him in thought under a description such as "the teacher of Alexander," or under a suitable combination of either/or descriptions. Similarly, there has been a tendency in the psychological literature to misinterpret Kripke's (1972) and Putnam's (1975) antidescriptionist views on the meaning of proper names and natural kind terms as invoking definite descriptions at one level removed. (No, Kripke did not claim that the referent of a proper name N is fixed in the user's mind by the description "whoever was originally baptized as N," nor did Putnam claim that the extent of a natural kind term is fixed for laymen by the description "whatever natural kind the experts have in mind when they use term T" [but see also Fumerton 1989].)

The theory that language categories are organized "probabilistically" (Medin 1989) by family resemblance or by reference to prototypes may combine realism with descriptionism. Families and prototypes are usually taken to center over highly correlated properties, and these correlations are taken to be empirically discovered. Thus prototype theory is naturally compatible with the view that many concepts end up paired with real kinds. But probabilistic theories are regularly interpreted as explaining how the learner's experience generates the category, the actual extension of the category being determined not by the real extension of the kind but by how the learner is inclined to classify new examples. The same is true of exemplar theories and for variations on these two views. Thus Billman suggests that we should compare and test psychological models of structure and processing of concepts by examining the function from "learning instances plus the target items to categorize" to "the set of possible *category judgments*" (Billman 1992, p. 415, my emphasis) and Ward and Becker state that "category structure" can mean "the set of items that the learner considers to be members of the category in question (i.e., the category extension)" (1992, p. 454). In other words, it is assumed that although experience with a natural kind may inspire the category, the category extent is determined by the

---

6. Whether it is supposed that the description is used rigidly or nonrigidly makes no difference in this context. In either case, the thinker entertains a prior description that determines the extent of his word or category.

thinker's potential decisions on exemplars. When all goes well, our psychologically determined kinds may contain the same members as the natural ones: that is all. Similarly, the realists Gelman and Byrnes tell us, explicitly making reference to Chomsky's theory of innate grammar, that "we can determine how languages and conceptual systems are constrained by examining the forms and meanings that children construct, and which errors they *fail* to make" (1991, p. 3), that is, it is the child's inclinations that constrain the concepts.

Most explicitly realist in their approach to concepts are contemporary researchers holding what Komatsu called an "explanation-based view" of concept structure. Komatsu characterizes this view by quoting Keil (1989, p. 1):

> No individual concept can be understood without some understanding of how it relates to other concepts. Concepts are not probabilistic distributions of features or properties, or passive reflections of feature frequencies and correlations in the world; nor are they simple lists of necessary and sufficient features. They are mostly about things in the world, however, and bear nonarbitrary relations to feature frequencies and correlations, as well as providing explanations of those features and correlations. If it is the nature of concepts to provide such explanations, they can be considered to embody systematic sets of beliefs— beliefs that may be largely causal in nature.

Note that the view is not just that concepts designate kinds for which there exist explanations of property correlations, but that the concept actually consists in essential part of an understanding; or, looking beyond page 1 of Keil's text, a partial understanding of these explanations. Of particular interest to the explanation theorists, for example, has been Medin's work showing that people behave as though believing that beneath their categories there are hidden essences making the things in the categories what they are (e.g., Medin and Ortony 1989). Keil, Carey, Gelman, and Markman are among those who have done very interesting work tracing the development of children's natural kind concepts and artifact concepts, for example, documenting the transition from reliance on superficial characteristic properties for identification of these kinds to use of rudimentary and then more sophisticated "theories" about the underlying causes of the unity of the kind. But these advocates of explanation-based views have remained strongly influenced by the characteristic mid-twentieth-century doctrine that the "meaning" of a term or concepts is a matter of its connections with other terms or concepts, so that introducing or changing theories threatens to change meanings:

> How can one be sure that one is even talking about the same concept at all if all concepts are relative to theories? ... We do not want every change in theoretical beliefs to make the concepts embedded in them completely different from those that were embedded before the change; yet no precise method is offered [by Smith et al. 1985] for making a decision.... These are difficult issues, and it is hardly surprising that they are not yet resolved. (Keil 1989, pp. 21–22)

Following Smith et al., Keil speaks of "'tracking' concepts across theory change" and agrees with them that probably "descent can be traced ... because of several properties of theories that stay fixed through change" (Smith et al. 1985, p. 182). And he agrees with Fodor that it is not obvious how the classical view could be true that "children and adults could have different kinds of concepts for the same terms," for that makes it seem as though (quoting Fodor 1972) "they must misunderstand each other essentially" (Fodor p. 88; Keil, pp. 15–16). Again, the view here is description-ist. There is no suggestion here that the extent of the concept, its "meaning" in the most fundamental sense, might be directly fixed by the extent of a natural unit in nature, reference remaining the same while conceptions change. (For an exception, see Gopnik and Meltzoff 1996.)

In the alternative to descriptionism that I am suggesting, having a concept of a substance is not having a defining description of it or a theory about it. To have a theory about a substance you have to be able to think of it, and it is this capacity that is the concept. To think of it one must be able to represent it in a stable representa-tional system, where what is in fact the same substance again is represented as being the same again. To maintain such a representational system requires that one have the capacity to recognize the substance under varying conditions so as to know what incoming information to store as information about the same thing. Thus the core of a substance concept is a (necessarily fallible) capacity to recognize what is objectively the same substance again as the same, despite wide variation in the faces it shows to the senses. The extension of one's concept is then determined, not by one's fallible dispositions to recognize portions of its extent, but by the real extent of the sub-stance that has governed the development of these dispositions.

The standard descriptionist view takes the substance concept to be an ability to *classify* instances of the substance. Forcing the distinction, perhaps, between these two for expository purposes, the difference between identifying and classifying lies both in purpose and in psychological structure. The purpose of a classification system is nicely captured by the following contemporary descriptions of "categorization" and of "concepts":

> Categorization ... is a means of simplifying the environment, of reducing the load on memory, and of helping us to store and retrieve information efficiently. (Markman 1989, p. 11)

> Without concepts, mental life would be chaotic. If we perceived each entity as unique, we would be overwhelmed by the sheer diversity of what we experi-ence and unable to remember more than a minute fraction of what we encoun-ter. And if each individual entity needed a distinct name, our language would be staggeringly complex and communication virtually impossible. (Smith and Medin 1981, p. 1)

> concepts are used to classify ... if you know nothing about a novel object but are told it is an instance of X, you can *infer* that the object has all or many of X's properties. (Smith and Medin 1981, p. 8)

A good classification system aids efficient information storage and transfer: the effi-cient organizing of what we already know (encyclopedias), putting things away where we can find them again (libraries, grocery shelves), communication (briefly telling enough about the object for someone else to identify it). The initial data for a paradigm classification task include a specification of all the properties of the object to be classified that are relevant to its classification. A librarian would not try to classify a book, for example, without carefully examining its contents. Similarly, in classical categorization experiments, all relevant properties of each "stimulus" and each "test item" are clearly exhibited to the learner.

Reidentifying is required, on the contrary, not for information storage and transfer, but for its acquisition and use. One needs to be able to identify a substance under diverse circumstances in order to *come to know* its properties, properties that happen not to be currently manifest. This one does by managing to recognize the substance on the basis of whatever properties do happen to be currently manifest, then applying one's prior knowledge of others of its properties to the current encounter. Only in this way can prior knowledge of the substance find a use.

The psychological structure of classification is the structure of subject-predicate judgment. To classify an item requires differentiating the item to be classified in thought and applying a predicate to it. For example, classifying animals as dogs, cats, or mice involves thoughts of Fidos and Spots, Amoses and brothers of Amoses, each individual to be judged a member of its proper category. But when the child recognizes Mama, "Mama" is not a predicate term: surely the child is not categorizing instances of Mama. Nor need the child conceive of mice as individuals in order to recognize the substance *mouse* again.

5. The Development of Substance Concepts

Viewing a substance concept as an ability to reidentify, which a mobile person comes to exercise within a supporting but changing environment, the study of concept development is also seen in a new light. What subskills are involved in this ability? What is the characteristic progression toward acquiring these skills? The answers here are mainly for psychologists to find, but I can try to make the questions clearer.

According to various estimates, children acquire from five to nine words daily between the ages of two and six (Byrnes and Gelman 1991; Clark 1991; Waxman 1991). Chomsky says, "about a word an hour from ages two to eight with lexical items typically acquired on a single exposure" (Chomsky 1995, p. 15). How is this possible? An obvious hypothesis here is that many concepts are developed prior to language, and indeed, at least some must be, for infants recognize their mothers and dogs recognize their masters. Each has the capacity to reidentify the relevant individual under diverse conditions, thus making it possible to learn how to behave appropriately in their presence.

Some of the skills needed to accomplish the task of reidentifying ordinary substances have traditionally been classified as "motor" and "perceptual" rather than "cognitive." Perhaps the most fundamental of these is the ability to track objects with the eyes, head, feet, hands, ears, and nose, and so forth. Objects tracked in this way are not merely conceived to be the same but are *perceived* as the same under certain conditions, the perception of sameness bridging, for example, over motions of perceived and perceiver, over changes in properties of the object, and over temporary disappearances of the object behind other objects. The mechanisms responsible for the ability to track and for perceptual "identity-" or "existence-constancy" may well be largely endogenous (Dodwell et al. 1987; Nelson and Horowitz 1987; Spelke 1993) and certainly are "cognitively impenetrable" (Shepard 1976; 1983). These basic abilities are surely the bottom layer on which conceptions of substances are built.

Tracking allows the accumulation of information about a substance over a period of time, information perceived as being about the same substance. Nor is it only individual objects that are tracked in this way. If I am tracking Fido, I am also tracking the species dog, and also fur and bone. Which of these I am tracking with my mind depends upon which I am learning about or registering information about as I go. And that is determined by which substance I identify on other occasions as the one this learning concerns—as being the same substance again. As I dissect my specimen frog in the zoology laboratory, whether I am conceptually tracking the individual, Kermit, or tracking just frogs depends on whether I attempt to apply what I have learned from my experience only to later meetings with Kermit or whether to frogs in general.

For the usefulness of one's knowledge of a substance to last, however, one must also know how to reidentify the substance after a lengthy break, say, next day or next week. Let us call this "conceptual tracking": one understands rather than perceives that the substance is the same one again. Out of what materials is it that our abilities conceptually to track substances are built?

By tracking a substance perceptually one can learn many different ways to recognize it: how it looks, how it sounds, how it feels, the way it moves and changes. The mechanisms of perceptual constancy for properties can then be brought into play. These mechanisms may be fashioned in part, and certainly are tuned, through experience, but much of their structure also may be endogenous (Dodwell et al. 1987; cf. Gallistel et al. 1993; Marler 1993). They cause distal qualities to appear as the same through wide variation in proximal manifestations. For example, they allow the same shape and size to be registered as the same despite alterations in angle of observation and distance, colors can appear as the same under widely varying lighting conditions, and voices can sound like the same voice through distortions and superimposed noise.

Involvement of the mechanisms of perceptual constancy should not be thought to imply, however, that actual concepts of properties are always involved in conceptual tracking of substances—not if having concepts of properties means being able to represent properties, as such, in thought. For example, being caused to token mental *squirrel* again when prompted by the same distal configuration of shape, color, texture, and motion is not, as such, to token any thoughts of the shapes, colors, or textures themselves. The thought of a property is not just a reaction caused by a property; it must play an appropriate representational role. This accords, of course, with the finding that children appreciate holistic similarities before appreciating separate property dimensions such as color and shape.

When perceptual tracking is coupled with exploratory manipulation, probing, and testing, this may reveal properties and dispositions that prove to be better trackers, better aids to achieving conceptual constancy. An easy example is the tool bag of tests and routines that chemists use in order to reidentify chemical stuffs. In the end, indeed, any knowledge at all that one has of a substance can help to identify it, if not positively, then negatively. "No," we think, "that can't be Sally after all because Sally doesn't know French," or "that can't be real gold in the window because real gold would cost more than that." It is because knowledge of the properties of substances is often used in the process of identifying them that it is easy to confuse having a concept of a substance with having knowledge of properties that would identify it.

But how do children know which aspects of the substances they are learning to track can be relied on for reidentification? And how do they know what questions they should expect to be answerable about each substance? Just as children have built-in perceptual tracking abilities and built-in perceptual constancies, we might expect them to have certain built-in conceptual tracking abilities.

There is evidence, for example, that infants may have inborn systems designed specifically to recognize human faces. And it is well known that they have a strong disposition from the earliest days to track and study human faces (e.g., Johnson et al. 1991). In addition, many species that recognize conspecifics as individuals instinctively use smell for this purpose; and (Dan Dennett has reminded me) human infants also know Mama by smell in the early months (MacFarlane 1977). It appears that innately the infant may know at least two good ways to track individual conspecifics conceptually. Faces and personal odors are indicative of individual identity; clothes, postures, and so forth, are not.

The mechanisms by which infants reidentify individuals perceptually do not appear to rely on the invariance of properties of the tracked object but upon common movement, spatial location, and trajectory (Gopnik and Meltzoff 1996). Xu and Carey (1996) have recently produced experimental evidence that 10-month-old infants, unlike 12-month-olds, are not surprised if an object of one kind apparently turns into an object of another kind, say, a yellow rubber duck into a white styrofoam ball, though they are surprised if an object they are tracking apparently turns into two objects. Tracking in this property-blind way would make it possible to observe, for various broad kinds of objects, what sorts of things tend to remain the same and what sorts may change within a short period, yielding clues for later conceptual tracking.

Whether we have built-in ways of conceptually tracking stuffs or real kinds of any particular sort, such as physical kinds, animal kinds, plant kinds, artifacts, social kinds, and so forth, is clearly a matter for empirical research—research of the sort that Spelke, Carey, Keil, Gelman, Markman, and others have recently been doing, though I am suggesting a somewhat different framework for interpretation of experimental results. Without doubt, the results of more traditional studies of concept formation may also cast light on how conceptual tracking develops. Examining "the function" from "learning instances plus the target items to categorize" to "the set of possible category judgments," as Billman put it (1992), should help us discern what kinds of traces are followed in attempting conceptual tracking at various ages and for different domains of real kinds. To be acutely sensitive to correlations among properties, probably among specific kinds of properties in specific domains (cf. Atran 1989; Carey 1985; Gallistel et al. 1993; Gelman and Coley 1991; Keil 1979; 1989; Markman 1989; Marler 1993; Spelke 1989; 1993) seems an obvious way to track many kinds of substances. But experiments need to be designed and interpreted bearing in mind that the cognitive systems are designed by evolution and tuned by experience to find real world substances, not random logically possible ones. Close attention should be paid to the details of real world ontology and to the principles that hold real substances together; and the relevance of experiments using artificial objects and kinds should be carefully justified.

The most accurate and sophisticated ways of tracking substances conceptually emerge only as insight is slowly gained into the ontological principles that ground them. The psychologists Medin, Gelman, Keil, and Gopnik and Meltzoff (1996), especially, have been interested in tracing the origin and development of children's understanding of these principles. I much admire this research. My suggestion is only that we should be clear that understanding of this sort is not necessary to having a concept of a substance, and that having or lacking such understanding need make no difference to the *extensions* of one's substance concepts.

A substance concept causally originates from the substance that it denotes. It is a concept of A, rather than B, not because the thinker will always succeed in reidentifying A, never confusing it with B, but because A is what the thinker has been conceptually, hence physically, tracking and picking up information about, and because the concept has been tuned to its present accuracy by causal interaction with either the members of A's specific domain or with A itself, during the evolutionary history of the species or through the learning history of the individual. If it is not definite which among various closely related, overlapping, or nested substances was the one primarily responsible for the information that has been gathered or for the tuning of the (would-be) tracking dispositions, then the concept is equivocal. For example, to have two people "mixed up" or "confused" in one's mind is to have an equivocal substance concept (Millikan 1984, Ch. 15; 1991; 1993a, Ch. 14; 1994; 1997).

We now move to a still more fundamental medium through which conceptual tracking is achieved, namely, language.

6. Substance Concepts and Language

The story I have been telling about substance concepts apparently runs headlong into the blatant fact that many of these concepts, both for children and adults, have been acquired without encountering the substances "themselves" but only by "hearing of them." With regard to these same substances, however, we are often in the position that Kripke (1972) and Putnam (1975) noted: knowing neither how to identify these substances in the flesh, nor by any unique or defining description. That is, neither verificationist nor descriptionist theories of concept extension explain these cases. This entire problem falls away, however, if we view speech as a direct medium for the perception of objects in the same way that, say, light is.

It is traditional to assume that gathering information by being told things is a radically different sort of process from gathering information directly through perception. There is reason to think, however, that the difference has been greatly exaggerated—that uncritically believing what one hears said is surprisingly like uncritically believing what one sees. For example, there is experimental evidence that what one is told directly generates a belief, unless cognitive work is done to prevent this, just as with what one perceives through other media. Loading the cognitive systems with other simultaneous tasks, such as having to count backwards by threes, has the effect of facilitating belief fixation regarding whatever one hears or reads (Gilbert 1993).

There are two things that distinguish direct perception quite sharply from the acquisition of information through language, but neither implies a difference in immediacy. In direct perception, the spatial and temporal relation of the perceiver to the object perceived is given, whereas it is not normally given through language. On the other hand, in watching television, the spatial relation of perceiver to perceived is not given either. Nor, unless the program is live, is the temporal relation. Yet one perceives that the newscaster frowns or smiles just as immediately as one would in his presence. The second feature that distinguishes perception is its near infallibility. For the most part, it takes a modern understanding of the mechanisms of perception and a substantial technology to manage materially to fool the human eye or ear. False appearances are easily arranged, however, using modern communications media, offering the most common (though generally overlooked) illustration of the persistence of perceptual illusion. Similarly, through language, persistent illusions are very easy to arrange, hence abundant. That is, sentences are often false, and even when you know they are false, they continue to present the same false appearances—they do not shift and appear to say something different. In sum, hearing sentences may be a lot like perceiving though the media, which in turn is a lot like directly perceiving the original.

Think of the matter this way. There are many ways to recognize, say, rain. There is a way that rain feels when it falls on you, and a way that it looks through the window. There is a way that it sounds falling on the rooftop, "retetetetet," and a way that it sounds falling on the ground, "shshshshsh." And falling on English speakers, here is another way it can sound: "Hey, guys, it's raining!" (Thanks to Crawford Elder for this example.) Nor should you object that it is not rain you hear in the last case but rather "a sentence." A sound? Is it then a sound that you hear rather than rain on the roof? Is it a television screen that you see rather than Dan Rather? A pattern of ambient light rather than the TV screen? Best of all, perhaps all you see is a visual impression. You can, if you like, hear or see any of these things. What you see when you look depends, first, on where you focus your eyes; second, it depends on where you focus your mind, your attention.

But there is no need to belabor this point here. In the present context, what really matters is that believing what one hears said is a way of picking up information about substances, and that it is by learning a language that a child becomes able to pick up information in this way. It sounds a bit queer to speak of learning a word for a substance as learning a way to identify that substance. But just as the relation of one part of the pattern on the television screen to another part can manifest the relation of one part of Dan Rather to another, the relation of a word to other words in a sentence can manifest the configuration of a substance in relation to other substances and properties in the world. The semantics of natural languages is productive; alterations performed upon sentences correspond systematically to alterations in what the sentences represent, just as in the case of pictures, although the mapping functions involved are of course far more abstract. So if learning what a substance looks like can be learning how to identify it, similarly, learning a word for the substance can be learning to identify it. In both cases, what one learns is to recognize or understand manifestations of the substance as manifestations of it; one learns how to translate information arriving in one more kind of sensory package into beliefs.

Learning a language is, in part, learning more ways to pick up information through the senses and put it away in the right boxes. A difference, of course, is that this way of picking up information is much more fallible than in the case of ordinary perception. But no human ability is infallible. Further, just as substances are sometimes look-alikes in the flesh (twin brothers), many substances are sound-alikes in words (John$_{(Doe)}$ and John$_{(Roe)}$). But substances are tracked through the medium of words, not merely by means of the same words manifesting the same substances. Like more direct manifestations of substances, words and sentences occur in context, allowing methods of tracking to be used that are analogous to more ordinary tracking in that they rely in large part on expected spatial, temporal, and causal relations (cf. trajectory) rather than persistence of properties. (How do I recognize that as John's elbow poking out over there behind the lamp? I saw John head that way with a book just a moment ago.) Some of these relations are natural, such as the natural relation of a speaker's experience and the context of his speech to his expressed knowledge. One will usually know which "John" a speaker is talking about in this way. Other such relations are conventional, as in the interpretation of certain anaphoric pronouns and certain indexicals.[7]

Recognizing a linguistic reference to a substance is just another way of reidentifying the substance itself. It is identifying it through one more medium of manifestation. Think of this medium as like an instrument that aids perception. Like a camera, a radio, a CAT scan, or a microscope, another person who talks to me picks up information-bearing patterns from his environment, focuses them, translates them into a new medium, and beams them at me. Or think of living in a language community as like being inundated in one more sea of ambient energy. Like the surrounding light, surrounding people transmit the structure of the environment to me in ways that, barring certain interferences, I can become tuned to interpret.

It is even possible, indeed it is common, to have a substance concept entirely through the medium of language, that is, in the absence of any ability to recognize the substance in the flesh. For most of us, that is how we have a concept of Aristotle, of molybdenum, and, say, of African dormice. There, I just handed you a concept of African dormice, in case you had none before. Now you can think of them at night if you want to, wondering what they are like on the assumption, of course, that you gathered from their name what sorts of questions you might reasonably ask about them (animal questions, not vegetable or mineral or social artifact questions). In many cases there is not much more to having a substance concept than having a word. To have a word is to have a handle on tracking a substance via manifestations of it produced in a particular language community. Simply grasping the phonemic structure of a language and the rudiments of how to parse it enables one to help oneself to an embryo concept of every substance named in that language. That, I suppose, is why it is possible for small children to learn a new word every hour. The basic phenomenon here is the same as that underlying Putnam's phrase, "The Division of Linguistic Labor" (Putnam 1975) and Burge's claim that the constitution of the very content of one's *thought* sometimes passes through the word usages of a surrounding language community (1979; 1982; 1986).

Acquiring adequate substance concepts involves learning to focus one's thought in such a way that all of the incoming information scattered over time about each substance is put into one slot, and associated with the right categories of properties (determinables). Earlier, I suggested that preschoolers who take tigers to be "kitties" may be confused, not about the meaning of the word "kitty," but about how to identify cats. From our present perspective, however, thinking tigers are "kitties," that is, putting tiger information away in the same slot as information gotten from hearing about "kitties," is being confused about tigers as well as about domestic cats (for a full discussion of equivocation in concepts, see Millikan 1993a, Ch. 14; 1993b; 1994). But Gelman and Coley (1991, p. 184) are surely right that "a word can serve to stake out a new category, which then must be explored in more depth" (see also Gopnik and Meltzoff 1993). Words are handles to hang onto, helping to stabilize concepts so as gradually to eliminate equivocation in thought, as long as those who speak to us have adequate concepts themselves.

But have we not overlooked an obvious distinction here between merely knowing a word and knowing what that word means? In the present view there is an interest-

---

7. For a full discussion of equivocation in concepts, see Millikan (1993, Chapter 14; 1993b; 1994; 1997).

ing question about what it is for a child to learn the meaning of a word that names a substance. Traditionally, this is supposed to involve coming to exercise the same concept in connection with the word as adults do. But since a concept is an ability, there is an ambiguity here in the notion "same concept," derived in turn from a natural ambiguity in the notion "same ability." Suppose, for example, that you tie your shoes by looping one lace into a bow, encircling it with the other, and pulling through, while I tie mine by looping each lace separately, then tying them together. The results that we get will be exactly the same, but do we exercise the same ability? Sometimes what counts as the same ability is what accomplishes the same outcome; other times it is what accomplishes the same outcome by the same means.

Similarly, both the organic chemist and the child identify sugar and collect knowledge about it. Does it follow that there is a concept that they both have, hence that they have "the same concept"? In one sense they do, for each has the ability, fallibly, to identify sugar. But in another sense they do not, for chemists have much more sophisticated and reliable means at their disposal for identifying sugar than do children. Similarly, we could ask, did Helen Keller have many of the same concepts as you and I, or did she have different ones, and again the answer would be equivocal. Suppose we say that children have the "same concept" as chemists, namely, the concept of sugar, but that their "conception" of sugar is very different from that of chemists, for children use very different methods to identify it. Similarly, Helen Keller had very many of the same concepts as you and I but quite different conceptions of their objects. This fits with the ordinary view that people having very different information or beliefs about a thing have "different conceptions" of it, for information one has about a substance is often used to help identify it.

What do we mean, then, when we speak of a child as coming to understand "the meaning of a word"? If the word denotes a substance, there is a sense in which its meaning is simply that it is referring to *that* substance. To know what the word means is just to have a concept of the substance that includes knowing how to reidentify it via the word. But of course the child may not be very good at identifying the substance. The child may make gross mistakes that an adult would not make. Is there then a richer sense in which a child can come to understand what adults mean by the word? Is there such a thing as *"the* adult conception," of a substance? Given the numerous and diverse methods by which it is possible to learn to identify almost any substance, it seems that there could not be.

On the other hand, for some (how many?) substances, it may be that there are core methods by which nearly every adult (the "nearly" is for Helen Keller) knows how to reidentify them. Or there may be certain conditions under which any adult would recognize the substance, or examples of the substance that any adult would recognize given a chance to examine them. Then there may be a sense in which children do not fully understand "the meaning" of the word for that substance until their competence at identifying the substance has been filled out to match adult standards. In this sense of "the meaning," knowing how to track a substance only by tracking its name would not be nearly enough for "knowing the meaning." But is it in this sense that you "know the meaning" of the word "molybdenum," or "brisket," or "African dormouse"? Indeed, *do* you know what these words mean? Best not to fall into a verbal dispute over what gets to count as "knowing the meaning."

References

Abbot, V., Black, J. B. and Smith, E. E. (1985) The representation of scripts in memory. *Journal of Memory and Language* 24:179–99.

Angelin, J. M. (1977) Classifiers. *Language* 53:285–311.

Atran, S. (1989) Basic conceptual domains. *Mind & Language* 4. nos. 1 and 2:7–16.

Barsalou, L. W. (1987) The instability of graded structure: Implications for the nature of concepts. In: *Concepts and conceptual development*, ed. U. Neisser. Cambridge University Press.

Bartlett, F. C. (1932) *Remembering*. Cambridge University Press.

Billman, D. (1992) Modeling category learning and use. In: *Percepts, concepts, and categories; The representation and processing of information*, ed. B. Burns. North-Holland.

Boyd, R. (1989) What realism implies and what it does not. *Dialectica* 43:5–29.

Boyd, R. (1991) Realism, anti-foundationalism and the enthusiasm for natural kinds. *Philosophical Studies* 61:127–48.

Burge, T. (1979) Individualism and the mental. In: *Studies in metaphysics: Midwest studies in philosophy IV*, ed. P. French, T. Uehling, and H. Wettstein. University of Minnesota.

Burge, T. (1982) Other bodies. In: *Thought and object*, ed. A. Woodfield. Clarendon.

Burge, T. (1986) Individualism and psychology. *Philosophical Review* 95:3–45.

Burns, B. ed. (1992) *Percepts, concepts, and categories; The representation and processing of information*. North-Holland.

Byrnes, J. P. and Gelman, S. A. (1991) Perspectives on thought and language: Traditional and contemporary views. In: *Perspectives on language and thought*, ed. S. A. Gelman and J. P. Byrnes. Cambridge University Press.

Carey, S. (1985) *Conceptual change in children*. The MIT Press.

Carey, S. and Gelman, R., eds. (1993) *The epigenesis of mind: Essays on biology and cognition*. Erlbaum.

Choi, S. and Gopnik, A. (1993) Nouns are not always learned before verbs: An early verb spurt in Korean. In: *The Proceedings of the Twenty-fifth Annual Child Language Forum*. Center for the Study of Language and Information.

Chomsky, N. (1995) Language and nature. *Mind* 104:1–61.

Clark, E. V. (1991) Acquisitional principles in lexical development. In: *Perspectives on language and thought*, ed. S. A. Gelman and J. P. Byrnes. Cambridge University Press.

Dodwell, P., Humphrey, K. and Muir, D. (1987) Shape and pattern perception. In: *Handbook of Infant Perception*, vol 2: *From perception to cognition*, ed. P. Salapatek and L. Cohen. Harcourt Brace Jovanovich.

Dromi, E. (1987) *Early lexical development*. Cambridge University Press.

Fodor, J. A. (1972) Some reflections on L. S. Vygotsky's *Thought and language*. *Cognition* 1:83–95.

Fumerton, R. (1989) Russelling causal theories. In: *Rereading Russell: Essays in Bertrand Russell's Metaphysics and epistemology, Minnesota Studies in the Philosophy of Science*, vol. 12., ed. C. W. Savage and C. A. Anderson. University of Minnesota Press.

Gallistel, C., Brown, A., Carey, S., Gelman, R. and Keil, F. (1993) Lessons from animal learning for the study of cognitive development. In: *The epigenesis of mind: Essays on biology and cognition*, ed. S. Carey and R. Gelman, Erlbaum.

Gelman, S. A. (1988a) Children's expectations concerning natural kind categories. *Human Development* 38:213–44.

Gelman, S. A. (1988b) The development of induction within natural kind and artifact categories. *Cognitive Psychology* 20:65–95.

Gelman, S. A. and Byrnes, J. P., eds. (1991) *Perspectives on language and thought*. Cambridge University Press.

Gelman, S. A. and Coley, J. D. (1991) Language and categorization: The acquisition of natural kind terms. In: *Perspectives on language and thought*, ed. S. A. Gelman and J. P. Byrnes. Cambridge University Press.

Gelman, S. A. and Markman, E. M. (1987) Young children's inductions from natural kinds: The role of categories and appearances. *Child Development* 58:1532–41.

Gentner, D. (1982) Why nouns are learned before verbs: Linguistic relativity versus natural partitioning. In: *Language, thought and culture; Language development*, vol. 2, ed. S. Kuczaj. Erlbaum.

Ghiselin, M. (1974) A radical solution to the species problem. *Systematic Zoology* 23:536–44.

Ghiselin, M. (1981) Categories, life and thinking. *Behavioral and Brain Sciences* 4:269–83.

Gilbert, D. (1993) The assent of man: Mental representation and the control of belief. In: *Handbook of mental control*, ed. D. M. Wegner and J. W. Pennebaker. Prentice-Hall.

Gopnik, A. and Meltzoff, A. (1993) Words and thoughts in infancy: The specificity hypothesis and the development of categorization and naming. In: *Advances in infancy research*, ed. C. Rovee-Collier and L. Lipsitt. Ablex.

Gopnik, A. and Meltzoff, A. (1996) *Words, thoughts and theories*. MIT Press.

Hacking, I. A. (1991) On Boyd. *Philosophical Studies* 61:149–54.

Hull, D. L. (1978) A matter of individuality. *Philosophy of Science* 45:335–360. Reprinted in *Conceptual issues in evolutionary biology*, E. Sober (1994). MIT Press.

Ingram, D. (1989) *First language acquisition; Method, description and explanation*. Cambridge University Press.

John, O. (1985) Actions, verbs and the role of context: Differences between categories of objects and those of actions and events. Unpublished manuscript, University of Oregon and Oregon Research Institute, Eugene.

Johnson, M. H., Dziuawiec, S., Ellis, H. D. and Morton, J. (1991) Newborns' preferential tracking of face-like stimuli and its subsequent decline. *Cognition* 40:1–21.

Johnson-Laird, P. N. (1983) *Mental models*. Harvard University Press.

Katz, J. (1972) *Semantic theory*. Harper & Row.

Katz, J. and Fodor, J. A. (1963) The structure of a semantic theory. *Language* 39:170–210.

Keil, F. C. (1979) *Semantic and conceptual development: An ontological perspective*. Harvard University Press.

Keil, F. C. (1983) Semantic inferences and the acquisition of word meaning. In: *Concept development and the development of word meaning*, ed. T. B. Seiler and W. Wannemacher. Springer-Verlag.

Keil, F. C. (1987) Conceptual development and category structure. In: *Concepts and conceptual development: Ecological and intellectual factors in categorization*, ed. U. Neisser. Cambridge University Press.

Keil, F. C. (1989) *Concept, kinds and cognitive development*. MIT Press.

Keil, F. C. (1991) Theories, concepts, and the acquisition of word meaning. In: *Perspectives on language and thought*, ed. S. A. Gelman & J. P. Byrnes. Cambridge University Press.

Komatsu, L. K. (1992) Recent views of conceptual structure. *Psychological Bulletin* 112.3:500–26.

Kornblith, H. (1993) *Inductive inference and its natural ground*. MIT Press.

Kripke, S. (1972) *Naming and necessity*. Harvard University Press.

Lakoff, G. (1987) *Women, fire, and dangerous things*. Chicago University Press.

MacFarlane, A. (1977) *The psychology of childbirth*. Harvard University Press.

Markman, E. (1989) *Categorization and naming in children*. MIT Press.

Markman, E. (1991) The whole-object, taxonomic and mutual exclusivity assumptions as initial constraints on word meaning. In: *Perspectives on language and thought*, ed. S. A. Gelman & J. P. Byrnes. Cambridge University Press.

Marler, P. (1993) The instinct to learn. In: *The epigenesis of mind: Essays on biology and cognition*, ed. S. Carey & R. Gelman. Erlbaum.

Medin, D. L. (1989) Concepts and conceptual structure. *American Psychologist* 44(12):1469–81.

Medin, D. L. and Ortony, A. (1989) Psychological essentialism. In: *Similarity and analogical reasoning*, ed. S. Vosniadou and A. Ortony. Cambridge University Press.

Medin, D. L. and Schaffer, M. M. (1978) Context theory of classification learning. *Psychological Review* 85:207–38.

Medin, D. L. and Smith, E. E. (1981) Strategies and classification learning. *Journal of Experimental Psychology: Human Learning and Memory* 7:241–53.

Medin, D. L. and Smith, E. E. (1984) Concepts and concept formation. *Annual Review of Psychology* 35:113–38.

Mervis, C. B. (1987) Child-basic categories and early lexical development. In: *Concepts and conceptual development*, ed. U. Neisser. Cambridge University Press.

Mervis, C. B. Crisafi, M. A. (1982) Order of acquisition of subordinate-, basic-, and superordinate-level categories. *Child Development* 53:258–66.

Millikan, R. (1984) *Language, thought and other biological categories*. MIT Press.

Millikan, R. (1991) Perceptual content and Fregean myth. *Mind* 100.4:439–59.

Millikan, R. (1993a) *White Queen psychology and other essays for Alice*. MIT Press.

Millikan, R. (1993b) On mentalese orthography. In: *Dennett and his critics*, ed. Bo Dahlbom. Blackwell.

Millikan, R. (1994) On unclear and indistinct ideas. In: *Philosophical Perspectives* vol. VIII, ed. James Tomberlin. Ridgeview Publishing.

Millikan, R. (1997) Images of Idenfity. *Mind* 106:499–517.

Millikan, R. (forthcoming) Historical Kinds and the Special Sciences. *Philosophical Studies*.

Minsky, M. (1975) A framework for representing knowledge. In: *The psychology of computer vision*, ed. P. H. Winston. McGraw-Hill.

Murphy, G. L. and Medin, D. L. (1985) The role of theories in conceptual coherence. *Psychological Review* 92:289–316.

Neisser, U. (1975) *Cognition and reality*. W. H. Freeman.

Neisser, U., ed. (1987) *Concepts and conceptual development*. Cambridge University Press.

Nelson, C. and Horowitz, F. (1987) Visual motion perception in infancy: A review and synthesis. In: *Handbook of Infant Perception*, ed. P. Salapatek and L. B. Cohen.

Nelson, K. (1974) Variations in children's concepts by age and category. *Child Development* 45:577–84.

Nelson, K. (1991) The matter of time: Interdependencies between language and thought in development. In: *Perspectives on language and thought*, ed. S. A. Gelman and J. P. Byrnes. Cambridge University Press.

Piaget, J. (1926) *The language and thought of the child*. Harcourt Brace.

Putnam, H. (1975) The meaning of "meaning." In: *Language, mind and knowledge*, Minnesota Studies in the Philosophy of Science, vol. 7, ed. Keith Gunderson. University of Minnesota Press.

Quine, W. V. (1960) *Word and object*. MIT Press.

Rifkin, A. (1985) Evidence for a basic-level in event taxonomies. *Memory and Cognition* 13:538–56.

Rosch, E. (1973) Natural categories. *Cognitive Psychology* 4:328–50.

Rosch, E. (1975) Universals and cultural specifics in human categorization. In: *Cross cultural perspectives on learning*, ed. R. Brislin, S. Bochner and W. Honner. Halsted.

Rosch, E. (1978) Principles of categorization. In: *Cognition and categorization*, ed. E. Rosch and B. B. Lloyd. Erlbaum.

Rosch, E. and Mervis, C. B. (1975) Family resemblances: Studies in the internal structure of categories. *Cognitive Psychology* 7:573–605.

Rosch, E., Mervis, C. B. Gray, W. D., Johnson, D. M. and Boyes-Braem, P. (1976) Basic objects in natural categories. *Cognitive Psychology* 8:382–439.

Rumelhardt, D. E. (1980) Schemata: The building blocks of cognition. In: *Theoretical issues in reading comprehension*, ed. R. J. Spiro, B. C. Bruce and W. F. Brewer. Erlbaum.

Schank, R. C. and Abelson, R. P. (1977) *Scripts, plans, goals and understanding*. Erlbaum.

Shepard, R. (1976) Perceptual illusion of rotation of three-dimensional objects. *Science* 191:952–54.

Shepard, R. (1983) Path-guided apparent motion. *Science* 220:632–34.

Smith, C., Carey, S. and Wiser, M. (1985) On differentiation; A case study of the development of the concepts of size, weight, and density. *Cognition* 21:177–237.

Smith, E. E. and Medin, D. L. (1981) *Categories and concepts*. Harvard University Press.

Spelke, E. (1989) The origins of physical knowledge. In: *Thought without language*, ed. L. Weiskrantz. Oxford University Press.

Spelke, E. (1993) Physical knowledge in infancy: Reflections of Piaget's theory. In: *The epigenesis of mind: Essays on biology and cognition*, ed. S. Carey and R. Gelman. Erlbaum.

Tversky, B. and Hemenway, K. (1984) Objects, parts and categories. *Journal of Experimental Psychology: General* 113:169–93.

Ward, T. B. and Becker, A. H. (1992) Intentional and incidental learning. In: *Percepts, concepts, and categories; The representation and processing of information*, ed. B. Burns. North-Holland.

Waxman, S. R. (1991) Semantic and conceptual organization in preschoolers. In: *Perspectives on language and thought*, ed. S. A. Gelman and J. P. Byrnes. Cambridge University Press.

Wettstein, H. (1988) Cognitive significance without cognitive content. *Mind* 97:1–28.

Winograd, T. (1975) Frame representations and the declarative-procedural controversy. In: *Representation and understanding: Studies in cognitive science*, ed. D. G. Bobrow and A. Collins. Academic Press.

Xu, F. and Carey, S. (1996) Infant metaphysics: The case of numerical identity. *Cognitive Psychology* 30:111–53.

Chapter 24

How to Acquire a Concept

Eric Margolis

1. Introduction

In cognitive science, theories of concepts tend to be constrained by an assumption that is so pervasive it is hardly ever challenged. This is the assumption that what makes a concept the very concept that it is is its relation to certain other concepts.[1] The difference between most theories of concepts consists in the character of the relation they impose. For example, while the classical theory of concepts says a concept C must decompose into a set of concepts that express necessary and sufficient conditions for the application of C, the prototype theory says that C must decompose into a set of concepts that express statistical conditions that govern the application of C. Similarly, the theory-theory—which is gaining attention in psychological circles—says that a concept C must participate in an inferential system of a certain sort and that C is inherently connected to the other concepts that constitute the system.[2] While defenders of each of these theories have emphasized their differences, from the present vantage point, the theories are all strikingly alike. In contrast, one can envision quite a different theory, according to which what makes a concept the very concept that it is is not how it is related to certain other concepts but how it is related to the world. Following current philosophical practice, I'll call theories in this spirit atomistic theories of concepts.[3]

Surely one of the more interesting questions in the history of cognitive science is why atomistic theories have received so little attention. This issue is especially pertinent given the difficulties that most theories of concepts are known to have.[4] My own suspicion is that the underlying motivation has always had something to do

---

1. The term 'concept' is used in a number of ways in philosophy and cognitive science. Throughout this paper, I'll follow standard psychological usage, according to which concepts are understood as mental representations that are largely individuated by their contents. In contrast, philosophers often insist that concepts are senses—Fregean abstract objects. For some discussion on the relation between these two views of concepts, see Laurence and Margolis (1999).
2. For a review of these and related theories, including the exemplar theory, see Smith and Medin (1981), Komatsu (1992), Medin (1989), and Laurence and Margolis (1999).
3. Note that, since definitional or statistical analyses can't go on forever, both the classical theory and the prototype theory are committed to the existence of a stock of concepts that aren't themselves subject to analysis. Thus both theories are incomplete, pending an account of what makes these unanalyzed concepts the very concepts that they are. Perhaps, at this point, one may want to say that connections to the world supplement the theories—that atomism is true at the most fundamental level of the conceptual system. Yet defenders of these theories rarely address this issue explicitly, leaving it an open question how exactly the unanalyzed concepts are to be treated.
4. On the classical theory, see Fodor et al. (1980), Fodor et al. (1975); on the prototype theory, see Osherson and Smith (1981), Armstrong et al. (1983), Rey (1983), Margolis (1994); on the theory-theory, see Margolis (1995).

with the issue of which concepts, if any, are innate. The problem is that, on the face of it, atomistic theories of concepts encourage extreme nativistic positions. This is because models of concept learning generally presuppose that learning a concept is a process in which previously available concepts are assembled in a way that reflects the conditions on the learned concept's identity. For instance, if the classical theory were right, then learning a concept might involve assembling the concepts that express the conditions that are necessary and sufficient for its application. In the same fashion, if the theory-theory were right, then learning a concept might involve learning the theory in which the concept is an essential participant. The trouble with atomistic theories of concepts is that, for any given concept C, there isn't a prescribed set of related concepts whose assembly would constitute having learned C. But if C can't be learned, then presumably it is innate.[5]

Despite the appeal of this line of reasoning, it's a shame that atomistic theories have received so little attention, first, because it's an empirical question which concepts are innate—just because a theory has a strong nativistic commitment doesn't mean we can rule it out from the start—and, second, because other theories of concepts are known to be highly problematic. Who could deny that we are in need of some new theoretical options?

In this paper, I propose to defend atomistic theories of concepts against the claim that they are inconsistent with plausible accounts of concept acquisition. The heart of my defense is a novel model of acquisition that I develop around an atomistic theory, focusing on natural kind concepts. The model I sketch is sensitive to a considerable amount of data that has come to constrain other theories of concepts yet, it should be said, the data look quite different from the perspective introduced by conceptual atomism. Since any learning model must take into account the nature of what is eventually acquired, I begin, in section 2, by presenting an atomistic theory of concepts—Jerry Fodor's asymmetric-dependence theory. In section 3, I turn to the specific concerns that natural kind concepts raise for the asymmetric-dependence theory. Then, in section 4, I present the model of acquisition. In the first instance, the model is developed around the central case where a concept is acquired by exposure to its instances. In section 5, I add a modification so that it covers the acquisition of concepts that depend upon deference to members of a linguistic community.

2. Concepts, Information-Based Semantics, and Sustaining Mechanisms

Before we can turn to the question of how concepts are acquired within an atomistic framework, we need to address the question of how an atomistic theory of concepts works. It's one thing to say that a concept's identity doesn't depend upon its relations to any other particular concepts; it's quite another to offer a positive account of what the alternatives are. In this section, I explain Jerry Fodor's asymmetric-dependence theory, since it is the most developed atomistic alternative (Fodor 1990). Because Fodor's theory is a variant on the information-bases semantics approach to content, we should begin with information-based semantics (IBS, for short).

IBS is a schematic semantic theory; it answers the question, what makes a given mental representation have the interpretation or content that it does? For example,

---

5. An inference that is notoriously endorsed in Fodor (1981).

what makes it the case that the mental representation BREAD expresses the property *bread* and not, say, the property *refrigerator*?[6] What unites IBS theories is that their answer to this question depends, in a crucial way, on the information a concept carries, where information is understood in terms of lawful (or reliable) correlations. The number of rings in a cross-section of a tree correlates with the age of the tree, so the rings are said to carry the information about how old the tree is. The expansion of mercury correlates with the local temperature, so the mercury is said to carry the information about the local temperature. Following these examples, we can say in general that a token or an event carries information about its reliable cause. Put in mental terms what this means is that the concept BREAD expresses the property *bread* because bread is the reliable cause of BREAD-tokenings. In other words, there is a law connecting the property of being bread with the property of being a BREAD-tokening, and it is in virtue of this law that the concept BREAD expresses the property *bread*.

In the philosophical literature, one difficulty with this sort of account has dominated the discussion—the problem of error. A fundamental constraint on any theory of content is that it must accommodate incorrect applications of a concept. The worry has been that information-based semantics may not be able to meet this constraint. The reason is straightforward. Information-based semantics says that effects carry information about their reliable causes. Yet surely some incorrect applications of a concept are reliable. If at night and at a certain angle and distance a crumpled bag looks like a cat, then you will be bound (at first) to token the concept CAT and not BAG. What's more, because under these conditions the bag looks like a cat, the mistake isn't gratuitous. It is a perfectly natural mistake and one that you ought to make not just once, but whenever similar situations arise. After all, bags in these situations look like cats. Here, then, is the problem. The concept CAT has at least two reliable causes. CAT-tokenings are elicited by cats but they are also elicited by crumpled bags. So they carry information about cats and about bags. So why does the concept CAT express the property *cat* and not the disjunctive property *cat-or-bag*? In short, if erroneous applications of concepts can be as reliable as correct applications, an unadulterated information-based semantics has no room for error. There are currently a number of proposals about how to accommodate error. In my view, Fodor's stands out because of the way it locates error within a more fundamental difficulty, which he calls the 'robustness' of meaning.

The problem with erroneous applications of a concept stems from their potential reliability. Yet there are other cases where a concept will be reliably elicited by something other than instances of the property it expresses. Thought is another obvious example. If thinking about fur reliably causes you to think about cats, then (for you) CAT carries information about fur-thoughts. But, of course, CAT doesn't express the property *cat-or-fur-thought*. CAT means *cat*. It just happens that its tokenings are indicative of whether you've been thinking about fur. Information, in other words, is intrinsically tied to etiology; in contrast, the robustness of meaning consists in the distinctness of a symbol's meaning from its cause. All tokens of a symbol mean the same thing however they are caused. Tokens of CAT express the property *cat*

---

6. To distinguish concepts from properties, I'll adopt a notation where the first are indicated by capitals and the second by italics. Mentioned words are indicated by single quotes.

whether they are caused by cats, by cat-looking things (in cases of mistaken identification), or by other thoughts. Hence if conceptual content is to be constructed out of information, content has to be information plus something else.

Fodor's theory is of special interest since it adds to information in a way that treats error as a special case of the robustness of meaning and not as a unique problem that requires its own, special solution. The theory has two parts:

(i) A concept stands in lawful relation to the property it expresses.

(ii) Other lawful relations involving the concept are asymmetrically dependent upon the lawful relation between it and the property it expresses.

(i) recapitulates the initial intuition that grounds information-based semantics; concepts express properties they carry information about. However, since they don't always express the properties they carry information about, (ii) distinguishes the cases where they do from the cases where they don't. Asymmetric dependence is a relation among laws. Suppose that a concept stands in lawful relations to two properties and hence caries information about both. Let us call these relations L_1 and L_2. Essentially, (ii) says that L_2 wouldn't hold but that L_1 holds and not vice versa. L_2 is asymmetrically dependent upon L_1.

The mechanics of the proposal are easiest to see in light of an example. Take the concept CAT again. According to the theory, CAT stands in a lawful relation with the property *cat*, whereby the presence of cats tends to elicit tokenings of the concept CAT. Yet tokenings of the concept CAT may be elicited in other, regular ways, as in the case of the crumpled bag spotted on a dark night. Then, we may suppose, there also exists a lawful relation between the concept CAT and the property *crumpled bag*. However, this lawful relation seems only to hold because the other one holds. If cats didn't cause CAT-tokenings, crumpled bags wouldn't either, but not the other way around. That's why CAT expresses the property *cat*, not the property *crumpled bag*.[7]

Again, this theory differs from most others in philosophy and cognitive science in that mind-world relations do the bulk of the work. On other accounts, conceptual content is largely a matter of how concepts figure in a conceptual system. As a result, other accounts tend to require that people have particular beliefs, or inferential dispositions, that are essential to a concept. In contrast, Fodor's theory says that the beliefs one has are irrelevant to conceptual content as such. To have the concept CAT, one needn't believe anything in particular about cats, so long as the concept stands in the right mind-world relation to the property *cat*. The difference between these two ways of looking at things is made vivid by picturing concepts in terms of a filing system. Think of a concept as a file whose label specifies which concept it is and whose entries count as knowledge structures that, in one way or another, are associated with the concept. The question at stake is what determines how a file is labeled. Why does one file receive the label 'cat' and another receive the label 'lamppost'? The usual answer is that the information in the file is essential in determining the file's label. It is because, for example, a file includes specific information about animals and other things that it gets the label 'cat'. The asymmetric-dependence theory, on the other hand, dissociates a file's contents from its label, so the entries of

7. The asymmetric-dependence theory isn't without its problems. I'll discuss several of these in the next section, when we turn to natural kind concepts and the various ways that the theory handles them. For other critical discussions, see Adams and Aizawa (1994) and the papers in Loewer and Rey (1991).

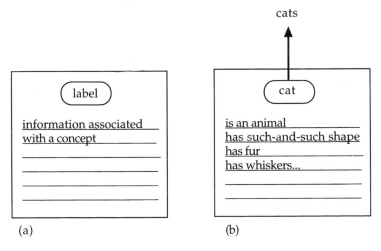

Figure 24.1
Concepts may be pictured along the lines of a filing system. (a) represents the general schema, Each file indicates a concept; the entries below a label indicate knowledge structures that are associated with the concept. The question 'What makes a concept express the property it does?' may be recast as the question 'What makes a file have the label it has?' Is it that the file has certain information encoded as an entry or is it that the file is suitably related to things outside of the filing system? In (b), e.g., the file could receive the label 'cat' because it has information specifically about animals, fur, and so on encoded as entries, or, instead, because it is suitably related to cats.

a file are, in a sense, inessential. For Fodor, it is because a file is related to things outside of the filing system (i.e., to properties in the world) that it is labeled as it is (see figure 24.1).

But it is one thing to think that a file's contents are inessential to how it is labeled and another to think that they are entirely irrelevant. No one, not even Fodor, thinks they are irrelevant. The reason he doesn't suppose this—indeed, the reason he can't—is that the mind-world relation that he thinks does determine conceptual content must be sustained by a mechanism, and generally the only available mechanism is the inferential apparatus that is associated with a concept. The reason the asymmetric-dependence relation requires a sustaining mechanism is that it isn't at all plausible that the laws in question are basic. Special science laws typically aren't—this is almost a point of definition—and the laws connecting concepts to the properties they express would appear to be on a par with other special science laws, including the laws of psychology.

Now in some cases the sustaining mechanism is going to be non-cognitive. This may be true in lower-level perceptual processing, where psychophysical laws are generally expected to have a biological source. But what about the concept TABLE or the concept WALKING or, worse, the concept PROTON? It is hard to see how biology alone could account for the lawful dependence of PROTON-tokenings on protons, that there is a psychophysical law, as it were, connecting PROTON with protons. Fodor recognizes this difficulty and suggests putting a twist on a characteristic idea of positivist philosophy of science. The idea, in brief, is to allow that much of what one believes, including the scientific theories one accepts, may be implicated in the mechanism that links, for example, one's PROTON-thoughts with protons.

The beliefs a person has endow her with specific inferential dispositions. If someone believes current physical theories and has a sufficient understanding of them, she will have the disposition to infer that a proton is present in certain carefully designed experimental situations where the evidence, in light of what she knows, points to the presence of a proton.

Here's the twist: For Fodor, unlike the positivists, our theoretical beliefs and other knowledge structures aren't constitutive of the concepts whose applications they sustain. So, in particular, one's beliefs about protons aren't constitutive of the concept PROTON. What *is* essential to the concept is that tokens of PROTON are connected to protons in the way the theory of asymmetric-dependence articulates. As long as tokens of PROTON are suitably connected to protons, it doesn't matter how the connection is sustained (see, e.g., Fodor 1990, note 6, p. 83). You can have your beliefs and I can have mine, and the differences in our beliefs won't in themselves entail that we are subject to conceptual differences. Whether our concepts are different depends upon their connections to the world.

In what follows, I'm going to rely quite heavily on Fodor's version of IBS. This isn't because I think Fodor's theory is entirely correct. Rather, what I find useful about the asymmetric-dependence theory is that it is the most developed and, in my view, the most plausible version of an atomistic theory of concepts. Remember: The question at hand is whether a conceptual atomist can explain the learning of a concept. In this context, Fodor's theory serves as heuristic in that it provides a set of concrete assumptions under which this question can be fruitfully posed.

3. Natural Kind Concepts

To keep the discussion focused, I want to concentrate on just one group of concepts. Partly because they have been prominent in the psychological literature, but also for reasons that will become clear later on, I want to focus on natural kind concepts. Our question, then, isn't how concepts in general are acquired but how natural kind concepts are acquired. And before we can take up the issue of acquisition in earnest, we need to get clear about the way that IBS handles natural kind concepts in an adult's mental life.

It should be clear from the last section that IBS doesn't require of a person who has a natural kind concept that she believes of the things the concept applies to that they are members of a natural kind. (This is for the simple reason that IBS doesn't require of a person that she have any particular beliefs about the things a concept applies to.) Rather, what makes a concept a natural kind concept is just that it tracks a natural kind in the world, that is, that it is related to a natural kind in the way that IBS requires. Still, this leaves a lot to be said about how it is that our concepts stand in this relation to natural kinds. We need an account of the typical sustaining mechanisms for concepts such as CAT and GOLD and WATER and PROTON. These will vary along several dimensions, including the type, amount, and accuracy of the knowledge associated with a concept.

One case that has already come up is where a person actually knows a scientific theory of a kind. Suppose, for example, that a person has had considerable training in physics and chemistry and has assembled a complex set of beliefs about atomic structure, essentially internalizing both the principles of contemporary physical science and the known procedures for manipulating physical particles. Then, because of her hard-earned intellectual resources, she would be in a position to infer the presence of a proton when the available evidence together with what she knows about protons compel the conclusion that a proton is present. In other words, her knowledge puts her in a state of mind where protons cause her to token the concept PROTON, the disposition that is at the heart of the IBS treatment of concepts. Let's call sustaining mechanisms of this kind *theory-based sustaining mechanisms*.

Theory-based sustaining mechanisms clearly have their place in an atomistic framework. Yet it would be unreasonable to maintain that people always have some theory or other that is rich enough to sustain the right mind-word relation between, as it might be, PROTON and protons. Another type of sustaining mechanism allows for people to have rather scarce knowledge about a kind, so long as they are prepared to exploit other people's more detailed knowledge. I call sustaining mechanisms of this second type *deference-based sustaining mechanisms*. These find their inspiration in Hilary Putnam's proposal that reference depends upon a 'division of linguistic labor' (Putnam 1975).

Putnam's aim is to rationalize the glaring fact that, for many terms, lots of people are apparently incapable of telling whether they apply in particular cases. He mentions, for example, that he himself is incapable of telling the difference between elms and beeches and hence that he is incapable of telling whether 'elm' or 'beech' applies to a given tree. What are we to make of this and similar examples? Putnam's reaction is to reject, but only partially reject, a verificationist semantics for these terms. He writes (Putnam 1975, pp. 227–8; emphasis in original):

> [E]veryone to whom gold is important for any reason has to *acquire* the word 'gold'; but he dose not have to *acquire the method of recognizing* if something is or is not gold. He can rely on a special subclass of speakers. The features that are generally thought to be present in connection with a general name—necessary and sufficient conditions for membership in the extension, ways of recognizing if something is in the extension ('criteria'), etc.—are all present in the linguistic community *considered as a collective body*; but that collective body divides the 'labor' of knowing and employing these various parts of the 'meaning' of 'gold'.

In other words, a person may be semantically competent with a range of terms, even if she doesn't know how to tell whether things fall in their extensions, so long as she is suitably related to people who do. You don't have to be able to tell whether this tree is an elm so long as you can depend upon someone who can—e.g., a botanist. Such people are said to be the experts, and the botanically ignorant are said to use 'elm' deferentially with respect to the experts, that is, to use 'elm' with an intention to be speaking of the things that the experts would identify as elms. In the philosophical literature, terms that are typically used with this sort of intention are said to be deferential terms. These can include natural kind terms, theoretical terms, and perhaps others, such as some social kind terms and artifact terms. By extension, the concepts that these terms encode are said to be deferential concepts.[8]

---

8. Whether deference pertains to just certain classes of terms/concepts or whether it is a more pervasive phenomenon is an interesting question, but one that is irrelevant to the present concern. All that matters is that natural kind terms/concepts are (often) deferential, though I suspect that nearly any term/concept is subject to principles of deference (see Burge 1979).

The notion of a deferential concept is somewhat peculiar. Though it may be true that we have policies about what we take the meaning of a word to be, it is hardly clear that the same thing can be said of the representations in which thinking takes place. Still, there seems to be something right about the appeal to experts in the explanation of concept possession. If we give up Putnam's residual verificationism, a plausible answer is that experts play much the same role as any other sort of evidence. Jerry Fodor has made the comparison especially vivid (Fodor 1994, pp. 34–5; emphasis in original):

> 'I can't tell elms from beeches, so I defer to the experts.' Compare: 'I can't tell acids from bases, so I defer to the litmus paper'; or 'I can't tell Tuesdays from Wednesdays, so I defer to the calendar.' These three ways of putting the case are, I think, equally loopy, and for much the same reason. As a matter of fact, I *can* tell acids from bases; *I use the litmus test to do so.* And I can tell elms from beeches too. The way I do it is, I consult a botanist.
>
> What I do with the litmus, and with the botanist, is this: I construct environments in which their respective states are reliable indicators of the acidity of the sample and the elmicity of the tree; in the one case, I dip the litmus into the fluid, in the other case, I point the expert at the tree. I construct these environments with malice aforethought; with the intention that what color the litmus turns (mutatis mutandis, what the botanist says about the tree) will cause me to have true beliefs about whether the sample is an acid (mutatis mutandis, whether the tree is an elm). In effect, I contrive to replace the problem of determining whether the sample is an acid with the (de facto easier) problem of determining whether the litmus turns red. Likewise, mutatis mutandis, I contrive to replace the problem of determining whether the tree is an elm with the (de facto easier) problem of determining whether the expert calls it one.

In other words, it is simply not true that ordinary people are incapable of telling whether an object is in the extension of a deferential concept. It's just that, in order to tell, they usually need to exploit a special kind of evidence, namely, expert testimony. While Putnam knows next to nothing about elms and beeches, still he has it within his cognitive resources to discriminate between the two.

The significance of these considerations is that we can imagine a class of sustaining mechanisms, for some natural kind concepts, that don't require complicated sets of beliefs about the kinds. With deference-based sustaining mechanisms, the agent need only know some superficial information about a kind (e.g., that its members are called 'elms' in English) and have a disposition to rely upon people who can reliably tell members of the kind from non-members.

So the range of knowledge that goes into a sustaining mechanism for natural kind concepts is quite broad. On the one hand, it could incorporate an internalized body of scientific knowledge and, on the other, it could include as little information as a single yet salient contingent fact about the kind taken together with enough knowledge to locate an expert.

Between these two cases there is another type of sustaining mechanism that is of considerable interest. I call sustaining mechanisms of this third type *syndrome-based sustaining mechanisms*. What I have in mind is a situation where someone, while ignorant of the nature of a kind, nonetheless knows enough contingent information about the kind to reliably discriminate members from non-members without relying upon anyone else's assistance. Take the concept CAT. The case we are imagining isn't one where the person just knows that cats are called 'cat', and it isn't one where the person has a theory of cats, such as a theory about their genetic structure or about the historical facts tying present-day cats to their ancestors. Instead, the proposal is that the person knows about what, for lack of a better term, one might call the cat-syndrome—a collection of salient properties that are readily open to inspection and are reliable indicators that something is a cat. These might include, for instance, the shape of a cat, the typical motions that a cat exercises when it walks or runs, the typical sounds that come out of a cat's mouth, and so on.

Now one of the more significant and problematic features of natural kinds is that their outward, commonly noticed properties aren't constitutive of them. Rather, category membership for natural kinds is determined to a large extent by the hidden, often structural, properties that are responsible for their readily noticed properties. Thus natural kinds are subject to a robust appearance/reality distinction. To take a simple example, a given toy may look tremendously like a skunk, but, even so, it is not a skunk; it's an artifact, a toy. Similarly, a (real) skunk may be altered to look like a cat, but, even so, it remains a skunk and doesn't thereby become a cat. Let's call cases like these *fakes*. A fake is a case where a syndrome that is a reliable indicator of a particular natural kind is instantiated in an item that isn't a member of the kind.

For our purposes, the question is, Given this peculiarity of natural kinds, what sorts of sustaining mechanisms will support a natural kind concept's standing in the mind-world relation that IBS says it does? If we return to the first two types of sustaining mechanisms, fakes don't seem to be a problem. A scientist who has a theory of a kind might be fooled by the appearance of an exemplar, but she would be disposed to correct herself were she to discover that the exemplar lacked the appropriate causal structure of the kind she had mistaken it for. Her theory tells her, for example, that a skunk that is made up to look like a cat isn't really a cat. Similarly, someone who relies upon experts may depend upon people who have such theories. But what about the case where someone has at her disposal only a syndrome of properties that are indicative of a kind?

The way to handle fakes in cases like these is to grant that, along with the syndrome for a kind, people know something else, some general knowledge that affects their cognitive dispositions, leaving them less governed by the appearance of things. The natural elaboration of this idea is a view that Douglas Medin and Andrew Ortony have aptly called 'psychological essentialism' (Medin and Ortony 1989). According to this view people believe, in general, that category membership for certain kinds of things is determined by the hidden, often structural properties, that cause their outward appearances.[9] To be an essentialist is to be disposed to look past the appearance of an exemplar in categorization judgments. The general picture, then, is one where a person's relation to a kind is mediated by two things.

(1) the person's knowledge of the syndrome for the kind
(2) the person's belief that membership within the kind is determined by possession of an essential property (or set of properties) and that this property is a reliable cause of the syndrome.

---

9. The status of psychological essentialism is controversial in psychological circles (Malt 1994, Braisby et al. 1996), though for reasons that I don't find particularly convincing. For a useful critical discussion of some of the arguments against psychological essentialism, see Abbott (1997).

Together, this information gives the agent the dispositions that asymmetric-dependence requires. Suppose, for example, that the agent were presented with a paradigmatic instance of a cat, where its syndrome is fully apparent. Then the agent would token the concept CAT because her knowledge of the syndrome leads her to infer that she is being presented with a cat. So far, then, we have a mechanism—an inferential mechanism—that mediates the relation between cats and CATs. At the same time, however, the same agent has a disposition to token CAT when presented with a fake cat, e.g., when presented with a skunk that, for one reason or another, looks like a cat. But there is this difference. Were she to find out more information about the latter item—that it lacked the essential property of which the cat-syndrome is a reliable effect—she would cease to apply the concept CAT to it.

Another difficulty that is related to the issue of fakes is owing to a set of examples that have become the focus of attention in philosophical circles—twin cases. Twin cases are instances where two distinct kinds are practically indistinguishable because they fortuitously (yet reliably) exhibit the same apparent characteristics (Putnam 1975). Here on Earth, H_2O reliably gives rise to the water syndrome, but XYZ, which is located on Twin-Earth, reliably gives rise to the water syndrome too. So a sample of XYZ would cause a normal Earthling to token the her concept WATER just as if it were a sample of H_2O. This wouldn't be a problem if it were simply accepted that the concept WATER has both H_2O and XYZ in its extension; then we could say that water has a disjunctive essential property. But the intuition that is widely accepted in philosophy is that XYZ falls outside of the extension of WATER.

I should say that I'm not sure about what to do with twin cases. There are currently a number of proposals in the literature. One is to add an extra clause to the asymmetric-dependence theory, so that reference to the actual world supplements the counterfactuals—since the actual world contains only H_2O, this may suffice to exclude XYZ (Fodor 1990). Another is to emphasize the rarity of twin cases (Fodor 1994). Still another is to argue that twin cases reveal inherent limitations in accounts like the asymmetric-dependence theory, and consequently that they should be abandoned (Adams and Aizawa 1994). I'm not happy with any of these, but to discuss them all would require a more detailed assessment of asymmetric-dependence—and Twin Earth—than would be warranted here. Instead, what I propose to do is put this difficult issue to the side, except to emphasize one aspect of the way asymmetric-dependence theory handles twin cases. This is the special case where an agent comes to know that, in fact, there are two essential properties that reliably cause a syndrome.

Take, for instance, the case where a scientist learns about XYZ and comes to distinguish it from H_2O. In this case, although both H_2O and XYZ would cause the scientist to token WATER, the latter is subject to the normal treatment of error. In other words, the XYZ/WATER connection is asymmetrically-dependent upon the H_2O/WATER connection. The asymmetry is evidenced by the fact that the scientist, were she to learn that a sample is XYZ, would cease to apply WATER to it, but not the other way around.[10]

10. On the other hand, if the scientist doesn't have a disposition to treat H_2O and XYZ differently even once she is able to discriminate the two, this is reason to think that, for her, WATER actually applies to H_2O and XYZ. In this case, it's the lack of asymmetry that confirms a disjunctive content. Cf. the standard intuition about jade—an actual case where a single syndrome is caused by two distinct properties (jadeite and nephrite), yet people tend to think that JADE applies to both.

4. Acquiring a Natural Kind Concept

Within the IBS framework, acquiring a concept involves establishing a sustaining mechanism that connects the concept with the property it expresses. So, to a large extent, the question of how concepts are acquired amounts to the question of how their sustaining mechanisms are acquired. Now that we've seen what sorts of sustaining mechanisms are involved in the possession of natural kind concepts, we are in a position to turn to the issue of how natural kind concepts, in particular, are acquired. In this section, I focus on the central case where, intuitively, it makes sense to say that a concept is learned, that is, where concept acquisition proceeds in the presence of members of the category that the concept picks out. One acquires the concept SQUIRREL and not BEE, for example, in the presence of squirrels. This principle isn't universal. Concept acquisition can be facilitated by representations or depictions of the category in the form of pictures, stories, or book-learning. What's more, there are any number of cases where acquired concepts refer to objects that, for one reason or another, the subject couldn't interact with. Nonetheless, an account of concept acquisition should be responsive to the fact that the experience leading to the acquisition of a concept is often related to the concept in ways that aren't entirely arbitrary. This is one place where standard, non-atomistic treatments of concept acquisition do well.[11] But atomistic theories of concepts can also explain the non-arbitrary relation between experience and acquisition, at least when the acquired concept depends upon a syndrome-based sustaining mechanism.

Recall the chief features of a syndrome-based sustaining mechanism. First, the person has to know a collection of salient, relatively accessible properties that are highly indicative of the kind. Second, the person has to have an essentialist disposition; she has to believe that what makes something a member of the category isn't that it exhibits the syndrome but that it possesses the essential property, or set of properties, that is constitutive of the kind and that is a reliable cause of the syndrome. With a little elaboration, the details of this account can be turned into an acquisitional model:

(1) Young children believe that certain categories are natural kinds and that these categories are subject to a principle of essentialism.

(2) This principle says that a kind's most accessible properties aren't what determine category membership; rather, it's the possession of an essential property (or set of properties) that reliably causes the syndrome.

(3) Young children are also predisposed to respond to the types of properties that enter into a kind-syndrome and consequently are highly indicative of a kind.

(4) There are, in fact, syndromes for some natural kinds.

Assuming all this, we can reconstruct one of the paradigmatic scenarios of concept acquisition, where it's experience of bees, say, that leads to the acquisition of the

---

11. Consider, for instance, the learning model that goes with the prototype theory of concepts. According to the prototype theory, the concept SQUIRREL decomposes into simpler concepts which together express properties that squirrels tend to instantiate. To learn the concept, then, one need only be able to detect the properties and to perform a statistical analysis that keeps track of how properties, in general, tend to cluster. Since the properties cluster in squirrels, it's exposure to squirrels that precedes acquisition of the concept SQUIRREL.

concept BEE. In the abstract, the way it works is this: The child sees some bees and notices that they have certain properties that suggest that the essentialist principle applies. So the child focuses on the salient accessible properties of the bees and, as a consequence, happens to assemble beliefs about bees that articulate the bee-syndrome. Finally, because of her essentialist disposition, she takes it that something is a member of the kind of which these items are instances so long as it has the same causal structure—the same essential property—that is a reliable cause of these salient and accessible properties. As a result, the child acquires a state of mind—a sustaining mechanism—that links her to bees in the way that the asymmetric-dependence theory requires for her to have the concept BEE. Consider the implications of this mechanism for bees that exhibit the bee-syndrome and for fake bees. Bees that exhibit the syndrome will elicit BEE tokenings simply because they have the right appearance. At the same time, however, fake bees will elicit BEE tokenings too. But, as with the child's adult counterpart, there will be this difference. Were she to find out more information about the fake—that it lacked the essential property that reliably causes the bee-syndrome—she would cease to apply the concept BEE to it.

Of course, from a psychological perspective, this is all very abstract. The model's prospects depend upon, among other things, the plausibility of principles (1)–(4). My own feeling is that they vary in plausibility. Perhaps the most secure is (2). Despite the empiricist tradition in developmental psychology, young children show many signs of an essentialist disposition (for a review, see Gelman and Coley 1991). First, they appear to be prepared to override gross perceptual similarity in simple induction tasks (Carey 1985, Gelman and Markman 1986, 1987). Second, they appear to understand that an object's insides may differ from its outsides and that, for certain kinds of things, the inside of an item is more pertinent to its identity than its outsides (Gelman and Wellman, 1991). Of course, these data are open to interpretation[12] and more studies need to be done, but, given the present state of the evidence, it's reasonable to conclude that children around the age of three or four have an essentialist disposition and that this disposition may emerge in children as young as two. The hard question that this research hasn't settled is, what are the properties that children take to license a special regard for the insides of a novel object? That is, what is it that triggers the essentialist disposition in children for clear cases of natural kinds and not for things like bottles? Also, to the extent that there are syndromes for natural kinds, we need an account of the properties that children are sensitive to such that they do turn out to be reliable indicators of kind membership.

I don't have much to say about the first problem, except to point out that children might depend upon rather coarse heuristics. For example, animate objects are all members of some natural kind or other. So if there were a reliable clue to animacy, this could be used to infer for a range of objects that their insides are especially relevant to their category membership. And, of course, there are some obvious heuristics for identifying animate objects. One of these has to do with their characteristic motion. Unlike chairs or balls, many animate objects don't require an external force to put them into motion. Their movement appears to be spontaneous or internally directed. But what of the syndromes? What are they, and are children really sensitive to the properties that enter into a kind's syndrome? I think a little more can be said on this point.

12. For a different perspective and some potentially conflicting data, see Keil (1989).

For some time now cognitive psychologists who have recognized the importance of categorical hierarchies have also recognized a battery of converging evidence for distinguishing a level of basic perceptual categories (Brown 1958, Rosch et al. 1976). The basic level in a taxonomy is the level that, intuitively speaking, is in the middle. For instance, in the hierarchy [*Fido, dachshund, dog, animal, physical object*, and *thing*], *dog* marks the basic level; *animal, physical object*, and so on are too abstract, and *dachshund, Fido*, and so on are too concrete. Among the chief features of basic perceptual categories is that, in a taxonomic hierarchy, they are the most abstract members whose instances share similar shapes. The notion of shape that's at stake is a matter of controversy. It would be fair to, say, however, that all hands agree that a fairly rich notion must be accepted, one that incorporates, for example, the prototypical angle from which the object is viewed. In any event, it is generally recognized that, at the basic level, shape correlates with kind. Thus shape is a prime candidate for a host of kind syndromes.

Moreover, the available evidence suggests that in certain categorization tasks young children are guided by their recognition of similarities of shape. The interpretation of these data is highly controversial, but I think a coherent picture is emerging. This takes a bit of explanation, starting with some background on the study of lexical acquisition.

In the past, the typical categorization study in developmental psychology would have children examine an object only to be asked which of two new objects it goes with. The notorious finding for young children has always been that they tend to group objects thematically. For instance, given a baseball, a volleyball, and a bat, young children might say that the baseball and the bat go together. This choice is considered to be thematic because the ball and bat are related by their typical uses and not by the taxonomic criteria that adults instinctively acknowledge. Under a taxonomic criterion, the two balls are supposed to go together because they are both the same type of thing: They are both balls.

Recently the conviction that young children's categorizations are dominated by thematic groupings has come under attack. Much of the supporting research for this shift in perspective comes from lexical acquisition studies. The main finding has been that when young children take themselves to be learning the meaning of a new word, thematic groupings give way to taxonomic ones. Ellen Markman has been at the forefront of this research (for an overview, see Markman 1989). In a landmark study undertaken with Jean Hutchinson, Markman presented two- and three-year-old children with groups of pictures, starting, in each case, with a target picture that was followed by two other pictures. For each triad, one of the follow-up pictures was taxonomically related to the target; the other was thematically related. For example, one triad consisted of a tennis shoe (the target), followed by a high-heeled shoe (the taxonomic choice) and a foot (the thematic choice). The study had two conditions, the 'no word' condition and the 'novel word' condition. The no word condition was just the usual sorting task. The children were asked which of the two pictures goes with the target. The wording used was '... See this? [pointing to the target] Find another one that is the same as this....' The novel word condition, on the other hand, involved labeling the target with a noun the children had never heard before. 'See this? [pointing to the target] It's a kind of dax. Can you find another kind of dax?' The results were that children in the no word condition opted for the taxonomic solution on average at a level no better than chance, while children in the novel word condition opted for the taxonomic solution 83% of the time on average (Markman and Hutchinson 1984).

This and related data have been the source for Markman's advancing the taxonomic assumption, a view about the biases that are inherent to the mechanism responsible for lexical acquisition. The taxonomic assumption says that children assume that a novel word refers to a type of thing rather than a group that is organized thematically. The problem with this proposal—a problem that Markman and her colleagues barely address—is that it can't be taken for granted that children automatically know that two items are of the same type. Indeed, without specific information about how to settle issues of categorical identity, the taxonomic assumption is no better than the economic advice "buy low, sell high".

Now as the evidence for the taxonomic assumption has accrued, so has a body of related evidence for a bias concerning shape. If children act as if they assume that novel words refer to types of things, they also act as if they assume that novel words (in particular, novel count nouns) refer to objects of the same shape (Landau et al. 1988). Thus developmental psychologists have had to consider a second constraint on lexical acquisition, the shape bias.

A common reading of the shape bias is that it competes with the taxonomic assumption and reflects an empiricist conception of children, where children are taken to be perceptually bound. (Shape, on this view, is supposed to be a high-level perceptual property of objects.) However, this reading is hardly mandatory. A preferred reading, one that Barbara Landau has stressed, is that the shape bias is in place as a heuristic that supports the taxonomic assumption. That is, while children assume that novel count nouns refer to categories that are organized taxonomically, they depend upon the shapes of objects in making decisions about how to project to new members of a category. The value of this heuristic is that it provides a partial answer to the difficult question of how children know that two objects are of the same type. As Landau puts it (Landau 1994, p. 297):

> If the object naming system is linked to object shape on the one hand and object kind on the other hand, then young learners might assume that objects of similar shape are also likely to be of similar kind. That is, the links among shape, name, and kind should allow learners to make a critical inference: Objects of similar shape are often also of similar kind.

Landau's suggestion, in other words, isn't that children are subject to the shape bias instead of the taxonomic assumption but rather that the two are integrated. Moreover, Landau takes the shape bias to be just one heuristic among potentially many others. Her proposal is that children have an evolving stack of diagnostics for making category decisions. At the top of the stack is the principle that shape is indicative of category membership, though it isn't decisive and can be overridden by other factors. Indeed, 'In this scheme, most of the burden of development would be placed on learning about other diagnostics for category membership, and thereafter (with increasing attentional and memorial resources), organizing and revising their weighting both relative to shape and to each other' (Landau 1994, p. 299).

So the stack is subject to change as a child comes to learn more about the sorts of things that count as evidence for category membership, and, as she matures, the expansion of cognitive resources gives her greater facility with the stack and the ability to alter it as her experience dictates. Some of the other diagnostics that Landau seems to think may be on the initial stack include things like texture and function, properties whose salience with respect to shape can be tested in the laboratory. Yet it is clear, on Landau's view, that eventually just about anything can be added as the result of explicit instruction or education. The difference between younger children and older children—or the difference between children and adults, for that matter— is that the older you are, the more beliefs you've accumulated about the properties you take to be diagnostic of category membership.

Landau's view of lexical acquisition is, I think, loaded with implications for broader issues of cognitive development. This is because her model of lexical acquisition co-opts a relatively general intellectual mechanism. The taxonomic assumption may be a bias of a language learning device, but the heuristics that support it look to be part of a child's understanding of the nature of objects.

If this is right, we may be able to use some of Landau's materials to fill in the gaps in the model of concept acquisition with which we began. The model was supposed to explain the acquisition of natural kind concepts by granting children the ability to accumulate beliefs about the syndromes for natural kinds, where these beliefs would interact with their tacit commitment to essentialism. We've already seen that there is some evidence that children are essentialists. So we've been focusing on the question of whether children are sensitive to the sorts of properties that may be indicative of kind membership. Shape is by far the most convincing candidate. Things like the texture, characteristic local motion, color, and a host of other properties may be involved as well.

At any rate, we have a first-pass sketch of a model of concept acquisition, and it's one that's responsive the common situation in which a concept is acquired through experience with an exemplar (see figure 24.2). According to the model, children have a disposition to acquire natural kind concepts. They understand that certain sorts of things are what they are by virtue of the causal structure that is responsible for their salient and accessible characteristics. They also have a batch of heuristics that are indicative of kind membership, including, importantly, the belief that shape is a good

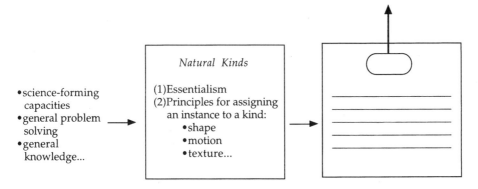

Figure 24.2
A model for the acquisition of natural kind concepts. Salient properties of a kind are recorded on the basis of perceptual contact. This information is put in association with a new mental symbol which, in conjunction with the essentialist principle, comes to constitute a sustaining mechanism linking the symbol with the encountered kind.

guide to kind membership. And finally, children's heuristics are malleable, changing as they gain more experience and education.

What happens under this model is that a child, in certain situations, takes herself to be confronted by a natural kind. As a result, she records information about the kind that her heuristics tell her is important and puts a record of this information in association with a dummy concept, that is, a previously unused mental symbol. This information together with the essentialist principle comes to constitute a sustaining mechanism that links the symbol with the kind she has encountered. The consequence is that she acquires a disposition under which members of the kind cause tokenings of the symbol. If it's bees she has encountered, the concept she will acquire is BEE; if it's cats that she has encountered, the concept she will acquire is CAT.

5. Concluding Remarks: The Nativism Dispute

At this point, it might prove useful to step back and look at the larger issue of whether the model I've been sketching is implausibly nativistic. The worry for many people has been that if conceptual atomism is correct, then all sorts of concepts that couldn't possibly be innate are innate. Some of the concepts that people keep returning to in the philosophical literature include CARBURETOR, PROTON, and BROCCOLI—concepts of artifacts, concepts associated with scientific theories, and concepts of ordinary natural kinds. Again, I should say that I'm not sympathetic with the claim that these concepts must be learned, since the innate structure of the mind is clearly an empirical question; and elsewhere I've argued against the chief reason that philosophers have offered for supposing that BROCCOLI and its ilk couldn't be innate, namely, that evolutionary theory wouldn't allow it (Margolis ms.).

Still, to the extent that there is something to the empiricist intuition, the present model of concept acquisition may suffice to temper some of the resistance to conceptual atomism. This is because the model doesn't entail that natural kind concepts themselves are innate. Rather, individual natural kind concepts are learned by exploiting a mechanism that is responsible for the acquisition of a whole class of concepts.

To see how this works, consider the question of why the child learns the concept BROCCOLI, given the model as it has been developed so far. It's not because the concept BROCCOLI is innate, just waiting to be elicited. Rather, it's because of two things. First, the child has a more general intellectual endowment—perhaps an innate intellectual endowment—that suits the purpose of acquiring natural kind concepts. Second, the child has experiences with broccoli. If she had experiences with a different kind, she would have acquired a different syndrome and hence a different concept. Thus the model has a distinctive Kantian flavor. It explains the acquisition of a range of concepts against the background of a disposition to view the world in terms of a distinctive human category.

Notice that this sort of explanation is quite different from the one that is usually associated with atomistic theories of concepts. Atomistic theories are generally thought to entail that concepts can only be acquired by a triggering process. This means, among other things, that unstructured concepts are innately specified, only to be made available to cognition when an innately specified 'trigger' is encountered. In contrast, the model I've been encouraging is hardly a triggering-theory. There may be constraints on which concepts can be acquired, but they are rather general constraints; they guide the acquisition of a certain type of concept. Moreover, specific concepts are acquired in a way that is responsive to the experience that the agent undergoes. It's not just that experience is a precursor to concept acquisition. Experience is crucial to the development of the syndromes that come to support concept possession. As a result, the model of acquisition has the spirit of a learning model. It explains how a concept, of a certain type, might be learned in the course of experience, even if it lacks internal structure.[13]

One of the virtues of this account is that it doesn't require that children know too much before acquiring a natural kind concept. Most important, they don't have to know the nature of a kind. What they have to know is some contingent information about a kind, information that is available given perceptual contact with one or more of its exemplars. But while perceptual contact is often a precursor to concept acquisition, it isn't a precondition. Certainly, people have the ability to acquire natural kind concepts without perceptual contact, and there is no reason to think that this ability is limited to an achievement of adult life. Here it pays to bear in mind one of the sustaining mechanism types that, with adults, allows for the possession of a natural kind concept in the face of gross ignorance—deference-based sustaining mechanisms.

Adults, we've seen, can exploit expert testimony, and consequently have the ability to discriminate members of a kind of which they know almost nothing. All they do have to know is some small amount of contingent information about the kind and some rather general information about how to locate a suitable expert. But if this is how it is for adults, why not for children? We can just add to Landau's stack of heuristics an entry that says to defer to expert testimony. Of course, children may not know who the experts are. That is something to be learned in the course of development. However, even if children start by assuming that their caretakers are the experts, this may do a lot to extend their conceptual repertory. Though the caretakers may not themselves be experts, they might be able to locate the real experts and consequently act as a medium of reliable discrimination. After all, the caretakers will be adults and will have acquired the experience and knowledge that's common within society.

What's more, children probably do have the disposition to rely upon adult testimony. One of the things that causes them to override perceptual similarity in an induction task is that the perceptually dissimilar items are referred to by the same name. By hypothesis, the reason children conclude that the dissimilar items have the same hidden properties is that they are following the taxonomic assumption and applying it backward: knowing that two items have the same name, children infer that they are of the same kind. But children aren't forced to accept this conclusion. They could infer, instead, that the experimenter or the puppet or whoever is talking is using the names incorrectly. Deference, then, can be used to supplement the core model by providing an entirely general disposition that helps to put in place specific sustaining mechanisms. Moreover, since deference may not be restricted to natural kind terms/concepts (see note 8), it may offer a way of explaining the acquisition of nearly any lexicalized concept where the child lacks sufficient experience of its instances.

---

13. Natural kind concepts constitute one type to be guided by a special acquisitional mechanism. Perhaps there are other types, and corresponding mechanisms, as well—a question I'll leave for another time.

In short, conceptual atomists have a number of resources to explain how concepts are learned. In each case the key to acquisition is a process that constructs a sustaining mechanism that effects the mind-world relation that is constitutive of conceptual identity. This orientation shows that one of the main arguments for rejecting atomistic theories of concepts is simply unfounded. Unstructured concepts needn't be innate.[14]

References

Abbott, B. 1997: A Note on the Nature of 'Water'. *Mind*, 106, 311–19.

Adams, F., and Aizawa, K. 1994: Fodorian Semantics. In S. Stich and T. Warfield (eds.), *Mental Representation: A Reader*. Cambridge, MA: Blackwell, 223–42.

Armstrong, S., Gleitman, L., and Gleitman, H. 1983: What Some Concept Might Not Be. *Cognition*, 13, 263–308.

Braisby, N., Franks, B., and Hampton, J. 1996: Essentialism, Word Use, and Concepts. *Cognition*, 59, 247–74.

Brown, R. 1958: How Shall a Thing Be Called? *Psychological Review*, 65, 14–21.

Burge, T. 1979: Individualism and the Mental. In P. French, T. Uehling, Jr., and H. Wettstein (eds.), *Midwest Studies in Philosophy, IV: Studies in Metaphysics*. Minneapolis: University of Minnesota Press, 73–121.

Carey, S. 1985: *Conceptual Change in Childhood*. Cambridge, MA: MIT Press.

Fodor, J. A. 1981: The Present Status of the Innateness Controversy. In *Representations: Philosophical Essays on the Foundations of Cognitive Science*. Cambridge, MA: MIT Press, 257–316.

Fodor, J. A. 1990: A Theory of Content. In *A Theory of Content and Other Essays*. Cambridge, MA: MIT Press, 51–87.

Fodor, J. A. 1994: *The Elm and the Expert: Mentalese and Its Semantics*. Cambridge, MA: MIT Press.

Fodor, J. A., Garrett, M., Walker, E., and Parkes, C. 1980: Against Definitions. *Cognition*, 8, 263–367.

Fodor, J. D., Fodor, J. A., and Garrett, M. 1975: The Psychological Unreality of Semantic Representations. *Linguistic Inquiry*, 6, 515–32.

Gelman, S., and Coley, J. 1991: Language and Categorization: The Acquisition of Natural Kind Terms. In S. Gelman and J. Byrnes (eds.), *Perspectives on Language and Thought: Interrelations in Development*. New York: Cambridge University Press, 146–96.

Gelman, S., and Markman, E. 1986: Categories and Induction in Young Children. *Cognition*, 23, 183–209.

Gelman, S., and Markman, E. 1987: Young Children's Inductions from Natural Kinds: The Role of Categories and Appearances. *Child Development*, 58, 1532–41.

Gelman, S., and Wellman, H. 1991: Insides and Essences: Early Understandings of the Non-Obvious. *Cognition*, 38, 213–44.

Keil, F. 1989: *Concepts, Kinds, and Cognitive Development*. Cambridge, MA: MIT Press.

Komatsu, L. 1992: Recent Views of Conceptual Structure. *Psychological Bulletin*, 112, 500–26.

Landau, B. 1994: Object Shape, Object Name, and Object Kind: Representation and Development. In D. Medin (ed.), *The Psychology of Learning and Motivation*. New York: Academic Press, 253–304.

Landau, B., Smith, L., and Jones, S. 1988: The Importance of Shape in Early Lexical Learning. *Cognitive Development*, 3, 299–321.

Laurence, S., and Margolis, E. 1999: Concepts and Cognitive Science. In E. Margolis and S. Laurence (eds.), *Concepts: Core Readings*. Cambridge, MA: MIT Press.

Loewer, B., and Rey, G. 1991: *Meaning in Mind: Fodor and His Critics*. Cambridge, MA: Blackwell.

Malt, B. 1994: Water Is Not H_2O. *Cognitive Psychology*, 27, 41–70.

Margolis, E. 1994: A Reassessment of the Shift from the Classical Theory of Concepts to Prototype Theory. *Cognition*, 51, 73–89.

Margolis, E. 1995: The Significance of the Theory Analogy in the Psychological Study of Concepts. *Mind and Language*, 10, 45–71.

14. I've benefited from many useful conversations with friends and colleagues. I'm especially grateful to Jerry Fodor, Alan Leslie, Barbara Landau, Stephen Laurence, and Kenneth Taylor. Thanks also to Elizabeth Shipley, Stephen Stich, Michael Strevens, and Jonathan Sutton.

Margolis, E. ms.: Why Evolution Can't Settle the Nativism Controversy. Under review.

Markman, E. 1989: *Categorization and Naming in Children: Problems of Induction.* Cambridge, MA: MIT Press.

Markman, E., and Hutchinson, J. 1984: Children's Sensitivity to Constraints on Word Meaning: Taxonomic vs. Thematic Relations. *Cognitive Psychology,* 16, 1–27.

Medin, D. 1989: Concepts and Conceptual Structure. *American Psychologist,* 44, 1469–81.

Medin, D., and Ortony, A. 1989: Psychological Essentialism. In S. Vosniadou and A. Ortony (eds.), *Similarity and Analogical Reasoning.* New York: Cambridge University Press, 179–95.

Osherson, D., and Smith, E. 1981: On the Adequacy of Prototype Theory as a Theory of Concepts. *Cognition,* 9, 35–58.

Putnam, H. 1975: The Meaning of Meaning. In K. Gunderson (ed.), *Language, Mind and Knowledge.* Minneapolis: University of Minnesota Press. Reprinted in H. Putnam (1975), *Mind, Language and Reality: Philosophical Paper, Vol. 2.* New York: Cambridge University Press, 215–71.

Rey, G. 1983: Concepts and Stereotypes. *Cognition,* 15, 237–262.

Rosch, E., Mervis, C., Gray, W., Johnson, D., and Boyes-Braem, P. 1976: Basic Objects in Natural Categories. *Cognitive Psychology,* 8, 382–439.

Smith, E., and Medin, D. 1981: *Categories and Concepts.* Cambridge, MA: Harvard University Press.

Concept Possession in Infants and Children

Chapter 25

The Object Concept Revisited: New Directions in the Investigation of Infants' Physical Knowledge

Renée Baillargeon

An important concern of cognitive psychology in recent years has been the description of children's and adults' physical knowledge. This research has focused on three important questions. First, investigators have sought to describe the *content* of children's and adults' knowledge. Physical domains that have been examined include astronomy (Vosniadou and Brewer, 1989), biology (Carey, 1985), and physics (Clement, 1982; D. Gentner and D. R. Gentner, 1983; Karmiloff-Smith and Inhelder, 1975; McCloskey, 1983; Siegler, 1978). Second, researchers have attempted to elucidate the *structure* of children's and adults' physical knowledge. Different models have been proposed, ranging from lists of local rules to naive models or "theories" organized around causal principles (Carey, 1985; Gelman, 1990; D. Gentner and Stevens, 1983; Keil, 1990; Siegler, 1978, 1983; Vosniadou and Brewer, 1989; Wellman, 1990). Finally, investigators have been concerned with the *development* of children's and adults' physical knowledge. Of particular interest has been the comparison of novices' and experts' representations of physical domains (Chi, Feltovitch, and Glaser, 1981; Larkin, 1983; Wiser and Carey, 1983).

In the realm of infancy research, investigators have also sought to characterize infants' physical world. Most of this research has focused on issues of content, and more specifically, on infants' understanding of occlusion events. When adults see an object occlude another object, they typically make three assumptions. The first is that the occluded object continues to exist behind the occluding object. The second is that the occluded object retains the spatial and physical properties it possessed prior to occlusion. The third is that the occluded object is still subject to physical laws; its displacements, transformations, and interactions with other objects do not become capricious or arbitrary but remain regular and predictable. Collectively, these assumptions are generally referred to in the developmental literature as a concept of *object permanence* or, more broadly, as an *object concept*.

Piaget (1954) was the first to investigate whether infants share adults' assumptions about occluded objects—or, in other words, whether infants possess a notion of object permanence. Detailed analyses of infants' performances on manual search tasks led him to conclude that the development of infants' beliefs about occluded objects progresses through six stages and is not complete until 2 years of age.

Piaget's theory of the development of infants' beliefs about occluded objects has occupied a central position in the field of infant cognition (e.g., Flavell, 1985; Harris, 1983). The acquisition of a notion of object permanence is often considered to be the cornerstone of cognitive development in infancy, and indeed, what could be more basic than the object concept? The realization that visible and occluded objects exist in the same objective space and obey the same physical laws constitutes one of the fundamental tenets on which our representation of the physical world is built. It is not surprising, therefore, that considerable effort has been expended since the publication of Piaget's theory to confirm and extend his conclusions (see Bremner, 1985; Gratch, 1975, 1976; Harris, 1987, 1989; Schuberth, 1983; Sophian, 1984; Spelke, 1988; and Wellman, Cross, and Bartsch, 1987, for reviews).

Since the early 1980s, my collaborators and I have conducted an extensive series of experiments on young infants' understanding of occlusion events. In these experiments, we have used visual tasks rather than the manual search tasks used by Piaget and his followers. The selection of visual tasks stemmed from a concern that infants might preform poorly in manual search tasks, not because their concept of object permanence was underdeveloped, but because their ability to plan search action sequences was limited. Some of the experiments we carried out were designed expressly as tests of Piaget's theory; others focused on hitherto unexplored aspects of infants' understanding of occlusion events. In general, the results of these experiments paint a radically different picture of infants' ability to represent and to reason about occluded objects than that bequeathed by Piaget and, until recently, adopted by most developmental psychologists. Indeed, the results suggest that young infants' understanding of occlusion events is strikingly similar to that of adults.

This chapter is divided into four sections. The first section presents Piaget's description of the sequence of changes in infants' beliefs about occluded objects, and the evidence on which this description was based. The second section reviews the experiments we have conducted to test Piaget's theory and to pursue new directions suggested by the results of these initial tests. The third section considers possible explanations for the marked discrepancy between search and non-search assessments of infants' understanding of occlusion events. Finally, the last section examines the implications of the present research for descriptions of the content, structure, and development of infants' physical knowledge.

1. Piaget's Theory

Piaget (1954) proposed that infants' beliefs about occluded objects develop through six stages. During the first three stages (0 to 9 months), infants do not realize that objects continue to exist when occluded: They assume that objects cease to exist when they cease to be visible and begin to exist anew when they come back into view. According to Piaget, the objects at the stage is "a mere image which reenters the void as soon as it vanishes, and emerges from it for no objective reason" (1954, p. 11). During the fourth stage (9 to 12 months), infants begin to view objects as permanent entities that continue to exist when masked by other objects. However, this permanence is still limited. Infants do not yet conceive of occluded objects as occupying objective locations in space. It is not until the fifth stage (12 to 18 months), Piaget maintained, that infants begin to systematically attend to visible displacements and to assume that occluded objects reside in whatever locations they occupied immediately prior to occlusion. The sixth stage (18 to 24 months), which is signaled by the emergence of symbolic representation, constitutes the final advance in the development of infants' beliefs about occluded objects. Because of their new representational capacity, infants become able to imagine invisible displacements and hence to infer, as opposed to merely represent, occluded objects' locations. According to Piaget, objects' appearances and disappearances are then no longer mysterious but follow known, predictable patterns. By the end of the sixth stage, the world of the infant is thus radically different from what it was in the beginning stages. It is a world that contains both visible and occluded objects, existing in a unitary, objective space, and obeying the same physical laws.

As was mentioned earlier, the main evidence for Piaget's description of the sequence of changes in infants' beliefs about occluded objects came from studies of the development of manual search behavior. Thus, Piaget's first claim, that it's not until about 9 months of age that infants begin to endow objects with permanence, was based on the finding that manual search does not emerge until this age. Piaget noted that, prior to Stage 4, infants do not search for objects they have observed being hidden. If a toy is covered with a cloth, for example, they make no attempt to lift the cloth and grasp the toy, even though they are capable of performing each of these actions. Beginning in Stage 4, however, infants do remove obstacles to retrieve hidden objects.

Why did Piaget select infants' willingness to search for hidden objects as marking the beginning of object permanence? This question is important because Piaget observed several behaviors prior to Stage 4 that are suggestive of object permanence. For example, he noted that, as early as Stage 1 (0 to 1 month), infants may look at an object, look away from it, and then return to it several seconds later, without any external cue having signaled the object's continued presence. In addition, Piaget observed that, beginning in Stage 3 (4 to 9 months), infants anticipate the future positions of moving objects. If they are tracking an object and temporarily lose sight of it, they look for it further along its trajectory; similarly, if they are holding an object out of sight and accidentally let go of it, they stretch their arm to recapture it.

Piaget held that although these and other behaviors seem to reveal a notion of object permanence, closer analysis indicates "how superficial this interpretation would be and how phenomenalistic the primitive universe remains" (1954, p. 11). Prior to Stage 4, Piaget maintained, infants lack a concept of physical causality and regard all of reality as being dependent on their activity. When acting on an object, infants view the object not as an independent entity but as the extension or the product of their action. If the object disappears from view, infants reproduce or extend their action because they expect that this action will again produce the object. Proof for Piaget that infants regard the object as being "at the disposal" of their action is that if their action fails to bring back the object, they do not preform alternative actions to recover it. Beginning in Stage 4, however, infants act very differently. For example, if a ball rolls behind a cushion and they cannot recapture it by extending their reach, they try alternative means for recovering it: They lift the cushion, pull it aside, or grope behind it. According to Piaget, such activities indicate that infants conceive of the object, not as a thing at the disposal of a specific action, but as a substantial entity that is located out of sight behind the cushion and that any of several actions may serve to reveal.

Piaget's second claim, that it is not until about 12 months of age that infants begin to conceive of occluded objects as occupying objective locations on space, was suggested by the finding that perseverative search errors do not disappear until this age. Piaget noted that when Stage 4 infants search for hidden objects, they often search in the wrong location. Specifically, if an object is hidden in a location A and, after infants have retrieved it, the same object is hidden in a new location B, infants tend to search for the object in A, where they first found it. Piaget took these errors to indicate that, although infants endow the object with permanence, as evidenced by their willingness to search for it, this permanence is not yet complete. Infants still regard the object as the extension of their action: When the object disappears at B, they search for it at A because they expect that by reproducing their action at A they will again produce the object. According to Piaget, "in all the observations in which the child searches in A for what he has seen disappear in B, the explanation should be sought in the fact that the object is not yet sufficiently individualized to be dissociated from the global behavior related to position A" (1954, p. 63). Beginning in Stage 5, however, infants do search for objects where they were last seen, rather than where they were first found. According to Piaget, infants are becoming aware that objects reside not in special positions linked to their own actions, but in objective locations resulting from the objects' displacements within the visual field.

Finally, Piaget's third claim, that it is not until about 18 months of age that infants begin to infer the location of occluded objects, was based on the discovery that it is not until this age that infants succeed at search tasks involving invisible displacements. In these tasks, an object is hidden, in full view of the infant, in a small container, which is then moved behind each of several screens. The object is surreptitiously left behind one of the screens, usually the last. Piaget found that when asked to find to object, Stage 5 infants typically search the container, the location where they last saw the object. Failing to find the object there, they make no attempt to search behind the screens. Beginning in Stage 6, however, infants do search behind the screens. Piaget speculated that because of their new-found representational abilities, infants are able to imagine or to infer the object's probable displacements. Piaget described the transition from Stage 5 to Stage 6 in these terms:

> A world [such as the world of the fifth stage infant] in which only perceived movements are regulated is neither stable nor dissociated from the self; it is a world of still chaotic potentialities whose organization begins only in the subject's presence.... [The] representation and deduction characteristic of the sixth stage result in extending the process of solidification to regions ... which are dissociated from action and perception; displacements, even invisible ones, are henceforth envisaged as subservient to laws, and objects in motion become real objects independent of the self and persisting in their substantial identity. (Piaget, 1954, p. 86)

2. Test of Piaget's Theory

Since the early 1980s, my collaborators and I have conducted an extensive series of experiments on young infants' understanding of occlusion events. This section summarizes the results of these experiments. The section is organized into three parts. The first reports experiments on young infants' ability to represent the existence of occluded objects; the second reviews experiments on young infants' ability to represent the spatial and physical properties of occluded objects; and the third presents preliminary experiments on young infants' ability to make inferences about the existence and properties of occluded objects.

2.1. Representing the Existence of Occluded Objects
During the 1960s and 1970s, Piaget's (1954) observation that young infants do not search for hidden objects was confirmed by many investigators (see Gratch, 1975,

1976, for reviews of this early work). Nevertheless, Piaget's interpretation of this observation was questioned. It was proposed that young infants might fail to search for hidden objects, not because of a lack of object permanence, but because of difficulties associated with manual search (e.g., Bower, 1974).

This analysis suggested that young infants might show evidence of object permanence if given tests that did not require manual search. Bower (1967, 1972, 1974; Bower, Broughton, and Moore, 1971; Bower and Wishart, 1972) devised several such tests and obtained three results that seemed indicative of object permanence in young infants. First, 7-week-old infants were found to discriminate between disappearances that signaled the continued existence of an object (e.g., gradual occlusions), and disappearances that did not (e.g., gradual dissolutions or sudden implosions; Bower, 1967). Second, 2-month-old infants were found to anticipate the reappearance of an object that stopped behind a screen, "looking to that half of the movement path the object would have reached had it not stopped" (Bower et al., 1971, p. 183). Finally, 5-month-old infants were found to show disruptions in their tracking when an object was altered while passing behind a screen: They tended to look back at the screen, as though in search of the original object (Bower, 1974; Bower et al., 1971).

Although suggestive, Bower's three results did not provide conclusive evidence of object permanence in young infants. First, methodological problems cast doubts on the validity of the results (e.g., Baillargeon, 1986, 1987b; Baillargeon, Spelke, and Wasserman, 1985; Goldberg, 1976; Gratch, 1975, 1976, 1982; Harris, 1987; Hood and Willatts, 1986; Meicler and Gratch, 1980; Muller and Aslin, 1987). Second, the results were open to alternative interpretations that did not implicate object permanence. In particular, the last two results could be explained by Piagetian theory in terms of the extension of an ongoing action or the reproduction of a previous action. When anticipating the reappearance of the object, the infants could simply have been extending a tracking motion begun prior to the object's disappearance. Furthermore, when looking back at the screen, after the novel object had emerged from behind it, the infants could have been repeating their prior action of looking in that direction, with the expectation that this action would again produce the original object.

The first of Bower's (1967) results could not the explained in terms of the extension or the reproduction of an action, but it, too, was open to alternative interpretations. One such interpretation was that the infants discriminated between the test disappearances on the basis of superficial expectations about the way objects typically disappear, rather than on the basis of a belief in object permanence. In their daily environment, infants often see objects occlude one another but they rarely, if ever, see objects implode or dissolve into the air. Hence, the infants could have responded differently to the occlusions than to the implosions or the dissolutions simply because the occlusions represented the only type of disappearance that was familiar to them.

Because of the difficulties associated with Piaget's and Bower's tasks, my colleagues and I sought a new means of testing object permanence in young infants (Baillargeon et al., 1985). Like Bower, we chose not to rely on manual search as an index of object permanence. However, we tried to find an index that did not depend on (a) the extension or reproduction of an action or (b) knowledge about superficial properties of object disappearances.

The method we devised focused on infants' understanding of the principle that a solid object cannot move through the space occupied by another solid object. We

Habituation Event

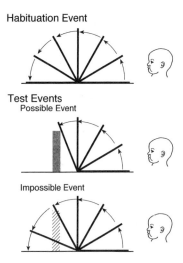

Test Events
Possible Event

Impossible Event

Figure 25.1
Schematic drawing of the events shown to the infants in Baillargeon et al. (1985) and in Baillargeon (1987a).

reasoned that if infants were surprised when a visible object appeared to move through the space occupied by another, occluded object, it would suggest that they took account of the existence of the occluded object.

In a series of experiments, $5\frac{1}{2}$-month-olds (Baillargeon et al., 1985) and $4\frac{1}{2}$-month-olds (Baillargeon, 1987a) were habituated to a screen that rotated back and forth through a 180° arc, in the manner of a drawbridge (see Fig. 25.1). Following habituation, a box was placed behind the screen and the infants saw a possible and an impossible test event. In the possible event, the screen stopped when it reached the occluded box; in the impossible event, the screen rotated through a full 180° arc, as though the box were no longer behind it. Both the $5\frac{1}{2}$- and the $4\frac{1}{2}$-month-old infants looked reliably longer at the impossible than at the possible event, suggesting that they (a) represented the existence of the box behind the screen; (b) understood that the screen could not rotate through the space occupied by the box; and hence (c) expected the screen to stop and were surprised in the impossible event that it did not.

There was, however, an alternative interpretation for the results. The infants could have looked longer at the impossible than at the possible event simply because they found the 180° screen rotation more interesting that the shorter rotation used in the possible event. To check this interpretation, we tested additional groups of infants in a control condition that was identical to the experimental condition except that no box was placed behind the screen. The infants now looked equally at the two screen rotations. This finding provided evidence that the infants in the experimental condition looked longer at the impossible event, not because they preferred the 180° screen rotation, but because they expected the screen to stop and were surprised that it did not.

In other experiments also reported in Baillargeon (1987a), $3\frac{1}{2}$-month-old infants were examined using the same paradigm. The results indicated that the infants who

Habituation Event

Test Events
Possible Event

Impossible Event

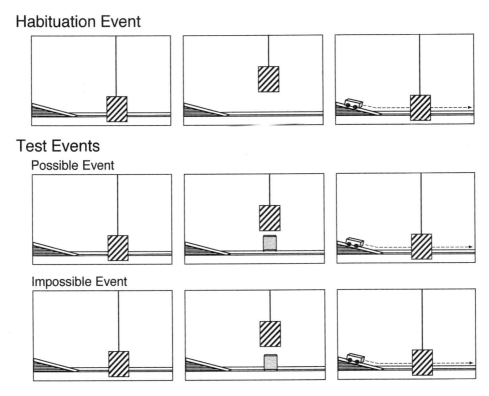

Figure 25.2
Schematic drawing of the events shown to the infants in Baillargeon (1986) and in Baillargeon and DeVos
(1991, Exp. 3).

were fast habituators[1] looked reliably longer at the impossible than at the possible
event, whereas the infants who were slow habituators looked equally at the two
events. These findings suggested that, like the $5\frac{1}{2}$- and the $4\frac{1}{2}$-month-old infants in the
initial experiments, the $3\frac{1}{2}$-month-old infants who were fast habituators expected the
screen to stop and were surprised in the impossible event that it did not. A control
condition conducted without the box supported this interpretation. The results of
these experiments thus indicated that, contrary to what Piaget had claimed, infants as
young as $3\frac{1}{2}$ months of age represent the existence of occluded objects.

2.2. Representing the Properties of Occluded Objects

Location   The results presented in the last section indicated that infants represent the
existence of occluded objects long before 9 months of age. Such a finding raised the

1. In this experiment, an infant received habituation trials until (a) the infant reached a criterion of habituation of a 50% or higher decrease in looking time on three consecutive trials relative to his or her looking
time on the first three trials, or (b) the infant completed nine trials without satisfying the habituation criterion. Therefore, the minimum number of habituation trials an infant could receive was six, and the maximum number was nine. Infants who took six or seven trials to reach the habituation criterion were classified
as *fast* habituators; infants who required eight or nine trials to reach the criterion or who failed to reach the
criterion within nine trials were classified as *slow* habituators.

possibility that infants represent the location of occluded objects—the next step in Piaget's (1954) developmental sequence—before the age of 12 months. To examine this possibility, $6\frac{1}{2}$- and 8-month-old infants were tested using a novel paradigm (Baillargeon, 1986). The infants sat in front of a screen; to the left of the screen was a long inclined ramp (see Fig. 25.2). The infants were habituated to the following event: The screen was raised (to show the infants that there was nothing behind it) and then lowered; a toy car then rolled down the ramp, passed behind the screen, and exited the apparatus to the right. Following habituation, the infants saw a possible and an impossible test event. These events were identical to the habituation event except that a box was placed behind the screen. In the possible event, the box stood in back of the car's tracks; in the impossible event, the box stood on top of the tracks, blocking the car's path.

The results indicated that the infants looked reliably longer at the impossible than at the possible event. A second experiment in which the box was placed in front (possible event) or on top (impossible event) of the car's tracks yielded similar results. Together, these results indicated that the infants (a) represented the location of the box behind the screen; (b) assumed that the car pursued its trajectory behind the screen; (c) understood that the car could not roll through the space occupied by the box; and hence (d) were surprised in the impossible event to see the car roll past the screen.

In subsequent experiments, 4-month-old infants were tested using a similar procedure, except that the box was replaced by a toy mouse (Baillargeon and DeVos, 1991). The results showed that the *male* infants tended to look equally at the test events; in contrast, the *female* infants looked reliably longer when the toy mouse stood on top of the car's tracks than when it stood either in back or in front of the tracks. (This is no doubt the first evidence of female superiority in reasoning about cars! See Baillargeon and DeVos, 1991, for interpretations of this unexpected sex difference.) The results obtained with the female infants indicated that, like the $6\frac{1}{2}$- and the 8-month-old infants in the original experiments, these younger infants were surprised to see the car reappear from behind the screen when the mouse stood in its path.

The results of these experiments thus indicated that, contrary to what Piaget had claimed, infants as young as 4 months of age assume that objects retain their locations when occluded.

Additional Properties   The experiments described in this section asked whether infants could represent not only the location but also the height and the compressibility of occluded objects.

The first experiment in this series examined $7\frac{1}{2}$-month-old infants' ability to represent the height and the location of a hidden object (Baillargeon, 1987b). The infants were habituated to a screen that rotated back and forth through a 180° arc (see Fig. 25.3). Following habituation, the infants saw a possible and an impossible test event. In both events, a box was placed behind the screen, which rotated back and forth through a 165° arc. The only difference between the events was in the orientation and location of the box behind the screen. In the possible event, the box lay flat 10 cm behind the screen and was 4 cm high; in the impossible event, the box stood upright 25 cm behind the screen and was 20 cm high. The 165° rotation of the screen was consistent with the horizontal orientation of the box (the screen stopped rotating when it reached the box), but not with its vertical orientation (the screen rotated through the space occupied by the top 14 cm or 70% of the box).

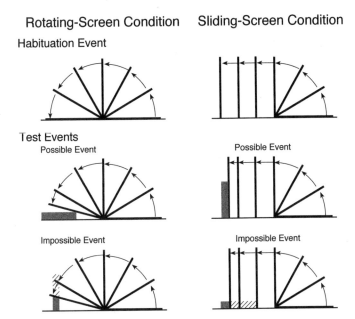

Figure 25.3
Schematic drawing of the events shown to the infants in Baillargeon (1987b, Exp. 1).

The infants looked reliably longer at the impossible than at the possible event, suggesting that they (a) represented the height and location of the box behind the screen; (b) used this information to estimate at what point the screen would reach the box; (c) understood that the screen could not rotate through the space occupied by the box; and therefore (d) were surprised when the screen continued to rotate after it reached the box. This interpretation was supported by a control condition in which the screen underwent a different motion (see Fig. 25.3). In the habituation event, the screen rotated upward 90° and then, remaining vertical, slid backward 30 cm. In the test events, the screen again rotated 90° but slid back 25 cm instead of 30 cm. As in the rotating screen condition, the box either stood upright 25 cm behind the screen (possible event), or lay flat 10 cm behind the screen (impossible event). The infants again looked reliably longer at the impossible than at the possible event. This result provided evidence that the infants in the rotating screen condition looked longer at the impossible event, not because they preferred the box in its vertical orientation, but because they were surprised that the screen continued rotating after it reached the box.

The next experiment (Baillargeon, 1987b) examined whether $7\frac{1}{2}$-month-old infants could represent the compressibility as well as the height and location of a hidden object. The infants saw a possible and an impossible test event in which a screen rotated back and forth through a 157° arc (see Fig. 25.4). In the possible event, a soft, compressible object (an irregular ball of gauze) stood behind the screen, and in the impossible event, a hard, non-compressible object (a wooden box) stood behind the screen (the infants were allowed to manipulate the test objects for a few seconds before the experiment began). The two objects were approximately the same color and size and they were placed at the same location behind the screen. The 157° rotation was consistent with the presence of the soft object (the screen could compress

Habituation Events

Soft Object (Fluff) Event

Soft Object (Plastic) Event

Test Events

Possible Event

Impossible Event

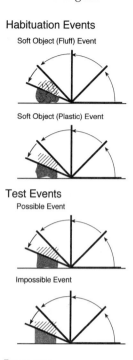

Figure 25.4
Schematic drawing of the events shown to the infants in Baillargeon (1987b, Exp. 2).

the object), but not with the presence of the hard object (the screen appeared to rotate through the space occupied by the top portion of the object). Prior to seeing the test events, the infants watched two habituation events that were identical to the possible event except that other soft objects were used (these were two irregular balls, one made of polyester stuffing and the other of plastic bags).

The infants looked reliably longer at the impossible than at the possible event, suggesting that they (a) represented the height and location of the object behind the screen, and used this information to decide at what point the screen would reach the object; (b) represented the compressibility of the object behind the screen, and understood that the screen could compress the soft but not the hard object; and hence (c) were surprised when the screen continued to rotate after it reached the hard object. This interpretation was supported by a control condition in which the screen rotated 112° instead of 157° and thus stopped before it reached the hard or soft object behind it. The infants in this condition tended to look equally at the test events. This finding provided evidence that the infants in the experimental condition looked longer at the impossible than at the possible event, not because they preferred the hard to the soft object, but because they were surprised that the screen continued to rotate after it reached the incompressible hard object.

Together, the results of these experiments suggested two conclusions. The first was that, by $7\frac{1}{2}$ months of age, infants can represent the physical (e.g., height, compressibility) as well as the spatial (e.g., location) properties of occluded objects. The second was that infants this age can make both qualitative and quantitative predictions about occluded objects. The infants in the experiments not only realized *that* the screen should stop when an object blocked its path (qualitative prediction): They

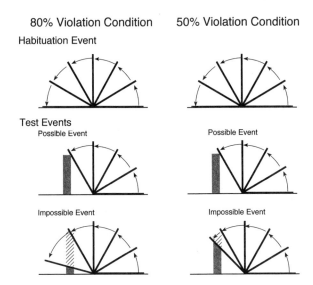

80% Violation Condition   50% Violation Condition

Habituation Event

Test Events

Possible Event   Possible Event

Impossible Event   Impossible Event

Figure 25.5
Schematic drawing of the events shown to the infants in Baillargeon (1991, Exp. 1).

also were able to judge *at what point* the screen should stop, depending on the object's height, compressibility, and location (quantitative prediction). Following the terminology used in computational models of everyday physical reasoning (e.g., Forbus, 1984), the second prediction is said to be quantitative because it required the infants to compute a quantitative estimate of the screen's stopping point. Specifically, the infants had to determine how high above the apparatus floor the screen would be when it came to a stop. In contrast, the first prediction is referred to as qualitative because it embodied no quantitative judgments.

Developmental Evidence The next experiments asked two questions (Baillargeon, 1991). First, would younger infants, $6\frac{1}{2}$- and $4\frac{1}{2}$-month-olds, also be able to represent and to reason quantitatively about the height and location of an occluded object? Second, how precise was infants' quantitative reasoning? In Baillargeon's (1987b) experiment (shown in Fig. 25.3), the screen rotated through the top 70% of the space occupied by the occluded box—to adults, an obvious violation. Would infants still detect that the screen rotated farther than it should if it rotated through a smaller portion of the occluded box? The experiments compared infants' performances with 80% and 50% violations.

In the first experiment, $6\frac{1}{2}$-month-old infants were habituated to a screen that rotated back and forth through a 180° arc (see Fig. 25.5). Following habituation, a box 25 cm tall was placed 12.5 cm behind the screen (as in Baillargeon, 1987a), and the infants saw a possible and an impossible test event. In the possible event, the screen stopped rotating before it reached the occluded box (112° arc); in the impossible event, the screen rotated through either the top 80% (157° arc) or the top 50% (135° arc) of the space occupied by the box.

The results indicated that the infants in the 80% rotation condition looked reliably longer at the impossible than at the possible event, whereas those in the 50% violation condition tended to look equally at the two test events. These results suggested that the infants were able to detect the 80% but not the 50% violation. A control

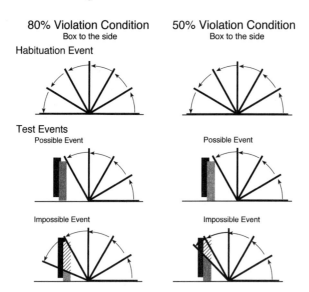

Figure 25.6
Schematic drawing of the events shown to the infants in Baillargeon (1991, Exp. 4).

condition conducted without a box behind the screen provided evidence that the infants in the 80% violation condition looked longer at the impossible event, not because they preferred the 157° rotation to the 112° rotation, but because they detected that the screen rotated farther than it should have given the box's height and location.

In a subsequent experiment, $4\frac{1}{2}$-month-old infants were tested in the 80% violation condition. The infants failed to show a reliable preference for the impossible over the possible event, suggesting that, in contrast to the $6\frac{1}{2}$-month-old infants, they were unable to detect the 80% violation.

The next experiments investigated whether infants would form more precise expectations about the screen's stopping point under different conditions. These experiments were identical to the last series with one exception: A second, identical box was placed 10 cm to the right of and in the same fronto-parallel plane as the box behind the screen (see Fig. 25.6). This second box stood out of the screen's path and so remained visible throughout the test trials.

With this second box present, (a) the $6\frac{1}{2}$-month-old infants now looked reliably longer when the screen rotated through the top 50% of the occluded box, and (b) the $4\frac{1}{2}$-month-old infants now looked reliably longer when the screen rotated through either the top 80% or the top 50% of the occluded box. These results suggested that the infants spontaneously made use of the second box to predict the screen's stopping point: They were able to detect with this box violations that they failed to detect without it. This interpretation was supported by control conditions in which the box behind the screen was removed, leaving only the box to the side of the screen. The infants in these control conditions tended to look equally at the different screen rotations. These findings provided evidence that the infants in the experimental conditions looked longer at the impossible events, not because they preferred the 157° or the 135° to the 112° screen rotation, but because they were surprised that the screen continued to rotate after it reached the occluded box.

How did the infants make use of the visible box to predict the screen's stopping point? At least two answers were possible. One was that the visible box facilitated the infants' *quantitative* reasoning by providing them with an exact reminder of the occluded box's height and distance from the screen. The other answer was that the visible box made it possible for the infants to offer a *qualitative* prediction about the screen's stopping point. That is, rather than computing the screen's approximate height at its stopping point, the infants could simply reason that the screen would stop when it was aligned with the top of the visible box. This prediction is said to be qualitative because it required no quantitative estimate of the screen's stopping point; the top of the visible box provided the infants with a direct reference point.

Did the infants in the experiments use the visible box to offer a quantitative or a qualitative prediction about the screen's stopping point? To decide between these two possibilities, experiments were conducted that were identical to the two-box experiments just described except that the visible box was no longer in the same fronto-parallel plane as the box behind the screen. The visible box now stood 10 cm to the right and 8.5 cm in front of the box behind the screen. Under these conditions, the infants still had a reminder of the occluded box's height and approximate distance from the screen, but they could no longer use an alignment strategy: The screen rotated past the top of the visible box in both the possible and the impossible events. The results indicated that (a) the $6\frac{1}{2}$-month-old infants were no longer able to detect the 50% screen violation, and (b) the $4\frac{1}{2}$-month-old infants were no longer able to detect the 80% and the 50% screen violations.

Together, the results of the experiments reported in this section revealed an interesting developmental sequence. At $6\frac{1}{2}$ months of age, the infants were able to predict both quantitatively and qualitatively at what point the screen would reach the occluded box and stop. Quantitative predictions were produced when only the box behind the screen was present; qualitative predictions were produced when the second box was placed to the right of and in the same plane as the box behind the screen. Not surprisingly, the infants' quantitative predictions were less precise than their qualitative counterparts: The infants could detect 80% violations when reasoning quantitatively, and smaller, 50% violations when reasoning qualitatively.

At $4\frac{1}{2}$ months of age, however, the infants were unable to predict quantitatively at what point the screen would stop. When only the box behind the screen was present, the infants detected 100% violations (Baillargeon, 1987a) but not 80% or 50% violations. They could reason *that* the screen should stop, and were surprised if it completed its 180° rotation without doing so; but they were unable to predict *at what point* the screen should stop.[2] The 112°, 135°, and 157° stopping points were all

2. An alternative interpretation might be that, like the $6\frac{1}{2}$-month-old infants, the $4\frac{1}{2}$-month-old infants could predict both quantitatively and qualitatively at what point the screen should stop, but that their quantitative reasoning was so poor that it enabled them to detect only the 100% violation. Recall that the screen rotated through all 25 cm of the box in the 100% violation, and through the top 20 cm and 12.5 cm of the box in the 80% and the 50% violation, respectively. Thus, one might propose that infants can initially detect only extreme (25 cm or greater) violations, and gradually improve with age. However, some additional data are inconsistent with this view. In an unpublished experiment, $4\frac{1}{2}$-month-old infants were found to detect a 100% violation in which a box only 12.5 cm high stood behind the screen. Similar results were obtained with $3\frac{1}{2}$-month-old fast habituators (Baillargeon, 1987a). Such findings suggest that young infants use a qualitative strategy to detect 100% violations. Specifically, infants take as their point of reference the apparatus floor and reason that if the screen rotates until it lies flat against the floor, then it rotates farther than it should, given the presence of the box in its path.

High Similarity

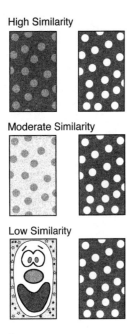

Moderate Similarity

Low Similarity

Figure 25.7
Schematic drawing of the boxes shown to the infants in Baillargeon (1992).

judged to be consistent with the box's height and location. When the second box was placed to the right of and in the same plane as the occluded box, however, the infants had no difficulty predicting qualitatively at that point the screen would stop, and now viewed both the 135° and the 157° stopping points as unacceptable.

Further Developmental Evidence   The experiments described in the last section pointed to important developments in infants' quantitative reasoning. Additional experiments indicated that there might be differences in infants' qualitative reasoning as well. These experiments tested whether $4\frac{1}{2}$- and $6\frac{1}{2}$-month-old infants would still be able to make use of the second box to detect 50% violations if it differed in appearance from the box behind the screen (Baillargeon, 1992). Technically, the superficial similarity of the two boxes is, of course, irrelevant: As long as the boxes are of the same height and are placed in the same plane, one can be used as a reference point for the other.

The infants were assigned to one of three conditions (see Fig. 25.7). The infants in the high-similarity condition saw two red boxes, one decorated with green dots and the other with white dots; the infants in the moderate-similarity condition saw a yellow box with green dots and a red box with white dots; the infants in the low-similarity condition saw a yellow box decorated with a brightly-colored clown face and a red box with white dots (boxes decorated with clown faces were used in all of the rotating screen experiments mentioned in the previous section). The results indicated that (a) the $6\frac{1}{2}$-month-old infants detected the 50% violation in the high- and the moderate- but not the low-similarity condition and (b) the $4\frac{1}{2}$-month-old infants detected the 50% violation in the high- but not the moderate- or the low-similarity conditions.

One possible interpretation for these findings was simply that, as the differences between the boxes increased, the infants became absorbed in the task of comparing

Familiarization Events

Short-rabbit Event

Tall-rabbit Event

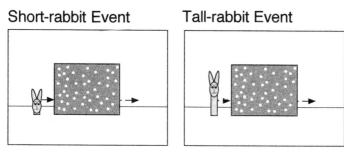

Test Events

Possible Event

Impossible Event

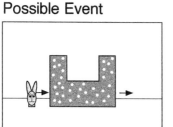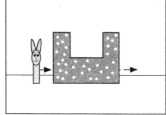

Figure 25.8
Schematic drawing of the events shown to the infants in Baillargeon and Graber (1987).

the two boxes and as a result paid little or no attention to the screen's motion. To address this possibility, an additional group of $6\frac{1}{2}$-month-old infants was tested using the low-similarity condition procedure. For these infants, however, the two boxes stood on either side of the screen throughout the habituation trials. The reasoning was that this prolonged exposure (the infants received a minimum of six and a maximum of nine habituation trials) would give the infants ample opportunity to peruse the two boxes. However, the results of the experiment were again negative: Despite their increased familiarity with the two boxes, the infants still failed to detect the 50% violation.

Two conclusions followed from the results of these experiments. One was that whether the infants used the visible box to predict when the screen would reach the occluded box depended on the perceptual similarity of the two boxes. The other conclusion was that the older the infants the less similarity they needed to make spontaneous use of the visible box. Whereas the $4\frac{1}{2}$-month-old infants used the visible box to predict the screen's stopping point only when it was identical or highly similar to the occluded box, the $6\frac{1}{2}$-month-old infants used the visible box even when it was only moderately similar to the occluded box. These results suggested that, with age, infants become better at dismissing irrelevant differences in objects they use as reference points in solving physical problems. One noteworthy aspect of these results is that they mirror findings from the analogical reasoning literature: Investigators have shown that children and adults are most likely to realize that the solution to a familiar problem may be of help in solving a novel problem when the superficial similarity between the two problems is high (Brown, 1989; D. Gentner and Toupin, 1986; Gick and Holyoak, 1980; Holyoak, Junn, and Billman, 1984; Ross, 1984).

Converging Evidence   The last set of experiments described in this section used a different paradigm than the rotating screen paradigm to gather converging evidence of young infants' ability to represent and to reason about the properties of occluded objects.

The experiments examined the ability of $5\frac{1}{2}$-month-olds (Baillargeon and Graber, 1987) and $3\frac{1}{2}$-month-olds (Baillargeon and DeVos, 1991) to represent and to reason about the height and trajectory of occluded objects. The infants were habituated to an object, such as a toy rabbit, that slid back and forth along a horizontal track whose center was hidden by a screen (see Fig. 25.8). On alternate trials, the infants saw a short or a tall rabbit slide along the track. Following habituation, the midsection of the screen's upper half was removed, creating a large window. The infants saw a possible and an impossible test event. In the possible event, the short rabbit moved back and forth along the track; this rabbit was shorter than the window's lower edge and thus did not appear in the window when passing behind the screen. In the impossible event, the tall rabbit moved back and forth along the track; this rabbit was taller than the window's lower edge and hence should have appeared in the window but did not in fact do so.

The infants looked equally at the short and the tall rabbit habituation events but looked reliably longer at the impossible than at the possible test event, suggesting that they (a) represented the height of each rabbit behind the screen; (b) assumed that each rabbit pursued its trajectory behind the screen; and hence (c) expected the tall rabbit to appear in the screen window and were surprised that it did not. This interpretation was supported by the results of another condition that was identical to the experimental condition with one important exception: Prior to the habituation trials, the infants received two pretest trials in which they saw two short or two tall rabbits standing motionless, one on each side of the windowless habituation screen. Half of the infants saw the two short rabbits in the first trial and the two tall rabbits in the second trial; the other infants saw the rabbits in the opposite order. Unlike the infants in the experimental condition, the infants in this pretest condition looked equally at the impossible and the possible events. One explanation for these results was that the infants were able to use the information presented in the pretest trials to make sense of the impossible event. Specifically, the infants understood that the tall rabbit did not appear in the screen window because it did not in fact travel the distance behind the screen: Instead, one rabbit traveled from the left end of the track to the left edge of the screen and stopped just inside this edge; a second, identical rabbit then emerged from the right edge of the screen and traveled to the right end of the track (see Baillargeon and DeVos, 1991, for a fuller discussion of these results).

How did the infants in the experimental condition determine whether the tall or the short rabbit should appear in the screen window? The most likely answer, we believed, was that the infants visually compared the height of each rabbit, as it approached the screen, to that of the window. Such a direct visual comparison process was of course qualitative, because it did not require the infants to compute estimates of how high each rabbit would extend above the window's lower edge. This account is analogous to that offered in the last section to explain infants' performances in the two-box experiments.

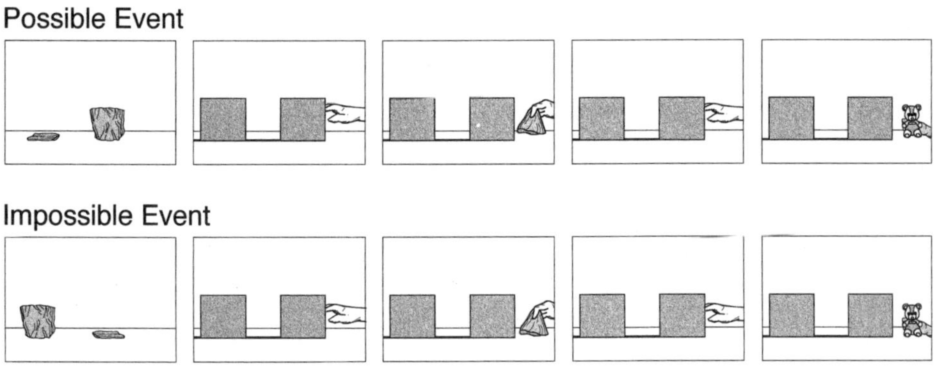

Possible Event

Impossible Event

Figure 25.9
Schematic drawing of the events shown to the infants in Baillargeon and DeVos (1992, Exp. 1).

Three conclusions followed from the present results. First, they confirmed the finding, reported earlier, that $3\frac{1}{2}$-month-old infants represent the existence of occluded objects (Baillargeon, 1987a). Second, the results indicated that infants this age are also able to represent and to reason about some of the physical (height) and spatial (trajectory, location) properties of occluded objects. This finding provided evidence against the hypothesis that the object concept develops in stages, with infants representing first the existence and only later the properties of occluded objects. Finally, the absence of significant differences (Baillargeon and DeVos, 1991) between the responses of the $3\frac{1}{2}$-month-old fast and slow habituators in the experimental condition indicated that both groups of habituators believed that objects continue to exist when out of sight. This finding ruled out one interpretation of the differences obtained in Baillargeon's (1987a) rotating screen experiment, namely, that only the fast habituators preferred the impossible event because only they had attained a notion of object permanence.

2.3. Inferring the Existence and Properties of Occluded Objects
The results reported in the last section indicated that infants represent the properties of occluded objects long before the age of 12 months. This finding suggested that infants might be able to make inferences about occluded objects—the last step in Piaget's (1954) developmental sequence—before 18 months of age. The experiments presented in this section examined infants' ability to infer the existence and the properties of occluded objects.

Existence The first experiment in this series tested 6- and 9-month-old infants' ability to infer the presence of a hidden object from the presence of a protuberance in a soft cloth cover (Baillargeon and DeVos, 1992). The infants were shown a possible and an impossible event (see Fig. 25.9). At the start of each event, the infants saw two covers made of soft pink fabric; one lay flat on the table, and the other showed a large protuberance. Next, two screens were pushed in front of the covers, hiding them from view. A hand then reached behind the right screen and reappeared first with the cover and then with a toy bear of the same height as the protuberance seen earlier. The only difference between the two test events was in the location of the two covers at the start of the trials. In the possible event, the flat cover was behind the left screen and the cover with the protuberance was behind the right screen; in the impossible event, the position of the two covers was reversed.

The results indicated that the 9-month-old infants looked reliably longer at the impossible event, suggesting that they (a) represented the appearance and location of the two covers behind the screens and (b) understood that an object could be retrieved from under the cover with a protuberance but not the flat cover. This interpretation was supported by a control condition in which the hand reached behind the left rather than the right screen so that the bear's position in the impossible and the possible events was reversed.[3]

In contrast to the 9-month-old infants, the 6-month-old infants looked equally at the impossible and the possible events, suggesting that they found it equally plausible for the bear to have been hidden under the cover with a protuberance or the flat cover. This negative result was replicated in another experiment conducted with a simpler procedure. In this experiment, the infants saw a single cover in each test event: the flat cover in the impossible event, and the cover with a protuberance in the possible event. After a few seconds, the cover was hidden by a screen. Next, the hand reached behind the screen and retrieved first the cover and then the toy bear. The infants again looked equally at the impossible and the possible events, suggesting that they believed that the bear could have been hidden under either the flat cover or the cover with a protuberance.

These negative results seemed inconsistent with the results of the first rotating screen task described earlier (Baillargeon, 1987a). In this task, $5\frac{1}{2}$-, $4\frac{1}{2}$-, and even $3\frac{1}{2}$-month-old infants were surprised to see the screen lay flat against the apparatus floor when the box stood behind it. In the present task, 6-month-old infants were *not* surprised to see the bear retrieved from under a cover that lay flat against the apparatus floor. Both tasks called upon the same general physical knowledge: In each case, the infants had to appreciate that objects continue to exist when hidden, and that objects cannot occupy the same space as other objects. Nevertheless, there was one important difference between the two tasks. In the rotating screen task, the infants saw the box and then were asked to predict its effect on the screen. In the present task, however, the infants did not see the bear but had to infer its presence from its effect on the cover. What this analysis suggests is that infants are able to reason about known objects several months before they are able to make inferences about unknown objects. Having formed a representation of an object, infants can use this representation to reason about the object after it has become hidden from view. However, infants cannot make inferences about an unknown object, even when the cues that point to the existence of the object call upon precisely the same knowledge infants would use to reason about a known object. We return to this issue at the end of the next section.

Size   The results described in the last section indicated that, by 9 months of age, infants could use the presence of a protuberance in a soft cloth cover to infer the existence of a object beneath the cover. Our next experiment investigated whether

---

3. These results have implications for explaining infants' perseverative search errors. Piaget (1954), Bower (1974), and others have noted that infants will return to a location, A, for an object they have seen disappear in a location B, *even when* the object creates a large protuberance or emits a sound under the B cover. The present results suggest that by 9 months of age infants have the cognitive ability to use such information to infer where the object is hidden. Why infants do not make this inference is addressed further on.

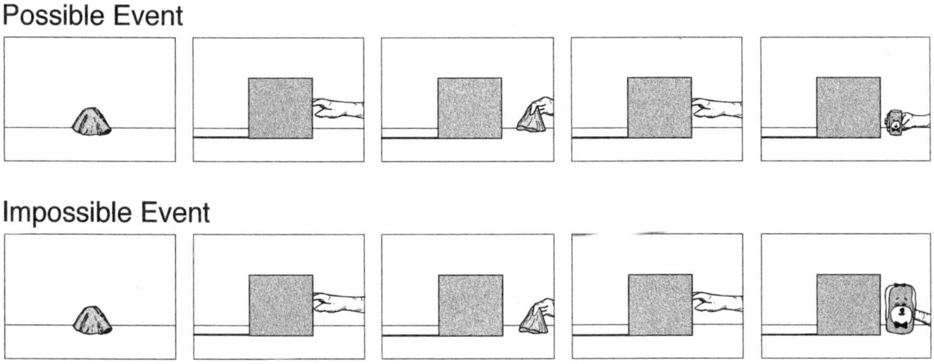

Possible Event

Impossible Event

Figure 25.10
Schematic drawing of the events shown to the infants in Baillargeon and DeVos (1992, Exp. 4).

infants could also use the size of a protuberance in a cloth cover to infer the size of the object beneath the cover (Baillargeon and DeVos, 1992).

In this experiment, $12\frac{1}{2}$- and $13\frac{1}{2}$-month-old infants watched two test events (see Fig. 25.10). At the start of each event, the infants saw a purple cloth cover with a protuberance approximately equal in size to that in the last experiment. Next, a screen was raised in front of the cover, hiding it from view. A hand then reached behind the screen twice in succession, reappearing first with the cover and then with either a small dog of the same size as the protuberance (possible event), or a large dog more than twice as large as the protuberance (impossible event).

The $13\frac{1}{2}$-month-old infants looked reliably longer at the impossible than at the possible event, suggesting that they (a) used the size of the protuberance in the cover to infer the size of the object under the cover, and hence (b) were surprised to see the hand reappear holding the large dog. Support for this interpretation came from a control condition in which a cover with a protuberance as large as the large dog was shown at the beginning of the test events. The infants in this condition looked about equally when the large and the small dogs were retrieved from behind the screen. This finding showed that the infants in the experimental condition looked reliably longer at the impossible event, not because they preferred the large dog, but because they realized that its size was inconsistent with the size of the protuberance shown at the start of the event.

Why did the infants in the control condition look equally when the small and the large dogs were retrieved from under the cover? The most likely explanation, we believed, was that the infants realized that neither event was impossible: Either dog could have been hidden under the cover. Something in addition to the small dog could have been hidden under the cover, such as a doghouse, to give the cover its large protuberance.

In contrast to the $13\frac{1}{2}$-month-old infants, the $12\frac{1}{2}$-month-old infants (in the experimental condition) tended to look equally at the impossible and the possible events, suggesting that they believed that the large or the small dog could have been hidden under the cover. Our next experiment examined whether infants would perform better when provided, as in the two-box rotating screen experiments described earlier (Baillargeon, 1991), with a second, identical cover that remained visible

Possible Event

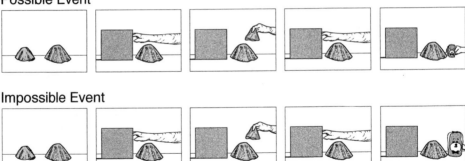

Impossible Event

Figure 25.11
Schematic drawing of the events shown to the infants in Baillargeon and DeVos (1992, Exp. 5).

throughout the experiment (see Figure 25.11). Subjects in the experiment were $12\frac{1}{2}$- and $9\frac{1}{2}$-month-old infants.

The $9\frac{1}{2}$-month-old infants tended to look equally at the two test events. In contrast, the $12\frac{1}{2}$-month-old infants looked reliably longer at the impossible than at the possible event, suggesting that they made use of the visible cover to judge that the small but not the large dog could have been hidden under the cover behind the screen. A control condition supported this interpretation. The infants in this condition were simply shown the hand holding the small or the large dog next to the visible cover, as in the right panels in Fig. 25.11. The infants in this condition looked about equally at the large and the small dog displays. This result provided evidence that the infants in the experimental condition looked longer at the impossible event, not because they preferred seeing the large dog next to the visible cover, but because they detected that this dog was too large to have been hidden under the cover behind the screen.

The $12\frac{1}{2}$-month-old infants in this last experiment clearly made use of the visible cover to determine which dog could have been hidden under the cover behind the screen: They were able to detect, with the help of this second cover, a violation that they failed to detect without it. How did the second cover help the infants' performance? As in the two-box experiments described earlier (Baillargeon, 1991), two answers were possible. One was that the second cover enhanced the infants' quantitative reasoning by providing them with an exact reminder of the size of the hidden cover's protuberance. Armed with this reminder, the infants were then in a better position to compute a quantitative estimate of the size of the object hidden under the cover. The other possibility was that the visible cover enabled the infants to use a qualitative approach to judging which dog could have been hidden under the cover behind the screen, by comparing each dog to the visible cover.

To decide between these two possibilities, an additional group of $12\frac{1}{2}$-month-old infants was tested in a control condition in which the visible cover was placed to the left rather than to the right of the screen. In this condition, the infants still had a reminder of the hidden cover's exact size, but because the dog was retrieved to the right of the screen they could no longer compare in a single glance the visible cover and the small or the large dog. The infants in this condition looked about equally at the two events. This finding provided evidence that the infants in the experimental condition detected that the large dog could not have been hidden under the cover behind the screen by directly comparing the size of the visible cover to that of the small and the large dogs.

The results of these experiments were in many ways strikingly similar to those of the rotating screen experiments discussed earlier (Bailargeon, 1991). Recall that the $6\frac{1}{2}$-month-old infants could predict quantitatively, but the $4\frac{1}{2}$-month-old infants only qualitatively, at what point the screen would reach the occluded box and stop. Similarly, in the present experiments, the $13\frac{1}{2}$-month-old infants could reason quantitatively, but the $12\frac{1}{2}$-month-old infants only qualitatively, about the size of the dog hidden beneath the cover behind the screen.

One explanation for these results is that, as infants become aware of specific variables affecting events' outcomes (e.g., the height and location of the box in the rotating screen task, or the size of the protuberance in the soft cover task), they are able to reason at first qualitatively and only later quantitatively about the effect of these variables. Why development should proceed in this manner is as yet unclear. However, the answer is unlikely to involve infants' memory for quantitative information. Recall that the infants in the rotating screen experiments failed to detect the 50% violation when the visible box was moved slightly forward of the hidden box, just as the $12\frac{1}{2}$-month-old infants in the present experiments failed to realize that the large dog could not have been under the hidden cover when the visible cover was placed to the left of the screen. Providing the infants with a reminder of the hidden object's size and location thus did not improve their performance, suggesting that a faulty memory was not the primary source of their difficulty.

Despite their similarity, the results of the experiments reported in this section differ from the results of the rotating screen experiments in one crucial respect: They involve much older infants. The décalages revealed by these experiments parallel the one discussed in the last section. Recall that infants were found to be able to reason about the existence of a known, hidden object several months before they were able to infer the existence of an unknown hidden object. The present results suggest that infants are also able to reason (qualitatively and quantitatively) about the properties of a known hidden object long before they can infer (qualitatively and quantitatively) the properties of an unknown hidden object. Why are infants very good, from an early age, at reasoning about what they know, but very poor, until late in the first year, at inferring what they don't know? We return to this question in the Conclusion.

Location Piaget (1954) held that infants less than 18 months of age are unable to infer the location of hidden objects because they are unable to infer displacements that occur behind occluders. We have recently begun experiments to examine this claim with infants aged $11\frac{1}{2}$ to $13\frac{1}{2}$ months. These experiments are too preliminary to be described here. The initial results we have obtained, however, tentatively suggest that by the end of the first year infants are already able to infer a hidden object's location. If valid, these results would indicate that Piaget underestimated the age at which infants begin to show evidence of this ability. In addition, the results would again point to a marked décalage between infants' ability to reason about locations and trajectories they have directly witnessed, even after these are hidden from view, and to infer novel locations and trajectories. Recall that in the rolling car experiments reported earlier, 8-, $6\frac{1}{2}$-, and even 4-month-old infants were able to reason about the location of the box and the trajectory of the car behind the screen (Baillargeon, 1986;

Baillargeon and DeVos, 1991). Similarly, in the sliding rabbits experiments, $5\frac{1}{2}$- and $3\frac{1}{2}$-month-old infants were able to reason about each rabbit's trajectory behind the screen (Baillargeon and Graber, 1987; Baillargeon and DeVos, 1991).

Piaget assumed that because young infants could not infer invisible displacements, they did not appreciate that occluded objects obey the same physical laws as visible objects. Although Piaget may have been right in claiming that young infants cannot infer hidden trajectories, there is reason to doubt that young infants do not understand that occluded objects follow the same predictable patterns as visible objects. The infants in the car and the sliding rabbits experiments clearly perceived the car's and the rabbits' displacements behind the screen to be constrained by the same laws that apply to visible displacements. In particular, the infants believed that the car and the rabbits moved along continuous paths behind the screen just as they did on either side of the screen; they understood that the car could not roll through the box in its path; and they assumed that each rabbit retained its height while traveling behind the screen. Such data support the notion that young infants' inability to make inferences about hidden objects stems not from a belief that hidden objects' displacements and interactions with other objects are arbitrary and unpredictable, but from an incapacity to reason without concrete representations of objects and their properties.

3. Why the Discrepancy between Search and Non-search Assessments of Object Permanence?

The experiments reported earlier indicated that infants represent the existence and the location of hidden objects at a very early age. Why, then, do infants fail to search for hidden objects until $7\frac{1}{2}$ to 9 months of age? And why do they search perseveratively when they begin to search for objects? These two questions are considered in turn.

3.1. Why do Young Infants Fail to Search for Hidden Objects?
If infants realize, at $3\frac{1}{2}$ months of age, that objects continue to exist when hidden, why do they fail to search for objects until $7\frac{1}{2}$ to 9 months of age (e.g., Diamond, 1985; Willatts, 1984)? It is not surprising that $3\frac{1}{2}$-month-old infants, whose motor abilities are very limited, do not engage in search activities, but what of older infants? Why do they fail to search of hidden objects?

One possibility is suggested by observations on the development of action in infancy. Researchers (e.g., Diamond, 1988; Piaget, 1952; Willatts, 1989) have noted that it is not until infants are $7\frac{1}{2}$ to 9 months of age that they being to coordinate actions directed at separate objects into means–end sequences. In these sequences, infants apply one action to one object so as to create conditions under which they can apply another action to another object. Examples of such sequences include pulling the near end of a cloth to bring within reach a toy placed on the far end of the cloth, pushing aside a cushion to get a toy visible on the other side of the cushion, or reaching around to the opening of a transparent box to get a toy placed inside the box. Thus, young infants might fail to search for hidden objects simply because this task typically requires them to coordinate separate actions on separate objects (e.g., lifting a cloth to get a toy hidden under the cloth).

Support for this hypothesis comes from reports that infants *do* search for hidden objects when they can find the objects by performing direct, as opposed to means–

end, actions. First, a number of authors (e.g., Bower and Wishart, 1972; Clifton, Rochat, Litovsky, and Perris, 1991; Hood and Willatts, 1986) have found that young infants readily search for objects "hidden" by darkening the room. For example, Hood and Willatts (1986) presented 5-month-old infants with an object on the left or the right side within reaching distance; the infants were restrained from reaching for the object. Next, the room lights were turned off, the object was removed, and the infant's hands were released. Infrared recordings indicated that the infants reached more often to the side where they had seen the object than to the opposite side.

Second, recall Piaget's observation that when young infants hold an object out of sight and accidentally let go of it, they often stretch their arm to recapture it. One of Piaget's protocols involved his son Laurent: "As early as 0;4(6) Laurent searches with his hand for a doll he has just let go. He does not look at what he is doing but extends his arm in the direction toward which it was oriented when the object fell" (Piaget, 1954, p. 23).

Finally, young infants search visually for objects, as when they anticipate objects' reappearance from behind occluders (e.g., Moore, Borton, and Darby, 1978; Piaget, 1954). In a similar vein, we have observed that infants who are shown impossible events involving an object hidden behind a screen sometimes lean to the side and attempt to look behind the screen, as if to verify for themselves the continued presence of the object.

Thus, it appears that young infants do search for hidden objects when they can search without producing means–end sequences, by groping for objects "hidden" by the dark or dropped out of sight, or by peering past or around screens that block their line of vision.

On the strength of this evidence, let us assume that young infants perform poorly on most search tasks because these tasks typically require them to produce means–end sequences. The next question we must address is: Why do infants less than $7\frac{1}{2}$ to 9 months of age have difficulty producing means–end sequences? Two general hypotheses come to mind. One is that infants are unable to *perform* such sequences because of poor motor control; the other is that infants are unable to *plan* such sequences because of limited problem solving ability.

Studies of young infants' actions provide little suport for the first hypothesis. The actions involved in the examples of means–end sequences I have listed (reaching for, grasping, pulling, pushing, lifting, and releasing objects) fall well within the behavioral repertoire of 4- to 7-month-old infants (Bushnell, 1985; Granrud, 1986; von Hofsten, 1980; Newell, Scully, MuDonald, and Baillargeon, 1989; Piaget, 1952, 1954). Furthermore, infants this age seem to have little difficulty performing series of actions in rapid succession. Piaget (1952) described in meticulous and delightful detail how his children, beginning at $3\frac{1}{2}$ months of age, would repeatedly kick, pull, swing, shake, or strike objects suspended from their bassinet hoods, at times systematically varying the speed and vigor of their actions, and at other times playfully intermingling bouts of different actions, such as pulling and shaking or striking and shaking. Such observations are inconsistent with the hypothesis that young infants' failure to produce means–end sequences stems from inadequate motor skills.

The second hypothesis was that young infants are unable to plan means–end sequences because of problem solving difficulties. Before discussing the potential source of these difficulties, let us define a few terms.

Problem solving is frequently described in cognitive psychology in terms of searching a *problem space*, which consists of various states of a problem. The goal pursued by the problem solver is referred to as the *goal state* and the initial situation that faces the problem solver as the *initial state; operators* are actions carried out by the problem solver to generate each successive *intermediate state* on the way to the goal (e.g., Anderson, 1985; Mayer, 1983; Newell and Simon, 1972).

Having established this terminology, we can now consider a typical search problem situation: A young infant watches an experimenter hide an attractive toy under a cover. To what should we attribute the infant's failure to search for the toy? A first possibility is that the infant's goal in the situation differs from what the experimenter has in mind. Instead of seeking to retrieve the toy, the infant may be pursuing a different, unrelated goal. A second possibility is that the infant's representation of the situations' initial state is inaccurate or incomplete, making it impossible for the infant to find a sequence of operators to retrieve the toy. For example, the infant may represent the existence but not the location of the hidden toy.

Neither of these two possibilities is likely, however. With respect to the first possibility, there is ample evidence that young infants reach readily for objects that are "hidden" by the dark (Clifton et al., 1991; Hood and Willatts, 1986), as well as for objects that are only partially visible (Piaget, 1954). Furthermore, young infants are sometimes distressed when desired objects are hidden before them and attempt to grasp the objects as soon as they are even partially uncovered, either by the experimenter's or by their own chance actions (Piaget, 1954). Such observations are inconsistent with the hypothesis that young infants do not search for hidden objects because they have no wish to possess them. With respect to the second possibility, it is difficult, given the results of the experiments I have summarized (e.g., Baillargeon, 1986, 1987a, 1991; Baillargeon and DeVos, 1991; Baillargeon et al., 1985; Hood and Willatts, 1986), to believe that young infants' representation of the initial conditions of search situations could be seriously flawed. The results of these experiments suggest that young infants are able to represent the existence and the location of hidden objects and to reason about these objects in sophisticated, adultlike ways. Such findings are not easily reconciled with the proposal that young infants fail to retrieve objects hidden behind obstacles because their representation of the objects, the obstacles, or the relations between them is deficient.

Young infants' representation of the goal state and initial state of means–end problem situations thus seems unlikely to be responsible for their lack of success in these situations. Another, more likely possibility is that this lack of success reflects difficulties in reasoning about operators—about the actions that are applied to transform the initial state into the goal state. Two general hypotheses can be distinguished. First, it may be that infants perform poorly in means–end situations because their knowledge of the relevant operators is lacking or incomplete. Infants may not be fully aware of the preconditions necessary for the application of an operator, or of the effects of an operator. For example, infants may realize that grasping an object will result in their possession of the object, but not that it will *also* alter the location of the object relative to other objects in the situation. Infants would thus be unable to appreciate why grasping the cover placed over a toy would bring them closer to achieving their goal of recovering the toy; to their minds, grasping the cover would result only in their holding the cover, not in their gaining access to the toy. Second, it may be that infants are unable to select or chain appropriate sequences of operators to achieve their goals, even when the relevant operators and their preconditions and effects are well-known to them.

Experiments were conducted to examine the first of the two hypotheses just mentioned, namely, that young infants are unable to plan means—end search sequences because they lack sufficient knowledge about the operators or actions involved in the sequences (Baillargeon, Graber, DeVos, and Black, 1990). In these experiments, $5\frac{1}{2}$-month-old infants were shown events in which a toy was placed in front of, behind, or under an obstacle. The experiments tested whether the infants could distinguish between actions (performed by an experimenter's hand) that *could* result in the toy's retrieval and actions that could *not*. We reasoned that evidence that the infants could identify correct and incorrect actions for the toy's retrieval would argue against the hypothesis that young infants cannot plan search sequences because their knowledge of the relevant actions is lacking or incomplete.

Our first experiment examined whether $5\frac{1}{2}$-month-old infants are aware that a direct reaching action is sufficient to retrieve a toy placed in front of an obstacle, but is not sufficient to retrieve a toy placed behind (barrier condition) or under (cover condition) an obstacle.

The infants in the barrier condition were shown a possible and an impossible test event (see Fig. 25.12). At the start of each event, the infants saw a toy bird and a barrier standing side by side at the center of a display box. After a few seconds, a screen was pushed in front of the objects, hiding them from view. Next, a hand reached behind the screen's right edge and reappeared holding the bird. The only difference between the two events was in the relative positions of the bird and the barrier at the start of the events. In the possible event, the barrier was on the left and the bird was on the right, directly accessible to the hand; in the impossible event, the bird was on the left and the barrier was on the right, blocking the hand's access to the bird. Prior to the test events, the infants saw familiarization events designed to acquaint them with various facets of the events (see Fig. 25.12).

The events shown to the infants in the cover condition were similar to those in the barrier condition except that the bird and the barrier were replaced by a bear and a clear rigid cover (see Fig. 25.13). In the possible event, the cover was on the left and the bear was on the right, where it could be retrieved by the hand; in the impossible event, the bear was under the cover and should therefore have been inaccessible to the hand.

The results indicated that the infants in the two conditions looked reliably longer at the impossible than at the possible event, suggesting that they (a) represented the existence and the location of the toy (bird, bear) and the obstacle (barrier, cover) behind the screen; (b) realized that the direct reaching action of the hand could result in the retrieval of the toy when it stood in front of, but not behind (barrier condition) or under (cover condition), the obstacle; and therefore (c) were surprised in the impossible event to see the hand reappear from behind the screen holding the toy. Support for this interpretation was provided by pretest trials which showed that the infants in the barrier condition did not prefer seeing the bird behind rather than in front of the barrier, and that the infants in the cover condition did not prefer seeing the bear under as opposed to in front of the cover.

The results of this experiment suggested that, by $5\frac{1}{2}$ months of age, infants are aware that a direct reaching action is insufficient to retrieve an objects placed behind or under an obstacle. Our next experiment examined whether infants this age know what actions *are* sufficient to retrieve an object placed under an obstacle.

The infants again saw a possible and an impossible test event (see Fig. 25.14). At the start of each event, the infants saw two covers placed side by side: On the left

Familiarization Events
Right Familiarization Event

Left Familiarization Event

Test Events
Possible Event

Impossible Event

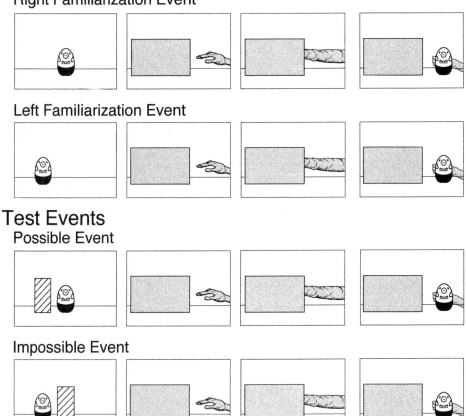

Figure 25.12
Schematic drawing of the events shown to the infants in the barrier condition in Baillargeon et al. (1990, Exp. 1).

was the clear cover used in the first experiment and on the right was a small cage. The toy bear used in the first experiment stood under one of the two covers. After a few seconds, a screen was pushed in front of the objects, hiding them from view. Next, a hand reached behind the screen's right edge and reappeared holding the cage. After depositing the cage on the floor of the apparatus, the hand again reached behind the screen and reappeared holding the bear. The only difference between the two test events was in the location of the bear at the start of the events. In the possible event, the bear was under the cage and hence could be retrieved after the cage was removed. In the impossible event, the bear was under the clear cover and hence should still have been inaccessible to the hand after the cage was removed. Prior to the test events, the infants saw familiarization events designed to acquaint them with different facets of the test situation.

A second group of $5\frac{1}{2}$-month-old infants was tested in a control condition identical to the experimental condition except that the clear cover was replaced by a shallow,

Familiarization Event

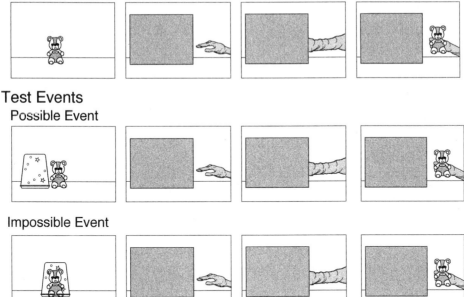

Test Events
Possible Event

Impossible Event

Figure 25.13
Schematic drawing of the events shown to the infants in the cover condition in Baillargeon et al. (1990, Exp. 1).

clear container. The bear's head and upper body protruded above the rim of the container (see Fig. 25.15). In this condition, the bear was always accessible to the hand after the cage was removed.

The infants in the experimental condition looked reliably longer in the impossible than at the possible event, whereas the infants in the control condition tended to look equally at the bear-in-container and the bear-in-cage events. These results indicated that the infants (a) represented the existence and the location of the bear, the cage, and the clear cover or container behind the screen; (b) understood that the hand's sequence of actions was sufficient to retrieve the bear when it stood under the cage or in the container but not when it was placed under the clear cover; and hence (c) were surprised in the impossible event when the hand reappeared holding the bear.

The results of these initial experiments indicated that young infants can readily identify what actions are and what actions are not sufficient to retrieve objects whose access is blocked by obstacles. Would young infants be as successful at reasoning about other means–end problems? To explore this question, we have begun experiments on another means–end sequence infants have been found not to produce until $7\frac{1}{2}$ to 9 months of age, namely, pulling one end of a support to bring within reach an object placed on the opposite end of the support (e.g., Piaget, 1952; Willatts, 1989).

Only one experiment has been completed to date. This experiment tested whether $6\frac{1}{2}$-month-old infants realize that pulling the near end of a support is sufficient to bring within reach an object placed on the far end of the support, but not an object placed next to the support (Baillargeon, DeVos, and Black, 1992). The infants

Familiarization Events
Cage Familiarization Event

Right Familiarization Event

Left Familiarization Event

Test Events
Possible Event

Impossible Event

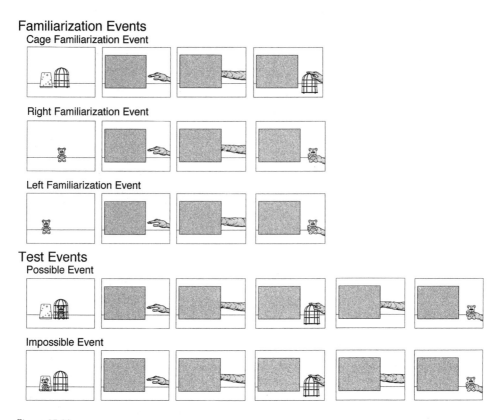

Figure 25.14
Schematic drawing of the events shown to the infants in the experimental condition in Baillargeon et al. (1990, Exp. 2).

watched a possible and an impossible test event (see Fig. 25.16). At the start of each event, the infants saw a rigid support (a long, narrow platform covered with brightly colored paper) lying across the floor of the apparatus, and a small toy bear. After a few seconds, a screen was pushed in front of the objects, hiding them from view. The upper right corner of this screen was missing, creating a small window. Next, a hand reached behind the screen's right edge, took hold of the support's right end, and pulled it until the bear's head became visible in the screen window. The hand then reached behind the screen, grasped the bear, and brought it out from behind the screen. The only difference between the two test events was in the location of the bear at the start of the event. In the possible event, the bear was placed on the left end of the support; in the impossible event, the bear was placed on the floor of the apparatus, to the left of the support.

The infants looked reliably longer at the impossible than at the possible event, suggesting that they (a) represented the existence and the location of the bear and the support behind the screen; (b) understood that pulling the support was sufficient to bring the bear to the window when the bear stood on, but not off, the support; and thus (c) were surprised in the impossible event to see the bear appear in the window. Support for this interpretation was provided by pretest trials that indicated

Familiarization Events
Cage Familiarization Event

Right Familiarization Event

Left Familiarization Event

Test Events
Bear-in-cage Event

Bear-in-container Event

Figure 25.15
Schematic drawing of the events shown to the infants in the control condition in Baillargeon et al. (1990, Exp. 2).

Possible Event

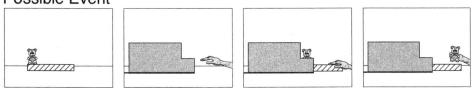

Impossible Event

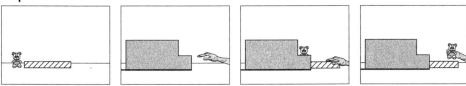

Figure 25.16
Schematic drawing of the events shown to the infants in Baillargeon, DeVos, and Black (1992).

that the infants had no reliable preference for seeing the bear off as opposed to on the support.

The findings of the experiments presented in this section indicate that infants aged $5\frac{1}{2}$ to $6\frac{1}{2}$ months have little difficulty (in some situations, at least) determining what actions can and what actions cannot result in the retrieval of an object placed out of reach beneath a cover or at the far end of a support. Evidence that young infants can readily identify valid means–end sequences argues against the hypothesis that infants fail to plan such sequences because their knowledge of the operators involved in the sequences is inaccurate or incomplete.

To what, then, should one attribute young infants' inability to plan means–end sequences? One possibility, already alluded to, is that young infants are unable to select or chain appropriate operators, even when these are well-known to them. At least two explanations could be advanced for this inability. One is that young infants lack a subgoaling ability—an ability to form sequences of operators such that each operator satisfies a subgoal that brings infants one step closer to their goal. This explanation seems unlikely given that young infants routinely perform what appear to be intentional series of actions directed at single objects. An example of such a goal-directed action sequence might be infants' reaching for and grasping a bottle, bringing it to their mouths, and sucking its nipple. Piaget (1952) described many sequences of this type. Several of his observations involve his children's responses to chains suspended from rattles attached to their bassinet hood. For example, Piaget noted the following: "At 0;3(14) Laurent looks at the rattle at the moment I hang up the chain. He remains immobile for a second. Then he tries to grasp the chain (without looking at it), brushes in with the back of his hand, grasps it but continues to look at the rattle without moving his arms. Then he shakes the chain gently while studying the effect. Afterward he shakes it more and more vigorously. A smile and expression of delight" (p. 163). It is very difficult to imagine how an infant might be capable of such clearly intentional actions and yet lack a subgoaling ability. Laurent's reaching for, grasping, and shaking the chain are all actions performed in the service of his goal, experienced from the start, of shaking the rattle.

A second explanation for young infants' inability to chain operators in means-end sequences is that young infants possess a subgoaling ability but have difficulty with situations in which the performance of the means would put them in apparent conflict with the achievement of their goal. That is, if infants want to grasp a toy placed under a cover, or at the far end of a cover, then grasping the cover puts them in apparent conflict with their goal of grasping the toy. Similarly, reaching around a screen to retrieve an object placed behind the screen may be difficult for infants because it puts them in the position of having to reach away from where they know the object to be.

Exactly why infants have difficulty with these conflict situations is unclear. However, it should be noted that adults often show similar difficulties. Klahr (personal communication, April 16, 1990) has found that naive adults who are given the Tower of Hanoi problem will avoid performing moves that are in apparent conflict with their goal, even though these counterintuitive moves are, in fact, the correct ones. According to this second explanation, then, infants would be in the same position as adults who, when faced with physical problems whose solutions require counter-intuitive actions, find themselves able to *identify* but not to *generate* correct solutions to the problems.

3.2. Why do Infants Search in the Wrong Location for Hidden Objects?
Piaget (1954) attributed infants' perseverative errors in the AB search task to limitations of their object concept. Infants, Piaget maintained, do not conceive of the hidden object as a separate entity whose displacements are regulated by physical laws, but as a thing "at the disposal" of their action: They return to A after watching the experimenter hide the object at B because they believe that by repeating their action at A they will again produce the object.

The results reported in the previous sections argued against Piaget's interpretation of infants' AB errors. These results indicated that infants aged 4 months and older are able to represent and to reason about the location of one or more hidden objects. Further evidence against Piaget's interpretation came from reports that AB errors rarely occur when infants are allowed to search immediately after the object is hidden at B; errors occur only when infants are forced to wait before they search (e.g., Diamond, 1985; Wellman et al., 1987). Furthermore, the older the infants, the longer the delay necessary to produce errors (e.g., Diamond, 1985; Fox, Kagan, and Weiskopf, 1979; Gratch, Appel, Evans, LeCompte, and Wright, 1974; Harris, 1973; Miller, Cohen, and Hill, 1970; Wellman et al., 1987). Thus, according to Diamond's (1985) longitudinal study, the delay needed to elicit AB errors increases at a mean rate of 2 seconds per month, from less than 2 seconds at $7\frac{1}{2}$ months to over 10 seconds by 12 months. There is no obvious way in which Piaget's theory can explain these findings.

In recent years, several interpretations have been proposed for infants' search errors (e.g., Bjork and Cummings, 1984; Diamond, 1985; Harris, 1987, 1989; Kagan, 1974; Schacter, Moscovitch, Tulving, McLachlan, and Freedman, 1986; Sophian and Wellman, 1983; Wellman et al., 1987). One hypothesis is that these errors reflect the limits of infants' recall memory, with increases in the delay infants tolerate without producing errors corresponding to increases in their retention capacity (e.g., Kagan, 1974). There is a long-standing assumption within the field of infant memory (e.g., Bruner, Olver, and Greenfield, 1966; Piaget, 1951, 1952) that recognition memory is present during the first weeks of life, whereas recall memory does not become operative until late in infancy. Investigations of recognition memory using habituation and preferential-looking paradigms have shown that by 5 months of age infants can recognize stimuli after delays of several hours, days, and even weeks (e.g., Fagan, 1970, 1973; Martin, 1975). These data contrast sharply with those obtained with the AB search task and, it would seem, give credence to the notion that recall memory emerges long after recognition memory and is at first exceedingly fragile, lasting at most a few seconds.

There are serious grounds, however, to doubt explanations of infants' search errors in terms of a late-emerging and easily disrupted recall capacity. Meltzoff (1988) recently reported experimental evidence that young infants can recall information after intervals considerably longer than those used in the AB search task. In Meltzoff's study, 9-month-old infants watched an experimenter perform three actions on novel objects; 24 hours later, they were given the same objects to manipulate. The results indicated that half of the infants spontaneously imitated two or more of the actions they had observed on the previous day. This finding (which was supported by findings from control conditions) suggested that by 9 months of age, if not before, infants can recall information after a 24-hour delay.

The hypothesis that infants' perseverative and random search errors reflect the general limits of their recall memory is thus unlively (because infants perform successfully in different circumstances with longer delays), but perhaps this hypothesis could be revised to render it more plausible. One could propose that infants' search errors stem from the absence or the immaturity of a *specific* recall mechanism that is critical for success on the AB task but not on Meltzoff's (1988) delayed imitation task. Comparison of the two tasks suggests several candidate mechanisms. For instance, the AB task requires infants to update the information they have in memory as the object's location is changed; no such updating is needed in Meltzoff's task. A difficulty with this particular candidate, however, is that infants perform well on the AB task with short delays, indicating that they have no trouble updating information.

A more likely candidate for the specific recall mechanism implicated in infants' search errors is an inability to hold updated information in memory. We have just seen that infants have little difficulty updating information, and we know from Meltzoff's data that they can hold information for long delays. Infants' search errors, it might be hypothesized, stem from an inability to correctly perform both of these tasks at once.

In recent years, several versions of this hypothesis have been put forth (e.g., Diamond, 1985; Harris, 1973, 1989; Schacter and Moscovitch, 1983; Sophian and Wellman, 1983; Wellman et al., 1987). For example, one account of infants' AB errors assumes that infants can update information about the object's hiding place but can retain this information only for brief delays because of an extreme sensitivity to proactive interference (e.g., Harris, 1973; Schacter and Moscovitch, 1983). According to this view, as infants grow older, they become able to withstand longer and longer delays before the B representation becomes supplanted by the A representation formed on the previous trial. Another account maintains that both the A and B representations remain available in memory. However, infants rapidly forget or dismiss the fact that the B representation represents the object's *current* location. When deciding whether the object is hidden at A or at B, before engaging in search, infants tend to choose the prior A location because of an inadequate selectivity rule (e.g., Sophian and Wellman, 1983), of a mistaken attempt to infer the object's current location from its prior location (e.g., Wellman et al., 1987), or of an undue reliance on long-term spatial information (e.g., Harris, 1989). In each case it is assumed that infants are more likely to choose the correct B location when there is no delay between hiding and search, and that increasing age, infants choose correctly over increasingly long delays.

Do infants' search errors stem from some deficient recall memory mechanism? A series of experiments were carried out to examine this hypothesis (Baillargeon and Graber, 1988; Baillargeon, DeVos, and Graber, 1989). We reasoned that if infants are unable to update, hold, and selectively attend to information about an object's current location, they should perform poorly in *any* task requiring them to keep track of trial-to-trial changes in an object's location. The task we devised was a nonsearch task (see Fig. 25.17). In this task, 8-month-old infants watched a possible and an impossible test event. At the start of each event, the infants saw an object standing on one of two identical placemats located on either side of the infants' midline. After a few seconds, identical screens were slid in front of the placemats, hiding the object from the infants' view. Next, a human hand, wearing a long silver glove and a bracelet of jingle bells, entered the apparatus through an opening in the right wall and "tiptoed"

Possible Event

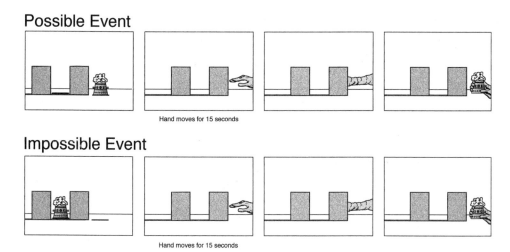

Hand moves for 15 seconds

Impossible Event

Hand moves for 15 seconds

Figure 25.17
Schematic drawing of the events shown to the infants in Baillargeon and Graber (1988).

back and forth in the area between the right wall and the right screen. After frolicking in this fashion for 15 seconds, the hand reached behind the *right* screen and came out holding the object, shaking it gently until the end of the trial. The only difference between the two test events was in the location of the object at the start of the trial. In the possible event, the object stood on the right placemat; in the impossible event, the object stood on the left placemat, and thus should not have been able to be retrieved from behind the right screen. The infants saw the possible and the impossible events on alternate trials (order was, as always, counterbalanced) until they had completed three pairs of test trials.

The results indicated that the infants looked reliably longer at the impossible than at the possible event. Furthermore, the infants showed the same pattern of looking on all three pairs of test trials. In a second experiment, the hand reached behind the *left* screen for the object; the position of the object during the possible (left screen) and the impossible (right screen) events was thus reversed. The infants again looked reliably longer at the impossible than at the possible event, and did so on all three test pairs. Together, the results of these two experiments suggested that the infants (a) registered the object's location at the start of each trial; (b) remembered this location during the 15 seconds the hand tiptoed back and forth; and (c) were surprised to see the object retrieved from behind one screen when they remembered it to be behind the opposite screen.

In our next experiments, we tested 8-month-old infants with delays of 30 and 70 seconds (Baillargeon, DeVos, and Graber, 1989). The infants again looked reliably longer at the impossible than at the possible event, indicating that they remembered the object's location during even the 70-second delay.

The results of these experiments revealed that 8-month-old infants have no difficulty remembering trial-to-trial changes in an object's hiding place after delays of 15, 30, and even 70 seconds. These results contrasted sharply with those obtained with the standard AB task: Investigators have found that 8-month-old infants typically search perseveratively after a 3-second delay (e.g., Butterworth, 1977; Diamond,

1985; Fox et al., 1979; Gratch and Landers, 1971; Wellman et al., 1987). The present results thus cast serious doubts on attempts to explain infants' search errors in terms of a deficient memory mechanism.

To what, then, should one attribute infants' search errors? One possibility (suggested by my husband, Jerry DeJong) is that these errors reflect problem solving difficulties caused by the demands of planning search actions. In order to describe this hypothesis, we must first distinguish between two types of problem solving, which may actually constitute opposite ends of a single continuum. One, *reactive* type corresponds to situations in which solutions are produced immediately, without conscious reasoning. Operators stored in memory and whose conditions of application are satisfied are simply "run off" or executed. An example of such problem solving might be reaching for an object whose location is known or driving home along a familiar route. The second, *planful* type of problem solving corresponds to situations in which solutions are generated through an active reasoning or computation process. An example of this second type of problem solving might be finding an object whose location can be deduced from available cues or planning a trip to a novel location. It is assumed that because the second type of problem solving is effortful, individuals use it only when no other avenues are available, preferring, whenever possible, to rely on previously computed solutions rather than generate new ones. Hence, when a problem situation is perceived to be similar to a previously experienced situation, individuals will attempt to apply the solution computed in the initial situation, thus engaging in reactive as opposed to planful problem solving (see Logan, 1988; Suchman, 1987, for interesting discussions of similar concepts).

To account for infants' performance in the AB search task, we must make two assumption. The first is that, with *short* delays, infants engage in reactive problem solving: they "run off" an already existing operator to retrieve the object on both the A and the B trials. The second assumption is that, with *long* delays, for reasons that are still unclear, infants cannot use the short-delay operator. This leads them to perform differently on the A and the B trials. On the A trial, infants engage in planful problem solving: They compute a solution (i.e., determine where and how to find the object) and store this solution in memory. On the subsequent B trial, instead of recomputing a solution, infants engage in reactive problem solving and simply execute the solution they have just stored in memory, leading to perseverative errors. It is plausible that the overall similarity of the task context in the A and B trials lures infants into thinking "Aha, I know just what to do here!" and into blindly applying what is no longer an appropriate solution.

Two pieces of evidence are consistent with the hypothesis that infants' search errors reflect not memory limitations but deficiencies in problem solving. One such piece is that infants produce perseverative errors in the AB search task even when the object is visible at B instead of being hidden at B (e.g., Bremner and Knowles, 1984; Butterworth, 1977; Nielson, 1982; see Wellman et al., 1987 for review and discussion). This finding creates serious difficulties for memory accounts but is easily explained by the notion that infants, instead of performing a close analysis of the task situation and computing the correct solution, are simply repeating a previously successful solution.

The other piece of evidence concerns data collected with tasks where no demands are made on infants' memory and yet perseverative errors very similar to those obtained in the AB task are found. Two such tasks are the locomotor detour tasks designed by Rieser, Doxsey, McCarrell, and Brooks (1982) and by Lockman and Pick (1984). Rieser et al. (1982) tested 9-month-old infants' ability to use auditory information to select an open as opposed to a blocked route to get to their mothers. Each infant and his or her mother sat on opposite sides of an opaque barrier; a side barrier stood perpendicular to the front barrier on the mother's left or right (the position of the side barrier on each trial was randomly determined). The front barrier was sufficiently high so as to hide both the mother and the side barrier from the infant. At the start of each trial, the mother asked the infant to join her behind the front barrier. The mother's calls were differentially reflected on her left and right sides because one side was open and the other side closed. The results indicated that on the initial trial the infants crawled or walked to the open side to find their mothers, suggesting that they detected the auditory cues that specified the location of the side barrier; on subsequent trials, however, the infants merely repeated the left or right direction of their first response. Lockman and Pick (1984) examined 12-month-old infants' ability to go around a barrier by the shortest route to get to their mothers. Each infant and his or her mother were positioned on opposite sides of one end of an opaque barrier (the left and right ends of the barrier were used on alternate trials). The infant could not step over the barrier but could see the mother above it. Lockman and Pick found that on the initial trial the infants chose the shortest route to go to their mothers; on subsequent trials, however, the infants tended to repeat their first response, going to their mothers via the same side across trials.

The results of these two detour tasks are very similar to those obtained in the AB search task with longer delays. On the initial trial, infants analyze the task situation and compute the correct solution (i.e., determine where to find the object hidden or visible at A, use auditory cues to decide which path to their mother is open and which path is blocked, and select the barrier end that constitutes the shortest route to their mother). On the subsequent B trial, however, instead of reanalyzing the situation and computing a novel solution, infants simply repeat the solution they performed successfully on the previous trial.

The account of infants' perseverative errors in terms of problem solving deficiencies possesses two additional advantages over alternative hypotheses. One is that it contradicts the view that these errors are peculiar responses characteristic of infancy but quite distinct from anything that occurs later in development. On the contrary, it leads us to view infants' perseverative errors on a continuum with or in the same light as errors produced by older subjects in other tasks. A number of tasks have been found in which adults perseverate by using in one context a solution devised or learned in another, superficially similar context. A well-known example of this phenomenon is the Luchins' water jar problem (A. S. Luchins, 1942; A. S. Luchins and E. H. Luchins, 1950; cited in Mayer, 1983). Another example is the "Moses illusion." Adult subjects who are asked, "How many animals of each type did Moses bring on the ark?" usually answer, "Two, a male and a female," without realizing that Moses was mentioned rather than Noah (e.g., Reder and Kusbit, 1991); Ross (1984) provided related evidence.

Children, too, can be lulled by context similarity into producing perseverative responses. An anecdote involving my son Antoine, aged 28 months, illustrates this point well. One morning I asked Antoine to play a guessing game with me; I would describe various objects and he would guess what they were. I said I was thinking of an animal with a very, very long neck, and Antoine correctly guessed a giraffe. I then said I was thinking of something he put on his feet to go outside to keep his toes warm, and Antoine correctly guessed boots. Later that day, I asked Antoine to play our guessing game a second time. I first said I was thinking of an animal with a very, very long neck, and Antoine again correctly guessed a giraffe. My next question was, "I am thinking of something you put on hour head when you go outside to keep your ears warm," and Antoine quickly responded "Boots." Because my son knew the difference between boots and hats and was familiar with both words, I concluded that he had been lulled by the similarity in context to repeat a previously correct but now inappropriate solution. Examples of this type are probably extremely common.

Two points about this anecdote are worth nothing. One is that my son was much quicker, during our second game session, at answering my questions; this is, of course, exactly what one would expect (shorter latencies) if answers are retrieved from memory rather than being computed on the spot. The second is that Antoine did not spontaneously realize he had erred in his answer to the second question. He did not behave as someone who knew full well the correct answer was *hat* but could not inhibit his prior response *boots*. He seemed perfectly satisfied with his answer, and did not change it until I repeated the question to him with appropriate exclamations and emphasis.

In brief, what I am claiming is that infants, like older children and adults, can be lured by overall context similarity into retrieving previously computed responses that changes in the context have rendered inappropriate. The main difference between infants and older subjects, in this account, is that infants are less likely to notice changes, or to integrate changes in the planning of future responses, and so are more prone to perseveration errors. Additional research is needed to specify the conditions under which infants are likely to notice contextual changes and to explain how this set of conditions is modified with age.

The second advantage that the problem-solving deficiency explanation has over alternative accounts of infants' AB errors is that it can be integrated relatively easily with the explanation, discussed in the previous section, of young infants' failure to search for hidden objects. Briefly, it is assumed that infants fail to search because they are unable to plan means–end sequences of actions; and that they search perseveratively, once they begin to search, because they are overly inclined (for reasons that are still unspecified) to rely on previously computed means–end sequences, rather than recompute or replan new ones. Furthermore, in both cases, infants show themselves better able to identify than to generate correct action sequences: as shown earlier, infants identify sequences that can result in the recovery of objects placed under obstacles or at the far end of supports long before they produce these sequences themselves (Baillargeon et al., 1990, 1992); in addition, infants identify context-appropriate searches after delays of 15, 30, and even 70 seconds long before they search correctly with similar delays (Baillargeon and Graber, 1988; Baillargeon et al., 1989).

4. Conclusion

The research summarized in this chapter has implications for at least three areas of infant development: object permanence, physical reasoning, and search. They are discussed in turn.

Object Permanence

When adults see an object occlude another object, they typically assume that the occluded object (a) continues to exist behind the occluding object; (b) retains its physical and spatial properties; and (c) remains subject to physical laws. Piaget (1954) proposed that infants initially do not share adults' beliefs about occlusion events, and adopt these beliefs one by one over the first two years of life.

The findings reported in this chapter clearly contradict Piaget's proposal. Consider the many experiments that obtained positive results with infants aged $3\frac{1}{2}$ to $5\frac{1}{2}$ months: the rotating screen experiments (Baillargeon, 1987a, 1991, 1992; Baillargeon et al., 1985), the rolling car experiments (Baillargeon and DeVos, 1991), the sliding rabbit experiments (Baillargeon and Graber, 1987; Baillargeon and DeVos, 1991), and the searching hand experiments (Baillargeon et al., 1990). The infants in these experiments seemed to have no difficulty representing the existence of one, two, and even three hidden objects. Furthermore, the infants represented many of the properties of the objects, such as their height, location, and trajectory. Finally, the infants expected the objects to behave not in capricious and arbitrary ways but in the same regular and predictable ways as visible objects. In particular, the infants realized that hidden objects, like visible objects, cannot move through the space occupied by other objects and cannot appear at two separate points in space without having traveled from one point to the other.

Thus, it appears that, far from adopting adults' beliefs about occlusion events in a stage-like manner over a protracted period of time, infants possess these beliefs from a very early age. Another way of stating this conclusion is to say that infants' understanding of occlusion events is qualitatively similar to that of older children and adults. This is not to say, of course, that no development remains to take place. Indeed, we saw several instances in which older infants' performance was distinctly better than that of younger infants. However, these differences seem to reflect improvements in infants' physical reasoning abilities, rather than changes in infants' conception of occluded objects.

Physical Reasoning

The research reported in this chapter suggests three hypotheses about the development of infants' physical reasoning. One is that in their first pass at understanding physical events, infants construct general, all-or-none representations that capture the essence of the events but few of the details (e.g., a rotating screen will stop when an obstacle is placed in its path; the presence of a protuberance in a soft cloth cover signals the presence of an object beneath the cover). These initial, core representations are progressively elaborated as infants identify variables that are relevant to the events' outcomes (e.g., the location, height, and compressibility of the obstacles in the path of a rotating screen can be used to determine at what point the screen will stop; the size of the protuberance in a cloth cover can be used to judge the size of the object beneath the cover). Infants incorporate this accrued knowledge into their reasoning, resulting in increasingly accurate predictions over time.

The second hypothesis is that, in reasoning about variables, infants can reason first qualitatively and only after some time quantitatively about the effects of these variables. Recall that the $4\frac{1}{2}$-month-old infants in the rotating screen experiments (Baillargeon, 1991) and the $12\frac{1}{2}$-month-old infants in the soft-cover experiments (Baillargeon and DeVos, 1992) were able to solve the two-box or the two-cover tasks before they were able to detect violations in the one-box or the one-cover task. It does not seem unreasonable that development should proceed in this manner. Indeed, infants' success in generating qualitative solutions to physical problems may facilitate their production of quantitative solutions to the same problems. For example, having determined, by using the visible box, at what point the screen will encounter the occluded box, infants might be in a better position, when the visible box is removed, to compute a quantitative estimate of when the screen should stop.

The foregoing discussion presupposes that infants' approach to learning about physical events—the representation of core events and the progressive identification of pertinent variables—reflects the operation of innate, highly constrained learning mechanisms that direct infants' attention to particular observations and guide the quantitative and qualitative analyses of these observations. The third hypothesis suggested by the present research is that, although infants' approach to learning about the physical world remains the same throughout infancy, which events are understood at which ages depends on a host of developmental factors. These include infants' visual abilities (what cannot be seen cannot be understood) and motoric capacities (some knowledge may arise from manipulations that cannot occur until infants can reach successfully, sit with support, and so on). In addition, there are undoubtedly cognitive factors having to do with the development of infants' memory and representational abilities. With respect to the latter factor, the present research suggests that infants can reason about objects they have seen, even after these objects are hidden from view, long before they can make inferences about hidden objects. The fact that young infants appear limited to physical reasoning based on concrete representations clearly must restrict the range of physical problems they can solve.

The three hypotheses described in this section suggest new directions for research on the development of infants' physical reasoning. How do infants go about forming representations of core events? How do they identify variables that are relevant to these events? How do they devise qualitative and quantitative strategies for reasoning about the effects of these variables? Do infants integrate their representations of events? If yes, how should these networks of representations be described? Finally, what are the sensorimotor and cognitive factors that interact with infants' approach to learning about the physical world to yield the knowledge revealed in the present experiments?

Search

Researchers have identified two distinct stages in the early development of infants' search behavior: Prior to about $7\frac{1}{2}$ months of age, infants do not search for objects they have observed being hidden, and prior to about 12 months of age, infants do search for hidden objects but their performance is fragile and easily disrupted by task factors, such as the introduction of a delay between hiding and retrieval. According to the arguments put forth in this chapter, both of these stages reflect limitations in problem solving. During the first stage, infants are unable to plan means–end sequences, such as search sequences, possibly because the performance of the means (e.g., grasping a cover) places them in an apparent conflict with the achievement of their goal (grasping the toy beneath the cover). During the second stage, infants become able to plan search sequences but are overly inclined, under certain conditions, to repeat previously planned sequences rather than to compute new and context-sensitive sequences. Interestingly, at each stage infants show themselves able to *evaluate* correct sequences even when they cannot *generate* them. Specifically, infants can identify correct sequences for the retrieval of a hidden object long before they spontaneously produce these sequences. Similarly, infants can identify context-appropriate searches after delays of 15, 30, and even 70 seconds long before they produce correct searches at comparable delays.

A salient aspect of the explanations proposed here is that they appeal to problem solving limitations that have already been identified in children and adults. Adults often have difficulty solving physical problems whose solutions depend on moves that are counterintuitive in that they appear to take one farther away from one's goal. Furthermore, adults can be lulled by overall context similarity in applying a previous solution that is no longer appropriate. Finally, in all these instances, adults typically have little difficulty recognizing accurate solutions, even when they have failed to generate them.

The general picture suggested by the present research is, thus, one in which the physical world of infants appears very similar to that of adults: Not only do infants and adults share many of the same beliefs and show many of the same physical reasoning abilities, but these abilities seem limited in the same ways.

Final Remarks
The research presented in this chapter is interesting for three reasons. One is that it yields a picture of infants as budding intuitive physicists, capable of detecting, interpreting, and predicting physical outcomes, which is radically different from the traditional portrayal of young infants as enclosed within a world in which an object is "a mere image which reenters the void as soon as it vanishes, and emerges from it for no objective reason" (Piaget, 1954, p. 11). Another reason is that it suggests several new directions for research on infants' acquisition and representation of physical knowledge and on the manifestation of this knowledge in tasks calling for manual and non-manual responses. The third reason is that, as we discover how infants attain, represent, and use physical knowledge, we come one step closer to understanding the central issue of the origins of human cognition.

Acknowledgments

The research reported in this manuscript was supported by grants from the National Institute of Child Health and Human Development (HD-21104 and HD-05951). I wish to thank Judy Deloache and Carl Granrud for their careful and discerning review of the manuscript, and Jerry DeJong and Joe Malpelli for insightful suggestions about the research.

References

Anderson, J. R. (1985). *Cognitive psychology and its implications* (2nd ed.). New York: Freeman.

Baillargeon, R. (1986). Representing the existence and the location of hidden objects: Object permanence in 6- and 8-month-old infants. *Cognition, 23*, 21–41.

Baillargeon, R. (1987a). Object permanence in 3.5- and 4.5-month-old infants. *Developmental Psychology, 23*, 655–664.

Baillargeon, R. (1987b). Young infants' reasoning about the physical and spatial properties of a hidden object. *Cognitive Development, 2*, 179–200.

Baillargeon, R. (1991). Reasoning about the height and location of a hidden object in 4.5- and 6.5-month-old infants. *Cognition, 38*, 13–42.

Baillargeon, R. (1992). *The role of perceptual similarity in infants' qualitative physical reasoning.* Unpublished manuscript.

Baillargeon, R., and DeVos, J. (1991). Object permanence in young infants: Further evidence. *Child Development, 62,* 1227–1246.

Baillargeon, R., and DeVos, J. (1992). *Qualitative and quantitative inferences about hidden objects in infants.* Manuscript submitted for publication.

Baillargeon, R., DeVos, J., and Black, J. (1992). *Young infants' reasoning abut the use of supports to bring objects within reach.* Unpublished manuscript.

Baillargeon, R., DeVos, J., and Graber, M. (1989). Location memory in 8-month-old infants in a non-search AB task: Further evidence. *Cognitive Development, 4,* 345–367.

Baillargeon, R., and Graber, M. (1987). Where is the rabbit? 5.5-month-old infants' representation of the height of a hidden object. *Cognitive Development, 2,* 375–392.

Baillargeon, R., and Graber, M. (1988). Evidence of location memory in 8-month-old infants. *Cognition, 20,* 191–208.

Baillargeon, R., Graber, M., DeVos, J., and Black, J. (1990). Why do young infants fail to search for hidden objects? *Cognition, 36,* 255–284.

Baillargeon, R., Spelke, E. S., and Wasserman, S. (1985). Object permanence in 5-month-old infants. *Cognition, 20,* 191–208.

Bjork, E. L., and Cummings, E. S. (1984). Infant search errors: Stage of concept development or stage of memory development? *Memory and Cognition, 12,* 1–19.

Bower, T. G. R. (1967). The development of object permanence: Some studies of existence constancy. *Perception and Psychophysics, 2,* 411–418.

Bower, T. G. R. (1972). Object perception in infants. *Perception, 1,* 15–30.

Bower, T. G. R. (1974). *Development in infancy.* Sam Francisco: Freeman.

Bower, T. G. R., Broughton, J. M., and Moore, M. K. (1971). Development of the object concept as manifested in the tracking behavior of infants between 7 and 20 weeks of age. *Journal of Experimental Child Psychology, 11,* 182–193.

Bower, T. G. R., and Wishart, J. D. (1972). The effects of motor skill on object permanence. *Cognition, 1,* 165–172.

Bremner, J. G. (1985). Object tracking and search in infancy: A review of data and a theoretical evaluation. *Developmental Review, 5,* 371–396.

Bremner, J. G., and Knowles, L. S. (1984). Piagetian Stage IV search errors with an object that is directly accessible both visually and manually. *Perception, 13,* 307–314.

Brown, A. L. (1989). Analogical learning and transfer: What develops? In S. Vosniadou and A. Ortony (Eds.), *Similarity and analogical reasoning* (pp. 369–412). London: Cambridge University Press.

Bruner, J. S., Olver, R. R., and Greenfield, P. M. (1966). *Studies in cognitive growth.* New York: Wiley.

Bushnell, E. W. (1985). The decline of visually guided reaching during infancy. *Infant Behavior and Development, 8,* 139–155.

Butterworth, G. E. (1977). Object disappearance and error in Piaget's Stage IV task. *Journal of Experimental Child Psychology, 23,* 391–401.

Carey, S. (1985). *Conceptual change in childhood.* Cambridge, MA: MIT Press.

Chi, M. T. H., Feltovitch, P. J., and Glaser, R. (1981). Categorization and representation of physics problems by experts and novices. *Cognitive Science, 5,* 121–152.

Clement, J. (1982). Students' preconceptions in introductory mechanics. *American Journal of Physics, 50,* 66–71.

Clifton, Rachel K., Rochat, P., Litovsky, R. Y., and Perris, E. E. (1991). Object Representation Guides Infants' Reaching in the Dark. *Journal of Experimental Psychology: Human Perception and Performance, 17,* 323–219.

Diamond, A. (1985). Development of the ability to use recall to guide action, as indicated by infants' performance on AB. *Child Development, 56,* 868–883.

Diamond, A. (1988). Differences between adult and infant cognition: Is the crucial variable presence or absence of language? In L. Weskrantz (Ed.), *Thought without language* (pp. 337–370). Oxford: Oxford University Press.

Fagan, J. F. (1970). Memory in the infant. *Journal of Experimental Child Psychology, 9,* 217–226.

Fagan, J. F. (1973). Infants' delayed recognition memory and forgetting. *Journal of Experimental Child Psychology, 16,* 424–450.

Flavell, J. H. (1985). *Cognitive development* (2nd ed.). Englewood Cliffs, NJ: Prentice-Hall.

Forbus, K. D. (1984). Qualitative process theory. *Artificial Intelligence, 24,* 85–168.

Fox, N., Kagan, J., and Weiskopf, S. (1979). The growth of memory during infancy. *Genetic Psychology monographs, 99*, 91–130.

Gelman, R. (1990). First principles organize attention to and learning about relevant data: Number and the animate–inanimate distinction as examples. *Cognitive Science, 14*, 79–106.

Gentner, D., and Gentner, D. R. (1983). Flowing waters or teeming crowds: Mental models. In D. Gentner and A. Stevens (Eds.), *Mental models* (pp. 99–127). Hillsdale, NJ: Lawrence Erlbaum Associates.

Gentner, D., and Stevens, A. (Eds.). (1983). *Mental models.* Hillsdale, NJ: Lawrence Erlbaum Associates.

Gentner, D., and Toupin, C. (1986). Systematicity and surface similarity in the development of analogy. *Cognitive Science, 10*, 277–300.

Gick, M. L., and Holyoak, K. J. (1980). Analogical problem solving. *Cognitive Psychology, 12*, 306–355.

Goldberg, S. (1976). Visual tracking and existence constancy in 5-month-old infants. *Journal of Experimental Child Psychology, 22*, 478–491.

Granrud, C. E. (1986). Binocular vision and spatial perception in 4- and 5-month-old infants. *Journal of Experimental Psychology: Human Perception and Performance, 12*, 32–49.

Gratch, G. (1975). Recent studies based on Piaget's view of object concept development. In L. B. Cohen and P. Salapatek (Eds.), *Infant perception: From sensation to cognition* (Vol. 2, pp. 51–99). New York: Academic Press.

Gratch, G. (1976). A review of Piagetian infancy research: Object concept development. In W. F. Overton and J. M. Gallagher (Eds.), *Knowledge and development: Advances in research and theory* (pp. 59–91). New York: Plenum.

Gratch, G. (1982). Responses to hidden persons and things by 5-, 9-, and 16-month-old infants in a visual tracking situation. *Developmental Psychology, 18*, 232–237.

Gratch, G., Appel, K. J., Evans, W. F., LeCompte, G. K., and Wright, J. A. (1974). Piaget's Stage IV object concept error: Evidence of forgetting or object conception. *Child Development, 45*, 71–77.

Gratch, G., and Landers, W. (1971). Stage IV of Piaget's theory of infants' object concepts: A longitudinal study. *Child Development, 42*, 359–372.

Harris, P. L. (1973). Perseverative errors in search by young children. *Child Development, 44*, 28–33.

Harris, P. L. (1983). Infant cognition. In M. M. Haith and J. J. Compose (Eds.), *Handbook of child psychology: Infancy and developmental psychobiology* (Vol. 2, pp. 689–782). New York: Wiley.

Harris, P. L. (1987). The development of search. In P. Salapatek and L. B. Cohen (Eds.), *Handbook of infant perception* (Vol. 2, pp. 155–207). New York: Academic Press.

Harris, P. L. (1989). Object permanence in infancy. In A. Slater and J. G. Bremner (Eds.), *Infant development* (pp. 103–121). HIllsdale, NJ: Lawrence Erlbaum Associates.

Hofsten, C. von (1980). Predictive reaching for moving objects by human infants. *Journal of Experimental Child Psychology, 30*, 369–382.

Holyoak, K. J., Junn, E. N., and Billman, D. O. (1984). Development of analogical problem-solving skill. *Child Development, 55*, 2042–2055.

Hood, B., and Willatts, P. (1986). Reaching in the dark to an object's remembered position: Evidence for object permanence in 5-month-old infants. *British Journal of Developmental Psychology, 4*, 57–65.

Kagan, J. (1974). Discrepancy, temperament, and infant distress. In M. Lewis and A. Rosenblum (Eds.), *The origins of fear* (pp. 229–248). New York: Wiley.

Karmiloff-Smith, A., and Inhelder, B. (1975). If you want to get ahead, get a theory. *Cognition, 3*, 195–212.

Keil, F. C. (1990). Constraints on constraints: Surveying the epigenetic landscape. *Cognitive Science, 14*, 135–168.

Larkin, J. H. (1983). The role of problem representation in physics. In D. Gentner and A. Stevens (Eds.), *Mental models* (pp. 75–98). Hillsdale, NJ: Lawrence Erlbaum Associates.

Lockman, J. J., and Pick, H. L. (1984). Problems of scale in spatial development. In C. Sophian (Ed.), *Origins of cognitive skills* (pp. 3–26). Hillsdale, NJ: Lawrence Erlbaum Associates.

Logan, G. D. (1988). Toward an instance theory of automatization. *Psychological Review, 95*, 492–527.

Luchins, A. S. (1942). Mechanization in problem-solving. *Psychological Monographs, 54*(6, Whole No. 248).

Luchins, A. S., and Luchins, E. H. (1950). New experimental attempts at preventing mechanization in problem-solving. *Journal of General Psychology, 42*, 279–297.

Martin, R. M. (1975). Effects of familiar and complex stimuli on infant attention. *Developmental Psychology, 11*, 178–185.

Mayer, R. E. (1983). *Thinking, problem-solving, cognition.* New York: Freeman.

McCloskey, M. (1983). Naive theories of motion. In D. Gentner and A. L. Stevens (Eds.), *Mental models* (pp. 299–324). Hillsdale, NJ: Lawrence Erlbaum Associates.

Meicler, M., and Gratch, G (1980). Do 5-month-olds show object conception in Piaget's sense? *Infant Behavior and Development*, *3*, 265–282.

Meltzoff, A. N. (1988). Infant imitation and memory: Nine-month-olds in immediate and deferred tests. *Child development*, *59*, 219–225.

Miller, D., Cohen, L., and Hill, K. (1970). A methodological investigation of Piaget's theory of object concept development in the sensory-motor period. *Journal of Experimental Child Psychology*, *9*, 59–85.

Moore, M. K., Borton, R., and Darby, B. L. (1978). Visual tracking in young infants: Evidence for object identity or object permanence? *Journal of Experimental Child Psychology*, *25*, 183–198.

Muller, A. A., and Aslin, R. N. (1978). Visual tracking as an index of the object concept. *Infant Behavior and Development*, *1*, 309–319.

Newell, K. M., Scully, D. M., McDonald, P. V., and Baillargeon, R. (1989). Task constraints and infant grip configurations. *Developmental Psychobiology*, *22*, 817–832.

Newell, A., and Simon, H. A. (1972). *Human problem solving*. Englewood Cliffs, NJ: Prentice-Hall.

Nielson, I. (1982). An alternative explanation of the infant's difficulty in the Stage III, IV, and V object-concept task. *Perception*, *11*, 577–588.

Piaget, J. (1951). *Play, dreams, and imitation in childhood*. New York: Norton.

Piaget, J. (1952). *The origins of intelligence in children*. New York: International University Press.

Piaget, J. (1954). *The construction of reality in the child*. New York: Basic Books.

Reder, L. M., and Kusbit, G. W. (1991). Locus of the Moses illusion: Imperfect encoding, retrieval, or match? *Journal of Memory and Language*, *30*, 385–406.

Rieser, J. J., Doxsey, P. A., McCarrell, N. S., and Brooks, P. H. (1982). Wayfinding and toddlers use of information from an aerial view of a maze. *Developmental Psychology*, *18*, 714–720.

Ross, B. H. (1984). Remindings and their effects in learning a cognitive skill. *Cognitive Psychology*, *16*, 371–416.

Schacter, D. L., and Moscovitch, M. (1983). Infants, amnesics, and dissociable memory systems. In M. Moscovitch (Ed.), *Infant memory: Its relation to normal and pathological memory in humans and other animals* (pp. 173–216). New York: Plenum.

Schacter, D. L., Moscovitch, M., Tulving, E., McLachlan, D. R., and Freedman, M. (1986). Mnemonic precedence in amnesic patients: An analogue of the AB error in infants? *Child Development*, *57*, 816–823.

Schubert, R. E. (1983). The infant's search for objects: Alternatives to Piaget's theory of concept development. In L. P. Lipsitt and C. K. Rovee-Collier (Eds.), *Advances in infancy research* (Vol. 2, pp. 137–182). Norwood, NJ: Ablex.

Siegler, R. S. (1978). The origins of scientific reasoning. In R. S. Siegler (Ed.), *Children's thinking: What develops?* Hillsdale, NJ: Lawrence Erlbaum Associates.

Siegler, R. S. (1983). Information processing approaches to cognitive development. In W. Kessen (Ed.), *Handbook of child psychology: History, theory, and methods* (Vol. 1, pp. 129–211). New York: Wiley.

Sophian, C. (1984). Developing search skills in infancy and early childhood. In C. Sophian (Ed.), *Origins of cognitive skills* (pp. 27–56). Hillsdale, NJ: Lawrence Erlbaum Associates.

Sophian, C., and Wellman, H. M. (1983). Selective information use and perservation in the search behavior of infants and young children. *Journal of Experimental Child Psychology*, *35*, 369–390.

Spelke, E. S. (1988). Where perceiving ends and thinking begins: The apprehension of objects in infancy. In A. Yonas (Ed.), *Minnesota symposia on child psychology: Vol. 20. Perceptual development in infancy* (pp. 197–234). Hillsdale, NJ: Lawrence Erlbaum Associates.

Suchman, L. A. (1987). *Plans and situated actions: The problem of human-machine interaction*. Cambridge: Cambridge University Press.

Vosniadou, S., and Brewer, W. F. (1989). A cross-cultural investigation of children's conceptions about the earth, the sun, and the moon: Greek and American data. In H. Mandl, E. DeCorte, N. Bennett, and H. F. Friedrich (Eds.), *Learning and instruction: European research in an international context* (Vol. 2.2, pp. 605–629) Oxford: Pergamon.

Wellman, H. M. (1990). *The child's theory of mind*. Cambridge, MA: Bradford Books/MIT Press.

Wellman, H. M., Cross, D., and Bartsch, K. (1987). Infant search and object permanence: A meta-analysis of the A-not-B error. *Monographs of the Society for Research in Child Development*, *51*(3, Serial No. 214).

Willatts, P. (1984). Stages in the development of intentional search by young infants. *Developmental Psychology*, *20*, 389–396.

Willatts, P. (1989). Development of problem-solving in infancy. In A. Slater and J. G. Bremner (Eds.), *Infant development* (pp. 143–182). Hillsdale, NJ: Lawrence Erlbaum Associates.

Wiser, M., and Carey, S. (1983). When heat and temperature were one. In D. Gentner & A. L. Stevens (Eds.), *Mental models* (pp. 267–297). Hillsdale, NJ: Lawrence Erlbaum Associates.

Chapter 26

Insides and Essences: Early Understandings of the Non-obvious

Susan A. Gelman and Henry M. Wellman

Introduction

In many ways adult cognition involves disregarding external appearances and instead penetrating to underlying realities, seeking deeper levels of analysis, and grasping (or inventing) non-obvious essences. This happens in everyday thought when we explain overt behaviors psychologically (by appealing to mental states, personality traits, and internal dynamics), when we categorize living kinds, such as mammals and birds, on the basis of non-obvious features (by appealing to their reproductive, genetic, and kinship relations), and when we go beyond observational appearances in countless other domains (acknowledging that the earth circles the sun, not vice versa, that fake diamonds are just glass, and so on). Attention to underlying, non-obvious realities also characterizes experts' knowledge in a broad range of fields, including scientific theories, map making, medical diagnosis, and impressionist art. Indeed, imagine the phenomenal world of an organism that regarded only external appearances—for example, an organism who understood people behavioristically, believed glass chips were diamonds, understood maps as merely decorated paper, or regarded having measles as nothing more than wearing red spots.

One traditional and powerful view of young children, articulated in detail by Piaget (1951) and others, is that young children are remarkably like this hypothetical organism. They are, in other words, externalists. More precisely, children are described as incapable of reasoning about a broad cluster of understandings. On this view, until roughly age 6 or 7 children are artificialistic, assuming that natural or mechanical events are caused by people rather than by intrinsic or internal mechanisms (Piaget, 1929). They are thought to have difficulty reasoning about what they cannot see, such as internal mechanisms of the human body (Carey, 1985; Gellert, 1962); dreams, thoughts, and other mental states (Piaget, 1929); or non-obvious concepts that conflict with surface perceptions (Bruner, Olver, and Greenfield, 1967). This child-as-externalist position suggests that a wide range of inabilities or conceptual confusions are interrelated and follow from the tendency to focus on the observable to the exclusion of other properties.

More recently, a number of findings in a variety of domains challenge this view, suggesting that children attend to non-obvious aspects of things well before school

This research was supported in part by NICHD grant HD-23378 and a Spencer Fellowship to S. Gelman and NICHD grant HD-22149 to H. Wellman. We are grateful to Catherine Givens for her assistance in Studies 1 and 2, and to Rebecca Stein and Michelle Wecksler for their assistance in Studies 3 and 5. We thank Grant Gutheil for helpful comments and for conducting Study 4, and two anonymous reviewers for suggestions on an earlier manuscript. We also gratefully acknowledge the children, teachers, and staff of the following schools for their participation: Ann Arbor "Y", Gretchen's House, St. Luke's Day Nursery, and University of Michigan Children's Centers.

age (see Wellman and Gelman, 1988, for review). For example, by 3 of 4 years of age children have a sensible understanding of the mind (Astington, Harris, and Olson, 1988; Wellman, 1990), of the appearance–reality distinction (Flavell, Flavell, and Green, 1983), and of the importance of non-obvious properties for reasoning about categories (Gelman and Markman, 1986; Gelman and O'Reilly, 1988). It has further been suggested that such understandings may serve as a mechanism for cognitive growth.

In the present paper we examine children's understanding of the non-obvious, looking closely at children's beliefs concerning two inherently non-obvious aspects of things: insides and essences. Our goal is twofold: first, to provide further evidence that the externalist view mischaracterizes young children's cognition; and second, to articulate more precisely what kinds of knowledge young children do have.

Insides and Essences

Concepts of insides and essences represent two distinct yet related understandings. Both insides and essences typically contrast with the outer appearance of an object. The insides of an item are the matter residing physically behind or under its outer layer (e.g., the bones, heart, and blood of a dog; the stuffing and wires of a chair). Insides are concrete and ultimately observable, yet typically remain unobserved. An essence is the unique, typically hidden property of an object that makes it what it is, without which it would have a different identity (e.g., the chemical composition of water, the DNA structure of an elephant).[1] Essences generally are never observed, and in fact may remain unknown (consider, for example, the essence of life, or the essential nature of humans). Locke (1894/1959) characterized essences this way: "Essence may be taken for the very being of anything, whereby it is what it is. And thus the real internal, but generally (in substances) unknown constitution of things, whereon their discoverable qualities depend may be called their essence" (p. 26).

Both insides and essences are difficult to define precisely. Do a dog's insides begin under the fur, under the skin, under the flesh, or indeed even interior to the skeletal framework? More troubling still, essences are typically unknown; those insensible parts or cores that enable or cause the sensible qualities of an object. Essences are often unspecifiable, and by their nature require an inference about some deeper organization or disposition. Nevertheless, adults certainly understand that objects have insides and outsides and can distinguish the two. Similarly, adults often distinguish essences from appearances and seem to believe that many objects have an essence. Medin and Ortony (1989), for example, suggest that adults "act as if their concepts contain essence placeholders" (p. 186)—they believe that things have an underlying reality or true nature that cannot be observed directly. For some objects, one kind of essence may be an internal part or substance (e.g., DNA structure); for other objects the essence may differ or remain unknown.

Although clearly different, insides and essences have a special affinity. On the one hand, for many objects insides are more essential to their identity or functioning than are outer appearances. On the other hand, many purported essences, such as the genetic code of an animal and the chemical structure of elements, are internal or

---

1. We are not making a metaphysical claim about the true existence of essences in the world. Rather, we are referring to "psychological essentialism" (Medin and Ortony, 1989), or people's *beliefs* that things have essences.

compositional in nature and so neither ʼexternal nor perceptible. Nonetheless, insides are not synonymous with essences; essential similarities may also take the form of behaviors, functions, parentage, psychological make-up, or even intangible qualities (e.g., a soul).

The inside–outside distinction seems a particularly promising vehicle for studying children's emerging ideas of the non-obvious. Internal parts (e.g., the seeds of an apple, the heart of a dog) are concretely present in everyday objects although intrinsically less obvious than outer surfaces. Children's grasp of the inside–outside distinction could be a stepping-stone to understanding a variety of non-obvious properties more generally. The insides of an object are often critical for its proper functioning (the spring of a watch) or for its appropriate use (the white and yolk of an egg). Even young children may grasp that internal parts of features can be more essential than outer coverings. Studies 1 and 2 focus on children's understanding of insides.

At first glance, essences would seem a more difficult concept than insides for children to grasp. Precise specification of a category essence certainly implies complex theoretical constructions. For example, an understanding of chemistry is required to realize that the essence of water is H_2O; an understanding of biology is required to posit that the essence of a tiger is its genetic structure. Nonetheless, as mentioned earlier, belief in some unspecified category essence may be frequent in adults and is possible even without such precise, scientific knowledge. Psychological essentialism—the psychological *belief* that certain kinds of objects or substances have something like a constitutive yet unknown essence—could thus also make an early developmental appearance. If it did, then such a belief could have important implications for children's subsequent knowledge acquisition and categorization. Studies 3, 4, and 5 of the present paper are designed to determine if and when children also hold the belief that categories encompass hidden essences.

1. Study 1: The Inside–Outside Distinction

Recent work demonstrates that children are somewhat knowledgeable about the insides of familiar objects by age 3 years. If asked to report the contents of various objects they offer different answers for animate and inanimate things, typically reporting that animates have blood, bones, and internal organs (such as hearts or muscles), whereas inanimates have either nothing or have material such as cotton, paper, hair, or "hard stuff" (Gelman, 1987). By age 4 years children assume that members of a particular category are likely to have the same internal parts and substance as one another, claiming for example that all dogs have "the same kinds of stuff inside" (Gelman and O'Reilly, 1988).

Although these demonstrations are informative, they provide only a preliminary picture of children's abilities. In particular, little work has examined whether children explicitly distinguish insides from outsides, and particularly whether they realize that insides can conflict with outer appearances. A critical component to understanding insides is to realize explicitly that they may differ from outsides.

Understanding this "inside–outside distinction," as we will refer to it, seems analogous to understanding the appearance–reality distinction. Even an organism that consistently apprehends reality faces grave difficulties if it confuses reality with appearance, or vice versa (cf. Flavell et al., 1983). When reasoning about the appearance–reality distinction, focusing exclusively on reality is an error referred to as "intellectual realism" (e.g., reporting that a sponge painted to resemble a rock not only *is* a sponge but also *looks like* a sponge). It is only when one can report that appearance and reality differ (e.g., "It's a sponge, but it looks like a rock") that one has a firm understanding of the distinction.

The only previous research shedding light on children's grasp of the inside–outside distinction was conducted by Gelman (1987). She asked 3-, 4-, and 5-year-old children to describe both the insides and outsides of a range of animate and inanimate objects. She found that for animate things, subjects typically described insides and outsides differently (e.g., saying "skin" for the outside of an animal but "bones" for its inside).

In Study 1 we investigate children's understanding of the inside–outside distinction more directly. It is possible, for example, that in a task like R. Gelman's children simply respond to the inside and outside questions with common associates, without comparing these two levels directly. Therefore, in Study 1 we included sets of pictures in which appearances and internal properties were placed in direct conflict with one another (e.g., children had to reason about triads of pictures representing an orange, a very similar-looking orange balloon, and a lemon). These items can reveal whether children are capable of reflecting on both outer appearances and internal properties in the same task. Rather than simply describe the insides and outsides of objects taken one at a time, children were asked to match up two objects at a time in terms of either appearances or insides. In order to answer correctly about insides, children had to select two items that looked very different on the outside as having the same insides (e.g., they had to select the orange and the lemon as having the same insides, even though the orange much more clearly resembled the orange balloon).

Method

Subjects   Twenty-three 3-year-olds (3;2 to 4;2, mean age 3;9) and 24 4-year-olds (4;4 to 5;2, mean age 4;8) participated. One additional 3-year-old was tested but did not complete the session. In addition, 10 adults participated in a pretest of the items (see below).

Items   Each child saw the six sets of items listed in Table 26.1. For each set, children saw three pictures at a time, consisting of one target picture and two comparison

Table 26.1
Items used in Study 1

Target	Same appearance	Same insides
Pig	piggy bank	cow
Hound dog	stuffed dog	sheep dog
Orange	balloon	lemon
Almond nut	rock	peanut
Glass of milk	glass of orange juice	carton of milk
Bowl of cereal	bowl of soup	box of cereal

pictures. The sets were constructed so that appearances and category membership conflict. For example, on one item children saw a pig (target picture), a piggy band, and a cow. The pig and the piggy bank look very similar, whereas the pig and the cow are both animals. As can be seen in Table 26.1, the target items were chosen to include two animals, two inanimate natural kinds (e.g., orange, nut), and two inanimate containers. All pictures were color photographs or realistic color drawings.

Adult Pretest   The purpose of the pretest was to validate that the pairs of pictures selected to be perceptually similar were indeed viewed that way, at least by naive adults. Adults saw each of the six triads, one at a time, with the three pictures arranged in a triangle. For each triad they were asked to choose the two pictures that "looked most similar." Performance was consistent with our predictions 90% of the time, which greatly exceeds chance performance of 33%, $t(9) = 703.0$, $p < .0001$.

Procedure   Children were tested individually in a small room apart from their regular classroom. The session began with a brief warm-up designed to clarity the task and remind children to think about both insides and outsides. In this warm-up children saw a pitcher of water with a handle and were asked whether the handle was inside or outside of the pitcher, and whether the water was inside of outside of the pitcher. On rare occasions when a child answered one of these questions incorrectly, he or she was corrected and asked the questions again. All children answered correctly at this point.

The experimental session included a series of eight questions asked of each triad. The two focal questions required the child to match the target with one of the two comparison pictures: (1) Which comparison picture *looks most like* the target? (e.g., "Which of these looks most like the pig, the piggy bank or the cow?"); and (2) Which comparison picture *has the same kinds of insides as* the target? (e.g., "Which of these has the same kinds of insides as the pig, the piggy band or the cow?"). Half the children were always asked the "looks like" question first; half were always asked the "insides" question first. In between the two focal questions, the "looks like" question and the "insides" question, children were asked to describe the insides and outsides of each picture in each triad (i.e., what do a pig, a piggy bank, and a cow "have inside" and "have outside").

Results
Each of children's choices on the focal "looks like" and "insides" questions were coded as either correct or incorrect , yielding a total score ranging from 0 to 6 per question, or 0 to 12 across both questions. When responses to both questions were combined to yield a single score (out of 12), children performed significantly above chance (a score of 6, or 50%) at both ages (3-year-olds: $M = 6.96$, $t(22) = 4.70$, $p < .0001$; 4-year-olds: $M = 8.80$, $t(23) = 5.94$, $p < .0001$).

We then coded the number of same-category responses given to each question at each age (e.g., responses claiming that the pig and the cow—rather than the pig and the piggy bank—looked most alike or had the same insides). The results are shown in Table 26.2. The data were analyzed by a 2 (age: 3 years, 4 years) ×2 (question type: looks like, insides) repeated-measures analysis of variance. There was a significant main effect for question type, $F(1, 45) = 51.95$, $p < .0001$, as well as a question type by age interaction, $F(1, 45) = 12.45$, $p < .001$. These results indicate that overall children at both ages appropriately distinguished between insides and looks like

Table 26.2
Study 1, mean number of same-category responses by age and question type (out of 6 total)

	Inside	Looks like
Age 3	3.61*	2.65[a]
Age 4	4.17*	1.37**[a]

* Significantly different from chance, $p < .01$
** Significantly different from chance, $p < .0001$
[a] The difference between responses to the inside the looks-like questions was significant at $p < .05$

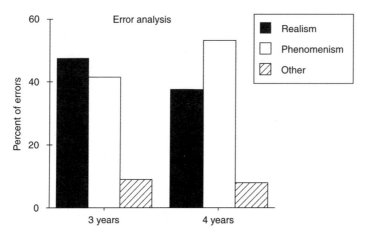

Figure 26.1
Mean percentage of realism, phenomenism, and other errors in Study 1.

probes, but the distinction became clearer with age. There were no other significant effects.

Of particular interest in this study were children's errors. We classified them into three types, based on Flavell et al.'s (1983) work on the appearance–reality distinction. First, there were errors in which children relied too much on appearances, or "phenomenism" errors. Here, children said that objects that looked alike also had the same insides (e.g., the pig and the piggy bank). Second, there were errors in which children relied too much on category membership, or "realism" errors. Here, children said that the objects that had the same insides actually looked alike (e.g., the pig and the cow). Finally, children could show uninterpretable errors—answering incorrectly on both the insides and looks-like questions. As shown in Figure 26.1, children showed as many realism errors as phenomenism errors. In other words, children's errors did not result from simply focusing on perceptual similarity. Note that some of children's errors (particularly phenomenism errors) would be very reasonable to make if children lack particular knowledge about the objects in question. (For example, a child who does not know what is inside a piggy bank may assume that pigs and piggy banks are internally similar.) Thus, children's above-chance performance and their failure to give overwhelming numbers of phenomenism errors are all the more impressive.

Table 26.3
Study 1, mean number of trials (out of 6 possible) on which subjects reported that the insides differed, as a function of pair type and age

Comparison type	(Age)	
	3 years	4 years
Insides for different-insides pair	4.22	5.46
Insides for same insides pair	2.04	2.25
Insides vs. outsides for target object	5.65	5.71

Descriptions of Insides and Outsides   Children's descriptions of the insides and outsides of each picture were transcribed. For each triplet, we coded (1) whether the insides attributed to the two different kinds of things (e.g., pig and piggy bank) were different, (2) whether the insides attributed to the two things of the same kind (e.g., pig and cow) were different, and (3) whether the insides attributed to each target item (e.g., bones for the insides of the pig) were different than the outsides attributed to that item (e.g., skin for the outside of the pig). In order for the descriptions to count as different, subjects had to supply two distinct and specific descriptions. We did not include in this tally any trials on which subjects said that they did not know what was inside or outside. A second person independently coded almost 20% of the items and agreed with the first coder on 90% of these decisions.

The purpose of this analysis was to provide converging evidence for the claim that children distinguish insides from outsides. Do children realize that the insides of objects can differ even when their surface appearances are strikingly similar, and that the insides and outsides of the same item differ? In one sense this is an easier task than the judgment task reported earlier, because children were asked to consider only one object at a time. The present task can provide additional useful information, however, because children were required to name particular internal contents. Whereas the judgment data tap children's knowledge *that* the insides differ, the descriptions can provide insight into their beliefs about *how* the insides differ.

Table 26.3 presents the mean number of trials (out of 6 possible) on which children reported that: (1) the insides differed, for the different-insides pairs; (2) the insides differed, for the same-insides pairs; and (3) the insides differed from the outsides, for the target items. These data were analyzed by means of a 2 (age: 3 years, 4 years) $\times$ 3 (comparison: insides different (insides-different pairs), insides different (insides-same pairs), insides versus outsides different (target items)) ANOVA. There was a main effect for age, $F(1, 45) = 6.80$, $p < .02$, a main effect for comparison type, $F(2, 90) = 187.16$, $p < .00001$, and an age by comparison type interaction, $F(2, 90) = 5.72$, $p < .005$. At both ages, children's description of the insides of a single object typically differed from their descriptions of the outsides of that object. Moreover, their descriptions were much more likely to differ when describing the insides of different kinds of things (e.g., pig and piggy bank) than when describing the insides of the same kind of thing (e.g., pig and cow). Finally, this last effect was slightly more pronounced in the older children.

One way of comparing these results to those from the judgment task is to say that the pictures that looked alike were typically described as having different insides.

Children readily overlooked misleading perceptual information when describing the insides.

It is important to note in this analysis that children did not have to be accurate in order to appreciate differences appropriately. For example, a child could say that an orange balloon has orange air inside and an orange has orange juice inside, or that an orange has orange skin outside and orange babies inside, and still be credited with appropriately reporting that insides are different in these cases. Indeed many incorrect responses occurred (e.g., rocks have nothing inside, peanuts have skin outside, a stuffed dog has blood but no bones inside, a soup bowl has tiny bowls inside, a balloon has little balloons inside) and many uninformative ones occurred as well (lemons have lemony stuff outside, piggy banks have colors outside, *everything* has skin outside, a stuffed dog has stuff inside). These sorts of inaccuracies are important for demonstrating that children do not require knowledge of particular insides in order to appreciate a general inside–outside distinction.

Indeed, a fully knowledgeable and precise responder might report that even those items that are "the same kinds of things" do *not* have the same kinds of insides. For example, although pigs and cows are alike inside at a general level (both having blood and bones), they differ in the details of their physiology and anatomy (e.g., cows but not pigs have multiple stomachs). Accordingly, children's successful performance on this task does not require having detailed domain-specific knowledge and reflects instead a more general appreciation of hidden similarities and differences.

Discussion

Altogether, there are two main findings from Study 1. First, children at both ages accurately distinguished insides from outsides, even though the task required them to consider both perspectives at once. In order to answer correctly subjects had to choose two items as having the same insides which, on a different part of the task, they judged as *not* looking alike. The second finding is that the children had some difficulty ignoring appearances to assess insides, particularly at age 3. Importantly, however, they also had some difficulty ignoring the insides to assess appearances. That is, when children made errors they showed no bias toward focusing on appearances; realism and phenomenism errors were equal even for 3-year-olds. What improves with age in this study is an ability to deal with conflict between insides and outer appearances, not a shift toward understanding insides at all. Young children readily attended to non-obvious internal similarities even though they conflicted with surface appearances.

2. Study 2: Are Insides Essential?

For adults an important aspect of understanding the inside–outside distinction is the realization that internal parts sometimes have a privileged status: they can be essential for defining an object or for its continued functioning. At the very least, insides can be relatively more essential than outer surfaces. Recent studies by Keil (1989) suggest that children may not have this appreciation till early elementary school age. His method was to describe an object that changed in outer appearance only, and to ask whether that change constituted a change in kind. For example, a skunk was altered, through surgery and dye, to look like a raccoon while its insides remained unchanged. Preschoolers tended to report that the creature was now a raccoon; second graders reported that the animal was a skunk that only looked like a raccoon.

Keil's studies are valuable for demonstrating that, with development, children become better able to focus on less obvious properties for judging identity. That is, success on Keil's task certainly seems to require an understanding of the importance of non-obvious insides, and as they get older children perform increasingly well on the task. However, failure on the task cannot be taken as demonstrating a clear lack of understanding, because the procedure does not seem sensitive for uncovering the abilities of the youngest age group.

One potential problem with the task concerns its reliance on questions about identity, and the relation of different criteria for determining identity. Both insides and outsides can figure into an object's identification and even into its conventionally agreed-upon identity, and it is often not clear how to resolve cases of discrepancy. For example, is a person who undergoes a convincing sex-change operation now a man, a woman, or some third kind of person? More generally, questions of identity (particularly borderline cases, such as the ship of Theseus; see Millikan, 1984) pose knotty philosophical conundrums that often have no clear intuitive (or psychological) solution. Insides can be *essential* to an object's identity without being the only relevant quality. Young children might know this and still fail Keil's task.

A related concern is that it seems more difficult to judge which of two identities (raccoon or skunk) applies after changes have been made, than to determine that such changes *influence* identity. It would be informative therefore to question children about items that posed less of an identity choice, for example to include animals in which the outsides were altered in such a way that they did not resemble another known species (e.g., a dog with no fur) and to ask *whether* identity was changed rather than *what* the identity was.

Note in addition that Keil's research failed to include items in which the animal's insides were altered but the outsides remained the same (e.g., a dog with no blood or bones). This comparison could be crucial for gauging the relative importance of insides versus outsides for the young child. It is possible that children believe that any kind of change affects an object's identity, but that changing the insides is more important than changing the outsides.

Method
Subjects   Children of two age groups participated: 17 4-year-olds (4;5 to 4;11, mean age 4;7) and 14 5-year-olds (5;0 to 6;2, mean age 5;7). There were approximately equal numbers of girls and boys at each age. An additional two children (one at each age) were tested but completed only half the task, and so were not included in these analyses.

Items and Questions   There were two kinds of test items: *insides-relevant* and *insides-irrelevant*. The insides-relevant items were ones for which the insides are critical to the identity and continued functioning of the object. Insides are not essential for all objects, so we selected items that would be clear-cut examples for adults. These included two animals (turtle, dog), two inanimate natural kinds (banana, egg), and three artifacts (book, pencil, car). As an example, the insides (yolk and white) of an egg are more critical than the shell for ordinary use of the item (e.g., cooking) or for its ordinary identification (without yolk and white it's "just a shell" rather than an egg). The insides-irrelevant items served as contrasts and included three containers (jar, toy box, and refrigerator), for which the insides (e.g., the jam in the jar) do not affect the object's identity and continued functioning. A realistic color drawing was used for each item.

We asked questions about both the insides and outsides of both the insides-relevant and insides-irrelevant items. In this, we proposed to the child three sorts of transformations and then asked the child whether each transformation of the item would change its identity and also an aspect of its ordinary functioning. More specifically, for each object children were asked to consider the following:

(a) *Inside removal* ("What if you take out the stuff inside of the dog, you know, the blood and bones and things like that and got rid of it and all you have left are the outsides?").

(b) *Outside removal* ("What if you take off the stuff outside of the dog, you know, the fur and got rid of it and all you have left are the insides?").

(c) *Movement* (e.g., "What if the dog stands up?"). This transformation served as a control to determine whether children have a bias to report that any change will result in a change of identity, given our task. If children have such a bias then the movement transformation can provide a baseline of correct responding against which to compare children's responses from the inside and outside removal questions.

All transformations are listed in Table 26.4. Following each transformation, children were asked two questions, always in the same order. One question concerned the identity of the transformed object (e.g., "Is it still a dog?"); a second concerned how the transformed object would function (e.g., "Can it still bark and eat dog food?").

Table 26.4
Items and transformations used in Study 2

Item	Insides removal	Outsides removal	Movement
Insides-relevant			
turtle	blood	shell	put in box
dog	blood and bones	fur	stands up
egg	runny stuff	egg shell	roll on table
banana	white part	peel	turn upside-down
car	motor	paint	turn around
book	pages	cover	turn over
pencil	black stuff (lead in middle)	paint	drop on table
Containers			
jar	food	label (paper with writing)	put in box
toy box	toys and games	paint	drag across room
refrigerator	food and shelves	paint	move to other side of kitchen

Note in Table 26.4 that for the outsides removal we took off only the outermost veneer of the object (e.g., paint, fur). We did this because we wanted to propose clear contrasts between the object's insides and outsides. If we had proposed taking off a deeper layer of "outsides" we risked taking off some essential insides. In this study we were concerned with whether children consider insides essential; we were not concerned with the exact point at which children draw the line between insides and outsides. Therefore, the outside removals were not included to test children's understanding of outsides, but rather to contrast with inside removal and test whether in such a clear contrast children consider insides (interior to the outermost surface and appearance of the object) critical.

Procedure   Children were tested individually in a small room apart from their regular classroom. The same warm-up was used as in Study 1. For each item, children first saw a picture of the standard (e.g., a dog) and were told its identity (e.g., "Here's a dog"), then were asked to consider the three transformations for that item, one at a time. For each transformation children were asked the identity and function questions. Thus, for each item, six questions were asked. The order of transformations (insides removal, outside removal, movement) was randomized across items and across children. For every transformation the two questions were asked in the same order: identity first, function second. Items were presented in one of two random orders, neither order beginning with a container. Approximately half the children at each age received each item order.

Results

We coded the proportion of trials on which each child said "no," that an item would no longer have the same identity or function as before. That is, the scores represent the proportion of trials that children affirmed that the object had *changed* identity or function. Our primary analyses concern the inside-removal versus outside-removal questions.

Inside-Removal versus Outside-Removal Questions   The results are presented in Table 26.5. Two analyses were conducted: one concerning the identity questions and one concerning the function questions.

IDENTITY   As evident in Table 26.5, *correct* responding to the identity questions for inside and outside removals averaged 73–69% for insides-relevant items and 78% for

Table 26.5
Study 2, mean percentage of responses affirming that identity or function changes (numbers in parentheses indicate mean percent correct)

	Insides removal	Outsides removal	Movement
Identity questions			
Insides relevant	72 (72)	35 (65)	12 (88)
Containers	17 (83)	28 (72)	10 (90)
Function questions			
Insides relevant	92 (92)	29 (71)	15 (85)
Containers	20 (80)	23 (77)	7 (93)

containers, collapsing across the insides-removal and outsides-removal questions. We conducted a 2 (age) ×2 (item type: inside-relevant items vs. containers) ×2 (question type: inside removal vs. outside removal) ANOVA on subjects' percentage "no" responses. There were no significant effects for age. There was a significant main effect for item type, $F(1,29) = 65.32$, $p < .0001$ and a significant main effect for question type, $F(1,29) = 17.89$, $p < .0002$. However, both of these effects were subsumed under the expected significant interaction between item and question type, $F(1,29) = 107.54$, $p < .0001$. As this finding indicates, children most often reported that identity changed when insides were removed from the inside-relevant items (e.g., when the insides of a turtle or egg were removed). On the relevant items, children considered insides more critical than outsides; on the containers, children considered both insides and outsides as irrelevant to the object's identity.

These findings for the insides-relevant items held up across all seven of the items tested. For example, correct performance on the insides-removal question (i.e., asserting that removing the insides does change identity) ranged from 81% for the egg to 65% for the car. Moreover, for each of the seven items, identity was judged to change more when the insides were removed than when the outsides were removed. Thus, the results appear to be widely generalizeable.

FUNCTION   As noted in the introduction, questions concerning identity might be especially difficult for adults as well as children. Therefore we also included questions about the objects' ordinary, characteristic functioning. As shown in Table 26.5, correct responding was marginally higher to function questions (80% correct overall, 82% for inside-relevant items and 79% for containers) than to identity questions. More importantly, however, the pattern of results closely parallels the pattern from the identity question, reported above. Again we conducted a 2 (age) ×2 (item type: inside-relevant items vs. containers) ×2 (question type: inside removal vs. outside removal) ANOVA. There was a significant main effect for item type, $F(1,29) = 115.04$, $p < .0001$ and a significant main effect for question type, $F(1,29) = 77.33$, $p < .0001$. Again, these main effects must be interpreted in light of the significant item type by question type interaction, $F(1,29) = 161.47$, $p < .0001$. These results demonstrate that children considered insides critical for object functioning, but only on inside-relevant items. On the containers, children considered both insides and outsides to be irrelevant.

Individual item analyses reveal that the advantage of insides held up on every one of the insides-relevant items. Across the seven items correct performance on the insides-removal question (i.e., asserting that removing the insides does change the item's characteristic functioning) ranged from 100% for the book to 87% for the turtle. And for each item, function was judged to change more when insides were removed than when outsides were removed. Again, this suggests that the results are broadly generalizeable.

Movement Questions
We included the movement questions as a control, to assess whether and to what extent, in our task, children answer that any change affects the identity and functioning of an object. This seemed possible since our format was to propose a *change* to the child (e.g., the outsides are removed) and then to ask whether a *change* had resulted (e.g., "Is it still a ...?"). The movement transformations ask the child to con-

sider patently irrelevant changes. The results are presented in Table 26.5. Overall, children were typically correct on these questions (89%). However, there was a slight tendency to answer that identity and functioning change with movement changes. To assess whether this tendency emerged under certain conditions more than others, the results were analyzed by means of a 2 (age: 4-year-olds, 5-year-olds) ×2 (question type: identity, function) ×2 (item type: insides-relevant, containers) ANOVA. There were no significant effects. Overall, children knew that location changes were irrelevant to the identity and functioning for all items.

The slight bias to report that change has occurred cannot account for our primary results. Children claimed that inside removal changed identity and function much more often than they claimed that movement did (72 vs. 12% for identity and 92 vs. 15% for function). More important still, in our prior analyses we compared children's judgments about insides removal with that for outsides; children were significantly more likely to say that insides removal changes identity than that outsides removal does. In sum, children understand insides as essential to an object's identity and functioning, and significantly more essential than the controls we included, namely, external parts and position.

Discussion

By age 4 years, children appreciate the special importance of insides for an object's identity and how it functions. These results contrast with Keil's (1989) findings, that children are misled by outer appearances until elementary school age. It may be that we were able to access an earlier understanding because we included no conflicting perceptual cues. All information about the hypothetical objects of interest were given by verbal descriptions. These may have allowed children to focus on the relevant features (insides versus outsides) without being caught up by misleading perceptual details.

A further difference between past work and the present study is that children were not simply asked to judge object identity. Even philosophers disagree as to what constitutes identity and what is sufficient to alter identity, and we had hypothesized that reliance on identity questions could have obscured children's knowledge in prior research. However, children in the present study considered insides critical to both identity and functioning. This constitutes a strong demonstration of young children's understanding that unseen insides can constitute privileged, even essential, qualities.

3. Study 3: Innate Potential of Animals

Study 2 focused on an overlap between insides and essences, demonstrating that even for preschoolers insides are considered essential to an object's identity and functioning. In the final studies we focus more closely on whether children have a grasp of essences even when they are not necessarily internal or spatially localizable. As noted in the Introduction, essences come in many varieties and may even be unknown. Psychological essentialism represents a belief that there are essences; it does not necessarily entail accurate knowledge about particular essences.

We approach the issue of psychological essentialism by focusing initially on innate or intrinsic category potential. For many living kinds, an individual can have a certain intrinsic potential even before it manifests that potential in any visible way. For example, a tiger cub has the potential to grow into something large and fierce, even though when born it is small and helpless. To explain developmental changes of this sort, we as adults often appeal to something like an intrinsic category essence. In other words, all tigers have an underlying nature or essence that is responsible for how they grow. If children, too, believe that immature creatures have intrinsic potentials that are not yet visible but will become manifested over time, then this would constitute evidence of one kind of essentialism, the belief in an essential nature or a determining but non-manifest predisposition.

To test this notion, we conducted a study that can be thought of as a "nature–nurture" study. On each of a series of items, children were told about an immature being, a baby animal that was brought up in an environment more suited to a different species. The question is how children believe this animal will grow. Will it show as yet invisible, undeveloped potentialities intrinsic in its category membership, or will it instead display the properties associated with its environment of upbringing?

Method

Subjects Fifty 4-year-olds participated. Twenty-five children were in the conflict condition, divided into older and younger groups (younger: $n = 12$, 4;0 to 4;7, mean age 4;3; older: $n = 13$, 4;8 to 5;7, mean age 5;0). In addition, there were two control conditions; same upbringing control ($n = 13$, 4;2 to 5;0, mean age 4;4) and same category control ($n = 12$, 3;11 to 4;10, mean age 4;4). Subjects in these control conditions were approximately the same age as the younger group in the conflict condition, to make certain that even our youngest subjects could pass these controls.

Items Five picture sets were used (see Table 26.6), all with realistic color drawings. Each set included a newborn animal of one species and a group of adult animals of another species (e.g., a newborn kangaroo and a group of adult goats). The newborn always had fewer prototypical features than the adults of its own species. For example, the baby kangaroo was hairless, pink, had closed-lidded eyes, and was curled into a small ball. For each set, the newborn animal picture was smaller than the picture of the adults.

Table 26.6
Items used in Study 3

Baby	Upbringing	Questions
Rabbit	monkeys	long or short ears?
		rather have carrots or bananas?
Tiger	horses	striped or plain fur?
		neigh or roar?
Cow	pigs	straight or curly tail?
		say "moo" or say "oink"?
Mouse	dogs	round or floppy ears?
		run away from or chase cats?
Kangaroo	goats	have pouch or no pouch?
		good at hopping or climbing?

Procedure   Children were tested individually in a small room. There were three conditions in this study, a conflict condition and two controls (same upbringing and same category controls). In the conflict condition, children first saw a picture of a baby animal which had few of the characteristics that the adult members of the species have. For example, they were shown a picture of a calf and were told that it was a cow. Children then learned that the baby had been brought up by another species (e.g., Edith had been taken to a pig farm when she was a baby, was cared for by pigs, and never saw another cow). Children were shown a picture of the environment of rearing when it was mentioned (e.g., a picture of the pigs on the pig farm). Both pictures—of the baby and of the contrasting context of raising—were left in view. The baby animal was always reared in the company of adults of a different species.

For example, on the cow/pig item, children heard the following:

> Now I'm going to tell you about a cow named Edith. Look, here's a picture of Edith when she was a baby. Right after Edith was born, when she was just a tiny baby cow, she was taken to a farm that had pigs—lots of pigs. See, here are the pigs on the farm. The pigs took care of Edith. Edith grew up on the farm with all the pigs, and she never saw another cow.

For each item set, children were asked four questions. The first two questions were simple checks to make certain that children remembered the information we had given: What kind of animal was, for example, Edith, and who raised her? (In this example, the correct answers would be "a cow" and "pigs," respectively.) If a child answered either of these questions incorrectly or incompletely, he or she was corrected. The next two questions were focal for this study, and concerned how the animal would be after it grew up. One question concerned a mature physical feature (e.g., "When Edith got to be a grown-up, what did her tail look like; was it straight or was it curly? Why?"). The other question concerned a mature behavior (e.g., "When Edith got to be a grown-up, what sound did she make; did she say 'moo' or did she say 'oink'? Why?"). Importantly, neither of these questions could be answered by looking at the picture of the baby; for example, the picture of Edith did not include her tail. So children were asked about non-visible attributes of the target that would develop in the future. Children were encouraged to justify their answers to the last two questions for each item set.

Preceding the five item sets, all children first received an easy warm-up item concerning a baby bear that grew up with other bears. Children were asked two questions about the bear after it grew up: would it like honey or ketchup, and would it be brown or purple.

Control Conditions   The two control conditions were included to ensure that the properties we used were ones that children of this age could answer correctly when there was no conflict—for example, we wanted to be certain that children would say that ordinarily cows say "moo" and have straight tails. In the same category control, children were presented with the picture of just the baby, and were told that it was raised in the environment appropriate to that species (e.g., they saw Edith, a baby cow, and were told that she was raised by other cows). In the same upbringing control, children were presented with the picture of just the environment of raising, and were told about a baby appropriately raised in that environment (e.g., they were told about a hypothetical baby pig, Edith, and were shown the other pigs she was raised

Table 26.7
Study 3, mean number of responses based on category membership (out of five), as a function of condition and age

Conditions	Behavior	Physical feature
Category control	4.50**	4.08*
Environment control	4.23**	4.23**
Conflict condition	4.32**	3.36*

$^*p < .01$
$^{**}p < .0001$

with). By including both control conditions, we could determine whether children knew not only that cows say "moo," but also that pigs say "oink" and do not say "moo."

In all three conditions, the order of items (except for the warm-up) was randomly determined for each subject. The order of the choices (e.g., "Did she have a straight tail or a curly tail?" vs. "Did she have a curly tail or a straight tail?") were counter-balanced both within and between subjects. All sessions were audiotaped.

Results
We scored how often children answered in accord with innate potential or essence; the data are summarized in Table 26.7. Scores could range form 0 to 5 per subject and question type (behaviors vs. physical features).

Control Conditions   The first analysis examined children's performance in the two control conditions to make certain that they could answer the questions accurately when there was no conflict, and that the behavior and physical feature questions were roughly equal in difficulty. The data were analyzed in a 2 (condition: category control, upbringing control) $\times 2$ (question type: behavior, physical feature) repeated-measures ANOVA. Results indicated no significant main effects or interactions due to either condition or question type (all $ps > .40$). Overall, children were correct a mean of 4.26 out of 5 items (85%) in the control conditions, which is significantly above a chance expectation of 50% or 2.5, $t(24) = 12.68$, $p < .0001$. Thus, the properties used in this study are ones that subjects of this age are familiar with and attribute to the appropriate species.

Conflict Condition   The primary results concern how children perform in the conflict condition when innate potential is in conflict with the environment of rearing. As shown in Table 26.7, children in the conflict condition nearly always answered on the basis of innate potential. For example, they said that a baby cow raised among pigs will grow up to say "moo" and have a straight tail. To examine the effects of age and question type more closely the results were analyzed by means of 2 (age: younger, older) $\times 2$ (question type: behavior, physical feature) repeated-measures ANOVA. There were no significant effects due to age. However, there was a main effect of question type, $F(1,23) = 17.45$, $p < .0005$. Children relied more on innate potential when the question concerned a behavior (e.g., what noise a cow will make) than a physical feature (e.g., whether a cow will have a straight tail). However, performance was above chance (50% correct or 2.5) in both cells, $p < .01$.

Discussion

The results of Study 3 suggest that children are essentialists, at least concerning how animals grow and mature. They assume that members of a category share something like an innate or intrinsic potential that will be realized even when an animal is reared by members of a different species.

The results of the conflict condition cannot be due to some bias simply to prefer some response alternatives (e.g., moo and straight tail) over others. In the same upbringing control, when children were shown just the picture of the rearing environment (e.g., pigs) and were asked about a baby raised in that environment, they appropriately predicted that that baby would, in this example, oink and have a curly tail after it grew up. More generally, in the control conditions children chose either alternative, as appropriate.

A deeper issue concerns whether children's answers reveal an understanding of non-manifest potential, or whether they simply reflect category associations (e.g., because the experimenter called the baby a kangaroo, it must hop and have a pouch). One piece of evidence against this latter interpretation is that children's answers differed according to the question type—behavior or physical feature. If children simply report category features or associations, they should do so equally for the two types of questions, but they did not. Children were more likely to grant the baby species-typical behaviors than species-typical physical features when it grew up, thus demonstrating that they considered each question separately and did not simply assume that the animals would have the properties normally associated with their names. We pursue this issue further in Study 4.

4. Study 4: Inborn Properties of Animals

In Study 4, children were asked which properties the infant animals of Study 3 had when they were babies. If children tend to presume that babies do not yet have their adult features, that would support our interpretation of the answers in Study 3 in two ways. First, it would provide converging evidence that children do not answer just by reporting category associations. Second, it would indicate that children in Study 3 correctly expected properties to develop that were not even yet present in the baby animals of the study.

Method

Subjects   Twelve children ranging in age from 3;10 to 4;3 participated (mean age 4;1). Again we sampled younger 4-year-olds to be sure the data would represent even the youngest children tested in Study 3.

Items   Each child was asked about the five baby animals used in Study 3 (see Table 26.6). For each, they were asked about four properties, the physical and behavioral features used in Study 3 (see Table 26.6) and also two new sorts of properties: inherent and impossible. Inherent and impossible properties serve as comparison items— the first are properties that all baby animals of the sort we included have from birth (e.g., legs, nose); the second are properties that members of these species never have (e.g., wings).

Procedure For each item, the experimenter showed the picture of the infant (from Study 3) with no specified environment. Its proper name and species were identified, as in Study 3. Then children were asked the species name (as a memory check), followed by the four questions in random order. For example, on one item children were asked whether Edith (a cow) says moo (behavioral property), has a straight tail (physical property), has eyes (inherent property), and has fins (impossible property). Each question was a yes–no question, e.g., "Does this baby kangaroo have a pouch?" The order of items was randomized separately for each subject.

Results and Discussion

Children attributed the behavioral properties to infant animals 87% of the time; they attributed the physical features only 40% of the time, $t(11) = 6.20$, $p < .0001$. Both kinds of properties were attributed more often than the impossible ones (mean of 7%), both $ps < .005$, but only the physical features were attributed less than the inherent ones (mean of 88%), $t(11) = 7.73$, $p < .0001$. That impossible properties were rarely if ever attributed to the infants shows that children's answers do not just reflect a response tendency to answer "yes."

Note that in this study children attributed specified physical features to infant animals only 40% of the time, whereas in Study 3 they attributed these same features to the same animal, *when it grew up*, 67% of the time, $t(35) = 2.67$, $p < .02$. This result provides critical evidence that children are not just reporting category associations. Physical features that are typically attributed to the adult are typically not attributed to the infant. It is striking that subjects anticipate that properties not currently possessed by the infants will inevitably develop, and will do so even in an environment of upbringing encompassing very different appearances. This is precisely the sort of belief that is consistent with an intrinsic potential or category essence. The final point of interest is that the behaviors we used in Study 3 were seen as applying to category members even as infants, and were thought to apply just as frequently as inherent body parts (such as eyes or tails). We cannot explain this difference between behaviors and physical features, but the impressive result with regard to physical features remains.

5. Study 5: Innate Potential of Seeds

One potential difficulty with Study 3 was that, in order to specify the innate nature of the animals, each animal was identified as a member of a certain species (e.g., children were told that Edith was a cow). This sort of species identification seems to imply an unchanging category membership which could bias children to attend to and report category associates (e.g., since cows have straight tails and say "moo," then so does Edith). It now seems unlikely that such an alternative explanation could account fully for the results, given the findings of Study 4. Nonetheless, Study 5 was designed in part to provide further evidence about this issue. In addition, we wished to extend our results beyond the domain of animals.

The format of Study 5 was the same as Study 3, except that the questions concerned seeds instead of baby animals. There are several advantages of this procedure. One can specify the nature and hence the innate potential of a seed (e.g., a seed that came from an apple) without giving it an unchanging category membership (i.e., an apple). Furthermore, a seed looks nothing like the mature plant or fruit it eventually

Table 26.8
Items used in Study 5

Seed	Environment	Question
Seed from apple	flower pot	apple or flower?
Seed from watermelon	corn field	watermelon or corn?
Seed from lemon	orange trees	lemon tree or orange tree?
Seed from flower	strawberries	flower or strawberry?
Seed from rose	dandelions	rose or dandelion?
Seed from grape	coconut trees	grapes or coconut tree?
Pit from peach	plum trees	peach tree or plum tree?

becomes, in contrast to infant animals, which share some perceptual features with their mature kin. A seed that came from an apple is not an apple or an apple tree, nor does it resemble an apple or apple tree.

Method

Subjects   Similar to Study 3, 25 4-year-olds participated, divided into two groups: a younger group ($n = 12$, 4;2 to 4;7, mean age 4;4) and an older group ($n = 13$, 4;9 to 5;4, mean age 5;1).

Items   Seven sets of items were included (see Table 26.8). Each set included a seed of one species and a plant or set of plants of another species (e.g., an apple seed and a pot of flowers). All items were presented as photographs, primarily in color.

Procedure   Children were tested individually in a small room. The session began with an easy warm-up question concerning a seed that came from a grapefruit and was planted with grapefruit trees. The remaining items posed a conflict between the innate potential of the seed and the environment in which it grew. For example, children saw a seed that came from an apple and was planted with flowers in a flowerpot. All questions concerned object identity (e.g., "When that seed grew, what popped up out of the ground, was it an apple tree or a flower?"). To imply unchanging category memberships as little as possible, the identity of the seed was never explicitly stated (e.g., an apple seed), but we referred only to "a seed that came from an apple."

Here is an example of the exact wording that children heard: "This seed came from a watermelon. A girl named Jennifer took this seed out of the watermelon. Then she planted the seed in a cornfield. See, here's the cornfield." In the pretest, we additionally said that the child "watered that place and made sure it got lots of sunshine, and the seed grew and grew. Now I'm going to ask you some questions."

The order of items (except for the warm-up) was randomly determined for each subject. The choices (e.g., "Was it an apple tree or a flower?" vs. "Was it a flower or an apple tree?") were presented in counterbalanced order both within and between subjects.

Results and Discussion

We scored how often children answered in accord with innate potential. Scores could range from 0 to 7 per subject. Given the two-choice answers, chance responding would be 50% or 3.50. The primary result is that there was a significant difference in performance between the two age groups, $t(23) = 1.90$, $p < .05$, one-tailed. The older children, as in the previous study, answered overwhelmingly on the basis of innate potential ($M = 6.0$ out of 7 correct, $t(12) = 6.657$, $p < .0001$). Only one child in this age group (out of 13) answered below the chance level of 3.5 items correct; indeed, over half of these children performed perfectly. In contrast, the younger children as a group performed at chance levels ($M = 4.17$, $t(11) = 0.725$, n.s.).

Although the younger children did not score above chance, they did not appear to be simply guessing. When individual response patterns were examined, we found that all 12 of the younger children answered consistently throughout the task. Specifically, seven children (58%) were correct on every item or all but one (out of 7), and five children (42%) were in error on every item or all but one (out of 7).

There are two points to make from this analysis. First, it is noteworthy that more than half the younger children consistently based their answers on innate potential on this particular task. The seeds as depicted were completely unrelated to any mature exemplar (e.g., the seed from an apple in no way looked like an apple or an apple tree). To the contrary, the only visible exemplars were those of the environment (e.g., the flower plant was visible, but not an apple tree). Thus, in comparison to Study 3, an environment-based response in this study would seem even more compelling. The fact that half the younger 4-year-olds and almost all the older 4-year-olds could ignore the salient environmental cues and answer on the basis of origins is significant.

The second point is that the younger children's bimodal pattern of responding suggests that around this age a change is taking place enabling children to advance from consistent errors to a basically correct understanding. Although we can only speculate as to what is changing during this period, we suggest that children may be learning about the nature of seeds. In particular, it seems likely that children are learning that seeds are the immature versions of plants—that seeds are the plant "babies," so to speak. Once children grasp that critical fact, then their understanding of innate potential can be applied to seeds as well as to young animals. Until that point, children may misconstrue the relation between seeds and plants (e.g., they may believe that seeds are plant food, or may simply know that seeds are found inside of plants), and so would have no reason to answer based on the seed identity.

The primary finding, therefore, is that in a very different domain (seeds versus animal babies) and in a task where an even firmer grasp of innate essences seems to be required to generate correct responses, 4-year-olds provided converging evidence of an understanding of non-visible, as-yet-undeveloped intrinsic potential.

One question these last three studies raise is when children can be said to possess biological concepts, for example an understanding of biological properties of animals beyond a physical conception of their bodies and a psychological conception of their behaviors. The present findings suggest that children may have sensible biological understandings by age 4 years (see also Keil, 1989). Most strikingly, children's appreciation of intrinsic properties (demonstrated in Studies 3 and 5) could be considered to reflect an initial understanding of something like genetics. In contrast, Carey (1985, 1988) argued that children do not initially understand biological concepts as biological, in the adult sense, but rather misunderstand such concepts physically or psychologically. For example, preschoolers consider "babies" to be behaviorally limited versions of bigger animals, rather than their offspring. It may be that there are important beginnings of genuinely biological knowledge during this preschool period. Our findings are consistent with such a possibility but do not test it directly.

6. General Discussion

The results from all five studies demonstrate that preschool children are not externalists, in contrast to the traditional view that their thinking is limited to phenomenal qualities. Instead, young children show an impressive ability to penetrate beneath surface appearances. These findings extend recent research showing that young children can sensibly describe the concrete insides of objects (Gelman, 1987) and expect categories to include features beyond those that are immediately perceptible (Gelman and Markman, 1986). Beyond this, we have shown that young children distinguish insides of objects from their outsides, even when the two conflict, and believe that insides can be more essential to an object's functioning and identity. Moreover, we provide evidence for an early understanding of innate potential, whereby immature living things are thought to possess a native essence that influences the nature of visible attributes, of non-visible attributes, and even of attributes not yet present in any form.

Throughout the chapter we have introduced several related notions, including not only insides and essences, but also innate potential, inborn features, and intrinsic characteristics. At this point we wish to clarify how these concepts interrelate, and to what extent the present studies provide evidence for each. To undertake this discussion it seems useful to focus momentarily on living kinds (e.g., tigers) which have internal, inborn, and intrinsic features (see also Gelman and Kremer, 1991). "Internal" features are those that are on the inside of the organism, as we discussed in the Introduction. By "inborn" we mean properties that are possessed at birth either congenitally or genetically (e.g., the whiskers of a tiger). "Intrinsic" properties are not necessarily apparent at birth but are typical of adults and so typically acquired during an organism's lifetime (e.g., tigers are intrinsically large and fierce, but are not actually large and fierce at birth). Thus, intrinsic properties are part of the innate *potential* of the organism, although the features themselves are often not inborn. These distinctions are not scientific ones, but rather part of our adult commonsense understanding. Commonsensically, internal, inborn, and intrinsic properties are separable notions. An internal feature (e.g., the defective heart of a tiger) may be neither intrinsic nor inborn; and, as just mentioned, intrinsic features (fierceness for tigers) need not be either inborn or internal in any literal, spatial sense. Internal, inborn, and intrinsic features can all be non-obvious and in some sense "essential."

The present studies examined children's understanding that internal and intrinsic properties exist and are essential. With regard to children's understanding that non-obvious properties exist, we tested first whether preschoolers understood that objects could have insides quite different from their obvious outsides. Three- and 4-year-olds know this. We tested second whether children understood that living things—animals and seeds—could have intrinsic properties that are not inborn. Four-year-old children understand that babies and seeds have intrinsic properties— ones that are not apparent at birth but that inevitably manifest themselves over time. This, too, shows an appreciation for the primacy of non-obvious qualities.

Beyond testing children's understanding of the presence of non-obvious properties, we tested whether children consider them essential in the sense of specially important. We showed, first, that 4-year-olds understand that insides are often critical to an object's identity and functioning. We showed, second, that 4-year-olds understand that essential aspects of an item's identity (e.g., whether it will be a watermelon or corn, whether it will have the physical features of a kangaroo or a goat) can be completely non-obvious before it matures.

In addition to what they reveal about the conceptual understandings of 4-year-olds, the present findings have implications for two interrelated issues: the course of development, and the concept of psychological essentialism.

Course of Development

Although our data concern mostly 4-year-olds, an intermediate preschool age tested in all four studies, we also provide some initial developmental findings. Before the fourth birthday, children have a clear albeit imperfect grasp of the inside-outside distinction (Study 1). They realize that such a distinction exists, and they can reflect on it even when insides directly conflict with outside appearances. The distinction may serve as a concrete precursor to the more refined understanding of insides and essences apparent in the older children.

Beyond the fourth birthday understanding in this area appears to be in part knowledge-dependent. Children's grasp of essences is partly limited by their knowledge of specific classes of objects. In particular, note that children appreciate the innate potential of animal babies at an earlier age than they appreciate the innate potential of plant seeds (Studies 3 and 5). Similarly, children's grasp of the privileged nature of insides (Study 2) rests on specific knowledge of the distinction between containers and insides-relevant items. Thus, children's understanding of insides and essences can only be revealed when they have some pertinent knowledge about the object in question (e.g., whether or not it is a container, or the nature of its developmental stages).

Nonetheless, the range of items, categories, and tasks used in the present studies document that children's grasp of insides and essences has significant generality. Our findings clearly demonstrate an early disposition to expect insides and outsides to differ (at least for relatively complexly structured items like turtles and eggs, if not rocks and water), and to expect some objects to have essence-like qualities. For example, although 3- and 4-year-olds are by no means accurate at identifying the specific insides of even common objects such as oranges and dogs (Study 1), they firmly grasp that insides and outsides differ. Thus, children may have a general presumption that insides and essences exist, before they have much domain-specific knowledge about an item. We turn to this issue next.

Psychological Essentialism

These findings stand on their own as demonstrating a grasp of the presence and importance of internal and intrinsic features by quite young children. Beyond this, however, the findings raise the question of whether or to what extent young children might not also be psychological essentialists.

Recently Medin (1989) has proposed that adults' concepts are framed by what he calls psychological essentialism (pp. 1476–1477):

The main ideas are as follows: People act as if things (e.g., objects) have essences or underlying natures that make them the thing that they are. Furthermore, the essence constrains or generates properties that may vary in their centrality....

It is important to note that psychological essentialism refers not to how the world is but rather to how people approach the world. Wastebaskets probably have no true essence, although we may act as if they do. Both social and psychodiagnostic categories are at least partially culture specific and may have weak if any metaphysical underpinnings (see also Morey and McNamara, 1987).

If psychological essentialism is bad metaphysics, why should people act as if things had essences? The reason is that it may prove to be good epistemology. One could say that people adopt an *essentialist heuristic.*

The notion of an essence if the hypothesis that objects possess constitutive natures that make them what they are, that such an underlying nature is *distinct from* but *responsible for* more obvious external features. Having stripes is not essential to being a tiger, but it may be the direct consequence of having a tiger essence. Positing that there are essences does not mean identifying what those essences are; in fact, essences are typically hidden and unknown.

The notion of an essence underlying an object's identity and character has been discredited in both philosophy and biology (Dupre, 1986; Mayr, 1988). But Medin's claim is that it remains a viable psychological phenomenon—that people tend to *believe* that objects have essences, even though that belief may be faulty. Medin argues that describing adults as psychological essentialists accounts for much of their performance on categorization tasks. Essentialism is a powerfully useful psychological disposition that directs adult induction and knowledge acquisition (including the sorts of hypotheses we entertain and attempt to confirm). Medin suggests that such an essentialist disposition constrains our sense of similarity and can even have a revolutionizing influence on it.

It may seem premature to ask when and to what extent children become essentialists when it is still unclear whether adults are. But we raise the question because psychological essentialism seems to be a plausible candidate for an important cognitive *pre*disposition. Medin's arguments about its usefulness as a disposition in adult cognition can be extended to argue for the usefulness of such a presumption in knowledge acquisition, induction, and concept building in development.

That is, we propose that something like an essentialistic disposition could propel knowledge acquisition and shape concept representation early in development—not just at the end. Consider children's understanding of insides as revealed in the present studies. Why would such young children have a clear and distinct understanding that the insides of such varied things as pencils, turtles, and cars differ from their outsides? Although children may have considerable experience with these objects (e.g., having discovered that pencils make lines, can be sharpened if broken, etc.; that turtles have shells, walk slowly, etc.), that sort of everyday experience would not clearly yield an early understanding of their insides, nor an understanding that the insides are crucial to object functioning and identity. This sort of understanding of insides would be less mysterious, however, if children—like adults—are predisposed to believe that insides are different from outsides (see also Gelman, 1987), and that insides are essential to an object's identity and functioning. Children's early grasp of the critical nature of insides is consistent with the view that early in the process of knowledge acquisition children are psychological essentialists. An essentialist disposition could help account for the burgeoning evidence that even young children construct considerable knowledge about the non-obvious (Wellman and Gelman, 1988), distinguish reality and appearances (Flavell et al., 1983), and form theories to organize and go beyond phenomenal observations (Carey, 1985; Wellman, 1990).

We believe that psychological essentialism is an attractive possibility for such a basic developmental cognition, though of course the present data do not provide a direct test. Our data simply document an early and impressive understanding of insides and essences. This leaves open the question of whether children's knowledge, demonstrated here, is derived from accumulated past knowledge, or whether instead manifests a belief brought to the task of acquiring knowledge. On the one hand, it is possible that children are acquiring numerous particular pieces of information about insides and essences—such as that pencils have lead inside, dogs have bones inside, apple trees are inherent in apple seeds, adult tiger behavior is intrinsic in tiger cubs. That is, a disposition toward essentialism in adults and, when it becomes present, in children may be the result of an accumulation of particular, acquired essentialistic beliefs of the sort studied here. If so, then the importance of the present findings is that they reveal the building blocks of an important adult acquisition.

On the other hand, something like psychological essentialism may be an early, basic cognitive predisposition revealed in (rather than built upon) young children's early understanding of insides and innate potentials. If so, then findings such as ours might have an even greater developmental significance, because such a basic disposition would have formative consequences.

We favor this second alternative, because in the present studies children seem prone to believe that insides are important even when knowing little about the insides in question. They also seem prone to believe that babies (or seeds) may have intrinsic properties even when knowing little about specific babies or seeds. Either alternative, however—that something like psychological essentialism emerges developmentally or that it frames knowledge acquisition developmentally—further underlines the importance of research on children's early developing notions of insides and essences.

References

Astington, J. W., Harris, P. L., and Olson, D. R. (1988). *Developing theories of mind.* New York: Cambridge University Press.

Bruner, J. S., Olver, R. R., and Greenfield, P. M. (1967). *Studies in cognitive growth.* New York: Wiley.

Carey, S. (1985). *Conceptual change in childhood.* Cambridge, MA: MIT Press.

Carey, S. (1988). Conceptual differences between children and adults. *Mind and Language, 3,* 167–181.

Dupre, J. (1986). Sex, gender, and essence. In P. A. French. T. E. Uehling Jr., and H. K. Wettstein (Eds.), *Midwest Studies in Philosophy XI, Studies in Essentialism* (pp. 441–457). Minneapolis: University of Minnesota Press.

Flavell, J. H. (1977). *Cognitive development.* Englewood Cliffs, NJ: Prentice-Hall.

Flavell, J. H., Flavell, E. R., and Green, F. L. (1983). Development of the appearance–reality distinction. *Cognitive Psychology, 15,* 95–120.

Gellert, E. (1962). Children's conceptions of the content and functions of the human body. *Genetic Psychology Monographs, 65,* 291–411.

Gelman, R. (1987, August). *Cognitive development: Principles guide learning and contribute to conceptual coherence.* Invited Address to Division 1, American Psychological Association. New York.

Gelman, S. A., and Kremer, K. E. (1991). Understanding natural cause: Children's explanations of how objects and their properties originate. *Child Development, 62,* 396–414.

Gelman, S. A., and Markman, E. M. (1986). Categories and induction in young children. *Cognition, 23,* 183–209.

Gelman, S. A., and O'Reilly, A. W. (1988). Children's inductive inferences within superordinate categories: The role of language and category structure. *Child Development, 59,* 876–887.

Keil, F. C. (1989). *Concepts, kinds, and cognitive development.* Cambridge, MA: MIT Press.

Locke, J. (1894/1959). *An essay concerning human, understanding,* Vol. 2. New York, NY: Dover.

Mayr, E. (1988). *Toward a new philosophy of biology.* Cambridge, MA: Harvard University Press.

Medin, D. L. (1989). Concepts and conceptual structure. *American Psychologist, 44,* 1469–1481.

Medin, D., and Ortony, A. (1989). Comments on Part I: Psychological essentialism. In S. Vosniadou and A. Ortony (Eds.), *Similarity and analogical reasoning* (pp. 179–195). Cambridge, UK: Cambridge University Press.

Millikan, R. G. (1984), *Language, thought, and other biological categories.* Cambridge, MA: MIT Press.

Morey, L. C., and McNamara, T. P. (1987). On the definitions, diagnosis, and DSM-III. *Journal of Abnormal Psychology, 96,* 283–285.

Piaget, J. (1929). *The child's conception of the world.* London: Routledge and Kegan Paul.

Piaget, J. (1951). *Plays, dreams, and imitation in childhood.* New York: Norton.

Putnam, H. (1977). Is semantics possible? In S. P. Schwartz (Ed.), *Naming, necessity, and natural kinds* (pp. 102–118). Ithaca, NY: Cornell University Press.

Sugarman, S. (1987). *Piaget's construction of the child's reality.* New York: Cambridge University Press.

Wellman, H. M. (1990). *The child's theory of mind.* Cambridge, MA: MIT Press.

Wellman, H., and Gelman, S. A. (1988). Children's understanding of the nonobvious. In R. J. Sternberg (Ed.), *Advances in the psychology of human intelligence* (Vol. 4, pp. 99–135). Hillsdale, NJ: Erlbaum.

Index

Abelson, R. P., 392–393, 397, 447
Abstracta, concepts as, 5–8, 336
Adjective modification, 359–363. *See also* Selective
  Modification Model for adjective-noun
  conjunctions
Adjective-noun conjunctions. *See* Selective
  Modification Model for adjective-noun
  conjunctions
Adkins, D. C., 108
Adverbs
  dual, 374–375
  Selective Modification Model for, 373–375
  test of, 375–383
  single, 373–374
Aggregation, 315, 320–323
Air/nothing concept, 479–480, 484
Ambiguity, semantic, 141–142
Analytic data, 53
Analytic Data Problem, 65–67, 71
Analytic inferences, 12–13
Analytic/synthetic distinction, 12–14, 18–21, 339–
  340
Analyticity
  in Classical Theory of Concepts, 12–13
  empiricism and, 153–163
    background for, 153–155
    definition of, 155–157
    interchangeability and, 157–160
    semantical rules and, 160–163
    synonymy and, 155–157, 160, 163–164
    syntheticity and, 153, 166–167
  horizontal challenge to, 339–341
  Kantian notion of, 144
  Problem, 18–21, 27
  Quinean critique of, 28
  vertical challenge to, 339
Anglin, J. M., 198, 211
Animals
  inborn properties of, 629–630
  innate potential of, 625–629
Anomaly, semantic, 143–144
Answerability, 345–346
Antonymy, 145–147
Aoki, H., 406
Archimedes, 111, 472

Argument structure of concepts, 315–318
Aristotelian principles, 405
Aristotle, 154, 471–473, 525–526
Armstrong, S., 14, 32–34, 327, 411, 418–420, 452
Artificial categories, 198
Artificial languages, 161–163
Asch, S. E., 114–115
ASL, 199
Assumptions, 208–209, 418
Asymmetric Dependence Theory
  acquisition of, 63–64
  argument against, 67–71
  information-based semantic theories and, 552–
    553, 558
  origin of, 60–61
  sustaining mechanisms and, 63–64, 552–553
Atomic concepts, 4
Atomic features, 4
Atomism, 413. *See also* Conceptual Atomism
Attribute matching and similarity insufficiency,
  general, 432–435
Attribute selection, 433–435, 437–438
Attribute-listing paradigm, 254–255
Attribute-value structure, 356–357, 383, 385–386
Attributes, common, 193–194
Aufbau (Carnap), 164–165
Austin, G., 101, 104, 106, 109, 112–113, 119–120,
  177

Bach, E., 310
Baillargeon, R., 575–577, 581–591
Barsalou, L. W., 384–385, 433–435, 441–442
Bartlett tradition, 447
Basic assumptions, 418
Battig, W. F., 198–199, 235
Bayes's theorem, 447
Beattie, 125
Becker, A. H., 535
Behavioral attainment, 108
Belief, concept of, 337
Bellugi, U., 196
Bentham, J., 164
Berlin, B., 196
Best-examples model, 210–213, 217
Billman, D., 535, 540

Bolinger, 412
Boundedness, 315, 320–323
Bouthilet, L., 108
Bower, G. H., 433–435, 440
Bower, T. G. R., 575
Bransford, J. D., 204
Brentano, 339
Brooks, P. H., 603
Brown, J. S., 447
Brown, R., 106
Bruner, J., 101, 104, 106, 109, 111–113, 119–120
Brunswick, E., 114
Bulmer, R., 445
Burge, T., 280, 541
Byrnes, J. P., 536

Callanan, M. A., 450
Camerer, C. F., 441
Carey, S., 44, 449–451, 464, 469–470, 475, 477–478, 480, 484, 536, 540, 632
Carlson, T. B., 447
Carnap, R., 10–12, 155, 161, 164–165, 168, 177, 181, 185, 339–340
Carroll, J. J., 449–450
Carrying information, 514
Categories and Concepts (Smith and Medin), 280
Categorization
  as attribute matching, 432–433
  of children, 559–564
  in Classical Theory of Concepts, 11, 72
  conceptual core in, 35
  consequences of specific, 105, 117–121
  in developmental psychology, 561
  errors, 31
  function of, 286
  general theory of, difficulty envisaging, 256–257
  horizontal dimensions, 196–201
  judgments, 31
  linear separability in, 441
  mental bases for, 225–227
  models of, 210–217
    best-examples, 210–213, 217
    context, 211, 213–217
  objects in events, 202–205
  principles, 190–191
  problematic issues, 201–202
  processes, 208–210, 448
  prototype effects and, 411–413
  in Prototype Theory of Concepts, 27–31, 46
  similarity computation in, 215–217
  stereotypes and, 398–400, 402–403
  subordinate, 192
  superordinate, 192, 199
  taxonomy and, 189–192, 561–562
  ultimate arbiters of, 75
  vertical dimensions, 191–196
Categorization theories insufficiency, 431–432
Category resemblance, 192

Category-chaining, 410
Causal covariance, 514
Cavendish, 461
Chapman, J. P., 440
Chapman, L. J., 440
Characteristic features, 453
Chi, M., 444
Chomsky, N., 54, 125, 177, 306, 311, 536, 538
Clark, E., 11, 445, 448–449, 451, 493
Clark, H., 445, 447, 449, 493
Clark, R., 387
Classical Theory of Concepts
  categorization and, 11, 72
  categorization theories insufficiency and, 431
  concept acquisition and, 10–11
  conceptual coherence and, 451–453
  constitutive structure of concepts and, 64–65
  empirical phenomena and, 212–213
  lexical concepts in, 9
  Neoclassical Theory of Concepts and, 54
  overview and definitions, 8–14
    analytic inferences, 12–13
    analyticity, 12–13
    categorization, 11
    concept acquisition, 10–11
    epistemic justification, 12
    reference determination, 13–14
  problems for, 14–27
    Analyticity Problem, 18–21, 26
    Conceptual Fuzziness Problem, 23–24, 26
    Ignorance and Error Problem, 21–23, 26, 75
    Plato's Problem, 14–16, 26
    Psychological Reality Problem, 17–18, 26
    summary of, 26
    Typicality Effects Problem, 24–27
  Smith and Medin and, 280–282, 287, 290–295
  Theory-Theory of Concepts and, 47–48
Cluster concept view, 225, 229–234. *See also* Prototype Theory of Concepts
Clusters of cognitive models, 394–396, 398
Cognitions, 133
Cognitive economy, 190
Cognitive fix, 533
Cognitive Grammar, 313–314
Cognitive Models Interpretation
  clusters of, 394–396, 398
  feature bundles vs., 394
  generators and, 404–405
  graded, 393
  hon category and, 407–411
  idealized character of, 393, 397–398, 442
  ideals and, 403–404
  metonymy and, 396–398, 401–402
  paragons and, 404
  prototype effects and, 391–392, 419–421
  radial structures and, 400–401, 406
  representativeness structures and, 400
  rules of language and, 411

salient examples and, 405–406
stereotypes and, 398–400, 402–403
study of, 392–393
submodels and, 405
typical examples and, 403
Cognitive models. *See specific types*
Cognitive Reference Points, 405
Cognitive Semantics, 313
Cohen, B., 385–386, 446
Coherence. *See* Conceptual coherence
Cole, M., 444–445
Coleman, L., 294, 394
Coleman-Kay study, 394
Coley, J. D., 527, 543
Collins, A., 226, 447
Competence, conceptual, 295–298
Completers Problem, 54–55, 59
Complex concepts, 4, 445–446
Componential organizational universals, 126
Composite concepts, 355–356, 359–363
Compositionality
  Conceptual Atomism and, 43, 74
  Dual Theories of Concepts and, 42–43
  Frege and, 137
  semantic theory and, 128–129
Compositionality Problem
  in Conceptual Atomism, 67–68, 71
  in Prototype Theory of Concepts, 37–43
Concept acquisition
  of children, 559–565
  Classical Theory of Concepts and, 10–11
  Conceptual Atomism and, 564–565
  information-based semantic theories and, 550–554
  Keil and, 525
  lexical concepts and, 308–309
  model of, 563–564
  nativism and, 564–566
  natural kind concepts, 554–564
  overview, 549–550
  Prototype Theory of Concepts and, 29
  sentential concepts and, 308–309
  study of, 525
  sustaining mechanisms and, 550–554
  The Standard Picture and, 491–506
Concept attainment
  behavior, conditions affecting, 105–122
    consequences of specific categorizations, 105, 117–121
    definition of task, 105–108
    imposed restrictions, nature of, 105, 121–122
    instances encountered, nature of, 105, 108–113
    validation, nature of, 105, 113–117
  investigation of, 102–105
  knowledge about, current, 101–102
  lexical, 249
Concept cores, 253–256, 277
Concept use and theories
  complex concepts, 445–446

correlated attributes, 439–441
cross-cultural research, 444–445
expertise, 443–444
linear separability in categorization, 441
linguistic innovations, 445–446
prototype structure and, 441–443
Concepts. *See also See also specific theories*
  as abstracta, 5–8, 336
  agents and, 279–280
  algebraic system and, 323
  of belief, 337
  Classical Theory of, 8–27
    overview and definitions, 8–14
    problems for, 14–27
  cluster view of, 225, 229–234
  complex, 4, 445–446
  composite, 355–356, 359–363
  Conceptual Atomism and, 59–71
    overview and definitions, 59–62
    problems for, 62–71
  conjunctive, 267–268
  controversies about, 3
  coreless, 251
  decomposition of, 225–227, 325–327, 502–505
  deferential, 555–556
  definitional view of, 227–229
  definitions of, 305, 335, 460, 525
  disjunctive, 212, 269–270
  Dual Theories of
    compositionality and, 42–43
    Prototype Theory of Concepts and, 33, 35, 42–43, 46–47
    Rips and, 49–50
    Theory-Theory of Concepts and, 46
  as embedded in theories, 436–437
  as equivalent to their components, 434–435
  Euthyphro-Socrates discussion and, 87–99
  functions of, 282–285
  further information about, 75–77
  general theory of, difficulty of envisaging, 256–257
  graded responses and, 247–250
  holisitc descriptions of, 225–227
  identification procedure of, 72, 250, 277–278, 288–289, 416
  importance of, 3
  knowledge in, representing more, 217–218
  learning, 502–505
  lexical
    in Classical Theory of Concepts, 9
    composition of, 327–330
    concept acquisition and, 308–309
    in Conceptual Atomism, 74
    creativity of language and, 306–309, 327
    definition of, 4
    decomposition of, 325–327
    grammar of, 308–309
    lexicon and, 314–315

Concepts (cont.)
  logically empty, 268–269
  logically universal, 268–269
  as mental representations, 5–8, 75–76
  natural kind
    concept acquisition and, 554–564
    fakes and, 557–558, 560
    kind syndrome and, 63–64
    knowledge acquisition and, 527
    nouns and, common, 177–180
    perceptual features and, 286–287
    stereotypes and, 185
    sustaining mechanisms for, 63–64
  Neoclassical Theory of, 52–59
    problems for, 54–59
    updating, 52–54
  nested, 213
  nondescriptionist theory of, 525–526
  normative character of, 337
  observational, 336
  origins of, theories of, 460
  partial definitions of, 52–53
  primitive, 4
  Prototype Theory of, 27–43
    emergence of, 27–31
    problems for, 32–43
  Smith and Medin and, 280–282, 297
    functions of, 282–285
  sentential, 307–309, 315
  similar, 49
  simple, 355, 357–359
  spurious, 338
  standard set theory of, 275
  stereotypes and, 279–298
  structure of
    aggregation and boundedness, 315, 320–323
    argument, 315–318
    constitutive, 63–65, 139–140
    encoding and, 310
    models of, 5, 18, 45
    semantic fields, 315, 318–320
    types of, 72–74
  of substances, 530–544
    development of, 538–541
    language and, 541–544
    primary, 530–534
  tension in, fundamental, 305–306
  Theory-Theory of, 43–52
    advantages of, 45–47
    overview and definitions, 43–47
    problems for, 47–52
  traditional theories of, 275
  world view of, 305
Conceptual Atomism
  category judgments and, 75
  compositionality and, 43, 74
  concept acquisition and, 564–565
  conceptual cores and, 74–75
  lexical concepts and, 74

  overview and definitions, 59–62
  problems for, 62–71
    Analytic Data Problem, 65–67, 71
    Compositionality Problem, 67–68, 71
    Empty and Coextensive Concepts Problem, 69–71
    Explanatory Impotence Problem, 64–65, 71
    Radical Nativism Problem, 62–64, 71
    summary of, 71
  reference determination and, 74–75
  stability and, 75
Conceptual coherence
  approaches to, 427–437
    attribute matching and similarity insufficiency, 432–435
    categorization theories insufficiency, 431–432
    correlated attributes insufficiency, 430–431
    embedded in theories, 436–437
    overview, 427–429
    similarity insufficiency, 427–429
    similarity-based measures of category structure insufficiency, 429–430
    summary of, 435–436
  Classical Theory of Concepts and, 451–453
  conceptual development, 448–451
  naturalness vs., 427
  overview, 453–455
  related ideas, 446–448
  role of theories in, 437–439
  theories and concept use, 439–446
    complex concepts, 445–446
    correlated attributes, 439–441
    cross-culture research, 444–445
    expertise, 443–444
    linear separability in categorization, 441
    linguistic innovations, 445–446
    prototype structure and theories, 441–443
Conceptual combination, prototype theory and
  adequacy, 264–265
  compatibility, 267–270
  fuzzy-set theory and, 261, 265–267
  issue, 264
Conceptual competence, 295–298
Conceptual constituents, 315–316
Conceptual contents, 279
Conceptual core, 35, 248
Conceptual development, 195, 448–451
Conceptual differentiation, 463–465
Conceptual Fuzziness Problem, 23–24, 26
Conceptual Semantics
  Cognitive Grammar and, 314
  concept structure and, 315–323
    aggregation and boundedness, 315, 320–323
    argument, 315–318
    semantic fields, 315, 318–320
  description of meaning and, 309–313
  Language of Thought Hypothesis and, 311–313, 327

lexical composition versus meaning postulates
   and, 327–330
model-theoretic semantics and, 310–311
organization of language and, 313–315
overview, 330–331
principles of, 306–309
problems of, 323–327
Conceptual tracking, 534–541
CONDUIT metaphor, 407, 410
Confirmation holism, 342–343, 346–348
Conjunction effects, 357, 383
Conjunction fallacy, 405
Conjunctive concepts, 267–268
Constancy, perceptual, 539
Constraints, lack of, 218–219
Constructivism, 460
Containment Model, 5, 18, 45
Context effects, 219
Context model, 211, 213–217
Continuous domain, focal values in, 325
Contradiction, 144–145
Contrast Principle, 30
Copernican system, 19
Core + Identification Procedure Proposal, 411–
   413
Core facts, 185–187
Core features, 286–287
Core procedures, 289–290, 416
Coreless concepts, 251
Correlated attributes, 438–441
   insufficiency, 430–431
Correlational structure, 430
Correspondence rules, 313
Covariance, 514
Covariation theory, 349–351
Creativity of language, 306–309, 327
Critical assumptions, 208–209
Cross-cultural research, 444–445
Crutchfield, R. S., 114–115
Cue validity, 192

Darwin, C., 19, 519
Davidson, 310
Davidsonian sense, 309–310
Decomposition of concepts, 225–227, 325–327,
   502–505
Default values, 327
Deference-based sustaining mechanisms, 555–556,
   565
Deferential concepts, 555–556
Defining features, 212, 452–453
Definition, analytic, 155–157
Definition of task, 105–108
Definitional view of concepts, 227–229
Definitions
   of concepts, 305, 335, 460, 525
   experimental investigation of, 491–492
   innateness vs., 510–511
   language theory and, 491–506

decomposition of concepts into elements, 502–
   505
   extension of word, 492–495
   summary, 505–506
   understanding word to recover its definition,
   499–502
   validity of informally valid arguments, 495–499
post-definitional era and, 492, 506–511
sentence comprehension without, 509–510
DeMorgan's law, 276–277
Dennett, D., 313
Derived readings, 132, 137, 140
Descartes, R., 504–505
Description of meaning models, 309–313
Descriptionism, 21, 525, 534–538
Determination theory, 335
Development, 195, 448–451
DeVries, R., 474–475
Dewey, G. I., 441
Dictionary, 131, 138–139, 186–187
Differentiation, 463–465
Disjointed text, 462
Disjunction Problem, 61
Disjunctive concepts, 212, 269–270
Distinctions, psychologically real, 287–288
Distribution of defaults, 385
Division of linguistic labor, 543
DNA structure, 614
Dougherty, J. W. D., 444
Douglas, M., 453
Downing, P., 406
Doxsey, P. A., 603
Dretske, F., 514
Dual Theories of Concepts
   compositionality and, 42–43
   identification procedure of concepts and, 72, 250
   Prototype Theory of Concepts and, 33, 35, 42–43,
   46–47
   Rips and, 49–50
   Theory-Theory of Concepts and, 46
Duhem, P., 19, 289

E-concepts, 305–306
E-language, 306, 310–311
Ebbinghaus tradition, 447
Edelson, S. E., 441
Effects = Structure Interpretation, 391, 412–415,
   419
Einstein, A., 473
Empirical phenomena, 212–213, 217
Empiricism
   analyticity, 153–163
   background for, 153–155
   definition, 155–157
   interchangeability and, 157–160
   Quine's skepticism about, 18
   semantical rules and, 160–163
   synonymy and, 155–157, 160, 163–164
   syntheticity and, 153, 166–167

Empiricism (cont.)
  incommensurability and, 467
  knowledge and, 19
  overview of dogmas, 153
  reductionism, 153, 163–166
  The Standard Picture and, 506
  truth of, 505, 564
  without dogmas, 166–168
Empty and Coextensive Concepts Problem, 69–71
Entry, dictionary, 131, 138–139
Epistemic differences, 342
Epistemic justification, 12
Epistemological function, 282, 284–285
Epistemology, 285–290
Error Problem. *See* Ignorance and Error Problem
Essences, 614–615. *See also* Non-obvious essences
Essentialism, psychological, 45, 557, 615, 634–636
Estes, D., 469, 474, 478
Euler, L., 472
Euthypro, 87–99
Events, 202
Evolution, theory of, 19
Exemplar view
  categorization theories insufficiency and, 432
  concept representations and, 208–210
  criticisms and problems of, 217–220
  models of categorization and, 210–217
    best-examples, 210–213, 217
    context, 211, 213–217
  process of categorization and, 208–210
  rationale for, 207–208
  test instance and, 212–213
Exemplariness, graded judgments of, 30–31
Experience, 336, 355
Expertise, 443–444
Explanatory Impotence Problem, 64–65, 71
Extension of word, 492–495
Externalized language (E-language), 306, 310–311

Facial recognition, infant, 540
Fakes, 557–558, 560
Falsity, truth versus, 273
Family resemblance description, 229
Featural substrate, 253–254
Feature bundles, 394
Feature descriptions, 250–256
Feature-based semantics
  limitations and failings of, 323–327
  structure of, 315–323
    aggregation and boundedness, 315, 320–323
    argument, 315–318
    semantic fields, 315, 318–320
Features, 4–5, 49, 250–253, 286–287, 449
Feltovich, P. J., 444
Feyerabend, 448
Field theory, 134
Fillmore, C., 393, 442, 452
Fisher, S. C., 111

Flavell, E. R., 618
Flavell, J. H., 618
Focal instances, 210
Focal values in continuous domain, 325
Fodor, J. A., 10, 14, 16, 35–36, 39, 41–42, 58–63,
    65, 67–68, 70, 226–227, 233, 252–253, 309,
    311–313, 327–330, 493–494, 504, 506, 519,
    550–554
Formal universals, 126
Formation rules, 313
Foss, D. J., 17
Foss, M. A., 428
Frege, G., 6–8, 69, 71, 73, 133, 137, 153, 164, 185,
    309, 336
Frege's Puzzle, 6
Fumerton, R., 535
Fuzziness, 23–24, 26, 31, 247, 294
Fuzzy inclusion, 271–273
Fuzzy-set theory
  Min rule and, 38
  Prototype Theory of Concepts and
    conceptional combination and, 261, 265–267
    truth conditions of thoughts and, 271–272
Fuzzy-truth remedy, 273

Garrett, M. F., 253
Gelman, R., 484, 536, 616
Gelman, S. A., 46, 527, 536, 540, 543
Generative grammar, 305–306, 310–311
Generators, 404–405
Generic instance, 111
Gentner, D., 447, 454
Geoghegan, W. H., 444
Gettier, E., 15
Gettier examples, 15, 54
Ghiselin, M., 530
Glaser, R., 444
Gleitman, H., 32, 327, 411, 418–420, 452
Gleitman, L., 32, 327, 411, 418–420, 452
Gödel's Incompleteness Theorem, 285
Goldbach's conjecture, 285, 292
Goldstein, K., 106
Goodman, N., 428
Goodnow, J., 101, 104, 106, 109, 112–113, 117,
    119–120
Gopnik, A., 47, 51, 540
Graded judgments of exemplariness, 30–31
Graded responses
  concepts and, 247–250
  Experiment I, 234–238
  Experiment II, 238–242
  Experiment III, 242–247
  feature descriptions and, 250–256
  not studying, thoughts in, 256–257
Graded speed of quick categorization judgments,
    31
Grammar
  Cognitive, 313–314

generative, 305–306, 310–311
innate, 536
of lexical concepts, 308–309
of sentential concepts, 307
Universal, 125, 308, 311, 323, 327, 329–330
Gravity, theory of, 19
Green, F. L., 618
Grice, H. P., 447
Grimshaw, J., 55–56
Grosslight, L., 470
Gruber, J. S., 315, 318–319

Halle, M., 125
Hampton, J., 41, 388
Harris, Z., 177
Heathcote, N. H. V., 463–464
Hedges, 199, 412
Helson, H., 111
Hemenway, K., 437–438
Herrnstein, R., 69
Heuristics, 560, 564
Hidden objects. *See* Occluded objects
Holistic descriptions of concepts, 225–227
Holistic similarities, 527
Homogeneity of matter, 480–483
Hon category, 407–411
Horizontal challenges, 339–341, 345–346, 348
Horizontal dimensions of categories, 196–201
Hovland, C. I., 109–110
Hull, C. L., 106, 108, 113, 530
Hume, D., 164, 285, 513
Hutchinson, J., 561–562
Hypothesis of External Definitions, 293, 295

I-concepts. *See* Conceptual Semantics
I-language, 306
IBSTs. *See* Information-based semantic theories
ICM, 393, 397–398, 442
Ideal epistemic circumstances, 342
Idealized Cognitive Model (ICM), 393, 397–398, 442
Ideals, 403–404
Identification features, 250–253
Identification function, 247–248
Identification procedures, 72, 250, 277–278, 288–289, 416
Ignorance and Error Problem
in Classical Theory of Concepts, 21–23, 26, 75
in Neoclassical Theory of Concepts, 55–56, 59
in Prototype Theory of Concepts, 34–35, 43
in Theory-Theory of Concepts, 47–48, 51
Illusory correlation, 440
Imagery, 195
Inborn properties of animals, 629–630
Inclusion, 271–273
Incommensurability
of children vs. adults, 465–468
evidence of, 468–469

empiricism and, 467
local, 461–465
nativism and, 467–468
weight, density, matter, and material kind and, 469–484
air/nothing concept, 479–480, 484
child's material/immaterial distinction, 474–477
material/immaterial distinction, 472–474, 477–478, 480
mathematical prerequisites, 483–484
matter's homogeneity, 480–483
physical objects occupying space, 478–479
undifferentiated concept, 469–472
weight and materiality, 477–478
Incompatibility, 145
Incomplete symbols, 164
Inductive logic, 274
Infant's physical knowledge
development of adults' and, 571, 607–608
occluded objects
failure to search for, 592–599
inferring existence and properties of, 587–592
representing existence and properties of, 574–587
wrong location for searching for, 599–605
Piaget's theory of, 572–574
test of, 574–606
search behavior and, 607–608
structure of adults' and, 571
Inferences, 447
Inferential Model, 5
Infinite-valued logic, 274
Information, 60–61, 514
Information sufficiency, psychological, 112
Information-based semantic theories (IBSTs)
alternative versions of, 514
Asymmetric Dependence Theory and, 552–553, 558
concept acquisition and, 550–554
Disjunction Problem and, 61
problem of, 513–518
representation and, nature of, 518–524
Inhelder, B., 483
Innate grammar, 536
Innate potential
of animals, 625–629
of seeds, 630–633
Innateness controversy, 510–511
Inside-outside distinction, 615–620
Insides. *See also* Non-obvious essences
definition of, 614–615
essentialness of, 620–625
inside-removal vs. outside-removal, 623–624
movement questions and, 624–625
outside and, distinction between, 615–620
Instances encountered, nature of, 105, 108–113

Insufficiency
  of attribute matching and similarity, 432–435
  of categorization theories, 431–432
  of correlated attributes, 430–431
  of similarity, 427–429
  of similarity-based measures of category structure,
    429–430
Intellectual realism, 616
Intentional Realism, 311–313
Interactional properties, 392
Interchangeability, 157–160
Internalized language (I-language), 306
Interpretation, 462
Intersentential relations, 495–499
Israel, D., 519

Jackendoff, R., 52–53, 55–59, 62, 73, 310–312,
    315, 318, 323–324, 326, 460
James, W., 504–505
Jammer, M., 472–473
Johnson, M., 204, 397, 402, 407
Johnson-Laird, P., 277, 416, 438, 446–447
Jones, L. E., 428
Judgment, 447

Kahneman, D., 204, 405–406, 447
Kant, I., 12, 285
Karam of New Guinea, 445
Katz, J., 11, 13, 144, 177, 181–182, 185, 253, 290,
    496, 502
Kay, P., 294, 394, 411, 413
Keil, F. C., 255, 282, 427, 442, 449–450, 525, 527,
    529, 536–537, 540, 620–621, 625
Keller, H., 544
Kempton, W., 411
Kepler, J., 472–473
Kind syndrome, 63–64
Kintsch, W., 17–18
Kitcher, P., 461–462
KL-ONE system of knowledge representation, 386
Klahr, 599
Knowledge acquisition. See also Infant's physical
    knowledge
  incommensurability and, 461–484
    of children vs. adults, 465–468
    empiricism and, 467
    local, 461–465
    nativism and, 467–468
    weight, density, matter, and material kind, 469–
      484
  innate representations and, 459
  natural kind concepts and, 527
  overview, 484–485
  physical, 571–572, 605–608
  scientific, 459–460
  Spelke and, 459–461, 467–459, 484–485
Knowledge independent operations, 446
Komatsu, L. K., 251, 255, 534

Korzybski, A., 106
Kripke, S., 3, 21–23, 48, 60, 250, 280, 285, 291–
    292, 294, 340–341, 525, 535, 541
Kuhn, T. S., 442, 448, 461–463

Lakoff, G., 373, 394, 397, 402, 407, 442, 533, 535
Landau, B., 249–250, 562–563, 565
Language, in vertical dimension of categorization,
    196
Language comprehension, 447
Language learning, 462
Language of Thought Hypothesis, 311–313, 327
Language-games, 171–174
Larkin, K. M., 447
Learning. See also Concept acquisition
  concepts, 502–505
  errors of children's, 450–451
  language, 462
  order of development in children's rate of, 198
  speed of, 198
Legitimation by application, 336–337
Leibniz, G., 155, 157
Lepore, E., 41–42, 67
Lerdahl, F., 311–312
Levin, B., 62
Leviticus, abominations of, 425, 453
Lewis, C. I., 168
Lewis, D., 309, 310
Lexical composition, 327–330
Lexical concepts
  in Classical Theory of Concepts, 9
  composition of, 327–330
  concept acquisition and, 308–309
  in Conceptual Atomism, 74
  creativity of language and, 306–309, 327
  decomposition of, 325–327
  definition of, 4
  grammar of, 308–309
  lexicon and, 314–315
Lexical items, 131, 139
Lexical readings, 132, 137, 140
Lexicon, 314–315
LF, 313
Linear separability in categorization, 441
Linguistic function, 282–284
Linguistic innovations, 445–446
Linguistic levels, 507
Linguistic theory. See Semantic theory
Linguistic universals, 125
Locke, J., 9–10, 14, 29, 164, 614
Locking theory, 349–351
Lockman, J. J., 605
Loftus, E. F., 226
Logical Form (LF), 313
Logical Positivists, 285
Logically empty concepts, 268–269
Logically true, 154
Logically universal concepts, 268–269

Luce's choice axiom, 447
Lyerly, S. B., 108

McCarrell, N. S., 605
McKie, D., 463–464
McNamara, T. P., 452–453
Margolis, E., 63
Marker language, 182
Markman, E., 450, 527, 536, 540, 561–562
Marr, D., 324
Masling, M., 440
Material/immaterial distinction, 472–474, 477–478, 480
 child's, 474–477
Mathematics, 19, 483–484
Matter's homogeneity, 480–483
Maxwell, J., 134, 466
Maxwell's field theory, 134
Meaning, 13, 131, 177, 181–182
Meaning postulates, 327–330
Mediating relation between two nouns, 446
Medin, D., 23–24, 26, 30, 44–46, 207, 209, 211, 213, 216–217, 230–231, 280, 363, 430–432, 438–439, 441, 534, 536, 540, 557, 614, 634–635
Meltzoff, A., 51, 540, 601–602
Memory research, 447
Mental categories. See Categorization; Concepts
Mental representations. See Concepts
Mentalese, 310
Mervis, C., 24–25, 28, 197, 200, 210, 254–255, 357, 364, 431, 437, 527
Metaphysical function, 282, 284
Metonymic models, 396–398, 401–402, 409
Michalski, R. S., 448
Mill, J. S., 434
Miller, G., 277, 416, 438, 446
Miller, J. G., 445
Millikan, R., 519, 543
Min Rule, 38
Minsky's frames, 392–393
Missing Prototypes Problem, 35–37, 39, 43
Mode of presentation, 6
Model-theoretic semantics, 310–311
Mohr, R. D., 442
Montague, W. E., 198–199, 235
Motor movements, common, 194
Murphy, G. L., 44, 385–386, 388, 440, 443, 446–447
Murphy, T., 441
"Mysteries of Science" Problem, 51–52

Nativism
 concept acquisition and, 564–566
 concept learning and, 504
 incommensurability and, 467–468
Natural kind concepts
 concept acquisition and, 554–564

fakes and, 557–558, 560
kind syndrome and, 63–64
knowledge acquisition and, 527
nouns and, common, 177–180
perceptual features and, 286–287
stereotypes and, 185
sustaining mechanisms for, 63–64
Naturalness, 427
Neoclassical Theory of Concepts
 Classical Theory of Concepts and, 54
 problems for, 54–59
  Completers Problem, 54–55, 59
  Ignorance and Error problem, 55–56, 59
  Regress Problem, 56–59
  summary of, 59
 updating, 52–54
Nested concepts, 213
Newport, E. L., 196
Newton, I., 19, 466, 472
Newtonian mechanics, 466
Nominalism, 534
Non-logical vocabulary, 495
Non-obvious essences
 concepts of, 614–615
 courses of development and, 634
 inborn properties of animals and, 629–630
 innate potential and
  of animals, 625–629
  of seeds, 630–633
 inside-outside distinction, 615–620
 insiders as essential, 620–625
 overview, 613–614
 psychological essentialism and, 615, 634–636
 results of studies of, 633–634
Nonconceptual representational content of experience, 336
Nondescriptionist theory of concepts, 525–526
Nondifferentiation, 464
Nonnecessary features, 213
Nonreferential semantic structure, 73–74
Nonsemantic conceptual structure, 72–74
Normativity of meaning, 13
Noun prototypes. See Selective Modification Model for adjective-noun conjunctions
Nouns, 177–180, 386, 446. See also Selective Modification Model for adjective-noun conjunctions
Nussbaum, J., 481

Object concept, 571
Object permanence
 adult's view of, 607
 definition of, 571
 search for occluded objects and
  failure, infants', 592–599
  wrong location, 599–605
Objectivist semantics, 413
Objects in events, 202–205

Observational concepts, 336
Occluded objects
  additional properties of, 578–581
  adult's view of, 607–609
  children's view of
    failure to search for, 592–601
    inferring existence and properties of, 587–592
    representing existence and properties of, 574–587
    search errors and, 604–606
    wrong location in searching for, 601–606
  converging evidence for, 585–587
  developmental evidence for, 581–585
  existence of, 587–588
  location of, 577–578, 591
  size of, 588–591
Oden, G. C., 276–277
Order, 198–199
Organization of language, 313–315
Organizational universals, 126
Ortony, A., 45–46, 428, 557, 614
Osherson, D., 38–40, 357, 363, 386, 411–421, 451–452

Palmer, S., 200
Paragons, 404
Parameter estimates, 379–381
Parkes, C., 253
Partial definitions of concepts, 53
Partial falsification, 273–274
Payoff matrix, 119–121
Peacocke, C., 75–77, 339–342, 346
Perceived attributes, 201–202
Perceived world structure, 190–191
Perception, 195
Perceptual constancy, 539
Perceptual features, 286–287
Perceptual tracking, 539
Performance, effects of advance information on, 199
PF, 313
Philosophical investigations of language, 171–174
Phonetic Form (PF), 313
Phonological theory, 126–127
Phonological universals, 126
Phrase markers, 140
Physical knowledge, 571–572, 606–608. *See also* Infant's physical knowledge; Knowledge acquisition
Physical objects occupying space, 478–479
Physical reasoning, 606–607
Piaget, J., 459–461, 474–475, 483, 571–609, 613
Pick, H. L., 603–605
Pinker, S., 52–53, 55, 62
Planful problem solving, 604
Plato, 10, 13–16, 87–99, 185, 491
Platonic universals, 442
Plato's Problem, 14–16, 26, 53

Polysemy, 58–59
Possession conditions
  answerability and, 345–346
  confirmation holism and, 346–348
  locking theory and, 349–351
  spurious concepts and, 338
  surface of psychology and, 348–349
Preference rule systems, 325–327
Pribram, K., 113
Priestly, J., 461
Primitive compulsions, 339–343, 345, 348
Primitive concepts, 4
Primitive semantic markers, 133
Principle of contact, 48
Probabilistic view, 431–432
Probability of item output, 198–199
Problem solving, 447, 604–605
Progressive Matrices Test, 108
Projection rules, 131, 141
Property lists, 31
Propositional models, 393
Prototype = Representation Interpretation, 391, 412, 415
Prototype effects
  categorization and, 411–413
  clusters of cognitive models and, 394–396, 398
  Cognitive Models Interpretation and, 391–392, 419–421
  existence of, 391, 411
  interactional properties, 392
  interpretation of, 391–392
  metonymic sources of, 398
  psychological dependent variables and, 198
  research on, 225
  stereotypes and, 398–400
Prototype Theory of Concepts
  argument against, 67–68
  Armstrong, Gleitman, and Gleitman's research on, 411, 418–420
  categorization in, 29–30, 46
  characterization, formal, 262–263
  cognitive models in
    clusters of, 394–396, 398
    feature bundles vs., 394
    generators and, 404–405
    graded, 393
    hon category and, 407–411
    idealized character of, 393, 397–398, 442
    ideals and, 403–404
    metonymy and, 396–398, 401–402
    paragons and, 404
    prototype effects and, 391–392, 419–421
    radial structures and, 400–401, 406
    representativeness structures and, 400
    rules of language and, 411
    salient examples and, 405–406
    stereotypes and, 398–400, 402–403
    study of, 392–393

submodels and, 405
typical examples and, 403
composite concepts and, 355–356
concept acquisition and, 29
conceptual combination and, 264–270
   adequacy, 264–265
   compatibility with prototype theory and, 267–270
   fuzzy-set theory and, 261, 265–267
   issue, 264
definitions, 411
Dual Theories of Concepts and, 33, 35, 42–43, 46–47
emergence of, 27–31
extension of present results to other versions of, 275–276
gaps in, 263–264
implications, 275–278
models of, 229–234
Osherson and Smith's research on, 411–421
overview, 261
problems for, 32–43
   Compositionality Problem, 37–43
   Ignorance and Error Problem, 34–35, 43
   Missing Prototypes Problem, 35–37, 39, 43
   Prototypical Primes, 32–34, 43
   summary of, 43
real-world attributes and, 392
Rosch's research on, 418
truth conditions of thought and, 270–274
   adequacy, 271
   compatibility with truth conditions and, 272–273
   fuzzy-set theory and, 271–272
   issue, 271
   partial falsification and, 273–274
Prototypes
aspects of, general, 356–357, 383
context in basic-level, 202
definitions, 355, 356, 391
exemplariness and, 247–250
horizontal dimensions of categories and, 196–201
structure of, 441–443
Prototypical Primes Problem, 32–34, 43
Proximity model, 209–210
Psychological essentialism, 45, 557, 615, 634–636
Psychological information sufficiency, 112
Psychological Reality Problem, 17–18, 26
Psychologically dependent variables, 198
Psychosemantics, 520–524
Putnam, H., 3, 21–23, 48, 60, 73, 280, 291–294, 331, 525, 535, 541, 543, 555–556

Qualitative prediction, 583
Quantitative reasoning, 583

Quine, W. V. O., 18–21, 28, 54, 182–185, 256, 289, 339–343, 346, 426–427, 450–451, 531
Quinn, N., 403

Radial structures, 400–401, 406
Radical Nativism Problem, 62–64, 71
Radical reductionism, 164
Rationalist-Empiricist debate, 505
Rationalistic theory, traditional, 125
Reaction time, 198
Reactive problem solving, 603
Readings, 132, 137, 139–140
Real-world attributes, 392
Reddy, M., 407
Reduced content problem, 337
Reductionism, 153, 163–166
Redundancy, 144
Reed, H. B., 106
Reference determination, 13–14, 72, 74–75
Reference of expression, 6–8
Reference-point reasoning, 417
Referential potential, mismatch of, 461–462
Regress Problem, 56–59
Relativity Theory, 339
Representation, nature of, 213–215, 518–524. See also Concepts
Representativeness structures, 400
Rescher, N., 274
Restrictions, nature of imposed, 105, 121–122
Revision, 167
Rey, G., 54, 65–66, 75–77, 343, 519
Rhodes, R., 397
Rieser, J. J., 605
Rips, L., 49–50, 403
Rodrigues, 111
Rosch, E., 24–25, 28–29, 197–200, 210, 225, 230–231, 234–237, 242–243, 254, 279, 327, 357, 364, 391, 418, 429–431, 437, 439–440, 444, 525, 534–535
Ross, B. H., 605
Roth, E. M., 385
Rules of inference, 314
Rules of language, 411
Rumelhart, D. E., 446–447
Rumelhart's schemas, 392–393, 446
Russell, 153, 164

Salient examples, 405–406
Schaffer, M., 207, 209, 211, 213, 216–217
Schank and Abelson's scripts, 392–393, 397
Schank, R. C., 392–393, 397, 447
Schwanenflugel, P. L., 432
Schwartz, S., 506
Scientific knowledge, 459
Scribner, S., 444–445
Search behavior, 608–609
Search errors, 602–605

Secondary assumptions, 418
Seeds, innate potential of, 630–633
Selection restriction, 137–138
Selective Modification Model for adjective-noun
    conjunctions
  adverbs and extension of, 373–375
  test of, 375–383
  first test of, 363–370
    overview, 383
    Part 1, 364–367
    Part 2, 367–370
  implications, 384–385
  limitations, 40–42, 386–388
  overview, 383–388
  rationale for, 356–363, 383
    adjective modification, 359–363
    aspects of prototypes, general, 356–357
    typicality and simple concepts, 357–359
  relations to other proposals, 385–386
  subsequent tests of, 370–372, 383–384
  summary of, 383–384
Selkirk, E., 315
Semantic component, model of, 129–142
Semantic content, 55
Semantic Feature Hypothesis, 448–449
Semantic field feature, 56–59, 319
Semantic fields, 315, 318–320
Semantic interpretation, 131, 141–142
Semantic markers, 132–137
Semantic similarity, 142
Semantic stability, 342
Semantic structure, 55
Semantic theory. See also Conceptual Semantics;
    Information-based semantic theories
  compositionality and, 128–129
  Frege's, 6–8, 309
  grammar theory and, 125–128
  possibility of, 187
  properties and relations, 142–149
  semantic component model, 129–142
  in sound-meaning correlations, 129
  structure of, 125–129
Semantic universals, 126
Semantical rules, 160–163
Sense of expression, 6–8, 131, 309
"Sense and Reference" (Frege), 309
Sentence comprehension, 499–502
  without definitions, 509–510
Sentential concepts, 307–309, 315
Shank, R. C., 204
Shapes
  identifiability of averaged, 195
  similarity in, 194–195
Shoben, E. J., 363, 385
Shweder, R. A., 445
Similarity insufficiency, 427–429
Similarity-based measures of category structure
    insufficiency, 429–430

Simmel, M. L., 107
Simple Account, 338
Simple concepts, 355, 357–359
Smedslund, J., 107
Smith, C., 469–470, 475, 477–478, 480, 484, 536
Smith, E., 26, 30, 38–42, 49, 230–231, 280, 357,
    363, 386, 411–421, 431, 438, 451–452, 534
Smith and Medin (Categories and Concepts)
  Classical Theory of Concepts and, 280–282, 287,
    290–295
  concepts and, 280–282, 297
    functions of, 282–285
  epistemology and, 285–290
Smoke, K. L., 108, 110
Snir, Y., 470
Socrates, 87–99
Sommers, F., 282
Spatial structure of objects and actions, 324–325
Speed of learning, 198
Spelke, E. S., 257, 459–461, 467–469, 484–485,
    540
Spreading activation model, 226
Spurious concepts, 388
Stability function, 282–283
Stability Problem, 49–51, 69
Stalnaker, R., 519
Stampe, D., 342
Standard inclusion, 271–273
Standard set theory, 275
Stereotypes
  categorization and, 398–400, 402–403
  Cognitive Models Interpretation and, 398–400,
    402–403
  concepts and, 279–298
  cultural expectations and, 402–403
  housewife, 398
  natural kind concepts and, 185
  prototype effects and, 398–400
  working mothers, 398–400
Sternberg, R., 452–453
Stevens, A. L., 447, 454
Stich, S., 3
Story Understanders, 202
A Study of Concepts (SoC) (Peacocke)
  horizontal challenges and, 345–346, 348
  primitive compulsions and, 341
  thesis of, 76, 335–338
  vertical challenges and, 345–346, 348
Subcategories, 405
Submodels, 405
Subordinate categories, 192
Substances
  category of, 525–530
  concepts of, 530–544
    development of, 538–541
    language and, 541–544
    primary, 530–534
    descriptionism vs., 534–538

Substantive universals, 126, 129
Substitutability into sentences, 199
Superordinate categories, 192, 199
Superordinates in ASL, 199
Suppe, F., 448
Surface of psychology, 348–349
Sustaining mechanisms
    Asymmetric Dependence Theory and, 63–64,
        552–553
    concept acquisition and, 550–554
    deference-based, 555–556, 565
    for natural kind concepts, 63–64
    structure, 73–74
    syndrome-based, 556–557, 559–560
    theory-based, 553–557
Sweetser, E. E., 394
Syndrome-based sustaining mechanisms, 556–557,
    559–560
Synonymy, 142–143, 155–157, 160, 163–164
Syntactic theory, 126–128
Syntactic universals, 126
Syntax of Thought Hypothesis, 312
Syntheticity, 147–148, 153, 166–167
Systematic organizational universals, 126–127

Tarskian sense, 309–310
Taxonomy
    of animal kingdom, 189–190
    basic level of, 561
    categorization and, 189–192, 561–562
    definition of, 191
Test instance, 212–213
Thagard, P., 385
The Standard Picture (TSP)
    concept acquisition and, 491–506
    dismantling, 511
    empiricism and, 506
    in post-definitional era, 492, 506–511
Thematic Relations Hypothesis, 318–320
Theory of language. See Semantic theory
Theory of meaning
    core facts and, 185–187
    difficulty of, 177
    Katz and, 181–182
    nouns and, common, 177–180
    Quine and, 182–185
Theory-based sustaining mechanisms, 553–557
Theory-Theory of Concepts
    advantages of, 45–47
    category judgments and, 75
    Classical Theory of Concepts and, 47–48
    Dual Theories of Concepts and, 46
    overview and definitions, 43–47
    problems for, 47–52
        Ignorance and Error Problem, 47–48, 51
        "Mysteries of Science" Problem, 51–52
        Stability Problem, 49–51, 69
        summary of, 51
Third Realms, 336

3-D model structure, 73, 324–325
Thurstone, L. L., 108
Tooke, J., 164
Tracking, conceptual and perceptual, 534–541
Translation, 462
Triggering theory, 505, 564
True of entity, 154
True Issues of Semantics, 312
Truth conditions of thoughts, prototype theory and
    adequacy, 271
    compatibility, 272–273
    fuzzy-set theory and, 271–272
    issue, 271
    partial falsification and, 273–274
Truth, falsity versus, 273
Truth values, 160, 273–274
Truth-conditional semantics, 309–310
TSP. See The Standard Picture
Tversky, A., 30, 192, 204, 358, 383, 405–406, 428,
    447
Tversky, B., 437–438
Tversky, S., 192
Twin Earth problem, 331
Typical examples, 403
Typical instance, 111
Typicality
    categorization errors correlated with, 31
    conjunctions and, 383–384
    correlates with property lists, 31
    data, 30–31
    determinants of, 213
    ratings, 384
    simple, 212
    simple concepts and, 357–359
Typicality Effects Problem, 24–27, 72

UG, 125, 308, 311, 323, 327, 329–330
Unclear cases, 212
Undifferentiated concept
    air/nothing concept, 479–480, 484
    weight/density, 469–471, 484
    weight/density concept functions, 472–473
Unger, C., 470
Universal Grammar (UG), 125, 308, 311, 323, 327,
    329–330

Vaina, L., 324
Valid arguments, informally, 495–499, 507–
    509
Validation, nature of, 105, 113–117
Verbal attainment, 108
Verification Principle, 285, 296
Verification theory of meaning, 153, 163–166
Verificationism, 288, 338
Verkuyl, H., 310–311, 323
Vertical challenges, 339, 345–346, 348
Vertical dimensions of categories, 191–196
Vocabulary, non-logical, 495. See also Words
Vondruska, R. J., 428

Walk, R. D., 108
Walker, E. T., 253
Wallas, G., 101
Wanner, E., 252
Ward, T. B., 535
Wattenmaker, W., 441
Weight/density, 469–471, 477–478, 484
 functions, 472–473
Weiss, W., 110
Wellman, H., 46, 469, 474, 478
Wettstein, H., 533
Wiser, M., 464, 469–470, 475, 477–478, 480, 484,
   536
Wisniewski, E. J., 440
Wittgenstein, L., 3, 15, 28, 171–174, 196, 225, 229,
   280, 327, 339, 451
Woolley, J. D., 469, 474, 478
Words
 extension of, 492–495
 meaning of, 131, 177, 181–182
 understanding, to recover its definition, 499–502
Wright, J. C., 443

Xu, F., 540

Zadeh, L. A., 265, 271, 274, 276–277, 393, 412
Ziff, P., 442–443
Zwarts, J., 310–311, 323